S N Johnson
Barrister at Law
Barton Mill House
Barton Mill Road
Canterbury 764899
Dx 5342 Canterbury

THE
LAW OF
INSOLVENCY

AUSTRALIA AND NEW ZEALAND
The Law Book Company Ltd
Sydney : Melbourne : Perth

CANADA
The Carswell Company Ltd
Agincourt, Ontario

INDIA
N. M. Tripathi Private Ltd
Bombay
and
Eastern Law House Private Ltd
Calcutta and Delhi
M.P.P. House
Bangalore

ISRAEL
Steimatzky's Agency Ltd
Jerusalem : Tel Aviv : Haifa

PAKISTAN
Pakistan Law House
Karachi

THE
LAW OF
INSOLVENCY

by

Ian F. Fletcher,
M.A., LL.M., M.C.L., PH.D., LL.D.
of Lincoln's Inn, Barrister, Professor of Commercial Law and Director of the Centre for Commercial Law Studies, Queen Mary and Westfield College University of London

Second Edition

With a chapter on Company Receivership
contributed by Letitia Crabb, LL.B., LL.M.,
Solicitor, Lecturer in Law, University of Reading

LONDON
SWEET & MAXWELL
1996

First edition 1990
Second edition 1996
Published in 1996 by
Sweet & Maxwell Limited of
South Quay Plaza, 183 Marsh Wall, London E14 9FT
Computerset by MFK Information Services Ltd
and printed and bound in Great Britain by
Hartnolls Ltd., Bodmin

No natural forests were destroyed to make this product; only farmed timber was used and re-planted.

ISBN 0 421 51140 0.
A CIP catalogue record for this book is available from the British Library

All rights reserved. UK statutory material in this publication is acknowledged as Crown Copyright.
No part of this publication may be reproduced or transmitted in any form or by any means, or stored in any retrieval system of any nature without prior written permission, except for permitted fair dealing under the Copyright, Designs and Patents Act 1988, or in accordance with the terms of a licence issued by the Copyright Licensing Agency in respect of photocopying and/or reprographic reproduction. Application for permission for other use of copyright material including permission to reproduce extracts in other published works shall be made to the publishers. Full acknowledgement of author, publisher and source must be given.

©
Ian F. Fletcher
1996

DEDICATION

For Daniel and Julian,
Matris pulchrae filii.

DEDICATION

For David and Julian,
Adam, Jesse, Eva

PREFACE
TO SECOND EDITION

The first edition of this book went to press in October 1989, less than two years after the entry into force of the legislative reforms centred upon the Insolvency Act 1986. At that date, the task of assessing the impact of the new law had to be undertaken on the basis of a relative handful of reported decisions, mostly at first instance. Much has happened since that time. The conditions of acute and prolonged economic recession in the years after 1989 provoked unparalleled levels of insolvencies of companies and individuals alike, and were accompanied by a veritable explosion in terms of insolvency-related litigation. With substantial sums of money sometimes at stake, as well as important issues of principle, a considerable number of cases were pursued as far as the Court of Appeal, and even beyond. The entire period, while amply qualifying as "interesting times", has served as a rigorous testbed for the new insolvency law, revealing both virtues and—alas, far too often—deficiencies.

This new edition therefore attempts to evaluate the law and its workings from the vantage point of 1995, taking into account both the case decisions and the extensive amendments to the primary and secondary legislation, of which the Insolvency Act 1994, and its less controversial companion, the Insolvency (No. 2) Act 1994, are merely the most conspicuous by virtue of their self-announcing titles. It is already apparent that further legislative attention will be required if the numerous, systemic shortcomings—now openly and almost universally acknowledged—are to be rectified ahead of the onset of the next cyclical decline in the domestic economy. Whether the necessary political impetus will be forthcoming in the near future remains unclear, however.

In preparing this second edition I have been influenced not only by the desire to reflect the matters touched upon above, but also by a wish to respond to the helpful and constructive suggestions made by many users of the first edition. To all of these, I am most grateful. In particular, I became persuaded that my original decision to exclude any treatment of company receivership had impaired the overall usefulness of the book from the standpoint of those requiring a comprehensive account of the insolvency procedures which are of most significance in practice. Hence, I resolved to include a chapter on receiverships, aiming to show its special significance in the context of company operations. I was delighted that Letitia Crabb agreed to contribute this chapter and thereby impart the benefits of her depth of learning in these areas of company law. It is doubly fitting that, as one who has hitherto sustained me in my academic endeavours in the

Preface

various roles of muse, counsellor and consort, she should in this instance receive the full credit of authorship for a discrete part of a work to which, once again, she has furnished vital intellectual and spiritual stimulus throughout.

Other debts of gratitude also need to be acknowledged. It has been a constant source of sustenance over the years to be able to draw upon the wisdom and insight of such learned friends as Professor Douglass Boshkoff, Neil Cooper, Michael Crystal Q.C., John Gibson, Professor Roy Goode Q.C., David Graham Q.C., Ron Harmer, Peter Totty, Nick Segal, Philip Wood, and Professor Jay L. Westbrook. As is customary, I absolve each and all of them of culpability for any shortcomings that are found in the book, final responsibility for whose contents rests with myself. During a happy and productive residence as Visiting Professor at the Law School of the University of Texas at Austin I experienced at first hand the fabled qualities of the Tarlton Law Library and the superb services provided by its Librarian, Professor Roy M. Mersky and his colleagues, of whom Jonathan Pratter claims special mention. Tony Cooke, of Cork Gully-Coopers & Lybrand, generously accorded me access to his invaluable database providing immediate information about reported and unreported cases. Particular thanks are due to Peter Joyce, Inspector General and Chief Executive of the Insolvency Service, and his colleagues, notably Desmond Flynn, Graham Hickling and Eamon Murphy, for much helpful guidance with regard to emerging developments in law-making and policy on the domestic and also the European fronts. In updating the statistical data in Appendix III I was greatly assisted by the members of the Statistical Division of the Department of Trade and Industry.

The attempt has been made to state the law as at the end of June 1995.

Centre for Commercial Law Studies Ian F. Fletcher
University of London, Queen Mary
and Westfield College
July 1995

PREFACE
TO THE FIRST EDITION

The insolvency law of England and Wales has undergone greater change and development during the past 10 years than it had during the previous 100. The investigative labours of the Cork Committee, culminating in their *Final Report* of 1982, provided the basis for the successive Insolvency Act of 1985 and 1986, whereby the law was first reformed and then consolidated. In consequence, nearly all the statutory provisions concerning both personal and corporate insolvency are for the first time contained within a single Act of Parliament. Simultaneously, fundamental changes have taken place in the work and organisation of insolvency practitioners, who now constitute an identifiable professional grouping in their own right.

These momentous developments make it appropriate to recast the traditional textbook treatment of this area of law, whereby personal bankruptcy and company liquidation have been generally regarded as distinct subjects, and thus have been dealt with in separate legal treaties. In this book, I have adopted the view that insolvency law is essentially a unitary subject. I have accordingly provided an account of each of the collective procedures which may be utilised in the case of insolvency of either an individual or a corporate debtor. Non-collective procedures or remedies, such as receivership, are omitted.

The nature and extent of the recent reforms have necessitated a careful consideration of the appropriate style of treatment to be adopted. Some entirely new procedures have entered the law (such as corporate and individual voluntary arrangements, and company administration orders) on which there is as yet no great abundance of settled case law. On the other hand, the recasting of many provisions relating to the established procedures of bankruptcy and company winding up have made it appropriate to question whether the accumulated body of past judicial decisions can safely be regarded as good law. For my part (save in those instances of clear legislative intention to reverse the former law and to depart from past principles) I have been inclined to make frequent reference to judicial precedent in the course of discussing the current statutory provisions. This reflects my personal belief that it is in the rich legacy of reported case decisions that the true spirit of our insolvency law is to be discovered and appreciated. Only by renewed study of these wellsprings of our legal tradition can we ensure that the best standards, and fundamental principles, are maintained in the process of administering the law of the present day. If hard cases sometimes make bad law, absence of

Preface

cases invariably makes for dull law, and robs the learning process of its more enjoyable features. I have tried to state the law as at September 30, 1989, with the addition of some references to the effects of the Companies Act 1989, which assumed its final form when the book was in proof.

In my exploration of the fascinating realm of insolvency law I have had the advantage over the years of receiving the active encouragement and assistance of many wise and respected friends and colleagues. It is not possible here to list the names of all those who have helped to shape my understanding of the subject. Nevertheless, I feel it would be an unpardonable discourtesy if I were to fail to acknowledge openly the special quality of the help and inspiration provided unstintingly by David Graham, Q.C., Professor Douglass Boshkoff, Professor Clive Schmitthoff, Muir Hunter, Q.C., and Philip Pink, formerly Senior Official Receiver. While none of these should be held accountable for any errors or defects in this book (for which I accept full and sole responsibility), they have greatly helped to enhance such worthwhile qualities as it may possess.

By no means for the first time, I find myself quite unable to express in adequate terms the true measure of any indebtedness to my wife and colleague, Letitia Crabb, for all that she has done to enable me to complete the task of writing this book. With her permission, I dedicate it to our two sons, for whom over many months their father's preoccupation has doubtless seemed near akin to a "brooding omnipresence in the sky", producing an almost total eclipse of the sunnier aspects of normal family life. *Fiat Lux*.

Aberystwyth
October 1989

Ian F. Fletcher

CONTENTS

	Page
Preface to the First Edition	ix
Preface to the Second Edition	vii
Table of Cases	xx
Table of Statutes	lxvii
Table of Statutory Instruments	xc
Table of County Court Rules	c
Rules of the Supreme Court	ci

1 The Nature and Incidence of Insolvency   1

    Distinction Between "Insolvency" and "Bankruptcy"   4
    Historical Development of the Law   6
    The Reform and Development of the Law in Modern Times   13

2 The Evolution of the Administrative Machinery of Insovency Law   23

    The Department of Trade and Industry; The Insolvency Service; Official Receivers   24
    Insolvency Practitioners   26

PART I   PERSONAL INSOLVENCY   33

3 Bankruptcy Law in Outline   35

4 Voluntary Procedures and Alternatives to Bankruptcy   41

    (A) Formal Procedures   41
       (1) Individual Voluntary Arrangements   41
          (A) Arrangements Prior to Adjudication   42
          (B) Arrangements Subsequent to Adjudication   53
          (C) The Current Validity of Cases Decided under Earlier Legislation   56
       (2) Deeds of Arrangement   59

	(3) Administration Orders	60
(B)	Informal Procedures	66

5 Who Can be Made Bankrupt?   69

(A)	Who is a "debtor"?	70
(B)	The Debtor's Personal Amenability to the Jurisdiction of the English Courts	74
(C)	Special Categories of Debtor	76

6 The Bankruptcy Petition   81

(A)	Who May Present a Petition?	81
	(1) Creditor's Petition	82
	(A) Who is a Creditor?	82
	(B) Creditors Who are Ineligible to Petition	94
	(C) The Petitioning Creditor's Debt	101
	(2) Debtor's Petition	110
	(3) Petition Following Default in Connection with a Voluntary Arrangement	122
(B)	Procedure and Jurisdiction	124
	(1) Proper Court for Bankruptcy Proceeding	124
	(2) Procedural Requirements for Presentation of Petition	127
	(3) Hearing of the Petition	130
	Further Powers of the Court—All Petitions	134
	Further Powers of the Court: Protection of the Debtor's Estate	140

7 The Bankruptcy Order and its Consequences: (I)— General and Procedural Aspects   143

(A)	The Making of the Order	143
	Personal Situation of the Bankrupt	150
(B)	Consequential Proceedings	152
	Private Examination	152
	Public Examination	157
	First Meeting of Creditors; and Creditors' Meetings Generally	160
	The Trustee in Bankruptcy: Mode of Appointment	166
	Remuneration	170
	Powers of the Trustee	171
	The Trustee's Duties	175
	Resignation, Removal or Vacation of Office by the Trustee	180
	Creditors' Committee	182

Contents

8 The Bankruptcy Order and its Consequences: (II)—Proprietary Effects   187

  (A) The Basic Principles Governing the Composition of the Bankrupt's Estate   188
    (1) Property Vesting in the Trustee   188
        Choses in Action (Including Rights of Action)   191
        The Bankrupt's Home   194
        After-Acquired Property   199
        The Bankrupt's Income   203
    (2) Property not Vesting in the Trustee   209
        Property Which the Bankrupt has Ceased to Own   212
        Reservation of Title Clauses   216
        Exempt Property and Family Assets   218
  (B) Extension of the Trustee's Title   221
      Transactions at an Undervalue   221
      Preferences   226
      Extortionate Credit Transactions   230
      Avoidance of Unregistered General Assignments of Book Debts   231
      Transactions Defrauding Creditors   232
  (C) Curtailment of the Trustee's Title   234
      Property Disclaimed by the Trustee   235
      Distress or Execution Levied   240
      Dispositions or Payments Approved by the Court Protected Transactions   244
      Payments Designed to Avert Bankruptcy   246

9 Proof of Debts   249

  (A) Which Debts may be Proved?   250
      The Rule against Double Proof   255
      Contingent Liabilities   262
      Guarantors (Sureties)   267
      Costs   269
      Set-Off   272
      Proof for Interest   279
  (B) Mode of Proof   279
      Secured Creditors   281
      Admission and Rejection of Proofs   285

10 Distribution of Assets   287

  (A) Priority of Distribution of Assets   288
  (B) Second Bankruptcy   299
  (C) Declaration and Payment of Dividend   301

Contents

    (D) Final Distribution and Final Meeting   303

11 Termination of Bankruptcy   307

    (A) Automatic Discharge   307
    (B) Discharge by Order of the Court   309
        Appeals   314
        The Effect of Discharge   317
    (C) Annulment of Bankruptcy   322
        Effect of Annulment   325

12 Special Cases   327

    (A) Summary of Administration of Small Bankruptcies   327
    (B) Administration of Insolvent Estates of Deceased Persons   330

13 Bankruptcy and the Criminal Law   335

    (A) Bankruptcy Offences   337
        (a) Offences Arising from Conduct Prior to Presentation of the Petition   337
        (b) Offences Arising from Conduct Between the Presentation of the Petition and the Commencement of Bankruptcy ("the Initial Period")   346
        (c) Offences Arising from Conduct after the Commencement of Bankruptcy   348
    (B) Criminal Bankruptcy   355
        Abolition of Criminal Bankruptcy   355

PART II   COMPANY INSOLVENCY   357

Section A. Non Liquidation Procedures   357

14 Receivers   359

    (A) Types of Receiver   360
    (B) Receivers Appointed by the Court   362
    (C) Receivers Appointed Out of Court   368
    (D) General Issues Affecting Receivers   382

Section B. Alternatives to Winding Up   399

15 Company Voluntary Arrangements in England and Wales   401

Contents

The Proposal for a Voluntary Arrangement	402
Meetings of the Company and of its Creditors	407
Effects of Approval	411
Implementation of the Proposal	413
Completion of the Arrangement	414
Review and Reform of the Law	415

16 Company Administration Orders History — 419

When May an Administration Order be Made	421
When May an Administration Order not be Made	426
Who May Apply for an Administration Order	430
Procedure on Application for an Administration Order	432
Effect of an Application for an Administration Order	435
Hearing of the Administration Order Petition and Making of the Order	438
Effect of the Administration Order	442
The Administrator, his Appointment, Replacement, Resignation and Removal	449
Discharge of Administration Order and Release of Administrator	468
Review and Reform of the Law	478

SECTION B(1). THE WINDING UP OF INSOLVENT COMPANIES — 483

17 Winding Up Law in Outline — 485

Voluntary Winding Up	486
Compulsory Winding Up	487

SECTION B(2). CREDITORS' VOLUNTARY WINDING UP — 491

18 When Can a Creditors' Voluntary Winding Up Take Place? — 493

Distinction Between Members' and Creditors' Voluntary Winding Up	493
Conversion of Mode of Winding Up	496

19 Creditors' Voluntary Winding Up: to the Appointment of the Liquidator — 499

The New Law—Major Reforms	500
The Resolution for Voluntary Winding Up	504
Commencement of Voluntary Winding Up, and Consequences Thereof	505

Contents

Meeting of Creditors	507
Appointment of Liquidator	509
Resignation or Removal of Liquidator: Vacation of Office	511
Powers and Duties of the Liquidator	513
Appointment of Liquidation Committee	514

Section B(3). Compulsory Winding Up (Winding Up by the Court) — 517

20 When Can a Compulsory Winding Up Take Place? — 519

The Grounds on which Winding Up may take Place	522
(a) Registered companies	522
Company Unable to Pay its Debts	523
(b) Unregistered companies	528
Company Unable to Pay its Debts	530
Application to Foreign Companies	531

21 The Winding Up Petition — 533

Who may Present a Petition?	533
Jurisdiction and Procedure	541
Presentation and Service of the Petition	543
Advertisement of the Petition	544
Hearing of the Petition	547
Appeals	549
Provisional Liquidators and Special Managers	550

22 The Winding Up Order and its Consequences — 553

Notice and Settling of the Order	553
Commencement of Winding Up	554
Effects of the Order	554
Steps to the Appointment of a Liquidator	558
Appointment of Liquidator	572
First Meetings of Creditors and Contributories—Nomination of Liquidator	577
Resignation or Removal of Liquidator; Vacation of Office and Release	580
The Status, Duties and Powers of the Liquidator	582
The Liquidator's Books and Accounts	587
The Liquidation Committee	589

Section B(4). Aspects Common to Both Forms of Insolvent Liquidation — 593

CONTENTS

23 Proof of Debts — 595

Provable Debts — 595
Mode of Proving — 598
Set-Off — 599
Secured Creditors — 600
Non-provable Debts — 601

24 Collection and Distribution of Assets — 603

Augmentation of the Available Assets — 603
Disclaimer of Onerous Property — 604
Priority of Distribution of Assets — 606
The *pari passu* Principle: Tradition and Reality — 613
Declaration and Payment of Dividend — 616

25 The Conclusion of the Winding Up: Dissolution and After — 617

Final Meeting Prior to Dissolution — 617
Dissolution of the Company: Compulsory Winding Up — 619
Dissolution of Company: Voluntary Winding Up — 621
Official Notification: Dissolution by Striking Off — 621
Effect of Dissolution — 622
Dissolution Declared Void — 623

26 The Effects of Winding Up on Creditors and Third Parties — 627

The Advent of Winding Up: Preserving the Status Quo — 628
Dispositions and Transfers after Winding Up: Validation Orders — 628
Distress or Execution Levied — 632
Secured Creditors — 633
Reservation of Title Clauses — 634
Trust Devices — 637
Recovery of Assets Previously Disposed of by the Company: Adjustment of Antecedent Transactions — 640
Transactions at an Undervalue — 641
Preferences — 642
Connected Persons — 643
The Relevant Time — 644
Extortionate Credit Transactions — 647

Avoidance of Certain Floating Charges 648
Transactions Defrauding Creditors 650

27 Liability of Directors and Others 653

(A) Criminal Offences Before and During Liquidation 653
(B) Civil Remedies and Penalties Applicable to Directors and Officers 657
(C) Prosecution of Delinquent Officers and Members; Disqualification of Directors 667

Matters for Determining Unfitness of Directors 670

PART III INTERNATIONAL INSOLVENCY 679

28 General Problems, and Issues of Principle 681

General Problems Associated with Bankruptcies Containing International Elements 682
General Problems Associated with Liquidations Containing International Elements 683
Conflicts of Principles: Unity Versus Plurality; Universality Versus Territoriality 684

29 Bankruptcies with an International Element: The English Law and Practice 691

Jurisdiction to Adjudicate 691
International Effects of an English Adjudication 703
The Recognition of Foreign Adjudications at English Law 718
Recognition in England of the Proprietary Effects of a Foreign Adjudication 720
The Effects in England of a Foreign Discharge from Bankruptcy 723
Concurrent Bankruptcies 727

30 Liquidations with an International Element 731

Jurisdiction to Wind Up Foreign Companies in England 731

Contents

	International Effects of an English Winding Up	749
	Recognition of Foreign Liquidations	758
	Effect of Foreign Liquidation over English Assets	763
	Concurrent Liquidations	765
31	**International Regulation of Cross-Border Insolvency**	**767**
	The Draft Bankruptcy Convention of the European Union	769
	The European Bankruptcy Convention of the Council of Europe: The Istanbul Convention	777
	Judicial Co-operation in Cross-Border Insolvencies: The Way Ahead?	782
	Co-operation by United Kingdom Courts: Section 426 of the Insolvency Act 1986	784

Appendices   791

Index   811

TABLE OF CASES

A.B. & Co., Re [1900] 1 Q.B. 541; affirmed sub nom. Cook v. C.A. Vogeler & Co. [1901] A.C. 102, H.L. 696
——, Re (No. 2) [1900] 2 Q.B. 429, 69 L.J.Q.B. 568; 82 L.T. 544; 48 W.R. 485; 16 T.L.R. 365; 44 S.J. 448; 7 Mans. 268, C.A. 101
A. & B.C. Chewing Gum, Re; Topps Chewing Gum Inc. v. Coakley [1975] 1 W.L.R. 579; [1975] 1 All E.R. 1017; (1974) 119 S.J. 233 550
A.T. & T. Istel v. Tully [1993] A.C. 45; [1992] 3 W.L.R. 344; [1992] 3 All E.R. 523; [1992] 136 S.J. (LB) 227; (1992) 142 New L.J. 1088, H.L.; reversing [1992] Q.B. 315; [1992] 2 W.L.R. 112; [1992] 2 All E.R. 28; (1992) 142 New L.J. 88, C.A. 566
Abidin Daver, The. see Las Mercedes (Owners) v. Abidin Daver (Owners)
Aboulouff v. Oppenheimer (1882) 10 Q.B.D. 295 .... 694, 716
Adams, ex p. Culley, Re (1878) 9 Ch.D. 307; 47 L.J.Bcy. 97; 38 L.T. 858; 27 W.R. 27, C.A. 84
——, ex p. Griffen, Re (1879) 12 Ch.D. 480; 48 L.J.Bcy. 107; 41 L.T. 515; 28 W.R. 208, C.A. 99
—— v. Cape Industries plc [1990] Ch. 433; [1990] 2 W.L.R. 657; [1991] 1 All E.R. 929; [1990] B.C.L.C. 479; [1990] B.C.C. 786, C.A. 694
—— v. National Bank of Greece S.A., Darling v. National Bank of Greece S.A. [1961] A.C. 255; [1960] 3 W.L.R. 8; [1960] 2 All E.R. 421; 104 S.J. 489; reversing [1960] 1 Q.B. 64; [1959] 2 W.L.R. 800; [1959] 2 All E.R. 362; 103 S.J. 431, C.A.; affirming [1958] 2 Q.B. 59; [1958] 2 W.L.R. 588; [1958] 2 All E.R. 3; 102 S.J. 251 .... 734, 758, 762
Adebayo v. Official Receiver of Nigeria [1954] 1 W.L.R. 681; [1954] 2 All E.R. 197; 98 S.J. 286, P.C. 539
Adelaide Electric Supply Co. Ltd v. Prudential Assurance Co. Ltd [1934] A.C. 122, H.L. 763
Adlords Motor Group Holdings Ltd, Re [1990] B.C.L.C. 68 564
Adviser (188) Ltd, ex p. Trachtenbers, see Arrows (No. 4), Re; Bishopsgate Management, Re; Headington Investments, Re
A.G. v. Jackson [1932] A.C. 365, H.L. 277, 332
Affleck v. Hammond [1912] 3 K.B. 162; 81 L.J.K.B. 565; 106 L.T. 8; 19 Mans. 111, C.A. 204
Agricultural Industries Ltd, Re [1952] 1 All E.R. 1188; [1952] W.N. 209, C.A. . 577
Aiden Shipping Co. v. Interbulk; Vimera, The [1986] A.C. 965; [1986] 2 W.L.R. 1051; [1986] 2 All E.R. 409; [1986] 2 Lloyd's Rep. 117; (1986) 83 L.S.Gaz. 1895; (1986) 136 New L.J. 514, H.L.; (1985) 1 W.L.R. 1222; (1985) 129 S.J. 812; (1985) 82 L.S.Gaz. 3529; (1985) 135 New L.J. 1165, C.A.; reversing (1986) 130 S.J. 429; [1985] 3 All E.R. 641; [1986] 1 Lloyd's Rep. 107; [1985] 2 Lloyd's Rep. 377 549
Air Ecosse Ltd v. Civil Aviation Authority [1987] S.L.T. 751; (1987) 3 B.C.C. 492 .... 436, 442, 443
Air Express Foods Pty. Ltd, Re [1977] Qd. R. 107 766
Airlines Airspares Ltd v. Handley Page Ltd [1970] 1 Chap. 193 .... 388, 389
Akerman, Re, Akerman v. Akerman [1891] 3 Ch. 212; 61 L.J.Ch. 34; 65 L.T. 194; 40 W.R. 12 277

Table of Cases

Alan (W.J.) & Co. Ltd v. El Nasr Import and Export Co. [1972] 2 All E.R. 127; [1972] 2 Q.B. 189; [1972] 2 W.L.R. 800; 116 S.J. 139; [1972] 1 Lloyd's Rep. 313 260
Alivon v. Furnival (1834) 1 C.M. & R. 277; 149 E.R. 1084; 4 Tyr. 751; 3 L.J. 241 720
Allen v. Bonnett (1870) 5 Ch.App. 577; 23 L.T. 437; 18 W.R. 874, L.C. & L.JJ. 245
Alliance & Leicester Building Society v. Ghahremani [1992] RVR 198; [1992] 142 New L.J. 313; *The Times*, March 19, 1992 340
Allied Dunbar Assurance plc v. Fowle [1994] B.C.C. 422 625
Allobrogia Steamship Corp., *Re* [1978] 3 All E.R. 423 .... 736, 737, 744
Aluminium Industrie Vaassen B.V. v. Romalpa Aluminium Ltd [1976] 1 W.L.R. 676; [1976] 2 All E.R. 552; 120 S.J. 95; [1976] 1 Lloyd's Rep. 443; affirming (1975) 119 S.J. 318 .... 217, 635, 636
Amalgamated Properties of Rhodesia, *Re* [1917] 2 Ch. 115; 33 T.L.R. 414, C.A. 526, 537
Amec Properties Ltd v. Planning Research & Systems plc [1992] 13 E.G. 109, C.A. 389
American Express Banking Corp. v. Hurley 1985 FLR 350; [1985] 3 All E.R. 564; (1985) 135 New L.J. 1034, D.C. 395, 396, 397
Anantapadmanabhaswami v. Official Receiver of Secunderabad [1933] A.C. 394; 102 L.J.P.C. 77; 149 L.T. 54; 49 T.L.R. 316, C.A. 720
Anderson, *Re* [1911] 1 K.B. 896; 80 L.J.K.B. 919; 104 L.T. 221; 18 Mans. 217 .... 206, 718
Andrabell Ltd, *Re* [1984] 3 All E.R. 407 635
Andrews, *Re* (1881) 18 Ch.D. 464 .... 50, 311
Araya v. Coghill, 1921 S.L.T. 321; [1921] S.C. 462; 58 Sc.L.R. 395 .... 720, 722
Archer, *ex p.* Archer, *Re* (1904) 20 T.L.R. 390 119
Arctic Engineering Ltd, (No. 2), *Re* [1986] 1 W.L.R. 686; [1986] 2 All E.R. 346; (1985) 130 S.J. 429; [1986] P.C.C. 1; (1986) 83 L.S.Gaz. 1895 .... 511, 672
Argentum Reductions (U.K.) Ltd, *Re* [1975] 1 W.L.R. 186 631
Armani v. Castrique (1844) 13 M. & W. 443; 2 Dow. & L. 432; 14 L.J. Ex. 36; 153 E.R. 185 .... 692, 710, 725
Armitage v. A.-G., Gilliq v. Gilliq [1906] P. 135; 75 L.J.P. 42; 94 L.T. 614; 22 T.L.R. 306 .... 693, 719, 723
Armour v. Thyssen Edelstahlwerke A.G. [1991] 2 A.C. 339; [1990] 3 W.L.R. 810; [1990] 3 All E.R. 481; (1990) 134 S.J. 1337; [1991] 1 Lloyd's Rep. 395; [1991] B.C.L.C. 28; [1990] B.C.C. 925 636
Armstrong, *ex p.* Lindsay, *Re* [1892] 1 Q.B. 327; 65 L.T. 464; 40 W.R. 159; 7 T.L.R. 749; 49 Cox C.C. 349; 8 Morr. 271 153
Army and Navy Hotel, *Re* (1886) 31 Ch.D. 644; 55 L.J.Ch. 511; 34 W.R. 389; 2 T.L.R. 349 545
Aro Co., *Re* [1980] Ch. 196, [1980] 2 W.L.R. 453; (1979) 124 S.J. 15; [1980] 1 All E.R. 1067, C.A.; reversing [1979] Ch. 613; [1979] 2 W.L.R. 150; [1979] 1 All E.R. 32; (1978) 122 S.J. 625, D.C. 556
Arrows (No. 2), *Re*, [1992] Ch. 545; [1992] 2 W.L.R. 923; [1992] B.C.C. 125; [1992] B.C.L.C. 126; [1991] NPC 114 .... 565, 568
Arrows, *Re* (No. 3) [1992] B.C.C. 131; [1992] B.C.L.C. 555 439
——, *Re* (No. 4); Bishopsgate Investment Management, *Re*; Headington Investments, *Re* [1993] Ch. 452; [1993] 3 W.L.R. 513; [1993] 3 All E.R. 861; [1993] B.C.C. 473; [1993] B.C.L.C. 1222; (1993) 143 New L.J. 688, C.A.; reversing [1993] B.C.L.C. 424; [1992] B.C.C. 987 566
——, *Re* (No. 4) [1994] B.C.C. 641 .... 566, 567, 568
Art Reproduction Co. Ltd, *Re* [1952] Ch. 89; [1951] 2 All E.R. 984; [1951] 2 T.L.R. 979; 95 S.J. 745 596
Arthur (L.P.) Insurance Ltd v. Sisson [1966] 1 W.L.R. 1384 364
Artola Hermanos, *ex p.* André Châle, *Re* (1890) 24 Q.B.D. 640; 59 L.J.Q.B. 254; 62 L.T. 781; 6 T.L.R. 271; 7 Morr. 80, C.A. 728
Ash & Newman Ltd v. Creative Devices Ltd [1991] B.C.L.C. 403 389
Ashby, *ex p.* Wreford, *Re* [1892] 1 Q.B. 872; 66 L.T. 353; 40 W.R. 430; 9 Morr. 77 215

Table of Cases

Ashwin, *ex p.* Ashwin, *Re* (1890) 25 Q.B.D. 271; 59 L.J.Q.B. 417; 7 Morr. 175, C.A.; *subsequent proceedings* (1891) 8 Morr. 130 151
Associated Dominions Assurance Society Pty. Ltd, *Re* (1962) 109 CLR 516 583
Associated Travel Leisure and Services (In Liquidation), *Re* [1978] 1 W.L.R. 547; [1978] 2 All E.R. 273; (1977) 121 S.J. 790 592
Astor-Chemical Ltd v. Synthetic Technology Ltd [1990] B.C.C. 97; [1990] B.C.L.C. 1 435
Atherton, *Re* [1912] 2 K.B. 251; 81 L.J.K.B. 791; 106 L.T. 641; 28 T.L.R. 339; 56 S.J. 446; 19 Mans. 126 158
Atlantic Computer Systems, *Re* (No. 1) [1992] Ch. 505; [1992] 2 W.L.R. 367; [1992] 1 All E.R. 476; [1990] B.C.C. 859; [1991] B.C.L.C. 606, C.A.; reversing [1990] B.C.C. 454; [1990] B.C.L.C. 729 .... 394, 444, 445, 470
Att.-Gen.'s Reference (No. 1 of 1981) [1982] Q.B. 848; [1982] 2 W.L.R. 875; [1982] 2 All E.R. 417; (1982) 126 S.J. 210; [1982] Crim.L.R. 512, C.A. ... 338
Attree, *ex p.* Ward, *Re* [1907] 2 K.B. 868; 77 L.J.K.B. 130; 97 L.T. 641; 23 T.L.R. 734; 51 S.J. 687; 15 Mans. 9, D.C. 285
Austin, *ex p.* Austin, *Re* (1876) 4 Ch.D. 13; 46 L.J. Bcy 1; 35 L.T. 529; 25 W.R. 51, C.A. 153
Australian Mutual Provident Society v. Gregory (1908) 5 C.L.R. 615 722
Autolook Pty. Ltd, *Re* (1983) 8 ACLR 419 583
Avatar Communications, *Re* (1988) 4 B.C.C. 473, D.C. 570
Ayerst v. C. & K. (Construction) Ltd [1976] A.C. 167, [1975] 3 W.L.R. 16; [1975] 2 All E.R. 537; 119 S.J. 424; [1975] S.T.C. 345; [1975] T.R. 117, H.L.; affirming [1975] 1 W.L.R. 191; [1975] 1 All E.R. 162; (1974) 119 S.J. 100; [1975] S.T.C. 1; [1974] T.R. 269, C.A.; affirming [1974] 1 All E.R. 676; [1974] S.T.C. 98; [1973] T.R. 303 .... 583, 751
Aylmer, *ex p.* Bischoffsheim, *Re* (1887) 20 Q.B.D. 258; 57 L.J.Q.B. 168; 36 W.R. 231; 4 T.L.R. 174, C.A. 57
Aylwin's Trusts, *Re* (1873) L.R. 16 Eq. 585; 42 L.J.Ch. 745; 28 L.T. 865; 21 W.R. 864 722
Ayres, *Re* (1981) 51 F.L.R. 395; (1981) 56 F.L.R. 235; (1981) 39 A.L.R. 129 .. 254
——— v. Evans (1981) 39 A.L.R. 707
Azoff-Don Commercial Bank, *Re* [1954] 1 Ch. 315; [1954] 2 W.L.R. 654; [1954] 1 All E.R. 947; 98 S.J. 252 .... 711, 734, 736, 737, 741, 744, 751, 761, 764

Baby Moon Ltd, *Re* (1985) P.C.C. 103; (1985) 1 B.C.C. 298 542
Bacon (M.C.) Ltd, *Re* [1990] B.C.C. 78; [1990] B.C.L.C. 324 ..... 218, 228, 233, 642
———, *Re* (No. 2) [1991] Ch. 127; [1990] 3 W.L.R. 646 .... 607, 643
Badcock, *Re* (1886) 3 Morr. 138 313
Bagley, *Re* [1911] 1 K.B. 317; 80 L.J.K.B. 168; 103 L.T. 470; 55 S.J. 48; 18 Mans. 1, C.A. 88, 91
Bailey v. Thurston & Co. Ltd [1903] 1 K.B. 137; 72 L.J.K.B. 36; 88 L.T. 43; 51 W.R. 162; 19 T.L.R. 75; 47 S.J. 91; 10 Mans. 1, C.A. 192
Bailey (A Bankrupt) (No. 25 of 1975), *Re*; Bailey v. Trustee of the Property of the Bankrupt [1977] 1 W.L.R. 278; [1977] 2 All E.R. 26, D.C. 195
Baillie, *ex p.* Cooper, *Re* (1875) L.R. 20 Eq. 762; 44 L.J.Bkcy. 125; 32 L.T. 780 .... 87, 88, 89
Baker, *ex p.* Baker, *Re* (1887) 5 Mor. 5; 58 L.T. 233; 36 W.R. 558 99
———, *ex p.* Lupton, *Re* [1901] 2 K.B. 628 238
———, *Re* (1890) 44 Ch.D. 262 331
Balfour's Settlement, Public Trustee v. Official Receiver, *Re* [1938] 1 Ch. 928; [1938] 3 All E.R. 259; 107 L.J.Ch. 429; 159 L.T. 83; 54 T.L.R. 895; 82 S.J. 493 214
Banco de Bilbao v. Sancha, Banco de Bilbao v. Rey [1938] 2 All E.R. 253; [1938] 2 K.B. 176; 107 L.J.K.B. 681; 159 L.T. 369; 54 T.L.R. 603; 82 S.J. 254, C.A. 758, 759, 760
Banco de Portugal v. Waddell (1880) 5 App.Cas. 161; 49 L.J. Bcy. 33; 42 L.T. 698; 28 W.R. 477, H.L. 713, 754
Bank of Credit and Commerce International SA, *Re* [1992] B.C.C. 83; [1992] B.C.L.C. 570 551

Table of Cases

Bank of Credit and Commerce International SA, (No. 2), *Re* [1992] B.C.C. 715; [1992] B.C.L.C. 579 .... 683, 786
—— (No. 3), *Re* [1993] B.C.C. 787; [1993] B.C.L.C. 106; *The Independent*, October 1, 1992, C.A. 786
—— *v.* B.R.S. Kumar Ltd [1994] B.C.L.C. 211 .... 360, 363
Bank of Ethiopia *v.* National Bank of Egypt [1937] 1 Ch. 513; [1937] 3 All E.R. 8; 106 L.J. Ch. 279; 157 L.T. 428; 53 T.L.R. 751; 81 S.J. 479 .... 759, 760, 761
Bank of South Australia (No. 2), *Re* [1895] 1 Ch. 578; (1895) 2 Mans. 148; 64 L.J.Ch. 397; 72 L.T. 273; 43 W.R. 359; 39 S.J. 314; 12 R 166; *sub nom. Re* Bank of South Australia Ltd, *ex p.* Union Bank of Australia 11 T.L.R. 265, C.A. 578
Banque des Marchands de Moscou (Koupetschesky), *Re*, Moscow Merchants' Trading Co., *Re* [1958] Ch. 182; [1957] 3 W.L.R. 637; [1957] 3 All E.R. 182; 101 S.J. 798 .... 735, 741, 758, 763, 764
——, *Re* (No. 2) [1954] 1 W.L.R. 1108; [1954] 2 All E.R. 746; 98 S.J. 557 ... 734, 758, 762, 763, 764
Banque des Marchands de Moscou *v.* Kindersley [1951] 1 Ch. 112; 66 T.L.R. (Pt. 2) 654; [1950] 2 All E.R. 549; affirming (1950) 66 T.L.R. (Pt. 1) 1147 ... 734, 736, 744, 761
Banque Industrielle de Moscou, *Re* [1952] 1 Ch. 919; [1952] 2 T.L.R. 406; [1952] 2 All E.R. 532 .... 734, 741, 764
Banque International de Commerce de Petrograd *v.* Goukassow [1925] A.C. 150, 93 L.J.K.B. 1084; 132 L.T. 116; 40 T.L.R. 837; 68 S.J. 841, H.L. ... 759, 761, 762
Barclays Bank Ltd *v.* Quistclose Investments Ltd [1970] A.C. 567; [1968] 3 W.L.R. 1097; [1968] 3 All E.R. 651; 112 S.J. 903, H.L. affirming *sub nom.* Quistclose Investments *v.* Rolls Razor (In Liquidation) [1968] Ch. 540; [1968] 2 W.L.R. 478; *sub nom.* Quistclose Investments *v.* Rolls Razor (In Voluntary Liquidation) [1968] 1 All E.R. 613; [1967] C.L.Y. 514 .... 209, 247, 637
—— *v.* TOSG Trust Fund [1984] A.C. 626; [1984] 2 W.L.R. 650; [1984] 1 All E.R. 1060; (1984) 128 S.J. 261; (1984) 81 L.S.Gaz. 1360; (1984) 134 New L.J. 656, H.L.; affirming [1984] 2 W.L.R. 49; [1984] 1 All E.R. 628, C.A., (1983) 127 S.J. 730 596
—— *v.* Willowbrook International Ltd [1986] B.C.L.C. 45; [1987] FTLR 386; [1987] B.C.L.C. 717, C.A. 456
Barclays Mercantile Business Finance Ltd *v.* Sibec Developments Ltd [1992] 1 W.L.R. 1253; [1993] 2 All E.R. 195; [1993] B.C.C. 148; [1993] B.C.L.C. 1077 446
Barker, *Re* (1890) 25 Q.B.D. 285 312
Barlow Clowes Gilt Managers Ltd, *Re* [1992] 2 W.L.R. 36; [1991] 4 All E.R. 385; [1991] B.C.C. 608; [1991] B.C.L.C. 750; [1991] N.P.C. 73; (1991) 141 New L.J. 999 567
Barn Crown Ltd, *Re* [1994] B.C.C. 381 630
Barne, *ex p.* Barne, *Re* (1886) 16 Q.B.D. 522; 54 L.T. 662; 3 Morr. 33, C.A. ... 700
Barnett *v.* King [1891] 1 Ch. 4; 60 L.J.Ch. 148; 63 L.T. 501; 39 W.R. 39; 7 T.L.R. 24; 7 Morr. 267, C.A. 263
Baroness Wenlock *v.* River Dee Co. (1883) 36 Ch.D. 674 734
Barr, *ex p.* Wolfe, *Re* [1896] 1 Q.B. 616; 65 L.J.Q.B. 504; 74 L.T. 555; 44 W.R. 586; 40 S.J. 518; 3 Mans. 97, D.C. 105
Barrow Borough Transport Ltd, *Re* [1990] Ch. 227; [1989] 3 W.L.R. 858; [1989] 3 W.L.R. 858; [1989] B.C.L.C. 653; (1989) 133 S.J. 1513; [1989] L.S.Gaz. November 22, 39 436
Bartley *v.* Hodges (1861) 1 B. & S. 375; 30 L.J.Q.B. 352; 4 L.T. 445; 8 Jur. (N.S.) 52; 9 W.R. 693; 121 E.R. 754 .... 692, 725
Bastable, *ex p.* Trustee, *Re* [1901] 2 K.B. 518; 70 L.J.K.B. 784; 84 L.T. 825; 49 W.R. 561; 17 T.L.R. 560; 45 S.J. 576; 8 Mans. 239, C.A. 236
Bateson (John) & Co. Ltd, *Re* [1985] B.C.L.C. 259 .... 368, 448, 514
Batey, *ex p.* Emmanuel, *Re* (1881) 17 Ch.D. 35; 50 L.J. Ch. 305; 44 L.T. 832; 29 W.R. 526, C.A. 172
Bath Glass Ltd, *Re* (1988) 4 B.C.C. 130; [1988] B.C.L.C. 329 672
Baughan, *ex p.* Official Receiver *v.* Bennett, *Re* [1947] 1 Ch. 313; [1947] 1 All E.R. 417; [1947] L.J.R. 805; 176 L.T. 396; 63 T.L.R. 203; 91 S.J. 116 298

Table of Cases

Baum, *ex p.* Baum, *Re* (1878) 7 Ch.D. 719; 47 L.J.Bcy. 48; 38 L.T. 367; 26 W.R. 568, C.A. 58
——, *ex p.* Evans, *Re* (1880) 13 Ch.D. 424; 49 L.J.Bcy. 25; 42 L.T. 384; 28 W.R. 500, C.A. 165
Beacon Leisure Ltd, *Re* [1990] B.C.C. 213 643
Beale, *ex p.* Board of Trade, *Re* [1939] Ch. 761; 108 L.J. Ch. 297; 160 L.T. 618; 83 S.J. 417; [1938–1939] B. & C.R. 117 169
Beall, *ex p.* Beall, *Re* [1894] 2 Q.B. 135; 63 L.J.Q.B. 425; 70 L.T. 643; 1 Mans. 203; 9 R. 475, C.A. 154
——, *ex p.* Official Receiver, *Re* [1899] 1 Q.B. 688; 68 L.J.Q.B. 462; 80 L.T. 267; 43 S.J. 226; 6 Mans. 163 200
Beauchamp, *Re* [1904] 1 K.B. 572; 73 L.J.K.B. 31; 90 L.T. 594; 52 W.R. 542; 20 T.L.R. 269; 11 Mans. 5 *sub nom. Re* Debtor, *ex p.* Debtor, 48 S.J. 297, C.A. 135
Bebro, *Re* [1900] 2 Q.B. 316; 69 L.J.Q.B. 618; 82 L.T. 773; 48 W.R. 561; 7 Mans. 284; *sub nom. Re* M.B., *ex p.* G., 44 S.J. 501, C.A. 98
Beckham *v.* Drake (1849) 2 H.L.C. 579; 9 E.R. 1213; 13 Jur. 921; affirming S.C. *sub nom.* Drake *v.* Beckham (1843), 11 M. & W. 315, Ex. Ch. 192
Beer, *Re* [1903] 1 K.B. 628, C.A.; 72 L.J.K.B. 366; 88 L.T. 344; 51 W.R. 422; 19 T.L.R. 319; 47 S.J. 367; 10 Mans. 136, C.A. 56
Beesley (A.) (A Bankrupt), *Re, ex p.* Beesley (T.J.) *v.* Official Receiver [1975] 1 W.L.R. 568; (1974) S.J. 10; *sub nom.* Beesley (Audrey), *Re, ex p.* Beesley (Terence Jack) *v.* Official Receiver [1975] 1 All E.R. 385 324
Beeston, *Re* [1899] 1 Q.B. 626; 68 L.J.Q.B. 344; 80 L.T. 66; 47 W.R. 475; 43 S.J. 300; 6 Mans. 27; C.A. 205
Behrend's Trust, *Re* Surman *v.* Biddell [1911] 1 Ch. 687; 80 L.J.Ch. 394; 104 L.T. 626; 55 S.J. 459; 18 Mans. 111 200
Bell *v.* Kennedy (1868) L.R. 1 Sc. & Div. 307, H.L. 700
Bellaglade Ltd, *Re* [1977] 1 All E.R. 319 .... 555, 632
Belton, *Re* (1913) 108 L.T. 344; 29 T.L.R. 313; 57 S.J. 343 137
Bendall *v.* McWhirter [1952] 2 Q.B. 466; [1952] 1 T.L.R. 1332; 96 S.J. 344; 1 All E.R. 1307; C.L.Y. 257, C.A. 195
Benjamin, *Re* [1943] 1 All E.R. 468; 168 L.T. 425; 112 L.J.Ch. 163 313
Bennett [1907] 1 K.B. 149; 76 L.J.K.B. 134; 95 L.T. 887; 23 T.L.R. 99; 51 S.J. 83; 14 Mans. 6 200
Benzon, Bower *v.* Chetwynd, *Re* [1914] 2 Ch. 68; 83 L.J.Ch. 658; 110 L.T. 926; 30 T.L.R. 435; 58 S.J. 430; 21 Mans. 8, C.A. 206, 252
Bergerem *v.* Marsh (1921) 125 L.T. 630; L.J.K.B. 80 [1921] B. & C.R. 195 718
Berkeley Securities (Property) Ltd, *Re* [1980] 3 All E.R. 513; [1980] 1 W.L.R. 1589; (1980) 124 S.J. 880 .... 13, 257, 595, 597
Berry *v.* British Transport Commission [1962] 1 Q.B. 306; [1961] 3 W.L.R. 450; 3 All E.R. 65 100
Berry (Herbert) Associates *v.* I.R.C. [1977] 1 W.L.R. 1437; (1977) 121 S.J. 829; [1978] 1 All E.R. 161; [1977] T.R. 247; (1977) 52 T.C. 113, H.L.; affirming [1977] 1 W.L.R. 617; [1977] 3 All E.R. 729; [1977] T.R. 137; *sub nom.* Berry (Herbert) Associates (In Liquidation), *Re* (1977) 121 S.J. 252, C.A., affirming [1976] 1 W.L.R. 783; 3 All E.R. 207; (1976) 120 S.J. 538, D.C. 632
Best, *Re* (1881) 18 Ch.D. 488, 51 L.J.Ch. 293; 45 L.T. 95, C.A. 162
Bettle, *ex p.*, (1895) 14 N.Z.L.R. 129 .... 708, 722
Betts, *Re* [1901] 2 K.B. 39; 70 L.J.K.B. 511; 84 L.T. 427; 49 W.R. 447; 17 T.L.R. 383; 45 S.J. 381; 8 Mans. 227, D.C. 118, 119, 120, 695
——, *Re* [1897] 1 Q.B. 50; 66 L.J.Q.B. 14; 75 L.T. 292; 45 W.R. 98; 13 T.L.R. 23; 41 S.J. 50; 3 Mans. 287, C.A. 137, 695
Betts and Block, *Re* (1887) 19 Q.B.D. 39; affirmed *sub nom.* Board of Trade *v.* Block (1888) 13 App.Cas. 570; 59 L.T. 734, H.L. 312
Biederman *v.* Stone (1867) L.R. 2 C.P. 504; 16 L.T. 415; 15 W.R. 811 507
Birch (Samuel) Co., *Re* [1907] W.N. 31 545
Bird, *ex p.* Hill, *Re* (1883) 23 Ch.D. 695; 52 L.J.Ch. 903; 49 L.T. 278; 32 W.R. 177, C.A. 227
—— *v.* I.R.C., *Re, ex p.* The Debtor [1962] 1 W.L.R. 686; [1962] T.R. 173; *sub nom. Re* Bird *ex p.* The Debtor *v.* I.R.C., 106 S.J. 507; [1962] 2 All E.R. 406; *sub nom. Re* Bird, 41 A.T.C. 137, C.A. 697

TABLE OF CASES

Birkin, *Re* (1896) 3 Mans. 291, C.A. 137
Bishop (E.) & Sons Ltd, *Re* [1900] 2 Ch. 254; 69 L.J.Ch. 513; 82 L.T. 756; 7 Mans. 342 538
Bishopsgate Investment Management Ltd (In Liq.) *v.* Maxwell (No. 2) [1994] 1 All E.R. 261; [1993] B.C.L.C. 1282; [1983] B.C.C. 120, C.A. 569
Bishopsgate Investment Management *v.* Homan [1994] 3 W.L.R. 1270; [1995] 1 All E.R.; (1994) 138 S.J. (LB) 176; [1994] B.C.C. 868 C.A.
Bishopsgate Investment Management (In Provisional Liquidation) *v.* Maxwell; Cooper *v.* Maxwell; Mirror Group Newspapers *v.* Maxwell [1993] Ch. 1; [1992] 2 W.L.R. 99; 2 All E.R. 856; B.C.C. 222; (1992) 136 S.J.(LB) 69 C.A.; affirming [1992] B.C.C. 214 and [1992] B.C.C. 218; [1992] B.C.L.C. 470 .... 154, 155, 158
Bishopsgate Investment Management Ltd *v.* Maxwell [1992] B.C.C. 214 . 565, 571, 696
Bissell *v.* Jones (1868) L.R. 4 Q.B. 49; 9 B. & S. 884; 38 L.J.Q.B. 2; 19 L.T. 262; 17 W.R. 49 57
Bissill *v.* Bradford Tramways [1891] W.N. 51 363
Blackpool Motor Car Co., *Re* Hamilton *v.* Blackpool Motor Co. Ltd [1901] 1 Ch. 77 95
Blain, *ex p.* See *Re* Sawyers 696, 719
Blake, *ex p.* Coker, *Re* (1875) 10 Ch.App. 652; 44 L.J.Bcy. 126; 24 W.R. 145, L.JJ. 147
Blithman, *Re* (1866) L.R. 2 Eq. 23; 35 Beav. 219; 35 L.J.Ch. 255; 14 L.T. 6; 12 Jur. N.S. 84; 55 E.R. 879 .... 214, 718
Blount *v.* Whitely (1898) 6 Mans. 48; 79 L.T. 635 145
Bloxwich Iron and Steel Co., *Re* [1894] W.N. 111; 38 S.J. 546 510
Boaler *v.* Power [1910] 2 K.B. 229; 79 L.J.K.B. 486; 102 L.T. 450; 26 T.L.R. 358; 54 S.J. 360; 17 Mans. 125, C.A. 135
Board of Trade *v.* Employers Liability Assurance Corp. Ltd [1910] 2 K.B. 645 . . 177
Bolton, *Re* [1920] 2 I.R. 324 706
——, *ex p.* North British Artificial Silk Ltd, *Re* [1930] 2 Ch. 48; 99 L.J. Ch. 209; 143 L.T. 425; [1929] B. & C.R. 141 258
Bonacina, *Re* [1912] 2 Ch. 394; 28 T.L.R. 508; 56 S.J. 667 319
Bond, *Re* (1888) 21 Q.B.D. 17; 57 L.J.Q.B. 501; 58 L.T. 887; 36 W.R. 700; 5 Morr. 146 .... 118, 119, 120, 695
Bond Worth Ltd, *Re* [1980] Ch. 228; [1979] 3 W.L.R. 629; (1979) 123 S.J. 216; [1979] 3 All E.R. 919 .... 217, 636
Bonham, *Re* (1885) 14 Q.B.D. 604; 54 L.J.Q.B. 388; 52 L.T. 17; 33 W.R. 628, C.A. 254
Bonus Breaks Ltd, *Re* [1991] B.C.C. 546 .... 501, 666
Borden (U.K.) Ltd *v.* Scottish Timber Products Ltd [1981] Ch. 25; [1979] 3 W.L.R. 672; (1979) 123 S.J. 688; [1979] 3 All E.R. 961; [1980] 1 Lloyd's Rep. 160, C.A.; reversing [1979] 2 Lloyd's Rep. 168; (1978) 122 S.J. 825 ..... 217, 635
Borland's Trustee *v.* Steel Brothers & Co. Ltd [1901] 1 Ch. 279 215
Borneman *v.* Wilson (1884) 28 Ch.D. 53; 54 L.J.Ch. 631; 51 L.T. 728; 33 W.R. 141; 1 T.L.R. 64, C.A. 173
Boston Timber Fabrications Ltd, *Re* [1984] B.C.L.C. 328, C.A. 548
Bottomley, *Re* (1893) 10 Morr. 262 58
——, *ex p.* Brougham, *Re* (1915) 84 L.J.K.B. 1020; 59 S.J. 366; [1915] H.B.R. 75 158
—— *v.* Bell (1915) 31 T.L.R. 591; 59 S.J. 703, C.A. 192
—— *v.* Brougham [1908] 1 K.B. 584; 77 L.J.K.B. 311; 99 L.T. 111; 24 T.L.R. 262; 52 S.J. 225 311
Bowes, *Re* Strathmore (Earl) *v.* Vane [1889] W.N. 53 713
—— *v.* Hope Life Insurance and Guarantee Co. (1865) 11 H.L.C. 389; 11 E.R. 1383; 35 L.J.Ch. 574; 12 L.T. 680; 11 Jur.N.S. 643; 13 W.R. 790, H.L. . . 526, 538
Boyd *v.* Lee Guiness Ltd [1963] N.I. 49 753
Boys *v.* Chaplin. See Chaplin *v.* Boys 723
Bradley *v.* Eagle Star Insurance Co. Ltd [1989] 1 All E.R. 961; [1989] 2 W.L.R. 568; [1988] F.L.R. 238; [1988] 2 Lloyd's Rep. 233 624
Bradley-Hole *v.* Cusen [1953] 1 Q.B. 300; [1953] 2 W.L.R. 193; 97 S.J. 45; *sub nom.* Hole *v.* Cuzen [1953] 1 All E.R. 87 .... 206, 275

Table of Cases

Brandon v. McHenry [1891] 1 Q.B. 538; 39 W.R. 372; 7 T.L.R. 325 326
—— v. Robinson (1811) 18 Ves. Jun. 429; 34 E.R. 379; 1 Rose 197 214
Branson ex p. Trustee, Re [1914] 2 K.B. 701; 83 L.J.K.B. 1316; 110 L.T. 940; 58 S.J. 416; 21 Mans. 160 172
Brassard v. Smith [1925] A.C. 371, P.C. 763
Brauch, Re [1978] Ch. 316, C.A. 697, 698, 699
Brickland v. Newsome (1808) 1 Camp. 474; 170 E.R. 1026 94
Brickwood & Co., Re Bracken & Co., ex p. Waring, Re (1815) 19 Ves. Jun. 345; 34 E.R. 546 L.C.; 2 Rose 182; 2 Gl. & J. 404 210
Brickwood v. Miller (1817) 3 Mer. 279; 36 E.R. 108 714
Brierley (A.W.), Re 145 B.R. 151 (Bankr S.D.N.Y. 1992) 789
Briggs & Co., ex p. Wright, Re [1906] 2 K.B. 209; 75 L.J.K.B. 591; 95 L.T. 61; 50 S.J. 514 212
Bright, Re (1901) 18 T.L.R. 37; affirmed (1903) 19 T.L.R. 203 .... 698, 699
Brightlife Ltd, Re [1986] 3 All E.R. 673; [1987] Ch. 200; [1987] 2 W.L.R. 197; (1987) 131 S.J. 132; 1987 P.C.C. 435; (1987) L.S.Gaz. 653 610
Brightmore, ex p. May, Re (1844) 14 Q.B.D. 37; 51 L.T. 710; 33 W.R. 598; 1 Morr. 253, D.C. 127
Brighton Club and Norfolk Hotel Co. Ltd, Re (1865) 35 Beav. 204; 55 E.R. 873; 6 New Rep. 80; 12 L.T. 84; 11 Jur.N.S. 436; 13 W.R. 733 536
Brighton Hotel Co., Re (1868) 6 Eq. 339 537
Brindley, ex p. Taylor & Sons & Co., Re [1906] 1 K.B. 377; 75 L.J.K.B. 46; 22 T.L.R. 115; 12 Mans. 387, C.A. 96
Bristol Airport v. Powdrill [1990] Ch. 744; [1990] 2 W.L.R. 1362; [1990] 2 All E.R. 493; [1990] B.C.C. 130; [1990] B.C.L.C. 585; [1990] L.S.Gaz. May 9, 28, C.A. 436, 443, 444
British American Continental Bank, Re (Goldzieher and Penso's Claim) [1922] 2 Ch. 575 258
——, Re (Lisser and Rosenkranz's claim) [1923] 1 Ch. 276 258
British and Commonwealth Holdings (Joint Administrators) v. Spicer and Oppenheim, sub nom. British and Commonwealth Holdings (Nos. 1 and 2), Re [1993] A.C. 426; [1992] 3 W.L.R. 853; [1992] 4 All E.R. 876; [1992] B.C.C. 977; [1993] B.C.L.C. 168; (1992) 142 New L.J. 1611; The Times, November 3, 1992, H.L.; affirming [1992] Ch. 342; [1992] 2 W.L.R. 931; [1992] 2 All E.R. 801; [1992] B.C.C. 165 and [1992] B.C.C. 172; [1992] B.C.L.C. 641, The Times, December 31, 1991, C.A.; reversing [1991] B.C.C. 651 and [1991] B.C.C. 658; [1992] B.C.L.C. 306 and [1992] B.C.L.C. 314; Financial Times, November 6, 1991; The Times, November 8, 1991; Financial Times, August 6, 1991 .... 562, 569
British and Commonwealth Holdings plc, Re (No. 1) and (No. 2) [1992] 3 W.L.R. 853, H.L.; [1992] 2 W.L.R. 931, C.A. 461
——, Re (No. 2) [1992] 2 All E.R. 801; [1992] 2 W.L.R. 931; [1993] A.C. 426; [1992] 3 W.L.R. 853, H.L. 562, 563
—— (No. 1) [1992] Ch. 342; [1992] B.C.C. 165 569
British Airways Board v. Laker Airways Ltd [1985] A.C. 58; [1984] 3 W.L.R. 413; (1984) 128 S.J. 531; [1984] 3 All E.R. 39; [1984] L.M.C.L.Q. 563; [1985] E.C.C. 49; (1984) 134 New L.J. 746; (1984) 81 L.S.Gaz. 2849, H.L. reversing [1984] Q.B. 142; [1983] 3 W.L.R. 544; (1983) 127 S.J. 646; [1984] E.C.C. 304; (1983) 80 L.S.Gaz. 2437; [1983] Com.L.R. 254, C.A. 755
British Eagle International Airlines Ltd v. Cie. Nationale Air France [1975] 2 All E.R. 390; [1975] 1 W.L.R. 758, H.L. 614
British Folding Bed Co. ex p. Trustee v. Woodwiss & Co., Re [1948] Ch. 635; 1948 2 All E.R. 216; [1948] L.J.R. 1748 247
British Goldfields of West Africa, Re [1899] 2 Ch. 7; 68 L.J.Ch. 412; 80 L.T. 638; 47 W.R. 552; 15 T.L.R. 363; 43 S.J. 494; 6 Mans. 334, C.A. 270
Broadhurst, ex p. (1852) 2 De G.M. & G. 953; 42 E.R. 1145 104
Broads Patent Night Light Co., Re [1982] W.N. 5 545
Brocklebank, Re (1877) 6 Ch.D. 358; 46 L.J.Bcy. 113; 37 L.T. 282; 25 W.R. 859, C.A. 83
Brocklehurst v. Lawe (1857) 7 El. & Bl. 176; 119 E.R. 1213; 26 L.J.Q.B. 107; 3 Jur.N.S. 436; 5 W.R. 311 241

Table of Cases

Brooke v. Hewitt (1796) 3 Ves. Jun. 253; 30 E.R. 997 193
Brown, Re (1886) 32 Ch.D. 597 207
Browne, ex p. The Official Receiver v. Thompson, Re [1960] 2 All E.R. 625; [1960] 1 W.L.R. 692; (1960) 104 S.J. 545 .... 253, 286
Brown, Gow, Wilson v. Beleggings—Societeit N.V. (1961) 29 D.L.R. (2d) 673 .... 734, 763
Brunner, Re (1887) 19 Q.B.D. 572; 56 L.J.Q.B. 606; 57 L.T. 418; 35 W.R.719; 4 Morr. 255 158
Bryant Investment Co. Ltd, Re [1974] 1 W.L.R. 826; (1974) 118 S.J. 441; [1974] 2 All E.R. 683 524
Buchanan v. Rucker (1808) 9 East 192; 103 E.R. 546 694
Buchanan (Peter) Ltd v. McVey [1955] A.C. 516n; [1954] I.R. 89 .... 254, 707
Bullen, Re (1888) 5 Morr. 243; 36 W.R. 836 .... 313, 314
——, Re [1930] I.R. 82 706
Bulmer, ex p. Greaves, Re [1937] Ch. 499; 106 L.J.Ch. 268; 156 L.T. 178; 53 T.L.R. 303; 81 S.J. 117; [1936–37] B. & C.R. 196, C.A. 183
Bumpus, ex p. White, Re [1908] 2 K.B. 330; 77 L.J.K.B. 563; 98 L.T. 680; 52 S.J. 395; 15 Mans. 103 241
Burgoyne, ex p. Burgoyne, Re (1891) 8 Morr. 139, D.C. 151
Burke, King v. Terry, Re (1919) 54 L.Jo. 430; 148 L.T. Jo. 175 718
Burn (J.), Re [1932] 1 Ch. 247 178
Burr, ex p. Board of Trade, Re [1892] 2 Q.B. 467, C.A.; 61 L.J.Q.B. 591; 66 L.T. 553; 8 T.L.R. 515; 9 Morr. 133, C.A. 58
——, ex p. Clarke, Re (1892) 67 L.T. 232; 40 W.R. 608; 8 T.L.R. 671; 36 S.J. 628 164
—— v. Anglo French Banking Corp. Ltd (1933) 49 T.L.R. 405; 149 L.T. 282; 77 S.J. 448 .... 760, 761
Burroughs-Fowler, Re Burroughs-Fowler's Trustee v. Burroughs-Fowler [1916] 2 Ch. 251; 85 L.J.Ch. 550; 114 L.T. 1204; 32 T.L.R. 493; 60 S.J. 538; [1916] H.B.R. 108 214
Burrows v. Jemino (1726) 2 Stra. 733; 93 E.R. 815; Cas temp. King 69; Dick. 48; Mos 1; 2 Eq. Cas Abr. 524, Pl. 7 .... 692, 723
Burrows (J.) (Leeds) Ltd, Re, [1982] 2 All E.R. 882; 1 W.L.R. 1177; (1982) S.J. 227 514
Burrs & Co., ex p. Fore Street Warehouse Co. Ltd, Re (1874) 30 L.T. 624 58
Burt, Boulton and Hayward v. Bull [1895] 1 Q.B. 276, C.A.; [1891–4] All E.R. Rep. 1116; 64 L.J.Q.B. 232; 71 L.T. 810; 43 W.R. 180; 11 T.L.R. 90; 2 Mans. 94; 39 Sol. Jo. 95; 14 R. 65, C.A. 366
Burton & Deakin Ltd, Re [1977] 1 W.L.R. 390; [1977] 1 All E.R. 631; (1977) 121 Sol. Jo. 169 629
Bushell, ex p. Izard, Re (1883) 23 Ch.D. 75; 52 L.J.Ch. 678; 48 L.T. 751; 31 W.R. 418, C.A. 240
Business Computers International Ltd v. Registrar of Companies and Alex Lawrie Factors [1987] 3 All E.R. 465; 3 W.L.R. 1134; (1987) 131 S.J. 1628; [1988] Ch. 229; 1988 P.C.C. 16; (1985) 85 L.S.Gaz. 35; (1987) 137 New L.J. 758; (1987) 3 B.C.C. 395 544
Business Properties Ltd, Re (1988) 4 B.C.C. 684, D.C. 430
Busytoday, Re Popely v. Lewis [1992] B.C.C. 480 550
Butler v. Broadhead [1975] Ch. 97; [1974] 3 W.L.R. 27; (1973) 118 S.J. 115; [1974] 2 All E.R. 401 598
Button, ex p. Voss, Re [1905] 1 K.B. 602; 74 L.J.K.B. 403; 92 L.T. 250; 53 W.R. 437; 49 S.J.; 12 Mans. 111, C.A. 108

Cadiz Waterworks v. Barnett (1874) L.R. 19 Eq. 182; 44 L.J. Ch. 529; 31 L.T. 640; 23 W.R. 208 525
Caidan, ex p. The Official Receiver v. Regis Property Co. Ltd, Re [1942] Ch. 90; 111 L.J. Ch. 33; 58 T.L.R. 68; 86 S.J. 7; [1941] 3 All E.R. 491; [1940–42] B. & C.R. 87 242
Calahurst, Re [1989] B.C.L.C. 140; (1989) 5 B.C.C. 318 550

TABLE OF CASES

Callender Sykes & Co. v. Lagos Colonial Secretary & Davies, Williams & Davies [1891] A.C. 460; 60 L.J.P.C. 33; 65 L.T. 297, P.C. 705
Calvert, Re [1899] 2 Q.B. 145; 68 L.J.Q.B. 761; 47 W.R. 523; 43 S.J. 480; 6 Mans. 256; sub nom. Re: Calvert, ex p. The Debtor v. Walker, 80 L.T. 504; 4 Tax Cas. 79 .... 254, 286
Cammell v. Sewell (1860) 5 H. and N. 728; 157 C.R. 1371; 29 L.J. Ex. 350; 2 L.T. 799; 6 Jur. N.S. 918; 8 W.R. 639, Ex. Ch. 710, 717
Campbell, Re (1884) 14 Q.B.D. 32 245
——, ex p. Seal, Re [1911] 2 K.B. 992; 81 L.J.K.B. 154; 105 L.T. 529; 19 Mans. 1, C.A. 252
Cannon Screen Entertainment Ltd v. Handmade Films (Distributors) Ltd (1989) 5 B.C.C. 207 525
Carden v. Albert Palace Association (1886) 56 L.J. Ch. 166; sub nom. Re Albert Palace Assocn. Ltd, Carden v. Albert Palace Assocn. Ltd 55 L.T. 831 631
Caribbean Products (Yam Importers) Ltd Re, Tickler v. Swains Packaging [1966] 1 Ch. 331; 2 W.L.R. 153; 110 S.J. 32; [1966] 1 All E.R. 181; [1965] C.L.Y. 490, C.A. 244, 315, 556
Carl Zeiss Stiftung v. Rayner and Keeler Ltd [1967] 1 A.C. 853, sub nom. Carl Zeiss Stiftung v. Rayner & Keeler [1966] 3 W.L.R. 125; 110 S.J. 425; [1966] 2 All E.R. 536; [1967] R.P.C. 497, H.L. 734, 759
Carnac, ex p. Simmonds, Re (1885) 16 Q.B.D. 308; 54 L.T. 439; 34 W.R. 421 sub nom. Re Rivett-Carnac, ex p. Simmonds 55 L.J.Q.B. 74; 2 T.L.R. 18, C.A. . 207
Carr, ex p. Jacobs, Re (1901) 85 L.T. 552; 50 W.R. 336, D.C. 96
—— v. British International Helicopters Ltd [1993] B.C.C. 855; [1994] I.R.L.R. 212; [1994] I.C.R. 18; [1994] 2 B.C.L.C. 474, E.A.T. 443
Carreras Rothmans Ltd v. Freeman Mathews Treasure Ltd [1985] Ch. 207; [1984] 3 W.L.R. 1016; (1984) 128 S.J. 614; [1985] 1 All E.R. 155; (1984) 81 L.S. Gaz. 2375; 1985 P.C.C. 222 637
Carter and Ellis, ex p. Sarill Brothers Ltd, Re [1905] 1 K.B. 735 238
Cases of Taff's Well Ltd, Re [1992] Ch. 179; [1991] B.C.C. 582 596
Castle, ex p. Haslam Brothers, Re [1917] 2 K.B. 725; 87 L.J.K.B. 753; 117 L.T. 792; [1917] H.B.R. 205 193
Caston Cushioning, Re [1955] 1 All E.R. 508; 1 W.L.R. 163; 93 S.J. 131 510
Cavco Floors Ltd, Re [1990] B.C.C. 589; [1990] B.C.L.C. 940 429
Celia (S.S.) v. Volturno (S.S.) [1921] 2 A.C. 544, [1921] All E.R. 173; 90 L.J.P. 385; 126 L.T. 1; 37 T.L.R. 969; 15 Asq. M.L.C. 374; 27 Com. Cas. 46 H.L. affirming S.C. sub nom. The Volturno [1920] P 447; 454, n; 36 T.L.R. 838 C.A. 258, 259
Central Sugar Factories of Brazil (Flack's Case), Re [1894] 1 Ch. 369; 63 L.J. Ch. 410; 70 L.T. 645; 42 W.R. 345; 10 T.L.R. 150; 38 S.J. 113; 1 Mans. 145; 8 R. 205 754
Centrebind Ltd, Re [1967] 1 W.L.R. 377; [1966] 3 All E.R. 899 .... 501, 502
Chancery plc, Re [1991] B.C.C. 171; [1991] B.C.L.C. 712; The Times, Feb. 27, 1991 429
Chapel House Colliery, Re (1883) 24 Ch.D. 259, C.A.; 52 L.J. Ch. 934; 49 L.T. 575; 31 W.R. 933, C.A. 535, 538, 548
Chaplin v. Boys [1971] A.C. 356; [1969] 3 W.L.R. 322; 113 S.J. 608; [1969] 2 All E.R. 1085, H.L.; affirming sub nom. Boys v. Chaplin [1968] 2 Q.B. 1; [1968] 2 W.L.R. 328; 111 S.J. 968; [1968] 1 All E.R. 283; affirming [1967] 3 W.L.R. 266; 11 S.J. 297; [1967] 2 All E.R. 665 723
Chapman, Re (1873) L.R. 15 Eq. 75; 42 L.J. Bcy. 38; 21 W.R. 104 712
——, Re (1894) 10 T.L.R. 449 241
——, ex p. Edwardes, Re (1884) 13 Q.B.D. 747; 51 L.T. 881; 33 W.R. 268; 1 Morr. 238, C.A. 246
Charles, ex p., (1811) 14 East 197; 104 E.R. 576 103
Charles Forte (Investments) Ltd v. Amanda [1964] Ch. 240 545
Charlewood, Re [1894] 1 Q.B. 643 246
Charnley Davies Business Services Ltd, Re (No. 2) [1990] B.C.L.C. 760; [1990] B.C.C. 605 .... 398, 453
——, Re (1988) P.C.C. 1; 4 B.C.C. 152 .... 463, 468

xxviii

Table of Cases

Charterland Gold Fields Ltd, *Re* (1909) 26 T.L.R. 132 .... 511, 584
Chatterton, *ex p.* Hemming, *Re* (1879) 13 Ch.D. 163; 41 L.T. 513; 28 W.R. 218 318
Chelmsford City Football Club, (1980) Ltd, *Re* [1991] B.C.C. 133 425
Chelsea Cloisters (In Liquidation), *Re* (1981) 131 N.L.J. 482; (1980) 41 P. & C.R. 98 638
Cherry *v.* Boultbee (1839) 4 My. & Cr. 442; 41 E.R. 171; 9 L.J. Ch. 118 ..... 276, 277
Chesterfield Catering Co., *Re* [1976] 3 All E.R. 294; 3 W.L.R. 879; (1975) 120 S.J. 817 535
Chesters, *Re* (1877) 6 Ch.D. 57; 36 L.T. 839; 25 W.R. 786 315
Chidley, *Re* (1875) 1 Ch.D. 177; 45 L.J.Bcy. 49; 33 L.T. 553; 24 W.R. 182, C.A. 56
Chohan *v.* Saggar (No. 2) [1994] B.C.C. 134, C.A.; affirming [1992] B.C.C. 306 234
Christie *v.* Taunton, Delmard, Lane & Co. [1893] 2 Ch. 175; 62 L.J.Ch. 385; 68 L.T. 638; 41 W.R. 475; 37 S.J. 304; 3 R. 404 205
Churchill Hotel (Plymouth) Ltd, *Re* (1988) 4 B.C.C. 112 673
Citro, *Re* [1990] 3 All E.R. 952; [1990] 3 W.L.R. 880; (1990) 134 S.J. 806; (1990) 154 New L.J. 1073; [1991] 1 F.L.R. 71, C.A. 195
City and County Bank, *Re* (1875) 10 Ch.App. 470 545
City of London Corporation *v.* Brown *The Times*, October 11, 1989, C.A.; (1990) 22 H.L.R.; 60 P. & C.R. 42 189
Civica Investments Ltd, *Re* [1983] B.C.L.C. 456 672
Clandown Colliery Co., *Re* [1915] 1 Ch. 369; 84 L.J.Ch. 420; 112 L.T. 1060; 59 S.J. 350; [1915] H.B.R. 93 538
Clark, *ex p.* (1884) 13 Q.B.D. 426, C.A. 58
——, *Re*, Clark *v.* Clark [1926] 1 Ch. 833; 95 L.J.Ch. 325; 135 L.T. 666; 70 S.J. 344; [1926] B. & C.R. 77 214
—— *v.* Smith [1940] 1 K.B. 126 172
——, *ex p.* Pope and Knowles, *Re* [1914] 3 K.B. 1095; 84 L.J.K.B. 89; 112 L.T. 873; 59 S.J. 44; [1915] H.B.R. 1, C.A. 697
Clarke (a bankrupt), *Re* [1975] 1 All E.R. 453 208
Clarke (L.G.), *Re* [1966] 3 All E.R. 622 96
Clasper Group Services Ltd, *Re* (1988) 4 B.C.C. 673 643
Clayton and Barclay's Contract, *Re* [1895] 2 Ch. 212; 64 L.J.Ch. 615; 59 J.P. 489; 43 W.R. 549; 39 S.J. 503; 13 R. 556; *sub nom.* Clayton *v.* Barclay, 72 L.T. 764; 11 T.L.R. 415, *sub nom.* Clayton and Beaumonts' Contract, 2 Mans. 345 .. 200
Clifton Place Garage Ltd, *Re* [1970] Ch. 477, C.A. [1970] 2 W.L.R. 243; (1969) 113 S.J. 895; [1970] 1 All E.R. 353, C.A.; reversing 113 S.J. 832; [1969] 3 All E.R. 892 629
Clough Mill Ltd *v.* Martin [1984] 3 All E.R. 982; [1985] 1 W.L.R. 111, C.A. (1948) 128 S.J. 850; [1984] 3 All E.R. 982; [1985] 82 L.S.Gaz. 116; [1985] L.M.C.L.Q. 15; reversing [1984] 1 All E.R. 721; [1984] 1 W.L.R. 1067; (1984) 128 S.J. 564; (1984) L.S.Gaz. 2375 .... 217, 636
Cloverbay Ltd, *Re* [1989] B.C.L.C. 724 461
——, *Re* (No. 2) [1990] B.C.C. 299; B.C.L.C. 449; *Financial Times*, January 24, 1990 461
—— *v.* Bank of Credit and Commercial International [1991] Ch. 90; [1990] 3 W.L.R. 574; [1991] 1 All E.R. 894; [1991] B.C.L.C. 135, C.A. 461
Cobham *v.* Dalton (1875) 10 Ch. App. 655 147
Cockerell *v.* Dickens (1840) 3 Moo. P.C.C. 98; 2 Moo. Ind App. 353; 1 Mont. D. & De. G. 45; 13 E.R. 45, P.C. 722
Cohen, *Re* [1961] 1 Ch. 246; [1961] 2 W.L.R. 237; [1961] 1 All E.R. 646 204
—— *v.* Mitchell (1890) 25 Q.B.D. 262; 63 L.T. 206; 38 W.R. 551; 6 T.L.R. 326; 7 Morr. 207, C.A. 199, 200
Coldunell *v.* Gallon [1986] Q.B. 1184, C.A.; 2 W.L.R. 466; (1986) 130 S.J. 88; [1986] 1 All E.R. 429; [1986] F.L.R. 183; (1986) 82 L.S.Gaz. 520, C.A. 231
Cole, Trustee in Bankruptcy *v.* Public Trustee, *Re* [1931] 2 Ch. 174 .... 135, 254
Cole *v.* Kernot (1872) L.R. 7 Q.B. 534; 41 L.J.Q.B. 221 149
Coles *v.* Coles [1956] 3 All E.R. 542; [1957] P. 68; [1956] 3 W.L.R. 361; 100 S.J. 842 .... 148, 206

Table of Cases

Colgrave, *Re* [1903] 2 Ch. 705 214
Collier, *Re* [1930] 2 Ch. 37; 143 L.T. 329; *sub nom. Re* Collier, *ex p.* Collier's Exors. 99 L.J.Ch. 241; [1929] B. & C. 173 201
Combined Weighing and Advertising Machine Co. (1889) 43 Ch.D. 99; 59 L.J.Ch. 26; 61 L.T. 582; 38 W.R. 67; 6 T.L.R. 7; 1 Meg. 393, C.A. 90
Commercial Bank of South Australia, *Re* (1886) 33 Ch.D. 174; 55 L.J.Ch. 670; 55 L.T. 609; 2 T.L.R. 714 732
—— (1886) 33 Ch.D. 174; 55 L.J.Ch. 670; 55 L.T. 609; 2 T.L.R. 714 ...... 752, 757, 766, 782
Compania Merabello San Nicholas S.A., *Re* [1973] 1 Ch. 75; [1972] 3 W.L.R. 471; 116 S.J. 631; [1972] 3 All E.R. 448 .... 736, 737, 743, 744
Company A, *Re* (May 16, 1950) 1 C.L.C. 1406; 94 S.J. 369 545
——, *Re* [1974] 1 All E.R. 256; [1973] 1 W.L.R. 1566; 117 S.J. 910 ..... 536, 539, 551
——, *Re* [1894] 2 Ch. 349 545
——, *Re* (No. 003729 of 1982) [1984] W.L.R. 1090; [1984] 3 All E.R. 78; (1984) 128 S.J. 580; (1984) 81 L.S.Gaz. 2133 524
Company (No. 00175 of 1987) A, *Re* [1987] B.C.L.C. 467 .... 429, 437, 438
Company (No. 001418 of 1988) A, *Re* [1990] B.C.C. 526; [1991] B.C.L.C. 197, D.C. 660
Company A, *Re* (No. 001992 of 1988) [1989] B.C.L.C. 9, D.C. 436
——, *Re* (No. 001448 of 1989) [1989] B.C.L.C. 715 545
Company (No. 00687 of 1991) A, *Re* [1991] B.C.C. 210; [1992] B.C.L.C. 133 .... 546, 629
Company (No. 003102 of 1991) A, *Re*, *ex p.* Nyckeln Finance Co. Ltd [1991] B.C.L.C. 539 737
Company (No. 004055 of 1991) A, *Re* [1991] B.C.L.C. 865; *sub nom.* Record Tennis Centres Ltd, *Re* [1991] B.C.C. 509; [1991] 1 W.L.R. 1003; [1991] B.C.L.C. 865 549
Company A, *Re* (No. 0010656 of 1990) [1991] B.C.L.C. 464 528
Company (No. 00751 of 1992) A, *Re*, *ex p.* Avocet Aviation Ltd [1992] B.C.L.C. 869 528
Company (No. 00962 of 1991) A, *Re*, *ex p.* Electrical Engineering Contracts (London) Ltd [1992] B.C.L.C. 248 545
Company (No. 006273 of 1992) A, *Re* [1992] B.C.C. 794; [1993] B.C.L.C. 131 525
Company (No. 008790 of 1990) A, *Re* [1992] B.C.C. 11; [1991] B.C.L.C. 561 .... 526, 545
Company (No. 0012209 of 1991) A, *Re* [1992] 2 All E.R. 797; [1992] 1 W.L.R. 351 .... 525, 528, 546
Company (No. 006273 of 1992) A, *Re* [1993] B.C.L.C. 131; [1992] B.C.C. 794 546
Company (No. 007946 of 1993) A, *Re* [1994] 2 W.L.R. 438, *sub nom.* Normandy Marketing Ltd, *Re* [1993] B.C.C. 879 530
Company (No. 009080 of 1992) A, *Re* [1993] B.C.L.C. 269 545
Company (No. 0022 of 1993) A, *Re*, Philex *v.* Golban [1993] B.C.C. 726, reversed, *sub. nom.* Ridehalgh *v.* Horsefield [1994] B.C.C. 390, C.A. 528
Compaq Computer Ltd *v.* Abercorn Group Ltd [1991] B.C.C. 484; [1993] B.C.L.C. 603 637
Condon, *ex p.* James, *Re* (1874) 9 Ch.App. 609; 43 L.J.Bcy. 107; 30 L.T. 733; 22 W.R. 937, L.JJ. 201, 207, 208, 255, 448, 453, 583
Consolidated South Rand Mines, *Re* [1909] W.N. 66; 1 Ch. 491; 78 L.J.Ch. 326; 100 L.T. 319; 16 Mans. 81, C.A. 549
Constellation (The) [1966] 1 W.L.R. 272; (1966) 110 S.J. 307; [1965] 3 All E.R. 873; [1965] 2 Lloyd's Rep. 538 633
Consumer and Industrial Press Ltd, *Re* [1988] B.C.L.C. 177; (1988) 4 B.C.C. 68 424
Cook, *Re* (1889) 6 Morr. 224; 233 61 L.T. 335 313
Cooke *v.* Eshelby (1887) 12 App.Cas. 271, H.L. 278
Cooper, *ex p.* Hall, *Re* (1882) 19 Ch.D. 580; 51 L.J.Ch. 556; 46 L.T. 549, C.A. 227
—— *v.* Pepys (1741) 1 Atk. 107; 26 E.R. 70 261

Table of Cases

Copecrest Ltd, *Re* [1993] B.C.C. 844, C.A.; [1993] B.C.L.C. 1118 676
Corballis, *Re* [1929] I.R. 266 706
Cornhill Insurance plc *v.* Cornhill Financial Services Ltd [1992] B.C.C. 818; [1993] B.C.L.C. 914, C.A. 435, 442
—— *v.* Improvement Services Ltd [1986] 1 W.L.R. 114; [1986] P.C.C. 204 527
Cotterell *v.* Price [1960] 3 All E.R. 315; [1960] 1 W.L.R. 1097; 104 S.J. 763 .. 149, 206, 252
Cotton *v.* Heyl [1930] 1 Ch. 510; 99 L.J.Ch. 289; 143 L.T. 16 212
Cottrell *v.* Jones (1851) 11 C.B. 713; 138 E.R. 655 100
Coulson, *Re* [1934] Ch. 45; [1933] All E.R. 544; 150 L.T. 5 320
Cove, *Re*, (a debtor) [1990] 1 All E.R. 949; 1 W.L.R. 708 47
Cracknall *v.* Jackson (1877) 6 Ch.D. 735; 46 L.J.Ch. 652; 37 L.T. 118; 25 W.R. 904 109
Cranley Mansions Ltd, *Re*, Saigol *v.* Goldstein [1994] B.C.C. 576; [1994] 1 W.L.R. 1610; [1994] E.G.C.S. 95; (1994) 14 New L.J. 673; *The Times*, June 23, 1994 .... 49, 50, 123, 409, 412
Craven Insurance Co. Ltd [1968] 1 W.L.R. 675; 112 S.J. 378; [1968] 1 All E.R. 1140; 1 Lloyd's Rep. 361 538
Crispin, *Re* (1873) L.R. 8 Ch.App. 374; 42 L.J.Bcy. 65; 28 L.T. 483; 37 J.P. 391; 21 W.R. 491; L.C. & L.J. 696, 719
Croftbell Ltd, *Re* [1990] B.C.C. 781; [1990] B.C.L.C. 844 .... 361, 429
Re Crompton & Co. Ltd, Player *v.* Crompton & Co. Ltd [1914] 1 Ch. 954; 83 L.J.Ch. 666; 110 L.T. 759; 21 Mans. 200; 58 S.J. 433 363
Crossmore Electrical and Civil Engineering Ltd, *Re* (1989) 5 B.C.C. 37; [1989] B.C.L.C. 137 629
Crow (E. and J.), *Re* (1907) 97 L.T. 140 96
Cryne *v.* Barclays Bank plc [1987] B.C.C. 548, C.A. 360
Cuckmere Brick Co. Ltd *v.* Mutual Finance Ltd [1971] 2 All E.R., C.A. 398
Cullen (R.A.) Ltd *v.* Nottingham Health Authority (1986) B.C.C. 368 276
Cunningham, *ex p.*, (1884) 13 Q.B.D. 418; 53 L.J.Ch. 1067; 51 L.T. 447; 33 W.R. 22; 1 Morr. 137, C.A. 700
Curtain Dream plc, *Re* [1991] B.C.C. 484 637
Curtis *v.* Curtis [1969] 2 All E.R. 207; 1 W.L.R. 422; (1969) 113 S.J. 242 148
Cutts (A Bankrupt), *Re* [1956] 2 All E.R. 537; 1 W.L.R. 728; (1956) 100 S.J. 449 227
Cyona Distributors Ltd, *Re* [1967] Ch. 889, C.A.; [1967] 2 W.L.R. 369; (1967) S.J. 943; [1967] 1 All E.R. 281; [1966] C.L.Y. 1451, reversing [1966] Ch. 462; 2 W.L.R. 761; (1966) 110 S.J. 329; [1966] 1 All E.R. 825 660

D.K.G. Contractors Ltd, *Re* [1990] B.C.C. 903 .... 643, 658, 662
Daintrey, *ex p.* Mant, *Re* [1900] 1 Q.B. 546; 69 L.J.Q.B. 207; 82 L.T. 239; 7 Mans. 107, D.C. 272, 274
Dairen Kisen Kabushiki Kaisha *v.* Shiang Kee [1941] A.C. 373, P.C.; (1941) 111 L.J.P.C. 6 746
Dallhold Estates (U.K.) Pty Ltd, *Re* [1992] B.C.C. 394; [1992] B.C.L.C. 621; [1992] E.G.C.S. 18 .... 361, 432, 785, 786
Daniels *v.* Fielding (1846) 16 M. & W. 200; 153 E.R. 1159 100
Davenport *ex p.* The Bankrupt *v.* Eric Street Properties, *Re* [1963] 1 W.L.R. 817; [1963] 2 All E.R. 350 .... 76, 136
David Meek Access Ltd, *Re* [1993] B.C.C. 175; [1994] B.C.L.C. 680 445
Davidson's Settlement Trusts (1873) L.R. 15 Eq. 383; 42 L.J.Ch. 347; 21 W.R. 454; 37 J.P. 484, L.J. 718
Davies *v.* Direct Loans Ltd [1986] 2 All E.R. 783 231
Davies Chemists Ltd, *Re* [1992] B.C.C. 697; B.C.L.C. 544 629
Davis, *Re* (1885) 3 Morr. 27 241
Dawson Print Group Ltd, *Re* (1987) 3 B.C.C. 322; [1987] B.C.L.C. 601 673
Day, *ex p.* Hammond, *Re* (1902) 86 L.T. 238; 50 W.R. 448; 18 T.L.R. 442; 46 S.J. 361, D.C. 96
De Courcy *v.* Clement [1971] Ch. 693; [1971] 2 W.L.R. 210; (1970) 115 S.J. 93; *sub nom.* De Courcy *v.* Clements [1971] 1 All E.R. 681 494

TABLE OF CASES

De Marney *ex p.* Official Receiver *v.* Salaman, *Re* [1943] Ch. 126; 168 L.T. 217; 59 T.L.R. 153; *sub nom.*, *Re* A Debtor (No. 8 of 1942) *ex p.* Official Receiver *v.* Salaman (1943) 87 S.J. 93 .... 149, 201
De Villiers, *ex p.*, *Re* Carbon Developments (Pty.) Ltd [1993] 1 S.A. 493 (A) ... 616
De Choisy *v.* Hynes [1937] 4 All E.R. 54; (1937) 81 S.J. 883 353
Debtor, A, *Re* [1903] 1 K.B. 705 136
——, A, *Re* [1909] 1 K.B. 430 273
——, A, *Re* [1927] 1 Ch. 97 698
——, A, *Re* [1929] 1 Ch. 125 135
——, A, *Re* [1944] Ch. 344 158
——, A, *Re* [1965] 3 All E.R. 453 224
——, A, *v.* Focus Insurance Co. Ltd (in Liquidation) *The Times*, July 12, 1993 .. 128
——, A, *Re*, *ex p.* Berkshire Finance Co. (1962) 106 S.J. 468 104
——, A, *Re*, *ex p.* Newburys Ltd [1926] B. & C.R. 23; (1926) 95 L.J.Ch. 199 ... 95, 96
——, A, *Re*, *ex p.* the Debtor *v.* Dodwell [1949] Ch. 236; [1949] L.J.R. 907; 65 T.L.R. 150; (1949) S.J. 148; [1949] 1 All E.R. 510 .... 173, 179
——, A (No. 20 of 1904), *Re* 91 L.T. 664; 53 W.R. 223; *sub nom. Re* Goldberg, 21 T.L.R. 2 D.C. 98
——, A (No. 3 of 1909), *Re* [1917] 1 K.B. 558 153
——, A (No. 7 of 1910) [1910], *Re* 2 K.B. 59; 79 L.J.K.B. 1065; 102 L.T. 691; 26 T.L.R. 429; 17 Mans. 263, C.A. 132
——, A (No. 68 of 1911), *Re* [1911] 2 K.B. 652; 80 L.J.K.B. 1224; 104 L.T. 905; 18 Mans. 311, C.A. 270, 271
——, A (No. 30 of 1914), *Re* [1915] 1 K.B. 287; 84 L.J.K.B. 254; 59 S.J. 130; *sub nom. Re* A Debtor (No. 30 of 1914), *ex p.* Petitioning Creditors [1915] H.B.R. 18, D.C. 85
——, A (No. 28 of 1917), *Re ex p.* Petitioning Creditors *v.* The Debtor [1917] 2 K.B. 808; 87 L.J.K.B. 783; [1917] H.B.R. 235, D.C. 85
——, A (No. 946 of 1926), *Re* [1939] Ch. 489 316
——, (No. 1507 of 1921), A *Re* [1922] 2 K.B. 109; 91 L.J.Ch. 471; 127 L.T. 344; 38 T.L.R. 574; 66 S.J. 472; [1922] B. & C. 9, C.A. 109
——, A (No. 199 of 1922), *Re* [1922] 2 Ch. 470 728
——, A (No. 82 of 1926), *Re* [1927] 1 Ch. 410; 136 L.T. 349; *sub nom. Re* Mumford, Debtor *v.* Petitioning Creditor, *ex p.* Official Receiver, 96 L.J.Ch. 75; [1926] B. & C.R. 165, D.C. 273
——, (No. 946 of 1926) A, *Re* [1939] Ch. 489 320
——, (No. 229 of 1927) A, *Re* [1927] 2 Ch. 367; [1927] All E.R. Rep. 282; [1927] 2 Ch. 367; 96 L.J.Ch. 381; 137 L.T. 507; [1927] B. & C.R. 127, C.A. 136
——, A (No. 883 of 1927), *Re* [1928] Ch. 199; [1927] All E.R. Rep. 267; 97 L.J.Ch. 120; 138 L.T. 440; 72 S.J. 85; [1928] B. & C.R. 1, C.A. 97, 98
——, (No. 549 of 1928) A, *Re* [1929] 1 Ch. 170; [1928] All E.R. Rep. 505; 98 L.J.Ch. 35; 140 L.T. 165; 45 T.L.R. 10; 72 S.J. 727; [1928] B. & C.R. 125, C.A. 103
——, (No. 737 of 1928) A, *Re* [1929] 1 Ch. 362 728
——, (No. 76 of 1929) A, *Re* [1929] 2 Ch. 146; 98 L.J.Ch. 334; 141 L.T. 250; 45 T.L.R. 403; 73 S.J. 299; [1929] B. & C.R. 48, C.A. 84
——, A (No. 11 of 1935), *Re* [1936] Ch. 165; 105 L.J.Ch. 146; 154 L.T. 397; *sub nom. Re* Debtor, *ex p.* Debtor & Official Receiver (No. 11 of 1935) [1935] All E.R. Rep. 615; [1934–35] B. & C.R. 322 D.C. 95
——, (No. 24 of 1935) A, *Re* [1935] All E.R. Rep. 744; [1936] Ch. 292; 105 L.J.Ch. 364; 154 L.T. 234; 80 S.J. 54; [1936–37] B. & C.R. 93, C.A. 98
——, (No. 490 of 1935) A, *Re* [1937] Ch. 237; 105 L.J.Ch. 129; 154 L.T. 44; 52 T.L.R. 70; 79 S.J. 839; [1934–35] B. & C.R. 329, C.A. 246
——, (No. 975 of 1937) A, *Re* Debtor *v.* Petitioning Creditor & Official Receiver [1938] 2 All E.R. 530; [1939] Ch. 145; (1938) 107 L.J.Ch. 310; 159 L.T. 377; 54 T.L.R. 1098; 82 S.J. 663; [1938–39] B. & C.R. 133, C.A. 84
——, (No. 382 of 1938) A, *Re ex p.* Debtor *v.* Petitioning Creditors & Official Receiver [1939] Ch. 145; [1938] 3 All E.R. 744; 107 L.J.Ch. 310; 159 L.T. 377; 54 T.L.R. 1098; 82 S.J. 663; [1938–39] B. & C.R. 133, C.A. 96
——, (No. 441 of 1938) A, *Re* [1939] Ch. 251; 108 L.J.Ch. 35; 159 L.T. 505; 55 T.L.R. 41; 82 S.J. 908; [1938–39] B. & C.R. 91, C.A. 129

TABLE OF CASES

Debtor, (No. 23 of 1939) A, *Re* Debtor *v.* Petitioning Creditor & Official Receiver [1939] 2 All E.R. 338; 160 L.T. 443; 55 T.L.R. 620; 83 S.J. 376; [1938–1939] B. & C.R. 163, C.A. 96
——, A (No. 400 of 1940) *Re ex p.* The Debtor *v.* Dodwell (The Trustee) [1949] Ch. 236; L.J.R. 907; 65 T.L.R. 150; 93 S.J. 148; [1949] 1 All E.R. 510 585
——, (No. 1 of 1941) A, *Re* [1941] Ch. 487; 110 L.J.Ch. 220; 165 L.T. 417; 57 T.L.R. 654; 85 S.J. 434; [1940–42] B. & C.R. 54 77
——, (No. 6 of 1941) A, *Re* [1943] Ch. 213; [1943] 1 All E.R. 553; 112 L.J.Ch. 246; 168 L.T. 401; 59 T.L.R. 333; 87 S.J. 192, C.A. 109
——, (No. 564 of 1949) A, *ex p.* Customs and Excise Commissioners *v.* The Debtor, *Re* [1950] Ch. 282; [1950] 1 All E.R. 308; 66 T.L.R. (Pt. 1) 313 76
——, A (No. 21 of 1950), *Re* (No. 2) [1951] Ch. 612 275
——, (No. 41 of 1951) A, *Re ex p.* The Debtor *v.* Hunter [1952] Ch. 192; [1952] 1 All E.R. 107; [1952] 1 T.L.R. 53 85
——, (No. 48 of 1952) A, *Re* The Debtor *v.* Richardson (J.T.) [1953] Ch. 335; (1953) 97 S.J. 151; [1953] 1 All E.R. 545; 51 L.G.R. 261; 46 R. & I.T. 140, C.A. 92
——, (No. 20 of 1953) A, *Re* The Debtor *v.* Scott & Official Receiver [1954] 3 All E.R. 74; [1954] 1 W.L.R. 1190, reversing [1954] 1 W.L.R. 393; [1954] 1 All E.R. 454 103
——, (No. 66 of 1955) A, *Re* The Debtor *v.* Trustee of the Property of Waite (a Bankrupt) [1956] 1 W.L.R. 1226; [1956] 3 All E.R. 225; affirming [1956] 1 W.L.R. 480; [1956] 2 All E.R. 94 103
——, A, *Re* (No. 12 of 1958) [1968] 2 All E.R. 425 .... 135, 321
——, A, *Re ex p.* The Debtor *v.* Allen (No. 17 of 1966) [1967] Ch. 590; [1967] 1 All E.R. 668 .... 70, 119, 122
——, (No. 819 of 1970) A, *Re ex p.* Biart *v.* Trustee of the Property of the Debtor [1974] 3 All E.R. 502; [1974] 1 W.L.R. 1475; 118 S.J. 829 286
——, A (No. 12 of 1970), *Re* [1971] 1 All E.R. 504; affirmed [1971] 2 All E.R. 1494, C.A. 119, 121
——, (No. 39 of 1974) A, *Re ex p.* Okill *v.* Gething [1977] 3 All E.R. 489; [1977] 1 W.L.R. 1308 109
——, (No. 2283 of 1976) A, *Re* [1978] 1 W.L.R. 1512 696
——, (No. 2 of 1977) A, *Re ex p.* the Debtor *v.* Goacher [1979] 1 All E.R. 870; [1979] 1 W.L.R. 1308 103
—— (No. 1 of 1987) A, *Re* [1989] 1 W.L.R. 271; [1989] 2 All E.R. 46; (1989) S.J. 290; [1989] L.S.Gaz. April 26, 35, C.A. 111, 115
——, A (No. 10 of 1988), *Re* [1989] 1 W.L.R. 405; (1989) 133 S.J. 568; [1989] 2 All E.R. 39 115
——, A (No. 2389 of 1989), *Re* [1991] Fam. 326; [1991] 2 W.L.R. 578; [1990] 3 All E.R. 984 .... 47, 133
——, A (No. 222 of 1990), *Re ex p.* The Bank of Ireland [1992] B.C.L.C. 137; *The Times*, June 27, 1991 .... 46, 49, 163, 408, 510
——, A *Re* (No. 259 of 1990) [1992] 1 W.L.R. 226; [1992] 1 All E.R. 641 51
——, A (No. 51/SD/1991), *Re* [1992] 1 W.L.R. 1294; [1993] 2 All E.R. 40 112
——, A (No. 32/SD/91), *Re* [1993] 2 All E.R. 991; 1 W.L.R. 314 314
——, A (No. 32/SD/1991), *Re* (No. 2) [1994] B.C.C. 524; *The Times*, May 3, 1994 116
——, A (No. 53 of 1991, Kingston upon Thames), *Re The Independent*, August 19, 1991 113
——, A (Nos. 234 and 236 of 1991), *Re The Independent*, June 29, 1992 112
——, A (No. 490–SD–1991), *Re* [1992] 2 All E.R. 664; 1 W.L.R. 507; [1993] B.C.L.C. 164; *The Times*, April 9, 1992 115
——, A (No. 517 of 1991), *Re The Times*, November 25, 1991 115
——, A (No. 657–SD–91), *Re ex p.* I.R.C. *v.* The Debtor [1993] B.C.L.C. 180, [1993] B.C.L.C. 180 115
——, A (No. 784 of 1991), *Re* [1992] Ch. 554; [1992] 3 All E.R. 376; [1992] 3 W.L.R. 119; [1992] S.T.C. 549 697
——, A (No. 64 of 1992), *Re The Times*, November 12, 1993; [1994] 1 W.L.R. 264; [1994] 2 All E.R. 177; [1994] B.C.C. 55 50

Table of Cases

Debtor, A (No. 68 of 1992), *Re The Times*, February 12, 1993; [1994] 1 W.L.R. 264 324
——, A (No. 90 of 1992), *Re The Times*, July 12, 1993 116
——, A (No. 1594 of 1992), *Re The Times*, December 8, 1992 116
——, A (No. 22 of 1993), *Re*, A Debtor *v.* Focus Insurance Co. Ltd [1994] 1 W.L.R. 46; [1994] 2 All E.R. 105 113
——, A (No. 162 of 1993), *Re* Doorbar *v.* Alltime Securities Ltd [1994] B.C.C. 994 .... 49, 123, 409, 412
Deering *v.* Bank of Ireland (1886) 12 App.Cas. 20, H.L. 256
Delhi Electric Supply and Traction Co. Ltd, *Re* [1954] Ch. 131, C.A.; affirmed *sub nom.* Government of India *v.* Taylor [1955] A.C. 491, H.L. 751
Denny's Trustee *v.* Denny and Warr [1919] 1 K.B. 583; 88 L.J.K.B. 679; 120 L.T. 608; 35 T.L.R. 238; [1918–19] B. & C.R. 139 224
Densham, *Re ex p.* Trustee of the Bankrupt *v.* The Bankrupt [1975] 3 All E.R. 726; [1975] 1 W.L.R. 1519 *sub nom. Re* Densham (A Bankrupt) 119 S.J. 774 .. 195, 224
Derwent Rolling Mills Co., *Re* (1904) 21 T.L.R. 81; affirmed (1904) 21 T.L.R. 701, C.A. 757
Descharmes, *ex p.* (1742) 1 Atk. 103; 26 E.R. 68 241
Detmold, *Re* Detmold *v.* Detmold (1889) 40 Ch.D. 585; 58 L.J.Ch. 495; 61 L.T. 21; 37 W.R. 442 214
Deutsche Bank and Disconto Gesellschaft *v.* Banque des Marchands de Moscou (unreported, December 14, 1931, C.A.) 763
Devaynes *v.* Noble, Clayton's Case (1816) 1 Mer. 572; 35 E.R. 781 .... 210, 211
Deverall *v.* Grant Advertising Inc. [1955] Ch. 111; [1954] 3 W.L.R. 688; 98 S.J. 787; [1954] 3 All E.R. 389 749
Devon and Somerset Farmers Ltd, *Re* [1993] B.C.C. 410; [1994] 2 B.C.L.C. 99; *The Times*, May 25, 1993 .... 362, 432, 786
Dewe *v.* Dewe [1928] P. 113; 97 L.J.P. 65; 138 L.T. 552; 92 J.P. 32; 44 T.L.R. 274; 72 S.J. 69; 26 L.G.R. 191 .... 265, 266
Dibbens (E.) & Sons Ltd, *Re* [1990] B.C.L.C. 577 638
Dickinson, *ex p.* Charrington & Co. *Re* (1888) 22 Q.B.D. 187; 58 L.J.Q.B. 1; 60 L.T. 138; 37 W.R. 130; 5 L.T.R. 82; 6 Morr. 1, C.A. 149, 242, 244
Diplock, *Re* [1948] 1 Ch. 465; affirmed *sub nom.* Ministry of Health *v.* Simpson [1951] A.C. 251, H.L. 211
D.P.P. *v.* Ashley [1955] Crim.L.R. 565 351
Display Multiples Ltd, *Re* [1967] 1 W.L.R. 571; 111 S.J. 130; [1967] 1 All E.R. 685 544
Distin, *ex p.* Ormiston, *Re* (1871) 24 L.T. 197 712
Dixon, *Re* (1884) 13 Q.B.D. 118; 53 L.J.Ch. 769; 50 L.T. 414; 32 W.R. 837; 1 Morr. 98, C.A. 136
D'Jan of London Ltd, *Re* [1993] B.C.C. 646 659
Dodds *ex p.* Vaughans, Exors., *Re* (1890) 25 Q.B.D. 529; 62 L.T. 837; 39 W.R. 125; 6 T.L.R. 293; 7 Morr., 199 .... 263, 264, 265
Doetsch, *Re* Matheson *v.* Ludwig [1896] 2 Ch. 836; 65 L.J.Ch. 855; 75 L.T. 69; 45 W.R. 57; 40 S.J. 685 717
Douglas, *ex p.* Wilson, *Re* (1872) L.R. 7 Ch.App. 490; 41 L.J.Bcy. 46; 26 L.T. 489; 20 W.R. 564, L.JJ. 713
——, *ex p.* Wilson, *Re* (1872) L.R. 7 Ch.App. 490; L.J.Bcy. 46; 26 L.T. 489; 20 W.R. 564, L.JJ. 754
——, *Re* Griggs Engineering Ltd [1963] 1 Ch. 19; [1962] 2 W.L.R. 893 526
——, *Re* (Griggs) Engineering Ltd [1963] Ch. 19; [1962] 2 W.L.R. 893; [1962] 1 All E.R. 498 631
Downs Distributing Co. Pty. *v.* Associated Blue Star Stoves Pty. Ltd (1948) 76 C.L.R. 463 583
Downsview Nominees Ltd *v.* First City Corp. Ltd [1993] 3 All E.R. 626; (1992) 136 L.J. 855; [1992] *Gazette* 19 February, 28 .... 397, 398
Dowse *v.* Gorton [1891] A.C. 190; 40 W.R. 17; 64 L.T. 809, H.L. 332
Drabble Bros. *Re* [1930] 2 Ch. 211; 99 L.J.Ch. 345; 143 L.T. 337; 74 S.J. 464; [1931] B. & C.R. 200, C.A. 226
Dramstar Ltd, *Re* (1980) 124 S.J. 807 545
Drinkwater *v.* Goodwin (1775) 1 Cowp. 251; 98 E.R. 1070 209

Table of Cases

Drucker, *Re* (No. 1) [1902] 2 K.B. 55 247
Dry Docks Corp. of London, *Re* (1883) 39 Ch.D. 306; 58 L.J.Ch. 33; 59 L.T. 763; 37 W.R. 18; 1 Meg. 86; *sub nom. Re* Dry Dock Corpn. of London, *ex p.* St. Anne Limehouse Overseers, 4 T.L.R. 737, C.A. 551
Duffield, *ex p.* Peacock, *Re* (1873) 8 Ch.App. 682; 42 L.J.Bcy. 78; 28 L.T. 830; 21 W.R. 755, L.JJ. 270
Duleep Singh, *ex p.* Cross, *Re* (1890) 7 Mor. 228; 6 T.L.R. 385, C.A. 700
Dulles' Settlement (No. 2), *Re* Dulles v. Vidler [1951] Ch. 842; *sub nom. Re* Dulles' Settlement Trusts, Dulles *v.* Vidler [1951] 2 T.L.R. 145; [1951] 2 All E.R. 69, C.A. 760
Dummelow, *ex p.* Ruffle, *Re* (1873) 8 Ch.App. 997; 42 L.J.Bcy. 82; 29 L.T. 384; 21 W.R. 932 164
Dunn, *Re, ex p.* [1949] 1 Ch. 640; [1949] 2 All E.R. 388; 65 T.L.R. 521 .. 119, 120, 122
Dynamics Corporation of America, *Re*, [1973] 1 W.L.R. 63; 117 S.J. 32; [1972] 3 All E.R. 1046 753
——, *Re* [1976] 1 W.L.R. 757; 120 S.J. 450; [1976] 2 All E.R. 669 259
Dyster *v.* Randall & Sons [1926] Ch. 932; 95 L.J.Ch. 504; 70 S.J. 797; [1926] B. & C.R. 113 201

E.A.B., *Re* [1902] 1 K.B. 457, 71 L.J.K.B. 356; 85 L.T. 773; 50 W.R. 229; 9 Mans. 105, C.A. 58
Eades Estate, *Re* (1917) 2 W.W.R. 65; 33 D.L.R. 335 705
Eastgate, *ex p.* Ward, *Re* [1905] 1 K.B. 465; 74 L.S.K.B. 324; 92 L.T. 207; 21 T.L.R. 198; 12 Mans. 11 *sub nom. Re* Eastgate *ex p.* Trustee 53 W.R. 432; 49 S.J. 205 206
Edgcome, *Re* [1902] 2 K.B. 403, C.A. Edgcome *Re, ex p.* Edgcome [1902] 2 K.B. 403 147
Edgington *v.* Fitzmaurice (1885) 29 Ch.D. 459 228
Edwards, *Re, ex p.* Chalmers, (1873) L.R. 8 Ch.App. 289; 42 L.J.Bcy. 37; 28 L.T. 325; 21 W.R. 349, L.C. & L.JJ. 393
—— *v.* Hood-Barrs [1905] 1 Ch. 20; 74 L.J.Ch. 167; 91 L.T. 766; 21 T.L.R. 89 268
—— *v.* Ronald (1830) 1 Knapp P.C. 259; 12 E.R. 317, P.C. 692, 710
Eilbeck, *Re* [1910] 1 K.B. 136 Eilbeck, *ex p.* "Good Intent" Lodge, No. 987 of the Grand United Order of Odd Fellows (Trustees), *Re* [1910] 1 K.B. 136; 79 L.J.K.B. 265; 101 L.T. 688; 26 T.L.R. 111; 54 S.J. 118; 17 Mans. 1 291
Elkins *v.* Capital Guarantee Society (1900) 16 T.L.R. 423, C.A. 638
Ellis *v.* M'Henry (1871) L.R. 6 C.P. 228; 40 L.J.C.P. 109; 23 L.T. 861; 19 W.R. 503 .... 692, 705, 710, 723
Ellis and Co.'s Trustee *v.* Dixon Johnson [1924] 1 Ch. 342; [1925] A.C. 489; 94 L.J.Ch. 221; 133 L.T. 60; 41 T.L.R. 336; 69 S.J. 395; [1925] B. & C.R. 54 H.L. 262, 273
Eloc Electro-Optieck and Communicatie B.V., *Re* [1981] 2 All E.R. 1111; [1982] Ch. 43; [1981] 3 W.L.R. 176; [1981] 1 C.R. 732; 125 S.J. 412 ...... 736, 737, 744
Emanuel *v.* Symon [1908] 1 K.B. 302; 77 L.J.K.B. 180; 98 L.T. 304; 24 T.L.R. 85, C.A. 694
Emerson's Case (1866) 1 Ch. 433 545
Emma Silver Mining Co. *v.* Grant (1880) 17 Ch.D. 122; 29 W.R. 481; 50 L.J.Ch. 449 318
Emmadart Ltd, *Re* [1979] Ch. 540; [1979] 2 W.L.R. 868; (1978) 123 S.J. 15; [1979] 1 All E.R. 599 .... 533, 534
Employers' Liability Assurance Corp. Ltd *v.* Sedgwick Collins & Co. Ltd [1927] A.C. 95, 95 L.J.K.B. 1015; 42 T.L.R. 749; *sub nom.* Sedgwick Collins & Co., Ltd *v.* Rossia Insurance Co. of Petrograd, 136 L.T. 72 H.L. 747, 759, 761
English, Scottish and Australian Chartered Bank, *Re* [1893] 3 Ch. 385 .... 757, 782
Enohin *v.* Wylie (1862) 10 H.L.C. 1; 31 L.J.Ch. 402; 2 L.T. 263; 8 Jur. N.S. 897; 10 W.R. 467; 11 E.R. 924, H.L. 728
Equiticorp International Ltd, *Re* [1989] 1 W.L.R. 1010; (1989) 5 B.C.C. 599; [1989] B.C.L.C. 597; [1989] L.S.Gaz. November 15, 36 .... 430, 534

Table of Cases

Eros Films Ltd, *Re* [1963] Ch. 565, [1963] 1 All E.R. 383; [1963] Ch. 565; [1963] 2 W.L.R. 496; 107 Sol. Jo. 155 273
Erskine, *Re* (1893) 10 T.L.R. 32; 38 S.J. 144, C.A. 698, 699
Esal (Commodities) Ltd, *Re* (1988) 4 B.C.C. 475, C.A. 562
Esal Commodities, *Re* (No. 2) [1990] B.C.C. 708 566
Evans, *Re* [1891] 1 Q.B. 143; 64 L.T. 242; 39 W.R. 98 333
—— *v.* Clayhope Properties Ltd [1988] 1 W.L.R. 358 367
—— *v.* South Ribble Borough Council [1992] 2 W.L.R. 429; [1992] Q.B. 757; [1992] 2 All E.R. 695; [1991] RA 191; 89 L.G.R. 1042; (1991) 135 S.J. (LB) 124; [1991] C.O.D. 465; [1991] N.P.C. 88; [1991] E.G.C.S. 74, *The Independent*, July 16, 1991; *The Times*, August 13, 1991 242
Evelyn, *Re* [1894] 2 Q.B. 302; 63 L.J.Q.B. 658; 70 L.T. 692; 42 W.R. 512; 10 T.L.R. 456; 38 Sol. Jo. 479; 1 Mans. 195; 10 R 238, D.C. 149
Exchange Securities & Commodities Ltd, *Re* [1983] B.C.L.C. 186 633
Exchange Travel Agency *v.* Triton Property Trust plc [1991] B.C.C. 341; [1991] B.C.L.C. 396 443
Expanded Plugs Ltd, *Re* [1966] 1 All E.R. 877 535
Ezekiel *v.* Orakpo [1976] 3 All E.R. 659, [1977] Q.B. 260; [1976] 3 W.L.R. 693; 120 Sol. Jo. 504, C.A. 148, 215

F.L.E. Holdings, *Re* [1967] 3 All E.R. 553; [1953] 1 W.L.R. 1409; 111 S.J. 600 227
FSA Business Software Ltd, *Re* [1990] B.C.C. 465 525
Fabric Sales Ltd *v.* Eratex Ltd [1984] 1 W.L.R. 863; 128 S.J. 330; (1984) 81 L.S.Gaz. 1597, C.A. 541
Fairway Magazines Ltd, *Re* [1992] B.C.C. 924 643
Falcon (R.J.) Developments Ltd, *Re* (1987) 3 B.C.C. 146; [1987] B.C.L.C. 437 .... 497, 535
Family Endowment Society, *Re* (1870) L.R. 5 Ch.App. 118; 39 L.J.Ch. 306; 21 L.T. 775; 18 W.R. 266, L.C. & L.J. 733, 744
Fancy Dress Balls Co., *Re* [1899] W.N. 109, 43 S.J. 657 537
Farley *v.* Housing and Commercial Developments Ltd [1984] B.C.L.C. 442 ... 274
Farmers' Mart Ltd *v.* Milne [1915] A.C. 106, H.L. 165
Farnham *v.* Milward & Co. [1895] 2 Ch. 730 173
Fearman (W.F.) Ltd, *Re* (1988) 4 B.C.C. 139 433
—— (No. 2) (1988) *Re* 4 B.C.C. 141 440
Federal Bank of Australia (1893) W.N. 77 732
——, *Re* [1893] W.N. 77 .... 752, 766, 782
Federal Commerce and Navigation Co. Ltd *v.* Tradax Export S.A. [1978] A.C. 1, H.L.; [1977] 2 All E.R. 849; [1977] 3 W.L.R. 126; 121 S.J. 459; [1977] 2 Lloyd's Rep. 301, H.L. 259
Felixstowe Dock and Railway Co. *v.* U.S. Lines Inc. [1988] 2 All E.R. 77; [1987] 2 F.T.L.R. 75; [1987] 2 Lloyd's Rep. 76 .... 689, 765, 766
Fenton, *Re* [1931] 1 Ch. 85; 99 L.J.Ch. 358; 143 L.T. 273; 46 T.L.R. 478; 74 S.J. 387; [1929] B. & C.R. 189, C.A. 95, 275
Ferguson *v.* Spencer (1840) 1 Man. & G. 987; 133 E.R. 632; 2 Scott, N.R. 229; 10 L.J.C.P. 20 .... 692, 724
Fiesta Girl of London *v.* Network Agencies [1992] 32 E.G. 55; *sub nom.* Company (No. 11102 of 1991) A, *Re* [1992] E.G.C.S. 79 546
Findlay *v.* Findlay [1947] P. 122; [1947] L.J.R. 1338; 63 T.L.R. 391; 91 S.J. 397; [1947] 2 All E.R. 969 266
Finley, *ex p.* Clothworks' Co., *Re* (1888) 21 Q.B.D. 475; 57 L.J.Q.B. 626; 60 L.T. 134; 37 W.R. 6; 4 T.L.R. 745 *sub nom. Re* Findley, *ex p.* Hanbury 5 Morr. 248, C.A. 238
Finney, *Re* (1878) 30 L.T. 620 233
First Express, *Re* [1991] B.C.C. 782 380
Firth, *Re, ex p.* Schofield, (1879) 12 Ch.D. 337; 40 L.T. 823; 27 W.R. 925 .... 286, 153
Fisher *v.* Raven [1964] A.C. 210; [1963] 2 All E.R. 389; [1963] 2 W.L.R. 1146; 127 J.P. 382; 107 Sol. Jo. 373; 47 Cr.App.Rep. 174, H.L. 352, 353

TABLE OF CASES

Fitness Centre (South East) Ltd, *Re* [1986] B.C.L.C. 518 497
Flatau, *Re* (1888) 22 Q.B.D. 83 .... 133, 134
Fleetwood & District Electric Light & Power Syndicate, *Re* [1915] 1 Ch. 486 ... 596
Flint (A Bankrupt), *Re* [1993] 2 W.L.R. 537, C.A.; [1993] Ch. 319; [1993] 1 F.L.R.
   763; (1992) 136 S.J. (L.B.) 221; *The Times*, July 16, 1992 198
Flint *v.* Barnard (1888) 22 Q.B.D. 90, C.A.; 58 C.J.Q.B. 53; 37 W.R. 185; 5 T.L.R.
   79, C.A. 50
Flower *v.* Lyme Regis Corporation [1921] 1 K.B. 488, C.A.; 90 L.J.K.B. 355; 124
   L.T. 463; 37 T.L.R. 145; 65 S.J. 133; [1920] B. & C.R. 138 56
Forder, *Re* [1927] 2 Ch. 291; [1927] All E.R. Rep. 324; 96 L.J. Ch. 314; 137 L.T.
   538; [1927] B. & C.R. 84, C.A. 214
Forster *v.* Wilson (1843) 12 M. & W. 191; 152 E.R. 1165; 13 L.J.Ex. 209 272
Forte's (Manufacturing) Ltd, *Re*; Pension Trust Ltd *v.* Registrar of Companies
   [1994] B.C.C. 84 624
Fortuna Holdings Pty. *v.* F.C.T. (1976) 2 A.C.L.R. 349 537
Fortune Copper Mining Co., *Re* (1870) L.R. 10 Eq. 390; 40 L.J.Ch.43; 23 L.T.
   650 526
Foster Clark's Indenture Trusts, *Re* [1966] 1 All E.R. 43 383
Foster, Yates and Thom Ltd *v.* H.W. Edgehill Equipment Ltd (1978) 122 S.J. 860;
   The Times, November 29, 1978, C.A. 624
Fothergill, *ex p.* Turquand, *Re* (1876) 3 Ch.D. 445; 45 L.J.Bcy. 153, C.A. 261
Four Point Garage Ltd *v.* Carter [1985] 3 All E.R. 12 .... 217, 636
Fowler *v.* Broad's Patent Night Light Co. [1893] 1 Ch. 724; 62 L.J.Ch. 373; 68
   L.T. 576; 41 W.R. 247; 37 S.J. 232; 3 R. 295 555
—— *v.* Commercial Timber Co. Ltd [1930] 2 K.B. 1; [1930] All E.R. Rep. 224; 99
   L.J.K.B. 529; 143 L.T. 391, C.A. 506, 555
Fraser, *ex p.* Central Bank of London, *Re*, [1892] 2 Q.B. 633; [1891–94] All E.R.
   Rep. 939; 67 L.T. 401; 36 Sol. Jo. 714; 9 Morr. 256, C.A. 135
Freeman *v.* Pope (1870) 5 Ch.App. 538; [1861–73] All E.R. Rep. Ext. 1785; 39 L.J.
   Ch. 689; 23 L.T. 208; 34 J.P. 659; 18 W.R. 906, L.C. & L.J. 221
Freevale Ltd *v.* Metrostore (Holdings) [1984] Ch. 199; [1984] 1 All E.R. 495;
   [1984] 2 W.L.R. 496 388
French, *Re* (1889) 24 Q.B.D. 63; 62 L.T. 93; 38 W.R.; 6 T.L.R. 1; 6 Morr. 258,
   C.A. 127
French's (Wine Bar), *Re* [1987] B.C.L.C. 499; (1987) 3 B.C.C. 173 631
Fryer, *Re* (1866) 17 Q.B.D. 718 84

Galbraith *v.* Grimshaw [1910] A.C. 508, H.L.; [1908–10] All E.Rep. 561; 79
   L.J.K.B. 1011; 103 L.T. 294; 54 Sol. Jo. 634; 17 Mans. 183, H.L. 720, 721
Gallard, *ex p.* Gallard, *Re* [1896] 1 Q.B. 68; 65 L.J.Q.B. 199; 73 L.T. 457; 44
   W.R.121; 12 T.L.R. 43; 40 Sol. Jo. 99; 2 Mans. 515 .... 172, 183
Gallidoro Trawlers Ltd, *Re* [1991] B.C.C. 691; [1991] B.C.L.C. 411 429
Gamelstaden plc *v.* Brackland Magazines Ltd [1993] B.C.C. 194 549
Gardiner *v.* Houghton (1862) 2 B. & S. 743; 121 E.R. 1247 .... 692, 723
Gardner, *Re* [1942] Ch. 50 320
Garrett, *Re* [1930] 2 Ch. 137 220
Garrud, *Re* (1880) 16 Ch.D. 552 205
Gaskell, *Re* [1904] 2 K.B. 313
William Gaskell Group *v.* Highley [1993] B.C.C. 200 359
Gasque *v.* Commissioners of Inland Revenue [1940] 2 K.B. 80; 109 L.J.B. 769; 56
   T.L.R. 683; 84 S.J. 478; 23 Tax Cas. 210 .... 734, 759
Gedney, *Re* [1908] 1 Ch. 804 273
Gee, *Re* (1889) 24 Q.B.D. 65 236
Geen, *Re* [1917] 1 K.B. 183 247
Geiger, *Re* [1915] 1 K.B. 439 172
General Rolling Stock Co., *Re* (Chapman's Case) (1866) L.R. 1 Eq. 346; 35 Beav.
   207; 12 Jur.N.S. 44; 55 E.R. 874 555
——, *Re* Joint Stock Discount Company's Claim (1872) 7 Ch.App. 646; 41 L.J.Ch.
   732; 27 L.T. 88; 20 W.R. 762, L.JJ. 596

TABLE OF CASES

General Steam Navigation v. Guillou (1843) 11 M. and W. 877; 152 E.R. 1061; 13
  L.J.Ex. 168 .... 734, 758
George v. Thompson's Trustee [1949] Ch. 322; 93 S.J. 217; [1949] 1 All E.R.
  554 244
Gertzenstein Ltd, Re [1937] Ch. 115 584
Gibbons, Re (1960) 26 Ir.Jur. 60 .... 706, 707
Gibbs and Sons v. La Société Industrielle et Commerciale des Métaux (1890) 25
  Q.B.D. 399; 63 L.T. 503; 6 T.L.R. 393 .... 319, 692, 725, 758, 762
Gilbert, ex p. Gilbert, Re [1898] 1 Q.B. 282; 67 L.J.Q.B. 229; 775; 46 W.R. 351; 14
  T.L.R. 125; 42 S.J. 118; 4 Mans. 337 .... 277, 332
Gill v. Barron (1868) L.R. 2 P.C. 157; 5 Moo. P.C.C.N.S. 213; 37 L.J.P.C. 33; 16
  E.R. 496, P.C. 692, 705, 710
Gilmartin, Re [1989] 2 All E.R. 835 133
Glaister-Carlisle v. Glaister-Carlisle (1968) 112 S.J. 215; *The Times*, February 22,
  1968, C.A. 213
Globe New Patent Iron and Steel Co., Re (1875) L.R. 20 Eq. 337; 44 L.J.Ch. 580;
  23 W.R. 823 527
Gluckstein v. Barnes [1900] A.C. 240, H.L.; 69 L.J. Ch. 385; 82 L.T. 393; 16
  T.L.R. 321; 7 Mans. 321, H.L.; affg. S.C. *sub nom*. Re Olympia Ltd [1898] 2
  Ch. 153; 67 L.J. Ch. 433; 14 T.L.R. 451; 5 Man 139; *sub nom* Re Olympia Ltd,
  ex p. Gluckstein 78 L.T. 629; 42 Sol. Jo. 290, C.A. 659
Godfrey v. Furzo (1733) 3 P.Wms 185; 24 E.R. 1022, L.C. 209
Goetze & Sohn v. Aders Preyer & Co. (1874) 2 R. 150; 12 Sc.L.R. 121 (Scot.) .. 728
Golden Chemical Products Ltd, Re [1976] Ch. 300; [1976] 3 W.L.R. 1; 120 S.J.
  401; [1976] 2 All E.R. 543 540
Gomba Holdings UK Ltd v. Homan [1986] 3 All E.R. 94; [1986] 1 W.L.R.
  1301 .... 395, 396
Gomersall, Re (1875) 1 Ch.D. 137; 45 L.J.Bcy. 1; 24 W.R. 257, C.A.; affd. *sub nom*.
  Jones v. Gordon (1877) 2 App. Cas. 616, H.L. 261
Gooch, ex p. Judd, Re [1921] 2 K.B. 593 135
Goring, ex p., (1790) 1 Ves. Jun. 168; 30 E.R. 284 176
Gorringe v. Irwell India Rubber Works (1886) 34 Ch.D. 128; [1886–90] All E.R.
  Rep. Ext. 1643; 56 L.J. Ch. 85; 55 L.T. 572; 35 W.R. 86, C.A. 629, 630
Goscott (Groundworks) Ltd, Re [1988] B.C.L.C. 363; (1988) P.C.C. 297; (1988)
  4 B.C.C. 372; [1988] 2 F.T.L.R. 80 440
Gosling v. Gaskell [1897] A.C. 575; 66 L.J.Q.B. 848; 77 L.T. 314; 46 W.R. 208; 13
  T.L.R. 544, H.L.; reversing S.C. *sub nom*. Gaskell v. Gosling [1896] 1 Q.B.
  669, C.A. 396, 555
Gould, ex p. Gould, Re (1890) 7 Morr. 215 .... 313, 314
Government of India, Ministry of Finance (Revenue Division) v. Taylor; see India
  (Government of), Ministry of Finance (Revenue Division) v. Taylor [1955]
  A.C. 491; [1955] 2 W.L.R. 303; 99 S.J. 94; [1955] 1 All E.R. 292; [1955] T.R.
  9; 48 R. & I.T. 98; *sub nom*. Re Delhi Electric Supply & Traction Co. 34 A.T.C.
  10, H.L. 254, 707
Governors of St Thomas's Hospital v. Richardson [1910] 1 K.B. 271 210
Goy & Co. Ltd, Re, Farmer v. Goy & Co. Ltd [1900] 2 Ch. 149; 69 L.J.Ch. 481; 83
  L.T. 309; 48 W.R. 425; 16 T.L.R. 310; 8 Mans. 221 507
Gozzett, Re, ex p. Messenger & Co, Ltd v. Trustee [1936] 1 All E.R. 79; 80 S.J. 146,
  C.A. 207
Graham, Re [1928] 4 D.L.R. 375; [1928] 3 W.W.R. 8; 10 C.B.R. 171 705
——, Re (No. 2) [1929] 3 D.L.R. 353; [1929] 1 W.W.R. 309; 23 S.L.R. 297; 10
  C.B.R. 340 .... 705, 706
—— v. Lewis (1888) 22 Q.B.D. 1 697
Grainger v. Hill (1838) 4 Bing (N.C.) 212; 132 E.R. 769; 1 Arn. 42; 5 Scott, 561; 7
  L.J.C.P. 85; *sub nom*. Grainger v. Hill 2 Jur. 235 100
Grason, ex p. Taylor, Re (1879) 12 Ch. D. 366; 41 L.T. 6; 28 W.R. 205, C.A. .. 297
Graydon, ex p. Official Receiver, [1896] 1 Q.B. 417 203
Gray's Inn Construction Co. Ltd, Re [1980] 1 All E.R. 814, C.A. 629, 630
Great Eastern Electric Co. Ltd, Re [1941] 1 Ch. 241; [1941] 1 All E.R. 409; 57
  T.L.R. 373; 165 L.T. 366 507

TABLE OF CASES

Great Orme Tramways, *Re* (1934) 50 T.L.R. 450 257
Green and Sons (Northampton) Ltd *v.* Morris [1914] 1 Ch. 562; 83 L.J.Ch. 559;
   110 L.T. 508; 30 T.L.R. 301; 58 S.J. 398 190
Greenstone Shipping Co. S.A. *v.* Indian Oil Corp. Ltd *Financial Times*, March 20,
   1987 635
Greenwood, *Re* [1900] 2 Q.B. 306 538
—— *v.* Algesiras Ry Co. [1894] 2 Ch. 205; 63 L.J.Ch. 670; 71 L.T. 133; 1 Mans.
   455; 7 R. 620, C.A. 365
Gregory, *ex p.* Norton, *Re* (No. 1) [1935] Ch. 65; All E.R. Rep. 429; 78 S.J. 550; 104
   L.J.Ch. 1; [1934] B. & C.R. 165; 152 L.T. 58, C.A. 135, 153, 254
Grey's Brewery, *Re* (1883) 25 Ch. D. 400; 53 L.J.Ch. 262; 50 L.T. 14; 32 W.R. 381;
   28 S.J. 104 153
Griffiths, Jones *v.* Jenkins, *Re*, [1926] 1 Ch. 1007; 95 L.J. Ch. 429; 136 L.T. 57; 70
   S.J. 735; [1926] B. & C.R. 56 214
—— *v.* Secretary of State for Social Services [1974] 1 Q.B. 468; [1973] 3 All E.R.
   1184; [1973] 3 W.L.R. 831; 117 Sol. Jo. 873 .... 367, 383
Grosvenor Metal Co. Ltd, *Re* [1950] Ch. 63; 93 S.J. 774; [1949] 2 All E.R. 948; *sub*
   nom. Re Grosvenor Metal Co., *ex p.* Bebb Industries, 65 T.L.R. 755 ...... 244, 556
Guedalla, *Re*; Lee *v.* Guedalla's Trustee [1905] 2 Ch. 331; 75 L.J.Ch. 52; 94 L.T.
   94; 54 W.R. 77; 12 Mans. 392 211
Gunsbourg, *Re* (1919) 88 L.J.K.B. 479; [1920] 2 K.B. 426; *sub nom. Re* Gunsbourg,
   ex p. Trustee, 89 L.J.K.B. 725; *sub nom.* Re Gunsbourg (A.) & Co. Ltd, *ex p.*
   Cook [1920] All E.R. Rep. 492; 123 L.T. 353; 36 T.L.R. 485; 64 S.J. 498;
   [1920] B. & C.R. 50, C.A. 189, 245
Gutta Percha Corp., *Re* [1900] 2 Ch. 665; 69 L.J.Ch. 769; 83 L.T. 401; 44 Sol. Jo.
   628; 8 Mans. 67 535
Guy *v.* Churchill (1888) 40 Ch.D. 481; 58 L.J.Ch. 345; 60 L.T. 473; 37 W.R. 504;
   5 T.L.R. 149 193

Hafna Mining Co. *Re* (1888) 84 L.T. (o.s.) 403 514
Halberstamm, *Re* (1881) 17 Ch.D. 518; 29 W.R. 621, C.A. 152
Hall, *ex p.* Official Receiver *Re*, [1907] 1 K.B. 875; 76 L.J.K.B. 546; 97 L.T. 33; 23
   T.L.R. 327; 51 S.J. 292; 14 Mans. 82, C.A. 207
Hall (William) (Contractors) (in liquidation) Ltd, *Re* [1967] 2 All E.R. 1150;
   [1967] 1 W.L.R. 948; 111 S.J. 472; *sub nom.* William Hall (Contractors) Ltd,
   Re [1967] 2 All E.R. 1150 284
Hallett & Co., *Re* [1894] 2 Q.B. 237 211
Hallett's Estate, Knatchbull *v.* Hallett, Cotterell *v.* Hallett *Re* (1880) 13 Ch.D. 696;
   492 J.Ch. 415; 42 L.T. 421; 28 W.R. 732, C.A. 211
Hancock, *ex p.* Hillearys, *Re* [1904] 1 K.B. 585; 73 L.J.K.B. 245; 90 L.T. 389; 52
   W.R. 547; 48 S.J. 260; 11 Mans. 1, C.A. 119, 122
Hans Place Ltd, *Re* [1992] B.C.C. 737 237
Hardy *v.* Fothergill (1888) 13 App.Cas. 351, H.L.; [1886–90] All E.R. Rep. 597;
   58 L.J.Q.B. 44; 59 L.T. 273; 53 JP 36; 37 W.R. 177; 4 T.L.R. 603, H.L.;
   affg. S.C. *sub nom.* Morgan *v.* Hardy (1887) 18 Q.B.D. 646; 35 W.R. 588,
   C.A. 263, 284
Harris, *Re* (1896) 74 L.T. 221; 3 Mans. 46 708
—— *v.* Truman (1882) 9 Q.B.D. 264; 51 L.J.Q.B. 338; 46 L.T. 844; 30 W.R. 533,
   C.A. 209
Harris Simons Construction Ltd, *Re* [1989] B.C.L.C. 202; [1989] 1 W.L.R.
   368 424
Harrison, *Re* (1880) 14 Ch.D. 19 216
Harrods (Buenos Aires) Ltd, *Re* [1992] Ch. 72, C.A. 703
Hart, *Re* (1884) 25 Ch.D. 716, 53 L.J.Ch. 618; 50 L.T. 651; 32 W.R. 396,
   C.A. 276
Hartlebury Printers Ltd, *Re* [1992] B.C.C. 428 463
Hastings, *ex p.* Dearle, *Re* (1884) 14 Q.B.D. 184; 54 L.J.Q.B. 74; 33 W.R. 440; 1
   Morr. 281, C.A. 84
——, *Re* (1892) 61 L.J.Q.B. 654 149

Table of Cases

Hawkins, *ex p*. Dearle, *Re* [1894] 1 Q.B. 25; 69 L.T. 234; 8 T.L.R. 683; 36 S.J. 733; 9 Morr. 234 148
———, *ex p*. Troup, *Re* [1895] 1 Q.B. 404; 64 L.J.Q.B. 373; 72 L.T. 41; 43 W.R. 306; 39 S.J. 115; 2 Mans. 130 135
Hay, *Re* [1915] 2 Ch. 198; 84 L.J.Ch. 821; 113 L.T. 923 331
Hayward, *Re* Hayward *v*. Hayward [1897] 1 Ch. 905; 66 L.J.Ch. 392; 76 L.T. 383; 45 W.R. 439; 41 S.J. 367; 4 Mans. 130 214
Headington Investments Ltd, *ex p*. Maxwell, *Re* [1993] B.C.C. 500 569
Health *v*. Tang; Stevens *v*. Peacock [1993] 1 W.L.R. 1421; [1993] 4 All E.R. 694; *The Times*, August 11, 1993; *The Independent*, October 14, 1993, C.A. 316
Heather & Son *v*. Webb (1876) 2 C.P.D. 1; 46 L.J.Q.B. 89; 25 W.R. 253 319
Hecquard, *Re* (1989) 24 Q.B.D. 71 .... 699, 700
Hedderwick, *Re* Morlen *v*. Brinsley [1933] Ch. 669 102 L.J.Ch. 193; 149 L.T. 188; 49 T.L.R. 381 267
Hemming *v*. Davies [1898] 1 Q.B. 660; 67 L.J.Q.B. 458; 78 L.T. 500; 14 T.L.R. 309; 42 S.J. 365; 5 Mans. 73, D.C. 173
Hendy Lennox (Industrial Engines) *v*. Grahame Puttick [1984] 1 W.L.R. 485; 128 S.J. 220; [1984] 2 All E.R. 152; [1984] 2 Lloyd's Rep. 422; (1984) 81 L.S.Gaz. 585 .... 217, 635
Henley, *ex p*. Dixon, *Re* (1876) 4 Ch.D. 133; 46 L.J.Bcy. 20; 35 L.T. 644; 25 W.R. 105, C.A. 278
Bill Hennessey Associates, *Re* [1992] B.C.C. 386 546
Herbert Berry Associates Ltd, *Re* [1976] 3 All E.R. 207; [1976] 1 W.L.R. 783 .. 557
Hercules Insurance Co., *Re* (1871) L.R. 11 Eq. 321; *sub nom*. *Re* Hercules Insurance Co. Ltd, *Re* International Life Assurance Society 40 L.J.Ch. 379 . 493
Re Hermann Loog Ltd (1887) 36 Ch.D. 502; 58 L.T. 47; 35 W.R. 687 753
Hester, *ex p*. Hester, *Re* (1889) 22 Q.B.D. 632; 8 I.L.T.Jo. 109 .... 119, 120
Hewitt Brannan (Tools), *Re* [1990] B.C.C. 354; [1991] B.C.L.C. 80 497
Hibernian Merchants, *Re* [1958] Ch. 76; [1957] 3 W.L.R. 486; 101 S.J. 647; [1957] 3 All E.R. 97 .... 752, 766
Hide, *ex p*. Llynvi Coal & Iron Co., *Re* (1871) 7 Ch.App. 28; 41 L.J. Bcy.5; 25 L.T. 609; 20 W.R. 105, L.JJ. 240
Higginson and Dean, *ex p*. A.-G., *Re* [1899] 1 Q.B. 325; 68 L.J.Q.B. 198; 79 L.T. 609; 20 W.R. 105, L.JJ. 758, 762, 763
Highway Foods International (in administrative receivership), *Re*, [1995] B.C.C. 271; *The Times*, November 1, 1994 636
Hill *v*. East and West India Dock (1884) 9 App. Cas. 448 239
——— *v*. Smith (1844) 12 M. & W. 618; 152 E.R. 1346; 13 L.J.Ex. 243; 2 L.T.O.S. 424; 8 Jur. 179 192
Hille India Rubber Co., *Re* [1897] W.N. 6 545
Hindcastle Ltd *v*. Barbara Attenborough Associates [1994] 3 W.L.R. 1100; [1994] 4 All E.R. 129; [1994] E.G. 154; [1994] E.G.C.S. 109; [1994] N.P.C. 86; *The Times*, July 6, 1994, C.A. 240
Hire Purchase Furnishing Co. Ltd, The *v*. Richens (1887) 20 Q.B.D. 387; 58 L.T. 460; 36 W.R. 365; 4 T.L.R. 184 507
Hoare, *ex p*. Nelson, *Re* (1880) 14 Ch.D. 41; 49 L.J.Bcy. 44; 42 L.T. 389; 28 W.R. 554, C.A. 149
Hockley (William), *Re* [1962] 1 W.L.R. 555; 106 S.J. 308; [1962] 2 All E.R. 111 537
Hodgson, *ex p*. Brett, *Re* (1875) 1 Ch. D. 151; 33 L.T. 711; 24 W.R. 101 342
Holliday, *Re*, *ex p*. Trustee of the Bankrupt *v*. Bankrupt [1981] 1 Ch. 405; [1981] 2 W.L.R. 996; 125 S.J. 411; [1980] 3 All E.R. 385, C.A. 195, 196
Holloway *v*. York (1877) 25 W.R. 627 193
Holmes, *ex p*. Ashworth, *Re* [1908] 2 K.B. 812; 77 L.J.K.B. 1129; 52 S.J. 728; 15 Mans. 331, C.A. 238
——— *v*. Watt [1935] All E.R. Rep. 496; [1935] 2 K.B. 300; 104 L.J.K.B. 654; 153 L.T. 58, C.A. 241
Eric Holmes (Property) Ltd [1965] 2 All E.R. 333; [1965] Ch. 1052; [1965] 2 W.L.R. 1260; 109 Sol. Jo. 251 227
Home and Colonial Insurance Co., *Re* [1930] 1 Ch. 102; *sub nom*. *Re* Home & Colonial Insurance Co., May *v*. Barham 99 L.J.Ch. 113; 142 L.T. 207; [1929] B. & C.R. 85 253

TABLE OF CASES

Home Remedies Ltd, *Re* [1943] Ch. 1; 112 L.J. Ch. 36; 167 L.T. 362; 59 T.L.R. 31 .... 497, 537
Home Treat, *Re* [1991] B.C.C. 165; [1991] B.C.L.C. 705 453
Home's Trustee *v.* Home's Trustees 1926 S.L.T. 214 .... 706, 718
Re Hone (Bkpt), *ex p.* Trustee *v.* Kensington B.C. [1950] 2 All E.R. 716; [1951] Ch. 85; 114 J.P. 495; 66 (pt. 2) T.L.R. 350 201
Hooley, *ex p.* Hooley, *Re* (1899) 79 L.T. 706; 6 Mans. 44 560
——, Rucker's Case, *Re* 5 Mans. 331; (1898) 79 L.T. 306; 15 T.L.R. 16 158
Horne *v.* Chester and Fein Property Developments Pty. Ltd (1987) 5 A.C.L.C. 245 616
Hosack *v.* Robbins [1918] 2 Ch. 339; 87 L.J.Ch. 545; 119 L.T. 522; 62 S.J. 681; [1918–19] B. & C.R. 54, C.A. 201
Houghton, *ex p.* Tayler, *Re* (1857) 1 De. G. & J. 302; 44 E.R. 740; 26 L.J. Bcy. 58; 29 L.T.O.S. 254; 3 Jur. N.S. 753; 5 W.R. 669 261
Houlder, *Re* [1929] 1 Ch. 205; [1929] All E.R. Rep. 336 269
Houlditch *v.* Donegall (1834) 2 Cl. & F. 470, H.L.; 6 E.R. 1232 .... 718, 720
House Property and Investment Co., *Re* [1954] Ch. 576; [1953] 3 W.L.R. 1037; 97 S.J. 862; [1953] 2 All E.R. 1525 285
Howard, *Re* (1884) 14 Q.B.D. 310 149
—— *v.* Crowther (1841) 8 M. & W. 601; 151 E.R. 1179; 10 L.J. Ex. 355; 5 Jur. 914 191
—— *v.* Fanshawe [1895] 2 Ch. 581; 64 L.J.Ch. 666; 73 L.T. 77; 43 W.R. 645; 39 S.J. 623; 13 R. 663 .... 191, 192
Hubbock *v.* Helms (1887) 56 L.T. 232 363
Huggins, *Re* (1882) 21 Ch.D. 85 220
Humberstone Jersey Ltd, *Re* (1977) 74 L.S.G. 711, C.A. 525
Hunt *v.* Fripp [1878] 1 Ch. 675; 67 L.J.Ch. 377; 77 L.T. 516; 46 W.R. 125; 42 S.J. 47; 5 Mans. 105 200
Hunter *v.* Potts (1791) 4 Term Rep. 182; 100 E.R. 962 714
Hutchins *v.* Chambers (1758) 1 Burr. 579; 97 E.R. 458 557
Hutton, *Re* (A Bankrupt), Mediterranean Machine Operations *v.* Hargh [1969] Ch. 201; [1969] 2 W.L.R. 661; [1969] 1 All E.R. 936 147
Hyde (N.H.) Ltd, *Re* [1900] W.N. 245 537

I.I.T., *Re* (1975) 58 D.L.R. (3d) 55 760
Imperial Anglo-German Bank, *Re* (1872) 26 L.T. 229 733
Imperial Motors (U.K.) Ltd, *Re* [1990] B.C.L.C. 29 426
Independent Air Travel Ltd, *Re* [1961] 1 Lloyd's Rep. 604 638
Independent Automatic Sales Ltd *v.* Knowles and Foster [1962] 3 All E.R. 27; [1962] 1 W.L.R. 974; 106 S.J. 720 231
Indian and General Investment Trust Ltd *v.* Borax Consolidated Ltd [1920] 1 K.B. 539; 89 L.J.K.B. 252; 122 L.T. 547; 36 T.L.R. 125; 64 S.J. 225 763
Industrial Insurance Association [1910] W.N. 245 537
Inland Revenue *v.* Highland Engineering Ltd, 1975 S.L.T. 203 .... 735, 736, 744
I.R.C. *v.* Lysaght [1928] A.C. 234 698
Instrumentation Electrical Services Ltd, *Re* (1988) 4 B.C.C. 301; [1988] B.C.L.C. 550; 1989, P.C.C. 101 .... 430, 534
International Bulk Commodities Ltd, *Re* [1993] Ch. 77; [1992] 3 W.L.R. 238; [1993] 1 All E.R. 361; [1992] B.C.C. 463; [1992] B.C.L.C. 1074 .... 361, 362, 432, 786
International Harvester Co. *v.* Kentucky, 234 U.S. 579 (1914) 749
International Harvester Export Co. *v.* International Harvester Australia Co. [1983] V.R. 539 365
International Pulp and Paper Co. Ltd, *Re* (1876) 3 Ch.D. 594 753
International Shoe Co. *v.* State of Washington, 326 U.S. 310 (1945) 749
International Tin Council, *Re* [1989] Ch. 309; (1988) 4 B.C.C. 653; 1989 P.C.C. 90, C.A. 738, 750, 751
International Westminster Bank *v.* Okeanos, *sub nom.* Company (No. 00359 of 1987) A, *Re* [1988] Ch. 210; [1987] B.C.L.C. 450; [1987] 3 All E.R. 137; [1987] 3 W.L.R. 339 737

Islington Metal and Plating Works Ltd, *Re* [1984] 1 W.L.R. 14; 128 S.J. 31; [1983] 3 All E.R. 218; (1984) 81 L.S.Gaz. 354; [1983] Com.L.R. 176; (1983) 133 New L.J. 847 597
Izod, *ex p.* Official Receiver, *Re* [1898] 1 Q.B. 241; 67 L.J.Q.B. 111; 77 L.T. 640; 46 W.R. 304; 14 T.L.R. 115; 42 S.J. 117; 4 Mans. 343, C.A. 119, 121

Jackson, *Re* [1932] A.C. 365 296
——, *Re* [1973] N.Ir. 67 706
Jackson & Bassford Ltd, *Re* [1906] 2 Ch. 467 649
Jacob (Walter L.) & Co., *Re* [1989] B.C.L.C. 345; 1989 P.C.C. 47, C.A. 540
Jacobson *v.* Frachon (1927) 138 L.T. 386; 44 T.L.R. 103; 72 S.J. 121, C.A. 694
Jakeman *v.* Cook (1878) 4 Ex.D. 26; 48 L.J.Q.B. 165; 27 W.R. 171; 43 J.P. 255, D.C. 50, 319
James, *Re* (1891) 8 Morr. 19 313
—— *v.* James [1964] P. 303; [1963] 3 W.L.R. 331; 127 J.P. 352; 107 S.J. 116; [1963] 2 All E.R. 465, D.C. 266
Jawett, *Re* [1929] 1 Ch. 108; 98 L.J.Ch. 7; 140 L.T. 176; [1928] B. & R. 78 158
Jennings' Trustee *v.* King [1952] Ch. 899; [1952] 2 T.L.R. 469; 96 S.J. 648; [1952] 2 All E.R. 608 193
John *v.* Mendoza [1939] 1 K.B. 141; [1938] 4 All E.R. 472 326
Johnson, *Re* [1904] 1 K.B. 134 214
——, *Re* (1914) 111 L.T. 165 246
—— *v.* Emerson & Sparrow (1871) L.R. 6 Exch. 329; 40 L.J. Ex. 201; 25 L.T. 337 100
—— *v.* Smiley (1853) 17 Beav. 223; 51 E.R. 1019; 1 Eq. Rep. 397; 22 L.J.Ch. 826; 22 L.T.O.S. 39; 1 W.R. 440 205
Johnson (B.) & Co. (Builders) Ltd, *Re* [1955] Ch. 634; [1955] 3 W.L.R. 269; 99 S.J. 490; [1955] 2 All E.R. 775 397
Joint Administrators of Cloverbay Ltd *v.* Bank of Credit and Commerce International S.A. [1991] Ch. 90; [1990] 3 W.L.R. 574, C.A.; *The Independent*, May 4, 1990 .... 562, 563
Jollet *v.* Deponthieu (1769) 1 Hy. Bl. 132; 126 E.R. 80 720
Jones, *Re* (1881) 18 Ch.D. 109; 50 L.J.Ch. 673; 45 L.T. 193; 29 W.R. 747, C.A. 76
——, *ex p.* Nichols, *Re* (1883) 22 Ch.D. 782; 52 L.J.Ch. 635; 48 L.T. 492; 31 W.R. 661, C.A. 149
——, *v.* Challenger [1961] 1 Q.B. 176; [1960] 2 W.L.R. 695; 104 S.J. 328; [1960] 1 All E.R. 785, C.A. 195
Jones Bros, *ex p.* Associated Newspapers Ltd, *Re* [1912] 3 K.B. 234; 81 L.J.K.B. 1178; 19 Mans. 349, D.C. 96
Jubb, *ex p.* Burman & Greenwood, *Re* [1897] 1 Q.B. 641 137
Jubilee Sites Ltd, (1897) Syndicate, *Re*, [1899] 2 Ch. 204; 80 L.T. 869; 47 W.R. 606; 15 T.L.R. 391 .... 497, 539
Judgment Summons, A, *Re* (No. 25 of 1952), *ex p.* Henleys [1953] Ch. 195; [1953] 2 W.L.R. 315; [1953] 1 All E.R. 424; reversing [1953] Ch. 1; [1952] 2 All E.R. 772 .... 97, 98, 99
Jukes, *ex p.* Official Receiver, *Re* [1902] 2 K.B. 58; 71 L.J.K.B. 710; 86 L.T. 456; 50 W.R. 560; 46 S.J. 452; 9 Mans. 249 245

Karnos Property Co. Ltd, *Re* (1989) 5 B.C.C. 14 536
Karsberg (B.) Ltd, *Re* [1956] 1 W.L.R. 57; [1955] 3 All E.R. 854 .... 497, 537, 538
Katherine et Cie Ltd, *Re* [1932] 1 Ch. 70 237
Kavanagh, *Re* [1950] 1 All E.R. 39; 66 T.L.R. (Pt. 1) 65 192
Kayford, *Re* [1975] 1 All E.R. 604; 1 W.L.R. 279; 118 S.J. 752 638
Kearley *v.* Thomson (1890) 24 Q.B.D. 742; 63 L.T. 150; 38 W.R. 614; 6 T.L.R. 267 311
Keenan Bros, *Re* [1985] I.R. 401 456
Keene, *Re* [1922] 2 Ch. 475 190

TABLE OF CASES

Keet, *Re* [1905] 2 K.B. 666; 93 L.T. 259; 54 W.R. 20; 21 L.T.R. 615 . . . . 323, 326
Keever, *Re* [1967] Ch. 182; [1966] 3 W.L.R. 779; 110 S.J. 847; [1966] 3 All E.R.
    631 245
Kennedy (C.A.) Co. Ltd and Stibbe-Monk Ltd, *Re* (1977) 74 D.L.R. (3d) 87 . . . 708
Kent County Gas Light and Coke Co. Ltd [1909] 2 Ch. 195; 78 L.J.Ch. 625; 100
    L.T. 983; 16 Mans. 185 . . . . 200, 256
Kenward, *Re* (1906) 94 L.T. 277 331
Ker, *Re* (1879) 13 Ch.D. 304; 41 L.T. 743; 28 W.R. 403, C.A. 164
Kerr *v.* Kerr [1879] 2 Q.B. 439; 66 L.J.Q.B. 838; 77 L.T. 29; 46 W.R. 46; 13 T.L.R.
    534; 41 S.J. 679; 4 Mans. 207, D.C. 266
Keypack Homecare, *Re* [1987] B.C.L.C. 409; (1987) 3 B.C.C. 588 511
Keypack Homecare Ltd, *Re* (No. 2) [1990] B.C.C. 117 674
King, *ex p.* Furber, *Re* (1881) 17 Ch.D. 191; 44 L.T. 319; 29 W.R. 524 104
—— *v.* Henderson [1898] A.C. 720; 67 L.J.P.C. 134; 79 L.T. 37; 47 W.R. 157; 14
    T.L.R. 490; 5 Mans. 308, P.C. 99
—— *v.* Hutton [1900] 2 Q.B. 504; 69 L.J.Q.B. 786; 83 L.T. 68; 7 Mans. 393,
    C.A. 209
—— *v.* Michael Faraday and Partners Ltd [1939] 2 K.B. 753; [1939] 2 All E.R. 478;
    108 L.J.K.B. 589; 166 L.T. 484; 55 T.L.R. 684; 83 S.J. 498 164
Kitchen's Trustee *v.* Madders [1950] Ch. 134; [1949] 2 All E.R. 1079, C.A. . . . 273
Kitson, *Re* [1911] 2 K.B. 109; 80 L.J.K.B. 1147; 55 S.J. 443 330
—— *v.* Hardwick (1872) L.R. 7 C.P. 473; 26 L.T. 846 . . . . 91, 92
Kloebe, *Re* (1884) 28 Ch.D. 175 . . . . 711, 717, 718, 751
Knight *v.* Lawrence [1991] 01 E.G. 105 398
Kooperman, *Re* [1928] W.N. 101; 72 S.J. 400 722
Kraut A.G. *v.* Albany Fabrics Ltd [1977] Q.B. 112; [1976] 3 W.L.R. 872; [1977] 1
    All E.R. 116; [1976] 2 Lloyd's Rep. 350 259
Kuenigl *v.* Donnersmarck [1955] 1 Q.B. 515 759
—— *v.* Donnersmarck [1955] 1 Q.B. 515; [1955] 2 W.L.R. 82; 99 S.J. 60; [1955] 1
    All E.R. 46 734
Kumar, *Re* [1993] 2 All E.R. 700 198
Kushler (M.) Ltd, *Re* [1943] Ch. 248 . . . . 227, 228

LHF Wools Ltd, *Re* [1970] Ch. 27 524
La Bourgogne [1899] A.C. 431, H.L. 748
Lacey, *Re* (1884) 13 Q.B.D. 128 . . . . 108, 282
—— *v.* Hill (1876) 4 Ch.D. 537 211
Laker Airways Ltd *v.* Pan American World Airways 559 F.Supp. 1124 (1983) . . . 755
Lamb, *Re* [1894] 2 Q.B. 805; 64 L.J.Q.B. 71; 71 L.T. 312; 10 T.L.R. 575; 38 S.J.
    667; 1 Mans. 373; 9 R. 636, C.A. 169
Lanaghan Brothers Ltd, *Re* [1977] 1 All E.R. 265 549
Lancashire Cotton Spinning Co., *Re* (1887) 35 Ch.D. 656; 56 L.J.Ch. 761; 57 L.T.
    511; 36 W.R. 305, C.A. 633
Land and Property Trust Co. plc, *Re* [1991] B.C.C. 446 424
——, *Re* (No. 2) [1993] B.C.C. 462, C.A. 439
Landau, *Re* [1934] 1 Ch. 549 204
Larard, *Re* (1896) 3 Mans. 317 118
Las Mercedes (Owners of the Ship) *v.* Abidin Daver (Owners of the Ship); Abidin
    Daver, The [1984] A.C. 398; [1984] 2 W.L.R. 196; [1984] 1 All E.R. 470;
    (1984) 128 S.J. 99; [1984] 1 Lloyd's Rep. 339; (1984) 134 New L.J. 235, H.L.;
    reversing [1983] 1 W.L.R. 884; [1983] 3 All E.R. 46; [1983] 2 Lloyd's Rep.
    279; [1983] Com.L.R. 181, C.A. 755
Lascomme Ltd *v.* United Dominions Trusts [1994] I.L.R.M. 227 387
Lathia *v.* Dronsfield Bros. Ltd [1987] B.C.L.C. 321 390
Laurence *v.* Hayes [1927] 2 K.B. 111 205
Lawrence *v.* European Credit Co. Ltd [1992] B.C.C. 792 315
Lawson's Trusts [1896] 1 Ch. 175 718
Laye, *Re* [1913] 1 Ch. 298; 82 L.J.Ch. 218; 108 L.T. 324; 54 S.J. 284; 20 Mans.
    124 214

TABLE OF CASES

Lazard Bros. v. Banque de Moscou [1932] 1 K.B. 617, C.A. 764
Lazard Bros. & Co. v. Banque Industrielle de Moscou [1932] 1 K.B. 617, C.A. . . 761
—— v. Midland Bank Ltd [1933] A.C. 289; 102 L.J.K.B. 191; 148 L.T. 242; 49
T.L.R. 94; 76 S.J. 888, H.L. 734, 735, 759, 761
Le Mesurier v. Le Mesurier [1895] A.C. 517; 64 L.J.P.C. 97; 72 L.T. 873; 11
T.L.R. 481; 11 R. 527, P.C. 719
Leach, Re [1900] 2 Q.B. 649; 83 L.T. 222; 49 W.R. 76 329
Lee, ex p. Good, Re (1880) 14 Ch.D. 82; 49 L.J. Bcy. 49; L.T. 450; 28 W.R. 553,
C.A. 283
—— v. Sangster (1957) 2 C.B.N.S. 1; 140 E.R. 310 172
Leeming v. Lady Murray (1879) 13 Ch.D. 123; 48 L.J.Ch. 737; 28 W.R. 338 ... 173
Leggatt, Re (1873) 8 Ch.App. 965; 42 L.J.Bcy. 87; 29 L.T. 125; 21 W.R. 874,
L.J. 210
Leitch (William C.) Bros. Ltd, Re [1932] 2 Ch. 71 659
Lennard, Re [1934] Ch. 235 .... 256, 277
Lennox, Re (1885) 16 Q.B.D. 315; 55 L.J.Q.B. 45; 54 L.T. 452; 34 W.R. 51; 2
T.L.R. 60; 2 Morr. 271, C.A. 134, 135
Leon v. York-O-Matic Ltd [1966] 3 All E.R. 277; [1966] 1 W.L.R. 1450; 110 S.J.
685 .... 173, 179, 237, 585
Leonard, Re [1896] 1 Q.B. 473; 65 L.J.Q.B. 393; 74 L.T. 183; 44 W.R. 438; 12
T.L.R. 257; 40 S.J. 338; 3 Mans. 43, C.A. 137
Leslie (J.) Engineering Co. Ltd (in liquidation), Re [1976] 1 W.L.R. 292 630
Levasseur v. Mason & Barry [1891] 2 Q.B. 73; 60 L.J.Q.R. 659; 64 L.T. 761; 39
W.R. 596; 7 T.L.R. 436, C.A. 720
Levene v. I.R.C. [1928] A.C. 217 698
Levitt (Jeffrey S.) Ltd, Re [1992] B.C.C. 137 565
Levy, ex p. Walton, Re (1881) 17 Ch.D. 746; 50 L.J.Ch. 657; 45 L.T. 1; 30 W.R.
395, C.A. 238
Levy (A.I.) (Holdings) Ltd, Re [1964] Ch. 19; [1963] 2 W.L.R. 1464; 107 S.J. 416;
[1963] 2 All E.R. 556 .... 555, 631
Levy's Trusts, Re (1885) 30 Ch.D. 119; 54 L.J.Ch. 968; 53 L.T. 200; 33 W.R.
895 722
Leyland Daf, Re; Ferranti International, Re [1994] B.C.C. 658 .... 376, 377, 474
Leyland Daf Ltd v. Automotive Products plc [1993] B.C.C. 389; [1994] 1
B.C.L.C. 245; (1993) 137 S.J. (L.B.) 133; The Times, April 9, 1993, C.A.;
affirming The Times, April 6, 1993 393
Leyton and Walthamstow Cycle Co. Ltd, Re [1901] 50 W.R. 93; 46 S.J. 71 537
Libyan Arab Foreign Bank v. Bankers Trust Co. [1989] Q.B. 728; [1989] 3 W.L.R.
314; (1989) 133 S.J. 568; [1989] 3 All E.R. 252 763
Lichtenstein (Herman) & Co. Ltd, Re (1903) 23 T.L.R. 424 538
Lines Brothers Ltd, Re [1982] 2 All E.R. 183; [1982] 2 W.L.R. 1010; 126 S.J. 197;
[1982] Com.L.R. 81, C.A., reversing (1981) 125 S.J. 426; [1981] Com.L.R.
214 259
Lind, Re, Industrials Finance Syndicate Ltd v. Lind [1915] 2 Ch. 345; 84 L.J.Ch.
884; 113 L.T. 956; 59 S.J. 651; [1915] H.B.R. 204, C.A. 213, 318
Lindsay v. Paterson (1840) 2 D.(Ct. of Sess.) 1373 713
L'Industrie Verrière Ltd, Re [1974] W.N. 222 545
Linton v. Linton (1885) 15 Q.B.D. 239; 54 L.J.Q.B. 529; 52 L.T. 782; 33 W.R.
714; 49 J.P. 597; 2 Morr. 179, C.A. 148
Lipe Ltd v. Leyland Daf Ltd [1993] B.C.C. 385; [1994] 1 B.C.L.C. 84; The Times,
April 2, 1993, C.A. 381, 391, 394
Lister, ex p. Bradford Overseers & Bradford Corpn., Re [1926] Chap. 149; sub nom.
Re Lister, ex p. Bradford Overseers & Corpn. v. Durrance 134 L.T. 178; 90 J.P.
33; 24 L.G.R. 67; [1926] B. & C.R. 5, C.A. 235
Lister (Henry) & Co., ex p. Huddersfield Banking, Re [1892] 2 Ch. 417; 61 L.J.Ch.
721; 67 L.T. 180; 40 W.R. 589; 8 T.L.R. 538; 36 S.J. 488 575
Lloyd Generale Italiano, Re (1885) 29 Ch.D. 219; 54 L.J.Ch. 748; 33 W.R.
728 736
Llynvi and Tondu Co., Re (1889) 6 T.L.R. 11 584
Lo-Line Electric Motors Ltd, Re [1988] Ch. 477; [1988] 3 W.L.R. 26; 132 S.J. 851;
[1988] 2 All E.R. 692; 1988 P.C.C. 236; [1988] 2 F.T.L.R. 107; (1988) 4
B.C.C. 415; [1988] B.C.L.C. 698; (1988) 138 New L.J. 119 673

TABLE OF CASES

Loftus-Otway, *Re* Otway *v.* Otway [1895] 2 Ch. 235; 64 L.J.Ch. 529; 72 L.T. 656; 13 R. 536; *sub nom. Re* Otway, Otway *v.* Otway, 43 W.R. 501, 39 S.J. 449 .. 214
London and Globe Finance Corp. Ltd., *Re* [1903] 1 Ch. 728; 88 L.T. 194; 51 W.R. 651; 19 T.L.R. 314 338
London and Paris Banking Corp., *Re* (1875) 19 Eq. 444; 23 W.R. 643 524
London and Provincial Pure Ice, *Re* [1904] W.N. 48 Sol.Jo. 589 545
London and South American Investment Trust Ltd *v.* British Tobacco Co. (Australia) Ltd [1927] 1 Ch. 107; 96 L.J.Ch. 58; 136 L.T. 436; 70 S.J. 1024; *sub nom.* Pass *v.* British Tobacco Co. (Australia) Ltd 42 T.L.R. 771 763
London Borough of Hounslow *v.* Peake [1974] 1 All E.R. 688 265
London Hamburg and Continental Exchange Bank, *Re* (1866) L.R. 2 Eq. 231; reversed (1866) L.R. 1 Ch.App. 433 545
London India Rubber Co., *Re* (1886) 14 C.T. 316; 12 Jur.N.S. 402; 14 W.R. 506 545
London Marine Assurance Association, *Re*, Andrews & Alexander's case, Chatt's case, Coon's case, Crew's case (1869) L.R. 8 Eq. 176; 20 L.T. 943; 17 W.R. 784 521
London Pressed Hinge Co. Ltd, *Re* [1905] 1 Ch. 576; 74 L.J.Ch. 321; 92 L.T. 409; 53 W.R. 407; 21 T.L.R. 322; 12 Mans. 219; 49 Sol.Jo. 334 363
London United Investments plc, *Re* [1991] B.C.C. 760; affirmed [1992] B.C.C. 202, C.A.; [1992] B.C.L.C. 285; [1992] 142 New L.J. 87; [1992] Gazette, 26 February, 27; *The Times*, January 1, 1992; *The Independent*, January 9, 1992; *Financial Times*, January 17, 1992; *The Guardian*, February 5, 1992, C.A.; affirming [1991] B.C.C. 760 565
London Wharfing and Warehousing Co. Ltd, *Re* (1865) 35 Beav. 37; 55 E.R. 808 524
London, Windsor and Greenwich Hotels Co. (Quartermaine's Case), *Re* [1892] 1 Ch. 639; 61 L.J.Ch. 273; 66 L.T. 19; 40 W.R. 298; 8 T.L.R. 204; 36 S.J. 185 284
London Wine Co. (Shippers) Ltd, *Re* (1986) P.C.C. 121 638
Long, *ex p.* Cuddeford, *Re* (1888) 20 Q.B.D. 316; 57 L.J.Q.B. 360; 58 L.T. 664; 36 W.R. 346; 4 T.L.R. 232; 5 Morr. 29, C.A. 102
Lord's Trustee *v.* Great Eastern Railway Co. [1908] 1 K.B. 195 191
Lorillard, *Re*, Griffiths *v.* Catforth [1922] 2 Ch. 638; [1922] All E.R. 500; 92 L.J.Ch. 148; 127 L.T. 613; 38 T.L.R. 666, C.A. 708, 711
Loteka Pty. Ltd, *Re* (1989) 7 A.C.L.C. 998 630
Love, *ex p.* Official Receiver, *Re* [1952] Ch. 138; [1951] 2 T.L.R. 1207; 96 S.J. 28; [1951] 2 All E.R. 1016 244
Lovegrove, *ex p.* Lovegrove & Co. (Sales) Ltd, *Re* [1935] 1 Ch. 464; [1935] All E.R. Rep. 749; 104 L.J.Ch. 282; (1934–5) B. & C.R. 262; *sub nom. Re* Lovegrove, *ex p.* Applestone *v.* Trustees 152 L.T. 480; 79 S.J. 145; *sub nom. Re* Lovegrove, *ex p.* Lovegrove & Co. (Sales) Ltd *v.* Trustees T.L.R. 248, C.A. 231
Lovell and Christmas *v.* Beauchamp [1894] A.C. 607, 63 L.J.Q.B. 802; 71 L.T. 587; 43 W.R. 129; 1 Mans. 467; 11 R. 45; *sub nom. Re* Beauchamp Brothers, *ex p.* Beauchamp, 10 T.L.R. 682, H.L. 76, 109
Lovell Construction Ltd *v.* Independent Estates plc [1994] 1 B.C.L.C. 31 639
Lowestoft Traffic Services Co. Ltd (1986) 2 B.C.C. 98, 945; [1986] B.C.L.C. 81 497
Lowrie, *Re, ex p.* The Trustee of the Bankrupt *v.* The Bankrupt [1981] 3 All E.R. 353 195
Lubin, Rosen and Associates Ltd, *Re* [1975] 1 All E.R. 577; [1975] 1 W.L.R. 122; 119 S.J. 63 540
Lundy Granite Co., *Re, ex p.* Heaven (1871) 6 Ch.App. 462; 40 L.J.Ch. 588; 24 L.T. 922; 35 J.P. 692; 19 W.R. 609 633
Lupkovics, *Re, ex p.* The Trustee *v.* Freville [1954] 1 W.L.R. 1234; 98 S.J. 590; [1954] 2 All E.R. 125 .... 244, 253
Lympne Investments Ltd, *Re* [1972] 1 W.L.R. 523; [1972] 2 All E.R. 385; 116 S.J. 332 .... 524, 526, 534, 537
Lyons, *Re* (1934) 152 L.T. 201 227

M.S. Fashions Ltd *v.* Bank of Credit and Commerce International S.A. [1993] B.C.L.C. 280; [1992] B.C.C. 571, C.A.; (1993) 143 New L.J. 651; *Financial Times*, June 12, 1992; *The Times*, June 23, 1992, C.A. 275

TABLE OF CASES

M.S. Fashions Ltd v. Bank of Credit and Commerce International S.A. (No. 2) [1993] Ch. 425; [1993] 3 W.L.R. 220; [1993] 3 All E.R. 769; (1993) 137 S.J. (L.B.) 132; [1993] B.C.C. 360; [1993] B.C.L.C. 120; affirming [1993] B.C.C. 70 275
M.C.M. Services Ltd., *Re* (1987) 3 B.C.C. 179; [1987] B.C.L.C. 535 .... 497, 535
MEPC plc v. Scottish Amicable and Eckley (1993) 67 P. & C.R. 314; [1993] 36 E.G. 133; (1993) 137 S.J. (L.B.) 108; [1993] N.P.C. 44; *The Times*, April 6, 1993, C.A. 239
McCarthy, A Bankrupt, *Re*; *ex p.* Trustee of the Property of the Bankrupt [1975] 1 W.L.R. 807; [1975] 2 All E.R. 857; *sub nom.* McCarthy (A Bankrupt), *Re*, 119 S.J. 391 171
McCarthy (M.) & Co. (Builders) Ltd, *Re* (No. 2) [1976] 2 All E.R. 339 549
Macartney, *Re*, Macfarlane v. Macartney [1921] 1 Ch. 522; 90 L.J.Ch. 314; 124 L.T. 658; 65 S.J. 435 .... 694, 716
Macaulay v. Guaranty Trust Co. of New York [1927] W.N. 308; 44 T.L.R. 99 720, 760
McCulloch, *Re* (1880) 14 Ch.D. 716; 43 L.T. 161; 28 W.R. 935, C.A. 727, 782
MacFadyen (P.) & Co., *Re* [1908] 1 K.B. 675 .... 729, 782
McGreavey, *Re*, *ex p.* McGreavey v. Benfleet [1950] Ch. 269; [1950] 1 All E.R. 442; 66 T.L.R. (Pt. 1) 389; affirming [1950] Ch. 150; [1950] 1 All E.R. 30 ..... 92, 93
McGuiness Bros. (U.K.) Ltd, *Re* (1987) 3 B.C.C. 571 631
MacJordan Construction Ltd v. Brookmount Erostin Ltd [1992] B.C.L.C. 350; *The Times*, October 29, 1991, C.A. 639
Mackenzie, *Re* [1889] 2 Q.B. 566 241
Mack Trucks (Britain) Ltd, *Re* [1967] 1 All E.R. 977 384
McKewan v. Sanderson (1875) L.R. 20 Eq. 65; 44 L.J.Ch. 447; 32 L.T. 385; 23 W.R. 607 58
Mackintosh, *Re* (1884) 13 Q.B.D. 235; 51 L.T. 208; 33 W.R. 140 147
—— v. Pogose [1895] 1 Ch. 505; 64 L.J.Ch. 274; 72 L.T. 251; 43 W.R. 247; 39 S.J. 218; 2 Mans. 27; 13 R. 254 214
McMahon, *Re*, Fuller v. McMahon [1900] 1 Ch. 173; 69 L.J.Ch. 142; 81 L.T. 715; 16 T.L.R. 73; 7 Mans. 38 258
McMullen & Sons Ltd. v. Cerrone (1993) 66 P. & C.R. 351; [1994] B.C.C. 25; [1994] 1 B.C.L.C. 152; [1994] 19 E.G. 134; [1993] N.P.C. 93; *The Times*, June 10, 1993 .... 43, 242
McMurdo, *Re*, Penfold v. McMurdo [1902] 2 Ch. 684; 71 L.J.Ch. 691; 86 L.T. 814; 50 W.R. 644; 46 S.J. 550, C.A. 283
Macoun, *Re* [1904] 2 K.B. 700; 73 L.J.K.B. 892; 91 L.T. 276; 53 W.R. 197; 48 S.J. 672; 11 Mans. 264, C.A. 84
Macrae (P. & J.) Ltd, *Re* [1961] 1 W.L.R. 229; 105 S.J. 108; [1961] 1 All E.R. 302, *sub nom.* Credit Enterprise v. Woodcocks Sussex [1961] 1 W.L.R. 328 537
Majory, *Re* [1955] Ch. 600, *sub nom.* A Debtor, *Re* (No. 757 of 1954) [1955] Ch. 600; [1955] 2 W.L.R. 1035; 99 S.J. 316; [1955] 2 All E.R. 65 99
Mal Bower's Macquarie Electrical Centre Pty. Ltd, *Re* (1974) C.L.C. 40 630
Mander, *Re*, *ex p.* Official Receiver v. Davis (1902) 86 L.T. 234 246
Mangles v. Dixon (1852) 3 H.L.C. 702; 10 E.R. 278, H.L. 278
Manlon Trading Ltd, *Re* (1988) 4 B.C.C. 455 .... 424, 433, 545
Manmac Farmers Ltd, *Re* [1968] 1 W.L.R. 572; 112 S.J. 131; [1968] 1 All E.R. 1150 576
Mann, *Re*, *ex p.* The Debtor v. Harrods [1958] 3 All E.R. 660; [1958] 1 W.L.R. 1272 103
—— v. Goldstein [1968] 1 W.L.R. 1091; 112 S.J. 439; [1968] 2 All E.R. 769 .. 524, 536
Manning, *Re* (1885) 30 Ch.D. 480; 85 L.J.Ch. 613; 54 L.T. 33; 34 W.R. 111, C.A.   145
—— v. Chambers (1847) 1 De G. & Sm. 282; 63 E.R. 1069; 16 L.J.Ch. 245; 9 L.T.O.S. 146; 11 Jur. 466 213
Mapleback, *Re*, *ex p.* Caldecott (1876) 4 Ch.D. 150; 41 J.P. 262; *sub nom. Re* Mapleback, *ex p.* Butt, 46 L.J.Bcy. 14; 35 L.T. 503; 25 W.R. 103 205
Mardon, *Re* [1896] 1 Q.B. 140; 65 L.J.Q.B. 111; 73 L.T. 480; 44 W.R. 111; 12 T.L.R. 53; 40 S.J. 70; 2 Mans. 511 169
Marlborough Club Co., *Re* (1886) L.R. 1 Eq. 216 545
Marr (Pauline) (a bankrupt), *Re* [1990] Ch. 773; [1990] 2 W.L.R. 1264; [1990] 2 All E.R. 880; (1990) 134 S.J. 1009, C.A.; reversing [1989] 3 W.L.R. 674 ... 78

Table of Cases

Marsden, *ex p.* Board of Trade, *Re* (1892) 9 Morr. 70; 36 S.J. 309	184
Martin, *Re* (1888) 21 Q.B.D. 29; 57 L.J.Q.B. 384; 58 L.T. 889; 36 W.R. 698; 5 Morr. 129	169
—— *v.* Port of Manchester Insurance Co. Ltd, 1934 S.C. 143	753
Maskellyne British Typewriters, *Re* [1898] 1 Ch. 133	364
Mason, *ex p.* Bing, *Re* [1899] 1 Q.B. 810; 68 L.J.Q.B. 466; 80 L.T. 92; 47 W.R. 270; 43 S.J. 227; 6 Mans. 169	297
Matheson Brothers & Co., *ex p.* Matheson, *Re* (1884) Ch.D. 225; 3 N.Z.L.R. 323	732, 765
Mathieson's Trustee *v.* Burrup, Mathieson & Co. [1927] 1 Ch. 562	275
Matthews *v.* Kuwait Bechtel Corp. [1959] 2 Q.B. 57; [1959] 2 W.L.R. 702; 103 S.J. 393; [1959] 2 All E.R. 345, C.A.	257
Maudslay, Sons and Field, *Re* Maudslay *v.* Maudslay, Sons & Field [1900] 1 Ch. 602; 69 L.J.Ch. 347; 82 L.T. 378; 48 W.R. 568; 16 T.L.R. 228; 8 Mans. 38	709, 754
Maughan, *Re* (1855) 14 Q.B.D. 956	236
Maunder *v.* Lloyd (1862) 2 J. and H. 718; 70 E.R. 1248; 1 New Rep. 123; 11 W.R. 141	733, 758
Mawcon, *Re* [1969] 1 All E.R. 188	542, 555
Maxson, *ex p.* Lawrence & Lawrence Ltd, *Re* [1919] 2 K.B. 330; 88 L.J.K.B. 854; 121 L.T. 616; [1918–19] B. & C.R. 276	164
Maxwell *v.* Bishopsgate Investment Management Ltd (in liquidation), *The Times,* February 11, 1993	111
Maxwell Communications Corp. plc, *Re* [1992] B.C.C. 372; [1992] B.C.L.C. 465	450
—— (No. 2), *Re,* Barclays Bank plc *v.* Homan [1992] B.C.C. 757; affirming [1992] B.C.C. 767, C.A.	459, 683, 689, 703, 754, 755, 756, 789
—— (No. 3) [1993] 1 W.L.R. 1402; [1994] 1 All E.R. 737; [1993] B.C.C. 369; [1994] 1 B.C.L.C. 1; *The Times,* April 1, 1993	615
—— (Case No. 91 B 15741) 170 Bankr. 800; 25 Bankr.Ct.Dec. (CRR) 1567 (Bankr. S.D.N.Y., August 5, 1994)	459, 789
——, Homan *v.* Vogel [1994] B.C.C. 732	564
Mead, *Re* [1916] Ir.Rep. 285	136
——, *ex p.* Cochrane, *Re* (1875) L.R. 20 Eq. 282; 44 L.J.Bcy. 87; 32 L.T. 508; 23 W.R. 726	148
Meade, *Re, ex p.* Humber *v.* Palmer (Trustee) [1951] Ch. 774; [1951] 2 T.L.R. 111; 95 S.J. 382; [1951] 2 All E.R. 168	297
Measures Bros. Ltd *v.* Measures [1910] 2 Ch. 248; 79 L.J.Ch. 707; 102 L.T. 794; 26 T.L.R. 488; 54 S.J. 521; 18 Mans. 40, C.A.	555
Medical Battery Co., *Re* [1894] 1 Ch. 444; 63 L.J.Ch. 189; 69 L.T. 799; 42 W.R. 191; 38 S.J. 81; 1 Mans. 104; 8 R. 46	539
Medisco Equipment Ltd, *Re* (1983) 1 B.C.C. 98, 944; [1983] B.C.L.C. 305; [1983] Com.L.R. 232	497
Meesan Investments Ltd, *Re* (1988) 4 B.C.C. 788, D.C.	444
Melbourn, *ex p.* (1870) L.R. 6 Ch.App. 64; 40 L.J.Bcy. 25; 23 L.T. 578; 19 W.R. 83, L.JJ.	254, 709, 717, 722, 727
Mellor *v.* Mellor [1992] 1 W.L.R. 517; [1992] 4 All E.R. 10; [1992] B.C.C. 513; [1993] B.C.L.C. 30	365, 367
Memco Engineering Ltd, *Re* [1986] Ch. 86; [1985] 3 W.L.R. 875; (1985) 129 S.J. 776; [1985] 3 All E.R. 267; 1986 P.C.C. 45; (1985) 82 L.S.Gaz. 3695	557
Mendelssohn *v.* Ratcliffe [1904] A.C. 456; 73 L.J.K.B. 1027; 91 L.T. 204; 53 W.R. 240; 20 T.L.R. 669; 10 Com.Cas. 14, H.L.	105
Mercantile Bank of Australia, *Re* [1892] 2 Ch. 204; 61 L.J.Ch. 417; 67 L.T. 159; 40 W.R. 440; 36 S.J. 363	732
Mercer *v.* Vans Colina [1900] 1 Q.B. 130n; 67 L.J.Q.B. 424; 78 L.T. 21; 4 Mans. 363	200
Merker *v.* Merker [1963] P. 283; [1962] 3 W.L.R. 1389; 106 S.J. 881; [1962] 3 All E.R. 928	760
Mersey Steel & Iron Co. *v.* Naylor, Benzon & Co. (1884) 9 App.Cas. 434; 53 L.J.Q.B. 497; 51 L.T. 637; 32 W.R. 989, H.L.	275

TABLE OF CASES

Metropolitan Bank Ltd v. Pooley (1885) 10 App.Cas. 210; 54 L.J.Q.B. 449; 53
  L.T. 163; 49 J.P. 756; 33 W.R. 709, H.L. 192
Michael, ex p. Michael, Re (1891) 8 Morr. 305 96
Michaelides v. Bank of Cyprus (London) Ltd, The Times, December 11, 1980 .. 91
Midland Bank plc v. Laker Airways Ltd (in liquidation) [1986] 1 Q.B. 689; [1986] 2
  W.L.R. 707; (1985) 129 S.J. 670; [1986] 1 All E.R. 526; [1986] E.C.C. 329,
  C.A.; reversing Financial Times, June 14, 1985, D.C. 754
Midrome Ltd v. Shaw [1993] B.C.C. 659 .... 314, 550
Miles Aircraft Ltd, Re, Application of Barclays Bank [1948] Ch. 188; [1948] L.J.R.
  1133; 64 T.L.R. 278; 92 S.J. 72; [1948] 1 All E.R. 225 631
Milford Docks Co., Re; Lister's Petition (1883) 23 Ch.D. 292; 52 L.J.Ch. 774; 48
  L.T. 560; 31 W.R. 715 .... 536, 537
Miliangos v. George Frank (Textiles) Ltd [1976] A.C. 443; [1975] 3 W.L.R. 758;
  119 S.J. 774; [1975] 3 All E.R. 801; [1975] C.M.L.R. 585; [1976] 1 Lloyd's
  Rep. 201, H.L. 259
Miller, Re [1893] 1 Q.B. 327 291
——, Re [1901] 1 K.B. 51; 70 L.J.Q.B. 1; 83 L.T. 545; 49 W.R. 65; 17 T.L.R. 9; 45
  S.J. 44; 8 Mans. 1, C.A. 105
Mills, Re [1906] 1 K.B. 389; 94 L.T. 41; 54 W.R. 322, C.A. 96
Millward (James) & Co. Ltd, Re [1940] Ch. 333 537
Milner, ex p. Milner, Re (1885) 15 Q.B.D. 605; 54 L.J.Q.B. 425; 53 L.T. 652; 33
  W.R. 867; 1 T.L.R. 553; 2 Morr. 190, C.A. 58
Minna Craig S.S. Co. v. Chartered Mercantile Bank of India, London and China
  [1897] 1 Q.B. 460 .... 710, 717, 757
Mixhurst Ltd, Re [1993] B.C.C. 748; [1994] B.C.L.C. 19 624
Mont de Piété, Re [1892] W.N. 166; 37 S.J. 48 545
Montefiore v. Guedalla [1901] 1 Ch. 435 213
Montgomery Moore Ship Collision Doors Syndicate, Re (1903) 72 L.J.Ch. 624; 89
  L.T. 126; 19 T.L.R. 554; 10 Mans. 327 .... 89, 536
Moon, Re (1886) 17 Q.B.D. 275 214
Moore v. Anglo-Italian Bank (1879) 10 Ch.D. 681 .... 713, 757
—— (Sir John) Gold Mining Co., Re (1879) 12 Ch.D. 325, C.A. 511
Morant, ex p. Trustees, Re [1924] 1 Ch. 79; 93 L.J.Ch. 104; 130 L.T. 398; [1923] B.
  & C.R. 145 226
More v. More [1962] Ch. 424; [1962] 2 W.L.R. 215; [1962] 1 All E.R. 125; 106 S.J.
  37 .... 148, 326
Morel (E.J.), Re [1962] Ch. 21; [1961] 3 W.L.R. 57; 105 S.J. 156; [1961] 1 All E.R.
  796 284
Morgan v. Swansea Urban Sanitary Authority (1878) 9 Ch.D. 582 210
Morgan Guaranty Trust Co. v. Lothian Regional Council, 1995 S.L.T. 299, Ct.S.,
  IH 207
Morris (D.) and Sons Ltd v. Jeffreys (1932) 49 T.L.R. 76; (1932) 148 L.T. 56 .. 239
Morton, ex p. Robertson, Re (1875) L.R. 20 Eq. 733; 44 L.J.Bcy. 65; 34 L.T. 303;
  24 W.R. 351, C.A. 713
Moss S.S. Co. Ltd v. Whinny [1912] A.C. 254 .... 365, 366, 367, 384
Mostyn v. Fabrigas (1774) 1 Cowp. 161; 98 E.R. 1021; affirming S.C. sub nom.
  Fabrigas v. Mostyn (1773) 2 Wm.Bl. 929 734
Muirhead, ex p. Muirhead, Re (1886) 2 Ch.D. 22; 45 L.J.Bcy. 65; 34 L.T. 303; 24
  W.R. 351; C.A. 84
Multi Guarantee Co. Ltd, Re [1987] B.C.L.C. 257, C.A. 638
Murphy v. Sawyer-Hoare [1993] 27 E.G. 127; [1994] 1 B.C.L.C. 59 239
Murrieta, ex p. South American & Mexican Co., Re (1896) 3 Mans. 35; 12 T.L.R.
  238; sub nom. Re Murretta, ex p. South American & Mexican Co. 40 S.J. 317,
  C.A. 137
Mutton, ex p. Board of Trade, Re (1887) 19 Q.B.D. 102 697
Myers, Re [1908] 1 K.B. 941; 77 L.J.K.B. 386; 15 Mans. 85 253

N.M.B. Postbank Groep N.V. v. Naviede (No. 1) [1993] B.C.L.C. 707 365
N.M.B. Postbank Groep (No. 2) [1993] B.C.L.C. 715 365

TABLE OF CASES

Naeem, a Bankrupt, Re (No. 18 of 1988) [1990] 1 W.L.R. 48; [1989] L.S.Gaz. December 20, 37 51
Naoroji v. Chartered Bank of India (1868) L.R. 3 C.P. 444; 37 L.J.C.P. 221; 18 L.T. 358; 6 W.R. 791 273
Nathan, *ex p.* Stapleton, Re (1879) 10 Ch.D. 586 193
National Bank of Greece and Athens S.A. v. Metliss [1958] A.C. 509; [1957] 3 W.L.R. 1056; 101 S.J. 972; [1957] 3 All E.R. 608; affirming *sub nom.* Metliss v. National Bank of Greece and Athens S.A. [1957] 2 Q.B. 33; [1957] 2 W.L.R. 570; 101 S.J. 301; [1957] 2 All E.R. 1; affirming *The Times*, July 13, 1956; [1956] C.L.Y. 1555 .... 725, 758, 762
National Permanent Building Society, Re (1869) 5 Ch.App. 309 536
National Provincial Bank Ltd v. Ainsworth [1965] A.C. 1175; [1965] 3 W.L.R. 1; 109 S.J. 415; [1965] 2 All E.R. 472, H.L. 195
National Trust Co. Ltd v. Ebro Irrigation and Power Co. Ltd [1954] 3 D.L.R. 326 .... 734, 750, 759, 761
National Westminster Bank Ltd v. Halesowen Presswork & Assemblies Ltd [1972] A.C. 785; [1972] 2 W.L.R. 455; 116 S.J. 138; [1972] 1 All E.R. 641; [1972] 1 Lloyd's Rep. 101, H.L.; reversing [1971] 1 Q.B. 1; [1970] 3 W.L.R. 625; [1970] 3 All E.R. 33 .... 245, 274, 275, 600, 614
Neale, Assignees of Grattan v. Cottingham (1764) 1 H.Bl. 132; 126 E.R. 81 ... 714, 721
Nelson, *ex p.* Dare & Dolphin, Re [1918] 1 K.B. 459; 87 L.J.K.B. 628; 118 L.T. 549; [1918–19] B. & C.R. 1; *sub nom.* Re A Debtor (No. 333 of 1917), *ex p.* Debtor 34 T.L.R. 277; 62 S.J. 348, C.A. 319, 692, 710, 724
—— v. Bridport (1845) 8 Beav. 527; 50 E.R. 207; 8 L.T.O.S. 18; 10 Jur. 871 ... 734
New Bullas Trading Ltd, Re [1994] B.C.C. 36; [1994] 1 B.C.L.C. 485; *The Times*, January 12, 1994, C.A.; reversing [1993] B.C.C. 251; [1993] B.C.L.C. 1389 359
New Gas Co., Re (1877) 5 Ch.D. 703; 37 L.T. 111; 25 W.R. 643, C.A. 545
New Oriental Bank Corp., Re (No. 2) [1895] 1 Ch. 753; 64 L.J.Ch. 439; 43 W.R. 523; 11 T.L.R. 291; 39 S.J. 347; *sub nom.* Re Oriental Bank Corp. Ltd, *ex p.* Hong Kong Land Investment & Agency Co. Ltd 72 L.T. 419; 2 Mans. 301; 13 R. 459 284
New Par Consols, Re [1898] 1 Q.B. 573; 67 L.J.Q.B. 595; 42 S.J. 98; 5 Mans. 273, D.C.; *subsequent proceedings* [1898] 1 Q.B. 669, C.A. 560
New, Prance and Garrard's Trustee v. Hunting [1897] 2 Q.B. 19, affirmed *sub nom.* Sharpe v. Jackson [1899] A.C. 419, H.L. 158, 228
New Zealand Banking Corp. (1867) L.R. 4 Eq. 226 210
New Zealand Loan and Mercantile Agency Co. v. Morrison [1898] A.C. 349; 67 L.J.P.C. 10; 77 L.T. 603; 46 W.R. 239; 14 T.L.R. 141; 5 Mans. 171 .... 705, 710, 751, 760, 763
Newdigate Colliery Ltd, Re [1912] 1 Ch. 468 .... 363, 366
Newey, *ex p.* Whiteman, Re (1912) 107 L.T. 832 135
Newhart Developments Ltd v. Co-operative Commercial Bank Ltd [1978] Q.B. 814; [1978] 1 W.L.R. 636; (1977) 121 S.J. 847; [1978] 2 All E.R. 896, C.A. 384, 386, 387, 388
Newport County Association Football Club Ltd, Re [1987] B.C.C. 635; [1987] B.C.L.C. 582 .... 433, 463
Newton, Re [1896] 2 Q.B. 403 282
Nicholas, Re (1890) 7 Morr. 54 317
Nicholl v. Cutts [1985] B.C.L.C. 322; 1985 P.C.C. 311, C.A. 367, 374, 383, 474
Nichols v. Nixey (1885) 29 Ch.D. 1005; 55 L.J.Ch. 146; 52 L.T. 803; 33 W.R. 840 211
Noble, Re, *ex p.* The Bankrupt v. Official Receiver [1965] Ch. 129; [1964] 3 W.L.R. 206; [1964] 2 All E.R. 522 .... 103, 133
Nordenfelt, Re, *ex p.* Maxim Nordenfelt Guns & Ammunition [1895] 1 Q.B. 151; 64 L.J.Q.B. 182; 71 L.T. 565; 11 T.L.R. 26; 2 Mans. 20; 14 R. 71, C.A. ... 699
Normandy Marketing Ltd, Re [1993] B.C.C. 879 739
Norris, *ex p.* Reynolds, Re (1888) 4 T.L.R. 452; 5 Morr. 111, C.A. 698
North Australian Territory Co. Ltd v. Goldsborough, Mort and Co. Ltd (1889) 61 L.T. 716 .... 757, 761

xlix

TABLE OF CASES

North Carolina Estate Co., *Re* (1889) 5 T.L.R. 328 754
North Yorkshire Iron Co., *Re* (1878) 7 Ch.D. 661 633
Nuthall, *Re* (1891) 8 Morr. 106 147

Obers v. Paton's Trustees (1897) 24 R. (Ct. of Sess.) 719; 4 S.L.T. 350 718
Odwin v. Forbes (1817) Buck. 57 (B.C.) 692, 710
Official Custodian for Charities v. Parway Estates Developments [1985] Ch. 151;
   [1984] 3 W.L.R. 525; 128 S.J. 549; [1984] 3 All E.R. 679; 48 P. & C.R. 125;
   1985 P.C.C. 133; 270 E.G. 1077; 81 L.S.Gaz., 2382, C.A. 554
O'Gorman, *ex p.* Bale, *Re* [1899] 2 Q.B. 62; 68 L.J.Q.B. 650; 80 L.T. 501; 47 W.R.
   543; 43 S.J. 480; 6 Mans. 204 . . . . 84, 94
O'Keefe, *Re*, Poingdestre v. Sherman [1940] 1 All E.R. 216; [1940] Ch. 124; 109
   L.J.Ch. 86; 162 L.T. 62; 56 T.L.R. 204; 84 S.J. 44 701
Okura & Co. Ltd v. Forsbacka Jernverks Akt [1914] 1 K.B. 715; 83 L.J.K.B. 56 1;
   110 L.T. 464; 30 T.L.R. 242; 58 S.J. 232, C.A. 748
Olympia and York Canary Wharf Ltd; American Express Europe v. Adamson
   [1993] B.C.C. 154; [1993] B.C.L.C. 453 443
Olympia and York Canary Wharf Holdings, *Re* [1993] B.C.C. 866; [1984]
   B.C.L.C. 702 . . . . 468, 478
Onassis v. Drewry S.A.R.L. (1949) 83 Lloyd's Rep. 249, C.A., reversing (1949) 82
   Lloyd's Rep. 565 . . . . 760, 761
Onslow, *ex p.* Kibble, *Re* (1875) 10 Ch.App. 373; 44 L.J.Bcy. 63; 32 L.T. 138; 23
   W.R. 433 . . . . 134, 135
Operator Control Cabs Ltd, *Re* [1970] 3 All E.R. 657 629
Ord v. Barton (1847) 9 Dunl. (Ct. of Sess.) 541 713
O'Reardon, *ex p.* James, *Re* (1873) 9 Ch.App. 74; 43 L.J.Bcy. 13; 29 L.T. 761; 22
   W.R. 196 728
Oriental Bank Corp., *ex p.* Guillemin, *Re* (1884) 28 Ch.D. 634; 54 L.J. Ch. 322; 52
   L.T. 167; 1 T.L.R. 9 . . . . 545, 555, 629
Oriental Commercial Bank, *Re* (1871) 7 Ch.App. 99; 41 L.J.Ch. 217; 25 L.T. 648;
   20 W.R. 82 256
Oriental Credit, *Re* [1988] Ch. 204; [1988] 2 W.L.R. 172; 132 S.J. 127; [1988] 1 All
   E.R. 892 562
Oriental Inland Steam Co., *ex p.* Scinde Ry. Co., *Re* (1874) 9 Ch.App. 557; 43
   L.J.Ch. 699; 31 L.T. 5; 22 W.R. 810 . . . . 583, 751, 754, 755
Osborn, *ex p.* Trustee, *Re* (1931–32) 15 B. & C. R. 189 722
Oswell, *ex p.* Board of Trade, *Re* (1892) 9 Morr. 202 317
Othery Construction, *Re* [1966] 1 W.L.R. 69; 110 S.J. 32; [1966] 1 All E.R.
   145 535
Otway, *ex p.* Otway, *Re* [1895] 1 Q.B. 812; 64 L.J.Q.B. 521; 72 L.T. 452; 2 Mans.
   174; 14 R. 389, C.A. 98, 136, 137, 695
Owen, *ex p.* Owen, *Re* (1884) 13 Q.B.D. 113; 53 L.J.Ch. 863; 50 L.T. 514; 32 W.R.
   811; 1 Morr. 93, C.A. 85
Owens Bank Ltd v. Bracco Nos 1 and 2 [1992] 2 A.C. 443; [1992] 2 W.L.R. 621;
   [1992] 2 All E.R. 193; *The Independent*, May 6, 1992, H.L.; affirming [1992] 2
   W.L.R. 127; [1991] 4 All E.R. 833; *Financial Times*, April 12, 1991; *The Times*,
   April 15, 1991; *The Independent*, May 15, 1991, C.A.; affirming *The Times*,
   January 8, 1991; *The Times*, August 29, 1990 694

Paddington Town Hall Centre (1979) 4 A.C.L.R. 673 583
Padstow Total Loss and Collision Assurance Association, *ex p.* Byant, *Re* (1882) 20
   Ch.D. 137; 51 L.J.Ch. 344; 45 L.T. 774; 30 W.R. 326 521
Paget, *ex p.* Official Receiver, *Re* [1927] 2 Ch. 85 158
Paine, *ex p.* Read, *Re* [1879] 1 Q.B. 122; 66 L.J.Q.B. 71; 7 S.L.T. 316; 45 W.R. 190;
   13 T.L.R. 30; 3 Mans. 309 267
Painter, *ex p.* Painter, *Re* [1895] 1 Q.B. 85; 64 L.J.Q.B. 22; 71 L.T. 581; 43 W.R.
   144; 11 T.L.R. 9; 39 S.J. 168; 1 Mans. 499; 15 R. 16, D.C. 119, 120

l

Table of Cases

Palk v. Mortgage Services Funding plc [1993] Ch. 330; [1993] 2 W.L.R. 415; [1993] 2 All E.R. 481; (1992) 65 P. & C.R. 207; (1992) 25 H.L.R. 56; [1992] N.P.C. 114; *The Times*, August 7, 1992; *The Guardian*, August 19, 1992; *The Independent*, August 25, 1992, C.A. 398

Palmer (Gavin) (Dec'd) (A Debtor), Re [1994] Ch. 316; [1994] 3 W.L.R. 420; [1994] 3 All E.R. 835; (1994) 68 P. & C.R. D13; (1994) 138 S.J.(L.B.) 72; [1994] N.P.C. 41; [1994] E.G.C.S. 52; *The Times*, March 30, 1994; *The Independent*, April 6, 1994, C.A.; reversing [1993] 3 W.L.R. 877; [1993] 4 All E.R. 812; [1993] 41 E.G. 179; [1993] E.G.C.S. 62; [1993] N.P.C. 55 331

Palmer v. Carey [1926] A.C. 703; 95 L.J.P.C. 146; 135 L.T. 237; [1926] B & C.R. 51 213

—— v. Day & Sons [1895] 2 Q.B. 618; 64 L.J.Q.B. 807; 44 W.R. 14; 11 T.L.R. 565; 39 S.J. 708; 2 Mans. 386; 15 R. 523 273

Palmer Marine Surveys Ltd, Re [1986] 1 W.L.R. 573; (1985) 1 B.C.C. 99, 557 497

Pannell, *ex p.* Bates, Re (1879) 11 Ch.D. 914; 48 L.J.Bcy. 113; 41 L.T. 263; 27 W.R. 927, C.A. 263, 264, 265

Paramount Airways, Re (In Administration), *sub nom.* Powdrill v. Hambros Bank (Jersey) [1992] 3 W.L.R. 690; [1992] 3 All E.R. 1; (1992) S.J. (L.B.) 97; [1992] B.C.C. 416; [1992] B.C.L.C. 710, C.A.; reversing [1992] Ch. 160; [1991] 3 W.L.R. 318; [1991] 4 All E.R. 267; (1991) 135 S.J. (L.B.) 76; (1991) B.C.C. 559; [1991] B.C.L.C. 767 .... 155, 445, 645, 696, 715, 729

Paramount Airways Ltd, Re (No. 3) [1995] 2 All E.R. 65, H.L.; [1995] B.C.C. 319; [1994] 2 All E.R. 513; [1994] B.C.C. 172, C.A.; [1993] B.C.C. 662 ..... 372, 375, 379, 448, 472, 473, 474, 476, 477

Pardo v. Bingham (1868) L.R. 6 Eq. 485; *subsequent proceedings* (1869) 4 Ch.App. 735 717

Paris Skating Rink Co., Re (1877) 5 Ch.D. 959; 37 L.T. 298; 25 W.R. 701, C.A.; *subsequent proceedings* (1877), 6 Ch.D. 731 536

Parker, Re Morgan v. Hill [1894] 3 Ch. 400; 64 L.J.Ch. 6; 71 L.T. 557; 43 W.R. 1; 38 S.J. 694; 7 R. 590, C.A. 268, 269

—— v. Norton (1796) 6 T.R. 695; 101 E.R. 777 257

Parker-Tweedale v. Dunbar Bank (No. 1) [1990] 2 All E.R. 577; (1990) 60 P. & C.R. 83; (1990) 140 New L.J. 169, C.A. 397, 398

Parkers, *ex p.* Sheppard, Re (1887) 19 Q.B.D. 84; 56 L.J.Q.B. 338; 57 L.T. 198; 35 W.R. 566; 3 T.L.R. 563; 4 Morr. 135 256

Pascal, *ex p.* Myer, Re (1876) 1 Ch.D. 509, C.A.; 45 L.J.Bcy. 81; 34 L.T. 10; 24 W.R. 263, C.A. 75, 695

Pascoe (No. 2) *ex p.* Bkpcy. Trustee v. H.M. Treasury Lords Comrs., Re [1944] Ch. 310; [1944] 1 All E.R. 593; 113 L.J. Ch. 203; 171 L.T. 170; 60 T.L.R. 380; 88 S.J. 232, D.C. 251

Patrick and Lyon Ltd, Re [1933] Ch. 786 .... 659, 660

Paul and Frank Ltd v. Discount Bank (Overseas) Ltd [1967] Ch. 348; [1966] 3 W.L.R. 490; [1966] 2 All E.R. 922 231

Pavlou, Re [1993] 3 All E.R. 955; [1993] Fam. Law 629 198

Pawson, Re [1917] 2 K.B. 527; 86 L.J.K.B. 1285; 117 L.T. 315; [1917] H.B.R. 87 ... 164

Payne, *ex p.* Castle Mail Packers Co., Re (1886) 18 Q.B.D. 154; 35 W.R. 89; 3 T.L.R. 67; 3 Morr. 270, C.A. 312, 315

Peachdart Ltd, Re [1984] Ch. 131; [1983] W.L.R. 878; 127 S.J. 839; [1983] 3 All E.R. 204; (1984) 81 L.S.Gaz. 204 .... 217, 635

Pearce, *ex p.* Official Receiver, Re [1919] 1 K.B. 354; 88 L.J.K.B. 367; 120 L.T. 334; [1918–1919] B. & C.R. 131, C.A. 109, 149

—— v. Bastable's Trustee in Bankruptcy [1901] 2 Ch. 122; 70 L.J.Ch. 446; 84 L.T. 525; 17 T.L.R. 366; 8 Mans. 287 .... 193, 236

Pearse, *ex p.* Bankrupt, Re (1912) 107 L.T. 859 .... 312, 313

Pearson, *ex p.* Pearson, Re [1892] 2 Q.B. 263; 61 L.J.Q.B. 585; 67 L.T. 367; 40 W.R. 532; 8 T.L.R. 622; 36 S.J. 573; 9 Morr. 185, C.A. 696

Peat v. Gresham Trust Ltd [1934] A.C. 252, H.L. 227

Pemberton v. Hughes [1899] 1 Ch. 781; 68 L.J.Ch. 281; 80 L.T. 369; 47 W.R. 354; 15 T.L.R. 211; 43 S.J. 365, C.A. 694

TABLE OF CASES

Pen-y-Van Colliery, *Re* (1877) 6 Ch.D. 477; 46 L.J.Ch. 390 536
Pennington & Owen Ltd, *Re* [1925] 1 Ch. 825; 95 L.J.Ch. 93; 134 L.T. 66; 41
  T.L.R. 657; 69 S.J. 759; [1926] B. & C.R. 39, C.A. 276
Performing Rights Society Ltd v. London Theatre of Varieties Ltd [1924] A.C. 1,
  93 L.J.K.B. 33; 40 T.L.R. 52; 130 L.T. 450; 68 S.J. 99, H.L. 87, 88
Perkins, *Re* (1890) 24 Q.B.D. 613 108
Perry v. Equitable Life Assurance Society of U.S.A. (1929) 45 T.L.R. 468 723
Peters, *ex p.* Lloyd, *Re* (1882) 47 L.T. 64 179
Peveril Gold Mines, *Re* [1898] 1 Ch. 122; 67 L.J.Ch. 77; 77 L.T. 505; 46 W.R. 198;
  14 T.L.R. 86; 42 S.J. 96; 4 Mans. 398, C.A. 534
Phillips, *Re* [1914] 2 K.B. 689; 83 L.J.K.B. 1364; 110 L.T. 939; 21 Mans. 144 . . 201
—— v. Allan (1828) 8 B. & C. 477; 2 Man. & Ry. K.B. 576; 7 L.J.O.S. K.B. 2; 108
  E.R. 1120 . . . . 692, 724
—— v. Eyre (1870) L.R. 6 Q.B. 1; 40 L.J.Q.B. 28; 22 L.T. 869, Ex.Ch. 723
Philpotts v. Reed (1819) 1 Brod. & Bing. 294; 3 Moore C.P. 623; 129 E.R.
  735 . . . . 692, 727
Phosphate Sewage Co. Ltd v. Molleson (1878) 5 1125 . . . . 722, 728
Pickering v. Stephenson (1872) L.R. 15 Eq. 322 734
Piers, *Re* [1898] 1 Q.B. 627; 67 L.J.Q.B. 519; 78 L.T. 314; 46 W.R. 475; 14 T.L.R.
  300; 42 S.J. 365; 5 Mans. 97, C.A. 164, 575
Pilling, *Re* [1903] 2 K.B. 50; 72 L.J.K.B. 392; 88 L.T. 667; 51 W.R. 465; 19 T.L.R.
  388; 47 S.J. 435; 10 Mans. 142, C.A. 58, 173, 179
Pinto Silver Mining Co., *Re* (1878) 8 Ch.D. 273; 47 C.J.Ch. 591; 38 L.T. 336; 26
  W.R. 622 521
Pitchford, *ex p.* Official Receiver V. Hall, *Re* [1924] 2 Ch. 260 271
Platts v. Western Trust & Savings Ltd E.G.C.S. 75: [1993] N.P.C. 58; *The Times*,
  April 7, 1993, C.A. 114
Pleatfire, *Re* [1983] B.C.L.C. 102 541
Podberry v. Peak [1981] Ch. 344, C.A. 315
Pogose, *ex p.* Vanderlinden, *Re* (1882) 20 Ch.D. 289; 51 L.J.Ch. 760; 47 L.T. 138;
  30 W.R. 930, C.A. 109
Pollard (H.E.), *Re* [1903] 2 K.B. 41; 72 L.J.K.B. 509; 88 L.T. 652; 51 W.R. 483; 47
  S.J. 492; 10 Mans. 152, C.A. 108, 149
Polly Peck International plc [1991] B.C.C. 503 466
——, *Re* Secretary of State for Trade and Industry v. Ellis (No. 2) [1993] B.C.C.
  890; [1994] 2 B.C.L.C. 574 676
Pooley, *Re* (1882) 20 Ch.D. 685; 51 L.J.Ch. 810; 47 L.T. 177; 30 W.R. 650,
  C.A. 99
Portman Provincial Cinemas Ltd, *Re* (1964) 108 S.J. 581 526
Post Office v. Norwich Union Fire Insurance Society [1967] 2 Q.B. 363; [1967] 2
  W.L.R. 709; 111 S.J. 71; [1967] 1 All E.R. 577; [1967] 1 Lloyd's Rep. 216,
  C.A. 194
Potter v. Brown (1804) 5 East 124; 1 Smith, K.B. 351; 102 E.R. 1016 692
—— v. Brown (1804) 5 East 124; 1 Smith, K.B. 351; 102 E.R. 1016 723
Potters Oils Ltd (in liquidation), *Re* [1986] 1 All E.R. 890; [1986] 1 W.L.R.
  201 236
——, *Re* (No. 2) [1986] 1 All E.R. 890; [1986] 1 W.L.R. 201 . . . . 370, 397
——, *Re* [1985] B.C.L.C. 203; (1985) P.C.C. 148; (1985) 1 B.C.C. 99 604
Potts, *Re* [1893] 1 Q.B. 648; 62 L.J.Q.B. 392; 69 L.T. 74; 41 W.R. 337; 9 T.L.R.
  308; 37 Sol. Jo. 306; 10 Morr. 52; 4 R 305, C.A. 149
——, *Re* [1934] Ch. 356 163
Poulson, *Re, ex p.* Granada Television Ltd, v. Maudling [1976] 2 All E.R. 1020; 1
  W.C.R. 1023; 120 S.J. 734 . . . . 154, 160
Powdrill v. Watson: Leyland Daf Ltd, *Re*; Ferranti International plc, *Re* [1995] 2
  All E.R. 65 . . . . 372, 376
—— v. Watson; Leyland Daf; Ferranti 378
Powell v. Lloyd (1828) 2 Y. & J. 372; 148 E.R. 962 215
Power v. Sharp Investments Ltd [1993] B.C.C. 609, C.A.; affirming *sub nom.* Shoe
  Lace Ltd, *Re* [1992] B.C.C. 367; [1994] 1 B.C.L.C. 111; *The Times*, June 3,
  1993, C.A. 649

TABLE OF CASES

Powles v. Hargreaves (1853) 3 De G.M. & G. 430; 43 E.R. 169	210
Practice Direction (Ch.D.) (Companies Court: Advertisement of Winding-up Petitions) (No. 1 of 1986), February 10, 1986 [1986] 1 W.L.R. 286; [1986] 1 All E.R. 704; 1986 P.C.C. 175	544
—— (Ch.D) (Companies Court: Contributory's Petitions), February 22, 1990, [1990] 1 W.L.R. 490; [1990] 1 All E.R. 1056; [1990] B.C.L.C. 452	629
—— (Ch.D.) (Companies Court: Hearing of Winding-up Petitions in London) (No. 2 of 1986), October 22, 1986 [1986] 1 W.L.R. 1428; [1986] 3 All E.R. 672; [1986] 1 W.L.R. 1428	548
—— (Ch.D.) (Companies Court: Insolvency Act 1986) (No. 3 of 1986), December 10, 1986 [1987] 1 W.L.R. 53; [1987] 1 All E.R. 107	547, 548, 581, 598
—— (Chancery Chambers) [1982] 1 W.L.R. 1189; [1982] 3 All E.R. 124	541
—— (Right of Audience) May 9, 1986 [1986] 1 W.L.R. 545; [1986] 2 All E.R. 226; (1986) 83 Cr.App.R. 6	548
Practice Note [1952] W.N. 170	747
—— (Ch.D.) (Bankruptcy: Statutory Demands) (No. 1/88), February 26, 1988 [1988] 1 W.L.R. 461; [1988] 2 All E.R. 126	112
—— (Ch.D.) (Bankruptcy: Orders Without Attendance) (No. 2 of 1992) February 6, 1992 [1992] 1 W.L.R. 379; [1992] 2 All E.R. 300	131
—— (Ch.D.) (Bankruptcy: Voluntary Arrangements) (No. 1 of 1991) December 13, 1991 [1992] 1 W.L.R. 120; [1992] 1 All E.R. 678	45
Pratt, Re, ex p. I.R.C. v. Phillips [1951] Chap. 225; 66 T.L.R. (pt. 2) 847; 94 S.J. 803; [1950] 2 All E.R. 994; [1950] T.R. 293; 43 R. & I.T. 964; 31 T.C. 506	293
Priestley v. Clegg (1985) (3) S.A. 955	254, 707
Primlaks (U.K.) (No. 2), Re [1990] B.C.L.C. 234	413, 424
Prince Blucher, Re [1931] 2 Ch. 70	43
Probe Data Systems Ltd, Re (No. 3), Secretary of State v. Desai [1992] B.C.C. 110; [1992] B.C.L.C. 405 C.A.: affirming [1991] B.C.C. 428; [1991] B.C.L.C. 586	676
Produce Marketing Consortium Ltd (No. 2), Re [1989] B.C.L.C. 520	662
Purpoint, Re [1991] B.C.C. 121; [1991] B.C.L.C. 491	658, 662
Quantock v. England (1770) 2 W.B. 1 703; 96 E.R. 413; 5 Burr. 2628; 98 E.R. 382	70
Quartz Hill Gold Mining v. Eyre (1883) 11 Q.B.D. 674; 52 L.J.Q.B. 488; 49 L.T. 249; 31 W.R. 688, C.A.	100
Quelin v. Moisson (1828) 1 Knapp 265; 12 E.R. 320	692, 723
R.-R. Realisations Ltd, Re (formerly Rolls Royce Ltd) [1980] 1 All E.R. 1019	514
R. v. Bolus (1870) 23 L.T. 339; 11 Cox C.C. 610	342
—— v. Brockley [1994] 99 B.C.C.; [1994] 1 B.C.L.C. 606: [1994] Crim.L.R. 671; (1994) 138 S.J. (L.B.) 5; The Times, November 25, 1993	322, 676
—— v. Clowes [1992] 3 All E.R. 440; [1992] B.C.L.C. 1158	567
—— v. Creese (1874) L.R. 2 C.C.R. 105; 22 W.R. 375; 12 Cox C.C. 539; 29 L.T. 897	338, 339
—— v. Dandridge (1931) 22 Cr.App.R. 136; [1931] B. & E.R. 40, C.C.A.	343
—— v. Director of the Serious Fraud Office, ex p. Smith [1993] A.C. 1; [1992] 3 W.L.R. 66; [1992] 3 All E.R. 456; (1992) 136 S.J. (L.B.) 182; [1992] B.C.L.C. 879; [1992] Crim.L.R. 504; [1992] C.O.D. 270; (1992) 142 New L.J. 895 [1992] Gazette; 15 July, 34; The Independent, June 12, 1992; The Times, June 16, 1992; Financial Times, June 17, 1992; The Guardian, July 1, 1992, H.L.; reversing [1992]] 1 All E.R. 730; (1992) 135 S.J. (L.B.) 214; (1992) 95 Cr.App.R. 191; [1992] 1 All E.R. 730; (1992) 135 S.J. (L.B.) 214; (1992) 95 Cr.App.R. 191; [1992] C.O.D. 188; [1992] Gazette 11 March, 33; The Independent, November 8, 1991; The Guardian, November 13, 1991; The Times, November 13, 1991, D.C.	571
—— v. Doubleday (1964) 49 Cr.App.R. 62	354

liii

TABLE OF CASES

R. v. Duke of Leinster [1924] 1 K.B. 311 351
—— v. Dyson [1894] 2 Q.B. 176 350
—— v. Ellis [1899] 1 Q.B. 230; 79 L.T. 532; 47 W.R. 188; 15 T.L.R. 57; 19 Cox
  C.C. 210, C.C.R. 352
—— v. Erdheim [1896] 2 Q.B. 260; 65 L.J.M.C. 176; 74 L.T. 734; 44 W.R. 607, 12
  T.L.R. 445; 40 S.J. 569; 18 Cox C.C. 355; 3 Mans. 142, C.C.R. 158
—— v. Fryer (1912) 7 Cr.App.R. 183 352
—— v. Godwin (1980) 71 Cr.App.R. 97; [1980] Crim.L.R. 427 351
—— v. Goodall (1958) 43 Cr.App.R. 24; 226 C.T. 301 352
—— v. Grantham [1984] Q.B. 675; [1984] 2 W.L.R. 815; (1984) 128 S.J. 331;
  [1984] 3 All E.R. 166; (1984) 79 Cr.App.R. 86; [1984] Crim.L.R. 492; (1984)
  81 L.S.Gaz. 660
—— v. Harris (Richard) [1970] 3 All E.R. 746; [1970] 1 W.L.R. 1252 158
—— v. Hartley [1972] 1 All E.R. 599; [1972] 2 Q.B. 1; [1972] 2 W.L.R. 101 ... 352
—— v. Hayat (1976) 120 S.J. 434; 63 Cr.App.R. 181 351
—— v. Humphris [1904] 2 K.B. 89; 90 L.T. 555; 52 W.R. 591; 20 T.L.R. 425; 20
  Cox C.C. 620 339
—— v. Ingram [1956] 2 Q.B. 424; [1956] 3 W.L.R. 309; [1956] 2 All E.R. 639 . 352
—— v. International Trustee for the Protection of Bondholders A.G. [1937] 2 All
  E.R. 164; [1937] A.C. 500; 106 L.J.K.B. 236; 156 L.T. 352; 53 T.L.R. 507; 81
  S.J. 316; 42 Com. Cas. 246 763
—— v. Juby (1886) 55 L.T. 788; 35 W.R. 168; 3 T.L.R. 211; 16 Cox C.C.
  160 352
—— v. Judge of the County Court of Surrey (1884) 13 Q.B.D. 963 153
—— v. Kansal [1992] 3 W.L.R. 494; [1992] 3 All E.R. 844; (1992) 136 S.J. (L.B.)
  146; [1992] B.C.C. 615; [1992] B.C.L.C. 1009; (1992) 142 New L.J. 715;
  [1992] Gazette, 15 July, 35; *The Independent*, May 14, 1992; *The Times*,
  May 15, 1992; *The Guardian*, June 3, 1992; *Financial Times*, June 5, 1992,
  C.A. 157, 158, 336
—— v. Lloyd (1887) 19 Q.B.D. 213; 56 C.J.M.C. 119; 56 L.T. 750; 52 J.P. 86; 35
  W.R. 653; 3 T.L.R. 701, C.C.R. 153
—— v. Lusty [1964] 1 All E.R. 960; [1964] 1 W.L.R. 606 337
—— v. Miller [1977] Crim.L.R. 562; [1977] 1 W.L.R. 1129; [1977] 3 All E.R.
  986 352
—— v. Mitchell (1880) 50 L.J.M.C. 76 348
—— v. —— [1955] 1 W.L.R. 1125; [1955] 3 All E.R. 263 345
—— v. Peters (1886) 16 Q.B.D. 636; 54 L.T. 545; 34 W.R. 399; 2 T.L.R. 359; 16
  Cox C.C. 36 352
—— v. Pike [1904] 1 K.B. 552 155
—— v. Pryce (1949) 34 Cr.App.R. 21 352
—— v. Robinson (1867) L.R. 1 C.C.R. 80; 36 L.J.M.C. 78; 16 L.T. 605; 31 J.P.
  469; 15 W.R. 966; 10 Cox C.C. 467 C.C.R. 158
—— v. Salter [1968] 2 Q.B. 793; [1968] 3 W.L.R. 39; [1968] 2 All E.R. 951 .. 350, 337
—— v. Seelig [1991] B.C.L.C. 869; (1992) 94 Cr.App.R. 17; (1991) 141 New L.J.
  638; *The Independent*, May 3, 1991; May 13, 1991, C.A. 565
—— v. Sinclair [1968] 3 All E.R. 241; 132 J.P. 527 338
—— v. Smith (1915) 11 Cr.App.R. 81 352
—— v. Theivendran (Sundranpillai) (1992) 13 Crim.App.R.(S.) 601, C.A. 322
—— v. Thomas (1870) 22 L.T. 138; 11 Cox C.C. 535 342
—— v. Widdop (1872) L.R. 2 C.C.R. 3; 42 L.J.M.C. 9; 27 L.T. 693; 37 J.P. 131; 21
  W.R. 176; 12 Cox C.C. 251, C.C.R. 158
—— v. Williams [1942] A.C. 541; 3 D.L.R. 1; [1942] W.W.R. 321 763
—— v. Wiseman (1901) 20 Cox C.C. 144; 85 C.T. 791; 50 W.R. 333; 18 C.T.R.
  177 337
—— v. Zeitlin (1932) 23 Cr.App.R. 163; [1933] B. & C.R. 69 351
Raatz, *ex p*. Raatz, *Re* [1897] 2 Q.B. 80; 66 L.J.Q.B. 501; 76 L.T. 503, D.C. 105
Radford and Bright, *Re* [1901] 1 Ch. 272; 70 L.J.Ch. 78; 49 W.R. 270; 17 T.L.R.
  81; 9 Mans. 98 576
Raeburn, *Re* (1982) 74 Cr.App.R. 21 356
Rainbow Tours Ltd, *Re* [1964] Ch. 66; [1963] W.L.R. 459; 107 S.J. 664; [1963] 2
  All E.R. 820 244

TABLE OF CASES

Ramsey v. Hartley [1977] 2 All E.R. 673; [1977] 1 W.L.R. 686; 121 S.J. 319 ... 91
—— v. Hartley [1977] 2 All E.R. 673, C.A. 193
—— v. Liverpool Royal Infirmary [1930] A.C. 588; 99 L.J.P.C. 134; 143 L.T. 388; 46 T.L.R. 465, H.L. 700
Real Estate Development Co., Re [1991] B.C.L.C. 210 738
Redman (Builders) Ltd, Re [1964] 1 All E.R. 851, [1964] 1 W.L.R. 541; 108 S.J. 376 .... 244, 556
Reed and Bower & Co., Re (1887) 19 Q.B.D. 174 179
Rees, ex p. National Provincial Bank of England, Re (1881) 17 Ch.D. 98; 44 L.T. 325; 29 W.R. 796, C.A. 268
Reid v. Explosives Co. Ltd (1887) 19 Q.B.D. 264; [1886–90] All E.R. Reports 712; 56 L.J.Q.B. 388; 57 L.T. 439; 35 W.R. 509; 3 T.L.R. 588, C.A. 367
Reilly, Re [1942] I.R. 416 706
Reis, ex p. Clough, Re [1904] 2 K.B. 769; 73 L.J.K.B. 929; 91 L.T. 592; 53 W.R. 122; 20 T.L.R. 547; 11 Mans. 229, C.A. 263
——, Re [1904] 2 K.B. 769; affirmed sub nom. Clough v. Samuel [1905] A.C. 442, H.L. 319
Reliance Properties, Re Waygood Otis & Co. v. Reliance Properties [1951] W.N. 351; 95 S.J. 609; [1951] 2 All E.R. 327n., C.A. 550
Reprographics Export (Euromat), Re (1978) 122 S.J. 400 549
Reuss (Princess) v. Bos (1871) L.R. 5 176; 40 L.J.Ch. 655; 24 L.T. 641, H.L.; affirming S.C. sub nom. General Co. for Promotion of Land Credit, Re (1870) 5 Ch.App. 363, L.J. 732
Rewe, ex p. Derenburg, Re [1904] 2 K.B. 483; 73 L.J.K.B. 594; 91 L.T. 220; 52 W.R. 628; 48 S.J. 475; 11 Mans. 130, C.A. 268
Reynolds, Re (1882) 21 Ch.D. 601; 52 L.J.Ch. 223; 47 L.T. 495; 31 W.R. 187, C.A. 153
Rhine Film Corp. (U.K.) Ltd, Re (1986) 2 B.C.C. 98 497
Rhoades, ex p. Rhoades, Re [1899] 2 Q.B. 347; 80 L.T. 742; 15 T.L.R. 407; sub nom. Re Rhoades, ex p. Official Receiver, 47 W.R. 561; 43 S.J. 571 332
Rhodes v. Dawson (1886) 16 Q.B.D. 548; 55 L.J.Q.B. 134; 34 W.R. 240, C.A. . 147
Rhodes (John T.), Re (No. 2) (1987) 3 B.C.C. 588 562
Rica Gold Washing Co., Re (1879) 11 Ch.D. 36; [1874–80] All E.R. Rep. Ext. 1570; 40 L.T. 531; 27 W.R. 715, C.A. 535
Richardson, ex p. Smart, Re (1872) 8 Ch.App. 220; 42 L.J. Bcy. 22; 28 L.T. 146; 21 W.R. 237, L.JJ. 210
——, St. Thomas's Hospital (Governors), Re [1911] 2 K.B. 705; 80 L.J.K.B. 1232; 105 L.T. 226; 18 Mans. 327, C.A. 193
Rickett, Re ex p. Insecticide Activated Products v. Official Receiver [1949] 1 All E.R. 737; 65 T.C.R. 258; sub nom., Re A Debtor 93 S.J. 218 164
Ridgway, ex p. Hurlbatt, Re (1889) 6 Morr. 277; 6 T.L.R. 21; 61 L.T. 647; 38 W.R. 432 184
Riggs, ex p. Lovell, Re [1901] 2 K.B. 16; 70 L.J.K.B. 541; 84 L.T. 428; 49 W.R. 624; 45 S.J. 408; 8 Mans. 233 215
Ringeisen v. Austria, Case 2614/65, 1 E.H.R.R. 455; 16 Y.B.E.C. H.R. 468; (1972) 21 I.C.L.Q. 377; (1974) 23 I.C.L.Q. 193 192
Risdon Iron and Locomotive Works v. Furness [1906] 1 K.B. 49; 75 L.J.K.B. 83; 93 L.T. 687; 54 W.R. 324; 22 T.L.R. 45; 50 S.J. 42; 11 Com.Cas. 35 758
River Steamer Co., Mitchell's Claim, Re (1871) 6 Ch.App. 822; 25 L.T. 319; 19 W.R. 1130 596
Riviera Pearls, Re (Practice Note) [1962] 1 W.L.R. 722; 106 S.J. 328; [1962] 2 All E.R. 194 n. 497, 537
Roberts, Re [1900] 1 Q.B. 122; 69 L.J.Q.B. 19; 18 L.T. 467; 48 W.R. 132; 16 T.L.R. 29; 44 S.J. 44; 7 Mans. 5, C.A. 203, 204
Robertson (A Bankrupt), Re [1989] 1 W.L.R. 1139 323
Robertson v. Richardson (1885) 30 Ch.D. 623; 55 L.J.Ch. 275; 33 W.R. 897 ... 214
Robinson, ex p. Robinson, Re (1883) 22 Ch.D. 816; 48 L.T. 501; 31 W.R. 553, C.A. 136, 695, 728
Rochford v. Hackman (1852) 9 Hare 475; 68 E.R. 597; 21 L.J.Ch. 511; 19 L.T.O.S. 5 214

Table of Cases

Roe & Hunter v. Galliers (1787) 2 Term.Rep. 133; 100 E.R. 72 215
Rogers, Re (1884) 13 Q.B.D. 438 58
Rolls Razor v. Cox [1967] 1 Q.B. 552; [1967] 2 W.L.R. 241; 110 S.J. 943; [1967] 1
    All E.R. 397; [1966] C.L.Y. 641, C.A. 273, 274, 275
Rome v. Punjab National Bank (No. 2) [1989] 1 W.L.R. 1211; [1989] B.C.L.C.
    328, (1989) 5 B.C.C. 785 747
Rondel v. Worsley [1969] 1 A.C. 191; [1967] 3 W.L.R. 1666; 111 S.J. 927; [1967] 3
    All E.R. 993; affirming [1967] 1 Q.B. 443 255
Rose, Re, Rose v. Rose [1904] 2 Ch. 348; sub nom. Re Rose, Hasluck v. Rose 73
    L.J.Ch. 726; 91 L.T. 254; 11 Mans. 347 211
—— v. Buckett [1901] 2 K.B. 449; 70 L.J.K.B. 736; 84 L.T. 670; 50 W.R. 8; 17
    T.L.R. 544; 8 Mans. 259, C.A. 191
—— v. Hart (1818) 8 Taunt. 499; 129 E.R. 477; 2 Moore, C.P. 547 273
Roselmar Properties Ltd (No. 2), Re (1986) 2 B.C.C. 99 497
Roselmar Properties Ltd, Re (1986) 2 B.C.C. 99 545
Rossano v. Manufacturers' Life Insurance Co. [1963] 2 Q.B. 352; [1962] 3 W.L.R.
    157; 106 S.J. 452; [1962] 2 All E.R. 214; [1962] 1 Lloyd's Rep. 187 707
Rother Iron Works Ltd v. Canterbury Precision Engineers [1974] Q.B. 1; [1973] 2
    W.L.R. 281; (1972) 117 S.J. 122; [1973] 1 All E.R. 394, C.A. 393
Rothermere, Re [1945] 1 Ch. 72 264
Roundwood Colliery Co., Re, Lee v. Roundwood Colliery Co. [1897] 1 Ch. 373; 66
    L.J.Ch. 186; 75 L.T. 641; 45 W.R. 324; 13 T.L.R. 175; 41 S.J. 240, C.A. .. 555
Rowbotham Baxter, Re [1990] B.C.L.C. 397; [1990] B.C.C. 113 .... 424, 429, 435
Rowe, ex p. West Coast Gold Fields Ltd, Re [1904] 2 K.B. 489; 73 L.J.K.B. 852; 91
    L.T. 101; 52 W.R. 608; 48 S.J. 545; 11 Mans. 272 .... 164, 282, 575
Roxburghe v. Cox (1881) 17 Ch. D. 520; 50 L.J.Ch. 772; 45 L.T. 225; 30 W.R. 74,
    C.A. 205
Royal Bank of Scotland v. Commercial Bank of Scotland (1882) 7 App.Cas. 366; 47
    L.T. 360; 31 W.R. 49, H.L. 210
—— v. Cuthbert (1813) 1 Rose 462 .... 692, 708, 710
Royal Exchange Assurance v. The Liquidator [1952] 1 All E.R. 1269 758
Royal Trust Bank v. Buchler [1989] B.C.L.C. 130 444
Rubber and Producers Investment Trust, Re [1915] 1 Ch. 382; 84 L.J.Ch. 534; 112
    L.T. 1129; 31 T.L.R. 253; [1915] H.B.R. 120 .... 511, 577, 584
Rushforth, ex p. (1805) 10 Ves. 409; 32 E.R. 903 268
Rushton, Re [1971] 2 All E.R. 937 282
Russian Bank for Foreign Trade [1933] 1 Ch. 745; 102 L.J.Ch. 309; 149 L.T. 65;
    49 T.L.R. 253; 77 S.J. 197; [1933] B. & C.R. 157 .... 734, 735, 761, 762, 763, 764
Russian Commercial and Industrial Bank, Re [1955] Ch. 148; [1955] 2 W.L.R. 62;
    99 S.J. 44; [1955] 1 All E.R. 75 .... 259, 734, 741
——, Re (1963) 107 S.J. 415 741
—— v. Comptoir d'Escompte de Mulhouse [1925] A.C. 112; 93 L.J.K.B. 1098;
    132 L.T. 99; 40 T.L.R. 837; 68 S.J. 841, H.L. 734, 735, 759, 761, 762
Russian and English Bank, Re [1932] 1 Ch. 663; 101 L.J.Ch. 226; 147 L.T. 57; 48
    T.L.R. 282; 76 S.J. 201; [1931] B. & C.R. 140 .... 734, 744, 745, 761, 764
—— v. Baring Bros. & Co. Ltd [1934] Ch. 276; 103 L.J.Ch. 111; 150 L.T. 353; 77
    Sol. Jo. 913; [1933] B. & C.R. 213 .... 741, 745
—— v. Baring Bros. [1935] Ch. 120 745
—— v. Baring Bros. [1935] Ch. 127, C.A. 745
Russian and English Bank and Florence Montefiore Guedalla v. Baring Bros. and
    Co. Ltd (1936) A.C. 405; [1936] 1 All E.R. 505; 105 L.J.Ch. 174; 154 L.T.
    602; 52 T.L.R. 393; [1936–7] B. & C.R. 28, H.L. 734, 740, 741, 744, 745, 752,
                                                                               761, 762, 764
Russell (J.) Electronics Ltd, Re [1968] 1 W.L.R. 1252; 112 S.J. 621; [1968] 2 All
    E.R. 559 .... 497, 539
Russo-Asiatic Bank, Russian Bank for Foreign Trade, Re [1934] 1 Ch. 720; 103
    L.J.Ch. 336; 152 L.T. 142; 78 S.J. 647; [1934] B. & C.R. 71 764
Ryder Installations, Re [1966] 1 W.L.R. 524; 110 S.J. 246; [1966] 1 All E.R.
    453n. 497, 539
Ryley, ex p. Official Receiver, Re (1885) 15 Q.B.D. 329; 54 L.J.Q.B. 420; 33 W.R.
    656; 1 T.L.R. 468; 2 Morr. 171 147

TABLE OF CASES

S.C.L. Building Services Ltd, Re [1990] B.C.L.C. 98; (1989) 5 B.C.C. 746 424
S.N. Group plc, Re [1993] B.C.C. 808 550
—— v. Barclays Bank plc [1993] B.C.C. 506 546
S.O.S. Motors Ltd, Re [1934] N.Z.L.R. 129 538
S.S. Titian, Re (1888) 36 W.R. 347; 58 L.T. 178 514
Sabatier v. The Trading Company [1927] 1 Ch. 495; 98 L.J.Ch. 211; 136 L.T. 574;
  71 Sol. Jo. 104 .... 747, 759
Sabre International Products Ltd, Re [1991] B.C.L.C. 470; [1991] B.C.C. 694 . 443
Saccharin Corp. Ltd v. Chemische Fabrik A.G. [1911] 2 K.B. 516; 80 L.J.K.B.
  1117; 104 L.T. 886, C.A. 748
Sacker, ex p. Sacker, Re (1888) 22 Q.B.D. 179; 58 L.J.Q.B. 4; 60 L.T. 344; 37 W.R.
  204; 5 T.L.R. 112, C.A. 84
Safety Explosives Ltd, Re [1904] 1 Ch. 266; 73 L.J.Ch. 184; 90 L.T. 321; 52 W.R.
  470; 11 Mans. 76, C.A. 164, 286, 575
Said v. Butt [1920] 3 K.B. 497; 90 L.J.K.B. 239; 124 L.T. 413; 36 T.L.R. 762 .. 390
St. Ives Windings, Re [1987] 3 B.C.C. 634 425
St. James' Club, Re (1852) 2 De G.M. & G. 383; 42 E.R. 920; 19 L.T.O.S. 307; 16
  Jur. 1075 738
Salaman v. Tod [1911] S.C. 1214; 48 Sc.L.R. 974; 2 S.L.T. 172 720
Salcombe Hotel Development Co. Ltd, Re (1989) 5 B.C.C. 807; [1991] B.C.L.C.
  44; The Times, November 25, 1988 509
Salisbury Railway and Market House Co. Ltd, Re [1969] 1 Ch. 349; [1967] 3
  W.L.R. 651; [1967] 1 All E.R. 813 514
Salmen, Re (1912) 107 L.T. 108; 56 Sol.Jo. 632, C.A. 332
Salmon, ex p. Official Receiver, Re [1916] 2 K.B. 510; 85 L.J.K.B. 1268; 115 L.T.
  155; [1916] H.B.R. 120, D.C. 184, 329
Salomon v. Salomon & Co. [1897] A.C. 22; 66 L.J.Ch. 35; 75 L.T. 426; 45 W.R.
  193; 13 T.L.R. 46; 41 Sol.Jo. 63; 4 Mans. 89, H.L. 10
Sandiford, Re (No. 2) [1935] Ch. 681; [1935] All E.R.Rep. 364; 104 L.J.Ch. 335;
  154 L.T. 7 255
Sarflax Ltd, Re [1979] Ch. 592; [1979] 2 W.L.R. 202; (1978) 123 S.J. 97; [1979] 1
  All E.R. 529 660
Sartoris's Estate, Re Sartoris v. Sartoris [1892] 1 Ch. 11; 61 L.J.Ch. 1; 65 L.T. 544;
  40 W.R. 82; 8 T.L.R. 51; 36 S.J. 41, C.A. 214
Sass, ex p. National Provincial Bank of England Ltd, Re [1896] 2 Q.B. 12; 65
  L.J.Q.B. 481; 74 L.T. 383; 44 W.R. 588; 12 T.L.R. 333; 40 S.J. 686; 3 Mans.
  125 268
Saunders, ex p. Leigh, Re (1896) 13 T.L.R. 108 153
Savundra, Re [1973] 3 All E.R. 406; [1973] 1 W.L.R. 1147; 117 S.J. 696; 58
  Cr.App.R. 54; [1973] Crim.L.R. 631, D.C. 251
Sawyers, ex p. Blain, Re (1879) 12 Ch.D. 522; [1874–80] All E.R. 708; 41 L.T. 46;
  28 W.R. 334; 7 T.L.R. 177, C.A. 696, 719
Scharrer, Re (1888) 20 Q.B.D. 518; 4 T.L.R. 627 .... 153, 208, 321
Scheibler, ex p. Holthausen, Re (1874) 9 Ch.App. 722; 44 L.J.Bcy. 26; 31 L.T.
  13 .... 206, 721
Schemmer v. Property Resources Ltd [1975] Ch. 273; [1974] 3 W.L.R. 406; 118
  S.J. 716; [1974] 3 All E.R. 451 .... 707, 718, 719, 720, 760
Schibsby v. Westenholz (1870) L.R. 6 Q.B. 155; 40 L.J.Q.B. 73; 24 L.T. 93; 19
  W.R. 587 694
Schorsch Meier GmbH v. Hennin [1975] Q.B. 416; [1974] 3 W.L.R. 823; 118 S.J.
  881; [1975] 1 All E.R. 152; [1975] C.M.L.R. 20; [1975] 1 Lloyd's Rep. 1,
  C.A. 259
Scott v. Commissioner of Police for the Metropolis [1975] A.C. 819; [1974] 3
  W.L.R. 741; [1974] 3 All E.R. 1032; affirming sub nom. R. v. Scott [1974] Q.B.
  733; [1974] 2 W.L.R. 379; [1974] 2 All E.R. 204 338
Scottish Exhibition Centre Ltd v. Mirestrop Ltd, 1993 S.L.T. 1034 444
Scanton's Trustee v. Pearse [1922] 2 Ch. 87; 91 L.J.Ch. 579; 127 L.T. 698; 38
  T.L.R. 629; 66 S.J. 503; [1922] B. & C.R. 52, C.A. 208
Sea Insurance Co. v. Rossia Insurance Co. of Petrograd (1924) 20 Lloyd's Rep.
  308 .... 760, 762

lvii

TABLE OF CASES

Seagull Manufacturing Co. Ltd, *Re* [1991] 3 W.L.R. 307; [1991] 4 All E.R. 257; [1991] B.C.C. 550; affirmed [1993] B.C.C. 241, C.A. 155, 571, 696
Seaman, *ex p.* Furness Finance Co., *Re* [1896] 1 Q.B. 412; 65 L.J.Q.B. 348; 74 L.T. 151; 44 W.R. 496; 40 S.J. 318; 3 Mans. 19 245
Searle *v.* Choat [1884] 25 Ch. 723; 53 L.J.Ch. 506, 50 L.T. 470; 32 W.R. 397, C.A. 364
Secretary of State for Trade and Industry *v.* Gray; Grayan Building Services Ltd, *Re* [1995] B.C.C. 554; [1995] 3 W.L.R. 1; (1994) 138 S.J. (L.B.) 227; *The Times*, November 24, 1994, C.A. 669, 673
Securities and Investment Board *v.* Lancashire and Yorkshire Portfolio Management Ltd [1992] B.C.C. 381; [1992] B.C.L.C. 281 497
Sedgwick, Collins and Co. *v.* Rossia Insurance Company of Petrograd [1926] 1 K.B. 1; 95 L.J.K.B. 7; 133 L.T. 808; 41 T.L.R. 663, C.A. 765
Seear *v.* Lawson, Chatterton *v.* Lawson (1880) 15 Ch.D. 426; 49 L.J.Bcy. 69; 42 L.T. 893; 28 W.R. 929, C.A. 173, 192
Selig *v.* Lion [1891] 1 Q.B. 513; 60 L.J.Q.B. 403; 64 L.T. 796; 39 W.R. 254, D.C. 173
Selkrig *v.* Davies (1814) 2 Dow. 230; 3 E.R. 848; 2 Rose 97, H.L. 713, 714, 754
Semenza *v.* Brinsley (1865) 18 C.B. (N.S.) 467; 144 E.R. 526 278
Semler *v.* Murphy [1968] Ch. 183; [1967] 2 W.L.R. 1171; 111 S.J. 154; [1967] 2 All E.R. 185 147
Sevenoaks Stationers (Retail) Ltd, *Re* [1991] Ch. 164; [1990] 3 W.L.R. 1165; [1991] 3 All E.R. 578; [1990] B.C.C. 765; [1991] B.C.L.C. 325; (1990) 134 S.J. 1367, C.A.; reversing [1990] B.C.L.C. 668 .... 673, 674
Seymour, *Re* [1937] 1 Ch. 668; *sub nom. Re* Seymour, Trustee *v.* Barclays Bank Ltd [1957] 3 All E.R. 499; 157 L.T. 472; 53 T.L.R. 940; 81 S.J. 629; [1936–37] B. & C.R. 178 245
Shackleton, *ex p.* Shackleton, *Re* (1889) 6 Morr. 304; 61 L.T. 648; 38 W.R. 288; 6 T.L.R. 125 313
Shamji *v.* Johnson Matthey Bankers Ltd [1991] B.C.L.C. 36, C.A. 397
Sharps of Truro Ltd, *Re* [1990] B.C.C. 94 .... 433, 435
Shaw, *ex p.* Gill, *Re* (1901) 83 L.T. 754; 49 W.R. 264; 45 S.J. 218, C.A. 98
——, *Re* [1917] 2 K.B. 734; 86 L.J.K.B. 1395 311
Shearing and Loader Ltd, *Re* [1991] B.C.C. 232; [1991] B.C.L.C. 764 429
Shears *v.* Goddard, *Re* Sills [1896] 1 Q.B. 406; 65 L.J.Q.B. 344; 74 L.T. 128; 44 W.R. 402; 3 Mans. 24, C.A. 245
Sherborne Associates Ltd, *Re* [1995] B.C.C. 40 662
Sheridan Securities Ltd, *Re* [1988] 4 B.C.C. 200 .... 425, 478
Shields, *ex p.* The Bankrupt, *Re* (1912) 106 L.T. 345 316
Shilena Hosiery Co. Ltd, *Re* [1980] Ch. 219; [1979] 3 W.L.R. 322; 123 S.J. 568; [1979] 2 All E.R. 6 541
Shine, *Re* [1892] 1 Q.B. 522; 61 L.J.Q.B. 253; 66 L.T. 146; 40 W.R. 386; 8 T.L.R. 279; 36 S.J. 295; 9 Morr. 40, C.A. 205, 220
Shipley *v.* Marshall (1863) 14 C.B. (N.S.) 566; 143 E.R. 567 231
Shoolbred *v.* Roberts [1900] 2 Q.B. 497; 69 L.J.Q.B. 800; 83 L.T. 37; 16 T.L.R. 486; 7 Mans. 388, C.A. 204
Sidaway *v.* Hay (1824) 3 B. & C. 12; 107 E.R. 639; 4 Dow. & Ry.K.B. 658; L.J.O.S. K.B. 215 .... 692, 710, 724
Sidebotham, *Re* (1880) 14 Ch.D. 458; 49 L.J.Bcy. 41; 42 L.T. 783; 28 W.R. 715, C.A. 179
Signland, *Re* [1982] 2 All E.R. 609 546
Silkstone & Haigh Moor Coal Co. *v.* Edey [1900] 1 Ch. 167; 69 L.J.Ch. 73; 48 W.R. 137; 44 S.J. 41 .... 584, 587
Sill *v.* Worswick (1791) 1 H.Bl. 665; 126 E.R. 379 714
Silver Valley Mines, *Re* (1882) 21 Ch.D. 381; 47 L.T. 597; 31 W.R. 96, C.A. . 583, 584, 587
Simanson, *ex p.* Ball, *Re* [1894] 1 Q.B. 433; 63 L.J.Q.B. 242; 70 L.T. 32; 1 Mans. 30; 10 R. 107 247
Simpson *v.* Mirabita (1869) L.R. 4 Q.B. 257; 10 B. & S. 77; 38 L.J.Q.B. 76; 20 L.T. 275; 17 W.R. 589 .... 692, 724
Sims, *ex p.* Official Receiver, *Re* [1907] 2 K.B. 36; 76 L.J.K.B. 849; 96 L.T. 713; 51 S.J. 345; 14 Mans. 169 177

lviii

TABLE OF CASES

Sinclair, Re (1885) 15 Q.B.D. 616 246
—— v. Brougham [1914] A.C. 398; 83 L.J.Ch. 465; 111 L.T. 1; 30 T.L.R. 315; 58 S.J. 302, H.L. 211
Singer & Co. v. Fry (1915) 84 L.J.K.B. 2025; 113 L.T. 552; [1915] H.B.R. 115 720
Sir John Moore Gold Mining Co., Re (1879) 12 Ch.D. 325; 28 W.R. 203, C.A. . 584
Sirdar Gurdyal Singh v. Rajah of Faridkote [1894] A.C. 670, P.C.; 10 T.L.R. 62; 11 R. 340 694
Skyline Associates v. Small (1974) 50 D.L.R. (3d) 217 758
Slater v. Jones (1873) L.R. 8 Ex. 186; 42 L.J.Ex. 122; 29 L.T. 56; 21 W.R. 815 . 50
—— v. Pinder (1871) L.R. 6 Exch. 228; 40 L.J.Ex. 146; 24 L.T. 631; 35 J.P. 744; 19 W.R. 778 242
"Slogger" Automatic Feeder Co. Ltd, Re [1915] 1 Ch. 478; 84 L.J.Ch. 587; 112 L.T. 579; 59 S.J. 272; [1915] H.B.R. 138 364
Slotlogic Ltd v. Leisure Casinos (1993) I.L. & P. 38 368
Small Re Westminster Bank v. Trustee, [1934] Ch. 541; 103 L.J.Ch. 305; 151 L.T. 200; [1934] B. & C.R. 1 .... 109, 164
Smallman Construction Ltd, Re (1988) 4 B.C.C. 784; [1989] B.C.L.C. 420; 1989 P.C.C. 433, D.C. 465
Smith, ex p. Brown, Re (1886) 17 Q.B.D. 488; 3 Morr. 202, C.A. 171
——, Re (1890) 25 Q.B.D. 536 238
——, ex p. Hildesheim, Re [1893] 1 Q.B. 323; 2 Ch. 1 .... 146, 147
——, Re [1947] 1 All E.R. 769; 91 S.J. 338 312
—— v. Braintree District Council [1990] 2 A.C. 215; [1989] 3 All E.R. 897, H.L. 43, 147
—— v. Buchanan (1800) 1 East 6; 102 E.R. 3 .... 692, 725
—— v. Director of Serious Fraud Office. See R. v. Director of Serious Fraud Office, ex p. Smith
—— v. Gronow [1891] 2 Q.B. 394; 60 L.J.Q.B. 776; 65 L.T. 117; 40 W.R. 46; 7 T.L.R. 596 215
—— v. Liquidator of James Birrell Ltd [1968] S.L.J. 174 638
Smiths Ltd v. Middleton [1979] 3 All E.R. 842 373
Sneezum, ex p. Davis, Re (1876) 3 Ch.D. 463; 45 L.J.Bcy. 137; 35 L.T. 389; 25 W.R. 49, C.A. 193
Snowdon, ex p. Snowdon, Re (1881) 17 Ch.D. 44; 50 L.J.Ch. 540; 44 L.T. 830; 29 W.R. 654, C.A. 269
Société Co-operative Sidmetal v. Titan International Ltd [1966] 1 Q.B. 828; [1965] 3 W.L.R. 847; 109 S.J. 777; [1965] 3 All E.R. 494; [1965] 2 Lloyd's Rep. 313 760
Société des Hotels le Touquet Paris–Plage v. Cummings [1922] 1 K.B. 451; 91 L.J.K.B. 288; 126 L.T. 513; 38 T.L.R. 221; 66 S.J. 269, C.A. 260
Société Nationale Industrielle Aerospatiale v. Lee Kui Jak [1987] A.C. 871; [1987] 3 W.L.R. 59; [1987] 3 All E.R. 510; (1987) 84 L.S.Gaz. 2048, P.C. 755
Solicitor, A, Re [1952] Ch. 328; 96 S.J. 59; [1952] 1 All E.R. 133 209
Solomon, Re, ex p. The Trustee of the Bankrupt [1967] Ch. 573; [1967] 2 W.L.R. 172; 110 S.J. 978; sub nom. Re A Debtor; ex p. Trustee v. Solomon [1966] 3 All E.R. 255 195
Solomons v. Ross (1764) 1 Hy.Bl. 131; 126 E.R. 79 720
Somers, ex p. Union Credit Bank, Re (1897) 4 Mans. 227 .... 136, 695
Somes, Re (1896) 3 Mans. 131 .... 710, 713
South Wales Atlantic Steamship Co., Re (1875) 2 Ch.D. 763, C.A.; 46 L.J.Ch. 177; 35 L.T. 294, C.A. 536
South Western Venezuela Ry Ltd, Re [1902] 1 Ch. 701; 71 L.J.Ch. 407; 80 L.T. 321; 50 W.R. 300; 46 S.J. 281; 9 Mans. 193 .... 367, 384
Southall v. British Mutual Life Assurance Society (1871) L.R. 6 Ch. 614; 19 W.R. 865; 40 L.J.Ch. 698 529
Southard & Co. Ltd, Re [1979] 1 W.L.R. 1198; [1979] 3 All E.R. 556, C.A.; affirming [1979] 1 W.L.R. 546; [1979] 1 All E.R. 582 .... 497, 538
Sowman v. Samuel (David) Trust Ltd [1978] 1 W.L.R. 22; (1977) 121 S.J. 757; [1978] 1 All E.R. 616; (1978) 36 P. & C.R. 123 396

lix

TABLE OF CASES

Specialised Mouldings Ltd, Re February 13, 1987 (unreported) 372, 375, 377, 472, 474
Specialist Plant Services Ltd v. Braithwaite [1987] B.C.L.C. 1, C.A. 637
Spiliada Maritime Corp. v. Cansulex Ltd [1987] A.C. 460; [1986] 3 W.L.R. 972; (1986) 130 S.J. 925; [1986] 3 All E.R. 843; [1987] 1 F.T.L.R. 103; [1987] 1 Lloyd's Rep. 1; [1987] E.C.C. 168; (1986) 130 S.J. 925; (1987) 84 L.S.Gaz. 113; (1986) 136 New L.J. 1137, H.L.; reversing [1985] 2 Lloyd's Rep. 116; (1985) 82 L.S.Gaz. 1416, C.A. 755
Spiller v. Turner [1897] 1 Ch. 911; 66 L.J.Ch. 435; 76 L.T. 622; 45 W.R. 549; 41 S.J. 452 763
Stacey v. Hill [1901] 1 Q.B. 660; 70 L.J.K.B. 435; 84 L.T. 410; 49 W.R. 390; 17 T.L.R. 311; 45 S.J. 325; 8 Mans. 169, C.A. 239
Stainton, ex p. Board of Trade, Re (1887) 4 Morr. 242 312
Standard Chartered Bank Ltd v. Inland Revenue Commissioners [1978] 1 W.L.R. 1160; (1978) 122 S.J. 698; [1978] 3 All E.R. 644; [1978] T.R. 45; [1978] S.T.C. 272 763
Standard Insurance Co. Ltd, Re [1968] Qd.R. 118 766
Standring and Co. Ltd, Re (1895) S.J. 603; [1895] W.N. 99 537
Stanford Services Ltd, Re [1987] B.C.L.C. 607; (1987) 3 B.C.C. 326 673
Stanhope Pension Trust Ltd v. Registrar of Companies [1994] B.C.C. 84; [1994] 1 B.C.L.C. 628; [1993] E.G.C.S. 206; [1993] N.P.C. 169, C.A.; reversing [1993] B.C.C. 603; [1993] 48 E.G. 129 240
Stanton (F. and E.) Ltd, Re [1928] 1 K.B. 464 542
Stapylton Fletcher Ltd, Re [1994] 1 W.L.R. 1181 638
State of Norway's Application, Re (Nos. 1 and 2) [1990] 1 A.C. 723; [1989] 2 W.L.R. 458; [1989] 1 All E.R. 745, H.L.; reversing [1989] 1 All E.R. 661, 701, C.A. 707
Steane's (Bournemouth), Re [1950] 1 All E.R. 21; 66 (Pt. 1) T.L.R. 71 629
Steel Wing Co., Re [1921] 1 Ch. 349; [1920] All E.R.Rep. 292; 90 L.J.Ch. 116; 124 L.T. 664; 65 S.J. 240; [1920] B. & C.R. 160 .... 89, 90, 525, 536
Stein v. Blake, The Times, May 19, 1995, H.L.; affirming [1994] Ch. 16; [1993] 3 W.L.R. 718; [1993] 4 All E.R. 225; [1993] B.C.C. 587; [1993] B.C.L.C. 1478, C.A. 91, 193, 274
—— v. Pope [1902] 1 K.B. 595; 71 L.J.K.B. 322; 86 L.T. 283; 50 W.R. 374; 18 T.L.R. 337; 9 Mans. 125, C.A. 215, 238
Stewart, ex p. Pottinger, Re (1878) 8 Ch.D. 621; 47 L.J.Bcy. 43; 38 L.T. 432; 42 J.P. 743; 26 W.R. 648, C.A. 257
—— v. Auld (1851) 13 Dunl. (Ct. of Sess.) 1337 713
Stokes, ex p. Mellish, Re [1919] 2 K.B. 256; 88 L.J.K.B. 794; 121 L.T. 391; 35 T.L.R. 345; [1918–19] B. & C.R. 208 201
Stone v. City and County Bank Ltd (1877) 3 C.P.D. 282; 47 L.J.Q.B. 681; 38 L.T. 9 505
Stotter v. Arimaru Holdings Ltd [1994] 2 N.Z.L.R. 655 615
Stray, Re (1867) 22 Ch.App. 374; 36 L.J.Bcy. 7; 16 L.T. 250; 15 W.R. 600; L.JJ. 95
Sturmey's Trustee v. Sturmey (1913) 107 L.T. 718 245
Suidair International Airways Ltd, Re [1951] Ch. 165; 66 T.L.R. (Pt. 2) 909; 94 S.J. 742; [1950] 2 All E.R. 920 .... 244, 556, 755, 757
Sullivan and Hughes, Re (1904) 20 T.L.R. 393 56
Sultzberger, ex p. Sultzberger, Re (1887) 4 Morr. 82 312
Summers, ex p. Official Receiver, Re [1907] 2 K.B. 166; 96 L.T. 791; 23 T.L.R. 465; 51 S.J. 430 316
Sunderland, Re [1911] 2 K.B. 658; 80 L.J.K.B. 825; 105 L.T. 233; 27 T.L.R. 454; 55 S.J. 568; 18 Mans. 123, C.A. 96
Surplus Properties (Huddersfield) Ltd, Re [1984] B.C.L.C. 89 497
Suse (No. 2), ex p. Deves, Re (1885) 14 Q.B.D. 611; 54 L.J.Q.B. 390; 53 L.T. 131; 33 W.R. 625, C.A. 210
Sussman (J. & P.) Ltd, Re [1985] 1 W.L.R. 519 545
Sutherland, Re [1963] A.C. 235 262
Sutters v. Briggs [1922] 1 A.C. 1; 91 L.J.K.B. 1; 125 L.T. 737; 38 T.L.R. 30; 66 S.J. 9, H.L. 208

lx

TABLE OF CASES

Sutton v. Rees (1869) 9 Jur. (N.S.) 456; (1863) 32 L.J.Ch. 437; 8 L.T. 343; 27 J.P. 388; 11 W.R. 413	364
Swabey, ex p. Swabey, Re (1897) 76 L.T. 534	313
Swain (J.D.) Ltd, Re [1965] 1 W.L.R. 909; [1965] 2 All E.R. 761; 109 S.J. 320, C.A.; affirming The Guardian, January 19, 1965	497, 537
Swift 736, Re; Secretary of State for Trade and Industry v. Ettinger [1993] B.C.C. 312; [1993] B.C.L.C. 896; The Times, February 18, 1993, C.A.; reversing in part [1992] B.C.C. 93; [1993] B.C.L.C. 1	674
Swiss Bank Corp. v. Boehmische Industrial Bank [1923] 1 K.B. 673; 92 L.J.K.B. 600; 128 L.T. 809; 39 T.L.R. 179; 67 S.J. 423, C.A.	710
Sykes, Re (1932) 101 L.J.Ch. 298; [1931] B. & C.R. 215	710, 713
Synthetic Technology Ltd, Re, Secretary of State for Trade and Industry v. Joiner [1993] B.C.C. 549	674
Syria Ottoman Railway Co., Re (1904) 20 T.L.R. 217	737
T.H. Knitwear Ltd, Re [1988] 4 B.C.C. 102	514
T.W. Construction Ltd, Re [1954] 1 W.L.R. 540	629
Tait, ex p. Harper, Re (1882) 21 Ch.D. 537	286
Tait and Co., ex p. Tait, Re (1872) L.R. 13 Eq. 311; 41 L.J.Bcy. 32; 20 W.R. 318	712
Tannenberg & Sons, ex p. Parrier, Re (1889) 60 L.T. 270; sub nom. Re Tannenberg & Sons, ex p. Parrier, 37 W.R. 480; 6 Morr. 49, D.C.	96
Tapster v. Ward (1909) 101 L.T. 503; 53 S.J. 503, C.A.	201
Tasbian Ltd, Re (No. 2) [1990] B.C.C. 322	442
——, Re (No. 3) [1992] B.C.C. 358; [1993] B.C.L.C. 297, C.A.; affirming [1991] B.C.C. 435; [1991] B.C.L.C. 792	676
Taylor, ex p. Crossley, Re (1872) L.R. 13 Eq. 409; 41 L.J.Bcy. 35; 20 W.R. 400	152
——, ex p. Taylor, Re [1901] 1 Q.B. 744; 84 L.T. 426; 49 W.R. 510; 45 S.J. 382	324
——, ex p. Norvell, Re [1910] 1 K.B. 562; 79 L.J.K.B. 610; 120 L.T. 84; 26 L.T.R. 270; 54 S.J. 271; 17 Mans. 145	273
—— v. Plumer (1815) 3 M. & S. 562; 105 E.R. 721; 2 Rose 457	209
Taylors Industrial Flooring Ltd v. M. & H. Plant Hire (Manchester) Ltd [1990] B.C.L.C. 216; (1990) B.C.C. 44, C.A.	527, 528
Taylor's Settlement Trusts, Re [1929] 1 Ch. 435; 98 L.J.Ch. 142; 140 L.T. 553; [1929] B. & C.R. 15	212
Tea Trading Co. K. and C. Popoff Bros, Re [1933] Ch. 647; 102 L.J.Ch. 224; 149 L.T. 138; 77 S.J. 215; [1933] B. & C.R. 120	746, 761
Tennant's Application, Re [1956] 1 W.L.R. 874; 100 S.J. 509; [1956] 2 All E.R. 753, C.A.	204
Thellusson, ex p. Alody, Re [1919] 2 K.B. 735; 88 L.J.K.B. 1210; 35 T.L.R. 732; 63 S.J. 788; 122 L.T. 35; [1918–19] B. & C.R. 249, C.A.	207
Theophile v. Solicitor General [1950] A.C. 186; 66 T.L.R. (Pt. 1) 441; 94 S.J. 208; [1950] 1 All E.R. 405; 43 R. & I.T. 180; affirming sub nom. Re A Debtor (No. 335 of 1947), ex p. R. v. The Debtor, 64 T.L.R. 446; [1948] 2 All E.R. 533	697
Thomas v. Patent Lionite Co. (1881) 17 Ch.D. 250; 50 L.J.Ch. 544; 44 L.T. 392; 29 W.R. 596, C.A.	241, 555
Thompson v. Cohen (1872) L.R. 7 Q.B. 527; 41 L.J.Q.B. 221; 26 L.T. 693; 36 J.P. 822	149
—— v. Freeman (1786) 1 T.R. 155; 99 E.R. 1026	227
Thompson and Cottrell's Contract, Re [1943] Ch. 97; [1943] 1 All E.R. 169; 112 L.J.Ch. 109; 168 L.T. 155; 59 T.L.R. 127; 87 S.J. 57	239
Thorne v. Silverleaf [1994] B.C.C. 109; [1994] 2 B.C.L.C. 637, C.A.	666
Thorne (H.E.) & Sons Ltd, Re [1914] 2 Ch. 438; 84 L.J.Ch. 161; 112 L.T. 30; 58 S.J. 755; [1915] H.B.R. 19	275
Throckmorton, ex p. Fyston, Re (1877) 7 Ch.D. 145; 47 L.J. Bcy. 62; 37 L.T. 447; 26 W.R. 181, C.A.	214
Thurso New Gas Co. Ltd, Re (1889) 42 Ch.D. 486; 61 L.T. 351; 38 W.R. 156; 5 T.L.R. 562; 1 Meg. 330	556, 753

Table of Cases

Thurburn v. Steward (1871) L.R. 3 (P.C.) 478 717
Tilley v. Bowman [1910] 1 K.B. 745; 79 L.J.K.B. 547; 102 L.T. 318; 54 S.J. 342; 17 Mans. 97 .... 272, 274
Times Life Assurance Co., Re (1869) 9 Eq. 382 537
Tobias & Co., Re, ex p. Tobias [1891] 1 Q.B. 463; 64 L.T. 115; 39 W.R. 399; 7 T.L.R. 296 316
Todd (L.) (Swanscombe) Ltd, Re [1990] B.C.C. 125 660
Toleman and England, ex p. Bramble, Re (1880) 13 Ch.D. 885; 42 L.T. 413; 28 W.R. 676 170
Tollemache, ex p. Anderson, Re (1885) 14 Q.B.D. 606; 54 L.J.Q.B. 383; 52 L.T. 786, C.A. 254
——, ex p. Edwards, Re (1884) 14 Q.B.D. 415, C.A. 155, 253
——, ex p. Revell, Re (1884) 13 Q.B.D. 720; 54 L.J.Q.B. 89; 51 L.T. 376; 33 W.R. 288 .... 253, 254
Tomkins v. Saffery (1877) 3 App.Cas. 213; 47 L.J.Bcy. 11; 37 L.T. 758; 26 W.R. 62, H.L. 233
Tomkins (J.G.) & Co., Re [1901] 1 Q.B. 476; 70 L.J.Q.B. 223; 84 L.T. 341; 49 W.R. 294; 17 T.L.R. 198; 45 S.J. 218; 8 Mans. 232, C.A. 85
Torkington v. Magee [1902] 2 K.B. 427; 71 L.J.K.B. 712; 87 L.T. 304; 18 T.L.R. 703 191
Tottenham Hotspur plc v. Edennote plc [1994] B.C.C. 681 536
Tout and Finch Ltd, Re [1954] 1 W.L.R. 178; [1954] 1 All E.R. 127 209
Tovarishestvo Manufactur Liudvig-Rabenek, Re [1994] Ch. 404; [1944] 2 All E.R. 556; 113 L.J.Ch. 250; 171 L.T. 66; 60 T.L.R. 467; 88 S.J. 262 .... 736, 761
Town Investments Ltd Underlease, Re [1954] Ch. 301; [1954] 2 W.L.R. 355; 98 S.J. 162; [1954] 1 All E.R. 585 239
Townreach Ltd, Re (No. 002081 of 1994) [1994] 3 W.L.R. 983 625
Tramways Building and Construction Co. Ltd, Re [1988] Ch. 293; [1988] 2 W.L.R. 640; (1988) 132 S.J. 460; 1988 P.C.C. 85; (1987) 3 B.C.C. 443; [1987] B.C.L.C. 632 631
Travel Mondial Ltd, Re [1991] B.C.C. 224; [1991] B.C.L.C. 120 674
Travellers' Chambers Ltd, Re (1895) 12 T.L.R. 529 659
Travers v. Holley [1953] P. 246; [1953] 3 W.L.R. 507; [1953] 2 All E.R. 794; reversing *The Times*, December 10, 1952; [1952] C.L.Y. 542 .... 718, 760
Trepca Mines Ltd, Re [1960] 1 W.L.R. 1273; 104 S.J. 979; [1960] 3 All E.R. 304n., C.A.; reversing [1960] 1 W.L.R. 24; 104 S.J. 32; [1959] 3 All E.R. 398n; [1959] C.L.Y. 2516 760
Trytel, Re, ex p. Trustee of the Property of the Bankrupt v. Performing Right Society and Soundtrac Film Co. [1952] 2 T.L.R. 32; [1952] W.N. 355 149
Tucker, Re (1974) 232 E.G. 715 171
——, Re [1988] 2 W.L.R. 748; (1988) 132 S.J. 497; [1988] 1 All E.R. 603; [1988] 1 F.T.L.R. 137, C.A.; reversing [1987] 1 W.L.R. 928; [1987] 2 All E.R. 23; (1987) 131 S.J. 938 .... 154, 155
——, Re [1990] Ch. 148, C.A. 696, 707
Tudor Grange Holdings Ltd v. Citibank N.A. [1992] Ch. 53; [1991] 3 W.L.R. 750; [1991] 4 All E.R. 1; (1991) 135 S.J. (L.B.) 3; [1991] B.C.L.C. 1009; *The Times*, April 30, 1991 .... 386, 387
Turner, Re A Bankrupt, ex p. Trustee of the Property of the Bankrupt [1974] 1 W.L.R. 1556; 118 S.J. 849; [1975] 1 All E.R. 5 .... 171, 195
Tweeds Garages Ltd, Re [1962] Ch. 406; [1962] 2 W.L.R. 38; [1962] 1 All E.R. 121 524
Tyler, ex p. Official Receiver, Re [1907] 1 K.B. 865; 76 L.J.K.B. 591; 97 L.T. 30; 23 T.L.R. 328; 51 S.J. 291; 14 Mans. 73, C.A. 201, 367
Tyneside Permanent Benefit Building Society, Re [1885] W.N. 148; (1885) 20 L.J.N.C. 130 549
Tynte, Re (1880) 15 Ch.D. 125; 42 L.T. 598; 28 W.R. 767 70

Udny v. Udny (1869) L.R. 1 Sc. & Div. 441 .... 700, 701
Unit 2 Windows (in liquidation) Ltd, Re [1985] 1 W.L.R. 1383; [1985] 3 All E.R. 647; 1986 P.C.C. 194 284

TABLE OF CASES

Usines de Melle's Patent, *Re* (1954) 91 C.L.R. 42; 284 L.J. 225	764
Utley, *Re* (1901) 17 T.L.R. 349	58
Vadala *v.* Lawes (1890) 25 Q.B.D. 310; [1886–90] All E.R. Rep. 853; 63 L.T. 128; 38 W.R. 594, C.A.	694, 716
Van Laun, *ex p.* Chatterton, *Re* [1907] 2 K.B. 23; 76 L.J.K.B. 644; 97 L.T. 69; 23 T.L.R. 384; 51 S.J. 344; 14 Mans. 91, C.A.	253
Vanlohe, *ex p.* Dewhurst, *Re* (1871) 7 Ch.App. 185; 41 L.J.Bcy.; 25 L.T. 731; 20 W.R. 172	200
Vaughan *v.* Halliday (1874) 9 Ch.App. 561; 30 L.T. 791; 22 W.R. 886, L.JJ.	210
Vautin, *ex p.* Saffrey, *Re* [1899] 2 Q.B. 549; 68 L.J.Q.B. 971; 48 W.R. 96; 43 S.J. 706; 6 Mans. 391	282
Vavasour, *Re* [1900] 2 Q.B. 309	171
Vernon Heaton Co. Ltd, *Re* [1936] Ch. 289	542
Victor *v.* Victor [1912] 1 K.B. 247; 81 L.J.K.B. 364; 105 L.T. 887; 28 T.L.R. 131; 56 S.J. 204; 19 Mans. 53, C.A.	250, 265
Videofusion Ltd, *Re* [1994] 1 W.L.R. 1548	545
Vimbos Ltd, *Re* [1900] 1 Ch. 470; 69 L.J.Ch. 209; 82 L.T. 597; 48 W.R. 520; 8 Mans. 101	395
Vint *v.* Hudspith (1885) 30 Ch.D. 24; 54 L.J.Ch. 844; 52 L.T. 774; 33 W.R. 738, C.A.	270
Viola *v.* Anglo-American Cold Storage Co. [1912] 2 Ch. 305; 81 L.J.Ch. 581; 107 L.T. 118; 19 Mans. 287	364
Vitoria, *ex p.* Vitoria, *Re* [1894] 2 Q.B. 387; 63 L.J.Q.B. 795; 71 L.T. 48; 42 W.R. 529; 10 T.L.R. 491; 38 S.J. 532; 1 Mans. 236; 9 R. 536, C.A.	134
Vocalion (Foreign) Ltd, *Re* [1932] 2 Ch. 196; 102 L.J.Ch. 42; 148 L.T. 159; 48 T.L.R. 525; [1933] B. & C.R. 1	754, 766
Von Dembinska, *ex p.* Debtor, *Re* [1954] 2 All E.R. 46; [1954] 1 W.L.R. 748; 98 S.J. 316, C.A.	160
Von Engel (a bankrupt), *Re*, *The Independent*, August 21, 1989	324
Von Hellfield *v.* E. Rechnitzer and Mayer Frères and Co. [1914] 1 Ch. 748; 83 L.J.Ch. 521; 110 L.T. 877; 58 S.J. 414, C.A.	758
Vuma Ltd, *Re* [1960] 1 W.L.R. 1283; 104 S.J. 980; [1960] 3 All E.R. 629	538
Wait, *ex p.* Collins, *Re* [1927] 1 Ch. 606; reversing [1926] 1 Ch. 962	213
Waite *v.* Bingley (1882) 21 Ch.D. 674; 51 L.J.Ch. 651; 30 W.R. 698	722
Walker, *Re* Public Trustee *v.* Walker [1939] 1 Ch. 974; [1939] 3 All E.R. 902; 109 L.J.Ch. 1; 161 L.T. 223; 55 T.L.R. 1092; 83 S.J. 731	214
——, *Re* The Trustee of the Property of the Deceased Debtor *v.* Department of Trade and Industry [1972] 1 All E.R. 1096	177
—— *v.* Mottram (1881) 19 Ch.D. 355; 51 L.J.Ch. 108; 45 L.T. 659; 30 W.R. 165, C.A.	190
Wallace, *Re* (1884) 14 Q.B.D. 22; 54 L.J.Q.B. 293; 51 L.T. 551; Morr. 246; *sub nom. Re* Wallace, *ex p.* Richards, 33 W.R. 66; 1 T.L.R. 17, C.A.	85
—— *v.* Universal Automatic Machines Co. [1894] 2 Ch. 547; 63 L.J.Ch. 598; 70 L.T. 852; 10 T.L.R. 501; 1 Mans. 315; 7 R. 316, C.A.	363
Wallace Smith Trust Co. Ltd, *Re* [1992] B.C.C. 707	571
Wallis, *ex p.* Sully, *Re* (1885) 14 Q.B.D. 950; 33 W.R. 733	697
——, *ex p.* Jenks, *Re* [1902] 1 K.B. 719; 71 L.J.K.B. 465; 18 T.L.R. 414; 9 Mans. 136	206
Walls (J.) *v.* Legge [1923] 2 K.B. 240	363
Walter, *ex p.* Slocock, *Re* [1929] 1 Ch. 647; 98 L.J.Ch. 403; 141 L.T. 319; [1928] All E.R. Rep. 640; [1929] B. & C.R. 63	203
Walter and Sullivan Ltd *v.* Murphy J. and Sons Ltd [1955] 2 Q.B. 584; [1955] 2 W.L.R. 919; 99 S.J. 290; [1955] 1 All E.R. 843	87, 89
Ward, *ex p.* (1882) 22 Ch.D. 132	105
——, *Re, ex p.* Hammond & Son *v.* Official Receiver [1942] Ch. 294; 111 L.J.Ch. 137; 58 T.L.R. 294; 86 S.J. 105; [1940–42] B. & C.R. 116; *sub nom. Re* Debtor (No. 1123 of 1929), 166 L.T. 236	299

TABLE OF CASES

Ward v. Aitken, in Re Oasis Merchandising Services Ltd, The Times, June 19, 1995 189
—— v. Fry (1901) 85 L.T. 394; 50 W.R. 72; 18 T.L.R. 2; 46 S.J. 11, C.A. 245
Warder v. Saunders (1882) 10 Q.B.D. 114; 47 L.T. 475, D.C. 173
Warren (F.B.), Re; Wheeler v. Mills [1938] Ch. 725; [1938] 2 All E.R. 331; 107 L.J.Ch. 409; 159 L.T. 17; 54 T.L.R. 680; 82 S.J. 394; [1938–39] B. & C.R. 1, D.C. 145
Washington Diamond Mining Co., Re [1893] 3 Ch. 95; 62 L.J.Ch. 895; 69 L.T. 27; 41 W.R. 681; 9 T.L.R. 509; 37 S.J. 559; 2 R. 523, C.A. 659
Waters, Re, ex p. Waters (1874) L.R. 18 Eq. 701; 43 L.J.Bcy. 128; 30 L.T. 766; 22 W.R. 796 151
Watson, ex p. Oram, Re (1885) 15 Q.B.D. 399; 52 L.T. 785; 33 W.R. 890; 1 T.L.R. 553; 2 Morr. 199, C.A. 136
—— v. Holliday (1882) 20 Ch.D. 780; 46 L.T. 878; 30 W.R. 747 257
Watts v. Midland Bank plc [1986] B.C.L.C. 15 387
Webb Electrical, Re (1988) 4 B.C.C. 230; 1989 P.C.C. 379 629
Weddell v. Pearce (J.A.) and Major [1988] Ch. 1; [1987] 3 W.L.R. 592; (1987) 131 S.J. 1120; [1987] 3 All E.R. 624; [1988] L.S.Gaz. September 7, 33 193
Wedgecraft Ltd, Re (unreported, March 7, 1986) 673
Welham v. D.P.P. [1961] A.C. 103; [1960] 2 W.L.R. 669; [1960] 1 All E.R. 805; affirming sub nom. R. v. Welham [1960] 2 Q.B. 445; [1960] 2 W.L.R. 333; [1960] 1 All E.R. 260 338
Wells, Re [1929] 2 Ch. 269; 98 L.J.Ch. 407; 141 L.T. 323; [1929] B. & C.R. 119 241
——, Re, Swinburne-Hanham v. Howard [1933] 1 Ch. 29; 101 L.J.Ch. 346; 148 L.T. 5; 48 T.L.R. 617, C.A. 763
—— v. Wells [1914] P. 157; 83 L.J.P. 81; 111 L.T. 399; 30 T.L.T.R. 545; 58 S.J. 555, C.A. 255
Welsh Brick Industries Ltd, Re [1946] 2 All E.R. 197; 90 S.J. 430 524
Welsh Development Agency v. Export Finance Co. Ltd [1992] B.C.C. 270; [1992] B.C.L.C. 148; Financial Times, November 27, 1991; The Times, November 28, 1991, C.A.; reversing in part [1990] B.C.C. 393; [1991] B.C.L.C. 936 ... 390, 637
West v. Baker (1875) 1 Ex.D. 44; 45 L.J.Q.B. 113; 34 L.T. 102; 24 W.R. 277 .. 56
West Cumberland Iron and Steel Co., Re [1893] 1 Ch. 713; 62 L.J.Ch. 367; 68 L.T. 751; 41 W.R. 265; 37 S.J. 213; 3 R. 260 .... 753, 757
West Hartlepool Ironworks Co., Re (1875) 10 Ch.App. 618; 44 L.J.Ch. 668; 33 L.T. 149; 23 W.R. 938 538
West Tech Ltd, Re [1989] B.C.L.C. 600 435
Westbury v. Twigg & Co. [1892] 1 Q.B. 77; 61 L.J.Q.B. 32; 66 L.T. 225; 40 W.R. 208, D.C. 555
Wester Wemyss, Re Tilley v. Wester Wemyss [1940] Ch. 1, 108 L.J.Ch. 668; 33 L.T. 149; 23 W.R. 938 .... 277, 332
Wethered, ex p. Salaman, Re [1926] Ch. 127; 134 L.T. 264; [1925] B. & C.R. 265 245
Whicher, ex p. Stevens, Re (1888) 5 Morr. 173 152
Whicker v. Hume (1858) 7 H.L.C. 124; 28 L.J.Ch. 396; 31 L.T.O.S. 319; 22 J.P. 591; 4 Jur. 933; 6 W.R. 813; 11 E.R. 50 .... 700, 701
Whitaker, Re, Whitaker v. Palmer [1901] 1 Chap. 9; 70 L.J.Ch. 6; 83 L.T. 449; 49 W.R. 106; 17 T.L.R. 24; 45 S.J. 43, C.A. 295
White v. Chitty (1866) L.R. 1 Eq. 372; 35 L.J.Ch. 343; 13 L.T. 750; 12 Jur. 181; 14 W.R. 366 .... 213, 214
White and Osmond (Parkstone) Ltd, Re (unreported, June 30, 1960) 659
Whitley, J.J.R., ex p. Mirfield Commercial Co., Re (1891) 65 L.T. 351; 7 T.L.R. 508; 8 Morr. 149, D.C. 137
Whitmore v. Mason (1861) 2 J. & H. 204; 70 E.R. 1031; 31 L.J.Ch. 433; 5 L.T. 631 216
Whittaker, Re (1884) 1 Morr. 36; 50 L.T. 510 185
Whitting, ex p. Hall, Re (1879) 10 Ch.D. 615; 48 L.J.Bcy. 79; 40 L.T. 179; 27 W.R. 385, C.A. 213
Wigzell, ex p. Hall, Re [1921] 2 K.B. 835 .... 144, 207
Wilcoxon, ex p. Griffith, Re (1883) 23 Ch.D. 69; 52 L.J.Ch. 717; 48 L.T. 450; 31 W.R. 878, C.A. 227

Table of Cases

Wild v. Tucker [1914] 3 K.B. 36; 111 L.T. 250; 30 T.L.R. 507; 21 Mans. 181 .. 319
Wilenkin v. The Liquidator [1952] 1 All E.R. 1269; [1952] 1 T.L.R. 739 ..... 741, 763
Wilkie v. Cathcart (1870) 9 M. 168 720
William Brandt's Sons & Co. v. Dunlop Rubber Co. [1905] A.C. 454; 74 L.J.K.B. 898; 93 L.T. 495; 21 T.L.R. 710; 11 Com.Cas. 1, H.L. 87, 207
Williams, Re (1891) 8 Mor. 65 .... 277, 332
—— v. Atlantic Assurance Co. [1933] 1 K.B. 81; 102 L.J.K.B. 241; 148 L.T. 313; 37 Com.Cas. 304; 18 Asp. M.L.C. 334, C.A. 89
Williams' Will Trusts, Re [1953] 1 Ch. 138; [1953] 2 W.L.R. 418; 97 S.J. 133; [1953] 1 All E.R. 536 698
Wills v. Wood (1984) 128 S.J. 222, C.A.; (1984) 81 L.S.Gaz. 1211, C.A. 231
Willson, ex p. Nicholson, Re (1880) 14 Ch.D. 243; 49 L.J.Bcy. 68; 43 L.T. 266; 28 W.R. 936, C.A. 153
Wilmot v. Alton [1897] 1 Q.B. 17; 66 L.J.Q.B. 42; 75 L.T. 447; 45 W.R. 113; 13 T.L.R. 58; 4 Mans. 17, C.A. 149
Wilson, ex p. Vine, Re (1878) 8 Ch.D. 364; 47 L.J.Bcy. 116; 38 L.T. 730; 26 W.R. 582, C.A. 92, 191
——, Re [1926] 1 Ch. 21 207
—— v. United Counties Bank Ltd [1920] A.C. 102; 88 L.J.K.B. 1033, H.L. 191
Winans v. Att.-Gen. [1904] A.C. 287; 73 L.J.K.B. 613; 90 L.T. 721; 20 T.L.R. 510, H.L.; reversing sub nom. A.-G. v. Winans (1901) 85 L.T. 508, C.A. ... 700, 701
Windle, Re, ex p. Trustee of the Property of the Bankrupt [1975] 3 All E.R. 987; [1975] 1 W.L.R. 1628; sub nom. Windle (A Bankrupt), Re 119 S.J. 808 224
Winkworth v. Christie, Manson and Woods [1980] Ch. 496; [1820] 2 W.L.R. 937; [1980] 1 All E.R. 1121 710
Winterbottom, Re (1886) 18 Q.B.D. 446; 56 L.J.Q.B. 238; 56 L.T. 168; 4 Morr. 5, D.C. 85
Wiskeman, ex p. Trustee, Re (1923) 92 L.J.Ch. 349; [1923] B. & C.R. 28 ..... 179, 711
Witney Town Football and Social Club, Re [1993] B.C.C. 874; [1994] B.C.L.C. 487 738
Witton, ex p. Arnal, Re (1883) 24 Ch.D. 26; 53 L.J.Ch. 134; sub nom. Re Whitton, ex p. Arnal; 49 L.T. 221, C.A. 240
Wolff v. Van Boolen (1906) 94 L.T. 502 173
Wolmershausen v. Gullick [1893] 2 Ch. 514; 62 L.J.Ch. 773; 68 L.T. 753; 9 T.L.R. 437; 3 R. 610 268
Wood, ex p. Nader, Re (1874) 9 Ch.App. 670; 43 L.J.Bcy. 121; 30 L.T. 743; 22 W.R. 936, L.JJ. 265
Wood Green & Hornsey Steam Laundry, Re [1918] 1 Ch. 423; 87 L.J.Ch. 171; 118 L.T. 501; 62 S.J. 349 367
Woodley v. Woodley (No. 2) [1994] 1 W.L.R. 1167; [1993] 4 All E.R. 1010; [1993] 2 F.L.R. 477; [1993] 2 F.C.R. 660; [1993] Fam.Law 471, C.A. 198, 251, 267, 601
Woodroff, Re (1897) 4 Mans. 46; 76 L.T. 502 96
Woodroffe's (Musical Instruments) Ltd, Re [1986] Ch. 366; [1985] 3 W.L.R. 543; (1985) 129 S.J. 589; [1985] 2 All E.R. 908; 1985 P.C.C. 318; (1985) 82 L.S.Gaz. 3170 607
Woods (L.H.F.) Ltd, Re [1970] 1 Ch. 27 526
Woolf, Re (1906) 22 T.L.R. 501 311
Workvale (in dissolution), Re, sub nom. Workvale (No. 2), Re [1992] 1 W.L.R. 416; [1992] 2 All E.R. 627; [1992] B.C.C. 349; [1992] B.C.L.C. 544; [1992] Gazette, 8 April, 28, C.A.; affirming [1991] 1 W.L.R. 294; [1991] B.C.L.C. 531; [1991] B.C.C. 109 624
World Industrial Bank Ltd, Re [1909] W.N. 148 537
Worsley, ex p. Lambert, Re [1901] 1 Q.B. 309; 70 L.J.Q.B. 93; 84 L.T. 100; 49 W.R. 182; 17 T.L.R. 122; 45 S.J. 116; 8 Mans. 8, C.A. 697
Wray, Re (1887) 36 Ch.D. 138; 56 L.J.Ch. 1106; 57 L.T. 605; 36 W.R. 67; 3 T.L.R. 708, C.A. 147
Wreck Recovery and Salvage Co., Re (1880) 15 Ch.D. 353; 43 L.T. 190; 29 W.R. 266 507
Wright, ex p. Willey, Re (1883) 23 Ch.D. 118; 52 L.J.Ch. 546; 48 L.T. 380; 31 W.R. 553, C.A. 153

TABLE OF CASES

Wright, Re, ex p. Landau v. The Trustee [1949] 1 Ch. 729; 65 T.L.R. 564; 93 S.J. 679; [1949] 2 All E.R. 606 206
Wyatt v. Palmer [1899] 2 Q.B. 106; 68 L.J.Q.B. 709; 80 L.T. 639; 47 W.R. 549; 43 S.J. 553, C.A. 100
Wyvern Developments Ltd, Re [1974] 1 W.L.R. 1097; (1972) 118 S.J. 531; [1974] 2 All E.R. 535 .... 208, 448, 583

XY, ex p. Haes, Re [1902] 1 K.B. 98; 71 L.J.K.B. 102; 85 L.T. 564; 9 Mans. 5; sub nom. Re Debtor, ex p. Petitioning Creditors, 50 W.R. 182, C.A. 132
Xyllyx plc, Re (No. 1) [1992] B.C.L.C. 376 548

Yarmarine, (I.W.) Ltd, Re [1992] B.C.C. 28; [1992] B.C.L.C. 276 239
Yeatman, ex p. (1880) 16 Ch.D. 283 133
Yeovil Glove Co. Ltd, Re [1965] Ch. 148; [1964] 3 W.L.R. 406; 108 S.J. 499; [1964] 2 All E.R. 849, C.A.; affirming [1963] Ch. 528; [1962] 3 W.L.R. 900; 106 S.J. 817; [1962] 3 All E.R. 400; [1962] C.L.Y. 385 650
York, Re (1887) 36 Ch.D. 233; 56 L.T. 704; 35 W.R. 609; sub nom. Re Neal, Atkinson v. Powell 3 T.L.R. 548 331
Yorkshire Woolcombers Association Ltd, Re [1903] 2 Ch. 284, C.A. 361
Young, Re [1955] St.R.Qd. 254 .... 708, 720

Zakon, ex p. Trustee v. Bushell, Re [1940] Ch. 263; [1940] Ch. 253; 109 L.J.Ch. 118; 162 L.T. 181; 56 T.L.R. 312; 84 S.J. 96; [1940–49] B. & C.R. 1 247
Zoedone Co. (No. 1), Re (1883) 53 L.J.Ch. 465; 49 L.T. 654; 32 W.R. 312 533

TABLE OF STATUTES

1376	Fraudulent Assurances of Land or Goods Act (50 Edw. 3, c.6)	6	1845	Companies Clauses Consolidation Act (8 & 9 Vict., c.16) 11
1542	Bankruptcy Act (34 & 35 Hen. 8, c.4)	6	1846	County Courts Act 24
	s.1	7	1847	Bankruptcy Act (10 & 11 Vict., c.102) 24
1571	The Fraudulent Conveyances Act (13 Eliz. 1, c.5) 7, 232		1848	Joint Stock Companies Act (11 & 12 Vict., c.45)— s.5(7) 733
	Bankrupts Act (13 Eliz. 1, c.7)	7		Winding Up Amending Act (11 & 12 Vict., c.45)—
1605	Stat. (3 Jac. 1, c.18)	10		s.5 12
1623	Bankruptcy Act (21 Jas. 1, c.19)	208	1855	Limited Liability Act 1855 (18 & 19 Vict., c.133) .. 11
1705	Bankruptcy Act (4 & 5 Anne, c.4)—		1856	Mercantile Law Amendment Act (19 & 20 Vict., c.5)—
	s.8	9		s.5 268
1706	Bankruptcy Act (6 Anne, c.22)	9		Joint Stock Companies Act (19 & 20 Vict., c.47) .. 11, 520
	Bankruptcy Act (10 Anne, c.25)	9		Pt. III. .... 12, 519 ss.59–105. .... 12, 519
1720	Bubble Act (6 Geo. 1, c.18)	10		s.76 12
1732	Bankruptcy Act (5 Geo. 2, c.30)—		1861	Bankruptcy Act (24 & 25 Vict., c.134) 8
	s.24	23		s.69 8
1824	Bankruptcy Act (5 Geo. 4, c.98)	9		s.69 719
1825	Bankruptcy Act (6 Geo. 4, c.16)	9	1862	Companies Act (25 and 26 Vict., c.89) ..... 11, 520, 745 s.81 .... 12, 24
1831	Bankruptcy Act (1 & 2 Will. 4, c.56)	23		s.199 .... 744 (3) 733
1838	Judgments Act (1 & 2 Vict., c.110)—		1869	Debtors Act (32 & 33 Vict., c.62) 99
	s.17. ...... 279, 611, 612, 796			s.5. .... 99, 266, 267
1842	Bankruptcy Act (5 & 6 Vict., c.122)	24		s.11(15) .... 342 s.13(1) 345
1844	Joint Stock Companies Act (7 & 8 Vict., c.110)	10		Bankruptcy Act (32 & 33 Vict., c.71) ... 10, 87, 91, 242
	Joint Stock Companies' Winding Up Act (7 & 8 Vict., c.111)	10	1872	s.72 .... 203 Bankruptcy (Ireland) Amendment Act (35 & 36 Vict., c.58)—
	s.1	11		s.71 706
	s.2	11	1873	Supreme Court of Judicature Act (36 & 37 Vict., c.66) 23, 88
	s.25	11		
	s.26	11		s.3 23
	s.27	11		s.4 23

lxvii

Table of Statutes

1874 Infants Relief Act (37 & 38 Vict., c.62)............ 76
1875 Supreme Court of Judicature Act (38 & 39 Vict., c.77) 23, 88
     s.9 23
1878 Bills of Sale Act (41 & 42 Vict., c.31)........ 149, 231
1882 Bills of Exchange Act (45 & 46 Vict., c.61)—
     s.44(2)................. 210
     s.48............. 210, 261
     s.49 261
     (10)................. 261
1883 Bankruptcy Act (46 & 47 Vict., c.52)....... 10, 23, 60
     Pt. 4.................. 12
     s.24 312
     s.92 23
     s.122 419
1890 Partnership Act (53 & 54 Vict., c.39)—
     s.2................... 297, 612
     s.3................... 297, 612
     s.33(1)................ 78
     Companies (Winding Up) Act (53 & 54 Vict., c.63) 12
     s.32(3)................ 732
1907 Limited Partnership Act (7 Edw. 7, c.24) 79
1908 Companies (Consolidation) Act (8 Edw. 7, c.69).. 11, 520, 745
     s.268(1)(iii) 733
1913 Bankruptcy and Deeds of Arrangement Act (3 & 4 Geo. 5, c.34)—
     s.8 696
1914 Deeds of Arrangement Act (4 & 5 Geo. 5, c.47).. 37, 59, 95
     s.2 59
     s.21 291
     Bankruptcy Act (repealed) (4 & 5 Geo. 5, c.59).... 93, 140, 144, 154, 704
     s.1(1)................. 69, 110
     (a) 59
     (g)............ 110, 117
     (2).................. 696
     s.3 140
     s.4(1)(c) 59
     (d).... 117, 697, 698, 699
     s.6(1)................. 140
     s.15 158
     s.16 42
     (1)................. 43
     s.18 704
     s.19(2)................ 169
     s.21 42
     (2)................. 56

1914 Bankruptcy Act (repealed) (4 & 5 Geo. 5, c.59)—*cont.*
     s.25 320
     s.26 309
     (2)................. 314
     (3)................. 309
     s.29................... 121, 324
     s.30 597
     (1)................. 256
     (3)................. 271
     s.31................... 95, 599
     s.33(1)(a) 93
     (6)................. 77
     s.37 189
     s.38(c) 219
     (2)................. 208
     s.41 92
     s.44 640
     (1)................. 227
     s.53 704
     s.54(1) 236
     s.63(1) 77
     s.80 179
     s.82(2) 170
     s.99 24
     s.108(2)................ 315
     s.119 77
     s.138(1)................ 166
     s.155(a) 353
     s.156(a) 345
     s.167................. 107, 704
     s.292(4)................ 169
     s.382(1)(b) 270
     Sched. 3............... 24
1925 Supreme Court of Judicature Act (15 & 16 Geo. 5, c.49)—
     s.56 24
     Law of Property Act (15 & 16 Geo. 5, c.20)—
     s.30 .... 195, 198
     s.53(1)(c) 209
     s.79 206
     s.91(2)................. 398
     s.101 360
     (1)(iii).......... 360, 369
     s.103 360
     (3)................. 360
     (4)................. 360
     s.109 360
     (2)................. 395
     (4)................. 360
     (6)................. 370
     s.136..... 86, 89, 209, 212, 278
     (1)................. 205
     s.172........... 232, 233, 641
     s.198 143
     s.205 360

Table of Statutes

1926	Bankruptcy (Amendment) Act (16 & 17 Geo. 5, c.7)—	
	s.4	144
1927	Moneylenders Act (17 & 18 Geo. 5, c.21).......	71, 280
	s.9(2).................	280
1928	Companies Act (18 & 19 Geo. 5, c.45)—	
	s.91.................	744, 745
1929	Companies Act (19 & 20 Geo. 5, c.23)....	11, 520, 745
	s.338	745
	(1)(d)......	733, 745, 746
	(2)...........	745, 746
	Sale of Goods Act—	
	s.25	636
1930	Third Parties (Rights against Insurers) Act (20 & 21 Geo. 5, c.25)—	
	s.1	194
	s.3	194
1932	Hong Kong Companies Ordinance—	
	s.313(2)................	746
1933	Foreign Judgments (Reciprocal Enforcement) Act (23 & 24 Geo. 5, c.13).....	694
	s.4(1)(a)(ii)	694
	(iv).........	694, 716
	(v)..........	694, 716
	(b)	716
	(2)................	694
	(3)................	694
1935	Law Reform (Married Women and Tortfeasors) Act (25 & 26 Geo. 5, c.30)—	
	s.1(d).............	8, 76, 719
1948	Companies Act (11 & 12 Geo. 6, c.38)....	11, 520, 557
	s.95	231
	s.188	672
	s.206	401
	s.221(5)(a)	760
	s.287	401
	s.293	501
	s.306	401
	s.317	13
	s.320(1)................	227
	s.332(1)................	660
	s.399(5)................	733
	(a)	743
1949	India (Consequential Provision) Act (12, 13 & 14 Geo. 6, c.92)—	
	s.1	706
1955	Army Act (3 & 4 Eliz. 2, c.18)—	
	s.203	220
1955	Air Force Act (3 & 4 Eliz. 2, c.19)—	
	s.203	220
1959	County Courts Act (7 & 8 Eliz. 2, c.22)—	
	s.148(1)	60
1965	Industrial and Provident Societies Act (c.12)	362
	Law Commissions Act (c.22)—	
	s.3(1)..................	16
1967	General Rate Act (c.9)—	
	s.96(1)	92
	Criminal Law Act (c.58)—	
	s.13(1)(a)	193
	Matrimonial Homes Act (c.75)................	195
1968	Theft Act (c.60)	157
	s.1	339
	ss.2–6	339
	s.4(1).................	353
	s.15...........	344, 346, 353
	(1)................	346
	(2)................	344
	(4)................	344
	s.16...........	344, 345, 346
	(1)..............	344, 346
	(2)................	345
	(a)	345
	(3)................	344
	s.17.............	344, 346
	(1)................	346
	ss.18–20	344
1969	Law of Property Act (c.59)—	
	s.24(1), (3)	143
	Family Law Reform Act (c.46)—	
	s.1	76
1970	Law Reform (Miscellaneous Provisions) Act (c.33)—	
	s.4	84
	s.5(a), (c).............	84
	Republic of the Gambia Act (c.37)—	
	s.1	706
1971	Administration of Estates Act (c.25)—	
	s.10(1), (2)	277
	Attachment of Earnings Act (c.32)—	
	s.1(2)(c)	64, 65
	s.3(4).................	267
	s.5	64, 65
	s.9	65
	Recognition of Divorces and Legal Separations Act (c.53)................	719
	s.6	760
	Tribunals and Inquiries Act (c.62)................	32

Table of Statutes

Year	Statute	Page
1972	Road Traffic Act (c.20)—	
	s.150(1)	194
	Civil Evidence Act (c.30)—	
	s.4	734
	Land Charges Act (c.61)—	
	s.2	206
	s.6	143
	s.8	143
	s.18(1)	206
	Sched. 3, para. 8(1)	206
	European Communities Act (c.68)—	
	s.9	545
	Local Government Act (c.70)—	
	s.80(1)(b)	321
	s.81	321
	Criminal Justice Act (c.71)	355
	s.6	355
	ss.7–10	355
	Sched. 1	355
1973	Matrimonial Causes Act (c.18)—	
	Pt. II	206
	s.21	266
	s.22	266
	s.23	266
	s.24	198
	s.27	265, 266
	s.31	266
	s.32	266
	Domicile and Matrimonial Proceedings Act (c.45)—	
	s.1	700
	Powers of Criminal Courts Act (c.62)	355
	ss.35–38	355
	ss.39–41	355
	s.39	356
	(1)	355
	(4)	355
	(6)	355
	Sched. 2	355
1974	Solicitors Act (c.47)—	
	ss.12(1)(h), (i)	322
	s.15	322
	ss.16(2), (3)	322
	s.17	322
	Consumer Credit Act (c.39)	71, 72, 280, 353
	s.8	71
	s.9	71
	(1)	71
	s.16	71
	ss.21–42	71
	s.21	71
	s.25	71
	s.26	71
	s.29	71
	s.32	71
	s.39	71
	s.40	71
1974	Consumer Credit Act (c.39)—*cont.*	
	ss.137–139	230, 647
	s.137	71, 136
	s.138	71
	(1)	231
	(2)(a)	71
	s.139	71, 72
	(1)(a)	230
	s.171(7)	648
	s.189(1)	71, 436
	Sched. 5, Pt. I	71
	Friendly Societies Act (c.46)—	
	s.59	291
	Trade Union and Labour Relations Act (c.52)—	
	s.2(1)	521
	s.30	521
1975	Social Security (Northern Ireland) Act (c.15)	800
	Recess Elections Act (c.66)—	
	s.1	321
	s.5	321
	Employment Protection Act (c.71)—	
	s.99	463
1976	Fatal Accidents Act (c.30)	624
	Police Pensions Act (c.35)—	
	s.9	220
	Insolvency Act (c.60)	15, 588
	s.6	158
	s.7	308
	s.8	308
	Sched. I	102
1977	Unfair Contract Terms Act (c.50)	386
1978	Domestic Proceedings and Magistrates Courts Act (c.22)—	
	Pt. I	265, 266
	Interpretation Act (c.30)—	
	s.5	676
	Sched. 1	676
	Theft Act (c.31)—	
	s.1	344, 345, 346
	(2)	345
	s.2	344, 345, 346
	(1)	345
	s.4	346
	Employment Protection (Consolidation) Act (c.44)	290
	s.12(1)	801
	s.19	295, 801
	s.27(3)	295
	s.31(3)	295, 801
	s.31A(4)	295, 801
	s.47	295, 801
	s.122	291, 294
	(1)	294
	(3)	294

Table of Statutes

1978 Employment Protection (Consolidation) Act (c.44)—*cont.*
   s.122(4) 294
   (5) 294
   s.125 .... 291, 294

1979 Charging Orders Act (c.53)—
   s.1 242
  Sale of Goods Act (c.54) ... 634
   s.17 216
   s.19 216
   s.20(1) 216
   s.25 217
   ss.38–46 206
   s.48 206
  Justices of the Peace Act (c.55)—
   s.63A 322

1980 Magistrates Court Act (c.43) 251, 318
   s.32(9) 676
   s.76 266
   s.87A 534
   s.143 676
  Limitation Act (c.58) 70, 596, 694
   s.24 694
   s.38(1) 596

1981 Supreme Court Act (c.54)—
   s.14 315
   s.37(1) 363, 368
   s.61(1) 541
   Sched. 1, para. 1 541
  Companies Act (c.62)—
   s.106 501
  Betting and Gaming Duties Act (c.63)—
   s.12(1) 799
   s.14 799
   Sched. 2 799

1982 Civil Jurisdiction and Judgments Act (c.27) 693
   ss.41–46 701
   s.42 759
   s.43 759
  Insurance Companies Act (c.50) 426
   s.53 533
   s.54 533

1983 Matrimonial Homes Act (c.19) 196
   s.1 .... 195, 196, 197
  Mental Health Act (c.20)—
   Pt. VII 28, 77
   s.99 77
  Value Added Tax Act (c.55) 799

1984 Foreign Limitation Periods Act (c.16)—
   s.1 254

1984 County Courts Act (c.28)—
   Pt. VI 60, 95, 129, 419
   s.40 542
   ss.112–117 419
   s.112(1) 60, 61
   (1A) 61
   (3) 62
   (4) 61, 63
   (5) 64
   (6) 61
   s.113(a) 62
   (b) 62
   (c) 62
   s.114(1) 61, 63
   (2) 63
   (3) 63
   s.115(1) 63
   s.116 63
   s.117(1) 61, 64
   (2) 65
   s.144(1) 95
  Mental Health (Scotland) Act (c.36)—
   s.125(1) 28
  Matrimonial and Family Proceedings Act (c.42) 251, 318
  Police and Criminal Evidence Act (c.60)—
   s.78 566

1985 Companies Act (c.6) .. 11, 19, 20, 361, 362, 453, 489, 493
   Pt. I 520
   Pt. XII 633, 636
   Pt. XIV 540, 565
   Pt. XIX 19
   Pt. XX 19
   Pt. XXI 19
   Pt. XXII 520
   Chaps. III and IV 500
   Pt. XXIII 731, 747
   Pt. XXVI 432
   ss.1–42 520
   s.42 545
   (1)(a) 554
   (2) 554
   s.117 522
   s.178(3)–(6) 612
   s.196 802
   s.221 670
   s.222 670
   s.226 671
   s.227 671
   s.233 671
   s.252(5) 666
   s.288 670
   ss.295–302 672
   s.300 672
   s.349 447
   s.352 670

TABLE OF STATUTES

1985 Companies Act (c.6)—cont.
s.353 670
s.363 670
s.369 504
   (3), (4) 505
s.378 504
   (1) 505
   (2) 504
   (3) 504, 505
   (6) 504, 505
s.380(1) 505
   (4) 505
   (5) 505
   (7) 505
ss.395–409 607
s.395 .... 217, 231, 390
s.396 .... 231, 637
   (1)(f) 217
s.397 231
s.398 231
s.399 671
   (1), (2) 637
s.405 369
   (1) 362, 370
   (2) 370
s.415 671
s.425 .... 401, 407, 423
s.431 668
s.432 668
s.456 660
s.458 .... 657, 659
s.493 447
s.518 422
   (1A) 422
   (1)(e) 527
s.519(1) 533
s.528 559
s.529 559
s.530 560
s.533 .... 572, 577
s.534 572
s.542 588
   (4) 588
s.546 589
s.547 589
s.548 589
s.563 .... 560, 570
   (1) 570
s.564 .... 560, 570
s.568 620
s.572 502
s.582 401
s.588 .... 501, 502, 503
s.601 401
s.611 595
s.612 .... 13, 595, 597, 599
ss.614–616 640
s.615A 427
s.615B 427
s.617 648

1985 Companies Act (c.6)—cont.
s.618 604
   (1) 604
   (3) 605
s.619 .... 604, 605
s.620 604
s.651 .... 521, 623, 624
   (1) 623
   (2) 623
   (4) 623, 625
   (5) 623, 624
   (6) 623, 624
   (7) 623
s.652 ..... 485, 522, 621, 625
   (1)–(3) 621
   (4) 622
   (5) 622
   (6) 622
s.653 .... 522, 625
   (2) 625
   (3) 625
s.654(1) 623
s.656(1)–(3) 623
s.657 623
s.666(5) 733
s.675 520
ss.690A–703R 731
s.691 ..... 531, 731, 746, 747,
                    748, 749
   (1)(b)(ii) 747
s.694A 747
s.695 .... 731, 747, 748
   (2) 732, 748
   (b) 748, 749
s.711 .... 545, 621
   (1)(q), (r) 621
   (2) 554
s.716(1) 521
   (2), (3) 521
   (5) 521
s.726(1) 549
s.727 453
s.730 505
s.735 .... 362, 493, 520, 732
   (1) 520
      (a) 362
      (c) 520
   (2) 520
   (3) 520
   (4) 362
s.741 .... 654, 669
s.744 .... 731, 432, 654
Sched. 17 589
Sched. 24 657
Companies Consolidation
   (Consequential Pro-
   visions) Act (c.9)—
s.1 522

Table of Statutes

1985	Reserve Forces (Safeguard of Employment) Act (c.17)	801	1985	Bankruptcy (Scotland) Act (c.66)—*cont.*
				Sched. 5 27
	Insolvency Act (c.65) 11, 13, 18, 19, 20, 26, 32, 56, 59, 157, 169, 215, 293, 354, 360, 402, 498, 571, 588, 589, 597, 599, 641			Sched. 7, para. 20 427
				Housing Act (c.68)—
				s.86 189
			1986	Drug Trafficking Offences Act (c.32)—
				s.1 .... 251, 319, 601
	Pt. II, Chap. II	401		Insolvency Act (c.45) vii
	Pt. II, Chap. III 60, 419			Insolvency Act 4, 11, 13, 19, 20, 26, 31, 35, 56, 59, 73, 77, 95, 140, 155, 157, 158, 169, 185, 189, 204, 354, 356, 360, 402, 415, 485, 498, 571, 597, 619, 757
	Pt. III	19		
	Pt. XXVI	520		
	s.8(6)	32		
	ss.20–26	401		
	ss.27–44	419		
	s.27(1), (3)	425		Pt. I ... 27, 28, 42, 79, 233, 401, 403, 485, 416, 419, 640
	s.108(3)	610		
	s.202(4)(a)	24		Pts. I–VII 432, 791
	s.215	20		Pt. II 26, 79, 361, 419, 420, 427, 615, 785
	s.217(4)	20		
	s.218	20		Pt. III 513
	s.219	20		Chap. I 26, 420
	s.220 .... 20, 61			Chap. II 420
	(2)	63		Pt. IV 89, 521, 528, 732, 733, 795
	(3)	63		
	(4)	63		Chap. II 494, 500
	s.235 .... 232, 599			Chap. III 494, 500
	(1)	20		Chap. IV 500
	(3)	595		Chap. V 494, 500
	s.236(1)	20		Chap. VI 519, 521
	(2) 19, 20			Chap. VII 519
	Sched. 1	32		Chap. VIII 500, 519
	para. 5	32		Chap. IX 500, 519
	para. 5(1)–(3)	20		Chap. X 421, 500, 519
	para. 6	20		Pt. V 78, 79, 89, 361, 362, 519, 520, 521, 528, 529, 531, 731, 732, 733, 738, 739
	Sched. 6,			
	para. 3	20		
	para. 4	20		
	para. 8	20		Pt. VI 458
	paras. 10–13	20		Pt. VII 519
	para. 18	20		Pt. VIII 27, 37, 41, 44, 53, 54, 56, 57, 59, 67, 81, 95, 118, 122, 126, 128, 130, 132, 138, 139, 233, 292, 415, 798
	para. 19	20		
	para. 23	20		
	para. 24	20		
	para. 27	422		
	paras. 45–47	20		Pts. VIII–XI 174
	Sched. 8 .... 20, 321			Pts. IX–XI 519
	Sched. 9	658		Pt. IX 69, 79, 796
	Sched. 10,			Pt. IX, Chap. IV 175
	Pt. II 560, 588, 595, 599			Pt. IX, Chap. VI .. 335, 336, 337
	Bankruptcy (Scotland) Act (c.66) 16, 28, 792			Pt. XII 797
				Pt. XIII 20, 26, 28, 44, 169, 179, 185, 402, 404, 498, 500, 539, 574
	s.2	27		
	s.3	27		
	s.6	28		Pt. XIV 25
	s.59	27		Pt. XVI 670
	s.67(9)	354		Pt. XVIII 791
	(10)	354		ss.1–7 .... 42, 401
	s.73(1)	28		ss.1–251 791
	s.74	427		

lxxiii

TABLE OF STATUTES

1986 Insolvency Act—cont.
    s.1 .... 402, 411
      (1) 402
      (2) 27, 402, 403
      (3) 403
    s.2 .... 404, 405
      (1) 406
      (2) 405
        (a) 404
        (b) 404
      (3) 406
      (4) 27, 405, 412, 413
    s.3 .... 407, 411, 413
      (1) 405, 406, 407
      (2) 405
      (3) 407
    s.4(1) 407, 411
      (2) 27, 411, 412, 413
      (3) 403, 411
      (4) 403, 411
      (5) 407
      (6) 408, 411
      (7) 411
    s.5 .... 403, 420
      (1) 411
      (2) 412
        (b) 409
      (4) 413
    s.6 413
      (2) 412
      (4) 412
      (5) 412
      (6) 412
      (7) 413
    s.7(2) 404, 413
      (3) 413
      (4) 413
      (5) 27, 414
    ss.8–27 419
    s.8 .... 431, 438
      (1) 421, 425, 426, 439
        (a) 422, 426, 431
        (b) 423, 424, 426, 431
      (2) 440, 461
      (3) .. 423, 424, 425, 433, 439
      (4) 426
    s.9 .... 361, 438
      (1) 422, 430, 432, 534
      (2) 428, 432
        (a) 432
        (b) 435
      (3) .. 427, 428, 437, 438, 459
        (a) 428, 438
        (b) 428, 438
      (4) 438, 439
      (5) 439
    s.10(1) 422, 435, 437, 442
        (a) 436
        (b) 436
        (c) 436

1986 Insolvency Act—cont.
    s.10(2)(a) 436
      (b) 436
      (c) 436
      (3) 437
      (4) 436, 442
      (5) 436, 442
    s.11 .... 435, 436, 442, 443, 446
      (1) 446
      (b) 382, 428, 437
      (2) 371, 446
      (3) 436, 442, 443, 444,
                             470
        (a) 442
        (b) 437
        (c) ... 442, 443, 444, 445,
                             446
        (d) 442, 443, 446
      (4) 371, 382, 446
      (5) 446
    s.12 447
      (1) 446, 447
      (2) 447
    s.13 462
      (1) 449
      (2) 449, 450, 451, 478
      (3) 450
    s.14 .... 420, 422, 448, 454,
                    455, 460, 466
      (1)(a) 454
        (b) 454
      (2) 420, 481
        (a) 448, 455, 480
        (b) 455
      (3) 456, 465
      (4) 453
      (5) 452
      (6) 453
    s.15 .... 381, 390, 420, 444,
                 448, 456, 457, 458
      (1) 456, 458
      (2) 457, 458
      (3) 456, 457
      (4) 456
      (5) 457
      (6) 457
      (7) 457
      (8) 457
      (9) 381, 457
    s.16 .... 448, 457
    ss.17–25 448
    s.17 .... 422, 460, 466
      (2) 461, 465
      (3) 452
        (a) 452, 468
        (b) 452
    s.18 .... 451, 468
      (1) 425, 468

Table of Statutes

1986	Insolvency Act—*cont.*	
	s.18(2)	468
	(a)	468
	(b)	468
	(3)	469
	(4)	469
	(5)	469
	s.19	473, 474, 475, 476, 477
	(1)	450, 451
	(2)	451
	(a)	27, 405
	(b)	469
	(3)	469
	(4)	464, 469, 471
	(5)	372, 374, 376, 378, 394, 464, 469, 471, 472, 473, 474, 476
	(6)	469, 471, 472, 473, 477
	(7)	469, 471, 473, 477
	(8)	469, 473, 477
	(9)	469, 473, 477
	(10)	469, 473, 477
	s.20	478
	(1)	478
	(2)	478
	(3)	478
	s.21	380, 441, 462
	(1)	461
	(a)	441
	(b)	441
	(2)	441, 461
	(3)	441
	s.22	380, 406, 407, 462, 559, 671
	(1)	462, 559
	(2)	462
	(3)	462
	(4)	462
	(5)(a)	462
	(5)(b)	462
	(6)	463
	s.23	461, 464, 466
	(1)	463
	(a)	463
	(b)	463, 464
	(2)	463
	(3)	464
	s.24	461, 464
	(1)	464
	(2)	464
	(4)	464
	(5)	465
	(6)	465
	s.25	461, 465, 466
	(1)	465
	(2)	465
	(3)	466
	(4)	466
	(5)	466

1986	Insolvency Act—*cont.*	
	s.25(6)	466
	s.26	450, 465, 466
	(1)	466
	s.26(2)	467
	s.27	376, 451, 452, 458, 467
	(1)	467
	(2)	451
	(4)	451
	(a)	451, 467
	(b)	451, 467
	(c)	451, 467
	(d)	451, 467
	s.29	361, 362, 368
	(1)(b)	369
	(2)	26, 360, 361, 362, 369, 420, 427, 432
	(3)	361
	s.30	362, 369
	s.31	368, 369
	s.32	364
	ss.33–36	369
	ss.33–38	368
	s.33(1)(a)	369
	(b)	369
	s.34	369, 374
	s.35	370, 386
	s.36	370
	s.37	371, 372, 373, 374, 379, 388, 394, 395
	(1)	371, 378
	(a)	371, 377, 384, 391, 394, 474
	(b)	371, 374, 394
	(2)	371
	(3)	372
	(4)	371, 374, 394
	s.38	372
	s.39	369, 447
	s.40	362, 368, 369, 370, 432, 446, 798, 802
	s.41	369, 362
	(1)(a)	370
	(b)	370
	s.42	362, 373, 385, 392, 394, 420, 454
	(2)	373
	(3)	373
	s.43	390, 420, 456
	(1)	381, 456
	(2)	381, 456
	(3)	382
	(4)	382
	(5)	382
	(7)	381
	s.44	374, 388, 391, 394, 395, 446, 474, 475, 476
	(1)	378, 452
	(a)	373, 383, 390, 395, 396

Table of Statutes

1986	Insolvency Act—cont.		1986	Insolvency Act—cont.	
	s.44(1)(b)	373, 376, 377, 384, 389, 394, 452, 472, 474		s.89(5)	495
				(6)	495
				s.90	485, 494, 495
	(c)	374, 394		ss.91–96	486
	(2)	374		s.91(2)	506
	(2A)	379		s.95	496
	(2B)	379		(1)	496
	(2C)	379		(2)	496
	(3)	374		(b)	507
	s.45(1)	382		(c)	507
	(2)	27, 382		(d)	496
	(3)	374, 382, 394		(3)	496
	(4)	382		(4)	496
	(5)	382		(5)	496, 507
	s.46(1)(a)	380		(6)	496, 507
	(b)	380		(7)	496, 507
	(4)	380		s.96	496
	s.47	380, 462, 486, 559, 671		ss.97–99	501
	(1)	462, 559		ss.97–100	498, 539
	s.48	380, 381		ss.97–106	486
	(2)	381		s.97	503
	(3)	381		(2)	496
	(4)	381		s.98	496, 502, 503, 506, 507, 508, 509, 599, 671
	(5)	380			
	(6)	381		(1)(a)	503, 507
	s.49	381		(b)	503, 507
	s.51	428		(c)	503, 507
	s.53(6)	798, 802		(2)	508
	s.54	428		(a)	27
	(5)	798, 802		(3)	507, 508
	s.55	456		(4)	507, 508
	s.57	474		(5)	507, 508
	(1), (2)	452		(6)	503, 504, 508
	s.59	446, 798		s.99	406, 407, 496, 502, 503, 506, 671
	s.61	456			
	s.62(2)	27		(1)	503
	s.66	406, 559, 671		(a)	508
	(1)	559		(b)	508
	s.73(1)	485		(c)	508
	s.74	534		(2)	508
	(1)(f)	612		(3)	504, 508
	s.76	535		s.100	504, 509, 510, 578
	s.79	534		(1)	509
	ss.84–96	494		(2)	509
	s.84	487, 502, 504, 534		(3)	509, 510, 578
	(1)(c)	505		s.101	504, 509, 514
	(3)	505		(1)–(3)	515
	s.85(1)	505		(3)(b)	515
	(2)	505		s.103	506, 515, 628
	s.86	505, 554, 597, 628		s.104	511
	s.87	506, 628		s.105	617
	(1)	507		(1)	514
	s.88	507, 628		(2)	514
	s.89	487, 494, 495, 496		(3)	514
	(2)	494		s.106	512, 617
	(a)	494		(2)	618
	(b)	494		(3)	512, 618
	(3)	495		(4)	618
	(4)	495		(5)	618

TABLE OF STATUTES

1986 Insolvency Act—*cont.*
    s.106(6) 618
    ss.107–116 . . . . 486, 494
    s.107 487
    s.108 . . . . 511, 512
    s.109(1) 511
       (2) 511
    s.110 . . . . 507, 515
    s.111 . . . . 507, 515
    s.112 . . . 506, 514, 555, 571, 633
       (1) 628
    s.114 . . . . . . 498, 501, 502, 503, 506, 628
       (4) 502
    s.115 . . . . 487, 607
    s.116 . . . . 497, 535
    ss.117–219 519
    s.117 543
       (1) 521, 541, 732
       (2) 24, 541
       (3) 541
       (4) 24, 542
       (5) 542
       (6) 542
    s.118 542
       (2) 543
    s.119 542
    s.120 542
       (1) 521
    s.122 . . . . 463, 486, 522, 529
       (1) 522, 523, 535
         (a)–(d) 523
         (a)–(e) 486
         (f) 486, 488, 523, 535, 536, 537, 742
         (g) . . 486, 523, 535, 743
    s.123 . . . . . . 416, 422, 431, 530, 537, 644, 742
       (1) 422, 524
         (a) 110, 422, 431, 488, 523, 524, 530, 536
         (b) 116, 422, 526, 527, 530, 531
         (c) 116, 422, 526, 527, 530
         (d) 116, 422, 526, 527, 530
         (e) 422, 527, 528, 530
       (2) 422, 423, 524, 527, 531
       (3) 523
    s.124 . . . . 430, 533, 537
    s.124A 522, 533, 539, 540
       (1) 533, 536
       (2) 535
       (3) 535
       (4) 533
       (5) 488, 497, 533, 539, 540, 572

1986 Insolvency Act—*cont.*
    s.125 548
       (1) 538, 548
       (5) 498
    s.126 . . . . 628, 633, 753
       (1) 555, 557
    s.127 . . . . . . 546, 554, 555, 628, 629, 630, 631, 671
    s.128 . . . 554, 555, 628, 633, 757
       (1) 633
    s.129 . . . . 597, 628
       (1) 498, 506, 554
       (2) 554, 596
    s.130(1) 553
       (2) 555, 556, 557, 614, 628, 633, 753
       (4) 554
    ss.131–133 25
    ss.131–134 488
    s.131 . . . . . . 406, 407, 488, 559, 560, 571, 640, 671
       (1) 558, 559
       (2) 559
       (3) 558
       (4) 560
       (5) 560
       (6) 559
       (7) 560
    s.132 . . . . 488, 560, 640
       (1) 462, 561
       (2) 561
    s.133 . . . 488, 570, 571, 572, 640
       (1) 570
       (2) 570
    s.134 . . . . 488, 570
    s.135 . . . . 488, 550, 551
       (1) 550
       (2) 550
       (4) 550
       (5) 550
    s.136–140 488
    s.136 . . . . 25, 488, 572, 577, 578
       (1) 278
       (2) 558, 574, 579
       (4) 572
       (5) 572
         (b) 573
         (c) 572
       (6) 573
    s.137 . . . . 558, 579
       (1) 572, 579
       (2) 573
       (3) 574, 579, 590
       (4) 579, 590
       (5) 579, 590
    s.139 . . . . 558, 572, 578
       (2) 573, 578
       (3) 573, 578
       (4) 573, 577, 578, 579

Table of Statutes

1986 Insolvency Act—*cont.*
    s.140.......... 558, 577, 579
        (1)............... 465
    s.141............... 589, 590
        (2)............... 590
        (3)............... 590
        (4)............... 592
        (5)............ 584, 592
    s.143 640
        (1)............... 584
        (2)............ 584, 587
    s.144 488
        (1)............... 584
    s.145........ 85, 489, 583, 587
    s.146....... 581, 584, 617, 619
        (1)............... 618
        (2)............... 618
        (3)............... 618
    s.153 598
    s.154............... 613, 758
    s.156 607
    s.160 584
    s.163 587
    s.164 576
    s.165–168 489
    s.165–170 640
    s.165............... 503, 513
        (1)............ 498, 539
        (2)............... 515
          (b) 584
        (3)............. 85, 584
        (4)............... 513
        (5)............ 513, 613
    s.166...... 498, 501, 503, 513,
                      539, 628
        (2)............. 85, 507
        (3)............. 85, 503
        (5)............ 503, 509
        (7)............... 503
    s.167.......... 513, 584, 590
        (1)(a)... 85, 513, 584, 592
          (b) 584
        (2)............... 587
        (3)............... 585
    s.168 78
        (2)............... 580
        (3)............... 597
        (5)........ 237, 585, 597
    s.170 587
    s.171(2)............... 511
          (b) 512
        (3)............... 512
        (4)......... 27, 405, 512
        (5)............... 511
        (6)............... 512
          (b) 618
    s.172(1)............... 580
        (2)............... 580
        (3)............... 580
        (5)......... 27, 405, 581

1986 Insolvency Act—*cont.*
    s.172(6)............... 581
        (8).... 582, 618, 619, 620
    s.173 487
        (2)(e) 618
    s.174............... 581, 582
        (2)............... 582
        (3)............ 582, 619
        (4)............... 582
          (d).......... 618, 619
        (5)............... 582
        (6)............... 582
    s.175...... 487, 488, 514, 584,
                      609, 795
        (1)............ 609, 795
        (2)............... 795
          (a).......... 607, 609
          (b) 610
    s.176............... 557, 609
        (3)............... 609
    s.177....... 488, 507, 551, 552
        (2)............... 551
        (3)............... 551
        (4)............... 551
    ss.178–182.......... 235, 604
    s.178............... 605, 631
        (2)............ 604, 605
        (3)............... 604
        (4)(a) 604
          (b) 604
        (5)............ 605, 631
        (6)............... 605
    s.179(1)............... 605
    s.181............... 605, 606
        (5)............... 605
    s.182 606
        (3)............... 606
    s.183.......... 556, 557, 632
        (2)(a).......... 556, 632
          (c).......... 556, 614
    s.184 632
    s.186 632
        (2)............... 632
    s.188(2)............... 558
    s.189 611
        (1)............... 611
        (2)............ 601, 611
        (3)............... 611
        (4)............... 611
    s.192 617
        (1)............... 617
        (2)............... 617
    s.195 577
        (1)............... 538
        (2)............... 538
    s.201............... 512, 621
        (2)............... 621
        (3)............... 621
        (4)............... 621
    s.202............... 617, 620

Table of Statutes

1986 Insolvency Act—*cont.*
- s.202(3) 620
- (4) 621
- (5) 620
- s.203 .... 620, 621
- (1) 620
- s.204 620
- s.205 620
- (1)(b) 620
- (2) 620
- (3) 620
- (4) 620
- (1)(a) 620
- (6) 620
- ss.206–211 653
- s.206 .... 653, 656, 657
- (a)–(f) 654, 655
- (1) 654
- (a) 654
- (b) 654
- (2) 655
- (3) 654
- (4) 654
- (5) 654
- (6) 655
- (7) 654
- s.207 655
- (2) 655
- (3) 655
- s.208 655
- (a) 655, 656
- (b)–(e) 656
- (1) 655
- (2) 656
- (3) 655, 656
- (5) 656
- s.209 656
- (2) 656
- s.210 656
- (2) 657
- (4) 657
- (5) 657
- s.211 657
- (3) 657
- ss.212–217 .... 604, 657
- s.212 .... 478, 489, 561, 582, 658, 786
- (3) 658
- (5) 658
- s.213 .... 612, 658, 659, 660, 664, 786
- (2) 660
- s.214 .... 189, 421, 431, 449, 485, 486, 489, 500, 561, 612, 658, 661, 662, 664, 786
- (1) 661, 662
- (2)(a) 661
- (b) 662, 663
- (c) 662

1986 Insolvency Act—*cont.*
- s.214(3) 421, 663
- (4) 662, 663
- (5) 663
- (6) 4
- (7) 662
- (9) 662
- s.215 .... 486, 489
- (4) 612
- s.216 .... 489, 500, 501, 664, 665, 666, 667
- (2) 665
- (3) 501, 665
- (4) 666
- (7) 4
- s.217 ...... 489, 501, 666, 667
- (3) 667
- (5) 667
- s.218 667
- (1) 667
- (2)(a) 667
- (3) 667
- (4) 667
- (5) 668
- (6) 667
- s.219(3) 668
- (4) 668
- ss.220–229 78
- s.220 .... 732, 738, 739
- (1)(a) 529
- (b) 739
- s.221 .... 530, 733, 739
- (1) 530
- (2) 529, 739
- (3) 529, 740
- (b) 529
- (4) 493, 529, 733
- (5) 529, 731, 733, 736, 738, 743, 744, 745, 746, 761
- (a) 732, 733, 734, 736, 743, 746
- (b) 742, 743
- (c) 743
- s.222 .... 530, 742
- (1) 742
- (a) 530
- s.223 .... 530, 742
- s.224 .... 530, 742
- (1) 530
- (a) 530, 743
- (b) 530, 743
- (c) 530, 743
- (d) 530, 743
- (2) 531, 743
- s.225 ...... 522, 531, 732, 744, 745, 746, 761
- s.226(1) 758
- s.230 27
- (1) 449

Table of Statutes

1986 Insolvency Act—*cont.*
s.230(2).............. 380
s.231(2).............. 449
s.232.......... 380, 452, 458
ss.233–237 368
s.233...... 379, 390, 393, 459, 460, 639
   (1)........ 379, 458, 640
   (c) 412
   (2).............. 460
   (3).............. 460
ss.234–237...... 380, 603, 640
s.234... 380, 460, 565, 584, 671
   (1).............. 458
ss.235–237.......... 458, 488
s.235...... 380, 460, 563, 564, 565, 567, 571, 671
   (2).............. 564
   (b) 560
   (3).............. 564
   (5).............. 565
s.236...... 460, 461, 561, 562, 563, 564, 565, 566, 567, 568
   (2)........ 561, 562, 563
   (5).............. 562
   (6).............. 562
s.237 565
   (1).............. 564
   (2).............. 564
   (4).............. 564
ss.238–240.. 438, 459, 554, 671
ss.238–241.. 221, 420, 427, 640
ss.238–243.......... 641, 645
ss.238–244.......... 488, 611
ss.238–246...... 380, 561, 603
s.238...... 232, 458, 607, 644, 645, 646, 648, 786
   (1).......... 458, 645
   (4).............. 641
   (5).............. 641
ss.239–241(1) 458
s.239...... 218, 233, 458, 459, 607, 639, 643, 644, 645, 646, 658
   (1).............. 645
   (4).............. 642
   (b)........ 642, 643
   (5).............. 642
   (6).............. 643
s.240.......... 458, 644, 648
   (1)(a) 644
   (b) 644
   (2).............. 644
   (3).............. 644
   (a) 427
s.241.............. 645, 648
   (2).............. 646
   (a) 646
   (b) 646

1986 Insolvency Act—*cont.*
s.241(2A).......... 646, 647
   (3).............. 646
   (3A) 647
   (3B) 647
   (3C) 647
s.242... 420, 427, 438, 648, 671
   (1)(b) 427
   (7).............. 427
s.243...... 420, 427, 438, 671
   (4)(b) 427
   (5).............. 233
   (8).............. 427
ss.244–246 .... 221, 640
s.244........ 71, 458, 612, 647
   (1)............ 458, 647
   (2).............. 647
   (3)............ 647, 648
   (4).............. 648
   (5).............. 648
s.245...... 427, 438, 459, 554, 611, 648, 650
   (2)........ 648, 649, 650
   (a) 649
   (b)........ 649, 650
   (3)............ 428, 650
   (4).............. 650
   (5)(a) 428
s.246(1)............... 458
s.247(1).............. 4
   (2).......... 427, 597
s.249...... 410, 464, 512, 587, 643, 648, 791
s.251...... 362, 420, 432, 436, 520, 610, 654
ss.252–263.......... 41, 401
s.252...... 42, 43, 54, 57, 139, 328, 415, 798
   (2).......... 43, 55, 242
s.253.......... 43, 44, 45, 49
   (1).............. 44
   (2).............. 44
   (3)(a)........ 53, 54, 140
   (b) 43
   (4).............. 54
   (5).............. 43
s.254................ 43, 415
   (1).............. 43
s.255(1)(a) 45
   (b) 45
   (c) 45
   (d)............ 27, 44
   (2).............. 45
   (6).............. 46
s.256................ 46, 126
   (1).............. 55
   (b) 47
   (2).............. 46, 47
   (3).............. 46
   (a)............ 27, 47

Table of Statutes

1986	Insolvency Act—*cont.*	
	s.256(4)	46
	(6)	47
	s.257	55
	(1)	47
	(3)	55
	s.258	292, 798
	(1)	49
	(2)	49
	(3)	27, 49, 139
	(4)	49, 51, 58, 106
	(5)	49, 58
	(7)	45, 49
	s.259	49
	(1)	50
	(2)	50
	s.260	415
	(2)	50
	(b)	123
	(5)	50, 57
	s.261	54, 55, 140
	(1)(a)	56
	(2)	55
	s.262	51, 55, 57, 58
	(1)	51
	(b)	51
	(2)	51
	(3)	51, 95
	(4)	51
	(5)	51
	(6)	51
	(7)	51
	(8)	51
	s.263	52, 57
	(1)	51
	(2)	51
	(3)	52
	(4)	52, 53
	(5)	52
	(6)	52
	ss.264–385	519
	s.264(1)	81
	(a)	74, 695
	(b)	45, 74, 125, 695
	(c)	53, 74, 122, 123
	(d)	74, 307, 356
	(2)	75, 98, 118, 138
	s.265	45, 70, 74, 715
	(1)	74, 75, 695, 699
	(a)	75, 695, 700
	(b)	75, 696, 702
	(c)	75, 696, 702
	(i)	698
	(ii)	696, 697, 698
	(d)	702
	(2)	75, 696
	(c)(ii)	75
	s.266	330
	(2)	118, 132
	(3)	75, 98, 119, 134, 136, 138, 703

1986	Insolvency Act—*cont.*	
	s.266(4)	356
	ss.267–271	82
	s.267	83, 88, 101, 330, 536, 691
	(1)	73, 88, 93, 94, 101
	(a)	102
	(2)	93, 101
	(a)	73, 488
	(b)	73, 83, 94, 103, 105, 106, 111
	(c)	60, 72, 89, 110, 111, 113, 116, 488, 696
	(d)	113
	(3)	356
	(4)	37, 73, 102
	s.268	60, 110, 112, 113, 128, 691, 696
	(1)(a)	111, 113, 488
	(b)	116
	(2)	83, 111, 488
	s.269	106, 128, 282
	(1)(a)	109, 106
	(b)	108
	(2)	105
	s.270	112, 113, 128
	s.271	331
	(1)	131
	(2)	112
	(3)	72, 132, 133
	(4)	131
	(5)	137, 332
	s.272	45, 54, 70, 330, 331, 691
	(1)	70, 121
	(2)	45, 151, 155
	s.273	37, 43, 44, 45, 118, 138, 139, 140, 168, 289, 328
	(1)	138, 139
	(b)	328
	(d)	328
	(2)	27, 130, 139
	s.274	37, 45, 138, 139, 168, 328
	(1)	139
	(2)	139
	(5)	139
	s.275	37, 138, 150, 160, 168, 308, 327
	(2)	328
	(b)	329
	(3)	328
	s.276	53, 161
	(1)	122, 123
	s.277	356
	ss.278–282	150
	s.278	82, 145, 146, 259, 307, 331

Table of Statutes

1986 Insolvency Act—*cont.*
    s.278(a) 189, 250, 348
    ss.279–282 .... 145, 307
    s.279 .... 299, 307, 308,
               317, 323, 325, 329
       (1) 307, 308
         (a) 298, 307
         (b) 117, 204
       (2)(a) 308, 329
         (b) 307
       (3) 308
    s.280 ...... 155, 298, 299, 307,
            309, 310, 316, 317, 323
       (1) 309
       (2) 311
       (3) 312
    s.281 .... 250, 318, 692, 710
       (1) 317
       (2) 317
       (3) 318
       (4) 318
       (5) 148, 262, 318, 319
       (6) 318
       (7) 318
       (8) 148, 251, 318
    s.282 .... 100, 298, 307,
                322, 324, 695
       (1) 298, 299,
             322, 323, 324
         (a) 119, 324, 351
         (b) 54, 72, 323, 325
       (2) 356
       (3) 322
       (4) 56, 325, 326
         (b) 56
    s.283 .... 166, 189, 191,
                331, 705, 751
       (1) 189
         (a) 189
         (b) 199
       (2) 219, 300
       (3)(a) 209, 210
         (b) 212
       (4) 191, 211, 212
    s.284 ...... 144, 145, 189, 190,
             240, 246, 247, 331
       (1) 244
       (2) 244
       (3) 244
       (4) 245, 246
         (a) 245, 246
         (b) 246
       (5) 144, 145
       (6) 245
    s.285 .... 112, 147, 240, 331
       (1) . 43, 140, 147, 250, 271
       (2) 140, 147, 271
       (3) 109, 240, 250
         (a) 147

1986 Insolvency Act—*cont.*
    s.285(3)(b) 147
       (4) 105, 109, 149
       (5) 174, 325
    s.286 ...... 100, 120, 140, 146,
              198, 292, 798
       (1) 116
       (2) 27, 140
       (3) 141
       (4) 141
       (5) 141
       (6) 147
    s.287 .... 25, 141, 146
       (2) 146
       (3)(a) 146
         (c) 146
       (4) 146
    ss.288–291 25
    s.288 .... 54, 331
       (1) 151, 155
       (3) 156
       (4) 156
    s.289 .... 329, 331
       (1) 150
       (5) 150, 329
    s.290 154
       (1) 151, 158
       (2) 159
       (3) 159
       (4)(a) 157
         (b) 158
         (c) 158
         (d) 158
       (5) 152, 159
    s.291 708
       (1) 150
       (2) 150
       (4) 150, 180
       (6) 151
    s.292(1)(a) 166
         (b) 166
         (c) 166
       (2) 27, 169
    s.293 .... 161, 183
       (1) 151, 160, 161,
              168, 329, 356
       (3) 161, 166, 167
       (4) 161
    s.294 .... 161, 162
       (1) 161
         (b) 168, 329
       (2) 161
    s.295 .... 25, 180
       (1) 167
       (2) 166, 167
       (3) 167
       (4) 166, 167
    s.296 .... 161, 180
       (1) 167, 328
       (2) 166, 167

Table of Statutes

1986	Insolvency Act—cont.		1986	Insolvency Act—cont.	
	s.296(3)	167		s.307	199, 201, 202, 205, 235, 304
	(5)(a)	183		(1)	199, 200
	s.297	146, 166, 168		(2)	202
	(1)	166, 356		(c)	202
	(2)	166, 168, 328		(3)	201, 202, 300
	(3)	168, 328		(4)	200, 202
	(4)	168		(b)	200
	(5)	168		(5)	203, 205
	(7)	168		s.308	219, 235
	(8)	168		(1)	220
	(a)	183		(3)	220
	s.298	181		(4)	220
	(1)	178, 180		s.309(1)	202
	(3)	180, 328		(2)	202
	(4)	181		s.310	203, 204, 205, 220, 300, 320
	(5)	181		(1)	203
	(6)	27, 181		(2)	204
	(7)	180, 182		(3)	203
	(8)	181		(b)	203
	(9)	181		(5)	203
	s.299	53, 179, 182, 304		(6)	204, 205
	(1)	181		(a)	204
	(2)	181		(b)	204
	(3)(a)	182		(7)	203
	(b)	182		s.311(1)	176
	(c)	182		(2)	171
	(d)	182		(3)	174
	(4)	182		(4)	86
	(5)	182		(5)	174
	s.300	25, 167, 180, 304		s.312	171, 176, 708
	(2)	166		s.313	198, 199
	(3)	166, 167		(2)	199
	(4)	166, 167		(3)	199
	(5)	166, 328		s.314	171
	(6)	166, 168		(1)(a)	166, 171, 184
	(7)	166, 168		(b)	166, 174
	ss.301–304	178		(2)	166, 171
	s.301	166		(a)	173
	(1)	182		(b)	173
	(2)	182, 329		(c)	173
	s.302(1)	182		(3)	171, 172
	(2)	172, 183		(4)	172
	s.303	78, 152, 175		(5)	175
	(1)	178, 179, 220, 237, 262		(6)(a)	175
	(2)	174		(b)	175
	s.304	179, 182		(7)	167, 174, 178, 183
	(1)	179		ss.315–320	332
	(2)	179		ss.315–321	190, 235, 604
	(3)	179		s.315	193, 236
	s.305(2)	175, 178, 192, 249		(1)	235
	(3)	176		(2)	235, 236
	(4)	169		(3)	235, 238
	ss.306–310	166		(4)	235
	ss.306–321	171		(5)	240
	s.306	145, 169, 188, 191, 705, 751		s.316(1)	193, 236
	(1)	188		(2)	236
	(2)	188		s.317	237

Table of Statutes

1986	Insolvency Act—*cont.*	
	s.317(1)	237
	(a)	237
	(b)	237
	s.318	237
	s.319	237
	s.320	237, 238
	(2)	238
	(3)	238
	(5)	240
	s.321	238
	(1)(a)	238
	(b)	238
	(4)	238
	s.322	251, 279
	(1)	250, 251
	(2)	251, 279, 296
	(3)	257, 262, 280
	(4)	262
	s.323	103, 272, 273, 274, 599
	(2)	272
	(3)	272, 600
	s.324(1)	176, 249, 287, 288
	(3)	302
	(4)	287
	s.325(1)	302
	(2)	302
	s.326	303
	s.327	356
	s.328	249, 609
	(1)	291, 488, 796
	(2)	291, 488, 796
	(3)	295, 296, 796
	(4)	279, 296, 796
	(5)	297, 796
	(6)	290, 291, 296, 796
	s.329	249, 296, 297, 796
	(1)	796
	(2)	796
	(b)	297
	s.330	303
	(1)	303, 304
	(2)	303
	(3)	304
	(4)	304
	(5)	73, 298, 299
	s.331	53, 181, 182, 199, 303
	(1)	199
	(b)	304
	(2)	199
	(3)	304
	s.332	199
	(2)	82
	s.333	708
	(1)	151
	(2)	202
	(3)	320
	(4)	151
	s.334	80, 137, 299
	(2)	301

1986	Insolvency Act—*cont.*	
	s.334(3)	300
	s.335	80, 137
	(1)	300
	(2)	300
	(3)	301
	(4)	300
	(5)	300
	(6)	300
	ss.336–338	148, 196
	s.336	195, 196, 199
	(1)	196
	(2)	196
	(b)	196
	(3)	196, 198
	(4)	196, 198
	(5)	197, 198
	s.337	196, 199
	(2)	197
	(b)	197
	(3)	197
	(4)	196
	(5)	197
	(6)	198
	s.338	199
	ss.339–342	215
	ss.339–343	488
	ss.339–344	155, 158, 190, 221
	ss.339–345	332
	s.339	195, 198, 221, 222, 223, 232, 246, 257, 297, 339
	(1)	221
	(2)	221, 225
	(3)	222, 232
	(c)	222
	s.340	95, 198, 218, 227, 228, 257
	(2)	229
	(3)	227
	(b)	218, 229
	(4)	218, 227, 229
	(5)	218, 229, 232
	(6)	228
	s.341	222, 223, 226, 227, 229
	(1)(a)	223, 339
	(b)	229, 232
	(c)	229
	(2)	223, 224, 229
	(b)	232
	(3)	223, 229
	(4)	225, 356
	(5)	225, 356
	s.342	221, 225, 226, 227, 230
	(1)(a)	225
	(b)	225
	(c)	225
	(d)	225
	(2)	226, 301
	(2A)	226

Table of Statutes

1986	Insolvency Act—*cont.*		1986	Insolvency Act—*cont.*	
	s.342(2A)(a)	226		s.354(3)	350
	(b)	226		s.355	337, 343
	(4)	226		(1)	348
	(5)	226		(2)	347
	s.343	71, 136, 230, 231, 279, 647		(a)	347
				(b)	339
	(1)	230		(c)	339
	(2)	230		(d)	339
	(3)	230, 231		(3)	347
	(4)	231		(a)	340
	(6)	72, 230		(b)	340
	s.344	231		s.356	324, 337
	(3)(a)	231		(1)	348
	(b)	231		(2)(a)	348
	s.345	194		(b)	340
	(2)	194		(c)	340, 347
	(3)	194		(d)	340, 347
	(4)	194		s.357	203, 337
	s.346	148, 149, 240, 244, 632		(1)	339, 346, 348
	(1)	242, 244		(2)	339
	(2)	243		(3)	338, 339, 347, 348
	(3)	243		s.358	337, 341, 347
	(4)(a)	243		(b)	340, 347
	(b)	243		s.359	337
	(5)	242		(1)	341, 347, 348
	(6)	243, 244		(a)	348
	(7)	244		(2)	341, 347, 348
	s.347	146, 148, 240, 241, 295, 632		(3)	342
				(4)	342
	(1)	148, 241		s.360	350
	(2)	241		(1)	350, 353
	(3)	242, 295		(a)	350, 351, 352, 353, 354
	(4)	242, 295			
	(5)	241		(b)	336, 354
	(9)	241		(2)(a)	353
	s.348	290		(b)	353
	(4)	290		(3)	336, 353, 354
	(5)	290		(4)	354
	(6)	290		s.361	232, 336, 337, 348
	s.349	171		(1)	343
	s.350(1)	336		(2)	343
	(2)	336, 351		(3)	343
	(3)	336		(4)	343
	(4)	337		s.362	337, 348
	(5)	336		(1)	343
	(6)	336		(b)	348
	s.351(b)	346		(2)	343
	s.352	337, 341, 346, 347, 348, 351		s.363	151
				(2)	175
	ss.353–357	156		(3)	175
	s.353	324, 337		s.364	151
	(1)	348		(2)(a)	151
	(2)	348		(b)	151
	(3)	348		(c)	151
	s.354	324, 337, 348		(d)	152
	(1)(a)	348		(e)	152, 159
	(b)	337, 346		s.366	152, 153, 154, 208, 320, 321
	(c)	337, 346			
	(2)	346		(1)	152, 153, 320

TABLE OF STATUTES

1986	Insolvency Act—cont.	
	s.366(2)	153
	(3)	153, 208
	(4)	153, 208
	s.367(1)	154
	(2)	154
	(3)	154
	(4)	153
	s.369	153
	s.370	101, 146, 185
	(2)	185
	(3)	185
	(4)	185
	(5)(a)	185
	(b)	185
	(c)	185
	s.371	152
	s.373	43
	(1)	23, 124
	(2)	124
	(3)	127
	(a)	23, 24, 125
	(4)	126, 127
	s.374	4, 23, 43, 125, 542
	(1), (2), (3)	125
	(4)(a)	24, 124
	(b)	125
	s.375	43, 100, 314
	(1)	119, 314, 315, 316, 695
	(2)	23, 119, 314, 315
	s.376	131, 193
	s.382	82, 83, 250, 251, 257, 317, 323
	(1)	83, 95, 250
	(c)	82, 251, 356
	(d)	251
	(2)	83, 251, 257
	(3)	83, 95, 251, 257, 262
	(4)	250
	s.383(1)	82
	(a)	83, 356
	(b)	82
	(2)	107, 109, 281
	(3)	106
	s.385(1)	204, 220, 356
	s.386	45, 49, 291, 370, 411, 487, 488, 514, 584, 609, 797, 798
	(1)	797
	(2)	797
	(3)	797
	s.387	292, 797
	(1)	797
	(2)	797
	(3)	797
	(4)	798
	(5)	292
	(6)(a)	292
	(b)	292

1986	Insolvency Act—cont.	
	ss.388–398	380, 449
	s.388	4, 27, 434, 440
	(1)	27, 321, 574
	Pt. 13,	
	s.388(1)(a)	20, 405, 551
	(b)	404, 413
	(2)	27, 139, 321
	(a)	27
	(b)	27
	(c)	44
	(2A)	27
	(3)	28, 139
	(5)	28
	s.389	27, 31, 44, 169, 321, 380, 405, 413, 434, 440, 551, 574
	(1)	404
	(2)	28
	ss.390–398	574
	s.390	28, 181
	(1)	28, 579
	(2)	28
	(a)	31, 404, 441
	(b)	31
	(3)	30
	(4)	321
	(a)	28
	(b)	28
	(c)	28
	s.391	29, 30, 31, 180, 441
	(1)	404
	(2)	404
	(4)	181
	(5)	181
	ss.392–398	441
	s.392	31
	(2)	29
	(3)	29
	s.393	31
	(1)	31
	(2)	29
	(3)	31
	(4)	31
	s.394(1)	31
	(2)	31, 32
	(3)	31
	s.395	31, 32, 636
	s.396	31, 32, 636
	(1)	32
	(2)	32
	(a)	32
	(b)	32
	(3)	32
	s.397(1)	32
	(2)	32
	s.398	32
	ss.399–401	25
	s.399	25
	(1)	26, 553

Table of Statutes

1986	Insolvency Act—*cont.*	
	s.399(2)	26
	(3)	25, 26
	(4)	25, 26, 553
	(5)	26
	(6)(a)	25
	s.400(2)	25
	(3)	25
	s.401(1)	26
	(2)	26
	s.402	356
	ss.403–410	176
	s.409	369, 370
	s.412	176
	s.414	608
	s.415	288
	s.416	523
	s.418(1)	328
	s.420	4, 37, 78
	s.421	4, 27, 37, 330
	ss.423–425	155, 158, 215, 221, 232, 234, 603, 640, 641, 651
	s.423	195, 232, 233, 458
	(1)	232
	(2)	234
	(3)	232
	(4)	234
	s.424(1)(a)	233
	(b)	233
	(c)	233
	(2)	233
	s.425(2)	234
	(a)	234
	(3)	234
	s.426	361, 687, 703, 704, 705, 706, 719, 720, 729, 758, 759, 766, 784, 785, 786, 787, 788
	(1)	703, 704, 753
	(2)	704, 753
	(3)	704
	(4)–(12)	704
	(4)	706, 760, 784, 785, 786, 787
	(5)	431, 704, 705, 706, 758, 760, 784, 785, 786, 787
	(6)	704
	(10)	4, 784, 785
	(11)	431, 706, 760
	s.427(1)–(6)	76
	(1)	321
	(4)	321
	(5)	321
	(6)	321
	(7)	76
	s.429	61, 65, 66
	(4)	65
	(5)	66

1986	Insolvency Act—*cont.*	
	s.430	457, 464, 505, 508, 511, 514, 558, 617, 618, 621, 655, 656, 657, 666
	s.433	155, 157, 565
	s.434(b)	293
	s.435	45, 172, 175, 183, 218, 224, 225, 410, 427, 464, 512, 587, 643, 648, 791
	(1)	224, 791
	(2)	224, 225, 792
	(3)	224, 792
	(4)	224, 792
	(5)	224, 792
	(6)	792
	(7)	224, 792
	(8)	224, 225, 792
	(9)	224, 792
	(10)	224, 793
	(11)	224, 793
	s.436	188, 191, 219, 340, 353, 698, 705
	s.438	20, 401
	s.440(2)(c)	703
	s.441	739
	(1)(a)	703
	(2)	739
	s.443	19
	Sched. 1	362, 373, 420
	paras. 1–9	454
	para. 5	385
	paras. 10–23	455
	para. 13	392, 394
	para. 21	533
	Sched. 2	420, 454, 456
	Sched. 4	489, 513, 584
	para. 4	752
	r.4	85
	Pt. I	513, 515, 584, 585
	Pt. II	513, 584, 585
	paras. 4, 5	513
	Pt. III	584, 586
	Sched. 5	171, 192
	para. 1	172
	para. 2	173
	para. 3	173
	para. 4	173
	para. 5	173
	para. 6	173
	para. 7	173
	para. 8	173
	para. 9	174
	para. 10	174
	para. 11	174
	para. 12	174
	para. 13	174
	r.9	91
	Pt. I	166, 171, 184
	Pt. II	174

Table of Statutes

1986 Insolvency Act—*cont.*
Sched. 5—*cont.*
Pt. III............ 171, 175
Sched. 6......... 93, 291, 292,
293, 332, 370,
487, 488, 514,
584, 609, 797, 798
para. 9 294
paras. 9–12........ 294, 295
para. 13 295
(2)(b), (c) 295
Sched. 7.................. 32
para. 3 32
para. 4 32
Sched. 9,
para. 21 176
r.9 91
Sched. 10........ 66, 336, 341,
441, 457, 464,
495, 505, 508,
511, 514, 558,
617, 618, 621,
655, 656, 657, 666
Sched. 11.............. 658
para. 13 307
para. 20 233
Sched. 12............ 20, 401
Sched. 14.............. 32
Sched. 24.............. 505
Company Directors Disqualification Act (c.46) . 20,
28, 79, 181,
421, 500, 561, 668
s.1 668
(1).................... 669
ss.1–5 672
ss.4–11 489
ss.6–10 668
s.6 25
s.6....... 431, 448, 449, 486,
664, 668, 669, 672, 675
(1).. 448, 449, 669, 673, 675
(2)................ 669, 675
(b) 449
(3)................... 669
(4)................... 672
s.7........... 431, 448, 449,
486, 664, 675
(1)(a)............. 449, 675
(b)............. 25, 675
(2)................ 675, 678
(3)................... 675
(c) 449
(4).............. 449, 675
s.8 500
ss.8–11 672
s.9(1)............... 669, 673
s.10................. 664, 676
s.11................. 322, 676
(3)................. 322
s.12 .... 65, 66
s.13............ 66, 322, 676

1986 Company Directors Disqualification Act (c.46)—*cont.*
s.13(a) 676
(b)................. 676
s.15................ 676, 677
(3)................. 677
(5)................. 677
s.25 20
Sched. 1........... 480, 668,
670, 672, 673
Pt. I 670
Pt. II............ 670, 671
Sched. 4............... 20
Building Societies Act (c.53)—
s.37 534
Family Law Act (c.55) 726
Pt. II 719
Financial Services Act (c.60)—
s.1(a) 252
s.3 252
s.6(3)(a)........... 252, 601
(b) 252
s.61(3)................ 252
(a) 601
(b) 252
s.72................ 522, 533
s.94 540
s.105 540
s.177 540
1987 Minors' Contracts Act (c.13).............. 76
s.1(1)(a) 76
Banking Act (c.22)........ 427
s.49 .... 252, 601
s.92................ 523, 533
Criminal Justice (Scotland) Act (c.41)—
s.1............ 251, 319, 601
Criminal Justice Act (c.33) . 571
s.2......... 566, 567, 568, 569
(2)................. 566
(3)................. 568
(8)................. 566
1988 Income and Corporation Taxes Act (c.1)—
s.203 798
s.559 798
Criminal Justice Act (c.33) . 225
s.39 307
s.40 307
ss.71–103 356
s.71............ 251, 319, 601
s.101 356
Sched. 16........... 82, 161,
225, 307, 356

Table of Statutes

Year	Statute	Page
1988	Local Government Finance Act (c.41)	93
	Pt. I	93
	Pt. III	93
	ss.1–3	93
	s.62	94
	s.117(11)	92
	Scheds. 1–4	93
	Sched. 9, para. 3(2)	94
	Sched. 13, Pt. 1	92
1989	Companies Act (c.40)	369
	Pt. IV	636
	s.23	670
	s.60	539
	s.83	540
	s.93	217, 390
	s.100	370
	s.139(4)	670
	s.141	623
	(3)	624
	ss.397–407	217
	Sched. 10, para. 35(1), (3)	670
	Statute Law (Repeals) Act (c.43)—	
	s.1(2)	322
	Sched. 2, para. 2	322
1990	Courts and Legal Services Act (c.41)—	
	s.13(1)	60, 61
1991	Child Support Act (c.48)	251, 318
	Criminal Justice Act (c.53)—	
	s.17	341, 676
	Sched. 4	341
1992	Social Security Contributions and Benefits Act (c.4)	800
1992	Social Security Administration Act (c.5)—	
	s.187(1)	220
	Local Government Finance Act (c.14)—	
	Pt. I	93
	ss.1–69	93
	s.14(3)	94
	s.100	93
	s.117(2)	93
	s.118(1)	93
	Sched. 14	93, 94
	Trade Union and Labour Relations (Consolidation) Act (c.52)—	
	s.169	801
	s.189	801
1993	Charities Act (c.10)	533
	s.63	533
	Trade Union Reform and Employment Rights Act (c.19)—	
	Sched. 8, para. 35	295
	Pensions Schemes Act (c.48)—	
	Sched. 4	797, 800
1994	Insolvency Act (c.7)	vii, 372, 378, 379, 474, 476
	s.1	379, 469
	(4)	477
	(6)	477
	(7)	477
	s.2(3)	379
	Insolvency (No. 2) Act (c.12)	vii, 234, 646
	s.2	226, 230
	(3)	226
	s.6(2), (3)	646
	Finance Act (c.9)—	
	Pt. III	799

TABLE OF STATUTORY INSTRUMENTS

1914	Bankruptcy Rules	154
1925	Deeds of Arrangement Rules (S.R. & O. No. 795)	59
1949	Companies (Winding Up) Rules (S.I. 1949 No. 330)—	
	r.134	510
1952	Bankruptcy Rules (S.I. 1952 No. 2113)	
	r.86	154
	rr.279–296	77
	r.285	78
1970	The Secretary of State for Trade and Industry Order (S.I. 1970 No. 1537)	25
1974	The Secretary of State (New Departments) Order (S.I. 1974 No. 692)	25
1979	Companies (Winding-Up) (Amendment) Rules (S.I. 1979 No. 209)	544
1982	Rules of the Supreme Court (Amendment No. 2) (S.I. 1982 No. 1111)	541
1983	Civil Courts Order (S.I. 1983 No. 713)	125
	para. 10	542
	Sched. 3	24, 124, 542
1984	Criminal Penalties etc. (Increase) Order (S.I. 1984 No. 447)	341
	Insolvency Proceedings (Increase of Monetary Limits) Regulations (S.I. 1984 No. 1199)	102
1985	Companies (Tables A to F) Regulations (S.I. 1985 No. 805)	534
	Bankruptcy (Scotland) Regulations (S.I. 1985 No. 1925)	427
1986	Insolvency Act 1985 (Commencement No. 1) Order (S.I. 1986 No. 6)	19
1986	Insolvency Act 1985 (Commencement No. 2) Order (S.I. 1986 No. 185)	19
	Insolvency Act 1985 (Commencement No. 3) Order (S.I. 1986 No. 463)	19
	Insolvency Act 1985 (Commencement No. 4) Order (S.I. 1986 No. 840)	19
	Insolvency Practitioners' Tribunal (Conduct of Investigations) Rules (S.I. 1986 No. 952)	32
	Companies (Northern Ireland) Order (S.I. 1986 No. 1032) (N.I.6)	520
	Insolvency Practitioners (Recognised Professional Bodies) Order (S.I. 1986 No. 1764)	29, 180, 404
	Insolvency (Scotland) Rules (S.I. 1986 No. 1915)	428
	r.2.3(3)	441
	Insolvent Companies (Reports on Conduct of Directors) (No. 2) (Scotland) Rules (S.I. 1986 No. 1916 (s.140))	449
	r.3(2)	488
	Insolvency Act 1985 (Commencement No. 5) Order (S.I. 1986 No. 1924)	19
	Insolvency Rules (S.I. 1986 No. 1925)	42, 77, 100, 111, 128, 129, 154, 155, 159, 169, 185, 220, 322, 406, 407, 410, 414, 434, 494, 515, 582, 589, 595
	Pt. I, Chap. 3	405
	Chap. 4	406
	Chap. 5	407

Table of Statutory Instruments

1986	Insolvency Rules (S.I. 1986 No. 1925)—*cont.*	
	Pt. 4, Chap. 6	608
	Pt. 6, Chap. 2	82
	Chap. 5	289
	Chap. 10	53
	Pt. 10	25
	Pt. 11	616
	r.1.6(1)	406
	(2)	406
	(3)	406
	r.1.7(2)	405
	r.1.8	405
	r.1.9(1)	407
	(2)(a)	407
	(b)	407
	r.1.11	407
	(1)(b)	407
	r.1.12(7)	407
	r.1.13(1)	407
	(3)	407
	(4)	407
	r.1.14	408
	r.1.15	410
	r.1.16(1)	408
	(2)	408
	r.1.17(3)	408, 409
	(4)	408
	(5)	408
	(6)	408
	(8)	408
	r.1.18(1)	409
	(2)	409
	r.1.19(1)	408, 409
	(2)	409
	(3)	409, 410
	(4)	409
	(5)	409
	(6)	409
	r.1.20(1)	410
	(2)	409, 410
	(3)	410
	r.1.21(1)	410, 411
	(2)	410
	(4)	410
	(6)	410
	r.1.24(1)–(4)	411
	(5)	411
	r.1.26(1)	414
	(2)	414
	r.1.27(1), (2)	414
	(3)	414
	r.1.29(1)	414
	(2)	414
	(3)	414
	rr.2.1–2.8	432
	r.2.1	433
	r.2.2	433, 434, 450, 480
	r.2.3	433
	(6)	433
	r.2.4(6)(b)	434
	r.2.6	432

1986	Insolvency Rules (S.I. 1986 No. 1925)—*cont.*	
	r.2.6(1)	435
	(2)(a)	428, 434
	(3)	434
	r.2.7(1)	428
	(2)(a)	435
	r.2.8	434
	r.2.9	439
	(1)	438
	(b)	431
	(c)	438
	(g)	431, 438
	r.2.10(2)	441
	(3)	441
	r.2.17	463
	r.2.18	463
	(4)	464
	r.2.19(1)	466
	r.2.20	464
	r.2.21	468
	r.2.22	464
	(4)	464, 466
	r.2.24	464
	r.2.28(1)	464
	(1A)	464
	r.2.29	464, 465, 466
	r.2.30	464
	r.2.32	466, 467
	r.2.33(5)	467
	r.2.41	467
	(2)	467
	r.2.45	467
	rr.2.47–2.50	469
	r.2.51	458
	r.2.53	450
	r.2.54	478
	r.2.55	450
	r.3.1	369
	r.3.2(3)	380
	rr.3.9–3.15	381
	rr.3.16–3.30A	381
	r.3.32	381
	r.3.33	382
	r.3.34	382
	r.3.35	382
	r.4.3	545, 550
	rr.4.4–4.6	523
	r.4.7	543
	(1)	543
	(2)	543
	(3)	543
	(4)	543
	(5), (6)	543
	r.4.8(1), (2), (3)	544
	(4)	544, 746
	(5)	544, 746
	(6)	544, 746
	(7)	544, 746
	r.4.9	544
	r.4.10	543
	r.4.11	546

Table of Statutory Instruments

1986 Insolvency Rules (S.I. 1986 No. 1925)—*cont.*

r.4.11(1)	544
(2)	544
(3)	544
(4)	544
(5)	546
r.4.12(1)	543
(2)–(7)	543
r.4.14	547
r.4.15	547
r.4.16	544
(1), (2), (3), (4)	547
(5)	548
r.4.17	547
r.4.18	547
r.4.19	537
(1)	548
(2)	548
r.4.20(1)	553
r.4.20(2), (3)	553
r.4.21(1), (2), (3), (4)	553
(2)	746
r.4.21A	414
r.4.25	550
(4)	550
r.4.26(1)	550
r.4.32(4)	560
r.4.33	558, 560
(4)	559
(6)	560
r.4.34	496, 508
r.4.36	559
r.4.37	560, 608
r.4.38	508
r.4.41	608
r.4.42	560
r.4.43	560
r.4.45	560
r.4.50	573
(2)	574
(3)	574
(4)	574
(5)	574
r.4.51	496, 508
r.4.52	496, 509, 577
r.4.53	496, 509
r.4.54(4)	574
r.4.55	574
r.4.56	496
r.4.58	574
r.4.63	510, 573, 576
(1)	509, 576
(2)	509, 576
(2A)	576
r.4.66	576
r.4.67(1)(a)	575
(b)	575
(3)	575
(4)	510, 575
(5)	575
r.4.70	576

1986 Insolvency Rules (S.I. 1986 No. 1925)—*cont.*

r.4.71	576, 587
rr.4.73–4.99	595
r.4.73	598
(6)	598
r.4.74	598
r.4.75	598
r.4.76	598
r.4.77	598
r.4.78	598
r.4.82(1)	598
(2)	598
r.4.83(1)	598
(2)	598
(3)	598
r.4.84	598
r.4.85	599
r.4.86	597
(2)	597
r.4.90	599
(1)	600
(3)	600
r.4.91	597
rr.4.95–4.99	600
r.4.95	575
r.4.96	575
r.4.97	575, 600
r.4.99	600
r.4.100	581
(2)	578
(3)	578
(4)	578
(5)	578
r.4.101	510
r.4.102	580
(2)	579
(3)	579
(4)	579
(5)	579
(6)	579
r.4.103	510
r.4.104	579
r.4.106	511, 512, 578
r.4.107	579
(5)	579
(7)	580
r.4.108	581
(2), (3)	581
(3)	511
(4)	511, 581
(5)	581
(6)	581
r.4.110(2)	511
(3)	511
r.4.111	581
r.4.112	581
r.4.113	580
(1), (2), (3)	580
(4), (5)	581
r.4.114	512
(3)	512

Table of Statutory Instruments

1986 Insolvency Rules (S.I. 1986 No. 1925)—*cont.*

r.4.115	512
r.4.117	512
r.4.118	512
r.4.119(2)	580
(3), (4), (5)	580
(6)	580
r.4.120	511
r.4.121	582, 619
r.4.124	582
(1)	619
(2)	619
(3)	619
r.4.125	582
(1)	618
(2)	618, 619
(3)	618, 619
(4)	619
(5)	619
r.4.125(6)	619
r.4.126(1)	618
(2)	618
(3)	618
rr.4.127–4.131	582
r.4.127	515
(2)	512
(3)	512
(4)	512
(5)	512
(6)	513
r.4.128	513
r.4.130	513
r.4.131	513
rr.4.132–4.138	582
r.4.135	512
r.4.150	576
r.4.151–4.172	515
r.4.151	5
r.4.152(1)(a)	590
(b)	591
r.4.154(1), (2)	591
(3), (4)	591
r.4.155	515
r.4.160	591
r.4.161	591
r.4.162	591
r.4.163	591
r.4.164	591
r.4.168	515, 592
r.4.169	608
r.4.170	591
r.4.172	584, 592
r.4.179	584
r.4.180(1)	606
(2)	606
(3)	606
r.4.181	607, 611
r.4.182(2)	598
r.4.186	616
(3)	616
rr.4.187–4.194	605

1986 Insolvency Rules (S.I. 1986 No. 1925)—*cont.*

r.4.191	605
r.4.202	592
r.4.205	592
r.4.206(3), (5)	551
rr.4.211–4.217	570
r.4.213	570
r.4.214	609
r.4.218	606, 607
para. (a)	607
paras. (b)–(p)	608
para. (l)	609
para. (m)	609
para. (q)	609
(1)(a)	614
(2)	609
(3)	609
r.4.219	607
r.4.223(1)	617
r.4.223(2)	617
rr.4.226–4.230	501
rr.4.228–4.230	665
r.4.228	665
r.4.229	665
r.4.230	666
r.5.1(2)	53
rr.5.2–5.4	46
rr.5.2–5.5	43
r.5.2	45
r.5.3	44
(1)	45
(2)(a)–(c)	45
(d)–(p)	45
r.5.4	44
(5)	54
r.5.5	43
r.5.5A	43, 126
(4)	45
(a)	54
(c)	54
r.5.6	45
r.5.7(1)	46
r.5.8	46
(1)	54
r.5.9	46
r.5.10(1)	46
(3)	47
(5)	55
r.5.11	46
r.5.12(1)	47
(2)	47
r.5.13(1)	47
(2)	47
(3)	48
r.5.14(1), (2)	47
r.5.14(3)	48
r.5.15	48
r.5.16	48
r.5.17(1)	48, 123
(2)	48
(3)	48, 123

Table of Statutory Instruments

1986 Insolvency Rules (S.I. 1986 No. 1925)—*cont.*

r.5.17(4)	49
(5)	49, 51
(6)	49
(7)	49
(8)	49
r.5.18(1)	48
(2)	48
(3)(a), (b), (c)	49
r.5.19	50
(2)	50
(3)	50
(5)	50
r.5.22	50
r.5.23	50
r.5.24	50
r.5.25	51
r.5.26	52
r.5.27	52
r.5.27(1)(b)	52
r.5.29(1)	52
(2)	52
(3)	53
(4)	52
r.5.30	45
rr.6.1–6.5	111, 525
r.6.1(5)	114
r.6.3(2)	111
(3)	112
r.6.4	89, 113
(1)	113
(2)	113
(3)	113
r.6.5(1)	113, 114
(2)	114
(4)	114, 115
(a)–(c)	115
(d)	115
(5)	114
(6)	113
r.6.7	127
r.6.8	101
(1)	128
(2)	128
r.6.9(1)(a)	125
(b)	125
(c)	125
(d)	125
(3)	124
(4)	124
(4A)	126
(5)	124
r.6.10(1)	128
(2)	128
(3)	128
r.6.11	112, 128
r.6.12(1)	128
(2)	129
r.6.13	128
r.6.14(1)	128
(2)	129

1986 Insolvency Rules (S.I. 1986 No. 1925)—*cont.*

r.6.14(3)	129
(4)	128
r.6.15	129
r.6.18(1)	130
(2)	130
r.6.21	130
r.6.22	109
r.6.23	130
(3), (4)	131
r.6.24	131
r.6.25(1)	132
(2), (3)	133
r.6.26	131
r.6.29	137
r.6.30	102, 103, 137
(2)(c)	102
r.6.31(1), (2)	137
(3)	138
r.6.32	132
rr.6.33–6.35	143
r.6.33(1)	143
(2)	143
r.6.34(1)	143
(2)(a)	143
(b), (c)	143
(3)	144
r.6.38	129
r.6.39(1), (2)	130
(3)	130
r.6.40	113
(1)(a)	125
(b)	125
(2)(b)	124
(c)	124
(3)	125
(3A)	126
(4)	124
r.6.41	130, 139
r.6.42(1)	130
(2)	130
(3)	130
(4)	130
r.6.43	130
r.6.44	139
(3)	139
(4)	139
rr.6.45–6.47	143
r.6.45(1)	143
(2)	143
r.6.46(1)	143
(2)(a)	143
(b), (c)	143
(3)	144
r.6.48	328
r.6.49(1)	328
(2)	329
r.6.50(1), (2)	328
r.6.56(3)(a)	101
(4)	101
r.6.57(2)	100

Table of Statutory Instruments

1986 Insolvency Rules (S.I. 1986 No. 1925)—*cont.*

r.6.58	155
r.6.59	151, 155
r.6.60(1)	151, 156
(2), (3), (4)	156
r.6.61	156
r.6.62	156
r.6.63(1)	156
r.6.67	156
r.6.69	157
r.6.72(1)	157
(2), (3)	157
r.6.74	157
r.6.75	157
r.6.79(1)	162
(2)	162
(3)	162
(4)	163, 165, 281
(5)	162
r.6.79(6)	161
r.6.80	162
(1)(a)–(f)	162
(b)	183
(e)	162
(g)	162
(2)	162
rr.6.81–6.95	167
r.6.81	174
(3)	165
r.6.82(1)	162
r.6.83	167, 178
(1)	161
r.6.84(1)	162
(3), (4)	162
r.6.85	162
r.6.87	162, 178
(2)	162
(3)	162
r.6.88	163
(1)	162, 163, 165
(4)	165
r.6.89	165
r.6.92	166
r.6.93	163
(1)	163
(b)	165
(2)	164
(3)	164
(4)	164, 282
(5)	282
r.6.94(1), (2)	163
(3)	163
(4)	163
r.6.95(1), (2)	165
(3)	165
rr.6.96–6.119	116, 280
r.6.96	280
(3)	280
r.6.97	280

1986 Insolvency Rules (S.I. 1986 No. 1925)—*cont.*

r.6.98	280
(1)(g)	164, 281
(2)	280
(3)	280, 285
r.6.99	280
(3)	280
r.6.100	280
(2)	280
r.6.101	281
r.6.102	280
r.6.104	285
r.6.105	257, 283, 301
(2)	285
r.6.106	285
r.6.107	265, 286, 301
(1)(b)	286
r.6.108	282
r.6.109	106
(1)	281
(2)	281
r.6.110	280
r.6.111	260
(1)	112, 511
(2)	511
(4)	511
r.6.112	284
(2)	281
r.6.113	102, 279
r.6.115	262, 282, 283, 302
r.6.116	281
(1)	164
(2)	164
r.6.117	108, 282, 283
(2)	282, 283
(4)	282
r.6.118	282
r.6.119	262, 283
r.6.120	169
r.6.121	169, 180
r.6.122	169
r.6.124	169
r.6.126	180, 182
r.6.127	180, 182
r.6.128	180
rr.6.129–6.132	180
r.6.129(4)	180
r.6.131	182
r.6.132	180
r.6.133	181
r.6.135(1)	182
(2)	182
(3), (4), (5)	182
r.6.136	181, 182
r.6.137	181, 182
rr.6.138–6.142	161
r.6.138	289
(1), (2)	170
(3), (4)	170

Table of Statutory Instruments

1986	Insolvency Rules (S.I. 1986 No. 1925)—cont.	
	r.6.138(5), (6)	170
	r.6.140	170
	r.6.141	170
	r.6.142	170
	r.6.147	172
	r.6.148	171
	r.6.150	183
	(3)	183
	r.6.153	174, 183
	r.6.154	184
	r.6.155	184
	r.6.156	183, 184
	r.6.157	184
	r.6.158	185
	r.6.159	184
	r.6.160	185
	r.6.161	184
	r.6.162	184
	r.6.163	184
	r.6.164	185, 289
	r.6.165	183
	(1)	183
	r.6.166	183
	(2)	172
	r.6.167(1)	185
	(2), (3), (4)	185
	r.6.168	185
	r.6.169	185
	r.6.170	185
	r.6.171	185
	r.6.173	159
	(2)	160
	r.6.174	288
	(1)	159
	(2), (3), (4)	160
	r.6.175(2)	157, 158
	(4)	158
	(5)	158
	(6)	160
	r.6.176	160
	(4)	308
	r.6.177	160
	r.6.178	235
	r.6.179	235
	(2)	237
	r.6.180	235
	r.6.183	236
	r.6.185	235
	r.6.186	238
	r.6.187	220
	r.6.188	220
	rr.6.189–6.193	203
	r.6.193	205
	r.6.200(1)	202
	(2)	202
	(4)	202
	(5)	202
	rr.6.203–6.205	322
	rr.6.206–6.214	324
	r.6.206(1), (2)	324

1986	Insolvency Rules (S.I. 1986 No. 1925)—cont.	
	r.6.206(4)	324
	r.6.207(2)	325
	(3)	325
	(4)	325
	r.6.209	323, 325
	r.6.211	323
	(3), (4)	323
	r.6.213	325
	r.6.215	308
	r.6.216	308
	r.6.217(1)	310
	(2)	310
	(3)	310
	(4)	310
	r.6.218	310
	(2)	311
	(3)	311
	(4)	311
	r.6.219(1)	316
	(2)	316
	(3)	317
	r.6.220(1)	317
	(2)	317
	(3)	317
	r.6.221	316
	r.6.223	319
	r.6.224	170, 288, 290
	(1)	288, 290
	(2)	288
	(3)	288
	(4)(a)	288
	(b)	288
	(5)–(16)	289
	(11)	288
	(12)	288
	(14)	290
	r.6.226	300
	r.6.227	300
	r.6.237	199
	rr.7.11–7.15	126
	r.7.11(1), (2), (3)	126
	(4)	126
	(5)	126
	r.7.12	126
	(b)	126
	r.7.15(1)(c)	127
	(2)	127
	(3)	127
	r.7.20	571
	r.7.21(2)	153
	r.7.23	153
	r.7.26	543
	r.7.27	158
	r.7.28	158
	r.7.30	158
	r.7.31	157, 158
	r.7.39	173
	rr.7.43–7.46	77
	r.7.45	314
	r.7.47	441, 442, 550

Table of Statutory Instruments

1986	Insolvency Rules (S.I. 1986 No. 1925)—cont.	
	r.7.47(1)	314, 442, 549
	(2)	442, 550
	(4)	550
	r.7.48	315
	r.7.49	316, 550
	r.7.51	442, 550
	r.7.55	129, 545
	r.7.61	157, 158
	rr.8.1–8.7	165, 576
	r.8.1(3)	165
	(4)	165
	r.8.4	165
	r.8.5	165
	r.8.6(1)	165
	r.9.5	569
	(4)	567, 568
	rr.10.1–10.4	25
	r.11.2	303
	(1)	301
	(1A)	301
	(2)	301
	r.11.3	301
	r.11.4	301
	r.11.5	301
	r.11.6(1)	302
	(2)	302
	(4)	303
	(5)	303
	r.11.7	304
	r.11.8	303
	(1)	203
	r.11.9	283, 303
	(3)	283
	r.11.10	281, 302
	r.11.11	303
	r.11.12	301
	r.12.2	549
	r.12.3	251, 595, 601
	(1)	262, 597
	(2)	147, 601
	(a)	148, 251, 266
	(2A)	252, 601
	(a)	252
	(3)	252, 254
	r.12.4	301
	r.12.4A	166, 167, 407, 510, 576
	(4)	166
	r.12.5	166, 587
	r.12.7(1)	543
	(2)	543
	r.12.9	428
	r.12.12	154, 572, 746
	(3)	154, 542, 645, 746
	r.12.15	157
	r.12.16	574
	r.12.17	157
	r.12.18	157, 560
	r.12.19	243
	r.12.20	143, 574
	r.13.12	536

1986	Insolvency Rules (S.I. 1986 No. 1925)—cont.	
	r.13.13(4)	143
	r.61(5)	106
	Sched. 2	125
	Sched. 4	553, 574
	Sched. 5	157, 336
	Insolvency Regulations (S.I. 1986 No. 1994)—	
	reg. 15	303
	Insolvency Proceedings (Monetary Limits) Order (S.I. 1986 No. 1996)	65, 138, 152, 243, 328, 337, 341, 343, 350, 654
	art. 4	294, 800
	Administration of Insolvent Estates of Deceased Persons Order (S.I. 1988 No. 1999)—	
	art. 3	330
	art. 4	330
	(2)	291, 332
	art. 5	330
	(2)	332
	Sched. 1	330
	Pt. II	332
	para. 2	330
	para. 3	330
	para. 5	331, 333
	para. 6	331
	para. 10	331
	para. 12	331
	para. 15	331
	para. 16	331
	paras. 18–28	332
	Sched. 2	330
	Sched. 3	331
	Insolvency Fees Order (S.I. 1986 No. 2030)	289
	art. 8	128, 543
	art. 9	128, 543
	(b)	130
	art. 11	128, 549
	Co-operation of Insolvency Courts (Designation of Relevant Countries and Territories) Order (S.I. 1986 No. 2123)	706, 760, 785
	Insolvent Companies (Reports on Conduct of Directors) (No. 2) Rules (S.I. 1986 No. 2134)	449, 675
	r.4(2)	448
	(5)	448

Table of Statutory Instruments

Year	Entry	Page
1986	Insolvent Partnerships Order (S.I. 1986 No. 2142)	78, 79
	Insolvency Practitioners (Amendment) Regulations (S.I. 1986 No. 2247)	587
	reg. 4(1)(f)	29
	Act of Sederunt (Sheriff Court Company Insolvency Rules) (S.I. 1986/2297)	428
	Rules of Court (Act of Sederunt) (Rules of Court Amendment No. 11) (Companies) (S.I. 1986 No. 2298)	428
1987	(S.I. 1987 No. 1917)	665
	Insolvency (Amendment) Rules (S.I. 1987 No. 1919)	125, 166, 414, 464, 466, 494, 578, 601, 665
	Sched., Pt. 3	125
	para. 144	576
	Insolvent Companies (Disqualification of Unfit Directors) (Proceedings) Rules (S.I. 1987 No. 2023)	675
1988	The Insolvency Fees (Amendment) Order (S.I. 1988 No. 95)	289
1989	Criminal Justice Act 1988 (Commencement No. 7) Order (S.I. 1989 No. 264)	356
	Banks (Administration Proceedings) Order (S.I. 1989 No. 1276)	427
	Insolvency (Northern Ireland) Order (S.I. 1989 No. 2405) (N.I.19)—	
	art. 381	785
	Sched. 9, para. 41(b)	785
	The Insolvency Act 1986 (Guernsey) Order 1989 (S.I. 1989 No. 2409)	760, 785
1990	Insolvency Practitioners Regulations (S.I. 1990 No. 439)	404
	regs. 4–9	29
	reg. 4(1)(a), (b), (c), (d), (e)	29
	reg. 10	31
	regs. 11–15A	30
	reg. 12(1)	30
	(c)	30
	(2)	30
	(3)	30
	reg. 14	30
	reg. 15A	30
1990	Insolvency Practitioners Regulations (S.I. 1990 No. 439)—*cont.*	
	regs. 16–20	29
	reg. 17	587
	Sched. 2	30
	Sched. 3	29, 587
	Insolvency Fees Order (S.I. 1990 No. 560)	289
1991	Insolvency Fees Order (S.I. 1991 No. 496)	289
1992	Insolvency Fees Order (S.I. 1992 No. 34)	289
	Employment Protection (Variation of Limits) Order (S.I. 1992 No. 312)	294
	The Criminal Justice Act 1991 (Commencement No. 3) Order (S.I. 1992 No. 333)	676
	The Civil Jurisdiction and Judgments Act 1991 (Commencement) Order (S.I. 1992 No. 745)	694
	Companies (Single Member Private Limited Companies) Regulations (S.I. 1992 No. 1699)	522
	Oversea Companies and Credit and Financial Institutions (Branch Disclosure) Regulations (S.I. 1992 No. 3179)	747
1993	Insolvency Practitioners (Amendment) Regulations (S.I. 1993 No. 221)	30, 404
	Judgment Debts (Rate of Interest) Order (S.I. 1993 No. 564)	279, 612
1994	Insolvent Partnerships Order (S.I. 1994 No. 2421)	27, 78, 79
	art. 2	79
	art. 4	79
	art. 5	79
	art. 6	79
	art. 7	78
	art. 8	78, 79
	art. 11	27, 78, 79
	art. 14(1)	78
	(2)	78
	art. 16	79
	Sched. 1	79
	Sched. 2	79
	Sched. 3	78
	Sched. 4	78, 79
	Sched. 7	78, 79
	Sched. 8	79

TABLE OF STATUTORY INSTRUMENTS

1994	Insolvency Regulations (S.I. 1994 No. 2507)....	170, 176, 582, 587
	Part 2..................	588
	Part 5..................	513
	regs. 5–9	589
	reg. 5(1)..............	589
	reg. 6	589
	reg. 9	184
	reg. 10............... 515,	588
	(5)..............	588
	reg. 11	587
	reg. 12............... 515,	588
	reg. 13............... 515,	588
	reg. 14	588
	reg. 15	588
	regs. 17–18	589
	regs. 19–31	176
1994	Insolvency Regulations (S.I. 1994 No. 2507)—*cont.*	
	reg. 20(1).............	176
	reg. 21	177
	reg. 22	176
	regs. 24–29	177
	regs. 33–36......... 161,	582
	Sched. 2........ 161, 513,	582
1994	The Insolvency Fees (Amendment) Order (S.I. 1994 No. 2541)....	289, 543
1995	Insolvency Regulations (S.I. 1995 No. 2507)—	
	reg. 31	305
	reg. 32	305
	regs. 33–36	289
	Sched. 2...............	289

TABLE OF COUNTY COURT RULES

1981 County Court Rules (S.I. 1981, No. 1987/L20)	
Ord. 39	60
r.2(1)	61
r.3	62
r.6	62
r.7(a)	62
(b)	62
r.8(1)	61
r.9	62
r.10	64
r.11	64
(2)	64

1981 County Court Rules (S.I. 1981, No. 1987/L20)	
Ord. 39—*cont.*	
r.12	63
r.13	61, 64
r.14	61, 64
(1)(a)	65
(b)	65
(c)	65
(d)	64, 65
r.16	61
r.18	64

RULES OF THE SUPREME COURT

Ord. 1, r.4	541	r.3	550
Ord. 29, r.10	111	r.4	550
Ord. 30	363	r.14	550
Ord. 59	316	r.19	550

Chapter 1

THE NATURE AND INCIDENCE OF INSOLVENCY

The essence of the concept of insolvency consists in a debtor's ultimate inability to meet his financial commitments: upon a balance of liabilities and assets, the former exceed the latter with the consequence that it is impossible for all the liabilities to be discharged in full at the time of falling due. This factual inability to pay debts must be distinguished from a mere refusal or omission by a debtor, who otherwise has the material means to do so, to pay one or more of his debts at their due time. In such cases, a variety of reasons may underlie the non-payment of the debt. These may include: a bona fide dispute about the amount, or about the very existence, of the debt; an accidental or careless failure to observe the obligation as to time of payment; or, at the farthest extreme, a deliberate intention to keep the creditor out of his money for as long as possible. Whatever the circumstances, the unpaid creditor may properly have recourse to a variety of steps and proceedings, both of an informal and of a formal nature. The selection of the appropriate course of action by the individual creditor will be mainly influenced by the wish to procure a settlement of the liability at the lowest personal cost in terms of time and expense.

The non-payment of a debt by a debtor who is otherwise solvent is traditionally regarded as an issue whose relevance is confined to the debtor and the individual creditor concerned, and the creditor is not required, either in principle or by law, to concern himself with the question of the rights or interests of other creditors of the same debtor. Where, however, the debtor's failure to pay occurs in the context of insolvency, this introduces a completely different dimension in terms of principle and justice. The fact of the debtor's present or potential inability to meet all liabilities in full has the consequence that the unpaid creditor's position, together with that of all other parties involved including the debtor, is affected by special rules of law, and special procedures, which are applicable in such cases.

In determining what approach is to be followed with respect to the phenomenon of a debtor's insolvency, the basic alternatives, in terms of legal policy are either to permit a race of diligence to take place (with consequential anomalies resulting from the various permutations of accidental circumstance and individual acumen in determining the outcome of a race whose prizes are to be enjoyed by the swiftest); or to require a strict observance of chronological priority by the debtor, so that debts are discharged (to the extent that the available assets allow) in the order in which they were incurred; or alternatively to impose a collective regime involving the abatement of all claims of creditors who are ranked in common together—the so-called *pari passu* principle of distribution of an insolvent estate. As we shall see, English insolvency law has aligned itself with the third of these alternatives, in order of listing here. The consequences of the application of the *pari passu* principle are extremely far-reaching, and exert an influence upon the debtor-creditor relationship long before the commencement of formal insolvency proceedings. Hence, even though a debtor's financial crisis may eventually be surmounted without any such procedures being utilised (and *a fortiori* in cases where they are utilised) it is necessary, for reasons which will hereafter become apparent, that all parties concerned should bear in mind the relevant provisions of the insolvency law whenever any steps are taken, or transactions take place, involving a debtor who is demonstrably or even probably insolvent.

Foremost among the characteristics of the developed law of insolvency is the principle of collectivity. Most of the procedures described in this book are based upon that principle in an integral way, but there are exceptions. The procedure now known as administrative receivership of companies is one example. Essentially it is still mainly concerned with the exercise of rights by a particular type of secured creditor, namely one in whose favour a floating charge has been created by a company, as security for a substantial indebtedness. In view of the widespread use of this security device, administrative receivership is of great practical importance in relation to debt default and insolvency of companies, and in modern times has become closely integrated with the operation of the other, fully collectivised procedures. It is a central tenet of the collectivity principle that the debtor's assets are administered, and creditors' claims processed, without any necessary regard for the chronological order in which assets were acquired or debts created. A further feature of the operation of insolvency law is that it purports to embody a distinctive philosophy regarding the ethical proprieties which are to be observed in relationships between the creditors and their insolvent debtor, and amongst the creditors themselves as a group. The law also expresses a number of value judgments about the relative priority of the various kinds of liabilities owed by an insolvent debtor, and of the order in which these groups of liabilities should be discharged out of the limited funds available for the purpose. Thus the general notion of "equality among creditors," sometimes expressed in the maxim *par est condicio omnium creditorum*, has in practice been modified by judicial and legislative interventions which have superimposed a system of stratification of liabilities, whereby certain groups of creditors are accorded preferential status or otherwise acquire some kind of privilege, and hence enjoy improved prospects of recovering full or partial payment of their debts. It is with these, and other special

The Nature and Incidence of Insolvency

characteristics of insolvency law, and with the rules and procedures whereby such historically evolved principles are given practical effect, that this book is concerned.

It is a hypothetical possibility, even today, that there could exist a social system from which the phenomenon of insolvency was totally absent. If all transactions within the community, both in commercial and in private matters, took place on a strictly cash basis—or by way of barter involving simultaneous exchange—it might be supposed that no individual would ever arrive at a state in his affairs where the sum of his unsatisfied liabilities exceeded the sum of his available assets. In such an imagined society, the absence of the element of credit, whereby a person may incur obligations which are not immediately discharged in full on his part, would ensure that the relationship of debtor and creditor was never deliberately created, and it would follow in consequence that no situation could arise in which a person, having entered into some kind of forward commitment, might discover that at a time when payment or performance became due his present or future realisable assets were insufficient to match his liabilities. Even in such a "credit-free" society however, economic ruin for the individual (or for a company) could still occur, for example as a result of adverse claims of a contractual nature which did not manifest themselves until some time after the initial contractual performance took place,[1] or as a result of the onset of liability to pay substantial compensation for tortious injuries to another.

In reality of course, civilised societies have for many centuries availed themselves of the additional convenience, and enhanced commercial and economic opportunities, which the creation and use of credit can impart.[2] Given that the overwhelming majority of such transactions are destined to reach a fully satisfactory conclusion, the associated risk of the debtor's later inability to fulfil his obligations has become accepted as one which is, on balance, worth running, both in social and in individual terms, by reason of the countervailing advantages to be enjoyed as a result of the provision of credit. Nevertheless, the relationship of debtor and creditor has its darker aspects, and in the absence of balanced and effective legal regulation there is a potential for hardship and oppression to be experienced on either side. This in turn can give rise to serious social tensions and disharmony, particularly in periods of economic recession when the incidence of financial failures tends to be at its height.[3]

---

[1] *e.g.* a house built and paid for, which is subsequently found to have been badly constructed; defective products giving rise to multiple claims from dissatisfied or injured consumers; a painting guaranteed as by a recognised Master, and priced accordingly, but later proved not to be authentic.

[2] Coinage appears to have originated in Lydia (a kingdom in Central Western Asia Minor, part of modern Turkey) in the second half of the seventh century B.C. Roman Law began to recognise transactions for the borrowing of money (*mutuum*) from early Republican times (after c. 509 B.C.) and from 100 B.C. onwards developed the consensual contract of sale under which both parties' obligations could be purely executory. Bankruptcy procedures were also known to Roman law from Republican times onwards.

[3] Some of the most famous instances of legislative reform in the ancient societies of both Greece (Laws of Solon, c. 594 B.C.) and Rome (Laws of the *XII Tables*, c. 450 B.C.) were in large part the product of acute social unrest generated by the oppressive nature of primitive legal provisions relating to debt.

Thus it has become usual for legal systems to make special provisions for dealing with the phenomenon of insolvency in accordance with the prevailing social ethos towards economic and financial failure. This has generally tended to evolve from an initial position of severity and inflexibility, maintained partly in the interests of overall deterrence against possible default or failure, and partly as a reflection of a sense of communal outrage against those very events when they occur. Over a period of time a position is usually reached in which some effort is made to treat individual cases on their merits and to explore the possibilities for rehabilitation of the debtor under a controlled and more humane legal process. More general, but related, problems concerned with the overall relationship of debtor and creditor, particularly with regard to remedies for enforcement of a debtor's obligation, have likewise undergone gradual evolution, although this has not always happened in step with that taking place in relation to the law of insolvency. Even in the most recent phase of its development, English Law has been conspicuous for its lack of an overall design for the regulation of credit and insolvency, and of the various remedies and procedures which pertain thereto.[4]

Distinction Between "Insolvency" and "Bankruptcy"

It was as a result of the uncoordinated, and indeed illogical, condition of the laws relating to debt and bankruptcy that the distinction arose historically between insolvency, as a factual condition, and bankruptcy as a legal condition or status. This antithesis, between the factual and the technical meanings of the terms most often employed, has tended to become obscured by popular usage, whereby the adjectives "bankrupt" and "insolvent" are treated virtually as synonyms for each other. When used as legal terms, however, and particularly when used as substantives, it is only appropriate to refer to a person as "a bankrupt" if that status has actually been imposed in consequence of a formal, legal process to which the debtor has been a party. Conversely, the expression "an insolvent" has no formal or technical significance in English law, although the terms "insolvent" (used adjectivally) and "insolvency" are employed frequently throughout the Insolvency Act 1986 and related legislation.[5]

Because the formal status of "adjudicated bankrupt" can only be incurred through legal process initiated by a person having the requisite standing, it has long been true of the English law of individual bankruptcy

---

[4] *e.g.* aspects of the debtor-creditor relationship at English Law were separately examined by the Payne Committee on the enforcement of judgment debts (reported 1969, Cmnd. 3909) and the Crowther Committee on consumer credit (reported 1971, Cmnd. 4596). It was not until January 1977 that a Review Committee was set up to examine insolvency law and practice (see note 9 *infra*).

[5] See, *e.g.* Insolvency Act 1986, ss.214(6), 216(7) ("insolvent liquidation" of a company); 247(1) ("insolvency" of a company); 374 ("insolvency districts" of courts); 388 ("insolvency practitioner"); 420 ("insolvent partnership"); 421 ("insolvent estate of deceased person"); 426(10) ("insolvency law").

that it does not inevitably follow that a state of factual insolvency will result in an adjudication of bankruptcy. On the other hand, an adjudication may under some circumstances be obtained without any necessity of proving the debtor's true insolvency. The paradox has thus become established that under English law a person may be insolvent, yet not be made bankrupt, while a solvent person may nevertheless undergo adjudication as a bankrupt. Despite the thorough revisions of English insolvency law which have taken place in recent years this paradox still applies to the law today. Of course, much depends upon the attitude of the creditors, especially those whose debts have already matured and are due for payment. It is possible that they may be prevailed upon, either separately or collectively, to refrain from resorting to legal proceedings in respect of their unsatisfied debts, either for a specified period or indefinitely. In addition to an agreed rescheduling of the debtor's payments, existing creditors may be willing to extend further credit, and others may be prepared to become creditors for the first time. The consequence of all this may be that the debtor is enabled to retrieve his financial equilibrium, and to resume a state of solvency, so that all creditors in due course receive full payment of their debts. If, on the other hand, the debtor's attempts at regaining solvency are of no avail the consequence of the delay may be that greater losses are inflicted upon all parties, including those who became creditors for the first time only after the debtor was already hopelessly insolvent. Hence, even at the risk of maintaining the paradox described above, the principle has become established under English law that a creditor to whom full payment is not made or tendered at a time when it ordinarily falls due is entitled, albeit subject to certain safeguards,[6] to initiate insolvency proceedings on the premiss that the debtor's insolvency is reasonably to be inferred under the circumstances.

It follows from what is said above that it is perfectly possible (if somewhat exceptional) for a person to be made bankrupt (or for a company to be wound up) merely on account of a perverse refusal to pay a single debt which the debtor could perfectly well afford to discharge. It is likewise possible (and not indeed unusual) for insolvency proceedings to take place against a debtor whose total assets are not sufficiently liquid to provide an adequate amount of cash to meet present liabilities as they fall due. Such a predicament, which is sometimes termed "short-term" or "practical" insolvency,[7] may be distinguished from the situation known as "absolute" or "balance sheet" insolvency, where the sum total of all debts—present, future and contingent—exceeds the total value of all assets, even at their most favourable realisation.[8] But it is still the case that, even where the debtor's state of insolvency is both absolute and irretrievable, this situation can only be transformed into a legally acknowledged status (bankruptcy in the case of an individual; winding up in the case of a company) through the

---

[6] As to which, see *post*, Chaps. 6 and 21 with regard to the matters which must be established by a petitioning creditor in individual and corporate proceedings respectively.
[7] Sometimes referred to as a "cash-flow" crisis.
[8] For a number of reasons the actual amount which is likely to be realised through the forced liquidation of a debtor's assets is usually well below what might have been obtainable from a more leisurely disposal of the same assets at times of the debtor's own choosing.

formality of the appropriate insolvency procedure commenced at the instance of a duly qualified party.

Historical Development of the Law

In order that the special nature and form of the insolvency law of the present day may be properly understood it is necessary to have some regard to the way in which the law has evolved historically. One of the principal characteristics of this branch of English law, in contrast to that of many other countries, is that a number of fundamental distinctions are maintained between the insolvency of individuals and the insolvency of artificial legal persons (chiefly companies). This division, which is largely the result of the accidents of legal development, is of continuing importance notwithstanding the attempts in recent years to gather together the disparate elements of our insolvency law into a more coherent and unified whole.[9]

The early history of insolvency law in England and Wales is concerned purely with individual insolvency (bankruptcy). Statutes dealing with the bankruptcy of individual debtors were enacted at intervals from the mid-sixteenth century onwards.[10] Originally the common law did not concern itself with bankruptcy, which was an institution of the Law Merchant, a distinct body of law developed by a network of medieval courts scattered across Europe. These courts, though locally based within the territory of different, sovereign countries, nevertheless exercised in those places a special jurisdiction over the dealings of merchants and matters relative to commerce. The Law Merchant became a body of common European usage, drawing extensively upon the customs and practices which had become established among merchants in their dealings with one another, but based principally upon the mercantile law of Italy, which was itself derived from Roman Law.[11] The procedures under the Law Merchant for cases of individual insolvency were adapted from the Roman Law procedures known as *Cessio Bonorum* (assignment of property for the benefit of creditors), *Distractio Bonorum* (forced liquidation of assets), and *Remissio* and *Dilatio* (compositions with creditors).[12] Special remedies were also available under Roman Law to nullify fraudulent alienations of

---

[9] *cf.* the original terms of reference of the Review Committee on Insolvency Law and Practice (hereafter referred to as the Cork Committee), reproduced below at p. 15.

[10] See *infra*, text to n. 15. The founding statute is usually considered to have been Statute 1542 (34 and 35 Hen. 8, c. 4) ("An Act against such persons as do make bankrupts"). See however Statute 1376 (50 Ed. 3, c. 6).

[11] On the medieval development of insolvency law in Europe, see J. Dalhuisen, *International Insolvency and Bankruptcy* (2 Vols., 1980–1986), Vol. 1, Part I, Chap. 2.

[12] On these insolvency procedures under Roman Law, see Dalhuisen, *ibid.*, Vol. 1, Part I, paras. 1.01–1.05; W.W. Buckland, *Textbook of Roman Law* (3rd. ed., 1963) pp. 642–645, 671–673; J.A.C. Thomas, *Textbook of Roman Law* (1976) pp. 109–110, 122.

property by debtors.[13] Despite their absorption into the Law Merchant, these Roman antecedents of many present-day systems of insolvency law were destined to enjoy only a limited influence upon the general law of England (as opposed to Scotland), and were confined in application to the ranks of the merchants themselves.

From the fourteenth century onwards the centralised jurisdiction exercised by the ordinary Common Law courts progressively superseded that of the local Courts Merchant and Courts Maritime, and a lengthy process occurred whereby a considerable part of the Law Merchant was absorbed into the Common Law on the premiss that it was "part of the lawes of this realm,"[14] until, by the close of the seventeenth century the courts were regularly taking judicial notice of mercantile custom. The year 1542 saw the enactment of the first English Bankruptcy Act, a limited and specific measure whose purpose was to deal with absconding debtors. The Act enabled any aggrieved party to procure the seizure and sale, and rateable distribution among his creditors, of the debtor's property:

"to every one of the said creditors, a portion rate and rate-like according to the quantity of their debts."[15]

Thus we encounter, even at this early date, the deployment of what have come to be two of the fundamental principles on which English insolvency law is based, namely collectivity of participation by the creditors, and *pari passu* distribution among them of the debtor's available property.

The repeated references in the statute to absconding debtors as "offenders" are also noteworthy, as signifying the close identification between bankruptcy and criminality at this period, a stigma which was to endure until relatively recent times and one which has not yet been totally relinquished. In 1571 two further statutes were enacted, one for the setting aside of fraudulent conveyances and the other making more detailed and extended provisions for dealing with bankrupts.[16] These statutory developments coincided with the burgeoning of commerce in Tudor

---

[13] Especially significant was the *Actio Pauliana*, an action available to creditors defrauded by the alienation. See Dalhuisen, *supra* n. 12, especially para. 1.02[2]; Buckland, *op. cit.*, p. 596; Thomas, *op. cit.*, 375–376. The *Pauline Action* has become a characteristic feature of the insolvency laws of many countries belonging to the Romanistic legal family and is still widely utilised: see *Avoidance of Fraudulent Transfers and Related Bankruptcy Crimes* (International Bar Association, Collected Papers delivered in Vienna, 1984) *passim*; *Report of the Advisory Committee on the EEC Preliminary Draft Convention on Bankruptcy* (1976, Cmnd. 6602) paras. 361–363; Dalhuisen, *op. cit.*, Vol. 1, Part II, para. 1.04[4].

[14] Co. Litt. 182(a): "... and this is *per legem mercatoriam* which (as hath been said) is part of the lawes of this realm, for the advancement and continuance of commerce and trade, which is *pro bono publico.*"
On the relationship between the Law Merchant and English Common Law, see R.M. Goode, *Commercial Law* (1982) pp. 31–37; W.S. Holdsworth, *History of English Law*, Vol. 1 pp. 562–573; Vol. 5 pp. 60–154; Vol. 8 pp. 99–300; T.F.T. Plucknett, *A Concise History of The Common Law* (5th ed. 1956), pp. 657–670.

[15] Stat. 34 & 35 (Hen. 8, c. 4), s.1.

[16] The Fraudulent Conveyances Act 1571, (13 Eliz. 1, c. 5), and the Bankrupts Act 1571, (13 Eliz. 1, c. 7).

England, and it is pertinent to note that the operation of these early statutes was confined to cases concerning "insolvent traders," a reflection of the fact that the institution of bankruptcy was historically rooted in the Law Merchant. Indeed, this restricted application of the English bankruptcy law to persons engaged in a trade or business persisted until as late as 1861, when the Bankruptcy Act of that year declared its provisions to be applicable to "all debtors, whether traders or not."[17] Thus ended the period when the law of bankruptcy was of purely mercantile application, a state of affairs which is still maintained in some continental European countries to the present day.[18] The form of words used in the Bankruptcy Act 1861 placed emphasis upon the concept of the "debtor," a term which was capable of applying to unmarried women but which, by long established rules of English law, could not apply to a woman during the subsistence of a lawful marriage. It had previously become established that a married woman who engaged in trade on her own account could be made bankrupt in her capacity of "trader." However, since the Act of 1861 did not have the effect of making married women amenable to the law of bankruptcy it remained a curiosity of English law, even after 1861, that a married woman could only be made bankrupt if she engaged in trade. This anomaly was ended only by the enactment of the Law Reform (Married Women and Tortfeasors) Act 1935.[19]

The basis of the distinction between traders and non-traders, while it retained any relevance under the English law of bankruptcy, was formerly dependent upon the notion of a person's being engaged in the manufacturing, or the buying or selling, of goods. "Non-traders" would thus be any persons in employment, or engaged in a recognised profession, or occupying the positions of landowner or farmer. For so long as the provisions of the bankruptcy law were excluded from applying to non-traders such persons, if they became insolvent, enjoyed no relief from the rigours of the common law procedures for enforcement of the payment of debts through seizure and imprisonment of the debtor's person as well as through the seizure and sale of his property. A principal feature of such procedures, quite apart from their severity, was their non-collective nature. This might result, on the one hand, in the debtor's undergoing committal to prison at the instance of a single creditor, regardless of the wishes or interests of the others. On the other hand, a so-called "race of diligence" could readily arise consisting of an unseemly, and potentially wasteful, competition between creditors endeavouring to trace and attach assets out of which to satisfy their individual claims as fully as possible. Chaos and paradox thus existed side by side, for it might well happen that an otherwise honest debtor, whose insolvency was the result of mere accident or misfortune, came to suffer the degradation and stigma of prolonged imprisonment through lack of the means to satisfy one especially implacable creditor, while another debtor, whose conduct

---

[17] Bankruptcy Act 1861, (24 and 25 Vict., c. 134) s.69 *et seq.*
[18] *e.g.* Belgium, France, Greece, Luxembourg, Italy, Portugal, and Spain. See the relevant Chaps. of H. Rajak and G. White (Eds.), *A Practitioner's Guide to European Insolvency Law* (1992/93 ed.).
[19] s.1(d).

might have been marked by calculating fraud, could conceivably fare no worse, and might in the event fare a good deal better, thanks to the leniency, or naivety, of his particular creditors.

By the eighteenth century the law of debt and bankruptcy was in lamentable disarray. Not only was the procedure for bankruptcy limited in its application, as we have seen, to those persons classified as "traders," but the early bankruptcy statutes of the sixteenth and seventeenth centuries were conspicuously inflexible and harsh in their structure and operation. Thus no provision was made for an insolvent trader to apply of his own accord to be made bankrupt while, conversely, once such an adjudication had been pronounced at the behest of his creditors no procedure existed whereby the bankrupt, having surrendered all his property, could afterwards apply for discharge from the status of bankruptcy, with its attendant stigma and wholesale disabilities. Although some provision for discharge was introduced by an Act of 1705,[20] the generally unfavourable policy of the law towards bankrupt traders, whereby they were considered as a species of criminal, continued to be reflected in the rigorous penalties to which they were subject including the death penalty, which was available in cases of fraud.[21] The law at this period was also conspicuous for its failure to make any proper distinction between the honest but unfortunate debtor on the one hand, and the dishonest or reckless one on the other. The sole method of attaining some measure of protection for the public from the consequences of commercial failure and debt default seems to have been the deployment of deterrent penalties imposed in a relatively indiscriminate fashion upon those who actually became insolvent. The law had yet to develop any concept of bankruptcy as a medium for procuring relief, and possibly rehabilitation, for the debtor from the oppressive burden of debt and from the disruptive forces of individual creditors' remedies. Similarly, the parallel concept of insolvency law as a vehicle for achieving a balance between a complex structure of interests—social as well as individual—lay far in the future.

During the nineteenth century a series of bankruptcy statutes laid the foundations of the modern law of bankruptcy, as we know it today. In 1813 a Court for the Relief of Insolvent Debtors[22] was established for the purpose of alleviating the plight of the non-trader, whom at that date the bankruptcy law itself still did not touch.[23] Reforms to the law of bankruptcy were effected by the Bankruptcy Act 1824, consolidated in 1825.[24] At this same period, as is explained below,[25] the formative developments of modern company law were taking place. It may be observed that the stimulus to much legal development in the field of insolvency law during the first half of the nineteenth century was the momentum imparted to the national economy by the Industrial

---

[20] (4 & 5 Anne, c. 4) s.8 amended and explained by (6 Anne, c. 22) (1706), see also (10 Anne, c. 25).
[21] For a concise history of the evolution of insolvency law in England before 1883, see the *Cork Report* (Cmnd. 8558), Chap. 2, paras. 26–49.
[22] 53 Geo. 3, c. 102 and c. 138 (Ireland), amended by (54 Geo. 3, c. 23 and c. 28.).
[23] See *supra* for the reforms of 1861 affecting non-traders.
[24] Bankruptcy Act 1824, (5 Geo. 4, c. 98); Bankruptcy Act 1825, (6 Geo. 4, c. 16).
[25] See next section *infra*.

Revolution, while the adverse effects of the Napoleonic Wars, in conjunction with the ordinary hazards afflicting all sectors of society both inside and outside the realm of trade and commerce, produced periods of great economic difficulty during which many debtors, together with those to whom they were indebted, experienced much distress with which the law was initially incapable of dealing in an appropriate manner. Hence for the remainder of the nineteenth century the Legislature quite frequently intervened to adjust and amend the law in the light of experience, sometimes veering quite radically in its attempt to find satisfactory solutions to acute and notorious problems.[26] Finally, in the Bankruptcy Act 1883, the law of personal insolvency attained a state of development which is still recognisable today, albeit the reforms of 1985–86 have more recently effected some important structural changes, as well as numerous alterations in matters of detail.

The Historic Division Between Personal and Corporate Insolvency Under English Law

It is now appropriate to introduce some words of explanation concerning a particularly distinctive feature of the insolvency law of England and Wales, namely the traditional division between the law governing insolvent individuals (the law of bankruptcy), and the law governing corporate insolvency. It was not until relatively modern times that there developed a proper concept of corporate legal personality, capable of incurring and acquiring legal liabilities and of engaging in commercial activities in its own right, and consequently capable also of undergoing insolvency in separation from those individuals who are its members or controllers.[27] As the concepts of the modern limited liability company emerged during the first half of the nineteenth century it began to be possible for the members of incorporated companies to limit their personal liability, and thus to create a distinction between corporate and individual insolvency. The authoritative confirmation of this vital aspect of commercial law came with the decision of the House of Lords in *Salomon*

---

[26] The Bankruptcy Act 1869 contained several particularly unfortunate innovations. *cf.* Cmnd. 8558, para. 48.

[27] The first modern commercial "companies" were created either by Royal Charter (*e.g.* the Russia Company, 1555; the East India Company, 1600) or, from the early 17th century onwards, by means of special Acts of Parliament (*e.g.* the New River Company, 1605: Stat. (3 Jac. 1, c. 18)). Development of corporate theory and of company law itself was impeded between 1720 and 1825 due to the effects of the Bubble Act of 1720. Following the repeal of that Act in 1825, rapid advances occurred in the evolution of the corporate form. The foundations of the modern law of companies were laid by the Joint Stock Companies Act 1844, (7 & 8 Vict., c. 110) which introduced the procedure for the creation of joint stock companies by registration. Corporate insolvency was first regulated by a separate Act of 1844, the Joint Stock Companies' Winding Up Act, (7 & 8 Vict., c. 111). For further historical information, see: *Palmer's Company Law* (25th ed., 1992) paras. 1.101–1.135; L.C.B. Gower, *Principles of Modern Company Law* (5th ed., 1992) Chaps. 2 and 3, and works there referred to at p. 19, n. 1; W.S. Holdsworth *History of English Law*, Vol. 8 pp. 192–222.

v. Salomon & Co.,[28] which was a case involving the liquidation of what was, in substance, a one-man company.[29] When the company's declining fortunes resulted in it being put into liquidation, it was argued on behalf of the unsecured creditors that Salomon himself ought to be personally liable to repay their debts. Vaughan Williams J., at first instance, and subsequently the Court of Appeal, held in favour of the creditors' contention, regarding the company as a mere alias or agent for Aron Salomon. This view of the law's application was overturned by the House of Lords, which ruled that the Companies Act 1862 contained no requirement that the subscribers to the company's memorandum should all take a substantial interest in the company in terms of shareholding, nor that they should be independent or unconnected. The essence of their Lordships' decision was that the company, when duly formed, was a distinct person in law, separate from the subscribers, and that the company's debts were separate and self-contained.

From 1844 onwards corporate insolvency became the subject of special statutory provisions, which were consolidated into the successive versions of the Companies Act enacted and in force up until 1986.[30] At first the Legislature sought to treat insolvent companies as though they were but one more species of bankrupt, and provision was made in section 1 of the Companies Winding Up Act 1844 to enable a creditor to proceed against an insolvent company "in like manner as against any other bankrupts," with the important proviso, contained in section 2 of the Act, that the bankruptcy of the company "in its corporate or associated capacity" was not to be construed to be the bankruptcy of any member of the company in his individual capacity.

Thus was proclaimed the essence of what was soon to become established as the concept of the limited liability of the members for the debts of the company, but at this early date it was not actually accorded by the law: under the 1844 legislation it was readily possible for the privileges of incorporation to be revoked where the business of the company had been conducted in an unsatisfactory manner, in which case the members were rendered liable for the debts of the company to the full extent of their personal means.[31] Only with the passing of the Limited Liability Act 1855 did the concept of the limited liability of the members for the debts incurred by the company become properly established in law. Never-

---

[28] [1897] A.C. 22.
[29] Salomon's wife and five children had each subscribed one share; Aron Salomon himself received an issue of 20,000 shares in the company he formed to take over his hitherto profitable leather business.
[30] After the Companies' Winding Up Act of 1844, referred to in n. 27, further Companies Acts were passed and periodically consolidated at intervals from 1845 onwards (8 & 9 Vict., c. 16). Principal instances were the Joint Stock Companies Act 1856 (19 & 20 Vict., c. 47); the Companies Act 1862 (25 and 26 Vict., c. 89); the Companies (Consolidation) Act 1908; and the Companies Acts of 1929, 1948 and 1985. The latter was the last Companies Act to include a statutory code regulating corporate insolvency: the Insolvency Acts of 1985 and 1986 effected the removal of those provisions from the Companies Act into a separate Act covering both individual and corporate insolvency, with effect from December 29, 1986.
[31] Joint Stock Companies Act 1844, (7 & 8 Vict., c. 111,) ss.25, 26 and 27.

theless, despite the fact that the original form and venue of insolvency proceedings brought by the creditors of an insolvent company lay under the bankruptcy law and in the Bankruptcy Court, an element of confusion was injected by the later provision in the Winding Up Amending Act 1848 which established a parallel procedure whereby the shareholders of a company could bring about its dissolution and winding up by means of a petition presented to the Chancery Court.[32] The unsatisfactory consequences of the conflicts of jurisdiction and procedure which thereafter ensued were ultimately resolved through the consolidation of all procedures concerned with corporate insolvency into the exclusive jurisdiction of the Chancery Court, a transfer which took place in 1862.[33] This transfer of jurisdiction over corporate insolvency proceedings provided further impetus to the development of specialised procedures, which began to be contained within the provisions of successive Companies Acts from 1856 onwards,[34] whereby the law governing company winding up developed along its own particular lines, away from the basic framework and substance of the law of bankruptcy.

It therefore came about that, by the later nineteenth century, insolvency law had evolved into specialised branches—individual and corporate—whose provisions were contained in two separate collections of statutes—the Bankruptcy Acts and the Companies Acts—administered judicially by different courts under different sets of procedural rules. Although many points of resemblance existed, and in some cases entire doctrines or legislative provisions were directly duplicated from the one branch of law to the other,[35] the divergences between the two types of insolvency became, and remain, substantial. This has resulted in a state of affairs, unknown to most other systems of law apart from those which have closely followed this country in the development of their company law,[36] whereby insolvent companies are not amenable to the law of bankruptcy but instead undergo the separate process known as liquidation, or winding up, administered under separate rules by a separate branch of the courts. Hence, from the point of view of an unsatisfied creditor wishing to initiate insolvency proceedings, the question of whether his debtor is an individual[37] or an incorporated company assumes a vital significance. Upon this distinction depend not merely such matters as the proper court in which to bring proceedings, and the appropriate procedural steps to be taken, but even the very form and substance of those procedures, the

---

[32] (11 & 12 Vict., c. 45) s.5. See generally C.A. Cooke, *Corporation, Trust and Company* (1950) Chap. 10.

[33] Companies Act 1862, (25 & 26 Vict., c. 89), s.81.

[34] Companies Act 1856, (19 & 20 Vict., c. 47), Pt. 3 ss.59–105.

[35] *e.g.* the doctrine of fraudulent preference, developed under bankruptcy law, was made directly applicable in the winding up of companies by s.76 of the Companies Act 1856. The public official known as the Official Receiver, whose office was created by the Bankruptcy Act 1883, Pt. 4, was given duties and functions in relation to company winding up by the Companies (Winding Up) Act 1890.

[36] Examples are Australia, New Zealand, and the Republic of Ireland.

[37] As explained below (p. 77), for the purposes of the distinction here being discussed the expression "individual" includes a partnership formed under the law of England and Wales.

preconditions to their availability, and in the final analysis the *quantum* of the assets which are ultimately available for the purpose of meeting the creditors' claims.

A failure to appreciate the full extent of the divergence between corporate and individual insolvency has at times led even the Legislature itself to formulate potentially unworkable procedures whereby the unmodified provisions of the bankruptcy law were incorporated by reference into company winding up, without proper regard to the practical consequences resulting from the incompatibility of the two bodies of legal rules.[38] Even after the momentous reshaping and consolidation of the entire law of insolvency which was accomplished by means of the Insolvency Act 1985 and the Insolvency Act 1986, it is still the case that the law of corporate insolvency and the law of individual insolvency are essentially separate from each other in their respective structures, and in many matters of detail, although the statutory provisions by which these branches of the law are respectively governed are now contained within a single, comprehensive statute and related secondary legislation. Although the recent legislative reforms were the occasion for an extensive harmonisation in many matters of detail, regarding both substance and procedure, between the two branches of insolvency law the fundamental dichotomies remain as significant as ever, and are reflected in the structure of the treatment of the law which will be found throughout the subsequent chapters of this book.

The Reform and Development of the Law in Modern Times

The historic divisions between corporate and personal insolvency continued to be reflected in the approach adopted until well into the twentieth century in relation to the review and reform of the law. Committees were established, and from time to time legislation was enacted, in respect of one or other branch of the law.[39] At other times, committees were established to consider aspects of the law of credit and security,[40] or the enforcement of judgment debts,[41] both of which subjects

---

[38] *cf.* the provision, formerly in s.317 of the Companies Act 1948 and briefly re-enacted as s.612 of the Companies Act 1985, whereby it was declared that the rules of bankruptcy law regarding creditors' rights, provable debts and related matters were to apply in company winding up. A brilliant demonstration of the futility and absurdity of any attempt at a literal application of these rules, under certain circumstances, was given by Vinelott J. in his judgment in *Re Berkeley Securities* [1980] 3 All E.R. 513 at 526–529.

[39] Committees appointed to review aspects of the bankruptcy law included: the Muir Mackenzie Committee (1906, Cd. 4068); the Hansell Committee, Cmnd. 2326 (1925); and the Blagden Committee, Cmnd. 221 (1957). Among the committees which inquired into the workings of company law were the Loreburn Committee (1906 Cd. 3052); the Greene Committee (1926, Cmnd. 2657); the Cohen Committee (1945, Cmnd. 6659), and the Jenkins Committee (1959, Cmnd. 1749). Chapter 14 of the *Jenkins Report* deals with winding up.

[40] The Crowther Committee (1968–1971) Cmnd. 4596.

[41] The Payne Committee (1965–1969) Cmnd. 3909.

are closely inter-connected with insolvency law. But no comprehensive review of the insolvency law itself was undertaken by an officially constituted committee before the setting up of the Cork Committee in January 1977. That event may be seen as the culmination of a protracted process of discreet agitation for a thorough and radical review of the law to be undertaken. For example in 1957 the Report of the Blagden Committee on the working of the law of bankruptcy and deeds of arrangement contained an emphatic assertion that, in relation to the primary objects which the committee considered should underlie the law relating to discharge from bankruptcy, the law was seriously unsatisfactory. As they put it:

> "Practical experience has shown that the present law fails and, it is suggested, fails badly in all these primary objects."[42]

Nevertheless no legislative initiative was pursued in response to the recommendations of the Blagden Report, so that its many and valuable proposals remained unenacted.

A renewed impetus to reform was imparted from 1973 onwards by the greatly increased incidence of corporate and individual financial failures brought about by the combination of prolonged economic recession and high levels of inflation.[43] During this period numerous defects and inadequacies of the law's provisions and machinery for dealing with insolvency became increasingly exposed, and public concern was correspondingly intensified. There was strong disquiet at the obvious severity of the impact of insolvency law upon "honest but unfortunate" debtors against whom the law appeared to work in precisely the opposite way to its ostensible purpose of providing a merciful release from the inexorable burden of debt, coupled with the prospect of rehabilitation with a "clean slate." Yet at the same time a series of notorious instances, involving both individual and corporate insolvencies, revealed clearly the law's inability to deal properly and effectively with cases of irresponsible or even precalculated misuse of the privileges of credit. The "undeserving" debtor or company manager, whose recklessness or dishonesty had brought unmerited loss upon those dealing with him or his company, was too readily able to exploit the law to personal advantage and so escape from carrying the full measure of the appropriate consequences of his conduct.[44] In 1975 a report by "Justice," the British section of the International Commission of Jurists,[45] called specific attention to numerous defects, complexities and anachronisms in the law of bankruptcy. The cogent and succinct recommendations of this timely Report, prepared and published

---

[42] Cmnd. 221, at para. 55.
[43] The annual statistics for company winding up orders and bankruptcy adjudications for the years 1960–1986 are shown in Table A of Appendix III.
[44] Some of these notorious cases are described in S. Aris, *Going Bust* (1985), see Chaps. 6, 7 and 9.
[45] *Bankruptcy*, published 1975 by Stevens and Sons. The chairman of the committee which prepared the report was Allan Heyman.

by a non-governmental association possessed of considerable authority and prestige, were quickly answered via the Insolvency Act 1976, a short measure of only fourteen sections and three schedules, whose purpose was essentially to provide an interim alleviation of some of the most serious shortcomings of the law of insolvency, pending the carrying out of a wholesale review.

At the same time as Parliament was concluding the process of enactment of the Insolvency Act 1976 a further contribution to the movement for reform was furnished through the publication of the Report of the Cork Advisory Committee.[46] This Committee had been established, under the chairmanship of Mr (later Sir) Kenneth Cork, in July 1973 to consider the terms of the Draft EEC Bankruptcy Convention and to advise the Department of Trade upon its implications for the United Kingdom, which had become committed to participating in the negotiations for the adoption of such a convention as a consequence of accession to the EEC with effect from January 1, 1973. The Report of the Cork Advisory Committee was an important catalyst in the process towards the undertaking of a comprehensive review of the insolvency law of England and Wales, since it was part of the thrust of the Report, taken as a whole, that such a review was urgently required both as a matter of practical necessity and also as a precondition to the United Kingdom becoming capable of participating effectively in the negotiations taking place at EEC level.

In recognition of the overwhelming force of the arguments in favour of revision and reform of the law, the Secretary of State for Trade announced in October 1976 that he was to set up a Review Committee on Insolvency Law and Practice.[47] The Committee was duly appointed on January 27, 1977, with Kenneth Cork once again serving as chairman. The remit of the Committee was framed in wide terms, as follows:

(1) To review the law and practice relating to insolvency, bankruptcy, liquidation and receiverships in England and Wales and to consider what reforms are necessary or desirable;
(2) To examine the possibility of formulating a comprehensive insolvency system and the extent to which existing procedures might, with advantage, be harmonised and integrated;
(3) To suggest possible less formal procedures as alternatives to bankruptcy and company winding up proceedings in appropriate circumstances; and
(4) To make recommendations.

It may be observed nevertheless that the terms of reference of the Cork Committee did not include a review of the general law of credit and security, nor of the area of remedies for debt enforcement, whose provisions are in many respects intimately linked with insolvency. Also a

---

[46] Cmnd. 6602 (1976).
[47] Hansard H.C. Vol. 918, October 1976, written answer no. 20.

matter for regret is the fact that, despite the unprecedented scope of the review which the Cork Committee was actually required to undertake, the resources placed at the Committee's disposal were relatively limited, and arguably insufficient for the purpose in hand. Consequently, little or no specially commissioned research or empirical study was conducted other than that which could be undertaken by the members of the Committee themselves or by those who voluntarily submitted evidence.[48] It is somewhat curious to observe that the Law Commission for England and Wales, despite having a standing responsibility for keeping under review "all the law . . . with a view to its systematic development and reform . . ."[49] has effectively been excluded from the province of insolvency law, and thus had no formal involvement in the process of revision of this area of law whose provisions and effect are of such profound importance for the working of the law generally.[50] This paradox is heightened by the fact that, almost simultaneously, the review of the Scottish Law of bankruptcy and related aspects of insolvency and liquidation was being undertaken by the Scottish Law Commission as part of their systematic programme of law reform.[51]

The work of the Cork Committee was considerably affected by the change of government in May 1979, when the incoming Administration embarked upon a programme of scrutinising the cost-effectiveness of most aspects of public expenditure. The Government made an approach to the Committee in August 1979 and asked for an early indication of their likely recommendations, with reference especially to the question of the amount of time which would be required to be spent by the staff of the Insolvency Service in performing their duties under the amended law. The Committee's response took the form of an Interim Report, submitted to the Minister in October 1979 and subsequently published in July 1980[52] simultaneously with a government Green Paper.[53] The latter was concerned almost exclusively with the question of the manpower implications of the operation of the Insolvency Service, and contained radical proposals for the effective privatisation of insolvency procedures, and for the virtual elimination of the close involvement of the Official Receiver. The proposals were unsatisfactory and unconvincing, and attracted generally adverse criticism.[54] The most effective refutation of the

---

[48] See Cmnd. 8558, Appendices 1 and 3 for the lists of co-opted members and consultants, and of those who submitted written evidence. The Committee's own circulated questionnaire is reproduced in Appendix 2. By contrast, the United States Bankruptcy Reform Act of 1978 was accomplished with the assistance of an extensive programme of well-funded research. For some discussion of the latter, see P. Shuchman in I. Ramsay (Ed.), *Debtors and Creditors* (1986) at pp. 293–316.

[49] Law Commissions Act 1965, s.3(1).

[50] The Law Commission is listed in Appendix 3 to the *Cork Report* among the bodies which submitted written evidence to the committee: Cmnd. 8558, at p. 455.

[51] See the Report of the Scottish Law Commission, published 1982 as H.C. Paper 176 (Scot. Law Com. No. 68). This report also contains the Draft Bill which was subsequently enacted as the Bankruptcy (Scotland) Act 1985. No Draft Bill was included in the *Cork Report*.

[52] Cmnd. 7968: *Bankruptcy: Interim Report of the Insolvency Law Review Committee*.

[53] Cmnd. 7967: *Bankruptcy: A Consultative Document*.

[54] See Fletcher (1981) 44 M.L.R. 77.

arguments advanced in the Green Paper was subsequently included in the Cork Committee's own Final Report, published in 1982.[55] This appears to have succeeded in securing the continuation of the traditional role of the Official Receiver in both corporate and personal insolvency procedures, and the government's subsequent White Paper of February 1984[56] was notable for the absence of any further reference to the possibility of effecting savings in public expenditure by such a drastic diminution in the centralised supervision of insolvency. Instead the government made a point of emphasising its acceptance of the paramount importance of the investigative role of the Official Receiver, and was content to suggest that economies in the operation of the Insolvency Service would be sought through other means.[57]

The Final Report of the Insolvency Law Review Committee (hereafter in this book referred to as the *Cork Report*), was a voluminous and epoch-making document, which will continue to provide a major point of reference for many years to come. Throughout the *Report* a vigorous case was argued for a fundamental reform of insolvency law. The central recommendations were that a unified Insolvency Code should be enacted in place of the diversity of statutes governing two distinct, if cognate, branches of the law, and that a unified system of insolvency courts should be created to administer the law.[58] Not only should the traditional role of the Official Receiver be maintained, but his powers and responsibilities should be sharpened.[59] At the same time, all insolvency practitioners belonging to the private sector should be the subject of professional regulation, to ensure appropriate standards of competence and integrity.[60] A range of new procedures was proposed, so as to offer a number of alternatives to outright bankruptcy or winding up, thereby affording some prospect of dealing with individual cases in the light of their particular circumstances and merits.[61] Very many detailed proposals were made for alteration to the substance of the law, and to its administrative and procedural regulations, and reference will be made to these at appropriate places later in this book. In conclusion, the authors of the Report declared that:

> "It has been demonstrated overwhelmingly that the law of insolvency is now so unsatisfactory that, unless fresh legislation is introduced soon, it will fall into even greater decay and be regarded with contempt by society and those whose needs it is supposed to serve. We believe that the need for reform is urgent and imperative."[62]

---

[55] Cmnd. 8558: *Insolvency Law and Practice*. See Chap. 14, paras. 695–731, and *cf.* Cmnd. 9175 at paras. 36–38. For comments on the *Report*, see Fletcher and Farrar [1983] J.B.L. 72–74; Fletcher [1983] J.B.L. 94–104 and 200–217.
[56] Cmnd. 9175: *A Revised Framework of Insolvency Law*. For comment see Fletcher [1984] J.B.L. 304–307.
[57] Cmnd. 9175, Chaps. 7 and 8, and also paras. 17–18, 71–74, 76–77, 82, 90–93, 96, 102, 105–107, 117–119, 120 and 124.
[58] Cmnd. 8558, Chap. 10, paras. 538–544; Chap. 20.
[59] Cmnd. 8558, Chap. 14.
[60] *ibid.*, Chaps. 15 and 16.
[61] *ibid.*, Chaps. 6, 7, 9, 11, 12 and 13.
[62] *ibid.*, at paras. 1981, 1982.

The initial atmosphere of expectation engendered by the publication of the *Cork Report* sadly proved premature. No official intimations were forthcoming of any legislative intentions on the part of Government and no steps were taken even to make the Report the subject of a formal debate in either House of Parliament. A sudden change of attitude appeared to occur early in 1984, following a further spate of financial scandals which served particularly to arouse public disquiet over the way in which those responsible for the mismanagement of companies were in most cases able to escape serious personal consequences of either a civil or a criminal nature. At relatively short notice the Government White Paper, referred to above, was published in February 1984 together with an indication that legislation was imminent. In consequence, very little time was allowed for interested parties to submit comments before the drafting of the Insolvency Bill was embarked upon, and the Bill itself was introduced in the House of Lords on December 10, 1984.

This regrettable mishandling of the period of preparation for the first major overhaul of insolvency law for over 100 years cannot but be lamented. The inadequate manner in which consultation was conducted, coupled with the near-total lack of any form of public debate about the issues of policy and principle at the heart of any radical recasting of insolvency law, were an inauspicious prelude to what was to become a most contentious and confused episode of legislative history. Thereby, what ought to have been a largely non-controversial, non-Party Bill became the subject of highly dramatic proceedings before both Houses,[63] and also in Committee,[64] and unquestioned damage was inflicted upon the ultimate quality of a highly technical piece of legislation whose detailed provisions were but vaguely understood by all but a minority of those participating in its enactment, but whose social and economic importance was nonetheless immense. The Bill's deficiencies, due to haste in preparation, together with the vicissitudes of the Parliamentary process, resulted in a quite exceptional number of amendments being tabled to the Insolvency Bill, estimated to have approached 1,200 by the time of Royal Assent. A high proportion of these amendments were tabled by the government itself, and many were adopted virtually without debate during the closing stages of the proceedings.

As enacted, the Insolvency Act 1985 did not constitute the unified code of insolvency law for which the *Cork Report* had so strenuously argued. Indeed, the Government's White Paper had in some ways been as unbalanced and monothematic as had been the unfortunate Green Paper, albeit the focus of attention in the later document was upon such then-topical matters as the misdeeds of company directors and the abuse of the privilege of incorporation with limited liability.[65] Many of the recom-

---

[63] For Parliamentary proceedings on the Insolvency Act 1985, see Hansard: H.L. Vol. 458, cols. 875, 894; Vol. 459, cols. 565, 833, 835, 906, 1212, 1233; Vol. 461, col. 711; Vol. 462, cols. 11, 123, 606; Vol. 467, cols. 1093, 1188; H.C. Vol. 78, col. 141; Vol. 83, col. 526; Vol. 84, col. 677.

[64] The Bill was considered in Committee by the House of Commons in Standing Committee E on May 14, 16, 21, 23, and on June 4, 6, 11, 13, 18, and 20, 1985.

[65] See Cmnd. 9175, Chaps. 2, 10 and 12 and at paras. 20, 71–74 and 90–94.

mendations contained in the *Cork Report* were either not adopted at all in the Insolvency Act 1985—as in the case of the proposal for a unified Insolvency Court[66]—or, if adopted, underwent considerable alterations in the process of statutory enactment. Nevertheless the Act which received Royal Assent on October 30, 1985 could fairly be described as of revolutionary stature, in that it had effected a necessary modernisation and streamlining of the entire law of bankruptcy, and had similarly implemented urgently needed reforms in the law of corporate insolvency. But whereas all of the statutory provisions relating to bankruptcy would henceforth be contained entirely within the Insolvency Act, the law of corporate insolvency would continue to be governed partly by the provisions of the Insolvency Act 1985 and partly by those of the Companies Act 1985, as amended by the Insolvency Act itself.

Happily, the above unsatisfactory state of affairs was soon to be resolved, even before the Insolvency Act 1985 was fully brought into force by means of the requisite Commencement Orders.[67] A newly-drafted Insolvency Bill was introduced in the House of Lords on May 13, 1986, and was designed to operate as a consolidating Act in relation to almost the whole of the Insolvency Act 1985 together with those parts of the Companies Act 1985 relating to the insolvency and winding up of companies.[68] The Insolvency Bill of 1986, in contrast to its precursor of 1984–85, enjoyed a tranquil and speedy passage through all its Parliamentary stages.[69] As a consolidation measure, the Bill was referred for its Committee stage to a Joint Committee of both Houses, and a mere handful of drafting corrections were made. Royal Assent was signified on July 25, 1986, and implementation was then arranged so as to enable the Act to come fully into force simultaneously with the extensive range of secondary legislation complementary to the Act, contained in a series of statutory instruments.[70] This synchronised implementation was facilitated by means of a specially-devised commencement provision in the Act of 1986, which had the unusual effect of bringing the whole of the Act into force immediately after the moment when Part 3 of the Insolvency Act 1985 (dealing with individual insolvency and bankruptcy) came into force for England and Wales.[71] Thus, unusually, the Act of 1986 was actually brought into effect by means of a commencement order made in relation to the Act of 1985, the operative date of which was December 29, 1986.[72]

---

[66] Cmnd. 8558, Chap. 20, paras. 1000–1032; *cf.* Cmnd. 9175, which makes no reference to this aspect of the *Report*'s proposals.

[67] See Insolvency Act 1985, s.236(2); (S.I. 1986, Nos. 6, 185, 463 and 840) (Commencement Orders Nos. 1–4, made between January and May 1986). See [1986] J.B.L. 169–171.

[68] Pts. 19, 20 (apart from Chap. 6) and 21 of the Companies Act 1985. The Companies Act, itself a consolidation Act, had received Royal Assent only on March 11, 1985, and came into force on July 1, 1985.

[69] For Parliamentary proceedings on the Insolvency Act 1986, see Hansard: H.L. Vol. 474, col. 1038; Vol. 475, cols. 711–714; Vol. 477, cols. 420–422, 758, 1036; H.C. Vol. 120, cols. 152, 153.

[70] See the Table of Secondary Legislation for the Statutory Instruments associated with the Insolvency Act 1986.

[71] Insolvency Act 1986, s.443.

[72] Insolvency Act 1985 (Commencement No. 5) Order 1986, (S.I. 1986, No. 1924).

As a consequence of the coming into force of the Insolvency Act 1986, very nearly all of the provisions of the Act of 1985 underwent immediate repeal,[73] so that they actually came into effect for practical purposes as part of the Act of 1986. A small group of provisions of the Insolvency Act 1985, all concerned with the disqualification of company directors, were separately consolidated together with cognate provisions drawn from the Companies Act 1985 and enacted as the Company Directors Disqualification Act 1986, which came into force simultaneously with the Insolvency Act 1986.[74]

Thus, almost as an afterthought, the consolidation of all the statutory provisions governing the insolvency of individuals and that of companies within a single Act, as recommended by the *Cork Report*, was finally brought about. However, although a high degree of harmonisation has been achieved between many parallel provisions belonging to the different branches of insolvency law, the traditional distinction survives between corporate and personal insolvency and the pre-existing procedures have retained their respective, and separate features. These will be treated separately in the succeeding parts of the present book. Moreover, the statutory unification of insolvency law has not been accomplished without a degree of attendant paradox, because it is now the case that the law relating to the winding up of solvent companies is contained within the Insolvency Act, where its provisions are commingled with those applicable to the winding up of insolvent companies. It is also the case that, as a consequence of the new regulation of all persons eligible to serve as liquidators of companies, the winding up of every company, including one which is solvent, must be carried out (if not by the Official Receiver), by a person known as an "authorised insolvency practitioner."[75]

The Continuing Need for Review and Reform of the Law

The newly revised law of insolvency was subjected to a prolonged and searching period of practical testing during the years of economic recession between 1989 and 1993. In many respects, the experience gave rise to justifiable concern at the apparent failure of some of the more innovative aspects of the Insolvency Act—such as the administration order procedure,[76] and the company voluntary arrangement[77]—to fulfil their intended roles. Judged by the bare statistical evidence, at least,[78] these two procedures did not prove attractive as vehicles for the mounting of

---

[73] Insolvency Act 1986, s.438 together with Sched. 12. A small number of provisions of the Insolvency Act 1985 were not repealed by the Act of 1986, namely ss.215, 217(4), 218–220, 235(1), 236(1), (2); Sched. 1, paras. 5(1)–(3), 6; Sched. 6, paras. 3, 4, 8, 10–13, 18, 19, 23, 24, 45–47; and Sched. 8.

[74] Company Directors Disqualification Act 1986, s.25. Sched. 4 to the Act effected consequential repeals of those sections of the Insolvency Act 1985 which were consolidated into the Disqualification Act.

[75] See Insolvency Act 1986, Pt. 13, s.388(1)(*a*).

[76] See Chap. 15, *post*.

[77] See Chap. 16, *post*.

[78] See Statistics in Appendix III, *post*.

attempts at rescue and rehabilitation of ailing companies. Other empirical evidence began to accumulate, suggesting that the new law was working less well than had been hoped.

In response to the specific anxieties aroused by the low incidence of use of the two procedures mentioned above, the Insolvency Service undertook a review of the law's working, and issued Consultative Documents in October 1993 and in April 1995.[79] This exercise may in due course result in some amendments to the law itself. Almost simultaneously, a new committee was established by "Justice" to carry out a broader review of the current state of insolvency law, slightly less than 20 years after the seminal report on Bankruptcy was published by that same, reformist body.[80] The new "Justice" report, published in 1994, strongly advocates the creation of a permanent, specialised committee, charged with the mission to devise and promote a national insolvency strategy, and to ensure that the law is constantly monitored and reviewed, so that it is both more flexible and in tune with evolving social needs, and keeps pace with the most effective developments in the law and practice of insolvency in other developed countries of the world.[81]

---

[79] "Company Voluntary Arrangements and Administration Orders: A Consultative Document" (October 1993); "Revised Proposals for a New Company Voluntary Arrangement Procedure" (April 1995).
[80] See n. 45, *supra*.
[81] See "Insolvency Law: An Agenda for Reform" ("Justice" Publication, 1994), esp. Chaps. 6 and 7.

CHAPTER 2

THE EVOLUTION OF THE ADMINISTRATIVE MACHINERY OF INSOLVENCY LAW

The Present Arrangement

Besides the developments in the substantive law of bankruptcy which took place during the nineteenth century, it was during this period that the administration of this area of the law was placed in the hands of courts specifically established to deal with bankruptcy business. In London itself, the original statutes of the sixteenth century had placed the administration of the law under the control of special commissioners appointed by the Lord Chancellor. This did not prove to be a successful arrangement, however, and in the eighteenth century the jurisdiction in bankruptcy was conferred upon the Court of Chancery,[1] where the suits were frequently heard by the Lord Chancellor in person. But the notorious delays with which proceedings in Chancery were beset rendered this arrangement particularly unsatisfactory for bankruptcy cases, where speed of administration is one of the most essential qualities. With a view to providing a more efficient and expeditious judicial service, a Bankruptcy Court was established in London in 1831, staffed by four judges and six commissioners.[2] In the course of the extensive reorganisation of the structure of the courts under the provisions of the Supreme Court of Judicature Acts 1873–1875, the London Bankruptcy Court, although originally scheduled to be merged with the Supreme Court of Judicature,[3] was for a time left separate.[4] However the merger was finally effected by the Bankruptcy Act 1883,[5] and the High Court acquired the jurisdiction in bankruptcy which it retains to the present day.[6] This jurisdiction was at first conferred upon the Queen's Bench Division of the High Court, but

---

[1] Bankruptcy Act 1732 (5 Geo. 2, c. 30), s.24.
[2] (1 & 2 Will. 4, c. 56): "An Act to establish a Court in Bankruptcy".
[3] Supreme Court of Judicature Act 1873, ss.3, 4.
[4] Supreme Court of Judicature Act 1875, s.9.
[5] ss.92, 93.
[6] Insolvency Act 1986, ss.373(1), (3)(a), 374, 375(2).

since 1921 the work has been allocated to the Chancery Division.[7] Although this same Division of the High Court has, since 1862,[8] exercised jurisdiction in company matters, including company winding up, the administration of personal and corporate insolvency has remained largely distinct, with bankruptcy matters being allocated at first instance to the High Court Registrars sitting in court rooms designated as "bankruptcy courts", while company winding up proceedings are heard by Masters or Judges of the Chancery Division, either in chambers or in the companies court. It is thus only on appeals—either to the Chancery Divisional Court or to the Court of Appeal—that cases from the two branches of the insolvency law are likely to be considered by members of the same group of judges.

Outside London, a statute of 1842[9] removed jurisdiction in bankruptcy from the hands of the country commissioners who were the provincial counterparts of the original bankruptcy commissioners in London, and with whose behaviour there was much public dissatisfaction verging upon scandal. Initially, jurisdiction in bankruptcy was vested in a system of District Bankruptcy Courts, but with the creation of the County Courts under the County Courts Act 1846 it became feasible to rationalise the administrative arrangements. Thus it came about that under the Bankruptcy Act 1847 certain County Courts acquired exclusive control over bankruptcy matters outside London. This jurisdiction has been retained ever since in bankruptcy proceedings taking place outside the area formerly known as the London Bankruptcy District, and renamed since 1986 as the London Insolvency District.[10] Within the latter area all jurisdiction in insolvency matters continues to be exercised directly by the High Court.[11] In addition to exercising jurisdiction in bankruptcy, those County Courts to which this function has been allocated also enjoy jurisdiction in company winding up, and thus operate within an insolvency district properly so-called.[12] However, the basis upon which these same County Courts exercise jurisdiction in company winding up is separately prescribed by section 117(2) of the Insolvency Act 1986.[13]

The Department of Trade and Industry; The Insolvency Service; Official Receivers

In the present day the overall responsibility for the administration of

[7] Supreme Court of Judicature Act 1925, s.56 (now repealed).
[8] Companies Act 1862, s.81 (see Chap. 1 *ante*, n. 33).
[9] (5 & 6 Vict., c. 122).
[10] Insolvency Act 1986, s.374(4)(a). The former London Bankruptcy District was previously defined in s.99 of the Bankruptcy Act 1914, together with Sched. 3 thereto. See *post*, Chap. 6. The current composition of the London Insolvency District is as specified in Sched. 3 to the Civil Courts Order 1983 (S.I. 1983, No. 713), as amended.
[11] Insolvency Act 1986, s.373(3)(a).
[12] The expression was introduced for the first time by the Insolvency Act 1985, s.202(4)(a). See now Insolvency Act 1986, s.374(4)(a), and Sched. 3 to the Civil Courts Order 1983 (referred to *supra*, n. 10) as amended.
[13] See also Insolvency Act 1986, s.117(4). See generally, Chap. 21, *post*.

insolvency law in England and Wales rests with the Department of Trade and Industry.[14] Within the Department this responsibility is discharged by members of the Insolvency Service under the overall direction of the Inspector General. The latter exercises a controlling and supervisory function with regard to all official receivers and insolvency practitioners.

The statutory provisions relating to official receivers are now contained in Part XIV of the Insolvency Act 1986.[15] Section 399 of the Act indicates that the official receiver's functions are to be performed, in relation to both personal and corporate insolvency, by persons appointed for this purpose by the Secretary of State. Every person holding the office of official receiver is attached either to the High Court or to one or more specific County Courts having an insolvency jurisdiction,[16] and is, on the basis of that attachment, the person authorised to act as the official receiver in relation to every bankruptcy or winding up falling within the jurisdiction of that court.[17] Thus, whenever statutory provisions specify that some action is to be performed by the official receiver, or that some responsibility is to be assumed by him, this means in practice that the official receiver attached to the court with jurisdiction in the case in question (or one of them, if more than one official receiver is attached to that court) will undertake the requisite functions. In all cases of bankruptcy or compulsory winding up the official receiver has important investigatory functions to perform, as well as serving as trustee in bankruptcy or liquidator (as the case may be) in the event that no private sector insolvency practitioner is appointed, or in the event that an unfilled vacancy arises in that office during the course of the bankruptcy or winding up.[18]

Section 400(2) of the Insolvency Act 1986 confers upon the official receiver the status of officer of the court in relation to which he exercises the functions of his office, while subsection (3) of the same section contains an important provision whereby, if any official receiver dies or ceases to hold office or is otherwise succeeded in relation to his current functions by another official receiver, any property vested in the former official receiver in his official capacity in relation to any bankruptcy or winding up shall automatically vest in his successor without any

---

[14] This is the current name of the Department of State originally known as the Board of Trade, and referred to as such in the insolvency legislation of former times. Between 1970 and 1974, the title "Department of Trade and Industry" (D.T.I.) was first used (see S.I. 1970, No. 1537) and (S.I. 1974, No. 692). After being known as the "Department of Trade" for some time, the Department has more recently resumed its more extensive title. Since March 1990, the Insolvency Service has been constituted as an Executive Agency within the D.T.I.

[15] ss.399–401. See also Insolvency Rules 1986, (S.I. 1986, No. 1925), Pt. 10 (rr. 10.1 to 10.4 inclusive).

[16] Insolvency Act 1986, s.399(3). There are currently some five official receivers and assistants attached to the High Court. 33 provincial offices exist with an official receiver responsible for each one, albeit some official receivers have responsibility for more than one provincial office.

[17] Insolvency Act 1986, s.399(4). Official receivers may be authorised by directions made by the Secretary of State to act in relation to cases falling within the jurisdiction of another court: s.399(6)(a).

[18] See especially Insolvency Act 1986, ss.131–133, 136, 287, 288–291, 295, 300. See also Company Directors Disqualification Act 1986, ss.6, 7(1)(b).

conveyance, assignment or transfer. The Insolvency Act authorises the appointment of deputy official receivers to assist in the disposal of the business of the official receiver attached to any court, and any references within the Act to "the official receiver" consequently include a person appointed to act as his deputy.[19]

Insolvency Practitioners

In Chapters 15, 16 and 17 of the *Cork Report* a cogent case was argued for the introduction of a system of centralised, ministerial control over all persons, other than the official receiver, who are appointed to hold office in insolvency proceedings. These recommendations were implemented by the Insolvency Acts 1985–1986, the relevant provisions being now contained in Part 13 of the Act of 1986. Formerly, although a certain degree of judicial and ministerial control was exercised with respect to appointments to the offices of trustee in bankruptcy, and of liquidator in a compulsory winding up, there was a complete absence of supervision or regulation of appointments to liquidatorships in either form of voluntary winding up,[20] or in relation to appointment of receivers where this was done out of court. The *Cork Report* advocated the adoption of a standardised regulation of all insolvency practitioners from the private sector who might undergo appointment as office holder in any type of insolvency proceedings. The primary requirement for all such persons should be membership of an officially recognised and properly regulated professional body, to whose disciplinary supervision the insolvency practitioner would accordingly be subject. In the alternative, insolvency practitioners not belonging to any recognised professional body would be required to obtain a personal licence to practice by direct application to the Department of Trade. In this way, it was suggested, it would be possible to ensure a generally high level of competence, skill and integrity on the part of all who are at any time to act as liquidator or provisional liquidator, trustee in bankruptcy, administrative receiver,[21] administrator,[22] or as supervisor of a voluntary arrangement entered into by a company or by an individual.

The proposal to subject all insolvency practitioners to proper regulation also formed part of the overall strategy of the *Cork Report* aimed at eradicating a number of abusive practices, especially in relation to voluntary liquidation and also floating charge receivership. At the same

---

[19] Insolvency Act 1986, ss.401(1), (2). (This extension of the term "official receiver" does not apply to references contained in s.399(1)–(5) inclusive: s.401(2), proviso).

[20] Voluntary winding up may be either a members' or a creditors' voluntary winding up: see Chap. 18, *post*.

[21] This is the term used in the Insolvency Act for the purpose of distinguishing a receiver whose appointment results from the creation of a floating charge, as opposed to one whose appointment arises from some other type of security: see Pt. III, Chap. 1 of the Act, especially s.29(2) discussed in Chap. 14, *post*.

[22] This is the name of the office holder appointed under the administration order procedure, first established under the insolvency legislation of 1985–1986. See Pt. II of the Insolvency Act 1986, discussed in Chap. 16, *post*.

time, this reform was directed at restoring public confidence generally in the fair and effective working of the system of insolvency law.[23] It was not unreasonably suggested that the implementation of this proposal would bring about concrete improvements in the overall standards of insolvency practice, and in the way in which the various private-sector office holders discharge their functions. Indeed, many of the other reforms in the substance and procedure of insolvency law recommended by the *Cork Report* were predicated upon the assumption that office holders would in future be persons whose competence and diligence could be safely assumed to meet certain predetermined standards.[24]

The present regulation of insolvency practitioners is derived from an inbuilt requirement within the Insolvency Act whereby eligibility to act as an office holder in any species of insolvency proceedings is restricted to persons who are "qualified" within the meaning of the Act.[25] This concept of eligibility for appointment is reinforced by means of a criminal sanction, whereby any person who acts as an insolvency practitioner at a time when he is not qualified to do so commits a criminal offence of strict liability.[26] The key concept underlying the new regulation is therefore that of "acting as an insolvency practitioner" within the meaning of the Insolvency Act. The statutory definition of this concept is supplied by section 388 of the Act, which refers to the tenure of any one of a series of specified offices under the various types of insolvency proceedings governed by the Act. Thus, by section 388(1) a person acts as an insolvency practitioner in relation to a company by acting as its liquidator, provisional liquidator, administrator or administrative receiver, or as supervisor of a voluntary arrangement approved by the company under Part I of the Act. Section 388(2) provides that a person acts as an insolvency practitioner in relation to an individual by acting as his trustee in bankruptcy or interim receiver of his property[27]; as trustee under a deed of arrangement made for the benefit of his creditors[28]; as supervisor of a voluntary arrangement proposed by the debtor and approved under Part 8 of the Act; or as administrator of the insolvent estate of a deceased debtor, pursuant to section 421 of the Act. Section 388(2A), inserted by the Insolvent Partnerships Order 1994, provides that a person acts as an insolvency practitioner in relation to an insolvent partnership by acting as its liquidator, provisional liquidator or administrator, or as trustee of the partnership under Article 11 of the 1994

---

[23] See also Cmnd. 9175, Chap. 1, for the Government's endorsement of these proposals. Some of the abusive practices are graphically described in S. Aris, *Going Bust* (1985), Chaps. 6 and 7.
[24] See, *e.g.* Cmnd. 8558, paras. 508, 793, 796, 811–818, 857, 956, 961, 965, 1771, 1806 (proposed draft clause).
[25] See Insolvency Act 1986, s.230 and also ss.1(2), 2(4), 4(2), 7(5), 19(2)(a), 45(2), 62(2), 98(2)(a), 171(4), 172(5), 255(1)(d), 256(3)(a), 258(3), 273(2), 286(2), 292(2) and 298(6).
[26] *ibid.*, s.389.
[27] Under Scottish law the relevant terms are the permanent or interim trustee in the sequestration of the debtor's estate, and the trustee of a trust deed for his creditors: Insolvency Act 1986, s.388(2)(a), (b) and Bankruptcy (Scotland) Act 1985, ss.2, 3 and 59, together with Sched. 5.
[28] See n. 27 for the Scottish equivalent terms.

Order, or as supervisor of a voluntary arrangement approved in relation to it under Part I of the Act of 1986. By virtue of section 388(3) references to an individual include references to any debtor within the meaning of the Bankruptcy (Scotland) Act 1985. Therefore the concept of acting as an insolvency practitioner attaches also to persons acting in relation to insolvent partnerships, or in relation to anyone who fulfils the definition of "debtor" for the purposes of the Scottish statute.[29] Care is taken by means of sections 388(5) and 389(2) to exclude the official receiver from the meaning of Part 13 of the Insolvency Act. As explained above, the office of official receiver is held by public officials who are appointed for the purpose by the Department of Trade, and whose competence to act in insolvency matters is independently established.

The Requisite Qualification

For the purpose of being qualified to act as an insolvency practitioner within the meaning of the Insolvency Act, a person must satisfy a number of criteria, some of which are negative in character while others are positive. The negative criteria, contained in section 390, consist of a series of attributes, any one of which will of itself disqualify a person from acting as an insolvency practitioner. Thus, a person who is not an individual is disqualified from so acting,[30] with the consequence that no company or other legal person may validly act as an insolvency practitioner within the meaning of the Act. Moreover, no person is qualified to act as an insolvency practitioner at any time when he or she is an undischarged bankrupt, (or, in Scotland, a sequestrated debtor[31]), or is subject to a disqualification order made under the Company Directors Disqualification Act 1986,[32] or is a "patient" with the meaning of the English or Scottish mental health legislation, namely one who has been judicially assessed as incapable, by reason of mental disorder, of managing and administering his affairs.[33]

Other disqualifying factors mentioned in section 390 of the Insolvency Act, although expressed in negative terms, essentially refer to the need to do or to obtain certain things of a positive character in order to acquire eligibility to act as an insolvency practitioner. The first of these concerns the need to hold a valid authorisation so to act.[34] Such authorisation may be obtained in one of two alternative ways: either by virtue of membership of the recognised professional body, or by virtue of a personal authorisation granted in response to a direct application to the Department of

---

[29] See Bankruptcy (Scotland) Act 1985, ss.6, 73(1) (the definition of "a debtor", and the application thereto of the law of sequestration).
[30] Insolvency Act 1986, s.390(1).
[31] *ibid.*, s.390(4)(a).
[32] *ibid.*, s.390(4)(b). On disqualification of directors, see Chap. 27.
[33] Insolvency Act 1986, s.390(4)(c). See Mental Health Act 1983, Pt. 7; Mental Health (Scotland) Act 1984, s.125(1).
[34] Insolvency Act 1986, s.390(2).

The Requisite Qualification

Trade. In the former case, the professional body of which the insolvency practitioner is a member must be recognised for this purpose by the Department of Trade. To date, seven such professional bodies have been recognised in this way.[35] To obtain authorisation by virtue of membership of any of these bodies a person must satisfy the rules of the body in question for the purpose of gaining permission to act as an insolvency practitioner.

The alternative mode of obtaining authorisation is through application made to the Secretary of State whose decision, based upon the information which the applicant is required to furnish, together with any other information obtained from other sources, must be taken on the ground that the applicant is a fit and proper person to act as an insolvency practitioner and that he meets the prescribed requirements with respect to education and practical training and experience.[36] In determining whether an applicant is a "fit and proper person" regard may be had, *inter alia*, to whether the applicant has been convicted of any offence involving fraud or other dishonesty or violence, and to whether he has contravened any provision of domestic or foreign insolvency law or engaged in business practices which appear to be deceitful or oppressive or otherwise unfair or improper, whether unlawful or not.[37] Further matters to be taken into account include the level of professional propriety maintained in the course of operation of the applicant's past, present or future insolvency practice, with reference to the independence, integrity and professional skills with which the practice will be carried on, and also to the adequacy of the systems of control and record keeping employed.[38]

A further, and potentially wide-ranging, provision is contained in regulation 4(1)(f) of the Insolvency Practitioners Regulations 1986, whereby the authorising authority is to take into account whether the applicant, in any case where he has acted as an insolvency practitioner, has failed to disclose fully to persons affected any circumstances giving rise to an actual or apparent conflict of interest between his so acting and any personal or financial interest of his own.[39] The significance of this provision is that it furnishes an avenue of complaint for those who feel retrospectively that the office holder in any insolvency proceedings in which they have been interested parties may have transgressed the

---

[35] See Insolvency Act 1986, s.391; Insolvency Practitioners (Recognised Professional Bodies) Order 1986 (S.I. 1986, No. 1764). The bodies recognised are: the Chartered Association of Certified Accountants; the Insolvency Practitioners Association; the Institute of Chartered Accountants in England and Wales; the Institute of Chartered Accountants in Ireland; the Institute of Chartered Accountants in Scotland; the Law Society; and the Law Society of Scotland.

[36] Insolvency Act 1986, ss.392(2), (3), 393(2) together with regs. 4–9 inclusive of the Insolvency Practitioners Regulations 1990 (S.I. 1990, No. 439). A special application form, I.A. 1, is available from the Department of Trade and Industry, together with Guidance Notes for persons seeking authorisation to act as an insolvency practitioner. The fee to accompany any application is £200: Reg. 9.

[37] Insolvency Practitioners Regulations 1990, reg. 4(1)(a), (b), (c).

[38] *ibid.*, reg. 4(1)(d), (e). On the records to be kept by insolvency practitioners in relation to each case in which they act, see regs. 16–20 together with Sched. 3 to the Regulations.

[39] See also the Guidance Notes on professional conduct and ethics for persons authorised by the Secretary of State to act as insolvency practitioners, issued by the Department of Trade and Industry in April 1987, reference I.A. 4.

fundamental principle whereby he should remain at all times free from any conflict of interest which may compromise his professional independence and impartiality. A party so aggrieved may now submit a reasoned complaint to the Department of Trade, which may subsequently take the matter into account in deciding whether the person in question is a fit and proper person to act as an insolvency practitioner. Conversely, if the office holder belongs to a properly organised professional body it would be appropriate for the aggrieved party to complain in the first instance to the professional body in question. If no satisfactory outcome results from such an invocation of the supervisory and disciplinary procedures of the professional body, consideration should be given to the making of a further complaint to the Department, since it is intended to be a basic principle underlying the administration of this aspect of insolvency law that the criteria applicable to the acquisition and retention of eligibility to act as an insolvency practitioner shall be equally stringent in the case of those who do and those who do not belong to a recognised professional body.[40] If a substantial body of evidence were to accumulate, suggesting that any of the professional bodies recognised under section 391 of the Insolvency Act was failing to uphold adequate standards of discipline and accountability among its membership, the continued inclusion of the body in question upon the list of recognised professional bodies could certainly fall into question.

The final legal requirement for being qualified to act as an insolvency practitioner is that the person who is so to act must furnish security for the proper performance of his functions, in accordance with the prescribed limits applicable to the case in which he is to act.[41] The appropriate means of compliance with this requirement is by effecting a fidelity bond whereby the surety or cautioner assumes liabilities for both general and specific penalties in respect of the practitioner acting in relation to a person or company. The general penalty sum is set at £250,000 and the specific penalty is determined by means of a procedure for estimating the value of the assets of the person in relation to whom the practitioner is to act, and must be for a sum not less than that estimated value.[42] Where the practitioner subsequently forms the opinion that the value of the assets comprised in the estate is greater than the initial estimate, he must ensure that a supplementary certificate of specific penalty is issued forthwith such that the penalty sum is not less than that higher value, up to a maximum ceiling of £5,000,000.[43] Practical convenience will invariably be best served by means of a comprehensive bond incorporating a provision for the automatic extension of supplementary cover up to the prescribed maximum amount, to operate according to the circumstances of each case in which the practitioner acts.

---

[40] See Hansard, H.C. Vol. 83, cols. 527–528.
[41] Insolvency Act 1986, s.390(3); Insolvency Practitioners Regulations 1990, regs. 11–15A and Sched. 2 (as amended by S.I. 1993, No. 221).
[42] Insolvency Practitioners Regulations 1990, r. 12(1), (2) together with Sched. 2. For the retention and filing requirements attaching to fidelity bonds and to the certificate issued thereunder, see regs. 12(3), 14 and 15A.
[43] *ibid.*, reg. 12(1)(c), as amended by (S.I. 1993, No. 221).

Grant, Refusal and Withdrawal of Authorisation

Where an insolvency practitioner's authorisation to practice is enjoyed as a consequence of membership of a recognised professional body,[44] the procedural and material provisions relating to the initial acquisition of such authorisation, and of its retention or renewal thereafter, will be discovered upon consultation of the rules and regulations of the particular professional body in question. The Insolvency Act, and the secondary legislation enacted pursuant to it, only lay down detailed provisions with respect to the alternative mode of acquiring authorisation, namely by application to the Secretary of State as the competent authority to grant authorisation under section 393 of the Insolvency Act.[45] The statutory criteria upon which the grant of authorisation is to be based have been described above. If authorisation is granted, the applicant must be sent written notice of this fact, specifying the date on which the authorisation takes effect.[46] Such an authorisation, unless previously withdrawn, continues in force for the period specified in the authorisation, up to a permitted maximum of three years.[47]

While the initial processing of applications submitted under section 392 of the Insolvency Act is an administration matter, the Insolvency Act contains provisions whereby an applicant for authorisation, or a person to whom such authorisation has previously been granted, may initiate proceedings to challenge a proposed refusal or withdrawal of authorisation, as the case may be. Section 393(1) contains the basic power to refuse, as well as to grant, authorisation to act as an insolvency practitioner. Withdrawal of authorisation may be effected by the Secretary of State pursuant to section 393(4), and may be based on the grounds either that the holder of the authorisation is no longer a fit and proper person to act as an insolvency practitioner,[48] or that he has failed to comply with the legal provisions and regulations attaching to the holders of such authorisation, or that in purported compliance with those provisions he has furnished the Secretary of State with false, inaccurate or misleading information.

Where the competent authority (currently the Secretary of State) proposes to refuse an application, or to withdraw an authorisation, the applicant or holder must be given written notice to this effect, setting out particulars of the grounds on which the proposed action is to be taken and, in the case of a proposed withdrawal, the date on which it would take effect.[49] The notice must also inform the party affected of the rights exercisable under sections 395 and 396 of the Insolvency Act. Under the

---

[44] Insolvency Act 1986, ss.390(2)(a), 391.
[45] *ibid.*, ss.390(2)(b), 392.
[46] *ibid.*, s.394(1).
[47] *ibid.*, s.393(3); Insolvency Practitioners Regulations 1990, r. 10.
[48] For the meaning of this expression, see the text to nn. 36–40, *supra*, and the Insolvency Practitioners Regulations 1990, reg. 4.
[49] Insolvency Act 1986, s.394(2), (3). Notice as to the date on which authorisation is to be withdrawn is especially important in view of the criminal consequences of any infringement of s.389.

former of these sections, the person on whom notice has been served under section 394(2) may within the following fourteen days make written representations to the Secretary of State who, in making his final determination in the case, is required to have regard to such representations as may have been made. This mode of recourse is essentially designed to enable relatively minor matters of misunderstanding or irregularity to be adjusted and, if possible, rectified. It is exercisable quite separately from the more substantial procedure under section 396, which involves reference of the case to the Insolvency Practitioners Tribunal. This Tribunal, initially established by the Insolvency Act 1985,[50] is maintained in being by section 396(1) of the Act of 1986, together with Schedule 7 thereto. Any person served with a notice under section 394(2) of the Act may respond by giving written notice requiring the case to be referred to the Tribunal. A time limit of 28 days is allowed from the date of service of notice under section 394(2), but if the person concerned has initially made representations under section 395, the period of 28 days effectively begins to run from the date of service of a notice by the Secretary of State to the effect that he does not propose to alter his decision in consequence of the representations made in this manner.[51]

Where the procedure for reference to the Tribunal is invoked by means of a notice given under section 396(2), the Secretary of State is legally obliged to refer the case unless, within seven days of the giving of notice to him, he takes a decision to grant the application or, as the case may be, not to withdraw the authorisation and gives written notice of that decision to the party concerned.[52] On a reference being made to it, the Tribunal must investigate the case and thereupon report to the Secretary of State saying what would in their opinion be the appropriate decision in the matter, with supporting reasons.[53] The reasoned opinion of the Tribunal, a copy of which must be sent to the person who had invoked the reference procedure,[54] is effectively decisive of the case since section 397(1) declares it to be the duty of the competent authority to decide the matter in accordance with the Tribunal's opinion. Appeal from the Tribunal's opinion as to the appropriate decision to be taken lies, either directly or by way of case stated, to the High Court or the Court of Session, pursuant to section 13 of the Tribunals and Inquiries Act 1971.[55]

If, following the serving of notice under section 394(2), no representations or requirements for reference to the Tribunal are made within the prescribed time limits the way is open for the Secretary of State to give formal notification in writing of his refusal or withdrawal of authorisation to practice as an insolvency practitioner.[56]

[50] Insolvency Act 1985, s.8(6), Sched. 1.
[51] Insolvency Act 1986, s.396(2)(a), (b).
[52] *ibid.*, s.396(3).
[53] *ibid.*, s.397(1). On the procedure to be followed in such investigations, see paras. 3 and 4 of Sched. 7 to the Act, together with the Insolvency Practitioners' Tribunal (Conduct of Investigations) Rules 1986 (S.I. 1986, No. 952).
[54] Insolvency Act 1986, s.397(2).
[55] As amended by Sched. 14 to the Insolvency Act 1986 and by para. 5 of Sched. 1 to the Insolvency Act 1985.
[56] Insolvency Act 1986, s.398.

PART I

Personal Insolvency

Chapter 3

BANKRUPTCY LAW IN OUTLINE

This Part is concerned with the law of personal (or individual) insolvency, known traditionally by the term "bankruptcy law." As will presently emerge however the institution known as "bankruptcy" is but one of a number of possible procedures which may be resorted to when a person's affairs have attained a position of actual or near-insolvency. It is therefore more appropriate to employ the expression "personal insolvency" to refer to that branch of insolvency law which applies to individuals, in contrast to that which applies to companies and other legal persons, for which the term "corporate insolvency" will be used in Part II and elsewhere in this book. This nomenclature is also consistent with that used in the drafting of the Insolvency Act 1986, and has the further advantage of promoting the harmonisation of what have hitherto been two separate and badly co-ordinated branches of the law.[1]

Although the term "bankruptcy" is familiar to the general public, its precise, technical meaning is not well understood. In everyday usage, the terms "bankruptcy" and "bankrupt" carry heavy connotations of personal disaster accompanied by social stigma, giving rise to the supposition that bankruptcy is a fate to be avoided at all costs. To the extent that bankruptcy constitutes a species of "ultimate" remedy importing sweeping and profound consequences for the debtor and his entire property, the popular conception of bankruptcy is indeed founded upon the truth. Moreover, the very fact that bankruptcy can entail these consequences for a debtor should serve, and is indeed intended to serve, as a powerful incentive for those who avail themselves of credit to behave responsibly and honestly towards their creditors. However, the philosophical foundations of English Bankruptcy Law also include a number of beneficent purposes, based upon the proposition that the interests of the individual debtor, and also those of society at large, are ultimately best served by the provision of a legal procedure whose aim is to relieve the debtor from the cumulative burden of debts which he has no realistic prospect of repaying, and hence to offer him hope for the future in the form of a fresh start consequent upon his rehabilitation.

---

[1] See Chap. 1.

It has to be admitted that both in our past, and also in our present, insolvency law the punitive and deterrent aspects of legal policy have seemed hard to reconcile with the rehabilitative philosophy with which they are supposed to co-exist. It would certainly appear to be the case that it is not very widely appreciated that the bankruptcy law is also designed in part to protect the honest but unfortunate debtor, as well as to discipline and if necessary punish one who has been incompetent or even dishonest. To this end, the law imposes certain constraints upon the conduct of creditors and requires them to behave with a degree of propriety towards their debtors. The widespread lack of understanding about the legal parameters of the debtor-creditor relationship has many unfortunate consequences. For example, debtors who are unaware of the protection which the law affords them against improper pressures from their creditors may needlessly submit to oppressive, or even extortionate, demands accompanied by their creditors' threats to resort to bankruptcy proceedings or other legal processes. Those, again, who are unaware that it is actually open to them as debtors to take the initiative in invoking the machinery of the insolvency law in one form or another, thereby gaining the law's protective assistance, may instead succumb to despair engendered by the inexorable burden of debts by which they feel hopelessly encumbered. Conversely, it must be said that there are certain opportunities for those who are closely familiar with the insolvency law to exploit its provisions to their advantage, and at the expense of their less knowledgeable creditors. In this area of the law, the aphorism that knowledge is power has an especially truthful ring to it.

Thus, in view of the two-sided aspects of insolvency law, which may serve as boon or bane to debtor or creditor alike, it is essential that both parties to the debtor-creditor relationship should have an understanding of the law's content and operation, so that unnecessary inconvenience, hardship or even material loss may be averted on both sides. The following chapters within Part I contain detailed consideration of the successive stages of the insolvency process. Here, by way of preparation, we shall provide a brief résumé of the phases into which the law of individual insolvency may conveniently be divided, together with an indication of the relevant chapters of this book in which each topic is discussed.

In the first place it must be emphasised that bankruptcy itself, in the proper and technical sense of that term, is neither the inevitable nor indeed the appropriate fate of every individual who is approaching, or who has entered, a state of financial insolvency. Provided that the debtor's position is not already irretrievable, the feasibility of a recourse to some form of solution which falls short of a bankruptcy adjudication should preferably be explored. Of the various alternatives available, the one to be chosen for possible implementation will be largely dependent upon the elements of the particular case, and may be either formal or informal in character. The formal alternatives to bankruptcy consist of various types of voluntary arrangement concluded between a debtor and his creditors, and enjoying legally binding force. Voluntary procedures of this kind may take the form of a composition or scheme of arrangement, and may be effected either under the Insolvency Act itself,[2] or under the Deeds of Arrangement Act 1914,[3] or under the separate provisions of common law.[4] A further form of statutory procedure for the gradual payment of debts under judicial control is the county court administration order, which is available where a debtor's entire indebtedness, and also his entire estate, are of relatively modest proportions.[5] Alternatively, a variety of less formal solutions may be employed in an effort to overcome a personal liquidity crisis, such as the rescheduling of debt payments by agreement with the creditors concerned. This practice—also known as an informal moratorium—is heavily dependent upon voluntary adherence on the part of the major creditors, each of whom retains the capability of resorting to such rights and remedies against the debtor and his property as he may already enjoy. Although informal moratoria, and the general province of debt counselling, will not be examined further in this book,[6] their practical significance—and frequent utilisation in every day life—should not be underestimated. Their use invariably entails a degree of risk, and hence an exercise of judgment, on the part of the creditors involved who must assess the prospects that their debtor will succeed in retrieving a position of overall financial stability within a reasonable space of time. The creditors must also reflect upon the material consequences to themselves if the moratorium fails to attain its objective.

If efforts at achieving a non-bankruptcy solution to the debtor's predicament prove unavailing, the only practical alternative at present lies by way of a bankruptcy order, to be sought by means of a petition presented to the appropriate court. Although the *Cork Report* recommended the development of a wider range of procedures both for debt enforcement and for individual insolvency, the better to meet the needs of particular cases,[7] these proposals have not been adopted for the present. Bankruptcy therefore remains a unitary procedure applicable to all debtors regardless of the reasons for, and extent of, their financial failure.[8]

The first question to consider is whether a given person is capable of being made bankrupt,[9] a question which in turn necessitates establishing whether the person in question is "a debtor" within the meaning of the Insolvency Act. The apparently self-evident nature of this latter precondition to the application of the bankruptcy law is belied by the need to have regard, first, to the special legal rules which determine the validity

---

[2] Insolvency Act 1986, Pt. VIII: see Chap. 4, *post*.
[3] See Chap. 4, *post*.
[4] *ibid*.
[5] *ibid*.
[6] For further information on this subject see I. Ramsay (Ed.), *Debtors and Creditors* (1986), Chaps. 1, 4 and 8–11 inclusive, and also the select bibliography therein at pp. 347–352.
[7] See the *Cork Report*, Chaps. 5–6 and 10–11, especially at paras. 550 and 584–590.
[8] There is however a modified procedure—known as "summary administration"—for use in so-called "small bankruptcies," *i.e.* cases of limited indebtedness: see sections 273–275 of the Insolvency Act, discussed in Chap. 12, *post*. Specially modified procedures are also applicable in cases of insolvent partnerships, and with regard to insolvent estates of deceased persons: see sections 420 and 421 of the Act, and Chap. 12, *post*.
[9] See Chap. 5.

of any alleged "debt" for the purposes of English Law,[10] and then to the further rules which determine whether the supposed "debtor" is personally amenable to the jurisdiction of the English Bankruptcy Court,[11] and likewise whether the creditor is technically eligible to invoke the bankruptcy law in the capacity of petitioner.[12]

If the foregoing requirements as to legal standing are met, the first stage of the proceedings consists of the presentation of a bankruptcy petition either by the debtor personally or by any creditor who satisfies the qualifying criteria prescribed by the law.[13] Foremost among these criteria, in the case of a creditor's petition, is the requirement that the petitioning creditor must be owed a debt of at least £750.00 by the debtor.[14] There is a formal hearing of the petition at which the circumstances of the case are examined and the court decides upon the appropriate course of action to take. This may involve the engagement of an insolvency practitioner to explore the feasibility of concluding a voluntary arrangement as an alternative to adjudication,[15] but otherwise the court may make a bankruptcy order unless the debtor is able to show good cause why this should not be done.[16] The making of the order marks the moment of commencement of bankruptcy for the individual in question, and he will not be released from the condition and status of being a bankrupt until either he gains his discharge or the bankruptcy order itself is annulled.[17]

Following the making of a bankruptcy order the official receiver becomes receiver and manager of the bankrupt's property—known as his estate—and has the duty of protecting and preserving it for the benefit of the creditors. In due course the estate may become vested in a trustee in bankruptcy appointed by the creditors from among the ranks of the insolvency practitioners belonging to the private sector, but in the absence of such an appointment the official receiver will himself become the trustee in bankruptcy.[18]

Pending the determination of the identity of the trustee in bankruptcy the official receiver undertakes a series of duties, including the investigation of the bankrupt's conduct and affairs with a view to ascertaining the reasons for his insolvency, and for the further purpose of establishing the value and whereabouts of all assets comprised in the bankrupt's estate and the validity and size of all alleged liabilities. To facilitate this investigation the bankrupt is required to prepare a statement of his affairs in the prescribed form and submit it to the official receiver.[19] The official receiver's report of his findings becomes an important part of the record and may be referred to for a variety of further purposes, including at any

---

[10] *ibid.*
[11] *ibid.*, and also Chap. 6.
[12] Chap. 6.
[13] *ibid.*
[14] This is the amount known as "the bankruptcy level": Insolvency Act 1986, s.267(4). See Chap. 5.
[15] See Chaps. 4 and 6.
[16] See Chaps. 6 and 7.
[17] See Chap. 11.
[18] See Chap. 7.
[19] *ibid.*

time when the bankrupt's discharge is under consideration. A more immediate purpose for which the official receiver's findings are employed is in relation to his decision whether to apply for the holding of a public examination of the bankrupt at a duly convened sitting of the court. At this examination the bankrupt is examined upon oath in order to obtain and place on record the fullest possible picture of the events and circumstances which have culminated in his insolvency.[20] The official receiver's other main responsibility is to decide whether the assets are sufficient to justify the summoning of a meeting of the bankrupt's creditors for the purpose of appointing a trustee in bankruptcy. If such a meeting is summoned a trustee may be appointed and, as a further step, the creditors may appoint a committee from among themselves to serve as their representatives for the duration of the bankruptcy administration.[21]

When a trustee in bankruptcy is duly appointed the bankrupt's estate, consisting of the entirety of his property apart from those items which are specifically exempted by law,[22] vests in the trustee whose duty it is to realise the estate and to divide the proceeds amongst the creditors in accordance with the relevant legal rules.[23] The powers of the trustee are inevitably very extensive in order that he may carry out his task effectively: they include the power to trace and recover property of the bankrupt which may have passed into others' hands, and also to set aside antecedent transactions, and recover property of which the bankrupt may have purported to dispose at some time prior to his adjudication.[24]

The money realised by the trustee of the bankrupt's estate is distributable rateably amongst all those creditors who succeed in establishing that they have a quantifiable claim against the bankrupt of a kind which is legally recoverable as a bankruptcy debt. The process of establishing such indebtedness is known as "proving" for the debt in question, and those debts which are legally recoverable in bankruptcy are accordingly known as "provable" debts.[25] The payments made by the trustee to the proving creditors are known as "dividends."[26]

When the estate has been fully administered and all available assets are distributed amongst the proving creditors there remains the question of the bankrupt's discharge from bankruptcy. The effect of discharge is to release the debtor from all debts which were provable in his bankruptcy, so that if there is any balance of indebtedness remaining after deducting the dividends which have been paid by the trustee, the creditors enjoy no further right to enforce these claims by means of any legal process. In the case of those who are regarded as "first time" bankrupts, discharge may come about as an automatic process occurring by operation of law after an interval of time measured from the commencement of bankruptcy. This interval may be of either two or three years' duration, depending on the

---

[20] *ibid.*
[21] *ibid.*
[22] See Chap. 8.
[23] See Chaps. 9 and 10.
[24] Chap. 8.
[25] Chap. 9.
[26] Chap. 10.

circumstances.[27] But in the case of those whose bankruptcy commences within 15 years of any time at which they were undischarged from a previous bankruptcy, discharge must be sought by means of an application to the court, which will grant an order of discharge only after satisfying itself that it is proper to do so. In particular if the bankrupt's conduct has been unsatisfactory either prior to or since his latest adjudication, the court may at its discretion refuse him a discharge, or alternatively may impose conditions as part of the terms on which a discharge is granted.[28] It is relevant to observe that the Insolvency Act contains provisions which create a considerable number of criminal offences which may be committed by a bankrupt through acts on his part taking place before or after adjudication.[29] Not only may the bankrupt be punished in respect of any of these bankruptcy offences, but the fact of his having committed them, or any other related offences belonging to the general criminal law, will be a factor to be taken into account in determining whether and when he will obtain his discharge.

Certain special situations require separate consideration. Where the aggregate amount of the bankrupt's unsecured debts is less than £20,000 a special procedure known as summary administration may be utilised whereby a less elaborate, and hence less costly, bankruptcy administration may take place,[30] Where an insolvent debtor has died, another special procedure exists whereby his creditors may apply to have his estate administered according to the law of bankruptcy.[31] Modifications to the standard procedures are also required in relation to insolvent partnerships,[32] and special rules are also applicable where a bankruptcy order is made against a debtor who is still undischarged from a previous bankruptcy.[33] It is also relevant to give special consideration to the legal and practical consequences of the presence within a case of some foreign element of a material kind, for example if the debtor is a citizen or resident of some foreign country, or if he or she has property abroad or has incurred some debts abroad or under circumstances such that they are subject to foreign law.[34] Of interest in this context is the possibility that the United Kingdom may in due course become a party to one or more international conventions which will facilitate collaboration in cross-border insolvency matters.[35]

---

[27] Chap. 11.
[28] *ibid.*
[29] Chap. 13.
[30] Chap. 12.
[31] *ibid.*
[32] Chap. 5.
[33] Chap. 12.
[34] See Pt. III, especially Chaps. 28 and 29.
[35] See Pt. III, Chap. 31.

CHAPTER 4

VOLUNTARY PROCEDURES AND ALTERNATIVES TO BANKRUPTCY

(A) Formal Procedures

An insolvent debtor, or one whose insolvency is imminent and predictable, need not necessarily undergo adjudication as a bankrupt. Provided that the consent of his creditors, or at least a majority of them, is forthcoming it is possible for the debtor to avoid bankruptcy, at least in the short term, by means of a legally binding voluntary arrangement. Thereby, through a collectively agreed scheme for gradual discharge of outstanding liabilities, combined with a statutory moratorium against individual debt enforcement, the debtor may gain the necessary time and opportunity to overcome his financial crisis, reorganise his affairs and eventually regain a state of overall solvency. Even if this objective proves to be unattainable under the circumstances prevailing, or if the arrangement breaks down for some reason, the creditors' position will have been safeguarded to a considerable extent throughout the period for which the voluntary arrangement is in force, and a relatively smooth transition into bankruptcy can take place.

Alternatively, a voluntary arrangement may be concluded even after a bankruptcy order has been made, thus providing a route out of bankruptcy which generally offers advantages for bankrupt and creditors alike. The voluntary procedure most likely to commend itself for adoption prior to adjudication, and the only one available where a bankruptcy order has already been made, is established by Part VIII of the Insolvency Act 1986. Brief reference will however be made to other statutory and Common Law procedures later in this Chapter.

(1) Individual Voluntary Arrangements

The provisions of Part VIII of the Insolvency Act, ss.252–263 inclusive, govern the making of voluntary arrangements by individuals.[1]

[1] For background to the legislative provisions, and analysis of their practical effects, see: *Cork Report* (Cmnd. 8558), Chap. 7; Williams (1986) 2 I.L. & P. 11; Pond (1988) 4 I.L. & P. 66

Traditionally arrangements between a debtor and his creditors have taken one of two possible forms, which are respectively termed a composition and a scheme of arrangement. In the case of a composition the debtor personally retains, or resumes, control of his assets and agrees to pay a certain sum to his creditors from the proceeds accruing to him. A scheme of arrangement on the other hand involves the debtor's making over his assets to a trustee who thereafter administers them in accordance with the terms of the scheme. In either event, the requirements of the new statutory regime for voluntary arrangements introduced by the Insolvency Act are uniform, and include the important safeguard that the debtor's proposal must undergo preliminary scrutiny by a qualified insolvency practitioner, who must report to the court stating whether in his opinion the proposals should be carried forward and submitted to a meeting of the debtor's creditors for possible approval. Only if the court is satisfied that it is appropriate to proceed in this manner will steps be taken to convene a creditors' meeting, and only if at that meeting the requisite minimum majority of creditors votes to approve the proposal will the voluntary arrangement actually take effect and be legally binding upon all assenting and non-assenting creditors alike.

A further safeguard incorporated into the statutory provisions is that the insolvency practitioner who originally appraised the proposal, or some other qualified insolvency practitioner acting in his stead, must assume responsibility for the implementation of the voluntary arrangement, thus ensuring that at all stages the procedure is closely supervised by an independent and competent professional person. The corollary to this is that the role played by the court is far less active or direct than that which was assigned to it under the now abrogated procedure for concluding compositions and schemes under sections 16 or 21 of the Bankruptcy Act 1914. In view of the fundamentally altered approach embodied in the new procedure, the authority of many of the cases decided under the former legislation must be regarded as questionable from the standpoint of interpreting the new statutory provisions. This problem is considered further below.

(A) *Arrangements Prior to Adjudication*

The first steps

Where no bankruptcy adjudication has taken place the debtor may initiate a proposal for a voluntary arrangement with his creditors at any appropriate time. The first step in the procedure consists of the making of an application to the court for an interim order under section 252 of the Act. The court to which application must be made in accordance with the provisions of the Insolvency Act and the Insolvency Rules, is one in which the debtor would be entitled to present his own petition in bankruptcy, and the application must contain sufficient information to establish that it is

and 104, and (1989) 5 I.L. & P. 73; Oditah [1994] L.M.C.L.Q. 210. *cf.* Insolvency Act 1986, Pt. I (ss.1–7), which governs voluntary arrangements by companies, dealt with in Chap. 15, *post.*

brought in the appropriate court.[2] An interim order has the effect that during the period for which it is in force no bankruptcy petition relating to the debtor may be presented or proceeded with, and no other proceedings, and no execution or other legal process, may be commenced or continued against the debtor or his property without leave of the court.[3]

A moratorium is thus put into force covering the period during which the feasibility of effecting a voluntary arrangement is being actively explored. It is important to note that the moratorium is not a rigid one, however, and that creditors, and especially those who may wish to enforce rights in security over the debtor's property, may seek the leave of the court to commence or continue any action or legal process, including executions. Furthermore, by virtue of section 254 of the Act the very making of an application for an interim order enables the court at its discretion to impose a total or partial moratorium with respect to the debtor's affairs. The section provides that while such an application is pending the court may stay any action, execution or other legal process against the property or person of the debtor. Likewise, any court in which proceedings are pending against the debtor in question may either stay the proceedings or allow them to continue subject to terms. In *Smith v. Braintree District Council*,[4] the House of Lords held that the bankruptcy court's powers under section 285(1), which are exercisable when proceedings on a bankruptcy petition are pending, include the power to order a stay of proceedings for committal of the debtor for non-payment of rates. In view of the fact that the material terms of section 285(1) are identical to those of section 254(1), the same possibility appears to exist at any time when an application under section 253 for an interim order is pending. If a bankruptcy petition presented by the debtor himself is currently pending, section 253(5) forbids the making of an application for an interim order if the court has already appointed a person, pursuant to section 273 of the Act, to inquire into the debtor's affairs and to report.

The application for an interim order may be made by the debtor personally, and it is possible that the law may also permit the application to be made by a duly-appointed representative acting on the debtor's behalf.[5] The application is predicated upon the debtor's intention to make a proposal for a voluntary arrangement, and that proposal must provide for a

---

[2] Insolvency Act 1986, ss.373, 374 and 375; Insolvency Rules 1986, r. 5.5A. The topic of jurisdiction is discussed in Chap. 2, *ante* and in Chap. 6, *post*. For other procedural requirements attaching to an application for an interim order see Insolvency Rules 1986, r. 5.5.

[3] Insolvency Act 1986, s.252(2).

[4] [1990] 2 A.C. 215; [1989] 3 All E.R. 897. See Fletcher (1990) 3 *Insolvency Intelligence* 73–75. *cf. McMullen & Sons Ltd v. Cerrone* (1993) 66 P. & C.R. 351; *The Times*, June 10, 1993, where a distinction was drawn with regard to the right of a landlord to exercise the common law self-help remedy of distress for arrears of rent, notwithstanding an interim order was in force under section 252.

[5] *ibid.*, s.253(3)(b). This merely states that the application may be made "by the debtor," and hence makes no clear provision for the application to be made on the debtor's behalf. The provisions of the Insolvency Rules 1986 (rr. 5.2–5.5 inclusive) refer exclusively to "the debtor," and clearly require a high degree of involvement on his part. On the other hand, the statutory drafting is less unequivocal than that of the former s.16(1) of the Bankruptcy Act 1914, which required the debtor's proposal to be "in writing signed by him": *cf. Re Prince Blucher* [1931] 2 Ch. 70.

named person, known as the "nominee," to act in relation to the voluntary arrangement either as trustee or otherwise for the purpose of supervising its implementation.[6] The nominee must necessarily be an insolvency practitioner duly authorised to act in that capacity in relation to the debtor in question for, otherwise, it would be a criminal offence for that person to act as supervisor of the arrangement following its approval.[7] Moreover unless it can be shown that the nominee is a person duly qualified to act in this way, and that he is willing to act in relation to the proposal, the court cannot make an interim order in response to the application.[8]

In practice, therefore, a debtor who is intending to apply to the court for an interim order should first ensure that the following steps have been taken before the date of the application, even though the Act and the Rules fail to make clear provision as to the timetable to be followed. In the first place, the debtor should ensure that the proposal he intends to make is one which, as explained above, will satisfy the criteria of section 253 together with r. 5.3, so as to constitute a voluntary arrangement within the meaning of Part VIII. This is best ensured through the very obvious preliminary step of taking qualified professional advice from someone who would be eligible to act as the supervisor of any scheme which may eventually be approved. That person will inevitably require to be supplied with a full disclosure of the debtor's finances before signifying his consent to act in relation to the proposal and will moreover need to be in possession of a formal statement of the debtor's affairs when subsequently preparing the report which he will be required to submit to the court (see below). The logic of the situation therefore indicates that the preparation of a statement of affairs should be undertaken during the stage of exploratory consultations with the insolvency practitioner who is destined to become the nominee in relation to the voluntary arrangement.

In cases where it is essential to move speedily to put in place a moratorium over the debtor's affairs, the Rules are sufficiently flexible as to allow the application for an interim order to be made even before the statement of affairs is fully prepared, but the contents of the proposal for the voluntary arrangement itself must already be properly finalised, in accordance with the terms of regulation 5.3 of the Insolvency Rules, for only when the nominee has been given written notice of the proposal, accompanied by a copy of the proposal itself, may he validly signify his assent to act by causing a copy of the notice of the proposal, accompanied by a copy of the proposal itself, to be endorsed to that effect, as required by regulation 5.4. As we have seen, the nominee's assent is a *sine qua non* of the making of an interim order, and hence for all practical purposes the debtor will need to furnish the nominee with all the information which would be required for the purposes of the statement of affairs, before the application for an interim order can properly be made.

If the insolvency practitioner's engagement takes place under section 273 of the Act in consequence of the presentation of a bankruptcy petition by the debtor himself, a fully prepared statement of affairs will perforce be

---

[6] Insolvency Act 1986, s.253(1), (2).
[7] *ibid.*, s.388(2)(c), 389. See generally Pt. XIII of the Act, discussed in Chap. 2, *ante*.
[8] Insolvency Act 1986, s.255(1)(d).

available immediately, since by section 272(2) the debtor is required to lodge a statement of affairs at the time of presenting the petition. Consequently, it is both appropriate and advisable that the preparatory work which needs to take place ahead of the presentation of a debtor's own bankruptcy petition, including the preparation of a statement of affairs, should include consideration of the possibilities for concluding a voluntary arrangement. Any insolvency practitioner whose professional services are engaged by a debtor for the purpose of preparing a debtor's petition in bankruptcy should therefore have regard to the implications of section 273 and 274 of the Act, whose effects are described in Chapter 6 below.

Other matters as to which the court must be satisfied, as a precondition to being empowered to made an interim order, are that the debtor intends to make a proposal for a voluntary arrangement in conformity with the terms of section 253 of the Act; that on the day of making the application the debtor is a person able to petition for his own bankruptcy; and that no previous application has been made by the debtor for an interim order in the period of 12 months ending with that day.[9] In addition, the Rules specify in detail the required contents of the debtor's proposal, which are to include a short explanation why, in the debtor's opinion, a voluntary arrangement is desirable and also the reasons why his creditors may be expected to agree to one.[10] The proposal's prescribed contents include statements as to the debtor's assets and their estimated value, the extent of any existing securities over the assets, and the extent to which any of the assets are to be excluded from the voluntary arrangement. Similarly, the proposal must describe the nature and amount of the debtor's liabilities, and must include a description of how it is proposed to deal with preferential and secured creditors, and how any associates of the debtor who happen also to be creditors of his are to be treated under the arrangement.[11] Where these conditions are met, the court enjoys a discretion whether or not to make the order sought.[12]

A 14-day interim order can be made by the court without the attendance of either party, provided there is no bankruptcy order in existence and (so far as is known) no pending petition.[13]

Procedure following the interim order

The court must send at least two sealed copies of the interim order to the person who applied for it, and that person is responsible for serving a copy

---

[9] Insolvency Act 1986, s.255(1)(a), (b) and (c). For a debtor's eligibility to petition for his own bankruptcy, see ss.264(1)(b), 265 and 272 of the Act, *post*, Chap. 6.

[10] Insolvency Rules 1986, rr. 5.2, 5.3(1). See also r. 5.30, whereby it is made a criminal offence for the debtor to make any false representation or to commit any other fraud for the purpose of obtaining creditors' approval of his proposal.

[11] Insolvency Rules 1986, r. 5.3(2)(a)–(c). See also subparas. (d)–(p) inclusive. For the meaning of the expressions "preferential creditor" and "associate," see ss.258(7) with 386 and s.435 of the Act, dealt with in Chaps. 10 and 8 respectively, and see Appendixes I and II *post*. For procedural requirements relating to the hearing of the application, see Insolvency Rules 1986, rr. 5.5(4), 5.6.

[12] Insolvency Act 1986, s.255(2).

[13] Practice Direction (Insolvency: Voluntary Arrangement) (Bankruptcy 1/91) [1992] 1 W.L.R. 120; [1992] 1 All E.R. 678.

on the nominee.[14] The initial duration of the order is for 14 days beginning with the day after it is made, but this period may be extended by the court on the application of the nominee.[15] In consequence of the making of the order section 256 imposes a duty upon the nominee to submit a report to the court before the order ceases to have effect. This report must state whether, in the nominee's opinion, a meeting of the debtor's creditors should be summoned to consider the debtor's proposal. The nominee's professional judgment, as an insolvency practitioner, must therefore be brought to bear upon the case and his opinion will primarily be based upon the information contained in two documents which the debtor is required by law to submit to the nominee, namely a full statement of the terms of the proposed voluntary arrangement (as indicated above) and a statement of his affairs.[16] Each of these documents must be prepared and delivered to the nominee in accordance with the Rules.[17] If the nominee concludes that he cannot properly prepare his report on the basis of the information contained in these two documents he can call on the debtor to provide him with further and better particulars as to the reasons for his current financial embarrassment and such other information with respect to his affairs as the nominee thinks necessary, and the nominee must also be given access to the debtor's accounts and records.[18]

It is vitally important in keeping with the modern law's emphasis on the role of the licensed insolvency practitioner, that the nominee should exercise an independent and objective professional judgment in evaluating the debtor's proposal and in formulating his recommendations upon which the court, and subsequently the creditors, will necessarily rely in taking their respective decisions as to what course to pursue. The nominee must therefore guard against any tendency to suspend critical judgment in relation to the affairs and conduct of the debtor on whose behalf he has been retained to act, and be mindful of the wider responsibilities which he is required to discharge at this stage.[19]

The nominee's report is required to be delivered to the court not less than two days before the interim order ceases to have effect.[20] If the nominee fails to submit any report, the debtor may apply to the court for an order replacing the nominee with some other qualified insolvency practitioner, and extending or renewing the interim order for a specified period of time.[21] If the nominee's report is to the effect that a meeting of creditors should be summoned, his report must be accompanied by his comments on the debtor's proposal and must state the time, place and date

---

[14] Insolvency Rules 1986, r. 5.7(1).
[15] ss.255(6), 256(4) of the Act.
[16] *ibid.*, s.256(2).
[17] See Insolvency Rules 1986, rr. 5.2–5.4 inclusive, and r. 5.8. Although the Rules contain no specific Form for use in preparing a statement of affairs in relation to a proposed voluntary arrangement, the example of Form 6.28, for use in relation to a debtor's petition for bankruptcy, will serve as a convenient model.
[18] Insolvency Rules 1986, r. 5.9.
[19] *Re A Debtor (No. 222 of 1990)* [1992] BCLC 137; (the same) *(No. 2), ex p. Bank of Ireland and others* [1993] BCLC 233.
[20] *ibid.*, r. 5.10(1).
[21] Insolvency Act 1986, s.256(3). The debtor must give at least seven days' notice of such application to the existing nominee: Insolvency Rules 1986, r. 5.11.

of the proposed meeting.[22] Conversely, the nominee may apply to the court for the discharge of the interim order if the debtor fails to supply him with both documents as required by section 256(2), or if the nominee concludes, for reasons which must be openly stated, that it would be inappropriate to summon a meeting of creditors to consider the proposal.[23]

Because the interim order establishes a moratorium which blocks the bringing of alternative proceedings against the debtor—including a bankruptcy petition—it is essential that matters progress as expeditiously as possible once the interim order is made. It would be intolerable if the preliminary stages of a voluntary arrangement could be employed as a device for holding creditors at bay through the debtor's procrastination or tardiness. Therefore, it has rightly been held that the court may subsequently refuse to continue an interim order if it is satisfied that the creditors' meeting will serve no useful purpose because there is a strong probability that the debtor will be unable to obtain a majority vote in favour of his proposals, or that the continuation of the interim order will delay and unduly prejudice the creditors' rights and interests.[24]

The creditors' meeting

If the nominee's report to the court is to the effect that a meeting of creditors should be summoned, section 257(1) provides that the nominee[25] must proceed to summon that meeting at the time, date and place proposed by him, unless the court otherwise directs. The court thus enjoys the right to override the nominee's judgment as to the worthwhileness of convening a meeting, but in the main it is probable that the exercise of this power will be addressed to the substitution of a more convenient time, date or venue for the holding of the meeting. The Rules make it clear that the court's consideration of the nominee's report is to take the form of a hearing at which the same persons as received notice of the preceding hearing of the application for the interim order may once again appear or be represented.[26] The persons to be summoned to the meeting are every creditor of whose claim and address the nominee is aware. The meeting should be held not less than 14, nor more than 28 days from that on which the nominee's report was filed in court.[27] Notices convening the meeting must be sent to all the creditors entitled to attend it, at least 14 days before the day fixed for it to be held.[28] The notice of the meeting must be accompanied by a copy of the debtor's proposal, a copy or

---

[22] Insolvency Act 1986, s.256(1)(b); Insolvency Rules 1986, r. 5.10(3). See also r. 5.14(1), (2) concerning the requirements for selection of venue and time of commencement of the meeting.
[23] Insolvency Act 1986, s.256(6); Insolvency Rules 1986, r. 5.10(3). *cf. Re A Debtor (No. 2389 of 1989)* [1991] Ch. 326, in which the debtor's failure to put all the relevant facts before the creditors was regarded as a strong reason for allowing a creditor to petition for a bankruptcy order.
[24] *Re Cove (a debtor)* [1990] 1 All E.R. 949.
[25] Or his replacement, if one has been appointed under s.256(3)(a).
[26] Insolvency Rules 1986, r. 5.12(1). See also r. 5.12(2) concerning the issue of sealed copies of the court's order, and giving of notice of the making of the order.
[27] Insolvency Rules 1986, r. 5.13(1).
[28] *ibid.*, r. 5.13(2).

summary of the statement of affairs, and the nominee's comments on the proposal.[29]

The meeting is required to be chaired by the nominee, but if for any reason he is unable to attend he may nominate another person to act in his place provided that the person in question is also a person qualified to act as an insolvency practitioner in relation to the debtor, or is an employee of the nominee or his firm and is experienced in insolvency matters.[30] Although there is no formal requirement that the debtor must attend the meeting, it is obviously desirable that he should be present if at all possible, not only for the purpose of answering any questions put by his creditors but also because his consent will be necessary if his proposal is to be adopted in a modified form. In principle every creditor who was given notice of the meeting is entitled to vote thereat and may do so by proxy if unable to attend in person.[31] For any resolution to pass approving the proposal or any modification of it there must be a majority in excess of three quarters in value of the creditors present in person or by proxy and voting on the resolution.[32] In relation to any other resolution the requisite majority must be in excess of one half of those voting on the resolution.[33] It is therefore necessary, before the meeting proceeds to consider and vote upon any resolutions, to establish the respective amounts of the debts attributable to each creditor who is entitled to vote. In this instance, when no adjudication has taken place, the votes are to be calculated according to the amount of the debt as at the date of the meeting.[34] A creditor must not vote in respect of a debt for an unliquidated sum, or any debt whose value is not ascertained, unless the chairman agrees to put an estimated minimum value upon the debt for voting purposes.[35] There are conflicting decisions at first instance regarding the approach to be adopted in a case where there is an irreconcilable difference between the chairman and a creditor as to the appropriate value to be ascribed to the latter's claim. The preferable view, it is submitted, is that of Knox J, whose reading of the phrase "agrees to put" placed emphasis on the last two words, thus narrowing the required area of agreement between chairman and creditor to the former's undertaking *to put* an estimated value on the claim. This has the consequence of depriving the creditor of any ground for avoiding becoming bound by the arrangement if it is eventually approved by the creditors, unless it can be shown that the chairman failed to exercise a genuine, professional judgment in arriving at his estimate of the claim's value. The alternative, and less satisfactory, approach was that of Ferris J. in a case involving a company voluntary arrangement (where, however, the same phrase is employed in the corresponding provision of the Insolvency Rules). The learned judge chose to place emphasis on the word "agrees", so as to import a requirement that there must be some element of bilateral

---

[29] *ibid.*, r. 5.13(3).
[30] *ibid.*, r. 5.15.
[31] *ibid.*, rr. 5.14(3), 5.17(1), 5.18(1). See also r. 5.16 limiting the chairman's powers in relation to the use of any proxy held by him. For cases of notice not received, or sent to the wrong address, see *Re A Company (No. 003932 of 1995), The Times,* July 25, 1995; *Re A Debtor (No. 64 of 1992)* [1994] BCC 55.
[32] Insolvency Rules 1986, r. 5.18(1).
[33] *ibid.*, r. 5.18(2).
[34] *ibid.*, r. 5.17(2).
[35] *ibid.*, r. 5.17(3).

concurrence between the chairman and the creditor as to the amount of the valuation itself: a unilateral determination of value by the chairman alone would then not suffice to render the creditor eligible to vote in respect of the amount of value put on the debt thereby (it is submitted) bestowing an unwarranted degree of bargaining power upon the creditor.[36]

It is the chairman's function to admit or reject a creditors' claim regarding his entitlement to vote, subject to the right of appeal to the court against the chairman's decision. Such an appeal must be made within 28 days of the chairman's report of the outcome of the meeting being given to the court under section 259 of the Act.[37] If any dispute arises as to voting entitlement the meeting may proceed with its business with the disputed claim duly marked as such by the chairman, with the consequence that if the creditor's vote is subsequently declared invalid the court may either affirm the outcome of any voting (where it can be shown that the invalid vote has made no difference to the outcome), or else order another meeting to be summoned.[38] The Rules further provide that a creditor's vote is to be left out of account in respect of any claim, or part thereof, of which written notice was not given at or before the meeting to the chairman or nominee, or where the claim is wholly or partly secured.[39]

It is for the creditors' meeting, voting in accordance with the foregoing provisions, to decide whether to approve the proposed voluntary arrangement.[40] The meeting may approve the proposal in its original form or with modifications, but in the latter instance the debtor must consent to each modification.[41] The permissible modifications include the substitution of another qualified insolvency practitioner to undertake the functions originally intended to be performed by the nominee. However, under no circumstances may the modifications be such that the proposal ceases to comply with the overall definition of a voluntary arrangement contained in section 253 of the Act.[42] Moreover no proposal or modification may be approved which affects the right of a secured creditor of the debtor to enforce his security, unless the creditor concerned actively concurs in this.[43] Similarly, without the open concurrence of the preferential creditor concerned, no proposal or modification may be approved under which any preferential debt would effectively be deprived of its preferential status, either in relation to debts of non-preferential status or in relation to other preferential debts.[44] If the original terms of the proposal contain no reference to the possibility that the debtor may become entitled to property

---

[36] *Re A Debtor (No. 162 of 1993) Doorbar v. Alltime Securities Ltd* [1994] BCC 994 (Knox J) *cf. Re Cranley Mansions Ltd, Saigol v. Goldstein* [1994] BCC 576 (Ferri's J.) These cases are also discussed in Chap. 15, *post*.

[37] Insolvency Rules 1986, r. 5.17(4), (5) and (8).

[38] *ibid.*, r. 5.17(6), (7). Note also para. 9. See also *Re A Debtor (No. 222 of 1990)* [1992] BCLC 137.

[39] Insolvency Rules 1986, r. 5.18(3)(a), (b). See also subparagraph (c) in relation to debts secured by a bill of exchange or promissory note.

[40] Insolvency Act 1986, s.258(1).

[41] *ibid.*, s.258(2).

[42] *ibid.*, s.258(3).

[43] *ibid.*, s.258(4).

[44] *ibid.*, s.258(5), (7). For preferential debts, see s.386, discussed in Chap. 10, *post*. See also text to n. 11, *above*.

at a future time while the voluntary arrangement is still in force, it may be prudent for the creditors to seek to have the terms of the proposal modified so that after-acquired property coming to the debtor within a specified period can be added to the assets which are to be made available under the composition or scheme.

The Rules permit the adjournment of the creditors' meeting from time to time, during the course of attempts to obtain agreement on the proposal.[45] The maximum interval allowed for the holding of adjournments is 14 days from the day on which the meeting was originally held, and if no agreement can be obtained by that stage the proposal is deemed to be rejected.[46]

After the creditors' meeting: effect of approval

Within four days after the conclusion of the creditors' meeting, the chairman of the meeting must report the result of it to the court, and thereafter give notice of the result to the Secretary of State, for entry in the register of individual voluntary arrangements which he is required to maintain.[47] If the report is to the effect that the meeting has declined to approve the debtor's proposal the court may discharge any interim order which remains in force in relation to the debtor,[48] who in consequence ceases to enjoy the benefit of the statutory moratorium already described. Alternatively, where the creditors' meeting approves the voluntary arrangement, either with or without modifications, section 260(2) of the Act declares that the approved arrangement takes effect as if made by the debtor at the meeting, and binds every person who had due notice of, and was entitled to vote at, the meeting as if he were a party to the arrangement, whether or not he was present or represented at the meeting.[49] Moreover by virtue of section 260(5), unless the court otherwise orders, any bankruptcy petition against the debtor which was previously pending, and on which proceedings were stayed while the interim order was in force, is deemed to have been dismissed simultaneously with the expiry of the interim order itself. Consequently an approved voluntary arrangement constitutes an effective bar to the enforcement of any debt by a creditor who is so bound, and may be pleaded as a good defence to any subsequent action. By the same token, any agreement entered into before the voluntary arrangement was concluded, whereby the debtor promised to pay any creditor in full, even if in return for further consideration such as the granting of fresh credit, will be unenforceable as being inconsistent with good faith.[50] However, this does not affect the rights of a secured

---

[45] Insolvency Rules 1986, r. 5.19.
[46] *ibid.*, r. 5.19(2), (3), (5).
[47] Insolvency Act 1986, s.259(1); Insolvency Rules 1986, rr. 5.22, 5.23 and 5.24.
[48] Insolvency Act 1986, s.259(2).
[49] *cf. Re Cranley Mansions Ltd, Saigol v. Goldstein* (*supra*, n. 36): if the claim of any creditor who is not bound by the arrangement turns out to be for a substantial amount, the viability of the arrangement itself may be fatally compromised. See also *Re A Debtor (No. 64 of 1992)*, [1994] 2 All E.R. 177; [1995] BCC 55.
[50] *cf. Slater v. Jones* (1873) L.R. 8 Ex. 186; *Flint v. Barnard* (1888) 22 Q.B.D. 90 (C.A.); *Re Andrews* (1881) 18 Ch.D. 464. Contrast *Jakeman v. Cook* (1878) 4 Ex.D. 26, where the debtor's promise was made *after* discharge, and was supported by fresh consideration.

creditor to realise his security in the usual way unless these rights have been validly altered in accordance with the terms of section 258(4) of the Act.

The decision of the creditors' meeting is subject to challenge during the period of twenty eight days beginning with the day on which the chairman's report is made to the court.[51] During this period either the debtor, or any person who was (or who was declared to be) entitled to vote at the meeting, or the nominee or his replacement, may apply to the court on one or both of the grounds specified in section 262(1), namely that the voluntary arrangement approved by the meeting unfairly prejudices the interests of a creditor or of the debtor, or that there has been some material irregularity at or in relation to the meeting. As a matter of construction, it has been held that "unfair prejudice" for the purposes of section 262 is a concept confined to unfairness brought about by the terms of the voluntary arrangement itself, and with respect to relationships between the creditors themselves. If the true basis of a creditor's objection is that votes have been cast in respect of debts whose validity is in question, the proper basis on which to proceed is to appeal against the chairman's decision on entitlement to vote, as is permitted by rule 5.17(5) of the Insolvency Rules.[52] Alternatively, it may be possible to base an appeal on section 262(1)(b), by alleging that there has been some material irregularity at or in relation to the meeting. To be successful, however, the applicant would need to show that, but for the vote or votes of the persons improperly allowed to participate, the outcome of the decision would have been different, for otherwise the irregularity cannot be correctly described as "material".[53]

If the court is satisfied that the applicant's allegation is well-founded it may either revoke or suspend any approval given by the meeting, or give direction for the summoning of a fresh meeting.[54] The court may also give supplemental directions with respect to anything done since the meeting under any voluntary arrangement which was then approved.[55] Unless a successful challenge of the meeting's decision is pursued under section 262, the fact that any irregularity has occurred at or in relation to a creditors' meeting does not *per se* serve to invalidate an approval given at the meeting.[56]

The supervisor of the arrangement

Where a voluntary arrangement takes effect in accordance with the provisions explained above the person who at the time in question is carrying out the functions conferred upon the nominee becomes known as the supervisor of the voluntary arrangement.[57] The task of implementation of the arrangement will thus be undertaken by a qualified insolvency

---

[51] Insolvency Act 1986, s.262(2), (3).
[52] *Re A Debtor (No. 259 of 1990)* [1992] 1 W.L.R. 226. (Hoffmann J.)
[53] *ibid.*
[54] Insolvency Act 1986, s.262(4), (5) and (6). See also Insolvency Rules 1986, r. 5.25. *cf. Re Naeem, a Bankrupt (No. 18 of 1988)* [1990] 1 W.L.R. 48.
[55] Insolvency Act 1986, s.262(7).
[56] *ibid.*, s.262(8).
[57] *ibid.*, s.263(1), (2).

practitioner, without any further involvement of the court unless its jurisdiction under section 263 of the Act is brought into operation by any party possessed of the requisite standing to invoke it. The terms of section 263(3) are widely drawn, and allow application to be made to the court by the debtor, or any of his creditors or *any other person* (emphasis added). The basis for the making of application is that the applicant is dissatisfied by any act, omission or decision of the supervisor, and the court's powers on such an application are either to confirm, reverse or modify the supervisor's act or decision, or to give him directions, or to make any other order at its discretion.[58] Section 263(4) also enables the supervisor himself to apply to the court for directions at any time. The court is also empowered to make an order appointing a duly-qualified person to be supervisor, either in substitution for an existing supervisor or to fill any vacancy, or to augment the number of supervisors.[59]

Accountability of the supervisor

The modern law of voluntary arrangements is constructed upon the principle that the procedure should wherever possible be placed under the control of a properly qualified insolvency practitioner, who can be relied upon to administer it competently without close or constant supervision by the court or by the Insolvency Service. Nevertheless, as seen above, a supervisor's acts and decisions may be challenged before the court under section 263, and in the event of seriously unsatisfactory performance of his functions a supervisor may be removed and replaced. In a more routine fashion, the supervisor is made accountable to the Secretary of State, who is empowered to require him at any time during the course of the voluntary arrangement, or after its completion, to produce his records and accounts for inspection.[60] Where the voluntary arrangement authorises or requires the supervisor to carry on the debtor's business or to trade on his behalf or in his name, or in other ways to realise or administer assets belonging to him, the supervisor must also keep accounts and records of all his acts and dealings and, at least annually, send copies of an abstract of his receipts and payments together with a progress report to the court, the debtor and all creditors who are bound by the arrangement.[61]

Completion of the arrangement

When the terms of the arrangement have been completely implemented the supervisor must, within a maximum of 28 days, send to the debtor and to all creditors who are bound by the arrangement a notice that it has been fully implemented, together with a report summarising all receipts and payments made in pursuance of the arrangement and explaining any difference between the proposal as approved by the creditors' meeting and the actual implementation.[62] Copies of the notice and the report must also

---

[58] *ibid.*, s.263(3).
[59] *ibid.*, s.263(5), (6).
[60] Insolvency Rules 1986, r. 5.27.
[61] *ibid.*, r. 5.26. See also r. 5.27(1)(b).
[62] *ibid.*, r. 5.29(1), (2). The court may extend the period of 28 days: *ibid.*, subpara. (4).

be sent to the Secretary of State and to the court.[63] There are no further statutory provisions to regulate this concluding stage of the voluntary arrangement, nor is there any prescribed form for the final notice of implementation.[64] There are no provisions requiring the supervisor to convene a final meeting of creditors, nor to regulate the manner in which the supervisor is to obtain his release from office.[65] A supervisor who entertains any doubts as to the appropriate way to proceed at this juncture may always apply to the court for directions under section 263(4) of the Act.

Default in connection with the voluntary arrangement

Although, as we have seen, a voluntary arrangement which has been accepted by creditors is binding upon all assenting and non-assenting creditors alike, the law's mantle of protection is kept in place only so long as the debtor continues to comply with his obligations under the arrangement. Therefore, by section 264(1)(c) provision is made for a bankruptcy petition to be presented against a debtor either by the supervisor of a voluntary arrangement which has been accepted under Part VIII of the Act, or by any person other than the debtor himself who is for the time being bound by the arrangement. Where a petition is presented under section 264(1)(c) however, the further provisions of section 276 of the Act become applicable. That section stipulates that the court must not make a bankruptcy order on such a petition unless it is satisfied as to at least one of three matters. The first two of these are that the debtor has failed to comply with his obligations under the voluntary arrangement, or that information which was false or misleading in any material particular, or which contained material omissions, was contained in any statement of affairs or other document supplied by the debtor under Part VIII of the Act to any person, or was otherwise made available by the debtor to his creditors at or in connection with a meeting summoned under that Part. The third, alternative basis on which the court is permitted to proceed to make a bankruptcy order is where the debtor has failed to do all such things as have been reasonably required of him by the supervisor of the arrangement. Thus the debtor is subject to a powerful sanction in the event of his failure to adhere to the terms of the arrangement, or to collaborate in a satisfactory manner with the supervisor, or where it subsequently transpires that he has succumbed to the temptation to mislead or deceive his creditors in an effort to gain their consent to his proposal.

(B) *Arrangements Subsequent to Adjudication*

The law allows a debtor to submit a proposal for a voluntary arrangement even after he has undergone adjudication as a bankrupt.[66] In this

---

[63] Insolvency Rules 1986, r. 5.29(3).
[64] *cf.* ss.299 and 331 of the Act, and Chap. 10 of Pt. 6 of the Insolvency Rules 1986, which apply to the trustee in bankruptcy.
[65] See n. 64 above.
[66] Section 253(3)(a) of the Act. See also Insolvency Rules 1986, r. 5.1(2).

instance if the proposal is successful the arrangement will provide the bankrupt with an expeditious way of putting an end to his status as a bankrupt, with all the disabilities and inconveniences which that status entails. Under section 261 of the Act the court is empowered to annul the bankruptcy order following the creditors' approval of the debtor's proposal for a voluntary arrangement. Hence this procedure not only offers the distinct attraction that the bankrupt will be spared from undergoing the full rigours of the bankruptcy administration as it progresses through its successive stages, but it also carries the prospect that the bankrupt can obtain an annulment of the bankruptcy order without being required to make provision for all the bankruptcy debts to be paid in full, as would be necessary for the purposes of an annulment sought under section 282(1)(b) of the Act.[67]

In most respects the procedure to be followed in the case of a proposal for a voluntary arrangement made subsequently to the debtor's adjudication is the same as that which has been described above in the case where the proposal precedes the making of a bankruptcy order. However, certain provisions in Part VIII of the Act and in the Rules apply exclusively where the debtor is an undischarged bankrupt at the time when the proposal is made, and it is those provisions which will be discussed here.

The first steps

The procedure is initiated, as already described in section (A) above, by means of an application to the appropriate court for an interim order under section 252 of the Act. Section 253(3)(a) provides that where the debtor is an undischarged bankrupt the application for the order may be made by the debtor himself or by his trustee in bankruptcy, or by the official receiver. However, an application under that subsection cannot be made unless the debtor has given notice of his proposal for a voluntary arrangement to the official receiver and, if there is one, to his trustee in bankruptcy.[68] The applicant must give at least two days' notice of the hearing of the application to whichever of the relevant three parties—namely the bankrupt, the official receiver and the trustee in bankruptcy—is not himself the applicant, and also to the nominee who has agreed to act in relation to the proposal.[69]

Procedure following the interim order

The additional or alternative provisions which apply at this stage are that, if the debtor has already delivered a statement of affairs in fulfilment of the requirements of his bankruptcy[70] he need not deliver a further statement unless the nominee so requires, with a view to supplementing or amplifying that which has already been submitted.[71] In this instance when

---

[67] See Chap. 11, *post*.
[68] s.253(4) of the Act. See also Insolvency Rules 1986, r. 5.4(5).
[69] Insolvency Rules 1986, r. 5.5(4)(a), (c).
[70] s.272 or s.288 of the Act.
[71] Insolvency Rules 1986, r. 5.8(1).

the nominee has prepared his report on the debtor's proposal, as required by section 256(1) of the Act, he must send copies of the proposal and his report and comments thereon, and also a copy or summary of the debtor's statement of affairs, not only to the court (as explained above) but also to the official receiver and the trustee (if any).[72]

The creditors' meeting

Where the debtor is an undischarged bankrupt the creditors who are entitled to be summoned to the meeting under section 257 of the Act include every person who is a creditor of the bankrupt in respect of a bankruptcy debt, and every person who would be such a creditor if the bankruptcy had commenced on the day on which notice of the meeting was given.[73] The effect of the latter proposition is that all persons who have become creditors of the debtor since the date on which the bankruptcy order was made, and who would otherwise not be eligible to lodge proof in that bankruptcy,[74] are nevertheless made competent parties to a voluntary arrangement effected as a means of concluding the bankruptcy. This is a point of some importance in view of the fact that, as persons who have received notice of and who were entitled to vote at the creditors' meeting, all post-adjudication creditors will be bound by the arrangement if it is duly approved by the meeting. Moreover while the interim order remains in force creditors belonging to this group are subject to the effects of the moratorium imposed by section 252(2).

Effect of approval of proposal

Section 261 applies exclusively to cases where a creditors' meeting approves a voluntary arrangement which has been proposed by a debtor who is an undischarged bankrupt. The section confers authority upon the court to do either or both of two things, namely to annul the bankruptcy order, and to give such directions with respect to the conduct of the bankruptcy and the administration of the bankrupt's estate as it thinks appropriate for facilitating the implementation of the approved voluntary arrangement. Thus appropriate directions may be given by the court to ensure an orderly transfer of property from the trustee in bankruptcy to the supervisor of the arrangement, and to ensure a smooth transition from one procedure to the other in conjunction with the annulment of the bankruptcy order. However, in order to allow proper time for any challenge under section 262 to the decision of the creditors' meeting, provision is made by section 261(2) preventing the court from annulling the bankruptcy order until after the elapse of the 28 day period, commencing with the day on which the chairman's report of the meeting is made to the court, or while any such challenge is pending or is subject to further appeal.

The fact that the exercise of the power to annul the bankruptcy order is

---

[72] *ibid.*, r. 5.10(5).
[73] s.257(3) of the Act.
[74] For commencement of bankruptcy and proof of debts, see Chaps. 7 and 9 respectively.

made a matter for the court's discretion under section 261(1)(a) is reminiscent of the former position under section 21(2) of the Bankruptcy Act 1914. Under the previous case law, it was established that the court's exercise of this discretion would be influenced by such factors as the debtor's conduct prior to and during the bankruptcy in question, as determined from reports of the official receiver or from other sources. Annulment of the bankruptcy would not therefore take place as a matter of course, but the court would have regard to the creditors' interests, and also to the public interest and commercial morality in general, when reaching its decision.[75]

If the bankruptcy is annulled section 282(4) preserves the validity of any sale or other disposition of property, or payment made by or under the authority of the official receiver or trustee in bankruptcy prior to the annulment. Any of the bankrupt's property which is vested in his trustee in bankruptcy at the time of the annulment will automatically revert to the bankrupt unless the court makes an express appointment in favour of some other person.[76]

A voluntary arrangement approved in respect of an undischarged bankrupt has the usual effect of binding assenting and non-assenting creditors alike. Therefore the annulment of the bankruptcy does not have the consequence that the non-assenting creditors become free to enforce their claims by other methods, and indeed they may be legally restrained from any attempt to do so, since their claims are not revived by virtue of the annulment of the bankruptcy.[77] Any rights of set-off which could have been invoked by those indebted to the bankrupt, if the bankruptcy had proceeded, will presumably continue, as under the former law, to be invocable against the supervisor of the voluntary arrangement in any action he may bring to recover money or property to which the debtor's estate is entitled.[78]

(C) *The Current Validity of Cases Decided under Earlier Legislation*

The voluntary arrangement procedure contained in Part VIII of the Insolvency Act 1986 was in many respects an innovation, and differs both in form and in substance from the previous procedures for effecting compositions and arrangements which were contained in the now-repealed provisions of former Bankruptcy Acts. It would therefore be unsafe to approach any case decided under the provisions of the former legislation on the footing that it is still good law and would necessarily be followed by a court of the present day when construing or applying the provisions of the Insolvency Act. However, certain fundamental principles, and considerations of policy, remain unaltered by the transformations in law and procedure brought about by the Insolvency Acts of 1985 and 1986. Among these are the principle of equal treatment

---

[75] *Re Sullivan and Hughes* (1904) 20 T.L.R. 393, *cf. Re Beer* [1903] 1 K.B. 628 (C.A.).
[76] s.282(4)(b) of the Act. *cf. Flower v. Lyme Regis Corporation* [1921] 1 K.B. 488 (C.A.).
[77] *cf. Re Chidley* (1875) 1 Ch.D. 177.
[78] *cf. West v. Baker* (1875) 1 Ex.D.44.

of creditors (*par est condicio creditorum*) and the necessity of ensuring the maintenance of public trust in the proper administration of legal procedures associated with debt and insolvency.

Under the new voluntary arrangement, the nominee (and in due course the supervisor) has a vital part to play, while the role of the court is less prominent than under the old law in that it does not have to give active approval of an arrangement after its acceptance by creditors. However the court retains ultimate control over the procedure through the various channels provided by sections 260(5), 262 and 263. Under the latter two sections the court is only enabled to exercise its controlling powers if properly seized by a qualified party. Section 260(5) on the other hand appears to enable the court to keep alive bankruptcy proceedings which have been stayed during the currency of the interim order made under section 252, which it would presumably do where the terms or circumstances of the arrangement gave some cause for concern.

In the light of the foregoing, it seems appropriate to recall certain aspects of the former case law relating to compositions and arrangements which may provide help by way of analogy in the approach to construction of the new law. This is a matter of particular concern to those, such as the creditors, the debtor or the nominee/supervisor, with whom the initiative principally rests in utilising the procedures for which sections 262 and 263 make provision.

In former times the bankruptcy courts were especially alert to the possibility that the creditors might have been induced to assent to an arrangement the terms of which were ultimately not in their own best interests. In theory this danger has been countered under the modern law by the requirement that a qualified insolvency practitioner, as the nominee, must evaluate and in effect endorse the terms of the debtor's proposal before they are put to the creditors. It must be remembered however that the nominee's involvement comes about through his being approached by or on behalf of the debtor, with whom the initiative consequently resides in selecting whom to approach in this capacity. Hence, the possibility cannot altogether be excluded that a person may be selected as nominee on the basis of an acquired reputation for helping debtors to resolve their financial predicaments on relatively favourable terms. Equally, it must be borne in mind that there is always a possibility that some of the creditors may be party to an impropriety of some kind, whether aimed at gaining a private advantage for themselves, or in conjunction with the debtor.[79] Therefore the somewhat paternalistic judicial views expressed in the old cases should not be treated as wholly redundant or inapposite under modern conditions. If the creditors can be shown to have assented to an arrangement in the unfounded belief that they would enjoy adequate control over the debtor, whereas in reality their presumed rights would be unenforceable, this would surely be a proper ground on which to challenge the meeting's decision under section 262.[80] Similarly, it is evident from the provisions of Part VIII of the Act, taken as a

---

[79] cf. *Bissell v. Jones* (1868) L.R. 4 Q.B. 49.
[80] cf. *Re Aylmer* (1887) 20 Q.B.D. 258 (C.A.).

whole, that the general principle of equality of treatment for all creditors is to be respected, whilst in the case of preferential or secured creditors section 258(4) and (5) carefully preserve their legitimate expectations, to the extent that these can only be modified with the concurrence of the creditor in question.

It ought therefore to be a sustainable ground of objection that the terms of an arrangement confer a disproportionate benefit upon one or more creditors in comparison with the others, or that there has been a secret bargain made by the debtor, or by a third party with the debtor's knowledge, whereby certain creditors are to enjoy favoured treatment.[81] In essence, the acquisition of a collateral advantage is a fraud upon the other creditors, and it was held in the past that any money paid under such an illicit agreement was recoverable for the benefit of the creditors generally, and that the agreement itself, if executory, was unenforceable.[82] The practice of effectively "bribing" some of the creditors by means of secret promises of advantages was formerly held to vitiate the entire assent of creditors to any composition or scheme, even where it could be shown that the requisite majority for approval could have been obtained even without counting the "tainted" votes.[83] Similarly, the tactic of "buying up" a debt for the purpose of obtaining eligibility to vote in favour of acceptance of a debtor's proposal was traditionally considered to amount to a fraudulent malpractice whose effect was to taint the entire proceedings and render them voidable at the suit of any non-assenting creditor.[84] It is submitted that the same principle should be upheld under the present law.

It used formerly to be the case, when the law required the court's positive approval of a composition or scheme, that such approval would be refused if the court concluded that the terms of the arrangement, or the accompanying circumstances, raised more general questions of public interest or commercial morality such that it would be against public policy to enable the debtor to avert bankruptcy, and the rigorous enquiry into his conduct and affairs which this would entail.[85] The altered provisions of the present law afford a greatly diminished scope for the court to impose the same type of discretionary control over the use of voluntary arrangements as an alternative to bankruptcy. However, in appropriate circumstances a qualified party, such as a creditor, could perhaps advance the argument, in an application to the court under section 262,[86] that the voluntary arrangement approved at the creditors' meeting will unfairly prejudice his interest because the expected rate of repayment of debt under the arrangement is significantly less than that which might result from a full and effective use of the powers of a trustee in bankruptcy to trace and recover the debtor's assets and to bring about the avoidance of antecedent

---

[81] cf. *Re Milner* (1885) 15 Q.B.D. 605, (C.A.); *Re Pilling* [1903] 2 K.B. 50, (C.A.); contrast *Re Utley* (1901) 17 T.L.R. 349; *Re E.A.B.* [1902] 1 K.B. 457 (C.A.).
[82] *McKewan v. Sanderson* (1875) L.R. 20 Eq. 65.
[83] *Re Baum* (1878) 7 Ch.D. 719 (C.A.).
[84] *Re Burrs & Co. ex p. Fore Street Warehouse Co. Ltd* (1874) 30 L.T. 624.
[85] cf. *ex p. Clark* (1884) 13 Q.B.D. 426 (C.A.); *Re Rogers* (1884) 13 Q.B.D. 438; *Re Burr* [1892] 2 Q.B. 467 (C.A.); *Re E.A.B.* [1902] 1 K.B. 457, 466 per Vaughan Williams, L.J.; *Re Bottomley* (1893) 10 Morr. 262, 269 per Vaughan Williams, J.
[86] See *supra*.

transactions whereby the current pool of assets became seriously depleted.[87] It is not likely that such an argument would succeed unless the applicant is able to show strong prima facia evidence of the existence of concealed assets, or of past transactions which would be susceptible to attack.

(2) Deeds of Arrangement

Alongside the new procedure for voluntary arrangements contained in Part VIII of the Insolvency Act, 1986 there remains in force the alternative type of formal arrangement with creditors known as the deed of arrangement, whose use is still governed by the Deeds of Arrangement Act 1914.[88] In practice such arrangements almost invariably involve the debtor's giving up virtually all his assets to a trustee for the benefit of his creditors, in return for a release from their claims. The provisions of the Act of 1914 were framed with a view to eliminating various abusive practices which had come to be associated with the use of deeds of arrangement, but not only were they less than entirely successful in this aim, but also they introduced a statutory requirement of registration of all such deeds within seven days of their execution, in the absence of which the deed automatically becomes void.[89] It was also the case, prior to the reforms of the law of bankruptcy brought about by the Insolvency Acts of 1985 and 1986, that the debtor's very act of executing an assignment of substantially the whole of his property for the benefit of his creditors was capable of being utilised by any non-assenting creditor as a basis for a bankruptcy petition, whereupon the deed of arrangement itself, and any collection or distribution of assets by the trustee, was liable to be invalidated.[90]

The cumbersome nature of the deed of arrangement procedure had resulted in its being used with diminishing frequency in practice, a matter to which the *Cork Report* drew attention.[91] To remedy the manifest need for a convenient and practical alternative to bankruptcy, the *Cork Report* made recommendations for a new form of voluntary arrangement in place of the deed of arrangement, and proposed the consequential repeal of the Deeds of Arrangement Act.[92] While the *Report's* principal proposal has been implemented in the form of the new procedure which has been described above, the Deeds of Arrangement Act was left on the statute book, and hence the procedure remains available for use. However deeds of arrangement would appear to offer few attractions, if any, by comparison with the new procedure and it may be expected that their use will be negligible in the future. Indeed it may be observed that although, as a consequence of the abolition of the concept of acts of bankruptcy,[93] the

---

[87] See Chap. 8, *post*.
[88] See also Deeds of Arrangement Rules 1925, S.R. & O. No. 795.
[89] Deeds of Arrangement Act 1914, s.2.
[90] Bankruptcy Act 1914, ss.1(1)(a), 4(1)(c) (repealed).
[91] See Cmnd. 8558, paras. 58–67, 350–362, at para. 359. See also Chap. 5 of the *Report* (paras. 242–271) on enforcement procedure.
[92] Cmnd. 8558, paras. 363–399.
[93] See Chap. 5, *post, Preliminary* paras.

mere execution of a deed of arrangement by a debtor is no longer *per se* a ground on which a bankruptcy petition may be presented by a non-assenting creditor, any would-be petitioner will in practice encounter little difficulty in demonstrating the debtor's insolvency for the purposes of satisfying section 267(2)(c) of the Insolvency Act 1986,[94] so that a bankruptcy adjudication remains a possibility.

In view of the likelihood that deeds of arrangement will henceforth be of relatively minor significance in the law of personal insolvency, detailed treatment of this topic has been omitted from the present work.[95]

(3) Administration Orders[96]

The special procedure known as the administration order was first introduced by the Bankruptcy Act 1883, and was intended to provide an alternative to bankruptcy for those individuals whose aggregate debts, and likewise their personal assets, are small, and who also have a regular wage or income from which, over time, their debts may be repaid.[97] The procedure has been several times modified, most recently in 1984, but has yet to evolve into a form in which the original purposes which underlay its inception can be fully and properly realised. Indeed, the *Cork Report* recommended that the administration order procedure should be replaced as a matter of urgency with a new procedure for dealing with the ordinary consumer debtor,[98] but this recommendation was not implemented in the course of the insolvency law reforms of 1985–1986. However, while the administration order procedure has been perpetuated, it has undergone a further modification in that it is no longer a requirement that judgment must first have been recovered against an insolvent debtor in the very County Court to which he presents an application for an administration order.[99]

The statutory provisions governing administration orders are currently contained in Part VI of the County Courts Act 1984 and in Order 39 of the County Court Rules 1981.[1] The procedure thus operates outside the

---

[94] See also s.268 of the Insolvency Act 1986, and generally Chap. 6, *post*.

[95] For up to date accounts of the law, see *e.g.* I.S. Grier and R.E. Floyd, *Personal Insolvency: A Practical Guide* (1987), pp. 59–63; C. Grenville, *Bankruptcy, the Law and Practice* (1987), pp. 322–335.

[96] This type of order, available since 1883 in cases of personal insolvency only, should not be confused with the similarly-named orders, applicable exclusively to companies, which were introduced for the first time in Chap. 3 of Pt. II of the Insolvency Act 1985. Company administration orders are dealt with in Chap. 16, *post*.

[97] For a brief history of the evolution of the administration order, see the *Cork Report*, Cmnd. 8558, at paras. 68–73.

[98] See Cmnd. 8558, Chap. 6 (the proposed Debts Arrangement Order).

[99] See County Courts Act 1984, s.112(1), and *cf.* County Courts Act 1959, s.148(1). See also Cmnd. 8558, paras. 72–73, 277 and 289. The retention in the current statutory provisions of the requirement that some form of judgment must have been first recovered against the debtor is puzzling: its removal was facilitated by an amendment to s.112(1) of the Act of 1984, substituted by s.13(1) of the Courts and Legal Services Act 1990. The latter provision has not yet been brought into force (as at June 1995).

[1] (S.I. 1981, No. 1987/L20) as amended. See the current edition of the County Court Practice.

ambit of the Insolvency Act, and jurisdiction to make an order is vested in every County Court, and not merely in those on which jurisdiction in insolvency matters has been specially conferred.[2]

The essence of the procedure is that any debtor who is unable to pay forthwith the amount of a judgment debt obtained against him, and whose whole indebtedness, inclusive of the debt for which judgment was obtained, does not exceed the prescribed limit (known as the "County Court limit," currently set at £5,000) may apply to a County Court for an administration order wherein provision may be made for the payment of his debts by instalments or otherwise, and either in full or to a specified extent.[3] While the order remains in force no creditor whose name is included in the schedule to the order may present or join in a bankruptcy petition against the debtor without the leave of the court which made the order, unless he satisfies certain special criteria.[4] At the same time all other creditors' remedies concerning debts covered by the order are rendered unenforceable save with the leave of the court.[5] The court which made the order, through its officers, administers and enforces it until its terms have been fully carried out, in which case the order becomes superseded and the debtor is discharged from the scheduled debts.[6] Alternatively if the debtor fails to comply with the order, or if a material change of circumstances has occurred, the court may revoke, suspend or vary the order and may impose certain disabilities on the debtor in the case where he has defaulted on any payment he was due to make by virtue of the order.[7]

Commencement of the procedure: the debtor's request

A debtor who satisfies the requirements of section 112(1) of the County Courts Act 1984 may make an application to the appropriate County Court in the form of a request for an administration order. The appropriate court for this purpose is the court for the district in which the debtor resides or carries on business.[8] In his request the debtor must state whether he intends to pay his creditors in full or whether he proposes in effect to pay a composition, and in the latter case he must further specify the amount in the pound which he proposes to pay and (in either case) he must indicate the amount of the monthly instalments by which he proposes to pay.[9] It is open to the court, if it sees fit, to make an order on terms which vary from those proposed in the debtor's request, and it is also possible for the court to make the order subject to periodical review.[10] The

---

[2] See Chap. 2, *ante*.
[3] County Courts Act 1984, s.112(1), (6). By s.112(1A), added by s.13(1) of the Courts and Legal Services Act 1990 but *not yet in force*, provision is made to enable an order to be made on the application of any judgment creditor of the debtor, or of the court's own motion during or on the determination of any enforcement or other proceedings.
[4] County Courts Act 1984, s.112(4), as amended by s.220 of the Insolvency Act 1985.
[5] *ibid.*, s.114(1).
[6] *ibid.*, s.117(1); County Court Rules, Ord. 39, r. 13.
[7] County Court Rules, Ord. 39, rr. 14, 16; Insolvency Act 1986, s.429.
[8] County Court Rules, Ord. 39, r. 2(1). See Forms N92 and N93, *ibid.*
[9] *ibid.*, Forms N92 and N93.
[10] *ibid.*, Ord. 39, r. 8(1). See also County Courts Act 1984, s.112(6).

Voluntary Procedures and Alternatives to Bankruptcy

prescribed form for the making of a request requires the debtor to list the names, addresses and descriptions of all his creditors including particulars and the estimated value of any security given in respect of any debt, and to furnish specific information regarding his employment, pay and income, and also his liabilities to dependents, and outgoings for rent, or mortgage and rates. The statements in the debtor's request, and the information contained in the list of creditors, must be verified on oath.[11]

Hearing of the request

When the debtor's request has been filed the Registrar or Chief Clerk must appoint a day for the hearing and send to the debtor and to all creditors mentioned in the list which the debtor has furnished at least 14 days' advance notice of the day and time of the hearing.[12] Before any administration order is made the court is required to send to every person of whose name the debtor has notified the court as being a creditor of his, a notice to that effect.[13] Any creditor who wishes to object to any debt included in the debtor's list, or to any terms of the debtor's proposals for payment, must send written notice of his objection to the Registrar, to the debtor, and to the creditor to whose debt he objects. At least seven days' notice of objection must be given and, in the absence of such notice, no creditor may object to a debt except with the leave of the court.[14]

At the hearing of the request any creditor, whether or not he is mentioned in the list furnished by the debtor, may attend and prove his debt and, subject to what is stated above, may object to any debt included in that list.[15] Every debt included in the list is taken to be proved unless it is objected to by a creditor or disallowed by the court, or required by the court to be supported by evidence. In the latter instance the creditor in question must prove his debt by active means, and every creditor who proves his debt becomes entitled to be scheduled as a creditor for the amount of his proof.[16] If an administration order is made, notice of the order must be sent to the Registry of County Court Judgments and to every person whose name the debtor has notified to the court as being a creditor of his, or who has proved. Copies of the notice must also be sent to the debtor himself and to every other court in which, to the knowledge of the Registrar, judgment has been obtained against the debtor or proceedings are pending against him in respect of any scheduled debt.[17]

Effects of the Order

Where an administration order is made by the court upon the debtor's

---

[11] County Courts Rules, Ord. 39, r. 3. See also Forms N92 and N93.
[12] *ibid.*, Ord. 39, r. 5. See Form N373.
[13] County Courts Act 1984, s.112(3).
[14] County Court Rules, Ord. 39, r. 6; County Courts Act 1984, s.113(c).
[15] *ibid.*, Ord. 39, r. 7(a).
[16] *ibid.*, Ord. 39, r. 7(b), (c); County Courts Act 1984, s.113(b).
[17] County Courts Act 1984, s.113(a); County Court Rules, Ord. 39, r. 9.

request no creditor may have any remedy against the person or property of the debtor in respect of any debt which the debtor has notified to the court, or which has been scheduled to the order, except with the leave of the court by which the order was made and subject to such terms as the court may impose.[18] Any county court in which proceedings, other than bankruptcy proceedings, are pending against the debtor in respect of any debt so notified or scheduled must stay proceedings although costs already incurred by the creditor may be allowed him, and these may be added to the debt.[19] Thus a debtor who is the subject of an administration order enjoys a considerable degree of immunity from process at the hands of his creditors, in much the same way as one who has been adjudicated bankrupt. There are however three important exceptions to this immunity.

First, section 112(4) of the County Courts Act does make provision for a creditor to present or join in a bankruptcy petition against the debtor. For this purpose, any creditor whose name is included in the schedule to the administration order will normally require leave of the court which made the order, but such leave will not be required where three conditions are jointly satisfied, namely that the creditor's name was notified to the court before the administration order was made; that the debt by virtue of which he presents the petition exceeds £1,500; and that the bankruptcy petition is presented within 28 days following the creditor's receipt of the notice from the county court informing him that the debtor has notified his name to the court as being a creditor of his.[20]

Secondly, there is express statutory provision that execution may be levied against the debtor's goods by the Registrar of the county court by which the order was made if at any time while the order is in force it is shown that the property of the debtor exceeds £50 in value and any creditor requests that execution be levied.[21]

Thirdly, there is statutory saving of the right of a landlord or other person to whom rent is due from the debtor to distrain upon his goods or effects either before or after the administration order is made, although in the latter case it may be done only for up to six months' rent accrued due prior to the date of the order, and is not available for rent payable in respect of any period after the date when distress was levied.[22] Where the remedy of distress is not available the landlord or other person to whom rent is due from the debtor may prove for the surplus under the order.[23]

There is provision for a subsequent objection to any scheduled debt, or objection to the manner in which payments are directed to be made under the order, to be brought by any creditor who did not receive prior notice of the hearing of the debtor's request. Provided that the creditor gives notice

---

[18] County Courts Act 1984, s.114(1).
[19] *ibid.*, s.114(2), (3).
[20] *ibid.*, s.112(4), as amended by s.220(2) of the Insolvency Act 1985. See also County Court Rules 1981, Ord. 39, r. 12.
[21] County Courts Act 1984, s.115(1), as amended by s.220(3), (4) of the Insolvency Act 1985. The amount of £50 may be varied by statutory instrument.
[22] County Courts Act 1984, s.116.
[23] *ibid.*

of objection within a reasonable time of his becoming aware of the administration order the court has power to allow, or dismiss, such a subsequent objection or to adjourn the matter for full hearing upon notice to interested parties.[24] Moreover the possibility exists that, after the order has been made, it may be discovered that the total amount of the debtor's liabilities is in excess of the statutory limit of £5,000, as currently prescribed. This contingency is the subject of a special provision in section 112(5) of the County Courts Act whereby it is declared that the administration order shall not be invalid by reason of this fact alone, but that in such a case the court has a discretion to set the order aside.

Implementation of the order

The court must appoint someone—either the chief clerk or some other officer of the court—to have the conduct of the order, and it is that person's duty to take all proper proceedings for enforcing its terms. If there is any default in payment of any instalment under the order he may apply to the court to exercise its powers to review the order under Order 39 Rule 14 of the County Court Rules. Additionally with the leave of the court any creditor whose debt is scheduled to the order may take proceedings to enforce it and any such creditor, or the debtor himself, may apply to the court to review the order.[25] It is also the duty of the person appointed to have conduct of the order to report to the court any other matters of which he becomes aware which may make it desirable to review the order. Additionally, the court may make an attachment of earnings order to secure payments under an administration order.[26]

Section 117(1) of the County Courts Act, 1984 provides that money which the debtor pays into court under an administration order shall be appropriated first in satisfaction of the costs of the administration, which must not exceed 10p in the pound on the total amount of the debts, and then in liquidation of debts in accordance with the order. All persons scheduled as creditors are to be paid *pari passu*.[27] Any person who becomes a creditor of the debtor after the date of the administration order, and who proves his debt before the Registrar, must be added to the list of scheduled creditors for the amount of his proof, but is not entitled to any dividend under the order until those scheduled as having been creditors before the date of the order have been paid to the extent provided therein.[28] If the debtor does not dispute such later claims they are deemed to be proved unless the court requires evidence.[29] It is noteworthy that there is no differentiation between so-called "preferential" and "ordinary" creditors in relation to administration orders, unlike bankruptcy.[30]

[24] County Court Rules, Ord. 39, r. 10.
[25] *ibid.*, Ord. 39, r. 13.
[26] Attachment of Earnings Act 1971, ss.1(2)(c), 5; County Court Rules, Ord. 39, r. 14(1)(d).
[27] Ord. 39, r. 18.
[28] Ord. 39, rr. 11, 18.
[29] Ord. 39, r. 11(2).
[30] See Chap. 10, *post*.

Discharge, revocation or variation of the order

Where the amount received from the debtor as payment under the order is sufficient to pay each scheduled creditor to the extent provided by the order, together with the costs of the plaintiff in the action in respect of which the order was made, plus the costs of the administration itself, the order becomes superseded and the debtor is discharged from his debts to the scheduled creditors.[31] This automatic release of the debtor may be compared with the process of automatic discharge which operates in relation to first-time bankrupts under the provisions of the Insolvency Act.[32] It may be noted that there is no requirement that the debtor must make application for an administration order to be superseded. If on any review of the order it appears that the debtor's inability to pay is attributable to illness or other unavoidable misfortune the court may suspend the operation of the order for an appropriate period of time, or vary any of its provisions.[33] If the court is satisfied that the debtor has failed without reasonable cause to comply with any provision of the order, or that it is otherwise just and expedient to do so, the court may revoke the order. This may be done forthwith, or may take place consequent upon the debtor's failure to comply with any condition which may first be specified by the court.[34] As a further alternative the court is empowered to make an attachment of earnings order if none was previously in force or it may vary or discharge any such attachment of earnings order already made.[35]

Upon the revocation of an administration order further disabilities may be imposed upon the debtor at the court's discretion by virtue of section 429 of the Insolvency Act 1986. These are that, for a period of up to two years,

(1) section 12 of the Company Directors Disqualification Act 1986 shall apply to the debtor, who in consequence will be disqualified from acting as director or as liquidator of a company, or from being directly or indirectly concerned in the management of a company, without the leave of the court; and

(2) he may not, either alone or jointly with another person, obtain credit to the extent of £250 or more, or enter into any transaction in the course of or for the purposes of any business in which he is directly or indirectly engaged, without disclosing to the other party (from whom he obtains credit or with whom he enters into the transaction) the fact that he is subject to the restrictions imposed by section 429.[36]

---

[31] County Courts Act 1984, s.117(2).
[32] See Chap. 11, *post*.
[33] County Court Rules, Ord. 39, r. 14(1)(a), (b).
[34] *ibid.*, Ord. 39, r. 14(1)(c); Form 95.
[35] *ibid.*, Ord. 39, r. 14(1)(d); Attachment of Earnings Act 1971, ss.1(2)(c), 5, 9.
[36] See Insolvency Act 1986, s.429(4) for the meaning of the expression "obtain credit" in the context of the section. The amount of £250 is variable by statutory instrument, the current figure being fixed by the Insolvency Proceedings (Monetary Limits) Order 1986 (S.I. 1986, No. 1996).

Any contravention of section 429, or of section 12 of the Company Directors' Disqualification Act, constitutes a criminal offence punishable by imprisonment or fine.[37] Thus, some of the principal disabilities which apply to an undischarged bankrupt may be retrospectively imposed upon a debtor who, having averted possible bankruptcy by means of an administration order, subsequently defaults upon his obligations under that order. This constitutes a salutary counter-measure against the possibility that a debtor may seek to use the administration order procedure as a delaying tactic against creditors. It has the interesting, incidental aspect that because of the wider deployment of jurisdiction to make an administration order these selective disabilities, created by the Insolvency Act and the Company Directors' Disqualification Act, may be imposed, in certain cases, by order of a County Court which does not itself enjoy a jurisdiction in bankruptcy and winding up.

(B) Informal Procedures

Mention was made in Chapter 3 of the fact that a variety of informal alternatives to bankruptcy exist, and are much used in practice.[38] Creditors who can be persuaded that the debtor is capable of overcoming a current liquidity crisis if he is allowed a suitable space of time, or a certain amount of additional credit, may agree to participate in an informal moratorium in the interests of averting the greater calamity, both for them and for him, which may be occasioned by their debtor's bankruptcy. These moratoria may consist of relatively simple agreements whereby one or more major creditors either grant the debtor further credit facilities with full knowledge of his insolvent condition, or grant him an extension of time in which to discharge liabilities which have already matured or are about to do so. Debtor and creditors may alternatively enter into more complex arrangements worked out by negotiation whereby the participating creditors agree to a re-scheduling of debts in conjunction with the imposition of certain constraints upon the debtor's conduct of his business or personal affairs, his dealings with his property, and so forth. Not only do these informal arrangements entail the running of a considerable commercial risk by the creditors concerned, but also they are inherently unstable in that all creditors, whether participating in the arrangement or not, retain their freedom to exercise all their normal legal remedies, including having recourse to a bankruptcy petition against the debtor.

Somewhat more stable, in relation to the creditors actually participating, is the non-statutory, contractual composition with creditors. A debtor may at any time enter into such a composition with some or all of his creditors without resorting to any of the formal procedures established by the various statutory provisions described above. In such cases the

---

[37] Insolvency Act 1986, s.429(5), together with Sched. 10; Company Directors' Disqualification Act 1986, s.13.
[38] See *supra*, p. 37.

composition takes effect as a multi-party contract governed by Common Law. The debtor thereby obtains release from the obligation to pay his debts in full, and the creditors correspondingly agree to forgo their full entitlements in consideration of the benefits promised to them in the alternative, and to be furnished either by the debtor himself or by a third party. The debtor may once again derive significant advantages from such a composition in that he may avoid the publicity and inconvenience of the strict regime of bankruptcy, to say nothing of the stigma and disabilities attaching thereto. As always however, such private arrangements contain an element of risk from the creditors' point of view, because not only may the debtor persuade the creditors to accept a less substantial settlement than he is really capable of paying, but also he will be spared the thorough investigation of his affairs and conduct which the bankruptcy law, and to a lesser extent the new voluntary arrangement under Part VIII of the Act,[39] would require to be carried out. Despite the fact that each participating creditor is effectively deprived of the right to invoke any legal process in an effort to enforce payment of the original amount of his debt (on the premise that to do so would represent an act of fraud by that creditor perpetrated against the others), no such restraint or incapacity attaches to any creditor who is not a party to the composition contract, with the consequence that the debtor's property remains vulnerable to any legal process—including bankruptcy—brought about by any such creditor.

---

[39] See *supra*, section A(1).

CHAPTER 5

WHO CAN BE MADE BANKRUPT?

Preliminary

If it proves to be the case that none of the various types of voluntary procedure which were described in the previous chapter is either practicable or acceptable, the only available alternative form of collective insolvency procedure is bankruptcy. Although the *Cork Report* advocated the development of a comprehensive range of insolvency procedures, to be selected according to the requirements of each case,[1] these recommendations were not implemented in the legislative reforms of 1985 and 1986. The law and procedure relating to bankruptcy itself were substantially modified, however, with considerable fidelity to many of the report's proposals in this respect.[2] In the context of the present chapter, the most important change in the law was the abolition of the concept of the "act of bankruptcy," which was formerly an indispensable pre-requisite to an individual's becoming liable to undergo a bankruptcy adjudication.[3] The law and procedure relating to the commencement of bankruptcy proceedings have now been harmonised as closely as possible with those relating to the compulsory winding up of companies,[4] although the actual procedures themselves remain completely distinct from each other.

The principal legislative provisions which apply in bankruptcy and which have the effect of determining which individuals are capable of undergoing a bankruptcy adjudication, are contained in Part IX of the Insolvency Act, 1986. The primary requirement in this regard is that the individual by or against whom a bankruptcy petition is to be presented must be "a debtor" within the established meaning of that term under the law of bankruptcy. Secondly, the debtor must be personally amenable to the insolvency law jurisdiction of the courts of England and Wales, a circumstance which may be established either by the debtor's voluntary

---

[1] Cmnd. 8558, Chaps. 10 and 11. See also the proposals for a "two tier" bankruptcy system contained in the "Justice" Report.
[2] See Cmnd. 9175, Chaps. 3 and 11.
[3] *cf.* Bankruptcy Act 1914, s.1(1) (repealed). See I.F. Fletcher, *Law of Bankruptcy* (1978) pp. 18–37.
[4] See Chaps. 20 and 21, *post.*

act of invoking that jurisdiction on his own behalf, or otherwise by virtue of the existence of at least one of the requisite "contacts" with the jurisdiction which are prescribed for this purpose.[5] This broader question of jurisdictional competence must be considered in addition to the rules of particularised jurisdiction, which have the effect of determining the court or courts within England and Wales in which a bankruptcy petition may properly be presented.

(A) Who is a "debtor"?

The general characteristics of the term "debtor" are closely associated with those pertaining to its cognate terms, "debt" and "creditor." In the eyes of the law, as distinct from the less precise usages of ordinary parlance, the concept of a debt, and the relationship of debtor and creditor, arises in the case where a legally enforceable liability has been constituted whereby the party who is known as the debtor may be compelled, by legal process if necessary, to render that which is due by way of performance at the instance of the party who is known as the creditor. The concept of the "natural obligation,"[6] familiar to many foreign systems of law, has no place in the English law of obligations and hence in the absence of any ultimately exerciseable right on the part of the alleged creditor to maintain an action at law to compel performance, it is not appropriate to employ the terms "debt" or "creditor" to the situation. This is also the case where a liability which was once enforceable has ceased to be so, for example by virtue of the operation of the Limitation Acts.[7] The relevance of the attribute of enforceability will be observed at numerous points of operation of the bankruptcy process, but it is of particular importance with regard to the very inception of that process when it must be determined whether the individual in question can be made the subject of a bankruptcy order. This is true both in the case where the debtor himself seeks to present the bankruptcy petition, and in the case of a creditor's petition. In the former case, section 272(1) of the Insolvency Act 1986 specifies that the sole basis on which such a petition may be presented is that the debtor is unable to pay his debts. Consequently, if it can be shown that the debtor is able to pay such of his debts as are legally enforceable against him, and are currently due for payment, he is ineligible to petition for his own bankruptcy.[8] In the latter case, where the petition is presented by a creditor, attention necessarily focuses upon the nature and quality of the state of indebtedness existing between the debtor and the petitioning

---

[5] See *infra* for consideration of s.272 (debtor's petition) and s.265 (creditor's petition) respectively of the Insolvency Act 1986.

[6] *cf.* the Roman Law concept of *naturalis obligatio*: Gaius, Inst. 3.119a; Justinian, D.4.5.2.2., 46.3.5.2. For modern French Law, see *Code Civil*, Art. 1235; J. Carbonnier, *Droit Civil* (12th ed., Paris 1985), Vol. 4, pp. 15–25; J. Ghestin & G. Goubeaux, *Traité de Droit Civil* (2nd ed., 1982) Vol. 1, paras. 667–691 (pp. 580–610); Amos and Walton, *Introduction to French Law* (3rd ed., 1967) p. 139.

[7] See Limitation Act 1980, and related legislation. *cf. Re Tynte* (1880) 15 Ch.D. 125; see also *Quantock v. England* (1770) 2.W.B.1 703; 96 E.R. 413.

[8] *cf. Re A Debtor, ex p. The Debtor v. Allen (No. 17 of 1966)* [1967] Ch. 590.

creditor, on which the latter's standing to present the petition is ultimately based. This debt—known as the petitioning creditor's debt—is the subject of detailed and exacting legal provisions which will be further discussed in Chapter 6, but for present purposes it will suffice to make the obvious-seeming point that, in order to serve as a petitioning creditor's debt, the liability must be one which admits of legal enforceability in such a manner as to give rise to an award of either pecuniary damages, or specific delivery or transfer of property with a quantifiable value.

The general law of contract contains numerous principles and doctrines under which contracts may be rendered unenforceable, or void, or voidable, according to the circumstances. For a full account of these matters, the reader is referred to the specialist works on the subject,[9] with the observation that whenever the rules of contract law produce the consequence that a particular contract is unenforceable by one of the parties at least, this fact will preclude that party from presenting a bankruptcy petition against the other. Special note should be taken of the potential impact of the Consumer Credit Act 1974 on the enforceability of transactions governed by the provisions of that Act. The sanction of unenforceability, or of officially-imposed limitations upon enforceability, is now capable of applying to persons who give credit in the course of their business. By virtue of section 21 of the Consumer Credit Act 1974, a licence is required to carry on a consumer credit business or a consumer hire business, which are respectively defined as businesses which comprise or relate to the provision of credit under regulated consumer hire agreements.[10] All licence holders must conduct their business in conformity with the Act of 1974 and with regulations made pursuant thereto, the withdrawal or non-renewal of their licence being one of the principal sanctions which may be imposed upon them for unfitness or misconduct.[11] Any person who engages in any activities for which a licence is required without being duly licenced to do so not only commits a criminal offence but also is unable to enforce the provisions of any regulated agreement against the debtor or hirer, unless the Director-General of Fair Trading has made an order which applies to the agreement in question.[12] Moreover, where any credit bargain is found to be extortionate, the court may re-open the credit agreement so as to do justice between the parties.[13] The court may re-open the agreement either upon

---

[9] For the various grounds on which contracts may be unenforceable, or void, or voidable, see Cheshire, Fifoot and Furmston, *Law of Contract* (12th ed., 1991) Chaps. 7–12 inclusive; on extinction of remedies, see *ibid.*, Chap. 21, pp. 636–644.

[10] See Consumer Credit Act 1974, s.189(1), together with ss.8, 9, 16, 21–42. The business of a moneylender is now regulated by the Act of 1974 (see s.9(1)), and the Moneylenders Acts 1900–1927 have been repealed: *ibid.*, Sched. 5, Pt. I.

[11] Consumer Credit Act 1974, ss.25, 26, 29, 32.

[12] *ibid.*, ss.39, 40.

[13] *ibid.*, s.137. See also s.138, which provides that a credit bargain is "extortionate" if it provides for payments which are "grossly exorbitant," or if it "otherwise contravenes ordinary principles of fair dealing." The court is instructed to have regard, among other factors, to interest rates prevailing at the time the bargain was made, in order to determine whether the bargain was extortionate: section 138(2)(a). *cf.* ss.244 and 343 of the Insolvency Act 1986, which become applicable in place of s.139 of the Act of 1974, once insolvency proceedings have commenced (*post*, Chaps. 8 and 26).

the making of an application for this purpose specifically, or in the course of any proceedings to enforce the agreement, or in other proceedings (except in the course of bankruptcy proceedings)[14] in any court where the amount paid or payable under the agreement is relevant.[15] In all cases in which the effect of the Consumer Credit Act 1974 is to render the original provisions of an agreement wholly unenforceable, it also follows that the creditor cannot resort to bankruptcy proceedings against the debtor on the basis of any indebtedness alleged to have arisen thereunder. It may also happen that in cases where the creditor is limited to the enforcement of his agreement in part only, the effect may be to reduce the debt in question below the level of the minimum permitted as the basis for a bankruptcy petition.[16]

Although the status of "debtor" is a *sine qua non* for the purposes of applicability of the bankruptcy law, it is not every such person who is liable to undergo adjudication as a bankrupt. Logically, the rigours of bankruptcy should be reserved for those debtors who have arrived at a position of insolvency and whose creditors are no longer prepared to indulge them for any further length of time. However, although an assertion of insolvency is required in the case of a debtor's petition, the law does not actually impose it as a condition in all cases that the debtor's insolvency, or even his actual inability to pay his current debts, must be definitively established before a bankruptcy order can be made. Indeed, most creditors would encounter considerable practical difficulty in satisfying such a requirement on the basis of the information which is likely to be available to them. Instead, what has traditionally sufficed, and is still retained as the basis of the law of the present day, is that there should be evidence before the court that the debtor has given an outward and visible appearance of insolvency, by exhibiting behavioural features characteristic of that condition. In consequence of the recent legislative reforms, the one characteristic feature now utilised for this purpose is the debtor's apparent inability to pay such of his debts as are sought to be utilised by one or more of his creditors as the basis for a bankruptcy petition.[17] As will be explained below, there is a special procedure, known as the service of a statutory demand, whereby the creditor may cause the debtor to provide objective evidence which the law will regard as establishing his apparent inability to pay, so as to fulfil this legal requirement.

Thus it is possible for a debtor who is actually solvent to undergo a bankruptcy adjudication by reason of his neglect or refusal to pay a debt which he has the means, but not the will, to pay. It is true that, in such cases, the law will also allow the debtor to apply for the annulment of the adjudication by belatedly establishing his solvency through the very action of paying all his debts.[18] It should be noted however that there is otherwise no necessity for the bankruptcy process to be halted or discontinued merely because the debtor turns out not to be insolvent. Indeed, provision

---

[14] Insolvency Act 1986, s.343(6).
[15] Consumer Credit Act 1974, s.139.
[16] See Chap. 6, *post*, section A(a)(iii) (*The petitioning creditor's debt*).
[17] Insolvency Act 1986, s.267(2)(c).
[18] *ibid.*, s.282(1)(b), discussed in Chap. 11 *post*. See also s.271(3), discussed in Chap. 6.

for just such a contingency is made in section 330(5) of the Act, whereby the bankrupt is entitled to receive any surplus which remains after payment in full of all his creditors, plus the costs of the bankruptcy administration itself. Where such a surplus arises it is of course indicative of the fact that, whether he knew it or not, the bankrupt was in reality solvent, and hence need not have undergone adjudication at all. The fact that the law openly countenances the possibility that an intransigent, yet solvent, debtor may be bankrupted upon the petition of an unpaid creditor means that this most drastic of civil remedies can be utilised as a species of ultimate sanction for the purpose of enforcing the payment of debts. Although this use of bankruptcy as a debt-collecting device is questionable in terms of the proper principles which should underly the operation of the law of bankruptcy, its continued toleration is perhaps understandable in view of the cogent, and still unanswered, criticisms of the *Payne Committee* in their report in 1969 on the enforcement of judgment debts, wherein the serious inadequacies of English law in providing cost-effective procedures for debt enforcement were conclusively demonstrated.[19]

It may appear somewhat paradoxical, in view of what has just been stated, that the mere fact that a debtor is actually insolvent does not of itself guarantee that he or she can be made bankrupt. This is because the commencement of bankruptcy proceedings must take place upon the petition of either the debtor himself or a duly qualified creditor. The meaning of this latter expression will be further explored below,[20] but it can here be noted that the Insolvency Act 1986 imposes conditions which effectively make it impossible for a debtor to be subjected to the processes of the bankruptcy law unless he is indebted to the petitioning creditor for the unsecured amount of at least £750, payable either immediately or at some certain, future time.[21] Thus, even a hopelessly insolvent debtor can only be made bankrupt involuntarily if a duly qualified creditor will undertake the task of presenting a petition for his adjudication. If no single creditor is owed as much as the minimum statutory figure of £750 it follows that none of them is individually qualified to do this, and hence the sole alternative is for two or more of them to join in presenting the petition on the basis that the aggregate amount of the debts owed to them equals or exceeds the bankruptcy level. It can therefore happen that an indubitably insolvent debtor nonetheless escapes adjudication simply because no properly qualified party is prepared to invoke the machinery of the bankruptcy law. This may be on account of any one of a variety of factors, ranging from inertia, or ignorance regarding the correct way to proceed, to benevolence or indulgence towards the debtor and his dependents, having regard to the severe consequences which the debtor's bankruptcy would entail for them.

---

[19] Cmnd. 3909, 1969. See comments in Chap. 5 of the *Cork Report*, Cmnd. 8558, at paras. 244 *et seq.*
[20] See Chap. 6, *post.*
[21] s.267(1), (2)(a), (b), (4) of the Act.

(B) The Debtor's Personal Amenability to the Jurisdiction of the English Courts

It is a fundamental requirement of the law of bankruptcy, as indeed is true of every type of legal procedure, that any person who is to be subjected to its process must satisfy certain criteria which are properly considered to render the person amenable to the jurisdiction of the court in question. Depending upon the type of proceedings, different sorts of forensic ties (known as connecting factors) are used to furnish the requisite link between a particular person and the jurisdiction of the courts of a particular place. With regard to bankruptcy, the different possible connecting factors, any one of which will suffice to render the debtor personally amenable to the jurisdiction of the English courts, are listed in section 265 of the Act. The provisions of this section are of considerable importance, because unless the debtor can be brought within them no bankruptcy petition can be presented to any court in England and Wales, even though it may be the case that the debtor is demonstrably insolvent, and is indebted to persons in this country under circumstances which would otherwise qualify them to serve as petitioning creditors in view of the amount and nature of the debts involved.[22]

In considering the provisions of section 265 it may be noted at once that there is no reference to the debtor's nationality, or citizenship, for this purpose. Thus, the mere fact that the debtor happens to be a citizen of the United Kingdom is of no relevance to the question whether the English bankruptcy court enjoys jurisdiction over him or her. By the same token, a person who is a citizen of a foreign country is not on that account immune from the bankruptcy jurisdiction of the English courts, and may be adjudicated here provided that at least one of the connecting factors specified in section 265 is established. The section therefore has the function of prescribing what kind and degree of "minimum contact" with this country will suffice for the purposes of our law, so as to confer jurisdictional competence upon our courts.[23] It specifies no less than five alternative types of forensic connection with the territory of England and Wales, one at least of which must exist in order that the English court may entertain a bankruptcy petition with respect to the individual in question. These jurisdictional criteria will be considered in more detail in Chapter 29, in their international setting.[24] For the present it will suffice to state that section 265 precludes the presentation of a bankruptcy petition by or against a debtor[25] unless the debtor is either:

(1) domiciled in England and Wales; or
(2) personally present in England and Wales on the day on which the petition is presented; or

---

[22] See preceding section *supra*, (section (A)), and also Chap. 6 *post*.
[23] Further questions of jurisdiction in an international context are considered in Part 3, *post*.
[24] See Chap. 29, *post*, at p. 695 *et seq*.
[25] s.265(1) refers to the presentation of a petition under s.264(1)(a) or (b). The exclusionary provision therefore has no application in cases where a petition is presented under section 264(1)(c) or (d), *q.v.*

(3) at any time in the period of three years ending with that day:
   (a) has been ordinarily resident, or has had a place of residence, in England and Wales, or
   (b) has carried on business in England and Wales.

Section 265(2) further provides that the reference in (c)(ii) to the carrying on of a business by the debtor includes the carrying on of business by a firm or partnership of which the debtor is a member, and the carrying on of business by an agent or manager for the debtor or for the firm or partnership to which the debtor belongs.

Although in the great majority of cases the debtor will be found to satisfy simultaneously two or even more of the grounds specified in section 265(1) of the Act, it can readily be perceived that the connecting factors listed in the section also have the effect of bringing within the scope of English bankruptcy law a very considerable number of persons whose current contact with the social economy of England and Wales may be of comparatively low intensity, as against their contact with that of some other jurisdiction. This is especially true for cases which fall within section 265(1)(b), whereby it suffices if the debtor is personally present in England and Wales on the day on which the petition is presented, a provision which would, in principle, enable the English court to assume jurisdiction in a case where the petition was presented on the occasion of the debtor's first and only visit to this country.[26] Moreover it can be observed that the English law concept of domicile[27] is sufficiently flexible for it to be possible for one who has never been physically within this country, even for an instant of time, to be legally domiciled here and hence to satisfy the criterion embodied in section 265(1)(a). Indeed, even the criteria contained in section 265(1)(c),[28] which involve the debtor's having a residential or business connection with England and Wales, are so expressed that it is unnecessary for the connection to be subsisting up to the date of the petition, or even close to that date, since all that is required is that such a link should have been in existence at some time during the period of three years before the date of the petition. Nor, with the exception of a connection based on the debtor's ordinary residence, do the criteria within section 265(1)(c) involve any consideration of the quality or duration of the debtor's former or subsisting contact with England and Wales in that particular capacity. The ambit of bankruptcy jurisdiction of the English court is thus potentially a wide one, but it must be remembered that the final discretion whether to exercise that jurisdiction in any particular case rests with the court,[29] which could resolve not to make a bankruptcy order if it took the view that the circumstances of the case overall are such as to render an English adjudication inappropriate.

---

[26] *cf. Re Pascal* (1876) 1 Ch.D. 509 (C.A.).
[27] The concept of domicile is more fully described in Chap. 29, *post*, at p. 700.
[28] See further Chap. 29, *post*, p. 696 *et seq.*
[29] See ss.264(2), 266(3) of the Act, considered in Chap. 6.

(C) Special Categories of Debtor

As already explained,[30] the distinction between traders and non-traders, still important in the insolvency laws of some foreign countries, was removed from English bankruptcy law in 1861. Furthermore, since 1935 married women have been subject to the bankruptcy law in precisely the same way as those who are unmarried.[31] Minors may also be the subject of bankruptcy proceedings, although only in respect of debts which are legally enforceable against them.[32] By virtue of the Minors' Contracts Act 1987,[33] the contractual liability of minors is left to be regulated by the rules of the common law, under which certain contracts, namely those for the supply of necessary goods or services to the minor and service contracts including any under which a minor is employed, are subject to a rule of qualified enforceability. Other contracts are either not binding at all, or else are voidable at the instance of the party who is under the age of legal majority.[34] Bankruptcy proceedings may therefore be brought against minors only for debts incurred through enforceable contracts for necessaries, or under service contracts otherwise deemed to be beneficial, or for debts arising out of proceedings in tort, or for liability created by statute such as a liability for taxation.[35] As a consequence of section 1(1)(a) of the Minors Contracts Act 1987, contracts which at the time they were entered into were unenforceable or voidable at the minor's option may now be ratified and rendered fully binding after he or she has attained the age of majority, without the need for fresh consideration to be furnished by the other party.

Members of Parliament and also members of the peerage, may be made bankrupt in exactly the same way as any ordinary type of debtor, it being expressly provided by section 427(7) of the Insolvency Act 1986 that privilege of Parliament or peerage confers no special immunity to bankruptcy proceedings.[36]

A person of unsound mind may be adjudicated bankrupt, albeit the proceedings are subject to the over-riding powers of the Court of

---

[30] Chap. 1, *ante*, p. 8.
[31] Law Reform (Married Women and Tortfeasors) Act 1935, s.1(d), also mentioned in Chap. 1, *ante*, at p. 8.
[32] *Re A Debtor (No. 564 of 1949)* [1950] Ch. 282, distinguished in *Re Davenport* [1963] 1 W.L.R. 817.
[33] Which repealed the Infants' Relief Act 1874, as recommended by the Law Commission in their report on Minors' Contracts (Law Com. No. 134). The age of majority is currently 18 years: Family Law Reform Act 1969, s.1.
[34] On the meaning of "necessaries," and other aspects of the legal liability of minors, see Cheshire, Fifoot and Furmston, *op. cit. supra.* n. 9, at pp. 427–443; Treitel, *The Law of Contract* (8th ed., 1991) pp. 481–501; *Anson's Law of Contract* (26th ed., 1984) Chap. 5, pp. 183–203; *Chitty on Contracts* (26th ed., 1989) Chap. 8, paras. 552–612; *Winfield and Jolowicz on Tort* (13th ed., 1989) pp. 667–673; *Clerk and Lindsell on Torts* (16th ed., 1989) paras. 2–33, 2–34.
[35] *Re A Debtor (No. 564 of 1949)*, *supra*; *Re Jones* (1881) 18 Ch.D. 109; *Lovell and Christmas v. Beauchamp* [1894] A.C. 607 (H.L.).
[36] For Parliamentary disqualifications consequent upon adjudication, see s.427(1)–(6), discussed in Chap. 11, *post*.

Protection.[37] That court may appoint a receiver to act for the mentally disordered person in bankruptcy matters,[38] and there is also provision in the Insolvency Rules 1986 that where in insolvency proceedings it appears to the court that a person affected by the proceedings is one who is incapable of managing and administering his own affairs (whether due to mental disorder or to physical affliction or disability) the insolvency court may appoint some fit person to appear for, represent or act for the incapacitated person.[39] One special question which may arise in relation to insolvency proceedings involving a person of unsound mind is whether the debt which is to be used as the petitioning creditor's debt (and, in due course, any other debt which is sought to be proved in the bankruptcy) is legally enforceable, in view of the debtor's possible lack of capacity at the relevant time.[40] In principle however a mentally disordered person may be made bankrupt on the basis of liabilities incurred by him, or on his behalf, either prior to the onset of his incapacity or during a lucid interval between separate periods of mental disorder.

Partnerships

The Legal Background

Under the law of England and Wales (in contrast to that of Scotland and of many foreign countries) a firm or partnership is not a legal entity and has no legal personality distinct from its individual members. However, where two or more persons operate as a legally constituted partnership, or where a person carries on business under a partnership name, it is a well established principle that such persons may take proceedings, or alternatively be proceeded against, in the name of the firm, and this principle has long been applied in the case of insolvency proceedings. Prior to the reforms of insolvency law during 1985–1986 the provisions for the winding-up of companies incorporated under the Companies Acts were traditionally excluded from applying to insolvent partnerships, so that it had long been the practice to deal with them under the law of bankruptcy, albeit with special modifications developed for this purpose.[41] The court was given power to order the disclosure of the names of all the partners, so that individual partners could not hide behind the firm name. It was always possible for bankruptcy proceedings to take place against one of the partners in his individual capacity and, if so, the adjudication of him as an individual did not bring about the collective

---

[37] Mental Health Act 1983, Part VII. *cf. Re A Debtor (No. 1 of* 1941) [1941] Ch. 487. See generally, Haywood and Massey, *Court of Protection Practice* (11th ed., 1985). *N.B.* this edition antedates the Insolvency Act 1986.
[38] Mental Health Act 1983, s.99.
[39] See Insolvency Rules 1986, rr. 7.43–7.46 inclusive.
[40] On the question of the legal capacity of mentally disordered persons, see Haywood and Massey, *op. cit. supra*, n. 37, Chap. 16; Clerk and Lindsell, *op. cit. supra*, para. 2–39; Cheshire, Fifoot and Furmston, *op. cit.* pp. 447–448; Treitel, *op. cit.*, pp. 501–503; *Anson, op. cit.*, pp. 207–208; Chitty, *op. cit.*, Chap. 8, paras. 615–626 (all *supra*, n. 34).
[41] See Bankruptcy Act 1914, ss.33(6), 63(1) and 119; Bankruptcy Rules 1952, rr. 279–296 (all now repealed).

bankruptcy of the partnership, although the partnership would thereby undergo dissolution by virtue of section 33(1) of the Partnership Act 1890 unless there was provision to the contrary in the deed of partnership. However, if collective proceedings in bankruptcy were brought against the partnership in its firm name, the making of a bankruptcy order also resulted in the individual bankruptcy of each of the persons who were members of the partnership at the date of the bankruptcy order.[42]

The Present Law

The special complexities of partnership insolvency were acknowledged in section 420 of the Insolvency Act 1986, which made provision for this area to become specially regulated by means of a statutory instrument whereby the provisions of the Act would be made applicable subject to prescribed modifications. Under this enabling provision the Insolvent Partnerships Order 1986[43] introduced a significant recasting of this area of law. The complexity of this innovative measure, combined with procedural shortcomings which emerged when its provisions were put into practice, led to the whole Order of 1986 being revised and replaced by the Insolvent Partnerships Order 1994 as from December 1, 1994.[43] A particular feature of the 1986 Order, continued under the modified terms of that of 1994, amounts to a major innovation of principle in that it became possible for an insolvent partnership to be wound up under Part V of the Insolvency Act as an unregistered company.[44] Such a winding up may occur either in conjunction with the insolvency of one or more of the partners, or without involving the insolvency of any of the partners.[45] As a third possibility, individual members of an insolvent partnership may be made the subject of insolvency proceedings without these being accompanied by the winding up of the partnership as an unregistered company. This latter type of proceeding may either take the form of a joint debtors' petition presented by the individual members themselves,[46] or it may develop out of bankruptcy or winding up proceedings initially commenced against an insolvent member of the partnership, whereupon the discovery of the fact that the person in question is a member of an insolvent partnership may induce the court to make an order converting the proceedings into a collective insolvency procedure involving the other members.[47] As a further variant of this, provision is also made in article 14(2) of the Insolvent Partnerships Order governing the case where bankruptcy petitions have been presented against more than one

---

[42] Bankruptcy Rules 1952, r. 285 (*repealed*).
[43] See S.I. 1994, No. 2421, replacing S.I. 1986, No. 2142. See also *Cork Report*, Chap. 39; Pennington (1987) 8 Co. Law 195.
[44] See Insolvency Act 1986, ss.220–229, discussed in Chap. 20, *post*.
[45] Insolvent Partnerships Order 1994 (S.I. No. 2421), arts. 7 and 8 together with Scheds. 3 and 4. See *Re Marr (Pauline) (a bankrupt)* [1990] Ch. 773 (C.A.), decided under the now-superseded provisions of the 1986 Order.
[46] Insolvent Partnerships Order 1994 (S.I. No. 2421), art. 11, together with Sched. 7. See Form 14.
[47] *ibid.*, art. 14(1), (2), amending ss.168 and 303 of the Act of 1986.

individual member of an insolvent partnership: here, the court may give appropriate directions for consolidating the proceedings.

From the above, it can be seen that an insolvent individual who is also a member of an insolvent partnership may become involved in proceedings whereby an insolvency petition against himself is presented in conjunction with one for the partnership to be wound up as an unregistered company under Part V of the Act.[48] The same insolvency practitioner will act both as liquidator in the winding up and as trustee in the bankruptcies of the individual partners. In that event, it should be noted, the provisions of the Company Directors Disqualification Act 1986 apply in modified form so that any officer or former officer of the partnership, and any other person who has or who has had control or management of the partnership business, are treated like an officer and director of a company for the purposes of the Disqualification Act.[49] The alternative possibility, where both the individual partner and the partnership are insolvent, is that the partners take the initiative in presenting a joint debtors' petition not involving the winding up of the partnership as an unregistered company. In that case, both the partnership assets and the estates of the individual partners will conveniently become vested in the same insolvency practitioner as trustee in bankruptcy, who will proceed to wind up the partnership and simultaneously to act as trustee in bankruptcy in respect of the individual partners. Such an administration will be conducted under the provisions of Part IX of the Act, modified in accordance with any directions contained in the order of the court.[50] This procedure appears to offer a certain advantage from the partners' point of view, in that the provisions of the Company Directors Disqualification Act do not thereby become applicable to them.

The 1994 Order introduced certain new procedures with respect to insolvent partnerships that were not available under the Order of 1986. Thus, Articles 4 and 5 together with Schedule 1 allow Partnership Voluntary Arrangements to be concluded under modified provisions of Part I of the Act, while Article 6 together with Schedule 2 to the Order enables an insolvent partnership to be the subject of an Administration Order under Part II of the Act. These procedures are discussed in Chapters 15 and 16 *post*, in relation to company insolvency.

Finally, if an individual debtor, who happens to be a member of a partnership, is personally insolvent albeit the partnership itself is not, that individual can undergo bankruptcy in the normal way without the partnership itself undergoing any form of insolvency procedure. However, as mentioned above, the bankruptcy of any of its members would ordinarily cause the partnership to become dissolved unless the deed of partnership made contrary provision, or unless the remaining partners resolved that it should continue.

Where a partnership is formed under the Limited Partnerships Act 1907 it is in most respects subject to the rules of insolvency law just like any other

---

[48] *ibid.*, art. 8 together with Sched. 4 to the Order. See also Forms 4–9.
[49] *ibid.*, arts. 2 and 16, together with Sched. 8. On directors' disqualification see Chap. 27, *post*.
[50] *ibid.*, art. 11 together with Sched. 7. See also Forms 14–18.

partnership. There is one vital distinction to be made however with respect to those members who are the limited partners because, in the event that the partnership becomes insolvent and consequently is wound up, the private estate of the limited partners may not be taken by the creditors of the firm, whereas the private estates of the general partners may be so taken.

Undischarged Bankrupts

An undischarged bankrupt may be the subject of further bankruptcy proceedings based upon any fresh debts which have been incurred after the date of the adjudication. Post-adjudication debts cannot be proved for in the existing bankruptcy, and there is no rule or principle whereby successive bankruptcies may undergo consolidation. In practice, the interests of the later creditors will best be safeguarded by their causing second, and subsequent, adjudications to take place.[51]

---

[51] For the relevant rules concerning second bankruptcies, see ss.334, 335 of the Act, discussed in Chap. 10, *post.*

CHAPTER 6

THE BANKRUPTCY PETITION

Preliminary

In the previous Chapter it was seen which criteria must be satisfied with respect to a given person in order that he or she may be the subject of a bankruptcy order. The first stage of the proceedings in bankruptcy is the presentation, to the court having jurisdiction in the matter,[1] of a petition for a bankruptcy order to be made against the debtor in question. Such a petition must be presented by a party with appropriate standing for this purpose, who may be the debtor himself, or one or more of his creditors, or one of a limited number of other qualified persons.[2] The present chapter will explore the question of eligibility to present a bankruptcy petition, and will thereafter describe the legal provisions relating to the presentation and hearing of the petition.

(A) Who May Present a Petition?

Section 264(1) of the Insolvency Act 1986 lists three types of person by whom a bankruptcy petition may be presented. These are:

(1) one of the debtor's creditors, or more than one of them petitioning jointly;
(2) the debtor himself; or
(3) the supervisor of, or any person (other than the debtor) who is for the time being bound by, a voluntary arrangement proposed by the debtor and approved under Part VIII of the Act.

These three cases will be considered in turn.

---

[1] On jurisdiction, see Chap. 2, *ante*, and also *infra*, section (B).
[2] Insolvency Act 1986, s.264(1).

The Bankruptcy Petition

(1) Creditor's Petition

By far the most usual mode of inauguration of bankruptcy proceedings is for one or more of the creditors to present a petition for a bankruptcy order to be made against the debtor. The principal statutory provisions which are in point are sections 267–271 of the Act.[3] These provisions differ in numerous important ways from their counterparts in the pre-1986 bankruptcy law, and as a consequence many cases which were decided under the provisions of the former Bankruptcy Acts have either ceased to be relevant, or else must be read making due allowance for the ways in which the law has been altered. This is especially true of any decisions in which the now-abolished concept of the act of bankruptcy played a material part. In many respects however, the law and procedure concerning creditors' petitions are carried over from the pre-1986 legislative provisions, and to that extent the former case law may safely be referred to in the course of exploring the meaning of the current Act.

(a) Who is a Creditor?

Section 383(1) of the Act supplies the statutory definition of the term "creditor" and declares it to mean, in relation to a bankrupt, a person to whom any of the bankruptcy debts is owed. "Bankruptcy debt" is defined in section 382 as meaning any of the following types of indebtedness, namely:

(1) any debt or liability to which the bankrupt is subject at the commencement of the bankruptcy;
(2) any debt or liability to which the bankrupt may become subject after the commencement of the bankruptcy (including after his discharge therefrom) by reason of any obligation incurred before the commencement of the bankruptcy;
(3) [*provision repealed*]; and
(4) any interest provable in bankruptcy by virtue of section 332(2) of the Insolvency Act.[4]

Having thus established a frame of reference for the term "creditor" in relation to a bankrupt, section 383(1) of the Act utilises it as the hypothetical basis on which to determine who is a creditor in relation to an individual to whom a bankruptcy petition relates: section 383(1)(*b*) declares that the term "creditor" then means "a person who would be a creditor in the bankruptcy if a bankruptcy order were made on that petition." In principle therefore, a person is "a creditor" within the meaning of the Act, and as such is eligible to present or join in a bankruptcy petition against his debtor, if the debt or liability which is owed to him

---

[3] See also Chap. 2 of Part 6 of the Insolvency Rules 1986.
[4] On commencement of bankruptcy, see s.278 of the Act, discussed in Chap. 7, *post*; on proof for interest, see Chap. 9. The provision in s.382(1)(c), which referred to the now-abolished procedure of criminal bankruptcy, was repealed by the Criminal Justice Act 1988, Sched. 16.

Creditor's Petition

satisfies the definition of "bankruptcy debt" contained in section 382(1). Moreover the other subsections of section 382 have the effect of further widening the concept of "bankruptcy debt" for this and other purposes. Thus, section 382(2) provides that, in relation to any liability in tort, the bankrupt is deemed to become subject to that liability by reason of an obligation incurred at the time when the cause of action accrued. Section 382(3) states that for the purposes of any statutory reference to a debt or liability, it is immaterial whether the debt or liability is present or future, whether it is certain or contingent, or whether its amount is fixed or liquidated, or is capable of being ascertained by fixed rules or as a matter of opinion. Taken in isolation, these provisions would give rise to the possibility that a bankruptcy petition may be presented in respect of a debt which has not yet accrued due for payment, nor even become properly quantified, but, as we shall see, the potentially wide scope for creditors to petition for their debtors' bankruptcy on the basis of future or contingent or unascertained liabilities is considerably cut down by reason of the special statutory requirements relating to the petitioning creditor's debt.[5]

In addition to the statutory definition of "creditor" to be derived from the provisions of the Insolvency Act, it can further be observed, as mentioned previously,[6] that there is a logical inter-dependence between the terms "debtor," "creditor" and "debt" in general, legal parlance, and that the quality of enforceability through legal process is a unifying thread linking all three terms together. In view of the various grounds on which an apparent debt or liability may be rendered irrecoverable by action at law, or again may not be recoverable by proceedings brought solely by or in the name of the person to whom the debt is apparently due, it is necessary to form a clear understanding of who, under given circumstances, is the party enjoying the necessary *locus standi* to present a petition.

A number of interesting cases have turned upon the question whether the petitioner was indeed a properly qualified creditor. In *Re Brocklebank*[7] it was held that a minor was fully competent to sue for breach of a contract of apprenticeship, and to issue a debtor's summons based upon the judgment: if this summons was not paid the minor was further competent to present a petition, and his ability to do so was not affected by the fact that, procedurally, a minor is required to institute proceedings through his guardian or "next friend," who must be of full legal age. An essential factor in the decision was that it was to the minor personally that the proceeds would ultimately go, whereas in some situations a person may be clothed with the right to receive or collect money owed by the debtor, but will subsequently be obliged to make over the proceeds to someone else. In such cases, the person concerned cannot be treated as a "creditor" for bankruptcy purposes, because the debt is not owed to him personally.[8] It

---

[5] See ss.267, 268(2) of the Act, discussed *infra*.
[6] Chap. 5, *ante*, p. 70.
[7] (1877) 6 Ch.D. 358. On the contractual capacity of minors, see works cited in Chap. 5, *ante*, n. 34.
[8] *cf.* the wording of s.383(1)(a) of the Act, to the effect that "creditor ... means a person *to* whom any of the bankruptcy debts is owed ... ," and of s.267(2)(b), whereby it is required that the petitioning creditor's debt must be " ... for a liquidated sum payable *to* the petitioning creditor ... " (emphasis added in each instance).

was partly for this reason that, in *Re Sacker*[9] the Court of Appeal ruled that a receiver, whose terms of appointment indicated that he was to collect and receive certain goods on behalf of others, did not stand in the position of "creditor" because he would not own whatever he collected, either at law or in Equity, and also because he lacked the capacity to sue for the goods. By contrast, in *Re Macoun*[10] a receiver appointed by the Chancery Division to wind up a partnership was found by the Court of Appeal to be a good petitioning creditor because the terms of his appointment entitled him to sue and recover a debt due originally to the firm, and *Re Sacker*[11] was distinguished on that footing.

It is well established by the case law that a person who is merely a trustee of a debt for some other absolute, beneficial owner cannot alone sustain a petition against the debtor, but must be joined by the beneficial owner as co-petitioner.[12] Where however the beneficial owner is a person under a disability which incapacitates him from managing his own affairs, the rule does not apply and the trustee can petition alone. Very similar criteria seem to lie behind the decisions in a line of cases established during the time when the law enabled a husband to recover damages from the co-respondent in divorce proceedings[13]: where the order of the Divorce Court was framed in terms which left the husband entirely free to appropriate the damages to himself, he could also be a good petitioning creditor in respect of the debt created by the judgment.[14] Where, on the other hand, the order indicated that the proceeds were to be applied at the Court's discretion[15]—for example, for the benefit of any children of the marriage—or where the ultimate direction as to payment was still to be made in some later order,[16] then the husband lacked the capacity to stand as petitioner himself, albeit he could prove for the debt in question in any bankruptcy proceedings based upon the petition of some other properly qualified creditor.[17] It is submitted that, despite the disappearance of the legal remedy out of which this series of decisions arose, the principle on which they were consistently based retains its validity and is applicable, *mutatis mutandis*, in analogous situations in the present day.

Companies and Partnerships as Creditors

The problem which inevitably arises in the case of companies which occupy the position of creditor is that, being artificial legal entities whose "personality" is purely a conceptual one bestowed by the law itself, companies must act through the medium of some human officer or agent. Such acts are only legally valid if, in accordance with the established

---

[9] (1888) 22 Q.B.D. 179.
[10] [1904] 2 K.B. 700.
[11] *Supra*, n. 9.
[12] *Re Adams, ex p. Culley* (1878) 9. Ch.D. 307; *Re Hastings, ex p. Dearle* (1884) 14 Q.B.D. 184.
[13] This remedy was abolished by the Law Reform (Miscellaneous Provisions) Act 1970, ss.4, 5(a) and (c).
[14] As in *Re A Debtor (No. 975 of 1937)* [1938] 2 All E.R. 530, distinguishing *Re Muirhead, infra*.
[15] As in *Re Muirhead* (1886) 2 Ch.D. 22; *Re Fryer* (1866) 17 Q.B.D. 718.
[16] As in *Re A Debtor (No. 76 of 1929)* [1929] 2 Ch. 146.
[17] *Re O'Gorman* [1899] 2 Q.B. 62.

principles of company law, the agent has been validly authorised in order that the company, as the proper party to the proposed proceedings, may be regarded in law as having duly accomplished the requisite procedural steps. A company may participate in bankruptcy proceedings by any of its officers authorised under the seal of the company to perform the requisite acts on its behalf. It has been held that any person, even a clerk, who is bona fide chosen by a limited company to be its agent, and who is duly authorised under seal to sign and present a petition in bankruptcy, thereby becomes "an officer" of the company for that purpose.[18] Careful attention must be paid however to the precise terms of authorisation, for they will be strictly interpreted by the court in considering the limits of the officer's capacity to act. It is perfectly possible for an officer to be endowed with very broad powers drawn in general terms, such as would enable him to present petitions on behalf of the company as and when necessary. But if the authority is, by its very terms, limited to some specific occasion or a named debtor, the officer will be unable to act on other occasions or against other debtors unless his authority itself is renewed.[19] In any event, the officer must at all times indicate that he is acting on behalf of the company he is authorised to represent, so that the petition is effectively presented in the corporate name.

Additional complexity will arise if a petitioning company should itself enter into liquidation during the course of presenting a bankruptcy petition against someone who is indebted to it. It has been held that, since the liquidator of a company is empowered to bring or defend any action or other legal proceedings in the name and on behalf of the company,[20] his powers include the bringing of bankruptcy proceedings. However, where a liquidator acts in this way he must clearly proceed "on behalf of" the company, and not in his own name as liquidator.[21]

The different legal nature of a partnership enables the partners collectively, or any one of them representing the firm through the operation of ordinary principles of agency, to present a petition in the firm's name in respect of debts owed to the firm. Where enforcement proceedings are in progress and one of the partners of the firm becomes bankrupt, his solvent partner or partners may continue the proceedings, but must join as co-petitioner the trustee in bankruptcy of the insolvent partner in order that the subsequently made bankruptcy order may enjoy validity.[22] If the partnership as a whole becomes insolvent during the course of bankruptcy proceedings against one of its debtors, the conduct of the petition will be taken over by the liquidator or trustee in bankruptcy

---

[18] *Re J.G. Tomkins & Co.* [1901] 1 Q.B. 476. It is also possible for an authorised agent to institute and carry on proceedings on behalf of a natural person, given a duly executed power of attorney: *Re Wallace* (1884) 14 Q.B.D. 22.

[19] See *Re A Debtor (No. 28 of 1917)* [1917] 2 K.B. 808, distinguishing *Re A Debtor (No. 30 of 1914)* [1915] 1 K.B. 287.

[20] Insolvency Act 1986, ss.165(3), 166(2), (3), 167(1)(a), together with Sched. 4, r. 4.

[21] *Re Winterbottom* (1886) 18 Q.B.D. 446, followed in *Re A Debtor (No. 41 of 1951)* [1952] Ch. 192. A possible distinction may arise if a vesting order has been made under s.145 of the Act, whereby the debt in question has become vested in the liquidator by his official name: see Chap. 22, *post*.

[22] *cf. Re Owen* (1884) 13 Q.B.D. 113.

appointed to wind up the partnership, depending upon which form of insolvency procedure is employed in relation to the partnership.[23]

Assignees

A debt or liability, being a chose in action, is under English law capable of undergoing assignment with the effect that the assignee replaces the assignor as the party entitled to claim payment of, and give a good discharge for, the debt in question. In view of the widespread use of assignments nowadays in many commercial transactions, such as credit factoring, the question of an assignee's capacity to present a bankruptcy petition is one of considerable importance.

Where a debt has been assigned by the original creditor to whom it was owed and payable, the assignee's capacity to present a bankruptcy petition in his own name is dependent upon the precise nature of the assignment itself. If the assignment was in conformity with the provisions of section 136 of the Law of Property Act 1925, the assignee is fully competent to petition alone. Section 136 declares that:

> "any absolute assignment by writing under the hand of the assignor (not purporting to be by way of charge only) of any debt or legal thing in action, of which express notice in writing has been given to the debtor ... is effectual in law (subject to equities having priority over the rights of the assignee) to pass and transfer from the date of such notice—(a) the legal right to such debt or thing in action; (b) all legal and other remedies for the same...."[24]

The powers of an assignee under a non-statutory assignment, that is, one not falling within the ambit of section 136 quoted above, will depend upon the still-operative ancillary rules of law relating to equitable assignments.[25] Of basic importance in this context is the rule that an equitable assignment of a legal chose in action—of which a debt is a foremost example—has the consequence that it is enforceable against the debtor only if the assignor is joined as a party in the action. This requirement is a survival from the times when there was a rigid distinction between the Courts of Common Law and Equity, and when only a Court of Equity would countenance the enforcement of assignments of any kind. Since "legal" choses in action, *ex hypothesi*, fell properly under the jurisdiction of the Common Law courts, a Court of Equity would only enforce an assignment of such a chose if all parties were before it, thus

---

[23] See Chap. 5, *ante*, at p. 77 *et seq.*

[24] For a fuller explanation of the meaning of this section and of the law of assignment generally, see: Cheshire, Fifoot and Furmston, *Law of Contract* (12th ed. 1991) Chap. 16, pp. 505–524; G.H. Treitel, *The Law of Contract* (8th ed., 1991) Chap. 16, especially pp. 576–602. For the deemed assignment of choses in action which takes place on the bankruptcy of the creditor to whom them are due, see Insolvency Act 1986, s.311(4).

[25] See Cheshire, Fifoot and Furmston *op. cit.*, pp. 506–514; Treitel, *op. cit.*, pp. 587–592.

ensuring that there was no possibility of a collateral action being taken out before one of the Common Law courts, whose judgment would of course take no cognisance of the equitable assignment. Despite the fusion of the rules of Common Law and Equity since 1875, this rule still survives,[26] although since its primary purpose was to protect the debtor from the possibility of being sued, and condemned to pay, twice over in respect of the same debt it is nowadays treated somewhat liberally. Therefore, if the debtor raises no objection to the assignee's failure to join the assignor in an action to enforce the debt, the court may be prepared to ignore this technicality and permit the assignee to proceed alone,[27] and equally it would seem permissible for the assignee to present a bankruptcy petition without joining the assignor provided that the debtor will acquiesce. Should the debtor raise any objection to this, however, joinder may still be necessary.[28]

In ordinary proceedings for enforcement of an assigned liability, any requirement that the assignor be joined as a party is generally satisfied by the assignor's being joined as co-plaintiff if he is willing to participate in the proceedings, and as co-defendant if he is not. Where the assignee wishes to resort to bankruptcy proceedings however, the assignor's refusal to join in as co-petitioner presents a seemingly insuperable obstacle, since it is not possible for the assignor to become joined with the debtor against whom the petition is to be presented. In consequence, attempts have been made to argue that, even in the case of an equitable assignment under which joinder of the assignor would normally be required, a bankruptcy petition may be presented against the debtor despite the non-participation of the assignor as joint petitioner. However, such arguments inevitably rely upon the sole authority of the first instance decision in *Re Baillie, ex parte Cooper*,[29] a case decided under the Bankruptcy Act 1869 and only briefly reported. The judgment of Bacon C.J.B. consists of but two sentences in the Law Reports:

> "In Equity the assignee is the person to whom the debt is due, and he could sue for it either in the name of the assignor or in his own. I think that the assignee is entitled to present the petition alone."

The statement contained in the first sentence provides the premise upon which is based the conclusion contained in the second sentence and yet, with respect, the accuracy of the first statement, as a proposition of the state of the law, must be seriously questioned. Although in certain circumstances equitable assignees were, and still are, able to sue alone and

---

[26] *Performing Rights Society Ltd v. London Theatre of Varieties Ltd* [1924] A.C. 1 (H.L.).
[27] See *William Brandt's Sons & Co. v. Dunlop Rubber Co.* [1905] A.C. 454, 462 *per* Lord MacNaghten, indicating that Dunlop had disclaimed any desire to insist upon joinder of the assignor.
[28] As in *Walter and Sullivan Ltd v. J. Murphy and Sons Ltd* [1955] 2 Q.B. 584 (not a bankruptcy case), in which in fact the assignors were purporting to be able to sue. The court ruled that the assignee must be joined in view of the debtor's declared objection.
[29] (1875) L.R. 20 Eq. 762, also reported in 44 L.J. Bkcy. 125, and 32 L.T. 780.

The Bankruptcy Petition

in their own name, this possibility only applies in cases where the thing assigned is equitable in nature, such as a benefit under a trust: where a legal chose has been subjected to an equitable assignment, joinder of the assignor remains necessary, and any lingering doubts which may have been present in the mind of a judge in 1875, that the passing of the Supreme Court of Judicature Acts 1873–1875 might have eliminated the necessity of joining the assignor in those instances where it was formerly essential, must surely be dispelled by the unequivocal pronouncements of the House of Lords in *Performing Rights Society Ltd. v. London Theatre of Varieties Ltd.*[30] In that case, Viscount Cave, L.C., referring to submissions of counsel that the fusion of Common Law and Equity had altered the position of an equitable owner, declared:

> "I am unable to take that view ... [W]hen a plaintiff has only an equitable right in the thing demanded, the person having the legal right to demand it must in due course be made a party to the action."[31]

This statement, it is submitted, effectively refutes the reasoning upon which Bacon C.J.B. seems to have founded his judgment in *Re Baillie, ex parte Cooper*, and hence his decision by itself must be considered of doubtful authority for the proposition that joinder of the assignor as a co-petitioner is not indispensable. However, the decision does not appear to have been challenged subsequently in the courts.[32] Furthermore, it is noteworthy that section 267 of the Insolvency Act 1986 specifies a number of conditions which must be satisfied with respect to the petitioning creditor's debt, and that foremost among these conditions is the requirement in section 267(1) that

> "the petitioning creditor or each of the petitioning creditors must be a person to whom the debt or (as the case may be) at least one of the debts is owed."

It would certainly be possible for a court of the present day to adopt a broad approach to the construction of these statutory words, and hold that an equitable assignee of a debt is to be regarded as "a person to whom the debt ... is owed," so that the assignee would to that extent be personally qualified to present a bankruptcy petition against the debtor notwithstanding that, if the assignee were simply to try to sue the debtor for non-payment, it would be necessary for the assignor to be joined as a party to those proceedings. However, it is probable that the debtor would, if he chose to do so, be capable of alleging that the petitioning creditor's debt is bona fide disputed on the ground that the assignee is exceeding his legal capacity by seeking to enforce payment without joinder: if the assignee seeks to make use of a statutory demand for the purposes of satisfying

---

[30] [1924] A.C. 1.
[31] [1924] A.C. 1, 4.
[32] It may be observed however that in *Re Bagley* [1911] 1 K.B. 317 (referred to below, n. 43) the petition in bankruptcy was presented jointly by the assignor and the assignee.

section 267(2)(c) of the Act,[33] the debtor could properly apply under rule 6.4 of the Insolvency Rules to have the demand set aside.

To conclude the consideration of the problems associated with non-statutory assignments, a further special case should also be noted, namely where only a part of a larger debt has been assigned. Such an assignment has been held not to be a valid statutory assignment on the ground that it is not "absolute" as required by section 136 of the Law of Property Act 1925, and consequently it takes effect as an equitable assignment only.[34] This entails, as has been explained, the joinder of the assignor as a party, at any rate if the debtor insists upon it, in any action to enforce payment of the debt. If, however, the debtor is a company it has been held that the assignee of a part of a debt is not precluded from petitioning alone for the winding-up of the company although he could not actually demand and enforce payment in direct proceedings without joinder of his assignor.[35]

Although the main legal provisions concerning the winding up of companies are contained in Parts IV and V of the Insolvency Act 1986,[36] and continue the practice of maintaining procedures for the liquidation of insolvent companies which are entirely distinct from the procedure under which natural persons may be made bankrupt, it can be observed that the underlying aim and policy of the Insolvency Act has been to bring about as close a harmonisation of the two historic branches of insolvency law as is practicable.[37] It would obviously be consistent with this legislative policy if an identical approach were to prevail regarding the eligibility of assignees to petition alone for the appropriate insolvency procedure against their debtor, whether corporate or individual. Given that the main objective of the general law, in imposing the requirement of joinder, was to protect the debtor from hardship or injustice through the risk of being twice sued for the same debt, it would seem that this protection can be adequately assured under the modern insolvency law without the need for dogmatic insistence upon joinder. This is because of the collective nature of both winding up and bankruptcy proceedings, so that the assignor's rights, if any, against the debtor would be extinguished through those very proceedings themselves. Moreover, if any special factors are present which would make it appropriate for the assignee to be restrained from petitioning alone for the debtor's bankruptcy or winding up, an early procedural opportunity will usually arise, as mentioned above,[38] if the assignee seeks to utilise a statutory demand as the means of establishing the debtor's inability to pay the debt on which the petition is based. The

---

[33] See *infra* (*The petitioning creditor's debt*), pp. 101, 110.
[34] *Re Steel Wing Co.* [1921] 1 Ch. 349; *Williams v. Atlantic Assurance Co.* [1933] 1 K.B. 81; *Walter and Sullivan v. J. Murphy & Sons Ltd, supra*, n. 28.
[35] *Re Steel Wing Co., supra*. In an earlier, undefended case involving the same point of law, in which the assignee of part of the debt owed by a company was held to be entitled to petition for the winding up of the company, reference was made to *Re Baillie, ex p. Cooper* (*supra*, n. 29) as showing that a *similar right* existed under the law of bankruptcy: Byrne, J. agreed that the earlier decision was "a very analogous case in bankruptcy": see *Re Montgomery Moore Ship Collision Doors Syndicate* (1903) 72 L.J. Ch. 624.
[36] See Pt. 2, *post*, Chaps. 17–27 inclusive.
[37] See Chap. 1, *ante*.
[38] *Supra*, text to n. 33.

debtor's proper course of action is then to apply to have the demand set aside (or to seek an injunction to restrain the assignee from presenting a winding up petition) on the ground that there is a bona fide dispute as to enforceability.[39]

Garnishee Orders

By means of a garnishee order a person who has obtained final judgment against another person may be given judicial authorisation to attach a debt owed to the judgment debtor by a third party, who is known as the garnishee. Such an order instructs the garnishee to pay his debt to the garnishor instead of to his immediate creditor. It is necessary to distinguish between the rights of a garnishor against a garnishee, and the rights against a debtor which are enjoyed by an assignee (who, as we have seen above, can be regarded as a "creditor" for the purpose of presenting a bankruptcy petition). A garnishee order does not create, as between garnishor and garnishee, any debt at law or in Equity, but is merely a process for the attachment of a debt owed by the garnishee to the judgment debtor. Similarly, a person who has obtained such an order against a company, attaching a debt due from the company to someone who is indebted in turn to the garnishor, does not thereby become a creditor of the company in any sense, and is not entitled to present a petition for the winding up of the company if it fails to obey the order.[40] And it may be noted that the making of a bankruptcy order against the garnishee has the effect of discharging the garnishee order itself.

Assignments by Trustees in Bankruptcy

In contrast to the legal position arising between garnishor and garnishee, a trustee in bankruptcy does, as will in due course be explained,[41] succeed to almost all of the rights which the bankrupt formerly enjoyed as a creditor *vis-à-vis* other persons indebted to him. Indeed, under the early law of bankruptcy the person in whom the bankrupt's estate was vested actually bore the title of "assignee in bankruptcy," and it remains correct even in the modern era to classify bankruptcy as one of the two species of involuntary assignment of contractual rights and liabilities (the other being upon the death of one of the contracting parties).[42] Among the powers enjoyed by a trustee in bankruptcy is that of validly effecting an assignment for value of some intangible asset hitherto owned by the bankrupt, such as any debt owed to him at the date of his adjudication. In principle, the assignee under such an assignment will enjoy the same rights as any other type of assignee with respect to the enforcement of his claim

---

[39] *cf. Re Steel Wing Co.* (*supra*, n. 34) at pp. 356–7 per P.O. Lawrence, J., where the learned Judge indicated that an equitable assignee of part of a debt would be unable to serve a statutory demand upon the company, and would have to establish the company's insolvency by some other means in order that his winding up petition might succeed.
[40] *Re Combined Weighing and Advertising Machine Co.* (1889) 43 Ch.D. 99.
[41] See Chap. 7, *post*.
[42] *cf.* Cheshire, Fifoot and Furmston, *op. cit.* above, n. 24, Chap. 17.

for payment against the person indebted originally to the bankrupt. Naturally, these rights include the right to petition for the bankruptcy of the person so indebted, based upon the latter's inability to pay the debt which has been assigned by the trustee in bankruptcy.[43]

While it is usually the case that some third party will be the assignee, it is also possible, and is legally permissible, for the trustee to conclude a valid sale back to the bankrupt by way of an assignment to him for value of a debt or other property which had formerly passed to the trustee by virtue of the assignee's bankruptcy. To constitute a genuine act of prudent administration by the trustee, the transaction should take place for value, furnished by or on behalf of the bankrupt, at a level which at least matches the anticipated return in the form of liquid funds, available for distribution in the bankruptcy, which might have accrued if the trustee had elected to seek to recover the debt by his own, direct efforts. Provided that this condition is satisfied, the general validity of such a practice of re-assignment back to the bankrupt of assets previously owned by him was upheld by the Court of Appeal in *Kitson v. Hardwick*,[44] and was reaffirmed at the same level in the more recent case of *Ramsey v. Hartley*.[45] In the former case the court dismissed the defendant's objections to an action brought by the bankrupt alone to recover the price of goods originally sold to the defendant before the plaintiff's bankruptcy occurred. Willes, J. could find nothing contrary to public policy in such a sale by the trustee, and even suggested that this might be the most desirable course in some cases where the bankrupt was prepared to offer a higher price than anyone else for the opportunity to recover his own business. Nor could the learned judge find any provision in the Bankruptcy Act 1869, then in force, which might preclude such a sale: the equivalent provision to that now contained in Rule 9 of Schedule 5 to the Insolvency Act 1986 empowered the trustee to sell all or any part of the property of the bankrupt to "any" person and this was held to be capable of including a sale to the bankrupt himself.[46]

Once such an assignment in favour of the bankrupt has taken place, he too will enjoy whatever rights of enforcement properly follow upon the type of assignment which has been effected, and hence he may sue, or present a bankruptcy petition, either in his own name or jointly with the trustee in bankruptcy, according to the circumstances as explained above.

Bankrupts

Not all of a bankrupt's property does in fact pass to his trustee in

---

[43] *Re Bagley* [1911] 1 K.B. 317 (C.A.).
[44] (1872) L.R. 7 C.P. 473.
[45] [1977] 2 All E.R. 673; [1977] 1 W.L.R. 686. *cf.* the unreported case of *Michaelides v. Bank of Cyprus (London) Ltd* (*The Times*, December 11, 1980; also noted in [1982] J.B.L. 227–231). See also *Stein v. Blake* [1993] 4 All E.R. 225, (a case concerned with set-off, *q.v. post*, Chap. 23) in which the trustee's power to assign rights of action back to the bankrupt was accepted as "trite law" by the Court of Appeal. The House of Lords, affirming the decision on grounds which differed with regard to the operation of set-off, confirmed that the trustee could assign the net balance back to the bankrupt: [1995] BCC 543.
[46] Rule 9 of Sched. 5 to the Insolvency Act 1986 does not contain any words to restrict the destination of the property which the trustee is empowered to sell.

bankruptcy,[47] and in addition to certain tangible items the category of exempted property includes some that are intangible, such as claims in respect of torts of a personal character committed against the bankrupt, and also any damages recovered on the basis of a cause of action of this kind. Since these remain the property of the bankrupt, he is the proper "creditor" to sue for them. Thus, in *Re Wilson*[48] where an undischarged bankrupt recovered £250 damages for slander in an action brought seven years after his adjudication, the Court of Appeal held that his trustee in bankruptcy could not intervene to intercept this money on behalf of the creditors. The ground for the decision was that if the bankrupt could not enjoy the freedom to sue in tort and receive any resultant damages, this would effectively render the courts closed to him so long as he remained undischarged, and would amount to a denial of justice and of the right to protect himself.

It is not certain whether a bankrupt could proceed further than the taking of direct action at law to claim a debt due to him, for there seems to be no reported case in which a bankrupt, in circumstances analogous to those which existed in *Kitson v. Hardwick*[49] or *Re Wilson*,[50] has sought to present a bankruptcy petition against his debtor, but it is submitted that there appears to be no objection in principle to his doing so, since it is accepted that in these special situations he enjoys the right to sue in person for the recovery of debts which are legally due to him. Of course, if the bankrupt has already completed the task of recovering damages from some person prior to the date of his own adjudication, all such sums which have accrued to him before that date will form part of his estate passing to his trustee in bankruptcy notwithstanding that, if payment had not been recovered until after the commencement of bankruptcy, the bankrupt would have been entitled to retain them by virtue of the principle explained above.

Liability for Rates

A special situation arises in the case where the debt in question is an unpaid demand for general rates. While it was always the case that, for example, water rates might be recovered as a civil debt in an action at law,[51] the recovery of general rates was formerly restricted to the exercise of the sanctions of distress or imprisonment.[52] In *Re McGreavy*,[53] however, the Court of Appeal decided that an unpaid demand for general rates was a "debt" within section 41 of the Bankruptcy Act 1914 (corresponding for

---

[47] See further *post*, Chap. 8.
[48] (1878) 8 Ch.D. 364.
[49] Above, n. 44.
[50] Above, n. 48.
[51] *Re A Debtor (No. 48 of 1952)* [1953] Ch. 335. See the interesting outcome of the case, *sub nom. Re A Debtor (No. 10 of 1953)* [1953] 1 W.L.R. 1050.
[52] General Rate Act 1967, s.96(1) repealed with effect from March 31, 1990 by Local Government Finance Act 1988, s.117(11) with Sched. 13, Pt. I. See, *e.g.* Fletcher (1988) 1 Insolvency Intelligence 9; Croft (1992) 5 Insolvency Intelligence 33 and 42, for discussion of the remedy of distress in relation to insolvency.
[53] [1950] Ch. 269.

this purpose to section 267(1), (2) of the Insolvency Act 1986), and so might be the basis of a bankruptcy petition presented by the local authority to whom the rates were owing. This rather exceptional decision was made by the Court of Appeal after due consideration of the fact that some species of debt are provable in a bankruptcy although they cannot themselves be utilised as a basis for a petition.[54] Although acknowledging the fact that unpaid rates could not be recovered by ordinary action (and that, under the law then in force, rates were included among the debts enjoying priority over "all other debts" in any distribution upon bankruptcy[55]) the court did not conclude that they should therefore fall into that category of debts which, although provable, will not support a petition. Rather they considered that the priority accorded to such debts under the Bankruptcy Act 1914 (now repealed), combined with a "common sense" approach to the meaning of the word "debt" as employed throughout the Act, constituted sufficient reason for permitting a rates debt to be available as a basis for a petition. From the point of view of local authorities who experience difficulty in enforcing rate demands, this decision was no doubt a welcome one, but it appears to be the only instance to date of the courts admitting an exception to the general principle that legal enforceability of a debt is an essential pre-requisite to its being available to support a petition in bankruptcy.

Although the removal of preferential status from all forms of rating liability, which took place in the legislative reforms of 1985–1986, may arguably have removed one of the principal reasons on which the Court of Appeal based its decision in *Re McGreavy*, the decision itself is probably now sufficiently well established to remain good law for the proposition stated. Anomalous though this special rule may be, it must be observed that the true seat of the anomaly itself is to be found in the curious omission previously to furnish Local Government with appropriate powers to enforce its demands arising from such an important aspect of its revenue-raising capacity. This omission was first remedied with the enactment of the Local Government Finance Act 1988, which had the effect of replacing domestic rates with community charges with effect from March 31, 1990.[56] These provisions were politically controversial and the basis of domestic rating was further recast by Part I of the Local Government Finance Act 1992, which replaced the community charge with the council tax in respect of dwellings from March 31, 1993 onwards.[57] The comprehensive powers for enforcement of liabilities in respect of the community charge were effectively re-enacted with respect to liability for the council tax. Moreover, although non-domestic rates continue to be charged, a new scheme for this purpose was introduced by Part III of the

---

[54] See Chap. 9, *post*.
[55] Bankruptcy Act 1914, s.33(1)(a) (now repealed): under the Insolvency Act 1986 rates are nowhere mentioned among the categories of preferential debts contained in Sched. 6. See Chap. 10, *post*.
[56] Local Government Finance Act 1988, Pt. I, ss.1–3; Scheds. 1–4. See Fletcher (1989) 2 Insolvency Intelligence 67.
[57] Local Government Finance Act 1992, Part I (ss.1–69), together with ss.100, 117(2), 118(1) and Sched. 14.

Act of 1988, (which remains in force), and the provisions for the enforcement of payment both of domestic and of non-domestic rates are in fact identical. These include the making of a liability order by a Magistrates' Court; distress and sale of goods; commitment to prison; and the presentation of a bankruptcy petition or a winding-up petition as appropriate. Thus, the Local Authority has a full range of enforcement remedies available, and express provision is made for an insolvency petition to be presented on the basis of an unpaid demand for council tax or local rates.[58]

Joint Creditors

Where a single debt is owed to two or more creditors jointly a bankruptcy petition can be brought in respect of the debt only if all the joint creditors join in the petition.[59] But if one of the joint creditors has died, the surviving joint creditors may nevertheless present the petition by themselves.

(b) Creditors who are Ineligible to Petition

In certain circumstances a creditor is precluded by law from presenting a bankruptcy petition against his debtor, although he may still be able to prove his debt and receive dividend in a bankruptcy brought about through the petition of some other creditor who is qualified to initiate proceedings. One example which could formerly occur was the case, already instanced, of a husband who had been awarded damages against a co-respondent in divorce proceedings, when the destination of the damages was yet to be determined by the court.[60] Although this particular situation cannot now arise, on account of the abolition of the particular remedy in question, the essential principle which underlay the husband's disqualification as a petitioning creditor is still operative in other cases, and it may be said that, as a general rule, wherever some obstacle would preclude the creditor from taking direct action at law to enforce his claim against the debtor, he will equally be precluded from resorting to the bankruptcy court as an alternative means of enforcement. For although he may loosely be termed a "creditor," such a claimant in reality is not yet personally owed any proper, legally enforceable "debt" which can become the basis of the petition.[61] This form of ineligibility to petition for bankruptcy is therefore attributable to that fundamental interdependence of the legal concepts of "debtor," "creditor" and "debt" which was referred to earlier, and which is further considered below.[62]

One illustration of the above principle arises where a person has become surety for another. Such a person incurs thereby a contingent liability for which he is entitled to prove in the bankruptcy of the person for whom he

---

[58] L.G.F.A. 1992, s.14(3) and Sched. 4; L.G.F.A. 1988, s.62 and Sched. 9, para. 3(2).
[59] *Brickland v. Newsome* (1808) 1 Camp. 474; 170 E.R. 1026.
[60] *Re O'Gorman* [1899] 2 Q.B. 62.
[61] See the words of s.267(1), (2)(b) of the Insolvency Act 1986, referred to *supra*, text to n. 33.
[62] *Supra*, pp. 70, 83; *infra*, p. 101.

stands as surety,[63] and indeed this entitlement has been separately held to justify his being termed a "creditor" for certain purposes within the operation of the Insolvency Act, such as the giving of a preference in his favour, contrary to section 340.[64] But, for the purpose of presenting a petition, the fact that no *actual* debt is owed to the surety until he has been called upon to make some payment to a third party in accordance with his undertaking means that, so long as his liability remains a contingent one, he is not qualified to be a petitioning creditor in respect of the amount for which he has undertaken to furnish surety. Equally, where a surety or guarantor has been called upon to pay but has not in fact done so, it cannot properly be said that any debt is as yet owed to him: it has accordingly been held that such a guarantor cannot claim to set off the amount of these unmade payments against any liability which he may owe to the party whose debts he has guaranteed.[65] Similar reasoning governs the question of liabilities arising between a surety and his co-surety: until the first surety himself has paid to the principal creditor more than the proportion for which he agreed to be liable he is not entitled to call upon his co-surety for contribution, and so cannot present a bankruptcy petition against the co-surety, since the final quantum of the latter's contribution has yet to be ascertained.

One further example of a factor which disqualifies a person from presenting a petition is where he is currently bound by the terms of a valid and subsisting voluntary arrangement concluded between the debtor and some or all of his creditors. This may arise in relation to either a voluntary arrangement[66] concluded under Part VIII of the Insolvency Act (by virtue of section 262(3) of the Act) or a deed of arrangement[67] concluded under the Deeds of Arrangement Act 1914, or an administration order[68] concluded under Part VI of the County Courts Act 1984 (by virtue of section 144(1) of that Act). Much of the case law relating to creditors who for the time being remain bound by the terms of a deed of arrangement was concerned with the now obsolete question of whether the creditor could utilise the making of the deed as an act of bankruptcy by the debtor. Although the abolition of acts of bankruptcy under the modern law as codified in the Insolvency Act 1986 appears to deprive these cases of their immediate relevance today, it may be suggested that the broader principle on which they were founded, namely that a creditor who is presently bound by the terms of a deed to which he has assented is estopped from presenting a bankruptcy petition against the debtor by whom it was executed, retains its validity.[69] According to the case law, dating from long before the enactment of the present Insolvency Act, a creditor's assent to a

---

[63] See the definition of "bankruptcy debt" in s.382(1), (3) of the Insolvency Act 1986, considered in Chap. 9, *post*, and the discussion of the petitioning creditor's debt, *infra*.
[64] *Re Blackpool Motor Car Co.* [1901] 1. Ch. 77.
[65] *Re Fenton* [1931] 1 Ch. 85, decided under s.31 of the Bankruptcy Act 1914 (repealed).
[66] See Chap. 4, *ante*, section (A)(1).
[67] *ibid.*, section (A)(2).
[68] *ibid.*, section (A)(3).
[69] *cf. Re Stray* (1867) 22 Ch. App. 374; *Re A Debtor (No. 11 of 1935)* [1936] Ch. 165; *Re A Debtor ex p. Newburys Ltd* [1926] B. & C.R. 23; (1926) 95 L.J. Ch. 199.

deed of arrangement might be signified at the time of execution of the deed or subsequently, and it was settled law that a creditor might be estopped from petitioning if by his conduct he has so much as signified his express or tacit acquiescence in the deed's execution. Examples of this extended principle of estoppel were where the creditor stood idly by for some 14 days after receiving from the trustee of the deed information as to its terms,[70] and where he implicitly acknowledged the trustee's title by such acts as supplying goods, and receiving payment from him.[71] In contrast, a creditor who has merely given preliminary assent to a deed which it is proposed to execute may revoke his assent at any time up until the moment of actual execution, and in that event will remain at liberty to present a bankruptcy petition against the debtor.[72] Likewise, a creditor who has originally assented to the deed may revoke his assent even subsequently to its execution if that assent was procured by fraud or misrepresentation.[73] And a creditor who, having been among a dissenting minority at the time of execution of the deed, has reluctantly participated in subsequent proceedings once the arrangement had become a *fait accompli*, may succeed in convincing the court that he should not be regarded as estopped from petitioning, provided that his conduct has been consistent with his professed opposition to any arrangement whereby he would be paid less than the full amount of the debt due to him.[74] On the other hand, passive acceptance of the events surrounding execution of the deed, even without actually becoming a party thereto, have formerly been held to suffice for the purposes of estopping the creditor from using the deed as grounds for a bankruptcy petition, for example where he had failed to express dissent at the creditors' meeting at which the arrangement was approved,[75] or where, as mentioned above, he had "sat on the fence" for even so short a time as two weeks, without signifying his reservation or dissent in any way.[76]

Given the altered state of the current law, it remains to be seen how far the doctrine of estoppel may be redrawn in relation to those who have merely acquiesced in, as opposed to assenting to, a deed of arrangement. It may be thought unduly harsh to declare creditors ineligible to petition for the debtor's bankruptcy where they have merely behaved passively when aware that an arrangement was being concluded. Indeed, a notable distinction was formerly made with regard to creditors who had acquiesced in the execution of the deed of arrangement, in that they were still free to petition for bankruptcy on the basis of other, independent evidence of the debtor's insolvency.[77] It is submitted that, where a creditor is not actually a party to the deed, he should be estopped from petitioning

---

[70] *Re A Debtor ex p. Newburys Ltd, supra.*

[71] *Re Michael* (1891) 8 Morr. 305; *Re Brindley* [1906] 1 K.B. 377; *Re Woodroff* (1897) 4 Mans. 46; *Re A Debtor (No. 23 of 1939)* [1939] 2 All E.R. 338; *cf. Re E. and J. Crow* (1907) 97 L.T. 140.

[72] *cf. Re Jones Bros.* [1912] 3 K.B. 234.

[73] *Re Tannenberg & Sons* (1889) 60 L.T. 270; *cf. Re L.G. Clarke* [1966] 3 All E.R. 622.

[74] *Re Sunderland* [1911] 2 K.B. 658.

[75] *Re A Debtor (No. 382 of 1938)* [1939] Ch. 145.

[76] *Re Carr* (1901) 85 L.T. 552; *Re A Debtor, ex p. Newburys Ltd, (supra); cf. Re Day* (1902) 86 L.T. 238.

[77] *Re Mills* [1906] 1 K.B. 389; *Re Sunderland (supra).*

only in cases where he has actively shown his acquiescence in its execution in some way which signifies recognition of the deed's effectiveness.

The Special Case of Creditors Guilty of Impropriety Towards the Debtor

Commercial morality, and respect for the rule of law, may be said to constitute the very bedrock upon which the law of bankruptcy is founded. This has been reinforced through the fact that the judicial administration of bankruptcy has been mainly associated with the Chancery Division and its historic predecessors, and by the close attention paid within the tradition of the equity side of our law to matters of proper conduct and good faith on the part of those who seek to invoke the law's remedies. It is therefore somewhat characteristic of the law of bankruptcy that, as a matter both of principle and of policy, it has developed powerful countermeasures to forestall the possibility that during the course of relations between debtor and creditor, the latter may have employed improper pressure, or even indulged in measures of extortion, before resorting to legal process for the enforcement of his claims. The sanction deployed by the law in the face of such improprieties is to deprive that creditor of his usual right of recourse to bankruptcy proceedings, even though in every other respect he might be duly qualified to present a petition against the debtor. The conduct and practices which are considered to warrant the imposition of this penalty span a broad gamut, and extend from the most blatant use of, or threats to use, physical violence against the person to the debtor or his family, through to more veiled and subtle, but still insidious, intimations of unpleasant and embarrassing consequences which the debtor will be obliged to undergo if he fails to pay up. The very threat to have recourse to bankruptcy proceedings, with the consequent inconvenience and inevitable stigma that such potent measures would occasion for the debtor, may be shown to have enabled the creditor to induce the debtor to agree to an alternative arrangement on terms which are in the circumstances extortionate or grossly favourable to the creditor.[78] Such behaviour by a creditor must be considered a particularly flagrant abuse of the legal process, and it would clearly be a negation of justice for the law to allow its processes to be finally invoked by one who has previously shown a perverse disregard, if not open contempt, for the very principles which the law exists to uphold. It is inconceivable therefore that the court, once aware of them, would allow such a creditor's tactics to succeed, for no debtor should be placed in terror of the operation of the very legal machinery whose purpose is to protect both him and his creditor alike, according to their needs and deserts.

Since there is every likelihood that the creditor's improprieties towards the debtor will not be apparent from the face of his petition alone, the fact that his petition is "tainted" and thereby inadmissible will usually only emerge during the course of the hearing of the petition by the court.[79] In

---

[78] *Re A Debtor (No. 883 of 1927)* [1928] Ch. 199; *cf. Re A Judgment Summons (No. 25 of 1952)* [1953] Ch. 195.
[79] See *infra*, section (B). Another possibility, where the creditor makes use of a statutory demand, is for the debtor to apply to have the demand set aside: see *infra*.

practice, a debtor who has been subjected to pressures of the kind referred to above should appear at the hearing and disclose what has occurred, thereby utilising his right to show cause why the court should exercise its discretion to dismiss the petition.[80] It should be emphasised that in such cases it is not even necessary that the creditor should actually have succeeded in his attempt to practise extortion: the fact that an attempt was made at all is sufficient to "taint" any subsequent petition he may present, even in respect of the debt in its original terms as distinct from whatever alternative "arrangement" was proposed. The court's discretionary powers in dealing with a "tainted" petition are apparent from the terms of section 264(2) of the Act, whereby the making of a bankruptcy order is made a matter of discretion, and not obligation, for the court, and also from the express terms of section 266(3) which confers a general discretionary power upon the court to dismiss a bankruptcy petition or to stay proceedings thereon

> "if it appears appropriate to do so on the grounds that there has been a contravention of the rules *or for any other reasons.*"[81]

It is worthwhile to furnish some examples of the various ways in which pressure may be brought to bear for the purposes described above. Thus, in one case, a creditor made it a condition, before he would assent to a proposed deed of assignment, that a collateral arrangement be made whereby he was to receive payment in full, thereby effectively defrauding the other creditors who had agreed to accept a dividend.[82] In another case,[83] having already presented his petition, the creditor agreed to allow it to be dismissed upon the debtor's giving an undertaking to pay the debt in full with all actual costs and rather more besides: although there is no prima facie objection to a creditor receiving more than he was originally owed, as agreed terms for settling an overdue debt,[84] the settlement was there made objectionable because of the illicit pressure, including the threat to invoke the bankruptcy machinery, which was employed by the creditor to compel the debtor to yield to terms containing elements of costs which the debtor would not ordinarily have had to bear.[85] But it is always a question of fact for the court to determine whether, in the circumstances of each particular case, the creditor has been guilty of extortion, for there is no hard and fast rule that arrangements, even under the shadow of impending bankruptcy proceedings, are automatically tainted because the creditor will in consequence receive more than the amount to which he is legally entitled: it may be, for example, that the initiative to make the arrangement actually came from the debtor himself, and so he cannot

---

[80] Insolvency Act 1986, s.266(3); *cf. Re Otway* [1895] 1 Q.B. 812; *Re Shaw* (1901) 83 L.T. 754.
[81] Emphasis added.
[82] *Re Shaw, supra*; see also *Re A Debtor (No. 20 of 1904)* (1904) 91 L.T. 664.
[83] *Re A Debtor (No. 883 of 1927), supra*, n. 78.
[84] See *Re Bebro* [1900] 2 Q.B. 316; *Re A Debtor (No. 24 of 1935)* [1935] All E.R. Rep. 744 (this point is not reported in [1936] Ch. 292).
[85] See also *Re A Judgment Summons (No. 25 of 1952), supra* n. 78.

subsequently accuse the creditor of extortion.[86] And while it is true that the finding that his petition is "tainted" has the effect of closing the Bankruptcy Court to the creditor, he of course remains free to utilise any other legal remedy to which he may be entitled. Thus it has been held that the fact that a Bankruptcy Court had exercised its discretion to dismiss the petition of a creditor because of extortion did not in itself provide any reason why another court, of ordinary civil jurisdiction, should exercise any discretion which it possessed and thereby refuse his application for an entirely separate remedy in the form of a committal order under section 5 of the Debtors Act 1869.[87] Besides the instances of extortion, there are other cases in which the creditor's behaviour amounts to an abuse of the legal process constituting ground for dismissal of his petition. So where a debt originally owed by the debtor to some third party was bought up by the creditor with a view to acquiring a means whereby to wield power over the debtor,[88] or in order to gain the right to vote for the appointment of a trustee in bankruptcy who was favourable to the creditor's interests,[89] there was held to be good reason for dismissing the creditor's petition for abuse of process. Such manoeuvres must be distinguished, however, from the bona fide expedient of buying up a debt in order to increase above the figure of £750 the total amount that is owing to the creditor from the debtor against whom he desires to institute bankruptcy proceedings: such behaviour does not amount to abuse of process, unless it happens to be accompanied by some additional attempt to put pressure upon the debtor as seen above, or by some attempt to gain an improper advantage over third persons.[90]

Debtor's Remedies for Creditor's Abuse of Process

The Insolvency Act itself provides no special remedies to be available to the debtor where he has been the victim of the creditor's abuse of the bankruptcy process, and hence the only immediate consequence of such behaviour is that the creditor may forfeit the right to have the debtor made bankrupt, and in addition the court may exercise in favour of the debtor its discretion as to the award of costs when the petition against him is dismissed. If the truth only comes to light at a later stage, the court's

---

[86] *Re Majory* [1955] Ch. 600, also reported *sub nom. Re A Debtor (No. 757 of 1954)* [1955] 2 All E.R. 65.

[87] *Re A Judgment Summons (No. 25 of 1952), supra* n. 78. See especially pp. 212–213, *per* Jenkins, L.J.

[88] *Re Adams* (1879) 12 Ch.D. 480.

[89] *Re Pooley* (1882) 20 Ch.D. 685. The provisions of the modern law with regard to eligibility to serve as a trustee in bankruptcy, and the overall control of insolvency practitioners, should in theory render such tactics futile: see Chap. 2, *ante*, and Chap. 7, *post*.

[90] *Re Baker* (1887) 5 Mor. 5. In *King v. Henderson* [1898] A.C. 720, the Privy Council held that it was neither fraud nor an abuse of process to present a petition against a debtor with the indirect motive of excluding him from a partnership. This somewhat extreme decision seems to rest upon a fine distinction between duress or extortion and the use of the legal process to accomplish additional purposes besides those for which the process is designed. For further valuable information concerning the problem of harassment of debtors, see the reports of the Payne Committee, 1969, Cmnd. 3909 (especially paras. 1238 *et seq.*) and of the Crowther Committee, 1971, Cmnd. 4596 (especially paras. 6, 10, 27–29).

discretion may similarly be exercised when the adjudication of bankruptcy is annulled following the debtor's appeal.[91]

The debtor may however have recourse in the ordinary courts to the established common law remedies for malicious proceedings, of which the first possibility is an action against the creditor for maliciously taking or instituting legal proceedings, sometimes described as an action for malicious prosecution. Since bankruptcy is now regarded as wholly civil in nature, the plaintiff will need to establish special damage above the costs incurred in defending the proceedings,[92] but the court may incline to the not unreasonable view that any person against whom bankruptcy proceedings are instituted is thereby injured in respect of his credit, even though he suffers no instantly tangible pecuniary loss.[93] In addition, however, the plaintiff will need to prove that the previous proceedings ended in his favour, and that the defendant acted without reasonable and probable cause.

Another possible action, particularly appropriate if the debtor was subjected to arrest during the course of the creditor's actions against him, is an action for "maliciously procuring something to be done under legal process." The plaintiff must again show want of reasonable and probable cause on the part of the defendant and must further show that the latter acted "maliciously," whether by employing falsehood or fraud in procuring what was done.[94]

A third form of action available to the debtor is one which alleges that the creditor has maliciously abused legal proceedings or the legal process. In this case the plaintiff does not need to prove that the earlier proceedings in which he was the defendant, actually ended in his favour, nor that the defendant, who stood as plaintiff in the former action, acted without reasonable or probable cause, but he may succeed simply by satisfying the court that the defendant's actions did amount to an abuse of process which has occasioned some special damage to him.[95] It should be noted that the Insolvency Rules 1986 contain a provision which is applicable wherever an order has been made under section 286 of the Insolvency Act, appointing either an insolvency practitioner or the Official Receiver to be interim receiver[96]: if the petition is subsequently dismissed, and the debtor has suffered damage in consequence of the appointment of the interim receiver, rule 6.57(2) would enable an application to be made to the court

---

[91] See Insolvency Act 1986, ss.282, 375, discussed in Chap. 11, *post.*

[92] In cases where criminal proceedings were brought against the plaintiff, the court will accept that any expenses incurred in defending those proceedings, going beyond such costs as may have been awarded, constitutes special damage: *Berry v. B.T.C.* [1962] 1 Q.B. 306. ("Special damage" is the term employed in law to indicate such damage as will not be presumed to have been sustained by a person, but must be shown to have followed from the wrong complained of.) On the need to prove special damage where the proceedings were of a civil nature, see *Wyatt v. Palmer* [1899] 2 Q.B. 106, and also *Cottrell v. Jones* (1851) 11. C.B. 713; 138 E.R. 655.

[93] See *Quartz Hill Gold Mining v. Eyre* (1883) 11 Q.B.D. 674. For earlier uncertainties as to the availability of the remedy see *Johnson v. Emerson & Sparrow* (1871) L.R. 6 Exch. 329.

[94] *Daniels v. Fielding* (1846) 16 M. & W. 200; 153 E.R. 1159. See also *Berry v. B.T.C.,* above, n. 91.

[95] *Grainger v. Hill* (1838) 4 Bing N.C. 212; 132 E.R. 769.

[96] See *post,* p. 140.

for it to give such directions as it thinks fit with regard to the appropriate way in which redress is to be afforded to the debtor for the loss sustained.[97]

(c) The Petitioning Creditor's Debt

In addition to fulfilling the foregoing, general requirements of being a creditor enjoying the right to enforce his debt by means of bankruptcy proceedings, a petitioning creditor must satisfy all the particular requirements of section 267 of the Act, in order to be properly qualified to present a bankruptcy petition. Section 267 lays down a number of strict conditions relating to the debt on which the creditor's petition is based. Only if all of these conditions are fully met will the debt in question be regarded as "a good petitioning creditor's debt," with the consequence that the creditor's eligibility to present a bankruptcy petition will be finally established.

The first requirement contained in section 267(1), is that a creditor's petition must be in respect of one or more debts owed by the debtor, and the petitioning creditor must be a person to whom the debt is owed. The Insolvency Rules complement this by requiring precise identification of the petitioning creditor's debt on the face of the petition.[98] Where two or more creditors petition jointly, each of the petitioning creditors must be a person to whom at least one of the debts is owed. This provision in section 267(1) reinforces what has been said above regarding the overall characteristics of the relationship of debtor and creditor and, when read in conjunction with the rest of section 267, has the important effect of excluding as a petitioner anyone who is not personally owed a debt which qualifies as a good petitioning creditor's debt. Thus a person who, though occupying a position of creditor in relation to the debtor, is not personally owed a debt which meets the requirements of section 267, cannot validly present a petition merely because it may happen to be the case that the debtor owes such a debt to someone else, who is not a party to the petition. The essential principle is therefore that only someone who is personally owed a good petitioning creditor's debt has the status of being a competent petitioning creditor.

Section 267(2) of the Act lists a series of technical requirements relating to the petitioning creditor's debt. These provisions, which will be examined in detail below in view of their importance, have the combined effect of making it an indispensable requirement that, at the time when the petition is presented, the petitioning creditor's debt: must be of a minimum value of £750; must be for a liquidated sum payable either immediately or at some certain future time; must be unsecured; must be a debt which the debtor appears to be unable to pay or to have no reasonable prospect of being able to pay; and must not be affected by any pending application to set aside a statutory demand served in respect of the debt.

---

[97] In such circumstances, however, the interim receiver, or any special manager appointed in accordance with the provisions of s.370 of the Insolvency Act, will not be treated as a wrongdoer, and may receive out of the property of the debtor both his expenses and any remuneration properly due to him in respect of the period for which his appointment was valid: *Re A.B. & Co. (No. 2)*, [1900] 2 Q.B. 429; Insolvency Rules 1986, r. 6.56(3)(a), (4).
[98] Insolvency Rules 1986, r. 6.8; Forms 6.7 to 6.13 inclusive.

"The Bankruptcy Level"

Section 267(1)(a) specifies that a creditor's petition may be presented to the court in respect of a debt or debts only if, at the time the petition is presented, the amount of the debt, or the aggregate amount of the debts, is equal to or exceeds the bankruptcy level. Section 267(4) provides that "the bankruptcy level" is £750, but also contains an enabling power for this amount to be adjusted by means of a statutory instrument whenever appropriate, so as to maintain the real level of this statutory threshold, taking account of the changing value of money.[99] As the wording of section 267(1)(a) indicates, it is possible for two or more creditors, to whom as individuals debts of less than £750 are separately owed by the debtor, to consolidate their petition so that it becomes based upon an aggregate sum equal to, or in excess of, the statutory minimum figure. In that case, each of the joint petitioners must in all other respects satisfy both the general requirements relating to being a good petitioning creditor, as already described, and also the further requirements relating to the petitioning creditor's debt, to be considered below. There is also provision in Rule 6.30 of the Insolvency Rules for the court to order the substitution of another creditor in place of the petitioner if he voluntarily withdraws from the proceedings or fails to appear in support of it at the hearing, or where the creditor who originally petitions is subsequently found not entitled to do so. There is an essential proviso in relation to this, namely that the creditor who is substituted as petitioner must, at the date on which the petition was presented, have been in such a position in relation to the debtor as would have enabled him, on that date, to present a bankruptcy petition in respect of a debt or debts owed to him by the debtor.[1]

In quantifying the amount of the petitioning creditor's debt for the purpose of establishing that it at least equals the prevailing bankruptcy level, it is permissible to include interest for periods before the date on which the petition is presented, provided that such interest was properly payable by virtue of the contract or, alternatively, if a written demand for payment had previously been made upon the debtor containing notice that interest would be payable from the date of the demand to the date of payment.[2] The possibility that interest may be added to the principal of a debt, thereby producing a liquidated sum in excess of the statutory minimum figure, does not furnish a general principle capable of being extended to cases of other ancillary expenses alleged to have been incurred by the creditor in the course of his dealings with the debtor. Thus, in *Re Long*,[3] it was held that the costs of an abortive attempt to execute a judgment against the debtor, whose indebtedness was marginally less than the minimum statutory amount, could not be added to the judgment debt to produce a good petitioning creditor's debt. And furthermore, where a

---

[99] From 1869 until 1976 the minimum level of a petitioning creditor's debt was maintained at £50. It was raised to £200 by the Insolvency Act 1976, Sched. I, and was further raised to the present level of £750 by (S.I. 1984, No. 1199).

[1] Insolvency Rules 1986, r. 6.30(2)(c).

[2] *cf.* Insolvency Rules 1986, r. 6.113 (proof for interest).

[3] (1888) 20 Q.B.D. 316.

debt originally greater than £750 comes to be reduced by some means[4] before the time that the creditor's petition is actually presented, the bankruptcy proceedings may continue only if the net amount of the debt which is unpaid remains in excess of £750. Where the debt is either diminished below the statutory limit or paid in full (even by a third party who makes payment on the debtor's behalf), the court can make a bankruptcy order only by resorting to the power conferred by Rule 6.30 of the Insolvency Rules 1986, as mentioned above, to substitute as petitioner some other properly qualified creditor if one exists.[5] If, as a result of mutual dealings between the debtor and the petitioning creditor, the debtor is entitled under section 323 of the Insolvency Act to claim a set-off against the amount he owes to the creditor, the court should first investigate in order to be certain that the balance outstanding in the creditor's favour is not less than £750, and in so doing the court may even go behind any prior judgment in the creditor's favour which is alleged to establish finally the magnitude of the debt.[6] Only when satisfied that the creditor is owed at least the statutory minimum amount should the court proceed to make a bankruptcy order. The same principle applies when the debtor is in the course of appealing against a judgment which constitutes the basis of the petitioning creditor's debt: if the appeal is successful the debt may be diminished or even extinguished, and therefore the court should not make a bankruptcy order until the appeal has been determined except in cases where the appeal appears to be wholly without merit or prospect of success.[7]

"Liquidated Sum"

Section 267(2)(b) of the Insolvency Act provides that the debt, or each of the debts, must be for a:

> "liquidated sum payable to the petitioning creditor, or one or more of the petitioning creditors, either immediately or at some certain future time...."

The requirement that the debt be a liquidated sum is one of considerable significance, and was originally established by the common law of bankruptcy long before becoming part of the express statutory provisions.[8]

---

[4] For example, by the action of a superior landlord in attaching rent owed by sub-tenants to his tenant who is in arrears: *Re A Debtor (No. 549 of 1928)* [1929] 1 Ch. 170. Contrast however *Re A Debtor (No. 2 of 1977) ex parte the Debtor v. Goacher* [1979] 1 All E.R. 870 (payment of money to the sheriff who has levied execution *held* not to amount to a payment to the creditor so as to reduce the debt below the statutory bankruptcy level (then £200) from the moment of payment).

[5] *Re Mann* [1958] 3 All E.R. 660.

[6] *Re A Debtor (No. 66 of 1955)* [1956] 1 W.L.R. 1226, a case whose actual decision rests upon very special facts. For the powers of the Bankruptcy Court to go behind any antecedent judgment, see *infra*, p. 134. s.323 of the Act is further considered *post*, Chap. 9.

[7] *Re Noble* [1965] Ch. 129. See also *Re A Debtor (No. 20 of 1953)* [1954] 3 All E.R. 74.

[8] See *Ex parte Charles* (1811) 14 East 197; 104 E.R. 576.

THE BANKRUPTCY PETITION

It is therefore vital to appreciate which species of claim can be classified as "liquidated," and which cannot, since this quality is so central to the concept of a good petitioning creditor's debt. The decisive hallmark of a liquidated claim is that the process of quantification is already complete, and there is an absence of any element of "penalty" to be imposed over and above the actual loss sustained. Thus, claims in tort are of their very nature unliquidated until judgment has actually been given, or until a binding settlement has been concluded between the parties, because until then the process of quantification of damages remains unfinished, albeit the plaintiff may furnish an indication of a sum of damages which he believes to be appropriate. Claims in contract, on the other hand, are generally liquidated in nature at all stages, but if the sum includes an element which is held to be "penal," this will render the claim an unliquidated one. Likewise if the true quantum of loss directly and naturally resulting from a breach of contract or a breach of covenant cannot be immediately and definitely established, the claim must be considered as unliquidated for the time being. The following cases demonstrate the implications of the rule.

In *ex parte Broadhurst*[9] the father of a continuing partner had covenanted with the incoming partner that the debts of the old firm did not exceed £1,199, and further that if they did exceed this amount he would on demand pay *to the firm* the sum in excess. When it transpired that the debts did exceed £1,199, it was held that the excess did not constitute a good petitioning creditor's debt owed to the covenantee, because the latter would only derive benefit indirectly following payment to the firm, and he would therefore have to prove the quantum of his actual damage in an action for breach of covenant. Another apparently liquidated sum was the object of the claim in Re A Debtor, *ex parte Berkshire Finance Co.*,[10] where the terms of a hire-purchase agreement relating to a car stipulated that if the hiring was terminated prematurely, the full price of the car, plus hire charges, would become payable to the finance company "as agreed compensation for damage and depreciation." Despite having repossessed and resold the actual car in question, the finance company succeeded in obtaining judgment for the sum of £451, being the balance unpaid by the hirer in respect of the full price of the car, and they subsequently sought to present a petition on the basis of this. Cross, J. held that the petition must be dismissed because the petitioners had recovered altogether far more than any possible damage suffered. Their claim in contract thus contained a penal element, and despite its having been the subject of a judgment it could not stand as a good petitioning creditor's debt for bankruptcy purposes. That result may be contrasted with the one in Re King, *ex parte Furber*,[11] where the terms of lending of a sum of £1000 at 7½ per cent interest included a provision for repayment of the whole amount at an agreed date. It was held that the terms of the contract were clearly to the effect that interest at 7½ per cent was to continue to run after the date agreed for repayment, if the debt thereafter remained undischarged, and hence any amount which accrued after that date could be included in the

---

[9] (1852) 2 De G.M. & G. 953; 42 E.R. 1145.
[10] (1962) 106 S.J. 468.
[11] (1881) 17 Ch.D. 191.

creditor's demand, which could properly be classed as being for a liquidated sum.

In the absence of express contractual terms regarding either the payment of interest or the calculation of damages in certain predetermined situations, it is sometimes possible to take advantage of the well-established principle of the law of contract that the rules of some established institutions, such as the Stock Exchange, may be imported into the terms of a contract, either expressly or by implication or custom. In such cases any provisions contained in those rules for ascertaining the amount payable in the event of any default are capable of converting what might otherwise be an unliquidated claim for breach of contract into a fully liquidated debt upon which the petition may be presented.[12]

"Immediately Payable"

In addition to the requirement that the petitioning creditor's debt must be a liquidated sum, section 267(2)(b) of the Act further provides that it must be a sum payable "either immediately or at some certain future time." In effect, this imposes the requirement that the liability giving rise to the petitioning creditor's debt must be existing, and not contingent. Thus, if the debtor has assumed a liability to pay a specific amount of money which will, however, only become payable provided that some event happens or fails to happen, or provided that certain steps are taken consequent upon that contingency, the requirements of section 267(2)(b) will in this respect be unfulfilled unless all those necessary developments have taken place before the petition is presented. This may be illustrated by the case of *Re Miller*[13] where T, an intending member of the Stock Exchange, paid £2,000 to M, a broker with whom he hoped to enter partnership, under the terms of an agreement between them which also provided that if T should not become a member of the Stock Exchange or be at liberty to enter the partnership by a certain date the agreement should be terminable at T's option and the money repayable. The Court of Appeal there held that the agreement, by its own terms, did not terminate automatically upon M's being "hammered" and informing T that he "could not pay anybody." It followed that T was not entitled to present a petition against M before formally terminating their agreement in order to render the £2,000 repayable. On the other hand, where it is an express term of the agreement under which credit was granted to the debtor that, upon the happening of certain, specified events, the credit agreement will automatically terminate with the consequence that all outstanding sums due under it become payable immediately, the happening of the events in question will give rise to a right on the creditor's part to present a bankruptcy petition on the basis of the debt.[14]

---

[12] *Ex p. Ward* (1882) 22 Ch.D. 132, foll. in *Mendelssohn v. Ratcliffe* [1904] A.C. 456 (H.L.). Contrast *Re Miller* [1901] 1 K.B. 51 (*infra*).
[13] [1901] 1 K.B. 51.
[14] *cf.* analogous circumstances in *Re Barr* [1896] 1 Q.B. 616; *Re Raatz* [1897] 2 Q.B. 80, where the event bringing about the automatic termination of credit was the now-obsolete one of the commission of an act of bankruptcy by the debtor.

"Unsecured"

The words of section 267(2)(b) of the Act impose a third, important condition concerning the petitioning creditor's debt, namely that the debt must be unsecured. It is a long established feature of the law of credit and insolvency that a creditor may gain additional protection by effecting some recognised form of security which will remain valid and enforceable in the event of the debtor's insolvency, and of any consequential proceedings such as bankruptcy.[15] In view of the fact that, in most bankruptcies, the creditors receive much less than the full amount owing to them, it can be seen that there is a decided advantage to be gained by the taking of security for a debt. Should the debtor subsequently become bankrupt the creditor may realise his security and thus pay himself in full, and moreover may avoid the delay which the unsecured creditors will experience before they receive any payment at all. Naturally, the prudent creditor will have done his best to satisfy himself, before giving credit, that the security offered by the debtor is worth at least as much as the amount of the debt to be incurred.

Careful statutory provision is made to ensure that a secured creditor remains free to enforce his security in the event of the debtor's bankruptcy.[16] As a necessary corollary to this, it is a well established principle of the law of bankruptcy that a creditor whose debt is protected in this privileged way cannot at the same time utilise the debt as a basis for a bankruptcy petition. Section 267(2)(b) gives formal expression to this principle, but the sub-section itself has to be read in conjunction with section 269 of the Act, which has an overriding role in this matter. By virtue of that section, a petitioning creditor's debt need not be unsecured if either:

(1) the petition contains a statement by the person having the right to enforce the security that he is willing, in the event of a bankruptcy order being made, to give up his security for the benefit of all the bankrupt's creditors; or

(2) the petition is expressed not to be made in respect of the secured part of the debt and contains a statement by that person of the estimated value at the date of the petition of the security for the secured part of the debt.[17]

In the latter event (as section 269(2) expressly provides) the secured and unsecured parts of the debt fall to be treated as separate debts for the

---

[15] For discussion of the general features of credit and security, see R.M. Goode, *Commercial Law* (1982) Chap. 25, and the same author's *Legal Problems of Credit and Security*, (2nd ed., 1988). See also the *Cork Report*, Cmnd. 8558, paras. 17–20 and Chap. 34.

[16] See, *e.g.* Insolvency Act 1986, ss.258(4) and 285(4).

[17] Provision is made concerning these two alternatives in the standard forms for creditors' petitions: see Insolvency Rules 1986, r. 61(5), and Forms 6.7. to 6.9 inclusive. See also s.383(3) of the Act for the legal effect of a creditor's statement under s.269(1)(a), in the event that a bankruptcy order is made on his petition, and Insolvency Rules 1986, r. 6.109.

purposes of determining the creditor's eligibility to present a bankruptcy petition.

The foregoing statutory provisions represent a sensible compromise with regard to the secured creditor's rights. The value of the asset over which a real security right subsists may fluctuate, as may the level of the liability in relation to which the security was taken. In many instances, the security may prove at the critical time to be of relatively little value in proportion to the total amount of the debt, due allowance being made for the difficulty and expense of realising the security in question. In view of this possibility it would be absurd if the mere fact of his being a "secured creditor" were capable of depriving a creditor of all rights of petitioning for his debtor's bankruptcy under all circumstances, even where the true value of his security was so low as to render it practically worthless. Hence it is made possible for such a creditor, in effect, to abandon his secured status altogether by a formal act of surrender for the benefit of all the creditors, including himself. Alternatively he may be able to establish that the unsecured balance of the debt, even after deducting the estimated value of the security which he holds, is still at or above the bankruptcy level. In that event, the creditor can be admitted as a petitioning creditor in respect of the unsecured balance, and thereby remains at liberty to realise his security and to recoup in full as though it were a separate indebtedness, as much of the debt as it proves capable of covering. It is for the creditor to calculate, according to the circumstances in which he is placed, whether it would on the whole be more advantageous for him to surrender his security, and thus render himself eligible in the course of the bankruptcy to receive dividend in respect of the full amount of the debt, or whether he should elect to recover the secured part of the debt in full and receive dividend only in respect of that part which is effectively unsecured.

Who is a Secured Creditor?

The effect of the above is that if the balance of the petitioning creditor's debt, after deduction of the value of any security which he holds, is less than £750, the creditor will be disabled from petitioning at all unless he is willing to give up his security, or unless other creditors join with him, and so it can be an issue of no little importance to establish whether the creditor is properly to be regarded as a "secured creditor" or not. To this end, section 383(2) of the Act furnishes the following definition:

> "... a debt is secured for the purposes of this Group of Parts to the extent that the person to whom the debt is owed holds any security for the debt (whether a mortgage, charge, lien or other security) over any property of the person by whom the debt is owed."

These words appear not to differ in substance from the definition of "secured creditor" supplied in previous bankruptcy legislation,[18] which

---

[18] *cf.* Bankruptcy Act 1914, s.167 (repealed).

received further interpretation from the courts. One point which merits comment at the outset is the fact that the creditor is allowed to place his own estimation of value upon the security which he holds, for the words of section 269(1)(b) require only an "estimate" and not a true and accurate valuation of the security. So, provided that the estimate is itself a genuine one, the courts have traditionally not inquired into its correctness financially even though the result of such an inquiry might be to show that the unsecured balance of the debt was not sufficiently large to support the petition.[19] It may also happen that the creditor has no real idea of the true value of the security he holds, and his estimate may be a pure guess[20]; nevertheless, provided that the undervaluation is not shown to be a total sham, such estimates have been allowed to stand.[21] The most effective sanction which operates in this matter is the collateral rule that the creditor's own estimate of the value of his security is thereafter binding upon him throughout the remaining stages of the bankruptcy, and if an adjudication is made the trustee in bankruptcy will be entitled to redeem the security from the petitioner at the amount of his original estimate of its value, and then proceed to realise it for the benefit of the creditors.[22] By this means, the creditor's gross undervaluation of his security would rebound as a windfall to the advantage of the body of creditors generally, when the trustee gathered his "profit" by first acquiring the security from the creditor for the price the latter had originally placed upon it, and then realising it at its true worth.

It can sometimes be a matter of dispute whether the creditor is really a secured creditor within the meaning of the Act. So, in *Re Perkins*,[23] a limited company was presenting a petition against a debtor who alleged that the company was a secured creditor *vis-à-vis* himself by virtue of a provision in the company's own Articles which declared that the company should have:

> "a first and paramount lien on all shares for the monies due to the company from the registered holder or other persons for the time being entitled thereto as against the company."

The debtor had previously obtained judgment against one of the company's registered shareholders, declaring the shareholder to be a trustee of some of his shares for the debtor, and so he sought to argue that this declaration, combined with the provision in the Articles, constituted the company a "secured creditor." To this a simple answer was forthcoming, for the company was not in law bound to recognise trusts of its own shares, and so the debtor was not a person "entitled to the shares as

---

[19] *Re Button* [1905] 1 K.B. 602.
[20] As in *Re Lacey* (1884) 13 Q.B.D. 128.
[21] See the remarks of Vaughan Williams, L.J., in *Re Button, supra*, n. 19, at pp. 605–606. The court seems to have been remarkably tolerant to the fact that the creditor's "estimate" conveniently left a balance of just £51 unsecured, which was then just above the minimum limit of a petitioning creditor's debt.
[22] *Re Lacey, supra*, n. 19; Insolvency Rules 1986, r. 6.117. See Chap. 10, *post*.
[23] (1890) 24 Q.B.D. 613. See also *Re H.E. Pollard* [1903] 2 K.B. 41.

against the company," whilst the company accordingly had no lien on the shares for the debt to them from him. Hence, the company were not secured creditors. To understand this decision fully, it is vital to bear in mind that an essential aspect of the definition of "secured creditor" to be inferred from section 383(2) of the Insolvency Act is that the security must be held in respect of a debt due to the creditor *from the debtor*: the mere fact that the creditor happens to enjoy a right of security in respect of some other debt due to him from some other party is irrelevant to the question of his status *vis-à-vis* the particular debtor against whom he is presenting his petition.[24]

When the creditor has omitted altogether to mention that he is a secured creditor, or has not made his election as required by section 269(1)(a), this is a ground upon which the petition may be dismissed[25]; or, if a bankruptcy order has been made before the truth comes to light, the debtor may appeal and seek an annulment.[26] However, if the creditor can satisfy the court that his failure to disclose the security was due purely to inadvertence, or that the security was in any case of little or no value, the court may permit the creditor to amend his petition, and all will not have been lost.[27] Indeed, it is well established in case law decided under legislation prior to 1986 that the court has power to enable such an amendment to be made to the original petition even after a bankruptcy order has already been made upon it, but whenever this is done the court has a discretion to compel the petitioning creditor to bear the costs which have been incurred in the action as a consequence of his inadvertence.[28]

Finally, it should be observed that where a secured creditor does give up his security under section 269(1)(a) so as to be allowed to petition for the full extent of his debt, the security passes to the trustee in the bankruptcy whose duty is to realise the security so that its value may be shared by all the creditors jointly. It was held in *Cracknall v. Jackson*[29] that where the petitioning creditor was a mortgagee, who had taken a first mortgage from the debtor as security, his surrender of his security had the effect of placing the trustee in bankruptcy in his place as first mortgagee, and did not accelerate the rights of any subsequent mortgagees: the first mortgage was consequently not annihilated, but passed into the trustee's hands for the benefit of all the creditors. On the other hand, if a secured creditor elects to retain his security and petition only in respect of the unsecured balance of the debt, he is entitled by the provisions of section 285(4) of the Act to realise or deal with his security free from any of the usual effects of the making of a bankruptcy order,[30] and in respect of his security he thus remains unaffected by the operation of section 285(3).

---

[24] See *Re Pearce* [1919] 1 K.B. 354 for a further illustration of this. Contrast *Re A Debtor (No. 6 of 1941)* [1943] Ch. 213.
[25] See further *infra*, p. 131.
[26] See further *post*, p. 314.
[27] Insolvency Rules 1986, r. 6.22. *cf. Re A Debtor (No. 1507 of 1921)* [1922] 2 K.B. 109; *Re Small* [1934] Ch. 541; *Re A Debtor (No. 39 of 1974)* [1977] 3 All E.R. 489.
[28] *Lovell and Christmas v. Beauchamp* [1894] A.C. 607 (H.L.); *Re A Debtor (No. 1507 of 1921)*, *supra*; *Re Pogose* (1882) 20 Ch.D. 289; *Re Small*, *supra*.
[29] (1877) 6 Ch.D. 735.
[30] See *post*, p. 206, and also Chap. 9, p. 281 *et seq*.

Debtor's Apparent Inability to Pay

Section 267(2)(c) of the Insolvency Act makes it a further requirement with respect to the petitioning creditor's debt—or with respect to each of the debts if the petition is based upon an amalgamation of several liabilities—that it must be "a debt which the debtor appears either to be unable to pay or to have no reasonable prospect of being able to pay." The meaning and significance of this provision becomes properly clear only when read in conjunction with section 268, which supplies the statutory definition of "inability to pay" for the purposes of section 267(2)(c). The definition is an exclusive one, being introduced by the words "if, but only if," and in effect creates two possible grounds upon which the debtor's apparent inability to pay the petitioning creditor's debt may be established, namely the debtor's non-compliance with a statutory demand, or an unsatisfied execution upon a judgment debt.

The "Statutory Demand"

The first of these alternatives is designed to provide the creditor with a formal procedure whereby to provoke the debtor into revealing his insolvent situation through failure to satisfy a written demand for payment of the debt upon which the bankruptcy petition is subsequently to be based. This formal demand—known as the "statutory demand"—is adapted from the procedure which has been long established in relation to the compulsory winding up of companies, and which is currently embodied in section 123(1)(a) of the Insolvency Act.[31] The introduction of this convenient procedure for the grounding of bankruptcy proceedings is one of the principal modifications to the law of bankruptcy to have been implemented in response to the recommendations of the *Cork Report*.[32] It not only has the benefit of effecting a substantial harmonisation between key provisions in the two forms of non-voluntary procedure which respectively apply to corporate and individual insolvency, but it also greatly simplifies and clarifies this area of the law of individual insolvency by replacing the numerous, and highly diversified, "acts of bankruptcy" under the former law[33] with a single, relatively uncomplicated procedure under which the initiative rests entirely with the creditor. Although it may be possible to discern a superficial resemblance between the modern procedure involving the statutory demand, and the former, and now obsolete, formal device known as the bankruptcy notice,[34] it is submitted that the policy and purposes of the new legislation would be best served by resisting any temptation to pursue possible analogies between the two. Such a "fresh start" approach to the interpretation of the legislative provisions concerning the statutory demand was judicially endorsed by the

---

[31] See further Chap. 20 *post*.
[32] Cmnd. 8558, Chap. 10 especially paras. 535–538.
[33] As to which, see Bankruptcy Act 1914, s.1(1) (now repealed), described in Fletcher, *Law of Bankruptcy* (1978), pp. 18–37.
[34] As to which, see Bankruptcy Act 1914, s.1(1)(*g*); Fletcher *op. cit. supra*, n. 33, at pp. 28–35.

Court of Appeal, affirming the judgment of Warner, J. in *Re A Debtor (No. 1 of 1987, Lancaster)*.[35]

The essence of the new procedure is expressed in section 268(1)(a) of the Act, whereby the debtor's apparent inability to pay the petitioning creditor's debt is legally established for the purposes of section 267(2)(c) if the debt is payable immediately and the petitioning creditor to whom the debt is owed serves on the debtor a statutory demand in the prescribed form[36] requiring him to pay the debt or to secure or compound for it to the satisfaction of the creditor. If not less than three weeks elapse from the service of the demand, and within that period it is neither complied with by the debtor nor set aside by the court, the creditor can petition for the debtor's bankruptcy on the basis that his apparent inability to pay the debt has been duly established. An order made under Order 29, rule 10 of the Rules of the Supreme Court, requiring a defendant to ongoing proceedings to make an interim payment, has been held to create a "debt" within the meaning of section 267(2)(b), and thus to entitle the party to whom it is immediately payable to utilise a statutory demand framed in terms of section 268(1)(a).[37]

In the case where the debt is not immediately payable, but is due at a certain, future time, an alternative form of statutory demand is provided for in section 268(2), whereby the debtor's apparent lack of any reasonable prospect of being able to pay the debt, when it does become due, may be established through service upon him of a statutory demand, again in the prescribed form,[38] requiring him to establish to the satisfaction of the creditor that there is a reasonable prospect that the debtor will be able to pay the debt when it falls due. If not less than three weeks have elapsed since the demand was served, and the demand has been neither complied with by the debtor nor set aside by the court the creditor can validly present a bankruptcy petition even though the due date for payment of the petitioning creditor's debt may not yet have arrived.

Further provisions relating to the two alternative types of statutory demand, as well as the prescribed forms, which are to be used by the creditor in serving such a demand upon the debtor, are contained in the Insolvency Rules 1986.[39] Care has been taken in designing the forms to make them as clear as possible, and to ensure that they provide the debtor with all essential information as to the legal significance of the demand, the time allowed for dealing with it and the steps which should or may be taken in order to comply with it, and the possible consequences of non-compliance. In serving the demand upon the debtor, rule 6.3(2) of the Rules requires the creditor to do all that is reasonable for the purpose of bringing it to the debtor's attention and, if practicable in the particular circumstances, he must cause personal service of the demand to be

---

[35] [1989] 1 W.L.R. 271; [1989] 2 All E.R. 46. The judgment of Warner, J. is reported at [1988] 1 W.L.R. 419; [1988] 1 All E.R. 959.
[36] See Insolvency Rules 1986 (as amended), Forms 6.1, 6.2.
[37] *Maxwell v. Bishopsgate Investment Management Ltd (in liquidation)* (1993) *The Times*, February 11, 1993, (Chadwick, J.).
[38] See Insolvency Rules 1986 (as amended), Forms 6.1, 6.2 and 6.3
[39] *ibid.*, rr. 6.1–6.5 inclusive.

effected. It has been held that a demand (unlike a bankruptcy petition) does not necessarily require to be served on the debtor personally, but that it may suffice for service to be effected on the solicitor who is acting for the debtor provided that it is thereafter quickly transmitted to the debtor himself.[40] Although there are prescribed forms for use in serving a statutory demand, the demand itself is not a document issued by the court, and there is consequently no requirement that leave be obtained for service to take place outside the jurisdiction.[41] Where the debt in respect of which the demand is served is owed in terms of a foreign currency, the demand may be made in that foreign currency, without the need to indicate any sterling equivalent.[42]

Where the statutory demand is used in relation to a judgment debt, and the creditor knows, or believes with reasonable cause, that the debtor has absconded or is keeping out of the way with a view to avoiding service, or that there is no real prospect of the sum being recovered by execution or other process, the demand may be advertised in one or more newspapers, and the three-week period for compliance begins to run from the date of the advertisement's appearance.[43] When bankruptcy proceedings commence following the use of a statutory demand, there must be filed in court, together with the petition, an affidavit proving service of the demand.[44]

Expedited Petition

Under certain circumstances it may be demonstrable that the deterioration in the debtor's financial position is taking place so rapidly that there is a serious possibility that his property, or the value of some of it, will be significantly diminished during the period of three weeks which would normally have to elapse between the service of the statutory demand and the date upon which the creditor who has served it can present a bankruptcy petition against the debtor. This possibility is the subject of a special provision in section 270 of the Act, which allows the petition to be presented before the end of the three-week period in those special circumstances. Where this is done, however, section 271(2) precludes the court from making a bankruptcy order until the three-week period specified in section 268 has fully expired, but the expedited presentation of the petition makes it possible for applications to be made for an interim receiver to be appointed under section 286, and for a judicial order to be made under section 285 staying any action, execution or other legal process against the property or person of the debtor. In this way, the further depletion of the assets available for distribution in the eventual bankruptcy of the debtor may be prevented.

[40] *Re A Debtor (No. 234 and 236 of 1991)* (1992) *The Independent*, June 29.
[41] Practice Direction (Bankruptcy) No. 1 of 1988 [1988] 2 All E.R. 126.
[42] *Re A Debtor (No. 51–SD–1991)* [1992] 1 W.L.R. 1294; [1993] 2 All E.R. 40. *cf.* Insolvency Rules 1986, r. 6.111(1), which requires conversion into sterling for the purpose of proving a foreign currency debt.
[43] *ibid.*, r. 6.3(3).
[44] *ibid.*, r. 6.11.

In the interests of ensuring that the protective purposes underlying this special procedure are not frustrated through delay, it has been held that a creditor may present an expedited petition under section 270 notwithstanding that there is a pending application by the debtor to set aside the statutory demand. In this instance, the provision in section 267(2)(d) is overridden.[45]

Application to Set Aside Statutory Demand

The combined operation of sections 267(2)(c) and 268 of the Act is affected by the important provision contained in section 267(2)(d), which precludes the presentation of a creditor's petition at any time when there is an outstanding application to set aside a statutory demand which has been served in respect of the petitioning creditor's debt. Such an application may be made under rule 6.4 of the Insolvency Rules 1986, but the debtor is allowed only a limited time within which to initiate this form of challenge to the statutory demand. By virtue of rule 6.4(1), the period allowed for making application is 18 days from the date of service of the statutory demand on the debtor or, where the demand is advertised in a newspaper, from the date of the advertisement's first appearance. An application for leave for extension of time to bring application to set aside a statutory demand, made after the 18- and 21-day periods set by rule 6.4(1) and section 268(1)(a) but before presentation of a bankruptcy petition, will give rise to a situation equivalent to that arising under section 267(2)(d) where an application to set aside the demand is currently pending. Unless summarily dismissed under rule 6.5(1), the application precludes the presentation of a bankruptcy petition by the creditor until it has been heard and determined by the court.[46]

In most cases the appropriate court to which to apply is the court in which the debtor would be eligible to present his own bankruptcy petition.[47] However, where a statutory demand has been issued by a Minister of the Crown or Government Department in respect of a judgment debt which at least equals the current bankruptcy level, and the demand also indicates the creditor's intention to present a bankruptcy petition against the debtor in the High Court, the appropriate court to which to apply to set aside the demand is also the High Court.[48] One important consequence of the filing of an application to set aside a statutory demand is that it causes the running of the time limited for compliance with the demand to cease as from that date. If the application is subsequently dismissed, the court must make an order authorising the creditor to present a bankruptcy petition either forthwith, or after a date to be specified.[49]

---

[45] *Re A Debtor (No. 22 of 1993), A Debtor v. Focus Insurance Co. Ltd* [1994] 1 W.L.R. 46. For section 267(2)(d) of the Act, see *infra* (Application to Set Aside Statutory Demand).
[46] *Re A Debtor (No. 53 of 1991, Kingston on Thames)* (1991) *The Independent*, August 19.
[47] Insolvency Rules 1986, r. 6.4(2) together with r. 6.40. See further *infra* (*Debtor's Petition*) and (*Jurisdiction*).
[48] *ibid.*, r. 6.4(2).
[49] *ibid.*, rr. 6.4(3), 6.5(6).

The Bankruptcy Petition

On receipt of the debtor's application to set aside the statutory demand, the court has power under rule 6.5(1) to dismiss the application without giving notice to the creditor if satisfied that no sufficient cause is shown for it. Moreover, upon such peremptory dismissal the running of the time limited for compliance with the demand resumes. This provision is designed to ensure that the debtor can obtain only a minimal advantage from any frivolous or insubstantial challenge to the statutory demand which he may lodge in an effort to "buy time." The Court of Appeal have endorsed the philosophy underlying this approach to the power of summary dismissal of the debtor's application, pointing out that any possibility of genuine injustice could be rectified by the court at the time of hearing the bankruptcy petition itself.[50]

If the application is not dismissed under the foregoing provision, the court must fix a hearing upon at least seven days' notice to the parties primarily interested, namely the debtor (or his legal representative), the creditor, and whoever has been named in the demand itself as the person with whom the debtor may enter into communication with reference to the demand.[51] Upon hearing the application the court must consider the available evidence and may either summarily determine the application or adjourn it while giving appropriate directions for the further pursuit of the matter. The *Cork Report*,[52] while recommending the retention of the principle that insolvency proceedings must not be brought upon a disputed debt, also acknowledged that in most instances the Insolvency Court is not the proper forum for trying such a dispute. The present rule confers an ample discretion upon the court to frame its directions in the light of the relevant circumstances.

Rule 6.5(4) of the Insolvency Rules 1986 authorises the court to grant the debtor's application on any one of four grounds. These are:

(a) if the debtor appears to have a counter claim, set-off or cross demand which equals or exceeds the amount of the debt or debts specified in the statutory demand; or

(b) the debt is disputed on grounds which appear to the court to be substantial; or

(c) it appears that the creditor holds some security in respect of the debt claimed by the demand, and either rule 6.1(5) is not complied with in respect of it, or the court is satisfied that the value of the security equals or exceeds the full amount of the debt[53]; or

(d) the court is satisfied, on other grounds, that the demand ought to be set aside.

The fourth of these grounds confers a broad discretion on the court to have regard to a variety of factors which may furnish a justification for, in effect,

---

[50] *Platts v. Western Trust & Savings Ltd* [1993] EGCS 75; *The Times*, April 7, 1993.
[51] Insolvency Rules 1988, r. 6.5(2).
[52] Cmnd. 8558, at para. 537.
[53] See above, with reference to secured creditors. See also r. 6.5(5) on the amendment of an under-valued security.

disentitling the creditor from using a statutory demand. This enables the court to have regard to the requirements of justice in relation to the regulation of conduct between debtor and creditor and thus, as has been suggested above,[54] a debtor who has been improperly harassed by his creditor could seek to obtain the dismissal of the latter's statutory demand on the basis of rule 6.5(4)(d). This same sub-rule also furnishes a ground for setting aside a statutory demand which, as completed and presented to the debtor, is so lacking in clarity as to confuse and mislead the debtor in a serious manner. This issue was judicially considered in *Re a Debtor (No. 1 of 1987, Lancaster)*,[55] where Warner, J., whose judgment was affirmed by the Court of Appeal, was careful to emphasise that the former, technical rules developed under the old bankruptcy law in relation to the setting aside of a bankruptcy notice should not be regarded as having been carried over into the new Rules and practice. The learned judge therefore declared that it is not enough merely for the debtor to show that the statutory demand served on him is defective, or that it is perplexing in purely objective terms: he must go further and show that he was actually misled by it. An important aspect of this ruling upon the interpretation of a key provision of the Insolvency Rules 1986 is the judicial insistence that the "other grounds" referred to in paragraph (d) must be of the same degree of substance as the grounds specified in paragraphs (a) to (c) inclusive of rule 6.5(4).[56]

The position was summed up by Nicholls L.J., giving the sole judgment of the Court of Appeal in that same case, when he indicated that the Court's discretion to set aside a statutory demand under rule 6.5(4)(d) will normally be exercised where the circumstances are such that it would be unjust for the statutory demand to give rise to the consequence that the debtor's inability to pay the debt is established for the purpose of enabling a bankruptcy petition to be presented.[57] In the case in question, the debt itself had been overstated by the creditor in drawing up the demand: nonetheless, Nicholls L.J. declared that "... the mere overstatement of the amount of the debt in a statutory demand is not, by itself and without more, a ground for setting aside a statutory demand."[58]

Although in one case[59] Ferris J. held that the court had power to make it a condition of granting the debtor's application to set aside a statutory demand, that the debtor paid the disputed amount into a blocked account pending determination of the uncertainty, the correctness of this approach

---

[54] See p. 97 *et seq*. For consideration of the question whether a debt was disputed on substantial grounds, see *Re A Debtor (No. 10 of 1988)* [1989] 1 W.L.R. 405 (Hoffmann J.) In a later judgment, the same judge stated that his earlier decision had been incorrectly reasoned, and had been impliedly overruled by the Court of Appeal in *Re A Debtor (No. 1 of 1987, Lancaster)* (*supra*, n. 35 and *infra*, next footnote): see *Re A Debtor (No. 490–SD–1991)* [1992] 2 All E.R. 664.
[55] [1988] 1 W.L.R. 419; [1988] 1 All E.R. 959 (Warner J.); [1989] 1 W.L.R. 271; [1989] 2 All E.R. 46 (C.A.).
[56] [1988] 1 W.L.R. at 421; [1988] 1 All E.R. at 960.
[57] [1989] 1 W.L.R. 271 at 276; [1989] 2 All E.R. 46 at 50.
[58] [1989] 1 W.L.R. at 279; [1989] 2 All E.R. at 52–53. See also *Re A Debtor (No. 490–SD–91)* [1992] 2 All E.R. 664 (Hoffmann J.); *Re A Debtor (No. 657–SD–91)* [1993] BCLC 180.
[59] *Re A Debtor (No. 517 of 1991)*, (1991) *The Times*, November 25, 1991.

must be doubted. In two subsequent cases, Knox J. and Vinelott J. have respectively concluded that there is no authority for the court conditionally to set aside the whole or a part of a statutory demand.[60] Neither the Act nor the Rules provide scope for any "grey area" to exist with regard to the process of establishing whether a debtor should be treated as unable to pay a debt immediately payable, and hence the court must either set aside the demand, or otherwise uphold it.

It is respectfully suggested that, commendable though it may be in most respects, the judicial approach to the task of establishing the principles on which to exercise the jurisdiction to set aside a statutory demand may contain the seeds of certain difficulties for the future. Thus, while the emphasis upon the question of *substantive* injustice, rather than mere technical defect, is to be welcomed, there is some cause for concern that the judicial dicta in relation to the relevance of material inaccuracies in the terms of the demand—including the quantification of the actual debt itself—may give rise to casual or shipshod practices on the part of certain creditors who utilise this highly potent and significant procedure. It may, therefore, be necessary at some future stage for the courts to reformulate their thinking with regard to the care and responsibility required to be taken by creditors in this and in related aspects of their dealings with their debtor: a judicious invocation of the *contra proferentem* rule of construction may be one way in which to deter creditors from exercising insufficient care to avoid ambiguity or confusion in the preparation of a legal document of this kind.[61] Such an approach could be linked to an appropriate exercise of discretion with regard to the award of costs in cases where the debtor's application has been reasonably made in an effort to clarify confusion for which the creditor can be held responsible.

Unsatisfied Execution

The second of the alternative ways in which, according to section 286(1) of the Act, the debtor's apparent inability to pay a debt which is payable immediately may be established for the purposes of section 267(2)(c) is if execution or other process issued in respect of the debt on a judgment or order of any court in favour of the petitioning creditor, or one or more of the petitioning creditors to whom the debt is owed, has been returned unsatisfied in whole or in part.[62] This provision, like that in relation to the use of the statutory demand, is closely modelled on a long established provision applicable in company winding up as one of the ways in which a company can be deemed unable to pay its debts.[63] There are however certain differences between the respective provisions which are applicable to the two different forms of insolvency proceedings, the most notable being the more restrictive drafting employed in section 268(1)(b) for the purposes of a bankruptcy petition, in that it is essential that the unsatisfied

---

[60] *Re A Debtor (No. 90 of 1992)*, (1993) *The Times,* July 12, 1993; *Re A Debtor (No. 32–SD–1991) (No. 2)*, [1994] BCC 524. See further Chap. 11, *post* ("Appeals").
[61] *cf. Re A Debtor (No. 1594 of 1992)* (1992) *The Times,* December 8, 1992.
[62] Insolvency Act 1986, s.268(1)(b).
[63] See now s.123(1)(b), (c), (d) of the Insolvency Act 1986, considered in Chap. 20, *post.*

execution should have taken place in respect of a judgment debt in favour of the petitioning creditor, or at least one of the petitioning creditors where the petition is presented jointly. This statutory limitation upon creditors' eligibility to utilise an unsatisfied execution as a basis for a bankruptcy petition has been carefully imposed so as to preclude any possibility of resurrecting the concept of the "available act of bankruptcy" by analogy with, for example, the now-repealed provision for the use of a bankruptcy notice,[64] non-compliance with which by a debtor formerly enabled any creditor, and not merely the judgment creditor, to ground a bankruptcy petition upon the debtor's default.

(2) Debtor's Petition

It has long been a feature of the English law of bankruptcy that an insolvent debtor may seek sanctuary within the bankruptcy procedure by undergoing adjudication upon his own petition. This possibility of voluntarily invoking the law's protection is the logical corollary to the underlying major premise upon which the English notion of bankruptcy is founded, namely that in return for the giving up of virtually the whole of his current property a debtor may obtain freedom from the accumulated burden of his debts, and enjoy the prospect of a fresh start with a "clean slate."[65] The debtor's act of presenting his own petition has the immediate effect of removing both himself and his property from any separate course of action to which his unsecured creditors might otherwise resort, and will thus put an end to the inconvenience and dissipation of resources caused by multiple executions and other forms of enforcement process. At the same time, the insolvent debtor who embarks upon this initiative is effectively ensuring that all his creditors will be dealt with in the most equitable way through the collective process of bankruptcy, whereby such assets as he has for distribution amongst his creditors will be rateably shared by them in proportion to the debts which they are owed.[66] Thus, the ends of justice are served by the debtor ensuring that the recoupment of debts will cease to be a question of which of his creditors happen to be in a position to trace and seize assets in satisfaction of their claims. Even though the debtor is thereby ensuring that he will undergo adjudication as a bankrupt, this course of action represents, for the debtor who is merely unfortunate rather than dishonest (and especially for the debtor who has not previously undergone bankruptcy)[67] the means whereby he may free himself from the otherwise inexorable burden of his accumulated debts

---

[64] See Bankruptcy Act 1914, ss.(1)(*g*), 4(1)(d) (now repealed).

[65] This concept derives from the ancient Roman concept of *novae tabulae*, or general public cancellation of private debts, whereby the "slates," or tablets, of creditors' accounts were ordered to be wiped clean, thus deleting the liabilities which they evidenced: Cicero, Phil. 6, 4, 11; *id.*, Att. 5, 21, 13; 14, 21, 4; *id.*, Off. 2.23, 84.

[66] Admittedly, this statement must be qualified in the light of the fact that ordinary, unsecured creditors may receive little or nothing by way of dividend, whereas some of them might have fared substantially better in a private "race of diligence" outside of bankruptcy. See further Chap. 10, *post*.

[67] By virtue of s.279(1)(b), (2) of the Insolvency Act 1986, discussed in Chap. 11, *post*.

and enjoy the prospect of eventual rehabilitation in the realms of credit and commerce.

A further reason militating in favour of the debtor's taking the initiative in presenting his own petition is that under section 273 of the Act, the court will then be required to have regard to the appropriateness of appointing an insolvency practitioner to explore the possibility of concluding a voluntary arrangement under Part VIII of the Act as an alternative to the debtor being adjudged bankrupt. This exploratory procedure, which is further discussed later in this chapter, does not form a required part of the procedure upon a creditor's petition for a bankruptcy order against the debtor.

Possible Abuse of the Right of Petition

Although the above assessment of the law's policy and purposes is felt to furnish a justification for allowing a debtor to present his own petition, this facility can obviously provide a means whereby the dishonest and undeserving may contrive to elude their creditors and even, prospectively, recommence their nefarious practices. Some of the ways in which the law seeks to inhibit such possibilities, namely by the assertion of powers to set aside dishonest or fraudulent transactions and by the provision of safeguards which must be met before the bankrupt can be granted his discharge, will be dealt with in due course.[68] There is also an extensive category of criminal offences which are applicable in cases of misconduct perpetrated by those who come to be adjudged bankrupt,[69] and it should be remembered moreover that section 266(2) of the Insolvency Act provides that once a bankruptcy petition has been presented it cannot be withdrawn except by leave of the court. This ensures that the court, rather than the debtor, enjoys the initiative once the petition has been presented, and therefore considerably restricts the ability of debtors to "buy time" through the expedient of commencing proceedings against themselves with the intention of withdrawing the petition before a bankruptcy order is made: the court may properly persist in making the order and at this point not only the civil, but also the potential criminal consequences may come into play.

In addition to these not inconsiderable sanctions against misuse of the bankruptcy machinery, the law provides an additional safeguard which is operative at the very beginning of proceedings, when the debtor first presents his petition. For the court has always had a residuary discretion to refuse to entertain a petition where its presentation amounts to an abuse of the legal process.[70] This discretion, as has already been explained,[71] is encapsulated in the permissive words of section 264(2) of the Act, whereby it is provided that the court "may make a bankruptcy order on

---

[68] See *post*, Chaps. 8 and 11.
[69] See *post*, Chap. 13.
[70] *Re Bond* (1888) 21 Q.B.D. 17, 20, *per* Cave, J., and *Re Betts* [1901] 2 K.B. 39 (both discussed, *infra*); *cf.* also *Re Larard* (1896) 3 Mans. 317 (concerning dismissal of a creditor's petition as being vexatious). The court's discretion to dismiss a creditor's petition is considered, *supra*, pp. 97–99.
[71] *Supra*, p. 97.

any such petition," and is further affirmed by the express terms of section 266(3) to the effect that the court has a general power, if it appears to it appropriate to do so on the grounds that there has been a contravention of the rules or for any other reason, to dismiss a bankruptcy petition or to stay proceedings thereon. Later provisions within the Insolvency Act itself confer upon the court the power to "review, rescind or vary" any order made by it under its bankruptcy jurisdiction,[72] thus providing scope for the review of any bankruptcy order without prescribing any limitations to the grounds upon which this may be done, and there are the usual possibilities for appeal from a decision of a court sitting at first instance.[73] A further statutory provision which is of relevance in relation to possible abuse of the right of petition is section 282(1)(a), which allows the court full discretion to annul a bankruptcy order where it is of the opinion that, on grounds existing at the time the order was made, the debtor ought not to have been adjudicated bankrupt.

It would seem logical that such wide discretionary powers as have been described above should not simply be reserved for use only after a bankruptcy order has been made, but that the court upon first hearing a debtor's petition should be able then and there to consider that it is unacceptable as being an abuse of process. However, the court may not become aware of any impropriety at the time the debtor first presents his petition, and so the usual sequence of events, reflected in many of the decided cases, is for a bankruptcy order to be made in the first instance and for any challenge alleging impropriety as regards the petition to be advanced by way of an appeal either by the creditors[74] or by the Official Receiver.[75] At the hearing of such an appeal the court can rule, in the words of the statute, that the bankruptcy order "ought not to have been made," and proceed to annul the adjudication by exercising the powers conferred by section 282(1)(a). In that event there is then the possibility of a challenge to the annulment, brought by the debtor alleging that the court ought not so to have exercised its discretion, and seeking to have the order of adjudication restored.[76] If the court's exercise of its discretion is upheld however, the practical effect is that the debtor's attempt to take refuge under the protective mantle of the bankruptcy law will have failed.

In reviewing the exercise of discretion by the lower court, it seems that the appellate court will regard the discretion, though lacking any express statutory limitations, as one to be exercised subject to a number of guiding considerations, and if it decides that these have been neglected by the Court below it may proceed to reverse the decision.[77] In order to ascertain

---

[72] s.375(1).
[73] Insolvency Act 1986, s.375(2). See Chap. 11, *post*.
[74] As in *Re Hester* (1889) 22 Q.B.D. 632, and *Re Dunn* [1949] Ch. 640.
[75] As in *Re Bond* and *Re Betts* (*supra*, n. 70) and also in *Re Archer* (1904) 20 T.L.R. 390 and *Re Hancock* [1904] 1 K.B. 585.
[76] See *Re Painter* [1895] 1 Q.B. 85; *Re Izod* [1898] 1 Q.B. 241, and *Re A Debtor (No. 17 of 1966)* [1967] 1 All E.R. 668.
[77] *Re A Debtor (No. 12 of 1970)* [1971] 1 All E.R. 504, 507–509, *per* Stamp, J. The case in fact involved a creditor's petition, but it is apparent that the remarks relating to the possibility of challenging an exercise of discretion by a lower court are equally applicable to cases of debtors' petitions. (The decision was affirmed by the C.A., see [1971] 2 All E.R. 1494).

the nature of these guiding considerations it is necessary to have regard to the decisions in the relevant cases. Thus, in *Re Hester*,[78] the Court of Appeal affirmed that the registrar of the County Court had possessed full power, if he chose, to rescind a receiving order originally made against a debtor whose creditors were at the later hearing joining with him in his request that the order be rescinded. Nevertheless, the court declared that the Registrar had been correct in refusing to rescind the order, because the creditors had not in fact been paid in full, the debtor was hopelessly insolvent and it emerged that debtor and creditors had come to some private arrangement among themselves which Fry, L.J. characterised as one of the evils to which the bankruptcy law seeks to put an end.[79] In *Re Bond*,[80] on the other hand, the Official Receiver revealed that the joint traders had, by petitioning jointly for a receiving order against themselves, deprived the Revenue of £5 in stamp duty and were additionally intending to pay the husband's debts out of the wife's assets: the joint receiving order could therefore be set aside, because their petition was tainted with these improprieties.

A clear case of abuse of process was disclosed in *Re Betts*,[81] where the debtor had on two previous occasions evaded committal orders by the expedient of presenting a petition against himself which placed him beyond the reach of the ordinary procedures for enforcing repayment of judgment debts: his third attempt to utilise this means of effectively defrauding his creditors was confounded when the court rescinded the receiving order which had originally been made, and he was thus left at last to face his creditors and their committal orders. But the court in *Re Betts* was careful to point out that a debtor is allowed by the law to present a petition against himself even though his sole objective is to escape his creditors: the distinguishing aspect in the case was simply the fact that the debtor was flagrantly abusing this legal privilege, as was evident from the manner in which he had established a habit of utilising this means of escape. In *Re Painter*[82] another debtor, who had also resorted to filing his own petition in the face of a judgment summons, was successful in persuading the Divisional Court to restore, albeit with reluctance, the receiving order which had been rescinded by the County Court in consequence of an appeal by the judgment creditor: Vaughan Williams J. concluded that it was the statutory policy to enable the debtor to invoke this process in order to protect himself when in debt. Perhaps the most candid assessment of the seemingly indulgent attitude which the law adopts was that presented by Lord Evershed, M.R. in his judgment in *Re Dunn*[83]:

---

[78] See *supra*, n. 74. The intermediate order, known as a receiving order, which was formerly a part of the bankruptcy process has been discontinued under the Insolvency Act 1986, and a court today would normally proceed directly to make a bankruptcy order. Note however, the power to appoint an interim receiver under s.286 of the Act.
[79] See *Re Hester* (1889) 22 Q.B.D. 632, 641.
[80] See above, n. 70.
[81] See above, n. 70.
[82] See above, n. 76, followed in *Re Archer*, above, n. 75.
[83] [1949] 1 Ch. 640, 647.

Debtor's Petition

"There is nothing, I think, in the policy of the Act which disentitles the debtor to say: 'I will go bankrupt and protect myself from these possibilities and get rid, whether or not they are provable debts, of any claims which are made against me.' I think there is no ground for saying that that attitude amounts to an abuse of the process of the court, and no ground for saying that (without it amounting to an abuse of process of the court) it can be treated as sufficient reason for the court exercising its powers under [s.29 of the Bankruptcy Act 1914] and annulling the order."

This indicates that the debtor is allowed considerable latitude, although it must be borne in mind that, by affirming the bankruptcy order and so keeping the debtor subject to the regime of the bankruptcy law, the court thereby reserves to itself the capacity to deal with him in an appropriate manner at a later stage, such as when he seeks to obtain an order of discharge.[84] Moreover, the courts are aware of their duty to the public in general and to the creditors in particular, and may conclude that this duty is best fulfilled by ordaining that the administration in bankruptcy shall run its course, for then the creditors may proceed to prove for their debts and receive repayment, perhaps in full and certainly on an equitable basis, whereas there is always the danger, if once the matter is released from the control of the court, that some improper settlement may pass without redress. Hence, in *Re Izod*,[85] the court emphasised that the discretion to discharge an order must be used with great caution to ensure that the best interests of all the creditors are safeguarded and that there has been no misconduct by the debtor in connection with his insolvency. In normal circumstances, and apart from abuse of process, it may be said, the courts have traditionally exercised the discretion to undo or halt the course of bankruptcy processes, once a bankruptcy order has actually been made, only if they are satisfied that an arrangement has been made which is equivalent to one which would have been arrived at under the provisions of the Act itself. Accordingly, the mere fact that, for example, the debtor is a solicitor who is in danger of losing his practising certificate unless the bankruptcy order against him is rescinded, is not likely to move the court to consider it a special case for exercising its discretion to discharge the order.[86]

A further basis upon which the debtor's petition, and any order ensuing from it, may be set aside is to be discerned in the opening words of section 272(1) of the Act:

"a debtor's petition may be presented to the court only on the grounds that the debtor is unable to pay his debts."

If it can be shown that the debtor can in fact pay those debts which are presently exigible against him, his action in presenting a petition can be

---

[84] See *post*, Chap. 11.
[85] Above, n. 76. The case was explained in *Re A Debtor (No. 12 of 1970)*, above n. 77, and further considered when that same case was before the C.A.: [1971] 2 All E.R. 1494.
[86] See *Re A Debtor (No. 12 of 1970)* [1971] 2 All E.R. 1494, *per* Russell, L.J.

challenged as an abuse of process, and any bankruptcy order which has already been made before a challenge is registered may again be annulled. In *Re A Debtor, ex parte the Debtor v. Allen (No. 17 of 1966)*[87] a judgment debtor owing £2,400 had been ordered by the court to pay the debt by instalments of £1.25 per week. On that footing the debtor could pay all his debts, yet he presented a petition against himself claiming that he could not pay a debt of £2,400, hoping thereby to bring about the discharge of the entire judgment debt through bankruptcy. The creditor's appeal was upheld, and the debtor's adjudication was annulled, because the debtor was not liable to pay that sum immediately, nor had he need to invoke the protection of the bankruptcy law, since the terms of the order for payment by instalments offered him sufficient protection already. It should further be noted that the Act does not lay down any minimum figure of indebtedness which the debtor must establish in order to be qualified to present his own petition: so long as he is unable to pay his debts presently due, he is entitled to present the petition whatever their amount. This may be contrasted with the £750 minimum requirement in the case of a creditor's petition.[88]

(3) Petition Following Default in Connection with a Voluntary Arrangement

As was explained in Chapter 4,[89] a voluntary arrangement under Part VIII of the Insolvency Act is intended to provide a formal alternative to bankruptcy. Consequently, while such an arrangement is in force and undergoing implementation no person who is bound by it may have recourse to a bankruptcy petition against the debtor. Where however, the debtor fails to comply with his obligations under the arrangement, or where it can be shown that the debtor has supplied false or misleading information during the course of concluding the arrangement, or where he fails to do all that may be reasonably required of him by the supervisor of the arrangement for the purposes of its implementation, the debtor forfeits the protection from bankruptcy adjudication which the law has thus far afforded him. Section 264(1)(c) of the Act allows a petition for a bankruptcy order to be presented by the supervisor of the voluntary arrangement, or by any person (other than the debtor himself) who is for the time being bound by it, but this is subject to the provisions of section 276(1), which requires the court to be satisfied that at least one of the three specified grounds of fault or violation instanced above are established.[90] Notably, the drafting of section 264(1)(c) precludes the possibility that the debtor himself may present a petition for a bankruptcy order, the underlying logic of this being apparently that it should not be open to a debtor who has induced his creditors to accept his proposal for a voluntary arrangement to render the entire exercise a futility by his own conduct in

---

[87] [1967] Ch. 590, distinguishing *Re Dunn* and *Re Hancock*, above, nn. 74, 75.
[88] See further, above p. 101.
[89] *Ante*, p. 41 *et seq*.
[90] See further, *ante*, p. 53.

first defaulting upon his obligations under the arrangement, and thereafter presenting a petition for his own adjudication. This is an important safeguard because the debtor might otherwise occupy a position of considerable tactical strength which he might exploit, in appropriate circumstances, to frustrate the objectives of the voluntary arrangement and thereby to flout the obligations into which he had previously entered with his creditors' approval. Therefore, if a debtor commits default in connection with a voluntary arrangement it is for the supervisor of that arrangement, or any of the creditors who are bound by it, to determine whether the entire arrangement shall be brought to an end, and a bankruptcy order applied for by way of a petition.

It is noteworthy that the restrictions upon eligibility to petition which arise by virtue of the combined effects of sections 264(1)(c) and 276(1) only apply, in the case of creditors, to those who are "for the time being bound by [the] voluntary arrangement". It follows, therefore, that any person who stands in the position of creditor but who, for some reason, is not for the time being bound by the arrangement, is potentially capable of defeating the entire exercise even though it may be the case that none of the circumstances mentioned in section 276(1) is operative. The relevant provision of the Act for determining which persons are bound by an arrangement that has been approved is section 260(2)(b), which states that it binds every person who in accordance with the results had notice of, and was entitled to vote at, the meeting, irrespective of whether that person was present or represented, and irrespective of whether he actively supported or opposed its adoption. Consequently, much depends upon the extent to which the rules for convening the creditors' meeting, and its actual conduct, have been complied with in the instant case. If the debtor, for example, fails to ensure that all existing creditors are included in the information supplied to the nominee, and on which the latter will base his administrative preparations, the consequence could well be that one or more creditors will not receive notice of the meeting at which they would have been eligible to vote, and hence will not be bound by the outcome.[91] Alternatively, a creditor of whose existence the nominee is aware, but whose eligibility to vote is in question because the debt is for an unliquidated amount, or is for a value which is not ascertained, will likewise escape being bound unless an agreement can be arrived at between that creditor and the nominee to put an estimated minimum value upon the debt for voting purposes.[92] In that event, it will not suffice, and can indeed be counterproductive of certainty, if the nominee unilaterally proceeds to allocate a virtually nominal value to the debt, for that will leave the protesting creditor outside the ranks of those bound by the arrangement.[93]

---

[91] Insolvency Rules 1986, r.5.17(1).
[92] *ibid.*, r. 5.17(3).
[93] See *Re. A Debtor (No. 162 of 1993), Doorbar v. Alltime Securities Ltd* [1994] BCC 994 (Knox, J), distinguishing *Re Cranley Mansions Ltd, Saigol v. Goldstein* [1994] BCC 576 (Ferris, J). Both cases are, discussed in Chapter 4, *ante*, at p. 48 *et seq.*

(B) Procedure and Jurisdiction

(1) Proper Court for Bringing Proceedings

Jurisdiction in bankruptcy, and in matters pertaining to individual insolvency, is exercised throughout England and Wales by the High Court and the County Courts.[94] In the exercise of this jurisdiction a County Court has, in addition to its ordinary jurisdiction, all the powers and jurisdiction of the High Court, and the orders of the County Court may be enforced accordingly as though they had emanated from the High Court.[95] A rationalised arrangement for the particularised allocation of jurisdiction by reference to court districts has been in operation since 1869, and its rules have the effect of determining the proper court for the bringing of bankruptcy proceedings, based upon the whereabouts of the debtor's place of residence or place of carrying on business within the six months immediately preceding presentation of the petition. This jurisdiction is a sole one as far as concerns the court which is thus identified by reference to the specified criteria, and in cases where the place of residence and place of business are located in different court districts, the business qualification predominates.[96] If during the relevant six months' period the debtor has carried on business in more than one insolvency district, the petition must be presented to the court for the insolvency district in which his principal place of business is, or has been for the longest period in those six months.[97] No statutory criteria are laid down for the purpose of determining which place of business is to be regarded as the principal one, and it must hence be a matter of judgment based upon a commonsense view of the facts of each case. Rules 6.9(5) and 6.40(4) of the Insolvency Rules 1986 require that the petition must contain sufficient information to establish that it is brought in the appropriate court.

High Court

As between High Court and County Court, the division of jurisdiction is based upon the historic fact that in modern times no jurisdiction in insolvency matters has been conferred upon County Courts within the Greater London area. In relation to this area—known as the London Insolvency District[98]—jurisdiction is exercised by the High Court, and it is there that any petition should be presented in relation to a debtor who has either resided or carried on business within that district for the greater part of the six months immediately preceding the presentation of the petition,

---

[94] Insolvency Act 1986, s.373(1).
[95] *ibid.*, s.373(2).
[96] Insolvency Rules 1986, rr. 6.9(3), 6.40(2)(b).
[97] *ibid.*, rr. 6.9.(4), 6.40(2)(c).
[98] Insolvency Act 1986, s.374(4)(a). The London Insolvency District comprises the county court districts of the following metropolitan County Courts: Barnet; Bloomsbury; Bow; Brentford; Clerkenwell; Edmonton; Ilford; Lambeth; Marylebone; the Mayor's and City of London Court; Shoreditch (amalgamated with the Whitechapel County Court); Southwark; Wandsworth; Westminster; the West London County Court (formerly Brompton); and Willesden: Civil Courts Order 1983 (S.I. 1983, No. 713), Sched. 3 (as amended).

or for a longer period in those six months than in any other insolvency district.[99] The High Court is also the proper venue in those cases where the debtor is not resident in England or Wales, or where the petitioner is unable to ascertain the residence of the debtor, or his place of business.[1] Finally, the High Court is the prescribed venue where the petition is presented by a Minister of the Crown or a Government Department, provided that either the creditor has indicated in the statutory demand on which the petition is based that it is his intention to present a petition to the High Court, or the petition is presented in respect of an unsatisfied execution on a judgment debt in favour of the Minister or the Department.[2]

County Courts

Not all of the provincial County Courts enjoy an insolvency jurisdiction. By long established practice, only the larger County Courts outside the London Insolvency District are given such jurisdiction, and this jurisdiction is consequently exercised over a designated area usually comprising several County Court districts. The allocation of jurisdiction in accordance with this system of arrangement, and the designation of those areas which are to be comprised in the insolvency district of each County Court to which insolvency jurisdiction is thus allocated, is performed by the Lord Chancellor acting by statutory instrument under powers conferred by section 374 of the Insolvency Act. The arrangements are variable within the terms of the enabling provision, and are revised periodically.[3] Not all of the County Courts upon which insolvency jurisdiction is conferred are in session on a fulltime basis: in cases where such a court proves to be the proper court for presentation of the petition, and the petition is one which is presented by the debtor himself under section 264(1)(b) of the Act, the Rules make provision for an expedited hearing of the petition by allowing it to be presented in a court specified as being, in relation to the debtor's own County Court, the nearest fulltime court.[4]

The general principle of jurisdiction is therefore that, in cases which fall outside the jurisdiction of the High Court, the petition must be presented to the County Court for the insolvency district in which the debtor has resided or carried on business for the longest period during the six months immediately preceding the presentation of the petition. There is one further, overriding rule of jurisdiction applicable exclusively to cases

---

[99] Insolvency Act 1986, s.373(3)(a); Insolvency Rules 1986, rr. 6.9(1)(b), 6.40(1)(a).
[1] Insolvency Rules 1986, rr. 6.9(1)(c), (d), 6.40(1)(b).
[2] *ibid.*, r. 6.9(1)(a).
[3] See s.374(1), (2), (3) of the Act. The primary provisions for allocation of insolvency jurisdiction are contained in the Civil Courts Order 1983 (above, n. 98 (as amended), together with Sched. 2 of the Insolvency Rules 1986, as substituted by the Insolvency (Amendment) Rules 1987 (S.I. 1987, No. 1919)). The jurisdictional arrangements in force on the commencement date of the Insolvency Act 1986 (December 24, 1986) were given continuity of effect by s.374(4)(b) of that Act.
[4] Insolvency Rules 1986, r. 6.40(3) together with Sched. 2 to the Rules, as substituted by Pt. 3 of the Sched. to the Insolvency (Amendment) Rules 1987 (S.I. 1987, No. 1919).

where a petition is presented at a time when a voluntary arrangement under Part VIII of the Act is in force for the debtor. In that case, the petition must be presented to the court to which the nominee's report under section 256 of the Act was submitted.[5] This ensures continuity of jurisdiction for the court which, at the beginning of the process leading to the making of a voluntary arrangement, was the court in which the debtor would otherwise have been entitled to present his own bankruptcy petition.[6]

Transfer of Proceedings Between Courts

The foregoing rules for allocation of jurisdiction are subject to the power of transfer of proceedings pursuant to the provisions of the Insolvency Rules.[7] The power is broadly drawn, and enables proceedings to be transferred from the High Court to a specified County Court, or from a County Court to the High Court, or to another County Court with jurisdiction in insolvency matters.[8] This power is exercisable by any court in which the proceedings are pending, to transfer proceedings away from itself. But there is a further power, vested in the High Court alone, to order proceedings which are pending in a County Court to be transferred to the High Court.[9] Any of these types of transfer may be ordered by the court in question of its own motion, or on the application of the Official Receiver or of a person regarded by the court as having an interest in the proceedings.[10] The general power of transfer may be used to relocate proceedings in the court in which they can be most suitably and conveniently administered.

A separate, and specific, power to transfer proceedings is available for use in cases where it transpires that the proceedings have commenced in the wrong court, having regard to the jurisdictional rules described above. Since a petitioning creditor is perforce obliged to base his choice of forum upon such information as is available to him regarding the debtor's residence or place of doing business, accidental errors of this kind are quite capable of occurring. Also, if less excusably, a debtor may mistakenly present his own bankruptcy petition to the wrong court. These situations are met under rule 7.12 of the Insolvency Rules, which makes provision for the court in which such proceedings have been wrongly commenced either to order the transfer of the proceedings to the court in which they ought to have commenced, or alternatively to order the proceedings to be struck out. A third, and notable, possibility however is that the court may order that the proceedings be continued in the court in which they have been wrongly commenced,[11] a rule which, if too freely employed, might appear to undermine the very basis of the jurisdictional arrangements themselves.

---

[5] Insolvency Rules 1986, rr. 6.9(4A), 6.40(3A). See Chap. 4, *ante*, p. 46.
[6] See Insolvency Rules 1986, r. 5.5A.
[7] Insolvency Act 1986, s.373(4); Insolvency Rules 1986, rr. 7.11–7.15.
[8] Insolvency Rules, r. 7.11(1), (2), (3).
[9] *ibid.*, r. 7.11(4).
[10] *ibid.*, r. 7.11(5).
[11] *ibid.*, r. 7.12(b).

However, the provision properly presupposes that the court will use such a power sparingly, and in the interest of justice, so as to minimise the wastage of resources under circumstances where no substantial hardship or injustice would result from proceedings which have been commenced in what is technically the wrong court, for example where it transpires that a change in the debtor's residence or place of doing business has given rise to an error regarding choice of venue for the proceedings. Important reinforcement to the operation of these rules concerning transfer or retention of proceedings is supplied by section 373(4) of the Act, which provides that nothing in section 373(3) (which specifies the jurisdictional competence of the High Court and County Courts respectively) invalidates any proceedings on the grounds that they were initiated or continued in the wrong court.

What has been said above with regard to the accidental commencement of proceedings in the wrong court could equally well apply in cases where proceedings have been wilfully so commenced, save that the courts are less likely in such circumstances to be indulgent with respect to the retention or continuation of proceedings in the wrong court. Although there is no express statutory provision to the effect that the wilful presentation of a petition to the wrong court is in itself sufficient to render the petition invalid, there are case decisions, albeit none of them recent, to the effect that such an act by the petitioner constitutes *per se* a ground for dismissal of the petition.[12]

Where bankruptcy proceedings have been transferred to the High Court from a County Court, an order may be made of his own motion by a judge of any Division of the High Court to transfer to that Division any proceedings which are pending against the debtor either in another Division of the High Court or in any other court in England and Wales, and which have been brought by or against the insolvent for the purpose of enforcing a claim against the insolvent estate.[13]

(2) Procedural Requirements for Presentation of Petition

Creditor's Petition

In the case of a creditor's petition, the petition must be on the appropriate Form,[14] and must properly identify the debtor by name, place of residence and occupation, including any alternative name in which he carries on business, the nature of that business and the address or addresses at which it is carried on.[15] The petition must also contain, with reference to every debt in respect of which it is presented, information as to the amount of the debt, the consideration for it (or if none, how the debt has arisen), and when the debt was incurred or became due. There must be statements both of the fact that the debt is due to the petitioner, and is

---

[12] *Re Brightmore, ex p. May* (1844) 14 Q.B.D. 37, approved in *Re French* (1889) 24 Q.B.D. 63 (C.A.).
[13] Insolvency Rules 1986, r. 7.15(1)(c), (2), (3).
[14] *ibid.*, see Forms 6.8 to 6.10 inclusive.
[15] *ibid.*, r. 6.7.

unsecured, and to the effect that the debt is for a liquidated sum payable immediately and that the debtor appears unable to pay it; or alternatively, that the debt is for a liquidated sum payable at some certain, specified, future time and that the debtor appears to have no reasonable prospect of being able to pay it.[16] Where the petitioning creditor's debt is one for which, under section 268, a statutory demand must have been served on the debtor, there must be specified the date and manner of service of the demand and it must be stated that, to the best of the creditor's knowledge and belief, the demand has neither been complied with nor set aside, and that no application to set it aside is outstanding.[17] The foregoing requirements admit of exception, however, when an expedited petition is presented pursuant to section 270 on account of the alleged jeopardy to the debtor's property.[18]

The main steps which a petitioning creditor must take are to file the petition, verified by affidavit as to the truth of all statements contained in it, in the office of the court which has jurisdiction to receive it.[19] Together with the filed application, at least two additional copies must be delivered to the court, one for service on the debtor and one to be later exhibited to the affidavit verifying that service: each of the copies is to have the court seal applied to it and is then issued to the petitioner.[20] The petition cannot be filed unless the petitioning creditor produces with it the official receipt for the deposit (currently fixed at £270) which is payable on presentation of a creditor's petition.[21] Where a statutory demand has been employed, there must also be filed in court an affidavit proving service of the demand.[22] If it is known that a voluntary arrangement under Part VIII of the Insolvency Act is in force for the debtor, and the petitioner is not himself the supervisor of that arrangement, a copy of the petition must be sent by the petitioner to the supervisor.[23] When the petition is filed, the court must forthwith send to the Chief Land Registrar notice of the petition together with a request that it be registered in the register of pending actions.[24]

Following the release of the sealed copies to the petitioner, the petition must be served personally on the debtor by an officer of the court or by the petitioning creditor or his solicitor, or by a person instructed by them for that purpose.[25] The act of service must be effected by delivery to the debtor of a sealed copy of the petition, but if the court is properly satisfied that prompt personal service cannot be effected because the debtor is keeping

---

[16] Insolvency Rules 1986, r. 6.8(1). See also above, section A(1)(c). See also s.269 of the Insolvency Act 1986 with regard to the giving up of security.
[17] Insolvency Rules 1986, r. 6.8.(2). See *supra*, pp. 110–112, for the statutory demand.
[18] Insolvency Rules 1986, *A Debtor v. Focus Insurance Co. Ltd (in Liquidation)* (1993) *The Times*, July 12, 1993. For *Expedited Petitions*, see *supra*, p. 112.
[19] Insolvency Rules 1986, rr. 6.10(1), 6.12(1); Form 6.13.
[20] *ibid.*, r. 6.10(3).
[21] *ibid.*, r. 6.10(2); Insolvency Fees Order 1986 (S.I. 1986, No. 2030), as amended, Art. 8, 9. (For circumstances in which fees and deposits are repayable, see art. 11.)
[22] Insolvency Rules 1986, r. 6.11; Forms 6.11 or 6.12.
[23] *ibid.*, r. 6.14(4).
[24] *ibid.*, r. 6.13; Form 6.14.
[25] *ibid.*, r. 6.14(1).

out of the way to avoid service of the petition or other legal process, it may order substituted service to be effected in some appropriate manner, and upon the carrying out of such an order for substituted service the petition is deemed to have been duly served on the debtor.[26] A further affidavit must be sworn and filed in court immediately after service of the petition attesting to the fact of service. The affidavit must have exhibited to it a sealed copy of the petition and, if substituted service has been ordered, a sealed copy of that order.[27]

Procedurally, the act of service is one of the most vital steps of all, and the court will scrutinise its execution, and the attendant circumstances, with the utmost strictness. So, where a sealed envelope was served on a debtor resident abroad, but there was no evidence to the effect that he had been informed as to the nature of its contents at the time when delivery was made, the Court of Appeal held that the act of service was bad, but went on to declare that the proper action for the court to take in such a situation is to allow time for a second act of service by the creditor, so that he may remedy this slip.[28] It is one of the purposes of the Insolvency Act and Rules of 1986 that the overly strict and rigid attitude towards the observance of formal requirements in bankruptcy matters, which was formerly a feature of the law, should be relaxed in favour of a more balanced regard to the requirements of justice and fairness. Hence, rule 7.55 of the Insolvency Rules provides that no insolvency proceedings shall be invalidated by any formal defect or by any irregularity, unless the court before which objection is made considers that substantial injustice has been caused by the defect or irregularity, and that the injustice cannot be remedied by any order of the court. When all formalities are properly completed, and the sealed copy of the petition with the affidavit of service is filed in court, a date can be fixed for the hearing of the petition.

Debtor's Petition

The Insolvency Rules require that a debtor's petition must be presented to the appropriate court, having regard to the jurisdictional rules already considered,[29] and that it must properly identify the debtor with reference to his name, place of residence and occupation (if any) and indicating any alternative name in which he carries on business, the nature of that business, and the address or addresses at which it is carried on.[30] The petition must contain a statement that the petitioner is unable to pay his debts, and a request that a bankruptcy order be made against him. In addition, if within the period of five years ending with the date of the petition the petitioner has been adjudged bankrupt, or has made a composition with his creditors or a scheme of arrangement of his affairs, or has entered into a voluntary arrangement or been subject to an administration order under Part VI of County Courts Act 1984, particulars of

[26] *ibid.*, r. 6.14(2), (3). For service outside England and Wales, see r. 6.12(2).
[27] Insolvency Rules 1986, r. 6.15.
[28] *Re A Debtor (No. 441 of 1938)* [1939] Ch. 251.
[29] Above, pp. 124–127.
[30] Insolvency Rules 1986, r. 6.38; Form 6.27.

these matters must be given in the petition.[31] If at the date of the petition there is in force for the debtor a voluntary arrangement under Part VIII of the Insolvency Act 1986, the petition must include a statement to that effect and the name and address of the supervisor of the arrangement.[32]

The debtor's petition must be accompanied by a statement of the debtor's affairs on the prescribed Form, verified by affidavit, and these must be filed in court together with three copies of the petition and two copies of the statement.[33] Of the three copies of the petition delivered to the court office, one must be returned to the petitioner, endorsed with any venue fixed; another, similarly endorsed, is retained by the court and sent (together with a copy of the statement of affairs) to the Official Receiver if he is appointed interim receiver or a bankruptcy order is made; and the remaining copy is retained by the court, to be sent (together with the other copy of the statement) to an insolvency practitioner if one is later appointed under section 273(2) of the Act.[34] The petition cannot be filed unless there is produced with it the receipt for the deposit (currently fixed at £135) which is payable on presentation of a debtor's petition.[35] When the debtor's petition has been duly presented the court may hear the petition forthwith or, alternatively, must fix a venue for the hearing.[36] The court must also send to the Chief Land Registrar notice of the petition for registration in the register of pending actions.[37]

(3) Hearing of the Petition

Creditor's Petition

In most cases a minimum of at least 14 days must elapse between service of the petition and the hearing of it.[38] However, if good cause is shown rule 6.18(2) of the Insolvency Rules does allow the court to hear the petition at an earlier date, for example if it appears that the debtor has absconded, or if the court is satisfied that it is a proper case for an expedited hearing, or if the debtor consents to a hearing upon a reduced period of notice. Where the debtor intends to oppose the petition, he must file in court a notice specifying the grounds on which he will object to the making of a bankruptcy order, and send a copy of the notice to the petitioning creditor or his solicitor. This must be done not less than seven days before the day fixed for the hearing.[39] Other creditors who intend to appear on the hearing of the petition must give the petitioning creditor notice of that intention in accordance with rule 6.23. Such notice can be given at any time up to 16.00 hours on the business day before that appointed for the hearing, and

---

[31] *ibid.*, r. 6.39(1), (2).
[32] *ibid.*, r. 6.39(3).
[33] Insolvency Rules 1986, rr. 6.41, 6.42(1); Form 6.28. See also Chap. 7, *post*, regarding the statement of affairs.
[34] Insolvency Rules 1986, r. 6.42(1), (3), (4).
[35] *ibid.*, r. 6.42(1); Insolvency Fees Order 1986 (S.I. 1986, No. 2030), Art. 9(b), as amended.
[36] *ibid.*, r. 6.42(2).
[37] *ibid.*, r. 6.43.
[38] *ibid.*, r. 6.18(1).
[39] *ibid.*, r. 6.21; Form. 6.19.

a person failing to give such notice may appear on the hearing only with the leave of the court.[40] In view of the lack of any formal requirement to advertise the hearing publicly in advance, it is submitted that the court's discretion in such matters should be used in a liberal way. As with all time limits specified in the relevant Parts of the Insolvency Act, or in the Rules, the court has an overriding discretion to extend the time for doing anything, either before or after it has expired, subject to any terms which the court may impose.[41] The petitioning creditor must prepare for the court a list of those creditors who have given notice of intention to appear, whether in support of the petition or in opposition to it, and hand the list to the court before the commencement of the hearing.[42]

The petitioning creditor must appear at the hearing: if he fails to do so, rule 6.26 provides that no subsequent petition against the same debtor, either alone or jointly with any other person, may be presented by the same creditor in respect of the same debt without leave of the court to which the previous petition was presented. With the written consent of both parties, however, it is possible for certain orders to be made without either the debtor or the petitioning creditor being in attendance. These are: (i) an order dismissing the petition, or (ii) if the petition has not been served, an order giving leave to withdraw the petition.[43]

There is no statutory requirement to the effect that the debtor must appear, although it is highly desirable that he should do so, especially if he wishes to mount any effective opposition to the making of a bankruptcy order. If the debtor does not appear however, the hearing may proceed and the court may make a bankruptcy order if all other legal requirements are met. These consist of a mixture of negative and positive provisions contained in the Act and in the Rules. Section 271(1) provides that the court shall not make a bankruptcy order on a creditor's petition unless it is satisfied that the debt, or one of the debts, in respect of which the petition is presented is either:

(1) a debt which, having been payable at the date of the petition or having since become payable, has neither been paid nor secured or compounded for; or
(2) a debt which the debtor has no reasonable prospect of being able to pay when it falls due.[44]

This provision must be read in conjunction with subsection (4) of section 271, which effectively requires the creditor whose petition is based upon a debt payable at a future time to show that circumstances have materially altered since he allowed the debtor to incur the liability, and that there was at that time a reasonable prospect, which has subsequently ceased to be operative, that the debt would be paid on time. Subsection (4) thus prevents a creditor from taking a calculated risk concerning the debtor's

---

[40] *ibid.*, r. 6.23(3), (4).
[41] Insolvency Act 1986, s.376.
[42] Insolvency Rules 1986, r. 6.24.
[43] *Practice Note* (Bankruptcy, No. 2/92) [1992] 1 W.L.R. 379; [1992] 2 All E.R. 300.
[44] See the discussion of the petitioning creditor's debt in section A(1)(c) *supra*.

continuing solvency, in the anticipation that it will be possible for him to resort to bankruptcy proceedings ahead of the repayment date if that assumption proves ill-founded: there is an irrebutable presumption that the prospect of repayment given by the facts and other matters known to the creditor at the time he entered into the transaction was a reasonable one.

Rule 6.25(1) of the Insolvency Rules provides that on the hearing of the petition the court may make a bankruptcy order if satisfied that the statements in the petition are true, and that the debt on which it is founded has not been paid, or secured or compounded for. The question of adequacy of proof for this purpose is to some extent influenced by the debtor's appearance or non-appearance, and by the extent to which the debtor advances arguments to challenge any statements in the petition. Early in the present century, it was observed by the Court of Appeal that the abandonment of the notion that bankruptcy proceedings possess a quasi-criminal aspect, together with the facility that a debtor may present his own petition, has made it acceptable that a debtor should now be compellable to appear as a witness at the hearing, so that allegations made by the creditor in his petition may be proved.[45] But it has also been held by the full Court of Appeal that the creditor is not entitled, in advance of the hearing itself, to claim discovery of documents or to require the taking of interrogatories from the debtor, both of which would normally be possible in civil actions.[46]

The hearing of the petition furnishes the opportunity for the court to exercise its extensive powers in the role of guardian of the wider interests which are at stake in the operation of the bankruptcy law. Moreover, the interests of the debtor himself are likely to be best served by his appearance at the hearing, for he may then avail himself of every opportunity to question any inexactness or inconsistency in the statements or allegations made by the petitioning creditor or by any other creditor. This is especially important in cases where any impropriety has been committed by the petitioning creditor, since there is a greater possibility of this being acknowledged by the court if the debtor is present to provide his own version of events.[47] The court's full control over the destiny of proceedings, once they have been commenced, is further emphasised by the provision in section 266(2) of the Act to the effect that a bankruptcy petition cannot be withdrawn except with the leave of the court. This must be for cause shown, and no order giving leave to withdraw a petition can be made before the petition is heard.[48] This can provide a vital safeguard against misuse of the legal machinery by a creditor in his relations with, and conduct towards, his debtor.

By section 271(3) of the Act the court may dismiss the petition if it is satisfied that the debtor is able to pay all his debts, or alternatively if it is satisfied as to three matters, namely,

---

[45] *Re XY* [1902] 1 K.B. 98.
[46] *Re A Debtor (No. 7 of 1910)* [1910] 2 K.B. 59, distinguishing *Re XY, supra*.
[47] See section A(1)(b) above with regard to creditors' impropriety.
[48] Insolvency Rules 1986, r. 6.32.

HEARING OF THE PETITION

(1) that the debtor has made an offer to secure or compound for a debt in respect of which the petition is presented, and

(2) that the acceptance of the offer would have required the dismissal of the petition, and

(3) that the offer has been unreasonably refused.

The subsection provides direction to the effect that in determining whether for this purpose the debtor is able to pay all his debts the court is to take into account his contingent and prospective liabilities, but on the other hand there is no explicit guidance as to the test to be applied in determining whether an offer to secure or compound for a debt has been "unreasonably" refused.[49] It has been held that a debtor's proposal for a voluntary arrangement pursuant to the provisions of Part VIII of the Act is not to be regarded as an offer to each creditor which is capable of being accepted or refused by the petitioning creditor with consequences which fall to be measured under the terms of section 271(3). The consequences of such a proposal fall within Part VIII alone, and a petitioning creditor whose debt was such that, had he elected to vote in favour of the debtor's proposal, he could have secured its approval, is not to be taken as thereby refusing his consent to "an offer to secure or compound for" his debt, for the purposes of section 271(3).[50]

Further provisions relating to the powers of the court at the hearing are contained in rule 6.25(2) and (3) of the Insolvency Rules. The former provision states that if the petition is brought in respect of a judgment debt, or a sum ordered by any court to be paid, the court may stay or dismiss the petition on the ground that an appeal is pending from the judgment or order, or that execution of the judgment has been stayed. It is important to note that the power to stay proceedings is once again a discretionary one, and that the mere fact that a debtor has lodged appeal against a judgment does not confer upon him the right to insist upon a stay of any bankruptcy proceedings founded upon that judgment. If the law were otherwise it would, as was observed by Lord Esher, M.R., in *Re Flatau*[51] furnish an intolerable means whereby the debtor might delay the hearing of the petition, perhaps for months or even years, by embarking upon purely frivolous appeals. As it is, if the bankruptcy court forms the opinion that the appeal is without merit it may make a bankruptcy order without more ado. In proper cases however, a stay will be granted.[52] If the outcome of the trial of a disputed debt is that the debt is declared invalid, the debtor may apply to have the stayed bankruptcy proceedings dismissed, with costs awarded against the petitioner. The provision in rule 6.25(3) is to the effect that a petition preceded by a statutory demand shall not be dismissed on the ground only that the amount of the debt was over-stated in the demand, unless the debtor, within the time allowed for complying,

---

[49] *cf.* Muir Hunter (1988) 1 Insolvency Law and Practice 30, at p. 32.

[50] *Re A Debtor (No. 2389 of 1989)* [1990] 3 All E.R. 984 (Vinelott, J.), see also *Re Gilmartin* [1989] 2 All E.R. 835 (Harman, J.), where the debtor's offers were held not to have been unreasonably refused by the petitioning creditor.

[51] (1888) 22 Q.B.D. 83, 84.

[52] *Ex p. Yeatman* (1880) 16 Ch.D. 283; *Re Noble* [1965] Ch. 129, *per curiam*.

gave notice to the creditor disputing the validity of the demand on that ground. In the absence of such notice however the debtor is deemed to have complied with the demand if he has, within the time allowed, paid the correct amount.

Further Powers of the Court—All Petitions

The general powers of the court at the hearing, particularly with regard to the principal alternatives of either making a bankruptcy order or dismissing the petition, are broadly drawn. Reference has already been made[53] to the provisions of section 266(3), whereby the court has discretion to dismiss a bankruptcy petition or to stay proceedings thereon on the grounds that there has been a contravention of the rules or for any other reason. The courts have traditionally regarded the purpose of these wide discretionary powers as being to ensure that all parties maintain a proper respect for the spirit, as well as the letter, of the law. A further, and very striking, example of their use may be found in the case law relating to those situations where the petitioning creditor's debt is a judgment debt which would, on the face of it, appear to possess the most convincing of credentials for use in a petition. Although it might be thought that the proper, and indeed probably the only, way in which to attack a judgment debt would lie through the medium of an appeal against the judgment itself, there is a well established, additional possibility of initiating a challenge before the Bankruptcy Court. This court, although of course unable to quash the effects of a judgment emanating from some other court, is nevertheless able to exercise total control over the admissibility of such a judgment for bankruptcy purposes, and therefore may "go behind" the judgment, and enquire into the circumstances in which it was obtained, and if it so decides it may refuse to accept the judgment debt, or to make a bankruptcy order in respect of any petition founded on it. The debt will naturally continue to be enforceable in any other way open to the creditor,[54] but the very potent machinery of the bankruptcy law will be closed to him.

The ability of the Bankruptcy Court to go behind a judgment where necessary was well-established by a series of nineteenth-century cases,[55] and although this species of scrutiny is not carried out as a matter of course, it is always possible for it to be done if it is expressly requested, whether by the debtor himself or by the trustee in bankruptcy.[56] Nor is it any obstacle to the invocation of this doctrine that the debtor has originally

---

[53] See section A(1)(b) *supra*.

[54] *Re Vitoria* [1894] 2 Q.B. 387. If, however, the Bankruptcy Court does not consider that the judgment debt is in any way tainted, and proceeds to adjudicate him bankrupt, the debtor has no further possibilities of challenging the judgment, assuming his rights to appeal against the judgment itself are exhausted or have lapsed, for the High Court will not entertain an application by a bankrupt to set aside on the grounds of fraud the judgment upon which he was ultimately made bankrupt: *Boaler v. Power* [1910] 2 K.B. 229.

[55] See *Re Onslow* (1875) 10 Ch. App. 373; *Re Lennox* (1885) 16 Q.B.D. 315; *Re Flatau* (1888) 22 Q.B.D. 83.

[56] The trustee's interest in scrutinising a judgment may be aroused when it is sought to prove in the bankruptcy for the judgment debt in question. *See post*, Chap. 9, p. 285.

consented to the very judgment against himself which he is now attacking, or that his earlier appeal from the judgment was dismissed.[57] One justification for the existence of this power is that a debtor might suffer a number of bogus default judgments to be entered against himself by "allies" who could rescue some of his estate on his behalf by later proving for the debts in his bankruptcy.[58] But the far more usual occasion for invoking this doctrine is when it is the debtor who will otherwise suffer injustice, and this is particularly capable of occurring when the judgment was obtained by a compromise of action or by default. A default judgment, by its very nature, involves a one-sided presentation of the facts which may lack objectivity and may even be inaccurate or unfair, whilst it may equally be possible to show that the terms upon which an action was compromised were unfair or unreasonable from the debtor's point of view. In either situation, if the court accepts that the result is unfair the petition may be dismissed.[59] However, if a debtor was properly represented by counsel at the negotiations which led to a compromise, it seems that the Bankruptcy Court will be less likely to rule in his favour unless the reasons are unusually compelling,[60] nor will the Bankruptcy Court have any truck with an attack which is merely in the form of a speculation whether the compromised action would really have succeeded if fought out to a finish, for to admit such attempts to reopen the original contest would undermine the very institution of the compromise of actions.[61] In every instance, the attack must be calculated to establish some defect in the actual consideration for the judgment debt in question, and accordingly it is not a fatal objection to a judgment that it or the antecedent proceedings contained some slight error of form, such as erroneously describing as a "married woman" someone who, between the issuing of the writ and the entry of the judgment, had had her decree of divorce made absolute.[62] Similarly, where the actual compromise is not being immediately impugned, the court will not entertain a mere "fishing" expedition into the background of the parties' dealings requested in the hope that something may be revealed which would be of use to the debtor.[63] In *Re Newey*[64] it was held that, where a judgment debt was founded upon the award of an arbitrator to whom the parties originally agreed to submit their dispute, the debtor could not be allowed to go behind the award and reopen before the Bankruptcy Court the arguments he wished to have presented at the arbitration, for he was not alleging that the arbitrator had been guilty of any fraud or improper conduct which might vitiate his award. It should be

---

[57] See *Re Lennox* (above, n. 55); *Re Fraser* [1892] 2 Q.B. 633.
[58] See *Re Onslow* (above, n. 55); and the judgment of Cotton, L.J. in *Re Lennox* (1885) 16 Q.B.D., 315, 325–328.
[59] *Re Hawkins* [1895] 1 Q.B. 404.
[60] *Re A Debtor* [1929] 1 Ch. 125.
[61] *Re Cole* [1931] 2 Ch. 174.
[62] *Re Beauchamp* [1904] 1 K.B. 572. See also *Re Gooch* [1921] 2 K.B. 593, where the debtor's attempt to raise technical objections, this time relating to the law of Bills of Exchange, failed to find favour with the Court of Appeal.
[63] *Re Gregory, ex p. Norton (No. 1)* [1935] Ch. 65, an extreme case which was distinguished in *Re A Debtor (No. 12 of 1958)* [1968] 2 All E.R. 425.
[64] (1912) 107 L.T. 832.

remembered however that the court is always on the alert whenever transactions with a moneylender have led to the creation of a judgment debt, and if in the original action the debtor omitted to claim any relief to which he might have been entitled by virtue of section 137 of the Consumer Credit Act 1974, the Bankruptcy Court may subsequently grant this relief at the time when the moneylender comes to present a petition based upon the judgment debt.[65]

Another situation in which the bankruptcy court may discover grounds for rejecting a judgment debt is where it is shown that the other court should not have entered judgment against the debtor for some technical reason, such as where the alleged debtor was a minor against whom the alleged debt was unenforceable, or because the alleged debt was in some other way vitiated so as to be unenforceable.[66] Once again, it may be seen that the petition is vulnerable both because, despite the previous judgment, there is in reality no good petitioning creditor's debt and also because, on a broad view of things, no bankruptcy order "ought" to be made. Likewise, wherever it happens that the petitioning creditor falls within the category of those who are disabled from presenting a petition,[67] the consequence of this fact coming to light must be that the court will declare that no bankruptcy order "ought" to be made, and the petition will be dismissed. This may come about if the debtor is able to establish at the hearing that the creditor either participated in or acquiesced in the execution of a deed of assignment, despite which he is seeking to petition for the debtor's bankruptcy, for then as we have seen the creditor is estopped from presenting a petition.[68] Conversely, provided that the petitioning creditor is not in any way implicated in its execution, the fact that the debtor did enter into such an arrangement with the bulk of his other creditors, no matter how beneficial it may have been to them, is not a "sufficient cause" why no bankruptcy order "ought" to be made upon the petition of a non-assenting creditor.[69]

Lack of Assets

One final, and separate, reason for which the court may dismiss a petition using its powers under section 266(3) of the Act is where it appears that continuation of the proceedings will be merely a waste of effort and expense, because it is established that there can be no assets, nor any hope of assets to accrue in the future, which would be available for distribution amongst the creditors.[70] This basis for refusal to make a bankruptcy order is held to be made out where for example, the debtor's

---

[65] cf. Re A Debtor [1903] 1 K.B. 705. See also Insolvency Act 1986, s.343 (discussed in Chap. 8, post), whereby extortionate credit transactions may be attacked by the trustee in bankruptcy.

[66] Re Davenport [1963] 1 W.L.R. 817; Re Mead [1916] Ir. Rep. 285; Re A Debtor (No. 229 of 1927) [1927] 2 Ch. 367.

[67] Above, section A(1)(b).

[68] Above, p. 95 et seq.

[69] Re Dixon (1884) 13 Q.B.D. 118; Re Watson (1885) 15 Q.B.D. 399.

[70] Re Robinson (1883) 22 Ch.D. 816; Re Otway [1895] 1 Q.B. 812; Re Somers (1897) 4 Mans. 227.

only asset will be extinguished by the very fact of his being made bankrupt,[71] or where, in view of the fact that the debtor has not yet obtained his discharge from a previous adjudication, there can be no question of any assets available.[72] But where it only appears *probable*, rather than being completely certain, that there are no assets, the court will make a bankruptcy order so that the true state of affairs can be revealed at the debtor's examination.[73] Similarly, where it appears possible that property may be acquired by the debtor at some later time and so become available for distribution, a bankruptcy order can be made.[74] Where it is merely shown that the costs of the bankruptcy proceedings will probably exhaust such assets as are available, this will not be considered a sufficient cause for refusing to make a bankruptcy order.[75] Nor will the court regard as "sufficient cause" the debtor's plea that his present inability to settle his debts arises because property out of which they might be met is tied up in a Chancery suit: this is treated as a misfortune which will not prevent a bankruptcy order being made against him.[76]

The court may utilise its power to adjourn the hearing of the petition, in order to enable any incidental issues to be determined.[77] Where it is ascertained that no bankruptcy order may properly be made on the basis of the existing petition, the court may authorise the creditor's petition to be amended by the omission of any creditor or debt, and to be proceeded with as if things done for the purposes of bringing the original petition had been done only by or in relation to the remaining creditors or debts.[78] The Rules also allow the court to authorise the substitution of a properly qualified petitioning creditor in place of one who is found to be not entitled to petition, or who consents to withdraw his petition or fails to appear at the hearing or to pursue his petition properly.[79] As an alternative, any creditor who has previously given notice of his intention to appear at the hearing may there apply to the court for an order giving him carriage of the petition in place of the petitioning creditor. Before the court can grant such an application it must be satisfied that the applicant is an unpaid and unsecured creditor of the debtor, and that the original petitioner either intends by any means to secure the postponement, adjournment or withdrawal of the petition, or does not intend to prosecute the petition properly.[80] Nevertheless, the court may not make a change of carriage order if it is proved that the petitioning creditor's debt has been paid, secured or compounded for by means of a disposition of property made by

---

[71] *Re Otway*, above. But see *Re Birkin* (1896) 3 Mans. 291, where the asset in question was not shown to be the debtor's *sole* asset.
[72] *Re Betts* [1897] 1 Q.B. 50. See however ss.334, 335 of the Insolvency Act 1986, discussed in Chap. 10, *post*.
[73] *Re Leonard* [1896] 1 Q.B. 473; *Re Birkin*, above, n. 71.
[74] *Re Murrieta* (1896) 3 Mans. 35; *Re Belton* (1913) 108 L.T. 344. Contrast *Re Somers*, above n. 70.
[75] *Re Jubb* [1897] 1 Q.B. 641.
[76] *Re J.J.R. Whitley* (1891) 65 L.T. 351.
[77] Insolvency Rules 1986, r. 6.29.
[78] Insolvency Act 1986, s.271(5).
[79] Insolvency Rules, r. 6.30.
[80] *ibid.*, r. 6.31(1), (2).

some person other than the debtor, or alternatively by means of a disposition of the debtor's own property made with the approval of, or ratified by the court.[81]

Unless the court deems it appropriate to dismiss the petition on the basis of any of its extensive discretionary powers, the court will proceed to make a bankruptcy order. The making of the order, and the immediate consequences thereof, are considered in Chapter 7.

Debtor's Petition

In most respects the hearing of a debtor's petition is a relatively straightforward matter, as compared to the hearing of a creditor's petition, because by definition the debtor is freely consenting to the making of a bankruptcy order against him. However, the court enjoys an equally full discretion whether or not to make a bankruptcy order upon a debtor's petition[82] and will, as was explained above, have regard to the overall requirements of justice including the question of whether the debtor's petition constitutes in any sense an abuse of legal procedure.[83]

There is one important procedural step which the court is required to undertake before ultimately exercising its discretion to make a bankruptcy order. This is the requirement, embodied in sections 273 and 274 of the Act, that the court give active consideration to the circumstances of every debtor who presents his own petition, in order to establish whether the possibility exists for the concluding of a voluntary arrangement between the debtor and his creditor under Part VIII of the Act. Even if this alternative procedure to the making of a bankruptcy order is not undertaken, the court must still have regard to the appropriateness of invoking the summary administration procedure through the issue of a certificate for this purpose under section 275.[84] By virtue of section 273(1) the court may not make a bankruptcy order on the hearing of a debtor's petition if the following four findings are made, namely:

(1) that if a bankruptcy order were made the aggregate amount of the bankruptcy debts, so far as unsecured, would be less than the amount known as "the small bankruptcies level" (currently set at £20,000)[85];

(2) that if a bankruptcy order were made, the value of the bankrupt's estate would be equal to or more than the amount known as "the minimum amount" (currently set at £2,000)[86];

(3) that the debtor has neither been adjudged bankrupt nor entered into a composition or scheme of arrangement within the period of five years ending with the presentation of the petition; and

---

[81] *ibid.*, r. 6.31(3).
[82] Insolvency Act, ss.264(2), 266(3).
[83] See above, section A(2).
[84] See also Chaps. 7 and 12, *post.*
[85] (S.I. 1986, No. 1996). This amount is variable by Order subsequently to be made.
[86] *ibid.* This amount is likewise variable by further Order.

Hearing of the Petition

(4) that in the court's estimation it would be appropriate to appoint a person to prepare a report under section 274 as to the practicality of embarking upon the procedure for concluding a voluntary arrangement.

It will be noted that the first three of the required findings relate to matters of fact, whereas the fourth essentially requires the court to form a judgment as to the appropriateness of making use of the voluntary arrangement procedure in the case before it. Most of the information on which the court will make all four of these findings will be obtainable from the statements contained in the debtor's statement of affairs which is required to accompany his petition.[87] If the conditions specified in section 273(1) are all met, the court must appoint a person who is qualified to act as an insolvency practitioner in relation to the debtor[88] to inquire into the debtor's affairs and, within a specified time, submit a report to the court stating whether the debtor is willing to make a proposal for a voluntary arrangement within the terms of Part VIII of the Act, and whether in the practitioner's opinion, a meeting of creditors should be summoned to consider the proposal.[89] The expenses of the insolvency practitioner undertaking this task will be met out of the deposit lodged by the debtor when his bankruptcy petition was presented. If in due course a voluntary arrangement is concluded, the insolvency practitioner whom the court appointed under section 273 will undertake the further steps necessary to bring about the possible conclusion of such an agreement, and if these are successful will subsequently perform the duties of trustee or supervisor of the arrangement unless some other qualified person is substituted for him by decision of the creditors taken under section 258(3). In the first instance, when the report of the insolvency practitioner is considered by the court the debtor is entitled to attend if he wishes, and must attend if so directed by the court.[90] The court must hear any representations which the debtor may make and is empowered of its own motion to make an interim order under section 252 of the Act so as to facilitate the consideration and implementation of the debtor's proposal.[91] If however the court concludes that it would be inappropriate to make such an order, it may make a bankruptcy order. Although this signals the abandonment of the officially-inspired effort to avoid the debtor's adjudication as a bankrupt, the professional work undertaken by the insolvency practitioner will not be entirely wasted since his report, together with the debtor's petition and statement of affairs, will be sent by the court to the official receiver who will assume an initial, and thereafter an overriding, responsibility for the further stages of the bankruptcy process.[92] It may also be observed that the provisions of Part VIII of the Act allow for the possibility that a proposal for a voluntary arrangement may be made by a bankrupt subsequently to his

---

[87] Insolvency Rules 1986, r. 6.41; Form 6.28.
[88] For the meaning of this expression see ss.388(2), (3), 390, discussed in Chap. 2, *ante*.
[89] Insolvency Act 1986, ss.273(2), 274(1), (2), (5); Insolvency Rules 1986, r. 6.44.
[90] Insolvency Rules, r. 6.44(3).
[91] See Chap. 4, *ante*, p. 42.
[92] Insolvency Rules, r. 6.44(4). See further Chap. 7, *post*.

adjudication.[93] However, where such a proposal has already once been unsuccessfully made by the debtor, there is little likelihood that a later initiative would be worthwhile unless the terms of the proposal can be radically improved.

Further Powers of the Court: Protection of the Debtor's Estate

The commencement of bankruptcy proceedings through the presentation of a bankruptcy petition by or against the debtor also marks the beginning of a court-controlled moratorium in favour of the debtor in respect of all kinds of action, execution or legal process brought against the person or property of the debtor. By virtue of section 285(1) of the Insolvency Act, at any time when proceedings on a bankruptcy petition are pending the court to which the proceedings are allocated may stay any action, execution or other legal process against the property or person of the debtor, and by virtue of section 285(2) any court in which proceedings are pending against any individual may, upon proof that a bankruptcy petition has been presented in respect of that individual, either stay the proceedings or allow them to continue on such terms as it thinks fit.

Additional provisions for the protection of the debtor's property during the period between the presentation of a bankruptcy petition and the making of a bankruptcy order are contained in section 286 of the Act. This empowers the court to appoint the official receiver to be interim receiver of the debtor's property if it is shown that such an appointment is necessary for its protection. This procedure replaces the stage in the former bankruptcy procedure contained in the Bankruptcy Act 1914 whereby a receiving order was initially made by the court as an intermediate step on the way to the making of an order of adjudication.[94] The elimination of the receiving order from the new bankruptcy procedure contained in the Insolvency Act 1986 has given rise to the necessity of making provision for those cases whose circumstances actually involve a need for protective arrangements to be put into operation before the making of a bankruptcy order. Although the official receiver will usually assume the responsibilities of interim receiver, alternative possibilities occur under section 286(2) for the court to appoint some other person in those cases where, on a debtor's petition, the court has appointed an insolvency practitioner under section 273 to prepare a report examining the prospects for a voluntary arrangement to be concluded. In such circumstances the insolvency practitioner in question may be appointed interim receiver instead of the official receiver.

When an interim receiver is appointed, he is required to take immediate possession of the debtor's property and his powers may be limited or restricted by any direction contained in the court's order of appointment. Subject to such limitations, an interim receiver has in relation to the debtor's property all the rights, powers, duties and immunities which are enjoyed by the official receiver when acting as a receiver and manager

---

[93] Insolvency Act, ss.253(3)(a), 261. See Chap. 4, *ante*, section A(1)(B).
[94] Bankruptcy Act 1914, ss.3, 6(1) (repealed).

under section 287 of the Act.[95] The debtor is legally obliged to give such inventory of his property to the interim receiver, and also such other information, as the latter may reasonably require for the purpose of carrying out his functions, and the debtor must attend on him as and when required.[96]

---

[95] Insolvency Act 1986, s.286(3), (4). For the effects of s.287, see Chap. 7, *post*.
[96] Insolvency Act 1986, s.286(5).

CHAPTER 7

THE BANKRUPTCY ORDER AND ITS CONSEQUENCES: (I)—GENERAL AND PROCEDURAL ASPECTS

(A) The Making of the Order

If the court at the hearing of the petition decides to make a bankruptcy order against the debtor a unitary procedure is set in motion, and the same material provisions are applicable regardless of whether the original petition was presented by a creditor or by the debtor himself.[1] The Registrar of the court settles the bankruptcy order and draws it up in the requisite form.[2] The order must state the date of the presentation of the petition on which it is made, and the date and time of the making of the order, and must contain a notice requiring the bankrupt, forthwith after the service of the order on him, to attend on the official receiver at a specified place.[3] The order may also include provision staying any action or proceedings against the bankrupt. At least two sealed copies of the order are sent by the registrar to the official receiver, who must forthwith send one of them to the bankrupt.[4]

The official receiver must notify the Chief Land Registrar, for registration of the order in the register of writs and orders affecting land, whereupon all persons are deemed to have actual notice of the order for all purposes connected with any land affected by it, as from the date of registration.[5] The official receiver must also cause the order to be gazetted (that is, officially published in the London Gazette),[6] and to be advertised in such newspapers as the official receiver thinks fit.[7] However, rules

---

[1] Insolvency Rules 1986, rr. 6.33 to 6.35 (creditor's petition) and 6.45 to 6.47 (debtor's petition) are worded in virtually identical terms.
[2] *ibid.*, rr. 6.33(1); 6.45(1); Form 6.25 or 6.30.
[3] *ibid.*, rr. 6.33(2); 6.45(2).
[4] *ibid.*, rr. 6.34(1); 6.46(1).
[5] *ibid.*, rr. 6.34(2)(*a*); 6.46(2)(*a*). See also Land Charges Act 1972, ss.6, 8; Law of Property Act 1925, s.198; Law of Property Act 1969, s.24(1), (3).
[6] Insolvency Rules 1986, rr. 12.20; 13.13(4).
[7] *ibid.*, rr. 6.34(2)(*b*), (*c*); 6.46(2)(*b*), (*c*), as amended.

6.34(3) and 6.46(3) provide for a postponement of those three decisive steps, namely gazetting, advertisement and notification of the Chief Land Registrar, upon an order of the court made pursuant to an application by the bankrupt or a creditor, pending a further order of the court. Such a stay is appropriate where, for example, the debtor intimates his intention to appeal against the making of the bankruptcy order, and will safeguard the debtor's social and commercial reputation which could be irreparably damaged by the publicity and notoriety which would attach to public advertisement of a bankruptcy order, even if the order were subsequently to be annulled.

The court will be exceedingly circumspect over the matter of ordering such a stay in view of the attendant risks, for innocent parties who thereafter have dealings with the debtor may suffer loss if he ultimately fails to obtain rescission of the bankruptcy order on appeal. Moreover, since any who become creditors after the date of the making of the bankruptcy order are excluded from participation in the assets being distributed in that bankruptcy administration,[8] the extent of their loss may be proportionately greater than that of the creditors in the bankruptcy whose advertisement is stayed. Since the bankruptcy order remains in force despite the stay of advertisement, and since the day on which it was made constitutes the date of commencement of the bankruptcy, the trustee in bankruptcy will later be able to assert that transactions which have taken place between the bankrupt and other persons after the commencement of bankruptcy are void as against him.[9] This danger was illustrated in the case of *Re Wigzell*,[10] where the debtor obtained a stay of advertisement pending the hearing of his appeal against the order of the bankruptcy court. The appeal was later dismissed but in the meantime the debtor had paid into his bank account £165 collected from persons indebted to him, and had drawn out £199. The bank had acted in good faith and without knowledge of the order, but it was held by the Court of Appeal that the £165 was claimable by the trustee on behalf of the creditors, while the bank were not entitled to credit themselves with the sums paid out as these had been taken out after the commencement of bankruptcy.

To alleviate potential hardships of this kind statutory provisions were first introduced in 1926,[11] and are continued under the present Insolvency Act by means of section 284(5). This provides a limited degree of protection to certain persons, including innocent third parties, where dealings have taken place between the bankrupt and other persons during the period between the presentation of the petition for a bankruptcy order

---

[8] See Chap. 10, *post*.

[9] Subject to the limited protection afforded to bankers by s.284(5): see *infra*. Note that, by virtue of the other provisions in s.284 any disposition of property made by a debtor in the period between the presentation of the petition for a bankruptcy order and the day when the debtor's estate vests in his trustee in bankruptcy is void unless subsequently ratified by the court.

[10] [1921] 2 K.B. 835, decided under the Bankruptcy Act 1914, and involving stay of a receiving order. It is submitted that the general principles applied in the case retain their relevance in relation to the new law.

[11] Bankruptcy (Amendment) Act 1926, s.4 (repealed).

and the date when his estate vests in his trustee in bankruptcy.[12] Where during that period, and after the commencement of his bankruptcy, the bankrupt has incurred a debt to a banker or other persons by reason of making of a payment which is void under the preceeding provisions of section 284, the debt is deemed for the purposes of the Insolvency Act to have been incurred before the commencement of the bankruptcy, and hence the creditor will be eligible to lodge proof for his debt although he will necessarily be obliged to surrender any property—including money paid—which he received under the void transaction. The protection of section 284(5) is not applicable if the banker or other person who dealt with the bankrupt had notice of the bankruptcy before the debt was incurred, or if it is not reasonably practicable for the amount of the payment made by the bankrupt to be recovered from the person to whom it was made.[13] The protection afforded by section 284(5) is thus at best a tenuous one, so that there is undoubtedly a considerable risk to third parties attendant upon any stay of advertisement ordered by the court.

The Effects of the Order

A bankruptcy order takes effect immediately on the day it is made. Being a judicial act it is deemed to be operative from the earliest moment of that day, and so takes precedence over all other non-judicial acts, such as private transactions of the debtor, which are done on the same day.[14] Moreover, once a judicial order has been pronounced it is deemed to have been "made" and so may take effect despite the fact that, through some oversight, the judge or registrar may allow some days to elapse before formally drawing up and signing the order.[15] Exceptionally it has been held that an order which had been pronounced was thereby "made" despite the fact that the judge subsequently forgot to draw up an order in proper form.[16]

The bankruptcy of the debtor against whom a bankruptcy order has been made commences with the day on which the order is made, in the sense just explained, and continues until either the bankrupt is discharged or the bankruptcy order is annulled, according to the provisions of sections 279–282 of the Insolvency Act.[17] The proprietary effects of a bankruptcy adjudication will be considered in detail in Chapter 8 when we will examine exactly which elements of the debtor's property—past, present and future—are capable of vesting in his trustee in bankruptcy, and which are not. For present purposes we must note that the legal process by which title to the debtor's estate is automatically transferred cannot take place

---

[12] On vesting of the bankrupt's estate see Insolvency Act 1986, s.306, discussed in Chap. 8, *post*.
[13] Insolvency Act 1986, s.284(5), proviso.
[14] *Re F.B. Warren* [1938] Ch. 725 (involving the now obsolete order known as a receiving order).
[15] *Re Manning* (1885) 30 Ch.D. 480.
[16] *Blount v. Whitely* (1898) 6 Mans. 48.
[17] Insolvency Act 1986, s.278. See Chap. 11, *post*.

until a trustee has been duly appointed.[18] Nevertheless, with the making of a bankruptcy order against him (if not, indeed, before then[19]) the debtor is deprived of the power to deal with his property because, by virtue of section 278 of the Act, the official receiver is constituted receiver and manager of the bankrupt's estate until such time as it vests in a trustee (who, as we shall see, may be the official receiver himself). The official receiver's managerial function may be transferred to a special manager appointed by the court under section 370. Application for such an appointment would be made by the official receiver upon his concluding that the nature of the estate, property or business of the bankrupt, or the interests of the creditors generally, require the appointment of another person to undertake close personal responsibility for managing affairs on a daily basis. If such a special manager is appointed the official receiver's functions and status in relation to the bankrupt's estate, pending the appointment of a trustee in bankruptcy, are reduced to those of a receiver only.

The function of the official receiver while acting as receiver or manager of the bankrupt's estate under section 287 is to protect the estate, and for this purpose he is endowed with the same powers as if he were a receiver or manager appointed by the High Court. The official receiver is accordingly entitled to obtain and keep possession of the bankrupt's property, and may sell or dispose of any perishable goods comprised in the estate, and any others whose value is likely to diminish unless they are disposed of.[20] The official receiver is further required to take all appropriate steps for protecting any property which is potentially part of the bankrupt's estate by virtue of the fact that the trustee, when appointed, may claim it for the estate.[21] If in the course of performing his functions as receiver or manager of the estate the official receiver seizes for disposal any property which is not comprised in the estate he enjoys a statutory immunity from liability in respect of any loss or damage resulting from his action, provided that he has acted in the bona fide and reasonable belief that he was entitled to seize or dispose of the property, unless the loss or damage has been caused by his negligence.[22] The official receiver may at any time summon a general meeting of the bankrupt's creditors, and he must do so if directed by the court.[23]

While the bankrupt retains title to his property, albeit without the capacity to deal with it, he remains technically the "occupier" of his business and private premises so that, for example, he remains personally liable to pay rates and other bills for the supply of services to the premises.[24] Similarly, the bankrupt remains the only person qualified to take legal

---

[18] See *infra*. In special cases governed by s.297 the bankrupt's estate vests in a trustee immediately on the making of the bankruptcy order—see *infra*, and also Chaps. 12 and 13.
[19] See Insolvency Act 1986, s.286, discussed in Chap. 6.
[20] *ibid.*, s.287(2).
[21] *ibid.*, s.287(3)(a). See also Chap. 8, p. 219.
[22] Insolvency 1986, s. 287(4).
[23] *ibid.*, s.287(3)(c).
[24] *cf. Re Smith* [1893] 1 Q.B. 323. On a landlord's right to distrain for up to 6 months' arrears of rent accrued prior to the commencement of bankruptcy, see s.347 of the Act, *post*, Chap. 8.

proceedings for recovery of what still belongs to him, although he may be required to give security for costs before any action will be entertained,[25] and if successful he must hand over what he has recovered to the official receiver for the eventual benefit of his creditors.[26] On the other hand, although the bankrupt may still sue he may not in most cases be sued because one of the principal consequences of the making of a bankruptcy order is that no person who is a creditor of the bankrupt in respect of debt which is provable in the bankruptcy may have any remedy against the property or person of the bankrupt in respect of that debt.[27] Nor, before the bankrupt obtains his discharge, may any such creditor commence any action or other legal proceedings against the bankrupt except with the leave of the court, while proceedings in respect of non-provable debts may also be stayed at the discretion either of the bankruptcy court or of the court before which they are commenced or pending.[28] It has become established practice however that the courts of bankruptcy will not restrain proceedings in respect of liabilities from which a debtor would not be released by virtue of a discharge following upon bankruptcy.[29] Furthermore, a distinction is made between proceedings which are designed to enforce a legal obligation owed by the debtor and those which are of a punitive character and are brought on account of his personal misconduct. In the latter type of case—for instance, proceedings for contempt of court or for committal of a defaulting trustee[30]—the court of bankruptcy will not intervene. In *Smith v. Braintree District Council*[31] the House of Lords provided a reformulation of the scope of the principle of non-intervention by the bankruptcy court in cases of punitive proceedings against the debtor. The actual case itself was concerned with the statutory power of committal for non-payment of rates, and raised the question whether there was jurisdiction under section 285(1) of the Insolvency Act to order the stay of committal proceedings as being within the ambit of the phrase "or other legal process" for the purposes of that subsection. Lord Jauncey, delivering the unanimous opinion of the House, identified the underlying purposes of section 285 as a whole as the protection of the bankrupt's estate for the benefit of all the creditors, and the prevention of any steps on the part of unsecured creditors with a view to obtaining advantages over the others by the application of pressure against the debtor.[32] While accepting that proceedings which are purely criminal lie

---

[25] *Semler v. Murphy* [1967] 2 All E.R. 185.
[26] *Rhodes v. Dawson* (1886) 16 Q.B.D. 548, 554 *per* Lindley, L.J.
[27] Insolvency Act 1986, s.285(3)(*a*); *Cobham v. Dalton* (1875) 10 Ch.App. 655; *Re Ryley* (1885) 15 Q.B.D. 329; *Re Nuthall* (1891) 8 Morr. 106. Note the effect of s.286(6) of the Act in cases where an interim receiver is appointed. See Chap. 9, *post*, in relation to provable and non-provable debts.
[28] Insolvency Act 1986, s.285(1), (2), (3)(b). Non-provable debts are defined in the Insolvency Rules 1986, r. 12(3)(2). See Chap. 9, *post*.
[29] *Re Blake* (1875) 10 Ch.App. 652; *Re Hutton* [1969] Ch. 201. *cf. Cobham v. Dalton* (*supra*). For discharge, see Chap. 11, *post*.
[30] *Re Mackintosh* (1884) 13 Q.B.D. 235; *Re Smith* [1893] 2 Ch. 1; *cf. Cobham v. Dalton, supra*, and *Re Wray* (1887) 36 Ch.D. 138.
[31] [1990] 2 A.C. 215, overruling *Re Edgcome* [1902] 2 K.B. 403 (C.A.). See Fletcher (1990) 3 Insolvency Intelligence 73.
[32] [1990] 2 A.C. at 229–230.

outside the scope of the section, as thus characterised, Lord Jauncey declared that proceedings which are quasi-criminal, such as those for committal in the instant case, are nevertheless capable of falling within the bankruptcy court's powers to order a stay if their predominant purpose is to coerce the defaulting ratepayer into making payment. Where proceedings are stayed the creditors' rights are suspended but not extinguished, and may revive, for example if the bankruptcy proceedings are later annulled.[33]

The position of estranged spouses in the event of the bankruptcy of one of them is affected by the fact that any obligation arising under an order made in family or domestic proceedings is not provable in the bankruptcy of the person against whom the order was made.[34] Moreover, by virtue of section 281(5) of the Act discharge from bankruptcy does not release the bankrupt from any bankruptcy debt which arises under any order made in family proceedings or domestic proceedings, except to such extent and on such terms as the bankruptcy court may direct. Thus, if a wife has obtained an award of periodical payments the husband's liability to continue these is not interrupted by his bankruptcy, although if he should fall into arrears the wife has no right to lodge proof in respect of the amount outstanding, and the only practical remedy available to her is to obtain an order for him to be committed for contempt.[35] If the husband has been ordered to transfer a capital sum to the wife to provide for her maintenance, but has not done so before a bankruptcy order is made against him, the net result is likely to be that the wife will have to wait until her husband's discharge from bankruptcy becomes effective before the order can be properly enforced because the onset of bankruptcy has removed the husband's assets from his personal ownership and control.[36]

One special exception to the general freezing of creditors' rights and remedies exists in favour of a landlord, who is empowered by section 347(1) to levy distress at any time upon the goods and effects of an undischarged bankrupt, but only for six months' rent accrued due before the commencement of the bankruptcy.[37] The court will not restrain a landlord from levying distress, or from recovering possession where a lease has been forfeited,[38] after a bankruptcy order has been made against his tenant, but any other creditor who seeks physically to interfere with the debtor's property risks punishment for contempt of court. Thus even though he may hold a valid bill of sale over the property a creditor should take the precaution of making application to the court to enforce his rights if possible.[39] In this context, great significance attaches to the specific

---

[33] *More v. More* [1962] Ch. 424, 430, *per* Cross, J.

[34] Insolvency Rules 1986, r. 12.3(2)(a). For the meaning of "family or domestic proceedings," see s.281(8) of the Act.

[35] *Linton v. Linton* (1885) 15 Q.B.D. 239; *Re Hawkins* [1894] 1 Q.B. 25; *Coles v. Coles* [1957] P. 68.

[36] *cf. Curtis v. Curtis* [1969] 2 All E.R. 207. On the matrimonial home in bankruptcy, see ss.336–338 of the Act, discussed in Chap. 8, *post*.

[37] See further Chap. 8, *post*, with regard to the effects of sections 346 and 347 of the Act on distress and other types of enforcement.

[38] *Ezekiel v. Orakpo* [1976] 3 All E.R. 659.

[39] *Re Mead, ex p. Cochrane* (1875) L.R. 20 Eq. 282.

The Effects of the Order

exception, whose application is assured by virtue of section 285(4) of the Act, whereby the restriction upon actions and remedies following the making of a bankruptcy order is declared not to affect the right of a secured creditor of the bankrupt to enforce his security. This is a further illustration of the significance attaching to the position of secured creditors, as has been referred to already.[40] It will suffice here to furnish some illustrations of the distinction between secured and unsecured creditors following their debtor's adjudication. Thus, a mortgagee of the debtor's property is a secured creditor and cannot be restrained from selling the mortgaged property, albeit he will hold any surplus from the proceeds, after satisfying his own secured debt and expenses, for the trustee in bankruptcy as the person legally entitled to them.[41] A mere assignee on the other hand will not be a secured creditor unless some charge has also been created so as to confer upon the creditor a proprietary interest which the court will recognise.[42] Such a charge may be created by means of a bill of sale appropriately drafted and duly registered,[43] but the required effect will not be achieved if the creditor's rights conferred by the bill of sale merely amount to a licence to seize and sell the debtor's after-acquired property, for no proprietary interest in the property is thereby conveyed.[44] For the same reason an assignment or charge of future earnings or trade debts, insofar as it is referable to monies which are earned after a bankruptcy order has been made against the assignor, cannot constitute the assignee a secured creditor.[45] A mere issue of a writ of sequestration against a debtor, and its service upon a person who is indebted to him or who is trustee of a fund for him, is not of itself sufficient to constitute the creditor at whose instigation this is done a secured creditor for the purposes of the Insolvency Act[46]: for this to occur, something further must be done under the sequestration so that it is rendered effectual, as by the actual seizure and sale of property, whereupon the creditor acquires title to the proceeds and thereby becomes secured.[47] A judgment creditor who has obtained an order appointing a receiver of the property of the debtor does not thereby become a secured creditor, for the receivership does not alter the title of the goods or property which are placed in the custody of the receiver, nor does it create a charge over them: they are simply held on behalf of the court until the rights of the plaintiff have been determined.[48]

---

[40] Chap. 6, *ante* (Section A(a)(iii)).
[41] *Re Evelyn* [1894] 2 Q.B. 302.
[42] *Cotterell v. Price* [1960] 3 All E.R. 315, 318, *per* Buckley, J.
[43] *i.e.* under the Bills of Sale Acts 1878–1882.
[44] *Thompson v. Cohen* (1872) L.R. 7 Q.B. 527; *Cole v. Kernot* (1872) L.R. 7 Q.B. 534.
[45] *Re Jones, ex p. Nichols* (1883) 22 Ch.D. 782; *Wilmot v. Alton* [1897] 1 Q.B. 17; *Re De Marney* [1943] Ch. 1266. *cf. Re Howard* (1884) 14 Q.B.D. 310; *Re Trytel* [1952] 2 T.L.R. 32.
[46] *Re Hoare* (1880) 14 Ch.D. 41.
[47] *Re Hastings* (1892) 61 L.J.Q.B. 654; *Re H.E. Pollard* [1903] 2 K.B. 41. For the position of creditors where an enforcement procedure is incomplete at the date of the bankruptcy order, see s.346 of the Act, *post*, Chap. 8.
[48] *Re Dickinson* (1888) 22 Q.B.D. 187; *Re Potts* [1893] 1 Q.B. 648; *Re Pearce* [1919] 1 K.B. 354.

The Effects of the Order: (I)

Personal Situation of the Bankrupt

From the date of the making of a bankruptcy order against him, and until such time as either the bankrupt is discharged or the bankruptcy order is annulled,[49] the status of undischarged bankrupt attaches to the person who is the subject of the order. This status carries numerous important consequences in terms of the capacities and freedoms of the bankrupt, including a number of specific disqualifications to which a bankrupt is subject. These personal disqualifications are described together in Chapter 11, and it may be noted that in several cases the sanction of criminal liability, which is discussed in Chapter 13, applies to an undischarged bankrupt who contravenes them.[50] Criminal liability may also be incurred by the bankrupt in various ways as a result of his dealings with property which was formerly his to dispose of, and which may for the time being remain in his physical possession or control although it now legally forms part of the bankrupt's estate and, as such, is destined for distribution among his creditors.[51] Other controls and constraints which are applicable to the bankrupt are designed to facilitate the administration of the bankruptcy process itself, and the bankrupt must accordingly comply with a series of requirements in this connection, and co-operate with any person or official who may be conducting the administration of the bankruptcy at any particular time. Criminal liability, or in several cases the possibility of committal for contempt, again constitute the sanctions underlying these further restrictions upon the bankrupt's freedom.

In the first place, it is the duty of the official receiver to undertake an investigation into the conduct and affairs of every bankrupt, and to make any reports to the court which he deems appropriate.[52] The bankrupt must collaborate fully in this investigation by supplying an inventory of his estate, together with such other information as may be required by the official receiver. The latter may also require the personal attendance of the bankrupt for private examination and inquiry at all reasonable times.[53] The bankrupt must also deliver up possession of his estate to the official receiver, together with all books, papers and other records of which he has possession or control and which relate to his estate and affairs. This includes any items which would be privileged from disclosure in ordinary proceedings.[54] Wherever the bankrupt's estate consists of intangible property, or other things which cannot be delivered into the possession of the official receiver at the present time (including any property which it may subsequently be possible for the trustee to claim for the bankrupt's estate) the bankrupt is under a duty to respond to the official receiver's requirement that he do whatever lies in his power to protect the assets in question.[55] Failure on the part of the bankrupt to comply with any of these

---

[49] See ss.278–282 of the Act, *post*, Chap. 11.
[50] See *post*, esp. pp. 348–354.
[51] See Chap. 8, *post*.
[52] Insolvency Act 1986, s.289(1). It is left to the official receiver's discretion whether to undertake an investigation in cases of summary administration governed by s.275: see s.289(5).
[53] Insolvency Act 1986, s.291(4).
[54] *ibid.*, s.291(1).
[55] *ibid.*, s.291(2).

obligations constitutes, unless he has a reasonable excuse, contempt of court for which he may be suitably punished.[56] When in due course a trustee in bankruptcy is appointed a further set of duties is imposed upon the bankrupt, namely to give the trustee requisite information as to his affairs, and to co-operate in every other reasonable way in order to enable the trustee to carry out his statutory functions. Once again this includes the duty of personally attending on the trustee at such times as may be required.[57]

Among the first matters to which the official receiver must attend upon assuming responsibilities in the first phase after the making of the bankruptcy order is to decide whether or not it will be worthwhile to summon a general meeting of the creditors for the purpose of appointing a trustee in bankruptcy.[58] In forming his judgment with regard to this the official receiver will be guided by the information contained in the bankrupt's statement of affairs, which the debtor must prepare in the prescribed form and submit to the official receiver within 21 days of the commencement of bankruptcy.[59] The official receiver must issue the bankrupt with instructions for the preparation of his statement of affairs, and supply him with the requisite forms.[60] A further matter for which the official receiver is primarily responsible is the taking of the decision whether to apply to the court for the holding of a public examination of the bankrupt.[61] The exercise of the official receiver's judgment in this instance will be guided by the information which emerges from the official receiver's investigation into the conduct and affairs of the bankrupt, supplemented by the indications which arise from the bankrupt's statement of affairs.

In addition to risking loss of his personal liberty in the event of non-compliance with the legal requirements which have been outlined thus far the bankrupt incurs liability to undergo arrest, and to experience the forcible seizure of any books, papers, records, money or goods in his possession, pursuant to a warrant issued by the bankruptcy court in a variety of circumstances.[62] These include where it appears probable that he has absconded, or is about to do so, in order to avoid, delay or disrupt the proceedings in bankruptcy or any examination of his affairs, and also if it appears probable that he is about to remove his goods to delay or prevent their seizure by the official receiver or trustee, or that he has concealed or destroyed any of his goods or any books or documents, or is about to do so.[63] Indeed, the bankrupt may be arrested if he removes any goods in his possession whose value exceeds £500, without the leave of the official

---

[56] *ibid.*, s.291(6). See also ss.363, 364.

[57] *ibid.*, s.333(1). Non-compliance is again punishable as a contempt of court: subsection (4). cf. *Re Waters* (1874) L.R. 18 Eq. 701; *Re Burgoyne* (1891) 8 Morr. 139; *Re Ashwin* (1890) 25 Q.B.D. 271.

[58] s.293(1) of the Act. See *infra*.

[59] Insolvency Act 1986, s.288(1). See *infra*. Where the bankruptcy order was made on the debtor's own petition, the statement of affairs will necessarily have been lodged with the petition itself: s.272(2).

[60] Insolvency Rules 1986, rr. 6.59, 6.60(1).

[61] Insolvency Act 1986, s.290(1). See *infra*.

[62] *ibid.*, s.364.

[63] *ibid.*, s.364(2)(a)–(c).

receiver or trustee.[64] Failure by the bankrupt to attend any examination ordered by the court can result in the making of an order for his arrest.[65]

A further personal constraint to which the bankrupt may be subjected following the making of a bankruptcy order against him derives from the possibility that the court may make an order under section 371 of the Act that for a period of up to three months at a time the Post Office shall redirect his mail to the official receiver or trustee, or even to some other appropriate destination. Application for the redirection of the bankrupt's mail may be made by the official receiver or trustee only: no creditor—not even the petitioning creditor—is qualified to make such an application, or to appeal if he thinks any order made is not sufficiently extensive.[66]

(B) Consequential Proceedings

The proceedings which are about to be discussed are all designed to facilitate the compilation of the fullest possible picture of the bankrupt's true situation, and his past conduct of his affairs. To a large extent the bankrupt's subsequent fate is dependent upon the impact of this information upon those by whom important future decisions are to be taken. These can include decisions regarding: the possible bringing of criminal proceedings against the bankrupt; the acceptance by the creditors of any proposal for a voluntary arrangement as a means of ending the bankruptcy; and the timing of the bankrupt's discharge from bankruptcy, and any conditions to be attached thereto.[67]

Private Examination

At any time after a bankruptcy order has been made the court may, in response to the application of the official receiver or trustee, summon before it the bankrupt or the bankrupt's present or former spouse or any person known or believed to possess any property belonging to the bankrupt or to be indebted to him, and also any other person whom the court may think capable of furnishing useful information concerning the bankrupt, his dealings, affairs or property.[68] Although the statutory provision under which this power of summons arises refers only to the official receiver and the trustee as eligible to make application for a private examination, it was held in *Re Taylor, ex parte Crossley*[69] that such applications may also be made to the court by a creditor, and that it is within the court's competence to order a trustee in bankruptcy himself to

---

[64] *ibid.*, s.364(2)(*d*); (S.I. 1986, No. 1996). The amount of £500 may be varied by statutory instrument.
[65] *ibid.*, s.364(2)(*e*). See also ss.290(5), 366.
[66] *Re Halberstamm* (1881) 17 Ch.D. 518 (a creditor may however prefer a complaint to the court in respect of the conduct of a trustee: see s.303 of the Act, *infra*). For discussion of the civil liberties aspects of the power of redirection of the bankrupt's mail, see Jaconelli (1995) 8 *Insolvency Intelligence* 1.
[67] See, respectively, Chaps. 13, 4 and 11.
[68] s.366(1) of the Act.
[69] (1872) L.R. 13 Eq. 409. See also *Re Whicher* (1888) 5 Morr. 173.

submit to examination as to his dealings with the bankrupt's estate. It has also been held that the bankrupt himself may make application for the examination of a creditor.[70] The court may allow creditors to attend the examination inquiring into the bankrupt's dealings and property, but in *Re Grey's Brewery Co.*[71] it was held that the court has a discretion to exclude any persons from these essentially private proceedings, such as creditors who are attending in the hope of gaining information which may be useful to them in bringing separate proceedings against the persons who are being examined. The court also enjoys a discretion in the matter of summoning persons for examination, and if an application has been refused the Court of Appeal will not readily intervene,[72] and in any case the applicant must generally show a prima facie probability that some benefit will result to the estate or that the person to be examined is capable of giving useful information.[73]

Any person summoned for private examination by the court must if required produce any documents in his possession or under his control relating to the bankrupt or the bankrupt's dealings, affairs or property, and if he refuses to do so, or if he fails to appear before the court when summoned, or appears to have absconded or to be about to abscond in order to avoid appearing before the court, a warrant for his arrest may be issued so that he may be kept in custody and brought before the court for examination.[74] Refusal to submit to examination when ordered by the court to do so constitutes a contempt of court for which the person concerned may be committed.[75] The person summoned may either be required to submit an affidavit to the court, or to undergo examination upon oath, but any such witness other than the bankrupt himself may refuse to answer any question on the ground that his answer would tend to incriminate himself,[76] or on the ground that the questions are of a "fishing" nature.[77] On the other hand, a mere denial by the witness that he has had any dealings with the debtor is not at once conclusive, for he may be further examined by the court in order to test his credibility,[78] and there is the possibility that he may be later convicted of perjury if it is shown that he has given false evidence during his examination by the court.[79] By section 369 of the Act the court is empowered to order the Inland Revenue to produce tax records relating to the bankrupt for the purpose of a private examination held under section 366.

---

[70] *Re Austin* (1876) 4 Ch.D. 13.
[71] (1883) 25 Ch.D. 400.
[72] *Re Willson* (1880) 14 Ch.D. 243.
[73] *ibid*. See also *Re Saunders* (1896) 13 T.L.R. 108; *Re A Debtor (No. 3 of 1909)* [1917] 1 K.B. 558.
[74] Insolvency Act 1986, s.366(2), (3), (4); Insolvency Rules 1986, rr. 7.21(2), 7.23.
[75] *R. v. Judge of the County Court of Surrey* (1884) 13 Q.B.D. 963. Parliamentary privilege may be pleaded as a defence to committal in such cases: *Re Armstrong* [1892] 1 Q.B. 327.
[76] *Re Firth, ex p. Schofield* (1877) 6 Ch.D. 230; Insolvency Act 1986, ss.366(1), 367(4). *cf. Re Reynolds* (1882) 21 Ch.D. 601 (a witness cannot be required to furnish an account in writing of his transactions with the debtor).
[77] *Re Gregory* [1935] Ch. 65. *cf. Re Wright* (1883) 23 Ch.D. 118, 128, *per* Jessel, M.R.
[78] *Re Scharrer* (1888) 20 Q.B.D. 518.
[79] See however *R. v. Lloyd* (1887) 19 Q.B.D. 213 where the accused was acquitted on account of a procedural irregularity at the examination.

The Bankruptcy Order and its Consequences: (I)

On the basis of a careful and thorough review of the operative principles under the past and present law, the Court of Appeal have affirmed that it is well settled that, so far as the bankrupt personally is concerned, no privilege against self incrimination can be invoked either at a private examination under section 366, or at a public examination under section 290.[80]

The proceedings at a private examination are recorded, and unless some special reason for preserving confidentiality causes a "stop order" to be made, they become part of the file of proceedings in the bankruptcy.[81] If the examination leads the court to conclude that any person has in his possession any property comprised in the bankrupt's estate or that any person is indebted to the bankrupt, the court may order him to deliver or to pay all or part of it to the official receiver or trustee.[82] The court also has a discretion to order that a person who, if within the jurisdiction, would be liable to be summoned to appear before it for private examination shall be examined in any part of the United Kingdom where he may be for the time being, or in any place outside the United Kingdom.[83] The potential utility of this power is restricted in practice by the difficulty of effecting a valid service of an order of summons in the case of a person who is neither resident nor personally present within the territorial jurisdiction of the court. Some confusion, as a result of recent case law, has added to these practical difficulties. In a case decided under the now-repealed provisions of the Bankruptcy Act 1914 and its related Rules, the Court of Appeal in *Re Tucker*[84] held that the power of summons was exercisable against a foreign resident only if he or she is physically present in England at the relevant time so that personal service of the summons can take place within the jurisdiction. To the extent that there was apparent provision in the Bankruptcy Rules authorising service outside the jurisdiction, the Court concluded that this had originally been made *ultra vires* when first added to the Rules in 1962.[85] It is respectfully submitted that, even if correctly advanced in relation to the provision in the former Rules, the *ultra vires* argument cannot be sustained with regard to the Insolvency Rules 1986, which were duly adopted by Parliament in place of the former Rules. Rule 12.12(3) of the 1986 Rules, which confers a discretion on the court to order service out of the jurisdiction of any process or order of the court, or other document, may thus be invoked as a valid basis for the authorisation of such steps to be taken in appropriate cases. It is noteworthy that, in cases falling under the post-1986 law, the *Tucker* case has been distinguished at

---

[80] *Bishopsgate Investment Management Ltd v. Maxwell, Cooper v. Maxwell* [1992] 2 All E.R. 856; [1992] BCC 222 (C.A.), at 864–873 and 228–234 respectively, *per* Dillon L.J. See Fletcher [1992] JBL 442.

[81] *Re Beall* [1894] 2 Q.B. 135. For judicial consideration of "stop orders" and their justification, see *Re Poulson, ex p. Granada Television Ltd v. Maudling* [1976] 2 All E.R. 1020, especially at pp. 1028–30 and 1032, *per* Walton, J.

[82] Insolvency Act 1986, s.367(1), (2).

[83] *ibid.*, s.367(3).

[84] [1988] 1 All E.R. 603; [1988] 2 W.L.R. 745. See Fletcher [1988] J.B.L. 168 and 341.

[85] The court was actually considering the amended version of r. 86 of the Bankruptcy Rules 1952, (S.I. 1952, No. 2113), which is identical in substance to r. 12.12 of the Insolvency Rules 1986.

First Instance,[86] and on at least two occasions the Court of Appeal has refrained from re-invoking the *Tucker* doctrine,[87] preferring instead to pursue a fresh approach to the question of extraterritorial reach of English insolvency law which, it is respectfully submitted, is more in keeping with the challenging realities of modern conditions. It is further submitted that, although not expressly overruled, the *Tucker* case cannot be considered a reliable authority in relation to the law generated by the Insolvency Act 1986 and related Rules.[88]

Statement of Affairs

Except in cases where bankruptcy proceedings have been begun by means of a debtor's petition (in which case a statement of affairs must accompany the presentation of the petition itself[89] the bankrupt must submit to the official receiver a statement of his affairs in the prescribed form not more than 21 days after the commencement of the bankruptcy.[90] The form thus prescribed requires the bankrupt to list systematically the particulars of his creditors and of his debts and other liabilities and of his assets together with debts and liabilities which are due to him. The scheduled lists which are standardised by the Insolvency Rules are intended to create a record of the bankrupt's affairs and dealings, and of his holdings of and transactions affecting property, so as to furnish both a detailed and comprehensive picture of his current state of affairs and of the causes of its coming into being. Since the period covered by the statement of affairs usually extends back to a point some two years before the bankruptcy order, it may become apparent that the bankrupt has, or may have, committed one or more criminal offences,[91] or at any rate that his conduct has been commercially or morally reprehensible to the extent that account should be taken of it, for example in relation to any application which the bankrupt may have to make in order to obtain his discharge.[92] The information about the bankrupt's affairs during the pre-bankruptcy period may also reveal that certain transactions were either voidable as made, or else have subsequently been rendered voidable due to the making of the bankruptcy order, thereby enabling the trustee to reclaim property for the benefit of the creditors.[93]

In *R. v. Pike*[94] it was held that a statement of affairs prepared by a bankrupt is admissible in evidence against him in criminal proceedings, and hence it is understandable that a bankrupt who has something to hide may be tempted to omit the incriminating information, or even to decline

---

[86] *Re Seagull Manufacturing Co. Ltd* [1991] 4 All E.R. 257 (Mummery J.).
[87] *Bishopsgate Investment Management Ltd v. Maxwell, Cooper v. Maxwell* (*supra*); *Re Paramount Airways Ltd* (*No. 2*) [1992] BCC 416.
[88] See Fletcher (1992) 5 Insolvency Intelligence 27–29.
[89] s.272(2) of the Act. See Chap. 6, *ante*.
[90] *ibid.*, s.288(1); Insolvency Rules 1986, rr. 6.58, 6.59; form 6.33.
[91] See Chap. 13, *post*.
[92] s.280 of the Act. See Chap. 11, *post*.
[93] See especially ss.339–344, 423–425 of the Act, considered in Chap. 8, *post*.
[94] [1902] 1 K.B. 552 *cf. Re Tollemache* (1884) 14 Q.B.D. 415. See now s.433 of the Insolvency Act 1986, discussed, *infra*.

to submit any statement of affairs at all. Neither alternative is to be recommended however, for section 288(4) of the Insolvency Act specifies that if the bankrupt fails without reasonable excuse to submit a statement of affairs, or if he submits one which does not comply with the prescribed requirements, he may be punished for contempt of court and may additionally be liable to other punishment. Specific criminal offences are created by other provisions of the Act and any material omissions from the statement of affairs, or any acts on the bankrupt's part which impede the investigation of his affairs, will generally amount to contravention of at least one of these provisions.[95] The fact that such offences have been committed may also be of relevance in relation to the bankrupt's prospects of gaining his discharge from bankruptcy.

In view of the complexity of the task of setting out the requisite information regarding his affairs, and also in view of the possibly severe consequences of his omitting to furnish such information in full, the bankrupt may well wish to avail himself of professional assistance. The official receiver is required to furnish the bankrupt with instructions for the preparation of his statement of affairs, and the necessary forms,[96] and is furthermore empowered by rule 6.63(1) of the Insolvency Rules to employ someone at the expense of the estate to assist in the preparation of the statement if the bankrupt cannot himself prepare it properly. Naturally, the preparation of the statement will be greatly facilitated if the bankrupt has previously kept full and proper books and records of his accounts and affairs.[97] Although the period of 21 days is specified as the time allowed for submission of the statement of affairs, section 288(3) of the Act confers a discretion upon the official receiver to extend the period, or alternatively to release the bankrupt from his duty to submit a statement. The latter course might be adopted in cases where the bankrupt is too ill to carry out his statutory obligation in relation to the statement of affairs. The exercise of the official receiver's discretion in these matters may be carried out on his own initiative, or at the bankrupt's request, and in the event that such a request is refused by the official receiver, the bankrupt may apply to the court for a release or extension of time, and the matter can be decided at a hearing upon due notice.[98] The official receiver can also make application to the court for an order of limited disclosure in respect of all or part of the statement of affairs.[99] This may be done in cases where disclosure may prejudice the conduct of the bankruptcy, and the court may order that the relevant parts of the statement be not filed in court, or that it be not open to inspection except by leave of the court.

When completed, copies of the statement of affairs, one of which must be verified by affidavit for filing in court, are to be delivered to the official receiver.[1] Any bona fide creditor of the bankrupt who so describes himself in writing has the right of access to the statement of affairs, and may inspect

---

[95] See ss.353–357 of the Act, *post*, Chap. 13.
[96] Insolvency Rules 1986, r. 6.60(1).
[97] Conversely, past failure to keep such records may involve the bankrupt in criminal liability in some cases, and may again affect the question of his discharge: see *post*, Chaps. 11 and 13.
[98] Insolvency Rules 1986, r. 6.62.
[99] *ibid.*, r. 6.61. See also r. 6.67.
[1] *ibid.*, r. 6.60(2), (3), (4).

it and take copies or extracts and, until the statement is filed in court, any creditor can require the official receiver or trustee to furnish him with a list of the bankrupt's creditors and the amounts of their respective debts.[2] It is however a criminal offence for a person, with the intention of seeing documents which he has no right to inspect, falsely to claim a status which would entitle him to inspect them.[3] After the statement has been filed in court it is the duty of the official receiver to send out to all known creditors a report containing a summary of the statement and such observations thereon as he thinks fit.[4]

In addition to the submission of the statement of affairs the bankrupt can be required by the official receiver to furnish him with accounts relating to his affairs as at any specified date, and for any specified period within three years prior to the date of presentation of the bankruptcy petition. If accounts are required relating to an earlier period the official receiver may apply to the court for an order to that effect.[5] Even after the filing of the statement the official receiver may at any time require the bankrupt to submit further information in writing amplifying, modifying or explaining any matter contained in his statement of affairs or in his submitted accounts.[6] The official receiver may require these further disclosures to be verified by affidavit, and lodged with him in duplicate so that one copy can be filed in court.[7] By virtue of section 433 of the Act the statement of affairs, and any other statement made in pursuance of a requirement imposed by or under any provision of the Insolvency Act 1986 which is derived from a provision of the Insolvency Act 1985, may be used in evidence against any person making or concurring in that statement, in any proceedings (whether or not those proceedings themselves take place under the Insolvency Act 1986).[8]

Public Examination

The process of investigating the bankrupt's affairs may culminate in the holding of his public examination by the court which made the bankruptcy order. The public examination has traditionally been regarded as one of the most important aspects of the bankruptcy process, for it is intended to serve one of the main purposes of the public policy associated with bankruptcy law, namely the protection of the public by the gathering of as much information as possible about the debtor and his affairs.[9] The debtor is required to answer upon oath questions as to his conduct, dealings and property put to him by the official receiver (or by counsel acting on his behalf[10]), by the trustee of the bankrupt's estate, by any creditors who have

---

[2] *ibid.*, rr. 7.31, 7.61, 12.15, 12.17.
[3] *ibid.*, r. 12.18; Sched. 5.
[4] *ibid.*, rr. 6.74, 6.75.
[5] *ibid.*, r. 6.69.
[6] *ibid.*, r. 6.72(1).
[7] *ibid.*, r. 6.72(2), (3).
[8] For the significance of this provision in relation to proceedings under the Theft Act 1968, see *R. v. Kansal* [1992] 3 W.L.R. 494; [1992] 3 All E.R. 844 (C.A.).
[9] *cf. Re Cronmire* [1894] 2 Q.B. 246.
[10] Insolvency Act 1986, s.290(4)(a), together with Insolvency Rules 1986, r. 6.175(2).

tendered a proof in the bankruptcy, and by any person who has been appointed as special manager of the bankrupt's estate or business (again, with the possibility that any of these parties may appear by solicitor or counsel).[11] Questions may also be put by the court itself. The debtor must answer all questions which the court allows to be put to him and cannot avoid doing so even though his answers may incriminate him.[12] A written record of examination is kept by the court and must later be read over to or by the bankrupt, signed by him and verified by affidavit.[13] The record may afterwards be used as evidence in any proceedings against the bankrupt, as well as being available for inspection by any creditor.[14] The bankrupt's answers may be utilised for a variety of purposes including the institution of criminal proceedings against him,[15] or for the purpose of establishing his motive in previously executing some deed or settlement which may be capable of avoidance in his bankruptcy.[16] The official receiver also makes use of the information obtained at the debtor's public examination in order to prepare the reports which it is his duty to make, including those in relation to the possible prosecution of the bankrupt for any alleged offences, and also in relation to the bankrupt's eventual discharge.

The public examination may thus be aptly summarised as a formal procedure whereby the bankrupt can be obliged to incriminate himself upon oath, in public and on the record. However, the bankrupt's answers at this public examination are not admissible in evidence against third parties, including the trustee in bankruptcy himself, although the bankrupt may be called as a witness in the later proceedings and examined directly.[17] It is a contempt of court, and punishable as such, for any person to offer money to a bankrupt to purchase his silence upon his public examination as to matters which it would be inconvenient for the briber to have disclosed.[18]

Section 290(1) of the Act enables the official receiver to apply to the court for the holding of a public examination at any time before the discharge of the bankrupt. This represents an important alteration to the law as it stood previously to the enactment of the Insolvency Act 1986, since formerly a public examination was obligatory in all cases unless the court by order dispensed with the requirement in response to a special application by the official receiver on limited grounds.[19] The new provision

---

[11] s.290(4), (b), (c), (d) of the Act, together with r. 6.175(2) of the Rules.

[12] *Re Atherton* [1912] 2 K.B. 251; *Re Paget* [1927] 2 Ch. 85; *Re Jawett* [1929] 1 Ch. 108. The full history, and current effect, of the modern law was authoritatively summarised by Dillon, L.J. in *Bishopsgate Investment Management Ltd v. Maxwell, Cooper v. Maxwell* [1992] 2 All E.R. 856 at 864–873; [1992] BCC 222 at 228–234 (C.A.). See Fletcher [1992] JBL 442.

[13] Insolvency Rules 1986, r. 6.175(4).

[14] *ibid.*, rr. 6.175(5), 7.27, 7.28, 7.30, 7.31, 7.61. *R. v. Widdop* (1872) L.R. 2 C.C.R. 3; *Re A Debtor* [1944] Ch. 344; *R. v. Harris* [1970] 3 All E.R. 746 (a company case); *R. v. Kansal, supra.*

[15] *R. v. Robinson* (1867) L.R. 1 C.C.R. 80; *R. v. Erdheim* [1896] 2 Q.B. 260.

[16] See ss.339–344 and 423–425 of the Act, *post*, Chap. 8. *cf. New, Prance and Garrard's Trustee v. Hunting* [1897] 2 Q.B. 19, affirmed *sub nom. Sharp v. Jackson* [1899] A.C. 419 H.L.

[17] *Re Brunner* (1887) 19 Q.B.D. 572; *Re Bottomley* (1915) 84 L.J.K.B. 1020.

[18] *Re Hooley, Rucker's Case* (1898) 5 Mans. 331.

[19] Bankruptcy Act 1914, s.15 as amended by Insolvency Act 1976, s.6 (both repealed).

is that a public examination will only take place if the official receiver makes application to the court for this to be done, and if the court accedes to his request. If the official receiver himself does not see fit to make application for the holding of a public examination, section 290(2) provides an alternative procedure whereby if not less than one half, in value, of the bankrupt's creditors concur in the giving of notice to the official receiver requiring him to make the necessary application, the official receiver is obliged so to act unless the court orders otherwise.[20]

The ending of the practice of holding a public examination in every case of bankruptcy has done much to establish the conditions necessary for achieving a more appropriate balance between the two, distinctive policy aims of the law of bankruptcy, namely to provide a constructive and protective process for affording relief to hard-pressed, but essentially honest, debtors on the one hand while ensuring the most rigorous and exacting investigation, in a suitably public manner, for those who have misused or abused the privileges of credit and acted reprehensibly in the conduct of their affairs. In exercising his professional judgment whether to make an application for an examination to be held the official receiver can have regard to these policy aims, and form an evaluation of the individual merits of the bankrupt in the light of the information which progressively becomes available. The fact that it is open to the official receiver to bring about the holding of a public examination at any time up until the bankrupt's discharge has the advantage of obviating the need for the official receiver to take any precipitate decision in this matter. There is thus reason to hope that, under the new insolvency law, the "honest but unfortunate" type of bankrupt who co-operates fully and willingly in the bankruptcy administration may be spared the traumatic and ignominious experience of undergoing a public examination. No formal guidelines have been introduced by either the Act or the Rules to influence the exercise of the official receiver's discretion in this matter, but it would be unrealistic to suppose that the holding of a public examination will be dispensed with except in those cases where the official receiver is completely satisfied that the bankrupt has made a full and candid disclosure of every relevant aspect of his affairs, and that the bankruptcy appears in no way to be a matter of public concern.

The bankrupt is obliged to attend his public examination and may be arrested for failure to do so.[21] The Rules do however empower the court to stay the order for the public examination, or to direct that it shall be conducted in a modified manner and at an alternative venue, if the bankrupt is suffering from some mental disorder or physical affliction or disability rendering him unfit to undergo or attend for examination in court.[22] In such cases application may be made to the court by the official receiver or by a person who has been judicially appointed to manage the bankrupt's affairs, or by a relative or friend of the bankrupt recognised by

---

[20] For procedure, see Insolvency Rules 1986, r. 6.173: the creditor seeking to requisition a meeting must furnish security for the expenses of the hearing, if ordered.
[21] ss.290(3), (5), 364(2)(e) of the Act.
[22] Insolvency Rules 1986, r. 6.174(1).

the court as a proper person to make the application.[23] In practice it is the Registrar of the court who presides at the public examination, which must be heard in open court and may be adjourned from time to time.[24] The power of adjournment may be exercised at the court's discretion to serve the needs of justice and also the convenience of all parties concerned, including the bankrupt.[25] The bankrupt is entitled to be legally represented, but this must be at his own expense.[26] The examination continues until the court is satisfied that the affairs of the bankrupt have been sufficiently investigated, and the written record of the proceedings is then settled and verified. Usually the costs of the public examination are borne by the estate, but where the examination has been requisitioned by the creditors the court may order that a proportion of the expenses are to be met out of the deposit paid in advance by the requisitioning creditor.[27]

Despite the recent, welcome reforms in this area of the law the public examination retains its place as one of the aspects of the law of personal insolvency which registers the most vivid impact upon the public imagination. The publicity attending the examination particularly in any *cause célèbre*, ensures that the workings of what is otherwise for the most part a somewhat obscure and impenetrable area of the administration of justice continue to command a degree of general attention. Occasionally, as an incidental effect of what has been said and reported during the oral exchanges in open court, the reputations of third parties who are not themselves present or represented at the hearing may be damaged through assertions or allegations made about them. This calls for much care on the part of those responsible for the conduct of the proceedings, and for the course of questioning pursued.[28]

First meeting of creditors; and creditors' meetings generally

Appointment of a trustee in bankruptcy

Where a bankruptcy order has been made it is the duty of the official receiver to decide whether to summon a meeting of the bankrupt's creditors for the purpose of appointing a trustee in bankruptcy. Section 293(1) of the Act requires the official receiver to take this decision as soon as possible in the period of 12 weeks beginning with the day on which the order was made. In cases where a certificate of summary administration has been issued under section 275, the official receiver will automatically become trustee in almost all cases,[29] and hence section 293(1) is so worded that the statutory requirement regarding the convening of a creditors'

---

[23] *ibid.*, r. 6.174(2), (3), (4).
[24] *ibid.*, r. 6.176.
[25] *ibid.*, r. 6.175(6); *Re Von Dembinska* [1954] 2 All E.R. 46.
[26] r. 6.175(3) of the Rules.
[27] *ibid.*, rr. 6.173(2), 6.177.
[28] *cf.* the political furore consequent upon the public examination of Mr. J.G.L. Poulson at Wakefield County Court during 1972. See, *e.g.* the statement of Lord Hailsham, L.C. Hansard (H.L.) February 8, 1973, cols. 1228 *et seq.*, and see also *Re Poulson, ex p. Granada Television Ltd v. Maudling* [1976] 2 All E.R. 1020.
[29] See Chap. 12, *post*.

meeting does not then apply.[30] The underlying purpose behind the official receiver's task of deciding whether or not to convene a creditors' meeting is that unnecessary expenditure should be eliminated from the insolvency procedures wherever possible. Where it is readily apparent from the bankrupt's statement of affairs that the net deficiency is so substantial as to afford little prospect of there being any assets to distribute among the unsecured creditors it is unlikely that a trustee in bankruptcy from the private sector could be engaged, since his professional fees and expenses would count as administrative costs in the bankruptcy, and as such would be payable ahead even of the preferential debts.[31] In such cases, as the Cork Committee sensibly concluded,[32] there is no practical alternative to the administration of the bankruptcy being undertaken by the official receiver, ultimately at public expense insofar as the realisable assets may not even suffice to cover his allowable charges according to the current statutory tables of fees and expenses.[33]

Although the official receiver is charged with the primary task of deciding whether any useful purpose is likely to be served by summoning a meeting of creditors, with the inevitable outlay of costs which will fall to be borne by the estate, it is open to the creditors to requisition a meeting in any case where the official receiver has decided not to convene one, except in cases where a certificate of summary administration is in force. In the first place, section 293(4) makes it incumbent upon the official receiver, if he decides not to summon such a meeting, to give notice of his decision to the court and to every known creditor of the bankrupt. This must be done before the end of the period of 12 weeks running from the date of the bankruptcy order. As from the date of his giving notice to the court of his decision not to summon a creditors' meeting the official receiver becomes trustee of bankrupt's estate and will remain as trustee unless replaced by some person duly appointed from the private sector.[34] Section 294 of the Act gives any creditor the right to requisition a meeting for the purpose of appointing a trustee, but makes this conditional upon the creditor's request being made with the concurrence of not less than one quarter, in value, of the bankrupt's creditors, including the creditor making the request.[35] On receipt of a properly made request under section 294 it is the duty of the official receiver to summon the requested meeting within not more than three months.[36] In addition to the problems of coordinating the necessary proportion of support for the requisitioning of a meeting contrary to the official receiver's declared intentions, any creditor wishing to make use of section 294 in this way is faced by the further requirement that those requisitioning a meeting of creditors must furnish a deposit as

---

[30] The proviso to s.293(1), which had the effect of preventing s.293 from applying in cases of criminal bankruptcy, has been amended by the Criminal Justice Act 1988, Sched. 16, in consequence of the abolition of criminal bankruptcy. See pp. 355–356, *post*.
[31] See Chap. 10, *post*.
[32] Cmnd. 8558, Chap. 14, especially at paras. 723–726. *cf.* Cmnd. 9175, paras. 75–84.
[33] Insolvency Regulations 1994 (S.I. 1994, No. 2507), regs. 33–36 inclusive, together with Sched. 2. *cf.* rr. 6.138–6.142 of the Rules.
[34] s.293(3) of the Act. See also ss.276, 296, *infra*.
[35] s.294(1), (2) of the Act; r. 6.83(1) of the Rules, and form 6.34.
[36] s.294(2) of the Act; r. 6.79(6) of the Rules.

security for the expenses of summoning and holding the meeting.[37] The level of deposit is left to be determined by the official receiver himself who, as the party whose prior judgment is in effect being challenged by the requisitioning creditors, should take care to avoid any suggestion that the level of deposit is being set unrealistically high, in a quasi-penal manner.[38] Where a requisitioned meeting is summoned however, rule 6.87(3) of the Insolvency Rules empowers the meeting to vote that the expenses of summoning and holding it shall instead be payable out of the estate as an expense of the bankruptcy. A resolution to that effect would require the support of a majority in value of the creditors voting at the meeting.[39]

Whether the meeting is summoned as a result of his own decision, or as a result of a valid requisition by creditors, the venue for the first meeting of creditors must be fixed by the official receiver who must give notice of the meeting to the court and to every known creditor of the bankrupt, and also to the bankrupt himself.[40] Creditors must receive at least 21 days' notice of the meeting, which must also be generally announced by means of a public advertisement.[41] The Insolvency Rules impose strict controls on the nature of the business which is allowed to be transacted at the first meeting of creditors. Rule 6.80 stipulates that no resolutions may be taken at the meeting other than one to appoint one or more named insolvency practitioners to be trustee in bankruptcy; a resolution to establish a creditors' committee or, alternatively, a resolution relating to the fixing of the trustee's remuneration; a resolution to determine, in the case where joint trustees have been appointed, the respective scope of authority to be conferred upon each of them, a resolution to adjourn the meeting for not more than three weeks; and, in the case of a meeting requisitioned under section 294, a resolution that the cost of summoning and holding the meeting shall be payable out of the estate.[42] Significantly, no resolution is allowed to be proposed with the purpose of appointing the official receiver as trustee but, on the other hand, a discretionary power is conferred upon the chairman of the meeting to allow "any other resolution which (he) thinks it right to allow for special reasons."[43] The chairman of the meeting is the official receiver by whom it was convened, or some person nominated by him in writing.[44] The official receiver may at his discretion give notice to the bankrupt that he is required to be present, or in attendance, and if the bankrupt is not present when the meeting takes place, and it is desired to put questions to him, the meeting may be adjourned with a view to obtaining his attendance.[45]

---

[37] r. 6.87 of the Rules.
[38] *ibid.*, r. 6.87(2).
[39] *ibid.*, rr. 6.80(1)(e); 6.88(1).
[40] *ibid.*, rr. 6.79(1), (2); 6.84(1). Forms 6.35, 6.36.
[41] *ibid.*, r. 6.79(3), (5). In the interests of economy, the court can order that notice of meeting shall be given by public advertisement only: r. 6.85.
[42] *ibid.*, r. 6.80(1)(a)–(f).
[43] *ibid.*, r. 6.80(1), (g), (2).
[44] *ibid.*, r. 6.82(1).
[45] *ibid.*, r. 6.84(3), (4). *cf. Re Best* (1881) 18 Ch.D. 488.

Resolutions and Voting

Rule 6.88(1) of the Insolvency Rules expresses a general rule which applies to all meetings of creditors, including the first one, with regard to the passing of resolutions. This states that a resolution is passed when a majority *in value* of those present and voting, in person or by proxy, have voted in favour of the resolution. It is thus perfectly possible for a resolution to be carried on the vote of a single creditor, to whom a large amount of money is owing, cast against the opposition of numerous creditors for small amounts. In the case of a resolution for the appointment of a trustee, rule 6.88 further provides that if on any vote there are two nominees for appointment, the person who obtains the most support is appointed, and if there are three or more nominees of whom one has a clear overall majority, that one is appointed. But in any other case the chairman must continue to take votes, eliminating at each stage the nominee who obtained the least support in the previous vote, until a clear majority is obtained for one nominee.

In view of the crucial role played by the value of the debt which is owing to each voting creditor, it is necessary before the business of the meeting begins to establish the extent of the debt in respect of which each creditor will be regarded as voting. For this purpose creditors are required to lodge proof of their debts by a time and date which must be stated in the notice of meeting, but which must not be more than four days before the date fixed for the meeting.[46] A person is only entitled to vote as a creditor if proof of debt has been duly lodged by the specified time and date and the claim has been admitted for the purpose of entitlement to vote.[47] The chairman of the meeting has power to admit or reject a creditor's proof for this purpose, subject to a right of appeal to the court which is exercisable by any creditor or by the bankrupt.[48] If the chairman cannot decide whether a claim should be rejected or admitted before the meeting is due to begin, he must mark the claim as objected to and allow the creditor to vote, subject to his vote being subsequently declared invalid if the objection to the proof is sustained.[49] This need not result in the invalidation of the proceedings themselves, or any decision arrived at, provided that the majority in favour of any particular resolution was sufficiently large to be unaffected by the removal of any support from creditors whose claims are later disallowed. The court has power, when deciding any appeal against the chairman's decision on admissibility of a claim, to order that another meeting be summoned or to make any other order which it thinks just.[50] The court may also, exceptionally, make an order declaring that the creditors, or any

---

[46] *ibid.*, rr. 6.79(4), 6.93.
[47] *ibid.*, r. 6.93(1), form 6.37. For the concept of the "provable debt," see Chap. 9, *post*.
[48] *ibid.*, r. 6.94(1), (2). On the procedure for proving, see rr. 6.96–6.119, and generally Chap. 9, *post*.
[49] *ibid.*, r. 6.94(3). *cf. Re Potts* [1934] Ch. 356. See also *Re A Debtor (No. 222 of 1990)* [1992] BCLC 137 (a case involving an Individual Voluntary Arrangement).
[50] *ibid.*, r. 6.94(4).

class of them, are entitled to vote at meetings without being required to prove their debts.[51]

It is an important principle that a secured creditor may only vote in respect of the unsecured balance (if any) of his debt after deducting the value of his security as estimated by him.[52] Therefore unless he has chosen to surrender his security altogether a secured creditor must include in his proof the particulars of any security he holds, the date when it was given and the value which he puts upon it.[53] If a secured creditor omits to disclose his security in his proof of debt, and hence purports to vote in respect of its whole value, he must surrender his security for the general benefit of creditors unless the court on application by the creditor relieves him from this penalty on the ground that the omission to disclose was inadvertent or the result of honest mistake.[54] The onus of proving inadvertence rests upon the creditor, and the court will in general not be easy to convince: excuses such as those based upon some alleged clerical error, as in *Re Safety Explosives Ltd*,[55] may encounter a sceptical reception, and the court will in each case require a thorough demonstration that the creditor's misapprehension was genuine and that it arose through inadvertence on his part and not, for example, by reason of some miscalculation which he is subsequently regretting.[56] If the court is convinced of the creditor's genuine inadvertence he may be allowed to retain his security subject to amending his proof so that the value of the security is fully taken into account in calculating the net value of his debt for voting and other purposes.[57]

There is a further rule to the effect that no creditor may vote in respect of a debt for an unliquidated amount, or any debt whose value is not ascertained, except where the chairman agrees to put upon the debt an estimated minimum value for the purpose of entitlement to vote, and admits his proof for that purpose.[58] In *Re Dummelow*[59] a creditor was not permitted to vote in respect of his estimation of the untaxed costs in an action in which he had already been awarded a verdict in his favour: it was explained that his proper course was to apply for leave to sign judgment and tax his costs, or else to limit his claim to such a sum as his costs would certainly amount to. Where an action by the creditor against the debtor is still unconcluded, the creditor's entitlement to vote in respect of the amount being sought through litigation will depend upon the nature of his claim in law. If the claim is in essence an unliquidated claim, as in *Re Rickett*[60] where the claim was for damages for misfeasance and breach of

---

[51] *ibid.*, r. 6.93(2).
[52] *ibid.*, r. 6.93(4). For the meaning of "secured creditor," see Chap. 6, *ante*, section A(1)(c).
[53] *ibid.*, r. 6.98(1)(g).
[54] *ibid.*, r. 6.116(1). See, *e.g. King v. Michael Faraday and Partners Ltd* [1939] 2 K.B. 753.
[55] [1904] 1 Ch. 266. *cf. Re Maxson* [1919] 2 K.B. 330.
[56] *Re Burr* (1892) 67 L.T. 232; *Re Piers* [1898] 1 Q.B. 627; *Re Rowe* [1904] 2 K.B. 489; *Re Pawson* [1917] 2 K.B. 527.
[57] r. 6.116(2) of the Rules. *Re Ker* (1879) 13 Ch.D. 304; *Re Small* [1934] Ch. 541.
[58] *ibid.*, r. 6.93(3). *cf.* the differing judicial approaches to construction of the phrase "agrees to put" in relation to voting entitlement of creditors under the voluntary arrangment procedures, discussed in Chap. 4, *ante*, at p. 48 and in Chap. 15, *post*, at p. 408.
[59] (1873) 8 Ch.App. 997.
[60] [1949] 1 All E.R. 737.

trust as director of a company, the creditor will not be entitled to vote in respect of it at a creditors' meeting notwithstanding that for the purpose of the litigation he may have specified a sum of money to be sought as damages. In law the "true" amount of the indebtedness will only be fixed by judgment itself. If, on the other hand, the claim is in essence a liquidated one the plaintiff may lodge proof ahead of the actual determination of the proceedings by judgment.

A creditor who is entitled to vote at a meeting may do so in person or by proxy, and forms of proxy must be sent out in every notice summoning a creditors' meeting, together with an indication of the time and date by which proxies must be lodged for voting purposes.[61] A proxy may be either general or special, and may be given to the chairman of the meeting, or to any other person over the age of majority.[62] Any person who is entitled to attend a meeting in his own right as creditor, and who is also authorised to act as proxy on behalf of another, must clearly indicate that he is acting in such dual capacity whenever he acts during the course of the meeting, for otherwise his acts will be treated as being done on his own account alone, and will not be reckoned as additionally counting as the acts of the creditor whom he is authorised to represent.[63] After use at the meeting proxies must be retained by the chairman and kept available for later inspection by the creditors and by the bankrupt.[64] In general no person acting under a general or special proxy may vote in favour of any resolution which would directly or indirectly place him or any associate of his in a position to receive any remuneration out of the insolvent estate, otherwise than as a creditor alongside the other creditors, unless the proxy specifically directs him to vote in that way.[65] And in any vote upon a resolution which affects a person in respect of his remuneration or conduct as trustee, or as proposed or former trustee, the vote of that person and of any partner or employee of his, whether cast in his capacity as a creditor or as a proxy for a creditor, shall not be counted towards the majority required for passing the resolution in question.[66]

The chairman at the first and subsequent meetings of creditors must ensure that proper, signed minutes are taken and kept by him as a record of the proceedings, and also that a list is made and kept of all the creditors who attended the meeting.[67] The minutes must include a record of every resolution passed, and it is the chairman's duty to ensure that certified particulars of all such resolutions are filed in court within 21 days of the date of the meeting.[68] A minute of proceedings at a creditors' meeting, signed by a person describing himself as or appearing to be the chairman of that meeting, is admissible in insolvency proceedings without further proof as prima facie evidence of the following:

[61] See rr. 6.79(4), 6.81(3), 6.88(1), 6.89, 6.93(1)(b), and also rr. 8.1–8.7 inclusive, of the Rules.
[62] *ibid.*, r. 8.1(3), (4).
[63] *Re Baum* (1880) 13 Ch.D. 424.
[64] rr. 8.4, 8.5 of the Rules.
[65] *ibid.*, r. 8.6(1). *cf. Farmers' Mart Ltd v. Milne* [1915] A.C. 106 (H.L.) (Sc.).
[66] *ibid.*, r. 6.88(4).
[67] *ibid.*, r. 6.95(1), (2).
[68] *ibid.*, r. 6.95(3).

(1) that the meeting was duly convened and held;
(2) that all resolutions passed at the meeting were duly passed; and
(3) that all proceedings at the meeting duly took place.[69]

The meeting must be quorate in order that its business may be validly transacted. By virtue of rule 12.4A of the Insolvency Rules,[70] a quorum at a creditors' meeting is constituted by the presence of at least one creditor entitled to vote, and for this purpose "presence" may be established through representation by proxy. The meeting is therefore competent to proceed to act even if the only person physically present is the official receiver himself as chairman, provided that he holds the proxy of at least one creditor authorising him to vote on the creditor's behalf. However, where such a minimum quorum is constituted by virtue of the presence of either the chairman alone, or one other person in addition to the chairman, and the chairman is aware, for example by reason of proofs and proxies previously received, that one or more additional persons would, if attending, be entitled to vote, the commencement of the meeting must be postponed for at least 15 minutes beyond the time appointed so as to allow for the possibility that persons eligible to vote may actually enjoy the opportunity to do so, despite the fact that they arrive late.[71]

The Trustee in Bankruptcy: Mode of Appointment

The principal proprietary effect of a bankruptcy adjudication is that, with only a limited number of exceptions, title to the bankrupt's property vests in a trustee and is thereafter divisible among his creditors.[72] In most cases the creditors have the right to select and appoint a trustee in bankruptcy, but in default of such appointment being made the official receiver acts as trustee in the bankruptcy.[73] The creditors are also empowered to establish a committee, known as "the creditors' committee," to perform a number of functions under the Act and Rules, including maintaining communications between the trustee and the general body of creditors and exercising the right to authorise the trustee to exercise those powers for which he requires the sanction of the committee.[74] In addition to the creditors' right to appoint a person other than the official receiver to be trustee, the Insolvency Act contains provisions whereby in certain circumstances a trustee may be appointed by the court or by the Department of Trade.[75]

---

[69] *ibid.*, r. 12.5. (Note: formerly s.138(1) of the Bankruptcy Act 1914 (now repealed) provided that the minute could be signed at the next ensuing meeting by the chairman of the later meeting. This is now precluded by the wording of the new rule, and only the actual chairman of the meeting to which the minute relates may provide the requisite signature authenticating the record).

[70] Added by (S.I. 1987, No. 1919), in place of the original r. 6.92 (repealed).

[71] r. 12.4A(4) of the Rules.

[72] ss.283, 306–310 of the Act. See *post*, Chap. 8 for full elaboration of this.

[73] *ibid.*, ss.292(1)(a), 293(3), 295(4), 297(1), (2), 300(2), (7). The office of official receiver is described in Chap. 2, *ante*.

[74] *ibid.*, ss.301, 314(1)(a), (b), (2), together with Sched. 5, Pt. I. See *infra*.

[75] *ibid.*, ss.292(1)(b), (c), 295(2), 296(2), 297, 300(6).

Trustee in Bankruptcy: Mode of Appointment

The exercise by the creditors of their right to appoint a trustee is usually accomplished at the first meeting of creditors which, as explained above, is convened primarily for this very purpose. If no first meeting of creditors is convened the official receiver becomes trustee of the bankrupt's estate.[76] If a meeting is summoned but no appointment of a person as trustee is made section 295(1) makes it the duty of the official receiver to decide whether to refer the need for an appointment to the Department of Trade. On the making of such a reference the Department, acting in the name of the Secretary of State, is free to make an appointment or not, and this decision is left as a matter for Ministerial discretion.[77] If the official receiver decides not to refer the need for an appointment to the Department, or if he does refer the matter but the Department declines to make an appointment, the official receiver is required to notify the court of this matter and, as from his giving of notice, the official receiver becomes trustee of the bankrupt's estate.[78]

If the official receiver, having become trustee in bankruptcy, subsequently decides that it would be appropriate for a trustee from the private sector to assume responsibility for the bankruptcy, section 296(1) of the Act enables him to apply to the Department of Trade and Industry for such an appointment to be made. However, it is once again made a matter of Ministerial discretion whether the official receiver's application will be answered by the making of the requested appointment.[79] The fact that the official receiver has already made one such application which has been unsuccessful does not preclude him from subsequently making a further application, and the Department is at liberty to adopt a different position, again acting in the name of the Secretary of State, on a later application.[80] A further occasion for the appointment of a trustee to be made by the Department arises where the appointment of any person as trustee in bankruptcy fails to take effect, or where after such an appointment has initially taken effect a vacancy arises in the office of trustee through the resignation, removal or death of the incumbent. In either event section 300 provides that the official receiver shall be trustee until the vacancy is filled, and that he may summon a general meeting of creditors for the purpose of filling the vacancy. It is also open to the creditors to requisition the calling of a meeting for this purpose by means of a request made with the concurrence of not less than one-tenth, in value, of the bankrupt's creditors.[81] Alternatively if no meeting of creditors has been summoned within 28 days from the day on which the vacancy first came to the official receiver's attention, section 300(4) makes it obligatory for the official receiver to refer the need for an appointment to the Department, but it is once again a matter of Ministerial discretion whether an appointment is made, and failing such an appointment the official

---

[76] *ibid.*, s.293(3).
[77] *ibid.*, s.295(2).
[78] *ibid.*, s.295(3), (4).
[79] *ibid.*, s.296(2).
[80] *ibid.*, s.296(3).
[81] *ibid.*, ss.300(3), 314(7); r. 6.83 of the Rules. See generally rr. 6.81–6.95 and 12.4A, discussed, *supra*.

receiver continues to be trustee in bankruptcy, while retaining the right to make a further reference to the Department for the substitution of a private sector trustee.[82]

Section 297 of the Act makes provision for a number of special cases in which the court may exercise a power to appoint a person other than the official receiver as trustee in bankruptcy. Where the court issues a certificate for summary administration, which is designed to minimise the costs of administration in cases where the amount of the unsecured debts is relatively small, the official receiver becomes trustee *ex officio* and there is no provision in this instance whereby the creditors may requisition a meeting for the purpose of substituting a trustee from the private sector.[83] However section 297(3) does empower the court, at its discretion, to appoint a person other than the official receiver as trustee where a certificate for summary administration is issued. A further instance upon which the court may make the appointment of the trustee is where the bankruptcy order has been made on the debtor's own petition and the court has acted in accordance with sections 273 and 274 to commission an insolvency practitioner to prepare a report on the prospects for the use of a voluntary arrangement as an alternative to bankruptcy.[84] If nevertheless a bankruptcy order is ultimately made, but no certificate for summary administration is issued, the court may at its discretion appoint as trustee the insolvency practitioner who made the report.[85] This is clearly a sensible and efficient way in which to make use of the resources which have already been spent in carrying out a professional investigation of the bankrupt's affairs. Similarly, where a bankruptcy order is made following the breakdown of a voluntary arrangement previously concluded between the debtor and his creditors, section 297(5) empowers the court, if it thinks fit, to appoint the supervisor of the arrangement as trustee in bankruptcy.[86] Where the trustee's appointment is made by the court the person appointed must normally notify the creditors of his appointment, although the court may authorise him to advertise his appointment as a less costly alternative means of giving notice.[87] The trustee must also indicate whether he will be convening a creditors' meeting for the purpose of establishing a creditors' committee and, if no such meeting is envisaged, he must inform the creditors of their power to requisition such a meeting.[88]

Validity and Commencement of Appointment

A most important and indispensable requirement attaching to all cases where a person other than the official receiver is appointed to be trustee in

---

[82] *ibid.*, s.300(6), (7).
[83] *ibid.*, ss.293(1), 294(1)(b), 297(2). See also ss.275 with 273 and generally Chap. 12, *post*.
[84] See *ante*, Chap. 4, section A(1)(A), and Chap. 6, section B(C).
[85] s.297(4) of the Act.
[86] On default in connection with a voluntary arrangement, see Chap. 4, *ante*, section A(1)(A).
[87] s.297(7) of the Act.
[88] *ibid.*, s.297(8). On the requisitioning of meetings, see *supra* (this section); for the creditors' committee, see *infra*.

bankruptcy is that the person in question must, at the date of appointment, be qualified to act as an insolvency practitioner in relation to the bankrupt.[89] The statutory meaning in the expression, "qualified insolvency practitioner," which is governed by the provisions of Part XIII of the Act, has already been explored in Chapter 2, and it will suffice here to observe that any person who acts as an insolvency practitioner in relation to any person at a time when he is not qualified to do so commits a criminal offence of strict liability by virtue of section 389 of the Act. The new statutory regulations of the activities of insolvency practitioners, which was one of the important innovations of the Insolvency Acts of 1985–86, has eliminated the need for validation of each individual appointment of a trustee in bankruptcy by the Department of Trade and Industry, as was formerly required.[90] In addition to fulfilling the criteria for being "qualified to act" under Part XIII of the Act, the person appointed as trustee must ensure that he does not contravene any of the principles of conduct laid down by the professional body to which he belongs. For example it is a long established principle that a person should not act as trustee in a case where he is himself an accounting party to the estate—as where he is indebted to the bankrupt—so that he would experience a conflict of interests in fulfilling his duties as trustee.[91] It is also arguable that a similarly compromised position would be occupied by any trustee who is simultaneously a creditor of the bankrupt, since one of the first acts which such a trustee will be required to perform will be to determine the admissibility to proof of his own debt.

The appointment of any person other than the official receiver as trustee in bankruptcy takes effect only if that person accepts the appointment in accordance with the Rules, but subject to this the trustee's appointment takes effect at the time specified in his certificate of appointment.[92] The Insolvency Rules take care to provide that, whether the appointment is made by a creditors' meeting or by the court, the certificate of appointment shall not be issued unless and until the person to be appointed has furnished a written statement to the effect that he is an insolvency practitioner duly qualified under the Act to be the trustee, and that he consents so to act.[93] Where the trustee is appointed by a creditors' meeting he must forthwith after receiving his certificate of appointment give notice thereof in an appropriate newspaper in order to ensure that it comes to the notice of the creditors.[94] By virtue of section 306 of the Act the bankrupt's estate vests in his trustee immediately on his appointment taking effect, and does so automatically without any conveyance, assignment or transfer. The full implications of this are considered in Chapter 8. Section 305(4) of the Act states that the official name of the trustee shall be "the trustee of the estate of ... , a bankrupt," (inserting the name of the

---

[89] *ibid.*, s.292(2).
[90] Bankruptcy Act 1914, s.19(2) (repealed).
[91] *cf. Re Martin* (1888) 21 Q.B.D. 29; *Re Lamb* [1894] 2 Q.B. 805; *Re Mardon* [1896] 1 Q.B. 140; *Re Beale* [1939] Ch. 761.
[92] s.292(4) of the Act.
[93] rr. 6.120, 6.121 of the Rules. For appointment by the Secretary of State, see r. 6.122.
[94] *ibid.*, r. 6.124.

bankrupt), but he may also be referred to more concisely as "the trustee in bankruptcy" of the particular bankrupt.

Remuneration

In addition to receiving reimbursement of his proper expenses incurred in the course of his administration,[95] the trustee is entitled to receive a remuneration for his services, fixed either as a percentage of the value of the assets in the estate which are realised or distributed, or as a percentage of those two values in combination, or alternatively fixed by reference to the time properly given by the insolvency practitioner and his staff in attending to matters arising in the bankruptcy.[96] Where someone other than the official receiver is trustee it is for the creditors' committee, if there is one, to determine which basis is to be used for fixing his remuneration, and also to determine any percentage figure which is to be employed in this context. The committee are required to have regard to such matters as the complexity of the case, the nature and degree of the responsibilities falling upon the trustee and the effectiveness with which he appears to discharge them, and finally the value and nature of the assets in the estate.[97] If there is no creditors' committee, or if the committee fails to make the requisite determination, the trustee's remuneration may be fixed in accordance with the foregoing criteria by a resolution of a meeting of creditors, and failing such a determination the trustee is to be paid according to a scale laid down for the official receiver in the Insolvency Regulations.[98] If the trustee is dissatisfied with the rate or amount of remuneration fixed by the creditors' committee he may request that it be increased by resolution of the creditors.[99] Thereafter if the trustee is still dissatisfied at the remuneration which has been determined for him he may apply to the court for an order increasing its amount or rate.[1] Conversely any creditor of the bankrupt who considers that the trustee's remuneration is excessive may apply to the court for an order bringing about its reduction, provided that he acts with the concurrence of at least one quarter, in value, of the creditors (including himself).[2] It is no longer possible, as was formerly the case, for the bankrupt himself to raise a challenge to the trustee's remuneration.[3]

There is a strict rule against the use of solicitation, whether directly or indirectly, in order to procure a trusteeship: if the court is satisfied that such impropriety has been perpetrated by or on behalf of the trustee in obtaining proxies or procuring his appointment, it has power by order to

---

[95] *ibid.*, r. 6.224. See Chap. 10, *post*.
[96] *ibid.*, r. 6.138(1), (2).
[97] *ibid.*, r. 6.138(3), (4).
[98] *ibid.*, r. 6.138(5), (6); Insolvency Regulations 1994 (S.I. 1994, No. 2507), regs. 33–36 inclusive, together with Sched. 2, Tables 1, 2 and 3. The scale provided by Table 1 is: on realisations, 20% on the first £5,000; 15% on the next £5,000; 10% on the next £90,000; 5% on all further sums realised. On distributions, the percentages are one half of those in the foregoing scale.
[99] r. 6.140 of the Rules.
[1] *ibid.*, r. 6.141. *cf. Re Toleman and England* (1880) 13 Ch.D. 885.
[2] *ibid.*, r. 6.142.
[3] *cf.* Bankruptcy Act 1914, s.82(2) (repealed).

disallow any remuneration payable to him out of the estate, and this power overrides any resolution of the creditors' committee or of the creditors generally.[4]

Powers of the Trustee

For the purpose of carrying out the duties allocated to him by law the trustee enjoys wide powers enabling him to acquire and retain possession of the property of the bankrupt, whether tangible or intangible, and whether currently held or after-acquired, and also to take possession of the bankrupt's books, papers and records.[5] In this respect the trustee is in the same position as if he were a receiver of the property appointed by the High Court, and he may therefore invoke the sanctions of the legal process, including orders for possession and warrants for breaking open buildings and seizure of property, in order to enforce his acquisition and retention of the bankrupt's property.[6] Moreover no person is entitled as against the official receiver or trustee to withhold possession of any of the books, papers or other records of the bankrupt or to set up any lien upon them except where the lienholder asserts a right to retain possession of documents which give title to property and which are held as such, as where a mortgage has been effected by a deposit of title deeds.[7]

Further powers of the trustee in relation to the realisation of the bankrupt's available property and the administration of his estate are discussed in Chapter 8, in which the proprietary effects of adjudication are considered at length. It may be useful at this point however to set out the powers which are exercisable by the trustee by virtue of Schedule 5 to the Act. These are divided into three groups: (i) those which are exercisable with sanction; (ii) general powers exercisable without sanction; and (iii) ancillary powers.

(i) Subject to Permission

The first group of powers, which are specified in Part I of Schedule 5, and in section 314(2), are exercisable only with the permission of the creditors' committee or the court.[8] Section 314(3) states that permission for these purposes must relate to a particular proposed exercise of the power in question, and cannot be granted in the form of a general authorisation.[9] On the other hand the fact that the trustee has obtained the specific permission of the committee or the court does not absolve him from responsibility for any action which he may take, and he remains under a duty to avoid acting unreasonably, or in a wasteful or vexatious manner.[10] Where no committee exists for the time being, and the trustee is

---

[4] r. 6.148 of the Rules.
[5] ss.306–321 of the Act, especially s.314 together with Sched. 5.
[6] *ibid.*, s.311(2). See also Part III of Schedule 5 to the Act; *Re Tucker* (1974) 232 E.G. 715; *Re Turner* [1975] 1 All E.R. 5; *Re McCarthy* [1975] 1 W.L.R. 807.
[7] *ibid.*, ss.312, 349.
[8] *ibid.*, s.314(1)(a). For the creditors' committee, see *infra*.
[9] *Re Vavasour* [1900] 2 Q.B. 309.
[10] *Re Smith, ex p. Brown* (1886) 17 Q.B.D. 488.

a person other than the official receiver, the functions of the committee including that of granting permission to the trustee are vested in the Secretary of State,[11] but by virtue of rule 6.166(2) of the Rules they may then be exercised by the official receiver. Although permission should be obtained in advance of the trustee's taking the action in question,[12] his omission to do so will not automatically render his action legally invalid, for the requirement is not designed to regulate relations between the trustee and third parties.[13] Section 314(3) expressly states that a person dealing with the trustee in good faith and for value is not to be concerned to enquire whether any required permission has in fact been given, while section 314(4) provides that where the trustee has done anything without the requisite permission the court or the creditors' committee may ratify what he has done, so as to enable him to meet his expenses out of the estate. This is subject to the proviso that the committee must be satisfied that the trustee has acted in a case of urgency, and has sought its ratification without undue delay. Even where the trustee has obtained specific permission he is under no obligation to carry out that which has been authorised, for he retains a discretion whether, and also when, to exercise the power in respect of which permission has been granted.

The following may be done by the trustee with permission of the committee of creditors:

(1) He may carry on the business of the bankrupt so far as may be necessary for the beneficial winding up of the business.[14] Business considerations must furnish the motivation for carrying on: the law does not sanction a continuation which is intended to serve the bankrupt's interests, as would be the case where the trustee's intention was to make a profit, or to try to save the bankrupt from losing his business in consequence of his failure.[15] These are objectives which must be pursued by way of a voluntary arrangement of the kind described in Chapter 4. The trustee, in carrying on the business, must keep a distinct account of the trading, and care must be taken to ensure that neither the trustee himself nor any associate of his, nor any member of the creditors' committee, derives any profit from the venture unless prior leave of the court has been obtained.[16]

(2) He may engage in litigation, either as plaintiff or defendant, in any proceedings relating to property comprised in the

---

[11] s.302(2) of the Act.
[12] *Re Gallard* [1896] 1 Q.B. 68; *Re Geiger* [1915] 1 K.B. 439.
[13] *Lee v. Sangster* (1957) 2 C.B.N.S. 1; 140 E.R. 310; *Re Branson* [1914] 2 K.B. 701; *Clark v. Smith* [1940] 1 K.B. 126. The trustee may be personally penalised in costs, however.
[14] Sched. 5, para. 1 to the Act.
[15] *Re Batey, ex p. Emmanuel* (1881) 17 Ch.D. 35. *cf. Clark v. Smith, supra.*
[16] r. 6.147 of the Rules, enables the trustee's transactions with associates to be set aside. "Associate" is defined in s.435 of the Act: see Appendix I, *post.*

bankrupt's estate.[17] He may also validly assign any rights of action which are vested in him as trustee if he is unwilling to pursue them himself,[18] but if he suffers any cause of action to become procedurally unenforceable the bar will apply equally to any assignee of the cause of action, including the bankrupt himself.[19]

(3) He may sell the assets of the bankrupt upon credit terms subject to such conditions and stipulations as to security as the committee or the court think fit.[20]

(4) He may raise money by means of a mortgage or pledge of property comprised in the estate.[21]

(5) He may, where any property is subject to a right, option or other power which forms part of the estate, make payments or incur liabilities with a view to obtaining that property for the creditors' benefit.[22]

(6) He may refer any dispute to arbitration and compromise upon agreed terms any debts, claims or liabilities, whatever their nature, which other persons may have incurred towards the bankrupt.[23] The court is usually content to let the trustee and the committee use their own judgment in this matter, and will not intervene unless the proposed terms are grossly unsatisfactory, or otherwise fraudulent.[24]

(7) He may make any suitable compromise or other arrangement with creditors, or persons claiming to be creditors, in respect of any bankruptcy debts.[25]

(8) He may make any suitable compromise or other arrangement with respect to any claim arising out of, or incidental to, the bankrupt's estate.[26]

(9) He may appoint the bankrupt to superintend the management of his estate or any part of it, or to carry on his business for the benefit of his creditors, or to assist in any other way in administering the estate subject to the trustee's direction.[27]

---

[17] Sched. 5, para. 2 of the Act. When he is made defendant in an action, or is made a party to proceedings on the application of any other party, the trustee will not be personally liable for costs unless the court so orders: r. 7.39 of the Rules; *Hemming v. Davies* [1898] 1 Q.B. 660. But see also *Borneman v. Wilson* (1884) 28 Ch.D. 53; *Farnham v. Milward & Co.* [1895] 2 Ch. 730.

[18] *Seear v. Lawson* (1880) 15 Ch.D. 426, but *cf. Wolf v. Van Boolen* (1906) 94 L.T. 502, and see *post*, Chap. 8, p. 191.

[19] *Warder v. Saunders* (1882) 10 Q.B.D. 114; *Selig v. Lion* [1891] 1 Q.B. 513.

[20] Sched. 5, para. 3 to the Act.

[21] *ibid.*, para. 4.

[22] *ibid.*, para. 5.

[23] *ibid.*, para. 6. This is distinct from the trustee's powers to compromise any proceedings he has instituted in his own right as trustee under case 2, *supra*: *Leeming v. Lady Murray* (1879) 13 Ch.D. 123.

[24] *Re Pilling* [1906] 2 K.B. 644; *Re A Debtor ex p. the Debtor v. Dodwell* [1949] Ch. 236; *Leon v. York-O-Matic Ltd* [1966] 3 All E.R. 277.

[25] Sched. 5, para. 7 to the Act.

[26] *ibid.*, para. 8.

[27] s.314(2)(a), (b), (c) of the Act.

(10) By virtue of section 303(2) of the Act he may apply to the court for directions in relation to any particular matter arising under the bankruptcy.

(ii) General Powers

The second group of powers, which are specified in Part II of Schedule 5, are of general nature and may be exercised by the trustee without any need for permission.[28] These enable the trustee to do the following:

(1) He may sell any part of the property for the time being comprised in the bankrupt's estate, including the goodwill and book debts of any business.[29]
(2) He may give valid receipts in return for any money received by him and thereby effectually discharge the person paying the money from all further liability in respect of its application.[30]
(3) He may prove, rank, claim and draw a dividend in respect of such debts due to the bankrupt as are comprised in his estate.[31]
(4) He enjoys a general power to exercise, in relation to any property comprised in the bankrupt's estate, any powers which vest in him by virtue of Parts VIII to XI of the Insolvency Act.[32]
(5) He may deal with any property comprised in the estate to which the bankrupt is beneficially entitled as tenant in tail in the same manner as the bankrupt might have dealt with it.[33]
(6) He may exercise, in relation to any part of the bankrupt's estate which consists of stock or shares in a company or shares in a ship, the same right of transfer as the bankrupt himself might have exercised if he had not become bankrupt.[34]
(7) He may, where any goods comprised in the estate are held by any person by way of pledge, pawn or other security, serve notice in the same way as the official receiver under section 285(5) of the Act, thereby gaining the right to inspect the goods and at the same time preventing the person who holds the goods from realising his security without the leave of the court. The trustee may also at his discretion exercise the bankrupt's right of redemption in respect of any such goods.[35]
(8) He may at any time, at his own discretion, summon a general meeting of the bankrupt's creditors.[36]
(9) He has the right to determine when and where the creditors' committee shall meet.[37]

---

[28] *ibid.*, s.314(1)(b).
[29] *ibid.*, Sched. 5, para. 9.
[30] *ibid.*, para. 10.
[31] *ibid.*, para. 11.
[32] *ibid.*, para. 12.
[33] *ibid.*, para. 13.
[34] *ibid.*, s.311(3).
[35] *ibid.*, s.311(5).
[36] *ibid.*, s.314(7); Insolvency Rules 1986, r. 6.81.
[37] r. 6.153 of the Rules.

(10) He may, in the exercise of the powers conferred on him under the Act, employ a solicitor to undertake any business associated with the administration of the estate, subject to the requirement that if there is for the time being a creditors' committee the trustee must give notice to it of this exercise of his powers. Similarly it is competent for the trustee to dispose of property comprised in the bankrupt's estate to an associate of the bankrupt, but again subject to the obligation to notify the creditors' committee.[38] The modern law operates upon the assumption that the trustee's integrity and independence can be virtually taken for granted, so that former abusive practices whereby a trustee might dispose of assets at a low price to persons connected with the bankrupt should in theory have been eradicated. The onus is therefore cast on the creditors' committee to maintain a degree of vigilance over such disposals and if abuse is suspect they may challenge the trustee's act by an application to the court under section 303 of the Act.

(11) He may at any time apply to the court for a direction that the bankrupt do specific things for the purposes of his bankruptcy, or for the administration of the estate, even after the bankrupt has become discharged.[39]

(iii) Ancillary Powers

The third group of powers, which are specified in Part III of Schedule 5 are expressed to be ancillary in nature, and are broadly drawn to ensure that there is no possibility of calling into question the trustee's capacity to undertake the actions which are essential to the proper discharge of this statutory functions. It is therefore provided that, by his official name, the trustee may hold property of every description; make contracts; sue and be sued; enter into engagements binding on himself and, in respect of the bankrupt's estate, on his successors in office; employ an agent; execute any power of attorney, deed or other instrument; and do any other act which is necessary or expedient for the purposes of, or in connection with, the exercise of his powers under the Act.[40]

The Trustee's Duties

The duties of the trustee in bankruptcy—including where this position is occupied by the official receiver in any given case—are principally to administer the estate of the bankrupt using such of the above-mentioned powers as may be necessary, and thus to "get in, realise and distribute the bankrupt's estate" in accordance with the provisions contained in Chapter IV of Part IX of the Insolvency Act.[41] Subject to those provisions the

---

[38] s.314(6)(a), (b) of the Act. "Associate" is defined in s.435: see Appendix I, *post*.
[39] *ibid.*, s.363(2), (3).
[40] *ibid.*, s.314(5), together with Pt. III of Sched. 5.
[41] *ibid.*, s.305(2).

trustee is entitled to use his discretion with regard to the way in which he shall discharge his functions. It is also the duty of the trustee, if he is not the official receiver, to furnish the latter with such information, and to produce to him for inspection such books, papers and other records as the official receiver may reasonably require for the purpose of discharging his own statutory functions in relation to the bankruptcy.[42] As soon as possible therefore the trustee must take possession of all the property of the bankrupt which is divisible among his creditors, and so administer it as to maximise the return upon realisation. He must also take possession of all books, papers and other records which relate to the bankrupt's estate or affairs, and these must be surrendered to him whether they are in the possession or control of the bankrupt himself or of the official receiver, or of any prior trustee in bankruptcy or former supervisor of a voluntary arrangement to which the bankrupt was a party.[43] If it proves to be possible to pay dividends to the creditor, or to any class of them, these are to be declared and distributed whenever the trustee has sufficient funds in hand after deducting a retainer to cover the necessary expenses of the bankruptcy.[44]

Records and Accounts

To facilitate the exercise of proper control by the creditors, by the creditors' committee and ultimately by the Department of Trade and Industry, the trustee is required to maintain financial records and to handle all monies and fees in accordance with the provisions of the Insolvency Regulations 1994.[45] As a general rule the trustee is not permitted to operate a local bank account for the purposes of his administration, but must pay all money received by him in the course of carrying out his functions directly into the Insolvency Services Account kept by the Secretary of State at the Bank of England.[46] It is a long established principle that the trustee must not keep money in his own hands, and the present Regulations require that money received by him must be remitted to the Insolvency Services Account once every 14 days, or forthwith if £5,000 or more has been received. The trustee is not allowed to make any deductions when paying into the Insolvency Services Account, but must reclaim all necessary disbursements and properly-incurred expenses by making application to the Department on the requisite form, whereupon he may be repaid out of any money in the account which is standing to the credit of the insolvent.[47] If the trustee at any time fails to pay money into the Account in accordance with the

---

[42] *ibid.*, s.305(3).
[43] *ibid.*, ss.311(1), 312.
[44] *ibid.*, s.324(1). See Chap. 10, *post*.
[45] *ibid.*, ss.403–410, 412, together with Sched. 9, para. 21; Insolvency Regulations 1994, (S.I. 1994, No. 2507), regs. 19–31.
[46] Insolvency Regulations 1994, reg. 20(1). The statutory provisions governing the Insolvency Services Account are contained in ss.403–410 of the Insolvency Act 1986.
[47] Insolvency Regulations 1994 (S.I. 1994, No. 2507), regs. 20(1), 22. *cf. Ex parte Goring* (1790) 1 Ves.Jun. 168; 30 E.R. 284.

regulations this can result, unless a satisfactory explanation is forthcoming, in his being reported by the Secretary of State to the licensing body which has responsibility for his authorisation to practise as an insolvency practitioner.[48] Exceptionally, if the trustee intends to exercise his power to carry on the business of the insolvent he may apply to the Secretary of State for authorisation to open a local bank account, and if such authorisation is granted he must open and maintain a clearly named account in the name of each separate insolvent of which he is the responsible insolvency practitioner, and must keep proper records relating to all payments of money into and out of a local account.[49] The trustee is required also to keep administrative records in relation to the bankruptcy containing the minutes of proceedings at all meetings of creditors, or of the creditors' committee, including a record of every resolution passed at any such meeting. He must also keep financial records relating to the bankruptcy and enter on a daily basis all the receipts and payments made by him, and if required send an account of his receipts and payments to the Secretary of State. These records must be submitted to the creditors' committee when required, and if the committee are not satisfied with the contents they may so inform the Secretary of State giving the reasons for their dissatisfaction, whereupon the Secretary of State may take such action as he thinks fit. This can include his requiring any account to be audited. The trustee must on request supply a free copy of the account of his receipts and payments to the bankrupt and to any creditor.[50]

The Cork Committee, in Chapter 17 of their *Report*, were critical of the manner in which money being administered in insolvency proceedings was for the most part kept under centralised control through the requirement that it be lodged in the Insolvency Services Account. Not only does this represent an administrative incumbrance for the trustee, by subjecting all financial transactions to costly and time-consuming formalities, but it also prevents the money standing to the credit of the insolvent from earning a full commercial rate of interest during the time it is on deposit pending distribution. Not only does the Insolvency Services Account not pay interest at full current rates upon such deposits, but also charges are levied in respect of transactions on the account, thus actually diminishing the amount of money available for distribution to creditors. The surplus revenue which is thus generated through investment of money deposited in the Insolvency Services Account is payable to the Consolidated Fund and is ostensibly appropriated to meet the overall cost of operating the Insolvency Service of the Department of Trade and Industry. In fact, the Cork Committee were able to demonstrate[51] that the annual revenue generated in this manner is comfortably in excess of the cost of providing a service which, as an integral aspect of the proper

---

[48] The revised Insolvency Regulations of 1994 abolished the former provision under which penal interest was payable to the bankrupt's estate: *Re Sims* [1907] 2 K.B. 36; see also *Board of Trade v. Employers Liability Assurance Corp. Ltd* [1910] 2 K.B. 645; *Re Walker* [1972] 1 All E.R. 1096, 1104, *per* Foster J.

[49] Insolvency Regulations 1994 (S.I. 1994, No. 2507), reg. 21.

[50] *ibid.*, regs. 24–29 inclusive.

[51] Cmnd. 8558, ch. 17, especially at paras. 842–846 and 856–863.

administration of the law regarding debt, credit and insolvency, ought in principle to be sustained as part of the overall costs of administration of justice, rather than being paid for, as now, by those who for the time being are involuntarily embroiled in the operation of the insolvency law through being the unpaid creditors of a bankrupt. Despite the important changes whereby private-sector insolvency practitioners have come under statutory regulation and professional control, no reforms were implemented in the insolvency legislation of 1985–86 to alter the pre-existing provisions governing the financial management of insolvency proceedings, or the method of funding the operation of the Insolvency Service.[52]

Control of the Trustee

The provisions of section 305(2) of the Act indicate that the trustee must function in accordance with the terms of the act itself, and that he is entitled to use his own discretion in carrying out his duties. Sections 301–304 express the concept of control of the trustee to be achieved by means of the setting up of a creditors' committee[53] (except where the official receiver is trustee); by the Secretary of State (where there is no creditors' committee, or where the official receiver is trustee); and by the court, acting upon the application of the bankrupt, the creditors and any properly interested persons. While provision is made by section 314(7) to the effect that the trustee may summon a meeting of creditors at any time, which thereby enables him to ascertain their wishes, the subsection further provides that the trustee must summon such a meeting if he is requested to do so by a creditor acting with the concurrence of not less than one-tenth in value of the bankrupt's creditors (including the creditor making the request).[54] At such a meeting, if the requisite majority is forthcoming, the ultimate control of the creditors over the trustee may be asserted by means of a resolution bringing about his removal from office.[55]

An alternative means of exercising effective control over the trustee is through the court, which has jurisdiction to confirm, reverse or modify any act, omission or decision of the trustee, to give him directions or to make such other order as it thinks fit.[56] This could, in an especially serious case, include the making of an order removing the trustee from office, as permitted by section 298(1). This jurisdiction may be invoked by the bankrupt or any of the creditors or any other person who is "dissatisfied"

---

[52] *cf.* Cmnd. 9175 (*The White Paper*), Chap. 8.
[53] See *infra*.
[54] See also Insolvency Rules 1986, rr. 6.83, 6.87. Since those requisitioning a meeting of creditors are now required to assume responsibility for the cost of doing so, it is submitted that the former decision in *Re J. Burn* [1932] 1 Ch. 247 (whereby the court would not compel the trustee to summon a meeting which it considered would serve no useful purpose) should not be followed in the present day.
[55] s.298(1) of the Act. For resolutions and voting at creditors' meetings, see *supra*.
[56] *ibid.*, s.303(1).

by the trustee's actions,[57] but it was well-established under the former bankruptcy legislation that the court would interfere only where the trustee is acting in manner which is absurdly unreasonable, or even fraudulent, and there is moreover no reported case in which the bankrupt himself successfully invoked the intervention of the court.[58] The trustee may likewise apply to the court for directions if he requires guidance in any matter, although the court will not normally tender its advice or guidance upon the routine aspects of daily administration of the bankruptcy.[59]

A special remedy for the assertion of judicial control over the trustee is provided by section 304 which establishes a summary procedure against the trustee in respect of loss to the estate caused by his misapplication or retention of property, or by his misfeasance or breach of duty. An application under this section may be made by the official receiver, the Secretary of State, a creditor of the bankrupt or the bankrupt himself, but the leave of the court is required for the making of an application by the bankrupt, or if the application is to be made after the trustee has had his release under section 299.[60] The court has wide discretionary powers to order the trustee to make restitution to the estate, with interest, or to pay compensation for loss caused. There is a protective provision to safeguard the trustee's position in case he happens to seize or dispose of any property which is not comprised in the bankrupt's estate: provided that at the time of so doing the trustee bona fide and reasonably believed that he was entitled to seize or dispose of the property, he is not liable in respect of loss or damage resulting from his action except to the extent that this has been caused by his negligence.[61] The final agents of control over the trustee are the Department of Trade and Industry and the professional body to which the trustee belongs, membership of which has enabled him to acquire his qualification to act as an insolvency practitioner.[62] Any instances of demonstrable professional incompetence or misconduct on the trustee's part should be reported both to the Department and to the relevant professional body. The latter should investigate the matter and take appropriate action pursuant to their internal disciplinary procedures, but in the event that these prove to be ineffectively administered in practice a further complaint should be made to the Department, which possesses the

---

[57] *ibid.*, the word "dissatisfied" is used in the present section in place of "aggrieved," which appeared in Bankruptcy Acts down to and including that of 1914 (s.80, now repealed). The latter expression was judicially explained by James, L.J. in *Re Sidebotham* (1880) 14 Ch.D. 458, 465 as denoting a person "against whom a decision has been pronounced which has wrongfully deprived him of something or wrongfully refused him something or wrongfully affected his title to something." *cf. Re Reed and Bowen & Co.* (1887) 19 Q.B.D. 174. It is submitted that the use of the word "dissatisfied" in the present s.303(1) has deliberately broadened the basis of individual standing to invoke the court's intervention, and that an applicant may now properly complain of the general manner in which the trustee is conducting his administration, without the need to show special prejudice to the applicant personally.
[58] *Re Peters* (1882) 47 L.T. 64; *Re A Debtor ex parte the Debtor v. Dodwell, supra*, n. 24; *Leon v. York-O-Matic Ltd*; above, n. 24.
[59] *cf. Re Pilling*, above, n. 24; *Re Wiskeman* (1923) 92 L.J. Ch. 349.
[60] s.304(2) of the Act.
[61] *ibid.*, s.304(1), (3).
[62] See Chap. 2, *ante*, and generally Part XIII of the Act.

ultimate sanction of removing the professional body from the list of those which are "recognised" for the purposes of section 391 of the Act.[63] The financial controls exercised by the Department in relation to each and every trustee in bankruptcy, both as a matter of routine and upon the instigation of the creditors' committee, have already been described.[64]

Resignation, Removal or Vacation of Office by the Trustee

Apart from natural factors, such as his death or disablement during the course of his administration, the vacation of his office by the trustee may come about in several ways, as follows:

(1) He may voluntarily resign his office by giving notice of his resignation to the court.[65] Before resigning the trustee must call a meeting of creditors for the purpose of receiving his resignation, and must also notify the official receiver. Resignation is only permitted on the grounds of ill health, or because the trustee intends ceasing to practise as an insolvency practitioner, or because there is some conflict of interest or change in personal circumstances which prevents him from further discharging the duties of trustee.[66] If at the creditors' meeting it is resolved that his resignation be not accepted the trustee may apply to the court for an order giving him leave to resign.[67]

(2) He may be removed from office by an order of the court or by a general meeting of creditors summoned specially for that purpose.[68] If a removal is effected by a creditors' meeting, the meeting may further resolve that a new trustee be appointed, and also that the removed trustee be not given his release.[69] Similarly where the court removes a trustee upon a hearing at which sufficient cause is shown for the application, it may appoint a new trustee in his stead.[70] If a trustee has been appointed by the Secretary of State under sections 295, 296 or 300, or if the official receiver is acting as trustee either because he formally decided not to convene a first meeting of creditors, or because no trustee was appointed by the creditors or by the Secretary of State, a general meeting of creditors for the purpose of replacing the trustee may only be convened if the trustee himself thinks fit, or if the court so directs, or if the

---

[63] See especially s.291(4) of the Act. See also the Insolvency Practitioners (Recognised Professional Bodies) Order 1986 (S.I. 1986, No. 1764).
[64] Above: *Records and Accounts*.
[65] s.298(7) of the Act.
[66] rr. 6.126, 6.127 of the Rules.
[67] *ibid.*, r. 6.128.
[68] s.298(1) of the Act; rr. 6.129–6.132 of the Rules. Note that when a certificate of summary administration is in force a general meeting of creditors may not be held for the purpose of removing the trustee: s.298(3).
[69] r. 6.129(4) of the Rules.
[70] *ibid.*, rr. 6.132, 6.121.

meeting is requested by creditors representing at least one quarter, in value, of the creditors.[71]

(3) He may be removed by a direction of the Secretary of State if the appointment was originally made by him. The trustee must be notified of the grounds on which this action is to be taken, and must be allowed an opportunity to make representations against implementation of the Secretary of State's decision.[72]

(4) He must vacate office if he ceases to be a person who is for the time being qualified to act as an insolvency practitioner in relation to the bankrupt. This would necessarily include any case in which the trustee himself undergoes a bankruptcy adjudication, or is made the subject of a disqualification order under the Company Directors Disqualification Act 1986.[73]

(5) He must vacate office if, having concluded that the administration of the bankrupt's estate is complete and having in consequence summoned a final meeting of creditors under section 331 of the Act, he has duly given notice to the court that a final meeting has taken place, and of any decision taken at that meeting.[74]

(6) He must vacate office if the bankruptcy order is annulled.[75]

A matter closely related to the trustee's removal from or vacation of office is that of his obtaining his release from liability for his acts or omissions in the administration of the estate and in relation to his conduct as trustee. This is governed by section 298, which makes a distinction between cases where the official receiver ceases to be trustee and those where a private sector trustee ceases to hold office. In the former case, if the official receiver ceases to be trustee because some other person is appointed to replace him in office, his release is effective from the time of his giving notice to the court that this has taken place, or, where the court itself appoints his replacement, at such time as the court may determine.[76] If the official receiver ceases to be trustee because the administration of the bankrupt's estate has been completed, his release is effective from a time to be determined by the Secretary of State upon receipt of the trustee's notice that the administration is complete.[77] In the case of any person other than the official receiver who ceases to be trustee, the timing of the trustee's release is dependent upon the circumstances in which his tenure of office has come to an end. Thus if he has been removed by a meeting of creditors which has resolved against his release, or if he has been removed by the court or by the Secretary of State, or if he has vacated office because he has ceased to be qualified to act as an insolvency practitioner in relation to the bankrupt, the trustee's release does not become effective until such time as

---

[71] s.298(4) of the Act.
[72] *ibid.*, s.298(5); r. 6.133 of the Rules.
[73] *ibid.*, s.298(6). See also ss.390, 391(4), (5).
[74] *ibid.*, s.298(8); rr. 6.136, 6.137 of the Rules.
[75] *ibid.*, s.298(9). See Chap. 11, *post.*
[76] *ibid.*, s.299(1).
[77] *ibid.*, s.299(2).

the Secretary of State may determine, on an application made by the former office holder himself.[78] Where, on the other hand, the trustee has been removed from office by a creditors' meeting that has not resolved against his release, or where the trustee has died, his release is effective from the time at which the requisite notice is given to the court that that person has ceased to hold office.[79] The release of the trustee who has resigned is effective from the time when his resignation itself becomes effective, namely the date when the official receiver files in court a copy of the notice which the resigning trustee is required to send to him, signifying acceptance of his resignation by the creditors' meeting.[80] Where vacation of office by the trustee occurs upon completion of his administration the timing of his release is dependent upon whether the final meeting of creditors, summoned under section 331 of the Act, resolves against his release. If the meeting so resolves, his release becomes dependent upon the decision of the Secretary of State made on an application by the former trustee, but if the meeting does not so resolve, his release is effective from the time when he vacates office by duly notifying the court of the holding of the final meeting, and its outcome.[81] Lastly, where a bankruptcy order is annulled the court may determine the time as of which the serving trustee shall have his release.[82] It is to be noted however that, despite his having had his release by virtue of the appropriate provision of section 299, the former office holder still remains subject to the court's powers under section 304 to impose an order that he make restitution, or pay compensation, in respect of money or property for which he is held accountable, or for loss caused through his misfeasance or breach of duty, during the course of his administration.[83]

Creditors' Committee

A creditors' committee may be appointed by resolution of the creditors at their first, or at any subsequent, meeting.[84] The purpose of such a committee is to act as representatives of the general body of creditors, and to scrutinise and control the trustee's administration to the extent permitted by the Act and the Rules. Section 301(2) prevents the setting up of a creditors' committee at any time when the official receiver is trustee of the bankrupt's estate, except at a meeting where the creditors validly appoint a person to be trustee instead of the official receiver. Similarly, section 302(1) deprives the creditors' committee of the capacity to function at any time when the official receiver is trustee, but provides instead that the functions of the committee shall then be vested in the

---

[78] *ibid.*, s.299(3)(b); Insolvency Rules, r. 6.135(3), (4), (5); form 6.49.
[79] *ibid.*, s.299(3)(a); Insolvency Rules, rr. 6.131, 6.135(2).
[80] *ibid.*, ss.298(7), 299(3)(c); Insolvency Rules, rr. 6.126, 6.127, 6.135(1). On resignation, see above.
[81] *ibid.*, s.299(3)(d); Insolvency Rules, rr. 6.136, 6.137; form 6.50.
[82] *ibid.*, s.299(4).
[83] *ibid.*, ss.299(5), proviso; 304 (see above, "Control of the Trustee").
[84] *ibid.*, s.301(1).

CREDITORS' COMMITTEE

Secretary of State. If no creditors' committee is appointed, and the trustee is a person other than the official receiver, the Department of Trade and Industry, usually acting through the person of the official receiver, performs all the functions which would otherwise be exercised by the committee.[85]

Although the most usual and convenient occasion for the appointment of a creditors' committee is at the statutory first meeting of creditors,[86] the trustee may convene a general meeting for this specific purpose at any later time, in accordance with the general authorisation contained in section 314(7) of the Act. Sections 296(5)(a) and 297(8)(a) also direct the trustee to have regard to the practicability of establishing a creditors' committee when notifying the creditors of his appointment under either of those sections.[87] If however the trustee takes no initiative to summon a meeting for this purpose he can be compelled to do so under the further provisions of section 314(7) if at least one tenth in value of the creditors concur in formally requesting him to summon one.

The membership of the committee is limited to no more than five, nor less than three, persons who must be creditors of the bankrupt. Any creditor, other than one who is fully secured, may be a member so long as he has lodged proof of his debt and his proof has neither been wholly disallowed for voting purposes, nor wholly rejected for the purposes of distribution or dividend.[88] It is expressly provided by the Rules that a body corporate may be a member of the committee, but it must act through a representative who is properly appointed by written letter of authority.[89] The members of the committee are in a fiduciary position and must not, without the prior leave of the court, derive any profit from the administration, or acquire any asset forming part of the estate or receive payment out of the estate for services given or goods supplied in connection with its administration.[90] The same restriction also applies to persons who are appointed to act as representatives of members of the committee, to persons who are associates of committee members or their representatives, and to persons who have been members of the committee at any time within the previous 12 months.[91]

Meetings of the committee are to take place when and where the trustee determines, but he must call a first meeting within three months of his own appointment or of the committee's establishment (whichever is later) and thereafter he must call a meeting within 21 days of being so requested by any serving member of the committee or his representative, or at any date on which the committee has previously resolved that a meeting shall be held.[92] Although the committee is ostensibly created as an organ of control over the trustee the ideal relationship is intended to be one of

---

[85] *ibid.*, s.302(2); Insolvency Rules, r. 6.166.
[86] Insolvency Act 1986, s.293; Insolvency Rules, r. 6.80(1)(b), discussed above.
[87] See above.
[88] r. 6.150 of the Rules.
[89] *ibid.*, rr. 6.150(3), 6.156.
[90] *ibid.*, r. 165. *Re Gallard* [1896] 1 Q.B. 68; *Re Bulmer* [1937] Ch. 499.
[91] *ibid.*, r. 6.165(1) "Associate" is defined in s.435 of the Act: see Appendix I, *post.*
[92] *ibid.*, r. 6.153.

collaboration, with exchange of information between the committee and the trustee. Meetings of the committee are in fact required to be chaired by the trustee or by a person appointed by him.[93] The prescribed quorum at a meeting of the committee is two members who are either present or represented. Any member of the committee may be represented by another person duly authorised by him in writing to act on his behalf in relation to the business of the committee.[94] Resolutions at any meeting of the committee are passed on the basis of a simple majority of the votes cast, each member, or his representative, having one vote.[95] To facilitate the conduct of business the Rules provide for the circulation of resolutions by post to the members of the committee, and in the absence of any request by a member for a meeting of the committee to be summoned the resolution is deemed to have been carried in the committee if and when the trustee receives written notification of concurrence from a majority of the members.[96] It has been held that the court has jurisdiction to declare invalid any decisions of the committee which are taken *ultra vires*, or which are too vaguely or imprecisely expressed.[97]

Foremost among the functions of the creditors' committee are the granting of permission to the trustee where this is required in order for him to be able to exercise any powers under the Act, and the scrutinising of the trustee's accounts and records.[98] A resolution of the general body of creditors may overrule any act of the committee in the matter of granting permission.[99] The committee also have the power to direct the trustee at any time (but not more than once in any period of two months) to send to every member of the committee a written report upon the progress of the bankruptcy and related matters, and in the absence of such directions the trustee is required to send such a report not less often than once in every period of six months.[1] It is also the duty of the trustee to report to the members of the committee all such matters as he considers to be of concern to them with respect to the bankruptcy, and he must also report on such matters as they have indicated to him as being of concern, provided that the request is not frivolous or unreasonable, and that compliance would not involve excessive cost.[2]

Members of the committee may resign by giving written notice to the trustee, and they may be removed at a meeting of creditors by resolution of which at least 14 days' notice has been given.[3] A person's membership of the committee is automatically terminated if he becomes bankrupt or enters into a composition or arrangement with his creditors, or if his absence from three consecutive meetings of the committee is not

---

[93] *ibid.*, r. 6.154.
[94] *ibid.*, rr. 6.155, 6.156.
[95] *ibid.*, r. 6.161.
[96] *ibid.*, r. 6.162.
[97] *Re Marsden* (1892) 9 Morr. 70; *Re Salmon* [1916] 2 K.B. 510.
[98] s.314(1)(a) of the Act, together with Sched. 5, Pt. I; Insolvency Regulations 1986, reg. 9. See *supra* (*The Trustee's Powers; Records and Accounts*).
[99] *Re Ridgway* (1889) 6 Morr. 277; 6 T.L.R. 21.
[1] r. 6.163 of the Rules.
[2] *ibid.*, r. 6.152.
[3] *ibid.*, rr. 6.157, 6.159.

condoned by resolution at the third such meeting, or if he ceases to be a creditor or is found never to have been one.[4] A vacancy in the membership of the committee need not be filled, provided that the number of members does not fall below the permitted minimum of three. With the agreement of a majority of the other members of the committee the trustee may appoint any consenting and qualified creditor to fill the vacancy, or alternatively the vacancy may be filled by resolution passed at a meeting of creditors.[5] No remuneration is paid to members of the committee but they are allowed to claim out of the estate any reasonable travelling expenses directly incurred in respect of their attendance at the committee's meetings, or otherwise on the committee's business.[6]

Special Manager

It was mentioned above that a special manager may be appointed following the making of a bankruptcy order and pending the appointment of a trustee in bankruptcy, in order to safeguard the creditors' interests by providing closer personal management of the bankrupt's business and affairs than could be undertaken by the official receiver.[7] Section 370 of the Act also enables the court to appoint a special manager at any subsequent time during the administration of the bankruptcy, should circumstances warrant this. It is thus provided that an application for the appointment of a special manager may be made by the official receiver or the trustee in any case where it appears to the applicant that the nature of the bankrupt's estate, property or business, or the interests of the creditors generally, require the making of an appointment of this nature.[8] The application must be supported by a report setting out the reasons why it is being made, which must include the applicant's estimate of the value of the estate, property or business in respect of which the special manager is to be appointed.[9] Under the new statutory provisions of the 1986 Insolvency Act and Rules, there is no longer any requirement that one or more of the creditors should initiate the process of procuring the appointment of a special manager. On the other hand all such appointments must now be made by the court, and there is no authority, as formerly, for the official receiver to make the appointment himself. Significantly however there is no provision whereby the creditors, or a proportion of them, may requisition the making of an application to the court by the official receiver or trustee and it would therefore appear that the previously established principle has been respected to this extent, namely that it is a matter for the office holder to form a personal judgment as to the necessity for seeking the appointment of a special manager.[10]

[4] *ibid.*, r. 6.158.
[5] *ibid.*, r. 6.160.
[6] *ibid.*, r. 6.164.
[7] Above, p. 145 (*Effects of the Order*); s.370 of the Act.
[8] s.370(2) of the Act.
[9] r. 6.167(1) of the Rules.
[10] *cf. Re Whittaker* (1884) 1 Morr. 36.

If a special manager is appointed he may be invested with such powers as the court in its order of appointment may entrust to him, and where he is appointed to undertake any of the functions of the official receiver, or of an interim receiver, or of the trustee (as the case may be) the court may entrust to him any of the powers which under the Insolvency Act can be conferred upon the office holder in question.[11] The order of appointment must specify its duration, and the court is also required to fix the special manager's remuneration.[12] The special manager must give security to an extent not less than the value of assets over which he is to exercise responsibility, and his appointment is not effective until such security has been given (or, with the court's approval, promised) to the person who has applied for the appointment to be made.[13] The special manager must produce three-monthly accounts for the duration of his appointment and submit them for the approval of the trustee.[14] The appointment may be terminated by the court at any time prior to the end of its designated period of duration. An application for the making of such an order may be made by the official receiver or trustee if he is of the opinion that the employment of the special manager is no longer necessary or profitable, and such an application must be made if a resolution of the creditors is passed requesting that the appointment be terminated.[15]

There is no statutory requirement that a person appointed as a special manager must be qualified to act as an insolvency practitioner in relation to the bankrupt, within the meaning of Part XIII of the Act: the criteria for suitability for this type of appointment are essentially the possession of business and administrative skills appropriate to the type of business, or other assets, which require to be managed. The bankrupt may be required to collaborate with a special manager in the same way as with the official receiver or with the trustee in bankruptcy.[16]

---

[11] s.370(3), (4) of the Act.
[12] Insolvency Rules, r. 6.167(2), (3), (4); form 6.54.
[13] *ibid.*, rr. 6.168, 6.169; s.370(5)(a) of the Act.
[14] *ibid.*, r. 6.170; s.370(5)(b), (c) of the Act.
[15] *ibid.*, r. 6.171.
[16] s.370(4) of the Act.

CHAPTER 8

THE BANKRUPTCY ORDER AND ITS CONSEQUENCES: (II)—PROPRIETARY EFFECTS

Preliminary

In accordance with the general proposition that the bankruptcy law enables the debtor to be freed from the claims of his creditors in return for giving up substantially the whole of his assets, the proprietary effects of adjudication, broadly speaking, are that the bankrupt will subsequently be divested of his property, which will automatically become vested in his trustee in bankruptcy upon the latter's appointment. In view of the complexities which can exist in relation to the holding and use of property, intricate and particularised provisions are necessary to ensure that this simple-sounding objective may be realised in practice. Moreover in the interest of ensuring that full justice is done, the trustee's right to claim the property of the bankrupt is not limited only to such assets as may happen to belong to the latter at the very moment of his adjudication, but is capable of extension both backwards and forwards from that moment in time. Conversely, certain items of the bankrupt's property are excluded from the effects of adjudication and remain his in law, whilst, under certain conditions, it is possible for the trustee's title to other assets to undergo curtailment.

Thus the actual extent to which property will become available for realisation and distribution to the creditors in the form of dividends is a matter which will depend upon the particular circumstances of each case. This chapter will therefore examine the basic principles which determine whether property does or does not vest in the trustee in consequence of adjudication, and will thereafter describe the circumstances in which the trustee's title may be either extended or curtailed.

The Bankruptcy Order and its Consequences: (II)

(A) The Basic Principles Governing the Composition of the Bankrupt's Estate

(1) Property vesting in the trustee

The basic principles controlling the proprietary effects of a bankruptcy adjudication are expressed in section 306 of the Act, subsection (1) of which states that:

> "the bankrupt's estate shall vest in the trustee immediately on his appointment taking effect or, in the case of the official receiver, on his becoming trustee."[1]

The vesting takes place automatically, by operation of law as provided by section 306(2), which states that:

> "where any property which is, or is to be, comprised in the bankrupt's estate vests in the trustee ... it shall so vest without any conveyance, assignment or transfer."

With regard to such of the bankrupt's property as is situated within the jurisdiction of the English courts, and is therefore directly affected by a bankruptcy order made by a court in England and Wales, the essential effect of adjudication is clear.[2] However, for a proper understanding of the full significance of the provisions of section 306 it is necessary to explore the meanings borne by two key terms, namely "property" and "the bankrupt's estate," which are used in the section. A very broad definition of "property" is supplied by section 436 of the Act, which declares that, except insofar as the context otherwise requires, the word, when it appears in the Act,

> "includes money, goods, things in action, land and every description of property wherever situated and also obligations and every description of interest whether present or future or vested or contingent, arising out of, or incidental to, property."

This comprehensive and general formulation of the concept of "property" is nonetheless a non-exclusive one, as a consequence of the use of the word "includes," and it would therefore be open to a court to construe some novel or unusual form of proprietary interest as constituting "property" for the purposes of the Insolvency Act even in the unlikely event that it did not correspond to any of the categories listed in section 436. Conversely, certain species of rights are properly to be classified as merely personal in

---

[1] See Chap. 7, *ante*, on the trustee's appointment and its commencement.
[2] See Chaps. 28 and 29 in Part III, *post*, for the position concerning property situated outside the jurisdiction.

nature and as such do not constitute "property" forming part of the bankrupt's estate.[3]

The composition of the bankrupt's estate is determined by reference to the complex provisions of section 283, and several related sections, of the Act which require close examination. Section 283(1) expresses the key principle that the bankrupt's estate for statutory purposes comprises:

(a) all property belonging to or vested in the bankrupt at the commencement of the bankruptcy; and
(b) any property which by virtue of the provisions elsewhere in the Insolvency Act is comprised in that estate or is treated as falling within paragraph (a).

Property Belonging to the Bankrupt at the Commencement of Bankruptcy

The reference in section 283(1)(a) to "all property belonging to or vested in the bankrupt at the commencement of the bankruptcy" fixes the precise point in time at which the "stocktaking," so to speak, is to be carried out in order to determine the basic *corpus* of the bankrupt's estate. Thus, although the actual vesting in the trustee of title to the bankrupt's estate does not occur until the time when, according to the Rules,[4] his appointment takes effect, the composition of the estate to which the trustee's title attaches is determined at the date of the making of the bankruptcy order which, by virtue of section 278(a), is the technical date of commencement of the bankruptcy.[5] This represents a change from the provisions in force prior to the enactment of the Insolvency Act 1986, and is attributable to the abolition of the concept of acts of bankruptcy as part of the recasting of the bankruptcy law. Under the former law a rule known as the "relation back" doctrine was applied so as to fix the date of commencement of bankruptcy as at the date of commission of the act of bankruptcy on which the order of adjudication was made.[6] This doctrine, which could operate so as to place the commencement of bankruptcy at a time several months before the date of the order, has ceased to be part of the law and the new rule expressed in section 278(a) has the decided merits of clarity and certainty with regard to its application. It should not be overlooked however, that section 284 contains important provisions to restrict a debtor's powers of disposal of property during the period following the presentation of a bankruptcy petition by or against him, until such date as the estate vests in his trustee in bankruptcy. The trustee may

---

[3] *City of London Corporation v. Brown* (1989) *The Times*, 11 October; (1990) 60 P. & C.R. 42 (C.A.). (Non-assignable, secure periodic tenancy arising by virtue of s.86 of the Housing Act 1985). *cf. Ward v. Aitken, in re Oasis Merchandising Services Ltd* (1995), *The Times*, June 19, 1995 (a case concerning the nature of the right to take proceedings under s.214 of the Act—wrongful trading—in cases of company insolvency).
[4] See Chap. 7, *ante*.
[5] *ibid.*
[6] Bankruptcy Act 1914, s.37 (repealed); *Re Gunsbourg* [1920] 2 K.B. 426.

therefore be able to augment the property forming the bankrupt's estate as at the date of the bankruptcy order by reclaiming property the disposition of which is made void by virtue of section 284, while the provisions of sections 339–344 may be used to bring about a further enhancement of the bankrupt's available estate through the adjustment of other transactions which have taken place prior to the presentation of the bankruptcy petition. These provisions will be considered below.[7]

Equitable Interests

Where the nature of the bankrupt's interest in any property is merely an equitable one, that interest forms part of his estate passing to his trustee. Where the interest carries a right to claim some payment, or to seek specific performance of a contract for the conveyance of the legal title to property, it may in due course yield considerable value for the creditors' benefit. If, however, the assertion of the equitable interest is dependent upon the completion of some onerous performance still remaining due from the bankrupt's side, such as the payment of the purchase price of property which the bankrupt had formerly contracted to buy, the prospective net yield upon realisation of this interest may be small, or even negative, from the creditors' point of view and the trustee in bankruptcy may well deem it expedient to disclaim the property under sections 315–321 of the Act.[8] Where the bankrupt's equitable interest consists of a beneficial entitlement under the terms of a trust or settlement that interest will likewise pass to his trustee in bankruptcy, subject to the possible operation of any forfeiture clause contained in the instrument of settlement which may have the effect of causing the bankrupt's interest to terminate with effect from a date prior to the commencement of bankruptcy.[9]

Intangible Property

The notion of "property" includes intangible as well as tangible assets, and hence the goodwill of a bankrupt's business, together with the title to any secret formulas, patents, trademarks, copyrights or other "industrial" or "intellectual" property, including entitlement to royalties and licence fees, passes to the trustee in bankruptcy and may be disposed of for value.[10] However the bankrupt is exempted from the application of the usual rule, operative in the case of voluntary sales of this kind of property, that a vendor of the goodwill of a business is prohibited from soliciting his former customers if he afterwards resumes his former trade.[11] It remains possible

---

[7] *Infra*, p. 221, *et seq.*
[8] *Infra*, p. 235.
[9] See *infra*, p. 213. See also p. 209 with regard to property which the bankrupt holds on trust for another person.
[10] *Re Keene* [1922] 2 Ch. 475 (the bankrupt may be compelled to reveal his secret formulas).
[11] *Walker v. Mottram* (1881) 19 Ch.D. 355; *Green and Sons (Northampton) Ltd v. Morris* [1914] 1 Ch. 562.

nevertheless for a bankrupt to enter into a voluntary covenant with the purchaser of his business, binding himself to forbear from competing with his successor. Such an arrangement will naturally enhance the value of the business from the purchaser's point of view. It must be added that such goodwill as is personal to a bankrupt will perforce be incapable of passing either to his trustee or to any purchaser of the business. Goodwill of this type is encountered especially in connection with the activities of professional men and women, such as solicitors, doctors, accountants and architects. Inevitably, the very fact that an individual has undergone bankruptcy will have a significant, and detrimental, effect upon the goodwill and commercial reputation attaching to the person in question.

Choses in Action (Including Rights of Action)

Among the forms of intangible property included in the definition supplied by section 436 there is express mention of "things in action"—alternatively known as "choses in action." These expressions are used to denote a personal *right* to *claim* property (including payment of money) as opposed to actual corporeal property itself. In the classic definition of the term "choses in action," Channell J. stated that:

> "Chose in action is a known legal expression used to describe all personal rights of property which can only be claimed or enforced by action and not by taking physical possession."[12]

It thus includes such proprietary rights as debts, negotiable instruments, shares, policies of insurance (subject to what is said below), bills of lading, legacies under a will, and rights of action resulting from a tort or breach of contract, as well as such intangibles as patents, copyrights, and interests under a trust which have been referred to already.

It might be presumed that all of the bankrupt's property existing in the form of choses in action will pass to his trustee through the combined effects of sections 283, 306 and 436 of the Act. This is true of most species of chose in action,[13] but an exception exists in respect of torts of a "personal" character, such as claims for defamation[14] or injury to credit or reputation or for "wounded feelings."[15] In such circumstances the bankrupt remains personally entitled to sue and may moreover retain the fruits of any success he may achieve in litigation, since otherwise his incentive to vindicate the legal wrongs done to him would be much diminished. The bankrupt also retains the right to sue in respect of such causes of action where they arise subsequently to his adjudication.[16] The

---

[12] *Torkington v. Magee* [1902] 2 K.B. 427, 430. See also s.283(4) of the Act, *infra*.
[13] *cf. Howard v. Fanshawe* [1895] 2 Ch. 581.
[14] *Re Wilson, ex p. Vine*, (1878) 8 Ch.D. 364; *Wilson v. United Counties Bank Ltd* [1920] A.C. 102 (H.L.).
[15] *Howard v. Crowther* (1841) 8 M. & W. 601; 151 E.R. 1179; *Rose v. Buckett* [1901] 2 K.B. 449; *Lord's Trustee v. Great Eastern Railway Co.* [1908] 1 K.B. 195.
[16] *Re Wilson, ex p. Vine, supra*.

same principle has been respected and applied by the European Court of Human Rights to enable a successful applicant, who had been the victim of a violation of one of the rights contained in the European Convention of Human Rights, to receive and retain the amount of money awarded to him under Article 50 of the Convention as "just satisfaction" for the wrong done to him: payment was ordered to be made in such a manner that the money could not become available to be claimed by the creditors in the applicant's bankruptcy in Austria.[17]

In contrast to the above, rights of action in respect of tortious wrongs to the bankrupt's *proprietary* interests pass to his trustee as do the proceeds of any such actions which the bankrupt may have successfully brought prior to his adjudication. Difficulties may sometimes arise concerning the correct characterisation of a claim as "personal" or "proprietary."[18] Further alternative possibilities arise in cases where the bankrupt enjoys a right of action in respect of breach of contract. Where the right of action has arisen before the date of adjudication it thereupon passes to the trustee.[19] However, if the breach of contract does not occur until after adjudication it has been held that the bankrupt retains the right to sue, at least in respect of such "personal" claims as an action for his wrongful dismissal.[20]

The trustee is empowered to take whatever steps are necessary to realise the value represented by any chose in action which has vested in him as a consequence of the bankrupt's adjudication.[21] This includes the right to recover payment of book debts and other receivables due to the bankrupt from other parties with whom he has had dealings. According to the circumstances the trustee may decide to claim the benefit directly from the indebted party, if necessary by bringing action against him, or he may instead deal with the chose in its existing form and dispose of it for value to an assignee who will in turn acquire full rights as purchaser of the chose in action.[22] A factoring arrangement of this kind may be the most cost-effective way for the trustee to achieve some worthwhile return for the creditors out of the bankrupt's book debts and receivables. Alternatively, it has been held that where the trustee has calculated that it is not economically worthwhile to bring an action to enforce a right of this kind he may legitimately assign the right to pursue the action to any creditor who is prepared to undertake the risk, subject to an agreement that the

---

[17] *Ringeisen v. Austria*, Case 2614/65, 1 E.H.R.R. 455, 504 and 513; 16 Y.B.E.C.H.R. 468; (1972) 21 I.C.L.Q. 377, 795; (1974) 23 I.C.L.Q. 193.
[18] *Re Kavanagh* [1950] 1 All E.R. 39 n. (where the court, in view of the unclear position, ordered that the bankrupt and the trustee should share the proceeds equally). *cf. Metropolitan Bank Ltd v. Pooley* (1885) 10 App.Cas. 210 (H.L.); *Bottomley v. Bell* (1915) 31 T.L.R. 591.
[19] *Beckham v. Drake* (1849) 2 H.L.C. 579; 9 E.R. 1213; *cf. Hill v. Smith* (1844) 12 M. & W. 618: 152 E.R. 1346.
[20] *Bailey v. Thurston & Co. Ltd* [1903] 1 K.B. 137.
[21] Insolvency Act 1986, s.305(2); Sched. 5. See Chap. 7, *ante*, p. 171.
[22] *Seear v. Lawson* (1880) 15 Ch.D. 426; *Howard v. Fanshawe, above*, n. 13.

trustee shall receive a share of any consequent proceeds.[23] Outside the law of bankruptcy such arrangements would fall foul of the legal rules against champerty and maintenance, and would be contrary to public policy.[24]

The bankruptcy of a party to a contract does not automatically discharge that contract,[25] nor can the act of presenting a petition for his own bankruptcy by one party be treated by the other as a repudiation of the contract, at least in cases where time is not of the essence.[26] Rather, the trustee in bankruptcy has the right to decide whether he will adopt the contract or disclaim it,[27] according to his estimation of its potential value from the creditors' point of view. Where the trustee does exercise his right to call for performance of a contract originally made by the bankrupt he must of course undertake performance of the bankrupt's part of the contract, for example by paying the outstanding purchase price for goods sold to the bankrupt. If the trustee fails to make due performance within reasonable time the other party may treat the contract as broken and, for example, resell goods originally contracted to be sold to the bankrupt.[28]

Where the contract is of a continuous nature the trustee, having originally elected to carry it on, may perhaps decide at a later date that the contract is unprofitable. It was held in *Re Sneezum*[29] that in such circumstances the trustee is still able to desist from further performance without personally becoming liable to the other party, whose rights are restricted to lodging proof in the bankruptcy for damages occasioned by the belated breach of contract.

Specific performance may be ordered against the trustee in cases where the bankrupt has formerly contracted to sell realty,[30] but not usually where the bankrupt has entered a contract to buy.[31]

Although the trustee in bankruptcy may elect to affirm a contract concluded by the bankrupt prior to his adjudication the other party to the contract is also able to claim relief. Firstly, he may apply to the court for rescission of the contract upon equitable grounds,[32] and secondly he may ascertain the trustee's intentions by writing to him formally to require him to decide whether he will disclaim the contract or not. If the trustee does not give notice of disclaimer within 28 days, he is deemed to have adopted the contract.[33] A further possibility, introduced for the first time by section

---

[23] *Guy v. Churchill* (1888) 40 Ch.D. 481. *Cf.* also *Re Richardson* [1911] 2 K.B. 705, *Ramsey v. Hartley* [1977] 2 All E.R. 673 (C.A.), and *Weddell v. J.A. Pearce and Major* [1987] 3 All E.R. 624; *Stein v. Blake* [1993] 4 All E.R. 225 (C.A.), affd. H.L. [1995] BCC 543, (upholding the lawfulness of the trustee's assignment of the cause of action to the bankruptcy plaintiff himself).

[24] Although they no longer give rise to criminal liability: Criminal Law Act 1967, s.13(1)(a).

[25] *Brooke v. Hewitt* (1796) 3 Ves.Jun. 253; 30 E.R. 997.

[26] *cf. Jennings' Trustee v. King* [1952] Ch. 899.

[27] For disclaimer under s.315, see *infra*, p. 235.

[28] *Re Nathan* (1879) 10 Ch.D. 586.

[29] (1876) 3 Ch.D. 463; *cf. Re Nathan*, above.

[30] *Pearce v. Bastable's Trustee* [1901] 2 Ch. 122.

[31] *Holloway v. York* (1877) 25 W.R. 627.

[32] *cf. Re Castle* [1917] 2 K.B. 725.

[33] s.316(1) of the Act. The period of 28 days may be extended by the court: s.376. The trustee's rights of disclaimer are further considered, *infra*, p. 219.

345 of the Insolvency Act 1986, enables any non-bankrupt party to the contract to apply to the court for an order discharging obligations under the contract on appropriate terms, such as payment by the applicant or by the bankrupt of damages for non-performance.[34] The court is empowered to formulate its order in terms which appear equitable, and if it is the bankrupt who is ordered to pay damages, these are provable as a bankruptcy debt.[35] Where the bankrupt is a joint contracting party together with any non-bankrupt person, the latter may sue or be sued in respect of the contract without joinder of the bankrupt.[36]

Insurance

There is a special statutory rule in relation to any contract of insurance which a bankrupt may have effected covering his potential liabilities to third parties. If any such liability is incurred by the insured either before or after he became bankrupt or makes a composition or arrangement with his creditors, his rights against the insurer under the contract of insurance do not vest in the trustee but are transferred to and vest in the third party to whom liability has been incurred.[37] A payment or agreement between insurer and insured, which is made after the commencement of the bankruptcy of the latter, is of no effect so far as concerns the rights of the third party to whom the insured's rights have been transmitted by virtue of this rule.[38] In the most usual case, namely that of the effecting of motor insurance, it has now been further provided that upon the transfer to the third party of any claim against the insurer consequential to the bankruptcy of the insured, the insured's liability to the third party shall nevertheless subsist.[39] If the issue of liability or of quantum of damage remains unsettled at the date of the insured's bankruptcy, the third party may be obliged to bring action against the insolvent wrongdoer in order to ascertain the extent of the claim which he is entitled to make against the latter's insurer.[40]

The Bankrupt's Home

In the majority of cases, the single most valuable asset belonging to a bankrupt is the home which he or she occupies. Even where the purchase of the house has been financed in part by means of a loan secured by a mortgage, the sale of the freehold with vacant possession is likely, under normal circumstances, to yield an appreciable surplus of money for distribution among the creditors, even after the mortgagee has been fully

---

[34] s.345(2) of the Act.
[35] *ibid.*, s.345(2), (3).
[36] *ibid.*, s.345(4).
[37] Third Parties (Rights against Insurers) Act 1930, s.1.
[38] *ibid.*, s.3.
[39] Road Traffic Act 1972, s.150(1).
[40] *Post Office v. Norwich Union Fire Insurance Society* [1967] 2 Q.B. 363.

repaid the outstanding balance of the loan.[41] In the case of leasehold property, the residual term of the lease may likewise prove to be an asset of considerable net value. The unavoidable corollary to this process however is that the bankrupt is presently rendered homeless, and that this fate is also experienced by any spouse, children and other dependents who may share the home.

The issues of policy and principle associated with the treatment of the matrimonial home in the case of the bankruptcy of either spouse have given rise to protracted controversy, since they involve attempts to reconcile two mutually exclusive interests. On one side is the claim of the unpaid creditors to recoup some of their losses from the principal available asset; set against this is the general concern that the hardship and indignity of homelessness should not be imposed upon persons who are, in the main, innocent victims of the bankrupt's financial failure. Two alternative situations need to be considered, namely where the bankrupt is sole owner of the matrimonial home (albeit there may be rights of occupation subsisting in favour of an occupying spouse) and where the bankrupt and his or her present or former spouse are joint owners of the home.[42] In the former case, the law prior to 1986 had veered between the positions of allowing or denying a deserted wife's right of occupation to prevail over the right of her husband's trustee to sell the property.[43] In the latter case, it was well settled before 1986 that execution of the trust for sale resulting from joint ownership of the matrimonial home could be ordered by the court in response to an application by the trustee in bankruptcy under section 30 of the Law of Property Act 1925. The courts had determined that they enjoyed a discretion whether to order the sale of property where a spouse and children were in occupation, but in practice the majority of reported cases indicated a tendency to regard the interests of the creditors as prevailing over those of the spouse and children of the bankrupt in all but the most exceptional of circumstances.[44]

---

[41] This proposition may be invalidated under certain conditions affecting the domestic property market, as where a period of severe price recession results in a position of "negative equity" in terms of the realisable value of the bankrupt's home, less the outstanding debt secured by the subsisting mortgage.

[42] Where the non-bankrupt is the sole owner of the matrimonial home the trustee has no title to the home as such, unless its acquisition was facilitated by means of any payment or transfer from the bankrupt which may be impeachable by the trustee under either s.339 or s.423 of the Act: see *infra*, section (B).

[43] The so-called "deserted wife's equity": *Bendall v. McWhirter* [1952] 2 Q.B. 466 (C.A.); overruled by (H.L.): *National Provincial Bank Ltd v. Ainsworth* [1965] A.C. 1175. The latter decision was reversed by statute: Matrimonial Homes Act 1967, consolidated by the Matrimonial Homes Act 1983, s.1.

[44] *Jones v. Challenger* [1961] 1 Q.B. 176; *Re Solomon* [1967] Ch. 573; *Re Turner* [1975] 1 All E.R. 5; [1974] 1 W.L.R. 1556; *Re Densham* [1975] 3 All E.R. 726; [1975] 1 W.L.R. 1519; *Re Bailey* [1977] 2 All E.R. 26; [1977] 1 W.L.R. 278; *Re Lowrie* [1981] 3 All E.R. 353. Contrast *Re Holliday* [1981] 1 Ch. 405 (C.A.) (a case with very special facts where sale of the matrimonial home was postponed for five years). The foregoing cases were further reviewed by the Court of Appeal in *Re Citro* [1990] 3 All E.R. 952, with the observation that, since s.336 of the Act of 1986 does not apply to cases of unmarried couples who cohabit, the former case law will continue to be applicable to them: *ibid.*, at p. 963, *per* Nourse, L.J.

The Bankruptcy Order and its Consequences: (II)

The *Cork Report* adopted a revised approach with regard to the balance to be struck between the conflicting interests attaching to the matrimonial home, whereby the enforcement of the creditors' rights would be delayed but not cancelled.[45] During the enactment of the Insolvency Act 1985, several vigorous debates took place in both Houses regarding the appropriate statutory provisions to be adopted,[46] and those now in force as sections 336–338 of the Insolvency Act 1986 were inserted at a late stage with a view to achieving an acceptable compromise. They have the effect of enabling the sale of the family home to be postponed for up to one year from the date when the bankrupt's estate first vests in his trustee, but thereafter the continued postponement of the sale may take place only in exceptional circumstances. An important improvement over the previous state of the law has been effected through the consolidation into the exclusive jurisdiction of the court of bankruptcy of all proceedings regarding the bankrupt's family home.[47]

Where the bankrupt is the sole beneficial owner of the matrimonial home, the provisions of sections 336 and 337 of the Act are relevant. Section 336(1) has the effect of preventing any right of occupation from arising in favour of the bankrupt's spouse at any time between the date of presentation of the bankruptcy petition and the moment when the estate vests in the trustee. Subject to this, section 336(2) provides that where a non-bankrupt spouse has acquired statutory rights of occupation under the Matrimonial Homes Act 1983 which give rise to a charge on the estate or interest of the bankrupt, the charge not only continues to subsist despite the bankruptcy, but also binds the trustee of the bankrupt's estate and persons deriving title through him. Thus, despite the lack of a beneficial interest in the matrimonial home, the non-bankrupt spouse is placed in a similar position with regard to protected rights of occupation, as a spouse with such an interest. Any application under section 1 of the Act of 1983 to evict an occupying spouse from the property must be made to the bankruptcy court, which is then endowed by section 336(4) of the Insolvency Act with the discretion to make such order as it thinks just and reasonable, having regard to the following factors:

(1) The interests of the bankrupt's creditors;
(2) The conduct of the spouse or former spouse, so far as contributing to the bankruptcy;
(3) The needs and financial resources of the spouse or former spouse;
(4) The needs of any children; and
(5) All the circumstances of the case *other than* the needs of the bankrupt (emphasis added).

---

[45] Cmnd. 8558, paras. 1114–1131. See Miller [1986] Conv. 393.
[46] See Hansard, H.L. Vol. 459, cols. 1262–1267; H.L. Vol. 462, cols. 160–171; H.L. Vol. 467, cols. 1265–1270; H.C. Standing Committee E, 18 June 1985, cols. 372–376 and 394–395; H.C. Vol. 83, cols. 545–549 and 601–602.
[47] Insolvency Act 1986, ss.336(2)(b), (3), 337(4). *cf. Re Holliday, above,* where two sets of proceedings in different divisions of the High Court could not be consolidated until the matter reached the Court of Appeal.

Property Vesting in the Trustee

The order in which the various factors are listed may be of significance in that the interests of the creditors stand first in the list while the needs of any children stand fourth in order of mention. There is moreover no express reference to any other dependents, apart from children, although it is possible that the impact of eviction upon, for example, any ailing or elderly adult members of the family, including parents or grandparents, might be taken into account by the court under the general heading of "all the circumstances of the case."[48] The court's discretion with regard to the order which it is empowered to make is an unfettered one during the period of 12 months beginning with the first vesting of the bankrupt's estate in his trustee, but after the end of that one year period, section 336(5) stipulates that on any application which is then made the court must assume, unless the circumstances of the case are exceptional, that the interests of the bankrupt's creditors outweigh all other considerations.

Given the tenor of the above provisions, the trustee in bankruptcy is himself in a position to exercise a degree of discretion with regard to the timing of any application for an order of eviction, secure in the knowledge that after one year he will in most instances be assured of a court order in his favour. The court, for its part, could reasonably infer that the legislative intention underlying these provisions was to allow up to a year's "period of grace" in which to enable the various parties to make reasonable and orderly arrangements for the yielding up of possession in a way designed to minimise the inevitable hardship and distress for those in the process of losing their home.

Where the bankrupt has an occupational interest in a dwelling-house by virtue of his or her beneficial estate or interest in the property, and there were any persons under the age of 18 occupying the premises as their home together with the bankrupt at the time when the bankruptcy petition was presented and at the commencement of the bankruptcy, the bankrupt has the following rights as against the trustee by virtue of section 337(2):

(1) If in occupation, a right not to be evicted or excluded from the property or any part of it except with the leave of the court; and
(2) If not in occupation, a right with the leave of the court to enter into and occupy the property.

These rights constitute a charge in the nature of an equitable interest binding the trustee, and amount to statutory rights of occupation for the purposes of the Matrimonial Homes Act 1983.[49] The trustee must therefore make application for leave to evict, (and the bankrupt, conversely, must apply for leave to occupy) under section 1 of the Act of 1983, whereupon section 337(5) of the Insolvency Act provides that the court may frame its order at its discretion, having regard to the interests of creditors, to the bankrupt's financial resources, to the needs of the children, and to all the circumstances of the case *other than* the needs of the

---

[48] *cf.* Cmnd. 8558, paras. 1120–1121.
[49] s.337(2)(b), (3) of the Act.

bankrupt (emphasis added). Once again, section 337(6) supplies a supplementary presumption to be operated in all cases where the application is made more than one year after the first vesting of the bankrupt's estate in his trustee, whereby, as under section 336(5), the court is required to assume unless the circumstances of the case are exceptional that the interests of the bankrupt's creditors outweigh all other considerations.

Where the matrimonial home is owned jointly by the bankrupt and his or her spouse or former spouse, so that a trust for sale has arisen, the provisions of section 336(3) maintain the effect of the pre-existing law whereby the trustee in bankruptcy must apply under section 30 of the Law of Property Act 1925 for an order authorising the sale of the property. The beneficial interest of the non-bankrupt spouse will attach to the proceeds of such sale, so that the proportion to which the trustee will be entitled will be that which represents the extent of the bankrupt's beneficial interest in the matrimonial home. If the non-bankrupt spouse has been in sole occupation of the property and has personally borne the burden of such expenses as mortgage instalments, repairs and improvements, the consequential increase in value attributable to that party's expenditure will be taken into account in calculating the respective shares of the property to which that spouse, and the trustee in bankruptcy, are respectively entitled.[50] Section 336(3) also provides that the trustee's application for leave to execute the trust for sale must be made to the bankruptcy court, and on such an application the provisions of subsections (4) and (5) of section 336 once again apply with regard to the exercise of the court's discretion as to the order it makes.[51]

It is by no means uncommon for a trustee in bankruptcy to discover that at some time prior to the commencement of bankruptcy a transaction took place whereby the bankrupt purported to transfer all or part of his or her interest in the matrimonial home to the still-solvent spouse. Such transactions will be carefully scrutinized by the trustee for potential impeachability as having been entered into at an undervalue, or as having amounted to the giving of a preference by the bankrupt, contrary to sections 339 and 340 of the Act.[52] It is also possible for the rules of transaction avoidance to be applied in cases where the transfer of property has been effected pursuant to a court order under section 24 of the Matrimonial Causes Act 1973: if the spouse against whom the transfer order was made was a person against whom a bankruptcy petition had already been presented, the order constitutes a "disposition" for the purposes of section 286 of the Insolvency Act and is void unless validated by the bankruptcy court.[53]

In relation to the above provisions section 313 of the Act is also of

---

[50] *Re Pavlou* [1993] 3 All E.R. 955.
[51] See *above*.
[52] *Re Kumar* [1993] 2 All E.R. 700. For avoidance of antecedent transactions, see section (B), *infra*.
[53] *Re Flint* [1993] 2 W.L.R. 537 (C.A.). On the interaction between bankruptcy proceedings and proceedings for committal of a spouse for non-payment of a judgment debt arising from matrimonial proceedings, see *Woodley v. Woodley* (No. 2) [1993] 4 All E.R. 1010 (C.A.).

relevance. This section provides that where the bankrupt's estate includes any property consisting of an interest in a dwelling-house which is occupied by the bankrupt or by his spouse or former spouse, and the trustee is, for any reason, unable for the time being to realise that property, he may apply to the court for a charging order to be made in respect of the property for the benefit of the bankrupt's estate. If such an order is made the benefit of the charge becomes comprised in the bankrupt's estate and attaches to the property in question until such time as it comes to be enforced, and in consequence of this the order must provide for the property itself to cease to be comprised in the bankrupt's estate, and to revest in him subject to the charge.[54] This procedure is of particular relevance in cases where sections 336 or 337 operate in such a way that the interests of the creditors are for the time being considered to be subordinate to the needs of the bankrupt's spouse or former spouse, or of the bankrupt himself together with any dependent children, to remain in occupation of the family home. Furthermore, the provisions of section 332 of the Act come into play whenever an application for such an order has been made under section 313, because the trustee is then permitted to summon a final meeting of creditors under section 331 despite the fact that he has been unable to realise this item of property due to the prevailing right of occupation enjoyed by the person or persons concerned. Irrespective of whether a charging order has been made by the court in response to the application under section 313, the trustee is enabled to present his concluding report upon his administration and to seek his release from the meeting of creditors.[55] Also of relevance in relation to the bankrupt's home is section 338, whereby if the bankrupt occupies premises comprised in his estate on condition that he makes mortgage payments or pays other outgoings in relation to the property, he is prevented from acquiring any interest in the premises by virtue of those payments.

After-Acquired Property

By virtue of section 283(1)(b) of the Act the bankrupt's estate not only comprises such property as is owned at the commencement of bankruptcy, but also may be augmented by property which other provisions of the Act cause to be included in the estate. Most of these provisions will be considered in Section B below, but one which may properly be discussed at this point is section 307, whereby the trustee is empowered to claim for the bankrupt's estate any property which is acquired by the bankrupt, or which devolves upon him, between the date of commencement of bankruptcy and the date of his eventual discharge. Section 307(1) contains the enabling provision whereby the trustee may by notice in writing claim such after-acquired property for the bankrupt's estate. The provision effectively codifies a principle originally of judicial innovation, known as the rule in *Cohen v. Mitchell*.[56] This rule includes the possibility

---

[54] s.313(2), (3) of the Act; see also r. 6.237 of the Rules.
[55] ss.331(1), (2), 332 of the Act.
[56] (1890) 25 Q.B.D. 262.

that the trustee's claim to the bankrupt's after-acquired property may be defeated under certain conditions. These conditions are that, first, the bankrupt must dispose of the property to a person dealing with him in good faith, for value, and without notice of the bankruptcy, but subject to this the transaction is capable of defeating the trustee's claim to the property, irrespective of whether it takes place before or after the trustee serves the requisite notice upon the bankrupt under section 307(1).[57] The requirement that the transaction must be bona fide and for value ought to ensure that in most cases the property disposed of is exchanged for some other asset, or for money, to which the trustee's title may attach. "Value" can, however, be furnished by marriage between parties to a marriage settlement.[58] But if any recipient is properly classified as a donee, that person, however honest, and however innocent personally of the fact that the donor is an undischarged bankrupt, will not be able to keep any property which the bankrupt has purported to dispose of.[59] Where value has been given however, it was formerly held that a person's bona fides was not necessarily impaired by virtue of his being aware that the person with whom he was dealing was an undischarged bankrupt.[60] The introduction into section 307(4) of the specific requirement that the third party with whom the bankrupt deals must be actually without knowledge of the bankruptcy has thus had the effect of overruling cases decided under the pre-1986 legislation to the extent that the decisions turned upon this point. The nature of the property may be real or personal,[61] and may vary from the tangible to the intangible: it may be a leasehold,[62] or a legacy[63] or even a chose in action.[64] In the case of money which the bankrupt has both received and paid away after his bankruptcy, even to a person with notice of the bankruptcy, it has long been accepted that the transaction may be treated as valid against the trustee, and that the latter, having failed to intercept the money initially, has no right to follow it into the hands of the other party, for otherwise it would be impossible to deal with an undischarged bankrupt even upon a cash basis.[65] Where the transaction in question consists of an assignment by the bankrupt of a chose in action the third party's title to such after-acquired property may be defeated by the trustee if the latter succeeds in giving notice before the assignee to the party by whom the debt or liability is owed.[66]

It is essential that the property which is the subject of the transaction

---

[57] s.307(4) of the Act.
[58] *Re Behrend's Trust* [1911] 1 Ch. 687. Transactions with a banker need not be for value, but the banker must act in good faith and without notice of the bankruptcy: s.307(4)(b).
[59] *Re Bennett* [1907] 1 K.B. 149.
[60] *Cohen v. Mitchell*, above, n. 56; *Hunt v. Fripp* [1878] 1 Ch. 675; *Re Bennett*, above.
[61] s.307(1) of the Act ("any property"). *cf. Re Kent County Gas Light and Coke Co. Ltd* [1909] 2 Ch. 195 (realty), and *Cohen v. Mitchell, above* (personalty).
[62] *Re Clayton and Barclay's Contract* [1895] 2 Ch. 212.
[63] *Hunt v. Fripp, above.*
[64] *Cohen v. Mitchell, above.*
[65] *Re Vanlohe* (1871) 7 Ch.App. 185. For criminal offences which the bankrupt may commit by disposing of after-acquired property in circumstances such that the trustee's claim thereto is defeated, see Chap. 13, *post.*
[66] *Mercer v. Vans Colina* [1900] 1 Q.B. 130n.; *Re Beall* [1899] 1 Q.B. 688.

should be after-acquired, in order for the third party to enjoy protection as against the trustee. Thus an assignment of future earnings, effected prior to bankruptcy, does not constitute a transaction affecting after-acquired property even as regards receipts accruing subsequent to the adjudication.[67] Similarly, a drawing upon a bank account which was already over-drawn at the commencement of bankruptcy, though made after adjudication, has been held not to bestow upon the sum withdrawn the character of "after-acquired" property.[68] Moreover the transaction must be one in which the bankrupt is involved as an active party and therefore the third party will not be able to invoke the protection of section 307 in a case where he has unilaterally purported to establish a claim to the bankrupt's after-acquired property. Thus in *Hosack v. Robbins*,[69] a judgment creditor of the bankrupt, who had sought to enforce his claim by means of a charging order on shares to which the bankrupt had become entitled since his adjudication, was held not to be entitled to the shares as against the trustee, albeit the latter had not intervened to seize the shares until almost three years after the charging order had been made absolute. Where property is disposed of by the bankrupt in circumstances such that the trustee's claim thereto is defeated it has been held that once he has accomplished this the bankrupt himself becomes qualified to enforce, if necessary by action for specific performance, any contract into which he has entered.[70]

An associated problem concerns those instances in which the bankrupt has, since his adjudication and unbeknown to the trustee, either effected a policy of insurance upon his own life or has succeeded in keeping on foot a policy actually effected prior to his adjudication. In either event a question will ultimately arise as to who is entitled to the policy monies at maturity. The answer is that the trustee is to be regarded as the true owner of the proceeds of the policy, just as with any other property which the bankrupt fails to disclose, and may therefore claim the policy or the proceeds as soon as he discovers their existence,[71] even though this may not occur until long after the bankrupt has obtained his discharge from bankruptcy.[72] If the trustee has relinquished his office the official receiver will qualify to claim the proceeds in his stead. Where however the premiums have been paid, in whole or in part, by some other person than the bankrupt upon whose life the policy was effected, that party will be entitled, at any rate if the trustee at some time had knowledge of the arrangement, to be repaid out of the proceeds the sums plus interest which have been paid to maintain the policy and thereby have conferred an enrichment upon the trustee for the benefit of the creditors in the bankruptcy.[73]

A further important principle is embodied in section 307(3), which provides that upon the trustee's service of notice claiming after-acquired

---

[67] *Re De Marney* [1943] Ch. 126.
[68] *Re Hone* [1951] 1 Ch. 85.
[69] [1918] 2 Ch. 339.
[70] *Dyster v. Randall* [1926] Ch. 932.
[71] *Tapster v. Ward* (1909) 101 L.T. 503; *Re Phillips* [1914] 2 K.B. 689.
[72] *Re Stokes* [1919] 2 K.B. 256; *Re Collier* [1930] 2 Ch. 37.
[73] *Re Tyler* [1907] 1 K.B. 865, applying the rule in *ex p. James*, *infra*, p. 207.

property for the estate the property to which the notice relates shall vest in the trustee as part of the bankrupt's estate with effect retrospective to the time at which the property was first acquired by, or devolved upon, the bankrupt. This is expressed to operate subject to subsection (4) which, as we have seen, enables a third party to acquire a title good against the trustee, subject to meeting the specified conditions. Apart from such cases however the doctrine of relation back of the trustee's title which is embodied in subsection (3) ensures that the trustee's claim to the property will prevail over that of the third party regardless of whether the latter's dealing with the bankrupt took place before or after the trustee gave notice of his claim to the property in question.

To ensure that the trustee has a suitable opportunity to decide whether or not to claim any after-acquired property under section 307 the bankrupt is made subject to a continuous duty, at all times throughout the duration of the bankruptcy, to notify the trustee whenever any property is acquired by or devolves upon him, or if there is an increase in the bankrupt's income.[74] This notice must be given by the bankrupt, within 21 days of his becoming aware of the relevant facts.[75] Having served such notice in respect of the after-acquired property the bankrupt must not dispose of it within the period of 42 days beginning with the date of the notice, unless he has the trustee's written consent to do so.[76] To avoid the absurdities which would ensue from the need to observe this requirement of giving notice in those cases where the bankrupt is carrying on a business it is provided in the Rules that the bankrupt does not have to notify the trustee of any property which he acquires in the ordinary course of a business carried on by him, but instead the bankrupt must furnish the trustee with a half-yearly report on his trading activities, showing the total of goods bought and sold and the profit or loss arising from the business.[77] The prohibition against disposal of property by the bankrupt for 42 days from his giving notice of its acquisition to the trustee is balanced by the provision in section 309(1) of the Act whereby the trustee requires the leave of the court in order to serve notice under section 307 after the end of the period of 42 days from the date on which it first came to his knowledge that the property in question had been acquired by or had devolved upon the bankrupt.[78]

Finally it should be noted that by virtue of section 307(2) the trustee is now allowed to claim any after-acquired property which is excluded by other legislative provisions from forming part of the bankrupt's estate, including so-called "exempted property."[79] Nor may the trustee claim any property which is not acquired by the bankrupt until after his discharge, except insofar as any order of discharge granted by the court may have imposed a condition to the effect that property acquired after discharge was to be made available for the benefit of the creditors.[80]

---

[74] s.333(2) of the Act.
[75] r. 6.200(1) of the Rules.
[76] *ibid.*, r. 6.200(2).
[77] *ibid.*, r. 6.200(4), (5).
[78] See s.309(2) of the Act with regard to the time at which the trustee is deemed to have the requisite knowledge.
[79] See *infra*, p. 218 *et seq.*
[80] s.307(2)(c) of the Act: see Chap. 11, *post.*

The Bankrupt's Income

Although in principle any money which constitutes the bankrupt's income is claimable as after-acquired property as and when it is paid to him, it is nevertheless the policy of the law of bankruptcy to encourage the bankrupt to continue to maintain himself and his family, both as an aspect of the desire to preserve the dignity and self-respect of the bankrupt and his dependents, and in the interests of avoiding the creation of a further burden for the resources of the state if the bankrupt's family are rendered destitute. A rule has therefore been adopted whereby the bankrupt is allowed to retain a proportion of his income to the extent deemed necessary to maintain him and his family in reasonable circumstances.[81] However, any surplus income above the figure set by the trustee would in theory be claimable, were it not for the practical difficulties of doing so in view of the bankrupt's capability to dissipate it through spending, thus rendering it unamenable to tracing.[82] The more effective way in which to secure the receipt of the bankrupt's "surplus income" for the benefit of the estate is by way of an income payments order under section 310 of the Act.

An income payments order may be made by the court on the application of the trustee.[83] The order directs that for the period for which it is in force either the bankrupt, or the person from whom the bankrupt receives his income, must pay a specified proportion of the salary or income to the trustee.[84] Sums received by the trustee under an income payments order form part of the bankrupt's estate.[85] If the bankrupt, in violation of the terms of the order, applies the money in some other way the trustee cannot follow that payment into the hands of its recipient, and it is to be noted that section 307(5) of the Act provides that references to "property" within that section do not include any property which, as part of the bankrupt's income, is the subject of an income payments order under section 310. The trustee is thus prevented from establishing an alternative claim to the sum of money in question on the premiss that it constitutes "after-acquired property."[86] The safer course for the court to adopt wherever practicable is to require the bankrupt's employer to pay the specific proportion of income direct to the trustee, as section 310(3)(b) allows, but this needs to be tempered with a regard to the possibilities that the bankrupt may change his employment, and also that the added inconvenience caused to the employer may have a detrimental effect upon the bankrupt's employment prospects. It must also be acknowledged that this more restrictive course is not open to the court in those cases where the bankrupt is self-employed.

The definition of "income" supplied by section 310(7) is a broad one, and includes every payment in the nature of income which is from time to

---

[81] *Re Graydon* [1896] 1 Q.B. 417; *Re Roberts* [1900] 1 Q.B. 122; *Re Walter* [1929] 1 Ch. 647.
[82] See *above*, text to n. 65.
[83] s.310(1) of the Act. For procedure, including variation and review of the income payments order, see the Rules, rr. 6.189–6.193; Forms 6.64–6.68.
[84] s.310(1), (3) of the Act.
[85] *ibid.*, s.310(5).
[86] See *above*. The bankrupt's improper disposal of the money may amount to a criminal offence under s.357: see Chap. 13, *post*.

time made to the bankrupt, or to which he from time to time becomes entitled. It is thus not an essential part of the concept of "income" for the purposes of section 310 that it be produced by means of a regular or systematic course of activity or business dealing, and so the test of whether a payment constitutes "income" is rendered largely a matter of common sense.[87] A practical threshold must eventually be encountered however, below which the bankrupt's earning activities are so infrequently performed or haphazard as to make it difficult for the court to draw up an order in the requisite manner. It has been specifically held that a bankrupt's winnings arising from gaming or wagering do not constitute "earnings,"[88] and it is also doubtful whether benefits in kind which the bankrupt may receive from an employer are properly to be treated as "income."[89] The concept of "income" does however include payments received under a maintenance order made against the bankrupt's former spouse.[90] By contrast, where the bankrupt is in receipt of an income by virtue of the fact that he has a vested life interest in settled estate, the right to receive the income will automatically vest in the trustee following the adjudication, because the life interest itself, being a species of property, thereupon passes to his trustee in the ordinary way.[91]

In making an income payments order the court must adhere to the principle laid down in section 310(2), whereby the effect of the order must not be such as to reduce the income of the bankrupt below what appears to the court to be necessary for meeting the reasonable domestic needs of the bankrupt and his family. It will be a question of fact in each case to establish what are to be considered the "reasonable domestic needs" of the bankrupt and his family, and hence what proportion of his income he should be allowed to retain in order to meet them. The term "family" is defined in section 385(1) as meaning persons (if any) who are living with the bankrupt and are dependent on him.

The law as presently framed by the Act of 1986 has the particular merit that the trustee remains free to ignore any item of after-acquired property that turns out to be onerous and uneconomic to administer. It also contains foundations on which the courts may, if they so choose, build a new policy with respect to the requirement that the debtor should pay off his debts from surplus future income: where an income payments order is made in relation to a bankrupt, section 310(6) contains provisions enabling the court to include a condition whereby the requirement to make the payments may continue even after the bankrupt's discharge. In the case where the bankrupt is granted a discharge by the court there is no prescribed limit to the length of time for which such an obligation may be continued, but in the case where discharge results from the expiration of the relevant period under section 279(1)(b) of the Act the income payments order cannot continue for longer than three years from the date on which the order itself is made.[92] In taking advantage of the possibilities

---

[87] cf. *Affleck v. Hammond* [1912] 3 K.B. 162, 169, per Buckley, L.J.
[88] *Shoolbred v. Roberts* [1900] 2 Q.B. 497.
[89] *Re Roberts*, above, n. 81.
[90] *Re Landau* [1934] 1 Ch. 549; *Re Tennant's Application* [1956] 2 All E.R. 753.
[91] *Re Cohen* [1961] 1 Ch. 246.
[92] s.310(6)(a), (b) of the Act. For discharge see Chap. 11, *post*.

offered by section 310(6) the courts would be acting within the spirit expressed in the *Cork Report* in advocating the adoption of a more humane and realistic attitude towards the position of the debtor and his family, and the more imaginative utilisation of the bankrupt's surplus future income.[93]

In respect of that portion of his earnings or income which he is allowed to retain in consequence of an order made under section 310 the bankrupt enjoys full freedom of control and disposition.[94] It may be that the amount of which he is in receipt will in the event, or with prudent management of the domestic economy, prove more than adequate to support the bankrupt and his family, and that in consequence he may succeed in accumulating a surplus. Although it might appear to be opportune that the trustee should seek to claim such an accumulation for the creditors' benefit this would appear to fly contrary to the provision in section 307(5), mentioned above. Since that portion of his income which the bankrupt is allowed to retain is also, logically, the subject of the order it may be argued that it is thereby excluded from the category of after-acquired property which is claimable under section 307. The appropriate course of action, whenever the trustee becomes aware that the bankrupt is succeeding in amassing a surplus out of the income he has been allowed to retain, is to apply to the court for a review of the order itself, whereupon a hearing will take place at which the court may revise the proportions of income which are respectively allocated to the bankrupt and to the trustee.[95]

Trustee Takes "Subject to Equities"

The trustees's acquisition of title to the property of the bankrupt is subject to an important qualification. This is to the effect that the trustee is essentially a *successor* to such title as the bankrupt actually had at the time of his adjudication, including any limitations or imperfections in that title, and can enjoy no better position in relation to the property than did the bankrupt himself formerly.[96] It is customary to allude to this qualification of the trustee's title by means of the expression that the trustee takes "subject to equities." This expression accords naturally with the former practice, historically, of treating and indeed describing the trustee in bankruptcy as an "assignee" of the bankrupt's property. For it is a well-known rule in the law of assignment that an assignee takes subject to equities.[97] One consequence of the application of this principle to bankruptcy is that the trustee, as we have seen,[98] is in general amenable to actions for specific performance to enforce contracts affecting his property

---

[93] Cmnd. 8558, paras. 591–598, 1158–1163. See Milman (1988) 4 I.L.P. 71–74.
[94] *Re Shine* [1892] 1 Q.B. 522.
[95] r. 6.193 of the Rules.
[96] *Johnson v. Smiley* (1853) 17 Beav. 223; 51 E.R. 1019; *Re Mapleback* (1876) 4 Ch.D. 150; *Re Garrud* (1880) 16 Ch.D. 552 (see especially at p. 531, *per* James, L.J.); *Re Beeston* [1899] 1 Q.B. 626 (see especially at p. 630 *et seq.*, *per* Lindley M.R.).
[97] See *e.g. Roxburghe v. Cox* (1881) 17 Ch.D. 520; *Christie v. Taunton, Delmard, Lane & Co.* [1893] 2 Ch. 175; *Laurence v. Hayes* [1927] 2 K.B. 111, and also s.136(1) of the Law of Property Act 1925.
[98] *See above*, p. 191 (choses in action).

which the bankrupt had previously concluded.[99] The scope of these rights of action available against the trustee includes the enforcement of security arrangements, such as mortgages of or charges upon property,[1] and the exercise of any right of set-off or reimbursement arising from previous transactions concerning the property,[2] and the enforcement of any restrictive covenant into which the bankrupt may have entered, such as a covenant not to assign a lease without the landlord's consent.[3] Similarly, if the bankrupt's interest in a part of his property was subject to a third party's right, as a vendor who had been induced to sell by means of the purchaser's fraud, to disaffirm the sale and retake possession of the property, such a right may be exercised even after the purchaser's bankruptcy.[4] Alternatively, if the bankrupt has bought, but not paid for, goods prior to his bankruptcy his trustee's title to the goods will be affected by any lien or right of stoppage in transit which the vendor is capable of exercising,[5] but where the vendor no longer has the possibility of exercising such rights his only recourse is to prove for the outstanding price as a debt due in the bankruptcy. All such rights as might have been exercised by third parties prior to bankruptcy may be exercised after adjudication, and no action by the trustee can be effective to gain priority over such vested rights: unless the property can be disclaimed, the rights remain undisturbed.[6]

For an "equity" of any kind to prevail against the trustee after adjudication it must be one which the law recognises as being valid and enforceable against the *property* itself. The special position of the family home, and of the rights of occupation arising in favour of various parties in the event of the bankruptcy of a spouse having a beneficial interest in the family home, have already been considered.[7] The "equity" of such a right of occupation is one which for the time being affects the trustee's freedom to deal with and dispose of the family home, albeit the "equity" is nowadays a defeasible one, in accordance with the principles which were described above, so that in due course the trustee may come to enjoy a title to the family home which is free from any such equity. However, there is also a possibility that a husband's property may previously have been "charged" by order of the court in order to make provision for the wife, and such a charge will affect the quality of title transmitted to the husband's trustee in bankruptcy.[8]

---

[99] *Re Scheibler* (1874) 9 Ch.App. 722. Note, however, the trustee's powers of disclaimer: *see supra*, p. 193 and *infra*, p. 235.
[1] *Re Wallis* [1902] 1 K.B. 719. But such rights may become time-barred: *Cotterell v. Price* [1960] 3 All E.R. 315; *Re Benzon* [1914] 2 Ch. 68.
[2] *Bradley-Hole v. Cusen* [1953] 1 Q.B. 300.
[3] *Re Wright* [1949] 1 Ch. 729 *cf.* Law of Property Act 1925, s.79. For further discussion of these issues, see L. Crabb, *Leases: Covenants and Consents* (1991) at 22–24 and 29–31.
[4] *Re Eastgate* [1905] 1 K.B. 465.
[5] Sale of Goods Act, 1979 ss.38–46; 48.
[6] *Re Anderson* [1911] 1 K.B. 896.
[7] *Above*, p. 203.
[8] See Matrimonial Causes Act 1973, Part II, and also Land Charges Act 1972, ss.2, 18(1) and Sched. 3, para. 8(1). *cf. Coles v. Coles* [1956] 3 All E.R. 542.

The Rule in ex parte James

A further requirement for any "equity" which is to prevail against the trustee is that it must have arisen prior to the commencement of bankruptcy, which is the moment at which the trustee's title to the property is fixed by law.[9] Certain pitfalls which may beset persons who have dealings with a bankrupt after the time at which his bankruptcy is technically regarded as having commenced have already been alluded to.[10] In certain cases the misfortunes of those who have had dealings with a bankrupt after the time at which the law renders him technically incompetent to dispose of title to his own property are mitigated, together with other potential injustices, by the application of the rule in *ex parte James*.[11] This rule is based upon the proposition that a trustee in bankruptcy, as an officer of the court, ought to act in an exemplary manner by forbearing to insist upon his legal entitlement to retain money or property which, morally, ought to be made over to some other person.[12] So in *Re Wilson*,[13] where the trustee had personally sanctioned the completion, after the bankrupt's adjudication, of a business promotion which the latter had been in the course of arranging when bankruptcy supervened, it was held that the trustee could not conscionably proceed to enforce his strict rights of recovery against those who had paid over to the bankrupt monies which they ought to have paid directly to the trustee, for everything had taken place in accordance with arrangements agreed to by the trustee himself.

Such is the force of this exceptional rule that a party may be enabled to recover a payment made under a mistake of law, for which English law usually fails to allow recovery.[14] The rule has its limits, however, and will be of no avail where the trustee himself has neither done nor omitted to do anything which could give rise to the suggestion that he is debasing the dignity of the court. Thus, where creditors,[15] or even the bankrupt himself,[16] have acted spontaneously in such a way that the bankrupt's estate has come to be enriched the persons at whose expense the enrichment has occurred may discover that they stand to be treated just like any other unsecured creditor of the estate.[17] Furthermore the existence of the rule has been held to create no obstacle to the trustee's recovery of payments by which the bankrupt has honoured obligations which are rendered unenforceable against him by virtue of statutory

---

[9] *Re Wigzell* [1921] 2 K.B. 835; see *above*, p. 188.
[10] See *above*, p. 144.
[11] *Re Condon, ex p. James* (1874) 9 Ch.App. 609.
[12] *ibid.*, at p. 614, *per* James L.J., and at p. 616, *per* Mellish, L.J. See also *Re Thellusson* [1919] 2 K.B. 735.
[13] [1926] 1 Ch. 21, distinguishing *Re Wigzell*, above.
[14] *Re Carnac* (1885) 16 Q.B.D. 308; *Re Brown* (1886) 32 Ch.D. 597. The position is otherwise under the law of Scotland: see *Morgan Guaranty Trust Co. v. Lothian Regional Council* 1995 S.L.T. 299 (C.S., I.H.).
[15] *cf. Re Hall*, [1907] 1 K.B. 875.
[16] *Re Wigzell*, above.
[17] *Re Gozzett*, [1936] 1 All E.R. 79.

provisions such as the Gaming Acts.[18] Although the rule in *ex parte James* may appear somewhat capricious in its operation, and may fairly be said to employ principles of natural justice rather than of "equity" in its formal, technical sense,[19] there can be no doubt that it retains its force in the present day and is capable at times of providing a providential remedy to nullify an unjustified enrichment of the bankrupt's estate.[20]

Power of Examination

It may be desirable for a variety of reasons to pursue enquiries into the state of the bankrupt's affairs so as to clarify matters which cannot be readily discerned solely from an examination of the bankrupt's books and documents. In this context the court may be invited to make further use of the power conferred by section 366 of the Act to summon for examination the bankrupt or the bankrupt's spouse or former spouse, or any person known or suspected to have in his possession any property belonging to the bankrupt's estate, or to be indebted to him, or to be capable of giving information respecting the bankrupt, his dealings or property.[21] A person liable to be summoned in this fashion may also be required to produce any relevant documents of which he has possession or control. If necessary the court may compel the attendance of a person whom it desires to examine,[22] and the witness may be questioned as far as is necessary to establish the credibility of his testimony.[23] The criminal consequences for the bankrupt of any attempt to conceal property are considered in Chapter 13.

Abolition of the Doctrine of Reputed Ownership

In chapter 23 of the *Cork Report* a powerful case was made out for the abolition of the doctrine of reputed ownership. This was a rule of statutory origin first introduced by the Bankruptcy Act 1623 whereby, under specially defined circumstances, property which was not owned by the bankrupt but which happened to be in his possession at the commencement of bankruptcy could be included in his estate for bankruptcy purposes. In its modern operation in relation to conditions of trade and business, to which it exclusively applied, the Committee accepted that the doctrine had become capricious and unjust, and merely constituted a trap for the unwary.[24] The recommendation that the doctrine of reputed ownership be abolished was duly implemented in the reforms of 1985–1986 and it now forms no part of the law of bankruptcy.

---

[18] *Scranton's Trustee v. Pearse*, [1922] 2 Ch. 87, applying *Sutters v. Briggs*, [1922] 1 A.C. 1 (H.L.).
[19] [1936] 1 All E.R. 79, 86, *per* Lord Wright, M.R.
[20] See *Re Clarke* (a bankrupt), [1975] 1 All E.R. 453, in which the cases are extensively reviewed, and see also *Re Wyvern Developments Ltd* [1974] 2 All E.R. 535.
[21] s.366(1) of the Act, considered *ante*, Chap. 7, at p. 152. See also *post*, Chap. 11, at p. 320.
[22] *ibid.*, s.366(3), (4).
[23] *Re Scharrer* (1888) 20 Q.B.D. 518.
[24] Cmnd. 8558 at para. 1086. The last embodiment of the doctrine was in s.38(c) of the Bankruptcy Act 1914 (repealed).

(2) Property not vesting in the trustee

The general rule that, upon bankruptcy, the entirety of a debtor's property vests in his trustee admits of a certain number of exceptions. Some of these exceptions arise by virtue of specific statutory provisions, others are the creation of the case law, while others again are dependent upon specific arrangements being made by the debtor or some other person.

Property Held on Trust

Section 283(3)(a) of the Act provides that property held by the bankrupt on trust for any other person is not included in the bankrupt's estate and hence does not pass to his trustee for division amongst his creditors. In addition to the relatively straightforward situation in which the bankrupt has been constituted trustee of an express trust there are numerous instances in which a person by his own conduct comes to occupy the position of trustee, as where a person who has attempted to effect an assignment which falls outside the provisions of section 136 of the Law of Property Act 1925 may in some circumstances be held to have constituted himself trustee for the intended assignee.[25] In other situations the law imposes a fiduciary responsibility on account of relationships existing between parties, with the consequence that certain monies in the bankrupt's hands may be impressed with a trust in favour of those to whom he stands in a fiduciary capacity.[26] Such is the case for example with solicitors, who may at any time have charge of clients' monies,[27] or with factors or with mercantile agents, bankers or paying agents who may possess goods or money for application on behalf of their client or principal. However a careful distinction must be made between situations in which goods or monies are impressed with a trust by virtue of the fact that they are destined to be applied to some other specific purpose and the situation in which the relationship of debtor to creditor exists between the bankrupt and his client: in the latter case, funds which the bankrupt was due to make over to his client, such as profits which a broker has made in dealings upon the Stock Exchange, form part of the bankrupt's general assets and pass to his trustee.[28] Moreover it is essential that the bankrupt should be merely a "bare" trustee of any property which is to escape transmission to his trustee in bankruptcy; if, in addition to being trustee, the bankrupt enjoys a beneficial interest in the trust estate, the property

---

[25] In this context, see *William Brandt's Sons & Co. v. Dunlop Rubber Co. Ltd* [1905] A.C. 454 (H.L.); Law of Property Act 1925, s.53(1)(c). *cf. Re Tout and Finch Ltd* [1954] 1 W.L.R. 178; [1954] 1 All E.R. 127.
[26] *cf. Harris v. Truman* (1882) 9 Q.B.D. 264.
[27] *Re a Solicitor* [1952] Ch. 328. See especially the remarks of Roxburgh, J. at p. 332 concerning the concept of "trust" under present-day conditions, and see also Cmnd. 221, paras. 103, 105 (The *Blagden Report*).
[28] *cf. Godfrey v. Furzo* (1733) 3 P.Wms. 185; 24 E.R. 1022, and *Taylor v. Plumer* (1815) 3 M & S. 562; 105 E.R. 721, with *King v. Hutton* [1900] 2 Q.B. 504. See also *Drinkwater v. Goodwin* (1775) 1 Cowp. 251; 98 E.R. 1070, and *Barclays Bank Ltd v. Quistclose Investments Ltd* [1970] A.C. 567.

does not come within the exemption created by section 283(3)(a), which relates to property held on trust for "any *other* person."[29]

The Rule in ex parte Waring

There is one further, and somewhat rarified, instance in which the English courts have declared that specific assets may come to be impressed with a trust. This is where the holder of a dishonoured bill of exchange, of which both the drawer and the acceptor are insolvent, is able to establish that, by virtue of a contract between drawer and holder, particular property, or a particular security, has been specifically appropriated by the acceptor to meet the bill at maturity. In such circumstances under the decision of Lord Eldon in *ex parte Waring*,[30] a holder of the bill is entitled to satisfy his claim directly out of the specified property or security, and is not confined merely to the remedy of lodging proof in the bankruptcies of the two parties who are liable upon the bill. This is allowed upon the footing that the asset in question is impressed with a trust in the hands of the acceptor,[31] and the consequence is that the property which is thus made available to the holder is excluded from transmission to the trustee in bankruptcy for the benefit of the creditors generally. The rule in *ex parte Waring* has acquired an established place in English law through its repeated application,[32] but its merits may be considered to be questionable since it creates a highly favourable exception from the usual operation of the bankruptcy regime in favour of the holder of a bill of exchange, yet it does so by means of a rule whose effects are dependent upon the almost fortuitous circumstances of the contractual relationship between drawer and acceptor, to whose contract the holder is by no means necessarily privy. The rule has undergone some restriction and refinement,[33] but has been accepted, albeit not without some voicing of dissatisfaction, by the House of Lords.[34] It has not, however, been adopted in Scotland.[35]

Mixed Funds

Special difficulties arise where funds which would be protected from passing to the trustee have been mixed with unprotected funds in one and the same banking account. The basic rules concerning the following of assets which have been paid into the mixed fund are derived from the rule in *Clayton's* case,[36] to the effect that where a running account is maintained

---

[29] *Morgan v. Swansea Urban Sanitary Authority* (1878) 9 Ch.D. 582; *Governors of St. Thomas's Hospital v. Richardson* [1910] 1 K.B. 271.
[30] *Re Brickwood, ex p. Waring* (1815) 19 Ves.Jun. 345; 34 E.R. 546. See Bills of Exchange Act 1882, ss.47(2); 48.
[31] See *Re Suse (No. 2)* (1885) 14 Q.B.D. 611 *at p.* 620, *per* Brett, M.R. and at p. 623, *per* Cotton, L.J.
[32] *Powles v. Hargreaves* (1853) 3 De G.M. & G. 430; 43 E.R. 169; *Re Richardson* (1872) 8 Ch.App. 220; *Re Leggatt* (1873) 8 Ch.App. 965; *Re Suse (No. 2), above.*
[33] *e.g.*, in *Re New Zealand Banking Corp.* (1867) L.R. 4 Eq. 226; *Vaughan v. Halliday* (1874) 9 Ch.App. 561.
[34] *Royal Bank of Scotland v. Commercial Bank of Scotland* (1882) 7 App.Cas. 366.
[35] *ibid.*
[36] *Devaynes v. Noble, Clayton's Case* (1816) 1 Mer. 572; 35 E.R. 781.

without specific instructions as to retention of any particular sums, it is to be presumed that monies have been withdrawn in the same chronological order as they were paid in. The rule has been refined in regard to cases where a person has mixed trust monies with his own money, for it was held in *Re Hallett's Estate*[37] that such a person must be taken to have drawn out his own money first in preference to the trust money. Prima facie therefore, any balance remaining in the account may be attributed to the in-payments of trust monies. However, if the trust funds were derived from more than one source it was held in that same case that as between the different trust funds the rule in *Clayton's* case applies, so that the first sum paid in will be held to have been the first to have been paid out. A further proviso to the application of this rule is that there must be a transfer of money in tangible form in order for it to be possible to follow the money: a mere paperwork transaction, such as the setting-off of balances between mutual debtors, will not suffice.[38] Moreover, the Court of Appeal has held that there can be no equitable tracing of trust money paid into an overdrawn bank account, whether overdrawn at the time of each payment in or subsequently overdrawn.[39]

Powers of Appointment

Somewhat similar to the situation where the bankrupt holds property on trust is the position where the bankrupt has been given a power of appointment in relation to settled property. The property in question will not be divisible among the creditors of the donee of the power and so will not pass to his trustee in bankruptcy.[40] Nor will the power itself pass to the trustee in bankruptcy so as to be exercisable by him instead of by the original donee of it,[41] and hence it is not possible for the trustee in bankruptcy, by purporting to exercise the power of appointment in favour of the bankrupt himself, or by releasing the power, to cause the property to pass to the bankrupt's estate and therefore to become available to creditors.[42] However, where a settlor has reserved to himself a power of appointment, or direction, of his settled property the position is somewhat different. If, by virtue of his reserved power, a bankrupt settlor would have been capable of causing either property or income to be paid over to himself exclusively, the provisions of section 283(4) of the Act become relevant. This subsection lays down the basic proposition that references to "property" in relation to the bankrupt include references to any power exercisable by him over or in respect of property. However the further provisions of subsection (4) thereafter exclude from such references any case where the power is exercisable in relation to property not for the time

---

[37] (1880) 13 Ch.D. 696, accepted and extended in *Sinclair v. Brougham* [1914] A.C. 398 (H.L.); *Re Diplock* [1948] 1 Ch. 465 affirmed *sub. nom. Ministry of Health v. Simpson* [1951] A.C. 251 (H.L.).
[38] *Re Hallett & Co.* [1894] 2 Q.B. 237. See also *Lacey v. Hill* (1876) 4 Ch.D. 537. See also Goode (1976) 92 L.Q.R. 360, 528; Kurshid and Matthews (1979) 95 L.Q.R. 79.
[39] *Bishopsgate Investment Management Ltd v. Homan* [1994] BCC 868.
[40] *Re Guedalla* [1905] 2 Ch. 331.
[41] *Nichols to Nixey* (1885) 29 Ch.D. 1005.
[42] *Re Rose* [1904] 2 Ch. 348.

being comprised in the bankrupt's estate, and which satisfies either of two further, alternative conditions. These are:

(1) that the power is so exercisable after the conclusion of the bankruptcy administration; or
(2) that the power cannot be so exercised for the benefit of the bankrupt.

It would then seem that, since the net effect of section 283(4) is to confer upon the trustee in bankruptcy the capacity to exercise all such powers over property as might have been exercised by the bankrupt for his own benefit at the commencement of his bankruptcy or before his discharge, his trustee in bankruptcy could indeed exercise the power so as to benefit the creditors. Where, however, the power is expressed to be exercisable by the settlor for the joint benefit of himself and another person, such an indivisible power will probably not vest in his trustee in bankruptcy.[43]

One special form of ecclesiastical patronage is the right of nomination to a vacant benefice or living, properly called an advowson. Section 283(3)(b) perpetuates a long-established rule whereby such a right of nomination does not form part of the bankrupt's estate.

Property Which the Bankrupt has Ceased to Own

It would appear almost a truism to state that the trustee in bankruptcy does not acquire title to property which the bankrupt has ceased to own at some time before the commencement of bankruptcy. Nevertheless the proposition merits some consideration, not least because it is only an imperfect statement of the true position in law. In several instances, which will be discussed in due course,[44] the trustee is able to impeach pre-bankruptcy transactions by which the bankrupt has divested himself of the title to property. It is therefore more accurate to assert that the trustee will not acquire title to such property as the bankrupt may have unimpeachably disposed of prior to bankruptcy. A further qualification, of considerable importance, concerns the nature of the transaction whereby the bankrupt is supposed to have relinquished his title to property. To be effective for this purpose of removing the property from the scope of the trustee's right of claim the transaction must somehow effect an outright transfer of title to some other party. Where the property in question is a chose in action it is essential that the bankrupt should have properly assigned the chose to the other party, either by means of a valid statutory assignment,[45] or at any rate by means of an effective equitable assignment.[46] One notable quality of equitable assignments is that they are equally capable of transferring interests in future property as well as in property owned by the assignor at

---

[43] *Re Taylor's Settlement Trusts* [1929] 1 Ch. 435.
[44] *See infra*, p. 221.
[45] See Law of Property Act 1925, s.136, referred to *above*, n. 97.
[46] *Re Briggs & Co.* [1906] 2 K.B. 209; *Cotton v. Heyl* [1930] 1 Ch. 510. For the law of assignment generally, see Treitel, *The Law of Contract* (8th ed., 1991), Chap. 16; Cheshire, Fifoot and Furmston's *Law of Contract* (12th ed. 1991), Chap. 16.

the date of assignment.[47] Other ways in which an outright transfer of title may be accomplished include a bona fide sale under which property passes to the buyer, and a formal conveyance of property even by way of donation.[48] Alternatively, in cases where the bankrupt, having contracted to purchase goods, has resold them to sub-buyers before they have actually been delivered to him and has thereafter become bankrupt, the sub-buyers may be able to claim specific performance of the contract, and thus succeed in obtaining the goods themselves, provided that the property in the goods was capable of passing to the sub-buyers. But if, for technical reasons such as want of appropriation from bulk, property in the goods had not actually passed to them before bankruptcy supervened, the sub-buyers will be limited to lodging proof in the bankruptcy.[49]

It may sometimes transpire that the true effect of a given transaction was merely to confer at best some lesser right, such as a licence to seize goods, upon the party who later claims them in opposition to the trustee.[50] Such a right will be insufficient to enable the claimant to resist the trustee's title to the property, as will any agreement which may be construed as constituting merely a revocable authority permitting him to receive some payment or performance which is legally owed to the bankrupt.[51]

Forfeiture Clauses

Where the bankrupt, prior to his adjudication, is beneficially entitled to an interest of some kind, or where he becomes so entitled at some time after adjudication, the instrument of settlement may contain a provision whereby the interest is to be forfeited if the beneficiary should become bankrupt. Such a forfeiture clause, if it is to be effective, must satisfy three particular conditions.

First, in view of the potential effects of the principle of "relation back" of the title of the trustee in bankruptcy to the date of the bankruptcy order, it is essential that the forfeiture clause be so expressed as to operate upon the presentation of a bankruptcy petition by or against the beneficiary, such as may lead to his adjudication.[52] For example, the settlement may employ a form of words to the effect that the interest shall be forfeited if the beneficiary shall "do or suffer anything whereby he would be deprived or liable to be deprived of the beneficial enjoyment thereof." A similar provision may be employed as a safeguard against the possibility that an intended beneficiary may have become bankrupt by the time that a will or settlement ultimately takes effect in relation to him.[53] Such a clause is certainly capable of achieving its desired effects of preventing the trustee

[47] *Re Lind* [1915] 2 Ch. 345.
[48] But see *infra*, p. 221 for impeachability of such donations. Further difficulties of the law regarding donations *inter vivos* are displayed in *Re Cole* [1964] 1 Ch. 175 and in *Glaister-Carlisle v. Glaister-Carlisle* (1968) 112 S.J. 215.
[49] *cf. Re Wait* [1927] 1 Ch. 606 reversing [1926] 1 Ch. 962.
[50] *cf. Palmer v. Carey* [1926] A.C. 703 (P.C.).
[51] *Re Whitting* (1879) 10 Ch.D. 615.
[52] *cf. Montefiore v. Guedalla* [1901] 1. Ch. 435.
[53] *Manning v. Chambers* (1847) 1 De G. & Sm. 282; 63 E.R. 1069. *cf. White v. Chitty* (1866) L.R. 1 Eq. 372.

from acquiring title to the interest of the beneficiary upon the latter's adjudication, at any rate if this takes place upon a creditor's petition,[54] and possibly also where the beneficiary presents his own petition.[55] There is an attendant disadvantage to the use of this device however, because the forfeiture will automatically occur whenever the beneficiary is the subject of a bankruptcy petition, irrespective of whether this actually leads to his being made bankrupt.[56] The same will be true of interests which fall into possession after either a bankruptcy petition has been presented or a bankruptcy order has been made: the forfeiture will occur notwithstanding that the petition may be subsequently dismissed or the bankruptcy order be annulled, provided that at some time before the dismissal or annulment the trustees of the settlement have had funds in their hands representing income which, but for the bankruptcy proceedings, might have been paid to the beneficiary.[57] On the other hand, slight variations in the form of forfeiture clause employed may produce a different outcome under some circumstances and several cases may be said to have turned upon their special facts.[58] There is authority to the effect that a bankruptcy occurring under foreign law will not accomplish a forfeiture under the terms of a settlement governed by English law, where the beneficiary is of English domicile.[59]

The second requirement is that the settlement should contain a gift over of the interest to be forfeited, otherwise the forfeiture clause will not have the effect of preventing the interest from vesting in the trustee in bankruptcy.[60]

Thirdly, no forfeiture clause can be validly expressed to operate upon the bankruptcy of the settlor himself, it being a fundamental principle that an owner of property cannot by way of settlement or contract qualify his own interest in the property by a condition determining or controlling it in the event of his own bankruptcy, so as to defeat his creditors' legal rights against that property.[61] However, if the settlement comprises additional property which does not belong to the settlor, a provision for cesser of the settlor's interest upon his bankruptcy will be valid to the extent of that other property.[62] Where the trustees of a settlement have themselves exercised any powers of termination of the beneficiary's absolute interest, such a termination will, if asserted prior to the commencement of the beneficiary's bankruptcy, defeat any claim of his trustee in bankruptcy.[63] If

---

[54] *Re Throckmorton* (1877) 7 Ch.D. 145.

[55] *Re Colgrave* [1903] 2 Ch. 705. This decision was doubted and distinguished in *Re Griffiths* [1926] 1 Ch. 1007, where the terms of the forfeiture clause were slightly different.

[56] *Re Sartoris's Estate* [1892] 1 Ch. 11; *Re Laye* [1913] 1 Ch. 298.

[57] *Robertson v. Richardson* (1885) 30 Ch.D. 623; *Re Loftus-Otway* [1895] 2 Ch. 235; *Re Forder* [1927] 2 Ch. 291; *cf. White v. Chitty*, above.

[58] *cf. Re Moon* (1886) 17 Q.B.D. 275; *Re Clark* [1926] 1 Ch. 833; *Re Walker* [1939] 1 Ch. 974.

[59] *Re Hayward* [1897] 1 Ch. 905, following *Re Blithman* (1866) L.R. 2 Eq. 23. See further *post*, Chap. 29.

[60] *Brandon v. Robinson* (1811) 18 Ves.Jun. 429; 34 E.R. 379 (see at pp. 433–435, *per* Lord Eldon, L.C.); *Rochford v. Hackman* (1852) 9 Hare 475; 68 E.R. 597; *Re Detmold* (1889) 40 Ch.D. 585.

[61] *Re Johnson* [1904] 1 K.B. 134. See also *Re Burroughs-Fowler* [1912] 2 Ch. 251.

[62] *Mackintosh v. Pogose* [1895] 1 Ch. 505.

[63] *Re Balfour's Settlement* [1938] 1 Ch. 928.

upon such a determination of an absolute interest the settlement provides for the beneficiary to continue to receive payments upon a discretionary basis, his right to retain such payments as may be due to him after his adjudication will be limited to an amount sufficient for his necessary maintenance, the surplus being claimable by his trustee in bankruptcy.[64]

Forfeiture clauses designed to operate in the event of bankruptcy are also encountered in other contexts. The insertion in a lease of a clause providing a right of re-entry by the landlord in the event that a bankruptcy petition is presented by or against the tenant will accomplish the purpose of preventing creditors of the tenant from acquiring an interest in the premises demised.[65,66] However, such a forfeiture clause will only be effective upon the bankruptcy of the tenant in possession of the term. Where the lessee has validly assigned the lease prior to his bankruptcy no forfeiture will be suffered by the assignee.[67] It has been held however that a lessee's act of presenting a bankruptcy petition against himself, upon which he is adjudicated, does not constitute a breach of his covenant not to assign the lease without the landlord's permission, because, technically, such an "assignment" takes place by operation of law despite the fact that it is the lessee's act which has initiated the legal process.[68] By a further paradox, if the assignment of the lease is effected as part of a general assignment of the lessee's property this may be impeachable as a transaction at an undervalue, or possibly as a preference or as a transaction defrauding creditors, in the event of the bankruptcy of the assigning tenant.[69] If such consequences do ensue the assignment itself will be rendered void and hence the landlord should be disabled from treating the abortive assignment as amounting to a breach of the covenant not to assign.[70] But until the assignment is rendered void by virtue of the adjudication the assignee incurs liability for any rent which falls due.[71]

It has been held that a provision in a company's articles whereby a shareholder may be compelled to sell his shares to the company's nominees at a fixed price in the event of his bankruptcy is a valid provision and in no way repugnant to the bankruptcy law, provided that the fixed price is a fair one and is fixed equally for all persons alike.[72] On the other hand a provision in a building lease whereby the landlord was to become

---

[64] *Re Ashby* [1892] 1 Q.B. 872. See also *above* p. 203.

[65] *Roe d. Hunter v. Galliers* (1787) 2 Term.Rep. 133; 100 E.R. 72. Contrast the separate type of provision in a lease for the right of re-entry by the landlord, and forfeiture of the lease, for non-payment of rent: *Ezekiel v. Orakpo* [1976] 3 All E.R. 669, (C.A.). See L. Crabb, *Leases: Covenants and Consents* (1991), p. 23.

[66] If the lease was drawn up before the enactment of the Insolvency Act 1985, it is likely to contain a reference to the now obsolete concept of the commission of an act of bankruptcy by the tenant. Unless the court is prepared to construe this as denoting the happening of any event capable of resulting in the tenant's bankruptcy—namely the presentation of a bankruptcy petition—it is possible that the clause may now be ineffective to achieve the purpose originally intended.

[67] *Smith v. Gronow* [1891] 2 Q.B. 394.

[68] *Re Riggs* [1901] 2 K.B. 16.

[69] ss.339–342 and 423–425 of the Act, *post*, p. 221.

[70] *Powell v. Lloyd* (1828) 2 Y. & J. 372; 148 E.R. 962.

[71] *Stein v. Pope* [1902] 1 K.B. 595. See further *infra*.

[72] *Borland's Trustee v. Steel Brothers & Co. Ltd* [1901] 1 Ch. 279.

entitled to the building materials on the land in the event of the builder's bankruptcy was held in *Re Harrison*[73] to be void as contrary to the bankruptcy law, so that the building material became the property of the trustee in bankruptcy. Likewise, a provision in a deed of partnership that, in the event of the bankruptcy or insolvency of a partner, his share in the partnership property was to vest in his co-partners was held in *Whitmore v. Mason*[74] to be void for the same reason, and with the same consequences.

Reservation of Title Clauses

Where goods of any kind are sold in circumstances where all or part of the purchase price is to be paid at a later date the seller assumes the role of creditor in relation to the buyer until the balance of the price is paid. If in the meantime the buyer becomes insolvent there is generally little prospect that the seller, along with the other non-preferential creditors, will receive payment in full. Conversely, the value represented by the goods supplied may either have been dissipated by the buyer prior to the onset of insolvency or else, if still extant within the insolvent's estate, it will in practice be transmitted to the buyer's secured and preferential creditors.[75] In the not unreasonable desire to mitigate these possibilities it has become a widespread practice for sellers of goods—particularly those who are serving as trade suppliers—to introduce a provision into the contract of sale whereby ownership of the thing sold will not be transferred to the buyer until such time as the purchase price is fully paid. Such a provision—known as a reservation of title clause—is fully compatible with the law governing contracts for the sale of goods, under which the parties are left free to determine that title to the goods shall be transferred at a separate time to the physical delivery of the goods themselves, and that it shall do so subject to specified conditions being fulfilled.[76]

In theory therefore a properly drafted reservation of title clause should leave the unpaid seller in a position to recover the goods themselves, insofar as they remain in the possession of the insolvent buyer and are physically identifiable and capable of severance and removal. Prior to the enactment of the Insolvency Act 1986 however the practical value of a reservation of title clause in any contract with an individual was questionable in view of the operation of the doctrine of reputed ownership under the law of bankruptcy: goods in the possession of the bankrupt for the purposes of his trade or business were in many instances capable of being assimilated to the bankrupt's estate, notwithstanding that he was not the legal owner of them at the commencement of bankruptcy.[77] The doctrine of reputed ownership did not apply to corporate insolvency, however, and a body of case law has grown up in relation to the efficacy of

---

[73] (1880) 14 Ch.D. 19.
[74] (1861) 2 J. & H. 204; 70 E.R. 1031.
[75] See Chap. 10, *post*.
[76] Sale of Goods Act 1979, ss.17, 19. The parties may also provide that the goods shall be at the buyer's risk even before either possession or title have been transferred from the seller: *ibid.*, s.20(1).
[77] See *supra*, p. 208.

reservation of title clauses—also known as *Romalpa* clauses[78]—in the context of receivership or winding up, where the principal issue has often been to determine whether the clause as drafted was capable of being construed as a species of charge, which would be void unless duly registered.[79] Subject to that possibility the general principles relating to the use of reservation of title clauses are now reasonably well established.

In view of the abolition of the doctrine of reputed ownership from the law of bankruptcy, and in the absence thus far of any statutory requirement of registration of reservation of title clauses as a precondition to their validity in the event of bankruptcy,[80] it would now appear to be possible for such clauses to play a more prominent role than hitherto in the law of individual insolvency. It should be possible for the seller not only to protect himself by means of a clause reserving the legal title to the goods, but also to provide that his interest shall attach to the proceeds of any sub-sales of the goods supplied, so that if identifiable and kept separately from other monies they should admit of tracing by the unpaid supplier.[81] Where the goods supplied to the bankrupt have been mixed with other goods or materials so as to lose their original identity, for example as part of a process of manufacture, this may serve to defeat the rights of the unpaid seller under the reservation of title clause.[82] If however the goods, though mixed with others not belonging to the supplier, have nonetheless retained their essential integrity and are capable of being detached or disconnected, even though the process of recovery may be costly, the supplier's rights may remain intact and enforceable.[83]

There is one additional possibility which requires some consideration, namely whether a reservation of title clause in a contract formerly entered into by the bankrupt as buyer is impeachable under any of the provisions of the Insolvency Act which are concerned with the adjustment of prior transactions, and in particular whether such a clause may amount to a voidable preference under section 340. The provisions referred to, including section 340, are discussed in detail below,[84] but for present purposes it should be observed that the essential question will be whether it can be held that, in assenting to the inclusion of the clause, the buyer was:

"influenced . . . by a desire to produce in relation to [the seller] the

---

[78] After the leading case of *Aluminium Industrie Vaassen B.V. v. Romalpa Aluminium Ltd* [1976] 2 All E.R. 552: [1976] 1 W.L.R. 676, (C.A.). See also *Clough Mill Ltd v. Martin* [1984] 3 All E.R. 982; [1985] 1 W.L.R. 111, (C.A.), for a discussion of the applicable principles.
[79] Companies Act 1985, ss.395, 396(1)(f) as originally enacted. These provisions have been amended by the Companies Act 1989, s.93 (not yet in force). See also *ibid.*, ss.397–407. Also Chap. 26, *post*, p. 634.
[80] *cf.* Cmnd. 8558, Ch. 37, especially *paras.* 1637–1641 and 1650.
[81] The sub-buyer will receive a title good against both the unpaid supplier and the trustee in bankruptcy by virtue of s.25 of the Sale of Goods Act, 1979: *cf. Four Point Garage Ltd v. Carter* [1985] 3 All E.R. 12.
[82] *cf. Re Bond Worth Ltd* [1980] Ch. 228; *Borden (U.K.) Ltd v. Scottish Timber Products Ltd* [1981] Ch. 25 (C.A.); *Re Peachdart Ltd* [1984] Ch. 131.
[83] *cf. Hendy Lennox (Industrial Engines) Ltd v. Graham Puttick Ltd* [1984] 2 All E.R. 152: [1984] 1 W.L.R. 485.
[84] *infra*, p. 226.

effect ... of putting [the seller] into the position which, in the event of [the buyer's] bankruptcy, will be better than the position he would have been in if the thing had not been done."[85]

This is an exceedingly broad definition of "preference" and it is scarcely deniable that the effect of a reservation of title clause is to improve the position of the seller in the event of the buyer's insolvency. It will however be a matter to be established by evidence whether the buyer was "influenced" by a "desire" to produce this effect, as the statute requires. Thus, if the seller has insisted upon the insertion of the term as the only basis upon which he would do business other than for cash, or if the clause forms one of the standard terms of business utilised by the seller, it may be arguable that the bankrupt was influenced by no other consideration than the desire, for his part, to obtain supplies on credit. In *Re M.C. Bacon Ltd,*[86] a case concerned with the alleged giving of a preference by a company, Millett, J. ruled that the connotation of the term "desire" in this context is that it be demonstrable that the debtor "positively wished" to improve the creditor's position in the event of the debtor's insolvency. The mere fact that, as an incidental consequence of the debtor's action (*in casu,* the creation of security in favour of a bank in return for maintaining overdraft facilities and financial support) the creditor's position will be materially improved would not in itself suffice to render the transaction voidable as a preference unless accompanied by the requisite, subjective motivation on the debtor's part.[87]

Where the seller is an associate of the bankrupt within the meaning of section 435 of the Act,[88] the validity of a reservation of title clause is much less certain because, by virtue of section 340(5), the court is required to presume, unless the seller can prove to the contrary, that the bankrupt was influenced by the desire to confer the requisite advantage on the seller when assenting to the inclusion of the clause in their contract of sale. The matter will undoubtedly require to be further tested in litigation.

Exempt Property and Family Assets

It has long been accepted that, in divesting the bankrupt of his property for the benefit of his creditors, the law should refrain from stripping him and his family of the last vestiges of dignity and comfort as represented by their personal clothing, their essential domestic furniture and equipment and the tools or equipment with which the bankrupt earns his living and thus supports himself and his family. A statutory exemption therefore removes certain items or categories of property from the estate which vests

---

[85] The words in parentheses are drawn from the provisions of s.340(3)(b) and (4) of the Insolvency Act 1986.
[86] [1990] BCC 78; [1990] BCLC 324. See Fletcher [1991] J.B.L. 71 and the further discussion in Chapter 26, *post,* and in section (B) *infra.*
[87] [1990] BCC at p. 87; [1990] BCLC at 334–336. Although the case was decided under section 239 of the Act, the drafting is identical to that of section 340 for the purposes of the matter here being considered.
[88] See p. 223, and Appendix I, *post.*

Property Not Vesting in the Trustee

in his trustee in bankruptcy. In its previous formulation,[89] the exemption had come to appear unduly rigid and somewhat arbitrary in its application, and the *Cork Report* made a number of important recommendations for reform which, while respecting the traditional spirit of the English law approach to such exemptions, would make the statutory provisions more flexible and reasonable in their operation.[90] These recommendations have been incorporated into section 283(2) of the Act which establishes two separate categories of exempt property. These are:

(1) Such tools, books, vehicles and other items of equipment as are necessary to the bankrupt for use personally by him in his employment, business or vocation; and

(2) Such clothing, bedding, furniture, household equipment and provisions as are necessary for satisfying the basic domestic needs of the bankrupt and his family.

The concept of "necessity" is thus applied in both categories, and will constitute a question of fact requiring the trustee to exercise his judgment in the light of actual circumstances.

In the case of the first category, to qualify for exemption it is required that the item in question must be *necessary* for the *personal* use of the bankrupt in the context of *earning his livelihood*: three criteria therefore have to be satisfied. On the other hand, the paragraph is expressed in broad terms which are apt to cover not only the tools of the workman's trade but also books and materials needed by those who earn their living by means of their intellectual skills, while business and office equipment of not inconsiderable value could quite properly be granted exemption as "items of equipment."[91] The exemption available in the case of vehicles, where the three criteria are properly met, is further evidence of the liberal philosophy which is now embodied in this provision.

The second category of exempt property, expressed in paragraph (b), allows the bankrupt and his family to retain such of the listed items as are necessary for satisfying their *basic, domestic* needs. Again, the exercise of common-sense judgment is called for, but the omission from the paragraph of any express reference to "vehicles" is significant and it would seem unrealistic to suppose that the retention of a vehicle could be allowed on the basis that it constitutes "household equipment."

It is especially noteworthy that the provisions of section 283(2) impose no monetary limit to circumscribe the total extent of the exemption which may be accorded in any given case. However, the provisions of section 308 are of relevance in that they enable the trustee to claim for the estate any item of exempt property which appears to have a higher intrinsic value than the cost of providing a reasonable replacement for the bankrupt or his

---

[89] Bankruptcy Act 1914, s.38(2) (repealed).
[90] Cmnd. 8558, Ch. 24.
[91] s.436 of the Act defines "business" as including a trade or profession.

family to use.[92] The trustee may claim the item in question by serving written notice upon the bankrupt, and the cost of providing the replacement is made a first charge upon the bankrupt's estate.[93] The Rules also provide for the possibility that a third party may undertake to provide the estate with a sum of money representing the surplus value of any item which the trustee might otherwise claim and sell under section 308, thereby enabling the bankrupt to be left in possession of the property.[94]

Inalienable Pension Rights

Where the bankrupt is in receipt of a salary or wages the trustee's right to claim the surplus of that income over and above the reasonable domestic needs of the bankrupt and his dependents has already been described.[95] Where the income is paid in the form of a pension the trustee's rights are subject to the application of any special statutory provision governing the pension in question. Some statutory provisions simply state that any assignments of the pension shall be void, but add that nothing is intended to prejudice any other enactment providing for payment to a bankrupt's trustee.[96] Other statutory provisions are so drafted as to contain an express indication that the benefit of the pension or allowance payable under the Act in question shall not pass to any trustee upon the bankruptcy of the beneficiary, as well as providing that any assignment of or charge upon the benefit shall be void.[97]

Although the latter type of provisions purport to render the relevant benefits inalienable, it has been held that they merely ensure that the pension does not automatically vest in the trustee as part of the bankrupt's estate, and that such an effect is not incompatible with the making of an income payments order by the court under what is now section 310 of the Act of 1986.[98]

A contrasting situation arises where the bankrupt has previously effected some kind of private, contractual arrangement with a view to providing a personal pension in the event of retirement or disability. The capital which has accumulated in the bankrupt's "private pension fund", it is submitted, is an asset to which the trustee in bankruptcy may properly lay claim, subject to such rights of retention as can legitimately be asserted by the party who had contracted to provide the pension, in the event of premature cancellation of the contract.

---

[92] A definition of "reasonable replacement" is offered in s.308(4), but effectively makes it a matter of judgment in the light of the circumstances. If there is disagreement, the bankrupt could challenge the trustee's decision by applying to the court under s.303(1). "Family" is defined in s.385(1) as meaning the persons (if any) who are living with the bankrupt and are dependent on him.
[93] s.308(1), (3) of the Act; r. 6.187 of the Rules. *cf.* Cmnd. 8558, para. 1109.
[94] r. 6.188 of the Rules.
[95] *Supra*, p. 203.
[96] *e.g.* Army Act 1955, s.203; Air Force Act 1955, s.203.
[97] *e.g.* Social Security Administration Act 1992, s.187(1); Police Pensions Act 1976, s.9.
[98] *Re Garrett* [1930] 2 Ch. 137, applying *Re Shine* [1892] 1 Q.B. 522 and *Re Huggins* (1882) 21 Ch.D. 85.

(B) Extension of the Trustee's Title

In certain circumstances the trustee is able to assert title to property of which the bankrupt was no longer the owner at the date of commencement of the bankruptcy. This will in some cases facilitate a considerable augmentation of the estate which is available for distribution among the creditors, since the course of a debtor's descent into a state of insolvency will sometimes be marked by transactions which have performed the role of catalyst, either on account of their grossly unfavourable terms so far as the debtor is concerned, or because their very objective was to bestow an advantage upon the other party at the expense, inevitably, of the general body of unpaid creditors.

Under the law prior to 1986 the trustee in bankruptcy was frequently unable to attack in a cost-effective way many types of transaction formerly entered into by a bankrupt whereby property, including money, was disposed of either for no consideration, or for a commercially inadequate consideration, even where this was done with a palpably fraudulent motive. The *Cork Committee* accordingly made constructive recommendations for the improvement of the law,[99] and these have formed the basis for an extensive recasting of the law under two general headings, namely the Adjustment of Prior Transactions (comprising transactions at an undervalue, preferences, extortionate credit transactions, and the avoidance of general assignments of book debts),[1] and Provisions against Debt Avoidance (relating to transactions defrauding creditors).[2] These provisions, which are complemented by parallel provisions applicable in corporate insolvency,[3] will be considered in turn.

Transactions at an Undervalue

Section 339 of the Act establishes a procedure for the retrospective avoidance of transactions at an undervalue entered into by a person who is subsequently adjudged bankrupt. The procedure may be invoked by the trustee through an application to the court, whereupon the court at its discretion may make an order to restore the position to what it would have been if the transaction had not been entered into.[4] The principle which underlies this procedure for the avoidance of such transactions has been judicially explained by the maxim that:

> "persons must be just before they are generous: debts must be paid before gifts can be made."[5]

Any liberality conferred by one person upon another, and also any transaction for value where anything less than a true commercial

---

[99] Cmnd. 8558, ch. 28. See also Cmnd. 9175 (*The White Paper*), paras. 61–69.
[1] ss.339–344 of the Act.
[2] *ibid.*, ss.423–425. These provisions apply to both individual and corporate insolvency.
[3] See ss.238–241, 244–246: Chap. 24, *post.*
[4] ss.339(1), (2), 342 of the Act.
[5] *Freeman v. Pope* (1870) 5 Ch.App. 538, 540, *per* Lord Hatherley, L.C.

equivalence is achieved, has the inevitable consequence of diminishing the amount of the property which will be available for creditors in the event of bankruptcy.

For the remedy under section 339 to be invocable two requirements must be satisfied: the transaction must have been entered into at an undervalue, within the meaning of section 339(3), and it must have been entered into at a relevant time, within the meaning of section 341. As to the former, section 339(3) states that an individual enters into a transaction with a person at an undervalue if:

(1) He makes a gift to that person or he otherwise enters into a transaction with that person on terms that provide for him to receive no consideration; or
(2) He enters into a transaction with that person in consideration of marriage; or
(3) He enters into a transaction in return for a consideration the value of which, in money or money's worth, is significantly less than the value, in money or money's worth, of the consideration provided by the individual.

It may be observed that there is no restriction as to the nature of the property of which the bankrupt may have disposed by means of a transaction caught by section 339: it may be money, or it may be any other item of value supplied from the bankrupt's side, including possibly an act or service performed in return for a token consideration, or gratuitously.[6] The term "transaction" is defined by section 436 as including "a gift, agreement or arrangement," and it is indicated that the references to "entering into a transaction" are to be construed accordingly. Where the circumstances of the transaction are such that it can be shown that some consideration was provided by the person with whom the bankrupt has dealt, the voidability of the transaction will depend upon the meaning which the court attaches to the word "significantly" for the purposes of section 339(3)(c). The word has clearly been chosen for its flexible properties, in order to avoid setting specific, yet inevitably arbitrary, limits for determining the impeachability of a given transaction. There is in consequence an element of uncertainty regarding the effect of this paragraph in relation to any particular transaction, but it should be safe to assume that where parties have dealt with each other on a genuinely commercial basis the fact that one of them has succeeded in driving a very good bargain ought not to render the transaction voidable in the event of the other's bankruptcy.

A relevant time

The second requirement imposed by section 339 is that the transaction

---

[6] *e.g.* a commercial entertainer performing without charging a fee, or a craftsman or professional person who waives or reduces his usual rate of charges, as an act of favour.

must have been entered into at a "relevant time," an expression which is defined by section 341 in such a way as to denote several different periods of time, varying according to the particular type of case being considered. The basic concept in each instance is of a specific period of time ending with the day of the presentation of the bankruptcy petition on which the individual is adjudged bankrupt: any transaction entered into within that period will have been entered into at "a relevant time" for the purposes of the operation of section 339 in that type of case. The drafting of section 341 is highly complex, and it is best to analyse the various types of case separately.

(i) The two-year case

A transaction at an undervalue which was entered into at any time in the period of two years ending with the day the petition is presented can be set aside under section 339 without any further enquiry as to the bankrupt's circumstances at the time at which it was entered into.[7] It follows therefore that any transaction at an undervalue is at its most vulnerable for the period of two years after it is entered into.

(ii) The two-to-five year case

A transaction at an undervalue which was entered into at any time more than two years before the day the petition is presented, but not more than five years before that day, can be set aside under section 339 provided that one of two additional criteria is satisfied. These are that the individual who has later become bankrupt was either insolvent at the time when the transaction was entered into, or became insolvent in consequence of the transaction itself.[8] Section 341(3) lays down the test of insolvency which is to be applied in this context, and it also comprises two, alternative criteria, namely that a person is insolvent if either he is unable to pay his debts as they fall due, or the value of his assets is less than the amount of his liabilities, taking into account his contingent and prospective liabilities.[9] Insolvency may thus be established for the purposes of section 341 on either a "commercial" (or "cash-flow") basis, or on a "balance sheet" basis.

Burden of proof; "associates"

The remaining question with regard to this case for avoidance of transactions is upon whom does the law impose the burden of proving the bankrupt's state of solvency, or otherwise, at a given, past moment in time? The proviso to section 341(2) is so worded as to create the inference that it is incumbent upon the trustee, in seeking the avoidance of any transaction entered into "at arms' length," to establish that the bankrupt either was insolvent at the time or became so in consequence of the transaction.

---

[7] s.341(1)(a), (2) of the Act.
[8] ibid.
[9] ibid., s.341(3).

However, where the transaction was entered into between the bankrupt and a person who is an "associate" of his (other than by reason only of being his employee) the onus of proof is reversed and it will be incumbent upon the party who seeks to uphold the validity of the transaction to rebut a statutory presumption that the bankrupt was, or became, insolvent at the time in question.[10] The statutory definition of "associate" is therefore of key significance in determining the incidence of the burden of proof of insolvency for this purpose. This is furnished by section 435 of the Act, which is applicable to every instance in which the word "associate" is used in the Act. It is an elaborately drafted provision, so designed that most forms of blood or marital relationship, and also association in partnership or business, and in employment, will produce the effect in law that the persons thus linked are associates of each other.[11] In the same manner, the relationship between trustee and beneficiaries under certain kinds of trust may give rise to the status of being "associates" if the bankrupt or his associates are capable of benefitting under the trust.[12] Therefore, when a trust is established for the benefit of the settlor's family or the other "associates," and *a fortiori* where the beneficiaries under the trust can include the settlor himself, the trust will be capable of avoidance if the settlor becomes bankrupt on a petition presented within five years of the constitution of the trust, unless the beneficiaries can prove that the settlor was, and remained, solvent at the time the trust was created.

Transactions entered into between a person and a company will also take place between "associates" if that person has control over the company, or if that person and persons who are his associates together have control of it.[13] The test for having control of a company is established by section 435(10) in alternative terms which cover cases of *de facto* and *de jure* control. The former type of control is exercised, directly or indirectly, by a person in accordance with whose directions or instructions any of the directors are accustomed to act,[14] while the latter type is established where a person is entitled to exercise, or control the exercise of, one third or more of the voting power at any general meeting of the company or of another company which has control of it.

The network of a given person's "associates" for the purposes of the Insolvency Act is therefore potentially very wide, and this will ensure that in many instances gifts, settlements, or transactions entered into in return for less than a true commercial consideration will be vulnerable for five years under the conditions described above. This will be the case, notably, with arrangements whereby the bankrupt has contrived to diminish the *corpus* of the property of which he is legal owner, either by himself paying for an asset which is registered and owned in the name of some relative, typically the spouse, or by disposing of property by means of a formal gift

---

[10] *ibid.*, s.341(2), proviso.
[11] *ibid.*, s.435(1), (2), (3), (4), (8), (9). The section is reproduced in Appendix I, *post*.
[12] *ibid.*, s.435(5).
[13] *ibid.*, s.435(7). "Company" is defined in subsection (11).
[14] *cf. Denny's Trustee v. Denny and Warr* [1919] 1 K.B. 583; *Re Densham* [1975] 3 All E.R. 726; *Re Windle* [1975] 3 All E.R. 987; *Re A Debtor* [1965] 3 All E.R. 453, 457, *per* Stamp, J.

inter vivos, or a purported "sale" at far below the true value of the asset.[15] It should be noted that the combined effect of section 435(2) and (8) is to include within the meaning of "associate" the bankrupt's husband or wife, or former husband or wife. It remains to be seen what construction the courts will place upon the words "reputed husband or wife," in particular in cases where persons are openly cohabiting without making any attempt to create the suggestion or inference that their relationship is to be equated with that of a lawfully married husband and wife, or where a close relationship is maintained between persons who, for whatever reason, refrain from entering into cohabitation with each other.[16,17]

The nature of the remedy

Where a transaction at an undervalue is successfully impeached by the trustee under section 339, the court is clothed with a broad discretion to make:

> "such order as it thinks fit for restoring the position to what it would have been if [the bankrupt] had not entered into that transaction."[18]

This general power is supplemented, without reduction or encroachment, by the provisions of section 342 whereby the court is given additional, specific powers to make orders of various kinds, as circumstances require. The court enjoys a substantial repertoire of powers to order the specific restitution of property transferred as part of the transaction, or alternatively to follow the proceeds of the sale of property so transferred, or of money so transferred, into the form in which it currently exists in any person's hands.[19] All such money or property will thereby come to be vested in the trustee as part of the bankrupt's estate. Other forms of order may include the imposition upon a person of a requirement to make a payment to the trustee in respect of benefits received from the bankrupt, or to release or discharge (in whole or part) any security given by the bankrupt.[20]

It is to be noted that the person affected by the court's order may be the person with whom the bankrupt initially dealt, or may equally be a third party who has acquired a derivative title or benefit from such a person. In

---

[15] *cf.* Cmnd. 8558, at paras. 1221–1240, 1278–1282, 1285, 1288. See also Australian Law Reform Commission, General Insolvency Inquiry, Report No. 45 (1988), Vol. 1, Chap. 14; Scottish Law Commission Report on Bankruptcy (Scot. Law Com. No. 68, 1982), paras. 12.1 to 12.32.

[16] *cf.* Cmnd. 8558, ch. 21, "Connected Persons." s.435 applies to Scotland, but it is doubtful whether the concept of "associate" as embodied in the section is apt to cover all cases formerly caught under Scottish Law by the expression "conjunct or confident person": Hansard, H.L. Vol. 459, cols. 1271–1272.

[17] The special provisions relating to criminal bankruptcy, contained in s.341(4), (5) of the Act, became redundant with the abolition of criminal bankruptcy under the Criminal Justice Act 1988. In consequence, s.341(4) and (5) have been repealed by Sched. 16 to the Act of 1988: see Chap. 13, *post*, p. 355.

[18] s.339(2) of the Act.

[19] *ibid.*, s.342(1)(a), (b).

[20] *ibid.*, s.342(1)(c), (d).

the latter case section 342(2) (as amended)[21] affords protection to anyone who was not a party to the original transaction, and who has acquired an interest in property or a benefit from the transaction in good faith and for value. Section 342(2A) introduces a rebuttable presumption to the effect that, in either of the alternative cases specified in paragraphs (a) and (b) of the subsection, absence of the requisite good faith is to be presumed with respect to such a third party who has acquired an interest in property from a person other than the individual who is subsequently adjudged bankrupt, or who has received a benefit from the transaction or preference. The alternative cases are: (a) that the third party in question had notice of the relevant surrounding circumstances and of the relevant proceedings, or (b) he was an associate of, or was connected with, either the individual adjudged bankrupt or the person with whom that individual entered into the transaction or to whom that individual gave the preference. Section 342(4) (as substituted)[22] explains that "the relevant surrounding circumstances" means, according to the context, either (a) the fact that the bankrupt entered into the transaction at an undervalue; or (b) the circumstances which amounted to the giving of the preference by that individual. Section 342(5) (also as substituted)[23] further provides that, for the purposes of subsection (2A)(a), a person has notice of the relevant proceedings if he has notice (a) of the fact that the petition on which the individual in question is adjudged bankrupt has been presented; or (b) of the fact that the individual in question has been adjudged bankrupt. The effect of the foregoing provisions of section 342, in their amended form, is to enhance the protection of third parties who purchase an interest in property which, it subsequently transpires, had been the subject of a voidable transaction entered into by an individual whose later bankruptcy occurred at a time such that the transaction took place at a "relevant" time within the meaning of section 341. Third parties are now protected against the risk to them of the transaction being set aside, provided that they were without notice of the actual or potential bankruptcy of the individual in question at the completion of the transaction whereby their interest in the property was acquired.

Preferences

The term "preference" is customarily applied to any act of a debtor[24] which confers upon a particular creditor, or upon a surety or guarantor for a debt due to a particular creditor, a material advantage relative to the position of other creditors in the event of the debtor's insolvency. Such preferences work in contravention of the basic principle of bankruptcy law whereby the bankrupt's estate is to be distributed *pari passu* among the creditors. The law prior to 1986 was unsatisfactory in many respects, but in their review of this topic the *Cork Committee* were not of one mind as to

---

[21] See Insolvency (No. 2) Act 1994, s.2.
[22] *ibid.*, s.2(3).
[23] *ibid.*
[24] Or of his agent who has authority to pay creditors at his own discretion: *Re Drabble Bros.* [1930] 2 Ch. 211. Contrast *Re Morant* [1924] 1 Ch. 79.

the appropriate way in which to recast the law.[25] The new provision contained in section 340 of the Act is aimed at enhancing the prospects for the trustee in bankruptcy successfully to impeach transactions which have resulted in advantage for the person preferred, but the drafting of the section gives rise to some uncertainty with regard to the nature and quality of the motive which must accompany the giving of the preference.[26] Section 340 operates in conjunction with sections 341 and 342, which have been discussed above in relation to transactions at an undervalue.

The central proposition embodied in section 340 is that where the bankrupt has, at a *relevant time*, given a preference to any person the trustee in bankruptcy may apply to the court for an order under the section, whereupon the court enjoys wide discretionary powers to effect a restoration of the position to what it would have been if the preference had not been given. The concept of "preference" for this purpose is defined in section 340(3), and consists of two components: the person to whom the preference is given must be one of the bankrupt's creditors, or a surety or guarantor for any of his debts or other liabilities; and the bankrupt must do something or suffer something to be done, which (in either case) has the effect of putting that person into a position which, in the event of the debtor's bankruptcy, will be better than the position he would have been in if that thing had not been done. This is a very broadly drawn definition involving reference to the hypothetical position of the person preferred, compared with the position he actually enjoys as an effect of the preference given.

Motive

Although an "effects" test is utilised in section 340(3), this operates in conjunction with section 340(4) which introduces an overlapping test based upon motive. The subsection has the effect that a preference is not impeachable unless the individual who gave it was *influenced* in deciding to give it by a *desire* to produce in relation to the recipient the effect described in subsection (3). Under the old law it was essential to show that the intention to give a preference was the dominant one, so far as the bankrupt was concerned,[27] and it was also settled law that where a debtor had acted in response to pressure, including the threat of legal process, from the creditor allegedly preferred, the presence of such pressure was capable of cancelling out any freedom of will on the debtor's part, and hence the payment would not constitute a voidable preference.[28] In effect, it was in a creditor's best interests to pressurise his debtor into making payment, at

---

[25] Cmnd. 8558, paras. 1241–1288, especially at 1252 and 1256.
[26] See s.340(4) of the Act.
[27] *Re Bird* (1883) 23 Ch.D. 695; *Peat v. Gresham Trust Ltd* [1934] A.C. 252 (H.L.); *Re Lyons* (1934) 152 L.T. 201; *Re Cutts* [1956] 2 All E.R. 537: *Re M. Kushler Ltd* [1943] Ch. 248. See also *Re Eric Holmes (Property) Ltd* [1965] Ch. 1052; *Re F.L.E. Holdings* [1967] 3 All E.R. 553 (both decided under s.320(1) of the Companies Act 1948, corresponding to s.44(1) of the Bankruptcy Act 1914—both repealed).
[28] *Thompson v. Freeman* (1786) 1 T.R. 155; 99 E.R. 1026; *Re Wilcoxon* (1883) 23 Ch.D. 69; *Re Cooper* (1882) 19 Ch.D. 580.

least so long as the pressure was kept within the permissible limits of the law. Under the modern formulation of the rule as to motive it seems clear that there is no necessity that the intention to prefer must be dominant, provided that it constituted one of perhaps a mixture of motives influencing the debtor's action. But what is less than clear is the extent to which the new law still embodies the rule that a creditor may retain a preference which he succeeded in extracting from his debtor by means of pressure of some kind. A majority of the *Cork Committee* reached the conclusion that genuine pressure by a creditor should continue to afford him a defence against impeachment of the preference by the trustee.[29] In the absence of any express provision to the contrary in section 340 itself it may perhaps be inferred that the former rule, which was a product of the case law, continues to apply, although it is to be observed that section 340(6) provides that the fact that something has been done in pursuance of a court order does not, without more, prevent the doing or suffering of that thing from constituting the giving of a preference.

The first instance decision of Millett, J. in *Re M.C. Bacon Ltd*,[30] already referred to above, lends support to the view that bargained-for advantages, which come about through orthodox commercial processes, are an acceptable means of defending a creditor's position where his willingness to maintain or increase his exposure in the event of the debtor's failure is crucial to the latter's efforts to stave off that very possibility. The emphasis placed upon the significance of the term "desire", as connoting a state of mind on the part of the debtor amounting to a "positive wish" to improve the creditor's position, leaves open the possibility that a creditor who is in a position to exert "proper" commercial pressure towards a debtor experiencing financial difficulties, can be reasonably confident that the ensuing transaction will not be set aside as a voidable preference if the debtor's bankruptcy is not after all averted.

In seeking to establish whether the requisite desire was present in the debtor's mind at the time of giving the preference the court must effectively determine a question of fact. In a well-known dictum, Lord Greene, M.R., echoing the language of Bowen, L.J. in an earlier case, asserted that

> "a state of mind is as much a fact as a state of digestion, and the method of ascertaining it is by evidence and inference. . . ."[31]

Now that the adjective "fraudulent" is no longer applied to the concept of "preference" it may be that the courts will be more ready to infer the presence of the requisite motive, since the insinuation of dishonesty has ceased to be an integral aspect of this ground for recovery of payments. In one particular situation however, the court is required to presume, unless

---

[29] Cmnd. 8558, paras. 1252, 1256.

[30] [1990] BCC 78; [1990] BCLC 324, referred to *supra*, p. 217 (*Reservation of Title Clauses*), and further discussed in Chapter 26, *post*, at p. 642.

[31] *Re M. Kushler Ltd* (*above*, n. 27) at p. 252; *cf. Edgington v. Fitmaurice* (1885) 29 Ch.D. 459, 483, *per* Bowen, L.J. (not a bankruptcy case); *New, Prance and Garrard's Trustee* v. *Hunting* [1897] 2 Q.B. 19, 27, *per* Lord Esher, M.R.

the contrary is shown, that the bankrupt was influenced by the requisite motive as expressed in subsections (3)(b) and (4) of section 340. This is where the preference has been given to a person who, at the time the preference was given, was an "associate" of the debtor (otherwise than by reason only of being his employee).[32] The rebuttable presumption which thus operates in those cases where a preference has been given to an associate of the bankrupt will render it incumbent upon the recipient to disprove the presence in the debtor's mind of *any* motive of preferring the creditor, or the guarantor within the meaning of section 340(3)(b).

A relevant time

A preference is only impeachable if it was given at a time which, in the circumstances, is a "relevant time" within the meaning of section 341. As in the case of transactions at an undervalue (for which provisions within section 341 also supply the meaning of the expression "relevant time"), the period of vulnerability is reckoned backwards from the date of presentation of the petition on which the debtor is subsequently adjudged bankrupt. In the case of a preference which is not a transaction at an undervalue this period is set at six months, but in the case where such a preference is given to a person who is an associate of the debtor (other than by reason only of being his employee) the period is set at two years.[33] The period of impeachability for preferences is considerably shorter than that which applies in the case of transactions at an undervalue, but where one and the same act of the debtor simultaneously constitutes both a transaction at an undervalue and a preference it may continue to be impeachable *qua* transaction at an undervalue even after it ceases to be impeachable *qua* preference.

In determining the meaning of "relevant time" with respect to preferences the provisions of section 341(2) must also be considered. This introduces the additional requirement that at the time of giving the preference the debtor must either have been insolvent or have become insolvent in consequence of the preference. As explained above the meaning of "an insolvent" is supplied by section 341(3), but what is to be noted, in contrast to the provisions of section 341 in their application to transactions at an undervalue, is that no presumption of insolvency is introduced in relation to preferences, even where the recipient is an associate of the bankrupt.[34] It is therefore incumbent upon the trustee in every case where he is attacking a preference under section 340 to establish that the requirement of section 341(2) with respect to the debtor's insolvency was met at the time the preference was given.

The nature of the remedy

In addition to the broad discretion conferred by section 340(2), a range of remedies available for use by the court in restoring the position to what it

---

[32] s.340(5) of the Act. The meaning of "associate" has been explained *above*.
[33] *ibid.*, s.341(1)(b), (c).
[34] See *supra*, p. 223.

would have been if the preference had not been given is again to be found in section 342 (as amended),[35] which applies with respect both to preferences and to transactions at an undervalue. What was said above regarding section 342 in the context of transactions at an undervalue may therefore be read as applying to preferences, *mutatis mutandis*.[36]

Extortionate Credit Transactions

Section 343 of the Act creates a remedy which may be invoked by the trustee in bankruptcy, who may make application to the court for the re-opening of any credit transaction entered into by the debtor up to three years before the date of the bankruptcy order. The transaction must be one for, or involving, the provision of credit to the person who has become a bankrupt, and the application may be made whether or not the agreement was still in force at the commencement of bankruptcy provided that it was first entered into within the three year limit.[37] Section 343 is modelled upon the provisions of sections 137–139 of the Consumer Credit Act 1974, which enable a debtor to apply to the court for the re-opening of any extortionate credit bargain. However, section 343(6) makes clear provision to the effect that, upon the debtor's insolvency, the remedy is to be pursued under the Insolvency Act by means of an application by the trustee to the court by which the bankruptcy order was made, and neither the trustee nor an undischarged bankrupt may make application under section 139(1)(a) of the Act of 1974. It will often be the case that an extortionate credit transaction will also constitute a transaction at an undervalue, and the administrative good sense of consolidating all remedies relating to the bankrupt's affairs is further enhanced by the concluding provision of section 343(6), to the effect that the powers conferred by section 343 are exercisable concurrently with any powers exercisable in relation to that transaction as a transaction at an undervalue.[38]

The court is empowered to re-open a credit transaction if it is or was extortionate. The meaning of "extortionate" in this context is supplied by section 343(3), namely that, having regard to the risk accepted by the person providing the credit, either:

(1) The terms of the transaction are or were such as to require grossly exorbitant payments to be made (whether unconditionally or in certain contingencies) in respect of the provision of credit, or

(2) The transaction otherwise grossly contravened ordinary principles of fair dealing.

The concept of "grossness" is therefore a key one and is left for the court to

---

[35] See Insolvency (No. 2) Act 1994, s.2, the effects of which are discussed *supra* in relation to Transactions at an Undervalue.
[36] See *supra*, p. 225.
[37] s.343(1), (2) of the Act.
[38] See *supra*.

Avoidance of Unregistered Assignments of Book Debts

determine in the light of the circumstances of each case, but in view of the identity of substance between the definitions employed by section 343(3) of the Insolvency Act and section 138(1) of the Consumer Credit Act 1974, it is to be expected that a consistent approach to interpretation will be maintained by the courts, irrespective of which provision happens to provide the basis for re-opening a given transaction.[39] The position of the trustee in attacking a transaction under section 343 is strengthened by the presumption introduced by the rider to subsection (3), which has the effect in all cases of casting on the party who occupies the position of creditor under the transaction the onus of proving that it was not extortionate.

The range of remedies available under section 343 is delineated in subsection (4), and may include the setting aside wholly or partly of any obligation created by the transaction; the re-writing of the terms of the transaction, or of the terms on which any related security is held; a restitutional order whereby money or property must be made over to the trustee; and provision for a taking of accounts.

Avoidance of Unregistered General Assignments of Book Debts

Section 344 of the Act re-enacts a long established ground for the avoidance of a certain type of transaction entered into by a person prior to bankruptcy. This is where a person who is engaged in any type of business makes a general assignment of his existing or future book debts, or any class of them, to another person. Unless the assignment has been duly registered under the Bills of Sale Act 1878 as if it were an absolute bill of sale it is void against the trustee in bankruptcy as regards book debts which were not paid before the presentation of the bankruptcy petition. It is expressly provided by section 344(3)(a) that the term "assignment" in this context includes an assignment by way of security or charge on book debts. On the other hand subsection (3)(b) has the effect of preserving the validity of any assignment of book debts due at the date of the assignment from specified debtors, or of debts becoming due under specified contracts, and of any assignment of book debts included in a transfer of a business made bona fide and for value[40] or in an assignment of assets for the benefit of creditors generally.

The courts have traditionally seemed to favour a fairly imprecise definition of the term "book debts,"[41] but the expression was held in *Shipley v. Marshall*[42] to mean such debts accruing in the ordinary course of business as are usually entered in the trade books, and hence a debt will not

---

[39] See, *e.g. Davies v. Direct Loans Ltd* [1986] 2 All E.R. 783, 789; *Coldunell v. Gallon* [1986] Q.B. 1184, (C.A.); *Wills v. Wood* (1984) 128 Sol. Jo. 222, C.A. See also Chap. 5, *ante*, pp. 71–72, text to nn. 10–16.

[40] For an example of such a transfer, see *Re Lovegrove* [1935] 1 Ch. 464.

[41] *cf. Independent Automatic Sales Ltd v. Knowles and Foster* [1962] 3 All E.R. 27, 34 *per* Buckley, J.

[42] (1863) 14 C.B.(N.S.) 566; 143 E.R. 567. See also *Paul and Frank Ltd v. Discount Bank (Overseas) Ltd* [1966] 2 All E.R. 922 (decided under s.95 of the Companies Act 1948, now replaced by ss.395–398 of the Companies Act 1985). *Cf. Re Lovegrove*, above.

lack the quality of being a "book debt" merely because the trader has omitted to enter it in his books. Failure to keep proper accounting records in relation to any business in which the bankrupt has engaged within two years prior to petition constitutes a criminal offence under section 361 of the Act.[43]

Transactions Defrauding Creditors

Sections 423–425 of the Act contain new provisions to replace the old law of fraudulent conveyances formerly contained in section 172 of the Law of Property Act 1925 which has been repealed.[44] The new provisions are also part of the general law, since there is no precondition of insolvency to the operation of the remedies they contain. In practice however it will seldom be necessary to invoke this means of avoiding a prior transaction unless the debtor actually becomes insolvent, even if formal adjudication does not take place.[45] The new provisions are applicable to all types of persons, individual or corporate, who enter into a transaction at an undervalue accompanied by the requisite motive. The same definition of "transaction at an undervalue" is employed as under section 339 already discussed,[46] but the key element of the debtor's motive which must accompany his entering into such a transaction for it to be impeachable under section 423 is prescribed in section 423(3). This requires the court to be satisfied that the transaction was entered into by the person concerned for the purpose of either:

(1) Putting assets beyond the reach of a person who is making, or may at some time make, a claim against him; or
(2) Of otherwise prejudicing the interests of such a person in relation to the claim which he is making or may make.

Significantly, the new provision does not embody the words "with intent to defraud," whose lack of a definite meaning under the old law formerly gave rise to considerable uncertainty. The essence of the required motive is therefore an intention to defeat or delay creditors, and it is noteworthy that the drafting of the modern provisions is sufficiently broad to make them applicable to payments of money as well as to transfers or conveyances of other types of movable or immovable property.

There is no inbuilt presumption with regard to the debtor's accompanying motive, even in cases where the transaction has been entered into with a person who is closely connected.[47] Hence it is always

---

[43] See Chap. 13, *post*.
[44] Insolvency Act 1985, s.235, together with Sched. 10, Part IV. s.172 of the Act of 1925 was evolved from the Fraudulent Conveyances Act 1571, (13 Eliz. I. c. 5.).
[45] *cf*. Cmnd. 8558, paras. 1200–1220, 1283–1284.
[46] Insolvency Act 1986, s.423(1). *cf*. s.339(3), *supra*, p. 221. See also s.238 in relation to corporate insolvency, *post*, Chap. 26.
[47] *cf*. the effect of dealing with an "associate" for the purposes of ss.340(5), 341(1)(b), (2)(b), proviso, discussed *above*.

incumbent upon the party seeking to impeach the transaction to prove that the requisite motive was present on the debtor's side. The legislature has refrained from adopting in express terms the recommendation of the *Cork Committee* that the court should be authorised to infer the requisite intent whenever this is the natural and probable consequence of the debtor's actions.[48] It is submitted nevertheless that it would be open to the court to utilise this presumption that a person is taken to intend the necessary consequences of his own acts: there were formerly precedents for its use in connection with the element of intent specified for certain acts of bankruptcy, and with regard to the old law of fraudulent preferences.[49] It would surely be appropriate to revive the application of this doctrine in order to ensure that section 423 achieves its intended effect. The Court of Appeal have ruled that documents relating to a transaction are not covered by legal professional privilege where there is a strong prima facie case that the transaction contravened section 423.[49a]

Applications under section 423

A person actually or potentially prejudiced by a transaction falling within the terms of section 423 is referred to as "a victim" of the transaction.[50] Section 424 specifies which persons have standing to make application under section 423 to impeach a transaction defrauding creditors. In the first instance, where the debtor has been adjudged bankrupt (or is a body corporate which is being wound up or in relation to which an administration order is in force) application may be made by the official receiver, or by the trustee in bankruptcy (or by the liquidator or administrator, in the case of a company) or, with the leave of the court, by a victim of the transaction.[51] Secondly, if a victim of the transaction is bound by a voluntary arrangement approved under Part I or Part VIII of the Insolvency Act, application may be made by the supervisor of the voluntary arrangement or by any person (whether or not so bound) who is such a victim.[52] Thirdly, in any other case any victim of the transaction has standing to impeach it.[53] Thus, where insolvency proceedings are in progress the office holder is given competence to apply under section 423, and is indeed the preferred party for this purpose. Where he declines to do so however—as well as in other cases where no insolvency proceedings are taking place—any victim of the transaction may make application. However, section 424(2) imposes a collective character upon such proceedings by providing that any application made by a competent party is to be treated as made on behalf of every victim of the transaction. Significantly, no time limits are laid down for the bringing of applications

---

[48] Cmnd. 8558, para. 1283(b).
[49] *cf. Re Finney* (1878) 30 L.T. 620; *Tomkins v. Saffery* (1877) 3 App.Cas. 213. *cf.* dicta by Millett, J. in the course of his judgment in *Re M.C. Bacon Ltd* [1990] BCC 78 at p. 87, involving impeachment of an alleged preference under s.239 of the Act, and referred to *supra*, p. 228.
[49a] *Barclays Bank plc v. Eustice* [1995] 1 W.L.R. 1238.
[50] s.423(5) of the Act.
[51] *ibid.*, s.424(1)(a).
[52] *ibid.*, s.424(1)(b).
[53] *ibid.*, s.424(1)(c).

to impeach a transaction under section 423.[54] The remedy belongs to the general law, and section 423(4) confers jurisdiction upon the High Court exercisable concurrently in some instances with any other court competent to exercise an insolvency jurisdiction in relation to the debtor in question.

The nature of the remedy

By virtue of section 423(2) the court enjoys wide discretionary powers to make any order:

(1) Restoring the position to what it would have been if the transaction had not been entered into; and
(2) Protecting the interests of persons who are victims of the transaction.

The collective character of the remedy is thus further emphasised. Section 425, without cutting down the generality of section 423(2), describes a range of specific orders which can be made either against a person who was an immediate party to the transaction or against one whose interest is of a secondary or derivative character. There is however the usual protection for innocent third parties who have dealt in good faith for value and without notice of the relevant circumstances (namely those which give rise to impeachability of the original transaction).[55] The Court of Appeal have affirmed that the power under section 423(2) is essentially a power to restore and protect so far as is practicable, having regard to the requirement under section 425(2)(a) that interests of third parties, who have acquired in good faith from someone other than the debtor must not be prejudiced by the order made by the court.[56]

(C) Curtailment of the Trustee's Title

It can happen that some of the debtor's property which is in theory available for distribution upon his bankruptcy will in practice not pass to his trustee. This may occur either because of action voluntarily taken by the trustee himself, or because of the actions of other persons whereby they may lawfully take and retain property of the bankrupt. We have already encountered examples of such a process, first in considering the capability of the bankrupt to make valid dispositions of after-acquired property or income,[57] and secondly in considering the operation of forfeiture clauses.[58] Other situations will now be considered.

---

[54] Transactions entered into before December 29, 1986 may only be set aside under the old law, *i.e.* s.172 of the Law of Property Act 1925: Insolvency Act 1986, Sched. 11, para. 20.
[55] s.425(2), (3) of the Act. *Note* that the provisions of the Insolvency (No. 2) Act 1994 (discussed *supra* in relation to Transactions at an Undervalue and Preferences) do not affect the operation of ss.423–425 of the Act of 1986.
[56] *Chohan v. Saggar* [1994] BCC 134 (C.A.), affirming [1992] BCC 306; 750.
[57] *Supra*, p. 199.
[58] *Supra*, p. 213.

Property Disclaimed by the Trustee

By utilising the powers and procedures established by sections 315–321 of the Act, the trustee may disclaim any onerous property (as defined in section 315(2)) which is comprised in the bankrupt's estate. As a means of saving the further costs and outgoings which would merely diminish the net assets available for distribution, the power of disclaimer is a most valuable one. Its present formulation embodies several significant reforms recommended by the *Cork Report*.[59] The disclaiming powers of a trustee in bankruptcy are parallel to those enjoyed by a liquidator in company winding up, by virtue of sections 178 to 182 of the Act. The latter powers are further referred to in Chapter 24 *post*, but the principles relating to their exercise are identical, *mutatis mutandis*, to those here described with regard to the bankruptcy of individuals.

The power of disclaimer is exercised by the simple formality of the trustee's executing a written and signed notice of disclaimer of the property in question and filing it in court together with a copy.[60] The copy of the notice, sealed and dated by the court, is returned to the trustee who must within seven days send copies to all persons with interests in the property, or whom he considers it is appropriate to inform.[61] The trustee is allowed to disclaim property classified as onerous even though he may have taken possession of it, have tried to sell it, or have otherwise exercised rights of ownership in relation to it, but on the other hand he is not allowed without the leave of the court to disclaim any property which he has previously claimed for the estate under section 307 as after-acquired property, or under section 308 as exempt property of the bankrupt which can be replaced by a less expensive substitute.[62] From the date of the disclaimer all the rights, interests and liabilities of the bankrupt and his estate in respect of the disclaimed property are terminated, and the trustee is discharged from all personal liability in respect of that property as from the commencement of his trusteeship.[63] Nevertheless, so far as the property is concerned the trustee's release only applies to such liabilities as would otherwise devolve upon him automatically by virtue of his having succeeded to the bankrupt's title to the property: he is not released from any related liabilities which he may have incurred through his own voluntary act since the date of the vesting. Thus in *Re Lister*[64] it was held that a trustee who had gone into voluntary occupation of the bankrupt's leasehold premises for a period prior to disclaiming the tenancy was liable to be assessed for rates as "occupier" during that period. It was pointed out

---

[59] Cmnd. 8558, Chap. 27. Note however that the former 12-month limit for disclaimer has been dropped, contrary to the view expressed in para. 1195.
[60] s.315(1) of the Act: r. 6.178 of the Rules; Form 6.61. There are parallel provisions in ss.178–182 of the Act, applicable in company winding up: see Chap. 24, *post*.
[61] rr. 6.179, 6.180 of the Rules. By r. 6185 a disclaimer is presumed valid and effective, unless it is proved that the trustee has been in breach of his duty with regard to the giving of notice.
[62] s.315(1), (4) of the Act. See *supra* for exempt and after-acquired property.
[63] *ibid.*, s.315(3).
[64] [1926] Chap. 149.

that the trustee had not been bound to go into occupation, but that having chosen to do so he had also become responsible for rates.[65]

The definition of "onerous property" supplied by section 315(2) is even broader under the new law than was formerly the case, and covers:

(1) Any unprofitable contract; and
(2) Any other property comprised in the bankrupt's estate which is unsaleable or not readily saleable, or is such that it may give rise to a liability to pay money or perform any other onerous act.

The previous requirement that the non-saleability of property must be attributable to some liability imposed upon the possessor to pay money or to perform some onerous act[66] has been abandoned, and the two components of this compound condition have become separate and independent grounds for the trustee being at liberty to disclaim the property. The word "property" appears in section 315 without any words to restrict it to property which is divisible among the bankrupt's creditors. Hence, the bankrupt's interest in premises under an agreement for a lease has been held to be disclaimable where there were onerous covenants attached to the agreement.[67] However, it has also been held that where the bankrupt has entered into a contract for the sale of a lease, his trustee cannot disclaim the contract unless he also disclaims the lease itself.[68] But where, prior to his bankruptcy, the lessee of the premises has already assigned them, for example by way of a mortgage, for the entire residue of the term, the fact that liability upon any onerous covenants attached to the lease will fall upon the assignee will obviate all necessity for the trustee to disclaim.[69]

Although no time limit is imposed upon the trustee within which he may exercise the right of disclaimer, a procedure is available whereby any person interested in property comprised in a bankrupt's estate may put an end to any uncertainty regarding the trustee's intention to disclaim the property. By making a written application to the incumbent trustee requiring him to decide whether he will disclaim or not, the person interested sets in motion a process by which the trustee must either exercise the power within 28 days of the making of the application, or lose altogether the right for himself or any successor in the office of trustee to disclaim the property affected.[70] In the case of any contract in respect of which such notice is served the trustee is deemed to have adopted it if he does not disclaim within the time permitted.[71]

---

[65] *ibid.*, at p. 166, *per* Sargant, L.J.
[66] *cf.* Bankruptcy Act 1914, s.54(1) (repealed), and see *Re Potters Oils Ltd (in liquidation)* [1985] P.C.C. 148; [1986] 1 All E.R. 890; [1986] 1 W.L.R. 201.
[67] *Re Maughan* (1855) 14 Q.B.D. 956.
[68] *Re Bastable* [1901] 2 K.B. 518. See also *Pearce v. Bastable's Trustee* [1901] 2 Ch. 122, *supra*, p. 193.
[69] *Re Gee* (1889) 24 Q.B.D. 65.
[70] s.316(1) of the Act, r. 6.183 of the Rules; Form 6.62.
[71] Insolvency Act 1986, s.316(2).

Property Disclaimed by the Trustee

In contrast to the former law prior to 1986, the trustee does not require authorisation from the court as a condition for exercising the power of disclaimer. Former case law concerned with the question of the granting of leave by the court is therefore no longer of direct relevance.[72] However, some of the arguments formerly deployed in cases where the trustee's application for leave was challenged by an interested party may resurface in the context of an application by such a party seeking to have the trustee's act of disclaimer set aside by the court.[73] It appears, however, that the reworking of the statutory provisions concerning the exercise of disclaimers has brought about a substantive alteration in the law, and that the office holder's exercise of discretion will only be interfered with by the court in cases where he can be shown to have acted with mala fides or perversely.[74] Failing that, the court is unlikely to venture to substitute its own discretionary appraisal for that of the trustee, even though the action of the latter may have worked counter to the interests of third parties.

Disclaimer of Leasehold Interests

The provisions of sections 317–319 apply in various cases where land is disclaimed. Where the property is of a leasehold nature the effect of disclaimer is postponed until the trustee has served notice on every person claiming under the bankrupt as underlessee or mortgagee.[75] Thereafter the disclaimer may only take effect in one of two alternative circumstances. The first is if no application is made to the court under section 320 by any party seeking a vesting order before the end of the period of 14 days from the day on which the last notice was served on an interested party by the trustee. The second is where such an application is duly made, and the court nonetheless directs that the disclaimer is to take effect.[76] Where the disclaimer relates to a dwelling house the further provisions of section 318 must be satisfied before the disclaimer can take effect. These similarly require the giving of notice to every person in occupation of or claiming a right to occupy the dwelling house, in order to afford them the opportunity to apply for a vesting order under section 320. Then the same conditions apply as under section 317 with regard to the disclaimer taking effect. Where land is disclaimed which is subject to a rentcharge section 319 confers protection upon the creditor or any other person in whom the land consequently vests by operation of law (referred to as "the proprietor"), and ensures that those parties are not liable for any sums becoming due under the rentcharge prior to the date when the proprietor first takes possession or control of the land, or enters into occupation of it.

As just referred to above, section 320 allows application for a vesting

---

[72] cf. *Re Katherine et Cie Ltd* [1932] 1 Ch. 70 (a company liquidation case).
[73] Section 303(1) of the Act. The equivalent provision in cases of challenge to acts of a company liquidator is s.168(5): see *Re Hans Place Ltd* [1992] BCC 737.
[74] *Re Hans Place Ltd, supra*, at pp. 745–749, per Judge Evans-Lombe, Q.C., invoking *Leon v. York-O-Matic Ltd* [1966] 1 W.L.R. 1450.
[75] Insolvency Act 1986, s.317(1); r. 6.179(2) of the Rules.
[76] Insolvency Act 1986, s.317(1)(a), (b).

order to be made to the court by a number of persons, namely anyone who claims an interest in the disclaimed property, anyone who is under liability in respect of it that will not be discharged by the disclaimer itself, and, in the case of a dwelling house, anyone occupying or entitled to do so.[77] The court by its order may vest the property in any person who is entitled to it, or in a trustee for that person, or (if it seems just to do so, by way of compensation) in any person who is subject to a liability in respect of the property, or in any person who was in occupation, or was entitled to be so, at the time when the bankruptcy petition was presented.[78] When the trustee disclaims a lease upon which the bankrupt has previously created a sub-lease, a mortgage or a charge, the original lessor's position is protected by the provisions of section 321 whereby the court must ensure that the terms of any vesting order provide that the person in whom the property becomes vested is subject to the same liabilities and obligations as the bankrupt was subject to under the original lease on the day the bankruptcy petition was presented.[79] Alternatively the court may at its discretion make a vesting order subjecting the person in whose favour it is made only to the same liabilities as if the lease had been assigned to him at the day of presentation of the petition.[80] If the sub-lessee or mortgagee declines to accept a vesting order under section 320 upon those terms, that person forfeits all interest and security in the property.[81]

Although disclaimer puts an end to the bankrupt's rights and liabilities concerning the property with effect from the disclaimer and discharges the trustee from personal liability from the date when his trusteeship commenced, other persons are only affected to the extent which is necessary for the purpose releasing the bankrupt, his property and his trustee from liability.[82] So, in *Re Levy, ex parte Walton*,[83] where the trustee disclaimed a lease of property on which the bankrupt had previously granted an underlease at a rent less than that payable under the terms of the original lease, the Court of Appeal held that the lessor's right to distrain on the property for the rent reserved in the original lease was not affected by the disclaimer. Nevertheless the court went on to rule that the underlessee thus distrained upon would be entitled to prove in the bankruptcy for a sum representing the difference between the two rents.

A further consequence of the fact that disclaimer leaves the rights and liabilities of other persons respecting the property substantially unimpaired is that a person who has taken a sub-lease from a lessee who has become bankrupt may, if the sub-lease so provides, remain liable to perform all the covenants of the head lease even if it is disclaimed by the trustee in bankruptcy. For this reason a disclaimed head lease has been likened to a dormant volcano, in that it retains its potency, in both a

---

[77] *ibid.*, s.320(2); r. 6.186 of the Rules.
[78] Insolvency Act 1986, s.320(3).
[79] *ibid.*, s.321(1)(a); see *Re Holmes* [1908] 2 K.B. 812.
[80] Insolvency Act 1986, s.321(1)(b); see *Re Carter and Ellis* [1905] 1 K.B. 735.
[81] Insolvency Act 1986, s.321(4); *cf. Re Finley* (1888) 21 Q.B.D. 475; *Re Smith* (1890) 25 Q.B.D. 536; *Re Baker* [1901] 2 K.B. 628.
[82] Insolvency Act 1986, s.315(3).
[83] (1881) 17 Ch.D. 746. *Cf. Stein v. Pope* [1902] 1 K.B. 595.

beneficial and a detrimental sense, so far as the sub-lessee is concerned.[84] This principle of the survival of liabilities of other persons does not apply to any persons who stand as guarantors or sureties of the original liabilities of the bankrupt himself: by virtue of the fact that the primary liability has been cancelled, the liabilities of such persons are determined as from the date of any disclaimer of the property to which their undertakings have been attached.[85] This is the case, provided that the lease remains vested in the original lessee at the time of disclaimer. Consequently, there is a distinct possibility that under certain circumstances the very purpose underlying the use of suretyship in relation to leases, namely to furnish protection for the lessor's economic interest in the event of the lessee's default or insolvency, may be defeated. The proper solution to this dilemma is to employ careful and precise drafting when framing the terms of the suretyship covenant itself, so that the surety expressly and unequivocally undertakes to become liable as primary obligor, and not merely as indemnifier, so as to continue to be liable to the original lessor notwithstanding the discharge of the principal debtor's liability by reason of a disclaimer, or on any other ground.[86]

Where it is an assignee of a leasehold tenancy who is adjudged bankrupt, and that party's trustee in bankruptcy exercises the right of disclaimer, the predicament of the original lessee, and also of any surety of that party, is readily apparent. Even if the assignment of the tenancy took place with the lessor's consent, the privity of contract which subsists between the lessor and the original lessee, ensures that the latter is subject to a continuing liability which is not determined by the subsequent events following upon the bankruptcy of the party in whom the lease has become vested.[87] The lease itself continues in existence, and in accordance with the principles stated above, the lessor's rights continue to be enforceable except as against the bankrupt and his estate (and as against any surety of the bankrupt). Nor, in this instance, can the original lessee claim to be released from liability in the same way as a guarantor or surety of the assignee, because this would be to fly in the face of the pristine character of the obligation contracted towards the original lessor. As a further consequence of this proposition, which is attributable to the enduring effect of the decision of the Court of Appeal in *Stacey v. Hill*,[88] the non-

---

[84] See *Re Thompson and Cottrell's Contract* [1943] Ch. 97, 100, *per*, Uthwatt J., and also *Re Town Investments Ltd Underlease* [1954] Ch. 301.

[85] *Stacey v. Hill* [1901] 1 Q.B. 660; *D. Morris and Sons Ltd v. Jeffreys* (1932) 49 T.L.R. 76; *Re Yarmarine (IW) Ltd* [1992] BCC 28.

[86] *cf. Murphy v. Sawyer-Hoare* [1993] 27 E.G. 127 at p. 129, *per* Judge A. Grabiner, Q.C.

[87] *MEPC plc v. Scottish Amicable and Eckley* [1993] NPC 44. *Note*: the same principle is true for cases where an assignee of a lease has entered into direct and continuing covenants with the original lessor, so that privity of contract is established between them. Such an arrangement is commonly required in cases of assignment of commercial leases, as a condition for gaining the lessor's consent. The rights thereby established will survive even in the event that, by reason of a further assignment of the lease, privity of estate between original lessor and intermediate assignee is subsequently lost. See further L. Crabb, *Leases, Covenants and Consents* (1991), at pp. 115–119. [*Note*: the statement in the text must be read subject to the provisions of the Landlord and Tenant (Covenants) Act 1995, ss.5 and 16, when brought into force].

[88] *supra*, n. 85. See also *Hill v. East and West India Dock Co.* (1884) 9 App.Cas. 448.

determination of the liability of the original lessee means that, in turn, the liability of any surety for that party is to be treated as a subsisting one, notwithstanding the effects of disclaimer by the trustee in bankruptcy of an assignee.[89]

Any person sustaining loss or damage in consequence of the trustee's disclaimer of property is deemed to be a creditor of the bankrupt to the extent of the injury, and may prove in the bankruptcy for the amount involved as a bankruptcy debt.[90] For example, in *Re Hide*[91] it was held that a landlord could prove for the difference between the rent provided for in the disclaimed agreement and the rent which was obtainable for the property from a new tenant. Where the trustee, having kept a landlord out of possession of property for a time, eventually disclaims it the court will order the trustee to pay compensation only where his occupation has actually resulted in a benefit to the bankrupt's estate, and in ordering him to pay compensation the court will also have regard to the question whether the trustee's retention of possession was done with a view to obtaining such a profit.[92]

Distress or Execution Levied

It is a general rule that with the making of a bankruptcy order the bankrupt's estate ceases to be directly accessible to those who seek to enforce any claims against it, or against the bankrupt personally: from then on claims must be pursued via the collective processes of the bankruptcy, by lodging of proof. In principle, indeed, the bankrupt is disentitled to deal freely with his property from the moment that bankruptcy proceedings commence through the presentation of a petition, and from that time on, as we have seen, the court may stay any proceedings and remedies which are in progress.[93] After the making of the bankruptcy order section 285 of the Act transforms this discretionary moratorium into a mandatory restriction on proceedings and remedies against the bankrupt's person or property. Section 285(3) expressly creates two exceptions from this restriction, namely enforcement procedures completed before the commencement of the bankruptcy, and the right of a landlord to distrain for rent due from the bankrupt. These cases are governed by sections 346 and 347 respectively.

(1) Distress for rent

A landlord enjoys a privileged position in the event of the bankruptcy of

---

[89] *Hindcastle Ltd v. Barbara Attenborough Associates Ltd* [1994] BCC 705 (C.A.). (This case also involved the upholding of liabilities on the part of intermediate assignees who had entered into direct covenants with the original lessor, of the kind mentioned in n. 87, *supra*.)

[90] s.315(5) of the Act. Note the effect of s.320(5), which requires the effect of an order made under that section to be taken into account in assessing the measures of loss or damage for the purposes of s.315(5). See also *Stanhope Pension Trust Ltd v. Registrar of Pensions* [1993] 48 E.G. 129; [1994] BCC 84.

[91] (1871) 7 Ch.App. 28.

[92] *Re Bushell, ex parte Izard* (1883) 23 Ch.D. 115, as modified by *Re Witton* (1883) 24 Ch.D. 26.

[93] ss.284, 285 of the Act, *ante*, Chaps. 6 and 7.

his tenant, in that section 347 of the Act permits him to distrain upon the goods and effects of the bankrupt for rent due. Distress may be levied either before or after the commencement of the bankruptcy, but in the latter event there is imposed a limitation to the effect that distress is available only for six months' rent accrued due prior to the date of the bankruptcy order, and that no distress may be levied for rent payable in respect of any subsequent periods after the date when distress is levied.[94] A landlord must prove in the bankruptcy for any surplus of rent for which distress cannot be levied.[95] In respect of rent for which he is entitled to levy distress the landlord effectively enjoys the alternative of lodging proof and receiving dividends thereon, or of distraining, and until such time as any dividend is actually paid to him the alternative remains open.[96] The right to distrain is exercisable even after the property comprised in the bankrupt's estate has vested in his trustee, but is not exercisable after the discharge of the bankrupt.[97]

A landlord's common law right to distrain arises by virtue of the presence of goods or effects upon the demised premises and he will lose that right if the goods are removed from the premises before distraint is effected.[98] It was held in *Re Mackenzie*[99] that the landlord will not lose his right if goods are removed by a sheriff who is levying execution upon a judgment against the tenant, and that the landlord may claim to be paid the arrears of rent by the sheriff out of the proceeds of sale of the goods in question. Where the right of distress is exercisable it may be asserted against any property to be found on the demised premises, whether it be property of the bankrupt or not, and if it should chance that the property distrained upon does not belong to the bankrupt, the protective rule which limits the landlord to the levying of distress for only six months' accrued rent will not be applicable.[1]

Several rules have a bearing upon the position of a landlord who levies distress before any bankruptcy order is made. In the first place, where distress is levied by a landlord at a time when a bankruptcy petition has already been presented against the individual from whom rent is due, then if a bankruptcy order is subsequently made, the landlord may only retain out of the amount recovered by way of distress a sum up to the value of six months' rent accrued due for a period prior to the date of distress. Any excess realised over and above that level of entitlement is by law to be held for the bankrupt as part of his estate.[2] Secondly, if any person[3] has levied distress upon an individual who is adjudged bankrupt within three months

---

[94] *ibid.*, s.347(1).
[95] *cf. Re Bumpus* [1908] 2 K.B. 330.
[96] *Holmes v. Watt* [1935] 2 K.B. 300.
[97] s.347(5), (9) of the Act.
[98] *ex p. Descharmes* (1742) 1 Atk. 103; 26 E.R. 68; *Thomas v. Patent Lionite Co.* (1881) 17 Ch.D. 250. *Cf. Re Chapman* (1894) 10 T.L.R. 449. See also *Re Davis* (1885) 3 Morr. 27.
[99] [1889] 2 Q.B. 566.
[1] *Brocklehurst v. Lawe* (1857) 7 El. & Bl. 176; 119 E.R. 1213; *cf. Re Wells* [1929] 2 Ch. 269.
[2] s.347(2) of the Act.
[3] This is not limited to landlords, but can include other persons entitled to levy distress, *e.g.* for unpaid rates (or community charges) or taxes: see Fletcher (1988) 1 Insol. Intell. 9; (1989) 2 Insol. Intell. 67.

of the date of distraint, then so much of the property, or the proceeds of its sale, as is not already held for the bankrupt by virtue of the foregoing rule is by law charged for the benefit of the bankrupt's estate with the preferential debts of the bankrupt, to the extent that the bankrupt's estate is for the time being insufficient to meet those debts.[4] The distraining party will thus have to surrender goods or money to the trustee to discharge the preferential debts, but is then accorded the status of a preferential creditor by subrogation, so that he enjoys a preferential claim against the rest of the bankrupt's estate in respect of the value of what he has surrendered to the trustee.[5]

An effective levying of distress of goods in a dwelling-house requires an entry into the premises. A bailiff who is unable to gain lawful entry does not levy effective distraint on a debtor's goods merely through the act of posting a written notice of distraint through the debtor's letterbox.[6] It has been held that a landlord's right of distress is an ancient and distinctive self-help remedy and, as such, does not constitute a "legal process" within the meaning of section 252(2) of the Act. Hence, the existence of an interim order, made under that section, does not prevent the landlord from carrying out a distress.[7]

(2) Execution

The rights of a judgment creditor to seize and sell the goods of a debtor in satisfaction wholly or partially of the judgment are less extensive than the rights which a landlord enjoys under the present law with regard to arrears of rent.[8] By virtue of the provisions of section 346(1) of the Act, a creditor who has issued execution against the goods or lands of the debtor, or who has attached any debt due to him from another person, is not entitled to retain the benefit of the execution or attachment (including any sums paid to avoid it), against the debtor's trustee in bankruptcy unless he has "completed" the execution or attachment before the commencement of the bankruptcy. A great deal therefore depends upon the answer to the question whether the execution or attachment was completed before the date on which the bankruptcy order was made. To this end, section 346(5) declares that an execution against goods is completed by seizure and sale,[9]

---

[4] s.347(3) of the Act. Preferential debts are discussed in Chap. 10.
[5] Insolvency Act 1986, s.347(4). See *Re Caidan* [1942] Ch. 90. See Cmnd. 221 (*The Blagden Report*), paras. 98–101, for criticism of this quasi-preferential claim accorded to a distraining landlord, and also of the right of any landlord to levy distress after a bankruptcy order is made. The same recommendation was made by the *Cork Report* (Cmnd. 8558, para. 1668), but was not adopted.
[6] *Evans v. South Ribble Borough Council* [1992] 2 W.L.R. 429.
[7] *McMullen & Sons Ltd v. Cerrone* (1993) 66 P. & C.R. 351; *The Times*, June 10 1993. The Law Commission has recommended the abolition of the landlord's right to levy distress for arrears of rent: Law Com. No. 194 (February 4, 1991, H.C. 138).
[8] See *above*, previous section, p. 240.
[9] Mere seizure will not suffice: *Re Dickinson* (1888) 22 Q.B.D. 187. Contrast *Slater v. Pinder* (1871) L.R. 6 Exch. 228, decided under the Bankruptcy Act 1869.

or by the making of a charging order under section 1 of the Charging Orders Act 1979; that an execution against land is completed by seizure or by the appointment of a receiver, or by the making of a charging order; and that an attachment of a debt is completed by receipt of the debt.

Where an execution has been commenced, but not completed in the sense defined above, before the date of the bankruptcy order, notice of the making of the order may be given under section 346(2) to the sheriff or bailiff charged with the execution, with the following effects.[10] First, the sheriff or bailiff must on request deliver to the official receiver or trustee the goods and any money seized or recovered in part satisfaction but, on the other hand, the costs of the execution are a first charge on these items of property and the sheriff may sell the goods to the extent necessary to satisfy that charge.[11] Secondly, if the sheriff levies execution for a judgment for a sum exceeding the currently prescribed amount of £500,[12] and the goods are sold or money is paid in order to avoid a sale, then if within 14 days from the date of the sale or payment notice is given to the sheriff that a bankruptcy petition has been presented in relation to the judgment debtor, and a bankruptcy order is subsequently made on that petition the balance of the proceeds of the sale or money paid, after deducting the costs of execution, become comprised in the bankrupt's estate and do so in priority to the claim of the execution creditor.[13] Accordingly, in the case of executions for sums above £500 the sheriff is forbidden to dispose of the balance of the proceeds of the execution, after deducting the expenses thereof, for a period of 14 days from the date of sale or from receipt of any payment "buying out" the execution, and *a fortiori* he must not dispose of the proceeds while there is a bankruptcy petition pending of which he has been given notice.[14] If a petition is successfully presented within the 14 days' "period of grace," or if any pending petition results in the making of a bankruptcy order, the sheriff must then pay the balance of the proceeds to the official receiver or trustee.[15]

One tenuous possibility of relief for the creditor whose attempted execution is capable of being overturned by the trustee in bankruptcy is to be found in the provisions of section 346(6) of the Act which enable the court to set aside to such extent, and on such terms as it thinks fit, the rights conferred upon the official receiver or trustee by virtue of the rules just described. In practice however the courts have been reluctant to exercise this widely-expressed discretionary power. Although applications for orders based upon the power now conferred by section 346(6) have

---

[10] Notice must be given in writing, and be delivered by hand at, or by recorded delivery to, the office of the under-sheriff or officer charged with the execution: r. 12.19 of the Rules. Note however r. 12.19(3) deems such notice to be given where the officer in charge of the execution is the Registrar of the court in which the insolvency proceedings are taking place.
[11] s.346(2) of the Act.
[12] So fixed by the Insolvency Proceedings (Monetary Limits) Order 1986, (S.I. 1986, No. 1996).
[13] s.346(3) of the Act.
[14] *ibid.*, s.346(4)(a).
[15] *ibid.*, s.346(4)(b).

occasionally succeeded,[16] it is clear that the courts are inclined to use it but sparingly, and it will only be in the most exceptional circumstances that they will disturb the operation of the normal principles applicable to both bankruptcy and liquidation.

The provisions of the statutory predecessors of section 346 have undergone a strict interpretation by the courts with consequences which in a variety of situations may seem regrettably arbitrary, but which are inevitable given the fundamental nature of the bankruptcy order and its necessarily far-reaching, and instantaneous, effects. Thus, the chance that the sheriff or bailiff by whom execution is levied may not receive timely notice of a bankruptcy order or of the presentation of a petition may enable the creditor to retain the benefit of an execution which was incomplete at the date of the order.[17] Conversely, any mishap which impedes the actual payment or delivery of money or property to the creditor or his agent until after the date of the bankruptcy order or until the requisite notice has been received will have the effect of depriving the creditor of the benefit of an execution which he would otherwise have completed in time.[18]

Section 346(7) safeguards the position of the person who purchases the goods at the sheriff's sale, so that any person who purchases the goods in good faith from the sheriff acquires a title good against the trustee in bankruptcy. Nevertheless, as far as the execution creditor is concerned a provision safeguarding the position of innocent third parties may not in every case furnish an answer to the basic provision of section 346(1) to the effect that the creditor who has issued execution before the commencement of bankruptcy is not entitled to retain the *benefit* of an incompleted execution as against the trustee. Essentially, the purport of section 346(1) is that the mere fact that a creditor may have commenced the process of attachment or execution against the bankrupt before the commencement of the latter's bankruptcy does not make the creditor a "secured" creditor if he was not one already.[19]

Dispositions or Payments Approved by the Court. Protected Transactions

Any disposition or payment made by the bankrupt beginning with the day of the presentation of the petition and ending with the vesting of his estate in the trustee in bankruptcy is void except to the extent that it either takes place with the consent of the court, or is subsequently ratified by the court.[20] A disposition is void by virtue of this rule notwithstanding that the

---

[16] See *Re Grosvenor Metal Co. Ltd* [1950] Ch. 63; *Re Suidair International Airways Ltd* [1951] Ch. 165; *cf. Re Redman (Builders) Ltd* [1964] 1 All E.R. 851; *Re Caribbean Products (Yam Importers) Ltd* [1966] 1 Ch. 331, overruling on another point *Re Rainbow Tours Ltd* [1964] Ch. 66, in which, however Buckley J. indicated that he would *not* have exercised his discretion in the creditor's favour, if he had felt it necessary to consider the application of s.325(1)(c) of the Companies Act 1948 (then the equivalent of the present s.346(6) of the Insolvency Act 1986).

[17] *Re Love* [1952] Ch. 138.

[18] See *George v. Thompson's Trustee* [1949] Ch. 322 for an exasperating illustration; *cf.* also *Re Lupkovics* [1954] 1 W.L.R. 1234.

[19] *Re Dickinson,* above n. 9.

[20] s.284(1), (2) (3) of the Act.

property is not, or would not be, comprised in the bankrupt's estate, although this extension does not apply to any disposition made by a person of property he holds on trust for another.[21]

The general rule therefore is that payments or dispositions made by the bankrupt during this "suspect period" will only be lost from the estate which vests in the trustee in bankruptcy if the court actively approves this result. There are however a limited number of exceptions to the rule that such dispositions are basically void. These are maintained by section 284(4), which has the effect of conferring protection upon two types of transaction.

The first type of protected transaction is where a person has received any property or payment from the debtor before the commencement of bankruptcy, and has done so in good faith, for value and without notice that the petition had been presented.[22] This is a long-established species of protection whose ultimate justification is the need to avert the disastrous consequences if parties could no longer safely deal with a person, even honestly and for value, if there was even a possibility that a bankruptcy petition had been, or was soon to be, presented concerning him.[23] Provided that the other party can establish that he lacked notice of the presentation of the petition, and that he dealt in good faith and for value, the transaction will receive statutory protection although it may be noted that the value received by the bankrupt will generally become available for creditors as part of his estate.

Consideration

The consideration in question must both be fully legal[24] and also, apparently, possess the character of "commerciality" in order to merit the protection sought.[25] The transaction itself must also be fully legal and respectable. Thus in *Ward v. Fry*[26] it was held that money paid by a bankrupt in settlement of a debt incurred through betting could not constitute a "contract, dealing or transaction" within the meaning of the then-current legislation, because the alleged liability, being founded upon a wagering contract, was null and void. On the other hand, in *Re Keever*[27] it was held that the lien which is created in favour of a bank when a customer hands over a cheque for collection did constitute a "contract, dealing or transaction" attracting statutory protection. In the case of an assignment by the bankrupt, even an equitable assignment is capable of enjoying protection provided it is made for valuable consideration.[28] If the amount

---

[21] *ibid.*, s.284(6).
[22] *ibid.*, s.284(4)(a).
[23] See *e.g.*, *Shears v. Goddard* [1896] 1 Q.B. 406; *Allen v. Bonnett* (1870) 5 Ch.App. 577; *Re Seymour* [1937] 1 Ch. 668; *Re Jukes* [1902] 2 K.B. 58 (decided under the equivalent provisions of former Bankruptcy Acts).
[24] *cf. Re Campbell* (1884) 14 Q.B.D. 32.
[25] See *e.g.*, *Sturmey's Trustee v. Sturmey* (1913) 107 L.T. 718; *Re Wethered, ex p. Salaman* [1926] Ch. 127; *Re Seaman* [1896] 1 Q.B. 412.
[26] (1901) 85 L.T. 394.
[27] [1967] Ch. 182 *cf. National Westminster Bank Ltd v. Halesowen Presswork & Assemblies Ltd* [1972] A.C. 785.
[28] *Re Gunsbourg* (1919) 88 L.J.K.B. 479.

of the consideration furnished by the party dealing with the bankrupt is disproportionately low the protection enjoyed for the purposes of section 284 will be of no avail if the transaction is challenged by the trustee under some other section of the Act, for example as a transaction at an undervalue.[29]

The second type of protected transaction is where a person obtains an interest in property from someone whose interest is already protected by virtue of section 284(4)(a) of the Act.[30] Such persons do not need to fulfil any further conditions in order to enjoy this derivative protection, and hence it is immaterial whether such third parties have dealt in good faith, for value, and without notice of the petition.

Payments Designed to Avert Bankruptcy

Where a bankrupt has paid money as part of a transaction intended to avert his adjudication the payment will in many cases be unprotected if bankruptcy is not averted, because the other party will frequently fail to fulfil all of the conditions imposed by section 284(4) when he receives the payment. Thus, in *Re Chapman, ex parte Edwardes*[31] it was held that sums of money received from the bankrupt by the petitioning creditor's solicitor as consideration for successive adjournments of the hearing of the petition were not protected transactions because the solicitor, acting as agent for the petitioning creditor, received the money with notice and so must refund all the money to the trustee. This creates a problem for any person who is called upon to act as a legal agent on behalf of a client whom he knows to be on the verge of bankruptcy. If it were the case that any legal fees paid by a debtor against whom a bankruptcy petition has been presented would be reclaimable by the trustee if bankruptcy should ensue, it can hardly be supposed that anyone in such circumstances would find it easy to obtain much-needed legal advice and assistance. Therefore, in deference to the requirements of justice that persons must not be left defenceless before the law,[32] an exception has been admitted in favour of those acting on behalf of a debtor in proceedings taken to avoid bankruptcy. Albeit they have actual knowledge that a bankruptcy petition has been presented against their client they are permitted to retain money paid to defray fees and legal expenses for services actually rendered up to the bankruptcy order.[33] This exception is strictly limited however, and a solicitor will not be permitted, for example, to retain money paid to him after the bankruptcy order for the costs of an appeal against that order.[34] If a solicitor receives money from a debtor in respect of both past and future

---

[29] s.339 of the Act, *supra*, p. 221.
[30] *ibid.*, s.284(4)(b).
[31] (1884) 13 Q.B.D. 747.
[32] *cf. Re Sinclair* (1885) 15 Q.B.D. 616, 618, *per* Cave J.
[33] *Re Charlewood* [1894] 1 Q.B. 643; *Re Mander* (1902) 86 L.T. 234; *Re Johnson* (1914) 111 L.T. 165 (These cases, decided well before 1986, refer to now-obsolete elements of the former law, namely acts of bankruptcy and receiving orders).
[34] *cf. Re A Debtor (No. 490 of 1935)* [1937] Ch. 92.

Payments Designed to Avert Bankruptcy

services he will only be entitled to retain so much of the money as represents the costs he thereafter incurs in striving to avoid bankruptcy for his client. Nevertheless, services rendered after the time when this special protection has ended may be adopted and paid for by the trustee in bankruptcy at his discretion, where the services have clearly resulted in a benefit or profit to the bankrupt's estate.[35] The trustee will, however, exercise great circumspection in awarding reasonable compensation for services so rendered, and it must be understood that a legal or professional agent proceeds at his own risk beyond the point at which the protection of section 284 is withdrawn.[36]

Occasionally a recipient of money may be able to retain it, irrespective of the applicability of section 284, if it is possible to show that the money did not emanate from the bankrupt, and never formed part of his estate. Thus, if a third person has attempted to avert the bankruptcy by offering some of his own money to the petitioning creditor if he will withdraw the petition, the creditor should be able to retain the money if adjudication later follows.[37]

---

[35] *Re Simonson* [1894] 1 Q.B. 433; *Re Geen* [1917] 1 K.B. 183; *Re British Folding Bed Co.* [1948] Ch. 635.
[36] cf. *Re Zakon* [1940] Ch. 253.
[37] *Re Drucker (No. 1)* [1902] 2 K.B. 55; *Barclays Bank Ltd v. Quistclose Investments Ltd* [1970] A.C. 567.

Chapter 9

PROOF OF DEBTS

Preliminary

Once he has performed the first two stages of his statutory function to get in and realise the bankrupt's estate the trustee in bankruptcy's third function is to distribute it in the form of dividends among the creditors who have proved their debts.[1] For the purposes of distribution the creditors are subdivided into different classes according to the nature of their claims against the bankrupt's estate, and in the distribution of that estate by way of dividends an order of priority is established which the trustee is obliged to follow, such that all the creditors within a class enjoying higher priority must be paid in full before any dividend can be distributed to creditors in a class of relatively lower ranking.[2] The details of the relevant provisions governing priority of distribution will be explained in Chapter 10, but for present purposes it will be apparent that the creditor's act of proving for a debt due from the bankrupt's estate has in fact a dual significance in that it determines not only the amount of the liability in respect of which his entitlement to dividend will be calculated, but also the relative ranking of his claim in the various classes which are destined to be repaid in serial fashion. Since in a case of true insolvency it is impossible for all creditors to be paid in full the question of priorities is one of great significance to all creditors. Furthermore, as was already seen in Chapter 7, a creditor's proof of debt has the additional effect of determining the amount of debt in respect of which he is qualified to vote at any meeting of creditors, and the relative weight of that vote when cast.[3]

The notion of "proof" of a debt in bankruptcy is a technical one involving for the creditor a two-fold task. First, he must establish that the debtor is truly and justly indebted to him, and secondly he must show what is the nature and character of that liability. The second aspect is of importance not merely because of the rules concerning priority of entitlement, but also because it must be shown, as a *sine qua non*, that the

---

[1] Insolvency Act 1986, ss.305(2), 324(1).
[2] *ibid.*, ss.328, 329.
[3] See Chap. 7 *ante*: creditors' meetings.

debt properly belongs within the overall statutory definition of "provable" debts, namely those claims which are subsumed under the bankruptcy process so that, when in due course the bankrupt's discharge becomes effective, all liabilities arising from those claims will be released irrespective of whether the creditors in question have received any degree of payment in the form of dividend, and irrespective also of whether they have succeeded in lodging proof during the currency of the bankruptcy.[4] This principle applies whether the creditor's failure consists of an omission to lodge any proof at all within the time available, or is the result of his proof having been ruled inadmissible, albeit the debt in question was by nature a *provable* one. In either event, the creditor will have lost all possibility of recovering his debt by legal proceedings in the event of the debtor's eventual discharge from bankruptcy.[5] Only if the debt is *not* a provable debt in the bankruptcy may the creditor still have recourse to such remedies against the debtor as may ordinarily be available, but this is subject as we have seen to the overriding power of the bankruptcy court, during the currency of the bankruptcy itself, to stay any action, execution or other legal process against the property or person of the bankrupt.[6]

In the present chapter we shall consider which debts are provable and which are not, and how the creditor is to make his proof.

(A) Which Debts may be Proved?

"Provable" and "Non-Provable" Debts

Section 322(1) of the Act makes provision for secured or unsecured creditors of the bankrupt to lodge "proof of any bankruptcy debt," and indicates that this process, and the admission or rejection of any proof, is to be governed by the Rules. The outermost limits of the concept of the "provable debt" are thus determined by the statutory meaning of the expression "bankruptcy debt," which is supplied by section 382. This provides, in subsection (1), that the expression means:

(1) Any debt or liability to which the bankrupt is subject at the commencement of bankruptcy (which, as we have seen, means the date of the bankruptcy order[7]);

(2) Any debt or liability to which the bankrupt may become subject after the commencement of the bankruptcy (including after his discharge from bankruptcy) by reason of any obligation incurred before the commencement of the bankruptcy;

[(3) Any amount inserted in a criminal bankruptcy order made

---

[4] See s.281 of the Act, and generally Chap. 11, *post.*
[5] See *e.g. Victor v. Victor* [1912] 1 K.B. 247 (C.A.).
[6] s.285(1), (3) of the Act. See Chap. 7, *ante*, p. 147.
[7] *ibid.*, s.278(a). The meaning of the term "liability" is supplied by s.382(4), which indicates that the essential concept is that of "a liability to pay money or money's worth."

against the debtor before the commencement of the bankruptcy[8];] and
(4) Any interest claimable in respect of the debt for any period prior to the commencement of bankruptcy.[9]

It is further provided by section 382(3) that for the purposes of any references to a debt or liability within those Parts of the Insolvency Act which are concerned with personal insolvency it is immaterial whether the debt or liability is present or future, whether it is certain or contingent or whether its amount is fixed or liquidated, or is capable of being ascertained by fixed rules or as a matter of opinion.

Insofar as they furnish an element of the concept of "provable debt" for the purposes of section 322, the broad terms in which the expression "bankruptcy debt" is defined in section 382 are susceptible to some attenuation by reason of any provisions within the Insolvency Rules, to which section 322(1) expressly refers. Rule 12.3, which applies both to bankruptcy and winding up, bears the heading "provable debts," and opens with an affirmative statement similar, but not identical, to the provision in section 382(3) of the Act, to the effect that:

"all claims by creditors are provable as debts ... whether they are present or future, certain or contingent, ascertained or sounding only in damages."

This expression of principle is subject to the further provisions within rule 12.3 itself, however, paragraph (2) of which (as amended) specifies that the following debts are not provable in bankruptcy:

(1) Any fine imposed for an offence,[10] and any obligation made under an order made in family proceedings or under a maintenance assessment made under the Child Support Act 1991[11]; and
(2) Any obligation arising under a confiscation order made under section 1 of the Drug Trafficking Offences Act 1986 or section 1 of the Criminal Justice (Scotland) Act 1987 or section 71 of the Criminal Justice Act 1988.

---

[8] *ibid.*, s.382(1)(c) (repealed); for the now-repealed provisions concerning criminal bankruptcy, see Chap. 13 *post*.
[9] *ibid.*, ss.322(2), 382(1)(d). For interest, see *infra*.
[10] This reverses the previous law, as determined in *Re Pascoe (No. 2)* [1944] Ch. 310; see also *Re Savundra* [1973] 3 All E.R. 406. The reform was recommended by the *Cork Report*: Cmnd. 8558, paras. 1319–1330.
[11] The meanings of the terms "fine," and "family proceedings" are supplied by s.281(8) of the Act, which incorporates by reference the meanings ascribed to those terms under the Magistrates Courts Act 1980 and the Matrimonial and Family Proceedings Act 1984. Note the critical observations regarding the non-provable nature of these kinds of debts under r. 12.3(2)(a) made by Balcombe L.J. in *Woodley v. Woodley (No. 2)* [1993] 4 All E.R. 1010, at p. 1021 (C.A.).

Proof of Debts

By rule 12.3(2A) a further group of debts are declared to be not provable in bankruptcy except at a time when all other claims of other kinds of creditors in the insolvency proceedings have been paid in full, with allowable interest. These are:

(1) Any claim arising by virtue of section 6(3)(a) or section 61(3)(a) of the Financial Services Act 1986, whereby persons may be ordered to repay profits resulting from the carrying on of an investment business in contravention of section 3 of that Act, or resulting from contravention of any provision mentioned in section (1)(a) of that Act[12]; and

(2) Any claim arising by virtue of section 49 of the Banking Act 1987, whereby the court may order repayment of profits arising from the acceptance of unauthorised deposits, within the meaning of that Act.

Finally, rule 12.3(3) is so expressed as to preserve the validity of any independently established rule of law or enactment under which a particular kind of debt is not provable, whether on grounds of public policy or otherwise. This sweeping, if un-specific, provision has the effect of excluding from the category of provable debts any debt or liability, established or alleged, which lacks the essential characteristic of being legally enforceable against the bankrupt as at the date of commencement of bankruptcy. This point was considered earlier in relation to the suitability of various types of debt to serve as a petitioning creditor's debt,[13] and it will suffice here to observe that no claim which could not have been validly enforced against the debtor outside of bankruptcy can be enforced through the bankruptcy process either. Accordingly, any debt which is for some reason unenforceable is inadmissible to proof.[14] It is important to remember that the criteria which determine whether a debt is provable in bankruptcy are not in every respect identical to those which determine whether a debt may be used as a petitioning creditor's debt in order to initiate bankruptcy proceedings. Thus, although the attribute of enforceability is a common requirement in both instances, the other technical and exacting requirements which together comprise the legal test of what constitutes a good petitioning creditor's debt are exclusively applied for that purpose, and it can hence be the case that a creditor whose debt could not serve as the basis of a bankruptcy petition may nevertheless prove for it if his debtor is made bankrupt on the petition of some properly qualified creditor.

---

[12] If the claim also arises under either s.6(3)(b) or 61(3)(b) of the Financial Services Act 1986 (namely because one or more investors have suffered loss as a result of the contravention), the exclusionary rule of the Insolvency Rules, r. 12.3(2A)(a) does not apply.

[13] Chap. 6, *ante*, p. 101.

[14] *Re Benzon* [1914] 2 Ch. 68; *Cotterell v. Price* [1960] 3 All E.R. 315 (limitation-barred debts; see *infra* however for possible rights of set-off in such cases); *Re Campbell* [1911] 2 K.B. 992 (dealings with unregistered moneylender); *Macdonald v. Green* [1951] 1 K.B. 594 (debt void under the Gaming Acts).

Which Debts may be Proved?

The trustee has power to go behind any apparently final judgment in favour of the creditor, and to reject a proof where he discovers the consideration for it to be inadequate.[15] Even where the bankrupt's sworn statement of affairs, prepared for use in his own bankruptcy, contains an admission of a debt for which proof is lodged, the creditor's claim is still capable of being questioned and, if found incorrect, may be rejected.[16] As always, the trustee and all bona fide creditors must be alert to detect any sham debts alleged to be due to persons who in reality are "accomplices" of the bankrupt as part of a subterfuge designed to rescue some of his assets. An illustration of the trustee's extensive powers of control in this type of situation may be drawn from the case of *Re Lupkovics*,[17] where a wife had recovered judgment against her husband for repayment of money advanced to him, and had sought to attach sums of money due to him. It was shown that the loans had in reality been made for the purpose of the husband's medical practice, and hence the wife's debt must be postponed to the claims of the other creditors.[18] Similarly, the case of *Re Myers*[19] demonstrates how a sham transaction conducted between the debtor and a confederate on the eve of the debtor's bankruptcy may be rendered void, and the property reclaimed by the trustees, whilst the confederate will pay the penalty for being party to a scheme devised in fraud of the general body of creditors by being left to sustain without redress any disadvantageous effects of his conduct, such as the loss of any money he may have paid in performing his part of the scheme.

Certain limits do operate to restrict the trustee's power to investigate claims lodged in the bankruptcy. Where a proof was initially admitted, and fresh funds have become available many years later, the court may decline to sanction the trustee's subsequently formed desire to scrutinise the debt (although it is technically still possible for it do so) if there are no circumstances sufficient to arouse suspicion. This disinclination to reopen matters already dealt with previously will be particularly pronounced when the material events took place many years prior to the date at which they are challenged by the trustee. The court may accordingly invoke the maxim *omnia praesumuntur rite et solemniter esse acta* and presume that a proof was initially properly admitted, so that it ought not to be expunged at a much later date.[20] But where the creditor has omitted for many years to lodge proof for his debt, and especially where he does not do so until after the bankrupt's death, the court will be highly suspicious of proofs which are lodged for the first time only after some new funds have become available to the bankrupt's estate. In such circumstances even a previous judgment of the High Court in favour of the proving creditor may be held

---

[15] *Re Van Laun* [1907] 2 K.B. 23; *cf. Re Home and Colonial Insurance Co.* [1930] 1 Ch. 102 (office holder's liability for misfeasance in not investigating the basis of an improperly admitted claim).

[16] *Re Tollemache, ex p. Revell* (1884) 13 Q.B.D. 720 (C.A.); *Re Browne* [1960] 2 All E.R. 625. See also *Re Tollemache, ex p. Edwards* (1884) 14 Q.B.D. 415 (C.A.).

[17] [1954] 1 W.L.R. 1234.

[18] See *post*, Chap. 10, p. 296 for an account of postponed debts.

[19] [1908] 1 K.B. 941.

[20] *Re Browne, above*, n. 16.

to be inadequate to support his proof, if it is too late to investigate the propriety of the judgment.[21]

It is also the case that where a previous action between the debtor and the creditor has been compromised, the resulting debt may not be reopened for scrutiny as to whether the action might have been successful if fought out to a finish.[22] Furthermore, the trustee cannot go behind a proof for assessed taxes lodged by the Inland Revenue,[23] although it is possible for the debtor to apply to the Inland Revenue if he disputes any assessment.

Foreign Tax Liabilities

Other principles of law whose operation is maintained by virtue of rule 12.3(3) include that whereby tax debts which are owed to any foreign state—including independent states of the Commonwealth—are not enforceable in the courts of England and Wales, and so are not provable in bankruptcy here.[24]

Mere Procedural Incapacity under Foreign Law

On the other hand, where a debt is based upon a contract validly made abroad and governed by the provisions of some foreign law, a provision by that law to the effect that the contract is to be unenforceable against creditors will not necessarily be fatal to the claim of any creditor who proves in a bankruptcy which is being administered in this country. This is because matters of procedure—such as questions involving the right to bring an action to enforce a claim which in itself is perfectly valid—are governed exclusively by the law of the place where the proceedings take place. Therefore, a procedural disability inflicted by a foreign law need not prevent enforcement at English law of a claim which is otherwise good, provided that the creditor possesses the capacity to enforce his claim according to the rules of English law.[25]

Barristers' Fees

Another rule of public policy whose effect is preserved by rule 12.3(3)

---

[21] *Re Tollemache, ex p. Revell*, above, n. 16; *Re Bonham* (1885) 14 Q.B.D. 604; *Re Tollemache, ex p. Anderson* (1885) 14 Q.B.D. 606 (C.A.).

[22] *Re Cole* [1931] 2 Ch. 174; *Re Gregory (No. 1)* [1935] Ch. 65. See also *ante*, Chap. 6, p. 134.

[23] *Re Calvert* [1899] 2 Q.B. 145. The observation of Wright J. in that case, that tax assessments differ from ordinary judgments in that there is not scope for fraud on creditors, may be correct as is stands, but it is respectfully submitted that injustice can nevertheless be inflicted upon the other creditors by an incorrect assessment, and so scrutiny should be possible. *See* the Blagden Report, Cmnd. 221, 1957, paras. 86–93.

[24] *Government of India v. Taylor* [1955] A.C. 491 (H.L.). *Cf. Peter Buchanan Ltd v. McVey.* [1955] A.C. 516n.; [1954] I.R. 89. Contrast *Re Ayres* (1981) 51 F.L.R. 395 and (1981) 56 F.L.R. 235, (1981) 39 A.L.R. 129; *Priestley v. Clegg* (1985) (3) S.A., 955.

[25] *Re Melbourn* (1870) L.R. 6 Ch.App. 64. *Note* however that statutes of limitation are now classified as matters of substantive law, rather than as matters of procedure. Hence, any claim which has become time-barred under the provisions of the applicable foreign law will also be inadmissible to proof in bankruptcy in England: see Foreign Limitation Periods Act 1984, s.1. See also *post*, Chap. 29.

Which Debts may be Proved?

concerns the non-recoverability of barristers' fees. The House of Lords, in its decision in *Rondel v. Worsley*,[26] confirmed the traditionally held principle that a barrister's fee for his work done on behalf of a litigant is payable to him by way of an honorarium, and not as a remuneration recoverable if necessary by action at law.[27] This decision implicitly reinforces the established rule in bankruptcy that a barrister cannot prove in the bankruptcy of a solicitor for fees due to him, even though the solicitor has received payment from the client by falsely representing to him that he had paid counsel's fee.[28] Various possibilities exist, however, whereby a barrister may succeed in retrieving his fee. First, the client who has paid the solicitor may prove in the latter's bankruptcy for repayment of the money he handed over in respect of counsel's fee, and may then pass on the proceeds directly to counsel, to whom they were intended to be transmitted.[29] Secondly, the trustee in bankruptcy, as an officer of the court, may be directed to pay to counsel the fees which he holds as part of the bankrupt solicitor's estate, despite the fact that counsel personally has no legal right to demand such payment. This solution rests on the basis of a rule formulated in *ex parte James*,[30] to the effect that the court and its officers ought to display exemplary honesty so that if money in the trustee's hands equitably belongs to someone else it should be handed over to that person. With respect, the same might be said of many debts due from the bankrupt to his creditors, and there seems to be no specially compelling reason why counsel should be favourably regarded and thus permitted to recover his fees in its totality, rather than by way of dividend. It is submitted that it would be a fairer solution to allow counsel to prove for fees, even though this might be thought to compromise a time-honoured tradition.[31] It should be understood that in any event counsel nowadays may always take steps, in the last resort, to avail himself of the arrangement whereby the Council of the Law Society, administering the Law Society Compensation Fund, may in its discretion make payment to counsel in respect of fees which a defaulting solicitor has received from a client but failed to pass on to him. As a sort of *quid pro quo* in return for this extra-legal safeguard, the Bar Council has issued a rule declaring that it is contrary to etiquette for counsel to seek to prove for fees in a solicitor's bankruptcy.[32]

The Rule against Double Proof

It is a well-settled rule that there cannot be two proofs against the same

---

[26] [1969] 1 A.C. 191 (H.L.).
[27] See, *e.g. Wells v. Wells* [1914] P. 157.
[28] *Re Sandiford (No. 2)* [1935] Ch. 681.
[29] Suggested in *Re Sandiford, supra*, at p. 692, *per* Clauson J.
[30] *Re Condon, ex p. James* (1874) 9 Ch.App. 609: see Chap. 8, *ante*, p. 207.
[31] In *Rondel v. Worsley, supra*, n. 26, the House of Lords declared that a barrister's immunity from liability for negligence in the conduct of a case in court did not rest upon the fact that he is unable to sue for his fees, but was established by reason of general public policy. It should follow therefore that the introduction of the possibility of proving for his fees would make no difference to the vital question of his legal liability for professional activities, and it is difficult to see what other valid objections could be raised in opposition to the change proposed in the text.
[32] Annual Statement, 1956, p. 31; Annual Statement 1958, p. 28.

estate in respect of one and the same debt, despite the fact that there may be separate contracts, each of which provides for payment of the debt.[33] This situation may arise, for example, where there has been a mortgage of an insurance policy coupled with a covenant by the mortgagor to continue to pay the premiums. Such a case was *Deering v. Bank of Ireland*,[34] where it was held that in the event of the mortgagor's bankruptcy the mortgagee could not prove both for the value of the covenant to pay premiums and also for the difference between the surrender value of the policy and the debt secured by the mortgage thereof. Another example of the operation of the rule concerns the position of sureties who, as we shall see,[35] usually have the right to prove in the bankruptcy of the principal debtor in respect of their contingent liability to satisfy the debt. However, where the creditor has already proved in the bankruptcy of the principal debtor, the surety's own liability is thereafter limited to the amount for which the creditor's proof has been admitted, less the value of any dividends that may have been paid to him, and accordingly the surety's proof may only be submitted in respect of the extent of his net remaining liability.[36]

Where there are distinct contracts upon which the debtor is liable, and in the case of one his liability is of an individual nature whilst the other is based on his membership of a firm, or where dual liability is derived from membership of two or more distinct firms, the rule against double proof does not operate and so there may be proof in respect of both contracts, although it may be that distinct funds may be required to bear the different claims. But where a partner misappropriates funds belonging to the firm there cannot be such double proof against both his personal estate and that of the firm, unless there is a distinct contract out of which personal liability arises, additional to the collective liability of the firm for the default of its members.[37] If there is no such distinct contract, the creditor must elect to prove against one estate only.[38]

Tort Claims as Provable Debts

Under the pre-1986 insolvency law the category of provable debts included claims arising either in contract or in tort, but with one important distinction. Whereas contractual claims were always provable, even if of a contingent or unliquidated nature, claims whose basis lay in the realm of tort were only provable provided that they had become liquidated—either through signing of judgment or through the conclusion of a binding settlement between the parties—before the date of commencement of bankruptcy.[39] Under certain circumstances, where a claim was capable of being based upon contract or tort, a creditor whose claim was unliquidated at the vital date could render the claim provable in bankruptcy through

---

[33] *Re Oriental Commercial Bank* (1871) 7 Ch.App. 99.
[34] (1886) 12 App.Cas. 20. (H.L.).
[35] See *Infra.* p. 267.
[36] *Re Lennard* [1934] Ch. 325.
[37] *Re Parkers* (1887) 19 Q.B.D. 84.
[38] *Re Kent County Gas, Light and Coke Co.* [1913] 1 Ch. 92.
[39] Bankruptcy Act 1914, s.30(1) (repealed).

exercise of the doctrine of election known as "waiver of tort."[40] In other respects however the effects of this special exclusionary rule were arbitrary and capricious, and became the object of criticism.[41] The reversal of the rule was recommended by the *Cork Report*,[42] and was duly implemented through the provisions of section 382 of the Act. The broad language of section 382(3), referred to above,[43] makes no distinction as to the legal basis on which a claim or liability is founded, and it is expressly declared to be immaterial

> "whether its amount is fixed or liquidated, or is capable of being ascertained by fixed rules or as a matter of opinion."

Further assistance is provided by section 382(2), which states that for the purpose of determining whether any liability in tort is a bankruptcy debt, the bankrupt is deemed to become subject to that liability by reason of an obligation incurred at the time when the cause of action accrued. Thus, provided that the cause of action had not become time-barred before the date of the bankruptcy order, a claim in tort may constitute a provable debt even though the person injured may not have begun proceedings through service of a writ before the commencement of the tortfeasor's bankruptcy. Moreover, section 322(3) requires the trustee to estimate the value of any bankruptcy debt which is of uncertain value, so as to permit it to be dealt with for purposes of proof, and his decision in this, as in other matters respecting proof, is susceptible of appeal to the court.[44]

Other Kinds of Provable Debts

Given the necessary attribute of enforceability, the list of the kinds of debt which are provable in bankruptcy is a long one. In addition to claims based upon contract or tort, those based on fraud or upon breach of trust have traditionally been provable whether or not they are liquidated at the commencement of bankruptcy. Nor does the law discriminate between debts incurred for valuable consideration and those assumed voluntarily. For example, claims based upon a deed of covenant entered into by the bankrupt may be admitted to proof along with claims lodged by the general body of creditors for value.[45]

---

[40] *cf. Re Great Orme Tramways* (1934) 50 T.L.R. 450; *Watson v. Holliday* (1882) 20 Ch.D. 780; *Matthews v. Kuwait Bechtel Corp.* [1959] 2 Q.B. 57 (not a bankruptcy case). Contrast *Parker v. Norton* (1796) 6 T.R. 695; 101 E.R. 777, where the creditor elected to frame the action in tort, in the hope that the tortfeasor would one day regain a solvent position.
[41] *cf.* Fletcher, *Law of Bankruptcy* (1978) at p. 390. See also *Re Berkeley Securities (Property) Ltd* [1980] 3 All E.R. 513; [1980] 1 W.L.R. 1589.
[42] Cmnd. 8558, paras. 1310–1318.
[43] *Above*, p. 251.
[44] r. 6.105 of the Rules.
[45] *Re Stewart* (1878) 8 Ch.D. 621. However, such transactions are especially susceptible to impeachment by the trustee under ss.339 and 340: see Chap. 8, *ante*, p. 251.

Calls on Shares

Where shares are not fully paid up as issued, their holder may be later called upon, either by the company or by its liquidator in a winding up, to contribute all or part of the unpaid balance outstanding in respect of the shares. If the shareholder has become bankrupt, proof may be lodged by or on behalf of the company for the estimated value of his liability in respect of future calls on the shares which he holds.[46] A company's articles of association usually provide for the forfeiture of shares in the event of non-payment of calls made upon the shareholder, and it may be further provided that the ex-shareholder shall still remain liable to pay all calls or other money owing upon the shares at the time of forfeiture. It has been held however that where a company has caused a shareholder to forfeit his shares, and has then re-allocated them to another person at a loss, the company may only prove in the bankruptcy of the ex-shareholder to the extent of the actual loss suffered, and that notwithstanding the provision in the articles any payment by the new allottee has the effect of reducing *pro tanto* the damages for which the ex-shareholder remains liable.[47]

Foreign Currency Debts[48]

A special problem arises whenever a creditor seeks to prove for a debt which, though claimed in this country, is expressed in terms of some foreign currency. In an English bankruptcy, proof for such a debt can only be entertained after it has been converted and expressed in terms of its equivalent value in sterling, but in view of the fact that currencies undergo fluctuations in their relative values, the exact moment to be selected for the purpose of calculating the sterling equivalent of the debt is of no little importance. The governing principle which was formerly employed by English law was the so-called "breach-date" rule, whereby the relevant moment in time, for the purpose of conversion from one currency into another, was taken to be the moment at which the debtor committed the act which gave rise to the creditor's right of action in law. Thus, for ordinary cases of claims for damages based upon a breach of contract on the part of the debtor, the moment for conversion into sterling was held to be the date of the breach.[49] Secondly, in claims for specific things, including specific amounts of foreign currency owed by the debtor to the creditor—such as money deposited with a bank, or the price of goods sold and delivered—the date for calculating the sterling equivalent was taken as being the date when payment was due to be made, either by the express terms of the agreement between the parties, or by virtue of the occurrence

---

[46] *Re McMahon* [1900] 1 Ch. 173.
[47] *Re Bolton* [1930] 2 Ch. 48.
[48] See also *post*, Chap. 29.
[49] *Re British American Continental Bank (Goldzieher and Penso's Claim)* [1922] 2 Ch. 575, applying *S.S. Celia v. S.S. Volturno* [1921] 2 A.C. 544 (H.L.). See also *Re British American Continental Bank (Lisser and Rosenkranz's Claim)*. [1923] 1 Ch. 276 for a particularly striking example of the significance which this principle can possess.

of some event which rendered payment due forthwith, such as the cessation of business and winding-up of a bank with which a customer's money had been deposited.[50] And thirdly, when a party's claim was based on a tort in consequence of which damages were payable in a foreign currency, the relevant date at which to ascertain the sterling equivalent of any sum of damages which might have been awarded was considered to be the date on which the injury was sustained.[51]

The validity of all three of the above rules was first put in question as a result of the decision of the House of Lords in *Miliangos v. George Frank (Textiles) Ltd.*,[52] although only in relation to one of the rules, namely the second as set out above, was the law expressly changed. In that case the majority of the House of Lords decided that in the case of "foreign money obligations," that is, obligations to pay foreign currency arising under a contract whose proper law is that of a foreign country, and where the money of account and payment is that of that country, or possibly of some other foreign country, the courts of this country may now award judgment expressed in terms of the foreign currency in question. As an alternative, the courts may award the sterling equivalent of the sum, to be converted at the date when the court authorises enforcement of the judgment in terms of sterling, which in the case of the lodging of proof in a bankruptcy or liquidation is to be taken as the date when the creditor's claim in terms of sterling is admitted by the trustee in bankruptcy or liquidator.[53] Their Lordships' decision was confined to the rule governing claims for specific things, such as specific foreign currency, and they expressly refrained from deciding what should be the rule regarding conversion in the two other situations, namely claims for breach of contract and claims based on tort. Moreover, the issue before the House of Lords on that occasion concerned the payment obligation of a solvent debtor.

In cases where the debtor's insolvency has supervened, the overriding principle of equality of treatment of creditors necessarily requires that the rights of all claimants must be determined and quantified as at the same fixed date. In the case of company winding up,[54] it has been held that the appropriate date for this purpose is the date of the winding up order, which is the date as at which all creditors' claims have to be quantified. It is respectfully submitted that this analysis was correct in relation to winding up, and that the same rule is now appropriate for bankruptcy purposes, since the date of commencement of bankruptcy by virtue of section 278 of

---

[50] As in *Re Russian Commercial Bank* [1955] Ch. 148, another case disclosing a dramatic depreciation in the sterling value of a debt, from £100 to 10p.
[51] *S.S. Celia v. S.S. Volturno*, above.
[52] [1976] A.C. 443. *Cf. Schorsch Meier GmbH v. Hennin* [1975] Q.B. 416.
[53] See [1976] A.C. 443, 467–469, *per* Lord Wilberforce, and at pp. 497–498, *per* Lord Cross.
[54] *Re Dynamics Corporation of America* [1976] 1 W.L.R. 757 (*dicta* of Lords Wilberforce and Cross, *loc.cit. supra.*, n. 53, not followed by Oliver J.) (the report in [1976] 2 All E.R. 682 has a misprint): the date of the winding up order was held to be the appropriate date for conversion because in principle the date of conversion must be the same for all creditors. See also Law Com. 80, Foreign Money Liabilities, p. 89 *et seq.* See also *Kraut A.G. v. Albany Fabrics Ltd* [1977] Q.B. 112; *Federal Commerce and Navigation Co. Ltd v. Tradax Export S.A.* [1978] A.C. 1, H.L.; *The Despina R* [1979] A.C. 685, H.L.; *Re Lines Brothers Ltd* [1982] 2 All E.R. 183 (C.A.). And see Libling (1977) 93 L.Q.R. 212.

the Insolvency Act 1986, is the date of the bankruptcy order. That principle has been duly embodied in the provision in rule 6.111 of the Insolvency Rules, which states that for the purpose of proving a debt incurred or payable in a currency other than sterling, the amount of the debt must be converted into sterling at the official exchange rate prevailing on the date of the bankruptcy order.

The recent alteration, originating via commercial case law, of what had been a long-established rule of English law was clearly effected in the interests of ensuring justice for creditors in an age of rapidly fluctuating exchange rates. It will be of special advantage to creditors, of course, in cases where sterling undergoes depreciation as against the foreign currency in question during the period between the time when payment was originally due and the time when the creditor's proof is admitted. In the converse situation, where sterling undergoes appreciation against the currency in question, the result will nonetheless be just, because the foreign creditor will still receive what he has bargained for, namely a specific amount of a specified foreign currency, notwithstanding the fact that when payment is made it may cost the debtor (or his trustee) less in terms of sterling to purchase the necessary foreign currency than if payment had been made at the proper time. Indeed, it has long been accepted that in cases where a debt, expressed in foreign currency and also payable abroad, has actually been paid in accordance with these conditions, the debtor will have obtained a good discharge from his obligation despite the fact that, by paying later than the time agreed, he may have derived a material advantage from a movement of exchange rates working in his favour between the time payment was due and the time payment was actually made.[55]

Cheques and Bills of Exchange Generally

Liability on the Bill

The widespread use nowadays of cheques—which are a particular kind of bill of exchange—makes it important to consider the general legal principles which are applicable to bills of exchange in the law of bankruptcy.[56] In view of the great commercial convenience which is served by the use of negotiable instruments such as bills of exchange, it has been found to be commercially expedient to facilitate their ready acceptability by providing the most extensive practicable legal guarantees that a person to whom a bill of exchange is negotiated will receive full payment of the value written upon its face. It is therefore established that such a person, who is termed the holder of the bill, may have recourse for payment against any of the parties to it, that is to say the acceptor (who is primarily liable) and also the drawer and any indorser of the bill (who are taken to stand as

---

[55] *Société des Hotels le Touquet Paris-Plage v. Cummings* [1922] 1 K.B. 451 (still apparently good law.) *Cf.* also *W.J. Alan & Co. Ltd v. El Nasr Import and Export Co.* [1972] 2 All E.R. 127.

[56] See *Chalmers and Guest on Bills of Exchange* (14th ed., 1991) esp. Part III (*'Cheques on a Banker'*) for a full exposition of the law relating to this species of negotiable instrument.

sureties for the acceptor to guarantee payment).[57] To the extent that the holder remains unsatisfied after action against one of these parties to the bill he is entitled to proceed against the others in order to recover the balance of the debt. Accordingly, if any of the parties liable upon a bill of exchange should become bankrupt the holder may prove in the bankruptcy to the extent of the bankrupt's liability on the bill. If this liability has already become established in the course of events, or if it is the acceptor himself who is bankrupt, there may be proof for the sum due as for a simple debt. But if the bankrupt is the drawer or an indorser of the bill, and there is no evidence at the time of the bankruptcy that the acceptor has refused to pay, the bankrupt's liability remains a contingent one and must be proved for as such by the holder.[58]

If one of the parties liable upon a bill has paid part of the amount due on it the holder may be admitted to proof in the bankruptcy of any other party to the bill only to the extent of the balance still outstanding.[59] However, after receiving his dividend in the bankruptcy the holder may go on to take proceedings against any other parties to the bill, until he has received full satisfaction of the debt to him.[60] It must be remembered that whenever a bill of exchange is dishonoured by non-acceptance or by non-payment, notice of dishonour must be given to the drawer and each indorser in accordance with section 48 of the Bills of Exchange Act 1882, thus alerting them to the possibility of their being called upon to meet their obligations upon the bill. Section 49 of the same Act further provides that notice must be given by or on behalf of the holder, or by or on behalf of an indorser who is himself liable on the bill. Where the drawer or an indorser is bankrupt, section 49(10) further provides that notice may be given to the bankrupt party himself or to his trustee. Thus, where a holder or an indorser of a bill of exchange learns of the bankruptcy of a person to whom he is obliged, under the provisions of section 48, to give notice of dishonour, the holder or indorser in question should ensure that he does give such notice, either to the bankrupt personally or to his trustee, in order to preserve his rights as holder against the party in question.

If one of the parties to a bill has been made to fulfil his obligation as surety to the acceptor by paying the holder, the party so paying may in turn proceed against the person who is primarily liable, if necessary lodging proof in that person's bankruptcy. But in such cases proof can be lodged only to the extent of the payment actually made.[61] Furthermore, when a person becomes the holder of a bill by paying for it a sum well below its face value he may be taken to have notice of any fraud associated with the execution of the bill, and although he will still be allowed to prove in the bankruptcy of any party liable on it, he will be able to do so only for the amount he actually paid for the bill, and not for its full face value.[62]

---

[57] For a discussion of the general position of sureties in bankruptcy, see *infra* p. 267.
[58] The manner of proving for contingent liabilities is discussed *infra* p. 262.
[59] *Cooper v. Pepys* (1741) 1 Atk. 107; 26 E.R. 70; *Re Houghton* (1857) 1 De. G. & J. 302; 44 E.R. 740.
[60] *Re Gomersall* (1875) 1 Ch.D. 137; *Re Fothergill* (1876) 3 Ch.D. 445.
[61] *Re Fothergill*, above.
[62] *Re Gomersall*, above.

Where a Bill is used as Security

A bill of exchange is often given as security for payment of a debt independently incurred, and in such cases the bill must be treated as a security, and the person to whom it is given must be treated as a secured creditor, in the usual way.[63] The creditor will therefore lodge proof in relation to the debt itself, not in relation to the bill of exchange by which the debt is secured, and if he is still the holder of the bill the creditor must either value it as a security and prove for the balance of the debt after deduction of the assessed value of the bill, or else surrender the bill to the trustee and prove for the whole debt. A third course of action would be to seek to realise the security by presenting the bill for payment: the creditor would thereafter be admitted to proof only in respect of any balance of the debt which remains unsatisfied after he has had recourse for payment against all parties liable on the bill. In the same way, if the creditor has already negotiated the bill for value this is tantamount to the realisation of his security, and he is again obliged to deduct any amount thus realised from the amount of the original debt, and to lodge his proof for the outstanding balance only.[64]

Contingent Liabilities

General Features

If at the date of the bankruptcy order the debtor's liability to the creditor is dependent upon the happening of some event which may or may not occur, his liability is said to be a contingent one.[65] Always provided that it was incurred before the making of the order, such a liability is declared, by the terms of section 382(3) of the Act and by rule 12.3(1) of the Rules,[66] to be provable in the debtor's bankruptcy, although naturally an allowance has to be made for the fact that the contingency may not happen and thus the liability may never be incurred. Accordingly, section 322(3) directs the trustee to estimate the value of such a liability, and any person who is aggrieved by that estimate may appeal to the court by application under section 303(1). Where the value of a bankruptcy debt is estimated in this way by the trustee or by the court, the amount provable in the bankruptcy is the amount of the estimate, and the subsequent discharge of the bankrupt will release the entire liability unless the court is in a position to direct otherwise by virtue of the particular nature of the liability itself.[67] It is established in law that a contingent claim for unliquidated damages is a debt provable in bankruptcy.[68] But it is essential that the debtor's contingent liability should involve him in the payment of money or

---

[63] See *infra.* p. 281 and also Chap. 6, *ante*, p. 107.
[64] See rr. 6.115 to 6.119 of the Rules, *infra* p. 282.
[65] For judicial elucidation of the concept of "contingent liability," see *Re Sutherland* [1963] A.C. 235, 239, *per* Lord Reid, and p. 262, *per* Lord Guest.
[66] This and the accompanying provisions are noted *above*, p. 251.
[67] See ss.322(4) and 281(5). The latter section is considered in Chap. 10, *post*.
[68] *Ellis and Co's Trustee v. Dixon Johnson* [1924] 1 Ch. 342, 356–357, *per* P. O. Lawrence J.

money's worth if the liability is incurred[69]: if, in the event of its being incurred, his liability will be of another kind, such as a liability for specific performance[70] or for specific restitution, or if an injunction would be capable of being made against him, there can be no proof based upon such a non-pecuniary contingency.

The leading case of *Hardy v. Fothergill*[71] indicates the manner in which contingent liabilities are to be dealt with for the purposes of proof. In that case, lessees had assigned their lease for a term of years, subject to a covenant on the part of the assignee to indemnify the lessees in respect of any damages recovered against them by the lessor for breach of their obligation to keep the property in repair. The assignee became bankrupt at a time when there were still eight years of the term unexpired, and it was held by the House of Lords that the assignee's contingent liability to indemnify the lessees during the course of the remaining eight years was capable of estimation in financial terms, and so was provable.

The mode of entering proof in relation to a contingent liability is for the creditor's claim to be stated as on the day of the making of the bankruptcy order, and if by the time proof is lodged the contingency has already happened, the task of assessing the true value of the claim at the date of the bankruptcy order is a relatively straightforward one. Accordingly, the longer the trustee's delay in finally admitting a proof of this kind, the greater will be the likelihood that the need for him to engage in an estimation will be overtaken by events which cause the true extent of the liability to become ascertained. A particularly striking illustration of this is *Re Dodds*,[72] where the debtor had covenanted to pay an annuity of £1,440 per annum to B for her life. When the debtor became bankrupt B lodged proof for the actuarial value of her annuity calculated as at the date of the [bankruptcy] order, at which date she was aged 75. Before the trustee had fully admitted her proof however, B died, and this event had the effect of reducing the debtor's liability on the covenant from an assessed value, as a contingent liability, of £7,240 to the actual value of the instalments due to B at the date of her death, a mere £240.[73]

If a creditor fails to appreciate that the debt owed to him by a bankrupt, although in the form of a contingent liability, is nevertheless provable in the bankruptcy it is possible that he may omit to lodge proof at all.[74] The unfortunate consequence of such an omission will be that if the contingency later occurs, the creditor's right to enforce his claim by action will have been lost, whilst his prospects of recovering anything under the bankruptcy at such a late stage will almost certainly be small, and indeed, if the bankrupt has already obtained his discharge it will be too late for proof to be lodged at all.[75] An illustrative case is that of *Barnett v. King*[76] in which

---

[69] See s.382(4) of the Act, *above*, n. 7.
[70] As in *Re Reis* [1904] 2 K.B. 769 (covenant by the debtor to settle after-acquired property).
[71] (1888) 13 App.Cas. 351 (H.L.).
[72] (1890) 25 Q.B.D. 529.
[73] For the converse situation, *see Re Pannell* (1879) 11 Ch.D. 914, discussed *infra*.
[74] This was so in the case of *Hardy v. Fothergill, supra*.
[75] For the lodging of proof late in time, see *infra*, pp. 283 and 302.
[76] [1891] 1 Ch. 4.

a party, who had covenanted for payment of a sum of money out of his estate after his death, became bankrupt. The covenantee knew of the bankruptcy but did not lodge proof in respect of the sum to which he was entitled under the covenant. After the covenantor's death, the covenantee's claim against the executors of the estate was held to be barred on account of the supervening bankruptcy, in which he should have proved.

Annuities

As indicated above by the case of *Re Dodds*[77] a debtor's liability to pay an annuity under the terms of a covenant is a liability provable in his bankruptcy. The precise manner in which such a liability is to be calculated for the purposes of a proof was explained by Vaisey J. in *Re Rothermere*,[78] where R had covenanted to pay B an annuity for life of £62 net of tax, but died insolvent. The learned judge ruled that the capital value of B's annuity must be calculated actuarially, and by reference to the market price of "consols" at the date of R's death. The idea was that the capital value would be assessed by determining first what sum would, if invested in consols at that date, provide interest, less tax, with resort as necessary to capital, so as to produce the annual net sum of £62. The "investment" sum thus determined would be converted into a capitalised valuation by the application of actuarial principles to establish the annuitant's life expectation. Although it was held to be permissible to allow for variations in the rate of income tax which had occurred between R's death and the date of making the calculation, no allowance was to be made for possible future changes in the rate of tax. As in *Re Dodds* therefore, certain material events occurring between the bankruptcy (or death insolvent), of the covenantor and the date of valuation and admission of the annuitant's proof will be taken account of in the trustee's calculation. It should however be emphasised that, unless of course the annuitant himself dies before his proof is fully admitted,[79] the capitalised value of the annuity is to be fixed as at the date of the bankruptcy order, or of the death of the covenantor, as the case may be. In *Re Pannell*,[80] the process of valuation of a life annuity, which was payable to trustees for the benefit of the bankrupt's wife, had been completed, and her trustees had made their proof and received a dividend of £698. The wife then died, and it was shown that, but for the bankruptcy of the husband which had necessitated the capitalisation of her claim, the wife would have actually been entitled to receive a total of only £401 in ordinary payments under the covenant up to the date of her death. The Court of Appeal held, however, that although as events had turned out there might appear to have been an overpayment of £297 to her trustees on the basis of the assessed value of her entitlement under the covenant, her trustees were not obliged to repay this "excess," because the effect of the husband's

[77] See *above* n. 72.
[78] [1945] 1 Ch. 72.
[79] *See Re Dodds, supra,* p. 263 for explanation of the consequence of that event.
[80] See *supra,* n. 73.

bankruptcy was, in law, to cause the whole of the assessed amount of the annuity to become immediately payable to the wife. Once proof for a claim has been fully admitted by the trustee in bankruptcy,[81] and a dividend has been distributed, it is impossible under the present law to disturb such payments as have been made, even where such an "overpayment" has in fact occurred. It is submitted that such cases, rare though they may be, do constitute an unnecessary anomaly, for there would seem to be little which could be said in favour of allowing the estate of a deceased annuitant to retain this windfall at the expense of the general body of creditors. Since the precise sequence of events in such cases will effectively determine upon what basis payment is initially made to the annuitant, it would seem fair to introduce a proviso to the effect that the annuitant's estate should be liable to repay to the trustee in bankruptcy any amount which has been overpaid in this way. Indeed, in his judgment in *Re Pannell* itself, Cotton L.J. stated that he had suggested during argument that the surplus might be declared to be held by the settlement trustees on a resulting trust for the covenantor, but he declined to employ this notion in his decision, remarking "we cannot decide that point now."[82] With respect, it would seem that some such principle of restitution would be preferable to the present rule of law, for the capitalised value of an annuity could well constitute one of the most substantial debts admitted to proof, and be instrumental in minimising the net return to the creditors for value in respect of the debts owed to them.[83]

Periodical Payments and Payments under a Separation Agreement

Where a husband and wife have separated the wife is entitled, formerly at common law and now by statute, to be provided for by her husband. Under the current law it is possible for either spouse to claim maintenance from the other.[84] If, on separation, the spouses conclude an agreement whereby the husband undertakes to pay his wife an income, this contractual undertaking has the effect, so long as it subsists, of suspending the wife's right to maintenance, and operates as an annuity which can be capitalised and proved for, in the way described above, in the event of the husband's bankruptcy.[85] Any payments which are in arrears at the date of the husband's bankruptcy are also provable as a debt actually due.[86] Since

---

[81] It may be noted that in *Re Dodds* the annuitant's claim had *not* been fully admitted by the trustee at the time of her death; *see above*, p. 263.
[82] (1879) 11 Ch.D. 914, 917.
[83] If the annuitant dies after proof has been fully admitted, but before any dividend has been paid, it is suggested that the trustee could successfully apply to expunge the proof: see r. 6.107 of the Rules, and generally *infra* p. 286.
[84] See Domestic Proceedings and Magistrates' Courts Act 1978, Part I; Matrimonial Causes Act 1973, s.27. See also P. M. Bromley and N. V. Lowe, *Bromley's Family Law* (8th ed. 1992) Chaps. 20, 21; S. M. Cretney and J. M. Masson, *Principles of Family Law* (5th ed. 1990), Part V. For confirmation that a husband continues to be liable at common law to maintain his wife, see *London Borough of Hounslow v. Peake* [1974] 1 All E.R. 688, 691, *per* Lord Widgery, C.J.
[85] *Re Wood* (1874) 9 Ch. App. 670. See Bromley and Lowe, *op. cit.*, Chap. 20, p. 656 *et seq.*; Cretney and Masson, *op. cit.*, Chap 21.
[86] *Victor v. Victor* [1912] 1 K.B. 247; *Dewe v. Dewe* [1928] P. 113.

the husband's future liability under a separation deed is provable in his bankruptcy as a contingent liability, the deed will be discharged by the event of the bankruptcy with the consequence that his wife will forfeit her future entitlement as well as any arrears which may be due to her, unless she proves for the value of both debts. It has been held, however, that in view of the fact that a husband's bankruptcy effectively causes a separation deed to be discharged, the wife's legal entitlement to maintenance is *ipso facto* revived, and that she may first prove, and receive dividend, in respect of the deed, and thereafter bring action against her husband alleging his wilful neglect to maintain her.[87]

A wife who, at the date of her husband's bankruptcy, is in receipt of judicially-awarded financial provision[88] is in a very different position from one to whom an income or a lump sum is payable under a separation agreement, because any obligation arising under an order made in family proceedings or under a maintenance assessment is expressly excluded from the category of provable debts by rule 12.3(2)(a) of the Insolvency Rules. The financial provision in question may be in the form either of maintenance pending suit or of periodical payments or a lump sum awarded in matrimonial proceedings. In the case first of maintenance awarded to the wife pending suit, since it is possible for the courts to vary any order in respect of future payments, and also to decline to enforce payments which may be in arrears,[89] it has been held that this inadmissibility to proof applies equally to arrears of maintenance as well as to any prospective future entitlement.[90] Naturally, since this species of liability is not a provable one it continues to be enforceable against the husband notwithstanding his bankruptcy, and a committal order may be made against him for failure to maintain his wife.[91]

The case, secondly, of unsecured periodical payments awarded to a wife in divorce proceedings is somewhat analagous to maintenance in that the wife enjoys no absolute entitlement either to arrears or to future payments.[92] All questions of enforcement again rest with the competent courts in the exercise of their discretion and consequently neither arrears of periodical payments which have accrued due before the husband's bankruptcy,[93] nor any payments alleged to be due afterwards,[94] are provable in the bankruptcy of the husband. In view of this, once again, the wife remains at liberty, despite the bankruptcy, to bring enforcement proceedings against her husband. The remedy available to her is an application for a committal order[95] under section 5 of the Debtors Act 1869, or for a distress or committal order under section 76 of the

---

[87] *Dewe v. Dewe*, above. See now Matrimonial Causes Act 1973, s.27.
[88] This may be either under the Matrimonial Causes Act 1973 (see ss.21, 22, 23 and 27) or under the Domestic Proceedings and Magistrates' Courts Act 1978 (Part I).
[89] Matrimonial Causes Act 1973, ss.31, 32.
[90] *James v. James* [1964] P. 303. See, however, *infra* for further aspects of the law regarding committal.
[91] See *above*, n. 90.
[92] See *above*, n. 89.
[93] *Kerr v. Kerr* [1879] 2. Q.B. 439.
[94] *Linton v. Linton* (1885) 15 Q.B.D. 239.
[95] *Findlay v. Findlay* [1947] P. 122.

Magistrates' Courts Act 1980, as appropriate. It must be remembered however that the enforcement of arrears is a matter residing within the court's discretion, and also that the current trend is away from the committal of persons for non-payment of civil debts. Accordingly it is now open to a court, in proceedings for committal, to take the alternative action of making an attachment of earnings order against the husband, as is provided for by section 3(4) of the Attachment of Earnings Act 1971. Although the court retains its power to order committal in these cases it should be noted that the remedy of committal ceases to be practicable upon the death of the husband, and that the wife thereafter lacks any means of recovering payments which are in arrears, irrespective of whether the husband's estate is solvent or insolvent.[96] Naturally, this same deficiency is equally the case with an attachment of earnings order.

Where a husband has sought to frustrate his wife's efforts at recovering payment of sums due to her under an order made in matrimonial proceedings, and has concealed property in an effort to defeat the wife's claims, there is a real possibility of his being committed to prison by the court in response to a summons under section 5 of the Debtors Act 1869. The Court of Appeal have held that, in principle, such punishment can be imposed despite the fact that, for part of the time when the husband was refusing to make payment as ordered, bankruptcy proceedings were pending against him so that enforcement processes were stayed. Nor does the fact that, by reason of his subsequent adjudication, his estate has become vested in his trustee in bankruptcy inevitably mean that the court is deprived of the power to punish his past contempt in failing to pay: a committal order can still be made in an appropriate case, although this is finally a matter for the court's discretion.[97]

Guarantors (Sureties)

Where a person, or several persons, has or have undertaken to guarantee payment of a debt incurred by another (the principal debtor), the nature of the liability of each guarantor (surety) is a contingent one whose vesting is dependent upon whether the principal debtor makes payment when the creditor lawfully requires him to. We shall proceed to examine the consequences of the bankruptcy of any party who has thus incurred liability, that is to say the principal debtor, a co-surety or the surety himself.

Bankruptcy of the principal debtor. Where the principal debtor becomes bankrupt every surety has a right of proof in respect of his contingent liability to make payment upon the debtor's failure to do so.[98] If a surety has already been obliged to fulfil this obligation his contingent liability has of course been converted into a vested claim for reimbursement for which he may lodge proof. Furthermore, if a surety has paid the full

---

[96] *Re Hedderwick* [1933] Ch. 669.
[97] *Woodley v. Woodley (No. 2)* [1993] 4 All E.R. 1010 (where the Court of Appeal, with some reluctance, decided not to order the belated committal of the obdurate husband.
[98] *Re Paine* [1879] 1 Q.B. 122.

amount of the debt himself he will have acquired as against the principal debtor all the rights previously enjoyed by the creditor, including any securities held by him, so that effectively the surety stands in the place of the creditor thereafter.[99] Where the surety is also bankrupt, his trustee will of course lodge proof on behalf of his estate in the bankruptcy of the principal debtor.

The creditor, for his part, is entitled to receive up to 100p in the pound in satisfaction of his debt, and is accordingly entitled to prove for his full debt in the bankruptcy of the principal debtor, besides seeking payment from any surety up to the limit for which that surety has engaged himself.[1] If any surety settles the debt in full, the creditor is obliged to make over to him any dividend he may already have received from the bankrupt's estate, since otherwise the creditor would have received payment in excess of 100p in the pound. Where a surety's liability is restricted to less than the full amount of the debt, or where, although liable up to the full amount, he effects a compromise with the creditor for less than its value,[2] the creditor continues to be entitled to lodge proof in the bankruptcy for the *full* value of the debt, and is not obliged to account for, or deduct from his proof, whatever sum may have been paid to him by the surety.[3] The creditor enjoys a similar right to prove in the bankruptcy of the principal debtor for the full amount of the debt if he has received some voluntary payment, not made by a party liable as a surety, of an amount which is less than the full debt,[4] although he is not permitted to *recover* more than 100p in the pound.

Bankruptcy of a co-surety. Where one of two or more co-sureties goes bankrupt, his co-sureties will have claims against him in respect of his contingent liability, in addition to any claim which may be preferred by the creditor to whom the debt is owed.[5] Since there exists between co-sureties a right to contribution in respect of payments made by any one of them in discharging their common liability, there may be proof in the bankruptcy of a co-surety in respect of his contingent liability to make contribution, even though the amount of that contribution is unascertained at the time of the bankruptcy, and irrespective of the fact that, at the date of lodging proof, the proving surety himself has paid nothing in fulfilment of his own liability.[6]

A surety who has effected a full settlement of the principal debt for which he and his co-surety are jointly liable is, as we have noted above,[7] placed in the position formerly occupied by the creditor, and enjoys the legal rights of the creditor in his stead. A surety is usually called upon to fulfil his liability in this manner as a consequence of the insolvency or default of the

---

[99] *ex p. Rushforth* (1805) 10 Ves. 409; 32 E.R. 903; *Re Parker* [1894] 3 Ch. 400. See also Mercantile Law Amendment Act 1856, s.5.
[1] *Re Sass* [1896] 2 Q.B. 12.
[2] As in *Edwards v. Hood-Barrs* [1905] 1 Ch. 20.
[3] *Re Rees* (1881) 17 Ch.D 98; *Re Sass above.*
[4] *Re Rowe, ex p. Derenburg* [1904] 2 K.B. 483.
[5] See *infra.*
[6] *Wolmershausen v. Gullick* [1893] 2 Ch. 514.
[7] See above, p. 267.

principal debtor, and therefore the most expeditious way in which such a paying surety can diminish the burden for himself is to seek contribution from his co-surety. If that co-surety is also bankrupt, the paying surety is entitled to prove in his bankruptcy for the *full* amount of the debt and not merely for the fraction for which the co-surety is liable to make contribution. But despite the enlarged figure which may be inserted in his proof, the paying surety is only entitled to *receive* dividend up to the amount which represents the just portion which, as between the sureties, the bankrupt co-surety is liable to *pay*.[8]

It should be noted finally that the right to prove in the bankruptcy of a co-surety is governed by different principles from those applicable to the question of a surety's right to bring action against a *solvent* co-surety to enforce contribution, for we have seen earlier[9] that a surety cannot bring such an action and also cannot present a bankruptcy petition against his co-surety, without first having paid more than his just proportion of the debt due.[10]

Bankruptcy of a surety. Where a surety becomes bankrupt the creditor to whom the debt is owed may prove in the bankruptcy on the basis of the surety's contingent liability to pay the principal debt. Once again, if the surety's undertaking extended to the full amount of the debt the creditor must be admitted to proof for that figure without allowance being made for anything he may have received from the principal debtor or from any co-surety, provided that the creditor does not ultimately *receive* a total in excess of 100p in the pound in respect of that debt.[11] Where the nature of the guarantee is such that it is restricted to the interest due upon the debt in question, the surety remains liable upon his guarantee in respect of future interest which may be payable and this liability is capable of estimation as a contingency. Liability of this kind remains effective even though, by virtue of the bankruptcy of the principal debtor, it is improbable that the principal debt will ever be repaid: the creditor may nevertheless prove in the surety's bankruptcy for the full estimated value of his entitlement to interest.

As mentioned above,[12] the trustee in bankruptcy of a bankrupt surety will pursue on behalf of the estate any claims which the surety may be entitled to make either against the principal debtor, or against any co-surety for contribution.

Costs

Where legal proceedings between the debtor and the creditor have taken place prior to the making of the bankruptcy order, and have led to an award of costs in the creditor's favour, the costs may be added to any sum awarded to the creditor in the judgment delivered in the proceedings in

---

[8] *Re Parker, above,* n. 99.
[9] *See ante,* Chap. 6, p. 94.
[10] *Re Snowdon* (1881) 17 Ch.D. 44.
[11] *Re Houlder* [1929] 1 Ch. 205.
[12] See *above* p. 268.

question. The creditor may thus lodge proof for the total sum in the debtor's bankruptcy.[13] This holds true even though the costs have yet to be taxed at the date of the bankruptcy order.[14] If the bankrupt has been the unsuccessful plaintiff in an action prior to his bankruptcy an award of costs in favour of the defendant in those proceedings will constitute a debt provable in the bankruptcy only if the bankrupt had been ordered to pay costs, or a verdict had been given against him, before the bankruptcy order was made.[15] The award of costs is usually dependent upon the outcome of the proceedings, although in interlocutory proceedings it is possible for an award of costs to be made "in any event," in which case the party failing in that application must pay the costs of the interlocutory proceedings whatever the ultimate outcome of the main action. It is however possible in such proceedings for the court to order that costs shall abide the eventual result of the action. Apart, therefore, from cases in which there have been interlocutory proceedings resulting in an award of costs "in any event," it may be said that there exists no provable debt to which costs may be attached at the date of the bankruptcy order, unless the proceedings in question have already reached their conclusion. So long as the proceedings remain in progress it is impossible to allege that there exists any liability to pay costs by reason of an obligation *incurred* by the bankrupt *before* the bankruptcy order was made[16] as is required by section 382(1)(b) of the Act.[17]

But if liability for costs cannot be considered a certainty so long as proceedings are unconcluded, neither can it be treated as a species of contingent liability for the purposes of proof in a party's bankruptcy. The Court of Appeal has held that the mere possibility that a person may lose an action in which he is a party at the date of his bankruptcy cannot form the basis of a speculative proof in respect of any costs which may be awarded against him.[18] The basis of this ruling was again considered by the Court of Appeal in *Re A Debtor (No. 68 of 1911)*,[19] where an order had been made for a new trial of an action between parties to previous proceedings, with a provision that the award of costs of the first trial should abide the event of the new one. Before the new trial took place the plaintiff in the proceedings became bankrupt, but the bankruptcy was annulled before the trial of the action, which was determined in the defendant's favour with an award of costs accordingly. When the defendant sought to recover the costs of the first trial in accordance with the order, the plaintiff alleged that they were irrecoverable because they had constituted a provable debt which had been discharged by his late bankruptcy. It was held that his objection could not succeed because at the date of his bankruptcy there had existed no order that the bankrupt *must* pay the costs, but there was merely a pending

---

[13] See the judgment of Lindley, M.R. in *Re British Goldfields of West Africa* [1899] 2 Ch. 7 at pp. 11–12 for a succinct expression of the applicable principles of law in such cases.
[14] *cf. Re Duffield, ex p. Peacock* (1873) 8 Ch.App. 682.
[15] *Re British Goldfields of West Africa*, above.
[16] *ibid.*, see p. 12, *per* Lindley, M.R.
[17] See above, p. 250.
[18] *Vint v. Hudspith* (1885) 30 Ch.D. 24: *Re British Goldfields of West Africa*, above. The rules concerning proof in respect of contingent liabilities are considered above, p. 262.
[19] [1911] 2 K.B. 652.

action with the attendant possibility that the plaintiff might as a consequence have to pay the costs of the earlier proceedings.[20] On this footing, the first trial was to be treated as analogous to any interlocutory proceedings, and the argument that the liability for costs should in such circumstances constitute a "contingent liability" was expressly rejected.[21]

Somewhat different in its circumstances, and in its result, was the case of *Re Pitchford*,[22] in which a creditor had commenced an action against a debtor for payment of a debt of £650. The action had been set down for trial when a receiving order was made against the debtor, and this was followed in due course by his adjudication. The plaintiff, having opted to lodge proof in respect of the debt in question, duly applied to stay the pending action. The Divisional Court held that although his claim for £650 was admissible to proof, the creditor was not entitled to prove for a further £46 in respect his untaxed costs in the stayed action, even though these had been incurred before the date of the receiving order, because the sum in respect of costs did not constitute a provable debt or liability within the meaning of section 30(3) of the Bankruptcy Act 1914 (the then applicable Act). Astbury J. observed that in *Re A Debtor*[23] there had been an order in relation to the first trial before the receiving order was made, and yet there could be no proof for the costs in that action because the terms of that order were operative in relation to an event which occurred after the making of the receiving order against the debtor. Since in the case of *Re Pitchford* itself there had been no order of any kind before the date of the receiving order, the learned judge was of the opinion that, *a fortiori*, there could be no proof in the bankruptcy for costs thus far incurred in the stayed proceedings. This decision has important implications for any creditor who is in the course of suing a debtor who becomes bankrupt, because he must remember that if he continues with the proceedings, and succeeds in obtaining judgment with costs against the bankrupt, there is no certainty that he will receive a full reimbursement of his costs, even assuming they are provable at all,[24] for the bankrupt's assets will usually be insufficient for all his debts to be paid in full. Yet if the creditor seeks to restrict his expenditure by staying the proceedings and lodging proof simply for the debt, any costs already incurred in the abortive proceedings are lost irretrievably. Thus, it will require a nice calculation on the part of the creditor to determine which of the alternative courses of action should prove, in the circumstances, to be less unprofitable.

Where legal proceedings remain uncompleted as at the date of the bankruptcy order (or even at the date of the petition) the bankruptcy court may exercise its powers under section 285(1) of the Act to stay the proceedings, or alternatively the court before which the proceedings are taking place may act under section 285(2) and either stay the proceedings or allow them to continue subject to such terms as the court may impose. In the light of what has been said above the issue of costs incurred prior to

---

[20] See p. 656, *per*, Fletcher-Moulton L.J.
[21] See pp. 655–656, *per* Cozens-Hardy, M.R., and p. 657, *per* Buckley, L.J.
[22] [1924] 2 Ch. 260.
[23] See *above*, n. 18.
[24] See *above*, p. 250.

Set-Off[25]

The possibility of effecting a set-off arises whenever the same two parties have engaged in two or more transactions, as a result of which each stands in the capacity of creditor *vis-à-vis* the other in respect of some of their dealings, and in the capacity of debtor in respect of the remainder. Such a situation would arise where each party has sold the other an item on credit, so that the price of each item is still outstanding. The simplest procedure in cases of this kind would be to set the one indebtedness off against the other, leaving the party to whom the greater amount is owed to seek payment of the balance. Where one of the parties has become bankrupt, the operation of such a set-off is especially desirable from the point of view of the solvent party, since the alternative would be for him to pay to the trustee in bankruptcy the full amount for which he stands indebted to the bankrupt, and thereafter to prove for the debt owed to him, of which no doubt he would receive but a fraction by way of dividend. By first effecting a set-off, and then limiting his proof to any balance still outstanding in his favour, the solvent party would receive full credit for what is owing to him, thus greatly minimising the loss he sustains as a result of the other's bankruptcy. However, since a consequence of the working of such a set-off is to deny the general body of creditors the benefit of a payment otherwise claimable on behalf of the bankrupt's estate, careful limits need to be set for the operation of the device.

Section 323 of the Act introduces the possibility of set-off into the situation where a bankruptcy order is made and there have previously been "mutual credits, mutual debts or other mutual dealings" between the bankrupt and any creditor of the bankrupt proving or claiming to prove for a bankruptcy debt. Section 323(2) provides that an account shall be taken of what is due from each party to the other in respect of the mutual dealings, and that the balance after set-off shall be paid or claimed on either side respectively. The critical moment in time at which the mutual liabilities must exist is the date of the bankruptcy order.[26] Detailed rules have been developed in the case law to provide for the application of this statutory right to claim a set-off in bankruptcy, and the law relating to this matter is now considerably refined.

The first qualification which may be noted is one expressly set forth in section 323 itself. It is there provided, by subsection (3), that no person is entitled to claim this statutory benefit of set-off if, at the time the sums became due from the bankrupt, that other party had notice that a bankruptcy petition was pending in relation to the bankrupt. Consequently it is not advisable to give credit to any person at a time when it is

---

[25] See R. Derham, *Set-off* (1987); Philip R. Wood, *English and International Set-off* (1989).
[26] *cf. Re Daintrey* [1900] 1 Q.B. 546; *Tilley v. Bowman* [1910] 1 K.B. 745. See also Derham, *op. cit.*, Chaps. 5, 6 and 7.

known that there is a bankruptcy petition pending in relation to him.[27] The logic and fairness of this rule is obvious, and requires no further comment.

The second noteworthy aspect of the law is that the operation of set-off in bankruptcy is wider than under the general law. The purpose of making set-off available in bankruptcy was explained by Park, B. in *Forster v. Wilson*[28] as being "to do substantial justice between the parties where a debt is really due from the bankrupt to the debtor to his estate." Under the general law the purpose of set-off is regarded as being to avoid cross-actions. But the case of *Forster v. Wilson* also illustrates one of the principles of limitation which are in practice applied in bankruptcy, for it was held that the proving creditor could set-off against the amount owed to him by the bankrupt only such debts as he owed to the bankrupt on account of property which he had received in his own right. Therefore, if a creditor was acting as agent or trustee for others when he received property from the bankrupt, no indebtedness was created such as is capable, after bankruptcy, of being set off against a debt due from the bankrupt to the creditor in his own right. There is equally a want of the essential mutuality where the debt of the proving creditor is owed directly to the trustee in bankruptcy in his own right as trustee and not by virtue of its being payable originally to the debtor himself. Such a debt cannot be set off against a debt owed by the bankrupt to the creditor in question.[29]

The requirement of mutuality, which is given specific emphasis by the wording of section 323 itself, must therefore be satisfied if there is to be a set-off.[30] It is essential that the mutual dealings are of a kind "such as will end on each side in a money claim,"[31] and therefore, if at the date of the bankruptcy order one of the parties enjoys a right to the specific restitution of property,[32] or to specific performance, no question of set-off can arise. It is not however necessary that the very transactions which gave rise to the mutual liabilities should themselves have been interrelated, nor need there have been any prior agreement to that effect between the parties to the set-off[33] provided that there is no indication of a positive intention on their part that the separate transactions should be incapable of being afterwards related for the purpose of settling accounts between them. But although such an active intention may be effective to remove the quality of mutuality from transactions not otherwise related, it is nevertheless well-settled that where the circumstances of the creation of the mutual liabilities are such that they are in fact related—as where they arise out of a single contract between the parties—it is impossible for the parties to exclude even by private agreement the statutory right to set-off which is created by section

---

[27] *cf. Re Eros Films Ltd* [1963] Ch. 565. If the creditor lacked knowledge of the bankruptcy petition, he may still claim a set-off: *cf. Re Taylor* [1910] 1 K.B. 562.
[28] (1843) 12 M & W. 191; 152 E.R. 1165 (see especially p. 1171).
[29] *Re A Debtor* [1909] 1 K.B. 430; *Kitchen's Trustee v. Madders* [1950] Ch. 134.
[30] See *e.g., Re Gedney* [1908] 1 Ch. 804, and *Re A Debtor (No. 82 of 1926)* [1927] 1 Ch. 410.
[31] *Palmer v. Day & Sons* [1895] 2 Q.B. 618, 622, *per* Lord Russell, C.J.
[32] *Ellis & Co's Trustee v. Dixon Johnson* [1925] A.C. 489, *above*, p. 262. See also *Rose v. Hart* (1818) 8 Taunt. 499; 129 E.R. 477, discussed in *Rolls Razor v. Cox* [1967] 1 Q.B. 552, 570, *per* Lord Denning, M.R.
[33] *Naoroji v. Chartered Bank of India* (1868) L.R. 3 C.P. 444, 452, *per* Montague Smith J.

323 of the Act.[34] Nevertheless, in *Stein v. Blake*[35] both the House of Lords and the Court of Appeal successively held that it remains possible for a trustee in bankruptcy, in the exercise of his power to effect an assignment for value of property, including rights of action, comprised within the bankrupt's estate, to assign to a third party a claim against a person who had a cross-claim against the bankrupt. However, the basis of the approach adopted by the House of Lords was fundamentally different from that of the Court of Appeal with respect to the impact of such an assignment upon the rights of set-off established by statute. In the single speech of Lord Hoffmann, with which the rest of the House concurred, it was carefully affirmed that the process of set-off is both mandatory and automatic, where the conditions for its application are met at the commencement of bankruptcy. In consequence of this self-executing process, only the net balance is owing as of the bankruptcy date. There is no need for any prior steps to have been taken—such as a lodging of proof or a quantification of the balance carried out by the trustee—in order to execute the set-off itself, although in practice such a calculation would need to be made in order to determine the value of the claim that is being assigned by the trustee. As a matter of principle, however, it was held that the trustee may assign the right to the net balance like any other chose in action. If the contrary had been held to be the case, the practical consequence would have been to deprive the general body of creditors of the value which would otherwise be gained by the bankrupt's estate.

In addition to the general requirement of "mutuality" as between the bankrupt and the proving creditor, it should be noted that the two statutory expressions "mutual credits" and "mutual debts" which are employed in section 323 possess special meanings, of which "mutual credits" represents the wider concept, for that expression facilitates the setting-off of debts which are immediately payable, against debts not payable until some future time. The rationale behind this possibility is that it is an essential feature, common to both debts, that credit has been given in each case.[36] But where one of the liabilities is a contingent one,[37] the position is altered: if the contingency has not yet occurred, and hence the liability has not become vested, at the date of the bankruptcy order, there cannot be a set-off because at the critical moment in time there is on the

---

[34] *Rolls Razor v. Cox*, above n. 32, *per* Lord Denning M.R. at pp. 569–570 ("the parties cannot contract out of the statute") This proposition was approved and applied by the House of Lords (Lord Cross dissenting), in *National Westminster Bank Ltd v. Halesowen Presswork and Assemblies Ltd* [1972] A.C. 785. *Cf.* Cmnd. 8558, Chap. 30 at paras. 1343–1348, 1362, where changes in the law were proposed which have not been implemented by the current legislation.

[35] [1993] 4 All E.R. 225, (C.A.); [1995] BCC 543 (H.L.) The House of Lords also stated that the Court of Appeal had taken a wrong view in *Farley v. Housing and Commercial Developments Ltd* [1984] BCLC 442. It may therefore be affirmed that the judgment of Neill J. in that case has been reinstated as good law. See Chap. 8, *ante*, for the treatment of rights of action forming part of the bankrupt's estate.

[36] *Rolls Razor v. Cox*, above, n. 32, following the ruling on this point in *Re Daintrey, above*, n. 26.

[37] Contingent Liabilities are discussed *above*, p. 262.

one side no actual debt, fixed as to amount and certain to be payable, which is capable of being set off.[38]

Given the necessary quality of mutuality, as explained above, there is scope for setting off claims of differing natures, always provided that liability is actually vested at the date of the receiving order. Therefore where a creditor has avoided a sale on the grounds of fraud, damages for the fraud of the bankrupt may be set off against the creditor's liability to repay to him the amount he has paid on account of the price of the goods.[39] Similarly, a claim for damages in respect of the bankrupt's failure to deliver goods may be set-off against the bankrupt's claim for the price of such goods as may have been delivered.[40] And an equitable debt may be set-off against a legal debt, where both were in existence before the bankruptcy order,[41] whilst a voluntary debt may be set-off against one which is contracted for value. At the court's discretion one party's claim for costs may be set-off against the other's claim either for costs or for a debt.[42] Further instances where a right to set-off has been successfully claimed include a case where a tenant was held entitled to deduct previous payments in excess of the permitted rent from subsequent payments which were due to his landlord, who had become bankrupt.[43] And in another case, previous transactions which had taken place between two companies, one of which was later being wound up, were held to give rise to a right of set-off.[44]

Where the right of set-off operates in respect of a surety's liability towards an insolvent creditor, the consequences are especially worthy of note. Where the surety stands in the position of creditor *vis-à-vis* the insolvent party, and is thereby able to invoke a set-off in respect of his liability owed under the terms of his suretyship, the effect is to bring about a reduction of debt itself, in that the insolvent debtor is taken to have received payment to the extent of the amount that was set off. This means that not only is the guarantor or surety discharged to the extent of the set-off, but so too is any other debtor who was liable in respect of the same sum.[45]

One situation in which set-off cannot take place is where a person is indebted to a firm, and debts are due to him from one of the members of that firm in his individual capacity, or where a person is indebted to one of

---

[38] *cf. Re Fenton* [1931] 1 Ch. 85.
[39] *Tilley v. Bowman*, above, n. 26.
[40] *Mersey Steel & Iron Co. v. Naylor, Benzon & Co.* (1884) 9 App.Cas. 434 (H.L.).
[41] *Mathieson's Trustee v. Burrup, Mathieson & Co.* [1927] 1 Ch. 562.
[42] *Re A Debtor (No. 21 of 1950) (No. 2)* [1951] Ch. 612. Proof for costs is discussed *above*, p. 269.
[43] *Bradley-Hole v. Cusen* [1953] 1 Q.B. 300.
[44] *Re H.E. Thorne & Sons Ltd* [1914] 2 Ch. 438. The bankruptcy law concerning set-off has been imported into the law governing winding up by a long series of legislative provisions, the most recent of which is r. 4.90 of the Insolvency Rules 1986. See *e.g. Rolls Razor v. Cox*, above, n. 32, and *National Westminster Bank Ltd v. Halesowen Presswork and Assemblies Ltd* [1972] A.C. 785, (H.L.).
[45] *M.S. Fashions Ltd v. Bank of Credit and Commerce International SA* [1993] BCLC 280; [1992] BCC 571 (C.A.). See also *M.S. Fashions Ltd v. B.C.C.I. SA (No. 2)* [1993] BCC 70; affd. (C.A.) [1993] BCC 360.

the members personally and is separately a creditor of the firm to which that member belongs.[46] In such cases, unless it is provided by the firm's articles that the firm is also to be liable for the individual debts of any of its partners, the lack of mutuality will preclude any set-off.[47] Moreover, although debts may be due to and from one and the same person, it may be that one debt has been incurred with him in his personal capacity, and the other incurred by him in some other capacity, (or vice-versa). This is possible because a person may act at some times on his own account, and at other times in some capacity such as executor, agent or trustee. Such a segregation of identities, for legal purposes, will preclude the operation of a set-off, albeit the two transactions were concluded by the person in question with the same other person. It should be noted however that a different attitude is adopted by the law when there exist mutual liabilities between the bankrupt and two different governmental departments, such as where a debt for taxes is owed to the Inland Revenue, and some other department is indebted to the bankrupt for goods supplied. As a result of the theory that the Crown is one and indivisible, the requirement of mutuality is taken to be satisfied in such cases, and the department which is in the position of creditor may invoke a set-off in respect of the debt owed by the other department and merely lodge proof for any balance which may still be owing to the Crown. An inter-departmental transfer of payment thereafter completes the recovery by the Crown of the entire amount thus set off. Both the *Blagden* and the *Cork Committees* observed that this privilege confers upon the Crown an even more extensive advantage than it already enjoys by virtue of the provisions of the Act relating to preferential debts,[48] and that it may be criticised as being unjustifiably favourable to the Crown at the expense of the general body of creditors. Accordingly, both Committees in their respective *Reports*, recommend that the law should be amended so as to prevent such a set-off from being invoked where different governmental departments are involved, but these recommendations have unfortunately never been implemented.[49]

The Rule in *Cherry v. Boultbee*

A further problem arises in relation to the so-called Rule in *Cherry v. Boultbee*,[50] which falls to be considered whenever a legatee himself owes money to the testator's estate. If the legatee becomes bankrupt before the death of the testator, the interest in the legacy never becomes vested in the legatee, but in his trustee in bankruptcy, and in view of the consequential

---

[46] *Re Hart* (1884) 25 Ch.D. 716.
[47] *Re Pennington & Owen Ltd* [1925] 1 Ch. 825.
[48] These are discussed, *post* Chap. 10, p. 291 *et seq.*
[49] See Cmnd. 221 (1957), paras. 83–85; Cmnd. 8558, paras. 1343–1348, 1362; Hansard H.L. Vol. 459, Cols. 1268–1270; H.C. Standing Committee E, June 18, 1985, Cols. 397–404; *ibid.*, June 20, Col. 545, where amendments which would have deprived the Crown of its privileged position were unsuccessfully moved during proceedings on the Insolvency Bill 1985. For an example of the pervasive and insidious operation of the "Crown set-off" rule see *R.A. Cullen Ltd v. Nottingham Health Authority* (1986) BCC 368.
[50] (1839) 4 My. & Cr. 442; 41 E.R. 171. See Derham, *op cit., supra.*, n. 25, Chap. 9.

lack of mutuality the administrators of the testator's estate cannot claim to set off the debt owed by the legatee before paying the legacy.[51] However, if the legatee's bankruptcy does not occur until after the death of the testator,[52] the interest in the legacy will for a time be vested in the legatee before passing to his trustee in bankruptcy along with the rest of his property.[53] In cases of this kind, the administrators of the testator's estate are entitled to set off the debt owed by the bankrupt, and to pay merely the balance of the legacy, if any, to the trustee in bankruptcy. The rule in *Cherry v. Boultbee* has the additional effect of facilitating the set-off even of a debt which, at the time of his death, the testator himself could not have recovered by action because of the Limitation Acts: since the debt, though irrecoverable by action, is nevertheless still "owed" to his estate, his administrators can effectively tell the legatee to "pay himself" the legacy out of the amount which he owes to the estate.[54]

Another matter which needs to be considered in the context of set-off is the former right of a personal representative or executor, to whom the deceased was personally indebted, to retain out of the estate a sum sufficient to pay the debt due to himself. This right was also formerly enjoyed by a widow, where she was the executrix of her husband's estate. If the deceased was insolvent, it was often the case that an application would later be made for the estate to be administered in bankruptcy,[55] but even in that event the executor's right of retainer could be exercised and would prevail against the claims of the trustee in administration of the estate,[56] and against creditors of equal degree to the executor and also against a claim for costs of the administration proceedings.[57] For this to happen, however, it was necessary that the executor assert his right of retainer before he had notice of the presentation of the petition for administration of the estate.[58] The right of retainer has now been drastically curtailed by the provisions of section 10 of the Administration of Estates Act 1971, subsection (1) of which states:

> "The right of retainer of a personal representative and his right to prefer creditors are hereby abolished."

However, subsection (2) goes on to provide protection for a personal representative, other than one who has been granted letters of probate solely by reason of his being a creditor of the deceased, who pays the debt of any person, including himself, who is a creditor of the estate. Such a personal representative will be protected from being made to account to

---

[51] This was so in the case of *Cherry v. Boultbee* itself.
[52] As in *Re Lennard* [1934] Ch. 235.
[53] This was explained, *ante*, Chap. 8, p. 190.
[54] *Re Akerman* [1891] 3 Ch. 212.
[55] *See post*, Chap. 12, p. 330.
[56] *Re Gilbert* [1898] 1 Q.B. 282.
[57] *Re Wester Wemyss* [1940] Ch. 1. The right of retainer did not prevail against the claims of any preferential creditors, such as the Crown: *A.G. v. Jackson* [1932] A.C. 365 (H.L.).
[58] *Re Williams* (1891) 8 Mor. 65.

Proof of Debts

creditors of the same degree as himself if the estate is subsequently found to be insolvent, provided that at the time of making the payment he acted in good faith and had no reason to believe that the deceased's estate was insolvent. It should be noted that this protection, though not available to those who are granted letters of administration solely in their capacity as creditors of the estate, may be invoked by those who, though creditors, qualify to be personal representatives in some other capacity as well, such as by virtue of being related to the deceased, or by being appointed executors of his will. Such "creditor administrators," provided that they act bona fide and without knowledge that the estate is insolvent, may pay even their own debts out of the estate and still enjoy protection.[59]

Equitable Set-Off

As an adjunct to the main principles of set off, there exists also a doctrine of equitable set-off, which is operative in some situations despite the apparent lack of mutuality as between the bankrupt and the party concerned. One such situation arises where goods have been sold by a factor selling in his own name, although in reality acting on behalf of a principal. The normal rules of agency[60] give rise to a debt directly owed by the buyer to the principal, but where the buyer was unaware that the factor was not acting exclusively on his own account, it has been held that the buyer may set-off any claim he may have against the factor before meeting the undisclosed principal's claim for the price, and in the same way the undisclosed principal's proof in the buyer's bankruptcy may be reduced by the amount of any such claim against the factor.[61] For such a set-off to operate, it is also required that the buyer must have been induced by the conduct of the principal to believe that the agent was selling on his own account, and he must have so believed in actuality.[62] Thus the doctrine may be said to rest upon a principle of equitable estoppel.[63]

The doctrine of equitable set-off is also operative in cases of assignment, and indeed it is expressly provided by section 136 of the Law of Property Act 1925[64] that even under a statutory assignment the assignee takes "subject to equities."[65] Thus the debtor may set up, against an assignee of the debt, claims against the assignor arising out of the contract by which the debt was created, and this is permissible even though such claims may not have ripened into a debt at the time of the assignment.[66] If the debtor is

---

[59] This alteration in the law is in accordance with the recommendations of the Law Commission in their Report on Administration Bonds and related matters, 1970 Cmnd. 4497 (Law Com. No. 31).

[60] See, *e.g. Bowstead on Agency* (15th ed. 1988), Chap. 7, pp. 353–386; Fridman, *Law of Agency* (6th ed. 1990) Chap. 12; B. Markesinis and R. J. C. Munday, *An Outline of the Law of Agency* (3rd ed. 1992), Chap. 4.

[61] *Semenza v. Brinsley* (1865) 18 C.B.(N.S.) 467; 144 E.R. 526, as explained in *Re Henley, ex p. Dixon* (1876) 4 Ch.D. 133, see especially. p. 138, *per* Brett, J.A.

[62] *Cooke v. Eshelby*, (1887) 12 App.Cas. 271 (H.L.).

[63] See *Cooke v. Eshelby, supra*, at pp. 278–279, *per* Lord Watson.

[64] Considered, *ante*, Chap. 6, p. 86.

[65] s.136(1).

[66] *Mangles v. Dixon* (1852) 3 H.L.C. 702; 10 E.R. 278 (H.L.).

bankrupt, his trustee may invoke the same right of set-off in respect of the assignee's proof for the debt assigned to him.

Proof for Interest

A proving creditor may wish to include a claim for interest in respect of the time elapsed since the debt was originally due to be paid. Here the law operates a distinction between the period prior to the date of commencement of the bankruptcy, and the period after that date, during which the administration of the bankrupt's estate is taking place.

Where a bankruptcy debt bears interest, that interest is provable as part of the debt except insofar as it is payable in respect of any period after the commencement of bankruptcy.[67] The creditor's claim for contractual interest under the terms of any agreement in which the rate of interest was specified is subject to any revision of the agreement which may come about through challenge by the trustee under the provisions of section 343 of the Act, concerning extortionate credit transactions.[68]

The act further provides, in section 328(4), that any surplus remaining after the payment of the preferential and ordinary debts is to be applied in payment of interest on those debts in respect of the periods during which they have been outstanding since the commencement of the bankruptcy. In this instance, no distinction is made between the preferential and non-preferential debts, and hence all are taken together for the purpose of distributing interest which has accrued due since the date of the bankruptcy order. The rate of interest which is payable by virtue of this provision in respect of any debt is whichever is the greater of the following:

(1) The rate specified in section 17 of the Judgments Act 1838 at the commencement of the bankruptcy[69] and
(2) The rate applicable to that debt apart from the bankruptcy.

Thus, if the rate of interest specified in the contract between the bankrupt and the creditor is higher than the rate specified under section 17 of the Judgments Act at the date of the bankruptcy order, it will be the former rate which will be applied in calculating post-adjudication interest on the debt in question, whereas if the reverse happens to be the case, the creditor will receive the statutory rate of interest as a "guaranteed" minimum rate.

(B) Mode of Proof

Section 322 of the Act declares that the proof of any bankruptcy debt by

---

[67] s.322(2) of the Act; see also r. 6.113 of the Rules. The law was recast by the 1985–1986 legislation, in line with recommendations in the *Cork Report*: Cmnd. 8558, ch. 31; Cmnd. 9175 (*The White Paper*), paras. 85–89. The meaning of the expression "commencement of the bankruptcy" is explained in Chap. 7, *ante*, esp. in section (1)(A).
[68] See Chap. 8, *ante*, p. 230.
[69] This rate is varied from time to time by statutory instrument. See Judgment Debts (Rate of Interest) Order 1993 (S.I. 1993, No. 564) (8%).

a secured or unsecured creditor, and related matters such as the admission and rejection of proofs, are to take place in accordance with the Insolvency Rules. Rules 6.96–6.119 inclusive cover numerous aspects of proof, including some which have already been considered in this present Chapter. We shall now examine these rules in detail.

Ordinary Cases

After the bankruptcy order has been made, every creditor should prove his debt as soon as possible,[70] and may do this by delivering or posting to the official receiver, or to the trustee if one has been appointed, a written claim to the debt in the form known as a "proof of debt," which must be verified by affidavit if the official receiver or trustee so requires.[71] An affidavit may be sworn before an authorised official of the court, who may be the trustee himself, or an official receiver or deputy official receiver, or an officer of the Department of Trade and Industry or of the court, who is duly authorised to swear affidavits.[72] The expression "officer of the court" includes any solicitor who is a Commissioner for Oaths. An affidavit or claim may be made by the creditor himself or by some person whom he authorises to do so on his behalf,[73] and it must contain or refer to a statement of account showing the particulars of the debt and also specify the documents by reference to which the debt can be substantiated.[74] The latter need not be submitted with the proof, but the trustee or the convenor or chairman of any meeting can at any time call for production of the documents where he thinks it necessary.[75] If the creditor is a moneylender, his affidavit or claim in respect of any moneylending transaction made before January 27, 1980 must also contain the extra details specified in section 9(2) of the Moneylenders Act 1927.[76]

Rule 6.100 declares that every creditor must bear the cost of proving his own debt unless the court specially orders otherwise: normally, the main expenses will be stamp duty and the fee for taking the oath. Costs incurred by the trustee in estimating the value of a bankruptcy debt under section 322(3) of the Act fall on the estate, as an expense of the bankruptcy.[77] In specifying the amount of his debt in his proof the creditor must deduct all trade and other discounts which would have been available to the bankrupt but for his bankruptcy, but need not deduct any discount which he may have agreed to allow for immediate or early settlement or for payment in cash.[78] Once he has lodged his own proof, a creditor becomes

---

[70] This will facilitate the creditor's participation in any creditors' meeting with full capacity to exercise voting rights. See Chap. 7, *ante*, p. 163.
[71] Insolvency Rules 1986, rr. 6.96, 6.99: Forms 6.37, 6.38, 6.39. Forms for use in proving bankruptcy debts must be sent out by the official receiver to all known creditors: r. 6.97.
[72] *ibid.*, r. 6.99(3); Form 6.39.
[73] *ibid.*, r. 6.96(3).
[74] *ibid.*, r. 6.98.
[75] *ibid.*, r. 6.98(2), (3).
[76] *ibid.*, r. 6.102. The Moneylenders Acts 1900–1927 were repealed in their entirety by the Consumer Credit act 1974: see *ante*, Chap. 6, pp. 135–136.
[77] Insolvency Rules 1986, r. 6.100(2).
[78] *ibid.*, r. 6.110.

entitled to see and examine the proofs of other creditors before the first meeting, and at all reasonable times, and thus he may keep himself informed of the extent of the claims to which the debtor is subject.[79] In his notice convening the first meeting of creditors the official receiver must specify a time limit for the lodging of proofs by creditors in order to be entitled to vote at that meeting.[80]

Secured Creditors

A most important provision relating to proof is that expressed in paragraph (g) of rule 6.98(1), which ordains that a creditor's proof of debt must state particulars of any security held, the date when it was given, and the value which the creditor puts upon it. This is completed by the provision in rule 6.116, which states that if a secured creditor omits to disclose his security in his proof of debt he shall surrender his security for the general benefit of creditors unless the court, on application by him, relieves him from the effect of this rule on the ground that the omission was inadvertent, or the result of honest mistake. If the court grants that relief, it may require or allow the creditor's proof of debt to be amended, on such terms as may be just.[81]

Section 383(2) of the Act states that a debt is secured, for the purposes presently under consideration, to the extent that the person to whom the debt is owed holds any security for the debt (whether a mortgage, charge, lien or other security) over any property of the person by whom the debt is owed. The significance of this definition has already been considered in relation to petitioning creditors,[82] but it must now be observed that such creditors are made the subject of further provisions governing the proof of debts. In addition to the sanction of forfeiture of his security for non-disclosure, a secured creditor who fails to comply with all the relevant provisions relating to the valuation of securities runs the risk under rule 11.10 of being wholly or partly excluded from participation in any dividend. This sanction may be imposed by the court upon the application of the trustee in bankruptcy, and it therefore behoves a secured creditor to pay special attention to the detailed provisions of the Insolvency Rules, and to observe them meticulously.

Effectively, the secured creditor has to choose one of three options which are open to him. First he may realise his security and prove for the balance, if any, which is due to him after deducting the net amount realised.[83] Secondly, he may surrender his security to the official receiver or trustee, and prove for the full amount of the debt as if it were unsecured.[84] Thirdly, if he does neither of these things, having stated in his proof the

---

[79] *ibid.*, r. 6.101. The bankrupt and his representative also have the right to see proofs which have been lodged.
[80] Insolvency Rules 1986, r. 6.79(4).
[81] *ibid.*, r. 6.112(2).
[82] Chap. 6, *ante*, p. 107.
[83] Insolvency Rules 1986, r. 6.109(1). See Anderson (1989) 5 I.L. & P. 180.
[84] Insolvency Rules 1986, r. 6.109(2).

PROOF OF DEBTS

amount at which he values his security, the creditor is entitled to rank for dividend in respect of the balance due after deducting the amount so assessed by him.[85] Unless the trustee otherwise allows, the creditor must produce any bill of exchange, promissory note, cheque or other negotiable instrument or security in respect of which he seeks to prove, before his proof can be admitted either for voting or for dividend.[86] This requirement that the creditor produce his security is a valuable adjunct to the provisions of rule 6.117, which empowers the trustee to redeem the security at any time on payment to the creditor of the assessed value. Thus if a creditor undervalues his security it may be required from him at that valuation, and will then become available for the benefit of the creditors generally. However, rules 6.115 and 6.117(2) provide that a secured creditor may, with the agreement of the trustee or the leave of the court, at any time alter the value which he has, in his proof of debt, put upon his security. However, this is subject to a special limitation in cases where the secured creditor, being the petitioner, put a value on his security, or has at any time voted in respect of the unsecured balance of his debt: in either of these cases the security may be re-valued only with leave of the court. There was formerly provision to the effect that a secured creditor might amend his valuation and proof upon his showing to the satisfaction of the trustee or the court that the valuation and proof were made bona fide on a mistaken estimate, or that the security had diminished or increased in value since its previous valuation. These provisions no longer appear in the current Insolvency Rules, but it is submitted that, where the leave of the court is required, the essential principles should remain identical to those established under the former provisions. Thus if the creditor's conduct is unimpeachable he should be able to amend his valuation,[87] but where the creditor is unable to plead bona fide mistake, or else to show that the value of the security itself has changed since his assessment was made, there are strong reasons in favour of holding a secured creditor irrevocably bound by his valuation throughout the bankruptcy, as a disincentive against any attempt at initially undervaluing a security, with a view to revaluing it in the event that the trustee discovers its true worth.[88]

A further course of action lies open to the trustee if he is dissatisfied with a creditor's valuation of his security, for by rule 6.118 he is empowered to require that the property comprised in any security be offered for sale. If the sale takes place by public auction, the creditor on his own behalf, and the trustee on behalf of the estate, may bid for or purchase the property. To a certain extent the creditor possesses the ability to force the trustee's hand in this matter, for rule 6.117(4) provides that the creditor may at any time

---

[85] *cf.* r. 6.93(4), regarding the voting rights of secured creditors, and also s.269 of the Act, regarding the position of a secured creditor when presenting a bankruptcy petition. *cf. Re Rushton* [1971] 2 All E.R. 937.

[86] Insolvency Rules 1986, r. 6.108. See also r. 6.93(5) with regard to voting rights at meetings.

[87] *cf. Re Newton* [1896] 2 Q.B. 403.

[88] *cf. Re Lacey* (1884) 13 Q.B.D. 128. The case of *Re Vautin* [1899] 2 Q.B. 549, which appears to hold to the contrary, may perhaps be distinguished on the grounds that the creditor in question was probably not correctly describable as a "secured" creditor at all, and furthermore had not taken the step of lodging proof at the time when the trustee sought to redeem the security. See also *Re Rowe, ex p. West Coast Goldfields* [1904] 2 K.B. 489.

give notice in writing to the trustee requiring the latter to elect whether or not he will exercise his power of redeeming the security, and if the trustee does not within six months signify in writing his election to exercise the power he may not thereafter exercise it.

If the creditor is able to effect an amendment of his valuation and proof, in accordance with rules 6.115 and 6.117(2), he automatically becomes subject to the provisions of rule 11.9, so that he is obliged to repay any surplus dividend which he may have received in excess of that to which he would have been entitled on the basis of the valuation as amended. Such a repayment will of course be a likelihood only where the creditor has substituted an increased valuation for his security: where the valuation has been reduced he will be entitled to be paid any dividend or share of dividend which he may have failed to receive by virtue of his original, incorrect valuation. But such payment can be made to him only out of any money available for dividend at the time of amendment of his valuation, for he is not entitled to disturb the distribution of any dividend declared before the date of amendment.[89]

Rule 6.119 provides that if the creditor, having originally opted to value his security for purposes of proof, subsequently realises it or if it is realised under the provisions of rule 6.117,[90] the net amount so realised is to be substituted for the amount of any valuation previously made by the creditor, and his valuation will for all purposes be treated as though it had been amended by him, so that the provisions of rule 11.9 will once again be applicable.

It is possible that the creditor may decide initially that he will rely upon his security, and that it will not be necessary to prove for his debt. If he later changes his mind and seeks to come in and prove, he will be allowed to do so provided that no injustice will be caused by his so doing. As in cases where an original valuation is amended, a creditor lodging proof for the first time after one or more dividends have already been declared in the bankruptcy will not be permitted to disturb any such previously-declared dividends.[91] In the final resort, wherever there is a dispute or doubt concerning the correctness of the trustee's decision with respect to proof, the creditor may appeal to the court within 21 days, and the court has power under rule 6.105 to reverse or vary the decision.[92]

It is a general principle of insolvency law that no creditor, secured or otherwise, should receive more than 100p in the pound upon his debt, plus such interest as is permitted by the Act. An exception is permitted to occur where the surplus recovery occurs as an incidental effect of the trustee's exercise of his powers under rule 6.117. Where a secured creditor himself realises his security, and a net balance is still left owing to him in respect of his debt, the assessment of the true extent of that balance, for purposes of lodging proof for it, is determined by applying the net proceeds from the realisation in payment of principal and interest due upon the debt at the date of the bankruptcy order. This procedure ensures that the creditor is

---

[89] Insolvency Rules 1986, r. 11.9(3).
[90] Discussed *above*, p. 282.
[91] Insolvency Rules 1986, rr. 11.8(1), 11.9(3). *Re McMurdo* [1902] 2 Ch. 684.
[92] See *e.g.*, *Re Lee, ex parte Good* (1880) 14 Ch.D. 82 (a case under the Act of 1869, s.72).

prevented from maximising the amount of principal for which he is able to lodge proof, which he might otherwise do by the simple expedient of purporting to apply the proceeds first towards payment of *all* interest, both before and after the bankruptcy order.[93] The creditor who realises his security is however permitted to apply the resulting proceeds towards the payment of *any* debt which may be owed to him by the debtor at the date of the bankruptcy order, and is not restricted to applying them to the debt actually secured. Therefore if he is owed several debts, some of which are preferential,[94] the creditor may properly apply the proceeds of realisation to the payment of any non-preferential or even non-provable debts, leaving himself free to lodge proof for such provable or preferential debts as may remain unsatisfied.[95]

Mention has already been made of the rule against double proof.[96] In relation to secured creditors it suffices to mention that the debt and the accompanying security are part of one and the same transaction, and are not two distinct transactions giving rise to two different claims. Accordingly, the extent to which the creditor may prove for the balance of the debt is at all times conditioned by the value of the security, whether realised or potential, since he is restricted to lodging proof for the balance only, as we have seen.

Periodical Payments

Rule 6.112 of the Insolvency Rules is designed to cover cases involving claims for rent or other payments of a periodical nature, and provides that whenever the making of the bankruptcy order does not coincide with the time for making one of those payments, the person entitled to the payment may prove for a proportionate part measured up to the day upon which the order is made, as though the rent or payment became due from day to day. Where there is a subsisting lease which has a fixed number of years to run, the future payments of rent may also be proved for.[97] If the lease is a subsisting one, it may be observed that the Rule in *Hardy v. Fothergill*[98] does not apply to cases where a lessor is proving in respect of the liability of his lessee,[99] and even where the lease has been assigned by the bankrupt lessee, and the lessor does not enjoy any absolute right to insist that a sum

---

[93] *Re London, Windsor and Greenwich Hotels Co. (Quartermaine's Case)* [1892] 1 Ch. 639. See *above*, p. 279.

[94] See *post*, Chap. 10. p. 291.

[95] *Re William Hall (Contractors) Ltd* [1967] 2 All E.R. 1150. Contrast the case of *Re E. J. Morel* [1962] Ch. 21 (where the facts were somewhat specialised, however); and also that of *Re Unit 2 Windows Ltd* [1985] 3 All E.R. 647 (a winding up case, in which a principle of "proportionate equity" was applied to the operation of set-off in relation to different types of debt, some preferential, owed to the same creditor of the company).

[96] See *supra*, p. 255.

[97] *Re New Oriental Bank Corp. (No. 2)* [1895] 1 Ch. 753.

[98] (1888) 13 App.Cas. 351, discussed *above*, p. 263. In that case the lessees were seeking indemnity from the assignee after the assignee's term had expired, but his liability was held, in the circumstances, to have been discharged by his bankruptcy which had occurred when his term had still eight years to run. The lessees had not lodged proof, and therefore lost all right to compensation.

[99] *Re New Oriental Bank Corp. (No. 2), above.*

Mode of Proof

be set aside by the trustee to cover the "contingent liability" that the assignee might default on the covenants. In such cases the proper course, as held by Roxburgh J. in *Re House Property and Investment Co.*,[1] is for the lessor to prove in the lessee's bankruptcy for the difference between the original value of the lease and the present value without the benefit of the original lessee's covenants.

Claims in Respect of Interest, and for Debts Payable in the Future

The provisions of the Act which entitle a creditor to prove for interest on his debt up to the date of the bankruptcy order, and also after that date provided that there are sufficient funds available, have been discussed already.[2] Similarly, the rules concerning proof for debts payable at a future time have been dealt with above.[3]

Admission and Rejection of Proofs

Rule 6.104 contains the general provision under which a proof may be admitted for dividend either for the whole amount claimed by the creditor, or for part of that amount. If the trustee rejects a proof in whole or in part, he must prepare a written statement of his reasons for doing so, and send it forthwith to the creditor. The official receiver or trustee examines every proof, and the grounds of the debt, and may require further evidence in support of it if he feels this is necessary.[4] We have already noted that a trustee who negligently admits to proof a debt not properly admissible may be subjected to a misfeasance summons preferred by any of the other creditors.[5] As mentioned above, rule 6.105 enables any creditor who is dissatisfied with the decision of the trustee in respect of a proof to appeal to the court. Rule 6.105(2) also allows an appeal to be lodged either by the bankrupt or by any of the other creditors who are dissatisfied by the trustee's partial or total acceptance of the proof of any particular creditor. Since the admission to proof of any creditor's debt effectively entails a diminution of the ultimate return which every creditor will be able to receive, it may be said that every admission to proof is a matter of common concern to all the creditors involved in the bankruptcy. There is also provision in rule 6.106 enabling a creditor's proof to be withdrawn or varied as to the amount claimed. This may be done at any time by agreement between the creditor and the trustee, and is the appropriate course for the creditor to adopt if, for example, he becomes aware that his original proof contains inaccuracies.[6] This may more readily be allowed at a time where the creditor's proof has not yet been admitted, or formally rejected, by the trustee. Also, if the trustee's position has been altered in reliance upon the original proof, or if the trustee is not convinced that there

---

[1] [1954] Ch. 576.
[2] See *above*, p. 279.
[3] See *above*, p. 262.
[4] Insolvency Rules 1986, r. 6.98(3).
[5] *Above*, pp. 179 and 252.
[6] *Re Attree* [1907] 2 K.B. 868.

was a bona fide mistake on the creditor's part, he may be refused leave to amend his proof.[7]

Expunging of Proof

It is further provided by rule 6.107, that if the trustee has admitted a proof which he later thinks may have been improperly admitted he may apply to the court which may, after notice to the creditor who lodged the proof, expunge it or reduce its amount. It was held in *Re Tait*[8] that a mere lapse of time is no bar to the trustee's right to apply to have the proof expunged, although the creditor will be entitled to retain any dividend which he may have previously received. In cases of exceptional delay however the trustee's application may be refused,[9] and there is also an established rule to the effect that the court will not go behind a proof for assessed taxes, and consequently if such a proof has been once admitted it cannot be expunged.[10] Where the trustee declines to interfere, an application to expunge or reduce a proof may be made to the court by a creditor.[11]

---

[7] *cf. Re Firth* (1879) 12 Ch.D. 337; *Re Safety Explosives Ltd* [1904] 1 Ch. 226.
[8] (1882) 21 Ch.D. 537.
[9] As in *Re Browne* [1960] 2 All E.R. 625, discussed, *supra*, p. 253.
[10] *Re Calvert* [1899] 2 Q.B. 145, *supra* p. 254.
[11] Insolvency Rules 1986, r. 6.107(1)(b). See also *Re A Debtor (No. 819 of 1970)* [1974] 3 All E.R. 502, for indications of the effect of annulment of the bankruptcy upon proofs which the trustee has omitted to process.

Chapter 10

DISTRIBUTION OF ASSETS

Preliminary

After the creditors have had the opportunity to lodge their proofs and these have been processed by the trustee,[1] the Act prescribes that the distribution of the first and any subsequent dividends should take place whenever the trustee has sufficient funds in hand for the purpose.[2] On each occasion when a dividend is declared and distributed the trustee is required to retain such sums as may be necessary for the expenses of the bankruptcy.[3] He must also make provision, in calculating a dividend, for any bankruptcy debts which appear to be due to persons who, by reason of the distance of their place of residence, may not have had sufficient time to tender and establish their proofs, and for any debts which are the subjects of claims which have not yet been determined, and likewise for disputed proofs and claims.[4]

It is by no means the case that all the funds in the trustee's hands will simply be distributed amongst all the proving creditors in equal proportions, for the law divides the debtor's liabilities into a number of separate categories, to each of which the funds of the estate are to be applied successively in a well-established order of priority. Since it is possible for the liabilities which enjoy first or early priority to be so large as to swallow up all the funds, the general body of ordinary creditors may in many cases receive little or nothing.

We shall consider in this chapter the rules governing priority of payment in bankruptcy, as well as the general provisions for the calculation and distribution of dividends.

---

[1] See *ante*, Chap. 9, p. 279.
[2] s.324(1) of the Act.
[3] *ibid.*, s.324(1).
[4] *ibid.*, s.324(4).

DISTRIBUTION OF ASSETS

(A) Priority of Distribution of Assets

The categories of liabilities to which the funds are to be applied are, in order of priority:

(1) The expenses of the bankruptcy;
(2) Pre-preferential debts;
(3) Preferential debts;
(4) Ordinary debts;
(5) Interest (accrued since the commencement of bankruptcy);
(6) Postponed debts;
(7) Surplus (payable to the bankrupt).

These will be considered in turn.

(1) The Expenses of the Bankruptcy

As mentioned section 324(1) of the Act states that the trustee is to retain "such sums as may be necessary for the expenses of the bankruptcy," before applying the funds of the debtor's estate towards meeting the debts of that estate. A more detailed description of the costs, fees and charges which are by law made payable out of the estate is contained in rule 6.224 of the Insolvency Rules 1986, where it is provided that the following expenses are payable out of the estate in the following order of priority:

(1) Expenses properly chargeable or incurred by the official receiver or the trustee in preserving, realising or getting in any of the assets of the bankrupt, including those incurred in acquiring title to after-acquired property[5];

(2) Any other expenses incurred or disbursements made by the official receiver or under his authority, including those incurred or made in carrying on the business of a debtor or bankrupt;

(3) The fees payable under any order made under section 415, including those payable to the official receiver (other than the fee referred to in sub-paragraph (4)(a) below), and any remuneration payable to him under general regulations;

(4)(a) The fee payable under any order made under section 415 for the performance by the official receiver of his general duties as official receiver;

---

[5] The expenses listed in para. 1 include the costs of employing a shorthand writer, if appointed by an order of the court made at the instance of the official receiver in connection with an examination: r. 6.224(2). The costs of employing a shorthand writer so appointed in any other case rank after the allowance mentioned in para. (11) and before the disbursements mentioned in para. (12).

Any expenses incurred in holding an examination under r. 6.174 (examinee unfit), where the application for it is made by the official receiver, also rank in priority with those specified in para. 1. (as numbered in the text above).

Priority of Distribution of Assets

    (b) Any repayable deposit lodged by the petitioner under any such order as security for the fee mentioned in sub-paragraph (a) (except where the deposit is applied to the payment of the remuneration of an insolvency practitioner appointed under section 273 (debtor's petition))[6];

(5) The cost of any security provided by an interim receiver, trustee or special manager in accordance with the Act or the Rules;

(6) The remuneration of the interim receiver (if any);

(7) Any deposit lodged on an application for the appointment of an interim receiver;

(8) The costs of the petitioner, and of any person appearing on the petition whose costs are allowed by the court;

(9) The remuneration of the special manager (if any);

(10) Any amount payable to a person employed or authorised, under chapter 5 of Part 6 of the Rules, to assist in the preparation of a statement of affairs or of accounts;

(11) Any allowance made, by order of the court, towards costs on an application for release from the obligation to submit a statement of affairs, or for an extension of time for submitting such a statement;

(12) Any necessary disbursements by the trustee in the course of his administration (including any expenses incurred by members of the creditors' committee or their representatives and allowed by the trustee under Rule 6.164 but not including any payment of capital gains tax in circumstances referred to in sub-paragraph (15) below);

(13) The remuneration or emoluments of any person (including the bankrupt) who has been employed by the trustee to perform any services for the estate, as required or authorised by or under the Act or the Rules;

(14) The remuneration of the trustee, up to any amount not exceeding that which is payable to the official receiver under general regulations[7];

(15) The amount of any capital gains tax on chargeable gains accruing on the realisation of any asset of the bankrupt (without regard to whether the realisation is effected by the trustee, a secured creditor, or a receiver or manager appointed to deal with a security);

(16) The balance, after payment of any sums due under sub-paragraph (14) above, of any remuneration due to the trustee.

In all the above cases, the claims for costs or expenses will be submitted by the person or persons who have initially incurred them in the course of

---

[6] See the Insolvency Fees Order 1986 (S.I. 1986, No. 2030), (as amended by S.I.'s: 1988, No. 95; 1990, No. 560; 1991, No. 496; 1992, No. 34; 1994, No. 2541).

[7] See the Insolvency Regulations 1995 (S.I. 1995, No. 2507), regs. 33–36, with Sched. 2. On the fixing of the trustee's remuneration, see r. 6.138 *et seq.* of the Rules, *ante*, Chap. 7.

performing their functions during the bankruptcy proceedings. Not all of the possible kinds of expenses will necessarily be incurred in the context of a single bankruptcy, of course, but the list contains all the possible categories of expenses which are likely to be met, and which constitute a first charge against the funds of the estate.

It is to be noted that rule 6.224 establishes an order or priority in which the respective expenses of the bankruptcy are to be paid. Each head of expenses, beginning with paragraph (1), must therefore be fully discharged before any payment is made in respect of a subsequent head of expenses. Therefore if the realisable assets are insufficient even to meet all the expenses of the administration, those items of expenditure which carry a low listing may not be paid fully, or at all: there is no provision to the effect that expenses abate *pro-rata* in the event of a shortfall in funds to discharge them. Significantly, the remuneration of the trustee is listed in paragraph (14), which may well render it inadvisable for a private-sector trustee to undertake an administration where the realisable assets are of a very small value.

(2) Pre-Preferential Debts

After the trustee has met the administrative costs of the bankruptcy, he is next required to apply the funds in his hands towards the payment of several categories of pre-preferential debts, whose priority is conferred by various statutory provisions especially designed to afford protection to the creditors in question. The effect and operation of these statutory provisions is secured by virtue of section 328(6) of the Act.

The first such protected category of creditors consists of any apprentices or articled clerks who may be articled to the bankrupt: their articles may be discharged when their master or principal is adjudicated bankrupt, and in that event any premium paid by the clerk or apprentice, or by anyone on his behalf, as a fee may be repaid by the trustee to the extent that he thinks reasonable.[8] Application for such repayment may be made by the apprentice or clerk himself, or by some person on his behalf, and in any event there is a right of appeal to the court from the trustee's decision in the matter. The trustee is empowered, as an alternative to repayment, to transfer the indenture of apprenticeship or articles of agreement to some other person.[9]

The provisions of the Employment Protection (Consolidation) Act 1978 contain an expeditious procedure for securing the reimbursement of any fee or premium paid by an apprentice or clerk whose employer has become insolvent. That Act provides that the Secretary of State shall, upon application by an employee, pay to him out of the National Insurance Fund (formerly known as the Redundancy Fund) such an amount as the trustee in bankruptcy or liquidator admits to be reasonable, by way of reimbursement of the whole or part of the sum which the employee

---

[8] Insolvency Act 1986, s.348: see especially subs. (4).
[9] *ibid.*, s.348(5), (6).

originally paid. Thereupon, the rights and remedies of the employee in respect of that debt are transferred to the Secretary of State.[10]

Special priority is also accorded to the claims of trustees of Friendly Societies in cases where an officer of such a Society has had in his possession money or property of the Society at the time of his being adjudicated bankrupt. By virtue of section 59 of the Friendly Societies Act 1974, whose provisions are enabled to enjoy priority of effect by virtue of section 328(6) of the Insolvency Act 1986, the trustees of the Society enjoy a first right of recovery against his estate in respect of the money or property in question.[11]

Article 4(2) of the Administration of Insolvent Estates of Deceased Persons Order 1986 (S.I. 1988, No. 1999) establishes a special case, applicable where the estate of a deceased insolvent is being administered in bankruptcy, whereby the reasonable funeral, testamentary and administration expenses enjoy pre-preferential status. A final species of pre-preferential debt is constituted by the claim for expenses of the trustee of any deed of arrangement which has been avoided by bankruptcy of the debtor.[12] This time, the relevant statutory provision which is in point is section 21 of the Deeds of Arrangement Act 1914.

(3) Preferential Debts

The next category of debts in order of priority is that of preferential debts, which are basically owed to the relevant public authorities in respect of certain forms of fiscal liability and contributions to occupational pension schemes and to the state social security system, and also claims for arrears for salary or wages owed to the bankrupt's present or former employees. The various categories of preferential debts are enumerated in Schedule 6 to the Act.[13] If there are sufficient funds to meet all these debts, they will of course be paid in full; otherwise, all debts ranking as preferential, irrespective of their type, will abate together in the same proportion, as a single group.[14] In the event of payment being made at a reduced rate, this will be effected by way of a dividend upon each debt at the same rate in the pound, the amount of the rate being determined by the amount of money available for distribution, in proportion to the total amount of the debts belonging to the preferential group. If the deficiency of assets in relation to debts is such that not even the preferential debts can be paid in full, it necessarily follows that debts belonging to the subsequent classes will not be repaid at all, even fractionally. Therefore, any creditor whose debt ranks among the class of ordinary, non-preferential debts will be well-advised to retain, and eventually to realise, any security he may have, rather than to surrender it to the trustee in order to become eligible to

---

[10] Employment Protection (Consolidation) Act 1978, ss.122, 125.
[11] See, *e.g. Re Miller* [1893] 1 Q.B. 327, followed in *Re Eilbeck* [1910] 1 K.B. 136.
[12] For administration of deceased insolvents' estates, see *post*, Chap. 11; for deeds of arrangement, see *ante*, Chap. 4.
[13] See also Insolvency Act 1986, ss.328(1), 386.
[14] *ibid.*, s.328(2).

prove for his debt in full,[15] for this act of surrender will in all likelihood merely serve to benefit the creditors who enjoy priority in the distribution.

The six categories of preferential debts listed in Schedule 6 to the Insolvency Act are as follows: (The provisions of Schedule 6, and related sections of the Act, are reproduced in full in Appendix II, *post*[16]; the repeated references in Schedule 6, to "the relevant date" involve further reference to section 387 as explained below).[17]

Category 1: Debts due to Inland Revenue;

Category 2: Debts due to Customs and Excise;

Category 3: Social Security contributions

Category 4: Contributions to occupational pension schemes, etc.

Category 5: Remuneration, etc., of employees;

Category 6: Levies on Coal and Steel Production;

"The Relevant Date"

To qualify as a preferential debt under the terms of Schedule 6, a sum must be shown to have fallen due within the relevant period of reference that is prescribed in the paragraph of the Schedule which confers preferential status upon that category of debt. The qualifying periods are determined with reference to a date—which can be objectively ascertained according to the circumstances of each case.

Section 387 of the Act provides that, in relation to a bankrupt, where at the time when the bankruptcy order was made there was an interim receiver appointed under section 286, the relevant date is the date on which the interim receiver was first appointed after the presentation of the bankruptcy petition.[18] In all other cases relating to a bankrupt, the relevant date is the date of the making of the bankruptcy order.[19] In cases where a voluntary arrangement under Part VIII of the Act is in force in relation to a person who is not an undischarged bankrupt, the relevant date for the purposes of section 258 is the date of the Interim Order made under section 252 with respect to his proposal.[20]

---

[15] See Chap. 9, *ante*, p. 281.
[16] See Appendix II, *post* at pp. 795–803.
[17] s.387 of the Act is reproduced in full in Appendix II, *post*, p. 797.
[18] s.387(6)(a).
[19] s.387(6)(b).
[20] s.387(5). See Chap. 4, *ante*, especially p. 42.

Further Comment

The categories of preferential debts now enumerated in Schedule 6 to the Act represent a considerable recasting of the law in comparison to its pre-1986 state. The current provisions reflect some of the arguments and recommendations made by the *Cork Committee* and indeed, in a more cautious spirit by the *Blagden Committee* a quarter of a century earlier.[21] Despite Government resistance during the successive Parliamentary stages of the enactment of the Insolvency Act 1985, reforms were implemented to abolish the Crown's privileged position as a preferential creditor for unpaid taxes assessed directly upon the insolvent debtor (individual or corporate) as taxpayer to the Inland Revenue, and also to abolish the preferential status formerly accorded to local rates. A further change in the law had the effect of restricting Crown preference in respect of outstanding payments of Value Added Tax to a period of six months, as against the period of 12 months which is applicable for other debts due to Customs and Excise. Although less extensive than the *Cork Committee's* original proposals, these reforms are doubly significant in that not only do they relegate to the level of ordinary debts a number of claims which are often among the largest items in an insolvency (such as arrears of income tax), and thus enhance the prospect that the other ordinary creditors will at least receive some dividend upon their claims, but also they symbolise an important change of attitude towards the traditional categories of preferential debt, whose status can no longer be regarded as sacrosanct. As the *Blagden Committee* so persuasively argued,[22] although taxes may be considered a specially deserving claim by virtue of the fact that they are owed to the community at large, the reality is that a disproportionate misery—tantamount to injustice—is inflicted upon the general body of ordinary creditors as a direct consequence of the Crown's ability to take maximum advantage of its privileged position. In particular, it may be observed, the Crown could in many cases be said effectively to have given a "false credit" to a debtor by failing either to claim and collect taxes promptly at the time when they fall due, or to take prompt steps to enforce payment of arrears.[23] Since a person's tax affairs are necessarily a confidential matter, other parties may become ordinary, unsecured creditors of the debtor at a time when, despite outward appearances to the contrary, he is already hopelessly insolvent due to the extent of his fiscal liabilities.

It should be noted that, by virtue of section 434(b) of the Insolvency Act 1986, the Crown is bound by the provisions of the Act relating to priorities of debts, so that all other debts owed by the debtor to the Crown, with the exception of those specific categories of debts mentioned in Schedule 6, will rank along with the ordinary debts owed to the general body of creditors.

---

[21] See Cmnd. 8558, Chap. 32, especially paras. 1409–1444, 1450; Cmnd. 221, paras. 88–93, 97.
[22] *Loc. cit. above*, n. 21.
[23] *cf. Re Pratt* [1951] Chap. 225.

Subrogation

In the insolvency of any person who has been an employer of others, the plight of the employees in the critical period around the commencement of bankruptcy is often especially acute. In addition to the customary rigours which accompany the onset of unemployment, a bankrupt's employees frequently experience additional hardship because there is no money available to pay any outstanding instalments of wages or salary for the period immediately prior to the making of the bankruptcy order. As we have seen,[24] paragraphs 9–12 of Schedule 6 to the Act confer preferential status upon such claims, within prescribed financial and temporal limits, but in practice a considerable time is likely to elapse before the trustee in bankruptcy is able to distribute the first of any dividends which the preferential creditors are destined to receive. To alleviate the most severe problems which can arise as a result of such delays in the making of payments to employees out of the assets of an insolvent employer, section 122(1) of the Employment Protection (Consolidation) Act 1978 requires the Secretary of State to pay to an employee out of the National Insurance Fund the amount to which he decides that employee is entitled in respect of a number of debts. The debts are listed in section 122(3) as follows:

(1) Any arrears of pay in respect of a period or periods not exceeding eight weeks;
(2) Any amount which the employer is liable to pay the employee for the relevant statutory period of notice;
(3) Any holiday pay in respect of a period or periods of holiday, not exceeding six weeks in all, to which the employee became entitled during the 12 months immediately preceding the employer's insolvency;
(4) Any basic award of compensation for unfair dismissal;
(5) Any reasonable sum by way of reimbursement of the whole or part of any fee or premium paid by any apprentice or articled clerk.[25]

Section 125 of the Act of 1978 provides that, where the Secretary of State makes any payment to an employee in pursuance of section 122, any rights and remedies of the employee in respect of that debt become vested in the Secretary of State. Accordingly, where any of the rights or remedies thus transferred were within the category of preferential claims contained in

---

[24] *Above*, p. 292, and Appendix II, *post*, p. 800.

[25] Case 5. has already been considered above, p. 290. See also s.122(4) (which defines the amounts which are to be treated as "arrears of pay" for the purposes of s.122; and s.122(5) (whereby the rate of payment which may be made to an employee by the Secretary of State is limited to a prescribed maximum, which is reviewed from time to time (fixed at £205 from 1.4.1992) to determine the amount per week which is applicable whenever the amount of the debt is referable to a period of time): see Employment Protection (Variation of Limits) Order 1992 (S.I. 1992, No. 312). (The maximum amount payable for arrears of pay is thus £2,460 at current rates, of which only a maximum of £800 can be preferential due to the combined effects of para. 9 of Sched. 6 to the Insolvency Act 1986 and Art. 4 of the Insolvency Proceedings (Monetary Limits) Order 1986 (S.I. 1986, No. 1996)).

paragraphs 9–12 of Schedule 6 to the Insolvency Act, the Secretary of State becomes entitled to be paid as a preferential creditor in respect of the preferential claims thus discharged. It is also to be noted that paragraph 13 of Schedule 6 to the Insolvency Act 1986 supplements and expands the meaning of the expression "sum payable by the debtor to a person by way of remuneration", for the purposes of the preferential entitlement to dividend conferred under the provisions of paragraphs 9 to 12 (set out in Appendix II, *post*). Included among the amounts so qualifying are remuneration on suspension on medical grounds, or on suspension on maternity grounds, under sections 19 and 47 respectively of the Employment Protection (Consolidation) Act 1978, and any payment for time off in respect of trade union duties, looking for work, or ante-natal care, under sections 27(3), 31(3) or 31A(4) of that Act.[26]

Finally, it may be noted that a process of subrogation also occurs in cases which are governed by section 347 of the Insolvency Act which, as has been explained earlier,[27] applies in cases where distress for rent is levied upon the goods and effects of a person who is, or who becomes, bankrupt. Where, by virtue of the charge created by section 347(3), any person is required to surrender the distrained property (or the proceeds of its realisation) to the trustee in bankruptcy so that it may be utilised towards the payment of the preferential debts, that person ranks, in respect of the amount of the proceeds of sale of the surrendered property, as a preferential creditor of the bankrupt in relation to the remainder of the bankrupt's available estate, apart from the surrendered property.[28]

(4) Ordinary Debts

Once the trustee has paid in full all the debts and expenses belonging to categories (1) to (3) as described above, he is next required to apply any remaining funds to the payment of the debts owed to the ordinary creditors. Once again, all creditors belonging to this category stand on an equal footing, irrespective of whether they gave value for their debts or not,[29] and section 328(3) of the Act ordains that all debts within this category shall rank equally between themselves and shall be paid *pari passu*. Thus if the funds are sufficient all the ordinary debts will be paid in full but if, as is usually the case, there is less than enough money to meet all the debts which have been admitted to proof, the ordinary debts will abate together in equal proportions between themselves. That is, each of the ordinary creditors will receive a dividend expressed as so many pence in the pound upon the debt in question.

(5) Interest

If there is any surplus remaining after the payment in full of all debts,

---

[26] Insolvency Act 1986, Sched. 6, para. 13(2)(b), (c), as amended by Trade Union Reform and Employment Rights Act, 1993, Sched. 8, para. 35. (See also *supra*, n. 16.)
[27] Considered in Chap. 8, *ante*, at p. 240.
[28] s.347(4) of the Insolvency Act.
[29] *Re Whitaker* [1901] 1 Chap. 9. See p. 12, *per* Rigby L.J.

down to and including the ordinary debts, the excess funds are to be applied in paying interest on the ordinary and preferential debts (which in this instance are all treated as a single category) in respect of the periods during which they have been outstanding since the commencement of the bankruptcy.[30] In view of the fact that, as we have seen,[31] section 322(2) of the Act allows creditors to prove for interest accrued due up to the commencement of bankruptcy, we are here concerned exclusively with the payment of dividend in respect of interest for the period during which the creditors have been kept out of their money since the date of the bankruptcy order. Thus, allowance must be made for any intermediate distribution of dividend which may have been received by creditors belonging to the respective categories, prior to their having been repaid the principal amount of their debts in full. These payments, as and when made, will have progressively reduced the outstanding amounts owing to each creditor, and in respect of which interest continues to be payable until repayment is fully accomplished.

(6) Postponed Debts

Section 328(6) of the Act specially preserves the effects of any statutory provision under which the payment of any debt is to be postponed in the event of bankruptcy until the claims of all preferential and ordinary creditors have been fully repaid, with interest. In certain cases such provisions have been enacted with a view to preventing the success of any fraudulent arrangements designed to defeat the claims of bona fide creditors, which is always a possibility wherever, for example, loans are alleged to have been made between a husband and wife, one of whom has later become bankrupt, or where the business associates of the bankrupt claim to be numbered among his creditors. Section 329 of the Act applies to cases where there have been loans between spouses. It is provided that where bankruptcy debts are owed in respect of credit provided by a person who (whether or not the bankrupt's spouse at the time the credit was provided) was the bankrupt's spouse at the commencement of bankruptcy, such debts shall rank in priority after the debts and interest required to be paid in pursuance of section 328(3) and (4).[32] The drafting of the section makes it irrelevant whether it is the husband or the wife who is the bankrupt party in any given case: the legal effect is identical. Nor is it material to the operation of the section whether the credit was provided in relation to the trade or business activities of the bankrupt's spouse, or for purely private purposes. In addition, the usual rule,[33] that an executrix enjoys a right of retainer in order to satisfy debts due to her from her deceased husband, was held in *Re Jackson*[34] to be exercisable only against debts of equal degree with that of the executrix, and could not be exercised in competition with

---

[30] s.328(4) of the Insolvency Act.
[31] Chap. 9, *ante*, p. 279.
[32] See sections (3), (4) and (5), *above*.
[33] See Chap. 9, *ante*, p. 277.
[34] [1932] A.C. 365.

debts enjoying priority to hers. In the majority of cases the funds available for distribution out of the bankrupt's estate will be exhausted before any payment of postponed debts can take place, but if this proves not to be the case, debts whose payment is postponed under section 329 are payable with interest in respect of the period during which they have been outstanding since the commencement of bankruptcy.[35]

If a person makes a loan to a trader who subsequently becomes bankrupt, it is provided by section 3 of the Partnership Act 1890[36] that where the terms of the lending are that the rate of interest on the loan is to vary with the profits of the business, or that a share of the profits is to be paid as interest, or where a share of the profits is to be paid in consideration of a sale, by the payee, of the goodwill of a business, the claims of other creditors for valuable consideration must be settled before the lender receives anything. Indeed, the lender's incapacity is even more extensive than the words of the section might at first suggest, for it has been held that such a lender is not entitled to prove in the bankruptcy of the borrower for any purpose at all, including even the right of voting, until all the other creditors have been paid in full.[37] And in *Re Meade*[38] it was held that where a person has authorised the use of his or her money for the purpose of a business which subsequently fails, the lender cannot prove in competition with the creditors of the business for the money so lent. This constitutes an even broader general principle than that established by section 3 of the Partnership Act, because it was expressly held in that case that it is irrelevant that the lender was not a partner and was not sharing directly in the profits of the business, provided that it may be said that the lender enjoys some indirect interest in the business as an "investment."[39]

It has further been held that an agreement for a loan which at its commencement is made on terms which fall within the provisions of section 3 of the Partnership Act is not taken out of the ambit of that section even by a subsequent dissolution of the partnership, if the loan is continued by one of the partners: the lender will be a postponed creditor in the bankruptcy of the continuing partner in respect of all advances made on a "profit" basis.[40] But if a lender who has formerly advanced money on a "profit" basis later advances further sums on terms that he is to receive a fixed rate of interest, the lender will stand as a postponed creditor only in respect of those sums advanced on a "profit" basis.[41]

A further category of postponed debts consists of any claims of the beneficiaries under settlements which have been avoided by the trustee in bankruptcy in the exercise of his powers under section 339 of the Insolvency Act.[42] The beneficiaries are entitled to prove in the bankruptcy

---

[35] s.329(2)(b) of the Act. See also s.328(5), discussed in Chap. 9, *ante*, p. 279, which regulates the rate of interest payable.
[36] See also s.2 of that Act.
[37] *Re Grason, ex p. Taylor* (1879) 12 Ch.D. 366.
[38] [1951] Ch. 774.
[39] *ibid.* See pp. 783–784, *per* Romer and Harman, JJ.
[40] *Re Mason* [1899] 1 Q.B. 810.
[41] *ibid.*
[42] See *ante*, Chap. 8, p. 221.

of the settlor for compensation for breach of covenant, but their claims are relegated to this sixth category,[43] and so will not be paid unless the funds which have become available are so ample as to render the insolvency of the bankrupt merely a marginal one.

(7) Surplus Payable to the Bankrupt

Section 330(5) of the Act declares that the bankrupt is entitled to any surplus remaining after full payment of all costs and expenses of the bankruptcy proceedings and after full payment with interest has been made to the creditors in the order we have described above in the first six categories. If such a surplus exists, it is clear that the bankruptcy has been only a technical one, occasioned by the debtor's having experienced a practical insolvency to a sufficient extent that a petition was successfully presented against him and an adjudication obtained. It may be that a debtor's inability to secure repayment to himself of debts which he was owed has been the sole cause of his failure to meet his own liabilities in due time, and hence the exercise by the trustee of his substantial and far-reaching powers to get in all debts owing to the bankrupt may have the most expeditious way of obtaining repayment, obviating the need for the bankrupt to litigate separately a number of small or even large claims. Nevertheless, although bankruptcy will in such cases have been something of a blessing in disguise, it may fairly be said that in a case of this kind the debtor "ought not to have been adjudged bankrupt," and certainly it can be proved *ex hypothesi*, that "the bankruptcy debts and the expenses of the bankruptcy have all been paid." Consequently, it may be thought that a clear case could be made out for annulment of the bankruptcy following an application under section 282 of the Act.[44] This might seem a more logical procedure in the circumstances than for an application to be made by the bankrupt seeking an early discharge from bankruptcy,[45] but it must be noted nevertheless that annulment of a bankruptcy is by no means an inevitable or automatic consequence of the bankrupt's solvency having been thus conclusively demonstrated. This is because the court's power under section 282(1) is a discretionary one, since the opening words of the section are permissive not mandatory. The court can therefore review the debtor's conduct before reaching its decision whether to annul the bankruptcy, just as it may do when considering an application for discharge under section 280. So, even where the sole reason for the creditor's having had to resort to bankruptcy proceedings was that the debtor, although fully solvent, simply refused to pay his debts so that bankruptcy effectively constituted the readiest means by which his creditors could compel him to pay, it is theoretically open to the court to "punish" the debtor for his intransigence by refusing to annul the order of the adjudication, so that the status of bankrupt, with its attendant disabilities and disqualifications,[46] will continue to attach to the debtor

---

[43] *Re Baughan* [1947] 1 Ch. 313.
[44] See Chap. 11, *post*, p. 322.
[45] *ibid.*, p. 309. Such an application could only be made where the bankrupt meets the condition specified in s.279(1)(*a*).
[46] See Chap. 11, *post*, p. 321.

until his discharge comes about under the appropriate provision of the Act, namely sections 279 or 280. In the past, the continuation of a bankruptcy even after the debtor's solvency had been established has been justified on the grounds that some creditor might not have proved his debt through inadvertence, and hence there remained a technical possibility that the debtor could turn out to be insolvent after all. Moreover, it was argued, by maintaining the bankrupt's subjection to the regime of the bankruptcy law a better opportunity was afforded to the trustee or official receiver to investigate the bankrupt's conduct thoroughly, with a view to discovering any offences which may have been committed. Despite some criticism,[47] the law has remained unchanged in this regard and no restrictions have been placed upon the court's discretion under section 282(1) with regard to the annulment of the bankruptcy order.

One other technical matter to be considered is the precise meaning of the word "creditors" in the context of section 330(5): is the requirement of the section satisfied if there has been payment in full to all creditors who have proved, or is it only satisfied if there has been payment in full to all known creditors of the bankrupt, whether they have proved or not? In *Re Ward*,[48] Farwell J. held that the former interpretation seemed the more appropriate, and hence a bankrupt will be entitled to receive any surplus despite the fact that there are creditors who have omitted to prove for their debts and will remain unpaid.

(B) Second Bankruptcy

Mention was made in Chapter 5 of the fact that a person may be the subject of a bankruptcy petition at a time when he is already undischarged from the effects of a previous bankruptcy order.[49] Where an undischarged bankrupt undergoes a second, or subsequent, adjudication important questions of principle arise regarding the proper manner in which to allocate priorities of entitlement as between the creditors in the earlier and the later bankruptcy. The current law, which is contained in sections 334 and 335 of the Act, represents a change from the provisions in force prior to 1986, and adopts the recommendations of the *Blagden Committee*,[50] which were subsequently endorsed by the *Cork Committee*.[51] The principal area of contention is the destiny of such assets as may have been acquired by the bankrupt since the date of the earlier bankruptcy order. In most cases these will have been acquired by means of credit provided by persons who, necessarily, cannot participate in the earlier bankruptcy on the basis of those debts but must, perforce, prove for them in the later bankruptcy. As the earlier bankruptcy will usually be the more substantial one, it would be grossly inequitable if the creditors in that bankruptcy were permitted to oust the creditors in the later bankruptcy from proper participation in the

---
[47] See Cmnd. 221 (1957), paras. 143–149.
[48] [1942] Ch. 294.
[49] *Ante*, p. 80.
[50] Cmnd. 221, para. 114.
[51] Cmnd. 8558, paras. 1164–1168.

rateable distribution of those assets which are in effect the product of the funds and credit which they have freshly provided.

It is well established that the second, and any subsequent, bankruptcy takes priority of effect over any previous bankruptcy from which the bankrupt remains undischarged and that the trustee in the earlier bankruptcy becomes a creditor in the later one in respect of any unsatisfied balance of debts provable in the bankruptcy of which he is trustee.[52] The creditors of the bankrupt in the earlier, or in any prior, bankruptcy do not themselves become creditors in the later bankruptcy in respect of the same debts, since their claims are administered collectively by the trustee in the bankruptcy of which they properly became proving creditors.[53] Section 335(6) of the Act provides that any amount provable in a later bankruptcy by the existing trustee in an earlier one ranks in priority after all the other debts provable in the later bankruptcy and interest on those debts. Accordingly, no payment can be forthcoming out of the assets comprised in the second bankruptcy, so far as the claims provable in the earlier bankruptcy are concerned, unless all the other debts provable in the second bankruptcy have been paid in full, together with interest and expenses payable.

Property which was comprised in the bankrupt's estate at the date of commencement of the earlier bankruptcy does not form part of the estate for the purposes of the later bankruptcy, and thus remains available for distribution to the creditors in the earlier administration.[54] However, any property which, as after-acquired property, has become vested in the trustee of the earlier bankruptcy by virtue of section 307(3) of the Act, and any money paid to that trustee in pursuance of an income payments order under section 310 (together with any property or money in the trustee's hands which represents the proceeds of sale or application of either of these categories of property) becomes comprised in the bankrupt's estate for the purposes of the later bankruptcy with effect from the commencement of that bankruptcy.[55] Where a bankruptcy order is made against an undischarged bankrupt the trustee in the earlier bankruptcy must, until such time as there is a trustee of the estate for the purposes of the later bankruptcy, assume responsibility for safeguarding the property which will in due course vest in the trustee in the later bankruptcy, and hold it in readiness for delivery up to the latter as and when requested to do so.[56] Indeed, from the time when he has notice of the presentation of a petition for a bankruptcy order against the bankrupt whose estate he is administering, a trustee must not distribute or otherwise dispose of any property which, if a bankruptcy order is in due course made, will become comprised in the bankrupt's estate for the purposes of the later

---

[52] Insolvency Act 1986, s.335(5).
[53] *ibid.*
[54] *ibid.*, s.335(4). (This expressly includes property which the bankrupt actually owned at the date of commencement of the earlier bankruptcy, but which was at the time exempted from his estate by virtue of s.283(2), while remaining subject to the right of the trustee under s.308 to claim an exempted item for the estate in exchange for providing a less expensive replacement: see Chap. 8, *ante*, p. 219.).
[55] Insolvency Act 1986, ss.335(1), (2), 334(3).
[56] *ibid.*, s.335(1); Insolvency Rules, rr. 6.226, 6.227.

bankruptcy: any such purported distribution or disposition is by section 334(2) rendered void except to the extent that it was made with the consent of the court or is subsequently ratified by the court. It may be noted however that any property which becomes comprised in a bankrupt's estate as a result of the operation of the statutory provisions which have been described is subject to a first charge in favour of the trustee in the earlier bankruptcy for any bankruptcy expenses incurred by him in relation to that property.[57]

(C) Declaration and Payment of Dividend[58]

Before declaring a dividend the trustee (or liquidator) must give notice of his intention to do so to all known creditors who have not proved their debts, and in the case of a first dividend, unless he has previously by advertisement invited the creditors to prove their debts, he must also give notice of the intended dividend by public advertisement.[59] The notice must specify a date, not less than 21 days from the date of the notice, which constitutes the last date for lodging of proof by creditors who are to participate in the dividend, and the trustee must state that it is his intention to declare an interim or final dividend (as the case may be) within the period of four months from the last date for proving.[60] All proofs lodged by creditors (insofar as not already dealt with) must be dealt with by the trustee within seven days from the last date for proving: the trustee is not obliged to deal with proofs lodged later than the specified date, but he may do so at his own discretion.[61] If a proof is rejected in whole or in part, application may be made to the court for the trustee's decision to be reversed or varied, or alternatively an application may be made for a proof to be expunged or for the amount of the claim to be reduced: in either event, if such an application is made within the period of four months from the last date for proving, the trustee may postpone or cancel the dividend.[62] If no such cancellation or postponement takes place the trustee must within the same four-month period proceed to declare the dividend of which he has given notice, but if any application to reverse or vary any decision of his on proof is pending before the court, the dividend may only be declared with the leave of the court itself.[63]

When a trustee has declared a dividend he is required to send to each

---

[57] *ibid.*, s.335(3). For bankruptcy expenses, see *above*.
[58] Note: the rules herein described apply in common to both bankruptcy and company winding up. The expression "the insolvent" is accordingly used to mean "the company in liquidation" or "the bankrupt," as the case may be. Where the word "trustee" is used in the text, the word "liquidator" can be understood as applying for the purposes of a company winding up.
[59] Insolvency Act, s.342(2); Insolvency Rules, r. 11.2(1), (1A). See however r. 11.12 for the more restricted requirements as to notice where a dividend is to be distributed to preferential creditors.
[60] Insolvency Rules, r. 11.2(2), (3). No special form for giving of notice is provided in the Rules, but under the general provision in r. 12.4 as to notices, notice must be in writing.
[61] *ibid.*, r. 11.3.
[62] *ibid.*, r. 11.4. On appeals against decisions on proof, see rr. 6.105, 6.107, *ante*, Chap. 9.
[63] *ibid.*, r. 11.5.

DISTRIBUTION OF ASSETS

creditor who has proved a notice showing the amount of the dividend, and how it is proposed to distribute it.[64] This notice must also include a number of particulars relating to the insolvency and the administration of the insolvent estate, namely:

(1) Amounts realised from the sale of assets, indicating (so far as practicable) amounts raised by the sale of particular assets;
(2) Payments which have been made during the course of administration of the estate;
(3) What provision, if any, has been made for unsettled claims, and any retention of funds for particular purposes;
(4) The total amount to be distributed, and the rate of dividend; and
(5) Whether, and if so when, any further dividend is expected to be declared.[65]

Although it is expressly provided by section 325(2) of the Act that no action lies against the trustee for a dividend, that sub-section goes on to declare, somewhat paradoxically, that if the trustee refuses to pay any dividend the court may, if it thinks fit, order him to do so and also to pay, out of his own money, interest on the dividend for the time that it was withheld. The correct procedure is therefore for the creditors to make application to the court for an order directing the trustee to pay a dividend, and if the application is successful the trustee will also be personally liable to bear the costs.

A creditor who has not proved his debt before the declaration of any dividend is not allowed to disturb the distribution of that, or any previous, dividend on the grounds that he has not participated in it, but, on the other hand, once he has proved his debt he is entitled to be paid, out of any money which remains or becomes available for distribution, any dividends which he has previously failed to receive, and he is entitled to "catch up" with the other creditors in this way before any money is applied in the payment of a further dividend to the creditors as a whole.[66]

If a creditor contravenes any statutory provision relating to the valuation of securities, the court may, on the application of the trustee (or liquidator), order that the creditor be wholly or partly disqualified from participation in any dividend.[67] On the other hand, a creditor may revalue his security in accordance with the Rules,[68] and if such revaluation occurs when a dividend has been declared and results in a reduction of the unsecured claim ranking for dividend, the creditor must repay to the estate any consequential excess which he has received as dividend above his proper entitlement. If, on the other hand, the revaluation results in an increase of the unsecured claim the creditor is entitled to receive an appropriate, supplementary dividend out of any money available for

---

[64] Insolvency Act, s.324(3); Insolvency Rules, r. 11.6(1).
[65] Insolvency Rules, r. 11.6(2).
[66] Insolvency Act, s.325(1).
[67] Insolvency Rules, r. 11.10.
[68] See r. 6.115 *et seq.*, *ante*, Chap. 9.

Declaration and Payment of Dividend

distribution, before any further dividend is distributed to the creditors generally.[69] In accordance with the principle applicable to late-proving creditors, however, a secured creditor who revalues his security is not entitled to disturb any dividend declared (even if not yet distributed) before the date of the revaluation. Similar rules apply in cases where a creditor alters his proof after payment of a dividend, whether in such a way as to increase the amount claimed or such that the proof is withdrawn or the amount of it reduced.[70]

Mode of Payment

Payment of dividend may be made by post, or arrangements may be made with any creditor for it to be paid to him in another way, or to be held for his collection. Where dividend is paid on a negotiable instrument, such as a cheque or other bill of exchange, it is necessary that the amount of the dividend be endorsed on the instrument, or on a certified copy of it, if required to be produced by the holder for that purpose.[71] The right to receive dividend can be assigned by the person who is entitled to it, provided he gives notice to the trustee (or liquidator) under rule 11.11 that he wishes the dividend to be paid to another person, or that he has assigned his entitlement to another person whose name and address must be specified in the notice.

Where any property comprised in the insolvent estate cannot be readily or advantageously sold, the trustee may, with the permission of the creditors' committee, divide it in its existing form among the bankrupt's creditors, according to its estimated value.[72]

(D) Final Distribution and Final Meeting

The Act declares, by section 330(1), that when the trustee has realised all the bankrupt's estate, or so much of it as can, in his opinion, be realised without needlessly protracting the trusteeship, he must give notice in the prescribed manner either:

(1) Of his intention to declare a final dividend or;
(2) That no dividend, or further dividend, will be declared.

In the case of a final dividend the giving of notice must take place in the same manner as for previous dividends which have been declared, as described above.[73] If the trustee (or liquidator) gives notice to the effect

---

[69] Insolvency Rules, r. 11.9.
[70] *ibid.*, r. 11.8.
[71] *ibid.*, r. 11.6(4), (5). See also Insolvency Regulations 1986, reg. 15 and Form 2.
[72] Insolvency Act s.326 (Note: this provision applies in bankruptcy only).
[73] *Above*, p. 301. See Insolvency Rules, r. 11.2, and also Insolvency Act, s.330(2). *Note:* the provisions of ss.330 and 331 are applicable only to bankruptcy.

that no dividend, or no further dividend, will be declared rule 11.7 of the Insolvency Rules makes it a requirement that the notice shall contain a statement to the effect either:

(1) That no funds have been realised; or
(2) That the funds realised have already been used up for defraying the expenses of the administration.

Where there is to be a final dividend, section 330(3) provides that the court may, on the application of any person, postpone the final date by which the trustee's notice requires claims against the bankrupt's estate to be established, but in the absence of such a postponement the insolvent administration enters its final phase, and the trustee will, after the final date has passed, defray any outstanding expenses of the bankruptcy (or liquidation) out of the funds remaining in his hands, and thereafter duly declare and distribute the final dividend among the proving creditors.[74] Thereafter, any creditor who has failed to establish his claim by lodging proof in time will receive nothing, although (in the case of bankruptcy) the debt, as one of the bankruptcy debts, will be discharged through the process of bankruptcy.

By section 331(3) the trustee may adopt the cost-saving procedure of sending out the notice of the final meeting of creditors at the same time as he sends out notice of final distribution as required by section 330(1). When the official receiver is acting as trustee (as is likely to be the case where the assets available for distribution are small) there is no requirement that a final meeting of creditors must take place.[75] Where a final meeting is held the trustee must present a report upon his administration of the bankrupt's estate, and the creditors must determine whether the trustee is to have his release under section 299 of the Act.[76]

Although the term "final dividend" may suggest that the distribution of assets is thereby concluded, the concept is a somewhat relative one because, until the bankrupt is discharged from bankruptcy, assets which become available as part of his estate are still capable of being claimed for the benefit of creditors as after-acquired property. Even if the trustee in bankruptcy has been granted his release, and has relinquished office, the provisions of section 300 of the Act ensure that the position of trustee remains occupied, technically by the official receiver, until the bankrupt's discharge takes effect. The official receiver is thus competent to serve notice under section 307, claiming the property for the estate, and may thereafter distribute a "post-final" dividend, although in practice such events are extremely rare.

Unclaimed Dividends

If at the date when the trustee vacates his office there are any funds left in

---

[74] Insolvency Act, s.330(4).
[75] *ibid.*, s.331(1)(b).
[76] On release, see Chap. 7, *ante*, p. 181.

Final Distribution and Final Meeting

his hands representing unclaimed dividends or undistributed assets of the bankrupt, the trustee must forthwith pay the money into the Insolvency Services Account at the Bank of England.[77] Any money of a similar character which comes into the hands of a former trustee after his vacation of office must be dealt with in the same manner. Once money has been paid into the Insolvency Services Account in this way, it becomes the responsibility of the creditor in whose favour the unclaimed dividend was declared to apply to the Secretary of State for payment, supporting his claim by such evidence of entitlement as the Secretary of State may require.[78] There is a right of appeal to the court exercisable by any person dissatisfied with the decision of the Secretary of State in respect of such a claim.

---

[77] Insolvency Regulations 1995, reg. 31 (S.I. 1995, No. 2507).
[78] *ibid.*, reg. 32.

Chapter 11

TERMINATION OF BANKRUPTCY

Preliminary

Section 278 of the Insolvency Act 1986 declares that the bankruptcy of an individual commences on the day on which a bankruptcy order is made against him, and continues until he is discharged under the provisions of sections 279–282 inclusive. These sections provide for two distinct processes whereby a bankrupt may become discharged: namely in section 279 an automatic discharge taking effect after a prescribed period of time from the commencement of bankruptcy, and in section 280 discharge by order of the court upon application made by the bankrupt. A third possibility also exists for bringing about the termination of a bankruptcy, since under section 282 the court has jurisdiction to annul a bankruptcy order in certain specified circumstances. These three procedures will be examined in turn, and in addition consideration will be given to the various restraints and incapacities which apply during bankruptcy, and in certain cases even after discharge.

(A) Automatic Discharge

Section 279(1) contains provisions whereby bankrupts who have not been previously bankrupt within 15 years of their current adjudication are automatically discharged from bankruptcy at the end of a prescribed period of time, running from the commencement of bankruptcy.[1] Such persons, whom we may term "first-time bankrupts," will obtain an automatic discharge after the elapse of three years from the date of the bankruptcy order,[2] but in cases where the summary administration

---

[1] s.279(1)(a), whereby automatic discharge did not apply to cases where a person was made bankrupt on a petition under s.264(1)(d), has been repealed in consequence of the abolition of criminal bankruptcy by the Criminal Justice Act 1988, ss.39, 40 and Sched. 16 (see also Chap. 13, *post*).

[2] Insolvency Act, s.279(2)(b). See also Sched. 11, para. 13 for transitional provisions applicable to bankruptcies which commenced before the Act came into force.

procedure is employed that period is shortened to two years.[3] The crucial date for the purpose of establishing the 15-year "clean sheet" is the date of the operation of discharge from any previous bankruptcy, and not the date of its commencement: the drafting of section 279(1) requires that the debtor must not have been an undischarged bankrupt at any time in the period of 15 years ending with the commencement of the current bankruptcy. Thus, it is technically possible for a debtor to be eligible for automatic discharge despite the fact that he or she is not, strictly speaking, a "first-time bankrupt", but in practice the later bankruptcy will need to commence at least 17 years, and possibly longer, after the earlier adjudication took place.

Where it transpires that an undischarged bankrupt who is eligible for automatic discharge in this way has failed, or is failing, to comply with the obligations to which he is currently subject by reason of his bankruptcy, the official receiver may apply to the court for an order that the relevant period—two or three years, as the case may be—shall cease to run. The order, made after a hearing of which the bankrupt and the trustee must have notice, may either specify a period for which the running of time shall cease for this purpose, or lay down certain conditions which must be fulfilled by the bankrupt before the running of time can resume.[4] Where such an order is made, the bankrupt may at any time apply for the discharge of the order, in which case a further hearing must be held upon 28 days' notice given to the official receiver and the trustee.[5]

The above arrangements are a further modification of the principle of automatic discharge which was introduced for the first time in 1976.[6] The new provisions are more simple in structure, and also more expeditious in their operation, in that the relevant period has been reduced from five years to three or even two. Although bearing no correspondence to the relevant recommendations of the *Cork Report*,[7] the provisions of section 279 concerning automatic discharge confirm that this mode of termination of bankruptcy is henceforth to be the norm for the majority of bankrupts, for whom adjudication is a first-time experience. The removal of the former requirement for such persons, in common with all other bankrupts, to make personal application to the court in order to obtain their discharge, and the substitution of the concept of a fixed, and relatively short, duration of the condition of bankruptcy for those debtors who respect their legal obligations while they remain undischarged, has undoubtedly marked the beginning of a fundamental adjustment in prevailing social attitudes towards bankruptcy, and towards those who undergo it. For the so-called "deserving" debtor, at any rate, the aura of menace and near-perpetual stigma which hitherto surrounded the institution of bankruptcy cannot but have been diminished by the clarified prospect of a finite, and relatively short, interruption of the individual's normal legal status.

[3] *ibid.*, s.279(2)(a). For summary administration, see s.275, discussed in Chap. 12, *post*.
[4] *ibid.*, s.279(3). For procedure, see Insolvency Rules, r. 6.215. see also r. 6.176(4).
[5] Insolvency Rules 1986, r. 6.216.
[6] Insolvency Act 1976, ss. 7, 8. See, *e.g.* Fletcher, *Law of Bankruptcy* (1978) Chap. 11, pp. 306–310.
[7] Cmnd. 8558, paras. 605–615; *cf.* the *White Paper*, Cmnd. 9175, paras. 117–119.

It may nevertheless be questioned whether the present law has succeeded in its commendable objective of mitigating the plight of the "honest but unfortunate" debtor only at the expense of providing enhanced opportunities for the "amoral calculator" to inflict considerable social and commercial harm at comparatively small personal cost and inconvenience. By making the operation of automatic discharge depend upon the sole criterion of the 15-year "clean slate" period, with the proviso that the bankrupt avoids provoking the trustee into taking steps to stop the clock, as it were, the law has refrained from making any attempt to evaluate the merits of the bankrupt's conduct prior to the commencement of bankruptcy itself. With respect, it must be urged that even a first-time bankruptcy may in some circumstances amount to a matter of serious social concern, either because of the magnitude of the debtor's overall deficiency, or because of the manner in which it has been generated, or because of a combination of these and other factors. In the absence of some procedure for bringing appropriate and effective sanctions to bear in such cases—for example by means of some process analogous to that under which company directors can be disqualified for unfitness for up to 15 years[8]—there is a danger of progressive erosion of the standards of commercial morality, to the extent that bankruptcy could in time be viewed as a mere rite of passage, or formative experience, carrying little or no connotation of moral opprobrium.[9]

(B) Discharge by Order of the Court

Where a person is adjudicated less than 15 years from the date of termination of a previous state of bankruptcy the automatic discharge provisions are not applicable. Bankrupts who belong to this category may be discharged from bankruptcy only by order of the court, for which application must be made under section 280. The earliest date at which such an application may be made is at the end of the period of five years beginning with the commencement of the bankruptcy.[10] It may be observed that the provisions of section 280 and the relevant Rules effect a drastic simplification of the law, by comparison with that in force prior to 1986.[11] Although the Rules still embody a requirement that the court have regard to the bankrupt's conduct prior to and during the bankruptcy, the subsidiary code of so-called "bankruptcy offences" has completely disappeared, thus leaving all cases to be dealt with on a uniform basis by the court.[12] As a result, much of the previous case law relating to discharge upon application to the court has been rendered obsolete, but it is tentatively suggested that courts may be inclined to maintain some sort of

---

[8] Disqualification of directors is dealt with *post*, Chap. 27.
[9] *cf.* the arguments in favour of a two-tier bankruptcy system advanced in Chap. 4 ("Bankruptcy Abuses") of the "Justice" Report (*Insolvency Law: An Agenda for Reform*), published in 1994.
[10] Insolvency Act 1986, s.280(1).
[11] *cf.* Bankruptcy Act 1914, s.26 (repealed).
[12] *cf.* Bankruptcy Act 1914, s.26(3); Fletcher, *op. cit.* above, n. 6, at pp. 291–298.

consistency in their approach to cases whose facts resemble those typically encountered and dealt with under the previous legislative provisions. In general, it may be supposed, the very fact that all bankrupts who have occasion to resort to the section 280 procedure will by definition be "repeat bankrupts" should dispose the courts to adhere to their traditional policy of rigorous appraisal of the merits of the bankrupt's case for reinstatement in commercial society.[13]

The Application

A bankrupt who intends to apply for discharge under section 280 must give the official receiver notice of the application and deposit with him such sum as the official receiver may require to cover the attendant costs.[14] If satisfied that this requirement has been complied with the court must fix a venue for the hearing and give at least 42 days' notice of it to the official receiver and the bankrupt, and the official receiver in turn must give at least 14 days' notice to the trustee and to every creditor who, to the official receiver's knowledge, has an unsatisfied claim outstanding against the estate.[15] As under the former law, the official receiver is required to prepare a report upon the bankrupt's conduct and to file it in court in advance of the hearing. Rule 6.218 now requires that the report be filed at least 21 days in advance of the hearing, and that it contain the following information with respect to the bankrupt:

(1) Any failure by him to comply with his obligations under the Insolvency Act;
(2) The circumstances surrounding the present bankruptcy, and those surrounding any previous bankruptcy of his;
(3) The extent to which, in the present and in any previous bankruptcy, his liabilities have exceeded his assets;
(4) Particulars of any distribution which has been, or is expected to be made to creditors in the present bankruptcy, or conversely (if such is the case) that there has been and is to be no distribution. Moreover, the official receiver is expressly directed to include in his report any other matters which in his opinion ought to be brought to the court's attention. The report thus contains the appraisal of an experienced officer of the court regarding the causes of the bankruptcy and the bankrupt's personal history insofar as bearing upon his financial failure. The official receiver's qualitative assessment of the bankrupt is thus of foremost significance, and has traditionally carried great influence with the court in making its decision regarding discharge.

Copies of the official receiver's report must be sent to the bankrupt and

[13] cf. Boshkoff (1982) 131 U. of Penn. Law Rev. 69.
[14] Insolvency Rules 1986, r. 6.217(1).
[15] ibid., r. 6.217(2), (3), (4).

the trustee so as to reach them at least 14 days before the date of the hearing.[16] The bankrupt is allowed to file notice in court specifying any statements in the report which he intends to deny or dispute. Such notice must be filed at least seven days in advance, with copies to the official receiver and the trustee.[17] In the past, a strict approach was adopted with regard to the bankrupt's right to challenge statements in the official receiver's report, and only those elements of which intention to raise objection had been precisely notified could be raised at the hearing itself. Indeed, a notable distinction was drawn between statements in the report and any conclusions which the official receiver might have based on those statements, and it was held that a notice of intention to dispute conclusions did not constitute notice of intention to dispute the statements on which those conclusions were founded.[18] For the purpose of ensuring that any such dispute can be properly examined at the hearing, it is suggested that this past policy should be maintained for the future also.

At the hearing of the application for discharge the official receiver, the trustee, and any creditor may appear and make representations, and put to the bankrupt such questions as the court may allow.[19] Although in most cases the official receiver will have discovered, and included in his report, all the information necessary to enable the court to decide whether to grant the bankrupt's application, there is much to be said in favour of a creditor's attending the hearing, and if he had any relevant evidence to adduce this may help to ensure that justice is done on the merits of the case. On the other hand, while there is no active obligation for any creditor to appear, any contract whereby a creditor agrees for a consideration not to appear, and not to oppose the application for discharge, will be illegal as tending to pervert the course of justice.[20] The trustee in bankruptcy, for his part, must maintain his objectivity and act in the interests of the creditors as a whole and of the public at large. He must certainly refrain from entering into any arrangement with the bankrupt whereby he effectively undertakes to connive at the latter's obtaining his discharge, upon whatever terms, for such improper arrangements may facilitate the perpetration of fraud upon creditors by the bankrupt or his associates.[21]

Powers of the Court

Section 280(2) provides that on an application for discharge the court may either:

(1) Refuse to discharge the bankrupt from bankruptcy; or

---

[16] *ibid.*, r. 6.218(2).
[17] *ibid.*, r. 6.218(3); Form 6.75.
[18] *Re Woolf* (1906) 22 T.L.R. 501. Reports of the Official Receiver have been held to enjoy absolute privilege: *Bottomley v. Brougham* [1908] 1 K.B. 584.
[19] Insolvency Rules 1986, r. 6.218(4).
[20] *Kearley v. Thomson* (1890) 24 Q.B.D. 742, in which it was held that any payment to the creditors, in part performance of the illegal agreement, was irrecoverable because the parties were not *in pari delicto*. *Cf.* also *Re Andrews* (1881) 18 Ch.D. 464.
[21] *Re Shaw* [1917] 2 K.B. 734.

(2) Make an order discharging him absolutely; or
(3) Make an order discharging him subject to specified conditions with respect to any income which may subsequently become due to him, or with respect to property devolving upon or acquired by him.

Subsection (3) further provides that in cases (1) and (2) the court may provide that the order is to have immediate effect, or alternatively that it is to have its effect suspended for a specified period, or until any specified conditions have been fulfilled. The court thus enjoys wide discretionary powers which have been so framed as to enable it to aim at striking a balance between rehabilitation and deterrence. It is especially notable that the court's powers can be so exercised as to require the bankrupt to undertake to contribute further to the repayment of creditors even after his discharge.[22] Appellate courts have traditionally been reluctant to interfere with the lower court's exercise of its discretion regarding the terms on which discharge is granted, and will do so only in cases where manifestly wrong conclusions have been formed by the judge on his way to making his decision.[23] A further ground for interference by the appellate court would be where it could be shown that statements in the official receiver's report, upon which the court's decision has been based at least in part, are either unfounded or capable of an alternative explanation.[24]

It is furthermore accepted that there are limits to the court's duty to take account of the bankrupt's behaviour outside the context of the bankruptcy itself, in taking its decision regarding his discharge. Thus, in *Re Barker*, Lord Esher M.R. expressed the opinion that the court need not take into consideration conduct of the debtor which could not have had anything to do with the bankruptcy, either in producing it or in affecting it in any way after its commencement,[25] while in the earlier case of *Re Betts and Block*,[26] a majority of the same Court of Appeal took the somewhat pedantic view that a bankrupt's refusal to cooperate in the effecting of insurance upon his life, so as to enhance the value of a contingent interest which was the principal asset, did not constitute a "misconduct in relation to the realisation of his property" which ought to influence the court's decision regarding his discharge.[27] A more readily accepted decision in favour of a bankrupt was *Re Pearse*,[28] in which it was held that delay in making the

[22] *cf.* Hansard, H.L. Vol. 459, Col. 1257; H.C. Standing Committee E, June 18, 1985, Col. 370.
[23] *Re Payne, ex p. Castle Mail Packets Co.* (1886) 18 Q.B.D. 154; *Re Stainton* (1887) 4 Morr. 242 (not reported on this point in 19 Q.B.D. 182), where the judge had taken an excessively lenient view of the debtor's conduct. *Cf.* also the remarks of Lord Greene, M.R., concerning interference with the use of discretion, in *Re Smith* [1947] 1 All E.R. 769, 771 *et seq.*
[24] *Re Sultzberger* (1887) 4 Morr. 82.
[25] (1890) 25 Q.B.B. 285, 293.
[26] (1887) 19 Q.B.D. 39, *affirmed sub nom. Board of Trade v. Block* (1888) 13 App.Cas. 570 (H.L.).
[27] See, however, the powerful dissenting judgments of Fry, L.J. in the Court of Appeal and of Lord Fitzgerald in the House of Lords. The case was decided under s.24 of the Bankruptcy Act 1883 (repealed).
[28] (1912) 107 L.T. 859.

Discharge by Order of the Court

application will not of itself constitute a justification for the unconditional refusal of a discharge, provided that the delay is not accompanied by any suggestion of fraud, such as the intention that lapse of time should blot out adverse evidence.

The Act itself lays down no explicit guidelines to indicate what are the objectives to be achieved through the court's controlled use of its discretionary powers in relation to discharge from bankruptcy. However, it may be logically inferred from the overall purposes attaching to the bankruptcy law that the court should be mindful of such questions as the debtor's suitability to recommence trading[29]; whether the creditors have been enabled to recover all that might reasonably be made forthcoming to them through the bankruptcy; and the essential consideration of the proper protection of the public.[30] Against such considerations must be balanced the need to avoid placing such a lingering burden upon the debtor as to destroy all motive for future exertion on his part, for it is a fundamental policy of the bankruptcy law that, in return for giving up his property, the debtor shall be made a free man again.[31] Likewise it would be regarded as unfair to accompany a refusal of discharge with a formulation of conditions as to the future payment of money to so great an amount that there is no reasonable chance that the bankrupt will ever qualify for his discharge.[32]

Of the alternatives open to the court, the most adverse decision, namely an unconditional refusal of discharge, is generally considered to be reserved for use in exceptional circumstances.[33] If the court is of the opinion that, while the bankrupt is not wholly irredeemable, it is desirable that he should undergo a further period of restriction in preparation for his fresh start, the appropriate admixture of discipline and encouragement may be achieved through the granting of an order of discharge whose operation is suspended for whatever period is deemed to be suitable. The periods of suspension range from the comparatively brief—six months or less—to the relatively extended—five years or, exceptionally, more. If an appellate court considers that the period of suspension which has been imposed is inappropriate in view of all the circumstances, it may vary the order in the interests of justice.[34]

In order to secure the interests of the creditors, who may well have received very little by way of dividend by the time that the application for discharge is made, the court may see fit to utilise its power of imposing terms upon the bankrupt as a condition of granting him his discharge. The Act accordingly allows the court to impose conditions with respect to the bankrupt's subsequent earnings or income, or with respect to his after-

---

[29] cf. Re Cook (1889) 6 Morr. 224, 233, per Field, J.
[30] Re Badcock (1886) 3 Morr. 138, 144, per Cave, J.
[31] See Re Shackleton (1889) 6 Morr. 304, 307 et seq., per Cave, J. and Re Gaskell [1904] 2 K.B. 478, 482, per Vaughan Williams L.J. Even if offences have been committed, it seems that this policy consideration will retain its validity cf. Re Bullen (1888) 5 Morr. 243; Re Gould (1890) 7 Morr. 215.
[32] Re James (1891) 8 Morr. 19.
[33] Re Pearse (1912) 107 L.T. 859; cf. Re Benjamin [1943] 1 All E.R. 468.
[34] Re Swabey (1897) 76 L.T. 534.

acquired property. The imposition of such a condition may be coupled with a reference to some minimum figure which is required to be made over to the creditors as dividend.[35] However, unless care is taken, such a condition may merely succeed in conferring upon the creditors an "expectation" of purely illusory value, for it may be that, either by accident or by design, the bankrupt never becomes entitled to any property, or to any income above what is required for the maintenance of himself and his family, and hence the condition will be rendered worthless so far as the creditors are concerned.[36]

Appeals (including appellate jurisdiction in general)

Appeal against the court's refusal to grant discharge, or against the terms upon which discharge is granted, lies in the way provided by section 375, which has general application to all aspects of bankruptcy. Section 375(1) provides that every court having jurisdiction in individual insolvency matters may review, rescind or vary any order which it has made in the exercise of that jurisdiction. Hence a possible first avenue of recourse is one in which an application is made to the court concerned, requesting it to reconsider and alter its own original decision in the light of new arguments or fresh information. Thereafter, an appeal properly so-called may take place. Strictly speaking, the jurisdiction conferred by section 375(1) does not constitute an appellate procedure, since the latter involves an exercise of jurisdiction by a hierarchically superior court to that whose original decision is being challenged. In practice the courts are cautious in exercising the jurisdiction to review their own decisions, since the effect of so doing is to allow what may amount to a second application for the order or relief which is being sought, possibly beyond the time limited for making the original application. The cases in which the court will exercise its discretion to entertain such an application will therefore be somewhat rare, and will normally involve the operation of exceptional circumstances, such as fresh and congent evidence such as would, if unanswered, furnish grounds for reversing or varying the original order of that court.[37] While not unmindful of the "floodgates" argument, the courts are aware that the costs of a full-scale appeal may be averted by appropriate use of the facility provided by section 375(1).[38]

Appeal from a decision by a county court or by a registrar in bankruptcy of the High Court lies to a single judge of the High Court, and a final appeal from a decision of that judge on such an appeal lies, with the leave of the judge or of the Court of Appeal, to the Court of Appeal.[39] It may be noted

---

[35] *cf.* the power formerly exerciseable by the court in special cases falling under s.26(2), proviso (iii), of the Bankruptcy Act 1914 (repealed).

[36] See *Re Bullen* (1888) 5 Morr. 243; *Re Gould* (1890) 7 Morr. 215.

[37] *Re A Debtor (No. 32–SD–91)* [1993] 2 All E.R. 991 (involving application to set aside a statutory demand).

[38] *cf.* the comparable power, in relation to the winding up of companies, provided by I.R., r. 7.47(1). The Court of Appeal have confirmed that s.375 of the Act and r. 7.45 of the Rules are intended to establish a uniform system of appeals in personal and corporate insolvency actions, so that it is permissible to draw analogies between their respective provisions: *Midrome Ltd v. Shaw* [1993] BCC 659 at pp. 660–661, *per* Bingham, M.R. and Hoffmann, L.J.

[39] Insolvency Act 1986, s.375(2). See Practice Direction No. 1 of 1995 (Insolvency Appeals: Individuals), announced July 28, 1995 (*The Times*, August 14, 1995).

that there is the further possibility (subject to leave being granted) of a final appeal to the House of Lords in bankruptcy matters where a point of law of general public interest arises. An appeal within the terms of section 375(2) of the Act may arise either as a challenge to the original decision taken by the lower court, or as a challenge to the refusal by that court to exercise its discretion under section 375(1) to review its own original decision. Where the grounds of an appeal to the Court of Appeal include a challenge to the refusal by the judge below to grant an extension of time for bringing an appeal at that level, difficult questions of statutory construction and procedure arise. This is because the terms of section 375(2) refer to an appeal from "a decision of that judge on such an appeal," whereas the essence of the appellant's complaint is that the precise effect of the decision of the judge has been to prevent any appeal from taking place. Although the drafting of the Insolvency Act appears to preclude the bringing of an appeal under section 375(2) in such cases, the Court of Appeal have held that the provisions of section 16 of the Supreme Court Act 1981, which empower the court to hear and determine appeals from "any judgment or order of the High Court" are sufficiently wide in their scope to confer a jurisdiction to entertain an appeal in these circumstances.[40]

Special provision is made by Rule 7.48 of the Insolvency Rules to enable an appeal to be preferred at the instance of the Secretary of State from any order of the court made on an application for the rescission or annulment of a bankruptcy order, or for a bankrupt's discharge. Other persons with the requisite interest and standing to appeal against the granting of an order of discharge are the official receiver or the trustee, and any creditor whose debt remains unpaid.[41] The basis of a creditor's appeal may be the undue leniency of the terms upon which the discharge has been granted, or the fact that the terms inflict some particular injustice upon the appellant personally so as to violate the principle that all equally-ranked creditors must be treated alike. In the latter instance, however, it would seem to be essential that the creditor should first have established his precise status in the bankruptcy by proving his debt, before he can properly claim to exercise a right of appeal.[42]

The standing of the bankrupt to initiate an appeal is necessarily limited to those matters in which the law regards him as retaining a personal interest in the outcome of the proceedings in question. This is manifestly the case where the decision appealed against concerned the bankrupt's own discharge, or the possible annulment of the bankruptcy.[43] The same is true of the limited range of personal rights of action which do not vest in the

---

[40] *Lawrence v. European Credit Co. Ltd* [1992] BCC 792. The decision confirms the correctness of the interpretative approach followed in *Podberry v. Peak* [1981] Ch. 344 (C.A.) in construing the effects of s.108(2) of the Bankruptcy Act 1914, whose material provisions are echoed by those currently contained in s.375(2) of the Act of 1986. The point concerning the separate jurisdiction arising under s.16 of the Supreme Court Act 1981 was not considered in the earlier case. For further comment on each decision see, respectively, Fletcher [1994] J.B.L. 279 and [1981] J.B.L. 387.

[41] *Re Payne* (1886) 18 Q.B.D. 154.

[42] *Re Chesters* (1877) 6 Ch.D. 57; *cf.* observations as to the principle of equal treatment in *Re Caribbean Products (Yam Importers) Ltd* [1966] 1 Ch. 331; [1966] 2 W.L.R. 153 (a company liquidation case).

[43] See Section (C) below, this chapter.

trustee in bankruptcy, and which the bankrupt is allowed to pursue on his own behalf despite undergoing adjudication.[44] But otherwise, according to long-established principle, a bankrupt cannot in his own name appeal from a judgment against him which is enforceable only against the estate vested in his trustee.[45]

In general, the procedure and practice of the Supreme Court is to be followed in relation to appeals in insolvency proceedings.[46] The notion attaching to the power of review now contained in section 375(1) is that it is perpetual and hence may be exercised at any time, notwithstanding the general maxim: *interest reipublicae ut sit finis litium*.[47] Hence there remains the possibility that at a later stage the court may form the view that the bankrupt has been punished enough by the provisions of its original order, which may consequently undergo alteration in a way favourable to the bankrupt. The court will be assisted to make such amendment by any evidence that the bankrupt has been of good conduct since the previous hearing.[48]

A qualified party may maintain an appeal, or even an application to review the granting of an order of discharge, even though the discharge itself has become effective. The court's general jurisdiction to revoke, or if appropriate to vary, any order of discharge is exercisable in addition to the court's particular power to revoke a discharge on account of the debtor's failure to fulfil any conditions which may have been attached to it, including the due satisfaction of any judgment which has been entered against him by the trustee.[49] Nevertheless, where the substance of the appeal consists of an objection to the manner in which a lower court has exercised a discretionary power, the established practice, as already stated, is that an appellate court will decline to interfere except upon the strongest of evidence that the decision below was wrongly arrived at.

The Order of Discharge

An order of discharge granted by the court under section 280 must bear the date on which it is made, but does not take effect until it is drawn up by the court.[50] When the order has been drawn up it has effect retrospectively to the date on which it was made.[51] The purpose of this inbuilt *hiatus* is to allow time for the lodging of any appeal against the order, and to avoid unnecessary confusion in case such an appeal is successful. Accordingly, rule 6.221 provides that the court's order must not be issued or gazetted until the time allowed for appealing has expired, or until the appeal, if there is one, has been determined. Moreover, the delay in drawing up the order

---

[44] See Chap. 8, *ante*, p. 191. Note also the possibility of assignment by the trustee bank to the bankrupt of rights of action of a proprietory character: *ibid.*
[45] *Heath v. Tang* [1993] 4 All E.R. 694 (C.A.), reviewing the previous case law.
[46] Insolvency Rules 1986, r. 7.49; see R.S.C., Ord. 59.
[47] *Re Tobias & Co.* [1891] 1 Q.B. 463.
[48] *Re Tobias & Co*, above; *Re Shields* (1912) 106 L.T. 345.
[49] *Re a Debtor (No. 946 of 1920)* [1939] Ch. 489; *Re Summers* [1907] 2 K.B. 166.
[50] Insolvency Rules 1986, r. 6.219(1).
[51] *ibid.*, r. 6.219(2).

allows time for the obtaining of any necessary consents to be given by the bankrupt as part of the conditions upon which discharge is granted. Copies of the order must be sent by the court to the bankrupt, the trustee and the official receiver, and the order must show the facts upon which the court has based its decision and also the reasons for that decision, for it is essential in the event of any appeal to have a clear indication of the findings which have influenced the exercise of the court's discretion.[52] Where discharge has come about automatically through expiration of time under the operation of section 279, the former bankrupt may find it useful to possess some officially-issued document as confirmation of this. The Rules therefore enable him to apply to the court for the issue of a certificate of discharge, which will indicate the date from which discharge is effective.[53] Furthermore, the discharged bankrupt may require the Secretary of State to give notice of the discharge, albeit at the former bankrupt's own expense, in the Gazette or in any newspaper in which the bankruptcy was advertised, or in both these publications.[54]

The Effect of Discharge

Whether discharge comes about automatically under the operation of section 279, or by order of the court under section 280, the effect is identical so far as the bankrupt is concerned. The general rule is that, from the date when it becomes operative, discharge releases the bankrupt from all the bankruptcy debts, and frees him from the disabilities and disqualifications to which he was personally subject while occupying the status of a bankrupt.[55] To this general proposition there are, however, a number of important exceptions.

In the first place, to allow for the possibility that a discharge may take effect in some cases before the completion of the task of administration and distribution of the bankrupt's estate, section 281(1) provides that discharge has no effect upon the functions of the trustee in bankruptcy, so far as they remain to be carried out, nor on the operation of the provisions of the Act which are relevant for this purpose. It is expressly stated that discharge does not affect the right of any creditor of the bankrupt to prove in the bankruptcy for any debt from which the bankrupt is released. Thus, further dividends may be distributed out of property realised or becoming available only after the bankrupt's discharge, and this will include anything which, as a condition imposed by the court in granting an order of discharge, he may be obliged to make over out of property acquired subsequently to the discharge itself being granted.

A further important, saving provision is contained in section 281(2) to the effect that discharge does not affect the right of any secured creditor of the bankrupt to enforce his security for any debt from which the bankrupt

---

[52] *ibid.*, r. 6.219(3); Form 6.76. See also *Re Nicholas* (1890) 7 Morr. 54; *Re Oswell* (1892) 9 Morr. 202.
[53] Insolvency Rules 1986, r. 6.220(1); Form 6.77.
[54] *ibid.*, r. 6.220(2), (3).
[55] Insolvency Act 1986, s.281(1). "Bankruptcy debts" are defined in s.382, discussed at p. 250, *ante*. The personal disqualifications of an undischarged bankrupt are discussed *infra*.

Termination of Bankruptcy

is released. This is in consequence of one of the fundamental principles of the law of security, namely that the security right itself is independent of the debt in respect of which it is created, and hence its validity is unimpaired by the process of discharge of that debt through bankruptcy. Cancellation of the security right only comes about as a consequence of the full repayment of the debt in question. Thus the secured creditor will be able to exercise his rights even after discharge, and will retain priority, for example, over others in whose favour the bankrupt may create fresh rights subsequently to his discharge.[56] By section 281(7) another essential principle is established, namely that discharge does not release any person other than the bankrupt from any liability, and thus any person who was jointly liable with the bankrupt for any debt, such as a partner or co-trustee, and likewise any person who had undertaken liability as surety for the bankrupt, is not thereby released.

The further provisions of section 281 furnish the exceptions to the general rule that the bankruptcy debts are released by discharge. Subsection (3) embodies a long-standing exception whereby no release operates in respect of any bankruptcy debt which the bankrupt incurred in respect of any fraud or fraudulent breach of trust to which he was a party. This also applies where forbearance in respect of any debt was secured by similar means. With regard to such debts, the discharged bankrupt remains liable to pay such balance as remains unpaid after deducting any dividends which have been received by the plaintiff.[57] The next excepted category, expressed by subsection (4), ensures that any liability in respect of a fine imposed for an offence, and any liability under a recognisance, will survive bankruptcy. However, a proviso is inserted in the subsection in respect of a penalty imposed for an offence under any enactment relating to the public revenue, and also any recognisance, to the effect that release may operate with the consent of the Treasury.

Next, section 281(5) (as amended) embodies a further group of exceptions whereby specified types of bankruptcy debt are not released by discharge except to such extent and on such conditions as the court may direct. The debts in question are, first, those which arise in respect of personal injuries to any person and result in a liability to pay damages for negligence, nuisance or breach of a statutory, contractual or other duty,[58] and secondly, those which arise under any order made in family proceedings or under a maintenance assessment made under the Child Support Act 1991.[59] Lastly, section 281(6) states that discharge shall not release the bankrupt from such other debts which are to be prescribed in the Rules as debts not provable in bankruptcy. It has long been a settled

---

[56] *Re Lind* [1915] 2 Ch. 345.

[57] *Re Chatterton, ex p. Hemming* (1879) 13 Ch.D. 163; *cf.* also *Emma Silver Mining Co. v. Grant* (1880) 17 Ch.D. 122.

[58] Thus adopting the approach of a minority of the *Cork Committee* Cmnd. 8558, paras. 1332, 1333. S.281(8) additionally provides that "personal injuries" includes death and any disease or other impairment of a person's physical or mental condition.

[59] s.281(8) as amended, supplies the meaning of the term "family proceedings," so that it bears the same meaning as in the Magistrates' Courts Act 1980 and the Matrimonial and Family Proceedings Act 1984.

principle that any debt or liability which is excluded from the category of provable debts is correspondingly excluded from the category of debts from which the bankrupt is released by his discharge.[60] The complementary categories of provable and non-provable debts were described in detail in Chapter 9, where it was observed that a major reform under the new insolvency law is that unliquidated tort claims have been transferred from the latter to the former category.[61] Consequently, all the bankruptcy debts which arise from tortious liability will be released by discharge, irrespective of whether they were liquidated or unliquidated at the date of commencement of bankruptcy, apart from any liability to pay damages in respect of personal injuries which, by virtue of section 281(5), will only be released to the extent indicated by the court. It may also be remarked that rule 6.223 of the Insolvency Rules expressly provides that discharge does not release the bankrupt from any obligation arising under a confiscation order made under section 1 of the Drug Trafficking Offences Act 1986, or under section 1 of the Criminal Justice (Scotland) Act 1987 or section 71 of the Criminal Justice Act 1988.

Where discharge has been effective to release a debt, the creditor's right of action is totally lost and will not revive merely because, after discharge, the debtor may utter a promise to pay.[62] However, if fresh consideration is furnished by the creditor in return for the debtor's promise to pay a debt from which he has been once released, the creditor's right of action will revive, and, because of the rule of English law that the courts will not inquire into the adequacy of consideration, this revival may be achieved with relative simplicity. Examples of the possible modes of effecting a revival of liability would be if the creditor were to extend further credit to the debtor, or if he were to make him a small loan.[63] Exceptionally, the need for consideration may be absent if the original contract was governed by some foreign law, and by that law no consideration is required to render enforceable a debtor's promise to pay a debt from which he has previously been released by a bankruptcy.[64] Conversely, as a result of a doctrine whose merits may be open to question.[65] English courts have asserted that a contract which was made and was to be performed in England will not be released at all by the debtor's bankruptcy and discharge where these occur under foreign law, and hence it has been held that in such cases the creditor may sue upon the original contract in the courts of this country.[66]

---

[60] *Re Reis* [1904] 2 K.B. 769, *affirmed sub nom. Clough v. Samuel* [1905] A.C. 442 (H.L.).
[61] See pp. 256–257, *ante*.
[62] *Heather & Son v. Webb* (1876) 2 C.P.D. 1.
[63] *Jakeman v. Cook* (1878) 4 Ex.D. 26; *Wild v. Tucker* [1914] 3 K.B. 36. The debtor's promise under seal would also be enforceable.
[64] *Re Bonacina* [1912] 2 Ch. 394.
[65] See *post*, Chap. 29, p. 723.
[66] *Gibbs & Sons v. La Société, etc., des Métaux* (1890) 25 Q.B.D. 399. *Cf. Re Nelson* [1918] 1 K.B. 459 in which it was held that a scheme of arrangement in Irish bankruptcy proceedings did not release the debts of English creditors who were not party to the composition. Paradoxically, in that case the Court of Appeal acknowledged that an Irish *discharge* would be effective in this country because the Irish bankruptcy legislation at that time had the force of an Imperial Statute. See, however, the judgment of Eve J. at p. 478, for his opinion of the law regarding discharge under a foreign bankruptcy.

Situation of the Bankrupt

The granting of his discharge has the effect of restoring the bankrupt, legally, to a state of near-normality, in that he becomes capable once again of freely entering into contractual relations, including those which involve his obtaining credit. He may also acquire and dispose of property on his own account, and may once again engage in trade. However, in several vital respects the discharged bankrupt is still subject to a number of controls and disabilities, and hence it must be confirmed that he does not, upon obtaining his discharge, acquire a character equal to that of one who has never been bankrupt.

In the first place, despite the fact that, after discharge, a bankrupt's income ceases to vest in the trustee in bankruptcy and reverts to the bankrupt absolutely, it is possible, in cases where an order has been made under section 310 of the Act,[67] for payment of a portion of the bankrupt's salary or pension to the trustee "during the bankruptcy," for the order of discharge to specify that these payments shall continue to be made even beyond the date upon which the discharge becomes effective.[68] Secondly, as seen above,[69] it is an integral condition of the granting of many orders of discharge that the bankrupt either consents to judgment being entered against himself or undertakes to make further payments to his creditors out of his subsequent earnings or after-acquired property.

Quite apart from any conditions attached to the order itself, the bankrupt after discharge remains under a duty, in consequence of section 333(3) of the Act, to give to the trustee such information as to his affairs, and to attend on the trustee at such times, as the trustee may reasonably require for the purpose of carrying out his functions under the Act. Failure to fulfil this duty amounts to a contempt of court on the part of the discharged bankrupt, for which he may be committed. Furthermore, even following his discharge a person who has once been bankrupt may be required to undergo examination as to his conduct, dealings or property as provided for by section 366 of the Act.[70] This section establishes a general power of judicial examination which is applicable also to a wide range of other persons associated with the bankrupt and his affairs, and is of considerable value in that it may become the medium for retrieving assets or income which have been illicitly concealed and retained during the bankruptcy. Not only may this power of examination be exercised after the bankrupt has been discharged, but it can also be employed after he is dead. This is because the court's power of summoning for examination is applicable to the spouse or former spouse of the bankrupt, and to any person known or believed to have any property comprised in the bankrupt's estate in his possession or to be indebted to the bankrupt, or who may be capable of giving information concerning the bankrupt, his dealings, affairs or property.[71] An especially striking example of the force of

---

[67] Discussed, *ante*, Chap. 8, at p. 203.
[68] *Re Gardner* [1942] Ch. 50; *cf. Re a Debtor (No. 946 of 1926)* [1939] Ch. 489.
[69] See *above*, p. 311.
[70] *cf. Re Coulson* [1934] Ch. 45, decided under s.25 of the Bankruptcy Act 1914 (repealed).
[71] Insolvency Act 1986, s.366(1).

this provision for inquiry into the bankrupt's affairs is furnished by *Re A Debtor (No. 12 of 1958)*,[72] in which a bankrupt who had disclosed liabilities of £131,000 and assets of £1,100 at the time of his adjudication was discovered, four years after he had satisfied all the conditions imposed upon him by the order of discharge, to have amassed a surplus of assets over liabilities of £45,000. Although the debtor himself died before he could be examined in the manner provided for under the equivalent of what is now section 366, it was held to be appropriate in the circumstances to order his three executors—who were respectively his former solicitor, accountant and partner—to submit to examination in the not unreasonable anticipation that they would be able to shed some light upon his affairs.[73]

Legal Restraints and Disqualifications to which an Undischarged Bankrupt is Subject

A most important aspect of reinstatement which is experienced by a bankrupt upon gaining discharge is the removal of the legal restraints and disqualifications to which he is subject while his status is that of undischarged bankrupt. It will be convenient here to list these legal disabilities, which are mostly self-explanatory.

(1) Section 390(4) of the Insolvency Act states that a person is not qualified to act as an insolvency practitioner at any time at which he is an undischarged bankrupt, or is undischarged from an order of sequestration of his estate. This disqualification prevents a person from holding any of the offices relating to insolvency proceedings which are mentioned in section 388(1) and (2) of the Act.[74]

(2) An undischarged bankrupt cannot be elected to, or sit or vote in, either House of Parliament, or sit or vote in a committee of either House.[75] The seat of a Member of the House of Commons becomes vacant if the disqualifications arising from his bankruptcy adjudication are not removed within six months of the date of the bankruptcy order.[76] This effectively means that a Member who becomes bankrupt must obtain an annulment of the bankruptcy (as described below) if he is to save his seat.

(3) An undischarged bankrupt cannot be elected to, or act as, a Member of a Local Authority.[77]

---

[72] [1968] 2 All E.R. 425.
[73] See also *Re Scharrer* (1888) 20 Q.B.D. 518 on the extent to which the examination of such witnesses may be pursued.
[74] See further, Chap. 2, *ante*, p. 27. *Note* that criminal liability is incurred under s.389 by any unqualified person who acts as an insolvency practitioner.
[75] Insolvency Act 1986, s.427(1).
[76] *ibid.*, s.427(4). See also subsections (5) and (6), and the Recess Elections Act 1975, ss.1, 5 (as amended).
[77] Local Government Act 1972, s.80(1)(b). See also s.81, as substituted by Sched. 8 to the Insolvency Act 1985.

(4) An undischarged bankrupt cannot be appointed, or act as, a Justice of the Peace.[78]
(5) An undischarged bankrupt cannot hold a solicitor's practising certificate.[79]
(6) It is a criminal offence for an undischarged bankrupt to act as a director of, or directly or indirectly to take part in or be concerned in the promotion, formation or management of, a company without leave of the court by which he was adjudged bankrupt.[80] The offence is an absolute one, from which the requirement of an element of *mens rea* has been omitted by the clear intention of Parliament. Accordingly, a person can be convicted upon proof of the *actus reus* of acting as a director while an undischarged bankrupt, even though he was unaware that he had not been discharged from his bankruptcy.[81]

In addition to the restraints and liabilities mentioned above, an undischarged bankrupt runs the risk of incurring criminal liability in several other situations in which, but for the fact of his bankruptcy, his conduct would be innocuous. These further penalties are described in Chapter 13.

(C) Annulment of Bankruptcy

Section 282 of the Act confers jurisdiction upon the court to annul a bankruptcy order at any time upon certain grounds which are there stated. The two principal grounds, as stated in section 282(1), are if it appears to the court:

(a) that, on any grounds existing at the time the order was made, the order ought not to have been made; or
(b) that, to the extent required by the Insolvency Rules, the bankruptcy debts and the expenses of the bankruptcy have all, since the making of the order, been either paid or secured for to the satisfaction of the court.[82]

It is further provided by section 282(3) that the court may annul a bankruptcy order whether or not the bankrupt has been discharged from the bankruptcy. Thus, broad scope is provided for the rectification of any injustice, and also to provide for those cases where the debtor seeks in the fullest way possible to expunge all the traces and connotations of

---

[78] Justices of the Peace Act, 1979, s.63A, inserted by Statute Law (Repeals) Act 1989, s.1(2); Sched. 2, para. 2.
[79] Solicitors Act 1974, ss.12(1)(h), (i), 15. *Note* also ss.16(2), (3), 17.
[80] Company Directors Disqualification Act 1986, s.11. See also s.13, concerning the penalties for contravention of s.11. For the procedural aspects of applications for leave to act as a director, see s.11(3), together with Insolvency Rules 1986, rr. 6.203–6.205. (See Chap. 27, *post*.)
[81] *R. v. Brockley* [1994] BCC 131 (C.A.). For the sentencing principles applied by the courts, see *R. v. Theivendran* (1992) 13 Crim.App.R.(S.) 601 (C.A.).
[82] Insolvency Act 1986, s.282(1)

bankruptcy from his established reputation. This latter objective may be accomplished through the debtor's act of fully paying or securing for all the debts and liabilities to which he was subject at the commencement of the bankruptcy.[83] A further reason why a bankrupt may seek to obtain the annulment of his adjudication in this way is in order to avert the onset of disqualifications to which he will be subject during bankruptcy, including the disqualification from certain categories of public office, which will inevitably take effect before any discharge from bankruptcy can come about under section 279 or section 280.[84] There has been a certain relaxation in the former strictness of the statutory requirement with regard to the full payment of the bankrupt's debts, in that it is no longer essential that all the debts must actually have been paid in cash before annulment of the order can take place, provided that the court is satisfied that all the debts and expenses of the bankruptcy are at least adequately secured for. The wording of section 282(1)(b) has the effect that it is no longer required that all the bankruptcy debts must have been paid in full. Nevertheless, the continued presence of the word "paid" in the relevant statutory provision, accompanied by the alternative possibility that the debts may be "secured for," may furnish sufficient basis for it to be arguable that it is still the legislative intention that actual payment of all the bankrupt's debts must be in prospect before the court can entertain an application for annulment. Thus, the former case law to the effect that a mere unconditional release of their debts by his unpaid creditors does not suffice to enable a debtor to apply for annulment may still remain good law.[85] Moreover, it will not suffice for the bankrupt to claim that all the bankruptcy debts and the costs of the bankruptcy have been directly paid off, or secured for, without the procedural formality of proving their debts having been first undergone by some or all of the creditors.[86]

The reference in section 282(1)(b) to the making of provision in the Rules as to the extent to which the bankruptcy debt must be paid for the purposes of seeking annulment is answered in rule 6.211. This expressly makes it a requirement that all bankruptcy debts which have been proved must have been paid in full, with the exception of any instances where a debt is disputed, or where a creditor who has proved can no longer be found. In such cases it is required that the bankrupt must have given such security in the form of money paid into court, or of a bond entered into with approved sureties, as the court considers adequate to satisfy any sum that may subsequently be proved to be due to the creditor concerned.[87]

Even where all the proved debts have been properly paid in full the court retains a discretion whether to annul the adjudication or not, for section 282(1) merely states that the court "may" annul the bankruptcy order under the circumstances described. Thus a bankrupt may still be denied

---

[83] "Bankruptcy debts" are defined in s.382 of the Act, discussed in Chap. 9, *ante*, p. 250.
[84] See above, previous section, and also sections (A) and (B) *above*.
[85] *cf. Re Keet* [1905] 2 K.B. 666.
[86] *Re Robertson* [1989] 1 W.L.R. 1139. In his judgment, Warner J. placed emphasis on the legislative intention to be inferred from rr. 6.209 and 6.211 of the Insolvency Rules (these are discussed *infra*).
[87] Insolvency Rules 1986, r. 6.211(3), (4).

an annulment if his conduct has been in some way improper as was the case in *Re Taylor*.[88] There the bankrupt had concealed the fact that he possessed a large sum of money, a portion of which he afterwards handed to the official receiver to pay his debts in full. The Divisional Court held that he was rightly to be refused an annulment, for he had committed two of the worst crimes which a bankrupt can commit, namely concealment of assets and the falsification of his statement of affairs.[89]

The other, and broader, basis for annulment furnished in section 282(1)(a) is where it appears to the court that the bankruptcy order "ought not" to have been made. Within the discretionary grounds upon which the court may act in accordance with this provision are to be found the general principles which have become established in the context of dismissal of a petition for "abuse of process."[90] The relevant facts may possibly not come to light until after adjudication has taken place, but this does not preclude the intervention of the court to rectify matters if the issue is raised on appeal. However, the drafting of section 282(1)(a) imposes a strict requirement that the court can only take into acount facts which were extant at the time the bankruptcy order was made.[91] The exercise of the court's discretion must therefore be based exclusively upon facts which meet this criterion, although there is no further requirement that the facts themselves should actually have been before the court on the occasion of making the bankruptcy order.[92]

If the court which originally made the bankruptcy order refuses to grant an annulment, an appeal against such refusal may be pursued, as described above.[93]

Procedure

Section 282 imposes no personal limitation upon the right to make application for the annulment of a bankruptcy order,[94] although in the majority of cases it will be the bankrupt who seeks this remedy, as the party with the greatest personal interest in the matter. The relevant procedure is laid down by the Insolvency Rules,[95] and includes the requirement that where an application is made under section 282(1) it must specify under which paragraph of the subsection it is made, and must be supported by affidavit stating the grounds on which it is made.[96] The official receiver and the trustee in bankruptcy must be given notice of the venue by the applicant, and in the case where the application is made under section 282(1)(a) notice must also be given to the person on whose petition the bankruptcy order was made.[97]

---

[88] [1901] 1 Q.B. 744.
[89] *ibid.*, p. 745, *per* Wright J. See now ss.353, 354 and 356 of the Act, *post*, Chap. 13.
[90] See Chap. 6, *ante*, pp. 97 and 118.
[91] *Re A Debtor (No. 68 of 1992)* (1993) *The Times*, February 12, 1993.
[92] *Re Von Engel (a bankrupt)* (1989) *The Independent*, August 21, 1989.
[93] *Above*, p. 314.
[94] *cf. Re Beesley* [1975] 1 All E.R. 385, involving the interpretation of the expression "person interested," formerly employed in s.29 of the Bankruptcy Act 1914 (repealed).
[95] Insolvency Rules 1986, rr. 6.206–6.214 inclusive.
[96] *ibid.*, r. 6.206(1), (2).
[97] *ibid.*, r. 6.206(4), as amended.

Annulment of Bankruptcy

Where annulment is sought on the basis that the debts and expenses of the bankruptcy are all paid or secured, the trustee, or otherwise the official receiver, must file a report in court not less than 21 days before the date fixed for the hearing. This report must describe the circumstances leading to the bankruptcy; must summarise the extent of the bankrupt's assets and liabilities at the date of the bankruptcy order and at the present time; must furnish details of any creditors known to have claims but who have not proved; and must include any other matters which the author of the report considers to be necessary for the information of the court.[98] Most importantly, the report must explain the extent to which, and the manner in which, the debts and expenses of the bankruptcy have been paid and secured, and in the latter aspect must indicate whether the security is considered to be satisfactory.[99] The applicant must be sent a copy of the report at least two weeks before the hearing and he may file further affidavits in answer to the statements it contains.[1] Where it is reported, in an application under section 282(1)(b), that there are known creditors of the bankrupt who have not proved, the court may direct the trustee or official receiver to send notice of the application to such of those creditors as the court thinks ought to be informed of it, with a view to their proving their debts within 21 days, and may also give direction for the making of the application to be advertised, so that creditors may prove within a specified time. In this event, the application may be adjourned for not less than 35 days.[2] The trustee must attend the hearing of the application, and the official receiver, if he is not the trustee, may attend but is not required to do so unless he has filed a report in the manner described above.

Where the bankruptcy order is annulled, the court must notify the Secretary of State of this fact, and the official receiver must forthwith send notice of the annulment to any creditors whom he has previously notified of the debtor's bankruptcy.[3] Although there is no longer any automatic requirement that the annulment shall be advertised or Gazetted, rule 6.213 contains a provision whereby the former bankrupt may require the Secretary of State to arrange for this publicity to be given of the annulment, at the applicant's expense.

Effect of Annulment

The most important effect of an annulment of a bankruptcy order is that, in principle, the person to whom the order relates is to be regarded in law as though the order had never been made. Thus, section 285(5) expressly declares that, in determining for the purposes of section 279[4] whether a person was an undischarged bankrupt at any time, any time when he was bankrupt by virtue of an order which was subsequently annulled is to be disregarded. Nevertheless, section 282(4) contains a

---

[98] *ibid.*, r. 6.207(2).
[99] *ibid.*, r. 6.207(3).
[1] *ibid.*, r. 6.207(4).
[2] *ibid.*, r. 6.209.
[3] *ibid.*, r. 6.212.
[4] See section (A), *above*.

saving provision to preserve the validity of any sale or other disposition of property, payment made or other thing duly done in accordance with the provisions of the Insolvency Act by, or under the authority of, the official receiver or trustee or by the court. However, if any of the bankrupt's estate is currently vested in the trustee it either vests in such person as the court may appoint or, failing such an appointment reverts to the bankrupt subject to any terms which the court may direct.[5]

There is one further, notable distinction between the ending of a bankruptcy by virtue of the bankrupt's gaining his discharge, and its ending by annulment. In the former case, the discharge has the effect of releasing the bankrupt from all provable debts, regardless of whether proof was in fact lodged by the creditors to whom they were owed.[6] In the case of annulment on the other hand, it was held in *More v. More*[7] that this does not have the effect of releasing the debtor from any provable debts for which proof may not have been lodged during the time that the bankruptcy was in force. Accordingly, a creditor who has omitted to lodge proof may maintain an action to enforce his debt after the bankruptcy has been annulled. However, a creditor who has lodged proof, but whose proof has been rejected by the trustee prior to the annulment of the bankruptcy, cannot thereafter enforce his debt because the rejection remains valid and the claim is consequently barred by virtue of the provision in section 282 (4), referred to above, which preserves the effects of all acts done by the official receiver or trustee.[8]

---

[5] Insolvency Act 1986, s.282(4)(b).
[6] See Chap. 9, *ante*, for the terms "proof" and "provable debt."
[7] [1962] Ch. 424. See also *Re Keet*, above n. 85; contrast *John v. Mendoza* [1939] 1 K.B. 141 (estoppel by record in a case where the plaintiff was guilty of collusion in refraining from proving for his debt).
[8] *Brandon v. McHenry* [1891] 1 Q.B. 538.

Chapter 12

SPECIAL CASES

Preliminary

Chapters 3 to 11 above explain the law and procedure which are applicable to ordinary cases of personal insolvency. In certain situations, special factors are present of which the law duly takes account by introducing special rules which partly replace the ordinary rules, or else modify their operation. These provisions are discussed in the present chapter.

(A) Summary Administration of Small Bankruptcies

Where the total amount of the unsecured liabilities of an insolvent debtor is comparatively small, the net worth of the assets comprising the estate in bankruptcy will be correspondingly low in value. In such cases the administrative costs entailed by the observation of the full formalities of a normal bankruptcy are likely to be disproportionately large, and may well absorb all the realisable funds in the estate so that there is no yield to the creditors. Estates of this kind are generally not profitable for a non-official trustee to administer, and any attempts to appoint such a person as trustee are likely to prove futile, and to waste the already slender resources of the estate. An alternative, and much simplified procedure, known as summary administration, has therefore been devised with a view to minimising the cost of the operation.

Section 275 of the Act specifies the circumstances in which the court may invoke the summary administration procedure where it regards this as the appropriate course to take. This is done through the issue of a certificate for the summary administration of the bankrupt's estate, which may take place if, upon the hearing of a debtor's petition,[1] the court makes a bankruptcy order and each of two facts is established. The first is that the aggregate amount of the unsecured debts in the bankruptcy is less than the

---

[1] See Chap. 6, *ante*, sections (A)2 and (B)2 and 3.

prescribed amount (currently set at £20,000)[2] known as the "small bankruptcies level," and the second is that within the period of five years ending with the presentation of the petition the debtor has neither been adjudged bankrupt nor made a composition with his creditors in satisfaction of his debts or a scheme of arrangement of his affairs.[3] Provided these two requirements are duly met a certificate of summary administration may be issued by the court, whether the bankruptcy order is made because the value of the assets comprised in the bankrupt's estate appears to be less than the "minimum amount" of £2,000 currently prescribed for the purposes of section 273(1)(b), or because it appears to the court not to be appropriate to appoint a person to prepare a report under section 274, or because the court thinks it would be inappropriate to make an interim order under section 252 to pave the way for attempts to conclude an individual voluntary arrangement.[4] Where a certificate is issued it may be included in the bankruptcy order, but if this is not done the court must forthwith send copies to the official receiver and to the trustee.[5] The court may at any subsequent time revoke a certificate for summary administration if it is demonstrated that, on any grounds existing at the time of issue, the certificate ought not to have been issued.[6] The court may revoke the certificate either of its own motion or on the application of the official receiver, of which the bankrupt must be given at least 14 days' advance notice.[7]

Where a certificate of summary administration is issued by the court section 297(2) of the Act specifies that the official receiver shall be the trustee of the bankrupt's estate as from the issue of that certificate. It is open to the official receiver to apply to the Secretary of State under section 296(1) for the appointment of another person as trustee in his place, and section 297(3) also confers upon the court a discretionary power to appoint some other person than the official receiver to be trustee, either at the time of issuing the certificate or at some later time while the certificate remains in force.[8] It is important to note that section 298(3) prevents the holding of any meeting of creditors for the purpose of removing the trustee at any time when a certificate for summary administration is in force.[9] If a trustee has already been appointed before the issue of a certificate for summary administration the official receiver must send him a copy of the certificate.[10] Also, insofar as he has not already done so, the official receiver

---

[2] (S.I. 1986, No. 1996): the Insolvency Proceedings (Monetary Limits) Order 1986, made under s.418(1) Insolvency Act 1986, for the purposes of s.273 of the Act.
[3] Insolvency Act 1986, s.275(2).
[4] *ibid.*, s.275(2) together with ss.252, 273(1)(b), (d). See further the discussion in Chap. 6, *ante*, of the *Hearing of the Petition* (pp. 130 *et seq.*), and in Chap. 4, *Individual Voluntary Arrangements* (pp. 41 *et seq.*).
[5] Insolvency Rules 1986, r. 6.48.
[6] Insolvency Act 1986, s.275(3).
[7] Insolvency Rules 1986, r. 6.50(1), (2); Form 6.31.
[8] For the procedure for filling any vacancy where the office of trustee is held by someone other than the Official Receiver, see s.300(5) of the Act.
[9] For removal of the trustee by the creditors in normal cases, see Chap. 7, *ante*.
[10] Insolvency Rules 1986, r. 6.49(1).

must give notice to creditors of the making of the bankruptcy order within 12 weeks of the issue of the certificate.[11]

Since the official receiver is constituted trustee and is not capable of being replaced by a trustee of the creditors' choosing, he is under no obligation to summon a meeting of creditors for the purpose either of appointing a trustee or of appointing a creditors' committee.[12] Moreover, section 294(1)(b) deprives the creditors of their usual power to requisition a meeting under that section. The investigatory responsibilities of the official receiver under section 289 are also limited, in that he is required to carry out an investigation into the conduct and affairs of the bankrupt only if he thinks fit.[13] Once the official receiver has completed his duties and obtained his release, or if a trustee has once been substituted and has later obtained his release, the residual duty of administration in a small bankruptcy thereafter vests in the official receiver alone. Therefore if fresh assets subsequently come into the bankrupt's estate before he is discharged the official receiver remains the sole person competent to act in relation to their administration and distribution to creditors: the creditors themselves still have no power to appoint a new trustee by resolution, and have no power to issue binding directions or recommendations to the official receiver with regard to the action he should take at this stage.[14]

A further important aspect of the summary administration procedure is that the bankrupt's discharge under section 279 will come about automatically after only two years from the commencement of bankruptcy, provided that the certificate for summary administration is not revoked before that time.[15] This means that the bankrupt's rehabilitation is brought forward by one year in comparison to other "first time" bankrupts, but it should be remembered that the summary administration procedure is not available for debtors whose unsecured liabilities exceed a total of £20,000, and likewise that the effect of section 275(2)(b) is to make summary administration unavailable to those debtors who have either been adjudged bankrupt or made a composition or arrangement with their creditors within the past five years.

---

[11] *ibid.*, r. 6.49(2).
[12] *cf.* Insolvency Act 1986, ss.293(1), 301(2).
[13] *ibid.*, s.289(5).
[14] *Re Leach* [1900] 2 Q.B. 649; *Re Salmon* [1916] 2 K.B. 510. For release of the trustee see Chap. 7, *ante*.
[15] Insolvency Act 1986, s.279(2)(*a*). For discharge generally, see Chap. 11, *ante*. The Civil Judicial Statistics for 1987 (Cm. 428) indicate that in 1987 there were a total of 6,784 adjudications of bankruptcy, and that summary administration certificates granted in that year numbered 1,532. Judicial statistics published for subsequent years supply less complete information. Figures supplied by the D.T.I. Insolvency Service indicate that for the years 1992–1994, the numbers of bankruptcies in England and Wales, and the numbers of summary administrations, were: for 1992, 32, 106 and 3,777; for 1993, 31,016 and 4,942; and for 1994, 25,634 and 3,936 respectively. The comparable statistics for the years 1983–1986 were: for 1983 (Cmnd. 9370): 5,346 and 3,347 respectively; for 1984 (Cmnd. 9599): 6,378 and 3,912; for 1985 (Cmnd. 9864): 5,556 and 3,402, and for 1986 (Cm. 173) 5,543 and 3,208.

(B) Administration of Insolvent Estates of Deceased Persons

Where a debtor dies during the course of bankruptcy proceedings which have been begun by or against him the proceedings are, unless the court orders otherwise, continued as if he were alive but are subject to special modifications.[16] Alternatively, a person may die insolvent before bankruptcy proceedings have commenced. This also calls for special regulation, because the powers of the court, and the rules of law applicable, in an ordinary administration of a deceased person's estate vary in several significant respects from the powers of the bankruptcy court and from the rules of law which are operative when an estate is being administered in bankruptcy.[17] For example, the rules concerning priority of payment of debts, and the right to disclaim onerous property,[18] are exclusive creations of the bankruptcy law, whilst the powers of the trustee and of the court to conduct an investigation of a bankrupt's affairs, and to recover property by the avoidance of antecedent transactions,[19] are far more extensive in the case of bankruptcy than any powers enjoyed by the Chancery Division in ordinary matters. Accordingly, section 421 of the Act sanctions the making of an order by statutory instrument whereby the provisions of the Act are made applicable in modified fashion to this type of special case.[20] The overall aim is that the unsatisfied creditors of a deceased insolvent should be enabled to receive such payment as might have been forthcoming to them by way of dividend if the debtor's adjudication had preceded his death. It goes without saying that the deceased's liabilities must be discharged in priority to any testamentary dispositions he may have made.

The first question to consider is the manner in which the proceedings may be brought under the control of the bankruptcy court. In effect, provision is made for proceedings to be begun analogously to the two alternative forms of petition, namely a creditor's or a debtor's petition, in normal cases. The former type of case is provided for by means of a rule whereby any creditor of a deceased debtor whose debt would have been sufficient to support a bankruptcy petition against the debtor had he been alive, may present to a court with bankruptcy jurisdiction a petition praying for an order for the administration of the deceased's estate according to the law of bankruptcy.[21] An insolvency administration petition must be served on the personal representative of the deceased debtor, and also upon such other persons as the court may direct.[22] The modified version of a debtor's petition consists of a petition in special form under section 272 of the Act, presented by the personal representative on

---

[16] Administration of Insolvent Estates of Deceased Persons Order 1986 (S.I. 1986, No. 1999) (hereafter referred to as "the A.I.E.D.P. Order"), Art. 5; Sched. 2.
[17] See *Re Kitson* [1911] 2 K.B. 109, 113, *per* Phillimore, J.
[18] See *ante*, Chap. 10, p. 288, and Chap. 8, p. 235, respectively.
[19] See *ante*, Chap. 7, p. 152, and Chap. 8, p. 221, respectively.
[20] See the A.I.E.D.P. Order, above, n. 16, Arts. 3, 4; Sched. 1.
[21] *ibid.*, Sched. 1, Pt. II, para. 3, modifying s.267 of the Act.
[22] *ibid.*, para. 2, modifying s.266 of the Act.

the grounds that the estate of the deceased debtor is insolvent.[23] Where proceedings have begun in any court for the administration of a deceased debtor's estate, no petition for an insolvency administration order may be presented to the bankruptcy court, but on the other hand the court in which the proceedings have commenced may, if satisfied that the estate is insolvent, transfer the proceedings to the bankruptcy court.[24] The proper procedure in cases of this kind is for the intending petitioner to make application to the court in which proceedings have already begun and, by satisfying that court that the estate is insolvent, induce it to make an order transferring the proceedings into the bankruptcy court. However, the transfer of proceedings in this way is a discretionary matter for the court to which the application is made.[25]

Where an insolvency administration order is made, the task of preparing a statement of affairs falls upon the debtor's personal representative, or if there is none, upon such person as the court may direct in response to application made by the official receiver.[26] The official receiver is under no duty to investigate the conduct and affairs of a deceased debtor unless he thinks fit.[27] The date of commencement of bankruptcy is the day on which the insolvency administration order is made.[28] However, for the purposes of determination of the bankrupt's estate and the property to be treated as comprised within it, sections 283 to 285 of the Act are specially modified so that the relevant point in time becomes that of the date of death of the deceased debtor.[29] Although this imports a "relation back" doctrine with regard to the proprietary effects of an order which, by definition, cannot be made until after the death of the debtor, the consequences of this provision must be assessed on the basis that it is not until the death of an insolvent person that the court has jurisdiction to make an insolvency administration order, and so as a matter of fact that person was not "a bankrupt" at the time of his or her death. This analysis of the true, historic sequence of events was employed by the Court of Appeal in *Re Palmer*[30] to formulate the conclusion that where a deceased insolvent had owned his matrimonial home jointly with his wife subject to a joint tenancy, the interest of the deceased passed upon his death directly to his widow by survivorship. The subsequent making of an insolvency administration order did not operate retrospectively as an impediment to the normal principle of survivorship, whose effect is instantaneous as at the moment of death.

The possibility exists, as in the case where the bankrupt is alive, of a creditors' meeting taking a decision to appoint a private sector trustee in place of the official receiver, and in other respects the statutory provisions regarding the administration of the estate by the trustee, including those in

---

[23] *ibid.*, para. 6, modifying s.272 of the Act; see also Form 6, set out in Sched. 3 to the Order.
[24] *ibid.*, para. 5, modifying s.271 of the Act.
[25] *Re York* (1887) 36 Ch. D. 233; *Re Baker* (1890) 44 Ch. D. 262; *Re Kenward* (1906) 94 L.T. 277; *Re Hay* [1915] 2 Ch. 198.
[26] The A.I.E.D.P. Order, Sched. 1, Pt. II, para. 15, modifying s.288 of the Act.
[27] *ibid.*, para. 16, modifying s.289 of the Act.
[28] *ibid.*, para. 10, modifying s.278 of the Act.
[29] *ibid.*, Sched. 1, Pt. II, para. 12.
[30] [1994] 3 All E.R. 835.

sections 339–345 of the Act concerning the adjustment of prior transactions, apply with minimal alteration.[31] There is one major adjustment to the rules regarding the sequence of distribution of the assets, in that the reasonable funeral, testamentary and administration expenses have priority over the preferential debts listed in Schedule 6 to the Insolvency Act.[32]

In an insolvent administration the official receiver or trustee may exercise the powers conferred by sections 315–320 of the Act to disclaim onerous property of the deceased bankrupt, just as in ordinary cases.[33] Furthermore, it has been held under previous legislation that the right of retainer, which is enjoyed by an executor to whom a debt was due from the testator,[34] is not affected by an insolvency administration order provided that the executor has received the money, from which he is to pay himself in this way, before the order is made.[35] Once the executor's right is duly constituted he does not forfeit it if by chance he inadvertently pays over to the official receiver all the assets which passed into his hands from the deceased: the executor may reclaim from the official receiver such a sum as he was legally entitled to retain.[36] It should be remembered that the right of retainer may not be exercised as against the claims of creditors whose debts enjoy a priority higher than that of the executor,[37] nor in respect of a claim for an expense which is not allowable against the claims of the creditors of the estate.[38] It is worth noting, however, that the right of retainer can be exceptionally favourable to the executor who claims it, and that where the debt owed to him is very large his exercise of the right is capable of exhausting all the assets of the estate at a single stroke.[39]

Where the executors of a deceased businessman carry on his business after his death, in accordance with the provisions of his will and with the assent of his creditors as well as of the beneficiaries, the executors enjoy a special right to be indemnified, out of the testator's estate, against the liabilities which they have properly incurred in carrying on the business.[40] This right is of considerable value where the business either was at the date of death of the testator, or has subsequently become, insolvent with the consequence that an insolvency administration order is made, but it is essential that the creditors actually assented to what was done, in the hope thereby of eventually receiving payment: if the creditors merely acquiesced tacitly in what was done the executors will not enjoy a right to indemnity in priority to the claims of the creditors in the administration of the estate.[41] Further, section 271(5) of the Act, as operative in this context, preserves

---

[31] The A.I.E.D.P. Order, Sched. 1, Pt. II, paras. 18–28. On the appointment of a trustee and the adjustment of prior transactions respectively, see Chaps. 7 and 8, *ante*.
[32] The A.I.E.D.P. Order, Arts. 4(2), 5(2). See further Chap. 10, *ante*.
[33] *ibid.*, Sched. 1, Pt. II, para. 23.
[34] See Chap. 9, *ante*, p. 276.
[35] *Re Williams* (1891) 8 Morr. 65.
[36] *Re Rhoades* [1899] 2 Q.B. 347; *cf. Re Wester Wemyss* [1940] Ch. 1.
[37] *A.-G. v. Jackson* [1932] A.C. 365 (H.L.).
[38] *Re Salmen* (1912) 107 L.T. 108.
[39] As in *Re Gilbert* [1898] 1 Q.B. 282.
[40] *Dowse v. Gorton* [1891] A.C. 190 (H.L.).
[41] *ibid.*, at p. 199, *per* Lord Herschell.

the validity of any payment made or any act or thing done in good faith by the personal representative before the date of the insolvency administration order.[42]

Jurisdiction

The appropriate court in which a petition for an insolvency administration order should be presented, or to which proceedings should be transferred from a court of ordinary civil jurisdiction, is that within whose jurisdiction the debtor resided or carried on business for the greater part of the six months immediately prior to his death.[43] If the debtor dies at a place outside England and Wales and if, though not resident in England during the six months prior to his death, he was nevertheless subject to the jurisdiction of the English court by virtue of his still being domiciled here, the proper court in which to present the petition is the High Court.[44]

---

[42] See the A.I.E.D.P. Order, Sched. 1, Pt. II, para. 5.
[43] *cf.* Chap. 6, *ante*, section (B)1.
[44] *Re Evans* [1891] 1 Q.B. 143.

CHAPTER 13

BANKRUPTCY AND THE CRIMINAL LAW

Preliminary

Chapter VI of Part IX of the Insolvency Act 1986 (comprising sections 350–362) consists of a miniature code of special criminal offences which are applicable to bankrupts. While it is appropriate here to reaffirm what was said earlier in this book, namely that a debtor who has been honest but unfortunate has no reason to be unduly apprehensive about the consequences of bankruptcy, it must be emphasised that the law necessarily contains provisions framed to deal in an appropriate way with those bankrupts who have been less than honest, or who have been imprudent to the point of recklessness, and have thus compounded the damage inflicted upon their trusting creditors. It is only through the maintenance of public confidence in the law's ultimate ability to punish those who abuse the privileges of credit that the overall social and commercial advantages derived from the widespread availability of credit on reasonable terms can be sustained.

The criminal offences established by the Insolvency Act, together with some of the provisions forming part of the general criminal law, operate both to punish wrongful conduct and also to deter those who might otherwise have embarked upon it. The *Cork Committee* observed that the factor of deterrence results at least as much from the public perception of the incidence of detection and successful prosecution of offenders as from the actual severity of the penalties which the law prescribes.[1] Effective deterrence is important in that it secures a corresponding degree of protection for all those who extend credit, and it thereby reduces the risks which they must take into account in deciding whether to do so, and if so on what terms. An additional purpose served by some of the criminal provisions in the Act is to secure the bankrupt's fullest cooperation throughout the course of the bankruptcy administration itself, in such matters as disclosing the whereabouts of property and in facilitating the tracing and recovery of assets which are properly claimable on the creditors' behalf. There are certain provisions which are applicable

---

[1] Cmnd. 8558, Chap. 48, para. 1900.

exclusively to bankrupts who are, or who have been, engaged in a trade or business.[2] The provisions of criminal law in relation to bankruptcy are also of relevance in the context of the formal interrogation of a bankrupt at his public examination.[3] He is there being compelled to utter, under oath, self-incriminating statements which will form part of the official record and thus facilitate his later prosecution and conviction for any offences which he is already suspected of having committed.[4] Alternatively, any denial by the bankrupt of a matter bearing upon his possible criminal liability will, if later shown to be untrue, amount in itself to the offence of perjury.

Any prosecution for bankruptcy offences will take place separately from the bankruptcy proceedings, for it must be brought before a court with criminal jurisdiction and so will be heard by a Magistrates' Court, in the case of a summary trial, or by the Crown Court in the case of a trial on indictment.[5] Proceedings for any criminal offence under the Insolvency Act or under the Rules can only be instituted by the Secretary of State, or by or with the consent of the Director of Public Prosecutions.[6] Persons convicted of any such offence are liable to imprisonment or a fine, or both.[7] The prescribed punishments for all offences are set out in the form of tables in Schedule 10 to the Act and in Schedule 5 to the Rules, respectively.

The criminal provisions of the Act may be conveniently analysed as having application to conduct during three separate periods of time, namely prior to the presentation of the petition, subsequent to the petition, and subsequent to adjudication. It is logically necessary that the debtor be adjudicated bankrupt in order that criminal liability may attach in accordance with the provisions of the Insolvency Act. If the bankruptcy order is subsequently annulled, criminal liability under Chapter VI still applies, but proceedings for an offence may not be instituted after the annulment.[8] Criminal proceedings may also be instituted against a discharged bankrupt for an offence committed before his discharge, but no offence may be committed through something done by a discharged bankrupt, at any rate for the purposes of his previous bankruptcy: if a further bankruptcy ensues, acts committed since he was last discharged from bankruptcy may then give rise to criminal liability.[9]

The fact that some criminal offences may be committed through conduct prior to the inception of bankruptcy proceedings means that it is necessary for a debtor to bear in mind that certain species of conduct—such as an omission to keep proper business records, or any indulgence in

---

[2] See ss.360(1)(b), 361, *infra*.
[3] See Chap. 7 *ante*.
[4] See *R. v. Kansal* [1992] 3 W.L.R. 494; [1992] 3 All E.R. 844 (C.A.), for a particularly forceful example.
[5] In the latter case there will first be committal proceedings before a Magistrates' Court. For a fuller discussion of the distinction between summary trial and trial on indictment, see J. C. Smith and B. Hogan, *Criminal Law* (7th ed., 1992), Chap. 3.
[6] Insolvency Act 1986, s.350(5).
[7] *ibid.*, s.350(6).
[8] *ibid.*, s.350(1), (2). See also s.360(3). For annulment, see Chap. 11, *ante*.
[9] *ibid.*, s.350(3). For discharge, see Chap. 11, *ante*.

gambling or speculative activities whereby he exposes himself to risk of losses which his financial position is inadequate to sustain—carry the seeds of potential criminal liability.[10] Such forms of conduct are capable of amounting to criminal offences if it should happen that the debtor is *subsequently* adjudicated bankrupt. A further point of general importance is the provision in section 350(4) of the Act whereby it is not a defence in proceedings for an offence under Chapter VI that anything relied on, in whole or in part, as constituting that offence was done outside England and Wales.

The bankruptcy offences will here be considered in three groups, corresponding to the three possible periods in time during which criminal conduct may take place. At the end of this chapter, a brief account will be given of the special procedure, formerly known as criminal bankruptcy, which was abolished in 1989.

(A) Bankruptcy Offences

(1) Offences arising from conduct prior to presentation of the petition

Investigation of the conduct of the bankrupt during the period prior to the presentation of the petition may reveal that he is guilty of one or more of the following offences.

(i) *Concealment or Removal of Property*

It is an offence for a debtor, at any time in the 12 months before the petition is presented, to conceal any property to the value of £500 or more, or to conceal any debt due to or from him, unless he proves that at the time of the conduct in question he had no intent to defraud, or to conceal the state of his affairs.[11] The provisions under which this offence, like several others,[12] arises are so worded that it is sufficient for the prosecution simply to prove the specified conduct on the part of the bankrupt, whereupon a burden of proof is cast upon him to exculpate himself by proving that he lacked any intention to defraud, referred to in the Act as the defence of "innocent intention." It is therefore unnecessary for the prosecution to allege, or to prove, fraud or a fraudulent intent on the part of the accused in order to procure his conviction of an offence of this type.[13] Given the severity of the task which the bankrupt is thus obliged to perform, it is considered to be improper for the court to exclude any evidence which he seeks to adduce in order to negative fraudulent intent, since this is the very essence of the defence which the law requires him to establish.[14]

---

[10] See ss.361, 362 of the Act, *infra*.
[11] s.354(1)(b), (c) of the Act, together with s.352. The figure of £500 is prescribed in the Insolvency Proceedings (Monetary Limits) Order 1986 (S.I. 1986, No. 1996).
[12] See ss.353, 354, 355, 356, 357, 358, 359, each of which refers to s.352 whereby the burden of proof of innocent intention is cast upon the bankrupt.
[13] *cf. R. v. Lusty* [1964] 1 All E.R. 960; *R. v. Salter* [1968] 2 Q.B. 793, 802, *per* Sachs, L.J.
[14] *R. v. Wiseman* (1901) 20 Cox C.C. 144.

The meaning of the expression "intent to defraud" has been examined frequently in relation to this type of legislative provision. Buckley J., in *Re London and Globe Finance Corp. Ltd* offered *obiter* an expression epitomising the distinction between fraud and deceit: "To deceive is by falsehood to induce a state of mind; to defraud is by deceit to induce a course of conduct."[15] This *dictum*, while enduring as a convenient formulation of the basic notion of fraud, has required subsequent explanation and expansion. Thus, in *Welham v. D.P.P.*,[16] the House of Lords were unanimously of the opinion that fraud might be perpetrated if *any* person might be prejudiced in any way by the conduct of the accused: it was not necessary that the victim should *personally* suffer an economic disadvantage, and it was equally possible that the "course of action" induced might in some instances take the form of the victim's *not* doing something he would otherwise have done. The House of Lords subsequently had occasion to review the concept of "fraud" in the case of *Scott v. Commissioner of Police for the Metropolis*,[17] in which Lord Dilhorne expressed a preference for replacing the notion of "deceit" with a more flexible one of "dishonesty." In this opinion, with which the rest of their Lordships concurred, the expression "to defraud" ordinarily means:

> "to deprive a person dishonestly of something which is his or of something to which he is or would or might, but for the perpetration of the fraud, be entitled."[18]

By section 357(3) of the Act it is an offence if the bankrupt has at any time before the commencement of bankruptcy concealed or removed any part of his property after, or within two months before, the date on which a judgment or order for the payment of money has been obtained against him, if the judgment or order has not been satisfied before the commencement of bankruptcy. Once again, it is made incumbent upon the bankrupt to establish the defence of innocent intention. The use of the words "his property" in section 357(3) has led to it being held that where a debtor, prior to his adjudication, has been divested of his title to the property in question, as by the execution of an assignment thereof, he cannot properly be convicted of this offence of fraudulent removal or concealment, even where he possessed the requisite intent and even though the assignment itself may be capable of being avoided as a consequence of his subsequent adjudication.[19] However, where such an assignment is intrinsically defective, so that no title passes initially from the debtor by virtue of it, he is still capable of committing the offences of

---

[15] [1903] 1 Ch. 728, 732.
[16] [1961] A.C. 103. See the speeches of Lord Radcliffe, p. 122 *et seq.*, and Lord Denning, p. 129 *et seq.*, *cf.* also the formulation offered by James J., in *R. v. Sinclair* [1968] 3 All E.R. 241, 246.
[17] [1975] A.C. 819.
[18] *ibid.*, at 839. The *dictum* was applied in *A.-G.'s Reference (No. 1 of 1981)* [1982] 2 All E.R. 417.
[19] *R. v. Creese* (1874) L.R. 2 C.C.R. 105.

fraudulent removal or concealment of "his" property.[20] On the other hand, if a prior divesting of title has duly taken place it should be remembered that although no offence may be committed under section 357(3), the fact that title to the property has become vested in some other person will render it probable that the debtor's act of removal will constitute theft, and hence be punishable as such.[21]

(ii) *Fraudulent Disposal of Property*

A bankrupt commits an offence under section 357(1) if he has in the period of five years ending with the commencement of the bankruptcy made or caused to be made any gift or transfer of, or any charge on his property. It is further provided by section 357(2) that in this context the making of a transfer of or charge on any property includes cases where the bankrupt has caused or connived at the levying of any execution against that property. To escape conviction of this offence, the bankrupt must establish the defence of innocent intention, as explained above. It is noteworthy that the period of five years, measured back from the date of the bankruptcy order, is commensurate with the period of time allowed under section 339 of the Act whereby gifts and undervalue transactions can be challenged if the bankrupt was insolvent at the time of the transaction.[22] The trustee's ability to trace and recover such assets is nonetheless a wholly separate issue, and the bankrupt's criminal liability under section 357(1) is not dependent upon whether the trustee is able to recover such assets as have been fraudulently disposed of.

(iii) *Offences relating to the Bankrupt's Books and Papers*

The bankrupt's books and papers are of considerable importance in the work of reconstructing the truth about the previous history of his affairs, and hence any act on his part which is calculated to conceal, destroy or falsify them is a serious matter. Three provisions render such acts punishable. First, it is an offence if, within the 12 months next before the presentation of the petition, the bankrupt conceals, destroys, mutilates or falsifies any books, papers or other records relating to his estate or affairs, and it is equally an offence for him to cause or permit any such act to be performed by someone else.[23] It is an offence, secondly, for the bankrupt within the 12 months before the petition to make or to cause or permit the making of, any false entries in any book, document or record relating to his estate or affairs.[24] The third offence concerning documents is committed where the bankrupt, during the 12 months before the petition, disposes of, or alters or makes any omission in, any book, document or record relating

---

[20] *R. v. Humphris* [1904] 2 K.B. 89, in which *R. v. Creese, above*, was distinguished on the facts.
[21] See the Theft Act 1968, s.1 and ss.2–6.
[22] See also s.341(1)(a) of the Act. For the avoidance of antecedent transactions, see Chap. 8, *ante*, p. 221.
[23] Insolvency Act 1986, s.355(2)(b), (d).
[24] *ibid.*, s.355(2)(c), (d).

to his estate or affairs, or if he causes or permits such an act to take place.[25] By section 436 of the Act it is provided that the expression "records" includes computer records and other non-documentary records.[26] This definition applies wherever the term "records" is used within the Act, unless the context otherwise requires.

In all three of the above offences the onus is cast upon the bankrupt to prove the defence of innocent intention. Such an opportunity for the bankrupt to explain his conduct is clearly necessary in the interests of justice, for otherwise some action performed for perfectly legitimate reasons, and at a time perhaps when the debtor had no intimations of bankruptcy, might subsequently be rendered criminal upon his becoming bankrupt within the following 12 months. Nevertheless, in the absence of an explanation which establishes his bona fides beyond all reasonable doubt, the bankrupt will suffer the adverse consequences of his action.

(iv) *False Statements to Creditors*

By section 356(2)(b) and (c), a bankrupt is guilty of an offence if, at any meeting of his creditors within the 12 months before the petition, he attempts to account for any part of his property by fictitious losses or expenses. The relevant paragraphs of the Act are so worded as to create an absolute offence, so that the bankrupt may be convicted upon simple proof of the conduct specified. All that is additionally necessary is that he is later adjudicated bankrupt on a petition presented within 12 months of the meeting at which the attempt was made to mislead his creditors. Furthermore, since the term "attempt" is employed in the statutory definition of the offence it is not even necessary that the debtor's attempt to deceive his creditors should have been successful. A further offence is created by section 356(2)(d), whereby an offence is committed if the bankrupt has at any time been guilty of any false representation or other fraud for the purpose of obtaining the consent of his creditors, or any of them, to an agreement with reference to his affairs or to his bankruptcy. The terms of this provision are in certain respects wider and more general than those of paragraph (b), since the precise nature of the representation is not specified, apart from the requirement that it be false. On the other hand, it appears to be an aspect of the offence that the consent of creditors be obtained to some agreement of the kind mentioned, as may be inferred from the absence of the word "attempts" from paragraph (d), in contrast to paragraph (b). It may nevertheless happen that a single course of illicit conduct by a debtor simultaneously gives rise to liability under both heads, as where a false story involving fictitious losses or expenses is used to induce creditors to agree to a composition or moratorium.

(v) *Absconding*

It is provided by section 358(*b*) of the Act that a bankrupt will have

---

[25] *ibid.*, s.355(3)(a), (b).
[26] *cf. Alliance and Leicester Building Society v. Ghahremani* [1992] RVR 198; *The Times*, March 19, 1992, (Hoffmann, J.).

committed an offence if, in the six months before the petition, he has left, or has attempted or made preparations to leave, England and Wales with any property the value of which is not less than £500,[27] and possession of which he would be required to deliver up to the official receiver or trustee in the event that a bankruptcy order were made against him. The Act casts upon the bankrupt the onus of proving innocent intention.[28] Since it is not unusual for a person to travel abroad—or even to journey to Scotland or Northern Ireland—taking more than £500 in money and other property which would if he became bankrupt be divisible among his creditors, any bankrupt who has travelled out of the jurisdiction of the English courts at any time during the year previous to his adjudication must be prepared to furnish a convincing explanation of his motives for making the journey in question.

(vi) *Fraudulent Dealing with Property Obtained on Credit*

If during the 12 months before petition the bankrupt disposed of any property which he had obtained on credit and, at the time he disposed of it, had not paid for it, a criminal offence will have been committed unless the bankrupt can satisfy the requirements of the defence of innocent intention.[29] In effect therefore, whenever the bankrupt has disposed of property before it was paid for, a presumption exists that the debtor's motives were fraudulent. It is a fairly common practice for debtors in financial difficulty to resort to this means of raising money, and it is worth remarking that, in common with the majority of the offences described in the present chapter, the prescribed maximum penalties for this offence are nowadays substantial. In the case of prosecution on indictment the court may impose punishment of up to seven years' imprisonment, or an unlimited fine, or both; whereas the respective maxima following conviction at a summary trial are six months' imprisonment or a fine of up to £2,000 or both.[30]

In addition to the offence committed by the bankrupt himself in disposing of property for which he has not paid, a further offence is committed by every person who acquires or receives property from a debtor within 12 months of the petition resulting in the latter's bankruptcy, either knowing or believing:

(1) That the bankrupt owed money in respect of the property, or
(2) That the bankrupt did not intend or was unlikely to be able to pay the money he so owed.[31]

---

[27] This is the figure currently prescribed for the purposes of s.358 under the Insolvency Proceedings (Monetary Limits) Order 1986 (S.I. 1986, No. 1996). *cf.* Cmnd. 8558, para. 1889, which recommended the removal of any arbitrary monetary limit in respect of this offence, as was also recommended in Cmnd. 221, paras. 200 and 202(d).
[28] See s.352 of the Act, and references *above*, to the defence of innocent intention.
[29] *ibid.*, s.359(1), together with s.352.
[30] See Sched. 10 to the Act: the "statutory maximum" therein referred to was formerly fixed by statutory instrument (S.I. 1984, No. 447), but is now mainly regulated through statutory provisions, esp. Criminal Justice Act 1991, s.17; Sched. 4.
[31] s.359(2) of the Act.

In this instance it is for the prosecution to prove the requisite *mens rea* on the part of the accused.

For the purposes of both the above offences, the concept of "disposing" of property includes the pawning of pledging of it, and persons who acquire or receive property under those circumstances are likewise within the ambit of the offence. A specific statutory exception to liability in each instance is provided by section 359(3) of the Act, whereby a person is declared not to be guilty of either type of offence if the disposal, acquisition or receipt of the property was in the ordinary course of a business carried on by the bankrupt at the time of the transaction in question. While this provision accords with the general policy of our mercantile law, which is to maintain confidence in businesses which are conducted in an orthodox way, it will be a question of fact whether the circumstances of the disposal in question were in conformity with the ordinary course of the business carried on by the bankrupt at the relevant time. One or two examples from decided cases may be illustrative. Thus it was not in the ordinary way of his trade for a toolmaker to sell in bulk, and unprocessed, six tons of steel which had been delivered to his tool factory as "raw materials" for his business.[32] Nor was it in the ordinary way of his trade for a grocer to dispose of the whole of his stock by way of a bill of sale, instead of selling it off piecemeal over the counter.[33] The underlying policy behind the original forerunners of the current statutory provision was once characterised by Mellish, L.J., thus: "the thing aimed at was the obtaining of goods on credit and then immediately selling them at a loss.[34] The court is provided with further guidance as to application of the modern provision by means of section 359(4), which states that in determining for the purposes of the section whether any property is disposed of, acquired or received in the ordinary course of a business carried on by the bankrupt, regard may be had to the price paid for the property. An accused's attempt to establish the defence referred to in section 359(3) is therefore unlikely to be successful where the price paid has been below the current market value of the property in question, due allowance being made for such factors as standard discounts and the operation of genuine, arms-length bargaining between the parties.

(vii) *Failure to Keep Proper Business Accounts*

Where a bankrupt has engaged in any trade, profession or business during any period in the two years immediately preceding the date of presentation of the bankruptcy petition, he will have committed an offence if any of the following matters is established:

    (1)   He has not kept proper accounting records throughout that period in which he was so engaged; or

---

[32] *R. v. Bolus* (1870) 23 L.T. 339.

[33] *R. v. Thomas* (1870) 22 L.T. 138 (see p. 139, *per* Lush J.).

[34] *Re Hodgson, ex p. Brett* (1875) 1 Ch.D. 151, 153 (discussing s.11(15) of the Debtors Act 1869).

(2) He has not preserved all the accounting records which he has kept.[35]

The statutory definition of the keeping of proper accounting records is supplied by section 361(3), whereby a person must in effect keep such records as are necessary to show or explain his transactions and financial position in his business, including records containing sufficiently detailed entries from day to day of all cash paid and received; statements of annual stock-takings in those cases where the business involves dealings in goods; and finally (except in the case of goods sold by way of retail trade to the actual consumer) records of all goods sold and purchased showing the buyers and sellers in sufficient detail to enable the goods and the buyers and sellers to be identified.

A businessman who has failed to keep proper accounting records may escape conviction upon either of two grounds.[36] The first is if his unsecured liabilities at the commencement of the bankruptcy did not exceed a prescribed amount, currently fixed at £20,000.[37] The second, alternative ground is if he proves that in the circumstances in which he carried on business the omission was honest and excusable. It was held in *R. v. Dandridge*[38] that the words "honest and excusable" indicate that there are two conditions to be met before the bankrupt satisfies this branch of the proviso, and that in some circumstances he may still be convicted despite his having demonstrated an "honest intent," because some species of honest conduct may yet be considered inexcusable. This would seem to follow from the premise that persons engaged in trade are under a duty to conduct their business responsibly, in the interests of all who extend credit to them and also in view of the general public interest in honest and responsible trading.

Lastly, as an additional deterrent against concealment, destruction or falsification of business records and accounts, section 361(4) provides that the offences created by section 355 relating to the bankrupt's books and papers (described in (iii) above) apply in relation to bankrupts who have engaged in business with the substitution of two years for the usual period of 12 months prior to petition.

(viii) *Gambling and Irresponsible Conduct*

The provisions of section 362(1) of the Act state that a bankrupt is guilty of an offence if, in the two years before petition, he materially contributed to, or increased the extent of, his insolvency by gambling or by rash and hazardous speculations. In determining whether any speculations were rash and hazardous, section 362(2) declares that the financial position of the bankrupt at the time when he entered into them must be taken into consideration. This implies that a certain ratio should be maintained between a person's speculations and his overall reserves at any time, so

---

[35] Insolvency Act 1986, s.361(1).
[36] *ibid.*, s.361(2).
[37] Insolvency Proceedings (Monetary Limits) Order 1986 (S.I. 1986, No. 1996).
[38] (1931) 22 Cr.App.R. 156.

that he only puts his resources to the hazard to the extent that he can properly and safely afford to do so. Naturally, the high profits which may accrue from speculative transactions may offer a particular attraction to those anxious to restore their declining fortunes, but the higher attendant risk is the very reason why such speculations ought not to be indulged in by those to whom an adverse outcome would be ruinous.

(ix) *Offences Under the General Criminal Law*

In addition to the above offences created by the Insolvency Act itself, it is appropriate to give an account of certain offences arising under the general criminal law which may be committed as a consequence of certain aspects of conduct which prove to be somewhat characteristic of those about to become, or who have recently become, bankrupt. The offences in point are created by sections 15, 16 and 17 of the Theft Act 1968, and sections 1 and 2 of the Theft Act 1978, which introduced provisions designed to punish fraudulent behaviour no matter by whom it may be committed.[39] A bankrupt may now face charges under one or more of the sections of the Theft Acts as a consequence of certain aspects of his conduct either before or after bankruptcy. In such cases, the actual fact of his bankruptcy is not an essential element of the offence, or offences, charged, although it may well be that the accused's bankruptcy, actual or impending, was a factor influencing his criminal conduct. It may also be the case that the offences with which he is charged have come to light, along with other "regular" bankruptcy offences, in the course of his examination in bankruptcy. A full discussion of the offences which form part of the general criminal law would go beyond the scope of this book, but it seems appropriate here to indicate their general purport, as the bankrupt may well be affected by them.[40]

Section 15 of the Theft Act 1968 creates the offence of obtaining by deception property belonging to another. The offence will be committed provided that the person obtaining the property has acted dishonestly, and with the intention of permanently depriving the other of it, and the element of "obtaining" will be satisfied if the accused has obtained ownership, possession or control of the property, either for himself or for the benefit of another person.[41] "Deception" is given a broad definition, and can be accomplished by words or conduct applying either to fact or to law, and can include a deception as to the present intentions of the person using the deception, or any other person.[42]

Section 16 creates the offence of obtaining a pecuniary advantage by deception. "Deception" is given the same broad meaning as in section 15,[43] and the offence may be made out regardless of whether the "advantage" was obtained for the accused himself or for some other person.[44] This

---

[39] See also ss.18–20 of the Theft Act 1968.
[40] For a full account of these offences, see Smith, *The Law of Theft* (6th ed. 1989), Chaps. 4, 5 and 6.
[41] See s.15(2) of the Theft Act 1968.
[42] *ibid.*, s.15(4).
[43] *ibid.*, s.16(3).
[44] *ibid.*, s.16(1).

provision replaces the former offence of obtaining credit by fraud, which was established by section 13(1) (now repealed) of the Debtors Act 1869, which also formed the model for the former section 156(a) of the Bankruptcy Act 1914 (also now repealed). The drafting of section 16 of the Theft Act 1968 is intended to eliminate certain loopholes which existed under the previous legislation.[45]

Section 17 of the Theft Act 1968 creates the offence of false accounting, which is committed by a person who, dishonestly and with a view to gain for himself or another, or with intent to cause loss to another, either:

(1) Destroys, defaces, conceals or falsifies any account or any record or document made or required for any accounting purpose; or
(2) In furnishing information for any purpose produces or makes use of any account, or any such record or document as aforesaid, which to his knowledge is or may be misleading, false or deceptive in a material particular.

Section 1 of the Theft Act 1978 makes it an offence for any person by any deception dishonestly to obtain services from another. Subsection (2) of that section indicates that it is an obtaining of services where the other is induced to confer a benefit on the understanding that the benefit has been or will be paid for. A further offence, established by section 2 of the Theft Act 1978, is that of evasion of liability by deception. There are three distinct offences created by the three paragraphs of section 2(1), namely:

(1) Dishonestly securing the remission of the whole or part of any existing liability to make a payment; or
(2) Dishonestly, and with intention of making permanent default, inducing the creditor or any person claiming payment on his behalf to wait for payment, or to forego payment; or
(3) Dishonestly obtaining any exemption from, or abatement of, liability to make a payment. Examples of circumstances in which an offence may be committed under one of the paragraphs of section 2(1) are where a debtor, by means of lies or deception, persuades his creditors to accept a composition in which they receive less by way of dividend than the debtor is actually able to pay; or where a debtor who is pressed for payment, and who wishes to gain time in which to abscond, gives his creditor a cheque in the knowledge that it will not be honoured by his bank when it is later presented for payment.

All the above provisions of the Theft Acts apply to bankrupts, just as much as to any other member of the public, and hence it may be that a

---

[45] Compare, *e.g.*, the provisions of s.16(2) of the Theft Act 1968 with those of s.13(1) of the Debtors Act 1869, under which the accused in *R. v. Mitchell* [1955] 3 All E.R. 263 escaped conviction. Nevertheless, the unsatisfactory operation of s.16(2)(a) of the Act of 1968 led to the repeal of that paragraph, and its replacement by the offence of obtaining services by deception, contained in s.1 of the Theft Act 1978.

bankrupt will face charges under these statutes, in addition to any which may be preferred under the Insolvency Act. It may happen that one and the same act by the bankrupt may constitute simultaneously offences under both the Theft Acts and the Insolvency Act. In such cases, the prosecution are likely to take into account, in framing their charges, that in many respects the onus of proof is cast upon the bankrupt by certain provisions of the Insolvency Act, thereby rendering a conviction simpler to achieve than it would be if, for example, a charge of false accounting were brought under section 17 of the Theft Act 1968 which, like sections 15 and 16 of that same statute, requires the prosecution to establish "dishonesty" on the part of the accused.[46] On the other hand, should the prosecution elect to frame charges under one of the provisions of the Theft Acts it should be noted that the maximum terms of imprisonment to which a convicted person may be sentenced are in certain instances greater under the Theft Acts than under the analogous provision within the Insolvency Act.[47]

(2) Offences arising from conduct between the presentation of the petition and the commencement of bankruptcy ("the initial period")

The presentation of a bankruptcy petition marks the beginning of the procedure which can lead to a debtor's adjudication. This is a sensitive and critical period, to which section 351(b) of the Act accords the special title of the "initial period." The following types of conduct are criminal offences if committed after a bankruptcy petition has been presented by or against a person who is subsequently adjudged bankrupt:

(i) Concealment or Removal of Property

It is an offence for the debtor to conceal any debt due to or from him, or any property to the value of £500 or more which he would be required to deliver to the trustee following his adjudication.[48] A further offence is constituted by section 354(2) of the Act, whereby it is an offence if the bankrupt, during the initial period, removed any property the value of which was not less than £500, and which he would be required to deliver up in the circumstances just referred to. This offence is one to which section 352 of the Act applies, and it is therefore incumbent upon the bankrupt to establish the defence of innocent intention in order to escape conviction.

(ii) Fraudulent Disposal of Property

The offence of fraudulent disposal is established by section 357(1) of the

---

[46] See *above*, pp. 345.
[47] The maxima prescribed for ss.15, 16 and 17 of the Theft Act 1968 are ten, five and seven years' imprisonment respectively, following conviction on indictment: see, ss.15(1), 16(1) and 17(1). The maxima for ss.1 and 2 of the Theft Act 1978 are five years' imprisonment: see s.4 of the Act.
[48] s.354(1)(b), (c) of the Act, discussed in section (1)(i) *supra*.

Act, which utilises a five-year reference period ending with the commencement of bankruptcy. Therefore this offence, which was discussed in section (1)(ii) above,[49] may also be committed through the making of any gift or transfer of, or charge on, the bankrupt's property during the initial period. The same is true of the offence under section 357(3) of fraudulent concealment or removal of property after, or within two months before, the date of any unsatisfied judgment, which was discussed in section (1)(i) above.

(iii) *Offences Relating to the Bankrupt's Books and Papers*

The offences created by section 355(2) and (3), concerning the concealment, destruction, mutilation or falsification of the bankrupt's books and papers, or the disposal or alteration of such documents, also apply in relation to the initial period.[50] A further offence, expressed in section 355(2)(a), becomes applicable from the beginning of the initial period onwards. This consists of the bankrupt preventing the production of any books, papers or records relating to his estate or affairs, and is thus an aspect of the requirement that the debtor must cooperate fully in the process of hearing and determining a bankruptcy petition relating to himself. The offence is one to which section 352 of the Act applies, so that the debtor must establish the defence of innocent intention if he is to avoid conviction.

(iv) *False Statements to Creditors*

The bankrupt commits an offence under section 356(2)(c) if during the initial period he attempts to account for any part of his property by fictitious losses or expenses, whether this occurs at any meeting of his creditors or on some other occasion.[51] The offence, created by section 356(2)(d), of obtaining creditors' consent to an agreement by means of a false representation or fraud, is also applicable to the initial period.

(v) *Absconding*

By section 358(b) of the Act, this offence also applies to the initial period.[52]

(vi) *Fraudulent Dealing with Property Obtained on Credit*

By section 359(1) and (2) of the Act, these offences also apply to the initial period.[53]

---

[49] *Above*, p. 339.
[50] See section (1)(iii) *above*, p. 339.
[51] s.356(2)(d) of the Act. See section (1)(iv) *above*, p. 340.
[52] See s.358 of the Act, discussed in section (1)(v) *above*, p. 340.
[53] See s.359(1), (2) of the Act, discussed in section (1)(vi) *above*, p. 341.

(vii) *Gambling and Irresponsible Conduct*

A bankrupt is guilty of an offence under section 362(1)(b) if he has, in the initial period, lost any part of his property by gambling or by rash or hazardous speculations. This offence is of broader scope than its counterpart, applicable to the pre-petition period,[54] whereby the bankrupt is punished if he has "materially contributed to, or increased the extent of, his insolvency" by the same species of conduct. Whereas the notion of "materiality" may call for the exercise of a subjective judgment, and thus allows some scope for argument from case to case, the post-petition period necessarily demands a stricter control over the debtor's dealings, and it is therefore made an offence for the debtor at this stage to lose *any* part of his estate in the manner prescribed.

(3) Offences arising from conduct after the commencement of bankruptcy

Apart from those offences which are expressed as applying purely in relation to the period before the commencement of bankruptcy,[55] all the offences which may be committed through the bankrupt's conduct during the initial period continue to be capable of commission by him after a bankruptcy order has been made, thereby marking the commencement of his bankruptcy.[56] Thus, the offences referred to within paragraphs (i), (iii), (iv) and (v) of section (2) above are all capable of being committed by the bankrupt if the relevant conduct takes place after the date of the bankruptcy order. In addition to these offences, some others become capable of commission from the time of bankruptcy onwards.

(i) *Non-Disclosure of Property*

As a sanction against any attempt by the bankrupt to keep secret the details of any property in which he has had an interest at some time, the Act provides that it shall be an offence if the bankrupt does not:

> "to the best of his knowledge and belief disclose all the property comprised in his estate to the official receiver or the trustee,"

or if he does not:

> "inform the official receiver or the trustee of any disposal of any property which but for the disposal would be so comprised, stating how, when, to whom and for what consideration the property was disposed of."[57]

---

[54] See s.359(1)(a) of the Act, discussed in section (1)(viii) *above*, p. 343.
[55] See ss.357(1), (3); 359(1), (2); 361; and 362, discussed *above*, in sections (1)(i) and (ii) and (2)(ii); (1)(vi); (1)(vii); and (1)(viii) and (2)(vii), respectively.
[56] See s.278(a) of the Act.
[57] Insolvency Act 1986, s.353(1).

The meaning of the word "property" in the context of this subsection is clearly "such property as he has had at some time or other," and which the trustee is capable of reclaiming for the estate through the exercise of his powers in relation to the bankrupt's antecedent transactions.[58] Thus, the bankrupt must frankly lay open the entire past record of his affairs to the trustee, who may therein discover items of property which are legally recoverable for the benefit of the creditors. An exception is conceded in the case of any part of the bankrupt's property which has been disposed of in the ordinary course of a business carried on by him, and also in the case of any payment of the ordinary expenses of the bankrupt or his family.[59] Where a bankrupt has omitted to disclose some item of property, or the disposal thereof, an onus is cast upon him of proving the defence of innocent intention, for otherwise he cannot escape conviction.[60]

(ii) *Non-Delivery of Property*

As a counterpart to the offence just described, the Act further renders punishable any failure by the bankrupt to deliver up possession to the official receiver or the trustee, or as he directs, of such of the property comprised in his estate as is in his possession or under his control, and which he is required by law to deliver up.[61] Once again, it is provided that the bankrupt may exculpate himself only by providing that his failure was unaccompanied by any intent to defraud.[62]

(iii) *Non-Delivery of Books and Papers, etc.*

The bankrupt commits an offence if he does not deliver up possession to the official receiver or the trustee, or as he directs, of all books, papers and other records of which he has possession or control, and which relate to his estate or affairs, unless he proves that he had no intent to defraud.[63]

(iv) *Omission in the Statement of Affairs, and Failure to Reveal Improper Proof*

It is an offence for the bankrupt to make any material omission from his statement of affairs, unless he proves that he had no intent to defraud.[64] It is an absolute offence if the bankrupt, knowing or believing that a false debt has been proved by any person under the bankruptcy, fails to inform the trustee of the matter as soon as practicable.[65]

---

[58] See Chap. 8, *ante*; *cf. R. v. Mitchell* (1880) 50 L.J.M.C. 76 (where it was suggested by Coleridge L.C.J., that there is no reason why property possessed up to five years previously should not be looked into).
[59] Insolvency Act 1986, s.353(2). The details of such transactions should be discoverable from the books which a trader is required to keep: see s.361 of the Act, discussed *above*, p. 342.
[60] Insolvency Act 1986, ss.352, 353(3).
[61] *ibid.*, s.354(1)(a).
[62] *ibid.*, s.352, 354.
[63] *ibid.*, s.355(1).
[64] *ibid.*, s.356(1).
[65] *ibid.*, s.356(2)(a).

(v) Failure to Explain Losses

Section 354(3) of the Act provides that a bankrupt is guilty of an offence if, on being required to do so by the official receiver or the court, he fails without reasonable excuse to account for the loss of any substantial part of his property incurred in the 12 months before petition or in the initial period, or fails to give a satisfactory explanation of the manner in which such a loss was incurred. It is to be observed that this offence is actually committed after bankruptcy, since it consists in the bankrupt's failure to furnish a satisfactory explanation when required, albeit the losses which are in question will have been incurred prior to adjudication. It was held in *R. v. Salter*[66] that the offence is an absolute one which will be committed even where the bankrupt's failure is unaccompanied by any intention to deceive, and that he may be convicted even where he has tried his best to furnish a satisfactory explanation.[67] The purpose of the provision under consideration was explained as being the protection of the rest of the business community by imposing criminal liability on the businessman who goes bankrupt without having so conducted his affairs as to be able satisfactorily to explain why some substantial loss has been made.[68]

(vi) Undischarged Bankrupt Obtaining Credit

The purpose of section 360(1)(a) of the Act is to protect the general public from unknowingly extending credit to an undischarged bankrupt. It is an offence for an undischarged bankrupt, either alone or jointly with any other person, to obtain credit to the extent of £250 or more from any person without informing that person that he is an undischarged bankrupt.[69] This constitutes one of the most severe continuing restrictions to which an undischarged bankrupt is subjected, and is applicable to all such persons regardless of how innocent their previous conduct may have been. Life is rendered extremely inconvenient and insecure, for unless the bankrupt meticulously notifies the other party that he is undischarged, a moment's thoughtlessness may easily suffice for there to occur an obtaining of credit to the extent of £250 or more. Section 360 re-enacts, with some modifications and with up-to-date drafting, a provision which is a long-established part of the law of bankruptcy.

The case law relating to this offence is extensive, and not without interest. In the first place, the offence has been held to be an absolute one, because there is no reference in section 360(1)(a) to the bankrupt's intent at the time of obtaining credit. Therefore, it will not excuse the bankrupt if he shows that he had no intent to defraud,[70] or that he duly instructed his

---

[66] [1968] 2 Q.B. 793.
[67] See the judgment of Sachs L.J., at p. 802 *et seq.*, discussing the variations in the requirement of *mens rea* in relation to the bankruptcy offences.
[68] The notion is thus put in layman's terms by Sachs L.J., at p. 810: "If you lose a substantial part of your estate and go bankrupt, you had better have, and give, a satisfactory explanation" (quoting remarks of counsel during argument).
[69] The amount of £250 is the figure currently prescribed for the purposes of s.360(1) by the Insolvency Proceedings (Monetary Limits) Order 1986 (S.I. 1986, No. 1996).
[70] *R. v. Dyson* [1894] 2 Q.B. 176.

agent for the transaction to inform the creditor as required by the Act, and that the omission was perpetrated by the agent rather than the bankrupt personally.[71] The purpose of the enactment is to protect any potential creditor by ensuring that he has the necessary information at the time of giving credit,[72] and to this end the state of mind of the bankrupt is irrelevant: innocence, at best, may serve as a factor to be considered in mitigation of sentence. This consequently explains the absence from section 360(1)(a) of any such words as "wilfully," "intentionally" or "fraudulently," and of any reference to the defence of innocent intention mentioned in section 352. It should be noted however that the Act does not go to the length of forbidding an undischarged bankrupt to obtain credit at all. Moreover, it has been held that the purpose of the section is achieved where the creditor is apprised of the necessary information at the moment of giving credit, so that it is an acceptable defence that the bankrupt, either personally or via his agent, had given the creditor the information a reasonable time *before* he obtained credit from him: there will then be no need to reiterate the warning at the very moment of obtaining credit.[73] What is plainly unacceptable is if notification is not communicated until after credit has been obtained.

The absolute nature of the offence has the additional consequence that a conviction can be brought in even though the bankruptcy itself may be annulled after the obtaining of credit.[74] Indeed, were the law to be otherwise it would be possible for a bankrupt to resort to the device of borrowing, without disclosure, an amount of money sufficient to pay all his debts in full, and thereupon to obtain an annulment.[75] In some cases where the bankruptcy has been annulled, and especially where the ground of annulment was that the court took the view that the bankruptcy order "ought not to have been made,"[76] it may be thought appropriate to utilise the discretion not to prosecute for the offence of obtaining credit.

While the absolute nature of the disclosure requirement has long been established, the concept of "obtaining credit" in this context has undergone a progressive elucidation. In *R. v. Hayat*[77] the Court of Appeal laid stress upon the essential requirement of an "obtaining" of credit, for which it is necessary that there should have been some conduct, either by words or otherwise, which amounted to an "obtaining" on the part of the person charged. It was settled at an early date that credit could be "obtained" for the purposes of what is now section 360(1)(a) without any

---

[71] *R. v. Duke of Leinster* [1924] 1 K.B. 311.

[72] *R. v. Zeitlin* (1932) 23 Cr.App.R. 163; *cf. R. v. Duke of Leinster, above,* at p. 316, *per* Hewart, L.C.J. See also the views of the *Cork Committee,* Cmnd. 8558 at paras. 132, 1840–1845, and 1882.

[73] *R. v. Zeitlin, above.*

[74] *D.P.P. v. Ashley* [1955] Crim.L.R. 565, but see s.350(2) of the Act, *above,* p. 336 (text to n. 8). *Note* also that no offence is committed where the bankrupt serves as the *agent* by whom credit is obtained for an independent principal whose status is not that of a bankrupt: *R. v. Godwin* (1980) 71 Cr.App.R. 97.

[75] *D.P.P. v. Ashley, above, per* Byrne J. (of course, a second bankruptcy might shortly afterwards ensue in such a case).

[76] *See* s.282(1)(a) of the Act, *ante,* Chap. 11, p. 322.

[77] (1976) 120 Sol.Jo. 434; 63 Cr.App.R. 181.

need for an express stipulation for credit in the contract between the parties.[78] Credit would be "obtained" whenever the bankrupt received goods without having to pay cash for them at the moment when payment could lawfully have been demanded, and for jurisdictional purposes it was held that the credit was "obtained" at the place where the goods were received.[79] Nor would it avail a bankrupt to plead that credit was "forced" upon him, in a situation where his order was for goods of less than £250 in value, and he had been sent, and had kept without protesting, goods of a greater value.[80] Moreover, it is well established that an offence is committed under section 360(1)(a) when the bankrupt has obtained credit to an aggregate amount in excess of £250, and hence the magnitude of the credit obtained upon each of several occasions is not in itself a decisive factor, provided that at some time the bankrupt's total, net indebtedness in respect of transactions in which his status was not disclosed exceeded £250.[81] Nor does the fact that the bankrupt has furnished collateral security prevent a transaction from involving an "obtaining of credit,"[82] although it has been suggested, *obiter*, that an exception might exist in a case involving pledge security, for example if an exceptionally valuable jewel were pledged for a sum less than its value.[83] Accordingly, it may be suggested that no crime will be committed by a bankrupt who pledges or pawns any property which is lawfully his, provided at least that he obtains less than the true value of the property employed as security.

The obtaining of "credit" is not confined to instances of the obtaining of goods without instantly effecting payment, for credit may also be obtained in other ways, such as by the bankrupt receiving services without having to pay for them immediately, or by his being permitted to occupy accommodation for which payment will be made in arrear.[84] Equally, a simple borrowing of money constitutes an obtaining of credit, for the bankrupt's consequent obligation is to repay the lender his money, plus interest if agreed. There is no substance to any pleading that the bankrupt is here obtaining "cash," not "credit," for in the case of a loan "there is no difference between getting money and getting goods from that point of view."[85] However, a less easy solution has been the case where the bankrupt obtains money from a person, or persons, by means of the promise to render services of some kind in return, which services he thereafter omits to perform. At one time this was also thought to be an obtaining of credit, but the House of Lords in *Fisher v. Raven*[86] held that this was a false conclusion. In that case, an undischarged bankrupt

---

[78] *R. v. Peters* (1886) 16 Q.B.D. 636.
[79] *R. v. Peters*, above; *R. v. Ellis* [1899] 1 Q.B. 230.
[80] *R. v. Juby* (1886) 55 L.T. 788.
[81] *R. v. Hartley* [1972] 1 All E.R. 599.
[82] *R. v. Fryer* (1912) 7 Cr.App.R. 183.
[83] *ibid.*, at p. 185, *per* Phillimore J.
[84] *R. v. Smith* (1915) 11 Cr.App.R. 81. See also *R. v. Miller* [1977] Crim.L.R. 562 (on the meaning of "credit" in the context of default on a contract of hire purchase).
[85] *R. v. Pryce* (1949) 34 Cr.App.R. 21, 22, *per* Goddard L.C.J.
[86] [1964] A.C. 210, overruling *R. v. Ingram* [1956] 2 Q.B. 424 and undermining the *obiter dicta* in *R. v. Goodall* (1958) 43 Cr.App.R. 24.

contracted with each of a number of persons to make paintings for them, and obtained part of the agreed price in advance. The paintings were never executed, but both the Court of Criminal Appeal and the House of Lords held that there could be no conviction under section 155(a) of the Bankruptcy Act 1914 (the relevant statutory provision then in force), ruling that in the context of that section the "credit" to be obtained is "credit in respect of the payment or repayment of money."[87] The anomaly resulting from this decision of the House of Lords has been reversed by the express terms of section 360(2)(b) of the Insolvency Act 1986, which provides that the reference in subsection (1)(a) to the bankrupt obtaining credit includes where he is paid in advance (whether in money or otherwise) for the supply of goods or services. Accordingly it is now an offence for an undischarged bankrupt to receive advance payments— whether in money or in another form—for the supply of goods or services without informing those concerned of his current status. In the interests of certainty, section 360(2)(a) further provides that "obtaining credit" includes where goods are bailed to the bankrupt under a hire purchase agreement or agreed to be sold to him under a conditional sale agreement.[88] It is further to be noted that a bankrupt who obtains money by promising to render future services and who, at the time of receiving any advance payment, did not intend to fulfill his promise to render those services, may be convicted of the offence of obtaining property by deception.[89]

Where it is established that a bankrupt has committed an offence under section 360(1)(a) in the course of entering into any particular contract under which he obtains credit, one further consequence is that the bankrupt himself cannot enforce the contract in question. He will therefore be denied an order for specific performance should he seek one, while the other party may apply for the equitable remedy of rescission of the contract.[90]

A further aspect of the modifications introduced into this statutory provision, when re-enacted in 1986, is the effecting of an integration between the separate jurisdictions of England and Wales, Scotland and Northern Ireland with regard to the essential elements which constitute the offence of obtaining credit without disclosure of status, or the separate offence of engaging in trade without disclosure of identity (see below). By virtue of section 360(3) a person whose estate has been sequestrated in Scotland, or who has been adjudged bankrupt in Northern Ireland, is guilty of an offence if he does anything in England which would be an offence under section 360(1) if he were an undischarged bankrupt by reason of a bankruptcy order made in England and Wales. The relevant information which must be given by, for example, a person who is

---

[87] [1964] A.C. 210, 232, *per* Dilhorne, L.C.
[88] On the meaning of the expressions "hire purchase agreement" and "conditional sale agreement," see Insolvency Act 1986, s.436, which incorporates the meanings borne by those terms in the Consumer Credit Act 1974.
[89] See Theft Act 1968, s.15 and also s.4(1) ("property" includes money and all other property). The offence is discussed *above*, p. 344.
[90] *De Choisy v. Hynes* [1937] 4 All E.R. 54.

undischarged from a Scottish sequestration, and who obtains credit in England, is in this instance the fact that he currently has the status incurred by reason of the Scottish proceedings.[91] Corresponding provisions are in force in the insolvency legislation applicable in Scotland and in Northern Ireland respectively, to render it an offence for a person who is undischarged from an adjudication in England and Wales to obtain credit or to engage in business in either of those jurisdictions without making the requisite disclosure.[92]

(vii) *Undischarged Bankrupt Engaging in Trade*

Section 360(1)(b) provides that it shall be an offence for an undischarged bankrupt to engage (whether directly or indirectly) in any trade or business under a name other than that under which he was adjudicated bankrupt, without disclosing to all persons with whom he enters into any business transaction the name under which he was adjudicated. The purpose of this section, as with section 360(1)(a) just discussed,[93] is the protection of the public, including other persons engaged in trade, who may unknowingly engage in dealings with an undischarged bankrupt who adopts a fresh business name in place of the one under which he has previously traded.[94] The offence is an absolute one, so that the bankrupt's subjective intentions are irrelevant to the question of guilt, and the effect is once again to render it exceedingly difficult for a bankrupt to recommence trading while he remains undischarged. Nevertheless, it is to be noted that the law does not prohibit the bankrupt from recommencing trading, but limits its concern to ensuring that every person who has dealings with him shall have the opportunity of first deciding whether to do business with one who is an undischarged bankrupt.

The words "whether directly or indirectly," which appear in parentheses in section 360(1)(b), were introduced for the first time by the Insolvency Acts of 1985 and 1986 in the course of re-enacting this long established statutory provision. The purpose behind these additional words is to make it also a criminal offence if an undischarged bankrupt utilises an agent to conduct business on his behalf, or if he in some other way contrives to control a business from behind the scenes. The other new aspect in the current statutory provision, as was mentioned above,[95] is the integration of the whole of the United Kingdom for the purpose of controlling the business activities of persons who have been adjudicated bankrupt, or undergone sequestration, in any part of the Kingdom: section 360(3) subjects all such persons to the criminal law of England and Wales if they do anything there which would be an offence under section 360(1)(b) if they were undischarged from an English adjudication.

---

[91] See Insolvency Act 1986, s.360(4).
[92] *cf.* Bankruptcy (Scotland) Act 1985, s.67(9), (10).
[93] See *above*, section (vi), p. 350.
[94] See, *e.g. R. v. Doubleday* (1964) 49 Cr.App.R. 62.
[95] See section (vi) *above*.

(B) Criminal Bankruptcy

It has frequently been a matter for complaint that our criminal law has hitherto made insufficient provision for the compensation of victims of crime, and correspondingly for the penalisation of the criminal in respect of the loss or damage he has inflicted. One approach to this question has been to confer upon the criminal courts powers to make compensation orders against convicted criminals, and also to make restitution orders in relation to stolen property.[96] But in many cases, the criminal is found to have no assets of value, and his victim's property will often have vanished without trace, so that orders for compensation to be paid, or for restitution to be effected, would accomplish little or nothing. To counter this, it was suggested that compensation of the victims, in whole or in part, might be most effectively facilitated by compulsorily subjecting the criminal's property to the same administration as it would undergo upon his bankruptcy. In such a "forced bankruptcy" the amounts of loss or damage inflicted upon the victims of crime would be treated as analogous to debts which are owed to creditors, and of course any true creditors, of the conventional sort, might join in and prove for their debts alongside them. For a brief period between 1972 and 1989, an institution known as criminal bankruptcy was implemented in the law in an attempt to supply such a remedy.

Criminal bankruptcy was first introduced into our law by the Criminal Justice Act 1972,[97] whose provisions were later re-enacted, in somewhat revised form, in the Powers of Criminal Courts Act 1973.[98] The power to make a criminal bankruptcy order was conferred upon any Crown Court before which a person was convicted of an offence as a result of which, either taken alone or in combination with any other offence or offences of which he was simultaneously convicted, or which were then taken into consideration, loss or damage[99] to an amount exceeding £15,000 had been suffered by one or more persons whose identity was known to the court.[1] Where persons were jointly convicted in respect of the same loss or damage, the criminal bankruptcy order might be made against all the offenders.[2]

Abolition of Criminal Bankruptcy

Despite the forcefully expressed disapproval by the *Cork Committee* of the criminal bankruptcy procedure,[3] and indications also of judicial

---

[96] The meaning of compensation orders is provided for in the Powers of Criminal Courts Act 1973, ss.35–38; restitution orders may be made under the provisions of s.6 of the Criminal Justice Act, 1972.
[97] ss.7–10 and Sched. 1.
[98] ss.39–41 and Sched. 2. This Act is referred to hereafter as "The Act of 1973."
[99] Except such as is attributable to personal injury (for which the victim may now seek compensation by applying to the Criminal Injuries Compensation Board).
[1] The Act of 1973, s.39(1). By s.39(6), the amount of £15,000 was made variable by statutory instrument.
[2] *ibid.*, s.39(4).
[3] Cmnd. 8558, Chap. 41, especially paras. 1718, 1722–1724.

dissatisfaction with it,[4] the procedure was initially retained, and its civil aspects fully incorporated into the structure of the Insolvency Act 1986. Nevertheless the low frequency of use of the procedure, and the poor rates of recoveries and realisations in those cases in which it was used, were already seen to furnish a strong case for the reconsideration of this unsuccessful experiment in using the law of bankruptcy as a means of helping to ensure that crime does not pay. Section 101 of the Criminal Justice Act 1988 abolishes the power of the Crown Court to make a criminal bankruptcy order under section 39 of the Powers of Criminal Courts Act 1973, and supersedes this by the power to make confiscation orders under sections 71–103 of the 1988 Act. These provisions came into force with effect from April 3, 1989.[5] Schedule 16 to the Act of 1988 effects the repeal of sections 39 and 40 of the Powers of Criminal Courts Act 1973, and of all those provisions within the Insolvency Act 1986 whose purpose was to provide the basis for the operation of the criminal bankruptcy procedure.[6]

---

[4] *cf.* Re Raeburn (1982) 74 Cr.App.R. 21.
[5] (S.I. 1989, No. 264).
[6] The following provisions of the Insolvency Act 1986 are repealed by Sched. 16 to the Criminal Justice Act 1988: ss.264(1)(d), 266(4), 267(3), 277, 282(2), 293(1)(part), 297(1), 327, 341(4) and (5), 382(1)(c), 383(1)(a)(part), 385(1) (definition of "criminal bankruptcy order"), 402.

PART II

Company Insolvency

Section A. Non-Liquidation Procedures

CHAPTER 14

RECEIVERS

The appointment of a receiver is one of the remedies available to a debentureholder or mortgagee[1] in respect of a company's default in complying with the terms of a loan.[2] The loan may be secured by fixed charge over some specific asset, *e.g.* land, plant and machinery,[3] or by floating charge over the company's fluctuating assets: goodwill, cash in hand and at the bank, book debts, work in progress. Often it will be secured by both.[4] A receiver takes the income from the assets and, after paying outgoings, accounts for it to the company. If the debt can be cleared in this way, the asset is ultimately returned to the company. Often, however, the "receiving" function is merely the precursor of a more expeditious discharge of the debt by a sale of the assets. Where, as in the case of a floating charge, the security includes a business, its preservation dictates an active managerial role, and it is in these circumstances that a receiver and manager is appointed. While there is a clear terminological and functional distinction between a *receiver* and a *receiver and manager*, where that distinction is not in issue it is very common to refer to the latter as simply a *receiver*.[5]

---

[1] See generally *Palmer's Company Law*, Vol. 2, paras. 14.301–14.313.
[2] It is impossible to do full justice to the volume and complexity of the law relating to receivers within the confines of a general work on corporate insolvency and this chapter should therefore be regarded as an introduction to the subject. More detailed accounts will be found in the standard works on the subject, namely, Lightman & Moss, *The Law of Receivers of Companies* (1994, 2nd ed.), Picarda, *The Law Relating to Receivers, Managers and Administrators* (1990, 2nd ed.) and *Kerr on Receivers* (1988, 16th ed.) to all of which the writer acknowledges her indebtedness.
[3] Or book debts, see *William Gaskell Group v. Highley* [1993] BCC 200; *Re New Bullas Trading Ltd* [1994] BCC 36. (C.A.).
[4] The appointment of a receiver causes a floating charge to crystallise: see *Palmer's Company Law*, Vol. 2, para. 13.129.
[5] See Picarda, *The Law Relating to Receivers, Managers and Administrators*, 2nd ed., p. 1.

(A) Types of Receiver

The appointment may be made by the court or under an express or implied power in the debenture. In the case of a fixed charge over land, the power if not express, can be implied under the terms of section 101(1)(iii) of the Law of Property Act 1925[6] (often referred to as an "*LPA Receiver*").[7] In other cases—floating charges or charges over fixed assets other than land—there will generally be an express provision permitting the appointment of a receiver and manager.[8] Such receivers are referred to in the Insolvency Act 1986 as *receivers appointed out of court* and also as receivers appointed "under powers contained in an instrument". In the absence of an express or implied provision (or if there is some doubt as to the validity of the debenture containing the power or, perhaps if it is considered that foreign courts would be more likely to recognise the appointment) a receiver can be *appointed by the court*. Court appointed receivers are not common[9]; the involvement of the court in the appointment of the receiver and in the operation of the receivership occasions delay and expense and, as will be seen, the status of a court appointed receiver differs in important respects from that of a receiver appointed out of court.[10] The Insolvency Act 1985 (now section 29(2) of

---

[6] The terms of s.101 of the Law of Property Act 1925 read with s.205 of the same Act make it clear that its application is not limited to land but reliance on the section alone would be inappropriate where the security includes a business because the section confers no power to appoint a manager. See also s.109, *ibid.* S.101 is employed in relation to charges of book debts. See *Lightman & Moss, op. cit.*, para. 3.106.

[7] The power arises where the mortgage is by deed (and, in the case of registered land, has been registered as a registered charge) and the mortgage money has become due. It becomes exercisable in the circumstances mentioned in s.103 of the Law of Property Act 1925: (i) notice requiring payment of the mortgage money has been served on the mortgagor and default has been made in payment of all or part of it for three months thereafter; or (ii) some interest under the mortgage is two months or more in arrear; or (iii) there has been a breach of some provision in the Act or the mortgage deed (other than the covenant for payment of the money or interest) which should have been observed or performed by the mortgagor or by someone who concurred in making the mortgage. It is a power to receive income from the charged property (or if the charged property is income, to receive that). The power can be varied or extended by the mortgage deed, *e.g.* to include a power to appoint a manager, and will not apply if a contrary intention is expressed (subsections (3) and (4)). A person paying money to the receiver is not concerned to enquire whether any case has happened to authorise the receiver to act (s.109(4) Law of Property Act 1925). The appointment, powers, remuneration and duties of such receivers are set out in s.109 Law of Property Act 1925. Some equitable mortgages will fall outside the terms of s.101 and in these cases the mortgagee can seek an appointment by the court. See Gray, *Elements of Land Law*, (1993, 2nd ed.) pp. 1027, 1032; *Megarry's Manual of the Law of Real Property*, (1993, 7th ed.), pp. 457, 459; Barclay, *To Possess or to Receive* (1992) 14 EG 114.

[8] The mortgage or charge will specify the circumstances in which such an express power is exercisable: these will usually be broader than those referred to in s.103 of the Law of Property Act 1925 (see supra n.7). They may specify the case where the security is in jeopardy but if they do not do so the court will not imply that the mortgageee has power in such circumstances, despite the fact that this is one of the circumstances where the court itself could appoint: *Cryne v. Barclays Bank plc* [1987] BCLC 548 C.A.

[9] For a recent example, see *B.C.C.I S.A. v. B.R.S. Kumar Ltd* [1994] BCLC 211.

[10] For an account of the disadvantages of court appointed receivers, see *Lightman and Moss, op. cit.*, para. 22.06.

the 1986 Act) defined a new type of receiver appointed out of court: the *administrative receiver*. He is:

(a) a receiver or manager of the whole (or substantially the whole) of a company's property appointed by or on behalf of the holders of any debentures of the company secured by a charge which, as created, was a floating charge, or by such a charge and one or more other securities; or
(b) a person who would be such a receiver or manager but for the appointment of some other person as receiver of part of the company's property.

It is crucial that the charge under which the receiver has been appointed was *as created* a floating charge. If it was floating at its inception it makes no difference that it subsequently became fixed on crystallisation.[11] Whether it was floating at its inception will depend upon its substance rather than its form.[12] The characteristics of a floating charge were identified in *Re Yorkshire Woolcombers Association Ltd*,[13] namely, (1) it is a charge on a class of assets of a company present and future, (2) that the class is one which in the ordinary course of business changes from time to time, (3) by the charge it is contemplated that until some future step is taken by or on behalf of the chargee the company may carry on its business in the ordinary way. If a charge has these features, it can be a floating charge, even if at the time the charge was created, the company had no assets which could fall within a floating charge and the grant of such a charge was to enable the chargee, who also had the benefit of a more substantial fixed charge, to appoint an administrative receiver, and thus to be clothed with power under section 9 of the Act to veto the making of an administration order.[14] The effect of section 29(2) & (3) is that the charge must extend to the whole, or substantially the whole, of the company's property; if it does, it is immaterial that the receiver's appointment does not extend to all the property charged because a prior chargee of some of that property has already appointed a receiver.

Section 29 refers to *company* receivers. It was held in *Re International Bulk Commodities Ltd*[15] that this includes a receiver of a foreign company which, though neither formed nor registered under the Companies Act 1985, would, as an unregistered company, have been amenable to winding up under Part V of the Insolvency Act 1986. There is no definition of "company" in section 29 itself or in the general definition section of the

---

[11] As to crystallisation see *Palmer, op. cit.*, paras. 13.129–13.130; *Farrar's Company Law*, 3rd ed., p. 263.
[12] See *Palmer, op. cit.*, paras. 13.110–13.115.
[13] [1903] 2 Ch. 284, per *Romer*, L.J. at p. 294.
[14] *Re Croftbell Ltd* [1990] BCC 781.
[15] [1992] BCC 463. In *Re Dallhold Estates (U.K.) Pty Ltd* ([1992] BCC 394) the question of the application of Part II of the Act (Administrators) to foreign companies in original proceedings was by-passed because the court was exercising its special jurisdiction under s.426 of the Act. See *infra*, Chaps. 16 & 31.

Act, section 251. However the latter does contain a cross-reference to the Companies Act 1985, section 735, subsection (1)(a) of which defines "company" as *excluding* foreign companies. This was not considered to be conclusive because section 735(4) provides that the definitions given are subject to contrary intention and Mummery, J. found that the content and purpose of the provisions relating to administrative receivers indicated that they were intended to apply to unregistered companies liable to be wound up under Part V of the 1986 Act. Therefore the receivers in this case had not merely their contractual powers but also, as administrative receivers, the statutory powers conferred by section 42 and schedule 1 of the Insolvency Act 1986. *Re International Bulk Commodities Ltd* was distinguished in *Re Devon and Somerset Farmers Ltd*[16] where His Honour Judge Hague considered the definition of "company" in section 40 of the Act, which imposes a duty on receivers generally to pay preferential debts out of the proceeds of a floating charge in priority to the claims of the chargee. This case also concerned a company not registered under the Companies Act 1985; here not a foreign company, but one registered under the Industrial and Provident Societies Act 1965. In reliance upon *Re International Bulk Commodities* and by analogy with section 29, it was argued that "company" in section 40 included unregistered companies generally. The Judge was not convinced by the reasoning in *Re International Bulk Commodities Ltd* and he distinguished it as a case concerning the *powers* of receivers of *foreign* companies. The case before him concerned the *duties* of a receiver of *an industrial and provident society*. Such societies were governed by their own legislation which included provisions relating to receivers and floating charges and he held that they were not within section 40. Whether foreign companies fall within section 29 remains uncertain.

It is also uncertain whether a receiver appointed by the court can fall within the definition of an administrative receiver in section 29(2).[17]

The position of court appointed receivers will be considered, followed by that of receivers appointed out of court including administrative receivers.

(B) Receivers Appointed by the Court[18]

The Appointment

The High Court has jurisdiction by order to appoint a receiver in all

---

[16] [1993] BCC 410.
[17] See *infra*.
[18] Certain provisions of the Act are applicable to all receivers, whether appointed by the court or not. They are: s.30 (disqualification of bodies corporate); s.39 (statements in invoices, etc.); s.40 (payment of preferential debts out of assets subject to a floating charge); s.41 (duty to make returns). See also s.405(1) Companies Act 1985 (notice of appointment to be given to the registrar of companies). These provisions are discussed, *infra.*, at pp. 369 & p. 370.

cases in which it appears to be just and convenient to do so.[19] The application may be by summons or motion.[20] The jurisdiction must only be exercised in aid of some legal or equitable right but an order appointing a receiver in respect of a fixed or floating charge clearly falls within its ambit. The court will not appoint a receiver if it would secure no legitimate advantage to the applicant, if it would unfairly prefer one creditor to another or if the property is incapable of beneficial realisation.[21] The court may have regard to any terms in the debenture which indicate when it was contemplated that the creditor should have the right to intervene but the existence of such terms does not limit the court's discretion.[22]

Orders have been made where there are arrears of principal or interest or the security is in jeopardy. A receiver may be appointed merely on the basis of arrears of interest, the principal not being due.[23] A receiver may be appointed even if there has been no default in the payment of principal or interest, and no other breach of contract by the company, if the security is seen to be in jeopardy. This was the situation in *Re London Pressed Hinge Co. Ltd*[24] where a receiver was appointed to protect the assets from execution by a judgment creditor. The jeopardy principle can also be seen operating in cases where companies, having granted a floating charge over their business and undertaking, then propose to dispose of the business and/or wind up. In either case the company will cease to carry on the business thus jeopardising the security. Thus a receiver can be appointed under a floating charge on the undertaking, prior to a fixed repayment date, if a resolution is passed winding up the company and its assets are transferred to a company formed to take them over.[25] The position is the same where the debenture states that the loan is to be repayable prematurely on winding up *unless* the winding up is for reconstruction; if, in furtherance of a reconstruction, the company passes a resolution for winding up and transfers its assets to a new company the court will appoint a receiver because of the jeopardy to the security.[26] The security under a floating charge is the business and if the company no longer carries on the business, having sold it, the rights of the debenture holders arise and they can ask for the appointment of a receiver.[27] In *B.C.C.I. S.A. v. B.R.S. Kumar Bros Ltd*[28] the court found it just and convenient to appoint a receiver of the transferee company. The plaintiff had a debenture secured by fixed and floating charges over the assets of B.R.S. The liquidators of the plaintiff appointed administrative receivers under the charge in

---

[19] s.37(1) Supreme Court Act 1981. The section does not expressly refer to the appointment of a receiver *and manager* but it is taken to confer such jurisdiction. See *Picarda, op. cit.*, Ch. 1. Where the court appoints a receiver and manager "it is with a view to sale; it is not a permanency": per Cozens Hardy, M.R. in *Re Newdigate* [1912] Ch. 468.
[20] Rules of the Supreme Court, Order 30.
[21] *J. Walls v. Legge* [1923] 2 K.B. 240.
[22] See *Lightman & Moss, op. cit.*, para. 22.07.
[23] *Bissill v. Bradford Tramways* [1891] W.N. 51.
[24] [1905] 1 Ch. 576.
[25] *Wallace v. Universal Automatic Machines Co.* [1894] 2 Ch. 547 C.A.
[26] *Re Crompton* [1914] 1 Ch. 954.
[27] *Hubbock v. Helms* (1887) 56 L.T. 232.
[28] [1994] BCLC 211.

November 1992. B.R.S. had previously transferred some of the charged assets and its business to B.R.S. International Ltd (with which it had a close but not completely defined relationship). The liquidators of the plaintiff company applied to the court for the appointment of a receiver of International there being no power to do so in the B.R.S. debenture (the validity of which was anyway challenged on the ground of illegality). Mervyn Davies, J. appointed a receiver of International. The B.R.S. debenture was not illegal in itself and to enforce it would not enable the liquidator to benefit from any illegal conduct by B.C.C.I. The enforcement of the debenture against a separate entity was justified upon two alternative grounds: International was a mere creature or nominee of B.R.S. or, if it was not, the transfer of its assets by B.R.S., and the consequent cessation of its business, crystallised the charge and International, not being bona fide purchasers for value without notice, took subject to it.

A receiver can be appointed by the court even though the debenture holder has already appointed one[29] and such a court appointment will displace the existing receiver.[30] The court selects the receiver having regard to the wishes of the company and the chargee; usually the nominee of the chargee, so long as he is independent, will be appointed. The appointee does not have to be a qualified insolvency practitioner.[31] Where the company is being wound up by the court, the court may appoint the official receiver.[32]

Status of a Receiver Appointed by the Court

Such a receiver is an officer of the court and a number of important consequences flow from this.

Suit

An officer of the court cannot sue or be sued without leave[33] but such leave may be given to enable an action to be brought against him by a person at whose instance he was appointed.[34]

Supervision

He acts under the close supervision of the court and in the course of the receivership many matters may have to be referred to the court.[35] In

---

[29] *Re "Slogger" Automatic Feeder Co. Ltd* [1915] 1 Ch. 478.
[30] *Re Maskellyne British Typewriters* [1898] 1 Ch. 133.
[31] See *supra*, p. 26.
[32] s.32 of the Act.
[33] *Viola v. Anglo American Cold Storage Co.* [1912] 2 Ch. 305; *Searle v. Choat* [1884] 25 Ch. 723 C.A.; *Sutton v. Rees* (1869) 9 Jur N.S. 456; (1863) 32 L.J. Ch. 437.
[34] *LP Arthur Insurance Ltd v. Sisson* [1966] 1 W.L.R. 1384.
[35] The receiver, not being a party to the action giving rise to his appointment, may have no standing to apply for supplementary directions unless it is conferred by the initial order: Totty and Jordan, *Insolvency*, D6.34.

principle he is entitled to remuneration, but the court controls the amount. That control extends to "disallowing claims for remuneration which have arisen from improper or misguided actions by the receiver and moderating such claims where they are adjudged to be excessive."[36] His accounts must be submitted to the court and he must apply to the court to obtain his discharge. Where the court appoints a receiver over disputed assets at the instance of a third party claimant, the claimant can ask the court to ensure that expenditure incurred defending the action is necessary and useful but is not entitled to monitor or ask the court to monitor every step in the litigation. In ordering the release of funds to meet such expenditure the court has to balance the claimant's interest in assets which may ultimately turn out to belong to him, against the public interest that a defendant should not be deprived of the means to fund a defence.[37]

Powers

These will be defined in the order appointing him and in any subsequent orders.[38] His powers, deriving from the court, are not limited by the debenture in respect of which the court appoints him or by the constitution of the company. Neither the company's capacity nor its authority have relevance to the validity of his acts. His powers are, of course, limited by the order of the court but the effect of a receiver exceeding the terms of the order, by for example acting outside the ordinary course of business, is uncertain. If a third party had no notice of any sort that the receiver was exceeding his authority, the transaction would seem to be enforceable by the third party.[39] If he did have notice, it is less clear. Lord Atkinson in *Moss SS Co. Ltd v. Whinny*[40] opined that he could not enforce: the receiver would be able to plead his own *ultra vires*. Lord Mersey in the same case considered that there was no duty on third parties to enquire whether the contract was in the ordinary course of business or not. If it was not, the receiver should still be liable and take the consequences of his own excesses by forgoing his right to an indemnity (see *infra*).[41] This implies that the third party would be unaffected at least by the concept of constructive notice.

If the receiver does act within the ordinary course of business, his acts are deemed to be sanctioned by the court and it may be that payments made by him cannot be challenged as an unlawful preference.[42]

---

[36] *Mellor v. Mellor* [1992] 4 All E.R. 10, 17. Michael Hart, Q.C. See also *Alliance & Leicester Building Society v. Edgestop (No. 2), The Times*, May 24, 1995, C.A.
[37] *N.M.B. Postbank Groep NV v. Naviede (No. 1)* [1993] BCLC 707 and, (No. 2) 715.
[38] For example, if he needs to borrow money to discharge his functions the court can authorise him to accord the lender priority over the debenture under which he was appointed. *Greenwood v. Algesiras Ry Co.* [1894] 2 Ch. 205 C.A.
[39] *Moss SS Co. Ltd v. Whinny* [1912] A.C. 254. This is implied in the judgments of Lord Loreburn, L.C., Lord Atkinson and Lord Mersey and would seem to be correct by analogy with the principles of agency by estoppel.
[40] See *ibid.*, at p. 267.
[41] *ibid.*, at p. 271.
[42] *cf. International Harvester Export Co. v. International Harvester Australia Co.* [1983] V.R. 539, 549.

Contracts

A receiver appointed by the court is not the agent of the company or of the debenture holders.[43] Thus his contracts do not bind them. He incurs personal liability[44] and may be entitled to an indemnity.[45] Not only is the company not liable on the receiver's contracts, it "becomes incapable of making contracts on its own behalf or exercising any control over any part of its property or assets."[46] It is superseded by the receiver.

Contracts which the company has concluded prior to the receivership do not bind the receiver.[47] He was not a party to them. They do, of course, bind the company. In general the receiver is under no duty to see that existing contracts are observed but *Re Newdigate Colliery Ltd*[48] establishes that such a duty may exist in some circumstances. It depends upon whether he has been appointed receiver and manager of the business. If he is merely a receiver of the assets, he can take those assets and sell them at the best price, even if this makes the performance of the company's existing contracts impossible. If he has been appointed receiver and manager of the business, he must, if possible, preserve the business; the court will not sanction a wholesale abandonment of existing contracts where:

> "it might well ruin the whole reputation of [the] company and destroy the value of the undertaking ... [t]he goodwill ... is part of that which is charged to them, and the receiver and manager has ... to do his best to preserve the whole of the property that is put in his care. It is not his duty to do what would ultimately sacrifice the value of the undertaking and consider it a sufficient justification that by so doing he would obtain somewhat more money for the sale of the specific assets of the company."[49]

The increased value of the goods "would be thrown into the security for the benefit of the mortgagees",[50] but the mortgagor's surplus assets would be subject not only to the claims of the existing unsecured creditors but also to the claims of persons who would become entitled to damages for breach of contract. As an officer of the court, the receiver has a duty to protect the business for the benefit of all those with an interest in it and not to sacrifice the interests of the unsecured creditors to those of the mortgagee. The court may authorise the receiver to disregard a particular contract if there are special circumstances.[51]

It follows from what has been said above that the receiver is not bound

---

[43] *Moss SS Co. Ltd v. Whinny, supra.*
[44] *Burt, Boulton and Hayward v. Bull* [1895] 1 Q.B. 276. (C.A.).
[45] See *infra*.
[46] *Moss SS Co. Ltd v. Whinny, supra.* See the *Earl of Halsbury* at p. 260 and also *Lord Mersey* at p. 271.
[47] Unless he novates.
[48] [1912] 1 Ch. 468.
[49] *Re Newdigate Colliery Ltd* [1912] 1 Ch. 468 per Fletcher Moulton, L.J. at p. 475
[50] *ibid.*, *per* Buckley, L.J. at p. 477.
[51] *Per* Cozens Hardy, M.R. at p. 475.

by existing contracts of employment. The company is bound by them but, on the court appointing a receiver, it is no longer carrying on business, even through an agent, and so this works an automatic dismissal[52] of its employees.[53] The employees are entitled as against the company to damages for breach of contract.[54] They may however be re-employed by the receiver and then their remuneration would reduce the damages recoverable.[55]

Indemnity

He is entitled to an indemnity out of the assets in his hands for liabilities properly incurred.[56] If his expenses exceed the value of the assets in his hands, the court will not order the company[57] or the debentureholders to meet them: the receiver is not their agent and they cannot be compelled to meet his expenses. He has a lien over all the assets in respect of which he has been appointed: not merely those of which he has possession. "Any other rule would place an undesirable premium on his taking precipitative action ... to commandeer assets not with a view to their preservation but with a view to protecting his own position."[58] This lien does not cease when, on discharge of the receivership, he passes the assets back to the company.[59]

Duties

Receivers, as officers of the court, have a duty to act not merely lawfully but in accordance with the principles of justice and honest dealing. In *Re Tyler*[60] on the bankruptcy of her husband, a wife, with the knowledge of the trustee in bankruptcy, kept up the premiums on a policy on his life. The husband died a few years later and the proceeds were paid to the mortgagee of the policy who, having discharged its own debt, passed the balance to the official receiver. The wife successfully claimed reimbursement of the premium money; if an officer of the court receives money which morally, if not legally or equitably, belongs to another he should repay it "because [it] would be insufferable for this court to have it said that it had been guilty by its officer of a dirty trick."[61] The operation of this principle involves a discretion which must be exercised upon judicial

---

[52] *Reid v. The Explosives Company Ltd* (1887) 19 Q.B.D. 264. Compare the position of a receiver and manager appointed out of court as agent of the company: *Griffiths v. Secretary of State for Social Services* [1974] 1 Q.B. 468; *Nicholl v. Cutts* [1985] BCLC 322.
[53] It does not affect the tenure of officers of the company or of employees in their capacity as officers: *Re South Western Venezuela Ry Ltd* [1902] 1 Ch. 701.
[54] *Reid v. The Explosives Co. Ltd, ibid.*, at p. 267.
[55] *ibid.* The position of employees is considered further, *infra*, p. 382.
[56] *Moss SS Co. Ltd v. Whinny, supra.* Where the court imposes a time limit upon him, liabilities incurred outside that time will not be the subject of indemnity: *Re Wood Green Steam Laundry* [1918] 1 Ch. 423.
[57] *Evans v. Clayhope Properties Ltd* [1988] 1 W.L.R. 358.
[58] *Mellor v. Mellor* [1992] 4 All E.R. 10 at p. 19, *per* Michael Hart, Q.C.
[59] *ibid.*
[60] [1907] 1 K.B. 865.
[61] *per* Vaughan Williams, L.J. at p. 871.

principles.[62] In *Re John Bateson & Co. Ltd*[63] it was held to be fair in the circumstances for an officer of the court[64] to take advantage of the fact that a company charge in favour of a third party had not been registered. There was a tacit understanding that the chargee would register it.[65]

As Administrative Receiver

It is not completely clear whether a receiver appointed by the court comes within the defintion of an administrative receiver in section 29; that section refers to a receiver or manager appointed *by or on behalf of the holders of any debentures* and, strictly, a court appointed receiver is neither. He is appointed by the court exercising its jurisdiction under section 37(1) of the Supreme Court Act 1981; the appointment, if made, is at the instance of the debentureholders but not by their agency. If this is so, receivers appointed by the court are excluded from the scope of sections 233–237 of the Act which reinforce the powers of office holders.[66] However, it is submitted that there is evidence within the Act that court appointed receivers were intended to fall within the ambit of section 29. Provisions intended to apply only to receivers appointed out of court refer, not to receivers "appointed by or behalf of the debentureholders", but to receivers "appointed under powers contained in an instrument."[67] Section 29 appears within a group of sections under the heading *Preliminary and General Provisions* and another section in this group, section 31, expressly provides that it has no application to a court appointed receiver. Furthermore if the wording of section 29 is to be taken as excluding court appointed receivers, then the similar wording in section 40 of the Act could have the effect of excluding court appointed receivers from the duty to pay preferential debts out of the proceeds of a floating charge despite section 40 appearing in a group of sections under the heading *Provisions applicable to every receivership*. While the wording of sections 29 and 40 is not particularly apt to describe the position of court appointed receivers, it would appear that, on balance, they should be construed as including them.

(C) Receivers Appointed Out of Court

Such receivers are appointed under a power in an instrument, whether under the express terms of the instrument or by virtue of a term implied by

---

[62] *ibid.*, at p. 870.
[63] [1985] BCLC 259.
[64] Possibly *obiter* because doubt was expressed whether a liquidator in a voluntary liquidation (*cf.* a compulsory liquidation) was an officer of the court.
[65] *cf.* receivers appointed out of court, see *e.g. Slotlogic Ltd v. Leisure Casinos* (1993) I.L. & P. 38. (The fiduciary nature of a receiver's obligation might oblige him to resile from a "subject to contract" agreement on receipt of a higher offer.)
[66] Lightman and Moss, *The Law of Receivers of Companies*, p. 3 and 244. But compare Totty and Jordan, *Insolvency* D6.34.
[67] See ss. 33–38 of the Act which follow the heading *Receivers and Managers appointed out of Court*.

statute into and having effect as if contained in an instrument.[68] They include both administrative receivers[69] and receivers who do not satisfy the definition of administrative receiver in section 29(2) of the Act, not having been appointed by the holders of debentures secured by a charge which *as created* was floating, for example LPA receivers, or not having been appointed in respect of property to which the definition refers. Some statutory provisions apply to both types: sections 30, 31, 33–36 and 39–41 of the Act and section 405 Companies Act 1985.[70] These will be considered first, followed by those applicable to out of court receivers (other than administrative receivers) and finally those applicable to administrative receivers.

Statutory Provisions Applicable to Out of Court Receivers (including Administrative Receivers)[71]

A number of these provisions relate to appointment. A body corporate is not qualified to act as a receiver of the property of a company and commits an offence by so doing (section 30 of the Act[72]). An undischarged bankrupt commits an offence by acting as receiver or manager of the property of a company on behalf of debentureholders (section 31). The appointment of a person as receiver or manager is of no effect unless it is accepted by that person before the end of the business day next following that on which the instrument of appointment is received by him or on his behalf. Assuming such acceptance, the appointment is deemed to be made at the time when the instrument of appointment was received (section 33(1)(a) and (b)[73]). Where an appointment of a person as receiver or manager under powers contained in an instrument turns out to be invalid (whether by virtue of the invalidity of the instrument or otherwise) the court can order the person by whom or on whose behalf the appointment was made to indemnify the person appointed against any liability arising solely by reason of the invalidity of the appointment (section 34). When a receiver or manager of the property of a company has been appointed, every invoice, order for goods or business letter issued by or on behalf of the company or the receiver or manager or the liquidator of the company, being a document on or in which the company's name appears, shall contain a statement that a receiver or manager has been appointed (section 39[74]). A person appointing a receiver or manager under powers contained in an instrument[75] must within seven days give notice of his appointment to the

---

[68] s.29(1)(b) of the Act. As to statutory implication, see *e.g.*, s.101(1)(iii) of the Law of Property Act 1925, *supra*.
[69] See *supra*, p. 360.
[70] An amended provision, s.409, was introduced by the Companies Act 1989 but has not been brought into force.
[71] Where these provisions also apply to court appointed receivers, the fact will be noted.
[72] Applies also to receivers appointed by the court.
[73] See also Insolvency Rules 1986, r. 3.1 which deals with the mode of acceptance and joint receivers.
[74] In the event of default, an offence is committed by the company, and also any officer, liquidator, receiver or manager knowingly and wilfully authorising or permitting the default. This provision also applies to receivers appointed by the court.
[75] Or obtaining an order of the court appointing a receiver.

registrar of companies who shall enter the fact upon the register of charges (section 405(1) Companies Act 1985[76]). Similar notice must be given by a receiver on cessation of office (section 405(2)).[77] Non-compliance with section 405 is punishable with a fine.

Other provisions having a common operation relate to the conduct of the receivership. Section 35 of the Act authorises a receiver or manager or the persons by whom or on whose behalf he was appointed to apply to the court for directions in relation to any particular matter arising in connection with the performance of his functions and the court can give directions or a declaration or such order as it thinks fit. A receiver appointed out of court has his remuneration fixed by agreement but the liquidator of the company can, notwithstanding, apply to the court to fix the receiver's remuneration.[78] It can be fixed retrospectively, even where the receiver or manager has died or ceased to act. Amounts already received which are in excesss of the amount fixed can be recovered from the recipient or his personal representatives but where the amount relates to a period prior to the application for the order the court should only exercise this power where there are special circumstances making it proper (section 36).[79] Section 40 of the Act applies to receivers appointed on behalf of the holders of any debentures of the company secured by a charge which, as created, was a floating charge[80] and requires the receiver to pay the preferential debts (defined in section 386 and Schedule 6 of the Act[81]) in priority to the claims of the chargee. To the extent that the proceeds of the charge are then insufficient to meet the claims of the chargee such claims may be recouped out of the assets available for payment of the general creditors. If the charge was floating at its creation the duty arises and it makes no difference that the charge crystallised prior to the appointment of the receiver. Section 41 provides that upon application the court can order the receiver to comply with a legal requirement relating to the filing, delivering or making any return or account or other document or the giving of any notice.[82] Where a receiver has failed to comply with a request by the liquidator of the company to render accounts of his receipts and payments and to vouch and pay over amounts due to the liquidator, the court can, on application by the liquidator, order the receiver to make good the default.[83]

---

[76] The form of this provision was amended by s.100, Companies Act 1989 and it was renumbered s.409 but the amendment has not been brought into force.

[77] See previous note. S.405(2) does not apply to receiver appointed by the court.

[78] This does not enable the court to interfere with the receiver's right to be indemnified for disbursements which have been properly incurred: *Re Potter's Oils Ltd* (No. 2) [1986] 1 All E.R. 890.

[79] As to the remuneration and expenses of "LPA" receivers, see s.109(6) of the Law of Property Act 1925.

[80] The application of this section to court appointed receivers is discussed, *supra*, at p. 368.

[81] See *infra*, p. 609.

[82] s.41(1)(a). This subsection applies also to receivers appointed by the court. Application can be made by any member or creditor of the company or by the registrar of companies.

[83] s.41(1)(b).

Statutory Provisions Applicable to Out of Court Receivers (other than Administrative Receivers)

Liability on Contracts[84] (Section 37)

A receiver or manager appointed under powers contained in an instrument (other than an administrative receiver) is, to the same extent as a receiver appointed by the court:

    (a) personally liable on any contract entered into by him in the performance of his functions (except in so far as the contract otherwise provides) and on any contract of employment adopted by him in the performance of his functions, and

    (b) entitled in respect of that liability to indemnity out of the assets (section 37(1)).

He is not to be taken to have adopted a contract of employment by reason of anything done or omitted to be done within 14 days after his appointment (section 37(2)).

Pre-receivership contracts

On general principles, a receiver is not liable on contracts entered into before he became receiver. A duty to ensure that the company complies with such contracts may arise and this is considered later (see, **(D) General Issues affecting Receivers**). In so far as a receiver expressly or impliedly novates an existing contract, he has entered into a new contract governed by section 37(1)(a) (see below). This subsection also introduces, in relation to existing contracts of employment, the concept of adoption.

Contracts made, and contracts of employment adopted, by the receiver

The instrument under which he was appointed will usually make the receiver the agent of the company and therefore contracts within his actual or apparent authority will bind the company. In these circumstances the agent himself would normally not incur personal liability but section 37(1)(a) imposes statutory liability upon him not only in relation to contracts entered into by him, but also contracts of employment adopted by him, in the performance of his functions. In respect of those liabilities he is entitled to an indemnity out of the assets (section 37(1)(b)) and when he vacates office this indemnity, along with his remuneration and expenses, is charged upon and payable out of any property of the company which is in his custody or under his control at that time in priority to any charge or other security held by the person by or on whose behalf he was appointed (section 37(4)[85]). These provisions do not limit any contractual

---

[84] It would seem inappropriate to refer to "contractual liability" in view of the apparently statutory basis of liability for contracts "adopted": see *infra*.

[85] As to vacation on the making of an administration order, see s.11(2) & (4) of the Act.

indemnity to which the receiver may be entitled against the debentureholders personally under the terms of his appointment (section 37(3)). Where the receiver has acted outside the performance of his functions, section 37 does not apply to impose personal liability but the receiver may nonetheless have accepted personal liability and in relation to such personal liability there is no statutory right of indemnity (section 37(3)).

Whether a contract has been entered into (or novated) by a receiver, falls to be decided in accordance with ordinary contractual principles. The principles upon which he can be held to have "adopted" a contract of employment are less straightforward. No definition of adoption is given in the Act. Section 37(2) merely makes it clear that, after 14 days have elapsed from his appointment, he may be held to have adopted by reason of anything done or omitted to be done. Contrary to the decision of Harman, J. in *Re Specialised Mouldings Ltd*[86] adoption cannot be avoided by service of a unilateral notice in which the receiver disclaims any intention to adopt or to assume personal liability: this practice was referred by the Court of Appeal in *Powdrill v. Watson, Re Paramount Airways Ltd (No. 3)*[87] as "mere ritual incantation[88]". The House of Lords, hearing consolidated appeals in *Powdrill v. Watson; Re Leyland Daf Ltd; Re Ferranti International plc*[89] considered the meaning of "adoption" in relation to the parallel provisions applicable to administrators[90] and administrative receivers[91] and held, affirming the decision of the Court of Appeal, that adoption arose inevitably if the administrator or receiver caused the company to continue the employment for more than 14 days after appointment.[92] The implications of this for the office holder and for employees are discussed in relation to administrative receivers below,[93] but it should be noted here that the Insolvency Act 1994, which was introduced to deal with the problems presented by the Court of Appeal decision in *Powdrill v. Watson, Re Paramount Airways Ltd (No. 3)*, applies only to administrators and administrative receivers[94]; it has no application to receivers governed by s.37.[95]

Receivership Accounts (Section 38)

A receiver (other than an administrative receiver) appointed under powers contained in an instrument must within one month after the expiration of 12 months from the date of his appointment and of every subsequent period of six months and on ceasing to act, deliver to the

---

[86] February 13, 1987 (unreported), see *infra*.
[87] [1994] BCC 172; [1994] 2 All E.R. 513.
[88] *ibid.*, at 179 and 520 respectively.
[89] [1995] 2 All E.R. 65.
[90] s.19(5) of the Act, considered further in Chap. 16, *post*, at p. 471.
[91] s.44 of the Act, see *infra*.
[92] *Per* Lord Browne-Wilkinson, at p. 84.
[93] In relation to administrators, see Chap. 16, *post*, at p. 471.
[94] And then only in relation to contracts of employment adopted on or after March 15, 1994.
[95] On May 26, 1994 the Government sought views on whether the Act should be extended to s.37 receivers.

registrar of companies the requisite accounts of his receipts and payments. In addition to this statutory duty, as the company's agent, he is bound to keep accounts and produce them to the company when required.[96]

Statutory Provisions Applicable to Administrative Receivers

Powers of Administrative Receivers

An administrative receiver has the general powers set out in Schedule 1 to the Act, subject to any express terms to the contrary in the debenture by virtue of which he was appointed; section 42. These powers are shared by an administrator and are set out elsewhere.[97] Section 42(2) of the Act adapts the powers in Schedule 1 to the position of an administrative receiver by making it clear that they only apply to the property actually covered by the charge under which he was appointed and not to the whole property of the company or to property subject to a prior charge under which a receiver has been appointed. It is further provided that a person dealing with an administrative receiver in good faith and for value "is not concerned to enquire whether the receiver is acting within his powers."[98]

Liability on Contracts (Section 44)

Pre-receivership contracts

As indicated above, in connection with section 37 of the Act, a receiver is not generally liable on contracts entered into before he became receiver but (i) he may have a duty to ensure that the company complies with such contracts (see *infra*, **(D) General Issues affecting Receivers**), (ii) he may become liable on such contracts by novation, and (iii), in relation to contracts of employment, he may become liable if he adopts.

Contracts made,[99] and contracts of employment adopted, by the administrative receiver

Background to the Legislation. Section 44(1)(a) provides that the administrative receiver is deemed to be the agent of the company unless and until the company goes into liquidation. The acts of the receiver within his actual or apparent authority will therefore bind the company— they would not usually bind the administrative receiver. Section 44(1)(b) however imposes statutory personal liability on him in relation to two classes of contract, namely on,

> "any contract entered into by him in the carrying out of his functions (except in so far as the contract otherwise provides) and on any

---

[96] *Smiths Ltd v. Middleton* [1979] 3 All E.R. 842.
[97] Chap. 16, *post*, p. 454.
[98] s.42(3) of the Act.
[99] This would include contracts novated.

contract of employment adopted by him in the carrying out of those functions."

Section 44(2) states that the administrative receiver is not to be taken to have adopted a contract of employment by reason of anything done or omitted to be done within 14 days after his appointment and section 44(1)(c) allows him an indemnity out of the assets of the company in respect of his personal liability.[1]

Whether a contract has been "entered into" by an administrative receiver, falls to be decided upon ordinary contractual principles. The concept of "adoption", which is introduced in relation to contracts of employment, has proved to be more difficult to conceptualise. As many of the issues which arise in this area are of relevance to non-administrative receivers (who are governed by section 37 of the Act) as well as to administrative receivers, the text will refer to "receivers" to encompass all receivers appointed under powers contained in an instrument, unless the contrary is stated.

The special provision for contracts of employment found in sections 44 & 37[2] was a response to *Nicoll v. Cutts*[3] which decided that, while a receiver who merely continued a managing director's contract of employment on behalf of the company could pay salary as an expense of receivership in priority to the claims of the secured creditors, he incurred no personal liability to do so and, if he elected not to, the managing director, in respect of services rendered post-receivership, merely had the status of an unsecured creditor. Thus such an employee may well remain, wholly or in part, unpaid and to that extent may find that he is funding the receivership. This was the mischief at which sections 44 and 37[4] of the Act were aimed. The mechanism used in sections 44 and 37[5] to rectify it and accord priority is the imposition of personal liability on a receiver who adopts a contract of employment and the conferment upon him, in respect of that liability, of an indemnity out of the assets.[6] Such indemnity, together with his expenses and remuneration, is a charge on and payable out of, the assets of the company in his custody or control at the time he vacates office in priority to any security held by the persons who appointed him.[7] The personal liability of the receiver is expressed to be a liability "on" the contract of employment and while its extent was initially uncertain, on a strict construction, it could have extended to all liabilities arising under the

---

[1] As with s.37, *supra*, p. 371, the statutory indemnity out of the assets of the company is additional to any other indemnity to which he may be entitled against the debentureholders personally under the terms of his appointment (or by virtue of an order of the court under s.34). Where the administrative receiver has acted outside the performance of his functions s.44 does not apply to impose any personal liability upon him but he may nonetheless have accepted such liability and in relation to that there is no statutory right to be indemnified (s.44(3)).
[2] And also in s.19(5) (administrators).
[3] [1985] BCLC 322 C.A.
[4] And s.19(5) (administrators).
[5] Compare s.19(5) of the Act.
[6] s.44(1)(c) and 37(1)(b) of the Act.
[7] s.45(3) and 37(4).

contract of employment whether they were incurred before, in the course of, or after the receivership.[8] Such were the potential consequences of adoption. On appointment therefore the receiver had just 14 days to make a very fine judgment: "to assess whether or not the increased price to be realised on a going concern basis will be greater than the increase in the imponderable liabilities consequent upon adoption of contracts of employment which will take priority over the secured rights of the debenture holder whose interest he was appointed to protect."[9] If he judged that it would not be, or found it impossible to make any judgment in the time, his best course would be to dismiss the employees and abandon any corporate rescue scheme. This unsatisfactory situation met with a pragmatic response. Receivers attempted to opt out of adoption by writing to key staff, within the 14 day post-appointment period, informing them that their employment by the company would continue but that their contracts were not adopted and that the receivers accepted no personal liability in respect of such contracts. This approach met with some success in the unreported decision of Harman, J. in *Re Specialised Mouldings Ltd*[10] where a letter in this form was held to be effective to avoid adoption and thus personal liability. Such letters subsequently became standard, not only in the case of receivership but also in relation to administration.[11] However while they enabled the receiver to get on with the job of rescuing the business without fear of incurring employment costs of uncertain extent, they also undid the reform; to the extent that the continuing staff were not paid for services rendered to the receiver, they ranked merely as unsecured creditors.

Adoption. It was in relation to administrators that the meaning of adoption, and the effectiveness of *Re Specialised Mouldings* letters, came under detailed examination. In *Powdrill v. Watson, Re Paramount Airways Ltd (No. 3)*[12] the Court of Appeal held that adoption is "a matter not merely of words but of fact."[13] The administrators had not dismissed the relevant employees: they hoped to keep the company, which operated a charter airline, in business over the peak summer season and sell it as a going concern. The employees were informed that the company would continue salary payments and other contractual entitlements but the letter stated:

> "the joint administrators act at all times as agents of the company and without personal liability. The administrators are not and will not at any future time adopt or assume personal liability in respect of your contracts employment."

---

[8] But see, *infra*, p. 378.
[9] *Per* Lord Browne-Wilkinson in *Powdrill v. Watson* [1994] 2 All E.R. 65 at p. 80.
[10] February 13, 1987. An account of the case can be found in Gordon Stewart, *Administrative Receivers and Administrators* (1987), at para. 512.
[11] As to which see Chap. 16, p. 471.
[12] [1994] BCC 172; [1994] 2 All E.R. 513 (C.A.).
[13] *ibid.*, at, respectively, p. 180 and p. 521, *per* Dillon, L.J.

No buyer was found and the employees were then summarily dismissed having been paid down to the date of their dismissal. Two employees petitioned under section 27 of the Act claiming that they were entitled to salary and other benefits (holiday pay, pension contributions) in lieu of the two months notice to which they were entitled under their contracts of employment. It was argued that the contracts had been adopted by the administrators, and consequently the amounts, being "in respect of debts or liabilities incurred while [they were] an administrator", had to be paid in accordance with section 19(5) out of property in the administrators' custody or control in priority to the administrators' expenses and remuneration and in priority to the claims under the floating charge. The petition was successful.

"It is submitted ... that to adopt a contract of employment the administrators must do something positive. It is said that here, by the original August letter, they said that they would not. As I see it, that does not do. If they continue substantially after the 14 days to employ staff and pay them in accordance with their previous contracts, they will be held impliedly to have adopted those contacts of employment."[14]

"The mere assertion by an administrator or receiver that he is not adopting the contract is mere wind with no legal effect ..."[15].

This interpretation of "adoption", was followed by Lightman, J. in *Re Leyland Daf Ltd; Re Ferranti International plc*[16] in relation to the liability of administrative receivers under section 44(1)(b). Adoption, "must be given the meaning 'treated as continuing in force' ".[17] If the receiver fails to dismiss the employee within the 14 day period, the statutory liability will arise and there is nothing the receiver can do unilaterally to prevent this. Adoption has since been defined by the House of Lords in consolidated appeals in *Powdrill v. Watson; Re Leyland Daf Ltd; Re Ferranti International plc*[18] in terms not dissimilar to those used in the lower courts. Lord Browne-Wilkinson refers to the need for "some conduct by the administrator or receiver which amounts to an election to treat the continued contract of employment with the company as giving rise to a separate liability in the administration or receivership"[19] and later in his judgment makes it clear that "causing the company to continue the employment for more than 14 days after his appointment"[20] constitutes such conduct. He also affirmed that it is not possible for an administrator or receiver to avoid adoption or its consequences unilaterally by informing the employees that

---

[14] *ibid.*, at, respectively, p. 178 and p. 520, *per* Dillon, L.J.
[15] *ibid.*, at, respectively, p. 180 and p. 521, *per* Dillon, L.J. Reliance was placed upon an extract from R.M. Goode, *Principles of Corporate Insolvency Law* (1990), at pp. 101–102.
[16] [1994] BCC 658.
[17] *ibid.*, at p. 670, *per* Lightman, J.
[18] [1995] BCC 319; [1995] 2 All E.R. 65.
[19] *ibid.*, at, respectively, pp. 334 and 83.
[20] *ibid.*, at, respectively, pp. 335 and 84.

he is not adopting or only doing so on terms.[21] It had been argued that because the company remained fully liable on the contract, there could be no objection to the administrator or receiver stating which contractual liabilities he would accept and which he would not. However, Lord Browne-Wilkinson rejected this reasoning because it would enable liability to be avoided for the very mischief which the provisions were enacted to cure: the non-payment of employees for services rendered to the administrator or receiver under contracts which he has continued. The "concept of adoption is inconsistent with an ability to pick and choose between different liabilities under the contract. The contract as a whole is either adopted or not ...".[22] In making these comments, it would appear that Lord Browne-Wilkinson was contemplating unilateral action on the part of the administrator or receiver. He does not appear to address the possibility of a new contract between the officeholder and the employee, though this was considered by Lightman, J. in *Re Leyland Daf Ltd; Re Ferranti International plc*.[23] In this case, it was argued on behalf of the administrative receivers that, even if the unilateral service of a *Specialised Mouldings* letter was ineffective to forestall adoption, it could constitute an offer to continue the employment in consideration of a release of personal liability, and that the employees had accepted that offer by continuing to provide their services. Lightman, J. had to decide whether it was possible to contract out of personal liability and, if so, whether this had happened in circumstances of the case. The difficulty here was in the drafting of section 44(1)(b) (and similarly section 37(1)(a)) which imposes personal liability for *entering contracts* "except in so far as the contract otherwise provides", but includes no such contracting out phrase in relation to the personal liability arising from adoption of contracts of employment. Lightman, J. did not however consider the absence of the contracting out phrase to be very significant and pointed out that if the receiver could not directly contract out of the personal liabilty which would attach to him by virtue of adoption, he could achieve the same end indirectly by terminating the contract of employment within the 14 day period and then entering a new contract with the employee in which he contracts out of the statutory liability. He did not consider that permitting the receiver to contract out of the personal liability consequent upon adoption would undermine the protection which the legislature intended employees to enjoy.

> "As it seems to me, the statutory policy is not to confer upon employees a basic right which they cannot contract out of, but to prevent receivers encouraging expectations of payment and then disappointing them; and in particular the unfair exploitation of employees by receivers, in the absence of the unequivocal agreement of the employees, taking the benefit of their services without at the same time accepting legal responsibility for payment."[24]

---

[21] *ibid.*, at, respectively, pp. 336 and 86.
[22] *ibid.*, at, respectively, pp. 334 and 84.
[23] [1994] BCC 658.
[24] At p. 671.

He stressed that there would have to be a contract between the employee and the receiver and that the court will be slow to infer one. In particular the fact that the receiver has served a notice "which had no immediate practical effect on the employee" and the employee has continued to work, as occurred in the *Leyland Daf* case, will not be construed as the acceptance of an offer by the employee. Full and informed consent is required. Thus there was no contractual exclusion of the statutory personal liability in the *Leyland Daf* case.

Extent of the Statutory Liability. In *Powdrill v. Watson; Re Leyland Daf Ltd; Re Ferranti International plc* the House of Lords not only considered the nature of adoption but also the extent of the statutory liability to which it gives rise. In relation to administration, the extent is limited by section 19(5) to "sums payable in respect of debts or liabilities incurred while he was administrator"; in relation to receivership the liability is simply "on" the contract which would appear much wider. Lord Browne-Wilkinson considered that even section 19(5) imposed a liability on administrators which was more extensive than was merited by the mischief, rendering them liable not only for services provided to the administrator but also for payments in lieu of notice, *viz* pension contributions and holiday pay in respect of months of employment after the appointment of the administrator. In relation to that however the anomaly, being unfortunate rather than absurd, did not justify departing from the literal meaning of the words.[25] The much more vague wording of section 44(1)[26] posed a more serious problem. Lightman, J., in *Re Leyland Daf Ltd; Re Ferranti International plc* had considered in some detail the extent of the statutory liability "on" the contract of employment. He identified three alternatives:

(i) a liability co-extensive with that of the company, *i.e.* for all liabilities whenever incurred and of whatever kind; or,
(ii) a liability restricted to those incurred while he was receiver; or,
(iii) a liability for services rendered to the company during the receivership.

The second alternative would have equated receivers with administrators, but the stark difference in drafting led him to the conclusion that the only tenable construction of the receivership provisions was the first alternative; he could find "no handle on which to fasten any limitation ...".[27] In the House of Lords, Lord Browne-Wilkinson, "to avoid the absurdity which Parliament cannot have intended"[28] held that section 44(1) must be given "a forced construction" and was therefore subject to the same restriction as applied to contracts adopted by an administrator and thus receivers' statutory liability was also restricted to liabilities incurred while he was receiver. In the case of administrative receivers and administrators, the Insolvency Act 1994 (see below) has, in effect, in

[25] See Chap. 16, *supra*, p. 472.
[26] And s.37(1).
[27] *ibid.*, at p. 673.
[28] *ibid.*, at respectively, p. 336 and p. 85.

relation to contracts of employment adopted on or after March 15, 1994, now reduced the extent of their liability to the third of the above alternatives. However, the House of Lords decision still governs the extent of the liability of a receiver under section 37 and also the extent of the liability of some 27,210 administrative receivers[29] in relation to contracts of employment adopted by them prior to March 15th, 1994.

Insolvency Act 1994. The 1994 Act was a speedy response to the Court of Appeal decision in *Powdrill v. Watson, Re Paramount Airways Ltd (No. 3)*[30] which was conceived as undermining the corporate rescue function of the administrative receivership and administration procedures. The purpose of the Act is to encourage rescue by curtailing the financial consequences, to the administrative receiver and his appointors, of adoption and it does this by limiting the liability of the administrative receiver to liabilities arising under the contract of employment[31] which fall within the definition of a "qualifying liability." In relation to administrative receivers[32] a liability is a "qualifying liability" if;

(a) it is a liability to pay a sum by way of wages or salary[33] or contribution to an occupational pension scheme,
(b) it is incurred while the administrative receiver is in office, and
(c) it is in respect of services rendered wholly or partly after adoption of the contract.[34]

Where the liability arises in respect of services rendered partly before and partly after the adoption, it is provided that only so much of it as relates to the post adoption period qualifies.[35]

Supplies of Utilities

Section 233 of the Act protects the supply of utilities[36] to office holders, including administrative receivers.[37] The extent of this protection is considered in Chapter 25.

---

[29] And the liability of administrators, see further Chap. 16, *supra*, p. 471, and also the statistical tables in Appendix III.
[30] *supra*, n. 12, p. 375.
[31] Not, it seems, by virtue of statute. Thus entitlements to redundancy pay or compensation for unfair dismissal arising from statute will not qualify.
[32] Similar provisions apply to administrators: s.1 of the 1994 Act.
[33] s.2(3) of the 1994 Act inserts into s.44 a new subsection (2C), which includes within the definition of wages and salary amounts payable in periods of absence due to holidays and sickness and also amounts payable in lieu of holiday.
[34] s.2(3) of the 1994 Act inserting a new subsection (2A) into s.44 of the Act.
[35] s.2(3) of the 1994 Act adding a new s.(2B) to s.44 of the Act.
[36] Gas, water, electricity and telecommunications.
[37] But not other receivers, see s.233(1). Supplies of other services, and goods, to an administrative receiver and supplies of goods and services to other receivers are considered, *infra*, p. 390.

Appointment

A person appointed as administrative receiver must be qualified to act as an insolvency practitioner in relation to the company.[38] On appointment, the administrative receiver must forthwith inform the company of his appointment and publish notice of it in the *Gazette* and a newspaper appropriate for ensuring that it comes to the attention of the company's creditors.[39] Within 28 days he must send notice of his appointment to all creditors of the company, so far as he is aware of their addresses.[40]

Ascertainment and Investigation of Company's Affairs

The administrative receiver must obtain forthwith a statement of affairs in prescribed form from some or all of the persons listed in section 47 of the Act. Section 47 is in identical terms to section 22 which imposes a parallel obligation upon an administrator.[41] An administrative receiver is assisted in the performance of his functions by sections 234 to 237 of the Act. These sections, which impose a duty on officers and others to cooperate with the administrative receiver[42] and enable him to apply to the court for an order for delivery of property etc.[43] and for examination of officers, etc., are discussed in Chapter 22.[44]

Administrative Receiver's Report

Under section 48, within three months of his appointment, unless the court allows an extension, an administrative receiver must report to the registrar, any trustees for the secured creditors and (so far as he is aware of their addresses) all secured creditors. The report must include details of (a) the events leading up to his appointment, so far as he is aware of them, (b) disposals or proposed disposals by him of company property and the carrying on or proposed carrying on by him of the company's business, (c) the amounts of principal and interest payable to the debentureholders who appointed him and the amounts payable to preferential creditors, and (d) the amount (if any) likely to be available for the payment of other creditors. It must also include a summary of the statement of affairs submitted to him under section 47, together with his comments.[45] It need not include anything which would "seriously prejudice" the carrying out of his

---

[38] s.230(2) of the Act. See also ss.388–398 of the Act, and Chap. 2, *supra*, p. 26. Acting without qualification is an offence (s.389) but does not affect the validity of the administrative receiver's acts (s.232).

[39] See s.46(1)(a) of the Act and r. 3.2(3) I.R. 1986. An equivalent provision applies to administrators: see s.21 of the Act.

[40] s.46(1)(b) of the Act. Fines are imposed in respect of default: see s.46(4) of the Act.

[41] See Chap. 16.

[42] s.235 of the Act.

[43] s.234 of the Act. An application should normally be made *inter partes*: *Re First Express* [1991] BCC 782.

[44] ss.238–246 of the Act which relate to adjustment of prior transactions have no application to receivership.

[45] s.48(5) of the Act.

functions.[46] In addition, within three months, an administrative receiver must also either send a copy of his report to all the company's unsecured creditors (of whose addresses he is aware) or publish an address to which they may write for copies to be sent to them free of charge. In either case he must also summon, on not less than 14 days notice, a meeting of the unsecured creditors before which he must lay a copy of the report.[47] The court may dispense with such a meeting if the report states that the administrative receiver intends to apply for a direction to that effect and the other requirements as to publicity are complied with at least 14 days before the application.[48] If the receivership is overtaken by a winding-up, the report must be sent to the liquidator within seven days.[49]

The Creditors' Committee

The meeting of unsecured creditors convened under section 48 may appoint a committee ("the creditors' committee") to exercise the functions conferred on it by or under the Act. The creditors' committee may summon the administrative receiver to attend before it and to give it such information as is reasonable, provided it gives him 7 days notice.[50]

Accounts

The administrative receiver must provide annual and final accounts of his receipts and payments to the registrar of companies, the company, the person who appointed him and each member of the creditors' committee (where there is one).[51]

Power to Dispose of Charged Property

By virtue of section 43(1) of the Act an administrative receiver can sell property[52] which is subject to a security having priority over the security of his appointor[53] free of that security if the court is satisfied that such a sale is likely to promote a more advantageous realisation of the company's assets.[54] The secured creditor whose security is thus overturned is

---

[46] s.48(6) of the Act.
[47] As to the creditors' meeting, see rr. 3.9–3.15 of the Insolvency Rules 1986.
[48] s.48(2) & (3) of the Act.
[49] s.48(4) of the Act.
[50] s.49 of the Act. As to the constitution, function and procedure of these meetings, see rr. 3.16–3.30A of the Insolvency Rules 1986.
[51] r. 3.32 I.R. 1986.
[52] Being property in relation to which he is the receiver or would be the receiver but for the appointment of a receiver by a prior chargee: s.43(7) of the Act.
[53] s.43(2) of the Act.
[54] Under s.15 of the Act an administrator has a similar power of disposal but it also includes disposal of goods in the possession of the company under a hire purchase agreement (which is defined by s.15(9) so as to include conditional sale agreements, chattel leasing agreements and retention of title agreements). Where an administrative receiver sells goods which are subject to a valid title retention clause in favour of third party he may be liable in conversion: *Lipe Ltd v. Leyland Daf Ltd and Ors* [1993] BCC 385 (discussed *infra*, p. 391).

protected by section 43(3); the net proceeds of sale must be used to discharge his debt together with, if the court regards such proceeds as less than the open market value of the property, such additional sums as are necessary to make good the deficiency.[55] The administrative receiver must send an office copy of any court order under this section to the registrar of companies within 14 days.[56]

Vacation of Office

An administrative receiver may only be removed from office by an order of the court but he may resign on giving due notice.[57] In addition, he must vacate office if he ceases to be qualified to act as an insolvency practitioner in relation to the company[58] or when an administration order has been made.[59] Whenever an administrative receiver vacates office otherwise than by death[60] he must inform the registrar of companies and is subject to a fine on default.[61]

Remuneration, Expenses and Indemnity

Upon vacation of office, the remuneration of, and expenses properly incurred by, an administrative receiver and any indemnity to which he is entitled out of the assets of the company, are charged on and paid out of any property of the company in his custody or under his control at that time in priority to any security held by the person by or on whose behalf he was appointed.[62]

(D) General Issues affecting Receivers

Employees

It has been noted[63] that upon a receiver being appointed *by the court*, employees are automatically dismissed. The company will be liable to pay damages for breach of contract. The receiver, not being a party to the contract, will not be liable. If he re-employs the worker, he will assume personal liability under the new contract of employment.[64] Any remuneration arising under the new employment will reduce the damages payable by the company for breach of the original contract.

The appointment of a receiver *out of court* does not, in general, terminate

---

[55] If there is more than one charge on the property they are to be repaid in order of priority: s.43(4) of the Act.
[56] s.43(5) of the Act.
[57] s.45(1) of the Act and r. 3.33 I.R. 1986.
[58] s.45(2) of the Act and r. 3.35 I.R. 1986.
[59] s.11(1)(b) of the Act.
[60] As to which see r. 3.34 I.R. 1986.
[61] s.45(4) and (5) of the Act.
[62] s.45(3) of the Act. See also s.11(4) of the Act which makes similar provision where he vacates under s.11(1)(b).
[63] *supra*, p. 366.
[64] See *supra*, p. 367.

contracts of employment. In the case of a court appointment, the company is no longer carrying on the business, even via an agent and it therefore ceases to employ. The business is being carried on by the receiver as an officer of the court and not as an agent of anyone. In contrast, where a receiver is appointed out of court he is usually the agent of the company which can therefore, through his instrumentality, continue to employ.[65]

> "The reason why the appointment of a receiver by the court has been held to operate as a dismissal of a company's employees is that the court's receiver does not operate on behalf of the company, but adversely to the company .... Where, however, the receiver is appointed out of court under a power in a debenture and the debenture provides that the receiver is to be the agent of the company, there is no change in the personality of the employer. The directors' powers to manage the company's business are displaced in favour of the receiver, but the business is still the company's business carried on by the company's agent."[66]

In the case of administrative receivers, the agency arises under section 44(1)(a) of the Act.

However, there are circumstances in which dismissal may occur, even in the case of an out of court appointment. In the rare case where the debenture does not provide that the receiver is to be the agent of the company, he will be the agent of the debentureholder and thus operate "adversely to the company", which will no longer be carrying on business. Dismissal will therefore result. Furthermore, as the shield against dismissal is the continued operation of the business by the company, *via* the receiver as its agent, if that agency ceases, dismissal results. In *Re Foster Clark's Indenture Trusts*[67] employees were entitled to benefit under a pension fund if the company terminated their employment before retirement age. A receiver was appointed under a debenture which provided that such receiver was the company's agent. On the day after his appointment, the receiver sold the business as a going concern to a wholly owned subsidiary, and he purported to transfer the employees into the employment of the wholly owned subsidiary. It was held by Plowman, J. that the employees were entitled to benefit under the scheme because the transfer of the business from one company to another, terminated the receiver's agency and operated as a dismissal.[68] A dismissal may also result if the continuance of a particular contract of employment would be inconsistent with the role and functions of a receiver and manager. This arises in connection with managerial appointments but only if there is a finding of inconsistency. In *Griffiths v. Secretary of State for Social Services*[69] Lawson, J. pointed out that though a person may hold a post labelled "managing

---

[65] *Nicholl v. Cutts* [1985] BCLC 322. C.A.
[66] *ibid.*, *per* Dillon, L.J., at p. 325.
[67] [1966] 1 All E.R. 43.
[68] The personal nature of contracts of employment meant that the attempt to transfer them was abortive.
[69] [1973] 3 All E.R. 1184.

director", it may be that he only acted under fairly stringent board control and that his role is therefore unimpaired by the assumption of managerial functions by a receiver. By the same token, many receivers are appointed "not with the intention that [they] should be employed full-time to conduct all the company's business but as someone who is going to exercise supervision and control of the way the company's business is run, particularly the financial implications of the way the company's business is run, as from the time when the receiver was appointed."[70] In the absence of a finding of inconsistency, the contract will not terminate.[71]

If, as is usually the case with a receiver appointed out of court, the employees are not dismissed, the company remains liable for remuneration and the receiver may also be liable on the basis of adoption.[72] Where the employees are automatically dismissed under one of the three exceptions referred to above, the company will be liable for breach of contract but there will be no question of the receiver having adopted that contract.

Directors

In so far as a director has a contract of employment, the position is considered above under *Employees*. Rather different issues arise in relation to his status as an officer of the company.

The effect of the appointment of a receiver *by the court* is to "practically [remove] the conduct and guidance of the undertaking from the directors appointed by the company and [place] it in the hands of a receiver and manager."[73] The directors remain in office but their powers cease.

In the case of a receiver appointed *out of court*, the directors may retain residual powers. The receiver's functions, though often very extensive in practice, are limited. They relate only to the assets in respect of which he has been appointed and in getting in and realising those assets the receiver's efforts are directed to the interests of those who appointed him. In relation to other assets and in relation to the interests of the company (and thus its other creditors and its shareholders) the directors still seem to have a role to play. In *Newhart Developments Ltd v. Co-operative Commercial Bank Ltd*[74] the assets in respect of which the receiver was appointed included an action for breach of contract which happened to be against the

---

[70] At p. 1199.
[71] A receiver and manager will have authority as agent of the company to dismiss employees. Thus, if "simultaneously or very soon after" his appointment he dismisses employees and re-employs them on the same terms, the old contract terminates and is replaced by the new one. *Re Mack Trucks (Britain) Ltd* [1967] 1 All E.R. 977, 982. This is not a result of the receiver's appointment but the operation of his agency.
[72] See ss.37(1)(a) and 44(1)(b), *supra* pp. 371 and 373.
[73] *Moss S.S. Co. Ltd v. Whinny* [1912] A.C. 254, *per* Earl of Halsbury at p. 260. The directors remain entitled to any fees specified in the articles of association, their obligation being merely "to do whatever there is to be done", *per* Buckley, J. in *Re South Western of Venezuela Railway* [1902] 1 Chap. 701, at p. 705.
[74] [1978] 2 All E.R. 896 C.A.

debentureholders who had appointed him.[75] This action was not pursued by the receiver, and the directors therefore, on behalf of the company, instituted proceedings against the debentureholders. The debentureholders applied to have the writ set aside on the ground that only the receiver had power[76] to bring such an action and his consent had not been obtained. The judge granted the application but the action was reinstated by the Court of Appeal, and Shaw, L.J. set out the position as follows:

> "It is only within the scope of its assets which are covered by the debenture, and only in so far as it is necessary to apply those assets in the best possible way in the interests of the debentureholders that the receiver has a real function. If in the exercise of his discretion he chooses to ignore some asset such as a right of action, or decides that it would be unprofitable from the point of view of the debentureholders to pursue it, there is nothing in any authority which has been cited to us which suggests that it is then not open to the directors of the company to pursue that right of action if they think it would be in the interests of the company. Indeed, in my view, it would be incumbent on them to do so, because, notwithstanding that the debentureholders have got the right to be satisfied out of the assets subject to the charge, other creditors are entitled to expect that those concerned with the management of the company should exercise their best efforts to ensure that, when the time comes, they too will find themselves in the position that there is a fund available to pay them, if not in full, at least something of what they are owed."[77]

Thus while the receiver in considering whether to realise assets is entitled to think only of the requirements of the debentureholders,

> "[n]ot so the company; not so therefore the directors of the company. If there is an asset which appears to be of value, although the directors cannot deal with it in the sense of disposing of it, they are under a duty to exploit it so as to bring it to a realisation which may be fruitful for all concerned."[78]

It was clear in this case that the action was in the interests of the company

---

[75] The action was in relation to a contract for the development of property under which the debentureholders were to provide finance. The company owed a substantial sum to the debentureholder and the latter refused further financial support and forfeited the company's interest in the venture. The company alleged that such withdrawal was a breach of the agreement and had deprived the company of its estimated profit from the development—a profit out of which it could have completely discharged its debt to the debentureholder.
[76] Clause 5 of the debenture empowered the receiver to take proceedings in the company's name for the purpose of collecting and getting in the charged property. Under s.42 and Sched. 1, para. 5 of the Act, an administrative receiver is deemed to have a general power to bring proceedings in the company's name unless this would be inconsistent with any provisions in the debenture.
[77] [1978] 2 All E.R. at p. 900.
[78] *ibid.*

and neither impinged prejudicially on the debentureholders, *qua* debentureholders, nor imperilled the assets which were the subject of the charge: a third party had agreed to indemnify the company, for its own costs and any costs awarded against it, in the event of the action being unsuccessful and, if it succeeded, the debentureholders, if still not fully satisfied, could attach the proceeds of the judgment. The action could therefore continue without their consent.

The *Newhart* case was followed in *Tudor Grange Holdings Ltd v. Citibank N.A.*[79] but it was distinguished on its facts and Browne-Wilkinson, V.-C., doubted its correctness. In this case, the banks which had provided the finance for the plaintiff companies' businesses, had appointed administrative receivers. The charge under which they had been appointed included causes of action and the administrative receivers had power to bring proceedings in the plaintiffs' name. The directors, without the consent of the administrative receivers, caused the plaintiffs to bring proceedings against the banks in order to impugn an agreement between the banks and the plaintiffs on the grounds of misrepresentation, duress and under the Unfair Contract Terms Act 1977. The banks counterclaimed for repayment of principal and interest and applied to strike out the plaintiffs' claim. Browne-Wilkinson, V.-C. followed *Newhart* but distinguished it on the ground that no outside party had provided an indemnity for costs and that therefore the proceedings could directly impinge on property subject to the charge. For this reason the directors had no power to bring the proceedings. He had "substantial doubts" whether the *Newhart* case was correctly decided and commented that it:

> "may have to be looked at again in the future. The decision seems to ignore the difficulty which arises if two different sets of people, the directors and the receivers, who may have widely differing views and interests, both have power to bring proceedings on the same cause of action. The position is exacerbated where, as here, the persons who have been sued by the directors bring a counterclaim against the company. Who is to have the conduct of that counterclaim which directly attacks the property of the company? Further the Court of Appeal in the *Newhart* case does not seem to have had its attention drawn to the fact that the embarrassment of the receiver in deciding whether or not to sue can be met by an application to the court for directions as to what course should be taken, an application now envisaged in s.35 of the Insolvency Act 1986."[80]

While this may be a solution for receivers embarrassed by the possibility of suing those by whom they were appointed, it is not very helpful to other creditors or to shareholders prejudiced by a decision neither to apply nor sue. Where a receiver has to be a qualified insolvency practitioner, that will no doubt make it likely that he will consult the court but non-

---

[79] [1991] 4 All E.R. 1.
[80] *ibid.*, at p. 10.

administrative receivers do not have to be so qualified. Both *Newhart* and *Tudor Grange* were considered by the High Court of Ireland in *Lascomme Ltd v. United Dominions Trusts*[81] where the problem of a receiver with a cause of action against those who appointed him arose again. Keane, J. preferred the *Newhart* approach; the directors' power to institute proceedings on behalf of the company continued despite the appointment of a receiver and could be exercised so long as it did not interfere with the receiver's ability to deal with or dispose of the assets charged or in any way adversely affect the debentureholders by threatening or imperilling the assets. If the action was unsuccessful and an order for costs was made against the company, this was unlikely to prejudice the recovery by the debentureholders of the debt due.[82] They may then fail to recover their costs from the company "but that cannot be a ground to stay the proceedings because otherwise the directors of the company would be unable to maintain a claim against the very persons who they say brought about the insolvency."

Whether or not the directors have power to institute an action on behalf of a company in receivership against the debentureholders who appointed the receiver,[83] it seems that they do have power to institute such corporate proceedings against the receiver himself for misconduct. *Watts v. Midland Bank plc*[84] establishes that the appointment of a receiver does not deprive the company, through its directors or majority shareholders, of its power to sue the receiver for the improper discharge of his duties. The action concerned a contract of sale by the receivers alleged to have been concluded at an undervalue and in breach of the self-dealing rule. An interlocutory injunction was sought to prevent the sale going ahead. The action had been commenced in the name of the directors and majority shareholders in derivative form on the ground that the appointment of a receiver made it legally impossible for the company to bring it in its own name. Peter Gibson, J. held that there was no such legal impossibility.[85] He cited the *Newhart* case and commented that the present case was *a fortiori* because the cause of action could not be said to constitute an asset subject to the charge: it only arose after the receivers had been appointed and could not be pursued by them. The company was substituted as plaintiff.[86] It remains to be seen whether it is necessarily improper for a receiver, appointed in respect of assets which include a cause of action against the debentureholders who appointed him, without application to the court, to

---

[81] [1994] I.L.R.M. 227.
[82] The security upon which they relied, a hotel, would have been sold and the proceeds used to discharge their debt before judgment was given in the action.
[83] Or indeed against anyone else.
[84] [1986] BCLC 15.
[85] He considered that the company in receivership must have some redress against a receiver who acted improperly and pointed out that a liquidator of a company in receivership can sue the receiver for misconduct: [1986] BCLC, at p. 21.
[86] As the derivative action was misconceived an order for costs down to the date of the amendment was made against the directors. The interlocutory injunction was not granted, damages being an adequate remedy. There seems to have been no indemnity as to costs given or required in relation to the continuance of the action by the company, though its finances were in a parlous state.

decide not to pursue an action against those debentureholders. If, as stated in *Newhart*, the receiver, in getting in and realising assets, is entitled to ignore the claims of anybody outside the debentureholders, there would appear to be no impropriety.[87]

Duty to comply with existing contracts[88]

The receiver is not liable for existing contracts.[89] The company remains liable and the question therefore arises whether there are any circumstances in which the receiver is under a duty to ensure that the company carries out the contract. Such a duty may well be for the benefit of the third party; however the receiver's duties have a wider focus. In *Airlines Airspares Ltd v. Handley Page Ltd*[90] H.P. Ltd had agreed to pay £500 for every "Jetstream" aircraft it sold. The benefit of the contract was assigned to the plaintiff. H.P. Ltd subsequently granted a debenture to the bank which in due course appointed a receiver and manager. The receiver formed a subsidiary, transferred the business and undertaking to it and was negotiating the sale of the subsidiary to an American company. He notified the plaintiff that he would not continue to pay the commission and the plaintiff sought an injunction restraining the sale and a declaration of entitlement to the commission. Both were refused. Graham, J. considered that the receiver had an overriding duty which was to realise the net assets of the company to the best possible advantage and in this case that duty was served by causing the company to off-load the commission agreement and leave the plaintiff to prove as an unsecured creditor. While this would harm the company's reputation "as a trustworthy company which can be expected to honour its contracts", in fact the company was not likely to trade in the future and so this was not an issue. To allow the plaintiff the remedies sought would be to prefer him to other unsecured creditors. It was common sense that the receiver should be able to discard company contracts "since otherwise almost any unsecured creditor would be able to improve his position and prevent the receiver from carrying out, or at least carrying out as sensibly and equitably as possible, the purpose for which he was appointed."[91] He concluded that the receiver was in a better position than the company itself in this respect, the only limitation being that such conduct does not adversely affect the realisation of the assets or the trading prospects of the company if it is to trade in future. A further limitation was identified in *Freevale v. Metrostore Holdings*[92] where Donald Rattee, Q.C. distinguished *Airspares* on the basis that some third parties were entitled to enforcement of their contracts against the receiver on the basis of a proprietary interest acquired. The plaintiff had the benefit of a specifically

---

[87] Per Shaw, L.J. [1978] 2 All E.R. at p. 900.
[88] For the position of receivers appointed by the court, see *supra*, p. 366.
[89] In the absence of novation or, where relevant, adoption: see s.37 and s.44 of the Act, *supra*, p. 371 and p. 373 respectively.
[90] [1970] 1 Chap. 193.
[91] *ibid.*, at p. 199.
[92] [1984] Chap. 199.

enforceable contract for the purchase of land which gave rise to an equitable interest in his favour and the judge refused to support the contention that "the mere appointment of the receivers *ipso facto* somehow destroyed the equitable interest in the land which the plaintiff already had and substituted for it the mere right to damages, a right which may well ... prove cold comfort when the affairs of the [company] are ultimately sorted out by the receivers."[93] In short, the receiver cannot refuse to accord creditors their proper priority merely because that priority happened to arise under a contract rather than a deed. In *Amec Properties Ltd v. Planning Research & Systems plc*[94] a point was raised concerning the receiver's liability on the completed transaction: did it amount to a contract entered into by him in the carrying out of his functions and so expose him to personal liability, under section 44(1)(b) of the Act, on the covenants it contained? Balcombe, L.J. pointed out that the section was subject to contrary intention and this might rule out personal liability in such cases. In case it did not, he ordered that the lease granted pursuant to the order should specifically provide that the receiver was not personally liable for performance of the contractual obligations which arose under it. A contract conferring a pre-emption over property does not confer a proprietary interest and therefore no priority principle can be called in aid. In *Ash & Newman Ltd v. Creative Devices Ltd*[95] Harman, J. nevertheless granted the third party an injunction to prevent the receiver dealing with the property other than in accordance with the agreement. The other principles upon which existing contracts can be enforced against receivers seem not to have been relied upon: whether the receiver sold to the third party or someone else the same price would be payable and so, unlike in the *Airspares* case, the performance of the contract had no impact upon realisation value. The "reputation" principle was not invoked by way of justification either. The fact that compliance was such a slight interference with the receiver's discretion did influence Harman, J. In *Airspares* the injunction was "in respect of the future conduct of the business which the receiver had to be free to carry on as he thought fit ... by a hive down of the business. ... The injunction here requires one specific act in the course of a sale of property which the receiver desires to effectuate." It caused no harm to the receiver and the balance of convenience dictated that the injunction be continued.[96] In view of the fact that one starts with the proposition that the receiver, not being party to the contract is

---

[93] At p. 210.
[94] [1992] 13 EG 109 C.A.
[95] [1991] BCLC 405.
[96] *ibid.* Another basis upon which a receiver could be required to implement a company contract may be the tort of wrongful interference with contract. It seems that this could only apply where the receiver was not the agent of the company; if he was his actions would be attributable to his principal, the company, which could not be guilty of wrongfully procur-

not bound by it, requiring compliance does perhaps need more precise justification.

Dealing with Suppliers

It has been seen above[97] that supplies of gas, electricity, water and telecommunications requested by an administrative receiver are protected by section 233 of the Act. Supplies of these services requested by non-administrative receivers fall outside section 233, as do supplies of other goods and services. A supplier will be concerned about amounts owing in respect of pre-receivership supplies and this will necessarily condition his attitude to a continuation of supplies. From the receiver's point of view it will be vital to ensure the continued supply of essential goods and services to maintain the business as a going concern with a view to its sale.

Amounts due in respect of pre-receivership supplies

In the case of goods, if the supplier has used a title retention clause and the goods are still in the possession of the receiver and are identifiable,[98] the supplier can repossess them rather than prove in any impending liquidation and risk receiving only a dividend. In relation to any balance the supplier, as an ordinary unsecured creditor, would have to prove.[99] If the validity of the title retention clause is challenged by the receiver, as would be likely where the repossession of the goods would force the

---

ing or intefering with its own contract with a third party (*Said v. Butt* [1920] 3 K.B. 497 (general agent); *Lathia v. Dronsfield Bros. Ltd* [1987] BCLC 321 (administrative receiver); *Welsh Development Agency v. Export Finance Co. Ltd* [1992] BCC 270 (administrative receiver)). As administrative receivers are deemed to be the agent of the company (s.44(1)(a) of the Act) and other receivers appointed out of court are usually expressly constituted such, the tort would appear to be limited to receivers acting outside the scope of their authority (*Lathia v. Dronsfield, supra, per* Sir Neil Lawson, at p. 324). However the reasoning in *Said* v. *Butt* is not without its critics (see the *Welsh Development Agency* case, *supra, per* Dillon, L.J. at p. 289) and furthermore it has been suggested that as receivers are agents of "an unusual kind being appointed by and owing a duty to a stranger" and it is by no means obvious that they should be regarded as the company's *alter ego* (*per* Staughton, L.J. in the *Welsh Development Agency* case at p. 305; but compare Dillon, L.J. at p. 289 of the same case).

[97] At p. 379.

[98] Where the goods have been incorporated into another product they cease to be identifiable and the supplier has no right to the composite product. In so far as he has attempted to reserve a charge over the composite product, it would require registration under s.395 of the Companies Act 1985. Section 93 of the Companies Act 1989 substitutes a new s.395 but the new section has not been brought into force.

[99] While an administrator can apply for an order authorising sale of goods subject to a title retention clause (s.15 of the Act) no such procedure exists in relation to receivers. Administrative receivers have a more limited right to apply for an order to sell property subject to a charge (s.43 of the Act).

company to cease trading, the supplier could seek an injunction restraining the company and the receiver from selling or dealing with the goods. The result of such an injunction would often be as drastic as an actual repossession. This would certainly have been the consequence in *Lipe Ltd v. Leyland Daf Ltd & Ors*[1] where the title retention claims of not only the plaintiff were at stake, but potentially those of 400 other suppliers. If the injunction was not granted and therefore the goods were not frozen, the suppliers, assuming the title retention was valid, might find that they had lost their proprietary claim against the company and were left with an unsecured claim against it for damages for conversion. The legitimacy of this fear had been recognised and the custom had developed for receivers to supplement the suppliers' damages claim with a personal undertaking to pay any damages in conversion, agreed in this case to be the invoice value (£93,000), in relation to any goods subject to a valid title retention claim which were used or sold during the receivership. Such an undertaking had been offered in this case but rejected by Lipe. The administrative receivers argued that, as a result of the undertaking, the supplier was certain to receive the value of the goods, and as they had no reason to wish to recover the goods *in specie*, they were adequately protected and no injunction should issue. Lipe argued that their interests were not fully protected on two main grounds. One was that no evidence had been provided as to the administrative receivers' personal resources and therefore there was a risk that they would be unable to fulfil the undertaking given to Lipe and also given to the 400 other suppliers; it was suggested that this risk should be eliminated by another undertaking, this time by the banks which had appointed the administrative receivers, to pay the value of the goods or, alternatively, by an agreement to pay the proceeds of sale into a joint account. Hoffmann, J. who refused to continue the interim injunction granted by Colman, J., considered that:

> "by concentrating on the personal resources of the receivers the judge ignored the realities of the way receiverships are conducted. Administrative receivers who carry on the business of an insolvent company will almost invariably incur personal liability under the contracts they make, sometimes in very large amounts: see s.44 of the Insolvency Act 1986.[2] The counterparties who deal with them are not concerned with their personal resources and do not rely upon such resources in giving them credit. They rely instead upon the fact that a receiver, acting as agent for the company, is entitled to be indemnified out of the company's assets under his control for all liabilities which he personally has incurred in exercising his powers as a receiver. Furthermore, they rely upon the fact that receivers, as sensible professional men, will not lightly risk personal bankruptcy and will therefore not incur liabilities unless they are satisfied that

---

[1] [1993] BCC 385.
[2] As will non-administrative receivers: s.37(1)(a).

there are sufficient assets to enable those liabilities, to say nothing of the receiver's personal expenses and remuneration, to be paid in full."[3]

The personal liability which the administrative receivers accepted by virtue of the undertaking[4] should be seen in the light of the same realities — assuming that the right to be indemnified extended to such liability. The second ground upon which Lipe asserted that the undertaking was inadequate to protect them was directed to this issue. It was argued that no right of indemnity would back up the undertaking because it consisted of an agreement to be answerable for damages in conversion, a wrongful act. Hoffmann, J. saw no force in this point; while there may turn out to have been a technically wrongful act against Lipe:

> "the question of whether the receivers will be entitled to their indemnity depends upon whether it would be wrongful as against the debentureholder, to whom the assets are equitably charged, and so far as there may be a surplus, as against the company. . . . I do not see how it could be wrongful against either of these parties. It would appear to me to be a prudent way of dealing to best advantage with assets which may or may not belong to the company and for which the company is in any event liable either to a contractual or a proprietary claim."[5]

It followed that in his view this was not a case in which an interlocutory injunction should be granted; a remedy in damages, backed up by the undertaking, which was itself backed up by an indemnity, would be an adequate remedy. He also referred to another factor, not mentioned by Colman, J., which he regarded as important, namely the receiver's right to pay liabilities out of assets of the company.[6] The balance of convenience also dictated that the injunction be discharged. If the injunction was discharged there was a remote risk that the claim against the receivers in relation to goods sold would turn out to be worthless. If the injunction was continued the goods would be frozen, along with those of other suppliers who obtained an injunction, and there was a substantial risk of damaging the business which the receivers were trying to sell.

The personal undertaking of the receivers does no more than secure, to the extent explained above, any title retention rights which the supplier is ultimately successful in substantiating. If such rights are not substantiated, the undertaking is worth nothing. Where this is a real possibility or even

---

[3] At p. 387.
[4] Apart from the undertaking they would not be personally liable for pre-receivership debts, though they would have power to pay them under s.42 and para. 13 of Sched. 1 of the Act.
[5] At p. 387.
[6] This is probably a reference to the power of an administrative receiver "to make any payment which is necessary or incidental to the performance of his functions"; see s.42 & para. 13 of Sched. 1 of the Act. The power is not applicable to non-administrative receivers. Quite why he regarded this as so important is not clear. If the administrative receiver had been prepared to pay for the goods already supplied there would not have been a problem.

where there was never any question of title retention, the supplier may be tempted to resort to normal commercial pressure and seek to ensure that pre-receivership debts are met by refusing to continue supplies to the receiver unless the debt is cleared. The receiver's response could be to obtain supplies elsewhere but in some cases the receiver will be unable to obtain alternative supplies and then the supplier is in a position of considerable strength. Before the rights of public utilities were restricted by section 233 of the Act they were able to pressurise officeholders in this way by virtue of their monopolistic powers. They can do so no longer, but the rights of other specialist suppliers to adopt this tactic remains. The matter was considered in *Leyland DAF Ltd v. Automotive Products plc.*[7] When Leyland went into administrative receivership it owed some £750,000 to Automotive Products plc in respect of brake and clutch parts. Automotive Products plc claimed the benefit of a title retention clause in respect of stocks held by Leyland to this amount. As in the *Lipe* case the administrative receivers gave an undertaking that to the extent that Automotive Products plc's claim was upheld by the courts, they would return the goods or, if they had been sold or used, pay for them. The administrative receivers had indicated that they did not accept the title retention claim and, in case the claim should fail, Automotive Products plc exploited their commercial advantage (there being no alternative supplier) by refusing to supply further parts unless the administrative receivers acknowledged the validity of the title retention clause anyway, and, in effect, paid the pre-receivership debt. The present action, for an interlocutory mandatory order compelling Automotive Products plc to continue to supply on their standard conditions for the next 3 months, was brought by Leyland on the basis that the demand made by Automotive Products plc, for payment by the receivers of the pre-receivership debt regardless of whether the title retention claim was sound, was unlawful. Nicholls, V.-C. examined the position at common law and under Article 86 of the Treaty of Rome but concluded that the demand by Automotive Products plc was lawful and refused the order. At common law:

> "in the absence of some statutory or contractual obligation, one person cannot be forced to trade with another. He cannot be forced to supply goods to someone else if he does not wish to do so. Further, even if a long term supply contract is in existence, and subject to the terms of the particular contract, the seller is not bound to continue to supply once the buyer has defaulted in making payment due for goods already supplied."[8]

Having examined the claim under article 86, he found that Leyland had no seriously arguable case that Automotive Products plc's conduct infringed the Treaty. On appeal Dillon, L.J., commented that at common law a

---

[7] [1993] BCC 389.
[8] *ibid.*, at p. 391, citing *Re Edwards* (1873) L.R. 8 Ch. App. 289 and *Rother Iron Works Ltd v. Canterbury Precision Engineers Ltd* [1974] Q.B. 1 (chargees and receivers appointed by them are in no better position).

supplier was entitled to stipulate for payment in full of his pre-receivership debts before making further supplies leaving the outcome to depend on "strength of will and strength of bargaining power." The specific legal question put to the Court of Appeal was whether such a stipulation was a breach of article 86 which prohibits abuse of a dominant position. It was held that there had been no breach, Dillon, L.J. and Rose, L.J. finding that Automotive Products plc did not occupy a dominant position and that there had been no abuse, Steyn, L.J. was prepared to assume that Automotive Products plc occupied a dominant position but again found that there had been no abuse. The court in refusing the mandatory injunction expressed its regret as to the consequences to Leyland and their workforce.

Post-receivership supplies

In relation to post receivership supplies, in so far as the receiver himself has contracted he will incur personal liability[9] and will be entitled to an indemnity out of the assets of the company in respect of that liability.[10] As pointed out by Hoffmann, L.J. in *Lipe Ltd v. Leyland DAF Ltd*,[11] in continuing to supply, suppliers do not primarily rely upon the receiver having the personal resources to meet their claims, but rather upon the receiver, having enough common sense not to incur liabilities which will attract an indemnity in excess of the company's assets. While the receiver's indemnity[12] is treated as an expense of the receivership to be met out of any property in the receiver's custody or under his control when he vacates office, in priority to any security held by the person by or on whose behalf he was appointed,[13] the liability to the supplier does not, directly at least, appear to have this status.[14] In practice, assuming that he has the power to do so[15] the receiver has every incentive to treat the liability as an expense of the receivership.

Where a receiver has not himself contracted, directly or by novation, for post-receivership supplies, he incurs no personal liability[16] and is entitled to no indemnity. This situation may arise in relation to contracts, typically leases of land or goods, which the receiver merely continues. One could say that he has adopted such contracts but that concept has relevance only in relation to contracts of employment.[17] The receiver is not liable to pay the rent or hire under an existing lease or hire purchase agreement. But as Nicholls, L.J. pointed out in *Re Atlantic Computer Systems plc*.[18]

[9] s.37(1)(a) (non-administrative receivers); s.44(1)(b) (administrative receivers).
[10] s.37(1)(b) (non-administrative receivers); s.44(1)(c) (administrative receivers).
[11] [1993] BCC 385, 387.
[12] Together with his remuneration and expenses properly incurred by him.
[13] s.37(4) (non-administrative receivers); s.45(3) (administrative receivers).
[14] Compare the different wording used in s.19(5) which relates to administrators.
[15] An administrative receiver, unless the debenture provides otherwise, would have such power under s.42 and para. 13 of Sched. 1 of the Act. Other receivers appointed to manage the business could be expected to have similar powers.
[16] Except in relation to contracts of employment "adopted" by him: see *infra*.
[17] ss.37 & 44.
[18] [1992] 1 All E.R. 476 at p. 486.

> "This is not a surprising conclusion. It does not offend against basic concepts of justice or fairness. The rent or hire charges were a liability undertaken by the company at the inception of the lease or hire purchase agreement. The land or goods are being used by the company even when an administrative receiver is in office. It is to the company that, along with other creditors, the lessor and the owner of the goods must look for payment."

Not only is the receiver not personally liable for these amounts, but the supplier cannot successfully claim that they are expenses of the receivership and should be treated as a prior charge on the assets. While this may be the case where a similar situation arises in the context of an administration or a liquidation, these insolvency procedures, unlike a receivership, trigger a statutory moratorium on proceedings. If a lessor is not paid by an administrative receiver, no moratorium applies and he may invoke his remedies under the agreement. Faced with this prospect, if the administrative receiver wishes to retain the land or goods for the purposes of the receivership, he will ensure that payment is made.[19]

Agency

A receiver appointed by the court is not an agent of the company or of the debentureholders at whose instance he was appointed.[20] An out of court receiver will usually be the agent of the company. In the case of a non-administrative receiver such agency results from the terms of the debenture under which he was appointed[21]; in the case of administrative receivers, section 44(1)(a) of the Act provides that the administrative receiver is deemed to be the agent of the company. For this reason it is normally the company, rather than the debentureholders, which is liable for his actions.[22] The agency is unusual because the control exercisable by the company as principal is circumscribed by the duty which the receiver owes to the debentureholders. As Hoffmann, J. pointed out in *Gomba Holdings UK Ltd v. Homan*[23]:

> "A receiver is an agent of the company and an agent ordinarily has a duty to be ready with his accounts and to provide his principal with information relating to the conduct of his agency. But these generalisations are of limited assistance because a receiver and manager is no ordinary agent. Although nominally the agent of the company, his

---

[19] *ibid.*
[20] See *supra*, p. 366.
[21] If the debenture is silent the receiver will be the agent of the debentureholders who will be liable for his acts; see s.109(2) Law of Property Act 1925; *Re Vimbos* [1900] 1 Ch. 470. The receiver may also become the agent of the debentureholder if the latter interferes or directs the receiver's activities; *American Express International Banking Corp. v. Hurley* [1985] 3 All E.R. 564.
[22] By reason of s.37 & 44 of the Act the receiver himself is also liable upon contracts entered into and contracts of employment adopted by him in the carrying out of his functions: see *supra*, p. 371 and p. 373.
[23] [1986] 3 All E.R. 94, at p. 97.

primary duty is to realise the assets in the interests of the debentureholder and his powers of management are really ancillary to that duty."

The board, having certain residual powers and duties,[24] may be entitled to demand information from the receiver, but its rights in this respect are qualified by the receiver's primary duty to the debentureholder to withhold information where he *bona fide* forms the opinion that disclosure would be contrary to the interests of the debentureholder in the realisation of the security. In *Gomba Holdings UK Ltd v. Homan* the company sought information concerning the assets which remained unsold because it claimed to have entered an agreement with a third party which involved the sale of these assets and the redemption of the security. Hoffmann, J. held that the receiver was not bound to disclose the information. The prospect of the agreement coming to fruition was uncertain and it was reasonable for the receivers to conclude that disclosure of future sales would be contrary to the interests of the debentureholders. The unusual nature of a receiver's agency is also recognised, on the discharge of the receiver, when determining the ownership of documents generated during the receivership. Those documents generated or received pursuant to the receiver's duty to manage the company's affairs and dispose of its assets belong to the company; those generated to enable the receiver to advise the debentureholder, belong the debentureholder; and those prepared by the receiver, not in pursuance of any duty to prepare them, but to assist him in the discharge of his duties, belong to the receiver.[25]

A receiver ceases to be the agent of the company when it is wound up[26] and consequently he can no longer create debts and liabilities binding on the company.[27] His powers with regard to the property are unaffected and he may continue to use the company's name for that purpose. Thus in *Sowman v. David Samuel Trust Ltd*[28] a receiver appointed over assets which included a mortgage debt could validly exercise the power of sale in the name of the company notwithstanding its liquidation. Having ceased to be the agent of the company, the receiver does not automatically become the agent of the debentureholders but may do so if the debentureholders treat him as such by directing or interfering with his activities,[29] or if the debenture so provides. If he does not become the agent of the debentureholders, it would appear that he carries on his functions as principal with personal liability.

---

[24] See *supra*, p. 384.
[25] *Gomba Holdings UK Ltd v. Minories Finance Ltd* [1989] 1 All E.R. 261 C.A.
[26] This is explicit in the case of administrative receivers: see s.44(1)(a). The relevant date is that of the winding-up order in the case of a compulsory winding-up; and the date of the resolution in the case of a voluntary winding-up. See Lightman and Moss, *op. cit.*, para. 11.11.
[27] *Gosling v. Gaskell* [1897] A.C. 575.
[28] [1978] 1 All E.R. 616.
[29] *American Express International Banking Corp. v. Hurley* [1985] 3 All E.R. 564, 588.

Equitable Duties

The duties of receivers appointed by the court are discussed, *supra*.[30] Receivers appointed out of court owe duties which derive from the intervention of equity in the enforcement of mortgages. They arise out of the relationship between mortgagor and mortgagee and they are owed to a limited class of person, namely, to the mortgagor, other persons interested in the equity of redemption (like subsequent encumbrancers) and to sureties of the debt.[31] The requirement of good faith is a fundamental element in these duties. It is good faith tempered by a recognition that the primary function of the mortgage is the discharge of the mortgage debt. The mortgagee must exercise his powers, *e.g.* to appoint a receiver, in good faith for the purpose of obtaining repayment[32] and if he complies with this rule it is no matter that the appointment of the receiver is disadvantageous to the mortgagor and others interested in the equity of redemption.[33] Thus while the power to appoint a receiver must be exercised in good faith to obtain repayment, that apart, it can be regarded as a contractual right of the debentureholder which he is entitled to exercise in order to protect his own interests as he sees them. Once appointed the receiver's duties are subject to the same duty of tempered good faith. In the case of a receiver and manager, it must be remembered that he is a "receiver with ancillary powers of management—for the debentureholders, and not simply a person appointed to manage the company's affairs for the benefit of the company."[34] He is under no obligation to carry on the business of the company at the expense of the interests of those who appointed him and may discontinue even if this would be detrimental to the company.[35] Furthermore, some authorities suggest that he commits no breach of duty to the company by a bona fide sale even though he might have obtained a higher price and the terms are disadvantageous from the point of view of the company.[36] However it now seems to be accepted that a mortgagee exercising a power of sale is not merely under a duty to act in subjective good faith but also must take reasonable care to obtain whatever was the

---

[30] p. 367.

[31] *American Express International Banking Corp. v. Hurley* [1985] 3 All E.R. 564. In particular no duty is owed directly to a person who claims to be a beneficiary under a trust of the mortgaged property; in such circumstances the duty is owed to the mortgagor as trustee. It is up to him to institute proceedings against the receiver to safeguard the trust property and only if he is guilty of misfeasance could the beneficiary intervene and take over the action on behalf of the trust: (*Parker-Tweedale v. Dunbar plc (No. 1)* [1990] 2 All E.R. 577).

[32] A breach of duty is committed where the receiver and manager exercises his powers for an improper purpose: *Downsview Nominees Ltd v. First City Corp. Ltd* [1993] 3 All E.R. 626 P.C. (for the purpose of preventing a subsequent encumbrancer from enforcing his security).

[33] *Shamji v. Johnson Matthey Bankers Ltd* [1991] BCLC 36 (where the appointment of receivers frustrated negotiations to obtain finance from a third party); *Re Potters Oils Ltd (No. 2)* [1986] 1 All E.R. 890 (where it was argued that the appointment of a receiver was unnecessary because the liquidator was doing all he could to protect the interests of the debentureholder and the appointment would cause unnecessary expense).

[34] *per* Jenkins, L.J., in *Re B. Johnson & Co (Builders) Ltd* [1955] 2 All E.R. 775, 790–791.

[35] *ibid.*

[36] *ibid.*

true value of the property at the moment when he chooses to sell it[37] and this specific duty is also owed by a receiver appointed by a mortgagee.[38] The manner in which this duty of care in relation to proper price was formulated in *Cuckmere Brick Co. Ltd v. Mutual Finance Ltd*[39] encouraged the belief for a time that a mortgagee owed a general duty of care in negligence in dealing with the assets of the company[40] but this view is not now generally favoured.[41] The Privy Council in *Downsview Nominees Ltd v. First City Corp. Ltd*[42] considered that such a general tortious duty would make it unsafe for the receiver to manage the affairs of the company at all and would encourage him to sell the assets as quickly as possible to discharge the mortgage debt.[43]

---

[37] *Cuckmere Brick Co Ltd v. Mutual Finance Ltd* [1971] 2 All E.R. 633 C.A. The mortgagee is entitled to give preference to his own interests in determining the time of the sale (compare an administrator: *Re Charnley Davies Ltd* (No. 2) [1990] BCLC 760), though if he delays, the mortgagee can apply for sale under s.91(2) of the Law of Property Act 1925 which gives the court an unfettered discretion: see *Palk v. Mortgage Services Funding plc* [1993] 2 All E.R. 481 (sale ordered where the mortgageee proposed to let the premises at a rental which would fall short of the interest which would be saved if the house was sold and where therefore the delay would cause manifest disadvantage to the mortgagor).
[38] *Downsview Nominees Ltd v. First City Corp. Ltd* [1993] 3 All E.R. 626 at p. 634 and p. 637 (P.C.).
[39] [1971] 2 All E.R. 633 C.A.
[40] See *e.g. Knight v. Lawrence* [1991] 01 E.G. 105 ("L.P.A." receiver, *supra*, p. 360).
[41] *China & South Sea Bank Ltd v. Tan* [1980] 3 All E.R. 839 (P.C.); *Parker-Tweedale v. Dunbar Bank plc* (No. 1) [1990] 2 All E.R. 577 C.A.; *Downsview Nominees Ltd v. First City Corp. Ltd* [1993] 3 All E.R. 626 P.C. See also *Mortgagee's Duties on Sale—No Place for Tort?*, Bentley, 1990 Conv. 431. Compare *Knight v. Lawrence* [1991] 01 EG 105.
[42] *supra* n. 38.
[43] The equitable duties of mortgagees and their receivers are discussed at length in Lightman & Moss, *op. cit.*, Chap. 7.

Section B. Alternatives to Winding Up

Chapter 15

COMPANY VOLUNTARY ARRANGEMENTS IN ENGLAND AND WALES

Preliminary

Part I of the Insolvency Act 1986 contains provisions to enable a company, including one for which an administration order is in force or which is being wound up, to enter into a voluntary arrangement with its creditors.[1] The need for a suitably simple procedure whereby a company may conclude a legally effective arrangement with its creditors had long been recognised. In Part II of Chapter 7 of their Final Report,[2] the Cork Committee surveyed the various procedures which were provided under the then-existing companies legislation,[3] and amply demonstrated that for a combination of technical and practical reasons each procedure proved to be cumbersome and unsuitable in the context of an attempt to rationalise the affairs of a company which is nearly or actually insolvent. In the opinion of the Committee, the complexity and expense of the requisite procedures were such as to preclude the majority of insolvent companies from effecting compositions with their creditors. Accordingly the Committee proposed, as a solution for this specific problem, a new form of voluntary arrangement which would be concluded without an order of the court but which would nevertheless constitute a formal and binding arrangement between the company and its creditors.[4] The procedure was envisaged as serving to complement the administration order procedure which, among numerous other points of distinction, notably involves the

---

[1] Pt. I of the Insolvency Act 1986 (ss.1–7 inclusive) corresponds in substance to Chap. II of Pt. II of the Insolvency Act 1985 (ss.20–26 inclusive). The provisions of the Insolvency Act 1985 were repealed without ever having come into force (Insolvency Act 1986, s.438 and Sched. 12). For the corresponding provisions regarding Individual Voluntary Arrangements, see ss.252–263 of the Act of 1986, discussed in Chap. 4, *ante*.

[2] Cmnd. 8558 (1982), paras. 400–430 inclusive.

[3] The relevant provisions referred to were ss.206, 287 and 306 of the Companies Act 1948, subsequently contained in ss.425, 582 and 601 respectively of the Companies Act 1985. ss.583 and 601 were repealed by Sched. 12 to the Insolvency Act 1986.

[4] Cmnd. 8558, paras. 419–422, 428–430.

obtaining of a court order.[5] The successive Insolvency Acts of 1985 and 1986 made provision for both types of procedure, and in the case of the new form of voluntary arrangement for companies the Committee's recommendations, deliberately based upon their parallel proposals for cases of individual insolvency, have been closely followed and implemented. In accordance with those recommendations, it is made a principal feature of the procedure under Part I of the Insolvency Act 1986 that any voluntary arrangement proposed and, in due course, concluded under that Part of the Act will be required first to be appraised and endorsed, and subsequently to be administered and implemented, by a qualified insolvency practitioner.[6]

The Proposal for a Voluntary Arrangement

Section 1 of the Insolvency Act 1986 indicates that the procedure for concluding a voluntary arrangement is commenced by the making of a proposal to the company and to its creditors for a composition in satisfaction of its debts or a scheme of arrangement of its affairs.[7] The proposal must provide for some person (known as "the nominee") to act in relation to the voluntary arrangement either as trustee or in some other capacity for the purpose of supervising its implementation.[8]

Who may make a proposal?

Important limitations are imposed by the provisions of section 1 both with regard to the persons who are eligible to make a proposal for a voluntary arrangement, and with regard to the persons who are eligible to serve as nominee. As to the former, section 1(1) indicates that the directors of the company may make the proposal, but that they may do so only provided that no administration order is in force in respect of the company, and that it is not being wound up. On the other hand, there is no requirement that it must be established that the company is insolvent, or unable to pay its debts, at the time of the proposal. The procedure may therefore be used in the context of an attempt to avert a threatened, or predictable, insolvency before it actually occurs. The subsection requires the directors to act collectively in making the relevant proposal and it may be observed that, unlike the situation which obtains under an administration order proceeding, the directors are not deprived of their powers of management during the implementation of a voluntary arrangement, nor do the company's property and affairs gain the benefit of any general and automatic moratorium either prior to the formal conclusion of the voluntary arrangement, or subsequently, save in so far as a wide circle of

---

[5] For a description of the Administration Order procedure see Chap. 16, *post*.
[6] *cf.* Cmnd. 8558, paras. 350–399, 428–430. The meaning of the expression "qualified insolvency practitioner," as governed by Pt. XIII of the Insolvency Act 1986, is explained in Chap. 2, *ante*.
[7] Insolvency Act 1986, s.1(1).
[8] *ibid.*, s.1(2).

parties, both assenting and non-assenting, become bound by the voluntary arrangement once it has been duly approved.[9]

Because of the absence of any comprehensive moratorium, operative from the very beginning of the voluntary arrangement procedure, it is not altogether surprising that in practice only a small number of companies have had recourse to this otherwise useful procedure.[10] The most effective way for an insolvent company to make use of the voluntary arrangement procedure is probably in conjunction with the administration order procedure. Where the company is already the subject of an administration order, or where it is being wound up, section 1(3) provides that a proposal for a voluntary arrangement may only be made by the administrator or the liquidator respectively, as the case may be. The question of eligibility to serve as nominee is considered below.

The terms of the proposal

Section 1 of the Insolvency Act 1986 prescribes only the barest essentials with regard to the required terms and substance of any proposal made for the purposes of Part I of the Act. The provisions of the section stipulate in effect that the proposal must embody the terms of a compact between the company and its creditors for a composition in satisfaction of the company's debts, or a scheme of arrangement of its affairs. In the absence of any statutory provisions regulating the permissible terms of such an arrangement, it becomes in effect a pure question of whether the terms themselves are capable of commanding the requisite measure of approval from the two respective sides so as to render the arrangement effective and binding. It is true that deliberate safeguards are contained in subsections (3) and (4) of section 4 to protect the positions of secured or preferential creditors, but even in this respect an overall policy of *laissez-faire* is adopted, and the rights of such creditors are permitted to be modified as part of the terms of the arrangement provided that in each instance this is done with the concurrence of the individual creditor who is thereby affected. Moreover, the absence of any restrictive provisions concerning the position of the ordinary, unsecured creditors makes it possible for the terms of the arrangement to provide for them to receive a different rate of return from that which would apply in a liquidation. For example, priority could be given to meeting the claims of the small creditors ahead of those whose claims are for large amounts.

The one express statutory requirement of a positive nature, with regard to the terms of the proposal, is that already referred to whereby section 1(2) requires provision to be made for a named person ("the nominee") to act in relation to the arrangement either as trustee or in some other way for the purpose of supervising its implementation. Section 1(2) imposes the further requirement that the nominee must be a person who is qualified to act as an insolvency practitioner in relation to the company. This is a

---

[9] *ibid.*, s.5 (discussed *infra.*). *cf.* Rajak, *Company Liquidations* (1988), para. 131(2).
[10] See the statistical information included in Appendix III, *post.*

further consequence of the implementation, via Part XIII of the Insolvency Act 1986, of one of the main recommendations of the Insolvency Law Review Committee with regard to the attainment of assured minimum standards of competence, integrity and experience with respect to every person, other than the official receiver himself, who is appointed to any of the key administrative positions in the various types of insolvency proceeding.[11] In addition to possessing the general qualifications prescribed by Part XIII of the Act, the nominee must ensure that he is not precluded on an *ad hoc* basis from accepting the appointment in question, for example by virtue of the guidelines and rules of conduct prescribed by any professional body to which he may belong, and by virtue of whose standing the nominee enjoys his own basic authority to act as an insolvency practitioner.[12] An exclusionary rule in point would be one which forbids or discourages members of the professional body in question from acting as insolvency practitioners in circumstances where an actual or potential conflict of interest may arise by reason of their personal association with a company or with any persons who are concerned in its management or who are creditors of the company.[13] No criminal sanction is prescribed in relation to any acts performed by a person in the capacity of nominee under a proposal for a voluntary arrangement, where it transpires that the nominee is not qualified to act as an insolvency practitioner in relation to the company. It should be borne in mind however that if such a person is in due course elevated to the position of supervisor of the arrangement[14] he will, by so acting at a time when he is unqualified to do so, commit a criminal offence of strict liability by reason of sections 388(1)(b) and 389(1) of the Insolvency Act 1986.[15]

Functions of the nominee

Where the nominee is not the administrator or liquidator of the company, his first function is to prepare a report upon the basis of his personal assessment of the soundness and fairness of the proposed voluntary arrangement. Section 2 of the Insolvency Act 1986 requires that the nominee shall submit his report to the court within 28 days after he is given notice of the proposal for a voluntary arrangement, or within such longer period as the court may allow. Although the nominee is under a statutory obligation to furnish the court with a report stating whether, in his opinion, meetings of the company and its creditors should be summoned to consider the proposal (and if so, when and where this should take place),[16] the Act does not establish any positive role for the court to

---

[11] See further, Chap. 2, *ante*.
[12] See Insolvency Act 1986, ss.390(2)(a), 391(1), (2). See also the Insolvency Practitioners Regulations 1990 (S.I. 1990, No. 439) (as amended by (S.I. 1993, No. 221)) and the Insolvency Practitioners (Recognised Professional Bodies) Order 1986, (S.I. 1986, No. 1764).
[13] *cf.* the concept of "associate," as defined in s.435 of the Insolvency Act 1986: see Appendix I, *post*.
[14] See Insolvency Act 1986, s.7(2).
[15] See p. 26, *ante*.
[16] Insolvency Act 1986, s.2(2)(a), (b).

Proposal for a Voluntary Arrangement

fulfil subsequently to having received the nominee's report. Although, by virtue of section 3(1) of the Act, it is effectively made a precondition to the nominee's proceeding to convene the requisite meetings of the company and its creditors that he shall first have reported to the court in favour of this course of action, his ability to convene the meetings is not dependent upon the making of any order to that effect by the court in question. On the contrary, section 3(1) provides that the nominee is obliged, as a consequence of his own report in favour of so proceeding, to summon those meetings for the time, date and place proposed in the report, unless the court otherwise directs. The court can become involved in a more positive sense as a consequence of the provision contained in section 2(4) if the nominee altogether fails to submit the report required by section 2. To overcome the possibility of a stultifying delay, or stalemate, subsection (4) enables the person intending to make the proposal for a voluntary arrangement to apply to the court for the original nominee to be replaced by another suitably qualified person. The original nominee must be given at least seven days' notice of such an application.[17] Rule 1.7(2) of the Insolvency Rules 1986 imposes the requirement that where the nominee's opinion is to the effect that meetings should not be summoned, he must in his report give reasons for that opinion.

The underlying purpose of the provisions contained in section 1(2) and section 3(1) is to ensure that no abortive or futile meetings are convened in an effort to conclude a voluntary arrangement. To this end the Insolvency Act imposes the requirement that every intended proposal for such an arrangement shall first be appraised and approved by an independent and properly qualified insolvency practitioner. In practice, the prudent course is for the directors of the company to prepare the draft proposal in consultation with the person who is to be named therein as the nominee. In cases where the company is either the subject of an administration order, or is being wound up, the office holder, who is the only party competent to make a proposal in the circumstances, will of necessity be a qualified insolvency practitioner.[18] Hence, it may be assumed that the requisite degree of professional judgment and discernment will be brought to bear by the office holder in formulating the terms of his proposal, and on that premise the office holder, if he provides for himself to be nominee, is permitted to summon meetings of the company and its creditors to consider the proposal at such time and place as he thinks fit, without the need to submit a report to the court as a prerequisite to the taking of this step.[19] If however an administrator or liquidator, while wishing to formulate a proposal for a voluntary arrangement, does not intend to nominate himself to serve as the person responsible for its implementation he must select as nominee someone who is personally qualified to act as an insolvency practitioner in relation to the company, and it is then necessary for such a nominee to fulfil the requirements of section 2(2) of the

---

[17] Insolvency Rules 1986 (S.I. 1986, No. 1925), r. 1.8. (references hereinafter are to "the Rules").
[18] Insolvency Act 1986, ss.388(1)(a), 389. *cf.* 19(2)(*a*), 171(4), 172(5).
[19] *ibid.*, s.3(2). *cf.* the Rules, Pt. I, Chap. 3.

Insolvency Act before proceeding to convene meetings pursuant to the provisions of section 3(1).[20]

Statement of Affairs

Essentially, the nominee's report must be based upon an informed professional judgment. For the purpose of enabling the nominee to form the requisite judgment, and to prepare his report, section 2(3) of the Insolvency Act requires that the person intending to submit the proposal must submit to him:

(1) A document setting out the terms of the proposed voluntary arrangement; and
(2) A statement of the company's affairs, together with other information, in correspondence with the requirements imposed by the Insolvency Rules 1986.

The latter contain detailed provisions concerning the information which is required to be comprised within the statement of affairs, which the directors are required to lodge with the nominee within seven days after their proposal is delivered to him.[21] The required contents of the statement of affairs are broadly identical to those of a statement of affairs which is to be prepared in the context of an administration or winding up of the company, or where an administrative receiver is appointed over a company.[22] Provision is made in the Rules to enable the nominee to oblige the directors to provide him with further and better particulars relating to the company's insolvent circumstances, and such other relevant information with respect to the company's affairs which he thinks necessary for the purpose of enabling him properly to prepare his report.[23] In this connection the directors must give the nominee access to the company's accounts and records, and must supply him with information relating to the business connections and financial circumstances of any past or present director or officer of the company who has been concerned with any other company which has become insolvent, or who has himself been adjudged bankrupt or entered into an arrangement with creditors.[24]

Where the proposal for a voluntary arrangement is made in relation to a company which is subject to an administration order or which is being wound up, the maker of the proposal (the administrator or liquidator, as the case may be) will have obtained the necessary information as to the company's affairs and circumstances, on which to formulate the terms of

---

[20] *cf.* Insolvency Act 1986, s.2(1), and see the Rules, Pt. I, Chap. 4.
[21] The Rules, r. 1.5. The nominee may allow a longer period of time than seven days for the lodging of the statement: *ibid.*, r. 1.5(1).
[22] *cf.* Insolvency Act 1986, ss.22, 47, 66, 99 and 131, together with the relevant provisions of the Insolvency Rules: See Chap. 22, *post.*
[23] The Rules, r. 1.6(1).
[24] *ibid.*, r. 1.6(2), (3).

Proposal for a Voluntary Arrangement

the proposed arrangement, as a consequence of the filing of the company's statement of affairs pursuant to sections 22, 99 or 131 of the Insolvency Act 1986.

Meetings of the Company and of its Creditors

Meetings to consider the proposal are summoned either by the nominee in accordance with section 3(1) of the Insolvency Act or (where there is one) by the liquidator or administrator in accordance with section 3(2). In the former case the date on which the meetings are held must be not less than 14, nor more than 28 days, from the date on which the nominee's report is filed in court.[25] The persons to be summoned to the creditors' meetings by means of notices sent at least 14 days in advance are every creditor of the company of whose claim and address the person summoning the meeting is aware, whether the nominee's knowledge of the creditor's identity results from the information included in the company's statement of affairs or from any other source.[26] Unlike the procedure for concluding a scheme of arrangement under section 425 of the Companies Act 1985, there is no requirement that separate meetings of different classes of creditor be held.

In the case of the meeting of members of the company, notices calling the meeting must be sent, at least 14 days in advance, to all persons who are, to the best of the belief of the person summoning the meeting, members of it.[27]

The purpose of the meetings summoned under section 3 of the Insolvency Act is to decide whether to approve the proposed voluntary arrangement, either in its original form or with modifications.[28] The conduct of the respective meetings is governed by the Insolvency Rules,[29] which impose upon the person summoning the meetings ("the convener") a duty to have regard primarily to the convenience of the creditors when fixing the venue for the meetings.[30] The meetings must be held on the same day, and in the same place, but the creditors' meeting must be fixed for a time in advance of the company meeting.[31] Voting by proxy is permitted at both meetings, and forms of proxy must be sent together with every notice summoning either meeting.[32]

At both the creditors' meeting and the company meeting, and at any combined meeting, the convener acts as chairman, but if he is unable to attend he may nominate another person to act as chairman in his place

---

[25] *ibid.*, r. 1.9(1).
[26] Insolvency Act 1986, s.3(3); the Rules, r. 1.9(2)(a). The same requirements are imposed where the proposal is made by an administrator or liquidator, whether or not he himself is the nominee: rr. 1.11, 1.12(7).
[27] The Rules, r. 1.9(2)(b). *cf.* also rr. 1.11(1)(b) and 1.12(7).
[28] Insolvency Act 1986, s.4(1).
[29] *ibid.*, s.4(5). See the Rules, Pt. I, Chap. 5.
[30] The Rules, r. 1.13(1).
[31] *ibid.*, r. 1.13(3).
[32] *ibid.*, r. 1.13(4). For the rules regarding quorum at meetings of creditors or contributories, see r. 12.4A.

provided that the person so nominated is either a person qualified to act as an insolvency practitioner in relation to the company, or is an employee of the convener or of his firm and is experienced in insolvency matters.[33] The convener must give to all directors of the company, and to any officers or any former directors or officers whose presence he thinks desirable, at least 14 days' notice to attend the meetings.[34] Conversely, the chairman of the meeting is empowered at his discretion to exclude any present or former officer from attendance at a meeting, regardless of whether notice to attend the meeting was sent to the person so excluded.[35]

Voting

Apart from the requirement that any resolution at a creditors' meeting approving the proposal or modification requires the approval of a majority in excess of three quarters in value of the creditors present in person or by proxy and voting thereon,[36] the general principles applicable to questions of voting rights, and the requisite majorities for any resolution to be validly passed at a meeting, correspond closely to those applicable to other kinds of insolvency procedure.

With respect to the voting rights of creditors, the basic rules are that every creditor who was given notice of the creditors' meeting is entitled to vote thereat, and that each creditor's vote is calculated according to the amount of his debt as at the date of the meeting or, where the company is being wound up or is subject to an administration order, the date of its going into liquidation, or the date of the administration order, as the case may be.[37] In the usual way the chairman of the meeting has the power to admit or reject a creditor's claim for the purpose of his entitlement to vote, and there is provision for appeal to the court against the chairman's decision.[38] The time limit for submitting application by way of appeal against the chairman's decision is the period of 28 days beginning with the first day on which each of the reports on the outcome of the meetings is made to the court in accordance with the requirements of s.4(6) of the Insolvency Act.[39] No creditor may vote in respect of a debt for an unliquidated amount, nor in respect of a debt whose value is not ascertained, except where the chairman of the meeting agrees to put an estimated minimum value upon the debt for the purpose of entitlement to vote.[40] The precise connotation of the word "agrees", as used in rule

---

[33] *ibid.*, r. 1.14.
[34] *ibid.*, r. 1.16(1).
[35] *ibid.*, r. 1.16(2).
[36] *ibid.*, r. 1.19(1).
[37] *ibid.*, r. 1.17(1), (2).
[38] *ibid.*, r. 1.17(4), (5). To avoid delay pending appeal, the creditor whose claim is objected to is allowed to vote at the meeting, subject to his vote being subsequently declared invalid if the objection to the claim is sustained: r. 1.17(6). See *Re A Debtor (No. 222 of 1990)* [1992] BCLC 137 (a case concerning an individual voluntary arrangement, but of considerable relevance also to cases of CVAs).
[39] *ibid.*, r. 1.17(8).
[40] *ibid.*, r. 1.17(3).

1.17(3), was the subject of divergent judicial rulings in *Re Cranley Mansions Ltd, Saigol v. Goldstein*, and in *Re A Debtor (No. 162 of 1993), Doorbar v. Alltime Securities Ltd.*[41] In the *Cranley Mansions* case, Ferris J. held that it connotes an element of bilateral concurrence between the chairman and the creditor in question. A unilateral or arbitrary determination of the estimated value, made by the chairman alone, would not suffice to render the creditor eligible to vote in respect of the amount of value put on the debt, or indeed to vote at all. Hence, that creditor would not be bound by the arrangement which the meeting may vote to adopt, since section 5(2)(b) of the Act has the effect of confining the effects of approval to those entitled to vote (see below). In the *Doorbar* case, however, Knox J. preferred to read the phrase "agrees to put" as meaning that it is the chairman's agreement to put a minimum value on the creditor's claim, and not the reaching of agreement between the two of them as to the amount at which the claim is valued, that determines whether or not the creditor is thereby rendered eligible to vote at the meeting and hence can be bound by its outcome. Knox J.—whose approach, it is respectfully suggested, is to be preferred—was careful to add the proviso that the chairman must approach the task of valuation in a genuine, professional way by making a real attempt to value the claim: a token or arbitrary "valuation" (such as the placing of a nominal, £1 value upon it) would be open to challenge by the aggrieved creditor.

At the company meeting the members vote according to the rights attaching to their shares respectively in accordance with the articles.[42] Where no voting rights attach to a member's shares he is nevertheless entitled to vote either for or against the proposal or any modification of it, subject to the overriding, and somewhat stultifying, rule that in determining whether a majority for any resolution has been obtained any vote cast on that basis is to be left out of account.[43]

As mentioned above, the prescribed majority at the creditors' meeting for any resolution to pass approving any proposal or modification is a majority in excess of three quarters in value of the creditors present in person or by proxy and voting on the resolution.[44] In respect of any other resolution proposed at a creditors' meeting the requisite majority is reduced to one in excess of one half of the creditors present and voting.[45] There are additional provisions in the Insolvency Rules where in certain cases a creditor's vote is to be left out of account, and whereby the chairman's misuse of a proxy may cause that proxy to be disregarded for the purpose of counting towards a majority.[46] Among these exclusionary rules is the highly significant provision in rule 1.19(4), which enhances the possibility for a resolution to be invalidated due to the opposition of those creditors who are both unsecured, and unconnected with the company.

---

[41] [1994] BCC 576 (Ferris, J.); [1994] BCC 994 (Knox, J.). Both cases are discussed above in Chap. 4, at p. 48.
[42] The Rules r. 1.18(1).
[43] *ibid.*, rr. 1.18(2) and 1.20(2).
[44] *ibid.*, r. 1.19(1).
[45] *ibid.*, r. 1.19(2).
[46] *ibid.*, r. 1.19(3), (4), (5) and (6).

The rule states that any resolution is invalid if those voting against it include more than half in value of the creditors, counting in these latter only those (a) to whom notice of the meeting was sent; (b) whose votes are not to be left out of account under rule 1.19(3); and (c) who are not, to the best of the chairman's belief, persons connected with the company.[47] This provision inevitably has far-reaching implications regarding the prospects for obtaining a valid approval of a given proposal, in view of the terms comprised therein.

The requisite majority for passing any resolution at a company meeting is if the resolution is voted for by more than one half in value of the members present in person or by proxy and voting on the resolution, and the value of votes cast by members is determined by reference to the number of votes conferred on each member by the company's articles.[48] This is subject however to the overriding effect of any express provision made in the company's own articles, and there are further exceptions whereby, in establishing whether a majority has been obtained, no account is to be taken of any vote cast by a member to whose shares no voting rights attach, nor of any purported exercise of a proxy by the chairman if the latter also misuses the proxy in order to vote for the increase or reduction of the remuneration or expenses of the nominee or supervisor of the proposed arrangement.[49]

The Rules make provision for the meetings to be adjourned from time to time on the day on which they are held, and for the two meetings to be consolidated at the chairman's discretion for the purpose of obtaining simultaneous agreement to the proposal.[50] If no requisite majority for approval of the proposal by both meetings is obtained on the day on which they are held the chairman may at his discretion adjourn them for not more than 14 days, and he must so adjourn them if a resolution to that effect is duly passed.[51] The Rules are silent as to whether it is sufficient if a resolution for adjournment is duly passed by only one of the meetings, or whether it is necessary that both meetings pass resolutions to the same effect. However, since it is forbidden to adjourn either meeting unless the other is also adjourned to the same business day[52] it would seem reasonable to expect the chairman to exercise his power to adjourn the one meeting if the other had duly passed a resolution for adjournment. There may be further adjournments, provided that the final adjournment is to a day not later than 14 days after the date on which the meetings were originally held, and if at the final adjournment of the meeting the proposal, in its original or in a modified form, is not agreed in identical terms by both meetings it is deemed rejected.[53]

---

[47] r. 1.19(3) [votes to be left out of account] provides that there is to be left out of account, *inter alia*, a creditor's vote in respect of any claim or part of a claim where the claim or part is secured. For the meaning of the expression "connected person", see Insolvency Act 1986, ss.249, 435, reproduced in Appendix I, *post*.
[48] *ibid.*, r. 1.20(1), as amended.
[49] *ibid.*, rr. 1.15, 1.20(1), (2) and (3).
[50] *ibid.*, r. 1.21(1).
[51] *ibid.*, r. 1.21(2).
[52] *ibid.*, r. 1.21(4).
[53] *ibid.*, r. 1.21(6).

Approval of the proposal

The meetings summoned under section 3 of the Insolvency Act must decide whether to reject the proposed voluntary arrangement, or to approve it as it stands or with modifications.[54] Any modification of the original proposal must be approved in identical form by both meetings, but no modification may be validly adopted whose effect is to take the substance of the proposal outside the ambit of section 1 of the Insolvency Act.[55] However, the modifications may include one substituting as eventual supervisor of the arrangement a person other than the nominee himself, provided always that the person substituted is qualified to act as an insolvency practitioner in relation to the company.[56]

Further limitations upon the extent to which it is competent for the meetings to approve proposals or modifications are imposed by subsections (3) and (4) of section 4 of the Insolvency Act. These limitations are designed to ensure that no alterations may be effected which disturb the legitimate expectations, and usual rights and remedies, of any secured or preferential creditor except with the concurrence of the creditor concerned. Thus, the right of any secured creditor of the company to enforce his security may not be affected except with his concurrence.[57] It is submitted that the statutory force of the word "concurrence" is such as to require the open and positive assent of the creditor concerned, rather than his merely tacit or passive acquiescence. Similarly, in the case of any preferential creditor no arrangement whereby any preferential debt is to lose its entitlement to be paid in priority to such of the company's debts as are non-preferential, or whereby a preferential creditor[58] is to be paid a smaller proportion pro rata than that which is to be paid to any other preferential creditor, may be approved without the concurrence of the creditor who is thus adversely affected. Once again, the significance of the term "concurrence" should be noted.

After the conclusion of each of the meetings the chairman is required within four days to report the result to the court, and immediately thereafter to give notice of the result to all those who were sent notice of the meeting in question.[59] If the voluntary arrangement has been approved by the meetings, the person who has thereby become supervisor of the arrangement must forthwith send a copy of the chairman's report to the registrar of companies.[60]

Effect of Approval

Where a voluntary arrangement is validly approved, whether with or

---

[54] Insolvency Act 1986, s.4(1).
[55] *ibid.*, s.4(2) proviso. See also s.5(1), and the Rules, r. 1.21(1).
[56] *ibid.*, s.4(2).
[57] *ibid.*, s.4(3).
[58] The terms "preferential debt" and "preferential creditor" are, by virtue of s.4(7), to be given the meaning conferred by s.386 of the Act: see Chap. 10, *ante*.
[59] Insolvency Act 1986, s.4(6); the Rules, r. 1.24(1)–(4) inclusive.
[60] The Rules, r. 1.24(5).

without modifications, by each of the meetings summoned for the purpose of considering it, the approved arrangement takes effect as if made by the company at the creditors' meeting, and binds every person who in accordance with the rules had notice of, and was entitled to vote at, that meeting as if he were a party to the voluntary arrangement, regardless of whether or not he was present or represented at the meeting.[61] The requirements of natural justice are thus satisfied since it is necessary that a person shall have been furnished with a reasonable opportunity to attend and to vote at the meeting at which, on a majority basis, a decision was taken to adopt a voluntary arrangement which thereby became binding also upon the non-assenting minority. Nevertheless, section 6 of the Insolvency Act provides a right to challenge either the approved voluntary arrangement itself or the manner by which its approval was obtained. This right is exercisable only within the period of 28 days beginning with the first day on which each of the reports of the outcome of the meetings is made to the court[62] and is exercisable only by one of the persons mentioned in section 6(2) of the Insolvency Act. These are:

(1) A person entitled, in accordance with the rules described above, to vote at either of the meetings; or
(2) The nominee or any person who has replaced him under section 2(4) or section 4(2); or
(3) If the company is being wound up or an administration order is in force, the liquidator or administrator.

The grounds on which an application may be made to challenge a voluntary arrangement under section 6 are either:

(1) That the voluntary arrangement as approved unfairly prejudices the interests of a creditor, member or contributory of the company; or
(2) That there has been some material irregularity at or in relation to either of the meetings.[63]

The court's powers on such an application include the power to revoke or suspend the approvals given by the meetings, or by the particular meeting at which any material irregularity is shown to have taken place, and to give directions for the holding of further meetings to consider any revised proposal, or to reconsider the original proposal.[64] The court may

---

[61] Insolvency Act 1986, s.5(2). See also s.233(1)(c) of the Act, whereby the provisions of that section (discussed in Chap. 16, *post*, at p. 459) become applicable where a voluntary arrangement has taken effect. For judicial consideration of the implications of a finding that a particular creditor was not "entitled to vote", see *Re Cranley Mansions Ltd, Saigol v. Goldstein* and *Re A Debtor (No. 162 of 1993), Doorbar v. Alltime Securities Ltd (supra*, n. 41, and text thereto).

[62] *ibid.*, s.6(3).

[63] *ibid.*, s.6(1)(a), (b). These grounds of challenge were examined in the course of the judgment delivered by Ferris, J. in *Re Cranley Mansions Ltd, Saigol v. Goldstein* [1994] BCC 576, at pp. 586–595. *cf.* Rajak, *Company Liquidations* (1988), paras. 126–129.

[64] *ibid.*, s.6(4). See also subs. (5) and (6).

grant discovery of relevant documents, and may order persons to attend for examination, if the party challenging the voluntary arrangement can show that this is necessary in the interests of justice, in order that the full facts and circumstances may be ascertained.[65]

Unless an application to challenge a decision is successfully brought under section 6 within the limited time allowed for this purpose, the decisions taken at any meeting, and in particular any approval thereby given to a voluntary arrangement, are unimpeachable notwithstanding any irregularity which may have occurred at or in relation to the meeting in question.[66]

If the company is being wound up or an administration order is in force, section 5(3) of the Insolvency Act empowers the court to make an order staying all proceedings in the winding-up or discharging the administration order, or alternatively to issue appropriate directions as to the further conduct of the winding-up or administration. By section 5(4) however the court is forbidden to make such an order until the expiry of the 28 day time limit for the bringing of a challenge under section 6, or until all proceedings and appeals in respect of any application under section 6 are finally completed.

Implementation of the Proposal

Where a voluntary arrangement has taken effect by virtue of its having been approved by meetings convened under section 3, responsibility for its implementation resides with the person identified for this purpose by the terms of the arrangement as finally agreed. This will in most instances be the nominee but may be some other person who has been substituted for the nominee under section 2(4) or section 4(2). In any event, the person who is for the time being carrying out the function of implementing an approved voluntary arrangement is known as "the supervisor of the voluntary arrangement."[67] It will be recalled that under sections 388(1)(b) and 389 of the Insolvency Act it is a criminal offence for a person to act as a supervisor of a composition or scheme at a time when he is not qualified to do so.[68] Provision is also made by section 7 of the Insolvency Act for any interested party to apply to the court in the event that the supervisor's conduct in office proves unsatisfactory, and the court enjoys overriding powers in relation to anything the supervisor may have done, and can issue directions to him as to his future conduct in discharge of his responsibilities.[69] Correspondingly, the supervisor may take the initiative in seeking directions from the court by way of an application, and is clothed with the potent right to apply for the company to be wound up or for an administration order to be made.[70] Finally the court enjoys the right

---

[65] *Re Primlaks (U.K.) Ltd. (No. 2)* [1990] BCLC 234.
[66] *ibid.*, s.6(7).
[67] *ibid.*, s.7(2).
[68] See nn. 11 and 15, *above*.
[69] Insolvency Act 1986, s.7(3).
[70] *ibid.*, s.7(4).

to replace any person as supervisor, and to appoint further persons to act in that capacity either instead of or in addition to any person who may previously have exercised the functions of supervisor.[71]

If the voluntary arrangement authorises or requires the supervisor to carry on the business of the company or to trade on its behalf or in its name, or to realise assets of the company, or otherwise to administer or dispose of any of its funds, he must keep accounts and records of his acts and dealings in discharging his allotted functions, including in particular records of all receipts and payments of money.[72] At least on an annual basis, the supervisor must prepare an abstract of his receipts and payments and send copies of it, together with his comments on the progress and efficacy of the arrangement, to the court, to the registrar of companies, to the company and to the company's auditors, to all creditors who are bound by the arrangement, and (unless the court in this particular dispenses with the need to do so) to the members of the company who are bound by the arrangement.[73] Upon being so required, the supervisor must at any time during the course of the voluntary arrangement or after its completion produce to the Secretary of State his records and accounts in respect of the arrangement and copies of the abstracts and reports which have been prepared in compliance with the Rules.[74] The Secretary of State may at his discretion cause any accounts and records which are thereby produced to him to be audited.[75]

Completion of the Arrangement

After the voluntary arrangement has been finally and fully implemented the supervisor must within 28 days of the completion send notice to that effect to all creditors and members of the company who are bound by the arrangement.[76] The notice must be accompanied by a copy of a report by the supervisor summarising all receipts and payments made by him in pursuance of the arrangement, and explaining any difference in the actual implementation of it as compared with the proposal which was approved by the creditors' and company meetings.[77] The notice and report must likewise be sent within the same 28 day period to the registrar of companies and to the court.[78] Rule 4.21A of the Insolvency Rules makes the expenses of the administration of a voluntary arrangement a first charge on the company's assets, where a winding up order is made and there is a voluntary arrangement in force at the time when the winding up petition is presented.[79]

[71] *ibid.*, s.7(5).
[72] The Rules, r. 1.26(1).
[73] *ibid.*, r. 1.26(2).
[74] *ibid.*, r. 1.27(1), (2).
[75] *ibid.*, r. 1.27(3).
[76] *ibid.*, r. 1.29(1).
[77] *ibid.*, r. 1.29(2).
[78] *ibid.*, r. 1.29(3).
[79] Rule 4.21A was added to the Insolvency Rules 1986 by the Insolvency (Amendment) Rules 1987 (S.I. 1987, No. 1919).

Review and Reform of the Law

The Company Voluntary Arrangement (CVA) was one of the innovatory additions to the repertoire of insolvency procedures introduced by the Insolvency Act 1986. The statistical profile of its operation, since first becoming available in 1987, show that the CVA has been by some way the least attractive of the new procedures introduced at that time.[80] Even during the period of severe recession in the British economy between 1989 and 1993, when the annual rate of company failures rose to well above 20,000, the annual average of concluded CVAs remained well below 100, and the highest number in any single year was a mere 137 (in 1991). This was in vivid contrast to the statistical success of the counterpart procedure for insolvent individuals, the Individual Voluntary Arrangement (or IVA), discussed in Chapter 4 above.[81]

As with the Administration Order procedure, to be discussed in Chapter 16, the low incidence of use during a period of steeply soaring levels of company insolvencies was widely regarded as demonstrative of a systemic failure on the part of the new insolvency legislation, and on the part of those responsible for administering the law, with regard to the development of a "rescue" culture to avert "unnecessary" liquidations of ailing companies. Although this proposition was not infrequently formulated in terms which were of a question-begging nature, the essential thrust of the underlying criticism was undoubtedly valid. Although there may be scope for debate in many instances as to the "necessity", or "inevitability", of ultimate liquidation of a given company and the consequential closure of its business, the very absence of any effective and affordable procedures, apart from administrative receivership (where available),[82] whereby rehabilitation can be attempted as an alternative to liquidation, means that in practice the option of an attempted rescue of the company is in many cases purely hypothetical.

Among analysts and commentators, a widespread consensus has emerged that the single most important reason for the near-negligible usage of the CVA is the lack of a statutory moratorium (sometimes referred to as an "automatic stay") to prevent creditors from enforcing remedies, including enforcement of security, during the period when active efforts are in progress to conclude an arrangement. This is in marked contrast to the IVA where, as described in Chapter 4, a moratorium on enforcement is an integral aspect of the process which takes place under Part VIII of the Act.[83]

In October 1993 the Insolvency Service of the Department of Trade and Industry issued a Consultative Document entitled *Company Voluntary Arrangements and Administration Orders*, as part of a process of review of the working of the 1986 legislation. Chapter 2 of the consultative document

---

[80] See the statistical data collected in Appendix III, *post*.
[81] See n. 80, *supra*.
[82] See Ch. 14, *ante*.
[83] See ss.252, 254 and 260 of the Act, discussed, *ante*, at pp. 42–51. For comments on the operation of the CVA, and generally unfavourable contrasts with the far more successful IVA, see, *e.g.* S. Hill (1990) I.L. & P. 47; J. Gibson (1992) 5 *Insolvency Intelligence* 60; J.B. Bannister (1994) 10 *Insolvency Lawyer* 5–8.

discusses the barriers to the use of the CVA under existing legislative provisions, and identifies the absence of a protective moratorium as a key matter for consideration. While emphasising that there are significant arguments in the opposite direction—such as the possibility that directors might use the threat of resorting to the procedure, if clothed with a moratorium, as a means of applying pressure against creditors when renegotiating terms of repayment of debts; or the possibility for abusive use as a means of postponing an inevitable liquidation—the suggestion is made, in paragraph 2.5, that on balance it would be advantageous to introduce a moratorium operative upon filing in court by the directors of an intention to set up a CVA. This suggestion is accompanied by several important safeguards, however. These would include, in addition to the nominee's advance consent to act (thereby assuring an acceptable level of supervision and due diligence throughout), the imposing of a strict limitation upon the period of duration of the moratorium, and it would furthermore be possible for creditors to take action with the leave of the court, thus enabling individualised relief against stay to be obtained upon suitable proof of hardship or injustice. The proposal is also advanced that secured creditors should be bound by the moratorium while it is in force, and that the levying of distress against the company or its property during that same period should not be possible except with leave of the court.[84]

In a further Consultative Document issued in April 1995 bearing the title *Revised Proposals for a New Company Voluntary Arrangement Procedure*, the Insolvency Service formulated an additional type of CVA which would exist alongside the one available under Part I of the Act of 1986. There would be a minimum of preliminary formalities, and a 28-day moratorium would be obtainable for the company by the filing of notice in court of a proposal for a CVA, supported by a statement by the directors that they have supplied correct information to the prospective nominee, whose consent to act would also have to be lodged at the time of filing. The guiding principle of this procedure would be that only viable businesses, adequately financed, should be accorded access to this mode of rescue, and that meetings of creditors and shareholders should be convened within 28 days (subject to limited possibilities for extension up to a maximum of two months) to vote upon the proposal and determine its fate. Non-acceptance could be followed by a smooth transition into winding up, on the basis that the company would be deemed to be unable to pay its debts within the meaning of section 123 of the Act.

Given that the documents containing the above proposals are merely consultative, it is an open question how closely they will prove to resemble such definitive amendments of, or additions to, the CVA procedure as are eventually enacted into law. It is submitted, however, that the case for

---

[84] Consultative Document, *Company Voluntary Arrangements and Administration Orders* (October 1993), paras. 2.41, 2.66. The proposed model of an additional CVA, incorporating the special features described above, is summarised in Chap. 4 of the Consultative Document. This approach would result in the directors having the option of using the existing procedure under Pt. I of the Insolvency Act 1986, for example in cases where the nature of the business is such that the very act of announcing a moratorium would be commercially disastrous (*e.g.* a travel company).

inclusion of a moratorium, with appropriate safeguards and exceptions, is well made and ought to be implemented as soon as practicable. It may be said that, in any serious attempt to nurture a "rescue culture" to complement the insolvency procedures properly so-called, an available and affordable means of entry into a CVA, embodying the interim protection of such a moratorium, is a *sine qua non*.

CHAPTER 16

COMPANY ADMINISTRATION ORDERS

History

The administration order procedure made its first appearance in the law of company insolvency as Chapter III of Part II of the Insolvency Act 1985 (ss.27–44 inclusive), and was consolidated as Part II of the Insolvency Act 1986 (ss.8–27 inclusive). The new procedure should not be confused with the completely different one, known unfortunately by the same name, which has been in use for more than 100 years to enable county court judgment debtors to pay all or part of their debts by instalments.[1] The new administration order procedure introduced by the Insolvency Act 1985, and consolidated in the Insolvency Act 1986 (hereafter in this Chapter referred to as "the Insolvency Act", or simply as "the Act"), is applicable exclusively to companies and is the result of proposals made in Chapter 9 of the *Cork Report*.[2] These proposals formed a part of the overall strategy advocated by the Committee for the provision of a variety of effective alternatives to the winding up of an insolvent, or near-insolvent, company where there are reasonable prospects of reviving the company as a going concern. One of the Committee's suggestions was for the introduction of improved provisions to enable an insolvent company to effect a voluntary arrangement with its creditors.[3] A further, and more radical, suggestion was that a completely new procedure should be introduced whereby a creative reconstruction of a failing company could be undertaken with a view either to procuring the rehabilitation and survival of the company as a going concern or, failing that, to securing a better realisation of the company's assets than would result from the winding up of a "gone" concern.

The administration order procedure, though comparable to some extent with procedures available under foreign systems of insolvency law

---

[1] Originally introduced by s.122 of the Bankruptcy Act 1883, the County Court Administration Order procedure has latterly been regulated by provisions in Pt. VI of the County Courts Act 1984 (ss.112–117). This procedure is described in Chap. 4, *ante*.
[2] Cmnd. 8558 (1982).
[3] See Cmnd. 8558, Chap. 7, paras. 400–430. Insolvency Act 1986, Pt. I, discussed in Chap. 15, *ante*.

to effect the rehabilitation of a company under the protective shield of a moratorium against creditors,[4] is largely inspired by the example of what has sometimes been achieved under the developed law of floating-charge receivership in England and Wales. In appropriate cases it has proved possible for a receiver and manager of a company's entire undertaking,[5] making full and imaginative use of the extensive powers conferred formerly by a well-drawn floating charge debenture, and nowadays arising under Schedule 1 to the Insolvency Act, to initiate a corporate rescue operation and thereby leave the company in a better economic condition than that in which he found it, while at the same time safeguarding the interests of the secured creditor by whom he was appointed. The *Cork Report* advocated the creation of a rehabilitative procedure that would be generally available, rather than being dependent first on the existence of a floating charge, and secondly upon the taking of appropriate initiatives by the receiver appointed thereunder. The consequence of this process of evolution by analogy with receivership is that, as will be seen, the general powers conferred upon the administrator, when appointed, are identical to those enjoyed by an administrative receiver by virtue of Chapter I of Part III of the Insolvency Act.[6]

The proposals expressed in Chapter 9 of the *Cork Report* were accorded a generally favourable and positive response in Chapters 6 and 14 of the Government White Paper *A revised Framework for Insolvency Law*,[7] although a number of points of divergence began to emerge between the Committee's conception of the new procedure and that of the Government. These indications were subsequently confirmed in the original terms of the relevant clauses of the Insolvency Bill when first presented to Parliament, and to an even greater extent in the final version of Part II of the Insolvency Act itself. Very substantial changes were made to the provisions within what is now Part II during the course of its first

---

[4] Chap. 11 of the U.S. Bankruptcy Reform Act 1978 is referred to as one possible model for the administration order procedure. There are however numerous differences of detail and of substance between the two procedures. One obvious example is that, under the Chap. 11 procedure, the board of directors remains in control of the company throughout.

[5] Nowadays such a receiver and manager is known in England and Wales as an administrative receiver: Insolvency Act 1986, ss.29(2), 251. In Scotland an "administrative receiver" continues to be known as a "receiver" (see Part III, Chapter II of the Act), and is one appointed under a floating charge which comprises the whole (or substantially the whole) of the company's property (Insolvency Act, s.251). The statutory powers of a receiver in Scotland are capable of achieving the result indicated in these comments.

[6] See Insolvency Act 1986, ss.14, 15 (administrators); 42, 43 (administrative receivers). The provisions of Sched. 1 to the Act apply in common to administrators and administrative receivers: see p. 454, *infra*. Note that in certain important respects an administrator enjoys powers not available to an administrative receiver, such as the right to challenge undervalue transactions and preferences (ss. 238–241, *infra*, p. 641).

The statements in the text refer to the situation in England and Wales. In Scotland the powers of receiver which, in fact, provided the model for these provisions, are very similar (Insolvency Act, s.5 and Sched. 2). As with England and Wales, an administrator in Scotland, unlike a receiver, has explicit power to challenge gratuitous alienations and unfair preferences (ss.242, 243), and a number of further powers not enumerated in Sched. 1 which are not available to a receiver (*e.g.* to remove directors or call meetings of members or creditors, under the Insolvency Act, s.14(2)).

[7] Cmnd. 9175 (1984).

enactment by Parliament.[8] Some scepticism was also apparent as to the likelihood that any appreciable amount of use would be made of the new procedure in practice. These doubts as to the suitability and acceptability of the new procedure have to a large extent been borne out by experience, although it may be suggested that some of the reasons for this are different from those which were anticipated by the sceptics. The problems of under-utilisation of the administration order procedure are considered later in this chapter. It should be noted, however, that the provisions elsewhere in the Insolvency Act, relating to liability and accountability of directors of insolvent companies, furnish cogent reasons why the administration order procedure ought to be used by the directors of ailing companies in more cases, and at an earlier stage, than currently tends to be the practice.

Directors' Personal Liability and the Administration Procedure

The provisions alluded to in the previous paragraph are contained in Chapter X of Part IV of the Insolvency Act, and are concerned with directors' personal liability for wrongful trading, embodied in section 214 of the Act.[9] In order to avail himself of the statutory defence established by section 214(3), each director of a company which has gone into insolvent liquidation will be required to satisfy the court that, from the moment when he had actual or constructive knowledge that there was no reasonable prospect that the company would avoid going into insolvent liquidation, he took every reasonable and practicable step with a view to minimising the potential loss to the company's creditors as, under the circumstances, he ought to have taken. It would seem to accord with the overall spirit and purpose of the Insolvency Act that in this context directors should be required to show that, during the critical period prior to the commencement of liquidation, they actively considered the possibility of recourse to the administration order procedure as one of the ways of minimising the ultimate loss to creditors. Thus, depending upon the extent to which courts are seen to lay emphasis upon the use of the pre-liquidation procedure as a factor which may help to save the individual directors from incurring personal liability for the company's debts, the practical importance of the administration order procedure could in time prove to be considerable. Similar considerations could, it is suggested, be employed by the courts in relation to the exercise of powers to disqualify unfit directors under the Company Directors Disqualification Act 1986, discussed in Chapter 27.

When may an Administration Order be made?

Section 8(1) of the Insolvency Act lays down two main conditions which

---

[8] The provisions were contained in Chap. II of Pt. II of the Insolvency Bill as first published on December 10, 1984, and then comprised clauses 15–33.
[9] Insolvency Act 1986, s.214, discussed in Chap. 27, *post*.

must be satisfied in order that the court may exercise the power to make an administration order in relation to a company.

(i) Company's inability to pay its debts

The first condition, imposed by section 8(1)(a), is that the court must be satisfied that the company is, or is likely to become, unable to pay its debts. For this purpose, the subsection incorporates by reference the definition of inability to pay debts contained in section 123 of the Act. Thus, any of the five alternative grounds described in section 123(1) of the Act together with the sixth ground added as section 123(2),[10] may furnish a basis upon which the court can find that the company is unable to pay its debts. These grounds include the demonstration that an attempt to enforce a judgment debt against the company by means of execution or similar process has been wholly or partially unsuccessful,[11] or the adducing of any other evidence which persuades the court that the company is unable to pay its debts.[12] However, by far the most convenient means of establishing a company's inability to pay its debts is that provided for in section 123(1)(a) of the Act, namely a creditor's service upon the company of a statutory demand for payment of a debt for a sum in excess of £750, which sum the company fails to pay or compound for within the period of three weeks from the date of service.[13] Although the statutory demand has traditionally been employed for the purpose of preparing the ground for presentation of a creditor's petition for a compulsory winding up, it will henceforth have an alternative function in relation to an application for an administration order. It should be observed that by virtue of section 10(1) of the Insolvency Act the presentation of a petition for an administration order has the effect of precluding both the making of an order for winding up of the company by the court, and the passing of a resolution for winding up. Thus the possibility arises that, when a company has failed to satisfy a statutory demand within the time permitted, the creditor by whom the demand was originally served may encounter an interruption of his expected progress towards the obtaining of an order for winding up, by reason of the presentation of a petition for an administration order by any party qualified to take this step.[14] As will be seen, however, directors of a company would not be well advised to present such a petition merely as a device for postponing winding up since the appointment of an administrator divests the directors of their powers of management, although it does not absolve them from all responsibility for the manner in which the company's affairs either have been or are henceforth conducted.[15]

---

[10] Formerly s.518 of the Companies Act, as amended and subs. (1A) added thereto, by Insolvency Act 1985, Sched. 6, para. 27. See Chap. 20, *post*.
[11] Insolvency Act 1986, s.123(1)(b). See also paras. (c) and (d) of the same subsection.
[12] Insolvency Act 1986, s.123(1)(e).
[13] See further Chap. 20, *post*.
[14] See Insolvency Act 1986, s.9(1), discussed, *infra*, p. 430.
[15] See Insolvency Act 1986, ss.14 and 17, discussed, *infra*, p. 454 *et seq.*.

Finally, the additional ground now contained in section 123(2) of the Act provides that a company is deemed to be unable to pay its debts where there is shown to be a balance sheet deficiency, taking into account the company's contingent and prospective liabilities.[16] This means that a petition for an administration order can be presented where, despite the fact that the company may have sufficient funds presently available to meet debts as they fall due, the contingent and prospective liabilities are such that the company's assets will in due course be exhausted leaving some creditors unpaid. It is in such circumstances that timely recourse to the administration order procedure should offer a particularly suitable means of retrieving the enterprise while this is still technically possible.

(ii) Likelihood of attainment of an authorised purpose

The second condition, imposed by section 8(1)(b) of the Insolvency Act, is that the court must consider that the making of an administration order would be likely to achieve one or more of the purposes mentioned in subsection (3). That subsection lists the following four purposes:

(1) The survival of the company, and the whole or any part of its undertaking, as a going concern;
(2) The approval of a voluntary arrangement under Part I of the Insolvency Act;
(3) The sanctioning under section 425 of the Companies Act 1985 of a compromise or arrangement between the company and any such persons as are mentioned in that section[17]; and
(4) A more advantageous realisation of the company's assets than would be realised on a winding up.

The foregoing list of authorised purposes for which an administration order may be made is an exhaustive one. Other possible purposes were suggested in the *Cork Report* as providing a suitable basis for use of the administration order procedure. These included: the reorganisation of the company with a view to restoring profitability or maintaining employment; the carrying on of a business in the public interest where the current management is unable to continue to function; and the undertaking of a feasibility study to explore the prospects for restoring the company to eventual profitability.[18] None of these purposes was expressly included in section 8(3) as finally enacted, although it may well be that some of them are effectively subsumed, to a certain extent, under its terms. What is clear, however, is that none of the unenacted expressions of purpose is capable, standing on its own, of furnishing a valid basis for the

---

[16] See n. 10, *above*.
[17] The persons mentioned in s.425 of the Companies Act 1985 as potential parties to a compromise or arrangement under that section are: the creditors of the company, or any class of them; and the members of the company, or any class of them.
[18] Cmnd. 8558, para. 498. *cf.* the White Paper, Cmnd. 9175, para. 150.

making of an administration order: it will need to be presented to the court as part of the incidental aspects of a proposal framed with reference to the actual terms in which section 8(3) is drafted.

The drafting of section 8(1)(b) is such that the very jurisdiction of the court to make an administration order hinges upon the court's own assessment of whether the order would be "likely to achieve" one or more of the purposes specified in subsection (3), as set out above. In practice, therefore, the judicial approach to the formulation of a test of "likelihood" is of crucial importance, since too exacting a standard would create a barrier to entry into administration which would render the entire procedure a dead letter, or virtually so. Initially, there was evidence of a divergence of approach as between different judges of the Chancery Division, sitting singly at first instance. Some of their Lordships inclined towards a particularly exacting requirement that it be established that attainment of an authorised purpose was "more likely than not" to occur.[19] On this approach, it would not suffice merely to show that there was a *possibility* that the purpose would be achieved; what was needed was demonstration of a strong *probability*. The view which in due course came to prevail however was that expressed by Hoffmann, J. in *Re Harris Simons Construction Ltd*,[20] in which he stated:

> "For my part ... I would hold that the requirements of s.8(1)(b) are satisfied if the court considers there is a real prospect that one or more of the stated purposes may be achieved."

This more liberal approach was endorsed by Vinelott, J. in *Re Primlaks (U.K.) Ltd*[21] with the salutary observation that the use of too strict a test would "stultify the Act and serve no useful purpose."

Later pronouncements by other judges of the Chancery Division indicate a broad consensus that the "real prospect" formulation of the test has become accepted.[22] There remains, however, the simple fact of human nature that some individuals—including members of Her Majesty's judiciary—may be less easily persuaded as to the existence of a "real prospect" of attainment of the purpose in question, given the unique circumstances of every case and the strength and substance of the evidence presented in court. This has been a powerful factor militating in favour of the allocation of substantial (and costly) resources to the pre-hearing preparation of administration order applications, in the hope of thereby rendering them "judge-proof". These problems are further discussed below.[23]

---

[19] See *e.g.*, *Re Consumer and Industrial Press Ltd* [1988] BCLC 177; (1988) 4 BCC 68 (Peter Gibson, J.); *Re Manlon Trading Ltd* (1988) 4 BCC 455 (Harman, J.).
[20] [1989] BCLC 202; [1989] 1 W.L.R. 368.
[21] [1989] BCLC 734; (1989) 5 BCC 710.
[22] See, *e.g.*, *Re S.C.L. Building Services Ltd* [1990] BCLC 98; (1989) 5 BCC 746 (Peter Gibson, J.); *Re Rowbotham Baxter Ltd* [1990] BCLC 397; [1990] BCC 113 (Harman, J.); *Re Land and Property Trust Co. plc* [1991] BCC 446 (Harman, J.).
[23] See *infra*. p. 432 (*Procedure on Application*) and p. 478 (*Review and Reform*).

When May an Administration Order be Made?

In deciding whether to appoint an administrator on the petition of a company's directors, the views of opposing creditors who also happen to be shareholders are likely to be disregarded, in so far as their objections are seen to be linked to their aspirations pursued in the latter capacity. Since the company is at or close to a state of insolvency, the members lack sufficient interest to be heard in that capacity and must therefore pursue their proposals, *e.g.* as to the refinancing of the company, with the administrator after his appointment.[24]

The administrator's subsequent proposals must match the purposes which are actually expressed in his order of appointment: proposals which fall outside the terms of the administrator's remit cannot be validly implemented unless the court first effects a variation of the terms of appointment.[25] An administrator would not be well advised to pursue purposes other than those for which the order has been made, lest he incur the accusation that time and money have been expended in an *ultra vires* manner, with possible consequences from the aspect of his obtaining his release, and recovery of his fee and expenses.[26] If the court decides to make an administration order, section 8(3) requires that the order must specify the purpose or purposes for which it is made. The drafting of the subsection imposes a clear requirement that the purpose or purposes to be specified must be selected from the list contained in section 8(3) itself. However, the drafting of the counterpart provision in the 1985 Insolvency Act (s.27(1) and (3)) was somewhat loose, and appeared to leave the court with more freedom of action. Undoubtedly, the drafting employed in the consolidation of this provision as s.8(1) and (3) of the Act of 1986 is effective to exclude such possibilities, but in doing so it arguably transgresses the accepted conventions with regard to the effects of consolidating legislation. On the premiss that the Insolvency Act 1986, as a consolidating measure, was not intended to alter the substance of the law, a possible argument might be advanced that, provided the court is satisfied that the making of an administration order would be likely to achieve one or more of the purposes which are mentioned in subsection (3), it is thereupon empowered to make an administration order in which additional purposes are specified beyond those contained in the subsection itself. This suggested construction, based upon a reference to the terms of the former section 27(1) of the Insolvency Act 1985, involves the resurrection of the original terms of repealed legislation, and it is perhaps unlikely to commend itself to a court unless no other practical means is available to accomplish some objective with which the court is otherwise completely in sympathy. An alternative approach, seemingly keeping within the parameters of the enacted law, may be offered by section 18(1), under which the administrator may at any time apply to the court for the administration order to be varied so as to specify an additional purpose. Since the terms of section 18(1) are open and unqualified—and in particular do not include any cross-reference to section 8(3) and the

---

[24] *Re Chelmsford City Football Club (1980) Ltd* [1991] BCC 133.
[25] *Re St. Ives Windings* [1987] 3 BCC 634. See also *Re Sheridan Securities Ltd* [1988] 4 BCC 200.
[26] *Re Sheridan Securities Ltd* (above).

purposes therein listed—this seems to leave open the possibility for the court to adopt an innovative response to the administrator's precisely formulated requirements.

The Exercise of the Court's Power is Discretionary

If both conditions specified in paragraphs (a) and (b) of section 8(1) are met, the court enjoys the power to make an administration order. The language of subsection (1) in this respect is permissive, not mandatory, and hence it is left as a matter for the court in the exercise of its discretion to decide whether to make an administration order. Accordingly the court may take into account any factors which are capable of off-setting the advantages expected to accrue if the administration order succeeds in achieving the purposes which would serve as the basis for making it. Here, in principle, the parties whose interest ought to receive the closest consideration are those who would still receive something under a distribution of the company's assets if a liquidation were immediately to take place. In most cases such persons might well derive some advantage from the achievement of the purposes instanced in the administration order, but it is equally possible that they may consider that such advantage would be marginal at best, and may not outweigh the disadvantage of being kept out of their money for the further period while the administration is carried through.

Where a petition is presented by a creditor who already holds adequate real and collateral securities to enable him to recover payment without recourse to insolvency proceedings, the court may have regard to the interests of the management of the company, especially where the company's balance sheet shows a surplus, even if it is the case that there is no money presently available to pay the petitioner's debt.[27]

When may an Administration Order not be Made?

The provisions of section 8(1) regarding the circumstances in which the court may exercise the power to make an administration order are in all cases subject to the overriding force of section 8(4), which precludes the making of an administration order in relation to a company in two cases. These are:

(1) After the company has gone into liquidation; and
(2) Where the company is an insurance company within the meaning of the Insurance Companies Act 1982;

While case 2 has the effect of excluding a certain category of company

---

[27] *Re Imperial Motors (U.K.) Ltd* [1990] BCLC 29.

from the administration order procedure for the time being,[28] case 1 is of general application. In this context the key concept of the time at which a company goes into liquidation is defined in section 247(2) of the Insolvency Act and means the date on which the company passes a resolution for voluntary winding up or alternatively, the date on which an order for its winding up is made by the court at a time when it has not already gone into liquidation by passing such a resolution.

A further case in which an administration order may not be made is supplied by section 9(3) of the Insolvency Act. By this provision the court is required to dismiss a petition for an administration order upon being satisfied that there is an administrative receiver[29] of the company, unless the court is also satisfied either that the person by whom or on whose behalf the receiver was appointed has consented to the making of the order, or that if an administration order were made, any security by virtue of which the receiver was appointed would be liable to be released or discharged or avoided under sections 238–241 or 245 of the Insolvency Act, or would be challengeable under sections 242 or 243,[30] or under any rule of law in Scotland. Sections 238–241 of the Insolvency Act make provision for the avoidance of transactions at an under value entered into, and preferences given by, a company within the period of up to two years before the onset of insolvency, which here denotes the date of presentation of the petition on which an administration order is made.[31] Section 242 makes provision for the reduction of a gratuitous alienation made by the company in favour of any person within two years of the making of the administration order, or within five years if in favour of an "associate."[32] Section 243 makes provision for the reduction of preferences created within six months of the making of an administration order. Both sections apply, whether the transaction challenged took place before April 1, 1986 (when the original provisions which are now these sections came into force) or later, but can only be invoked by the administrator (or liquidator) (Insolvency Act 1986, ss.242(1)(b) and 243(4)(b)).

Common law grounds of challenge are preserved by the Insolvency Act, ss.242(7) and 243(8). In general, they apply to administration procedure as to liquidation and are discussed in Chapter 26, *post*. Section 245 of the

---

[28] There is a possibility that the administration order procedure, or a closely analogous procedure, may be made available for insurance companies in due course following a full review of all the implications of such a development: *cf.* Cmd. 9175, para. 35. The former exclusion of administration order proceedings from applying to banks and to authorised institutions under the Banking Act 1987 was ended with effect from August 23, 1989 by the Banks (Administration Proceedings) Order 1989, S.I. No. 1276. Pt. II of the Insolvency Act now applies to banks, with the modifications contained in the Order.

[29] This term is defined in s.29(2) of the Insolvency Act 1986.

[30] ss.242 and 243 provide for the challenge of gratuitous alienations and unfair preferences in Scotland. They were originally added to the Companies Act 1985 as ss.615A and 615B by the Bankruptcy (Scotland) Act 1985, Sched. 7, para. 20. ss.238–241 of the Insolvency Act 1986 do not apply in Scotland, but s.245 does.

[31] Insolvency Act 1986, s.240(3)(a). See further, *infra*.

[32] The Insolvency Act, s.242(3)(a) requires this term to be defined by reference to the Bankruptcy (Scotland) Act 1985, s.74, as applied to companies by the Bankruptcy (Scotland) Regulations 1985, and not the Insolvency Act, s.435, but the two provisions are to the same effect. For the meaning of "associate," see Appendix I, *post*.

Insolvency Act is the provision under which a floating charge created by a company within a period of up to two years before the presentation of the petition for an administration order may be rendered invalid under certain circumstances.[33] The overall effect of the provisions in section 9(3) is therefore to furnish safeguards for the legitimate expectations of a secured creditor who has taken a valid floating charge over the whole of the company's property. If such a creditor, in the exercise of the rights conferred on him by the terms of the debenture (or in Scotland under the Insolvency Act, ss.51 or 54), has already appointed a receiver before the court hears the application for an administration order to be made, the court may not entertain the application unless the debentureholder has positively consented to the making of an order whose effect will be to oust the receiver.[34] However, where the status of the debenture holder as a secured creditor is capable of being impugned, section 9(3)(b) appropriately ensures that he is not enabled to forestall the making of the very order under which, in due course, steps may be taken to invalidate his security.

The specially protected position enjoyed by a debenture holder under the provisions of section 9(3) is not accorded to other types of creditor, whether secured or unsecured. Nor does the subsection confer any power to veto upon a debenture or charge holder who, although entitled to appoint an administrative receiver, has not yet actually done so by the time that the application for an administration order is heard by the court. However by section 9(2) where a petition for an administration order is presented to the court, notice of the petition must be given forthwith to any person who has appointed, or who is or may be entitled to appoint, an administrative receiver of the company. Rules 2.6(2)(a) and 2.7(1) together impose the requirement that such a creditor must be given five clear days' notice before the date fixed for the hearing of an application for the appointment of an administrator. It has been held that the court nevertheless enjoys an unrestricted power by virtue of r. 12.9 to abridge this period of notice where the affairs of the company are parlous, provided that the person entitled to appoint an administrative receiver is aware of the petition so as to have an opportunity to consider whether to exercise his

---

[33] Insolvency Act 1986, s.245(3), (5)(a). See further p. 648, *infra*.

[34] See Insolvency Act 1986, s.9(3)(a), where the words "has consented" are significant. *Semble* it would not be enough for the petitioner to show merely that the debenture holder has not expressed *dissent* to the making of the order. The consent of the chargeholder may be given in writing to the court. This interpretation does not appear to be valid in Scotland. Neither the Insolvency (Scotland) Rules 1986 nor the Act of Sederunt (Rules of Court Amendment No. 11) (Companies) Rules 1986 (Court of Session); nor the Act of Sederunt (Sheriff Court Company Insolvency Rules) 1986 require such consent to be demonstrated before such a petition is presented, or indeed before it is granted. They merely provide for the petition to be intimated to any person who has appointed or may be entitled to appoint an administrative receiver, or to such a receiver. The ouster of a receiver following the making of an administration order occurs by virtue of a s.11(1)(b) of the Act.

power before it is extinguished.[35] This requirement enables those with floating charges capable of leading to the appointment of an administrative receiver to be heard or represented at the hearing of the petition, when they may present arguments aimed at persuading the court as to the appropriate way in which to exercise its discretionary powers. One possibility is that the court may decide to refrain from making an administration order, subject to an undertaking by the charge holder to proceed to appoint an administrative receiver without further delay. It must be emphasised however that the charge holder who has not yet appointed a receiver enjoys no statutory right to prevent the making of an administration order. Accordingly, in many cases there may be strong arguments in favour of the charge holder taking appropriate steps to consolidate his legal position in advance of the hearing by appointing an administrative receiver following service upon him of notice of the presentation of a petition for an administration order.

In view of the restraints imposed upon all types of secured creditor (including one whose security is in the form of a floating charge) to impede their ability to realise their security during the period the administration order is in force, and likewise in view of the rights of the administrator to dispose of secured property free from encumbrance (to be discussed below), the incentives for exercising the right to appoint an administrative receiver are substantial and, in many cases, prove irresistible. It is a matter for calculation on the part of the secured creditor, however, whether the long term prospects of corporate recovery (and hence, the survival of a business client or customer) are such as to outweigh the more immediate advantages of asserting control over the process of recouping such value as can be extracted from recourse to receivership. In the case of institutional lenders—such as banks—there may be also a wider concern to demonstrate to other current and potential borrowers, and to the community at large, that the lender is sympathetic to the plight of cash-squeezed debtors and is prepared to allow rescue attempts *via* administration to be embarked upon, in suitable cases.

The special position occupied by a floating charge holder under the statutory provisions governing administration orders can thus be seen to give rise to valuable options with regard to the course of action to be followed. The strategic importance, in commercial terms, of these options has given fresh enhancement to the established arguments in favour of taking this form of security, either on its own or (preferably) in combination with some kind of fixed security. The decision of Vinelott, J. in *Re Croftbell*[36] has supplied judicial confirmation that the so-called "lightweight" floating charge confers all these privileges in full measure, including the power to block the appointment of an administrator, despite the fact that, at the time the charge was created, there were negligible

---

[35] *Re A Company (No. 00175 of 1987)* [1987] BCLC 467. For other examples of "short notice" orders, see: *Re Cavco Floors Ltd* [1990] BCC 589; [1990] BCLC 940; *Re Shearing and Loader Ltd* [1991] BCC 232; [1991] BCLC 764; *Re Chancery plc* [1991] BCLC 171; [1991] BCLC 712; *Re Gallidoro Trawlers Ltd* [1991] BCC 691; [1991] BCLC 411, cf. *Re Rowbotham Baxter Ltd* [1990] BCLC 397; [1990] BCC 113.

[36] [1990] BCC 781. See *Oditah* [1991] J.B.L. 49.

assets, or even none at all, which could have been subject to it (as where all items of value were already the subject of prior incumbrances).

One further demonstration of the role of the court's discretion in the development of this novel jurisdiction concerns the issue of the suitability of administration to be used in certain, typical sets of circumstances. For example, where there has been a breakdown of trust and confidence among those managing the company, so that corporate affairs are deadlocked, it has been held that the court would not normally appoint an administrator, but would regard a winding up as the appropriate course to adopt.[37] This may be questioned, however, in a case where an otherwise viable and profitable company stands in peril of being destroyed through personality clashes within the boardroom. The insertion of an outside figure, in the person of an administrator, with power to remove all or any of the incumbent directors, could be an effective means of severing the Gordian knot of discord without having recourse to the ultimate step of liquidation.

Who may Apply for an Administration Order?

Section 9(1) of the Insolvency Act lists the persons who are eligible to present a petition for an administration order. These are: the company itself or the directors; or a creditor or creditors (including any contingent or prospective creditor or creditors); or all or any of those parties acting together or separately.

It is significant that the Act requires the directors to act collectively in presenting a petition for an administration order. The use in section 9(1) of the expression "the directors," and the omission of any alternative reference to "director" in the singular form, has the effect of denying to an individual director, or indeed to a group of directors forming a minority on the board, the standing to present a petition for an administration order.[38] On the other hand, where a decision to seek administration for the company is duly passed by a majority of those board members who are present, any dissenting or absent members become bound by the resolution and a petition can properly be presented in the name of "the directors."[39] Moreover, any director or directors who happen also to be creditors of the company could properly present a petition in the latter capacity.

Where the board of directors acts collectively (including where the directors act on the basis of a majority of their number in accordance with the company's own articles) there is no requirement within the Insolvency Act that the directors must obtain the prior endorsement of a general meeting of the members before they may validly present a petition. On the other hand, the separate reference in section 9(1) to "the company" itself as an eligible petitioner indicates that it is open to the members, acting at a general meeting, to resolve that the company shall apply for an

---

[37] *Re Business Properties Ltd* (1988) 4 BCC 684.
[38] *cf. Re Instrumentation Electrical Services Ltd* (1988) 4 BCC 301 (decided under s.124 of the Act).
[39] *Re Equiticorp International Ltd* [1989] 1 W.L.R. 1010, (1989) 5 BCC 599.

administration order. Where such a resolution is carried and put into effect in the face of opposition by the board of directors, it is unclear whether the directors can be heard or represented before the court in order to oppose the making of an order.[40] However, directors who show themselves to be firmly opposed to the company's application for an administration order should be mindful of the personal consequences for themselves under section 214 of the Insolvency Act and under the provisions of sections 6 and 7 of the Company Directors Disqualification Act 1986 in the event that the company subsequently goes into insolvent liquidation.[41] Conversely, the fact that any director is on record as having advocated the use of the administration order procedure could be instrumental in ensuring a favourable outcome of any subsequent proceedings concerning his possible disqualification from company management, or the imposition upon him of responsibility for wrongful trading.

In relation to a creditor's petition it is noteworthy that no figure has been included in the statutory provisions to impose a minimum sum of indebtedness which must be owed by the company to the petitioning creditor as a precondition to his being able to apply for an administration order. However, in the majority of cases a petitioning creditor will encounter the practical difficulty of obtaining sufficiently conclusive evidence of the company's inability to pay its debts. By far the most convenient means by which a creditor may establish the company's inability to pay its debts, and may thus satisfy the requirements of section 8(1)(a), is by the use of a statutory demand for payment in accordance with section 123(1)(a) of the Act.[42] In that event, it will be necessary for the company to owe the creditor a sum exceeding £750 which is currently due.

It has been held that an English court has jurisdiction to make an administration order in respect of a company incorporated under the laws of a foreign country, where the matter arises in the context of a request for judicial assistance made by a court exercising jurisdiction in relation to insolvency law in a "relevant country or territory," within the meaning of section 426(11) of the Act. The provisions of section 426(5) empower the English court in such cases "to apply, in relation to any matters specified in the request, the insolvency law which is applicable by *either court* in relation to comparable matters falling within its jurisdiction (emphasis added). Upon the demonstration of the fact that the company in question met the conditions in section 8(1)(a) and (b), the court, being satisfied that an

---

[40] The Rules make no express provision for the directors to be heard, although conversely the company itself may be heard or represented at the hearing of a creditor's or directors' petition: Insolvency Rules 1986, r. 2.9(1)(b). Under para. (g) of r. 2.9(1), with the leave of the court "any other person who appears to have an interest justifying his appearance" may be heard.
[41] With regard to s.214 of the Insolvency Act and ss.6 and 7 of the Company Directors Disqualification Act 1986, see Chap. 27, *post*.
[42] s.123 of the Insolvency Act 1986 is made applicable for the purpose of s.8 of the Insolvency Act by virtue of s.8(1)(a).

Company Administration Orders

administration order was the most appropriate form of assistance in the circumstances of the case, exercised its discretion to that effect.[43]

Procedure on Application for an Administration Order

Court to which petition should be presented

Section 9(1) of the Insolvency Act states that an application for an administration order shall be by petition presented to the court. The Insolvency Act contains no further elucidation of the meaning of the term "court" in this context, but by virtue of section 251 any expression within Parts I–VII of the Insolvency Act for whose interpretation no provision is made therein is to be construed in accordance with any provision for its interpretation which is made in Part XXVI of the Companies Act 1985. In section 744 of the Companies Act, "court" is defined as "the court having jurisdiction to wind up the company." Accordingly a petition for an administration order may be presented to any court which, in the circumstances, has such jurisdiction.[44]

Steps to be taken on presentation of a petition

The statutory provisions relating to the presentation of a petition for an administration order are limited to those contained in section 9(2) of the Insolvency Act. Paragraph (a) of that subsection imposes the requirement that where such a petition is presented to the court, notice thereof shall be given forthwith to any person who has appointed, or is or may be entitled to appoint, an administrative receiver of the company and to such other persons as may be prescribed in the Rules. The special care which has been taken to protect the position of the floating charge holder in relation to the administration order procedure has already been referred to, and will be further considered in due course.[45] There is no statutory requirement that notice be given to any creditor who has a fixed charge over specific assets. Other provisions with regard to the parties to whom notice of the petition should be given, together with all other procedural requirements relating to the presentation of the petition, are accordingly contained in the Rules relating to the administration order procedure.[46] In general, these follow the analogous rules for winding up,[47] but with the following additions or modifications.

(1) In order for the court to be in a position to decide whether the company is, or is likely to become, unable to pay its debts and

---

[43] *Re Dallhold Estates (U.K.) Pty Ltd* [1992] BCC 394. See also. *Re International Bulk Commodities Ltd* [1993] Ch. 77, and *Re Devon and Somerset Farmers Ltd* [1993] BCC 410, for contrasting approaches to the interpretation of the term "company" for the purposes of ss.29(2) and 40 of the Act, respectively. (See the discussion of these cases in Chap.14, *ante*, p. 361.)
[44] See Chap. 21, *post*.
[45] See p. 427, *above*, and pp. 437 and 438, *infra*.
[46] Rules 2.1–2.8, especially r. 2.6.
[47] *cf.* Chaps. 20–22, *post*.

Procedures on Application for an Administration Order

that the making of the order would be likely to achieve one or more of the purposes mentioned in section 8(3) of the Insolvency Act, the petitioner is responsible for ensuring that an affidavit, containing appropriate statements by the deponent in support of the making of the order, is sworn and filed in court in support of the petition.[48] The affidavit must provide a statement about the financial position of the company, details of any security known or believed to be held by any company creditors, and also, if it is the case that an administrative receiver has been appointed or any petition for the winding up of the company has been presented, statements of these relevant facts. There is further provision, in Rule 2.2 of the Insolvency Rules, for the preparation of a report by an independent person to the effect that the appointment of an administrator for the company is expedient. The report may be by the person proposed as administrator (and, in practice, this has proved to be the most convenient and efficient approach), or it may be by any other person having adequate knowledge of the company's affairs, other than a director, secretary, manager, member or employee of the company, all of whom are expressly made ineligible to perform this task. The report, which must be exhibited to the affidavit in support of the petition, must specify which of the purposes within section 8(3) may, in the opinion of the person preparing it, be achieved for the company by the making of an administration order.

The preparation of a so-called "Rule 2.2. report" is clearly intended to be an optional matter, as is shown by the use of the permissive word "may" in each of the three paragraphs of the Rule itself. However, this is somewhat offset by the provision in rule 2.3(6) that, if no report under rule 2.2 has been prepared for the company, the affidavit must provide an explanation why not. Thus, from the very earliest days of the operation of the administration order procedure, the courts evolved a practice of openly attaching much weight and importance to the Rule 2.2 Report, to the extent that it came to be regarded as a *sine qua non* of a successful application.[49] The response to these judicial signals was unfortunate, if predictable, namely a proliferation of costly preparations in advance of the hearing of the petition, essentially aimed at ensuring that the supporting documentation rendered the application "judge-proof." The cumulative effect of this development, as noted in the Consultative Document issued by the Insolvency Service in 1993,[50] was to erect a significant "barrier to entry," effectively

---

[48] Rules 2.1, 2.3.
[49] See, *e.g. Re Newport County Association Football Club Ltd* [1987] BCC 635, at 635 per Harman, J.; *cf. Re W.F. Fearman Ltd* (1988) 4 BCC 139, and also *Re Manlon Trading Ltd* (1988) 4 BCC 455; *Re Sharps of Truro Ltd* [1990] BCC 94.
[50] *Company Voluntary Arrangements and Administration Orders* (October, 1993). See esp. paras. 5.2–5.3.

precluding access to the procedure in many cases on account of the high front-end costs.

A timely (and, it is to be hoped, effective) correction to the tendencies towards excess of zeal in the compilation of Rule 2.2 reports was forthcoming in the form of a *Practice Note* issued on behalf of the judges of the Chancery Division by Nicholls, V.-C. on January 17, 1994.[51] While acknowledging the value of such reports as a safeguard in assisting the court to see whether the application has a sound basis, it is emphasised that the contents of reports are sometimes unnecessarily elaborate and detailed, and that the preliminary investigation will often have been unduly protracted and extensive and, hence, expensive. In the normal case, it is suggested, what the court needs is a concise assessment of the company's situation and of the prospects of an administration order achieving one or more of the statutory purposes. There is a firm admonition that "Every endeavour should be made to avoid disproportionate investigation and expense," and the further suggestion that, where the proposed administrator is in court, oral evidence, followed if necessary by a supplemental report, can be resorted to as a means of providing the court with any additional information which proves to be necessary for the purpose of arriving at its decision. Finally, practitioners are reminded that in straightforward cases it may not be necessary to prepare a report at all, because it would provide little assistance, and that such an approach is within the letter and spirit of the Insolvency Rules.

(2) The petition must include the name or names and addresses of a nominated administrator or administrators, each of whom must be a person qualified to act as an insolvency practitioner in relation to the company.[52] Each nominated administrator should furnish a letter indicating willingness to act, together with an indication of the basis upon which he will charge his remuneration.[53]

(3) The petitioner must also take necessary steps to verify the personal service of the petition upon all known creditors who have appointed or who are or may be entitled to appoint an administrative receiver, on the administrative receiver (if appointed), and on any person who has presented a winding up petition, and also upon the person proposed as administrator.[54]

(4) In addition, when the petition is presented by a creditor the petition must be served upon the company itself.[55] Where the petition is served upon the company or upon any creditor in accordance with the foregoing requirements, it must be

---

[51] [1994] 1 All E.R. 324.
[52] Insolvency Act 1986, ss.388, 389.
[53] r. 2.4(6)(b).
[54] r. 2.6(2)(a) (as amended), together with r. 2.8; Form 2.3.
[55] r. 2.6(3).

accompanied by the supporting documents and the report on the company which has been prepared as previously described.[56]

Unlike a winding up petition, there is no advertisement of a petition for an administration order, but a prescribed deposit is payable by the petitioner, just as in the case of a petition for a winding up order. By section 9(2)(b) of the Insolvency Act, where a petition has been presented to the court it cannot be withdrawn except with the leave of the court. This provision enables the court to deal in an appropriate manner with any petitions which prove to be vexatious or frivolous, and is of particular relevance in cases where directors may be tempted to resort to the presentation of a petition with the intention of withdrawing it before the application is heard.[57] This might take place in an attempt to forestall action by creditors, including steps aimed at putting the company into liquidation, but the court could well respond to this tactic by imposing exacting conditions before giving leave for the petition to be withdrawn.

The very fact that applications for an administration order can be made *ex parte* gives rise to a forceful requirement that those who are responsible for presenting a petition in such circumstances should scrupulously observe the duty of candour owed to the court, and fully disclose all facts relevant to the exercise of the court's discretion to appoint an administrator, even though such revelations may prove embarrassing to the applicant or be detrimental to his case. Where material non-disclosure is found to have occurred, this can be an important factor in any subsequent application to the court to rescind the administration order, and may induce the court to direct the administrators to apply for their discharge.[58]

Effect of an Application for an Administration Order

The presentation of a petition for an administration order marks the commencement of a statutory moratorium over the company's affairs. Under the terms of section 10(1) of the Insolvency Act the initial phase of the moratorium ends when the court, having heard the application, either makes the order sought or dismisses the petition. In the latter event the moratorium comes to an end, but if the court makes an administration order section 11 of the Insolvency Act has the effect of extending the moratorium for the duration of the period for which the order is in force.

The following are the effects of the moratorium during the first phase, from the presentation of the petition until the conclusion of the hearing before the court.

---

[56] rr. 2.6(1); 2.7(2)(a).
[57] *cf. Re West Tech Ltd* [1989] BCLC 600 (where the director's petition for an administration order was suspected of being an attempt to "buy time" in the face of a winding up petition).
[58] *Astor Chemical Ltd v. Synthetic Technology Ltd* [1990] BCC 97, 107 *per* Vinelott, J. approved in *Cornhill Insurance plc v. Cornhill Financial Services Ltd*: [1992] BCC 818, 856 (C.A.). See also *Re Rowbotham Baxter Ltd* [1990] BCC 133, 114 *per* Harman, J., and *Re Sharps of Truro Ltd* [1990] BCC 94.

Company Administration Orders

(1) No resolution may be passed, or order made, for the winding up of the company. This does not however preclude the presentation of a petition for the winding up of the company, although the winding up petition will not be disposed of unless and until the petition for an administration order is dismissed, or any such order eventually discharged.[59] Advertisement of any winding up petition may also be restrained by the court, lest the adverse publicity should so harm the company as to defeat the purpose of the administration petition before the latter can be heard and disposed of.[60]

(2) No steps may be taken to enforce any charge on or security over the company's property, or to repossess goods in the company's possession under any hire purchase agreement, conditional sale agreement, chattel leasing agreement or retention of title agreement, except with the leave of the court and subject to such terms as the court may impose.[61]

(3) No other proceedings, and no execution or other legal process, may be commenced or continued, and no distress may be levied, against the company or its property except with the leave of the court and subject to such terms as the court may impose.[62] The reference to "other proceedings" has been construed strictly by the courts, and in a way which is *eiusdem generis* with the provisions of paragraphs (a) and (b) of section 10(1) of the Act. Under this approach the statutory moratorium will not apply to "proceedings" which are not similar to those which bring about the winding up of a company, the appointment of an administrative receiver, or the enforcement of a security.[63] In Scotland, diligence cannot be carried out or continued without leave of the court and subject to such conditions as the court may impose (Insolvency Act, s.10(5)).

Any creditor who applies to the court for leave to do anything which would constitute an exception to the moratorium whose effects are described above must serve prior notice of the application upon the company and the petitioner. However, section 10(2)(b) and (c) expressly excludes two important matters from the need to obtain leave of the court.

---

[59] Insolvency Act 1986, s.10(1)(a), (2)(a).
[60] *Re A Company (No. 001992 of 1988)* [1989] BCLC 9.
[61] *Ibid.* s.10(1)(b), (4). For the definitions of "hire purchase agreement" and "conditional sale agreement" see Consumer Credit Act 1974, s.189(1). For the definitions of "chattel leasing agreement" and "retention of title agreement" see Insolvency Act 1986, s.251. For the modified form in which the terms of ss.10(1) and 11(3) apply to Scotland, see s.10(5).
[62] Insolvency Act 1986, s.10(1)(c).
[63] *cf. Air Ecosse Ltd v. Civil Aviation Authority* [1987] S.L.T. 751; (1987) 3 BCC 492 (revocation by statutory authority of the company's operational licence); *Re Paramount Airways Ltd, Bristol Airport plc v. Powdrill* [1990] Ch. 744 (C.A.) (exercise of a lieu by unpaid creditor amounts to enforcement of a charge by way of security); *Re Barrow Borough Transport Ltd* [1990] Ch. 227 (application to register a charge out of time); (*Note*: these cases involved the construction of the phrase "other proceedings" as used in s.11 of the Act).

Effect of an Application for an Administration Order

These are the appointment of an administrative receiver of the company, or the carrying out by such a receiver (whenever appointed) of any of his functions. Thus, the first phase of the moratorium does not extend to the exercise by a floating charge holder of his right to appoint a receiver, nor does it extend to the proper actions of any receiver so appointed. Only if an administration order is actually made, thus marking the commencement of the second phase of the moratorium, does the charge holder's right to appoint a receiver become suspended for the duration of the order, and any receiver who has previously been appointed become required to vacate office.[64]

Where special circumstances warrant the taking of immediate steps to protect the company's assets, interim relief may be obtained through the court's exercise of its power to appoint a person to manage the company's affairs while the hearing of the petition is pending, or while a floating charge holder is deciding whether or not to appoint an administrative receiver.[65] Although there is no power under the Act or Rules whereby the court (at any rate in England) could appoint a provisional administrator as such, the point is made in the *Practice Note*[66] issued in January 1994 that in suitable cases the court may appoint an administrator but require him to report back to the court within a short period so that consideration can take place whether to allow the administration to continue or to discharge the order. It is further stated that in some cases the court may require the administrator to hold a meeting of creditors before reporting back to the court, both within a relatively short-period.

Postponed commencement of the moratorium

What has been said above with respect to the commencement of the moratorium over the company's affairs from the date of presentation of the petition admits of an important exception in the case where there is already an administrative receiver of the company at the date in question. Section 10(3) of the Act provides that in such a case the moratorium imposed by subsection (1) of that section will not apply if the person by or on whose behalf the receiver was appointed has not consented to the making of the order, and will not begin to apply unless and until that person so consents. This provision is further affirmation of the legislative policy of maintaining the basic legal position of such a charge holder, and is functionally complementary to the provision in section 9(3) whereby the court is required to dismiss the petition for an administration order if the charge holder's consent has not been given by the time of the hearing of the application.[67]

---

[64] *ibid.* s.11(1)(b), (3)(b).
[65] *Re A Company (No. 00175 of 1987)* [1987] BCLC 467.
[66] January 17, 1994, [1994] 1 All E.R. 324; [1994] 1 W.L.R. 160 (mentioned, *supra*, p. 434).
[67] See p. 427, *above.*

Hearing of the Administration Order Petition and Making of the Order

Procedure

At the hearing of the petition, the following persons may be heard or represented: the petitioner; the company (if it is a creditor's or directors' petition); those with floating charges capable of leading to the appointment of an administrative receiver; the administrative receiver where one has been appointed; and the nominated administrator.[68] The rules also enable the person who prepared the report on the company's affairs (discussed above) to be present or represented, if that person is not also proposed for appointment as administrator.[69] This may be the administrator-elect or some other person. The court is also empowered to give leave for any other person it considers appropriate to appear at the hearing. This could, for example, include the directors in a case where the petition is presented by the company as a consequence of a resolution carried, despite opposition from the board, at a general meeting of the members.

One necessary focal point of the hearing concerns the position of any floating charge holder, and likewise the position of any administrative receiver who may already have been appointed. Since, if an administrative receiver has already been appointed, the court is required by section 9(3) to dismiss the petition unless the person by or on whose behalf the receiver was appointed has consented to the making of the order, the court must be satisfied in such cases that the requisite consent has been actively and validly given. Only then may the court properly proceed to consider whether to make the order sought. The consent of the charge holder, for the purposes of section 9(3)(a), may be given in writing to the court.[70] Where no valid consent has been given by the charge holder, the court must proceed to satisfy itself that the security under which the receiver was appointed would not be released or avoided under either sections 238–240 or section 245 of the Insolvency Act, or in Scotland be challengeable under section 242 or 243 of the Act.[71]

If no administrative receiver has been appointed, but there are nevertheless holders of floating charges capable of leading to the appointment of such a receiver, the court must be satisfied that all such charge holders were given timely and effective notice of the presentation of the petition, so as to have enabled them to exercise their right of appointment in advance of the hearing if they had so wished.[72]

Once it has established that all the requirements of sections 8 and 9 of the Insolvency Act are satisfied so that the power to make an administration order is in principle exerciseable, the court may proceed to take its decision regarding the application itself. Section 9(4) states that on

---

[68] r. 2.9(1).
[69] r. 2.9(1)(g). See p. 433, *supra* (text to nn. 49–51).
[70] The charge holder is entitled to appear or be represented at the hearing: r. 2.9(1)(c).
[71] s.9(3)(b).
[72] *Re A Company (No. 00175 of 1987)* [1987] BCLC 467.

hearing a petition the court may dismiss the petition, or adjourn the hearing conditionally or unconditionally, or make any interim order or any other order that it thinks fit. The court's discretionary powers are thus amply framed to enable the case to be disposed of in the manner which seems best, having regard to all the legitimate interests involved. The court's available options are reinforced by section 9(5), which provides that an interim order under subsection (4) may restrict the exercise of any powers of the directors of the company, whether by reference to the consent of the court or of a person qualified to act as an insolvency practitioner in relation to the company, or otherwise.

In one case where the petition for administration was opposed by a majority in value of the company's creditors, and there were serious questions concerning the company's insolvency which required thorough investigation, the court refused to make an administration order on the ground that a compulsory liquidation was the appropriate option under the circumstances.[73]

Should the court decide to make an administration order, the order will be settled in accordance with procedural guidelines modelled on those employed in winding up.[74] The order will stipulate how the costs of the petition are to be met, and here again the practice in winding up is closely followed. Although there is a possibility that directors who have initiated an administration order application, in a vain attempt to postpone an inevitable liquidation, may be made personally liable to bear the associated costs, this is by no means the inevitable consequence of an unsuccessful application unless additional factors are present. Thus, if the directors are found to have acted in good faith and in response to appropriate professional advice, the mere fact that the court ultimately concludes that an administration order should not be made does not in itself warrant the imposition of a personal order for costs upon the directors resulting from what may be characterised as an error of judgment.[75]

The main purport of the order is, as indicated by the terms of section 8(1) of the Insolvency Act, to direct that, during the period for which the order is in force, the affairs, business and property of the company shall be managed by the person, to be known as "the administrator," appointed for this purpose under the order itself.

The concluding words of section 8(3) impose the requirement that the administration order must specify the purpose or purposes for whose achievement it is made. This is clearly intended to refer to the list of purposes contained in subsection (3) itself.

If the court decides not to make an administration order, it will dismiss the petition, leaving winding up as the likeliest alternative for the company. The costs of the application may then have to be borne by the party by whom the application was presented, but where an administration order petition has been presented reasonably and on appropriate professional advice, in parallel with a winding up petition, it

---

[73] *Re Arrows (No. 3)* [1992] BCC 131.
[74] r. 2.9 and Form 2.4; *cf.* Form 4.11.
[75] *Re Land and Property Trust Co. plc (No. 2)* [1993] BCC 462 (C.A.).

has been held that the costs incurred in the administration order application, down to the hearing at which it was dismissed, could be treated as allowable costs in the winding up.[76] Part of the rationale underlying this decision is that it would otherwise be difficult for directors, solicitors or accountants who have acted in good faith in preparing and presenting an administration order petition to recover the costs thereby incurred. This would work contrary to the legislative intention that this course of action should be pursued wherever practical as a means of averting the winding up of an insolvent company.[77]

The administrator's role in the presentation of the petition

The administrator's appointment, status and powers, and duties will be considered in later paragraphs of this Chapter but it is necessary to deal already here with his role in the presentation of the administration petition.

The above-mentioned, almost incidental, reference to the administrator which is contained within the definition of "administration order" supplied by section 8(2) is the nearest that the Insolvency Act comes to supplying a formal definition of the term "administrator." However, it is to be understood from what has already been stated in this Chapter, and from what follows hereafter, that the task of nominating a suitably qualified person to be appointed as administrator is one which falls to the petitioner to perform. From the time when the intention is formed to present a petition for an administration order, if not before then, the intending petitioner will be well advised to retain the services of a person capable of eventually acting as an administrator. Such a person must be qualified to act as an insolvency practitioner in relation to the company,[78] and as such could competently undertake the preparation of the report upon the company's affairs, and of the other supporting documents which are required (or, in Scotland, normally required) to accompany the petition itself.[79] Indeed, the administrator-elect, as a qualified insolvency practitioner, will be ideally placed to supervise the entire process of presentation of the petition on behalf of the petitioner, and in the latter's name, and should further be able to ensure that the petition itself is served, and requisite notice thereof is given, to all parties in accordance with the law's requirements.[80] In selecting an insolvency practitioner to nominate as administrator, the petitioner must bear in mind the need to avoid any transgression of the principles of *ad hoc* disqualification which may arise on account of a personal link or association between the insolvency practitioner and the company in

---

[76] *Re Goscott (Groundworks) Ltd* [1988] BCLC 363; (1988) P.C.C. 297; (1988) 4 BCC 372. Contrast *Re W.F. Fearman Ltd (No. 2)* (1988) 4 BCC 142.
[77] *Re Goscott (Groundworks) Ltd (supra)*: see [1988] BCLC at 366–367; (1988) P.C.C. at 302, *per* Mervyn Davies, J.
[78] Insolvency Act 1986, ss.388, 389.
[79] See p. 432, *above*.
[80] On the giving of notice see, *supra*.

relation to which he is to act. These principles will be found within the rules of professional conduct applicable to members of the professional body to which the administrator belongs, and by virtue of which he enjoys current authorisation to practise as an insolvency practitioner.[81] Alternatively if the insolvency practitioner does not belong to any professional body recognised for this purpose by the Secretary of State, analogous principles of professional conduct will have been made applicable to the person in question as part of the conditions attaching to his authorisation to practise as an insolvency practitioner granted under the provisions of sections 392 to 398 of the Insolvency Act.[82]

Transmission and advertisement of the order

Where an administration order has been made section 21(1)(a) requires the administrator who is appointed thereunder to send notice forthwith to the company, and to publish a notice of the order in the prescribed manner. The rules prescribe that the order is to be gazetted and advertised in such newspaper as the administrator thinks most appropriate for ensuring that the order comes to the notice of the company's creditors.[83]

Further duties of notification are imposed upon the administrator under the provisions of section 21 of the Insolvency Act. Section 21(1)(b) contains the requirement that within 28 days after the making of the order, unless the court otherwise directs, he must send a notice of the order to all creditors of the company, so far as he is aware of their addresses. Section 21(2) also requires the administrator, within 14 days after the making of the order, to send an office copy of the order to the Registrar of Companies and to such other persons as may be prescribed in the rules. The latter prescribe that notice is to be sent forthwith to any person who has appointed an administrative receiver, or has power to do so; to the petitioner in any pending petition for the winding up of the company; to any administrative receiver and to the registrar of companies.[84] Failure by the administrator without reasonable excuse to comply with the requirements of section 21 constitutes a criminal offence for which he is liable upon summary conviction to incur a fine of up to £400 and, for continued contravention, a daily default fine of up to £40.[85] Similar provisions as to the giving of notice are in force in Scotland.[86]

Appeals against the decision of the court

Appeals by a party aggrieved may be pursued according to the provisions of rule 7.47 of the Insolvency Rules 1986. The first avenue of

---

[81] Insolvency Act 1986, ss.390(2)(a), 391.
[82] See Chap. 2, *ante*, p. 26 *et seq.*
[83] r. 2.10(2).
[84] r. 2.10(3), as amended.
[85] s.21(3) of the Act, together with Sched. 10.
[86] Insolvency (Scotland) Rules 1986, r. 2.3(3).

recourse therefore lies by way of application to the court which has heard the petition, to invoke the power of the court to "review, rescind or vary its own order by virtue of rule 7.47(1). An appeal from a decision of a court in the exercise of that jurisdiction lies to a single judge of the High Court, and further appeal lies with leave to the Court of Appeal (rule 7.47(2)). Rule 7.51 provides that the practice and rules of the High Court apply in cases being heard on appeal by the High Court or Court of Appeal.

Among the parties eligible to maintain an appeal as "persons aggrieved" are not only the company, or the administrator, but also a creditor who can demonstrate that the original order operates in an oppressive way with respect to himself.[87]

Effect of the Administration Order

The making of an administration order has the effect of maintaining in force the moratorium over the company's affairs whose first phase commenced with the presentation of the petition for the order. In its second phase, however, the moratorium is extended in certain vital respects. Section 11(3) of the Insolvency Act stipulates that during the period for which an administration order is in force no resolution may be passed or order made for the winding up of the company; no administrative receiver of the company may be appointed; no other steps may be taken to enforce any security over the company's property, or to repossess goods in the company's possession under any hire purchase agreement, conditional sale agreement, chattel leasing agreement or retention of title agreement,[88] except with the consent of the administrator or the leave of the court and subject (where the court gives leave) to such terms as the court may impose.

The principal addition to be found in the provisions of section 11(3), when compared to those of section 10(1), is that it is rendered impossible for an administrative receiver to be appointed during this second phase of the moratorium. Thus if a floating charge holder has not exercised his right to appoint a receiver before, at the latest, the date of hearing of the petition, he is thereafter denied the right to do so while the administration order remains in force. The other notable modification to the rules governing the moratorium during its second phase is that the administrator is authorised to give consent to the taking of steps to enforce security, or to repossess goods, or to commence or continue proceedings or execution or the levying of distress (in Scotland, to carry out or continue diligences (Insolvency Act, s.10(5)) against the company or its property.[89] This

---

[87] *Cornhill Insurance plc v. Cornhill Financial Services Ltd* [1992] BCC 818 at 852–862 (C.A.), following *Re Tasbian Ltd (No. 2)* [1990] BCC 322. *cf.* the case law relating to appeals in winding up proceedings, which are also governed by r.7.47: Chap. 21, *post*, p. 549.

[88] The four types of agreement are included by virtue of s.10(4). See pp. 435–437, *above*, at n. 61.

[89] The expression "other proceedings" in s.11(3)(d) is to be strictly construed, *eiusdem generis* with paras. (a) to (c) of that subsection: *Air Ecosse Ltd v. Civil Aviation Authority* 1987 S.L.T. 751 (courses of action which may be open to persons who are not creditors—such as competitions—will therefore not be restrained under s.11).

authority is enjoyed by the administrator concurrently with the court, but is exerciseable by him independently and of his own initiative.

Several cases have involved points of interpretation arising from the provisions of section 11(3). In *Re Paramount Airways Ltd*[90] the Court of Appeal upheld a ruling to the effect that the assertion by a lien holder of a statutory right to retain goods or property subject to the lien constitutes the taking of steps to enforce security, within the meaning of section 11(3)(c), and therefore consent or leave is required. Likewise, a landlord's right of re-entry for non-payment of rent is to be regarded as a species of security for the payment in question, and as such amounts to a "legal process" falling within the ambit of section 11(3) where it is to be used against a company in administration.[91] On the other hand, the service of contractual notice purporting to make time of the essence, or for the purpose of terminating a contract by reason of the repudiatory breach by the company which has gone into administration, has been held not to amount to judicial steps of the kind to which section 11(3)(d) applies, so that consent or leave is not required before the notice is served.[92]

It was held in *Air Ecosse Ltd v. Civil Aviation Authority*[93] that the moratorium imposed by section 11 only applies in respect of the actions of creditors of the company. Hence, commercial competitors of the company are not debarred from taking steps aimed at enhancing their business position. In that case, it was held that a rival airline would not be restrained from making application to the licensing authority, aimed at bringing about the revocation of the operating licenses of the company undergoing administration. This case was distinguished in *Carr v. British International Helicopters Ltd*,[94] in which the Employment Appeal Tribunal held that a complaint to an industrial tribunal, alleging unfair selection for redundancy by the administrators in the course of reducing the number of the company's employees, falls under the description of "other proceedings" within the meaning of section 11(3)(d). Accordingly, the employee required the consent of the administrator or leave of the court to bring a complaint against the company, although the Tribunal suggested that only in rare cases would it be reasonable for consent to be refused to the bringing of cases for unfair dismissal or redundancy.

Lifting the Moratorium (Relief against Stay)

There is a growing body of case law concerning the granting of leave under section 11(3)(c) to enable a secured creditor to enforce his security, or to enable an owner to repossess goods in the possession of the company, during the period when an administration order is in force. It has been emphasised that the court must balance the interests of the secured

---

[90] [1990] Ch. 744; [1990] BCC 130, (C.A.). See also *Re Sabre International Products Ltd* [1991] BCLC 470.
[91] *Exchange Travel Agency v. Triton Property Trust plc* [1991] BCC 341.
[92] *Re Olympia and York Canary Wharf Ltd, American Express v. Adamson*, [1993] BCC 154.
[93] 1987 S.L.T. 751; (1987) 3 BCC 492 (Court of Session, Inner House).
[94] [1993] BCC 855. See also *Re Paramount Airways Ltd (No. 3)* [1993] BCC 664.

creditor as against those of the other creditors, and in the light of what the administrator's proposals, and progress made towards their implementation, seem destined to achieve.[95] On the other hand, it is not a precondition to the granting of leave to a secured creditor or an owner that the administrator's conduct should be capable of being criticised in some legitimate way.[96]

The process of balancing the competing interests as between a secured creditor or owner of goods on the one hand, and the general body of creditors on the other, arises both under section 11(3)(c) and also under section 15, when an administrator proposes to deal with secured property free from encumbrance.[97] Cases decided under either of these sections may therefore be instructive in relation to the operation of the other provision, although the two lines of authorities remain distinguishable from each other in the final analysis. The leading decision to date decided under section 11(3), is *Re Atlantic Computer Systems plc*. In that case,[98] the Court of Appeal made a number of important, general observations regarding cases where leave is sought to exercise existing proprietary rights, including security rights, against a company in administration. These may be summarised as follows[99]:

(1) In every case the onus is on the person who seeks leave to make out a case for this to be given.

(2) If granting leave to a lessor of land or the hirer of goods (a "lessor") to exercise his proprietary rights and repossess his land or goods is unlikely to impede the purpose for which the administration order was made, leave should normally be given.

(3) Where the giving of leave would impede the achievement of the purpose for which the order was made, the court has to carry out a balancing exercise, balancing the legitimate interests of the secured creditor/lessor and the legitimate interest of the other creditors of the company. The exercise is not a mechancial one, but calls for the exercise of judicial judgment in the light of all the circumstances of the case, having regard to the overall objectives of the administration order, and the possible inequity of any refusal of leave.

(4) In carrying out the balancing exercise great weight is to be given to the proprietary interests of the lessor or secured creditor. The Court of Appeal approved the *dicta* of Browne-

---

[95] *Re Meesan Investments Ltd* (1988) 4 BCC 788, also reported as *Royal Trust Bank v. Buchler* [1989] BCLC 130; *Re Paramount Airways Ltd* [1990] BCC 130, also reported as *Bristol Airport plc v. Powdrill* [1990] BCLC 585.
[96] *ibid.*
[97] See further, p. 456, *post*.
[98] [1990] BCC 859; [1992] 2 W.L.R. 367; [1992] 1 All E.R. 476 (C.A.).
[99] [1990] BCC 859 at 880. These guidelines also apply in Scotland: *Scottish Exhibition Centre Ltd v. Mirestop Ltd* 1993 S.L.T. 1034. In this case, landlords were granted leave to commence proceedings to irritate (*i.e.* terminate) a lease after the administrators had spent 18 months unsuccessfully endeavouring to dispose of the company's business carried on in the leased premises.

Wilkinson, V.-C., in *Re Paramount Airways Ltd*,[1] to the effect that: "... so far as possible, the administration procedure should not be used to prejudice those who were secured creditors when the administration order was made in lieu of a winding-up order." The same underlying principle is applicable in relation to the proprietary interests of the lessor; namely that an administration for the benefit of unsecured creditors should not be conducted at the expense of those who have proprietary rights, save to the extent that this may be unavoidable.[2]

(5) Therefore, leave will normally be granted if significant loss would be caused to a lessor or secured creditor by a refusal. For this purpose loss comprises any kind of financial loss, direct or indirect, including loss by reason of delay, and may extend to loss which is not financial. But if substantially greater loss would be caused to others by the grant of leave, or loss which is out of all proportion to the benefit which leave would confer on the lessor or secured creditor, that may outweigh the argument in favour of granting leave.

(6) In assessing these respective losses, the court will have regard to matters such as: the financial position of the company, its ability to pay the rental arrears, the administrator's proposals, the period for which the administration order has already been in force and is expected to remain in force, the effect on the administration if leave were given, and the effect on the applicant if leave were refused, the end result sought to be achieved by the administration and the prospects of its attainment, and the history of the administration thus far.

(7) The court will often have to take account of probabilities, assessing virtual certainties and remote possibilities in relation to the various factors under consideration.

(8) The foregoing list is not exhaustive. The conduct of the parties may also be a material consideration. All of these factors may be relevant not only to the decision whether to grant or refuse leave, but also whether to impose terms if leave is granted, or indeed if it is refused.

A further point of considerable importance was ruled upon by the Court of Appeal in the *Atlantic Computers* case, namely the question of whether goods are to be treated as being "in the company's possession" for the purposes of section 11(3)(c) in a situation where, under the terms of the headleases with the funders of a commercial activity, the company is permitted to enter sub-leases under which the end-users of the goods will take them to their own sites for the purpose of utilisation. The Court

---

[1] *Supra*, n. 95.
[2] For an example of the application of the foregoing principles in a case involving goods subject to hire-purchase agreements, see *Re David Meek Access Ltd* [1993] BCC 175. (Leave was given to two creditors who had sought unsuccessfully to repossess on the day before presentation of the administration order petition.)

declared that section 11(3)(c) contemplated the position as between the owner of the goods and the company in administration, and that as between these parties the location of the goods was irrelevant. Hence, the goods were still "in the company's possession" within the meaning of section 11(3)(c), so that the owner of the goods could not repossess them without obtaining either the consent of the administrator, or the leave of the court.[3]

It is important to emphasise that the effect of section 11(3)(c) and (d) is merely to impose a moratorium on the enforcement of the secured creditor's legal rights, and not to alter or destroy those rights altogether. Therefore, the judgment of the administrator, in deciding to refuse leave to the owner of goods on lease or hire purchase to retake them, may be reviewed in the light of its subsequent impact upon the creditor in question and, if found to have been wrongful in some respect, may give rise to a claim for compensation.[4]

Further important effects of the making of an administration order occur under section 11(1), which provides that any petition for the winding up of the company shall thereupon be dismissed, and that any administrative receiver of the company shall vacate office. No automatic requirement to vacate his office is imposed upon any receiver of part only of the company's property, but section 11(2) provides that such a receiver shall also vacate office on being required to do so by the administrator. The provisions of subsection (4) of section 11 further specify that where any administrative receiver or receiver of part of the company's property vacates office in accordance with the requirements of the section, his remuneration and any expenses properly incurred by him, and any indemnity to which he is entitled out of the assets of the company, shall be charged on and paid out of any property of the company which was in the custody or under the contol of the administrative receiver or receiver at that time, in priority to any security held by the person by or on whose behalf he was appointed. This provision thus provides the displaced administrative receiver with a continuing indemnity out of the charged assets in respect of his own remuneration and costs. Vacation of office by an administrative receiver or receiver pursuant to the provisions of section 11 of the Insolvency Act also has the effect of releasing the person concerned from any duty to pay preferential creditors under section 40 or 59 of the Act.[5]

Notification of order

In order that all parties dealing with the company at a time when an administration order is in force may have notice of this fact, section 12(1) of the Insolvency Act imposes the requirement that every invoice, order for goods or business letter, being a document on or in which the company's

---

[3] [1990] BCC at 871.
[4] *Barclays Mercantile Business Finance Ltd v. SIBEC Developments Ltd* [1992] 1 W.L.R. 1253.
[5] Insolvency Act 1986, s.11(5). For administrative receivership generally, and for the indemnity enjoyed by an administrative receiver under ss.40 and 44 of the Act, see Chap. 14, *ante*.

name appears[6] and which is issued by or on behalf of the company or the administrator during that period, must also contain the administrator's name and a statement to the effect that he is for the time being managing the company's affairs, business and property. If default is made in complying with this requirement strict criminal liability is imposed upon the company, and in addition if the administrator or any officer of the company has without reasonable excuse authorised or permitted the default, that person also commits a criminal offence.[7]

Although evidently modelled upon what is now section 39 of the Insolvency Act (formerly section 493 of the Companies Act 1985), which imposes notification requirements where a receiver or manager is appointed in relation to a company, the drafting of section 12(1) of the Insolvency Act is far from comprehensive or exhaustive in its coverage of the variety of means by which a company may have dealings with third parties. Thus the omission from the subsection of any reference to oral communications, or to those conveyed in the form of a telegram, telex or fax, or by other electronic means, appears to give rise to important exceptions under which contact or dealings with outside parties may avoid violating the letter, if not the spirit, of section 12. Other significant means of business documentation, such as catalogues or brochures, receipts or even company cheques, may also be found to be outside the ambit of the phrase "invoice, order for goods or business letter," and so escape the requirement that they carry the special information that the company is in the hands of an administrator.

Further problems may arise in practice concerning the precise meaning and effect of the word "issued" within the context of section 12(1). For an offence to be committed under this section, the document in question must be "issued" at a time when an administration order is in force. Although the Act supplies no definition of the term "issued," it is likely to be construed strictly in view of its function in relation to the imposition of criminal liability under the section being considered. Thus, where documents are dispatched before the administration order enters into force (albeit this may be at a time when a petition has been presented and a hearing is pending) it would seem that no offence is committed under section 12 even though the administration order has entered into force by the time the documents are received, read or acted upon by any third party for whom the administration order might well be a relevant factor for consideration. It may be expected however that an administrator would seek to ensure that the company's dealings with all parties are conducted with candour and integrity, even in cases apparently falling outside the limits of the notification requirement imposed by section 12. Indeed, as an office holder whose appointment arises under an order of the court, it would seem appropriate to regard the administrator as subject to a general and overriding duty to display exemplary standards of good faith in his

---

[6] Failure to include the company's name on or in any of the documents in question would constitute an offence by the company under s.349 of the Companies Act 1985.

[7] Insolvency Act 1986, s.12(2). The maximum fine which may be imposed for each offence is expressed as one fifth of the statutory maximum, and is therefore currently £400.

dealings with all parties, just as is required of a liquidator in a winding up by the court, or of a trustee in bankruptcy. This has been confirmed by the Court of Appeal in their ruling in Re Paramount Airways Ltd (No. 3), Powdrill v. Watson,[8] indicating that the rule in Ex parte James[9] is fully applicable to an administrator.

General effects of the order; the position of directors

In addition to the matters described above, which constitute the principal effects resulting from the making of an administration order, several other effects ensue as a necessary consequence of the administrator's taking over management of the affairs, business and property of the company, and thereafter exercising his general and specific powers under sections 14 to 16 of the Insolvency Act, for the purpose of fulfilling the statutory duties imposed principally by sections 17 to 25 of the Act. These matters will be discussed in the ensuing paragraphs of this chapter, but one which deserves special mention here is the effect of the administration order upon the position of the directors of the company. Although the directors are not automatically dismissed from office as a consequence of the making of the order, the corollary to the transfer of all managerial power to the administrator is that the powers of the directors are suspended for the duration of the administration order. Despite being deprived of their powers however, the directors remain liable to perform their statutory duties in relation to the company's fulfilment of any requirements imposed upon it by law, such as the proper filing of annual returns by the company. However, the administrator has power under section 14(2)(a) to remove any director of the company and to appoint any person to be a director of the company, whether to fill any vacancy or otherwise. Thus, during the period of an administration order, the composition of the board of directors may be changed through the administrator's exercise of his personal judgment regarding the company's needs, and the best way in which to achieve the purposes for which he himself was appointed.

A further consequence of the making of an administration order, from the directors' point of view, is that the provisions of sections 6 and 7 of the Company Directors Disqualification Act, under which persons may be disqualified from company management by order of the court, become applicable to all persons who are, or who have been, directors of the company.[10] The power of the court to make a disqualification order under section 6(1) arises where the person in question is or has been a director of

---

[8] [1994] 2 All E.R. 513, 524; [1994] BCC 172, 182, per Dillon, L.J.
[9] (1874) 9 Ch. App. 609. See also Re Wyvern Developments Ltd [1974] 2 All E.R. 535 (a case on compulsory winding up); contrast Re John Bateson & Co. [1985] BCLC 259 (a case on voluntary winding up).
[10] Under the Insolvent Companies (Reports on Conduct of Directors) (No. 2) Rules 1986 (S.I. 1986, No. 2134), r. 4(2), (5), the office holder is required to report upon the conduct of all persons who have been directors of the company at any time within the three years prior to the commencement of the insolvency proceedings. In Scotland, a similar duty arises under the Insolvent Companies (Reports on Conduct of Directors) (No. 2) (Scotland) Rules 1986 (S.I.1986, No. 1916 (S.140)), r. 3(2)).

a company "which has at any time become insolvent," an expression whose meaning includes, by virtue of subsection (2)(b), the case where an administration order is made in relation to the company. Moreover, a duty is cast upon the administrator by the terms of section 7(3)(c) of that Act to report to the Secretary of State forthwith if he becomes aware of matters which constitute a *prima facie* case for the making of a disqualification order under section 6(1).[11] Thus the possibility arises that proceedings may be initiated against one of more of the directors by means of an application for a disqualification order made by the Secretary of State under section 7(1)(a) of the Company Directors Disqualification Act 1986.[12] Although the further possibility of the imposition of responsibility for the company's wrongful trading under section 214 of the Insolvency Act will not arise unless the company subsequently goes into insolvent liquidation, the information gathered by the administrator, and submitted by him to the Secretary of State in fulfilment of the afore-mentioned reporting requirement, will inevitably be of considerable significance in any proceedings which may subsequently be brought by the liquidator under section 214 if the Company is later wound up.[13]

The Administrator: his Appointment, Replacement, Resignation and Removal

The holder of the office of administrator of a company must be a person who is qualified to act as an insolvency practitioner in relation to the company.[14] The appointment of an administrator is made either by the administration order itself, in accordance with section 13(1) of the Insolvency Act, or subsequently, under section 13(2), by an order of the court to replace an administrator who has died, resigned or vacated office for any other reason. It is permissible for more than one person to be appointed or nominated to the office of administrator so that the position is held jointly, but in that event the appointment or nomination must declare whether any act required or authorised to be done by the office holder is to be done by all or any one or more of the persons for the time being holding the office.[15]

Where different nominations are submitted for appointment to the office of administrator—for example, by the company and by a group of

---

[11] See also s.7(4) concerning the power of the Secretary of State to require the administrator to furnish information. More detailed requirements concerning the duties of an administrator, as an office holder within the meaning of the Insolvency Act, to report upon past and present directors of the company are contained in the Insolvent Companies (Reports on Conduct of Directors) (No. 2) Rules 1986 (S.I. 1986, No. 2134). The rules for Scotland are to be found in the Insolvent Companies (Reports on Conduct of Directors) (No. 2) (Scotland) Rules 1986 (S.I. 1986, No. 1916) (S.140)).

[12] On directors' disqualification generally, and with regard to ss.6 and 7 of the Company Directors Disqualification Act 1986 in particular, see Chap. 27, *post*.

[13] Liability for wrongful trading is discussed in Chap. 27, *post*.

[14] Insolvency Act 1986, s.230(1). For the statutory requirements attaching to qualification to practice as an insolvency practitioner see ss.388–398 of the Act.

[15] Insolvency Act 1986, s.231(2).

creditors respectively—the court must decide which of the nominees to appoint. Assuming that there is parity of professional experience and integrity, the court is unlikely to attach any special weight to the fact that each of the nominating parties may be said to have an interest to serve, since the office holder is required to act in an impartial and professional way once appointed. What is likely to influence the court in making its final choice is the extent to which one or other of the nominees is already thoroughly acquainted with the details of the company's affairs, so as to be able to act quickly upon gaining appointment, and without there being a costly duplication of investigative work which has already been carried out by one of the nominees prior to the hearing.[16] Inevitably, this results in an increased probability that the appointment will go to the nominee who was initially enlisted by or on behalf of the company itself, and to whom maximum access to information and records will have been accorded for the purpose, *inter alia*, of preparing the "Rule 2.2 report" mentioned above.[17] In a case of serious and irreconcilable disagreement between the interests involved, a joint appointment is a possible compromise solution, but this inevitably increases the overall costs of the administration.

In the event that a vacancy occurs in the office of administrator, application to the court for an order under section 13(2) of the Insolvency Act to fill the vacancy may be made by any continuing administrator (if there has been a joint administratorship); or failing such, by any committee of creditors established under section 26 of the Act[18]; or in the absence of both of the foregoing, by the company or the directors or by any creditor or creditors of the company.[19] Where a change occurs in the incumbent of the office of administrator the incoming administrator must advertise the fact and notify the registrar of companies of his appointment.[20]

An administrator of a company may at any time resign his office, in the prescribed circumstances, by giving notice of his resignation to the court.[21] The Rules prescribe that an administrator may resign office in any of the following circumstances:

(1) Ill health;
(2) If there is some conflict of interest which precludes him from further discharging the duties of administrator;
(3) In the case of a joint appointment, where it is no longer considered to be expedient that both or all should continue in office; or
(4) if the court is satisfied that there are good reasons why the resignation should be permitted.[22]

In addition to those cases where the administrator resigns for personal

---

[16] *Re Maxwell Communications Corporation plc* [1992] BCC 372.
[17] *Supra*, p. 433.
[18] See p. 466, *infra*.
[19] Insolvency Act 1986, s.13(3).
[20] r. 2.55 (as amended).
[21] Insolvency Act 1986, s.19(1).
[22] r. 2.53.

reasons, or for reasons of expediency falling within the circumstances prescribed in the Rules, there is a statutory requirement in section 19(2) of the Insolvency Act that the administrator must vacate office if he ceases to be qualified to act as an insolvency practitioner in relation to the company,[23] or if the administration order is discharged.[24]

Unfair Prejudice Applications

Section 19(1) of the Insolvency Act provides that the administrator of a company may at any time be removed from office by the order of the court. Such an order may be made by the court in consequence of proceedings brought under section 27 of the Act, which provides that at any time when an administration order is in force a creditor or member of the company may apply to the court by petition alleging that the company's affairs, business and property are being or have been managed by the administrator in a way which is unfairly prejudicial to the interest of its creditors or members generally, or of some part of its creditors or members (including at least the petitioner himself). Alternatively a petition under section 27 may complain that any actual or proposed act or omission of the administrator is or would be prejudicial to the interest of the parties in question. The court is empowered by section 27(2) to make such order as it thinks fit for giving relief in respect of the matters complained of, and various particular matters are mentioned in sub-section (4) in respect of which the order may make provision. These include the laying down of precise instructions to regulate the future management by the administrator of the company's affairs, business and property,[25] or the imposition of more particular requirements upon the administrator either to refrain from doing an act complained of, or to do an act which the petitioner has complained he has omitted to do.[26] The court may also order the summoning of a meeting of creditors or members for the purposes of considering matters in accordance with the court's directions,[27] and in the face of the most extreme evidence of unsatisfactory circumstances, the court may discharge the administration order and make whatever consequential provision it thinks fit.[28] Where the evidence suggests that the personal shortcomings of the administrator are mainly the cause of the dissatisfaction expressed in a petition under section 27, the court may invoke its widely drawn powers to make "such order as it thinks fit," and make an order under section 19(1) removing the administrator from office. If no nomination of a suitable alternative administrator has been made in the petition itself, it may be expected that the court will take the necessary steps under section 13(2) to fill the vacancy before the conclusion of the hearing.[29]

---

[23] See n. 14, *supra*.
[24] Discharge of an administration order is governed by s.18 of the Insolvency Act. See p. 468, *infra*.
[25] Insolvency Act 1986, s.27(4)(a).
[26] *ibid.*, s.27(4)(b).
[27] *ibid.*, s.27(4)(c).
[28] *ibid.*, s.27(4)(d).
[29] See above. On the administrator's release following his vacation of office, see p. 468, *infra*.

Finally it should be noted that under section 17(3) of the Insolvency Act an administrator may be compelled to summon a meeting of the company's creditors in two specified cases. The first is when he is requested to do so by creditors representing at least one-tenth in value of the company's debts, and the second is when the administrator is directed to do so by the court. Therefore, if a sufficient number of creditors wish to oblige the administrator to explain his conduct before a general meeting, and to hear the creditors's views, this can be brought about in a direct manner. On the other hand, if the requisite one-tenth of the creditors cannot be gathered in support of any proceeding under s.17(3)(a), the aggrieved minority could petition the court under section 27, including in their petition the suggestion that the court should order the administrator to convene a meeting pursuant to the direction under section 17(3)(b).

The Administrator: his Status and Powers

It has been explained above[30] that the general conception of the administration order procedure was inspired by certain aspects of the beneficent operation of the procedure for appointing an administrative receiver under a floating charge. The status and powers of an administrator are therefore modelled closely upon those of an administrative receiver, but in certain respects the powers with which an administrator is invested are more extensive than those enjoyed by an administrative receiver.

A principal aspect of the legal status of an administrator is that, by virtue of section 14(5) of the Insolvency Act, in exercising his powers he is deemed to be acting as an agent of the company. This places the administrator in a position identical to that of an administrative receiver,[31] and has the consequence that the company is both bound by, and liable in respect of, all acts validly performed by the administrator. Moreover, by virtue of section 232 of the Insolvency Act the acts of an individual as administrator are valid in law notwithstanding any defect in his appointment, nomination or qualifications.

It has been held that there is no analogy between an administrator and an administrative receiver, or between an administrator and any other species of receiver, as far as concerns the right of the administrator not to fulfil outstanding contracts entered into by the company.[32] A major reason underlying this distinction is the so-called "duality of capacities" existing in the person of an administrative receiver, who is simultaneously the agent of the company (and not of the debentureholder), while owing a duty to the latter as appointing creditor.[33] Conversely, an administrator is

---

[30] See p. 419, *supra*.
[31] *cf.* Insolvency Act 1986, s.44(1), discussed in Chap. 14, *ante*. However, an administrator does not incur personal liability for his acts in the way that an administrative receiver does by virtue of s.44(1)(b). In Scotland, the same comments apply by reference to the Insolvency Act, s.57(1) and (2).
[32] [1990] BCC 97; [1990] BCLC 1 (Vinelott, J.).
[33] See Chap. 14, *ante*, at p. 395.

appointed to manage the affairs of the company and not to realise them for the benefit of one of the creditors. The overriding duty of an administrator may be characterised as that of exercising responsible care for the company whose property and affairs have been entrusted to him.[34] Viewed in that light, it would seem reasonable to suggest that under some circumstances, the company's best interest might be advanced by the act of breaking a particular contract, rather than in fulfilling it, even at the cost of incurring liability in damages. An administrator forming such a view, if acting *bona fide* and on a sound professional basis, might avoid being restrained by injunction from following that course of action. However, it is well to bear in mind the consequences of the administrator's status as an officer of the court, and as a person subject to the principles of conduct established in *ex parte James*[35]: the exceptional powers vested in such an office holder should not be exercised in such a way as to cause the company to reap windfall benefits at others' expense, nor should there be any exploitation of legal advantages to evade obligations which the company ought morally to perform.

On the other hand, in *Re Home Treat Ltd*[36] an administrator was held to occupy a position analogous to that of a liquidator for the purpose of being entitled to apply for relief under section 727 of the Companies Act 1985 in respect of any potential allegation of negligence, default or breach of duty. It was held that an administrator is an "officer of the company" for this purpose, and may thus seek relief against possible liabilities resulting from a discovery that the company's business was being run in contravention of the objects clause of the memorandum of association.

A further aspect of the legal provisions associated with the office of administrator arises under section 14(6) of the Act, whereby a person dealing with the administrator in good faith and for value need not be concerned to enquire whether the administrator is acting within his powers. This protection for third parties dealing with an administrator in the manner specified has the effect of precluding either the administrator or the company for which he acts from raising the defence of *ultra vires* in relation to acts performed by the administrator. However, no presumption is imported into the drafting of section 14(6), and it is therefore incumbent upon the party who seeks to rely upon its provisions to prove that the conditions imposed therein were satisfied in the particular case.

A further statutory safeguard operates against any attempt by means of provisions in the company's memorandum or articles of association to create an obstacle to the administrator's ability to exercise to the full powers conferred upon him under the Insolvency Act. Section 14(4) of the Act provides that any power conferred on the Company or its officers either by the Insolvency Act or by the Companies Act 1985, or by the company's own memorandum or articles, which could be exercised in such a way as to interfere with the exercise by the administrator of his powers, shall not be exercisable except with the consent of the

---

[34] *Re Charnley Davies Ltd (No. 2)* [1990] BCLC 760; [1990] BCC 605.
[35] (1874) L.R. 9 Ch.App. 609. See *supra*, text to paras. 8 and 9.
[36] [1991] BCC 165.

administrator himself. Such consent may be given by the administrator in general terms or in relation to particular cases. The effect of this provision is thus to confirm the overriding nature of the status and legal powers of the administrator in relation to the company and its directors throughout the period for which the administration order is in force.

General powers

The general powers conferred upon an administrator are contained in section 14 of the Insolvency Act together with Schedule 1 thereto. The powers listed in the Schedule are by section 42 of the Act made applicable also to an administrative receiver in England and Wales, and the powers of a Scottish receiver under Schedule 2 are virtually identical, thus underlining the close connection between these two kinds of office holder. Section 14(1)(a) is drafted in extremely wide terms, so that the administrator is expressly empowered to do "all such things as may be necessary for the management of the affairs, business and property of the company." Moreover in paragraph (b) of that subsection, whereby the powers specified in Schedule 1 are made applicable to an administrator, it is stated that the powers contained in the Schedule are enjoyed "without prejudice to the generality of paragraph (a)." Therefore the fact that any given matter has not been included within the powers conferred by the Schedule cannot of itself constitute a basis for denying that the administrator has and can exercise such a power. Provided, at any rate, that the thing which the administrator proposes to do can be reconciled with the broad language of section 14(1)(a), as quoted above, it follows that the administrator enjoys the power to do it.

By virtue of Schedule 1 to the Act, the administrator has the following powers:

> "1. Power to take possession of, collect and get in the property of the company and, for that purpose, to take such proceedings as may seem to him expedient.
> 2. Power to sell or otherwise dispose of the property of the company by public auction or private contract or, in Scotland, to sell, feu, hire out or otherwise dispose of the property of the company by public roup or private bargain.
> 3. Power to raise or borrow money and grant security therefor over the property of the company.
> 4. Power to appoint a solicitor or accountant or other professionally qualified person to assist him in the performance of his functions.
> 5. Power to bring or defend any action or other legal proceedings in the name and on behalf of the company.
> 6. Power to refer to arbitration any question affecting the company.
> 7. Power to effect and maintain insurances in respect of the business and property of the company.
> 8. Power to use the company's seal.
> 9. Power to do all acts and to execute in the name and on behalf of the company any deed, receipt or other document.

Administrator: His Status and Powers

10. Power to draw, accept, make and endorse any bill of exchange or promissory note in the name and on behalf of the company.
11. Power to appoint any agent to do any business which he is unable to do himself or which can more conveniently be done by an agent and power to employ and dismiss employees.
12. Power to do all such things (including the carrying out of works) as may be necessary for the realisation of the property of the company.
13. Power to make any payment which is necessary or incidental to the performance of his functions.
14. Power to carry on the business of the company.
15. Power to establish subsidiaries of the company.
16. Power to transfer to subsidiaries of the company the whole or any part of the business and property of the company.
17. Power to grant or accept a surrender of a lease or tenancy of any property of the company, and to take a lease or tenancy of any property required or convenient for the business of the company.
18. Power to make any arrangement or compromise on behalf of the company.
19. Power to call up any uncalled capital of the company.
20. Power to rank and claim in the bankruptcy, insolvency, sequestration or liquidation of any person indebted to the company and to receive dividends, and to accede to trust deeds for the creditors of any such person.
21. Power to present or defend a petition for the winding up of the company.
22. Power to change the situation of the company's registered office.
23. Power to do all other things incidental to the exercise of the foregoing powers."

The following further powers of a general nature are conferred upon an administrator by section 14 of the Insolvency Act. By section 14(2)(a) he may remove any director of the company and appoint any person to be a director of the company, whether to fill any vacancy or otherwise. By means of this most sweeping power, the administrator may take appropriate action to rebuild the management team of the company in a view to leaving it in capable hands when the administration order expires or is discharged. Under section 14(2)(b) the administrator may at any time call a meeting of members or creditors of the company. This allows the administrator, at his discretion, to consult the relevant sector of interest in a direct manner on matters of importance, and on which their assent or support is judged to be desireable. Such a step could be taken, for example, when the administrator concludes that the company is in a position to be handed back to its management, as reconstituted by means of the powers just referred to. If the meetings of the members and creditors were in effect to pass votes of confidence in the new board and in the administrator's achievements in office, this would help to ensure that the ending of the administratorship could take place under the most favourable conditions.

The right to make direct contact with creditors or members of the company via a general meeting is supplemented by the right conferred on the administrator by section 14(3), whereby he may at any time apply to the court for directions in relation to any particular matter arising in connection with the carrying out of his functions.

Power to deal with charged property

By virtue of section 15 of the Insolvency Act, important and specific powers are conferred upon the administrator in relation to property of the company which is subject to any floating charge or other security. The purpose of section 15 is to enable the administrator to deal with or dispose of encumbered property free from the encumbrance in question, subject to the provision that the rights of the secured creditor shall be transferred and attached to any property which is substituted for the charged asset, or to the net proceeds of any disposal therof. The commercial advantages of the administrator's ability thus to deal with encumbered property are considerable and should in the majority of cases ensure that the rationalisation of the company's business is efficiently carried through, and that the disposal value of assets is duly maximised. The powers of disposal accorded to an administrator under section 15 are in some ways comparable to those accorded to an administrative receiver under section 43 of the Insolvency Act,[37] but in certain respects are more extensive since an administrator is empowered to dispose of property encumbered by a floating charge without any need to obtain authorisation from the court.[38]

Under subsection (1) of section 15, where there is property of the company which is subject to a security which, as created, was a floating charge the administrator may dispose of or otherwise exercise his powers in relation to that property as though it were not subject to the security. Subsection (4) supplies the necessary protection for the holder of the security in question by providing that where property is disposed of under subsection (1) the charge holder shall have the same priority in respect of any property directly or indirectly representing the property disposed of as he would have had in respect of the property subject to the security in its original form. The greater freedom of the administrator to dispose of property which is subject to a floating charge, as opposed to a fixed charge, is a further instance of the vital importance of the essential distinction between these two forms of security. Since the test of the nature of a charge as created is ultimately a functional one, the mere use of the words "fixed charge" will not of itself be conclusive as to the nature of the security being created, but it will be necessary to examine the substance of the arrangement between the debtor and creditor in question.[39]

---

[37] For the similar provisions applicable to Scottish receivers see s.61 of the Insolvency Act 1986. For the general powers of a Scottish receiver, see s.55 and Sched. 2.

[38] Insolvency Act 1986, s.15(1), (3). *cf.* s.43(1), (2) which applies to administrative receivers and Insolvency Act 1986, s.61, which applies to receivers in Scotland.

[39] *cf. Re Keenan Bros.* [1985] I.R. 401 (a charge on present and future book debts due to the debtor company was held to be a fixed charge as created, since the substance of the arrangement with the creditor was to deprive the company of the free use of the proceeds of the asset in question). See also *Barclays Bank plc v. Willowbrook International Ltd.* [1986] BCLC 45.

Under subsection (2) of section 15 the administrator may apply to the court for an order authorising him to dispose of any property of the company which is subject to a security other than one which, as created, was a floating charge, or of any goods in the possession of the company under a hire purchase agreement, conditional sale agreement, chattel leasing agreement of retention of title agreement.[40] The court may authorise the disposal (either alone or in conjunction with other assets) of property or goods which are the subject of such application provided that the court is satisfied that the disposal would be likely to promote the purpose, or one or more of the purposes, specified in the administration order.[41] The order of the court authorises the administrator to dispose of secured property as if it were not subject to the security, or to dispose of goods which are subject to a credit agreement as if all the rights of the owner under the agreement were vested in the company.[42] Any order made by the court under subsection (2) is subject to the mandatory condition that the net proceeds of the disposal shall be applied towards discharging the sums secured by the security or payable under the credit agreement.[43] Where the proceeds, net of the costs and expenses incurred in making the sale, are less than the notional amount determined by the court to be that which would be realised on sale of the property or goods in the open market by a willing vendor, the amount actually realised must be augmented by such other sums derived from the company's funds as may be required to make good the deficiency below the notional minimum return on the disposal.[44] Where there are two or more securities attaching to the same item of property, the net proceeds of disposal, augmented where necessary under the requirements just described, are to be applied towards discharging the sums secured by the securities in the order of their respective priorities.[45] Where property is disposed of under these provisions in Scotland, the granting of the appropriate disposition, transfer, assignation, etc., and the completion of the purchaser's title has the effect of disencumbering the property of the security. The disposal under the Insolvency Act, s.15 of goods subject to hire-purchase agreements, etc., also extinguishes the rights of the owner as against the purchaser (Insolvency Act, s.16).

Where the court makes an order under section 15(2) authorising disposal of property or goods by the administrator, the latter must send a copy of the order to the registrar of companies within 14 days. Failure on his part to do so without reasonable excuse constitutes a criminal offence punishable by a fine of up to £400 plus, for a continued contravention, a daily default fine not exceeding £40.[46]

When an administrator makes application to the court for an order

---

[40] Insolvency Act 1986, s.15(2), (3) and (9). For the statutory definitions of the various types of credit agreement referred to, see references on p. 436, *supra*, n. 61.
[41] See p. 423, *supra*.
[42] Insolvency Act 1986, s.15(2).
[43] *ibid.*, s.15(5).
[44] *ibid.*
[45] *ibid.*, s.15(6).
[46] *ibid.*, ss.15(7), (8), 430; Sched. 10.

under section 15(2), notification of the hearing must be given to any charge holder or other person affected, and the latter has the right to be represented and to oppose the application.[47] In the application the administrator should include an indication of the market value of the property to be sold or, failing that, should indicate how its value is to be determined. It may be observed that, even where the administrator is by section 15(1) empowered to dispose of property without first having to seek the authorisation of the court, it will always be open to any interested and duly qualified parties to make an application under section 27 in respect of any matters affected by the operation of section 15.[48]

Avoidance of antecedent transactions, etc.

As an "office holder" within the meaning of Part VI of the Insolvency Act,[49] an administrator enjoys significant powers under that Part to bring about the avoidance of antecedent transactions to which the company is or has been a party, to assist him in carrying out the investigation of the company's affairs, and to obtain control or possession of property or records belonging to the company. These powers, being common to administrators, liquidators, trustees in bankruptcy and (in some respects) administrative receivers, are fully described elsewhere and it will suffice here to refer to other parts of this work where the relevant statutory provisions are considered. With respect to antecedent transactions, the administrator in England and Wales may apply to the court under section 238 of the Insolvency Act for an order avoiding any transaction at an undervalue entered into by the company with any person, or any preference given by the company to any person, at a relevant time as defined in section 240.[50] The administrator may apply to the court under section 239 for an order avoiding any preference given by the company to any person at a relevant time, also defined for this purpose in section 240. If it can be shown that the company has previously entered into a transaction whose purpose was to defraud creditors, the administrator in England and Wales[51] may apply to the court under section 423 of the Act for an order avoiding the transaction and restoring the position to what it otherwise would have been.[52] The administrator in England and Wales or in Scotland[53] may also apply to the court under section 244 of the Act for an order reopening any extortionate credit bargain whereby credit has been provided to the company, which was entered into within the period of three years ending with the day on which the administration order was made.[54] Mention has already been made above of the fact that at the time of

---

[47] r. 2.51.
[48] Creditors' and members' rights of petition under s.27 are discussed at p. 451, *above*, and p. 467, *infra*.
[49] See Insolvency Act 1986, ss.232, 233(1), 234(1), 235–237, 238(1), 239–241(1), 244(1), 245(1), 246(1).
[50] The avoidance of transactions under ss.238 and 239 of the Insolvency Act is considered in Chap. 8, *ante*, and Chap. 26, *post*.
[51] The section (Insolvency Act, s.423) does not apply in Scotland.
[52] On s.423 of the Insolvency Act, see Chap. 8, *ante*.
[53] The section (Insolvency Act, s.244) applies in Scotland.
[54] On s.244 of the Insolvency Act, see Chap. 8, *ante*, and Chap. 26, *post*.

hearing the application for an administration order the court will inevitably have to examine whether any floating charge or security which has been created by the court is liable to be released or discharged under sections 238–240, or would be avoidable under section 245 of the Act, or under the equivalent statutory provisions applicable in Scotland.[55]

In the hitherto unprecedented circumstances arising in *Re Maxwell Communications Corporation plc (No. 2), Barclays Bank plc v. Homan*,[56] where an English company was placed simultaneously under the Administration Order procedure of English law and the Chapter 11 protective bankruptcy procedure of American law, the administrators wished to take proceedings to recover as a preference a payment of some US $30m made by M.C.C. to an English bank shortly before the administration order was made. The sum in question was derived from disposal of an American asset of M.C.C., and the administrators proposed taking proceedings in the U.S. Bankruptcy Court, invoking the avoidance provision of the U.S. law, rather than seeking to avoid the preference under section 239 of the Insolvency Act 1986 in proceedings in England. The bank to which the payment was made was unsuccessful in its attempt to persuade the English courts to issue an anti-suit injunction enjoining the administrators from proceeding other than under English law: both Hoffmann J. and the Court of Appeal concluded that the American court had subject-matter jurisdiction which it could be relied upon to exercise in a fair and prudent manner. Despite the fact that the U.S. legal provision afforded the administrators a better prospect of success, due to the absence of any requirement to establish the debtor's positive desire to prefer, the proposed U.S. proceedings were neither vexatious nor oppressive under the circumstances, particularly in view of the fact that the administrators were simultaneously subject to the jurisdiction of the U.S. court, by which they were recognised as the corporate governance of the debtor company for the purposes of Chapter 11.

Supplies by utilities

Where, as in most cases, the continuation of the company's business is dependent upon the continued availability of any of the following services supplied by public utilities, namely gas, electricity, water, or telecommunication services, the administrator may invoke the special protection conferred upon office holders by section 233 of the Insolvency Act. By this section, if a request is made by or with the concurrence of the administrator for the giving after the date on which the administration

---

[55] Insolvency Act 1986, s.9(3), discussed at p. 438, *supra*.
[56] [1991] BCC 757 (Hoffmann, J.); and 767 (C.A.). The U.S. Bankruptcy Court subsequently declined to hear the substantive action for preference avoidance, principally on the grounds that the transaction in question was properly governed by English law, and that the interest of England in having its avoidance law apply to transfers made in England by an English corporation to recipients found in England, on account of a debt incurred there, was greater than the U.S. interest in applying U.S. law: *Re Maxwell Communication Corporation* (Case No. 91B 15741) 170 Bankr. 800; 25 Bankr Ct. Dec (CRR) 1567 U.S. Bkcy. Ct., S.D.N.Y., August 5, 1994 (Brozman, J.).

order was made of any of the supplies referred to,[57] the supplier may make it a condition of the giving of the supply that the administrator personally guarantees the payment of any charges in respect of the supply, but may not make it a condition of the giving of the supply, or do anything which has the effect of imposing such a condition, that any outstanding charges in respect of a supply given to the company before the date of the administration order are paid.[58] The purpose of this provision, whose enactment was recommended in the *Cork Report*,[59] is to ensure that the public utilities are not enabled to exploit the advantage resulting from the essential nature of the services which they are legally obliged to provide, so as to impose terms for the continuation or resumption of supplies which have the effect of enhancing the supplier's rights or status in relation to the outstanding charges in respect of previous supplies to the company. Thus the imposition of any specially increased tariff or surcharge for the reconnection or resumption of supplies, or in respect of the rate of charge for supplies, would contravene section 233 and be consequently invalid.

The Administrator: General Duties

Section 17 of the Insolvency Act requires the administrator on his appointment to take into his custody or under his control all the property to which the company is or appears to be entitled. To assist him in accomplishing this task, the administrator not only may avail himself of the general powers vested in him as administrator by virtue of section 14 of the Act,[60] but also may invoke the assistance of the court by seeking an order under section 234 in respect of any person who has in his possession or control any property, books, papers or records to which the company appears to be entitled. The person in respect of whom the order is made may thereby be required to pay, deliver, convey, surrender or transfer the items in question to the administrator.

In his efforts to trace and take control of the company's property, and to investigate the company's affairs, the administrator may derive further assistance from section 235 of the Insolvency Act which imposes upon a wide circle of persons, presently or formerly connected with the company in a variety of capacities, the duty to co-operate with the administrator. This duty consists of an obligation to give the administrator such information concerning the company and its promotion, formation, business, dealings, affairs or property as the administrator may at any time reasonably require, and an obligation to attend on the administrator for private examination at any time when he may reasonably require it.[61] The administrator may further avail himself of the assistance of the court by making an application for an order under section 236 of the Insolvency

---

[57] The formal description of the supplies to which s.233 of the Insolvency Act relates is given in subs. (3).
[58] Insolvency Act 1986, s.233(2).
[59] Cmnd. 8558, Chap. 33, especially paras. 1451–1462.
[60] See p. 454, *supra*.
[61] s.235 of the Insolvency Act is further considered in Chap 22, *post*.

The Administrator: General Duties

Act, whereby persons may be summoned to appear before the court, or may be required to submit an affidavit, for the purpose of furnishing sworn evidence on any matter relating to the company's affairs.[62] The same statutory provision may be used by the administrator to obtain from such parties as the company's bankers the disclosure and production of books, documents and records relating to the company.[63]

In *Re British and Commonwealth Holdings plc (No. 2)*,[64] the Court of Appeal by a majority, and the House of Lords unanimously, confirmed the principles which apply in relation to the court's power to order discovery of information under section 236 on the application of the office holder in insolvency proceedings. The court enjoys an unfettered and general discretion in the exercise of this extraordinary power, and must balance the requirements of the office holder against possible oppression to the person from whom information is sought. On the other hand, there is no rule of limitation to the effect that the office holder is confined to reconstituting that knowledge which the company once had and was entitled in law to possess.[65] The terms of section 236 itself, and the logical requirements of the office holder's statutory role and function, admit of a broader approach to the exercise of the court's power, with a view to discovering relevant information with as little expense and as much ease as possible.

A further duty of the administrator, and one which is the very *raison d'être* of his administratorship, is to manage the affairs, business and property of the company.[66] This is to be done, in the first instance, in accordance with any directions given by the court, but after the administrator's proposals have been approved under section 24 of the Insolvency Act the administrator is required to carry out his managerial functions in accordance with those proposals, as from time to time revised by means of the procedures established for this purpose.[67]

Other duties which the administrator is required to perform without delay following the making of the administration order are concerned with the sending out of notice of the order,[68] the investigation of the company's affairs and the preparation of a statement of proposals to be submitted in due course to a meeting of the company's creditors in accordance with the requirements of sections 23 and 24 of the Insolvency Act.[69]

---

[62] s.236 of the Insolvency Act is further considered in Chap 22, *post*.

[63] *Re Cloverbay Ltd* [1989] BCLC 724. See however *Re Cloverbay Ltd (No. 2)* [1990] BCC 299, where attempts to obtain still more information from the same bankers in the same case were disallowed by the court as superfluous, and oppressive to the party concerned.

[64] [1992] 2 W.L.R. 931 (C.A.); [1992] 3 W.L.R. 853 (H.L.). See also the judgments of the same courts in the linked appeal arising out of the same case: *Re British and Commonwealth Holdings plc (No. 1)* reported together at the same citations, respectively).

[65] On this point, the Court of Appeal has ruled that a statement to the contrary in the judgment of Browne-Wilkinson, V.-C. in *Cloverbay Ltd v. Bank of Credit and Commercial International* [1991] Ch. 90 at p. 102 was an *obiter dictum* and incorrect.

[66] Insolvency Act 1986, s.17(2). *cf.* s.8(2).

[67] For approval of the administrator's proposals under s.24 of the Insolvency Act, and for revision or modification of the proposals under s.25, see p. 464, *infra*.

[68] See Insolvency Act 1986, s.21(1), (2), discussed at p. 441, *supra*.

[69] See p. 463, *infra*.

Statement of affairs

A central aspect of the administrator's duties at the outset of his tenure of office is the obtaining of a statement of the company's affairs as is required by section 22 of the Insolvency Act. Under this section the administrator must require some or all of the persons mentioned in subsection (3) thereof to make out and submit to him a statement in the prescribed form as to the company's affairs. Although a considerable standardisation has taken place with regard to the statutory provisions under which, in various circumstances, a statement of a company's affairs is required to be prepared,[70] the mandatory terms in which section 22(1) is drafted are such as to deprive the administrator of any discretion as to whether a statement of affairs shall be required at all.[71] Subject to that qualification however, the administrator does possess certain discretionary powers, both with regard to the extension of the period of 21 days within which the statement of affairs must be submitted by those persons on whom the requirement has been imposed by him,[72] and with regard to the releasing of any such person from the obligation to submit the statement within the prescribed time.[73]

The persons upon whom the obligation of submitting a statement of the company's affair may be imposed by the administrator are:

(1) Those who are or have been officers of the company;
(2) Those who have taken part in the company's formation at any time within one year before the date of the administration order;
(3) Those who are in the company's employment or have been in its employment within that year, and are in the administrator's opinion capable of giving the information required; and
(4) Those who are or have been within that year officers of or in the employment of a company which is, or within that year was, an officer of the company.[74]

Any of the foregoing persons on whom the administrator elects to serve a requirement under section 22(1) of the Insolvency Act must submit a statement of the company's affairs in the prescribed form and verified by affidavit. Section 22(2) specifies that the statement must show:

(1) Particulars of the company's assets, debts and liabilities;
(2) The names and addresses of its creditors;
(3) The securities held by the creditors respectively;

---

[70] *cf.* Insolvency Act 1986, s.47 (concerning receivership), and s.13 (concerning compulsory winding up), discussed in Chap. 22, *post*.

[71] *cf.* Insolvency Act 1986, s.132(1), where the material phrase reads: "the official receiver *may* require …" (emphasis added). On the other hand, s.47(1) of the Act is drafted in mandatory terms which are effectively identical to those of s.22(1).

[72] Insolvency Act 1986, s.22(4), (5)(b).

[73] *ibid.*, s.22(4), (5)(a).

[74] *ibid.*, s.22(3). It is expressly provided that the term "employment" here includes employment under a contract for services.

(4) The dates when the securities were respectively given; and
(5) Such further or other information as may be prescribed.[75]

Failure without reasonable excuse by any person (including the administrator himself) to fulfil any obligation imposed by section 122 of the Insolvency Act constitutes a criminal offence punishable by fine.[76]

The administrator's proposals; meeting of creditors

The primary duty of the administrator upon entering into office is to devise the most appropriate means of achieving the purpose or purposes which are specified in the administration order under which he was appointed, and whose attainment is the ultimate objective of the making of the order itself. To this end, section 23(1) of the Insolvency Act requires the administrator within three months after the making of the order to formulate his proposals for achieving the purpose or purposes specified therein. If it proves to be impracticable for the administrator to complete this task within the three month period, the court is empowered by the subsection to grant an extension of time. Although the company has standing to make the application for an extension, it has been held to be preferable if the application is made by the administrator, since he is the person on whom the statutory duty to report is laid, and who is liable to criminal proceedings should he fail to report. He is also in a position to offer an independent and detached view of the company's affairs.[77]

The administrator is required within the specified period to send a statement of his proposals to the registrar of companies and (so far as he is aware of their addresses) to all creditors. He must also lay a copy of the statement before a specially convened meeting of the company's creditors, summoned on not less than 14 days' notice.[78] The further requirements imposed upon the administrator by section 23(2) are that within the same time limit he must either send a copy of this statement of proposals to all members of the company of whose addresses he is aware, or alternatively publicise by advertisement a notice stating an address to which members of the company should write for copies of the statement to be sent to them free of charge.[79] The administrator may well deem it expedient to postpone, as far as the rules will allow, the incurring of expenditure in relation to the giving of notice to members until he is assured of the support of the creditors for the proposals he has devised.

Where the implementation of the administrator's proposals will involve the dismissal of employees of the company, the proper consultation procedures under section 99 of the Employment Protection Act 1975 must be undertaken just as in the case of redundancies which result from a company going into liquidation.[80]

---

[75] See Form 2.9, Insolvency Rules 1986.
[76] Insolvency Act 1986, s.22(6).
[77] *Re Newport County Association Football Club* [1987] BCLC 582. *cf. Re Charnley Davies Business Services Ltd* (1988) P.C.C. 1, 5–6 *per* Harman, J.
[78] Insolvency Act 1986, s.23(1)(a), (b).
[79] rr. 2.17, 2.18.
[80] *cf. Re Hartlebury Printers Ltd* [1992] BCC 428.

If the administrator fails without reasonable excuse to comply with any of the requirements of section 23, he commits a criminal offence which is punishable by a fine in accordance with the provisions of section 23(3) of the Act.[81]

Section 24 of the Insolvency Act contains the statutory requirements pertaining to the consideration of the administrator's proposals by a creditors' meeting convened under section 23(1)(b). The rules provide that the administrator, or a representative appointed by him, shall act as chairman of the meeting.[82] For the purpose of voting on a resolution approving the proposals in accordance with section 24(1) of the Act, the Rules provide that the resolution may be passed by a simple majority in value of those present or represented.[83] Creditors' votes are assessed according to the amounts of their respective debts at the date of the administration order.[84] Those creditors whose debts have arisen during the course of the administration may attend and speak at the meeting, but will normally be excluded from voting in respect of any part of the debt which has arisen after the administration order since, by virtue of section 19(5), this constitutes a secured debt enjoying first priority of entitlement to be paid out of any property of the company which is in the custody of the administrator when he vacates his office.[85] Apart from those whose secured status results from the operation of section 19(5), secured creditors are only permitted to vote at the meeting in respect of the unsecured balance (if any) of their debt, the amount of which must have been agreed in advance between the chairman and the creditor concerned.[86] Other creditors who are entirely debarred from voting are any who are, in relation to the company, associated companies or connected persons within the meaning of sections 249 and 435 combined of the Insolvency Act.

If the meeting is not prepared to approve the administrator's proposals in the form in which they are tabled, section 24(2) of the Act allows the proposals to be approved with modifications, provided that the administrator assents to each modification. If no majority can be obtained for the approval of the proposals either in their original or in modified form, the chairman may, and must if a resolution is passed to that effect, adjourn the meeting for not more than 14 days.[87]

When the meeting is concluded, the administrator must report the result of the meeting to the court within four days and give notice of the result to the registrar of companies.[88] The report must set out the proposals

---

[81] Insolvency Act 1986, ss.23(3), 430; Sched. 10.

[82] r. 2.20.

[83] r. 2.28(1). Note the effect of para. (1A), added by (S.I. 1987, No. 1919), whereby any resolution is invalid if those voting against it include more than half, in value, of the creditors to whom notice of meeting was sent, and who are not persons connected with the company.

[84] r. 2.22(4).

[85] See p. 468, *infra*. Creditors whose position is protected under s.19(4) or (5) of the Insolvency Act may be permitted to vote when the administrator's proposals will directly affect them.

[86] rr. 2.22, 2.24.

[87] r. 2.18(4).

[88] Insolvency Act 1986, s.24(4); rr. 2.29 (as substituted by (S.I. 1987, No. 1919)), and 2.30.

in the form in which they have been approved (if such is the case) and attached thereto should be a list of the names and addresses of the members of the committee of creditors, if one has been established.[89] If the report is to the effect that the meeting has declined to approve the administrator's proposals (even in modified form) the court may discharge the administration order, or may adjourn the proceedings or make an interim order, or otherwise dispose of the case in the exercise of its discretion.[90] These widely drawn powers enable the court to respond in a flexible way to the creditors' refusal to endorse the administrator's proposals. However unless there is persuasive evidence to suggest that the purposes for which the administration order was made may yet be attained, possibly through the substitution of a new or additional administrator, the court is likely to deploy its discretionary powers in such a way as to ensure the smoothest possible transition to the next appropriate form of insolvency proceedings, such as a voluntary or compulsory winding up.[91] Where the court discharges the administration order the administrator must, within 14 days, send an office copy of the order effecting the discharge to the registrar of companies.[92]

Revision of administrator's proposals

If the administrator's proposals are approved by the creditors he is thereafter required to manage the affairs, business and property of the company in accordance with the proposals as so approved, or as from time to time revised in accordance with the provisions of section 25 of the Insolvency Act.[93] The latter section operates upon the premise that the administrator enjoys a certain latitude in carrying out his duty to implement his proposals, and hence may of his own initiative validly effect such minor and incidental revisions as may prove to be expedient, in his judgment, in the interests of achieving the ultimate purpose for which the proposals were devised. Where, however, the administrator wishes to make revisions of his proposals which he perceives to be of a substantial nature, section 25 renders it obligatory for him to submit his fresh proposals to the same procedure as that whereby the original proposals were approved. He is therefore required to circulate all creditors with a statement in the prescribed form of his proposed revisions, and to lay a copy of the statement before a creditors' meeting summoned for that purpose on not less than 14 days' notice.[94] Only if the proposed revisions are approved by the meeting may the administrator make them and put

---

[89] rr. 2.29, 2.33 (as amended). On the committee of creditors, see s.26 of the Insolvency Act, discussed, *infra*, p. 466.
[90] Insolvency Act 1986, s.24(5).
[91] See s.140(1) of the Insolvency Act, which makes provision for the appointment of a liquidator by the court following the discharge of an administration order.
[92] Insolvency Act 1986, s.24(6).
[93] *ibid.*, s.17(2).
[94] *ibid.*, s.25(1), (2). In cases of genuine urgency, where the spirit and substance of the terms originally approved is fully respected, the court may grant authority to the administrator under s.14(3) to implement modifications without recourse to creditors' approval: *Re Smallman Construction Ltd* (1988) 4 BCC 784.

them into effect. In addition to submitting a statement of his fresh proposals to the creditors, the administrator must either send a copy of the statement to all members of the company of whose addresses he is aware, or publish by advertisement a notice of the fact that such a statement has been prepared, stating an address to which members of the company may write for copies of the statement to be sent to them free of charge.[95]

The conduct of a meeting of creditors convened under section 25 follows the same course as that of a meeting summoned under sections 14, 17 and 23.[96] The creditors, voting on the same basis as at the previous meeting, may by resolution approve the proposed revisions as submitted, or with modifications.[97] In the latter event, however, no modification may be approved unless the administrator assents to it. Once again, the administrator is required to report the outcome of the meeting to the court and to the registrar of companies.[98]

Creditors' committee and protection of creditors' and members' interests

The foregoing account of the procedures by which the administrators' proposals are to be approved and, if necessary, revised involves the active participation of the creditors, and the ultimate assent of a majority in value of the unsecured creditors. The close and active involvement of creditors in this, as in other forms of insolvency proceedings, and the maintenance of a steady supply of information about the administrator's conduct in office was seen by the *Cork Committee* as an important aspect of the revised basis for the operation of insolvency law.[99] Although the provisions of the Insolvency Act fall well short of the high ideals expressed in the *Cork Report*, section 26 of the Act makes provision for the creditors to take the initiative of establishing a committee of their number to maintain contact with the administrator and to keep themselves, and the body of the creditors on whose behalf they serve, informed of his progress and intentions. The creditors' decision to establish such a committee may be taken at the meeting convened under section 23 for the purpose of approving the administrator's proposals.[1] The committee may consist of between three and five members, elected by the general meeting on the basis of a vote by value of those present or represented at the meeting. The value of each creditor's vote is taken as the amount of the debt due from the company at the date of the administration order.[2] The names and addresses of the person originally elected to serve must be notified by the administrator to the court and to the registrar of companies at the same

---

[95] *ibid.*, s.25(3).
[96] *ibid.*, s.25(5); r. 2.19(1).
[97] *ibid.*, s.25(4).
[98] *ibid.*, s.25(6); r. 2.29 (as substituted by (S.I. 1987, No. 1919)).
[99] Cmnd. 8558, Chap. 19, especially paras. 930–967.
[1] Insolvency Act 1986, s.26(1).
[2] Rules 2.22(4), 2.32. On the principles governing the electoral procedure for constituting the committee, see *Re Polly Peck International plc* [1991] BCC 503.

time as he reports to them upon the result of the creditors' meeting. Subsequent changes in the composition of the committee should be notified as and when they occur.[3] Committee members may resign at any time by notifying the administrator in writing, and may be replaced through co-optation by the continuing members of the committee.[4] The minimum number of members with which the committee may continue in being is three.[5] The members of the committee may be paid travelling expenses as agreed by the administrator, such expenses being payable out of the assets of the company.[6]

The creditors' committee has no coercive or directory powers which may be exercised in relation to the administrator. The extent of the powers invested in the committee consists of the right to require the administrator to attend before it at any reasonable time, upon seven days' notice, and to furnish it with such information relating to the carrying out of his functions as it may reasonably require.[7] Although this appears to give the creditors' committee a somewhat neglible role, the regular supply of information which the committee should be capable of obtaining from the administrator should enable the general body of creditors to monitor the extent to which the administration order is fulfilling its intended purposes. On the basis of the information which is periodically revealed any creditor may at any time see fit to invoke the intervention of the court under section 27 of the Insolvency Act. This is equally the case if, in his relationship and dealings with the committee, the administrator falls under suspicion of being less than candid about his actions and intentions.

The provisions of section 27 of the Insolvency Act, which is expressed to be for the protection of the interests of creditors and members, are quite widely drawn. Under section 27(1) any creditor or member may at any time petition the court for an order on the ground that the company's affairs, business and property are being or have been managed by the administrator in a manner which is unfairly prejudicial to the interest of its creditors or members generally, or of some part of its creditors or members (including at least the petitioner personally), or that any actual or proposed act or omission of the administrator is or would be so prejudicial. As has been explained above.[8] The court's powers under section 27 are wide ranging, and include the ability by order to issue specific directions to the administrator and to regulate his exercise of his managerial powers for the future.[9] Additionally, the administrator may be required by the court to convene a meeting of creditors or members, and in an extreme case the court could discharge the administration order and make any consequential provisions it thinks fit.[10]

An alternative approach may be adopted by the creditors in a case where

---

[3] r. 2.33(5).
[4] r. 2.41.
[5] rr. 2.32, 2.41(2).
[6] r. 2.45.
[7] Insolvency Act 1986, s.26(2).
[8] See p. 451, *above*.
[9] Insolvency Act 1986, s.27(4)(a), (b).
[10] *ibid.*, s.27(4)(c), (d).

their dissatisfaction is attributable to the terms in which the administration order itself is expressed. This entails the use of the power established by section 17(3)(a) of the Insolvency Act whereby upon the request of one tenth in value of the creditors the administrator can be compelled to convene a creditors' meeting. At the meeting a resolution may be moved to the effect that the administrator should apply to the court for an order varying the original administration order by specifying an additional purpose. If such a resolution is duly passed, the provisions of section 18(2)(b) oblige the administrator to apply to the court for the making of such an order. The same approach may be adopted where a majority of creditors conclude that the administration order is no longer serving a useful purpose and should be discharged: by means of a suitably worded resolution passed at a creditors' meeting, the administrator may be compelled (in accordance once again with s.18(2)(b)) to apply to the court for an order discharging the administration order, as described in the paragraph next following.

Discharge of administration order and release of administrator

Section 18(1) of the Insolvency Act permits the administrator at any time to apply to the court for the administration order to be discharged.[11] One situation in which such an application may take place is where the company's exit from administration is to be synchronised with the coming into force of a company voluntary arrangement or a scheme of reconstruction, especially where the sanction of the court is required or where a dissenting minority of creditors or members, or other interested parties, seek to oppose its implementation.[12] While the terms of section 18(1) have the effect of making the timing of such an application a matter for the administrator's personal judgment and discretion, section 18(2) renders it obligatory for him to make an application under the section if either of two alternative circumstances arises. The first of these is if it appears to the administrator that the purpose, or each of the purposes, specified in the order either has been achieved or is incapable of being achieved.[13] The second, alternative circumstance is if the administrator is required to make the application to the court by a meeting of the company's creditors summoned for the purpose in accordance with the Rules.[14]

The court's powers upon hearing an application under section 18 are as usual very widely drawn: it may by order discharge or vary the administration order and make such consequential provision as it thinks

---

[11] s.18(1) of the Insolvency Act 1986 also permits the administrator to apply to the court for an order varying the administration order so as to specify an additional purpose: see pp. 423 and 425, *above*.

[12] *cf. Re Olympia and York Canary Wharf Holdings Ltd* [1993] BCC 866, where the objectors included tenants of property leased from the restructured companies.

[13] Insolvency Act 1986, s.18(2)(a). *cf. Re Charnley Davies Business Services* (1988) P.C.C. 1; (1987) 3 BCC 408.

[14] *ibid.* s.18(2)(*b*). On general provisions relating to the convening of creditors' meetings, and on voting threat, see pp. 463 and 464, *above*, and r. 2.21.

Discharge of Administration Order and Release of Administrator

fit, or adjourn the hearing conditionally or unconditionally, or make an interim order or any other order it thinks fit.[15] If the administration order is discharged or varied, the administrator must within 14 days send an office copy of the order to the registrar of companies. Failure on the part of the administrator to comply with the requirement of sending notice constitutes a criminal offence punishable by fine, unless a reasonable excuse can be shown.[16]

Administration Expenses

If the administration order is discharged the administrator must vacate office.[17] In that event section 19(3)—(10) of the Insolvency Act (as amended)[18] contains important provisions controlling the manner in which, and the assets from which, the administrator's own fees and expenses, and also any debts or liabilities incurred during the administration, are to be paid. With regard to the administrator's remuneration and his expenses properly incurred,[19] section 19(4) provides that these shall be paid out of, and shall enjoy a first charge against, any property of the company which is in his custody or under his control at the time he ceases to be administrator of the company. Subsection (4) is so drafted as to confer upon the charge thereby created a priority ahead of any security which, as created, was a floating charge. However any other form of charge or security may still enjoy priority, if suitably expressed.

With regard to any sums payable in respect of debts or liabilities incurred during the time when the administration order has been in force, section 19(5) provides that any sums thus incurred under contracts entered into or contracts of employment adopted by the administrator or a predecessor of his in the carrying out of his or the predecessor's functions shall be charged on and paid out of the same property as is available for meeting the administrator's own claim for remuneration and expenses, but in priority to these latter claims. Thus, persons dealing with an administrator during the period of his stewardship of the company's assets and affairs may do so in confidence of the fact that any debts which become due to them from the company enjoy priority ahead of both the administrator's own fees and expenses and the rights of any floating charge holders.

Apart from the "super-priority" arising under section 19(5) with respect to post-administration debts incurred under new contracts or adopted contracts of employment (as to which, see below), the standard priority attaching to the administrator's own remuneration and expenses by virtue of subsection (4) constitutes an important, further incursion into the entitlement of the company's creditors to receive payment out of the

---

[15] Insolvency Act 1986, s.18(3).
[16] *ibid.*, s.18(4), (5).
[17] *ibid.*, s.19(2)(b).
[18] See Insolvency Act 1994, s.1, and discussion below.
[19] On the fixing of the administrator's remuneration, and on the expenses properly allowable to him in the performance of his functions, see rr. 2.47–2.50 (as amended).

assets. The question therefore arises as to what items of expenditure are properly to be classed as "administration expenses" so as to entitle persons claiming in respect of that item to be repaid from property controlled by the administrator, ahead of any right of a floating charge holder, or of any unsecured creditors, to receive payment. This was one of the issues considered by the Court of Appeal in Re Atlantic Computer Systems plc[20] with particular reference to cases where land or goods belonging to other parties are being used by the company which undergoes administration, as part of the course of its business which it is one of the purposes of the administration to enable to continue. In the instant case, the question was whether the hire charges relating to goods in the company's possession under hire purchase agreements, which the lessor was unable to repossess an account of the moratorium imposed under section 11(3) of the Act,[21] should rank as expenses of the administration and as such be payable ahead of the claims of the pre-administration creditors. The court concluded, in the circumstances, that they should not.

Delivering the judgment of the Court, Nicholls L.J. drew a careful distinction between the settled principles regarding the concept of "expenses" in the case of the two established forms of insolvency procedure, namely liquidation and administrative receivership.[22] In the case of the former, the concept of liquidation expenses is a reflection of the fact that, the company's life being at an end, it is vital to respect the distinction between, on the one hand, the rights of third parties to retake their own property which has been in the possession of the company (or to enforce proprietary rights validly created in their favour by way of security, as in the case of a mortgage), and on the other hand, the claims of unpaid creditors, seeking to exercise some remedy over the company's property. In the second type of case, the principle of collectivity generally precludes the exercise of such remedies, save in the most exceptional of circumstances.[23] The concept of "liquidation expenses" is thus reserved for cases where fresh debts are incurred by the liquidator for the purposes of the liquidation, or cases where the possession and use of property of third parties is retained for those self-same purposes, as where property occupied under an existing lease continues to be utilised after the commencement of winding up. By contrast, the concept of expenses in receivership does not attach to claims or charges resulting from the retention and use by an administrative receiver of land or goods belonging to third parties, the reason being that there is no statutory moratorium resultant upon the appointment of an administrative receiver, so that a lessor or owner of goods is at liberty to exercise rights and remedies unless the receiver is prepared to pay rent or hire charges as they accrue.

In his appraisal of the contrasting processes of liquidation and receivership, Nicholls L.J. sought the most apt analogy to apply to the operation of the new procedure for administration of companies.[24] While

---

[20] [1992] 1 All E.R 476; [1992] 2 W.L.R. 367; [1990] BCC 859.
[21] Discussed, *supra*, p. 435.
[22] [1992] 1 All E.R. at 481–486.
[23] See further, Chap. 24, *post*.
[24] [1992] 1 All E.R. at 481–491. The entire passage is instructive.

observing that, as has been shown above, there are close and deliberate parallels between administration and administrative receivership, his Lordship concluded that the closest affinity for the purpose in hand was between administration and liquidation. The moratorium triggered by the making of an administration order is comparable to the prohibition on proceedings being brought or continued against a company when a winding-up order is made. Hence the "liquidation expenses" model was chosen as the basis of the approach to be followed in administration, but with the important qualification that the very nature and purpose of administration necessitates a less dogmatic approach to individual cases. Hence, the question whether those whose land or goods are being used during administration, (and for the purpose of securing the ultimate success of the process), should be given leave to enforce their proprietary rights or, in atonement for being denied leave, should enjoy the consolation of being paid ahead of everyone else, will be a matter for the exercise of a judgment by the administrator—or failing that, the court—in individual cases. Thus, there is no rigid principle to the effect that, if land or goods in the company's possession under an existing lease or hire-purchase agreement are used for the purposes of an administration, the continuing rent or hire charges will rank automatically as expenses of the administration and as such qualify for payment under section 19(4).[25] It follows from this, as Nicholls L.J. readily acknowledged, that the exercise of discretion to grant or withhold leave to enforce proprietary rights should duly reflect the specially invidious predicament of the owner of an asset whose continued availability to the company may be vital to the prospects of success for the administration. The administrator, as an officer of the court, may properly agree to pay current rents or hire charges as an appropriate atonement for the interference with the lessor's proprietary rights and commercial interests, thereby assuaging what might otherwise be a disproportionate and inequitable detriment suffered by the party concerned.[26]

Adoption of contracts of employment

The provisions originally enacted as subsections (4) and (5) of section 19 of the Insolvency Act 1986, and now comprising subsections (4) to (7) inclusive, have the effect of conferring distinct advantages upon the employees of a company whose contracts of employment are adopted by its administrator. First, they are accorded a priority of entitlement to payment of any sums payable under their contracts of employment, taking precedence ahead of the administrator's own entitlement to payment of remuneration and expenses properly incurred as office holder, and also ahead of the entitlement of any holder of a floating charge security. Secondly, these contractual entitlements are charged on and payable out of any property of the company in the administrator's custody or under his control. These important rights, and safeguards, in favour of the

---

[25] *ibid.*, at pp. 488–489.
[26] *ibid.*, at p. 490. See also pp. 498–503, whose purport has already been considered, *supra*, at p. 444.

employees are predicated upon their contracts of employment having been adopted by the person serving as administrator at the time in question, and in this context it is significant that section 19(5) (as originally enacted) contained a proviso, now embodied in the second paragraph of subsection (6), to the effect that the administrator is not to be taken to have adopted a contract of employment by reason of anything done or omitted to be done within 14 days after his appointment.

To the extent therefore that an administrator's acts or conduct are held to constitute the adoption of any contract of employment the consequence is that the entitlements of the floating charge holder, and of the administrator, undergo a corresponding subordination with respect to the finite resources—the company's remaining assets—from which all liabilities will ultimately fall to be discharged. In the absence of any statutory definition of the term "adopted", a practice evolved between 1987 and 1994 whereby administrators would issue letters to those employees of the company whom it was not considered necessary or expedient to dismiss, pending the outcome of any attempts to rescue the business or to sell it as a going concern. The essential purport of such letters—whose legal effectiveness had been upheld in an unreported decision of Harman J. of February 13, 1987[27]—was to the effect that the administrator was not adopting any or all terms of any contract of employment or service between the company and the addressee, but that the latter was reassured that the company would continue for the time being to pay wages or salary, plus other contractual entitlements, in return for continued "co-operation" from the employee's side. In this way, after the expiry of the 14 days' "grace period", administrators endeavoured to preserve the company's business as a going concern without conceding the status of super-priority, with security over the company's assets, to any claims by employees in respect of periods of service falling after the commencement of administration.

The Paramount Case

The validity of the above practice was judicially re-examined, together with the meaning and effect of the word "adopted" when used in section 19, in *Powdrill v. Watson*, also known as *Re Paramount Airways Ltd (No. 3)*.[28] At first instance Evans-Lombe J. expressed the view that the word "adopted" should have the same meaning in section 19(5) (as it then was) as it has in section 44(1)(b) with regard to administrative receivers, and that in both instances the word means "has procured the company to continue to carry out." The learned judge accepted the proposition that adoption may be effected by "any act or acquiescence (after expiry of the 14-day period) which is indicative of his intention to treat the contract as

---

[27] *Re Specialised Mouldings Ltd* (unreported), summarised by G. Stewart in *Administrative Receivers and Administrators* (1987), para. 512; see also R.M. Goode, *Principles of Corporate Insolvency Law* (1990), at p. 101.

[28] [1993] BCC 662 (Evans-Lombe J.); [1994] BCC 172 (C.A.); [1995] BCC 319, [1995] 2 All E.R. 65 (H.L.).

on foot,"[29] and he proceeded to rule that an administrator who seeks to contract out of the effect of adoption of contracts of employment, so as to prevent claims arising under such contracts from ranking in priority to his own remuneration and expenses, must employ a clear and specific form of drafting to signify that this effect is intended. It would be insufficient for this purpose for an administrator's letter to an employee merely to state that no personal liability is being adopted or assumed by the administrator in relation to the contract of employment.[30]

In relation to the question of which debts or liabilities were in principle capable of becoming secured under section 19(5), Evans-Lombe J. construed the words of the subsection in a literal and natural sense as denoting debts or liabilities of all kinds, provided they properly arise *under* a contract of employment adopted by the administrator. Thus any claim or entitlement exclusively attributable to an independent source—such as statutory entitlement to compensation for unfair dismissal, or a separate promise of bonus payments made by the administrator himself—would not attract the protection of section 19(5) notwithstanding that it arose in the context of an employment whose contractual foundation had been the subject of an act of adoption by the administrator.[31]

The Court of Appeal[32] affirmed the judgment of Evans-Lombe J. in all aspects which are here material. In so doing, they emphasised that the question of whether an administrator has adopted a contract of employment is essentially one of fact and of substance. The carrying on of the company's business necessarily involves the use of employees. If existing staff are used, the administrators must either adopt the existing contracts or negotiate new ones, and if the latter approach is adopted the process of negotiation must be genuine and not a sham. What Dillon L.J. castigated as "a ritual incantation" in a standardised letter in which the administrator or receiver merely asserts that he is not adopting the pre-existing contract is "mere wind with no legal effect" where the essential substance of what is taking place is that the employee's employment is being continued on the same basis as previously.[33] Thus Dillon L.J. asserted that "If [the administrators] continue substantially after the 14 days to employ staff and pay them in accordance with their previous contracts, they will be held

---

[29] *ibid.*, at 672, adopting the proposition stated in R.M. Goode, *Principles of Corporate Insolvency Law* (1990) at p. 101. See however the further formulation of the concept of "adoption" provided by the House of Lords, as explained below.

[30] *ibid.*, at 672–674.

[31] *ibid.*, at 674–675. It is submitted that these comments remain applicable to the acts of administrators after March 15, 1994, from which date the amended provisions of section 19 of the Insolvency Act become operative. These provisions (in force as subss. (6) to (10) inclusive) are discussed below.

[32] [1994] 2 All E.R. 513; [1994] BCC 172 (Dillon, Leggatt and Henry L.J.J.. The main judgment is that of Dillon L.J.).

[33] *Re Paramount Airways Ltd (No. 3)* [1994] 2 All E.R. 513 at 519–521; [1994] BCC 172 at 178–180, *per* Dillon L.J.

impliedly to have adopted those contracts of employment.[34] In his concurring judgment, Leggatt L.J. indicated that his interpretation of the statutory meaning of the word "adopted" as used in section 19 of the Insolvency Act was that it "connotes, in relation to contracts of employment ... 'the continuance of which is expressly or impliedly accepted'," and that in their use of the standardised letter to employees the administrators had unequivocally accepted such continuance.

The final stage of the *Paramount* case took place before the House of Lords in the form of consolidated appeals from three separate proceedings, all of which turned upon the meaning to be attributed to the word "adopt" when used in sections 19 and 44 respectively of the Insolvency Act 1986. The two conjoined appeals, concerned with the interpretation of section 44 of the Act, are considered above in Chapter 14 in the discussion of receiverships. The House of Lords delivered judgment on March 16, 1995,[35] by which time the provisions of the Insolvency Act 1994 (discussed next below) had been in force for almost one year. Since those statutory reforms were not given retrospective effect, the House of Lords was required to address the rights of persons affected by company administrations (and administrative receiverships) which commenced between December 29, 1986 (the date on which the Insolvency Act of that year came into force), and March 15, 1994 (when the Insolvency Act 1994 took effect). Approximately 1,200 administrations were commenced during that time, and there was a candid recognition by Lord Browne-Wilkinson, who delivered the sole speech on behalf of a unanimous House of Lords, that very large sums were at stake in the event that it was confirmed that the rights of employees had been dealt with on the wrong basis.

The House of Lords, by dismissing the administrators' appeal, duly confirmed that the practice developed on the basis of the unreported decision in *Re Specialised Mouldings Ltd*[36] had been equivalent to the proverbial building of a house upon sands. Lord Browne-Wilkinson, despite arriving at the same ultimate conclusion as had been reached in both courts below—*viz*, that the contracts of employment of the employees in question had been adopted by the administrators—did so by means of a different line of approach. Calling in aid the "mischief" rule of statutory interpretation, he recalled that the provisions subsequently enacted as sections 19(5), 44(1)(b), 37(1)(a) and 57 of the Insolvency Act 1986 were originally introduced as amendments to the Insolvency Bill 1985 to correct an injustice which had then recently been disclosed in the decision of the Court of Appeal in *Nicoll v. Cutts*,[37] whereby an employee who had rendered services during a receivership was held to be unable to recover the balance of any wages remaining unpaid at the time of

---

[34] *ibid.*, at pp. 520 and 178, respectively. *cf.* the observations of Lightman, J. in *Re Leyland Daf Ltd*; *Re Ferranti International plc* [1994] BCC 658 at 670: "... in the context of s.44, the word 'adopted' must be given the same meaning as 'treated as continuing in force'". This case is further considered in Chap. 14, *ante*.
[35] [1995] BCC 319; [1995] 2 All E.R. 65.
[36] *supra*, fn. 27.
[37] [1985] BCLC 322.

termination of his employment, whereas any wages actually paid to him would automatically have qualified as expenses of the receivership, with the consequence that the receiver could recoup those costs out of the company's assets. Reasoning from this relatively narrow basis for the introduction of a statutory concept of "adoption" of contracts of employment by administrators and by administrative receivers, coupled with a recourse to the presumption that it was "most improbable" that Parliament had intended to generate unfair anomalies between the position of employees under a receivership or under an administration, or between employees who are dismissed within the first 14 days after the office holder take appointment and those who are dismissed later, Lord Browne-Wilkinson concluded that the meaning of the term "adopt" must necessarily be interpreted in a special way, paying due regard to its context and to the canons of statutory construction.[38] He expressly rejected what he termed the "all or nothing" approach followed by the Court of Appeal, under which the continuation of employment and the payment of wages inevitably meant that the contract as a whole had been adopted and nothing said to the contrary in the administrators' letters could alter that fact.[39] Observing that neither the making of an administration order nor the appointment of an administrative receiver has the effect of dismissing any employee of the company in question, Lord Browne-Wilkinson stated the proposition that the mere continuation of the employment by the company—through continued payment of wages—does not lead inexorably to the conclusion that the contract has been adopted by the receiver or administrator. Nor could a mere "failure to disclaim" on the part of the office holder give rise to the consequence that he was, in law, taken to have adopted any contracts of employment remaining extant. In his judgment, "... adoption in sections 19 and 44 can only connote some conduct by the administrator or receiver which amounts to an election to treat the continued contract of employment with the company as giving rise to a separate liability in the administration or receivership."[40]

Having advanced this forthright, if non-specific, definition of the term "adoption" for the purpose in hand, Lord Browne-Wilkinson refrained from venturing any further by way of illustration or example of the type of conduct which would amount to the election of which he spoke. Instead, he next addressed the question whether it is open to the office holder to adopt a selective approach towards the act of adoption, by expressly showing that he only intends to adopt some aspects of the contract of employment. Here, deference to the force of his own logical premises ultimately compelled the learned Lord to conclude—"with regret"—that there could be no concession to the possibility of "cherry picking" by the office holder without there being a simultaneous violation of the mischief-rule basis on which this approach to the statutory construction had been carried out. This necessitated that in adopting a contract the administrator

---

[38] [1995] BCC at 327–331, and at 333–335; [1995] 2 All E.R. at 75–79, and at 82–89.
[39] [1995] BCC at p. 330; [1995] 2 All E.R. at 78–79.
[40] [1995] BCC at pp. 333–334, [1995] 2 All E.R. at 82–84.

must at the very least accept liability for payment for services rendered to the administrator under that contract.[41] With great respect, it is submitted that such a proposition can be accommodated without the further necessity that the administrator should be rendered liable—on the "all or nothing" basis—for an extended range of collateral benefits to which the employee was entitled under the terms of the original contract, such as substantial compensation for eventual termination of the contract if the office holder subsequently has to resort to this, or if liquidation ensues. Moreover, in his final summation of the effect of his own analysis of the law's effect, Lord Browne-Wilkinson concluded that: "if the contract of employment is continued for more than 14 days after the appointment of the administrator or receiver, there seems to be no escape from the conclusion that the whole contract has been adopted".[42] This, again with respect, appears indistinguishable from the statement of the law previously formulated by the court of Appeal and already quoted above. It thus transpires, very much after the event, that the only safe approach, prior to March 1994, for any administrator desirous of minimising the extent of the claims enjoying "super-priority" by virtue of section 19(5) (as originally enacted) would have been to dismiss all the workforce before the expiry of the 14 days' period of grace, and thereafter to have selectively re-engaged all or some of them on suitably amended terms, as he is perfectly free to do. Such cumbersome, and wasteful, manoeuvres should now be unnecessary as a consequence of the statutory amendments to section 19 (and also to section 44) that will next be described.

The Insolvency Act 1994

Even before the proceedings in the *Paramount* Case came on for hearing before the House of Lords, rapid Parliamentary steps had been taken to try to correct the deficiencies shown to have been present in the originally enacted law. The provisions of the Insolvency Act 1994, enacted within a little more than one month following the judgment of the Court of Appeal in *Re Paramount Airways Ltd (No. 3)*,[43] have remodelled the provisions of section 19 of the Insolvency Act 1986 so far as relating to contracts of employment adopted by administrators. The essential principle embodied in that section as originally enacted has not, however, been disavowed and it therefore remains the case that the contractual entitlements of employees whose contracts are adopted by an administrator enjoy the same advantageous position as before, to the extent that they are

---

[41] [1995] BCC at p. 334. See also the affirmation, in the concluding *Summary* at p. 336, that it is not possible for the office holder to avoid the results of adoption, or to alter them unilaterally, by communications of the type employed in the *Specialised Mouldings* case. (The corresponding references are found in [1995] 2 All E.R. at 83–84 and at 86).

[42] [1995] BCC at 334, reiterated in proposition (1) of the *Summary* at p. 336; [1995] 2 All E.R. at 84, reiterated at p. 86, as proposition (a) of the *Summary*.

[43] [1994] 2 All E.R. 513; [1994] BCC 172. Judgment was delivered on February 22, 1994; the Insolvency (No. 2) Bill was published on March 18, 1994 and received Royal Assent (as the Insolvency Act 1994), March 24, having passed through all its Parliamentary stages inside two days.

THE INSOLVENCY ACT 1994

"qualifying liabilities" as now expressly defined by section 19(7)–(10) inclusive.[44]

These provisions specify that for this purpose a liability under a contract of employment is a qualifying liability if (a) it is a liability to pay a sum by way of wages or salary or contribution to an occupational pension scheme, and (b) it is in respect of services rendered wholly or partly after the adoption of the contract.[45] However, it is expressly provided that the sums eligible to enjoy the priority, secured status conferred upon qualifying liabilities by section 19(6) of the Act are limited to such payments as are attributable to services rendered after the adoption of the contract.[46] For the purpose of establishing qualifying liabilities in accordance with the provisions of subsections (7) and (8), section 19(9) provides that: (a) wages or salary payable in respect of a period of holiday or absence from work through sickness or other good cause are deemed to be wages or (as the case may be) salary in respect of services rendered during that period, and (b) a sum payable in lieu of holiday is deemed to be wages or (as the case may be) salary in respect of services rendered in the period by reference to which the holiday entitlement arose.

The modified provisions of section 19 of the Insolvency Act have effect in relation to contracts of employment adopted on or after March 15, 1994.[47] It is noteworthy that their essential effect is to confirm the basic dichotomy identified by Evans-Lombe J., in his first instance judgment in *Re Paramount Airways Ltd (No. 3)*, as noted above,[48] to the effect that any benefits or entitlements to which employees lay claim by virtue of statutory provisions alone, as opposed to those attributable to the terms of their contract of employment, are not classifiable as "qualifying" liabilities for the purposes of section 19. Thus, any statutory liabilities arising by virtue of unfair dismissal or redundancy of an employee would be outside the protective scope of section 19(6), but conversely any redundancy payment or other compensation for which provision is made in any contract of employment which qualifies to be treated as "adopted" by the administrator is in principle within the ambit of section 19(6) as a "liability incurred ... *under* [the contract] of employment ..." (emphasis added).

It is further to be noted that the amended version of section 19 still contains no statutory definitions of the terms "adoption" and "adopted" for the purposes of the section. Consequently, the judicial *dicta* delivered in the successive stages of the *Paramount (No. 3)* case[49] are likely to continue to provide valuable guidance to administrators in the discharge of their functions. This view is reinforced by the terms of the ministerial remarks delivered by Mr Neil Hamilton during the House of Commons Proceedings on the Insolvency (No. 2) Bill, when he declared that "Adoption of a contract means that a person procures the performance of a contract. In effect, therefore, the person refrains from repudiating it. In

---

[44] Insolvency Act 1986, s.19(6), as inserted by Insolvency Act 1994, s.1(4).
[45] *ibid.*, s.19(7), as inserted by Insolvency Act 1994, s.1(6).
[46] *ibid.*, s.19(8).
[47] Insolvency Act 1994, s.1(7).
[48] *Supra*, text to n. 31.
[49] See above, text to nn. 29, and 32 to 34 inclusive.

such circumstances, the person can be said to adopt the contract. A contract may be adopted by words—'express' adoption—or by conduct—'applied' (*sic*) adoption.[50] The conduct constituting the adoption may be payment of wages, for example."[51]

The release of the administrator following his vacation of office occurs pursuant to the provisions of section 20. Where the vacation of office occurs through the death of the incumbent, his release is effective from the time at which notice is given to the court in accordance with the Rules that that person has ceased to hold office.[52] In all other cases, including the most usual case where the administration order itself is discharged, the administrator's release takes effect from such time as the court may determine.[53] This is one of the matters which the court will usually resolve in the course of settling the order discharging the administration order itself, although it could if necessary be held over to enable the administrator's conduct to be properly investigated before his release is made effective. In this context it may be noted that a person who has acted as administrator of a company remains liable, notwithstanding he has obtained his release, to proceedings brought under section 212 of the Insolvency Act to obtain a summary remedy against a person who has misapplied or retained or become accountable for any money or other property of the company, or been guilty of any misfeasance or breach of duty in relation to the company.[54] Apart from this continuing liability to proceedings under section 212, which is expressly preserved by section 20(3), the release of an administrator has the effect of discharging him from that time onwards from all liability in respect of acts or omissions of his in the administration, and otherwise in relation to his conduct as administrator.[55]

The court has discretion to fix a date upon which the administrator's release shall take effect. If there is any suggestion that the administrator has acted improperly during the course of the administration, his release may be postponed to enable the official receiver and the creditors to consider whether any claim may be pursued against him.[56]

Review and Reform of the Law

The first eight years of experience with the administration order procedure, since its introduction from the beginning of 1987, were disappointing. The raw statistics indicate that the average number of administration orders made, on a yearly basis, was only 166, with a maximum number—just 211—attained in 1990, a year in which there

---

[50] The word "applied" is presumably a misprint for "implied".
[51] *Hansard*, March 21, 1994, Vol. 240, col. 40.
[52] Insolvency Act 1986, s.20(1). On the filling of a vacancy caused by the death of an administrator, see s.13(2) of the Act, discussed at p. 449, *supra*. On the giving of notice to the court following the death of an administrator see r. 2.54.
[53] Insolvency Act 1986, s.20(1).
[54] On the further aspects of liability imposed by s.212 of the Insolvency Act, see Chap. 22, *post*.
[55] Insolvency Act 1986, s.20(2).
[56] *Re Sheridan Securities Ltd* (1988) 4 BCC 200.

were 15,051 company liquidations and 2,634 administrative receiverships.[57] As with the company voluntary arrangement, described in Chapter 15, the abnormally low incidence of usage indicates that the new procedures are failing to provide appropriate means of attempting the rescue and rehabilitation of potentially viable companies. While there is some evidence to suggest that, among the relatively small number of cases where administration has been resorted to, there have been worthwhile instances of successful rescues accomplished,[58] there are also plentiful indications from the empirical data that administration is often employed merely as a convenient means to an altogether different end, namely the delayed breakup and liquidation of a business where immediate liquidation is either impractical or commercially inexpedient. Despite some highly published examples of successful rescues of very large asset-rich companies *via* administration,[59] the conclusion is inescapable that the administration procedure in its originally enacted form does not offer an appropriate and affordable vehicle for the rescue of small- to medium-sized companies.

Mention has already been made in this chapter, and also in Chapter 15, of the review of the new insolvency procedures undertaken by the Insolvency Service, and of the Consultative Document, "Company Voluntary Arrangements and Administration Orders" issued in October 1993. In relation to administration, as was indicated above,[60] a number of barriers to the use of the procedure were identified. These include: the time and cost involved (particularly at the stage of preparation for the court hearing of the application for an order); the unduly exacting standards set by the courts in determining whether any of the authorised purposes of an administration is "likely" to be achieved[61]; the existence of the administrator's power to remove directors, and the obligation to report upon directors' conduct with the consequential possibility of their incurring disqualification and/or personal liability; and the possibility that any floating charge holder may exercise the powers of veto conferred by that form of security, and so frustrate the attempts to obtain an administration order.[62] In the latter eventuality, the considerable expenditure on preparation for the hearing of an administration order petition will have been wasted.

It is submitted that there is no single, simple solution to the problem of under-utilisation of administration in its current form. The reasons for its

---

[57] For the statistical data for the years 1987–1994, see Appendix III, *post*.
[58] See the studies conducted by: M. Homan, *Administration Orders under the Insolvency Act 1986: the Results of Administration Orders Made in 1987* (1989, Institute of Chartered Accountants in England and Wales); J. Goldring (1989) 5 I.L. & P. 2–8; M. Phillips (1987) 8 Company Lawyer 273–277; H. Rajak in J.S. Ziegel (Ed.) *Current Developments in International and Comparative Corporate Insolvency Law* (1994, Clarendon Press, Oxford) Chap. 8 (191–213).
[59] *e.g. Olympia and York/Canary Wharf; Maxwell Communications Corporation*. The latter case was however an example of an orderly disposal of non-insolvent subsidiaries of an insolvent parent company.
[60] *supra*, p. 433. See, generally, Chap. 5 of the 1993 Consultative Document.
[61] See *supra*, p. 423, and para. 5.4 of the 1993 Consultative Document.
[62] See *supra*, p. 428, and para. 5.7 of the 1993 Consultative Document.

neglect, despite the severity of the economic recession between 1989 and 1993, are complex, and in many respects are rooted in the human and psychological aspects of corporate management. Thus there is an inbuilt aversion to the taking of any step which amounts to relinquishing the reigns of power, even potentially, through the appointment of an office holder accountable to judicial, professional and regulatory authorities, rather than being an agent or amanuensis engaged by the company and its board. Hence, it may be suggested, the adjustment of some of the procedural—and cost-generating—aspects of administration, such as the lessening of the requirement to compile a "Rule 2.2 report", or the relaxing of the test to be applied in deciding whether a purpose is "likely to be achieved", while undoubtedly worthwhile in themselves, are unlikely to supply a complete answer to the problem of under-usage. A more compelling inducement to the *timely* recourse to administration which is vitally needed (so that rescue is embarked upon at a sufficiently early stage to provide realistic prospects for its success) would be imparted through the establishing of demonstrable advantages for directors themselves, to be secured through the taking of this initiative, balanced by significant sanctions to be encountered by those failing to do so. Thus, the requirement for the administrator to report on directors' conduct should be specifically excluded from applying in those cases where administration results in the survival of the company itself.[63] Conversely, it is submitted, there should be more explicit provision in the legislation relating to directors' disqualification to ensure that, in the event of liquidation, directors' failure to take timely and genuine steps towards obtaining an administration order can be treated as an indication of unfitness to be involved in company management.[64]

The above suggestions may still not suffice to overcome the undoubted aversion of many directors to the possibility that an administrator (even one who was initially consulted, and enlisted as nominee, by the company board itself) may utilise the powers of dismissal conferred by section 14(2)(a) and remove most if not all of them from office. This problem represents the essential conflict inherent in the aspiration of English insolvency law to nurture a "rescue" culture, while continuing to uphold the established social and commercial concerns that the privileges of limited liability should not be capable of being abused with impunity. There is thus a deep-seated mistrust of the concept of "debtor-in-possession", in the form of a retention by existing management of their full powers throughout the conduct of a "rescue" procedure, such as that offered by Chapter 11 of the United States Bankruptcy Code.[65] In recent years, indeed, a debate has developed amongst American authors as to the inherent soundness of many features of their Chapter 11 procedure, including the debtor-in-possession concept and the excesses to which it

---

[63] See paras. 5.9, 5.10 of the 1993 Consultative Document.
[64] See further, Chap. 27, *post*. The suggested introduction of an explicit incentive to seek administration could be achieved by a suitable provision inserted in Sched. 1 to the Company Directors Disqualification Act 1986 (*"Matters for Determining Unfitness of Directors"*).
[65] 12 U.S.C. (1988). For an accessible amount of the principal features of this procedure, and comparison with administration, see Westbrook (1990) I.L. & P. 86–90.

undoubtedly can give rise.⁶⁶ Such manifestations of concern and self-questioning from the spiritual homeland of the debtor-orientated approach to insolvency only serve as confirmation, from the English standpoint, of the perils engendered by leaving "old management" in control of a failing company. Yet it is self-evidently the case that, in the absence of satisfactory assurances as to the security of their own position, and even in the face of increased risk that they will incur personal liabilities and penalties by so doing, many directors will prefer to postpone the fateful decision to embark on administration until well after the point of no return has been exceeded.

Several different models have been devised, and introduced by legislation, in various countries seeking to address the challenge of providing a workable and satisfactory procedure for corporate rescue.⁶⁷ While these may furnish inspiration for fresh attempts to modify the English procedure, it is submitted that the most expeditious way of amending our law, so as to allay directors' personal anxieties without simultaneously abandoning all effective means of addressing genuine cases of directoral incompetence or impropriety where they are found to exist, would be to amend section 14(2) so that the removal of any director would require the approval of the court, with the opportunity for the administrator's arguments to be challenged by the party affected. Thus judicial judgment of the merits of the case for removal would be substituted for that of the office holder himself, at any rate in a contested case. This would amount to the adoption of the approach embodied in the Irish counterpart of the administration order procedure, known as Examinership.⁶⁸ Arguably, it is the solution which maintains the closest fidelity to the core values of the commercial tradition of the United Kingdom also.

---

⁶⁶ See *e.g.* Bradley and Rosenzweig (1992) 101 Yale L.J. 1043; Lopucki (1992) 91 Mich. L. Rev. 79 and (1993) Wisc L. Rev. 729; Warren (1992) 102 Yale L.J. 437. For a concise account of the debate on Chap. 11, see Boshkoff (1993) 2 International Insolvency Review 173.

⁶⁷ Among the countries of the common-law tradition to have introduced variations on the administration order procedure in recent years, the examples of Canada, Australia, and the Irish Republic may be mentioned. For accounts of these, see *e.g.* Tay (1993) 2 I.I.R. 44; Ogilvie [1994] J.B.L. 304; Harmer (1993) 2 I.I.R. 74; Fruchtman (1994) 3 I.I.R. 33; G. McCormack (1990) 1 I.L. & P. 94, and the same author: *The New Companies Legislation* (1991), Chap. 11; M. Forde, *Company Law* (1992), Chap. 17. For comparative observations, see Fletcher (1994) 2 *Insolvency Law Journal* 110–125.

⁶⁸ Companies (Amendment) Act 1990 (Ir.), s.9.

Section B(1). The Winding Up of Insolvent Companies

CHAPTER 17

WINDING UP LAW IN OUTLINE

If a company is insolvent, either in the absolute ("balance sheet") sense, or in the sense of being unable to meet its liabilities as they fall due, the winding up procedure will in most cases be resorted to as the means of bringing about its orderly liquidation and dissolution. Where the company is experiencing a liquidity crisis which is demonstrably of a temporary nature, it may prove possible to avoid liquidation by means of a voluntary arrangement under Part I of the Insolvency Act, as described in Chapter 15 above. In other cases, recourse to the administration order procedure as described in Chapter 16 may be undertaken with the objective of enabling the insolvent company to survive, but it is equally the case that the administrator procedure can be utilised so as to provide for a controlled transition into liquidation in such a way that everything possible is done to diminish the final loss suffered by the creditors, once the company's ultimate fate has become apparent to those in charge of its affairs.[1]

The law offers two separate modes of winding up procedure, namely voluntary or compulsory winding up.[2] The latter form is known technically as "winding up by the court." In fact, the two forms of winding up are applicable to solvent as well as to insolvent companies, and it is therefore necessary for those who wish to bring about the liquidation and dissolution of a solvent company to refer to the provisions of the Insolvency Act 1986, and to engage the services of a qualified insolvency practitioner to serve as liquidator of the company. In most respects the procedure to be followed is the same, irrespective of whether the company is solvent or not, but in the case of a voluntary winding up of a solvent company the reality of the members' ultimate interest in the return of their invested capital is acknowledged through the special designation of this mode of voluntary winding up as a *members'* voluntary winding up,[3] to which a number of

---

[1] For the importance of such a manifestation of concern to protect creditors' interests when liquidation is imminent, see Chap. 27, *post*, in relation to s. 214 of the Act (wrongful trading).
[2] Insolvency Act 1986, s.73(1). The only other mode of dissolution of a registered company is by striking off the register as a defunct company under s.652 of the Companies Act 1985.
[3] See Insolvency Act 1986, s.90 for the statutory distinction between a "members' " and a "creditors' " voluntary winding up.

special provisions of the Insolvency Act apply exclusively.[4] Where the voluntary winding up of an insolvent company takes place, the company's financial deficiency precludes the return of capital to the members, and the parties primarily interested are therefore the creditors, to whom ultimate control is duly accorded. This state of affairs is once again acknowledged by the nomenclature employed, whereby the winding up is designated as a *creditors'* voluntary winding up. A number of provisions of the Insolvency Act are exclusively applicable to this type of voluntary liquidation.[5]

No special designation is employed to identify the case where a solvent company undergoes a compulsory winding up, and all the procedural steps will be identical to those applicable in an insolvent liquidation of this kind, except for the fact that the originating ground upon which the proceeding is based cannot, for obvious reasons, be the one which is employed especially for the purposes of insolvent liquidation, namely that the company is unable to pay its debts.[6] However, section 122 of the Insolvency Act offers a variety of alternative grounds upon which the compulsory winding up of a solvent company may take place,[7] and one at least of these may therefore be used according to circumstances. The significance of these various grounds, and other general aspects of the winding up of solvent companies, are matters which fall outside the scope of this book, but are discussed in detail in treatises on company law.[8]

Voluntary Winding Up

The mode of winding up which is the most convenient and attractive from the point of view of those involved in the management of the company, and that which is the most frequently used in practice, is voluntary winding up.[9] This is because neither the court nor the official receiver are directly or immediately involved in the procedure, and will generally only become involved either if some major disagreement arises between interested parties which leads one of them to invoke the court's jurisdiction, or if the liquidator discovers some major improprieties in the past conduct of the company's affairs which necessitate the bringing of direct proceedings against those involved.[10] In the first instance however the initiative and timing of the resort to a voluntary liquidation rests with

---

[4] Insolvency Act 1986, ss.91–96. See also ss.107–116 (provisions applicable to both kinds of voluntary winding up).
[5] See Insolvency Act 1986, ss.97–106.
[6] *ibid.*, s.122(1)(f): see *infra*, p. 523 and *post*, Chap. 20.
[7] *ibid.*, s.122(1)(a)–(e) and (g). See Chap. 20, *post*.
[8] See, *e.g.*, *Palmer's Company Law* (25th ed., 1992) Part 15, especially paras. 15.108 to 15.113; and 15.205 to 15.231.
[9] In the years 1982–1985, the respective numbers of voluntary, as opposed to compulsory, liquidations, in England and Wales were: compulsory liquidations: 10,768; voluntary liquidations: 19,408 (source: D.T.I.). See also the statistical information in Appendix III, *post*.
[10] See, *e.g.* Insolvency Act 1986, ss.214, 215 (wrongful trading); and the Company Directors Disqualification Act 1986, ss.6 and 7 (disqualification of unfit directors), discussed in Chap. 27, *post*.

Voluntary Winding Up

the company, and in particular with those capable of controlling the official conduct of the company's affairs. The procedure commences with the passing of a resolution at a duly convened company meeting, to the effect that the company be wound up voluntarily.[11] If the company is insolvent it will not be possible for the directors to make a statutory declaration of the company's solvency,[12] and in the absence of such a declaration the winding up will take the form of a creditors' voluntary winding up.

The winding up will be conducted by a liquidator appointed from the private sector whose appointment is accomplished through resolutions passed at meetings of the company itself, and of the company's creditors.[13] The dominant role in the appointment of the liquidator is accorded to the creditors, who may also resolve to establish a liquidation committee to act on their behalf in relation to the conduct of the liquidation. The appointment of the liquidator brings about the displacement of the directors from the exercise of their powers. Although the legal title to the company's property remains vested in the company itself, the liquidator assumes control of it and administers it for the benefit of the creditors, distributing the proceeds of realisation in accordance with the statutory regime, which specifies the sequence in which the different categories of expenses and liabilities are to be paid.[14] Creditors are required to prove their debts for the purpose of establishing their entitlement to receive dividend, and the same process is also employed as a means of determining creditors' eligibility to vote at meetings, and also the respective weight to be borne by the votes they cast.[15] At the conclusion of the winding up process the company is dissolved and its legal personality extinguished, and the liquidator may obtain his release from office.[16] It is therefore to be noted that in company winding up, in contrast to the bankruptcy of individuals, there is no concept of rehabilitation or discharge to be operative at the conclusion of the procedure: the commencement of a winding up, whether it is voluntary or compulsory in nature, signals the beginning of the end of the company's legal existence.

Compulsory Winding Up

The principal differences between the voluntary and compulsory modes of winding up are ultimately attributable to the fact that a compulsory winding up is initiated by means of a court order, and is thus subject to more exacting, and more closely-applied, judicial and public administrative control. The public aspect of the procedure is manifested particularly through the involvement of the official receiver in a continuous manner from the making of the winding up order onwards,

---

[11] Insolvency Act 1986, s.84: see Chap. 19, *post*, at p. 504.
[12] *ibid.*, s.89: see Chap. 18, *post*, at p. 494.
[13] See Chap. 19, *post*, at p. 509.
[14] Insolvency Act 1986, ss.107, 115, 175, 386 and Sched. 6: *post*, Chap. 24.
[15] See Chaps. 19 and 23, *post*.
[16] Insolvency Act 1986, s.173: see Chap. 25, *post*.

and in some respects even prior to that event.[17] Although it is possible for the office of liquidator in a compulsory winding up to be held by an insolvency practitioner from the private sector, it can equally be the case that the official receiver will function in this capacity, either in default of any appointment of a private practitioner or in the event of any vacancy which arises subsequently.[18] In all cases, an investigation into the company's affairs, and the reason for its failure, is carried out by the official receiver during the course of the compulsory winding up.[19]

The first matters to be considered are the circumstances in which a compulsory winding up of an insolvent company can take place, and by whom, and in which court, a petition for a winding up order may be presented.[20] Some broad parallels may be drawn with the law of personal insolvency at this point, for example with regard to the procedure known as the service of a statutory demand for payment, whereby a creditor may establish the company's inability to pay its debts.[21] It is also the case that the same monetary amount—currently £750—is specified as the minimum level of indebtedness for the purposes of the use of the statutory demand procedure in relation to a company, and also in relation to an individual.[22] In other respects however the two procedures are distinct from each other, and differ in numerous ways. Only at the more advanced stages of the winding up procedure (as in the provisions which establish the categories of preferential debts, and in many of those relating to the adjustment of prior transactions[23]) is there full harmonisation with the law of bankruptcy.

The investigative functions of the official receiver, following the making of a winding up order, are combined with a number of administrative duties in relation to both the control and preservation of the company's assets, and to the assembling of an accurate statement of the company's assets and liabilities by requiring the directors and officers of the company to prepare and submit the company's statement of affairs.[24] The official receiver also decides whether to bring about the public examination of any past or present officers of the company, and must decide whether to convene meetings of the company's creditors and contributories with a view to choosing a private-sector liquidator to serve as office holder under the winding up.[25] When the identity of the office holder is finally resolved, that person thereafter has conduct of the winding up throughout its

---

[17] For example if a voluntary winding up is converted into a compulsory one by the official receiver himself presenting a petition for this purpose under s.124(5) of the Act, *infra*.
[18] See *infra*, pp. 579 and 581.
[19] See Insolvency Act 1986, ss.131–134, 235–237, *post*, Chap. 22.
[20] See Chaps. 20 and 21, *post*.
[21] Insolvency Act 1986, ss.122(1)(f), 123(1)(a), *post*, Chap. 20. *cf.* ss.267(2)(c), 268(1)(a), (2), *ante*, Chap. 6.
[22] *Note* however that s.123(1)(a) requires that a company must be "indebted in a sum *exceeding* £750," whereas s.267(2)(a) states that the debt in the case of a bankruptcy petition should be one which "*is equal to or exceeds*" the bankruptcy level of £750 (emphasis added in each case).
[23] See Insolvency Act 1986, ss.175, 328(1), (2), 386 together with Sched. 6: Chap. 10, *ante*, and Chap. 22, *post*; and ss.238–244 and 339–343, Chap. 8, *ante*, and Chap. 24, *post*.
[24] See *ibid.*, ss.131–132, 135–136, 144, 177, *post*, Chap. 24.
[25] See *ibid.*, ss.133–134, 136–140, *post*, Chap. 22.

remaining stages. The principal tasks of the liquidator are to take control of the company's assets, and to administer them for the benefit of the company's creditors through realisation and distribution in accordance with the statutory scheme, paying the company's debts in the prescribed order of priority insofar as the assets will allow. For this purpose, the liquidator is endowed with a wide range of statutory powers which are identical in substance to those enjoyed by the liquidator in a voluntary winding-up, (albeit there are procedural differences regarding the manner in which certain of those powers are to be exercised.[26] In contrast to the position in the bankruptcy of an individual, the assets of the company in winding up do not vest automatically in the liquidator, although he may apply to the court for a vesting order in respect of any or all of the company property if it should prove necessary or expedient.[27] The process of distribution of the company's realised assets takes place on the basis of creditors' lodging of proof for the unsecured balance of such debts or liabilities as are shown to be due to them from the company.[28] When this process is complete the company's legal personality is extinguished through dissolution, and the liquidator may obtain his release from office.[29]

In parallel to the process of winding up the company, the investigative process regarding the past management of the company's affairs continues, and may culminate in criminal or civil proceedings against one or more of the company's directors and other officers. These proceedings may include applications to require personal contributions towards the company's assets to be made by those who have had responsibility for its affairs, and applications for the making of disqualification orders against persons found to be unfit to be concerned in company management.[30] The criminal proceedings may include prosecution for offences under the Companies Act, committed prior to the commencement of the winding up, which have been discovered by the official receiver or liquidator, and for offences committed under the Insolvency Act itself, either by virtue of the conduct of directors and others prior to the company's liquidation, or in respect of acts or omissions during the course of the winding up itself.[31] Special new provisions restricting the re-use of the names of companies which have gone into insolvent liquidation have been introduced to combat the abusive practice known as the "Phoenix syndrome": a combination of civil and criminal sanctions is deployed against persons who are involved with a company bearing a name closely similar, or even identical, to that of a failed company with which they have previously been associated.[32] As advocated by the *Cork Report*, much emphasis is currently placed upon the efficient detection and subsequent prosecution, of offenders who have abused the privileges of incorporation with limited

---

[26] See *ibid.*, ss.165–168, together with Sched. 4: *post*, Chaps. 19 and 22.
[27] *ibid.*, s.145, *post*, Chap. 22.
[28] Chaps. 23 and 24, *post*.
[29] Chap. 25, *post*.
[30] See Insolvency Act 1986, ss.212, 214–215; and Company Directors Disqualification Act 1986, ss.4–11, *post*, Chap. 27.
[31] See generally, *post*, Chap. 27.
[32] Insolvency Act 1986, ss.216, 217, *post*, Chap. 27.

liability, or who have failed to bring to the performance of their responsibilities in company management the degree of competence, skill and diligence regarded as appropriate in the present day. The raising of standards of behaviour in the conduct of the affairs of companies is seen to be a matter of general public interest, as well as being of immediate concern to all who are involved in commerce.[33]

---

[33] See Cmnd. 8558, Chaps. 43–45 and 48, especially paras. 1891–1901.

Section B(2). Creditors' Voluntary Winding Up

CHAPTER 18

WHEN CAN A CREDITORS' VOLUNTARY WINDING UP TAKE PLACE?

When the directors of a company become aware that it is, or is likely soon to be, insolvent, they may take the initiative in bringing about the liquidation of the company by means of a voluntary winding up. This is a procedure whereby the company itself undertakes the task of bringing about its own dissolution, pursuant to a resolution to that effect passed by the company. To accomplish this objective the company acts through a liquidator appointed either by the members themselves, or by the creditors. The voluntary winding up procedure is applicable only to registered companies which are governed by the provisions of the Companies Act.[1] Section 221(4) of the Insolvency Act prohibits the voluntary winding up of an unregistered company, and it has been held that, if a petition for the compulsory winding up of an unregistered company has been presented, it is thereafter too late to effect the valid registration of the company for the purpose of rendering it eligible to undergo a voluntary winding up.[2] However, with the exception of "unregistered companies" within the combined meanings of the Companies Act 1985 and the Insolvency Act 1986, it may be stated that the procedure of voluntary winding up is applicable in principle to any company formed under and governed by English law.[3]

Distinction between members' and creditors' voluntary winding up

Before 1929 all voluntary liquidations were left largely in the hands of the members, acting through the liquidator, but since the enactment of the Companies Act of that year a distinction has existed between members'

---

[1] *See* Companies Act 1985, s.735, for the definitions of "company" and related terms. For the winding up of unregistered companies, see Chap. 20, *post*.
[2] *Re Hercules Insurance Co.* (1871) L.R. 11 Eq. 321.
[3] For the winding up of foreign companies, see Chaps. 20 and 30, *post*.

and creditors' voluntary winding up. The distinguishing characteristic of the former is that it is predicated upon the assumption that the company is ultimately solvent, and that this fact has been duly attested to by means of a formal, statutory declaration to that effect furnished by the directors in accordance with section 89 of the Insolvency Act 1986. If no such declaration of solvency is furnished within the permitted interval of time prior to the passing of the resolution for winding up,[4] the winding up will be a creditors' voluntary winding up.[5] Although the substantive provisions of the law governing the members' voluntary winding up are not strictly of relevance in a work devoted to insolvency, and hence will not be dealt with in detail here,[6] there are two matters which logically require to be considered. The first concerns the exact requirements relating to the formal declaration of solvency, since this effectively determines whether the winding up will be a members' or a creditors' voluntary winding up. The second matter concerns the possibility that a members' voluntary liquidation may undergo conversion to a creditors' voluntary liquidation upon discovery of the fact that the company is in reality insolvent. Both these matters are considered in turn.

Declaration of Solvency

The statutory requirements relating to a formal declaration of solvency are as follows. Where it is proposed to wind up a company voluntarily the directors of the company or, in the case of a company having more than two directors, the majority of them, may at a meeting of the directors make a statutory declaration to the effect that they have made a full enquiry into the affairs of the company and that, having done so, they have formed the opinion that the company will be able to pay its debts in full within a stated period not exceeding 12 months from the commencement of the winding up.[7] Such a declaration has no effect unless it is made within five weeks immediately preceding the date of the passing of the resolution for winding up the company, or on the same day but before the passing of the resolution,[8] and it must contain a statement of the company's assets and liabilities as at the latest practicable date before the making of the declaration.[9] The statement of assets and liabilities is valid as long as it can reasonably and fairly be described as such a statement and the company is solvent, even if it subsequently appears that the statement contains inaccuracies.[10] It is a matter for regret that there is no statutory provision to impose a more stringent requirement as to the nature and quality of the financial statement: there is a strong case for suggesting that a set of properly audited, up-to-date accounts ought to be filed as a requirement for the company to be able to enter a members' voluntary liquidation.

---

[4] See Insolvency Act 1986, s.89(2), *infra*.
[5] *ibid.*, s.90. See also s.89.
[6] See Insolvency Act 1986, Pt. IV, Chaps. II, III and V (ss.84–96 and 107–116).
[7] *ibid.*, s.89(1); Insolvency Rules 1986, Form 4.70 (as substituted by (S.I. 1987, No. 1919)).
[8] *ibid.*, s.89(2)(a).
[9] *ibid.*, s.89(2)(b).
[10] *De Courcy v. Clement* [1971] Ch. 693.

The declaration must be delivered to the registrar of companies within the period of 15 days following the date of the passing of the resolution for winding up: failure to lodge the declaration within the prescribed time limit results in the commission of an offence by the company and by every officer in default, and renders those concerned liable to a fine.[11] A criminal offence is committed by any director who makes a statutory declaration of the company's solvency without having reasonable grounds for the opinion that the company will be able to pay its debts in full, together with interest at the official rate, within the time specified in the declaration.[12] Moreover, if the company is wound up in pursuance of a resolution passed within five weeks after the making of the declaration, and its debts are not paid or provided for in full within the specified period, a statutory presumption is raised, which it is incumbent upon the accused director to rebut, that the director did not have reasonable grounds for his opinion.[13]

Conversion of mode of winding up

(a) Conversion from members' to creditors' voluntary winding up

In principle, the distinction between the two types of voluntary winding up should be made on the basis of a functional test, namely whether or not the company is insolvent. In the case of a creditors' winding up, the creditors' interest is rightly given pre-eminence in view of the company's inability to pay its debts in full, whereas in the case of a members' winding up, the procedure can, subject to appropriate safeguards, be left to be handled purely between the company and its members. Strictly speaking however, the criterion which determines whether a voluntary liquidation will be a members' or a creditors' voluntary winding up is a purely formal one in which the company's solvency or otherwise is only indirectly of relevance. Section 90 of the Insolvency Act simply states that where a directors' statutory declaration of the company's solvency has been duly made under section 89, the winding up is a "members' voluntary winding up," and in the case where such a declaration has not been made the winding up is a "creditors' voluntary winding up." It is hence quite possible for a solvent company to undergo a creditors' voluntary winding up through the directors' failure to lodge the requisite declaration properly, or even at all. Conversely, a company may be put into a members' voluntary liquidation despite the fact that (whether this is known or not) the company is in reality insolvent. In the latter case, naturally, the possibility exists that one or more of the directors who have made the declaration will be guilty of a criminal offence by virtue of the provisions just described.[14] But these additional factors do not in themselves invalidate the type of procedure which has been embarked upon, nor cause it to be automatically converted into the type which, in principle at least, should properly have been it from the outset. For such a

---

[11] Insolvency Act 1986, s.89(3), (6). For the rate of fine, see Sched. 10.
[12] *ibid.*, s.89(4).
[13] *ibid.*, s.89(5).
[14] See Insolvency Act 1986, s.89(4), (5), *supra*.

conversion to come about, formal steps must be taken by the liquidator of the company in accordance with section 95 of the Act.

Where the liquidator is of opinion that the company will be unable to pay its debts in full within the period stated in the directors' declaration of solvency he is required to take the following steps.[15] First, he must summon a meeting of creditors within 28 days of the day on which he formed the "motorising" opinion. He must send notice of meeting to the creditors at least seven days in advance of the day on which it is to be held, and must advertise the meeting in the Gazette and in at least two newspapers circulating in the locality (or in each locality) where the company's principal place of business in Great Britain was situated during the six months prior to the sending out of notices of the company meeting at which the resolution for voluntary winding up was passed.[16] In advance of the meeting the liquidator must furnish the creditors with information, free of charge, as to the company's affairs and the notice of meeting must inform the creditors of the liquidator's duty to respond to reasonable requests for such information.[17] It is incumbent upon the liquidator to make out a statement of the company's affairs in the prescribed form, to lay that statement before the creditors' meeting, and himself to attend and preside at that meeting.[18] As from the day on which the creditors' meeting is held section 96 of the Insolvency Act causes the other provisions of the Act to operate as if the directors' declaration of solvency had not been made, and as if the company meeting at which it was resolved that the company be wound up voluntarily, and the creditors' meeting which has taken place under section 95, were the meetings mentioned in section 98 in relation to the initial stages of a creditors' voluntary winding up.[19] Accordingly, the winding up becomes a creditors' voluntary winding up from that moment onwards, and without the need for any fresh start or reiteration of steps already undertaken.[20] At their meeting held under section 95 the creditors may resolve that a different liquidator be appointed, and a creditors' committee may likewise be established, just as though the meeting were taking place in accordance with section 98.[21]

(b) Conversion from voluntary winding up to compulsory winding up

Even in the case where the directors of a company make a statutory

---

[15] *ibid.*, s.95(1). *Note* that the liquidator is required to take the prescribed course of action even though his opinion may later turn out to have been ill-informed.

[16] Insolvency Act 1986, s.95(2), (5), (7); Insolvency Rules 1986, r. 4.51 (as amended). Where the company had no principal place of business in Great Britain during the relevant period, the locality of reference for the purposes of notice by advertisement is to be the company's registered office: s.95(6).

[17] Insolvency Act 1986, s.95(2)(d).

[18] *ibid.*, s.95(3), (4); Insolvency Rules 1986, r. 4.34 (as amended); Forms 4.18–4.20.

[19] Insolvency Act 1986, s.98 is discussed in Chap. 19, *post*.

[20] Accordingly, ss.98 and 99 do not apply where a members' voluntary winding up is converted into a creditors' voluntary winding up: s.97(2).

[21] Insolvency Act 1986, s.98 is discussed in Chap. 19, *post*. See also Insolvency Rules 1986, rr. 4.51 and 4.52 with 4.53, 4.56.

declaration of solvency prior to the passing of a resolution for voluntary winding up, and thus bring it about that the proceedings take the form of a members' voluntary winding up, the declaration of solvency has no binding consequences for creditors of the company, who are entirely free to present a petition for winding up by the court if they can prove that the company is actually insolvent. *A fortiori*, where no declaration of solvency is made, so that the proceedings become constituted as a creditors' voluntary winding up, the possibility exists for a duly-qualified party to petition for compulsory winding-up.[22] These possibilities are preserved by section 116 of the Act which provides that the voluntary winding up of a company does not bar the right of any creditor or contributory to have it wound up by the court. The section further provides however that in the case of an application by a contributory the court must be satisfied that the rights of the contributories will be prejudiced by a voluntary winding up. Although under the modern law there is no requirement that prejudice must be shown in the case of a creditor's petition, the court will in practice have regard to the wishes of the majority of creditors and will exercise its discretion in an unfettered way so as to take account of the overall merits of the case.[23] Suspicion that the liquidator appointed in a voluntary winding up is insufficiently impartial—or that his appointment may have been tainted through the exercise of improper influence on behalf of the directors—may incline the court to make a winding up order so as to supplant the office holder and ensure that an independent investigation of the company's affairs will take place.[24]

A further possibility for conversion of a voluntary into a compulsory winding up arises under section 124(5) of the Act which allows a winding up petition to be presented by the official receiver. The court may not make a winding up order on such a petition unless it is satisfied that the voluntary winding up cannot be continued with due regard to the interests of the creditors or contributories. Whether this condition is met in any given case is a matter for the court to determine on the balance of probabilities.[25] The possibility that the initial appointment of the liquidator may have been subject to the undue influence of a controlling

---

[22] *cf. Re Surplus Properties (Huddersfield) Ltd* [1984] BCLC 89. For compulsory winding up, see Chap. 20 *et seq.*

[23] *Re J.D. Swain Ltd* [1965] 2 All E.R. 761; [1965] 1 W.L.R. 909; *Re Southard & Co. Ltd* [1979] 1 All E.R. 582; [1979] 1 W.L.R. 1198 (C.A.); *Re Medisco Equipment Ltd* (1983) 1 BCC 98, 944; [1983] BCLC 305.

[24] *Re Lowestoft Traffic Services Co. Ltd* (1986) 2 BCC 98, 945; [1986] BCLC 81; *Re Palmer Marine Surveys Ltd* [1986] 1 W.L.R. 573: (1985) 1 BCC 99, 557; *Re Rhine Film Corp. (U.K.) Ltd* (1986) 2 BCC 98, 949; *Re Fitness Centre (South East) Ltd* [1986] BCLC 518; *Re Roselmar Properties Ltd* (No. 2) (1986) 2 BCC 99, 155. *cf. Re Home Remedies Ltd* [1943] Ch. 1; *Re B. Karsberg Ltd* [1956] 1 W.L.R. 57; *Re Riviera Pearls Ltd* [1962] 1 W.L.R. 722; *Re Falcon (R.J.) Developments Ltd* (1987) 3 BCC 146; [1987] BCLC 437; *Re M.C.M. Services Ltd* (1987) 3 BCC 179; [1987] BCLC 535. For analysis of the principles established by the foregoing cases, see Rajak (1990) 3 Insolvency Intelligence 41–42; 49–52. See also *Re Hewitt Brannan Tools* [1990] BCC 354; *Securities and Investment Board v. Lancashire and Yorkshire Portfolio Management Ltd* [1992] BCC 381; [1992] BCLC 281.

[25] See *Re Jubilee Sites Ltd* (1897) Syndicate [1899] 2 Ch. 204; *Re Ryder Installations Ltd* [1966] 1 All E.R. 453 n; [1966] 1 W.L.R. 524; *Re J. Russell Electronics Ltd* [1968] 2 All E.R. 559; [1968] 1 W.L.R. 1252.

shareholder, or of a dominant, major creditor, are certainly factors to be taken into account but will not necessarily give rise to the conclusion that the voluntary liquidation cannot be continued with due regard to the interests of all parties. An important consequence of the implementation of the Insolvency Acts of 1985 and 1986 is the reform of several aspects of the law and practice concerning voluntary liquidations. Foremost among these are the requirement that only a qualified insolvency practitioner may act as liquidator of a company,[26] and the imposition of strict limitations on the exercise of powers, first by the directors and subsequently by the liquidator at successive, crucial stages in the voluntary winding up process.[27] These reforms should help to ensure that the very real risks to creditors' interests, and also to those of the contributories, which formerly arose under the then existing law of voluntary liquidations, should be greatly diminished. As a consequence there should be fewer occasions on which it will be possible to satisfy the court that the voluntary winding up cannot be continued with due regard to the interests of the creditors or contributories, as is required by section 125(5).

Where a voluntary winding up is converted into a compulsory one all proceedings taken in the voluntary winding up are deemed to have been validly taken unless the court, on proof of fraud or mistake, directs otherwise.[28]

---

[26] Insolvency Act 1986, Part XIII, discussed in Chap. 2, *ante*.
[27] See Chap. 19, *post*, with reference to the Insolvency Act 1986, ss.97–100, 114, 165(1) and 166.
[28] Insolvency Act 1986, s.129(1).

CHAPTER 19

CREDITORS' VOLUNTARY WINDING UP: TO THE APPOINTMENT OF THE LIQUIDATOR

Preliminary

As indicated in the previous Chapter, a creditors' voluntary winding up is brought about by the passing of a resolution to this effect by the company itself. Hence the initiative in embarking upon the voluntary winding up rests entirely with the company. Moreover, as will emerge in the course of the present Chapter, the conduct of the proceedings in a voluntary winding up is placed in the hands of a liquidator appointed from the private sector, and there is no direct involvement of either the official receiver or the court unless deliberate steps are taken to invoke their intervention. The voluntary liquidation procedure thus represents a particularly attractive option from the point of view of those involved in the management of an insolvent company, in that the more rigorous and exacting process of a compulsory winding up may be avoided, provided that the requisite steps are taken in good time.[1] These self same attributes contain elements of danger however, in that the interests of creditors—and even of the company's members—may be adversely affected in the absence of adequate controls and safeguards. Prior to the implementation of the Insolvency Acts of 1985 and 1986 the cumulative effect of numerous inadequacies in the statutory provisions bearing upon voluntary liquidations had given rise to a serious incidence of abusive practices associated with corporate insolvency, to which the *Cork Report* rightly addressed much attention.[2] Before examining the law in detail it is as well to furnish an overall summary of the recent reforms introduced in response to the *Report's* recommendations.

---

[1] For compulsory winding up, see Chaps. 20–22, *post*.
[2] See Cmnd. 8556, especially Chaps. 13, 15, 16, 19, 43–45 and 52.

CREDITORS' VOLUNTARY WINDING UP: APPOINTMENT OF LIQUIDATOR

The New Law—Major Reforms

Under the provisions of the Insolvency Act 1986 several important reforms have been implemented which directly or indirectly affect the voluntary winding up of companies. The direct changes have been brought about through the repeal of the provisions previously embodied in Chapters III and IV of Part XXII of the Companies Act 1985, and their replacement by the provisions contained in Chapters II to V and VIII to X of Part IV of the Insolvency Act 1986. The indirect changes occur mainly as a result of the provisions in Part XIII of the Insolvency Act 1986, and in the Company Directors Disqualification Act 1986.

Under Part XIII of the Insolvency Act, as we explained in Chapter 2 above, all persons who occupy the position of liquidator of a company must fulfil various requirements as to experience or qualifications, and are subject to administrative and disciplinary control. These provisions apply to all liquidators in both a creditors' and a members' voluntary winding up. Provisions of the Company Directors Disqualification Act 1986, and also the provisions of Chapter X of Part IV of the Insolvency Act 1986, introduce a range of new sanctions applicable to directors whose conduct shows them to be unfit to be concerned in the management of a company, or unworthy to retain the protection of limited liability. These powers, which are discussed in Chapter 27 below, enable the court to make a disqualification order against a person found unfit to be a director, and to make a declaration under section 214 of the Insolvency Act that a director is to bear civil liability for a company's wrongful trading. The powers are exercisable only in cases where the company has gone into insolvent liquidation, and hence will only be of relevance, in the case of voluntary liquidation, if the company undergoes a creditors' voluntary winding up. However, it should be noted that the court's power to make a disqualification order under section 8 of the Disqualification Act is not made pre-conditional upon the company's undergoing any form of insolvency procedure, and hence the power could be invoked against a person who is or has been a director of a company undergoing a members' voluntary winding up.

Misuse of Company Names: "Phoenix" operations

A further provision within the Insolvency Act 1986 which has an important bearing upon practices which have traditionally been associated with winding up is contained in section 216. The purpose of the section is to contribute towards the eradication of the so-called "Phoenix syndrome," whereby companies are successively allowed to run down to the point where they are either compulsorily or voluntarily wound up as insolvent, only to be replaced by a new company formed and managed by an almost identical group of persons, conducting a business closely resembling that of its failed predecessor and utilising a company name closely similar to that under which the former company was trading. Section 216 is designed in such a way as to curb the abusive re-use of company names by persons who have been directors or shadow directors of a company within the 12 months prior to the commencement of its insolvent liquidation. During the next five years following the commencement of the liquidation the persons to whom this provision applies must not, without prior leave of the court, be involved in any other company which uses the same or a very similar name including the trading style used by the liquidated company. Any person who contravenes this prohibition against the use of a restricted company name is guilty of a criminal offence of strict liability established by section 216(3), and by virtue of section 217 that person is personally liable for all the debts and other liabilities of the new company which are incurred during the time when he is involved in its management.

It may be observed that section 216 of the Act does not prevent the legitimate transfer of a company name to a company formed or managed by one or more of the directors of a failed company: if that were the case, the creditors in the winding up would be deprived of the benefit which might accrue from the disposal of the name and goodwill of the company as a worthwhile asset. But where the acquisition and use of the company name will be carried out by a company with which any of the directors of the failed company is or are directly or indirectly involved, all such persons will have to obtain the prior approval of the court, which will need to be convinced of the bona fide nature of the proposed transactions.[3] Without such prior authorisation not only will each director who falls within the terms of section 216 commit a criminal offence, but he will also personally forfeit all protection of limited liability with respect to the new company with which he is involved. Section 216(3) contains an enabling provision to allow some scope to be created under the Insolvency Rules for the granting of permission to be involved in a company whose name is currently a "prohibited name" on some other basis than by the making of application to the court. The relevant provisions for this purpose are contained in rules 4.226–4.230 inclusive, and are described in Chapter 27 below.[4]

"Centrebinding" operations

The provisions of sections 97–99 of the Insolvency Act are designed to operate in close connection with those of sections 114 and 166. One of the principal objectives of these reforms is to remove from the voluntary winding up procedure some of the more notorious possibilities for abusive practices, particularly those associated with the exploitation of the judicial interpretation of the statutory predecessor to section 588 of the Companies Act 1985 (now repealed) which was embodied in the decision of Plowman J. in *Re Centrebind Ltd*.[5]

The nature of the principal threat posed by the provisions of the

---

[3] *cf. Re Bonus Breaks Ltd* [1991] BCC 546.
[4] *Post*, p. 664.
[5] [1967] 1 W.L.R. 377; [1966] 3 All E.R. 899. The case was decided under s.293 of the Companies Act 1948, which was subsequently amended by s.106 of the Companies Act 1981. Even in its amended form, however, the section failed to provide an effective obstacle to the practice of "Centrebinding."

CREDITORS' VOLUNTARY WINDING UP: APPOINTMENT OF LIQUIDATOR

pre-1986 law to the interests of creditors and members of a company entering upon a voluntary liquidation lay in the potential for dissipation or disposal of the surviving assets of the company during the period following the passing of a resolution for voluntary winding up under what is now section 84 of the Insolvency Act (formerly section 572 of the Companies Act 1985). In the first instance, disposal of assets might take place through the actions of the directors themselves prior to the appointment of a liquidator under the appropriate section of the prevailing legislation, depending upon whether the winding up was a members' or a creditors' voluntary winding up. The potential for such abuses has now been curtailed by section 114 of the Insolvency Act, which provides that where no liquidator has been appointed or nominated in a voluntary winding up the powers of the directors of the company shall not be exercised except with the sanction of the court or (in the case of a creditors' voluntary winding up) so far as may be necessary to comply with the requirements of sections 98 and 99 regarding the convening of a meeting of creditors and the preparation of a statement of affairs. The only acts in exercise of directors' powers which are exempted from the need to obtain the sanction of the court are those which are carried out to dispose of perishable goods and other goods whose value is likely to diminish if they are not immediately disposed of, and all other acts necessary for the protection of the company's assets. Any purported exercise of directors' powers which under the circumstances amounts to a contravention of section 114 will therefore be invalid, and moreover the directors are guilty of a criminal offence under section 114(4).

The second instance in which, under the law hitherto in force, the assets of the company might be disposed of in a manner detrimental to creditors' interests was capable of occurring through the exploitation by the directors and the members of the initiative which they inevitably enjoy in a voluntary winding up with regard to the matter of timing. In particular, the fact that the members will normally have had the chance to meet and to nominate a person to be liquidator, before the convening of the meeting of creditors, effectively confers a strong tactical advantage upon the members in this matter of choice. Where, in the past, this enabled the directors to secure the appointment as liquidator of an individual whom they themselves had deliberately selected for his willingness to collaborate with the directors, a clear threat was posed to creditors' interests. In certain cases however such a nomination of a liquidator by the members was coupled with a failure to comply with the requirements of section 588 of the Companies Act 1985 (now repealed) regarding the giving of at least seven days' notice of the company meeting and the summoning of a creditors' meeting on the same day as, or the next day following, the company meeting. In the *Centrebind* case it was held that, although in such circumstances an offence was committed by the company, the subsequent actions of the liquidator nominated by the members were capable of being rendered valid by a retrospective resolution to that effect passed at a belatedly convened meeting of creditors. In consequence of this decision the way was left open for flagrantly abusive, and pre-calculated, schemes to be put into effect. By means of such schemes the creditors could be deprived of all effective participation in what was ostensibly a creditors' winding up, and could be presented with a *fait accompli* by the liquidator through his disposing of all worthwhile assets before any steps were taken to assemble a meeting of creditors. Section 166 of the Insolvency Act 1986, which partly replaces section 588 of the Companies Act 1985, is designed to put an end to the so-called "Centrebinding" schemes. It does so by the simple expedient of declaring the powers which a liquidator ordinarily enjoys by virtue of section 165 of the Insolvency Act to be incapable of being exercised, except with the sanction of the court, during the period before the holding of the requisite meeting of creditors under section 98. The only matters in respect of which a liquidator nominated by the company is able to make use of his powers without the need for the court's sanction to be obtained are in relation to the preservation and protection of the company's assets, and the disposal of perishable goods and other goods whose value is likely to diminish if they are not disposed of.[6] The liquidator who has been nominated by the company only is therefore, for the time being, in the effective position of a provisional liquidator, with a purely conservative function.

In addition to inhibiting the freedom of action of a liquidator pending the holding of the meeting of creditors, section 166 of the Insolvency Act also imposes an active responsibility upon a liquidator so nominated to ensure that the necessary meeting of creditors is convened as the Act requires. Section 166(5) provides that if default is made by either the company or by the directors in complying with their respective obligations under section 98 or section 99, the liquidator must within seven days of the date of his own nomination by the company, or of his first becoming aware of the default (whichever is the later) apply to the court for directions as to the manner in which the default is to be remedied. Failure on the part of the liquidator to comply with the requirements of section 166 constitutes a criminal offence by virtue of subsection (7) of that section.

The strategy behind sections 114 and 166 of the Insolvency Act is thus to generate an impetus in favour of the convening of a meeting of creditors at the earliest practicable date. The provisions of sections 97–99 govern the convening of the meeting, and replace section 588 of the Companies Act which is repealed. The company is required to cause the creditors' meeting to be summoned for a day not later than the 14th day after the date of the company meeting at which the resolution for voluntary winding up is to be proposed.[7] Further details of the provisions relating to the creditors' meeting are given below.[8]

The directors of the company are required to make out a statement of affairs for the company in the prescribed form, and to cause that statement to be laid before the creditors' meeting. They must also appoint one of their number to preside at the meeting.[9] Any failure on the part of the company or the directors to comply with their respective duties imposed under the provisions of sections 98 and 99 constitutes a criminal offence

---

[6] Insolvency Act 1986, s.166(3).
[7] *ibid.*, s.98(1)(a).
[8] See especially s.98(1)(b), (c), (6), *infra*, p. 507.
[9] Insolvency Act 1986, s.99(1).

for the party or parties concerned, and unless reasonable excuse can be shown for the non-compliance, is punishable by a fine.[10] Having embodied more effective provisions designed to ensure that the creditors' meeting will be convened at the earliest practicable date, the law now incorporates improved provisions whose purpose is to secure the proper exercise by the creditors' meeting of the powers vested in it with regard to the choice of the liquidator, and the appointment of a liquidation committee.[11]

The Resolution for Voluntary Winding Up

Section 84 of the Insolvency Act prescribes the circumstances in which a company may be wound up voluntarily. Three different cases are stated, each of which is linked to the passing of a specific resolution at a company meeting. These are as follows:

(1) When the period (if any) fixed for the duration of the company by the articles expires, or the event (if any) occurs on the occurrence of which the articles provide that the company is to be dissolved, and the company in general meeting passes a resolution requiring the company to be wound up voluntarily. An ordinary resolution (that is to say one which is passed by a simple majority), will suffice in this case, although it is not one which occurs often in practice[12];

(2) When the company resolves by special resolution that it be wound up voluntarily. A special resolution, as defined by section 378 of the Companies Act, is one which is passed by a majority of not less than three-quarters of the members entitled to vote (in person or by proxy) at a meeting of which not less than 21 days' clear notice has been duly given, specifying the intention to propose the resolution as a special resolution.[13] It may be noted that under this second case the resolution need not refer to the company's state of solvency or otherwise, and this course of procedure may be employed as a means of embarking on either a solvent or insolvent liquidation, including one for the purpose of carrying out a reconstruction;

(3) When the company resolves by extraordinary resolution to the effect that it cannot by reason of its liabilities continue its

---

[10] *ibid.*, ss.98(6), 99(3).
[11] See especially ss.100 and 101 respectively, discussed, *infra*, at pp. 509 and 514.
[12] On the length of notice for calling meetings, see Companies Act 1985, s.369. On ordinary resolutions (which are nowhere defined in the Companies Act) see *Palmer's Company Law* (25th ed., 1992), para. 7.701 *et seq.*, at para. 7.704.
[13] Companies Act 1985, s.378(2). (See also *Palmer, op. cit.*, above, para. 7.706. *Note* that the full, 21-day notice period may be dispensed with by means of the exacting provision in s.378(3). Notice is deemed to be duly given for the purposes of s.378 when given in the manner provided by the Companies Act or by the company's own articles: s.378(6). See generally *Palmer, op. cit.*, at para. 7.501 *et seq.*)

business, so that it is advisable to wind up. An extraordinary resolution is defined by section 378(1) of the Companies Act as one which has been passed by a majority of not less than three-quarters of such members as (being entitled to do so) vote in person or (where proxies are allowed) by proxy at a general meeting of which notice specifying the intention to propose the resolution as an extraordinary resolution has been given.[14] It will be observed that in this third case the resolution constitutes a formal admission of the company's present, or imminent, insolvency, but that it has the convenience of speed in that the length of notice of meeting and of motion need be no more than 14 days if the company meeting is convened as an extraordinary general meeting. It is further possible for a meeting called by shorter notice to be deemed to be duly called if it is so agreed by those attending the meeting, provided that those so assenting represent not less than 95 per cent of the total voting rights of those eligible to attend.[15] Where the company is insolvent and is being pressed by creditors, this third case thus offers the most expeditious way of putting the company into a voluntary liquidation.

Whichever of the above alternatives is utilised, the notice of meeting must also contain notice of the terms of the motion which it is intended to propose, otherwise the resolution will not be valid. For this purpose it has been held that sufficient notice of motion will be furnished by a notice which states that it is intended to propose a resolution in the terms of a specified subsection of the Insolvency Act, such as section 84(1)(c).[16]

A copy of the resolution for winding up must be lodged with the registrar of companies within 15 days,[17] and must also be advertised in the London Gazette within 14 days of being passed.[18] Failure to comply with either of these requirements constitutes a criminal offence on the part of the company and of every officer of it who is in default.[19]

Commencement of Voluntary Winding Up, and Consequences Thereof

A voluntary winding up is deemed to commence at the time of the passing of the resolution for voluntary winding up.[20] If the voluntary

---

[14] On the due giving of notice, see Companies Act 1985, s.378(6) (previous note). See also *Palmer, op. cit.*, para. 7.705.
[15] Companies Act 1985, ss.369(3), (4), 378(3).
[16] *Stone v. City and County Bank Ltd* (1877) 3 C.P.D. 282.
[17] Insolvency Act 1986, s.84(3), together with Companies Act 1985, s.380(1), (4).
[18] Insolvency Act 1986, s.85(1).
[19] Companies Act 1985, s.380(5), (7); Insolvency Act, 1986 s.85(2), respectively. Note that in each case the statutory provisions expressly state that the liquidator of a company is for such purposes deemed to be an officer of the company. For the levels of fines applicable, see Insolvency Act, 1986 s.430 and Sched. 10; Companies Act 1985, s.730 and Sched. 24.
[20] Insolvency Act 1986, s.86.

CREDITORS' VOLUNTARY WINDING UP: APPOINTMENT OF LIQUIDATOR

winding up is subsequently converted into a compulsory one, the date of commencement remains that of the passing of the resolution.[21] From the commencement of the winding up the company must cease to carry on its business, except so far as may be required for its beneficial winding up, but the corporate state and corporate powers of the company continue until dissolution, notwithstanding anything to the contrary in its own articles.[22] Property in the company's assets remains with the company unless a vesting order is made under section 112.

As was explained above, section 114 of the Act has the effect that where a voluntary winding up has commenced, but no liquidator has been appointed or nominated by the company, the powers of the directors cease to be fully exercisable. While they remain competent to dispose of perishable goods and other goods whose value is likely to diminish if they are not immediately disposed of, and to do all other things which may be necessary for the protection of the company's assets, the directors may not otherwise exercise their powers except with the sanction of the court, other than for the purpose of doing whatever may be necessary to secure compliance with sections 98 and 99 of the Act (regarding the summoning of a meeting of creditors and the preparation of a statement of the company's affairs).[23] The purpose of this limitation on the directors' powers is to strengthen the protection of the company's assets during the critical period between the passing of the resolution for winding up and the appointment of a liquidator, upon which latter event all the powers of the directors cease except so far as the liquidation committee (or, in the absence of such a committee, a general meeting of the creditors) sanctions their continuance.[24]

Although the directors' powers cease to be fully and freely exercisable after the passing of a resolution for winding up, the directors and also the company's employees and agents are not automatically dismissed as a consequence of the commencement of a voluntary liquidation.[25] This is in contrast to the position which obtains in a compulsory winding up.[26] After the liquidator's appointment the conduct of the voluntary winding up is largely subject to the same provisions as those which apply during the same stages of a compulsory winding up, and it is thus open to the voluntary liquidator to exercise his powers, including those relating to the termination or continuation of contracts between the company and its employees and agents, in accordance with his judgment as to the best way to achieve an optimum realisation of the company's assets, including its business.[27] Thus, if the prospect exists of selling the company's business as a going concern the liquidator may retain the services of the workforce, or a

---

[21] *ibid.*, s.129(1).
[22] *ibid.*, s.87.
[23] See *infra*, with respect to ss.98 and 99.
[24] Insolvency Act 1986, s.103 (the same rule applies in a members' voluntary winding up, by virtue of s.91(2)).
[25] *cf. Fowler v. Commercial Timber Co. Ltd* [1930] 2 K.B. 1 (involving a members' voluntary winding up).
[26] See Chap. 22, *post.*
[27] The powers of liquidators are described in Chap. 22.

Commencement of Voluntary Winding Up, and Consequences

sufficient number of them, while efforts are made to this end. To do so is not incompatible with the requirements of section 87(1) of the Act, provided that the liquidator bona fide and reasonably believes that the carrying on of the business is necessary for the beneficial winding up of the company.[28] Indeed, if the circumstances are such as to warrant the appointment of a special manager of the business, the liquidator may apply to the court under section 177 for such an appointment to be made.[29] However, the liquidator must not carry on the business with a view to its financial reconstruction.[30]

One further consequence of the commencement of a voluntary winding up is that any alteration in the status of the company's members made after this point in time is void, and any transfer of shares made after commencement of liquidation is void unless made to, or with the consent of, the liquidator.[31] The liquidator may give his consent without the necessity of getting the court's permission. It may be noted that a transfer made without the liquidator's consent is void, but not illegal,[32] and that the prohibition only applies to transfers of shares, and not to transfers of debentures.[33]

Meeting of Creditors

Section 98 of the Insolvency Act imposes an obligation on the company to cause a meeting of its creditors to be summoned for a day not later than the 14th day after that of the holding of the company meeting at which the resolution for voluntary winding up was passed.[34] The creditors must be sent postal notices of the meeting so that they receive a minimum of seven days' notice that it is to take place, and there must also be advertisement of the meeting both in the London Gazette and in at least two newspapers circulating in the locality in which the company's principal place of business in Great Britain was situated during the six months immediately preceding the day on which the notices were sent out summoning the company meeting which passed the resolution marking the commencement of the voluntary liquidation.[35] Provided that the sending out of notice to creditors, and the advertisement of the meeting, is properly

---

[28] *Re Great Eastern Electric Co. Ltd* [1941] 1 Ch. 241. *Note* that the liquidator cannot exercise his powers in this manner unless the creditors' meeting required by s.98 has been held, unless his action is sanctioned by the court: s.166(2). See also ss.110, 111 with regard to the sale of the company's business or other property in the course of a winding up.

[29] For special managers, see Chap. 22, *post*.

[30] *Re Wreck Recovery and Salvage Co.* (1880) 15 Ch.D. 353. The onus of proof that a matter is not necessary for the beneficial winding up of the company is on the party objecting to it: *The Hire Purchase Furnishing Co. Ltd v. Richens* (1887) 20 Q.B.D. 387 (C.A.).

[31] Insolvency Act 1986, s.88.

[32] *Biederman v. Stone* (1867) L.R. 2 C.P. 504.

[33] *Re Goy & Co. Ltd, Farmer v. Goy & Co. Ltd* [1900] 2 Ch. 149.

[34] Insolvency Act 1986, s.98(1)(a).

[35] *ibid.*, s.98(1)(b), (c), (5). Note the effects of subsections (3) and (4) where the company's principal place of business has been moved within the relevant six months, or where the company had no place of business in Great Britain during that period. These provisions are in parallel with those of s.95(2)(b), (c), (5), (6) and (7) (conversion of members' to creditors' voluntary winding up), considered in Chap. 18, *ante*.

CREDITORS' VOLUNTARY WINDING UP: APPOINTMENT OF LIQUIDATOR

co-ordinated in advance it is quite possible, and will generally be found convenient, for the creditors' meeting to be held very soon after the company meeting at which it is resolved to wind up. The notice of meeting must either identify by name and address a qualified insolvency practitioner who, during the period prior to the meeting, will upon reasonable request furnish creditors, free of charge, with information concerning the company's affairs,[36] or the notice must indicate a place in the relevant locality (determined by the whereabouts of the company's principal place of business) where a list of the names and addresses of the company's creditors will be available for inspection free of charge during the two business days prior to the date of the meeting.[37] If there is any failure, without reasonable excuse, to comply with any of the requirements of section 98 the company is guilty of an offence and is liable to a fine.[38] The considerations underlying the provisions for the timing of the creditors' meeting and the safeguards against disposal of company assets either by the directors or by the company's nominee as liquidator, until the creditors' meeting has been held, were explained earlier in the present chapter.[39]

In preparation for the creditors' meeting the directors of the company must make out a statement of the company's affairs in the prescribed form, and lay it before the meeting.[40] The statement must give particulars of the company's assets, debts and liabilities, the names and addresses of its creditors, and details of all securities held by any creditors, including the dates when the securities were respectively given.[41] The reasonable and necessary expenses of preparing the statement of affairs constitute an expense of the liquidation, and payment may be made out of the company's assets in respect of such expenses.[42] The directors must also appoint one of their number to preside at the meeting of creditors, and it is his duty to attend the meeting and perform this function.[43] Once again default on the part of any director in complying with any of the above requirements constitutes a criminal offence punishable by a fine in the absence of any reasonable excuse for the accused's failure to comply.[44] In addition, it has been held that in the event of failure on the part of the person who should preside at the meeting to attend it and discharge this

---

[36] Typically, this person will be the insolvency practitioner who has been nominated as liquidator of the company at the meeting which resolved on the winding up.

[37] Insolvency Act 1986, s.98(2). See also subsections (3), (4) and (5) with regard to the matters mentioned in n. 35 above. Further provisions regarding the contents of the notice of meeting are contained in the Insolvency Rules 1986, r. 4.51 (as amended). No particular Form is specified, but Form 4.22 (applicable in compulsory winding up) may be taken as a model.

[38] Insolvency Act 1986, s.98(6). For the penalties, see s.430 and Sched. 10.

[39] *Above*, pp. 501–503.

[40] Insolvency Act 1986, s.99(1)(a), (b), (2); Insolvency Rules 1986, r. 4.34; Forms 4.18–4.20.

[41] *ibid.*, s.99(2).

[42] Insolvency Rules 1986, r. 4.38.

[43] Insolvency Act 1986, s.99(1)(c).

[44] *ibid.*, s.99(3). For the penalties, see s.430 and Sched. 10.

function, those present may proceed to appoint their own chairman and the meeting may validly conclude its appointed business on that basis.[45]

The central business at a meeting of creditors convened under section 98 is concerned with the exercise of the creditors' rights under sections 100 and 101 with respect to the appointment of the liquidator, and the appointment of a liquidation committee.[46]

Appointment of Liquidator

Section 100(1) states that the creditors and the company at their respective meetings may nominate a person to be liquidator for the purpose of winding up the company's affairs and distributing its assets. The company's nomination is thus made through a resolution tabled as part of the business at the meeting at which the resolution for winding up is passed. As has been explained above, the liquidator must meet the legal requirements of being an insolvency practitioner qualified to act in relation to the company,[47] but invariably the directors of the company have the advantage of being able to take thought in advance as to the choice of whom to propose for nomination as liquidator at the members' meeting. The Rules specify that a resolution, including one for the appointment of a liquidator, is passed on the basis of a majority measured in terms of value, which in the case of a shareholders' meeting is determined by reference to the number of votes conferred on each shareholder by the company's articles.[48] If more than one nominee is proposed for appointment, there may need to be a series of votes until a clear majority is obtained for one of them.[49]

The second phase of the process of appointment of the liquidator comes with the meeting of creditors. The provision in section 100(2) is aimed at giving a positive emphasis to the fact that the creditors enjoy the pre-eminent right to determine who shall be appointed as liquidator. Section 100(2) provides that the liquidator shall be the person nominated by the creditors or, where no person has been so nominated, the person (if any) nominated by the company. However, in the event of different persons being nominated it remains possible under section 100(3) for any director, member or creditor of the company to apply to the court for an order either directing that the company's nominee shall be liquidator instead of or jointly with the person nominated by the creditors, or that some other person shall be liquidator instead of the creditors' nominee. An application under section 100(3) must be made within seven days after the date on which the nomination was made by the creditors.

As a further means of ensuring that creditors are enabled to play a more

---

[45] *Re Salcombe Hotel Development Co. Ltd* (1989) 5 BCC 807. See also s.166(5) of the Act.
[46] Insolvency Rules 1986, r. 4.52, as applicable to meetings under Insolvency Act 1986, s.98 by virtue of r. 4.53, imposes a limitation on the resolutions which may be taken at the meeting.
[47] See *above*, p. 500, and also Chap. 2, *ante*.
[48] Insolvency Rules 1986, r. 4.63(1).
[49] *ibid.*, r. 4.63(2).

influential role in the conduct of a creditors' voluntary winding up, the new insolvency law incorporates changes in the rules governing voting procedure at creditors' meetings. In place of the compound majority requirements (*i.e.* a majority in number and in value) formerly specified under the Winding Up Rules of 1949,[50] the new Insolvency Rules provide that a resolution at a creditors' meeting is passed when a majority in value of those present and voting, in person or by proxy, have voted in favour of the resolution.[51] This change in the voting procedure should greatly enhance the ability of the creditors to act in a decisive way and so take advantage of their right, subject to the court's overriding powers where these are properly invoked, to determine who shall be the liquidator. The serious problem of low attendance at creditors' meetings has been addressed by a special rule to the effect that a quorum is constituted by the presence of at least one creditor entitled to vote. This can include a person represented by proxy by any person (including the chairman).[52] Thus a creditors' meeting may take place at which the chairman is the only person physically present.

Proof of debts for voting purposes

The fact that the method of voting at a creditors' meeting is based upon the value of debt means that it is necessary, before the business of the meeting commences, for each creditor to establish the value of his debt for voting purposes. This is done through the process of lodging proof which, since the same process is involved in cases of compulsory winding up, will for the sake of convenience be explained in a later chapter.[53] For the present, it will suffice to emphasise that a creditor is entitled to vote only in respect of that portion (if any) of his debt which is unsecured after deducting the estimated value of any security he may hold.[54] This rule has the merit of according the right of determination to those who must perforce look to the process of liquidation itself for such return on their outstanding debts as they are destined to receive.

Where a person is appointed as liquidator through the procedure contained in section 100, the chairman of the meeting at which his appointment takes place must so certify, but may not do so until the person appointed has furnished a written statement to the effect that he is duly qualified to hold office as liquidator under the Act, and that he consents so to act. Subject to this, the liquidator's appointment takes effect upon the passing of the resolution for that appointment.[55] The liquidator is

---

[50] (S.I. 1949, No. 330), r. 134 (*repealed*). For illustrations of the difficulties formerly caused by the "compound majority" rule, see *Re Caston Cushioning* [1955] 1 All E.R. 508. See also *Re Bloxwich Iron and Steel Co.* [1894] W.N. 111.

[51] Insolvency Rules 1986, r. 4.63.

[52] Insolvency Rules 1986 (as amended), r. 12.4A.

[53] See Chap. 22, *post*, p. 574.

[54] Insolvency Rules 1986, r. 4.67(4). *cf. Re A Debtor (No. 222 of 1990)* [1992] BCLC 137, on the procedure to be followed where a creditor's entitlement to vote is disputed at the meeting.

[55] Insolvency Rules 1986, r. 4.101 (as amended); Forms 4.27, 4.28. See also r. 4.103, which applies where the liquidator is appointed by the court following application made under s.100(3) of the Act (above).

required, within 14 days, to publish a notice of his appointment in the Gazette and to deliver a formal notification of his appointment to the registrar of companies.[56] Non-compliance with either of these requirements constitutes an offence of strict liability for which the liquidator is punishable by fine.[57] The Rules also require the liquidator to advertise his appointment suitably in a newspaper, so as to ensure that it comes to the notice of the company's creditors and shareholders.[58]

Resignation or Removal of Liquidator: Vacation of Office

Once appointed, the liquidator's appointment continues until he either resigns or is removed from office, or until he vacates office, or is released therefrom upon completion of his administration.

A liquidator may resign his office only on grounds of ill health or because he intends ceasing to be in practice as an insolvency practitioner, or because there is some conflict of interest or change in personal circumstances which furnishes an impediment to his further discharging his duties in office.[59] Before resigning the liquidator must call a meeting of creditors for the purpose of receiving his resignation, and must send with the notice of meeting an account of his administration, accompanied by a summary of his receipts and payments and a statement that he has reconciled his account with that which is held by the Secretary of State in respect of the winding up.[60] If the creditors' meeting resolves to accept the liquidator's resignation he must forthwith give notice of his resignation to the registrar of companies, as required by section 171(5).[61] The creditors may proceed to fill the vacancy by means of a resolution passed in the same manner as that which brought about the original appointment.[62]

If the creditors' meeting resolves not to accept the liquidator's resignation,, the liquidator may apply to the court for an order giving him leave to resign. If such an order is granted the court may make any appropriate provision with respect to matters arising in connection with the resignation and must determine the date from which the liquidator's release is effective.[63] The court is also empowered to appoint a liquidator if at any time there is none acting, and also has jurisdiction to remove a liquidator on cause shown, and appoint another in his place.[64]

---

[56] Insolvency Act 1986, s.109(1).
[57] *ibid.*, s.109(2). For the penalties, see s.430 and Sched. 10.
[58] Insolvency Rules 1986, r. 4.106.
[59] *ibid.*, r. 4.108(4).
[60] *ibid.*, r. 4.108(3).
[61] *ibid.*, r. 4.110(2).
[62] Insolvency Act 1986, s.104, together with Insolvency Rules 1986, r. 4.110(3).
[63] Insolvency Rules 1986, r. 6.111(1), (2); see also para. (4) with respect to notification of the registrar of companies.
[64] Insolvency Act 1986, ss.108, 171(2). For procedure on removal by the court, see Insolvency Rules 1986, r. 4.120. On the degree of unfitness justifying removal, see *Re Sir John Moore Gold Mining Co.* (1879) 12 Ch.D. 325 C.A.; *Re Charterland Gold Fields Ltd* (1909) 26 T.L.R. 132; *Re Rubber and Produce Investment Trusts* [1915] 1 Ch. 382. *cf.* also *Re Arctic Engineering Ltd (No. 2)* [1986] 1 W.L.R. 686; [1986] 2 All E.R. 346 (persistent default in submitting annual returns); *Re Keypack Homecare* [1987] BCLC 409 (failure to display sufficient vigour in carrying out his duties).

Creditors' Voluntary Winding Up: Appointment of Liquidator

Other than where he is removed by the court, a liquidator in a creditors' voluntary winding up may be removed only by a general meeting of the company's creditors summoned specially for that purpose.[65] The liquidator himself is obliged to summon the meeting for his own removal, if he is so requested by 25 per cent in value of the company's creditors, excluding those who are connected with the company.[66] At the meeting a person other than the liquidator or his nominee may be elected chairman, but it is also competent for the liquidator to chair the meeting, subject to the proviso that he may not adjourn the meeting without the consent of at least one half of the creditors present or represented, and entitled to vote.[67] If the creditors resolve that the liquidator be removed, the chairman of the meeting must forthwith send the certificate of removal to the registrar of companies, but if another liquidator is appointed at the meeting the chairman delivers his certificate of appointment to the new liquidator, whose first duty is thus to send it to the registrar.[68]

In addition to the termination of his office through death, vacation of office by the liquidator occurs in two cases. The first is if at any time he ceases to be a person who is qualified to act as an insolvency practitioner in relation to the company.[69] The second is where final meetings of the company and of its creditors have been held under section 106 of the Act, marking the conclusion of the administration and leaving the way open for the company's dissolution to take place under section 201.[70] In the latter case, the liquidator must vacate office as soon as he has sent the registrar of companies a copy of the account of the winding up together with a return of the holding of the final meetings, as required by section 106(3).

The Liquidator's Remuneration

The amount or rate of the liquidator's remuneration is fixed by the liquidation committee, if there is one (see below), or failing that is fixed by resolution of a meeting of creditors.[71] The remuneration is to be fixed either as a percentage of the value of the assets which are realised or distributed, or of the two values in combination, or else is to be fixed by reference to the time properly given by the liquidator and his staff in attending to the matters arising under the winding up.[72] If for any reason

---

[65] Insolvency Act 1986, s.171(2)(b). Any creditor may apply to the court for directions as to the mode of summoning the meeting, or the conduct thereof: Insolvency Rules 1986, r. 4.115. On the special restrictions which apply where the liquidator has been appointed by the court under s.108, see s.171(3).

[66] Insolvency Rules 1986, r. 4.114. On the meaning of "connected with the company," see Insolvency Act 1986, ss.249 and 435, reproduced in Appendix I, *post*.

[67] *ibid.*, r. 4.114(3).

[68] *ibid.*, r. 4.117. The new liquidator must also advertise his appointment, stating that his predecessor has been removed rr. 4.106, 4.118.

[69] Insolvency Act 1986, s.171(4); see also Insolvency Rules 1986, r. 4.135. On the meaning of the qualification referred to, see Chap. 2, *ante*, p. 28.

[70] *ibid.*, s.171(6). For dissolution of the company and release of the liquidator see Chap. 25, *post*.

[71] Insolvency Rules 1986, r. 4.127(3), (5).

[72] *ibid.*, r. 4.127(2). See also r. 4.127(4) for the guidelines to be followed by the committee.

the liquidator's remuneration is not fixed by the foregoing process, rule 4.127(6) of the Rules specifies that his remuneration shall be in accordance with the scale of fees laid down for the official receiver by general regulations.[73]

If the liquidator considers that the remuneration fixed for him by the committee is inadequate he may request that it be increased by resolution of the creditors, and if he considers that the amount fixed either by the committee or by resolution of the creditors is insufficient, he may apply to the court for an order increasing its amount or rate.[74] Correspondingly, any creditor of the company who considers the liquidator's remuneration to be excessive may, with the concurrence of at least 25 per cent in value of the creditors (including himself) apply to the court for an order that the remuneration be reduced.[75]

Powers and Duties of the Liquidator

Schedule 4 to the Insolvency Act sets out in detail the powers which are conferred upon liquidators in both the voluntary and the compulsory modes of winding up. Although a common formulation is employed in respect of the two modes, a distinction in the liquidator's freedom to exercise those powers results from the contrasting provisions of sections 165 and 167 of the Act. The former, which relates to voluntary winding up, indicates that the liquidator there enjoys a greater degree of freedom in that he may exercise the powers specified in Part II of the Schedule,[76] as well as the general powers specified in Part III, without requiring the sanction of the court or the liquidation committee (if there is one) or of a creditors' meeting in order to do so. A voluntary liquidator thus requires sanction only for the exercise of the powers specified in Part I of the Schedule, whereas a compulsory liquidator requires sanction in order to exercise any of the powers specified in both Part I and Part II.[77] The powers themselves are described in Chapter 22 below.

The exercise of his powers by a voluntary liquidator is subject to overriding provisions of section 166, which have already been considered.[78] Additional powers are conferred upon a voluntary liquidator by virtue of section 165(4) and (5), which authorise the liquidator to exercise the court's power of settling the list of contributories, to exercise the court's power of making calls, to summon general meetings of the company for the purpose of obtaining its sanction by special or extraordinary resolution or for any other purpose he may think fit, and to pay the company's debts and adjust the rights of the contributories among themselves.

A liquidator in a voluntary winding up is not an officer of the court and is

---

[73] As to which, see the Insolvency Regulations 1994 (S.I. 1994, No. 2507), Part 5, with Schedule 2. See also Insolvency Rules 1986, r. 4.128.
[74] Insolvency Rules 1986, r. 4.130.
[75] *ibid.*, r. 4.131.
[76] Part II of Sched. 4 consists of paras. 4 and 5, which are listed in Chap. 22, *post*, p. 585.
[77] Insolvency Act 1986, s.167(1)(a).
[78] *Above*, p. 503.

not subject to those duties which exclusively pertain to those office holders who have that status.[79]

Subsequent Course of Liquidation

After appointment, the duties of a voluntary liquidator, and the course of administration to be undertaken, are broadly identical to those which are applicable in a compulsory winding up. The basic principle of *pari passu* distribution of the realised assets of the company in satisfaction of its liabilities is common to both modes of winding up,[80] and the rules as to preferential debts likewise apply in common.[81] All of these matters are considered in the relevant parts of the Chapters dealing with winding up by the court.

Following completion of the administration the company undergoes dissolution and the liquidator obtains his release: the respective provisions governing these matters in the two modes of winding up are dealt with together in Chapter 25. If a voluntary winding up continues for more than one year the liquidator must summon a general meeting of the company and a meeting of creditors at the end of the first year, and of each successive year, and lay before the meetings an account of his acts and dealings and of the conduct of the winding up during the preceding year.[82] The liquidator is liable to a fine for failure to comply with this requirement.[83]

In case any uncertainty or difficulty is encountered in the course of a voluntary liquidation section 112 contains a wide and useful power whereby the liquidator or any shareholder or creditor may apply to the court to determine any question arising in the winding up, and the court is given a wide discretion to make such order as it thinks fit, or to exercise all or any of the powers which the court might exercise if the company were being wound up by the court.[84] In an appropriate case, for example where an arrangement with creditors is concluded, the court has power under section 112 to stay a voluntary winding up so that the company may resume business.[85]

Appointment of Liquidation Committee

Section 101 allows the creditors at the meeting held under section 98, or at any subsequent meeting, if they so decide, to have a liquidation committee (formerly known as a committee of inspection) and to appoint not more than five persons to be members of the committee. The company may then appoint not more than five persons to be members of the committee, subject to the power of the creditors to disapprove of any

---

[79] *Re John Bateson & Co.* [1985] BCLC 259; *Re T.H. Knitwear Ltd* [1988] 4 BCC 102.
[80] Insolvency Act 1986, s.105(1), (2).
[81] Insolvency Act 1986, ss.175 and 386, with Sched. 6, discussed in Chap. 24, *post*.
[82] Insolvency Act 1986, s.105(1), (2).
[83] *ibid.*, s.105(3). For the level of fine, see s.430 and Sched. 10.
[84] For illustrations of the scope of s.112, see *Re Salisbury Railway and Market House Co. Ltd* [1969] 1 Ch. 349; *Re R.-R. Realisations Ltd (formerly Rolls Royce Ltd)* [1980] 1 All E.R. 1019; *Re J. Burrows (Leeds) Ltd* [1982] 2 All E.R. 882.
[85] *Re S.S. Titian* (1888) 36 W.R. 347; *Re Hafna Mining Co.* (1888) 84 L.T.(O.S.) 403.

persons so appointed.[86] If the creditors do disapprove of the persons so appointed the latter may not act unless the court orders otherwise. The court has power to appoint other persons to act in place of those to whose appointment the creditors have objected.[87]

The powers of the liquidation committee are partly laid down by provisions within the Insolvency Act, and are partly expressed in the Insolvency Rules, as follows:

(1) To fix the remuneration of the liquidator or liquidators[88];
(2) To sanction continuance of the powers of directors[89];
(3) To sanction payment of any class of creditors in full or to make compromises with creditors or contributories in respect of calls[90];
(4) To sanction a reconstruction under sections 110 and 111 of the Insolvency Act;
(5) To direct the liquidator periodically to send a written report to every member of the committee indicating the progress of the winding up and any matters arising from it to which the liquidator considers that the committee's attention should be drawn[91];
(6) To direct the liquidator as to the keeping of financial records of the company and to receive such records when submitted by the liquidator for inspection.[92]

Detailed provisions are contained in the Insolvency Rules with regard to the procedure and conduct of the liquidation committee: these matters are discussed in Chapter 22 below.[93]

---

[86] Insolvency Act 1986, s.101(1)–(3).
[87] *ibid.*, s.101(3)(b).
[88] Insolvency Rules 1986, r. 4.127.
[89] Insolvency Act 1986, s.103.
[90] *ibid.*, s.165(2) and Sched. 4, pt. 1.
[91] Insolvency Rules 1986, r. 4.168. See also r. 4.155.
[92] Insolvency Regulations 1994 (above, n. 73), reg. 10, in conjunction with regs. 12 and 13.
[93] See Insolvency Rules 1986, rr. 4.151–4.172, *post*, p. 590.

Section B(3). Compulsory Winding Up (Winding Up By The Court)

CHAPTER 20

WHEN CAN A COMPULSORY WINDING UP TAKE PLACE?

Since the introduction in 1856 of a separate system of company winding up distinct from the law of bankruptcy[1] successive statutory enactments have carefully ensured that those companies which have been duly formed under the law of England and Wales, or which are governed by its provisions, cannot be the subject of bankruptcy proceedings but, instead, are liable to be wound up by the court in certain circumstances. This form of winding up—commonly known as compulsory winding up—is now principally governed by the provisions of Chapters VI-X of Part IV of the Insolvency Act 1986,[2] within the First Group of Parts of the Act, which apply exclusively to the insolvency of companies. On the other hand, the provisions governing bankruptcy are to be found in the Second Group of Parts of the Act, which govern the insolvency of individuals.[3] Thus, the established distinction between the two insolvency regimes—winding-up of companies, and bankruptcy of individuals—has been maintained within the structure of the new Insolvency Act, although it is to be noted that the provisions within the Third Group of Parts of the Act are of general application and bear upon both company and individual insolvency.

Field of Application of the Law

In England and Wales, jurisdiction in winding up is exercisable in relation to two kinds of company, namely those registered in England and Wales, which may be wound up by the court in accordance with Chapter VI of Part IV of the Insolvency Act, and those companies which are unregistered, within the meaning of the Insolvency Act and the

---

[1] See Joint Stock Companies Act 1856 (19 and 20 Vict., c. 47), Pt. III (ss.59–105). See also Chap. 1, *ante*, p. 10 *et seq.*
[2] Comprising ss.117–219 inclusive. Pts. V to VII are also of relevance.
[3] See Pts. IX to XI of the Act (ss.264–385), dealt with in Pt. I of this book.

When Can a Compulsory Winding Up Take Place?

Companies Act, which may be wound up by the court in accordance with Part V of the Insolvency Act. Under the latter group of provisions, the English courts enjoy a jurisdiction to wind up companies formed and registered under the law of foreign countries, since these companies come within the definition of "unregistered companies" for the purposes of the Insolvency Act.[4] It is thus appropriate to establish the precise meaning of the terms "company" "registered company" and "unregistered company" for the purposes of the legislation which is our present concern.

Section 251 of the Insolvency Act supplies the definitions of several terms for the purposes of the First Group of Parts, and the section further provides that any expression for whose interpretation provision is made by Part XXVI of the Companies Act 1985, other than an expression defined in section 251 itself, is to be construed in accordance with that provision. Hence it is section 735 of the Companies Act which supplies the statutory meaning of the key term "company" for the purposes of the Insolvency Act also. Section 735(1) states that the expression "company" means either a company formed and registered under the Companies Act 1985 itself,[5] or an "existing company". The latter expression, in turn, is defined as meaning: "a company formed and registered under the former Companies Acts," but it is expressly provided that this does not include a company registered under the Joint Stock Companies Acts, the Companies Act 1862, or the Companies (Consolidation) Act 1908 in what was then Ireland. Thus the juridical separateness of both the Republic of Ireland and of Northern Ireland is recognised, and companies formed and registered in either of those jurisdictions do not constitute "companies" within the meaning of the Companies Act 1985.[6] The "chain" of definitions in section 735(1) is completed with the provision supplying the statutory meaning of the expression "the former Companies Acts," which means: the Joint Stock Companies Acts,[7] the Companies (Consolidation) Act 1908, the Companies Act 1929 and the Companies Acts 1948–1983.[8]

The definition of existing companies is given further substance by section 675 of the Companies Act 1985, which provides that in its application to an existing company (as defined above), the Act applies in the same manner as if it had been formed and registered under Part I of the Companies Act 1985. Thus, all companies which have been formed and registered under companies legislation for the time being in force are accorded equal standing in the eyes of the law. Any company which has

---

[4] See *infra*.

[5] As to which, see Companies Act 1985, ss.1–42 (Pt. I) on formation and registration of companies.

[6] *cf.* also s.679 of the Companies Act 1985, which prevents the provisions in Pt. XXII of the Act from applying to companies registered in Northern Ireland or the Republic of Ireland. Nevertheless, the companies legislation of Northern Ireland is closely modelled on that of England and Wales and Scotland: see the Companies (Northern Ireland) Order 1986 (S.I. 1986, No. 1032) (N.I. 6). The company law of the Republic of Ireland, while nowadays contained in statutes enacted since Ireland became independent, still displays a close similarity to that of England.

[7] s.735(3) of the Companies Act 1985 supplies the full meaning of the expression "the Joint Stock Companies Acts."

[8] Companies Act 1985, s.735(1)(c).

undergone such formation can properly be described as a "company registered in England and Wales" (or in Scotland) and as such is capable of undergoing a winding up by the court under Chapter VI of Part IV of the Insolvency Act.[9] Conversely, any company which does not satisfy the factual criterion of having been formed and registered under United Kingdom companies legislation must necessarily be classified as an "unregistered company" for the purposes of the Companies Act and the Insolvency Act. As such, it may be possible for the company to undergo a winding up by the court under Part V of the Insolvency Act, provided that the further conditions imposed by the provisions within that Part of the Act are met in the case in question.[10] Mention may also be made of the fact that, as was explained earlier in this book,[11] the new law enables an insolvent partnership to be wound up as an unregistered company under Part V of the Act, with or without the simultaneous operation of insolvency proceedings involving the bankruptcy of one or more of the partners.

It may be noted that the following lie outside the ambit of the provisions of the Insolvency Act regarding winding up by the court:

(1) Trade unions, with the exception of the now closed category of "special register bodies," as defined by section 30 of the Trade Union and Labour Relations Act 1974[12];

(2) Illegal associations whose formation is prohibited by law unless they undergo registration as a company under the companies legislation[13];

(3) Municipal and ecclesiastical corporations, and societies incorporated by Royal Charter, such as the Royal Society for the Advancement of Science;

(4) Companies which have been dissolved. Such companies cannot be wound up unless the dissolution is first set aside.[14] Application to have the dissolution declared void must in most cases be made to the court within two years of the date of dissolution, although there are certain exceptions to this.[15] This requirement does not apply to unregistered companies which have been dissolved, nor to foreign companies which, as

---

[9] Insolvency Act 1986, Pt. IV bears the main heading: "Winding Up of Companies Registered under the Companies Acts." *Note* the provisions of ss.117(1), 120(1), further considered in Chap. 21, *post*.

[10] See *infra*.

[11] Chap. 5, *ante*, p. 77.

[12] Trade Unions are unincorporated associations whose status is specially defined by s.2(1) of the Trade Union and Labour Relations Act 1974 so as to deny them corporate identity, although by that same provision some attributes usually enjoyed by bodies corporate are expressly conferred on trade unions. Special register bodies, which are few in number, include the British Medical Association and the Royal College of Nursing.

[13] *cf. Re London Marine Assurance Association* (1869) L.R. 8 Eq. 176; *Re Padstow Total Loss and Collision Assurance Association* (1882) 20 Ch.D. 137. s.716(1) of the Companies Act 1985 prohibits the formation of any company, association or partnership consisting of more than 20 persons for the purpose of carrying on any business for gain, unless it is registered as a company under statute (see however the exceptions provided for in s.716(2),(3) and (5)).

[14] *Re Pinto Silver Mining Co.* (1878) 8 Ch.D. 273.

[15] Companies Act 1985, s.651. See Chap. 25, *post*.

will be described below, may be wound up here although dissolved in their country of formation, if there are assets in England[16];

(5) Companies which have been struck off the register under section 652 of the Companies Act 1985. Such companies cannot be wound up unless they are first restored to the register. Application to have the company restored to the register must be made to the court within 20 years of the publication of the notice of striking off.[17]

The Grounds on which Winding Up may take Place

(a) Registered Companies

Section 122(1) of the Insolvency Act lists the following seven, alternative grounds as supplying a basis for the making of a winding up order by the court:

(a) the Company has by special resolution resolved that the company be wound up by the court;
(b) being a public company which was registered as such on its original incorporation, the company has not been issued with a certificate under section 117 of the Companies Act 1985 (public company share capital requirements) and more than a year has expired since it was so registered;
(c) the company is an old public company within the meaning of section 1 of the Companies Consolidation (Consequential Provisions) Act 1985;
(d) the company does not commence its business within a year from its incorporation, or suspends its business for a whole year;
(e) (except in the case of a private limited company limited by shares or by guarantee)[18] the number of members is reduced below two;
(f) the company is unable to pay its debts;
(g) the court is of the opinion that it is just and equitable that the company should be wound up.

In addition to the grounds set out in section 122, the Department of Trade and Industry has powers, first, under section 72 of the Financial Services Act 1986 to petition for the winding up of an authorised person or appointed representative within the meaning of that Act, and secondly, under section 124A of the Insolvency Act to petition where, as a result of an inspector's report or its powers of investigation under the Companies Act 1985 or other legislation, it appears to the Department that it is in the

---

[16] Insolvency Act 1986 s.225. See *infra*, p. 531, and Chap. 30, p. 731.
[17] See Companies Act 1985, ss.652, 653, discussed in Chap. 25, *post*.
[18] The words in brackets were added by the Companies (Single Member Private Limited Companies) Regulations 1992, S.I. No. 1699.

public interest to wind up the company. The Bank of England is empowered by section 92 of the Banking Act 1987 to petition for the winding up of an authorised institution, if it is unable to pay sums due and payable to its depositors or is able to pay such sums only by defaulting on its obligations to its other creditors.

The majority of the grounds listed in section 122(1) of the Insolvency Act make no particular reference to the company's state of solvency. So far as the grounds contained in paragraphs (a) to (d), and also paragraph (g), are concerned, the company may be wound up on the basis of the facts therein specified, regardless of whether it is solvent or not. It may sometimes happen to be the case that the company is insolvent, but this will be of incidental relevance at the commencement of the proceedings. Conversely, it is part of the statutory scheme of things that a compulsory winding up may take place in respect of a company which is fully solvent, provided that one of the established grounds for winding up is made out. The compulsory winding up of a solvent company is a matter outside the concerns of the present work however, and will not be considered further. We shall instead concentrate upon the ground which is self-evidently applicable to cases of insolvent liquidations, namely that contained in section 122(1)(f), that the company is unable to pay its debts.

Company Unable to Pay its Debts

In practice, the ground for a petition which is most frequently employed by creditors is that specified in section 122(1)(f). The law now utilises two, alternative concepts of insolvency as supplying the basis of this ground for winding up, namely the company's demonstrable inability to pay its debts as they fall due (the "cash-flow" test), or the proven deficiency of the company's assets as compared with its liabilities, thus amounting to a state of absolute insolvency (the "balance sheet" test). These concepts are expressed in the provisions of section 123, subsection (1) of which states that a company is deemed unable to pay its debts in any one of the following circumstances:

(a) if a creditor, by assignment or otherwise, to whom the company is indebted in a sum exceeding £750[19] then due has served on the company, by leaving it at the company's registered office, a written demand (in the prescribed form)[20] requiring the company to pay the sum so due and the company has for three weeks thereafter neglected to pay the sum or to secure or compound for it to the reasonable satisfaction of the creditor; or

(b) if, in England and Wales, execution or other process issued on a judgment, decree or order of any court in favour of a creditor of the company is returned unsatisfied in whole or in part; or

(c) if, in Scotland, the induciae of a charge for payment on an

---

[19] s.123(3) of the Act provides that the money sum specified for the time being in subsection (1)(a) is subject to alteration by order under s.416.

[20] For the required form and content of the statutory demand, see Insolvency Rules 1986, rr. 4.4 to 4.6, and Form 4.1.

extract decree, or an extract registered bond, or an extract registered protest, have expired without payment being made; or

(d) if, in Northern Ireland, a certificate of unenforceability has been granted in respect of a judgment against the company; or

(e) if it is proved to the satisfaction of the court that the company is unable to pay its debts as they fall due.

The above five paragraphs of section 123(1) thus establish five alternative criteria, or methods, for determining that a company satisfies the "cash-flow" test of insolvency. The alternative, "balance sheet" test is expressed in section 123(2), which provides that a company is also deemed to be unable to pay its debts if it is proved to the satisfaction of the court that the value of the company's assets is less than the amount of its liabilities, taking into account its contingent and prospective liabilities.

The Statutory Demand

With regard to section 123(1)(a), it has been held that the use of the words "is indebted" ... "then due" ... and "so due" have the consequence that a debt can only furnish the basis for a statutory demand served under this provision if the debt is presently due at the date when the creditor seeks to utilise it for this purpose.[21] If the debt itself is bona fide disputed by the company upon substantial grounds, the company's failure to pay will not supply the creditor with a basis for petitioning for a winding up order, since it has been held that the words "neglected to pay" are to be understood to mean "omitted to pay without reasonable excuse."[22] In determining whether a debt is one which is "bona fide disputed" by the company, it has been held that a simple dispute as to the precise amount of the debt is not a sufficient answer by the company, and it has also been held that the mere fact that the company has been given unconditional leave to defend an action relating to the debt is not in itself conclusive evidence of the fact that the debt is disputed on substantial grounds.[23] The contrast between a dispute as to the very fact of indebtedness itself, and a dispute merely as to the quantum of an indebtedness, means that in the latter case, provided that the balance of the indebtedness which is undisputed stands above the minimum threshold of £750, the creditor may legitimately resort to the use of a statutory demand, with the presentation of a winding up petition a further prospect in the event of non-compliance.

There is no express provision in the Act or the Rules to enable an application to be made by the debtor company for the setting aside of a

---

[21] *Re Bryant Investment Co. Ltd* [1974] 1 W.L.R. 826.
[22] *Re London Wharfing and Warehousing Co. Ltd* (1865) 35 Beav. 37, 55 E.R. 808; *Re London and Paris Banking Corp.* (1875) 19 Eq. 444; *Mann v. Goldstein* [1968] 1 W.L.R. 1091; *Re Lympne Investments Ltd* [1972] 1 W.L.R. 523; [1972] 2 All E.R. 385; *Re A Company (No. 033729 of 1982)* [1984] W.L.R. 1090; *Re LHF Wools Ltd* [1970] Ch. 27.
[23] *Re Tweeds Garages Ltd* [1962] Ch. 406; *Re Welsh Brick Industries Ltd* [1946] 2 All E.R. 197 (C.A.).

The Grounds on which Winding Up may take Place

statutory demand which has been served upon it.[24] The appropriate course of proceeding, where indebtedness is disputed, is for the company to apply for an injunction restraining the creditor from presenting a winding up petition pending resolution of the question of indebtedness.[25]

The cases establish a general principle that it is an abuse of the process of the court to petition for a winding up with a view to enforcing payment of a genuinely disputed debt. Conversely, if a debt is undisputed it is an acceptable use of the winding up procedure for the creditor to present a petition with the object of forcing the company to pay. Although the individual circumstances of each case are of relevance, it has been held that an undisputed debt could be utilised as the basis of a petition, following non-compliance with a statutory demand, even though the company was apparently solvent and had a cross-claim which, though not established by litigation, substantially overtopped the debt due to the prospective petitioner.[26]

Further conditions attaching to the use of the statutory demand are, first, that the creditor's claim must be for a liquidated sum based upon contract or tort.[27] This is so regardless of the magnitude of the claim. Additionally, the creditor who serves the formal demand must be the person who is legally entitled to recover payment of the debt and to give a full and valid discharge for it. This may either be the original creditor, or an assignee of the entire indebtedness under an effective, legal assignment granted by that creditor, or by an intermediate assignee who so acquired the entitlement to the debt. Consequently, an equitable assignee of part of a larger indebtedness cannot serve a statutory demand for payment, although this disability does not extend to the potential act of presenting a petition for the winding up of the company, provided that the equitable assignee can succeed in establishing the company's inability to pay its debts by some alternative means than the use of a statutory demand.[28]

It should be noted that it is not necessary that the creditor who utilises the statutory demand procedure should first have recovered judgment in respect of the debt upon which the demand is based. On the other hand, if the creditor has already obtained judgment against the company, it is not normally a valid objection to an application for winding up on his petition that the defendant company disputes the claim, or is making a claim for an even larger amount against the petitioning creditor, or even that an appeal against the judgment is pending (unless, in that instance, the company is able to furnish security for the amount of the debt and costs pending the

---

[24] *cf.* Insolvency Rules 6.1–6.5, which apply in relation to the use of a statutory demand as a paving mechanism in the bankruptcy of individuals. See Chap. 6, *ante*, at p. 110.

[25] *cf. Cannon Screen Entertainment Ltd v. Handmade Films (Distributors) Ltd* (1989) 5 BCC 207; *Re A Company (No. 0012209 of 1991)* [1992] 2 All E.R. 797; [1992] 1 W.L.R. 351. See also *Cadiz Waterworks v. Barnett* (1874) L.R. 19 Eq. 182.

[26] *Re A Company (No. 006273 of 1992)* [1992] BCC 794. See esp. at p. 795, *per* Millett, J. See also *Re FSA Business Software Ltd* [1990] BCC 465, at 469, *per* Warner, J.

[27] *Re Humberstone Jersey Ltd* (1977) 74 L.S.G. 711 (August 31, 1977) (C.A.).

[28] *Re Steel Wing Co. Ltd* [1921] 1 Ch. 349 (where it was suggested, *obiter*, by P. O. Lawrence, J. that the petitioner might be required to join the party entitled to sue for the remainder of the debt).

outcome of the appeal).²⁹ To raise a valid plea of bona fide dispute in relation to a judgment debt, the defendant company would need to advance the allegation that the judgment itself was obtained by fraud.³⁰ Even though the position of a judgment creditor is basically a strong one, in that the law regards him as being in principle entitled to invoke immediate remedies for the purpose of satisfying the judgment, the making of a winding up order remains at all times a matter for the court's discretion, and it is possible for the court to order the petition to stand over if it is satisfied that there are valid reasons for awaiting the outcome of some collateral proceedings, provided at lease that the petitioning creditor will not be prejudiced by the delay.³¹

With regard to the service of the statutory demand, which must normally take place at the registered office of the company, it has been held that where no such registered office exists the demand may be validly served by being left at the company's actual place of business for the time being.³² The demand may be sent by registered post, rather than being delivered to the company's registered office by the petitioner (or a duly employed agent) in person, but if the post is utilised it will be necessary to prove that the demand was left at the requisite location for it to be accepted by the court that the demand has been properly served.³³

The period of three weeks is calculated in accordance with the rule that, for the purpose of establishing the running of a prescribed legal time limit, fractions of a day are ignored. Therefore, the day on which the demand is served on the company is ignored, and the period of 21 days begins to run from the beginning of the following day. Moreover, the time limit does not properly expire, and hence a petition for winding up may not be competently presented, until a full 21 days have completely elapsed since time began to run.³⁴ The earliest day on which a petition may be presented is thus the 22nd day after the commencement of the allotted period.

Unsatisfied Execution

Paragraphs (b), (c) and (d) of section 123(1) furnish alternative grounds for establishing the company's failure to pass the "cash-flow" test of solvency, so that it is deemed to be unable to pay its debts. These grounds presuppose that a creditor of the company has previously recovered judgment against it, and has proceeded to seek enforcement of that judgment by levy of execution on the company's property. If such a process fails to realise sufficient value of assets to satisfy the judgment debt (to which amount must be added the costs of the execution process itself),

---

[29] *Re Amalgamated Properties of Rhodesia* [1917] 2 Ch. 115; *Re Douglas Griggs Engineering Ltd* [1963] 1 Ch. 19.
[30] *Bowes v. Hope Life Insurance and Guarantee Society* (1865) 11 H.L.C. 389; 11 E.R. 1383.
[31] *Re L. H. F. Woods Ltd* [1970] 1 Ch. 27 (in which the two cases cited in n. 29 were distinguished). See also *Re Portman Provincial Cinemas Ltd* (1964) 108 Sol.Jo. 581.
[32] *Re Fortune Copper Mining Co.* (1870) L.R. 10 Eq. 390.
[33] *Re A Company (No. 008790 of 1990)* [1992] BCC 11.
[34] *Re Lympne Investments Ltd* (*above*, n. 22.)

this event in itself is to be treated as signifying the company's insolvent state. Section 123(1)(b) defines the circumstances in which such a return of *nulla bona* will be operative in cases of enforcement in England and Wales, while paragraphs (c) and (d) make parallel provisions for cases arising in Scotland and Northern Ireland respectively.

Proof of inability to pay debts falling due

A fifth version of the "cash-flow" test is supplied in section 123(1)(e), whose near-tautologous drafting specifies that a company is deemed unable to pay its debts if it is proved to the satisfaction of the court that the company is unable to pay its debts as they fall due. This provision, unlike its statutory predecessors,[35] omits any reference to the company's contingent and prospective liabilities, which logically have no part to play in the context of a "cash-flow" evaluation of the company's affairs, but are very properly included in the "balance-sheet" test of insolvency within section 123(2), as mentioned above.[36] What is of the essence, for the purposes of section 123(1)(e), is the demonstration, by suitable and credible evidence, that the company is failing to pay its mature liabilities within a reasonable time of their becoming due, provided that the company has no bona fide basis on which to dispute any debt whose non-payment is invoked by way of example of this state of affairs. The most usual, and indeed convenient, way of invoking this ground for petitioning for a winding up order is for the petitioner to utilise a debt due from the company to himself, of whose circumstances he is naturally in the best position to be fully informed. It has been consistently held by courts up to the level of the Court of Appeal that failure to pay even a single debt which is due and not disputed is of itself evidence of insolvency on which a winding up order can be made.[37] This proposition holds good even where it can be shown that the company does in fact have a substantial surplus of assets over liabilities, so that it would meet the "balance-sheet" test of solvency.[38]

The tactical advantage of a creditor being able to resort to section 123 (1)(e) as a basis for establishing the company's inability to pay its debts is that there is no necessity to wait for the elapse of the three-week period associated with the service of a statutory demand, before a winding up petition can be presented. During that interval of time, many things can occur which may have a detrimental and irreversible impact on the petitioning creditor's prospects of deriving any personal benefit from a winding up, in terms of repayment of debt. Yet the very act of serving the formal demand deprives that creditor of the ability to utilise other forms of direct action against the company's property, a course which remains open

---

[35] *e.g.* Companies Act 1985, s.518(1)(e) (repealed).
[36] *Supra*, p. 523.
[37] *Re Globe New Patent Iron and Steel Co.* (1875) L.R. 20 Eq. 337; *Cornhill Insurance plc v. Improvement Services Ltd* [1986] 1 W.L.R. 114; *Taylors Industrial Flooring Ltd v. M. & H. Plant Hire (Manchester) Ltd* [1990] BCLC 216, (1990) BCC 44 (C.A.).
[38] *Cornhill Insurance plc v. Improvement Services Ltd, supra.*

to other creditors to pursue. Thus, when the company's non-compliance with the demand becomes an accomplished fact, the creditor who served it may have cause to reflect ruefully on the capricious effects of the present law, which fixes the commencement of the liquidation at the date of presentation of the petition, rather than backdating its effect to the date of service of the demand.[39] This helps to explain the considerable attractions of subsection (e), from the petitioning creditor's point of view, since it allows him to use the winding up petition in a pre-emptive way. As proof of the debtor company's state of illiquidity, it will suffice to exhibit to the court some evidence—conveniently, often, in the form of correspondence—showing an unequivocal request for payment made by the creditor, and an absence of any bona fide dispute as to indebtedness on the part of the debtor. The Court of Appeal have carefully affirmed that there is no requirement under the insolvency law that a statutory demand must be used by a creditor pressing for payment of a due debt, nor is it necessary that the creditor should first recover judgment against the debtor as a precondition to resorting to a petition for winding up.[40] However, where the company can show that there are substantial grounds for disputing liability to pay the petitioner's debt, it then becomes inappropriate to invoke section 123(1)(e), and it has been declared to be an abuse of process of the court to present a winding up petition against a *solvent* company as a means of putting pressure on it to pay money which is bona fide disputed: the court may issue an injunction to restrain presentation of the petition and may penalise the petitioner (and possibly the legal advisor conducting the proceedings), in costs.[41]

(b) Unregistered companies

The principal heading of Part IV of the Insolvency Act indicates that the provisions of that Part apply to the winding up of companies registered under the Companies Acts. From this it follows that any corporate entity which does not fulfil the statutory definition for being a registered company cannot be wound up under that Part of the Act.[42] Nevertheless, a compulsory winding up by the court in England and Wales (or, in appropriate circumstances, by the court in Scotland) may take place under the provisions of Part V of the Act, which bears the heading: "Winding up of unregistered companies." This part of the legislation relating to company liquidations is in fact a survival from the early state of the companies legislation of the mid-19th century, when very many

---

[39] For the commencement of liquidation, and effects thereof, see *post*.
[40] *Taylors Industrial Flooring Ltd v. M. & H. Plant Hire (Manchester) Ltd* (*supra*, n. 37).
[41] *Re A Company (No. 0010656 of 1990)* [1991] BCLC 464; *Re A Company (No. 0012209 of 1991)* [1992] 1 W.L.R. 351, [1992] 2 All E.R. 797. For the principles regarding the use of "wasted costs" orders in insolvency proceedings, see *Re A Company (No. 0022 of 1993), Philex v. Golban* [1993] BCC 726 (Knox, J.), revsd. *sub nom. Ridehalgh v. Horsefield, and related appeals* [1994] BCC 390 (C.A.). On the award of costs on an indemnity basis against an unsuccessful petitioner, see *Re A Company (No. 00751 of 1992), ex p. Avocet Aviation Ltd* [1992] BCLC 869.
[42] See *above*, p. 520 on the statutory meaning of "registered company."

companies existed which had not been formed under any of the Companies Acts, nor been registered under the Acts subsequently to formation. In the present day, the concept of "unregistered companies" effectively embraces statutory companies formed by private Act of Parliament (with the exception of railway companies),[43] and foreign companies which have carried on business in Great Britain, whether or not they have established a place of business in this country.

Section 221(5) of the Insolvency Act specifies the circumstances in which an unregistered company may be wound up, as follows:

(a) if the company is dissolved, or has ceased to carry on business, or is carrying on business only for the purpose of winding up its affairs;
(b) if the company is unable to pay its debts;
(c) if the court is of the opinion that it is just and equitable that the company should be wound up.

The grounds for winding up set out above are more limited in number than those listed in section 122 of the Insolvency Act in relation to the winding up of registered companies.

An unregistered company may only be wound up by the court: the voluntary mode of liquidation is expressly declared to be inapplicable to unregistered companies.[44] Limitations upon the exercise of judicial jurisdiction to wind up unregistered companies are imposed by section 221(2), which provides that if the company has a principal place of business situated in Northern Ireland it shall not be wound up under the provisions of Part V unless it has a principal place of business situated in either England and Wales or Scotland, or both England and Wales and Scotland. Further, by section 221(3), for the purposes of determining winding up jurisdiction as between the English and Scottish courts in any given case, an unregistered company is deemed to be registered in the one or the other part of Great Britain, according as its principal place of business is situated in England and Wales or Scotland. If the company has a principal place of business in both countries, it is deemed to be registered in both.[45] The principal place of business of the company which is situated in that part of Great Britain in which proceedings are instituted is, for all purposes of the winding up, deemed to be the registered office of the company. Thus, all references in the Act or in the Rules to the company's registered office are to be applied with that modification in the case of the winding up of an unregistered company. In other respects, the winding up

---

[43] Insolvency Act 1986 s.220(1)(a), which excludes any railway company incorporated by Act of Parliament from the definition of "unregistered company".

[44] See Insolvency Act 1986, s.221(4). The company could register under the Companies Act, in order to enable a voluntary winding up to take place, but this must be done before any winding up proceedings are commenced: *Southall v. British Mutual Life Assurance Society* (1871) L.R. 6 Ch. 614.

[45] *ibid.*, s.221(3)(b).

follows the same course as that of a registered company, and all the provisions of the Insolvency Act and the Companies Act apply.[46]

Company Unable to Pay its Debts

The close identity between the insolvent winding up of registered and unregistered companies is emphasised through the provisions of section 222 of the Insolvency Act, which enable a creditor of the company to make use of the procedure for serving a statutory demand upon the company for payment of a debt which is presently due.[47] If the company neglects to pay the sum, or to secure or compound for it to the satisfaction of the creditor, within three weeks after the date of service upon the company, the company is deemed for the purposes of section 221 to be unable to pay its debts. The same amount—namely a sum exceeding £750—is specified in the case of section 222 as is specified by section 123 in relation to the use of the statutory demand against a registered company. In each instance, a creditor must be owed the specified amount, or more, by the company in order to be eligible to serve a formal statutory demand for payment. Service upon the company is effected by leaving at the company's principal place of business a written demand in the prescribed form, requiring the company to pay the sum due. Alternatively, the demand may be delivered to the Secretary or some director, manager or principal officer of the company, or by otherwise serving in a manner approved and directed by the court.[48]

As an alternative to the use of the statutory demand, sections 223 and 224 establish other ways in which the company can be placed in a situation where it is deemed to be unable to pay its debts for the purposes of section 221. Under section 223, this may result from the institution of an action against any member for any debt or demand actually or allegedly due from the company, or from the defendant in his character of member. If notice of the action has been served on the company at its principal place of business, or in some other manner pursuant to the court's directions, and the company does not within three weeks thereafter pay, secure or compound for the debt, or procure the staying of the action, the company is deemed unable to pay its debts. Under section 224(1), four alternative grounds are specified in paragraphs (a) to (d), corresponding in substance to the grounds contained in paragraphs (b) to (e) of section 123(1), which applies to registered companies.[49] A point of interest in relation to section 224(1)(a), which is concerned with unsatisfied executions levied against the company, is the inclusion of references to parties other than the company itself, against whom execution by a judgment creditor may be

---

[46] *ibid.*, s.221(1). For a case where a company registered in Northern Ireland was wound up in England under s.221 by virtue of having a principal place of business in England, see *Re A Company (No. 007946 of 1993)* [1994] 2 W.L.R. 438, also reported *sub nom. Re Normandy Marketing Ltd* [1993] BCC 879. See further Chap. 30, *post*, p. 739.
[47] *cf.* s.123(1)(a) of the Act, discussed *above*.
[48] Insolvency Act 1986, s.222(1)(a).
[49] See *above*, p. 523.

levied.[50] These additional references arise first from the possibility that a member may be liable for the debts of an unregistered company (which is generally not the case in relation to a registered company), and secondly, from the requirement under section 691 of the Companies Act 1985 that any company incorporated outside Great Britain must, within one month of establishing a place of business here, lodge various documents with the registrar of companies including a list supplying names and addresses of one or more persons resident in Great Britain authorised to accept service of process on the company's behalf. Finally, section 224(2) supplies a provision, identical in every respect to section 123(2), to enable the "balance sheet" test of insolvency to be employed as an alternative basis for establishing the company's inability to pay its debts.

Application to Foreign Companies

Although the number of extant companies of domestic origin which qualify as "unregistered companies" has steadily diminished since the last century, the provisions now contained in Part V of the Insolvency Act have during the present century assumed a special importance due to their ready application to companies formed under foreign law. Such companies, either by virtue of having established a place of business here or through having done business in this country, are in principle liable to be wound up by the court in England and Wales (or in Scotland) if the requisite grounds can be established. Indeed, an additional provision, specifically to enable the courts in Great Britain to wind up a foreign company after it has already been dissolved or otherwise ceased to exist as a company under the law of its original incorporation, has been embodied in our law since 1928 and is currently enacted as section 225 of the Insolvency Act. The exercise of this jurisdiction to wind up foreign companies is dealt with in Chapter 30 below, alongside other aspects of liquidations with a foreign element.

---

[50] *cf.* Insolvency Act 1986, s.123(1)(b) (*above*), which refers only to the case of execution against the company itself.

Chapter 21

THE WINDING UP PETITION

Who may Present a Petition?

In the case of an insolvent company, the petition for a winding up order will typically be presented to the court by one or more of the company's unpaid creditors. But the full range of persons eligible to present a winding up petition is considerably wider. By virtue of section 124 of the Insolvency Act, and of certain other statutory provisions, the following are eligible to present a winding up petition:

(1) The company[1];
(2) The directors[2];
(3) Any creditor or group of creditors (including any contingent or prospective creditor or creditors)[3];
(4) Any contributory or group of contributories[4];
(5) The official receiver under section 124(5) of the Act[5];
(6) The Secretary of State under sections 124(4) and 124A of the Insolvency Act[6]; or under section 72 of the Financial Services Act 1986; or under sections 53 and 54 of the Insurance Companies Act 1982;
(7) The Bank of England under section 92 of the Banking Act 1987;
(8) The Attorney-General, in the case of charitable companies[7];

---

[1] Insolvency Act 1986, s.124(1). If the company is already in voluntary liquidation, the liquidator is competent to present the petition. *Cf. Re Zoedone Co.* (1884) 53 L.J. Ch. 465. If the company is in administration (see Chap. 16 *ante*), or if an administrative receiver has been appointed (see Chap. 14 *ante*), the office holder is empowered to present a petition for the winding up of the company by virtue of para. 21 of Sched. 1 to the Insolvency Act 1986.
[2] Insolvency Act 1986, s.124(1). *Cf. Re Emmadart Ltd* [1979] Ch. 540 (decided under s.519 (1) of the Companies Act 1985, which contained no reference to the directors of the company as being eligible to present a petition).
[3] *ibid.* See further, *infra*.
[4] *ibid.* See further, *infra*.
[5] See further, *infra*, and also Chap. 18, *ante*.
[6] See further, *infra*.
[7] Charities Act 1993, s.63.

(9) The Building Societies Commission, in the case of certain defaults by a building society.[8]

(10) The clerk of the Magistrates' Court in the exercise of the power conferred by section 87A of the Magistrates' Court Act 1980.

The right to petition is a statutory right, and cannot be excluded by any c0lause in the company's articles of association.[9]

Petitions by the Company or by the Directors

Petitions of this kind are uncommon, since if the company wishes to wind up it is more likely to favour the voluntary mode of liquidation, and can readily pass a resolution for this purpose.[10] The directors would in any case require the authorisation of a general meeting in order to be entitled to present a petition for winding up, unless such a power is expressly conferred on the directors by the company's articles. The fact that the articles usually delegate the management of the company to the directors has been held not to include an authorisation to present a winding up petition without the sanction of a general meeting, and it is significant that Article 70 of Table A does not confer any such authority.[11]

Contributory's Petition

Outside of those cases where the company is solvent (which are not dealt with here), this type of petition is a rarity, since the forum of the company meeting will normally afford the shareholders an opportunity to decide for themselves whether the company should be put into liquidation, and if so they are readily able to pass a resolution for voluntary winding up, or alternatively they may resolve that a petition shall be presented to the court by the company or by the directors.[12]

Section 79 of the Insolvency Act defines the expression "contributory" as meaning "every person liable to contribute to the assets of a company in the event of its being wound up," and includes, in this context, any person alleged to be a contributory. Section 74 of the Act expressly provides that every present and past member of the company is included within the expression "contributory", even though—as where the shares held by a member are or were fully paid up—the amount of money actually payable

---

[8] Building Societies Act 1986, s.37.

[9] *Re Peveril Gold Mines* [1898] 1 Ch. 122.

[10] See Chap. 19, *ante*. The petition must be presented by all the directors: *Re Instrumentation Electrical Services Ltd* (1983) 4 BCC 301. However, a decision validly taken by a majority of the board at a duly convened meeting can bind the dissenting, or absent, directors so that a petition may then be presented: *Re Equiticorp International plc* (1989) 5 BCC 599 (a case involving a petition for administration under s.9(1) of the Act).

[11] See *Re Emmadart Ltd* (*above*, n. 2); Companies (Tables A to F) Regulations 1985 (S.I. 1985 No. 805).

[12] See Insolvency Act 1986, s.84, and generally Chap. 19, *ante*.

Who May Present a Petition?

by that member is zero. The right of a contributory to present a petition is a restricted one, the main controlling provision being section 124(2) of the Insolvency Act, which states that a contributory is not entitled to present a petition unless either:

(1) The number of members is reduced below 2, or
(2) The shares in respect of which he is a contributory were originally allotted to him, or have been held by him and registered in his name for at least six months during the 18 months before the commencement of the winding up, or have devolved on him through the death of a former holder.

The object of these provisions is to prevent a person from buying shares in order to qualify himself to harass or wreck the company. The case law also reinforces this policy, through the general requirement that a contributory must make out a special case in order to obtain a winding up order.[13] This invariably involves the petitioner in establishing a financial interest in the obtaining of an order, and hence a contributory whose shares are fully paid up will need to establish that the company is probably *solvent*, so that there is a prospect of a return of capital to the members at the conclusion of the winding up.[14] Where the petitioner is faced with a prospect of personal liability to contribute towards the company's debts and liabilities—as where his shares are not fully paid up, or where he is a shareholder of a company limited by guarantee, or of an unlimited company—he will have *locus standi* to present a petition. Furthermore, section 124(3) of the Act states that a person who is liable under section 76[15] to contribute to a company's assets in the event of a winding up may petition on either of the grounds set out in section 122(1)(f) and (g),[16] and the restriction in section 124(2) does not then apply.

The fact that a voluntary liquidation is in progress is prima facie a bar to the winding up of a company on a shareholder's petition, but it does not furnish an absolute bar in law. Section 116 of the Act expressly safeguards the ultimate right of any creditor or contributory to have the company wound up by the court, thus displacing the voluntary liquidation, but this is subject to the proviso that in the case of an application by a contributory the court must be satisfied that the rights of the contributories will be prejudiced by a voluntary winding up.[17]

---

[13] *cf. Re Gutta Percha Corp.* [1900] 2 Ch. 665; *Re Othery Construction Ltd* [1966] 1 All E.R. 145; *Re Expanded Plugs Ltd* [1966] 1 All E.R. 877; *Re Chesterfield Catering Co. Ltd* [1976] 3 All E.R. 294.

[14] *Re Rica Gold Washing Co.* (1879) 11 Ch.D. 36. *Cf. Re Chapel House Colliery* (1883) 24 Ch.D. 259 (C.A.), applying the same principle of "want of interest personally" to dismiss a petition by a fully secured creditor whose petition was opposed by the vast majority of debenture holders and supported by none.

[15] Insolvency Act 1986, s.76 deals with the liability of past directors and shareholders for certain payments received from the company within one year of the commencement of the winding up.

[16] On s.122(1), see Chap. 20 *ante*.

[17] See Chap. 18, *ante*. See also *Re Falcon (R.J.) Developments* [1987] BCLC 437; *Re M.C.H. Services* [1987] BCLC 535.

The Winding Up Petition

Creditor's Petition

To be eligible to present a creditor's petition under section 124(1), it is logically essential that the petitioner must properly occupy the position of creditor in the eyes of the law, *vis-à-vis* the company in question. This in turn presupposes that the company is truly and justly indebted to the petitioner and that the petitioner is personally entitled to claim the amount alleged to constitute the "debt," and to enforce his claim by legal process if necessary. Thus a claim arising from an illegal transaction does not constitute a debt for this purpose,[18] and likewise a statute-barred debt cannot serve as a basis for a petition.[19] The debt must exist in a liquidated form as at the date of presentation of the petition, albeit the debt may be either payable immediately or at a future date or subject to a contingency.[20] Consequently, a person claiming unliquidated damages in contract or in tort, but who has not yet obtained judgment, lacks standing to petition.[21] Similarly, a person whose debt is bona fide disputed on substantial grounds will not be regarded as eligible to petition, pending the resolution of the issue in dispute.[22] An order for costs, made against the company at the conclusion of abortive proceedings it has brought against another party, has the effect of constituting the latter "a creditor" of the company for the certified amount of costs, so that it has standing to petition for the company's winding up.[23]

Subject to what is stated above, it is not necessary that the person seeking to stand as petitioning creditor should be the original party to whom the debt was due from the company: a creditor by subrogation,[24] or one to whom the debt has been legally or equitably assigned[25] (including an assignee of part of a debt)[26] may properly petition for winding up.

It is to be noted that—in contrast to the law of bankruptcy[27]—there is no statutory provision imposing a minimum amount of indebtedness which must be owed by the company to the petitioning creditor. Where the creditor needs to have recourse to the service of a statutory demand in order to establish the company's inability to pay its debts for the purposes of section 122122(1)(f), the statutory requirement in section 123(1)(a),

---

[18] *Re South Wales Atlantic Steamship Co.* (1875) 2 Ch.D. 763 (C.A.).

[19] The crucial date for this purpose is the time of presentation of the petition, not that of the hearing. *Cf. Re Karnos Property Co. Ltd* (1989) 5 BCC 14.

[20] *Re Milford Docks Co.* (1883) 23 Ch.D. 292.

[21] *Re Pen-y-Van Colliery* (1877) 6 Ch.D. 477; *Re Milford Docks Co., above*; but *cf. Re A Company* [1974] 1 All E.R. 256, 260.

[22] *Re Brighton Club and Norfolk Hotel Co. Ltd* (1865) 35 Beav. 204; 55 E.R. 873; *Re Lympne Investments Ltd* [1972] 2 All E.R. 385; *Mann v. Goldstein* [1968] 1 W.L.R. 1091. See also Chap. 20, *ante* with regard to dispute as to the debt on which a statutory demand is based for the purpose of Insolvency Act 1986, s.123(1)(a).

[23] *Tottenham Hotspur plc v. Edennote plc* [1994] BCC 681, in which reference was made to the definition of "a debt" given in r. 13.12 of the Insolvency Rules 1986.

[24] *Re National Permanent Building Society* (1869) 5 Ch.App. 309.

[25] *Re Paris Skating Rink Co.* (1877) 5 Ch.D. 959; *Re Montgomery Moore Ship Collision Doors Syndicate* (1903) 72 L.J. Ch. 624.

[26] *Re Steel Wing Co.* [1921] 1 Ch. 349. Joinder of the assignor as co-petitioner may be necessary, if the company insists.

[27] As to which, see Insolvency Act 1986, s.267, discussed in Chap. 6, *ante*.

that the company must be indebted to the creditor in a sum exceeding £750, effectively serves as a monetary threshold for the purposes of eligibility to petition, in the event that the statutory demand is not complied with.[28] But in the absence of a need for the creditor to utilise the statutory demand, there is nothing within the statutory provisions to impose such a monetary threshold in a general way. Nevertheless, the principle has become established through the case law that, in the absence of special circumstances, a winding up order will not normally be granted where the petitioning creditor's debt is less than the amount fixed for the time being as the minimum indebtedness associated with the use of a statutory demand.[29] This is based upon the judicial view that winding up should not be turned into a procedure for collecting relatively small debts.

Payment or Tender

If the company pays the debt before the petition is presented the creditor ceases to be a creditor for the purposes of sections 122(1)(f), 123 and 124.[30] If the debt is paid after presentation the court may allow the substitution of another creditor under rule 4.19 of the Insolvency Rules 1986.[31] If no other creditor comes forward then the petition will be dismissed. A more difficult question arises when the company has tendered payment. This has sometimes led to dismissal of the petition[32] or adjournment[33] but the better view is that tender does not lead to automatic dismissal but is one of the factors to be taken into account by the court.

Opposition by Other Creditors

In principle, where a petition is presented by a creditor to whom at least a debt corresponding to the current level of minimum indebtedness is due, the court will regard him as enjoying a prima facie right to an order. The starting point in argument is that an unpaid creditor is entitled to a winding up order, as against the company, *ex debito justitiae*.[34] Nevertheless, the principle must be respected that winding up is a collective procedure, and the court will accordingly have regard to the wishes and interests of the majority of creditors, in order to determine the most appropriate way in which to dispose of the petition.[35] This establishes a contrast in law

---

[28] See Chap. 20, *ante*.
[29] *Re Milford Docks Co., Lister's Petition* (1883) 23 Ch.D. 292, 295; *Re Standring and Co. Ltd* (1895) Sol. Jo. 603; [1895] W.N. 99; *Re Fancy Dress Balls Co.* [1899] W.N. 109; *Re W.H. Hyde Ltd* [1900] W.N. 245; *Re Leyton and Walthamstow Cycle Co. Ltd* [1901] W.N. 225; *Re World Industrial Bank Ltd* [1909] W.N. 148; *Re Industrial Insurance Association* [1910] W.N. 245. See also *Re Lympne Investments Ltd.* (*above*, n. 22).
[30] *Re William Hockley Ltd* [1962] 1 W.L.R. 555.
[31] *cf. Fortuna Holdings Pty. v. F.C.T.* (1976) 2 A.C.L.R. 349.
[32] *Re Times Life Assurance Co.* (1869) 9 Eq. 382; *Re Amalgamated Properties of Rhodesia Ltd* [1917] 2 Ch. 115.
[33] *Re Brighton Hotel Co.* (1868) 6 Eq. 339.
[34] *Re James Millward & Co. Ltd* [1940] Ch. 333.
[35] *Re Home Remedies Ltd* [1943] Ch. 1; *Re B. Karsberg Ltd* [1956] 1 W.L.R. 57; *Re Riviera Pearls Ltd* [1962] 1 W.L.R. 722; *Re J.D. Swain Ltd* [1965] 1 W.L.R. 909, especially at 915, per Diplock L.J.; *Re P. & J. Macrae Ltd* [1961] 1 W.L.R. 229.

between the rights of the petitioning creditor as against the company, and his rights as against the body of creditors as a whole.[36] The court may direct the convening of meetings under section 195(2) of the Insolvency Act for the purpose of ascertaining the wishes of the creditors or contributories, and may have regard to those wishes as subsequently reported to it.[37] The court takes account of numerical majority as well as majority in value, but the latter carry greater weight.[38] Ultimately, however, the court will proceed to exercise an unfettered discretion, and the views of the majority of creditors will not necessarily be decisive. Thus, if the court regards the majority view as clearly erroneous,[39] or as inspired by personal benefit,[40] or if the petitioning creditor can demonstrate that he will suffer actual injustice in consequence of a refusal to make a winding up order,[41] an order may be granted.

The absence of assets capable of being distributed in a winding up was formerly regarded as a good reason for the court to refuse to make an order.[42] It is to be noted however that there is now a statutory provision in section 125(1) of the Act to the effect that the court must not refuse to make a winding up order on the ground only that the assets of the company have been mortgaged to an amount equal to or in excess of those assets, or that the company has no assets from which to pay its debts.

In exercising its discretion whether to make an order or not, the court will also have regard to the wider interests of commercial morality. If the facts reveal strong evidence of matters which would warrant further investigation regarding the formation or promotion or running of the company, the court will override creditors' opposition and make a compulsory order as the best means of ensuring a thorough inquiry into all aspects of the case.[43] On the other hand, the courts have declined to make it a consideration militating against the making of a winding up order that there is an arguable public interest in the company's business being continued, or that the employees of the company will inevitably be put out of work if the business is closed down.[44]

One powerful factor which will incline the court to refuse an order, and to strike out the petition, is if the petition amounts to an abuse of the process of the court. This would be the case if the petition is tainted by falsehood or misrepresentation, for the higher principle concerned with maintaining respect for the legal process will outweigh the factor that the

---

[36] *Bowes v. Hope Life Assurance and Guarantee Co.* (1865) 11 H.L.C. 389; 11 E.R. 1383, as explained in *Re Chapel House Colliery* (1883) 24 Ch.D. 259; *Re Greenwood* [1900] 2 Q.B. 306; *Re Southard & Co. Ltd* [1979] 3 All E.R. 556 (C.A.).
[37] Insolvency Act 1986, s.195(1).
[38] See cases cited *above*, n. 35. The views of unsecured creditors may also carry more weight than those of creditors whose debts are secured.
[39] *Re Vuma Ltd* [1960] 1 W.L.R. 1283.
[40] *Re S.O.S. Motors Ltd* [1934] N.Z.L.R. 129; *Re Greenwood*, above, n. 36.
[41] *cf. Re West Hartlepool Ironworks Co.* (1875) 10 Ch.App. 618; *Re B. Karsberg Ltd* [1956] 1 W.L.R. 57.
[42] *Re Chapel House Colliery Co.* (1883) 23 Ch.D. 259.
[43] *Re Bishop & Sons Ltd* [1900] 2 Ch. 254; *Re Lichtenstein* (1903) 23 T.L.R. 424; *Re Clandown Colliery Co.* [1915] 1 Ch. 369.
[44] *Re Craven Insurance Co. Ltd* [1968] 1 W.L.R. 675.

company may well be demonstrably insolvent, and in other respects liable to be wound up.[45]

Petition by Official Receiver

Section 124(5) of the Insolvency Act provides that where a company is being wound up voluntarily in England and Wales, a petition may be presented by the official receiver attached to the court having jurisdiction to wind up the company, as well as by any other person authorised in that behalf under the other provisions of the section, but the court shall not make a winding up order on the petition unless it is satisfied that the voluntary winding up cannot be continued with due regard to the interests of the creditors or contributories. This is to be determined on a balance of probabilities.[46]

It does not necessarily follow that, because a company was controlled by one shareholder of whom a liquidator in a voluntary winding up might be regarded as the nominee, a voluntary winding up cannot be continued with due regard to the interests of the creditors; whether that is so depends on the facts of each case which have to be considered in the light of the evidence before the court.[47]

A consequence of the implementation of the Insolvency Acts 1985 and 1986 is the reform of several important aspects of the law and practice concerning voluntary liquidations. Foremost among these reforms are the requirement that only a qualified insolvency practitioner may act as liquidator of a company (Insolvency Act 1986, Pt. XIII), and the imposition of strict limitations upon the exercise of powers by a liquidator in a creditors' voluntary winding up, prior to the convening of a creditors' meeting to confirm or to challenge the members' choice of liquidator.[48] These reforms should ensure that the very real risks to creditors' interests, and also to those of the contributories, which formerly arose under the law prior to 1986 should be greatly diminished. As a consequence, there should be fewer occasions on which it will be possible to satisfy the court that a voluntary winding up cannot be continued with due regard to the interests of the creditors or contributories.

Petition by the Secretary of State

The Secretary of State has power under section 124A of the Insolvency Act (inserted by section 60 of the Companies Act 1989) to petition the court for a winding-up order if it appears to him:

---

[45] *cf. Re A Company* [1974] 1 All E.R. 256. See also the discussion of the judicial response to abusive petitions in bankruptcy, Chap. 6 *ante*.
[46] *Re Jubilee Sites Syndicate* [1899] 2 Ch. 204; *Re Ryder Installations Ltd* [1966] 1 All E.R. 453n; [1966] 1 W.L.R. 524; *Re J. Russell Electronics Ltd* [1968] 2 All E.R. 559.
[47] *Re Medical Battery Co.* [1894] 1 Ch. 444; *Adebayo v. Official Receiver of Nigeria* [1954] 1 W.L.R. 681 P.C.
[48] See further Chaps. 17 and 18, *ante*, especially with reference to the Insolvency Act 1986, ss.97–100, 165(1) and 166.

The Winding Up Petition

(1) From an inspector's report made or information obtained under Part XIV of the Companies Act 1985; or
(2) From any report made under section 94 or 177 of the Financial Services Act 1986 or any information obtained under section 105 of that Act;
(3) From any information obtained under section 2 of the Criminal Justice Act 1987 or section 52 of the Criminal Justice (Scotland) Act 1987 (fraud investigations); or
(4) From any information obtained under section 83 of the Companies Act 1989 (powers exercisable for purposes of assisting overseas regulatory authorities);

that it is expedient in the public interest that the company should be wound up. If the court thinks it just and equitable for the company to be wound up, it will make a winding up order.

Although a petition by the Secretary of State cannot be presented against a company which is already in compulsory winding up it can be presented against a company in voluntary winding up.[49] Such a petition does not require the personal attention of the Secretary of State; it is sufficient that it is presented in his name by one of his officers.[50]

In *Re Lubin, Rosen and Associates Ltd*[51] Megarry J. indicated the special considerations which apply to a winding up petition by the Secretary of State in the following passage.[52]

> "It seems to me that a petition presented by the Secretary of State under [s.124A of the Insolvency Act 1986] is in a somewhat different category from a petition presented by a creditor or contributory. Creditors and contributories petition in their own interests as members of a class; under the section the Secretary of State petitions under a special statutory provision which comes into operation only when it has appeared to him that it is expedient in the public interest that the company should be wound up. The Secretary of State is necessarily acting not in his own interests but in the interests of the public at large. ... I think that the court, without in the least abdicating any of its judicial and discretionary powers, ought to give special weight to his views."

Accordingly, the special conditions contained in section 124(5), relevant to cases where a petition is presented by the official receiver, do not apply where a petition is presented by the Secretary of State.

---

[49] *Re Lubin, Rosen and Associates Ltd* [1975] 1 W.L.R. 122; [1975] 1 All E.R. 577.
[50] *Re Golden Chemical Products Ltd* [1976] Ch. 300.
[51] *Above*, n. 49.
[52] [1975] 1 W.L.R. at 128–129; [1975] 1 All E.R. at 583. *Cf. Re Walter L. Jacob and Co.* [1989] BCLC 345.

Jurisdiction and Procedure

Courts having jurisdiction to wind up

Section 117(1) of the Insolvency Act states that the High Court has jurisdiction to wind up any company registered in England and Wales. The jurisdiction of the High Court under the Act is exercisable by every judge of the High Court: there is no separate and distinct court known as the "Companies Court," although that term is used as a term of convenience to describe the High Court when exercising its jurisdiction under the Companies Act and the Insolvency Act.[53] Companies business, including the hearing and determination of petitions for winding up, is allocated to the Chancery Division of the High Court.[54]

Outside London, the High Court operates through District Registries in eight cities: Birmingham, Bristol, Cardiff, Leeds, Liverpool, Manchester, Newcastle-upon-Tyne, and Preston. The District Registries have the same powers, and unlimited jurisdiction in relation to winding up, as the Central Office of the High Court in London, and the District Registrars have the same function, and the same powers, as the Chancery Masters.[55] It is important to note that the District Registries are not limited to exercising jurisdiction merely over those companies whose registered offices are situated within the circuit or area in which the particular Registry is located. There are thus nine different locations in which winding up proceedings at High Court level may possibly be commenced, which is a fact to be taken into account by any creditor who intends to present a petition. Priority is by law accorded to the proceedings which are chronologically first in order of being commenced through presentation and advertisement.[56] Once a petition has been advertised, this constitutes constructive notice to the whole world regarding the fact of its presentation and service, and hence any other petition which is subsequently presented against the same company may be dismissed without any order as to costs if a winding up order has been, or is later, made upon the earlier petition. It is therefore vital that any intending petitioner should effect a search of the Central Index of Petitions, which is maintained at the Companies Court in London.[57]

In certain cases, a winding up petition may be presented in the County Court. Section 117(2) of the Act states that where the amount of the company's share capital paid up or credited as paid up does not exceed £120,000,[58] then the County Court of the district in which the company's registered office is situated has concurrent jurisdiction with the High

---

[53] *Fabric Sales Ltd v. Eratex Ltd* [1984] 1 W.L.R. 863; see also *Re Shilena Hosiery Co. Ltd* [1977] 2 All E.R. 6.
[54] Supreme Court Act 1981, s.61(1) and Sched. 1, para. 1. See also Chap. 2, *ante*.
[55] See R.S.C., Ord. 1, r. 4, as amended by (S.I. 1982, No. 1111), Practice Direction July 29, 1982 [1982] 3 All E.R. 124. See also *Re Pleatfine* [1983] BCLC 102.
[56] See *infra*.
[57] The Index may be searched by telephone (0171–936 7328).
[58] This amount is subject to variation by statutory instrument: s.117(3).

The Winding Up Petition

Court to wind up the company. By virtue of section 117(6), the company's "registered office" for this purpose is the place which has longest been its registered office during the six months preceding the presentation of the petition for winding up. Not all County Courts are endowed with jurisdiction in insolvency matters: for administrative convenience, the Lord Chancellor is empowered by section 117(4) to exclude any County Court from having winding up jurisdiction, and to attach all or part of its district to any other County Court, which thus becomes the administrative centre of an insolvency district comprising the territory so designated.[59] Furthermore, the County Courts within the London metropolitan area have no jurisdiction in insolvency matters, and so the High Court is necessarily the venue for all proceedings concerning companies whose registered office is situated within what is known as the London Insolvency District.[60]

Where a County Court enjoys jurisdiction to wind up a company, that jurisdiction is concurrent with that of the High Court, and by virtue of section 117(5) of the Act the powers of the County Court are for this purpose coextensive with those of the High Court, and the court can deal with all matters arising in the winding up—such as the setting aside of debentures, or the adjustment of other transactions—even though the amount involved may be very large.[61] A winding up commenced in the High Court can be transferred to the County Court, even if the paid-up capital exceeds £120,000.[62]

Where the company is registered in Scotland, the courts of relevant jurisdiction are the Court of Session or (in cases within the £120,000 limit on paid up capital) the Sheriff Courts.[63] In determining, as between England and Wales and Scotland, the appropriate jurisdiction in which to institute proceedings for winding up, the decisive criterion is thus the whereabouts of the Companies Registry (*i.e.* Cardiff or Edinburgh) at which the registration of the company was effected, and not the whereabouts of the company's registered office. Where a company had been registered in England and Wales, but had a registered office improperly located in Scotland, it was held that it could be wound up in England and Wales, with service of the petition upon the company ordered to take place outside the jurisdiction.[64]

Section 119 of the Act makes it possible for questions to be referred from a County Court in which winding up proceedings are taking place, to the High Court for determination on a case stated basis.[65] There is also a general safeguard provision in section 118, whereby proceedings are declared not to be rendered invalid by reason of being taken in the wrong

---

[59] See Civil Courts Order 1983, (S.I. 1983, No. 713), Para. 10 and Sched. 3, as periodically amended. See also Chap. 2 *ante*, (text to nn. 9–13).

[60] See Insolvency Act 1986, s.374. For the background, see Chap. 2 *ante* (n. 10 and text thereto).

[61] *Re F. and E. Stanton Ltd* [1928] 1 K.B. 464.

[62] County Courts Act 1984, s.40. *Re Vernon Heaton Co. Ltd* [1936] Ch. 289.

[63] Insolvency Act 1986, s.120.

[64] *Re Baby Moon Ltd* (1985) P.C.C. 103; (1985) 1 BCC 298. See Insolvency Rules 1986, r. 12.12(3).

[65] *Cf. Re Mawcon* [1969] 1 All E.R. 188.

court, so far as the provisions of section 117 require. Moreover, section 118(2) allows for the retention of any proceedings in the court in which they were commenced, even though it may not be the court in which they ought to have commenced. This provision gives rise to a discretionary power for the court to exercise as it sees fit, and it is therefore possible for an innocent or excusable mistake to be dealt with sympathetically, but without prejudice to the court's power to deal in a more severe manner—for example by dismissing the petition without award of costs—where it appears that the creditor's use of the wrong court has been the result of inexcusable carelessness, or even of a wilful calculation on his part.

Presentation and Service of the Petition

The principal provisions bearing upon this stage of the proceedings are contained in the Insolvency Rules. The petition should be presented for filing at the office of the Registrar of the court by which it is to be heard, being a court of competent jurisdiction according to the rules which have been considered above. The petition should be in the prescribed form,[66] which may be adapted as circumstances require.[67] The petition which is presented for filing must be verified by an affidavit that the statements in the petition are true, or are true to the best of the deponent's knowledge, information and belief.[68] The affidavit must be made by the petitioner (or by any one of them, in the case of a joint petition), or by some person, such as a director or officer of the company, who has been concerned in the matters giving rise to the petition, or by some responsible, and duly authorised, person who has requisite knowledge of the matters involved.[69] The petition cannot be filed unless there is produced with it the receipt for the deposit payable by a petitioner for winding up.[70]

Unless the petition is presented by the company itself, the petitioner must deliver two copies to the court, together with the petition for filing. The first of these copies is for service on the company, and the second is to be exhibited to the affidavit verifying such service.[71] Additional copies will be required if the company is already in the course of voluntary liquidation, or is the subject of an administration order, or if an administrative receiver has been appointed or a voluntary arrangement is in force. The additional copies of the petition are for service upon the office holder in the proceedings which are in progress.[72] Each of the copies of the petition has the court seal affixed to it, and is issued to the petitioner for service on the company and on any other parties, as necessary, and the Registrar also endorses on each copy the venue which has been fixed for the hearing of the petition.[73]

---

[66] Insolvency Rules 1986, r. 12.7(1); Forms 4.2, 4.3. See also rr. 7.26 and 4.7.
[67] *ibid.*, r. 12.7(2).
[68] *ibid.*, rr. 4.7(1), 4.12(1), and (2)–(7).
[69] *ibid.* r. 4.12(4).
[70] *ibid.* r. 4.7(2). The current deposit is £600: Insolvency Fees Order 1986, (S.I. 1986, No. 2030), Articles 8, 9, as amended by S.I. 1994, No. 2541.
[71] *ibid.*, r. 4.7(3).
[72] *ibid.*, r. 4.7(4). See also r. 4.10.
[73] *ibid.*, r. 4.7(5), (6).

Except where the petitioner is the company itself, the petition must be served upon the company. Service of the petition is to be effected at the company's registered office, either by handing it to a person who there and then acknowledges himself to be a director or other employee or officer of the company, or by handing it to a person who acknowledges that he is authorised to accept service of documents on the company's behalf, or otherwise by depositing it at or about the registered office in such a way that it is likely to come to the notice of a person attending at the office.[74] If service at the registered office is not practicable, or if the company has no registered office, or it is an unregistered company,[75] the petition may be served at the company's last known principal place of business in England and Wales, or at some place in this country at which it has carried on business.[76]

It is essential that the petitioner files proof of service of the petition in court immediately after service. Service is proved by affidavit specifying the manner of service, together with which there must be exhibited a sealed copy of the petition and, if substituted service has been ordered, a sealed copy of the order.[77]

Advertisement of the Petition

Unless the court otherwise directs, every petition is to be advertised in the *Gazette* seven clear days (excluding Saturdays, Sundays and public holidays)[78] after it has been served on the company and not less than seven clear days before the day fixed for the hearing.[79] A copy of the advertisement must be lodged with the court as soon as possible.[80] The former requirement of advertisement in a national or local newspaper was abolished by the Companies (Winding-Up) (Amendment) Rules 1979, but advertisement in a newspaper may still be directed by the court as an alternative to the *Gazette*, if advertisement in the latter is not reasonably practicable.[81] Every advertisement of a petition is to contain a note at the foot thereof stating that any person who intends to appear on the hearing of the petition, either to oppose or support, must send notice of his intention to the petitioner or his solicitor.[82] Notice of intention to appear must be given by any person intending to do so, and must contain his name and address.[83]

Any error in the title, name, day or place for hearing may render the

---

[74] *ibid.*, r. 4.8(1), (2), (3). On service at the wrong address, see *Business Computers International Ltd v. Registrar of Companies* [1987] 3 All E.R. 465.
[75] See Chap. 20, *ante*.
[76] Insolvency Rules 1986, r. 4.8(4). See also (5), (6) and (7).
[77] *ibid.*, r. 4.9; Forms 4.4, 4.5.
[78] *Re Display Multiples Ltd* [1967] 1 W.L.R. 571.
[79] Insolvency Rules 1986, r. 4.11(1), (2). This effectively means that service on the company must take place at least 14 days before the date set for hearing.
[80] Practice Direction (No. 1 of 1986) [1986] 1 W.L.R. 286; [1986] 1 All E.R. 704.
[81] Insolvency Rules 1986, r. 4.11(3). See also (S.I. 1979, No. 209).
[82] *ibid.*, r. 4.11(4). For the form of advertisement, see Form 4.6.
[83] *ibid.* r. 4.16; Form 4.9.

advertisement useless[84]; but a trifling formal defect where no one is misled will not invalidate the petition.[85] In addition, under rule 4.3 of the 1986 Rules the court is given power to extend the time for doing any act or taking any proceeding and this includes advertising. Further, under rule 7.55 it is provided that no proceedings shall be invalidated by any formal defect or irregularity unless the court before which an objection is made is of the opinion that substantial injustice has been caused thereby and that the injustice cannot be remedied by any order of the court. The court in practice will only exercise its discretion under these rules where there are special circumstances.[86]

The advertisement has been held to be notice to the world of the presentation of the petition but only from the time when they may reasonably be supposed to have seen it.[87] This is unaffected by sections 42 and 711 of the Companies Act (formerly section 9 of the European Communities Act 1972).[88]

The court will restrain the issuing of the advertisements when the petition is an abuse of the process of the court,[89] and may also decide to restrain advertisement when the petitioner's debt is shown to be disputed.[90] Cases arising from applications to restrain advertisement call for the exercise of an extremely delicate judgment, because the court must balance the potential for the company to suffer prejudicial publicity, against the prospects of detrimental consequences for the petitioner if the normal procedure for advertisement is postponed.[91] In the absence of any challenge to the presentation of the petition, and assuming that the petition itself has been correctly presented and that there is no administration order petition simultaneously pending, it is doubtful whether a judge has power *ex officio* to order that the winding up petition should not be advertised.[92] In a case where the debt itself was undisputed and there was merely an untested cross-claim against the petitioner by the

---

[84] *Re Army and Navy Hotel* (1886) 31 Ch.D. 644; *Re London and Provincial Pure Ice* [1904] W.N. 136; *Re City & County Bank* (1875) 10 Ch.App. 470; *Re Mont de Piete* [1892] W.N. 166; *Re Hille India Rubber Co.* [1897] W.N. 6; *Re Samuel Birch Co.* [1907] W.N. 31. *Re l'Industrie Verrière Ltd* [1914] W.N. 222; *Re J. & P. Sussman Ltd* [1985] 1 W.L.R. 519; *Re Roselmar Properties Ltd* (1986) 2 BCC 99, 156; *Re Broads Patent Night Light Co.* [1982] W.N. 5. As to errors in spelling see *Re Videofusion Ltd* [1994] 1 W.L.R. 1548.

[85] *Re London India Rubber Co.* (1886) 14 C.T. 316. A strike in the printing industry would probably suffice.

[86] *Emerson's Case* (1866) 1 Ch. 433; *Re Marlborough Club Co.* (1886) L.R. 1 Eq. 216; *Re New Gas Co.* (1877) 5 Ch.D. 703; *Re Oriental Bank Corp.* (1885) 28 Ch.D. 634. *Cf. Re Dramstar Ltd* (1980) 124 S.J. 807.

[87] *Re London, Hamburg and Continental Exchange Bank* (1866) L.R. 2 Eq. 231 (reversed on other grounds (1866) L.R. 1 Ch.App. 433).

[88] Presentation of a petition is not subject to official notification within s.711 of the Companies Act and is not within s.42 of that Act.

[89] *Re A Company* [1894] 2 Ch. 349; *Re A Company* (May 16, 1950) 1 C.L.C. 1406; 94 S.J. 369; and see *Charles Forte (Investments) Ltd v. Amanda* [1964] Ch. 240.

[90] *cf. Re A Company (No. 00962 of 1991), ex p. Electrical Engineering Contracts (London) Ltd* [1992] BCLC 248; *Re A Company (No. 008970 of 1990)* [1992] BCC 11.

[91] *Re A Company (No. 009080 of 1992)* [1993] BCLC 269. For the principles applicable to "public interest" petitions brought under s.124A of the Act, see *Re A Company (No. 007923 of 1994)* [1995] BCC 634 (C.A.).

[92] *Re Manlon Trading* [1988] 4 BCC 455. Contrast *Re A Company (No. 001448 of 1989)* [1989] BCLC 715, where the debtor company undertook to petition for an administration order.

company, this was held not to amount to an abuse of process on the part of the petitioner, and the court refused to restrain advertisement.[93] In another case, where part of the debt was disputed on bona fide grounds but an undisputed balance remained which was well in excess of the prescribed minimum figure relating to service of a statutory demand, the petition was allowed to be presented and to progress without interruption.[94]

For the purposes of any stay of advertisement which is granted by the court, pending the resolution of any challenge to the pursuit of the proceedings, the courts sometimes contrive to combat any tendencies towards abuse on the part of the petitioner by declaring that the concept of "advertisement" is a wide one extending to any informal communication to third parties.[95] Thus, the petitioner's act of sending a faxed copy of the winding-up petition to the company's bank on the same day as the petition was served on the company was considered by the court in *Re Bill Hennessey Associates Ltd*[96] to justify dismissal of the petition. The faxing of the copy was held to have been an advertisement in violation of rule 11(2), which requires a minimum of seven business days to elapse from the date of service of the petition, and the ulterior purpose of this targeted publicity was judged to have been the putting of pressure on the company to pay the sum demanded. This rigorous approach is understandable, given the commercial harm which can be inflicted upon a company through the improper use against it of the presentation of the winding-up petition. However, where the petitioner is innocent of all impropriety of purpose or conduct, and is presenting a petition with a view to the recovery of a debt which is not disputed, a valid distinction may be drawn by the court, in order to deprive the insolvent debtor of a technical basis for making an application to dismiss the petition. Thus, the fact that the petitioner may have notified the debtor's bank of the presentation of the petition may be explained as having been carried out for the purpose of minimising the risk of wasteful depletion of assets through the bank allowing the company's account to operate at a time when, by virtue of section 127 of the Act, the disposition of the company's property will be void. In that event, a more restricted notion of the meaning of "advertisement" was adopted in *S.N. Group plc v. Barclays Bank plc*,[97] confining it to the formal act of advertising the petition in the *Gazette*, as required by rule 4.11(1).

If the petition is not duly advertised in accordance with rule 4.11 of the 1986 Rules, the judge may order that it shall be removed from the file.[98] Where a winding up petition is advertised prior to service, in breach of rule 4.11 of the Insolvency Rules 1986, it will ordinarily be struck out.[99]

---

[93] *Re A Company (No. 006273 of 1992)* [1993] BCLC 131; [1992] BCC 794.
[94] *Fiesta Girl of London v. Network Agencies* [1992] 32 EG 55 (also reported as *Re A Company (No. 11102 of 1991)* [1992] EGCS 79). For the use of a statutory demand, see Chap. 20.
[95] *Re A Company (No. 00687 of 1991)* [1991] BCC 210.
[96] [1992] BCC 386. *Cf. Re A Company (No. 0012209 of 1991)* [1992] 1 W.L.R. 351; [1992] 2 All E.R. 797, referred to in Chap. 20, *ante* at p. 525.
[97] [1993] BCC 506.
[98] Insolvency Rules 1986, r. 4.11(5); *Re Signland* [1982] 2 All E.R. 609.
[99] *ibid.*

Compliance

At least five days before the hearing of the petition, the petitioner or his solicitor must file in court a certificate of compliance with the Rules relating to service and advertisement: non-compliance with this requirement is a ground on which the court may dismiss the petition.[1]

Withdrawal of Petition

The circumstances in which a petitioner may seek leave to withdraw his petition are as follows. If, at least 5 days before the hearing, the petitioner on an *ex parte* application satisfies the court that:

(1) The petition has not been advertised; and
(2) no notices, either in support or in opposition, have been received by him regarding the petition; and
(3) the company consents to an order for withdrawal being made, the court may order that the petitioner has leave to withdraw, on terms to be agreed.[2]

Thus a petitioning creditor whose debt has been paid, or who for some other reason does not wish to proceed with the petition, may discontinue the proceedings. If the petition has been advertised, application to withdraw must be made at the hearing of the petition itself.

Notice of appearance

Every person who intends to appear on the hearing of the petition must give the petitioner notice of that intention by means of a written notice sent to him at his designated address, or to his solicitor.[3] The notice must be sent so as to reach the addressee not later than 16.00 hours on the next business day before that appointed for the hearing, and must indicate the name, address and any telephone number of the person giving it, the amount and nature of his debt, and whether he intends to support or oppose the petition.[4] The petitioner must prepare for the court a list of those persons who have given notice of appearance, and hand it to the court before the commencement of the hearing.[5] If the company intends to oppose the petition, its affidavit in opposition must be filed not less than seven days before the date fixed for hearing.[6]

Hearing of the Petition

The petition is heard in open court, irrespective of whether it is opposed

---

[1] Insolvency Rules 1986, r. 4.14. See Form 4.7.
[2] *ibid.*, r. 4.15; Form 4.8. See Practice Direction [1987] 1 All E.R. 107.
[3] *ibid.*, r. 4.16(1), (3); Form 4.9.
[4] *ibid.*, r. 4.16(2), (4).
[5] *ibid.*, r. 4.17; Form 4.10.
[6] *ibid.*, r. 4.18.

or unopposed.[7] Opposed petitions are heard by a judge of the court, but unopposed petitions and related applications are heard by the registrar.[8] Solicitors, properly robed, are permitted rights of audience before the registrar of the Companies Court of the High Court.[9]

Only the petitioner and the company are entitled to be heard as of right, but the court will also hear submissions by or on behalf of persons who have given prior notice of appearance in the manner explained above. A person who has not given notice of appearance may appear on the hearing only with the leave of the court.[10]

The powers of the court on hearing the petition are defined in broad terms by section 125 of the Act. The court may dismiss the petition with or without costs, or adjourn the hearing conditionally or unconditionally, or make an interim order or any other order that it thinks fit.[11] But the court will not as a rule order a petition to stand over for a lengthy period, as it would not be fair to the company to do so.[12] If the petitioner neither appears nor is represented on the hearing, the petition will normally be dismissed. Alternatively, the court may exercise its power to substitute as petitioner any creditor or contributory who, in its opinion, would have a right to present a petition and who is prepared to prosecute it.[13] The power of substitution may also be exercised where the petitioner fails to advertise his petition within the time allowed, or where he withdraws his petition or, though appearing, fails to prosecute it properly.[14]

Mention has been made above of the proviso to section 125(1) whereby the court may not refuse to make a winding up order only on the ground that the company has no assets, or that its assets have been mortgaged to an extent equal to or in excess of their value. Subject to this, the court enjoys an unfettered discretion whether to make a winding up order or not. Factors which are taken into account by the court in exercising its discretion in various typical situations were discussed earlier in this chapter. The form and contents of the winding up order, if made, are considered in Chapter 22 together with the effects thereof.

Costs

If the petition is dismissed, costs will normally be awarded to the

---

[7] Practice Direction (No. 3 of 1986), December 10, 1986 [1987] 1 All E.R. 107; [1987] 1 W.L.R. 53.
[8] Practice Direction (No. 2 of 1986) October 22, 1986 [1986] 3 All E.R. 672; [1986] 1 W.L.R. 1428.
[9] Practice Direction (Right of audience) May 9, 1986 [1986] 2 All E.R. 226; [1986] 1 W.L.R. 545.
[10] Insolvency Rules 1986, r. 4.16(5).
[11] Insolvency Act 1986, s.125(1).
[12] *Re Chapel House Colliery Co.* (1883) 24 Ch.D. 259, 267; *Re Boston Timber Fabrications Ltd* [1984] BCLC 328.
[13] Insolvency Rules 1986, r. 4.19(2). See *Re Xyllyx plc (No. 1)* [1992] BCLC 376, where the court declined to allow contributories to be substituted as petitioners when the original petitioner (the Secretary of State) decided not to pursue the petition on grounds of public interest.
[14] *ibid.*, r. 4.19(1).

company against the petitioner, and creditors or contributories who joined in the opposing of the petition may also receive one set of their costs. On the other hand, costs will not be awarded against the petitioner if the company's own prior conduct is considered by the court to have induced him reasonably to have pursued the course he took initially in presenting the petition, or in subsequently withdrawing it, for example as a consequence of payment by the company of the debt owed to him.[15] Upon dismissal of the petition, however, the petitioner is entitled to the return of the deposit paid by him upon issue of the petition.[16]

If the petition is successful, the petitioning creditor and the company are awarded costs out of the company's assets,[17] and likewise one set of costs of contributories or creditors who supported the petition are awarded out of the company's assets as costs in the winding up. Where the company appeals from a winding up order, the court may order that sufficient security must be given for costs.[18]

It has been held that the court, having jurisdiction in exceptional circumstances to order costs against persons not parties to proceedings, may in appropriate cases order that costs be paid by the directors personally, rather than by the company, where an unsuccessful application is made to strike out a creditor's petition on the ground of disputed debt.[19] *A fortiori*, where directors have caused costs to be thrown away by instructing counsel for the company to procure an adjournment of hearing by maintaining that there is some real prospect of being able to furnish material upon which the application to appoint provisional liquidators might subsequently be opposed, the eventual exposure of the false basis on which the directors' instructions were issued will render them liable to be ordered to bear the ensuing costs personally.[20]

Appeals

Rule 7.47(1) of the Insolvency Rules 1986 states that every court having jurisdiction under the Act to wind up companies may review, rescind or vary any order made by it in the exercise of that jurisdiction. The first avenue of recourse against the making of a winding-up order thus lies by way of application to the judge or registrar by whom the order was made, inviting him to exercise the powers conferred by rule 7.47(1). Strictly speaking, such an application, and any hearing in relation to it, does not constitute an appeal. The exercise of appellate jurisdiction by some hierarchically superior court may take the form either of an appeal from the original decision at first instance, or of an appeal from a decision of the

---

[15] See *Re McCarthy & Co. (Builders) Ltd* (No. 2) [1976] 2 All E.R. 339; *Re Lanaghan Brothers Ltd* [1977] 1 All E.R. 247, *Re Tyneside Permanent Benefit Building Society* [1885] W.N. 148.
[16] See Insolvency Rules 1986, *above*; Insolvency Fees Order 1986, (S.I. 1986, No. 2030), Art. 11.
[17] *ibid.*, r. 12.2.
[18] Companies Act 1985, s.726(1); *Re Consolidated South Rand Mines* [1909] W.N. 66.
[19] *Re A Company (No. 004055 of 1991)* [1991] BCLC 865; *sub. nom. Re Record Tennis Centres Ltd* [1991] BCC 509, decided in the light of *Aiden Shipping Co. Ltd v. Interbulk Ltd* [1986] A.C. 965. See also *Re Reprographics Export (Euromat) Ltd* (1978) 122 S.J. 400.
[20] *Gamelstaden plc v. Brackland Magazines Ltd* [1993] BCC 194.

registrar or judge sitting at first instance to refuse to review his original decision.[21]

An appeal against a winding up order, or from a decision made in the exercise of the court's jurisdiction to review its own decision made by a County Court or by a registrar of the High Court, lies to a single judge of the High Court, and an appeal from a decision of that judge on such an appeal lies, with the leave of that judge or the Court of Appeal, to the Court of Appeal.[22]

An application for rescission of a winding up order must be made within seven days after the date on which the order was made.[23] An appeal is made by notice of motion which must be served within four weeks.[24] The appeal is treated as though it were an interlocutory appeal, in order to facilitate a speedy hearing of the case,[25] although a winding up order is properly to be regarded as final. The court will not usually grant a stay on the winding up order itself, pending disposal of the appeal, since this would impede the official receiver in the performance of his duties should the appeal be dismissed.[26] To minimise the commercial damage to the company, the court usually orders postponement of advertisement of the order, but it is an inescapable fact that the petition will have been advertised prior to the hearing.

Provisional liquidators and special managers

Provisional Liquidator

Under section 135 of the Insolvency Act the court has power to appoint a liquidator provisionally at any time after the presentation of a winding-up petition.[27] The appointment of a provisional liquidator may be made at any time before the making of a winding up order and either the official receiver or any other fit person may be appointed.[28] The court may limit and restrict his powers by the order appointing him.[29]

The procedure is set out in rule 4.25 of the Insolvency Rules 1986. Besides the petitioner himself, any creditor or contributory of the company may apply, as may the company itself, or the Secretary of State, or any person who would be entitled to present a winding up petition. Upon proof by affidavit of sufficient grounds the court may make the appointment if it thinks fit and on such terms as it thinks just and necessary.[30]

---

[21] *Re SN Group plc* [1993] BCC 808.
[22] Insolvency Rules 1986, r. 7.47(2); *Re Calahurst* [1989] BCLC 140; (1989) 5 BCC 318; *Re Busytoday Ltd* [1992] BCC 480; *Midrome Ltd v. Shaw* [1993] BCC 659 (C.A.), esp. at 660–661, *per* Bingham, M.R.
[23] *ibid.*, r. 7.47(4).
[24] Rules of the Supreme Court, Ord. 59, rr. 3, 4, 14, 19; Insolvency Rules 1986, rr. 7.47, 7.49, 7.51. The court may extend the time under r. 4.3.
[25] *Re Reliance Properties Ltd* [1951] 2 All E.R. 327 (C.A.).
[26] *Re A. & B. C. Chewing Gum Ltd* [1975] 1 All E.R. 1017, 1029.
[27] Insolvency Act 1986, s.135(1).
[28] *ibid.*, s.135(2).
[29] *ibid.*, s.135(5).
[30] *ibid.*, s.135(4), (5); Insolvency Rules 1986, rr. 4.25(4), 4.26(1).

An appointment can only be made if there is an effective subsisting petition pending for otherwise the section would apply to a company in perpetuity merely because there had been an unsuccessful petition to wind it up.[31] If the company makes, consents to, or is shown not to oppose, the application, the appointment is almost a matter of course when it is asked that the official receiver be appointed. However, where the company opposes the application or does not appear, an order may be made if there are special circumstances such as danger to the assets, or obvious insolvency. Section 135 confers a general power which the court will exercise on the basis of the view it takes of the requirements in the case before it. In practice, the official receiver is nearly always appointed as the provisional liquidator, although the court has power to appoint some other fit person, who must however be qualified to act as an insolvency practitioner in relation to the company.[32]

The primary object of appointing a provisional liquidator is to preserve the assets and maintain the *status quo*, and to prevent anybody from getting priority ahead of the general body of creditors.[33] The appointment is thus made for the purpose of protecting the company's property for equal distribution in the event of an order for winding up being subsequently made; if no such order is made, the appointment ought not then to interfere with the rights of third persons.[34] The provisional liquidator does not have authority to wind up the company or to distribute its assets, and the "provisional" character of his appointment may be said to refer both to its temporary duration and to its restricted purpose.

Special Manager

Where a company has gone into liquidation or a provisional liquidator has been appointed, application may be made to the court under section 177 of the Act for the appointment of a special manager. Application may be made by the liquidator or provisional liquidator, as the case may be.[35] The grounds for such an application are that it appears that the nature of the business or property of the company, or the interests of the creditors or contributories or members generally, require the appointment of another person to manage the company's business or property.

The special manager is an officer of the court with such powers and functions as the court may entrust to him.[36] The court also has power to fix the remuneration of the special manager and to specify the duration of his appointment.[37] There is no statutory requirement to the effect that a

---

[31] *Re A Company* [1974] 1 All E.R. 256, 261; *per* Megarry J.
[32] See Insolvency Act 1986, ss.388(1)(a), 389. *Cf. Re Bank of Credit and Commerce International SA* [1992] BCC 83, esp. at pp. 90 *et seq.*, *per* Browne-Wilkinson V.-C., where private-sector practitioners were appointed as provisional liquidators in a very large, multi-jurisdictional insolvency.
[33] *Re Dry Docks Corp. of London* (1883) 39 Ch.D. 306, 309, *per* Kay J.
[34] *Re Dry Docks Corp. of London, above*, at p. 314, *per* Fry L.J. (on appeal).
[35] Insolvency Act 1986, s.177(2).
[36] *ibid.* s.177(3), (4).
[37] Insolvency Rules 1986, r. 4.206(3), (5).

special manager must be a person who is qualified to act as an insolvency practitioner, either generally or in relation to the company, and it is possible for the existing directors (or some of them) to be appointed special managers by the court under section 177, since their powers are otherwise terminated upon the appointment of a provisional liquidator, or upon the making of a winding up order.

Chapter 22

THE WINDING UP ORDER AND ITS CONSEQUENCES

Notice and Settling of the Order

The winding up order is made by the court using the prescribed form,[1] whose purport is that the company whose full name is stated therein is to be wound up by the court under the provisions of the Insolvency Act 1986. When the order has been made, the court must forthwith give notice of the fact to the official receiver attached to the court.[2] The petitioner and every other person who has appeared on the hearing of the petition must, not later than the business day following that on which the order is made, leave at the court all the documents required for enabling the order to be completed. It is not necessary for the court to appoint a venue for any person to attend to settle the order unless the special circumstances of the case make this necessary.[3]

The next procedural steps fall to be performed by the official receiver, who assumes primary responsibility for the conduct of the liquidation according to the law's requirements. The court is required to furnish the official receiver with three sealed copies of the winding up order, one of which he must cause to be served upon the company by prepaid letter addressed to it at its registered office (if any), or otherwise at its principal or last known principal place of business.[4] The official receiver must forward another copy of the order to the registrar of companies, in fulfilment of the requirement imposed by section 130(1) of the Act,[5] and he must also cause the order to be officially notified in the Gazette and advertise the order in a local paper selected by himself.[6] There is no doctrine to the effect that, upon the completion of gazetting of the order, constructive notice is

---

[1] Insolvency Rules 1986, Sched. 4, Forms 4.11 and 4.12 (the latter is for use when the winding up order is made following upon discharge of an administration order).
[2] *ibid.*, r. 4.20(1); Form 4.13; Insolvency Act 1986, s.399(1), (4). On the official receiver see Chap. 2, *ante*.
[3] *ibid.*, r. 4.20(2), (3).
[4] *ibid.*, r. 4.21(1), (2).
[5] *ibid.*, r. 4.21(3).
[6] *ibid.*, r. 4.21(4).

deemed to have been given to the whole world of the fact that the company is in liquidation. While it is the case that the company cannot rely upon the winding up notice if it has not been gazetted, the Court of Appeal has held that the converse does not follow, since there is no positive statutory provision to the effect that the doctrine of constructive notice is imported through notification in the Gazette.[7] It will therefore be necessary to show actual notice on the part of persons dealing with the company after the order is made, although the point appears to be open whether the doctrine of constructive notice applies following registration of the order at the Companies Registry.

Commencement of Winding Up

The moment in time fixed by law as the commencement of winding up is of considerable importance, since it is in relation to this date that many other matters are determined, including the validity of actions, dealings or dispositions affecting the company's assets or its shares.[8] Section 129(2) provides that, in the majority of cases, the winding up of the company is deemed to commence at the time of the presentation of the petition for winding up. However, if the company had passed a resolution for voluntary winding up prior to the presentation of the petition, section 129(1) has the effect of backdating the commencement of winding up to the date of the passing of the resolution. It is further provided that, unless the court directs otherwise on proof of fraud or mistake, all proceedings in the voluntary winding up are deemed to have been taken validly. Thus, where a voluntary winding up is converted into a compulsory one,[9] the time which, according to section 86 of the Act, constitutes the commencement of winding up as originally constituted remains applicable in relation to the liquidation in its transformed state.

Effects of the Order

An order for winding up a company has effect with regard to all creditors of the company, and all contributories, in a collective manner, and is expressed to operate "as if made on the joint petition of a creditor and of a contributory."[10] The effects of winding up in relation to third parties are more fully considered in Chapter 26, but the following matters are to be noted.

First, the winding up order has the effect of terminating the employment

---

[7] Companies Act 1985, ss.42(1)(a), (2), 711(2). See *Official Custodian of Charities v. Parway Estates* [1984] 3 All E.R. 679; [1985] Ch. 151 (C.A.).
[8] See, *e.g.*, Insolvency Act 1986, ss.127, 128, 238–240 and 245, and generally Chaps. 24 and 26, *post.*
[9] See Chap. 18, *ante.*
[10] Insolvency Act 1986, s.130(4).

of all employees and agents of the company.[11] The directors are automatically dismissed, and their powers to act on behalf of the company cease, as of the date of the order.[12] The effect of the order is to avoid all dispositions of the company's property, and any transfers of shares or alteration in the status of the company's members, that have been made since the commencement of the winding up, unless the court orders otherwise by means of a validation order made upon application.[13] Likewise any attachment, sequestration, distress or execution put in force against the estate or effects of the company after the commencement of winding up is void.[14]

After the making of a winding up order (or the appointment of a provisional liquidator)[15] no action or proceeding may be proceeded with or commenced against the company or its property, except by leave of the court.[16] While the staying of all proceedings is automatic after the making of the order, the company's assets can be protected during the interim period between the presentation of the petition and the making of the order through the court exercising its power under section 126 to stay or restrain actions or proceedings against the company which are pending. An application for the stay of any action pending in the High Court or Court of Appeal in England and Wales or Northern Ireland is made to the court in which the matter is pending, while application in respect of proceedings pending in any other court is made to the court having jurisdiction to wind up the company.[17] Application may be made by the company, or any creditor or contributory. This procedure may be used also for the purpose of restraining the commencement or continuance of any non-litigious procedures for the enforcement of a claim, such as the levying of execution in enforcement of a judgment debt,[18] or the levying of distress for rent, rates or taxes.[19]

Leave to commence or continue proceedings against the company

Although it is one of the principal consequences of the making of a winding up order that all proceedings and actions by individual creditors in enforcement of their claims against the company are suspended, the court has an important, discretionary power under section 130(2) of

---

[11] *Re General Rolling Stock Co. (Chapman's Case)* (1866) L.R. 1 Eq. 346; *Re Oriental Bank Corp., ex p. Guillemin* (1884) 28 Ch.D. 634; *Re Mawcon Ltd* [1969] 1 All E.R. 188; *Gosling v. Gaskell* [1897] A.C. 575, (H.L.).

[12] *Measures Brothers Ltd. v. Measures* [1910] 2 Ch. 248; *Fowler v. Broad's Patent Night Light Co.* [1893] 1 Ch. 724; *Re Mawcon Ltd.* (*supra*); see also *Fowler v. Commercial Timber Co. Ltd* [1930] 2 K.B. 1 (in the case of insolvent, voluntary liquidation).

[13] Insolvency Act 1986, s.127; *Re A. I. Levy (Holdings) Ltd* [1964] Ch. 19. See further, Chap. 26, *post* (*Dispositions and Transfers after Commencement of Winding Up*).

[14] *ibid.*, s.128.

[15] See Chap. 21, *ante*.

[16] Insolvency Act 1986, s.130(2). See *infra*.

[17] *ibid.*, s.126(1).

[18] *Thomas v. Patent Lionite Co.* (1881) 17 Ch.D. 250; cf. *Westbury v. Twigg & Co.* [1892] 1 Q.B. 77 (in relation to voluntary liquidation: see Insolvency Act 1986, s.112).

[19] *Re Roundwood Colliery Co.* [1897] 1 Ch. 373; *Re Bellaglade Ltd* [1977] 1 All E.R. 319 (restraint will only be imposed in special circumstances, such as fraud or unfair dealing).

the Act to grant dispensation from this moratorium in favour of those who establish special reasons for being allowed to continue, or commence, an action or proceeding against the company or its property. There is a further discretionary power vested in the court under section 183(2)(c) with respect to the rights of creditors who had failed to complete an execution or attachment which was in progress at the date of commencement of winding up. Although the basic thrust of section 183 is to the effect that a creditor is not entitled to retain the benefit of such an incomplete execution or attachment against the liquidator, subsection (2)(c) creates the possibility for exceptions to be made, in the sense that the liquidator's rights may be set aside to such extent and on such terms as the court thinks fit. In exercising their discretionary powers—which can be invoked in relation to voluntary winding up, as well as in a winding up by the court[20]—the courts have evolved an approach which aspires to balance the collective interest against the relative hardship, and injustice, which may be experienced by the individual creditor, under circumstances where it is inevitable that any mitigation of that person's loss will be at the expense of the general body of creditors, and hence will amount to a judicially-sanctioned exception to the *pari passu* principle. Considerable judicial emphasis has been placed upon the desire to do what is "right and fair in the circumstances", with a particular regard for the invidious predicament of a creditor who can fairly claim to have been endeavouring to respect the requirements of established legal procedure and in consequence refrained from completing an execution process that would otherwise have been put through in time.[21] Courts have also been prepared to alleviate the plight of a creditor who would have completed a process of execution or attachment but for the perpetration of some act of deception or evasion by the debtor company.[22] However, the court has to be persuaded that there are compelling reasons for disturbing the operation of the *pari passu* regime, and the mere fact that a creditor has refrained from pressing home an available process of enforcement, on account of what may be termed the "standard repertoire" of excuses for non-payment or of entreaties for further indulgence, may result in the court failing to find sufficiently weighty grounds for setting aside the principle of uniform treatment of all unsecured creditors.[23]

Distress as an "action or proceeding"

Although in certain respects it is possible to draw lines of analogy between sections 130(2) and 183(2)(c), in terms of the principles underlying the exercise of judicial discretion to relieve the plight of an

---

[20] *cf.* s.183(2)(a), which expressly refers to the application of the section's provisions to the circumstances of a voluntary liquidation. See also *Re Thurso New Gas Co. Ltd* (1889) 42 Ch.D. 486.
[21] *Re Aro Co.* [1980] Ch. 196 (C.A.).
[22] *Re Grosvenor Metal Co. Ltd* [1950] Ch. 63; *Re Suidair International Airways Ltd* [1951] Ch. 165.
[23] *Re Redman (Builders) Ltd* [1964] 1 All E.R. 851; *Re Caribbean Products (Yam Importers) Ltd* [1966] 1 Ch. 331 (C.A.).

individual creditor, it must be emphasised that the drafting of the two sections places them somewhat apart in terms of their scope of application. Section 130(2) refers to the commencement or continuation of any "action or proceeding" against the company or its property, whereas section 183 relates to an "execution or attachment" which is issued against the goods or land of the company, or the attachment of any debt due to it. From time to time, cases arise in which it is necessary to define precisely whether some particular species of remedy or process falls within the ambit of either—or both—of these provisions. The long-established remedy of distress has been the subject of such definitional exercises on several occasions. Part of the difficulty may be attributed to the antique origins of the remedy, and to its peculiar diversity. Thus, the landlord's remedy of distress for rent was originally developed at Common Law, with subsequent statutory encrustations, whereas the remedies of distress for unpaid rates or taxes are wholly statutory in origin and have on that account tended to be viewed in a separate light by the court.[24] This approach formerly resulted in a judicial inclination to regard distress for rates or taxes as analogous to an execution, and hence to be affected by any statutory provision so expressed as to relate to an "execution". In recent times however there has been a change of approach, and courts have regularly declined to regard distress as a species of execution, and have further declined to accept that there is any material distinction between distress for rent and distress for rates or taxes.[25] It can also be observed that the drafting of section 128(1) of the present Act (following the phrasing used in previous legislation) appears to differentiate between "distress" and "execution" by listing them as alternatives, separated by the disjunctive "or", in the reference to "any attachment, sequestration, distress or execution."[26]

On the other hand, the remedy of distress is plainly capable of being held to lie within the ambit of the more general expression "action or proceeding", as used in section 130(2) (and also in section 126(1)). Accordingly, it has been held that any type of distress (whether for rent, rates or taxes) is affected by the provisions of section 130(2) unless it has been completed by the sale of the distrained goods before the winding up order is made.[27]

Publicity to third parties

In order to avoid loss or inconvenience to parties who may have dealings with the company after it has gone into liquidation, section 188 of the Act imposes the requirement that every invoice, order for goods or business letter issued by or on behalf of the company or the liquidator after the

---

[24] See, *e.g. Hutchins v. Chambers* (1758) 1 Burr. 579; 97 E.R. 458 (Lord Mansfield). See also Fletcher (1988) 1 Insolvency Intelligence 9–11.
[25] *Re Herbert Berry Associates Ltd* [1976] 1 W.L.R. 783; [1976] 3 All E.R. 207 (decided under the equivalent provisions of the Companies Act 1948). For the position of any creditor who has distrained upon the goods or effects of the company within three months of the date of a winding up order, see s.176 of the Act.
[26] s.128 is further considered in Chap. 26, *post* (*loc. cit. supra*, n. 13).
[27] *Re Memco Engineering Ltd* [1986] Ch. 86.

The Winding Up Order and its Consequences

winding up order must contain a statement that the company is in liquidation. A criminal penalty, in the form of a fine, is imposed upon the company and any of its officers, or the liquidator, who knowingly and wilfully authorise or permit default in respect of this requirement.[28]

Steps to the Appointment of a Liquidator

The Official Receiver's Duties

On the making of the winding up order, the official receiver by virtue of his office becomes liquidator of the company and continues in office until such time as another person becomes liquidator in accordance with the prescribed procedures.[29] Although this means that, in a certain sense, the official receiver is functioning as a provisional liquidator pending his possible replacement by a liquidator appointed from the private sector, his responsibilities throughout all ensuing phases of the liquidation are substantial, and may include his continuing to serve as liquidator to the conclusion of the winding up, either through lack of any displacing appointment or because a vacancy subsequently arises in the office of liquidator.[30]

After carrying out his initial duties with regard to the service and notification of the winding up order, the official receiver must perform a series of tasks relating to the investigation of the company's affairs, the preparation of information to be placed at the disposal of the creditors and shareholders at their meetings to be convened in due course, and the convening of those meetings, according to his personal judgment.

Statement of Affairs

Where a winding up order has been made or a provisional liquidator appointed,[31] the official receiver may require some or all of the following persons to submit to him a statement of the company's affairs, prepared in the prescribed form and verified by affidavit[32]:

(1) Present and past officers of the company;
(2) Persons who have taken part in the formation of the company within one year before the relevant date;
(3) Persons who are employees of the company, or who have been in its employment within that year, and are considered by the official receiver to be capable of giving the information required;
(4) Persons who are or have been within that year officers or

---

[28] Insolvency Act 1986, s.188(2). See also s.430 and Sched. 10.
[29] *ibid.*, ss.136(2), 137, 139, 140. See *infra*.
[30] See *infra*.
[31] See Chap. 21, *ante*.
[32] Insolvency Act 1986, s.131(1), (3), Insolvency Rules 1986, r. 4.33; Form 4.17.

employees of a company which is, or within that year was, an officer of the company.

In this context, the expression "the relevant date" means the date of the winding up order except where a provisional liquidator is appointed, when "the relevant date" is the date of his appointment.[33]

Section 131 of the Insolvency Act 1986 replaces sections 528 and 529 of the Companies Act 1985 with a new provision dealing with the preparation and submission of the company's statement of affairs. In fact, the matters formerly governed by section 529 of the Companies Act are now provided for in the new Insolvency Rules. As part of the strategy for harmonising and simplifying the insolvency law, the new provisions relating to the statement of affairs to be submitted by a company undergoing winding up by the court are in substance identical to those applicable in cases where a company is required to furnish a statement of affairs to an administrator[34] or to an administrative receiver[35] or to a receiver appointed in Scotland.[36] The forms of statement to be used in the various situations are prescribed in the Rules, and are identical for all types of procedure, apart from the inevitable variations in terminology to be employed in each particular case.

In one respect a notable distinction is made between a compulsory winding up and the other types of insolvency proceeding mentioned above, since in each of the latter it is made obligatory for the office holder to require the company to furnish a statement of affairs,[37] whereas in a compulsory winding up this is left to the discretion of the official receiver.[38] The purpose behind the maintenance of this discretion for the official receiver (or, in Scotland, for the liquidator or provisional liquidator) to elect whether to require the company to produce a statement of affairs in the case of a compulsory winding up is to avoid the possibility that the official receiver might become subject to a statutory duty which it might not lie within his power to perform, as where the directors cannot be found, or where there is insufficient information to enable a statement to be prepared, or where the director concerned is incapable of performing the task on account of illness or incapacity.

The statement must give particulars of the assets, debts and liabilities, the names, addresses and occupations of its creditors, their securities and such further information as may be required.[39] In practice the official receiver supplies forms and instructions.[40] The statement must be made out in duplicate and one copy verified by affidavit by the above persons.[41] It

---

[33] *ibid.*, s.131(6).
[34] *ibid.*, s.22.
[35] *ibid.*, s.47.
[36] *ibid.*, s.66.
[37] *ibid.*, ss.22(1), 47(1), 66(1).
[38] *ibid.*, s.131(1) ("the official receiver *may* require..." (emphasis added)). On the exercise of the official receiver's discretion, see Insolvency Rules 1986, r. 4.36.
[39] *ibid.*, s.131(2).
[40] The Department of Trade and Industry has issued guidance notes for completion of the statement of affairs.
[41] Insolvency Rules 1986, r. 4.33(4).

must be submitted to the official receiver within 21 days following the day on which the prescribed notice of the requirement is given by the official receiver to the persons concerned.[42] The official receiver may, at his discretion, either release a person at any time from the obligation of submitting a statement of affairs, or at any time extend the period within which the statement must be submitted.[43] If the official receiver refuses to exercise a power conferred on him by s.131(5), application may be made to the court, which has an overriding jurisdiction.[44] The official receiver then files the statement of affairs with the Registrar of the court.[45]

The official receiver may hold personal interviews with any of the above persons for the purpose of investigating the company's affairs and it is their duty to attend on the official receiver at such time and place as he appoints and give him all the information which he requires both before and after submission of the statement of affairs.[46] Any reasonable costs incurred in the making of the statement will be reimbursed by the official receiver or provisional liquidator out of the assets of the company.[47]

Any default in complying with section 131 without reasonable excuse is punishable with a fine.[48] In addition the official receiver can apply to the court for an order directing co-operation, and failure to comply will then be contempt of court. Any person who states in writing that he is a creditor or contributory is entitled to inspect the statement of affairs and to receive a copy of it on payment of the prescribed fee, but a false statement for this purpose is an offence.[49] Comments on a statement of affairs may be contempt of court[50] but the court will be reluctant to commit a person unless an attempt is made to interfere with the proper course of the winding up.[51]

Rule 4.45 of the Insolvency Rules 1986 requires the official receiver to send out to creditors and contributories a report containing a summary of the statement of affairs and such observations, if any, as he thinks fit with respect to it, or to the affairs of the company in general.[52]

Investigation by Official Receiver

Sections 530, 563 and 564 of the Companies Act 1985 were repealed by the Insolvency Act 1985. Schedule 10, Part II to the Insolvency Act 1985 effected the repeal of the provisions of the Companies Act which formerly imposed a requirement upon the Official Receiver to prepare reports upon the company's management and the causes of its failure. The new provision, contained in section 132 of the Insolvency Act 1986, imposes a

[42] Insolvency Act 1986, s.131(4); Insolvency Rules 1986, r. 4.33.
[43] *ibid.*, s.131(5).
[44] *ibid.*, s.131(5), proviso.
[45] Insolvency Rules 1986, r. 4.33(6).
[46] Insolvency Act 1986, s.235(2)(b); Insolvency Rules 1986, rr. 4.32(4) and 4.42.
[47] Insolvency Rules 1986, r. 4.37
[48] Insolvency Act 1986, s.131(7).
[49] Insolvency Rules 1986, r. 12.18.
[50] *cf. Re Hooley* (1899) 79 L.T. 706 (a bankruptcy case).
[51] *Re Hooley,* above, at p. 707. *cf. Re New Par Consols* [1898] 1 Q.B. 573 (C.A.).
[52] See also Insolvency Rules 1986, r. 4.43.

duty upon the official receiver, in every case where a winding up order is made by the court, to investigate the causes of the company's failure (where the company has failed), and in all cases to investigate the promotion, formation, business, dealings and affairs of the company.[53] Having completed his investigation, the official receiver is required to make such report to the court as he thinks fit. The official receiver thus has a discretion whether to submit any report at all, and if his investigations unearth no traces of misconduct worthy of report it is clearly sensible to avoid the trouble and expense of a purely formal report to the court. On the other hand, where a report is submitted by the official receiver, section 132(2) of the Act provides that, in any proceedings, the report shall be prima facie evidence of the facts stated therein. Thus the report could play a significant part in proceedings taking place under the Company Directors Disqualification Act 1986, or under section 214 of the Insolvency Act (concerned with the imposition of personal liability for wrongful trading), or under section 212 of the same Act (which provides a summary remedy against delinquent directors and others),[54] or in proceedings in which application is made to the court to adjust or set aside any transaction at an undervalue to which the company has been a party, or any voidable preference which it has given, or any extortionate credit transaction to which it has become a party.[55] The official receiver's report may also be used as evidence in any prosecution of officers of the company in respect of any criminal offences which may have been committed under the relevant provisions of the Companies Act.

Private Examinations of Officers of the Company and Others

The investigative process whereby the official receiver scrutinises the company's management and affairs may be reinforced through the use of the procedure contained in section 236 of the Insolvency Act. This enables the office holder—a term which may refer to the official receiver when occupying the position of liquidator—to apply to the court for the summoning before it of any officer of the company, or of various persons who may have relevant information regarding the promotion, formation, business, dealings, affairs or property of the company, or who may have in their possession any property of the company or who are supposed to be indebted to the company.[56]

The persons who may be summoned before the court under section 236 are listed in subsection (2). These are, any officer of the company; any person known or suspected to have in his possession any property of the company or supposed to be indebted to the company; or any person whom the court thinks capable of giving information concerning the promotion, formation, business, dealings, affairs or property of the company. The court may also require any of those persons to submit an affidavit

---

[53] Insolvency Act 1986, s.132(1).
[54] See Chap. 27, *post*.
[55] See Insolvency Act 1986, ss.238–246, *post*, Chap. 26.
[56] Insolvency Act 1986, s.236(2).

containing an account of his dealings with the company, or to produce any books, papers or other records in his possession or under his control which relate to the company or to matters germane to the court's investigation. A person who fails to appear before the court when summoned may be compelled to do so by means of an arrest warrant, and warrants may also be issued for the seizure of relevant books, papers, records, money or goods in that person's possession.[57]

Section 236—Principles of application

There has been a vigorous exploration of the provisions of section 236 in a series of cases, some of which have been appealed all the way to the House of Lords. It is indeed possible, and not unlikely, that some aspects of the section's application will in due course attract the involvement of the European Commission and Court of Human Rights, in view of their potential conflict with the principles of due process, and right to a fair trial, in criminal proceedings involving persons who have held directorships, or other positions, in relation to insolvent companies.

It may be observed that the courts, in their approach to section 236, have been conscious of the need to balance a variety of different principles and divergent interests, including the consensus of society at large to maintain credible sanctions against those who abuse the privileges of limited liability, which in practice are heavily dependent on the ability to pursue effective investigations in the face of determined and sophisticated resistance on the part of those whose conduct is under scrutiny. On the other hand, it cannot be denied that the extensive powers conferred by section 236, if applied without some degree of sensitivity, have the capability at times of posing an impossible dilemma for persons under investigation, and thereby put in question the prospect of a "fair" trial on matters which may be technically distinct from, although practically related to, the actual insolvency process itself.

In *Joint Administrators of Cloverbay Ltd v. Bank of Credit and Commerce International S.A.*,[58] the Court of Appeal formulated guidelines for the exercise of the court's discretion to order examinations of persons under section 236(2). These guidelines were re-examined very soon afterwards, and further elaborated, by the Court of Appeal and House of Lords respectively in *Re British and Commonwealth Holdings plc (No. 2)*,[59] on the basis of a full review of the case law relating to the current section and its statutory predecessors. Ralph Gibson L.J., whose judgment was later endorsed by the House of Lords, affirmed that seven principles were clearly established by authority:

[57] *ibid.*, s.236(5), (6). For early judicial decisions relating to the power of examination under s.236, see *Re John T. Rhodes (No. 2)* (1987) 3 B.C.C. 588; *Re Oriental Credit* [1988] 1 Ch. 204; *Re Esal (Commodities) Ltd.* (1988) 4 B.C.C. 475.
[58] [1991] Ch. 90; [1990] 3 W.L.R. 574 (C.A.).
[59] Decided by a majority of the Court of Appeal (Nourse L.J. dissenting): [1992] 2 W.L.R. 931; [1992] 2 All E.R. 801; and unanimously by the House of Lords: [1993] A.C. 426; [1992] 3 W.L.R. 853.

(1) the discretion conferred on the court by section 236(2) is an unfettered and general one;
(2) that discretion nevertheless involves balancing the requirements of the office-holder against possible oppression to the person from whom information is sought;
(3) the power conferred by the section is an extraordinary one whose existence is due to the fact that the office holder usually comes as a stranger to the relevant events;
(4) the power can be used not merely to obtain general information but to discover facts and documents related to contemplated claims, whether proceedings have been started or not, against the proposed witness or someone connected with him;
(5) the power is directed to enabling the court to help the office holder to complete his function as effectively and with as much expedition as possible, and to discover with as little expense and as much ease as possible, the facts surrounding any possible claim;
(6) great weight is to be given to the views of the office holder, who will have detailed knowledge of what problems exist and what information he needs;
(7) matters relevant to the balancing exercise will include that:
 (a) the case against a former officer will usually be stronger, since he owes both a fiduciary duty to the company and a duty under section 235 of the Act to assist the office-holder;
 (b) to ask a third party to expose himself, by giving information, to liability involves an element of oppression;
 (c) an order for oral examination is more likely to be oppressive than one to produce documents;
 (d) to require a person suspected of wrongdoing to prove the case against himself on oath prior to proceedings being brought, is oppressive.

In formulating the above statement of the law, Ralph Gibson L.J. confirmed to a certain extent the pronouncements previously made in the *Cloverbay* case (above). At the same time, however he expressly excluded from the list of principles in his own judgment the factor which had been formulated by Browne-Wilkinson V.-C. in *Cloverbay* that "the purpose of section 236 is to enable the office-holder to get sufficient information to reconstitute the state of knowledge that the company should possess."[60] In the judgment of Ralph Gibson L.J., such a restrictive rule of application of this statutory provision had never been laid down during more than 110 years of judicial consideration of the section's predecessors, and had not formed any part of the *ratio* of the *Cloverbay* decision. Consequently, that proposition in the guidelines stated in the earlier case, must be read in the light of the later pronouncement by a majority of the Court of Appeal in the *British and Commonwealth (No. 2)* case.

[60] [1991] Ch. at p. 102D (*supra*, n. 58).

An order for examination under section 236 is unlikely to be made where there is no prima facie evidence that a substantial case exists which warrants investigation, nor any real prospect of recoveries for the benefit of the creditors.[61] A person who is summoned before the court may be examined upon oath, and in the light of the information thereby disclosed the court may on the application of the office holder make further orders to require any person to deliver up any property of the company which is in that person's possession, or to pay to the office-holder a sum of money in full or partial discharge of any debt which that person owes to the company.[62] Although an application by the office-holder under section 236 may be made *ex parte*, this should only be done where the circumstances justify it, and for reasons that are suitably compelling. The court will be mindful of the possibilities that oppression and injustice may ensue from the over-zealous invocation of the power of examination, and of the power to compel production of documents, and will be reluctant to relax the general rule that a person is entitled to be heard before such a far-reaching order is made against him.[63] It is essential to avoid the creation of procedural opportunities for an office-holder to engage in a "fishing expedition" in the hope of acquiring potentially useful information.

Section 235—Non-judicial examinations

A further form of investigative process may be conducted by the office holder himself, utilising the powers conferred upon him by section 235 of the Insolvency Act 1986. This section imposes a duty upon each of the persons mentioned in subsection (3) to co-operate with the office holder in any insolvency proceedings relating to a company.[64] The persons upon whom this duty is imposed are:

(a) Those who are or have at any time been officers of the company;
(b) Those who have taken part in the formation of the company at any time within one year before the date of commencement of the insolvency proceedings;
(c) Those who are in the employment of the company, or have been in its employment within that year, and are in the office holder's opinion capable of giving information which he requires; and
(d) Those who are, or have within that year been, officers of, or in the employment of, another company which is, or within that year was, an officer of the company in question.[65]

Each of the persons mentioned above is placed under the following obligations:

---

[61] *Re Adlards Motor Group Holdings Ltd* [1990] BCLC 68.
[62] Insolvency Act 1986, s.237(1), (2) and (4).
[63] *Re Maxwell Communications Corporation plc, Homan v. Vogel* [1994] BCC 732, esp. at 747, *per* Vinelott J.
[64] *ibid.*, s.235(2).
[65] *ibid.*, s.235(3).

Steps to the Appointment of a Liquidator

(1) To give to the officer holder such information concerning the company and its promotion, formation, business, dealings, affairs or property as the office holder may at any time after the commencement of the insolvency proceedings reasonably require; and

(2) To attend on the office holder at such times as the latter may reasonably require.

It is a criminal offence punishable by a fine for a person to fail to comply with any obligation imposed by section 235, unless he has a reasonable excuse for his non-compliance.[66]

By means of private examinations carried out in the exercise of the powers conferred on him by section 235, reinforced by the right to apply for a judicial examination to take place under section 236, the official receiver (and, subsequently, the office holder who has responsibility for carrying through the remaining phases of the liquidation) can take prompt and effective steps to investigate the company's affairs and dealings, and to try to trace the whereabouts of assets which may have been dispersed, or disposed of, under circumstances which render them legally recoverable.[67]

Discretion-influencing factors: self-incrimination; confidentiality

There is a considerable body of case law relating to the nature and extent of the powers conferred under sections 235 and 236. As a basic proposition, it is established that a person who is required to give information to the office-holder under section 235, or an officer of an insolvent company who is summoned to appear before the court to be examined under section 236, cannot refuse to answer questions on the ground that to do so might tend to incriminate him or her, because the clear purpose of those sections, read in conjunction with sections 234 and 237, is to establish a class of persons on whom, by virtue of their relationship to the failed company, there is laid a statutory duty to furnish all relevant information, without being entitled to invoke the privilege against self-incrimination.[68] Moreover, the wide terms of section 433 have the effect that any statement made by a person during examination under section 236 (or any other provisions of the Insolvency Act) is admissible in evidence against him or her in any proceedings, whether civil or criminal, and whether or not under the insolvency Act.

The House of Lords have reviewed and restated the legal position

---

[66] *ibid.*, s.235(5).
[67] See further, *post*, Chaps. 24, 26 and 27.
[68] *Bishopsgate Investment Management Ltd v. Maxwell* [1992] BCC 214, (C.A.). See also *Re Jeffrey S. Levitt Ltd* [1992] BCC 137. *cf. R. v. Seelig* [1991] BCLC 869 (C.A.), in which it was held that the privilege against incrimination cannot be invoked by an officer of a company who is undergoing examination by inspectors appointed by the Department of Trade and Industry under Part XIV of the Companies Act 1985. See also *Re London United Investments plc.* [1991] BCC 760 (Scott J.), aff'd. C.A. [1992] BCC 202; *Re Arrows Ltd (No. 2)* [1992] BCC 446 (Vinelott J.).

regarding the right to silence in the context of the investigative powers of the Serious Fraud Office under section 2 of the Criminal Justice Act 1987. In *Smith v. Director of Serious Fraud Office*,[69] their Lordships affirmed that no right of silence is invokable by persons undergoing such investigation even after they have been formally charged, because the investigative process extends beyond that point in time, and Parliament has indicated by clear words in the Act of 1987 that the public interest in relation to the investigation of complex or serious fraud must override the ancient privilege against self-incrimination. However, in their subsequent decision in *Re Arrows (No. 4)*,[70] the House of Lords took the opportunity to observe that a person required to answer questions put directly by the Serious Fraud Office as a consequence of a notice under section 2(2) is protected to a substantial extent against the consequences of giving self-incriminating answers, due to the provision in section 2(8). The latter subsection effectively prevents the answers being used by the prosecution unless, at the criminal trial, the accused elects to give evidence.[71] No comparable protection is conferred by the Act of 1987 in respect of self-incriminating statements made in other investigations to which the privilege against self-incrimination does not attach, such as those conducted under section 236 of the Insolvency Act. The only safeguard appears to consist in the discretion of the judge at the criminal trial, by virtue of section 78 of the Police and Criminal Evidence Act 1984, to refuse to allow the prosecution to rely on transcripts obtained under a section 236 examination if the admission of the evidence would have such an adverse effect on the fairness of the proceedings that the court concludes it ought not to admit it.[72]

Information and documents obtained as a result of a private examination should normally be used only for the purposes of the winding up, but leave of the court may be obtained to allow their use for related purposes, such as the bringing of proceedings for fraudulent trading, or upon other justifying grounds concerned with the proper attainment of justice or the statutory regulatory process over companies and directors.[73]

In a number of cases, the question has arisen whether the circumstances under which the information was originally obtained may give rise to restrictions upon its being made more widely available, on the grounds of confidentiality. For example, if the office holder has given assurances of confidentiality to the persons from whom information was being obtained, the transcripts of those interviews may come to be regarded as "material

---

[69] [1993] A.C. 1; [1992] 3 All E.R. 456; [1992] 3 W.L.R. 66. *cf. A. T. and T. Istel Ltd v. Tully* [1993] A.C. 45 (H.L.). See also *Re Adviser (188) Ltd, ex p. Trachtenberg* [1993] BCC 492 (C.A.).

[70] [1994] BCC 641 (further considered below). The principal speech is that of Lord Browne-Wilkinson.

[71] *ibid.*, at p. 645, *per* Lord Browne-Wilkinson.

[72] *ibid.*, at pp. 644–645 and 654–656, *per* Lord Browne-Wilkinson, and at p. 657, *per* Lord Nolan.

[73] *cf. Re Arrows (No. 4)* [1994] BCC 641 at 651 (H.L.), affirming that the principle formulated by Millett J. in his judgment in *Re Esal Commodities (No. 2) Ltd* [1990] BCC 708, at p. 723H, was too wide. See also the comments in the Court of Appeal stage of *Re Arrows (No. 4)*, [1993] BCC 473 at pp. 480–481, *per* Dillon L.J. and at p. 487, *per* Steyn L.J.

evidence" for the purposes of criminal proceedings involving other persons who have been involved in the management of the company in question. It was held in *Re Barlow Clowes Gilt Managers Ltd*[74] that neither the accused persons in such proceedings, nor the prosecuting authorities, enjoy an automatic right of access to the transcripts and that the office holder should respect the interviewee's right of privacy by refraining from making voluntary disclosure. However, the Crown Court might subsequently form the view that the availability of the transcripts is necessary for the purposes of securing fairness in the context of the criminal trial, and on that basis issue a witness summons against the office holder under section 2 of the Criminal Justice Act 1987. In that event, the force of the statutory duty to which the office holder is thereby subjected is such as to override any assurances of confidentiality which may previously have been given to persons questioned under sections 235 or 236 of the Insolvency Act. It is possible however that a distinction may be drawn in the case of information obtained by a liquidator on an informal basis as a result of the duty imposed on persons by section 235. Although his comments were of the status of *obiter dicta* in the context in which they were uttered, Lord Browne-Wilkinson in delivering the principal judgment of the House of Lords in *Re Arrows Ltd (No. 4)*[75] indicated that he would be prepared to regard the public interest in ensuring the free flow of informally obtained information under section 235 as much greater than it is in relation to transcripts of formal examinations under section 236. This question may require further consideration by the courts in future, but in the meantime it may be submitted that it is not advisable for an office holder to give unqualified assurances of confidentiality without adding the proviso that this is subject to any statutory obligation with which he may subsequently be obliged to comply, such as that contained in section 2 of the Act of 1987. The interaction between the latter provision and the provisions of the Insolvency Act 1986 is a subject of considerable importance, and touches upon questions of legal policy and fundamental liberties.[76]

When application is made to the court under section 236 for a private examination to be conducted, the court is empowered by rule 9.5(4) of the Insolvency Rules to issue directions "as to the custody and inspection" of the documents containing the written record of that examination, thereby limiting access to the transcripts. During the sequence of judicial decisions

---

[74] [1991] 4 All E.R. 385. (See the further progression of this case in the Central Criminal Court: *R. v. Clowes* [1992] 3 All E.R. 440). The cautiously formulated principle regarding authorised disclosure and use of information obtained under s.236, as expounded by Millett J. at [1991] 4 All E.R. pp. 391–392; [1991] BCC 608 at p. 614, must be regarded as of doubtful authority in view of its disavowal by the Court of Appeal in *Re Arrows Ltd (No. 4)* [1993] BCC 473 (discussed below). See especially the judgment of Dillon L.J. at pp. 480–481.
[75] [1994] BCC 641 at 650–651, expressly disagreeing with the views revealed in the judgments of the Court of Appeal in those same proceedings, [1993] BCC 473, whereby sections 235 and 236 were seen as giving rise to equivalent considerations from the standpoint of public interest in ensuring the free flow of information.
[76] See Fletcher [1992] J.B.L. 442–450; [1994] J.B.L. 282–283; McCormack [1993] J.B.L. 425–443.

delivered in the context of the *Arrows* case, it was initially ruled that the power under rule 9.5(4) may be exercised in such a way as to deny access to other investigative bodies, such as the Serious Fraud Office, if the court is convinced that the absence of such protective restrictions would be counter-productive, in that the interviewee would then be unlikely to divulge any useful information to the liquidator, even at the risk of being punished for contempt of court.[77] However, in consequence of the decision of the House of Lords, confirming the unanimous decision of the Court of Appeal, in *Re Arrows Ltd (No. 4)*,[78] this proposition is no longer valid, at any rate with regard to the right of the Serious Fraud Office to exercise the powers conferred by section 2 of the Criminal Justice Act 1987 and thereby demand the release of information obtained by means of a private examination under section 236 of the Insolvency Act. The judgment of the Court of Appeal included a ruling to the effect that liquidators (and, by implication, other types of office holder in insolvency proceedings) are "persons" within the meaning of section 2(3) of the Act of 1987, and that transcripts and affirmations in their possession, resulting from private examinations under section 236, constitute "documents" within that same subsection 2(3), which the liquidators can be required to produce.[79] These findings were not challenged in the proceedings before the House of Lords, which were concerned with the issues of whether the judge in the civil proceedings taking place under the Insolvency Act has any discretion to refuse to permit the liquidators to hand over the transcript save upon the giving of an undertaking by the Director of the S.F.O. restricting the use to be made of its contents, and, if so, how such a discretion ought to be exercised. On these issues their Lordships' conclusion, expressed via the speech of Lord Browne-Wilkinson, was ultimately in agreement with that of the Court of Appeal, namely that it was not for the Companies Court judge to exercise any discretion so as to prevent the prosecuting authorities (including the S.F.O.) from obtaining and leading in evidence the transcripts of the section 236 examination.[80] The House of Lords did however diverge from the views of the Court of Appeal on the issue of the existence of a discretion for the Companies Court to exercise, and emphasised that the purpose of the provision in rule 9.5(4) is to ensure that the information extracted under compulsion using section 236 should not be generally available but should be used only for the purposes for which the power of examination was conferred.[81] Outside those areas where an overriding statutory power has been established, as in the case of the Criminal Justice Act 1987, it is therefore within the capacity of the Companies Court to exercise a discretion to decide who shall have

---

[77] *Re Arrows Ltd (No. 2)* [1992] BCC 125 (Hoffmann J.); [1992] BCC 46 (Vinelott J.), affd. C.A. (unreported). See also *Re Arrows Ltd (No. 4)* [1992] BCC 987 (Vinelott J.), a judgment subsequently reversed on appeal, as discussed in the text.
[78] [1994] BCC 641 (H.L.); [1993] BCC 437 (C.A.).
[79] [1993] BCC at 477, *per* Dillon L.J.; *ibid.* at 484, *per* Steyn L.J.
[80] [1994] BCC at 653–654; *cf.* [1993] BCC at 480–483, *per* Dillon L.J., and at 484–489, *per* Steyn L.J.
[81] [1994] BCC at 652–653; *cf.* the differing views expressed at [1993] BCC 483, *per* Dillon L.J., and at 488–490, *per* Steyn L.J.

access to the information thus obtained. In relation to the activities of the prosecution authorities pursuant to their designated, statutory functions, it is now established that there is no basis for excluding such statements from being available for use in subsequent criminal proceedings, whether on the basis of a private law right of confidentiality, or on the ground of public interest immunity.[82]

Viewed from the standpoint of the liquidator, therefore, the immediate public interest consists of the need to ensure a proper investigation into the affairs of the failed company. But this is capable of being overtaken by a further, and pre-eminent, public interest in the free flow of information from the official receiver and liquidators to prosecuting authorities about the commission of offences.[83]

The exercise of the court's power under rule 9.5 is usually based upon its perusal of the contents of a confidential statement which will have been filed in court, according to established practice, by the party who either wishes to deny access to other potentially interested persons, or conversely, by such persons seeking to have the restriction removed so far as applying to themselves. In the latter case, an application for a disclosure order is made *ex parte*, and it can become a further contested issue whether the contents of the applicant's confidential statement can themselves be inspected by the party whose records or transcripts of information would cease to be protected by complete confidentiality if the *ex parte* application is granted. In *Re British and Commonwealth Holdings plc (No. 1)*,[84] the Court of Appeal concluded that to withhold such information from the very party against whose interest in maintaining confidentiality it was being used could effectively deny that party the opportunity to challenge the contents of the statement in a proper and timely manner. Important guidance was issued by the court for the benefit of practitioners who in future lodge confidential statements in support of applications for disclosure of information obtained using powers contained in the Insolvency Act. The arguments and reasons which are submitted to the court in support of the application for disclosure should be set out in such a fashion that material which can uncontroversially be made accessible to the other party is separated from any arguments for which the applicant would, if challenged, argue for the maintenance of confidentiality even as against that party if the latter in due course seeks to challenge the order for disclosure. It follows that the uncontested material would normally be

---

[82] [1994] BCC at 648–652; *cf.* [1993] BCC at 478–479, *per* Dillon L.J., and at 486–487, *per* Steyn L.J.

[83] [1994] BCC at 651, *per* Lord Browne-Wilkinson, *cf.* [1993] BCC at 481–484, *per* Dillon L.J., and at 487–488, *per* Steyn L.J. See also the contemporaneous decision, by the same Court of Appeal, in *Re Headington Investments Ltd, ex p. Maxwell* [1993] BCC 500, to the effect that there is no parallel right enjoyed by the accused person to compel simultaneous disclosure to himself of all the documents obtained by the SFO by means of s.2 of the 1987 Act: the accused person's rights in this regard arise on a separate basis in the context of the criminal proceedings themselves and are a matter for the criminal, not the civil, court to administer.

[84] [1992] Ch. 342; [1992] BCC 165. See further: *Re Bishopsgate Investment Management Ltd (No. 2)* [1994] BCC 732, in which the confidentiality of the liquidator's annexure was maintained.

made available to the other party, but that the question of whether to allow inspection of the "reserved" material must be a matter of judgment for the court in the light of the nature of the material itself, having regard to the overall requirements of natural justice in affording a party adequate opportunity to contest matters which are of crucial significance in the determination of his legal rights or interests.

Public Examination of Officers of the Company

In place of the repealed sections 563 and 564 of the Companies Act 1985, the Insolvency Act 1986 makes new provision, in sections 133 and 134, for the public examination of the officers of a company being wound up by the court. In accordance with the strong recommendation of the *Cork Committee*,[85] the public examination in cases of company insolvency is intended to undergo a revival, and will operate analogously to the public examination of individuals in cases of bankruptcy. A public examination may take place whenever a company is being wound up by the court, irrespective of whether the company is insolvent or not, and it is no longer a precondition to the holding of a public examination that the official receiver should first make a report alleging fraud, as was formerly required under section 563(1) of the Companies Act 1985.

Section 133 of the Insolvency Act 1986 enables the official receiver or, in Scotland, the liquidator of a company, at any time before the dissolution of the company, to apply to the court for the public examination of any person who:

(1) Is or has been an officer of the company; or
(2) Has acted as liquidator or administrator of the company or as receiver of manager; or
(3) Is or has been concerned, or has taken part, in the promotion, formation or management of the company.[86]

The official receiver may be coerced into making an application for a public examination if he is formally requested to do so by one-half, in value, of the company's creditors, or by three-quarters, in value, of the company's contributories. However, the court may override the wishes of the creditors or contributories by ordering that no public examination shall be held.[87] A warrant of arrest may be issued against any director failing to attend a public examination, and he risks further punishment via the costs in relation to any proceedings disputing the steps taken against him for contempt.[88]

---

[85] Cmnd. 8558, Chap. 12, especially paras. 653–657.
[86] Insolvency Act 1986, s.133(1). See also Insolvency Rules 1986, rr. 4.211–4.217. See also s.134 of the Act, regarding penalties for non-attendance at the public examination, and the court's power to order the arrest of a person who absconds.
[87] *ibid.*, s.133(2). For the procedure for requisitioning of an application by creditors or contributories, see Insolvency Rules 1986, r. 4.213; Forms 4.62, 4.63.
[88] *cf. Re Avatar Communications* (1988) 4 BCC 473.

It has been authoritatively affirmed by the Court of Appeal that, under the modern law of insolvency, the privilege against self-incrimination cannot be invoked by any person who is undergoing a public examination conducted under section 133 of the Insolvency Act 1986 (in the case of a winding up by the court), or under section 112 of the Act (in the case of a voluntary winding up). In *Bishopsgate Investment Management Ltd v. Maxwell*,[89] the judgment of Dillon L.J. contains a thorough review of the history of the statutory provisions concerning public examinations in personal bankruptcy and in company liquidation cases respectively. Given the express Parliamentary intention that the Insolvency Acts of 1985 and 1986 should effect a harmonisation between individual and corporate insolvency, to the greatest practicable extent, it followed that the established principle of compulsion, which had long been a feature of the law of bankruptcy, must apply equally to public examinations in companies liquidation. Accordingly, Parliament was declared to have exercised its undoubted capacity to abrogate the privilege against self-incrimination in cases falling under either section 133 or section 112. This evaluation of the legislative policy in relation to the curtailment of the privilege against self-incrimination was reinforced by the decision of the House of Lords in *R. v. Director of the Serious Fraud Office, ex parte Smith*,[90] in which it was held that the SFO was entitled to require S to attend and answer questions on pain of conviction of an offence under the Criminal Justice Act 1987, notwithstanding that he had already been charged with other criminal offences in relation to the matters about which it was desired to question him. It would appear that, notwithstanding the imminence of a criminal trial itself, an accused company officer or director could be required to undergo public examination under section 133 of the Insolvency Act, or to fulfil other obligations to co-operate under that Act, although the court could have regard to the ultimate impact of such acts of compliance from the standpoint of justice to the accused at his pending trial.[91]

It has been held that a public examination may be legitimately used as a means of obtaining information which ought to have been furnished in a statement of affairs required under section 131 of the Act or in the course of an informal attendance upon the office holder or the official receiver for the purpose of complying with the duty arising under section 235.[92] But, although thus available as a weapon of last resort, a public examination should not be pursued for such a purpose ahead of the making of application under rule 7.20 of the Insolvency Rules 1986 for specific orders enforcing compliance with the obligations in question.[93]

It was held in *Re Seagull Manufacturing Co. Ltd*[94] that the power to order

---

[89] [1992] BCC 214.
[90] [1993] A.C. 1; [1992] 3 W.L.R. 66, discussed, *supra*, p. 566.
[91] *Re Wallace Smith Trust Co. Ltd* [1992] BCC 707, at pp. 709–710, *per* Ferris J. (this case also concerned the same person whose case was the subject of the ruling by the House of Lords cited in the previous footnote).
[92] *Re Wallace Smith Trust Co. Ltd, supra*.
[93] *ibid.*
[94] [1991] 3 W.L.R. 307; [1991] BCC 550, aff'd. (C.A.), [1993] BCC 241.

a public examination under section 133 may be exercised with extraterritorial effect. In that case, it was ordered that a British subject, then resident in the Channel Islands, could be the subject of an order requiring him to attend for public examination in England, and that the order could be served on the director abroad pursuant to rule 12.12 of the Insolvency Rules 1986. This conclusion was arrived at on the basis of a careful analysis of the relevant legislative provisions, and produces the effect that any person who becomes an officer of any company which is liable to undergo a winding up in England thereby becomes liable to be summoned for public examination in the event of that company's failure, even though he may have no other ties with this country which would otherwise make him amenable to the jurisdiction of English courts.

The power to examine a former liquidator of a company may be of particular significance in cases where a voluntary liquidation is converted into a compulsory winding up under section 124(5) of the Insolvency Act 1986. This represents a further component in the overall strategy aimed at eradicating the potential for the procedure for voluntary winding up to lend itself to various malpractices involving complicity on the part of the liquidator nominated by the company.[95]

First Meetings of Creditors and Contributories—Nomination of Liquidator

The provisions of sections 533 and 534 of the Companies Act have been repealed and replaced by sections 136 and 139 of the Insolvency Act 1986. Section 136 implements the proposal, advanced in Chapter 19 of the *Cork Report*, that it should become a matter of judgment for the official receiver to decide whether it is worthwhile to convene meetings of the company's creditors and contributories for the purpose of electing a private-sector liquidator in place of the official receiver himself. Section 136(4) of the Insolvency Act therefore confers upon the official receiver the discretion to decide whether to convene such meetings. In the alternative section 137(1) enables the official receiver to make direct application to the Secretary of State for the appointment of a person as liquidator in his place. Section 136(5) renders it a matter of duty for the official receiver to decide upon his preferred course of action under subsection (4) as soon as practicable within the period of 12 weeks beginning with the day on which the winding up order is made. However, subsection (5)(c) establishes the right of any creditor, if representing at least one quarter in value of the company's creditors, to serve a formal request upon the official receiver and thereby render it obligatory for him to convene the meetings.

The reason which underlies the new statutory provision regarding the convening of meetings of creditors and contributories is the wish to save the unnecessary wastage of expense in summoning such meetings where the company's anticipated deficiency is such that it is unlikely that any private-sector liquidator would be prepared to act in the matter. The *Cork Committee* was of the opinion, borne of experience, that in many cases where the available assets are not expected to yield any worthwhile return

---

[95] See Chaps. 18, 19, *ante*.

to the ordinary, unsecured creditors, few if any are likely to take the trouble to attend a creditors' meeting, the convening of which is thus rendered an empty formality which further depletes such assets as are realisable. Therefore, if the official receiver concludes that any meetings are likely to be sparsely attended, or that they could serve no useful purpose under the circumstances, he may elect not to hold them, but it is nevertheless open to the creditors to take steps to compel him to convene the meetings, even against his own better judgment. Furthermore, it is made incumbent upon the official receiver, upon his electing not to convene meetings, to give notice of that decision to the court and to all the company's creditors and contributories. The notice must be sent before the end of the period of 12 weeks from the making of the winding up order, and must include an explanation of the creditors' power to require the official receiver to summon meetings of creditors and contributories, in the way which has been described.[96]

Where meetings of creditors and contributories are summoned for the purpose of choosing a person to be liquidator of the company, section 139 of the Insolvency Act becomes applicable. The creditors and the contributories, at their respective meetings, may nominate a person to be liquidator, but priority is given to the person who is the creditors' nominee. Only if the creditors do not succeed in making a valid nomination, or where in fact the person whom they nominate is the same person as is nominated by the contributories, will the latter succeed in gaining the appointment of their nominee.[97] Formerly, there was considerable potential for the creditors' meeting to become deadlocked on account of the compound requirement attaching to the passing of resolutions at their meetings, whereby it was necessary for a resolution to be supported by both a majority in number and a majority in value of the creditors present or represented.[98] The new Insolvency Rules adopt the recommendation made in the *Cork Report* at paragraphs 921–922 that voting at creditors' meetings should be on the basis of a majority in value only.[99]

Although in principle the creditors enjoy priority in the matter of choice of liquidator, section 139(4) of the Insolvency Act establishes a right for any creditor or contributory of the company to apply to the court within seven days of the date of the creditors' nomination of a person different from the person nominated by the contributories. The purpose of the application is to obtain an order of the court either appointing the contributories' nominee to be liquidator instead of, or jointly with, the creditors' nominee, or appointing some other person to be liquidator instead of the person nominated by the creditors. Finally, if meetings of creditors and contributories are held, but fail to result in the appointment of any person as liquidator, the official receiver is placed under the duty of deciding whether to refer the need for an appointment to the Secretary of State.[1] However, whenever an application or reference concerning the

---

[96] Insolvency Act 1986, s.136(5)(b), (6); Insolvency Rules 1986, r. 4.50.
[97] *ibid.*, s.139(2), (3).
[98] *cf.* Chap. 19, *ante*, p. 510, with regard to voluntary liquidations (text to n. 50).
[99] Insolvency Rules 1986, r. 4.63.
[1] Insolvency Act 1986, s.137(2).

appointment of a liquidator is made to the Secretary of State, the latter is at liberty to elect to make no appointment, in which case the official receiver will continue as liquidator *ex officio*.[2]

A further matter of relevance in relation to the selection of a person to replace the official receiver as liquidator is that the person so appointed must be properly qualified to act as an insolvency practitioner in relation to the company, within the meaning of Part XIII of the Insolvency Act 1986.[3] It is a criminal offence, of strict liability, for a person to act as liquidator of a company at a time when he is not qualified to do so.[4] The provisions of sections 390–398 of the Insolvency Act are primarily applicable to determine whether a person is qualified to act as an insolvency practitioner at any given time, and in relation to any given company.

Procedure

Procedural requirements regarding the meetings of creditors and contributories are contained in the Insolvency Rules 1986. Notice of the date of the meetings must be forwarded by the official receiver to the court.[5] Notice of the meetings must be given by public advertisement and not less than 21 days' notice must be given by post to persons appearing from the company's books to be creditors or appearing in the company's books or otherwise to be contributories.[6] Notice must be given in accordance with Forms 4.22 and 4.23 in Schedule 4 to the 1986 Rules and the notice to creditors must state a time within which they must lodge their proofs in order to entitle them to vote at the meeting.[7]

Where a meeting of creditors or contributories is summoned by notice the proceedings and resolutions thereat shall, unless the court otherwise orders, be valid notwithstanding that some creditors or contributories have not received the notice sent to them.[8] As to proof of notice, see rule 12.20.

The official receiver must also give 21 days' notice to each of the officers of the company who, in his opinion, ought to attend the meeting.[9] If so required it is the officer's duty to attend and the official receiver must report to the court any failure to comply.

Conduct of the Meeting; Resolutions and Voting

The official receiver, as convener of the meetings, is designated chairman of the meetings of creditors and contributories, but he may nominate another qualified person to be chairman in his place.[10] At a creditors' meeting, a person is entitled to vote only if there has been duly lodged, by

---

[2] *ibid.*, ss.136(2), 137(3).
[3] See generally, Chap. 2, *ante*.
[4] Insolvency Act 1986, ss.388(1), 389.
[5] Insolvency Rules 1986, r. 4.50(2).
[6] *ibid.*, r. 4.50(3), (5).
[7] *ibid.*, rr. 4.50(4), 4.54(4).
[8] *ibid.*, r. 12.16.
[9] *ibid.*, r. 4.58.
[10] *ibid.*, r. 4.55.

the time specified in the notice of the meeting, a proof of the debt claimed to be due to him from the company, and the claim has been admitted by the chairman for the purpose of entitlement to vote.[11] Where a person is to act as proxy on behalf of a creditor who is unable to be present in person, not only must the creditor's claim have been proved and admitted, but also the proxy form must be lodged by the time specified.[12]

No creditor may vote in respect of any unliquidated or contingent debt or any debt whose value is not ascertained.[13] No creditor may vote in respect of any debt on or secured by a current bill of exchange or promissory note unless he is willing to treat the liability of every person who is liable thereon antecedently to the company as a security and to deduct the estimated value from his proof for the purposes of voting but not of dividend.[14]

A secured creditor, unless he surrenders his security, must state in his proof particulars of his security and the value at which he assesses it, and is only entitled to vote in respect of the balance (if any) of the debt owing to him. If he votes in respect of the whole debt he will be deemed to have surrendered his security unless the court is satisfied that the omission to value the security arose from inadvertence.[15] Where a creditor mistakenly believed his security to be a collateral one, failed to value it and proved for the full amount it was held that this was inadvertence and the court allowed the amendment on terms as to costs.[16] A mistaken belief that a security was worthless, if mentioned in the proof, does not amount to an omission to disclose that security. The onus of proof of inadvertence is cast upon the creditor, however, and the court will be alert to detect any indications that the creditor is belatedly seeking to take advantage from an undisclosed security whose true value has subsequently been appreciated.[17]

The official receiver may serve notice on a secured creditor that he proposes, at the expiration of 28 days, to redeem the security at the value put upon it in the creditor's proof. The creditor then has 21 days in which to exercise his right to revalue his security, whereupon the official receiver (or, subsequently, the liquidator) may only redeem at the new value.[18] The Rules allow a secured creditor at any time, with the agreement of the liquidator or the leave of the court, to alter the value which he has placed upon his security in his proof of debt. In the case where the secured creditor was also the petitioner, and has consequently valued his security in the petition itself, or where the creditor has voted in respect of the unsecured balance of his debt, revaluation may only be effected with leave of the court.[19]

---

[11] *ibid.*, rr. 4.67(1)(a), 4.70. See Form 4.22.
[12] *ibid.*, r. 4.67(1)(b).
[13] *ibid.*, r. 4.67(3).
[14] *ibid.*, r. 4.67(5).
[15] *ibid.*, rr. 4.67(4), 4.96.
[16] *Re Henry Lister & Co.* [1892] 2 Ch. 417.
[17] *Re Piers* [1898] 1 Q.B. 627; *Re Safety Explosives Ltd* [1904] 1 Ch. 226; *Re Rowe, ex p. West Coast Goldfields* [1904] 2 K.B. 489.
[18] Insolvency Rules 1986, r. 4.97.
[19] *ibid.*, r. 4.95.

At the meeting the chairman has the power to admit or reject proofs for the purpose of voting but his decision is subject to appeal to the court. If he is in doubt he must mark it "objected to" and allow the creditor to vote subject to the vote being declared invalid in the event of the objection being sustained.[20] Proper minutes must be kept of the meeting and a list of creditors and contributories present must be made in accordance with the requirements of the Rules.[21] At a meeting of the creditors a resolution is deemed to be passed when a majority in value of the creditors have voted in favour of the resolution.[22] At a meeting of the contributories a resolution is deemed to be passed when a majority in value of the contributories present vote in favour of the resolution, the value of the contributories being determined in accordance with the number of votes conferred on them by the regulations of the company.[23] In the case of each type of meeting—whether of creditors of contributories—the concept of a "majority" is based upon the aggregate of value represented by those present and voting, in person or by proxy, on the resolution in question. Hence, those who abstain from voting at a meeting, or those who fail to attend or to arrange proxies, cannot influence the outcome or validity of any voting on resolutions that are put. In the case of a resolution for the appointment of a liquidator, if on any vote there are two nominees for appointment, the person who obtains the most support is appointed, provided that the support for that person represents a majority of all those present (in person or by proxy) at the meeting and entitled to vote.[24]

The quorum, in the case of a creditors' meeting, is at least one creditor entitled to vote, and in the case of a meeting of contributories, at least two contributories so entitled, or all the contributories if their number does not exceed two.[25] A creditor or contributory may vote either personally or by proxy which may be general or special.[26] Where it appears to the court that there has been any solicitation by or on behalf of a liquidator to obtain proxies or procure his appointment the court may order that no remuneration out of the assets shall be allowed to the person concerned notwithstanding any resolution of the liquidation committee or the creditors or contributories to the contrary.[27] In addition, any person who gives or agrees to give any member or creditor of the company any valuable consideration with a view to securing his appointment or securing or preventing the appointment of someone else as the liquidator of the company is liable to a fine.[28]

Where a substantial creditor has not been represented at the first meeting[29] or a change of circumstances makes it desirable[30] the court will

---

[20] *ibid.*, r. 4.70.
[21] *ibid.*, r. 4.71.
[22] *ibid.*, r. 4.63(1).
[23] *ibid.*
[24] *ibid.*, r. 4.63(2), (2A).
[25] *ibid.*, r. 12.4A (substituted by (S.I. 1987, No. 1919), Sched., para. 144, in place of former r. 4.66 (deleted)).
[26] *ibid.*, rr. 4.63, 8.1–8.7; Forms 8.4, 8.5.
[27] *ibid.*, r. 4.150.
[28] Insolvency Act 1986, s.164.
[29] *Re Radford and Bright* [1901] 1 Ch. 272 and 735.
[30] *Re Manmac Farmers Ltd* [1968] 1 All E.R. 1150.

Steps to the Appointment of a Liquidator

order the meeting to be reconvened for the purpose of considering whether an application should be made to the court for the appointment of a liquidator. This may be effected through the exercise of the court's powers under section 195 of the Act to direct that meetings be held for the purpose of ascertaining the wishes of the creditors and contributories.

Only the following resolutions may be taken at the first meeting of creditors[31]:

(1) A resolution to appoint one or more named insolvency practitioners to be liquidator, singly or jointly;
(2) A resolution to establish a liquidation committee[32];
(3) A resolution specifying the terms on which the liquidator is to be remunerated (unless there is to be a liquidation committee);
(4) In a case where joint liquidators have been appointed, a resolution specifying whether acts are to be done by both or all of them, or by only one;
(5) (Where the meeting has been requisitioned under section 136) a resolution authorising payment out of the assets, as an expense of the liquidation, of the cost of summoning and holding the meeting;
(6) A resolution to adjourn the meeting for not more than 3 weeks;
(7) Any other resolution which the chairman thinks it right to allow for special reasons.

Appointment of Liquidator

Where a compulsory winding up takes place immediately after the discharge of an administration order, or at a time when a voluntary arrangement is in force, section 140 of the Insolvency Act 1986 empowers the court to appoint as liquidator the displaced administrator, or supervisor of the voluntary arrangement, as the case may be. Otherwise, by reason of the reforms to the ordinary procedure for appointing a liquidator, the court will not become involved in the process of appointment unless, following the nomination of different persons by the creditors and contributories, any qualified party elects to apply to the court under section 139(4) to have the appointment resolved by order pursuant to that subsection. It remains to be seen whether the past case law will furnish any guide to the way in which the court will exercise its new discretionary power. Formerly, in exercising its discretion under section 533 of the Companies Act (repealed) the court would have regard to the solvency or otherwise of the company. If the company was solvent it would pay greater attention to the wishes of the contributories.[33] If it was insolvent it would pay greater attention to the wishes of the creditors.[34]

---

[31] Insolvency Rules 1986, r. 4.52.
[32] See *infra*, p. 589.
[33] *Re Agricultural Industries Ltd* [1952] 1 All E.R. 1188.
[34] *Re Rubber and Producers Investment Trust Ltd* [1915] 1 Ch. 382.

Ordinarily, as Vaughan Williams J. said in *Re Bank of South Australia (No. 2)*, "the grant ought to follow the interest."[35]

In most cases, the appointment of the liquidator will come about as the consequence of resolutions passed at the meetings of contributories and creditors, convened by the official receiver under section 136.[36] The relevant statutory provision is section 139, which states that at their respective meetings the creditors and the contributories may nominate a person to be the liquidator.[37] The higher priority which is accorded to the creditors' interest, as against that of the members, is manifested in the terms of section 139(3), which provides that the liquidator shall be the person nominated by the creditors. Thus, only where no valid or effective nomination ensues from the creditors' meeting does the person, if any, whom the contributories have nominated become the liquidator. To this extent, the effect of section 139 is analogous to that of section 100, which is applicable to voluntary liquidations.[38] However, an important distinction arises with respect to the rights of parties to invoke the intervention of the court in the event of different persons being nominated by the respective meetings. Under section 139(4), the persons who may apply to the court within seven days of the nomination are any creditor or contributory: unlike section 100(3), there is no mention of any right for a director to make application to the court. This is a consequence of the fact that the making of an order for compulsory winding up terminates the directors' authority to act in relation to the company, and they are accordingly excluded from the category of interested persons with standing to apply to the court on the question of who is to be liquidator.

Where application is made under section 139(4), the court may either appoint the person nominated by the contributories to be a liquidator instead of, or jointly with, the creditors' nominee, or appoint some other person to be liquidator instead of the person nominated by the creditors.

Where a person is appointed as liquidator either by a meeting of creditors or by a meeting of contributories, the chairman of the meeting must certify the appointment.[39] Before the chairman may certify the appointment, the person appointed must first provide him with a written statement to the effect that he is an insolvency practitioner duly qualified under the Act to be the liquidator and that he consents so to act.[40] Where the chairman of the meeting is not the official receiver he must send the certificate to him, and the official receiver must send the certificate to the liquidator and file a copy thereof in court.[41] The liquidator's appointment is effective from the date on which the appointment is certified, and that date is to be endorsed on the certificate.[42]

---

[35] [1895] 1 Ch. 578; (1895) 2 Mans. 148, 149 (during argument).
[36] See above.
[37] Insolvency Act 1986, s.139(2).
[38] See Chap. 19, *ante*.
[39] Insolvency Rules 1986, r. 4.100(2); Forms 4.27, 4.28.
[40] *ibid.*
[41] *ibid.*, r. 4.100(4), (5) (as substituted by (S.I. 1987, No. 1919)).
[42] *ibid.*, r. 4.100(3) (as substituted: see previous footnote). See also r. 4.106, concerning advertisement and registration of the liquidator's appointment.

APPOINTMENT OF LIQUIDATOR

Where the liquidator is appointed by the court under section 139(4), as described above, or under section 140,[43] the court's order may not issue unless and until the person appointed has filed in court a statement averring to his being duly qualified to be the liquidator, and that he consents so to act.[44] The liquidator's appointment takes effect from the date of the order, two copies of which must be sent by the court to the official receiver, who in turn must send a sealed copy of the order to the person appointed as liquidator.[45] The liquidator must, within 28 days of his appointment, give notice of it to all creditors and contributories of the company of whom he is aware in that period, or alternatively he may if the court allows advertise his appointment in accordance with the court's directions.[46]

In the absence of any appointment of a liquidator by the respective meetings (if held), or by the court (if its jurisdiction is invoked), the official receiver by virtue of his office continues to be the liquidator of the company.[47] Section 137 of the Act enables the official receiver, at any time when he is the liquidator of the company, to apply to the Secretary of State for the appointment of a person as liquidator in his place.[48] The Secretary of State is obliged to take a decision in response to this application, but is allowed to elect between making an appointment and declining to do so.[49] If an appointment is made, the liquidator must give notice of his appointment to the company's creditors or, with the court's permission, may advertise his appointment.[50] The Secretary of State must send two certificates of appointment to the official receiver, who transmits one such copy to the person appointed, the appointment being effective from the date to be specified in the certificate itself.[51]

A corporate body cannot be appointed liquidator to another company, since only an individual can be a person qualified to act as an insolvency practitioner.[52]

When the liquidator's appointment takes effect the official receiver must forthwith put the liquidator into possession of all the property of the company.[53] The official receiver has a charge on the company's assets for unpaid expenses.[54] "Property of the company" does not include notes and memoranda representing information obtained by the official receiver from officers of the company. However it is the duty of the official receiver, if so requested by the liquidator, to communicate to him:

"all such information relating to the affairs of the company and the

---

[43] See above, (beginning of this section).
[44] Insolvency Rules 1986, r. 4.102(2); Forms 4.29, 4.30.
[45] *ibid.*, r. 4.102(3), (4).
[46] *ibid.*, r. 4.102(5). For the contents of the notice, see para. (6).
[47] Insolvency Act 1986, s.136(2).
[48] *ibid.*, s.137(1).
[49] *ibid.*, s.137(3).
[50] *ibid.*, s.137(4), (5).
[51] Insolvency Rules 1986, r. 4.104.
[52] Insolvency Act 1986, s.390(1). See Chap. 2, *ante.*
[53] Insolvency Rules 1986, r. 4.107.
[54] *ibid.*, r. 4.107(5).

course of winding up as he (the official receiver) considers to be reasonably required for the effective discharge by the liquidator of his duties as such."[55]

Resignation or Removal of Liquidator; Vacation of Office and Release

In a compulsory winding up, the liquidator may be removed from office only by an order of the court or by a general meeting of the company's creditors summoned specially for that purpose in accordance with the Rules.[56] A provisional liquidator may be removed from office only by an order of the court.[57]

Application to the court for removal of the liquidator, or for an order directing the liquidator to summon a meeting of creditors for the purpose of removing him, involves the applicant showing sufficient cause for removal. There may be an *ex parte* hearing upon at least seven days' notice, at which the court may dismiss the application if there appears to be no arguable case for removal.[58] If the application is not dismissed at this preliminary stage, a full hearing will take place of which both the liquidator and the official receiver must receive at least 14 days' notice. The court may require the applicant to make a deposit or give security for the costs to be incurred by the liquidator on the application, since costs are not payable out of the assets unless the court orders otherwise.[59] The net effect of these arrangements is to make it difficult for a single creditor, or a small and unrepresentative group of creditors, to harass the liquidator in the discharge of his functions. If the court removes the liquidator as a consequence of the hearing, it may make appropriate provisions in its order with respect to the effects of that removal, and may appoint a new liquidator to assume charge of the liquidation.[60]

Apart from where the court directs that a creditors' meeting be held for the purpose of replacing the liquidator, such a meeting may be held at the liquidator's own initiative, or in certain circumstances may be requisitioned by not less than one quarter, in value, of the creditors.[61] The meeting must be duly summoned with notice to creditors, indicating the purpose of the meeting, and a copy of the notice must be sent to the official receiver. A person other than the liquidator may be elected to act as chairman, but if the liquidator or his nominee does chair the meeting, and a resolution for removal is duly proposed, the chairman must not adjourn the meeting without the consent of at least one half (in value) of the creditors present or represented, and entitled to vote.[62] This rule is

---

[55] *ibid.*, r. 4.107(7).
[56] Insolvency Act 1986, s.172(1), (2).
[57] *ibid.*
[58] Insolvency Rules 1986, r. 4.119(2).
[59] *ibid.*, r. 4.119(3), (4), (5).
[60] *ibid.* rr. 4.119(6), 4.102.
[61] Insolvency Act 1986, ss.168(2), 172(3); Insolvency Rules 1986, r. 4.113.
[62] Insolvency Rules 1986, r. 4.113(1), (2), (3).

designed to prevent the creditors' wishes being frustrated through a procedural manoeuvre whereby the meeting is adjourned before the resolution is formally voted upon. If the resolution is put and carried, the creditors may resolve that a new liquidator be appointed, and can also resolve that the removed liquidator shall not be given his release.[63] The chairman of the meeting must, within three days, send to the official receiver a copy of any resolution which has been passed, including a certificate to the effect that it has been resolved to remove the liquidator, if such is the case, and the certificate of appointment of any new liquidator chosen by the meeting.[64]

Other than by removal, the liquidator may leave office either in consequence of his resignation, or through being required to vacate office upon the happening of certain events. A liquidator may resign office only on grounds of ill health, or because he intends ceasing to be in practice as an insolvency practitioner, or because there is some conflict of interest or change of personal circumstances which impedes the proper discharge of his duties as liquidator.[65] Before resigning, the liquidator must call a meeting of creditors for the purpose of receiving his resignation, and must send with the notice of meeting an account of his administration, accompanied by a summary of his receipts and payments and a statement that he has reconciled his account with that which is held by the Secretary of State in respect of the winding up.[66] If the creditors' meeting resolves to accept the liquidator's resignation, it may also resolve that a new liquidator be appointed, in which case the chairman of the meeting must send copies of the resolution and appropriate certificates to that effect to the official receiver within three days.[67] The resigning liquidator is thereupon required to give notice of resignation to the court, as required by section 172(6) of the Act, and must send a copy of the notice to the official receiver for filing in court.[68] The liquidator's resignation is effective as from the date on which the official receiver files the copy notice in court.[69]

If the creditors' meeting resolves not to accept his resignation, the liquidator may apply to the court for an order giving him leave to resign.[70] If such an order is granted the court may make any appropriate provision with respect to matters arising in connection with the resignation, and must determine the date from which the liquidator's release is effective.

A liquidator's office becomes vacant in the event of his death, and it is also provided by section 172(5) of the Act that he must vacate office if he ceases to be a person who is qualified to act as an insolvency practitioner in relation to the company. The other circumstance under which a liquidator vacates office is when a final meeting has been held under section 146 to

---

[63] *ibid.*, r. 4.113(4), (5), 4.100; on release, see Insolvency Act 1986, s.174 (*infra*).
[64] *ibid.*, r. 4.113(4), (5); Form 4.37.
[65] Insolvency Act 1986, s.172(6); Insolvency Rules 1986, r. 4.108(4).
[66] Insolvency Rules 1986, r. 4.108.
[67] *ibid.*, r. 4.108(2), (3).
[68] *ibid.*, r. 4.108(4), (5).
[69] *ibid.*, r. 4.108(6). See also r. 4.112 on the new liquidator's duty to advertise his appointment.
[70] *ibid.*, r. 4.111. See Practice Direction [1987] 1 All E.R. 107, para. 4(1).

receive the liquidator's report on completion of the winding up. After giving notice to the court and to the registrar of companies of the holding of the meeting, and of the decisions of the meeting, the liquidator must vacate office.[71]

Release of Liquidator

Upon completion of his duties in relation to the winding up, the liquidator requires to obtain his release under section 174 of the Act. The significance of this technical process is that, as from the moment when his release takes effect, the liquidator is discharged from all liability both in respect of acts or omissions during the winding up and otherwise in relation to his conduct as liquidator.[72] Section 174 indicates the timing of the moment of the release in relation to each of the ways in which the functions of the official receiver or liquidator may come to an end in relation to a company.[73] Notwithstanding the broad terms in which the effect of release is expressed in section 174(6), the proviso to that subsection preserves the operation of section 212 in relation to a person who has had his release under section 174, and hence the summary remedy in respect of misfeasance by a liquidator (among others), giving rise to a remedy in damages, continues to be available even after the liquidator's release has become effective.

The Liquidator's Remuneration

The provisions within the Insolvency Rules which apply to the fixing of the liquidator's remuneration were discussed in Chapter 19, in relation to voluntary liquidations.[74] The same provisions are also applicable in relation to a compulsory winding up. Where the official receiver acts as a liquidator, he does not receive a personal remuneration for his services, which are performed in the course of his duties as a salaried public official. However, a scale of charges is prescribed by the Insolvency Regulations 1994, representing the fees payable out of the assets, as an expense of the liquidation, for the services provided by the official receiver in this context.[75]

The Status, Duties and Powers of the Liquidator

The legal status of the liquidator is of considerable interest, being in several respects unique. The liquidator displaces the directors, and

---

[71] Insolvency Act 1986, s.172(8). See also Insolvency Rules 1986, rr. 4.132–4.138.
[72] *ibid.*, s.174(6). The provisions of s.174 also apply to a provisional liquidator.
[73] See s.174(2), (3), (4) and (5); see also Insolvency Rules 1986, r. 4.121, 4.124, 4.125.
[74] See Insolvency Rules 1986, rr. 4.127–4.131, *ante*, Chap. 18, p. 414.
[75] See Insolvency Regulations 1994 (S.I. 1994, No. 2507), regs. 33–36, together with Sched. 2 (as amended).

therefore his position closely resembles theirs, but the degree of skill and care he must display, and the nature of the overriding duty to which he is subject, are at a higher level.

The courts have sometimes utilised the language of the law of trusts in describing the nature of the role played by a liquidator in the course of a winding up. James L.J., during his judgment in *Re Oriental Inland Steam Co.*[76] observed that the assets of a company in liquidation are "fixed by the Act of Parliament with a trust for equal distribution amongst the creditors." However, it would be incorrect to conceive of the liquidator as a trustee in the full and literal sense of the word, since the legal title to the company's assets does not (in the absence of a vesting order made upon application under section 145 of the Act) vest in the liquidator. The company retains the legal title to its assets until they are disposed of, and their proceeds distributed as the law directs. But it is nevertheless the case that the beneficial title to the assets of the company in winding up passes to its creditors, and that the company's affairs are administered by the liquidator for the creditors' benefit according to the statutory régime for an insolvent winding up. An apt summary of the liquidator's status was provided by Cotton L.J., in *Re Silver Valley Mines*,[77] namely that he is an agent of the company, occupying a fiduciary position, who is employed for a remuneration to carry out a particular statutory task to whose performance he is bound to bring reasonable, professional skill. He must act honestly and impartially, serving the interests of the general body of creditors, but be mindful also of the residual interests (if any) of the contributories. He must afford all interested parties reasonable assistance and information so as to enable them to ascertain and exercise their rights.

In a compulsory winding up the liquidator is an officer of the court by virtue of his appointment, an attribute of status reflecting the fact that formerly the act of appointing the liquidator in this mode of winding up was performed by the court. In this respect the compulsory liquidator occupies a position analogous to that of a trustee in bankruptcy, and is subject to a special duty to deal fairly, and in an exemplary manner, in all aspects of the performance of his functions. This results from the application to the compulsory liquidator of the so-called "rule" in *ex parte James*,[78] which is applicable whether the liquidator is the official receiver himself or a practitioner from the private sector.

The general duties of the liquidator are inherent to the special status

---

[76] (1874) L.R. 9 Ch.App. 557, 559. For confirmation that the conceptual approach adopted in this classic decision of 1874 is still appropriate to the modern-day working of insolvency law, see *Ayerst v. C & K (Construction) Ltd* [1976] A.C. 167 (H.L.).

[77] (1882) 21 Ch.D. 381, 392.

[78] (1874) 9 Ch.App. 609 C.A.; see *Re Wyvern Developments Ltd* [1974] 2 All E.R. 534. On the origins and effects of the rule itself, see *ante*, Chap. 8, p. 207. The Australian Law Reform Commission recommended the abolition in Australia of the application of the rule in *ex p. James* in respect of company liquidations: see General Insolvency Inquiry (Report No. 45, September 1988), Vol. 1, paras. 909–911; Vol. 2 (Draft Legislation), clause M1 (p. 173). See, however, *Downs Distributing Co. Pty. Ltd v. Associated Blue Star Stores Pty. Ltd* (1948) 76 CLR 463; *Re Associated Dominions Assurance Society Pty. Ltd* (1962) 109 CLR 516; *Re The Paddington Town Hall Centre* (1979) 4 ACLR 673. *Cf. Re Autolook Pty. Ltd* (1983) 8 ACLR 419, 421, *per* Needham J.

which is invested in him by the law, as explained above. He must therefore act at all times in good faith, in strict accordance with the purposes of the liquidation, and with complete impartiality and the absence of any conflict of interest affecting him personally.[79] The principal, specific functions of the liquidator are laid down by the Insolvency Act, as follows:

(1) To secure that the assets of the company are got in, realised and distributed to the company's creditors and, if there is a surplus, to the persons entitled to it[80];
(2) To take control of the company's assets and papers[81];
(3) To ascertain the liabilities and discharge them in the proper order[82];
(4) To summon a final meeting of the company's creditors when he is satisfied that the winding up of the company is for practical purposes complete[83];
(5) (If he is not the official receiver) to furnish the official receiver with such information, and to allow him access to such books, papers and records for the purpose of inspection, as the official receiver may reasonably require, and to assist him generally in the performance of his official functions.[84]

To carry out his duties and functions, the liquidator is given a range of powers by virtue of section 167 of the Act together with Schedule 4. The powers listed in the Schedule are arranged in three groups, which are respectively allocated to Parts I, II and III of the Schedule. These powers are identical in substance to those enjoyed by a voluntary liquidator since Schedule 4 applies in common to both modes of winding up.[85] An important distinction arises however in relation to the liquidator's right to exercise certain of these powers of his own initiative, in that a compulsory liquidator requires the sanction of the court or the liquidation committee[86] to exercise any of the powers in Part I or Part II of the Schedule, whereas a voluntary liquidator requires sanction only in relation to the powers in Part I.[87] The powers in Part III are exercisable without sanction in any winding up.[88] In relation to the exercise of any of his powers, the liquidator is subject to judicial review at the instance of any creditor or contributory, or

---

[79] *Re Silver Valley Mines (above,* n. 77); *Re Llynvi and Tondu Co.* (1889) 6 T.L.R. 11; *Silkstone Coal Co. v. Edey* [1900] 1 Ch. 167; *Re Charterland Goldfields Ltd* (1909) 26 T.L.R. 132; *Re Gertzenstein Ltd* [1937] Ch. 115; *Re Sir John Moore Gold Mining Co.* (1879) 12 Ch.D. 325; *Re Rubber and Produce Investment Trust* [1915] 1 Ch. 382.
[80] Insolvency Act 1986, s.143(1).
[81] *ibid.*, ss.144(1), 160, 234; Insolvency Rules 1986, r. 4.179.
[82] *ibid.*, ss. 175, 386, Sched. 6.
[83] *ibid.*, s.146.
[84] *ibid.*, s.143(2).
[85] See Chap. 19, *ante*, p. 513.
[86] For the liquidation committee, see *infra*. If there is no liquidation committee, and the compulsory liquidator is someone other than the official receiver, the committee's functions are vested in the Secretary of State, on whose behalf they are exercised by the Official Receiver: Insolvency Act 1986, s.141 (5); Insolvency Rules 1986, r. 4.172.
[87] Insolvency Act 1986, ss.167(1)(a), 165(2)(b), (3).
[88] *ibid.*, ss.167(1)(b), 165(3).

of any person aggrieved, but the court will in practice only intervene if it is shown that the liquidator has not exercised his powers in good faith, or has acted in a way no reasonable liquidator could have acted.[89] The provisions of Schedule 4 are as follows:

PART I

Powers Exercisable with Sanction

(1) Power to pay any class of creditors in full.
(2) Power to make any compromise or arrangement with creditors or persons claiming to be creditors, or having or alleging themselves to have any claim (present or future, certain or contingent, ascertained or sounding only in damages) against the company, or whereby the company may be rendered liable.
(3) Power to compromise, on such terms as may be agreed—
 (a) all calls and liabilities to calls, all debts and liabilities capable of resulting in debts, and all claims (present or future, certain or contingent, ascertained or sounding only in damages) subsisting or supposed to subsist between the company and a contributory or alleged contributory or other debtor or person apprehending liability to the company, and
 (b) all questions in any way relating to or affecting the assets or the winding up of the company,
and take any security for the discharge of any such call, debt, liability or claim and give a complete discharge in respect of it.

PART II

Powers Exercisable without Sanction in Voluntary Winding Up, with Sanction in Winding Up by the Court

(4) Power to bring or defend any action or other legal proceeding in the name and on behalf of the company.

---

[89] *ibid.*, ss.167(3), 168(5); *Leon v. York-o-Matic Ltd* [1966] 3 All E.R. 277; *Re a Debtor (No. 400 of* 1940) *ex p. The Debtor v. Dodwell* [1949] Ch. 236.

(5) Power to carry on the business of the company so far as may be necessary for its beneficial winding up.

Part III

Powers Exercisable without Sanction in any Winding Up

(6) Power to sell any of the company's property by public auction or private contract with power to transfer the whole of it to any person or to sell the same in parcels.
(7) Power to do all acts and execute, in the name and on behalf of the company, all deeds, receipts and other documents and for that purpose to use, when necessary, the company's seal.
(8) Power to prove, rank and claim in the bankruptcy, insolvency or sequestration of any contributory for any balance against his estate, and to receive dividends in the bankruptcy, insolvency or sequestration in respect of that balance, as a separate debt due from the bankrupt or insolvent, and rateably with the other separate creditors.
(9) Power to draw, accept, make and indorse any bill of exchange or promissory note in the name and on behalf of the company, with the same effect with respect to the company's liability as if the bill or note had been drawn, accepted, made or indorsed by or on behalf of the company in the course of its business.
(10) Power to raise on the security of the assets of the company any money requisite.
(11) Power to take out in his official name letters of administration to any deceased contributory, and to do in his official name any other act necessary for obtaining payment of any money due from a contributory or his estate which cannot conveniently be done in the name of the company.

In all such cases the money due is deemed, for the purpose of enabling the liquidator to take out the letters of administration or recover the money, to be due to the liquidator himself.
(12) Power to appoint an agent to do any business which the liquidator is unable to do himself.
(13) Power to do all such other things as may be necessary for winding up the company's affairs and distributing its assets.

Where the liquidator is someone other than the official receiver, and in the exercise of the powers set out above he disposes of any property of the company to a person who is connected with the company, or employs a solicitor to help him in the carrying out of his functions, he must give notice of that exercise of his powers to the liquidation committee, if there is one.[90] If the liquidator is found to have been personally interested in any sale and purchase, the transaction may be set aside.[91]

Where the company's assets have been vested in him by order of the court under section 145, the liquidator is competent to bring action in his own name in relation to them. He should, nevertheless, style himself properly as "the liquidator of (the company in question)" or (if appropriate) "the official receiver and liquidator of (the company)," and should not describe himself simply by an individual name.[92] In other cases, litigation conducted by the liquidator to recover or protect assets of the company, or to enforce liabilities owed to it as creditor, must be brought in the company's name as plaintiff by the liquidator acting in his capacity as agent of the company.[93] It is to be noted that the liquidator's position as agent is one which is imposed upon the company by law, and not by any voluntary act on its part, but it is nevertheless the case that the liquidator is thereby able to bind the company by his acts performed within the compass of his powers, and will not incur personal liability provided that he makes it clear that he is acting as liquidator for the purpose in question. Liabilities which result from such acts by the liquidator must be discharged out of the assets of the company.

The Liquidator's Books and Accounts

The liquidator must keep proper books of account and minute books, and any creditor, contributory or director may, subject to the control of the court, inspect them.[94] The Insolvency Regulations 1994 and the Insolvency Practitioners Regulations 1986, in addition to the Insolvency Rules, specify the books and records which he must keep. These are:

(1) Sufficient records which are consistent with proper administration of the case in question.[95] These include the proper keeping of minutes, and records of attendance and of resolutions passed, in relation to every meeting of creditors or contributories of which he, or someone nominated by him, acts as chairman.[96]

(2) Financial records in which he must enter particulars of receipts and payments on a daily basis. The liquidator must submit the

---

[90] Insolvency Act 1986, s.167(2). "connected" person is defined by ss.249 and 435: see Appendix I, *post* p. 629.
[91] *Silkstone Coal Co. v. Edey* (*supra*, n. 79).
[92] Insolvency Act 1986, s.163.
[93] *Re Silver Valley Mines* (*above*, n. 77).
[94] Insolvency Regulations 1994 (S.I. 1994, No. 2507), regulation 11; *cf.* Insolvency Act 1986, ss.143(2), 170.
[95] Insolvency Practitioners Regulations 1990 (S.I. 1990, No. 439), reg. 17 together with Sched. 3.
[96] Insolvency Rules 1986 (S.I. 1986 No. 1925) (as amended), r. 4.71. See also r. 12.5.

financial records to the liquidation committee when required.⁹⁷ If the committee are not satisfied with the contents of the records they may so inform the Secretary of State, giving the reasons for their dissatisfaction, and the Secretary of State may take such action as he thinks fit.⁹⁸ The liquidator must if required by him at any time, send an account of receipts and payments for any specified period to the Secretary of State, who may require any such account to be audited. More generally, the liquidator must produce on demand to the Secretary of State, and allow him to inspect, any accounts, books or other records kept by him, including any passed to him by a predecessor in office.⁹⁹

(3) If the liquidator carries on the business of the company he must keep a separate account of trading and must incorporate in the financial records the total weekly amounts of the receipts and payments on the trading account.¹

All the liquidator's records must be retained by him for six years following his vacation of office, unless he delivers them to another qualified insolvency practitioner who succeeds him in the office of liquidator, or to the official receiver where the winding up is practically complete and it is the latter who succeeds him in office.²

The Insolvency Act 1976 created a single Insolvency Services Account which replaced the Companies Liquidation Account and Bankruptcy Estates Account. Under the provisions of successive Companies Acts, the liquidator was required to pay monies received by him into the Insolvency Services Account at the Bank of England unless the committee of inspection could persuade the Department of Trade that it would be to the advantage of creditors and contributories for the liquidator to keep an account with another bank.³ If the liquidator retained more than £100 for upwards of 10 days without the authority of the Department of Trade, then unless he could explain the retention to the satisfaction of the Department he was obliged to pay interest at the rate of 20 per cent. and was liable to disallowance of the whole or part of his remuneration. He might also be removed from office and be liable for expenses occasioned by reason of his default.⁴

The Insolvency Act 1985⁵ effected the repeal of section 542 of the Companies Act 1985. No alternative provision is substituted by the Insolvency Act 1986 in place of the repealed section 542, but the former system of centralised banking of insolvency funds in the Insolvency Services Account is continued by the virtue of provisions in Part 2 of the

---

⁹⁷ Insolvency Regulations 1994, reg. 10.
⁹⁸ *ibid.*, reg. 10(5).
⁹⁹ *ibid.*, regs. 14, 15.
¹ *ibid.*, reg. 12.
² *ibid.*, reg. 13.
³ Companies Act 1985, s.542 (repealed).
⁴ *ibid.*, s.542(4).
⁵ Insolvency Act 1985, Sched. 10, Part II.

Appointment of Liquidator

Insolvency Regulations 1994.[6] There is a contrast between the compulsory and voluntary modes of winding up in terms of the relative stringency of the constraints relating to the handling of moneys. In the case of a compulsory liquidation, Regulation 5(1) obliges the liquidator to pay all money received in the course of carrying out his functions without deduction into the Insolvency Services Account (I.S.A.) once every 14 days, or forthwith if £5,000 or more has been received. In the case of a voluntary liquidator, the requirement to pay funds into the I.S.A. applies only at intervals of six months, is limited to the balance of any funds in his hands, and admits of the deduction of money required for the immediate purposes of the winding up. In the case of a compulsory winding up, Regulation 6 enables the Secretary of State to authorise the liquidator to open a local bank account under limited circumstances. This represents only a partial implementation of the recommendation, made by the *Cork Committee* in their *Report*, that the liquidator should be able to deposit funds not immediately required for distribution in an interest-bearing account with a recognised bank in the United Kingdom.[7] The criticisms in the *Cork Report* of the adverse way in which the I.S.A. affects the efficiency of the working of the insolvency process, from the standpoint of the return to creditors in particular, were revived and reaffirmed in the 1994 Report by *Justice*, entitled *Insolvency Law: An Agenda for Law Reform*,[8] where it was observed that the discrepancy between the rates of interest payable on balances in the I.S.A. and the income derived by the Government from the commercial return on the sums invested is substantially greater than the annual costs of running the Insolvency Service. It can be argued that these windfall profits are gained at the expense of the ordinary creditors, who thus are made to be the involuntary funders of the entire cost of providing the public administration and regulation of the insolvency system.

The Liquidation Committee

The provisions of successive Companies Acts formerly enabled the creditors and contributories, if they so decided at their first meetings, to decide to have a committee known as a committee of inspection, consisting of a joint body of creditors and contributories, whose function was to assist the liquidator and supervise his proceedings. The relevant provisions under the Companies Act 1985 were contained in sections 546, 547 and 548, together with Schedule 17 to the Act. These provisions were repealed by the Insolvency Act 1985. The current statutory provisions replacing those which have been repealed are contained in section 141 of the Insolvency Act 1986, supplemented by further provisions in the Insolvency Rules 1986. Section 141 replaces the repealed provisions, but does not effect major alterations of substance as against the pre-existing law. The committee is no longer known as the "Committee of

---

[6] Above, n. 94, regs. 5–9, 17–18.
[7] Cmnd. 8558, paras. 842–863.
[8] See the Report at paras. 5.7–5.11.

Inspection," but is simply referred to as the liquidation committee. The discontinuance of the more imposing title formerly in use is intended to reflect the abandonment of any pretence at the exercise of a controlling power by the creditors in relation to the liquidator. In view of the new requirements whereby all persons who act as liquidators must be qualified to act as insolvency practitioners, it was considered unrealistic to try to maintain the myth of "creditor control" as a theoretical safeguard against misconduct or incompetence on the part of the liquidator. The main provisions which prescribe the functions to be performed by the liquidation committee are contained in section 167 of the Insolvency Act 1986. It is no longer necessary for the liquidator to obtain the sanction of the liquidation committee if he wishes to appoint a solicitor to assist him in the performance of his duties but in all other respects the matters for which the liquidator was formerly required to obtain the sanction of the committee of inspection (where one had been appointed) will henceforth require the sanction of the liquidation committee or, where none exists, the sanction of the court.

Section 141(2) of the Insolvency Act makes provision for cases where a private sector liquidator takes up office, in place of the official receiver, before it has been determined whether a liquidation committee is to be appointed. The liquidator is given a discretion to convene meetings of the creditors and contributories at any time for the purpose of deciding whether such a committee shall be established, and it can be rendered obligatory for him to convene such meetings if a formal request to this effect is made by one tenth in value of the creditors. The same process may be involved following the direct appointment of a liquidator by the Secretary of State, pursuant to section 137(3), since section 137(4) and (5) together oblige the liquidator who is thus appointed to notify all creditors whether he intends to summon meetings of creditors and contributories for the purpose of deciding whether a committee is to be established. The notice sent out by the liquidator must also inform the creditors of their power to compel him to summon such meetings if he is not otherwise intending to do so.

Where meetings of creditors and contributories are held pursuant to section 141 of the Insolvency Act, a liquidation committee will be established even if only one of the meetings effectively resolves that one should be set up. However, if only one of the meetings is in favour of the establishing of a liquidation committee, it is open to the court to overrule that decision and to order that no committee shall be set up.[9]

The membership of the committee is to consist of at least three, and not more than five, creditors of the company, elected by the meeting of creditors at which it is resolved to establish the committee.[10] Only in the case where the winding up is a solvent one may the contributories exercise a right, at their meeting, to elect up to three of their number to be members of the committee. A solvent winding up is specially defined for this purpose as one where the company is being wound up on grounds which do not

---

[9] Insolvency Act 1986, s.141(3).
[10] Insolvency Rules 1986, r. 4.152(1)(a).

include the assertion that it is unable to pay its debts.[11] If however the creditors' meeting does not decide to establish a liquidation committee, but the contributories' meeting does so decide, the contributories may authorise one of their number to apply to the court for an order to the liquidator to summon a further creditors' meeting in the hope that a different view will prevail with respect to the establishing of a committee.[12] If the second meeting of creditors does not establish a committee, a further meeting of contributories may do so, and it will then consist of between three and five contributories and will function in every respect as though composed of creditors.[13]

Members of the committee may resign by notice in writing to the liquidator, and may be removed by resolution of a meeting of the body by which they were appointed.[14] A person's membership of the committee is automatically terminated if he becomes bankrupt or concludes an arrangement or composition with creditors, or if he is absent from three consecutive meetings of the committee, unless at the third occasion his absence is condoned by resolution of those present.[15]

On a vacancy occurring the liquidator may, with the concurrence of the other members of the committee, appoint a qualified person to fill the vacancy, or he may decide to leave the vacancy unfilled, provided that the total number of members does not fall below the permitted minimum of three. Alternatively, a meeting of creditors or contributories may resolve to fill the vacancy.[16]

No member of the liquidation committee, nor any representative or associate of a member, nor anyone who has been a member of the committee at any time within the last 12 months, can receive any payment for services given or goods supplied in connection with the administration, or become a purchaser of any asset belonging to the company's estate, unless he has the prior leave of the court or of the liquidation committee itself, having demonstrated that he will be giving full value in the transaction.[17]

In addition to their functions in fixing the liquidator's remuneration,[18] and in sanctioning the exercise by the liquidator of those of his powers which he may not exercise upon his own initiative alone,[19] it is the function of the committee to oversee the conduct of the liquidation on behalf of those interested parties whom they respectively represent. They are empowered to direct the liquidator, as and when they see fit (but not more often than once in every two months), to send them a written report setting out the position generally as regards the progress of the winding up, and matters relating to it. In the absence of such directions from the committee

---

[11] *ibid.*, rr. 4.151, 4.152(1)(b).
[12] *ibid.*, r. 4.154(1), (2).
[13] *ibid.*, r. 4.154(3), (4).
[14] *ibid.*, r. 4.160, 4.162.
[15] *ibid.*, r. 4.161.
[16] *ibid.*, r. 4.163, 4.164.
[17] *ibid.*, r. 4.170.
[18] See *above*.
[19] See *above*.

the liquidator must send to its members such a report at least once in every period of six months.[20]

At any time when the official receiver is the liquidator, the committee is suspended from performing its functions, which are vested in the Secretary of State, although made exercisable by the official receiver himself.[21] Where there is no liquidation committee and the liquidator is a person other than the official receiver, the functions of the committee are vested in the Secretary of State for Trade and Industry, except to the extent that the Rules otherwise provide.[22] Once again, rule 4.172 provides that such powers may, when so vested in the Secretary of State, be exercised by the official receiver. The breadth of section 141(5) is, however, cut down by rules 4.202 to 4.205, which provide that in such a situation the liquidator may not make a call without obtaining the leave of the court.

The court has power to give a retrospective sanction in a proper case to action taken under section 167(1)(*a*) without the prior sanction of the liquidation committee or the court.[23]

---

[20] Insolvency Rules 1986, r. 4.168.
[21] Insolvency Act 1986, s.141(4); Insolvency Rules 1986, r. 4.172.
[22] *ibid.*, s.141(5).
[23] *Re Associated Travel, Leisure & Services Ltd* [1978] 2 All E.R. 273.

Section B(4). Aspects Common to Both Forms of Insolvent Liquidation

CHAPTER 23

PROOF OF DEBTS

When the assets of the company have been realised, the liquidator will proceed to distribute the proceeds in discharge of the company's debts and liabilities, in so far as this can be achieved in view of the inevitable deficiency that is present in a case of insolvency. The prescribed sequence of distribution of the assets will be discussed in Chapter 24. The present chapter is concerned with the rules which determine which creditors are eligible to participate in the process of distribution, and the procedure by which they establish that entitlement for the purposes of the liquidation process. This is the procedure known as proof of debt, and is substantially the same whether the liquidation is voluntary or compulsory, although there are certain procedural distinctions between the two modes which should be noted. The legal provisions governing proof of debts in a liquidation are now contained in the Insolvency Rules.[1] These rules constitute a new, self-contained code for the purposes of winding up, and the former statutory provisions whereby the rules of the law of bankruptcy with regard to provable debts were incorporated by reference into winding up, with some unfortunate and confusing consequences,[2] have been repealed.[3]

Provable Debts

Although the legislative provisions applicable to proof of debts in a winding up are now for the most part framed with specific reference to this type of insolvency proceeding, it is nevertheless true to state that the fundamental principles which underlie the concept of the provable debt are common to both bankruptcy and winding up. Thus, the claim or liability in respect of which proof is lodged must be one which is legally due, in the sense of being enforceable by legal process if necessary, and it must be demonstrable that the company itself is the party which, in law, is

---

[1] Insolvency Rules 1986, rr. 4.73–4.99; 12.3
[2] See Companies Act 1985, ss.611, 612; *cf. Re Berkeley Securities (Property) Ltd* [1980] 3 All E.R. 513, especially at 525–530, *per* Vinelott J.
[3] Insolvency Act 1985, s.235(3), Pt. II, Sched. 10.

liable to satisfy the claim.[4] Where, for example, an alleged debt or liability arises from a contract which is vitiated by fraud or illegality, rendering it unenforceable against the company, this same want of legal enforceability will preclude the lodging of proof for the amount in question in the company's liquidation. So, too, if the debt, though at one time valid and enforceable, has become statute-barred through lapse of time the creditor will be equally unable to lodge proof in the insolvent winding up of the company, albeit the company might have voluntarily discharged the liability, as a matter of moral duty, but for the onset of insolvency.[5] A winding up order stops the running of time for limitation purposes, so that if a debt was not time-barred at the date of the order, proof may be lodged even though the limitation period would otherwise have expired by the time that this is effected.[6] There is first-instance authority to the effect that, for the purposes of the interruption of the running of time under the Limitation Act 1980, it is the actual date of the making of the winding up order, and not the date of presentation of the petition on which that order is eventually made, that constitutes the crucial point in time.[7] An exception was declared to exist in favour of the petitioning creditor, or the premise that the act of petitioning for winding up constitutes the initiating process of a "proceeding in a court of law", within the meaning of section 38(1) of the Act of 1980. Hence, the petitioning creditor is *ipso facto* bringing action founded on the debt owed to him, and in this way can avoid the elapse of the period of limitation applicable to the cause of action in question. The court however took the view that no comparable benefits are thereby conferred upon the other creditors, despite the express provision of section 129(2) of the Insolvency Act whereby "the winding up of a company by the court is deemed to commence at the time of the presentation of the petition for winding-up". The learned judge declined to accept the argument that the presentation of a petition should be regarded as a species of class remedy brought on behalf of all the creditors. Yet, with respect, it must be observed that the remedy sought by the petitioner is the very embodiment of the principle of collectivity and so, by anticipation at least, implicates the entire body of the company's creditors. The matter surely warrants a further consideration at a higher judicial level, in view of the important issues of principle, as well as the practical consequences, which are at stake. Pending such a review of the law, any creditor whose claim is based on a cause of action which is near to becoming time-barred should prudently protect his position by issuing a writ, even though it is known that another creditor has presented a petition for winding up, because the unpredictable course and duration of the proceedings down to the making

---

[4] See the discussion of the general principles concerning provable debts in Chap. 9, *ante*. The rule against double proof was discussed by the Court of Appeal and House of Lords in *Barclays Bank Ltd v. T.O.S.G. Trust Fund Ltd* [1984] 1 All E.R. 628 (C.A.); [1984] 1 All E.R. 1060 (H.L.); [1984] A.C. 626.

[5] *Re General Rolling Stock Co., Joint Stock Discount Company's Claim* (1872) 7 Ch.App. 646; *Re River Steamer Co., Mitchell's Claim* (1871) 6 Ch.App. 822; *Re Fleetwood & District Electric Light & Power Syndicate* [1915] 1 Ch. 486; *Re Art Reproduction Co. Ltd* [1952] Ch. 89.

[6] *Re General Rolling Stock Co., Joint Discount Company's Claim, supra*.

[7] *Re Cases of Taff's Well Ltd* [1992] Ch. 179; [1991] BCC 582 (Judge Paul Baker Q.C.).

of a winding up order may exceed the time remaining before the limitation period fully expires.

The vital principle is that, to be provable, a liability must *exist* at the date of commencement of the winding up[8]: it is not necessary that the debt should have become due for payment by that date, however, and hence proof may be lodged in respect of debts which are present or future, certain or contingent, ascertained or sounding only in damages.[9] The Rules provide for the liquidator to attribute an estimated value to any debt which, by reason of its being subject to a contingency or for any other reason, does not bear a certain value.[10] In difficult or disputed cases, the task of valuation may be referred to the court under section 168(3) or (5) of the Act.

Formerly, if the company was insolvent, demands in the nature of unliquidated damages were not provable unless they arose by reason of a contract, promise or breach of trust, and hence unliquidated claims based upon torts committed by the company were excluded from the category of provable debts.[11] This exclusionary principle was abrogated as part of the reforms introduced by the Insolvency Acts 1985 and 1986, and there is no provision now in force whereby such debts are necessarily to be excluded from admission to proof. As indicated above, the liquidator is now required to estimate the value of any claim which for some reason does not bear a certain value, and the amount provable in the winding up in the case of that debt is that of the estimate for the time being.[12] The estimation may be periodically revised.

Foreign Currency Debts

In the case of a debt incurred or payable in a currency other than sterling, the amount of the debt must be converted into sterling at the official exchange rate prevailing on the date when the company went into liquidation.[13] This is a technical expression signifying the date of the passing of a resolution for voluntary winding up, or the date when an order for winding up by the court is made in the case of a company which is not already undergoing a voluntary liquidation.[14] In this way, the principle is upheld whereby all creditors' liabilities must be fixed as at the same date.

---

[8] On the technical concept of commencement of winding up, see Insolvency Act 1986, ss.86, 129, *ante*, Chaps. 19 and 22.
[9] Insolvency Rules 1986. r. 12.3(1).
[10] *ibid.*, r. 4.86.
[11] s.612 of the Companies Act 1985 and Bankruptcy Act 1914, s.30 (both repealed). However it was held at first instance that s.612 did not exclude a claim for damages for tort which had not become liquidated by judgment before the commencement of the winding up but only excluded from proof a claim not so liquidated at the date when the claimant came in to prove. There were differences in this respect between bankruptcy and insolvent winding up: *Re Berkeley Securities (Property) Ltd*, *supra*, n. 1 (Vinelott J.), not followed in *Re Islington Metal and Plating Works Ltd* [1984] 1 W.L.R. 14 (Harman J.).
[12] Insolvency Rules 1986, r. 4.86(2).
[13] *ibid.*, r. 4.91.
[14] See Insolvency Act 1986 s.247(2) (meaning of "goes into liquidation"); see also n. 8, *supra*. See also Chap. 9, *ante*, especially at pp. 259–260: "foreign currency debts."

Proof of Debts

Mode of Proving

The court may fix the time limit within which creditors are to prove their debts or claims, and creditors who fail to prove in time are excluded from distributions made before proof of their debts.[15] A creditor who subsequently seeks to lodge proof may do so up until the company's dissolution, but is not allowed to disturb any distributions made before his proof was admitted.[16]

A document by which a creditor seeks to establish his claim is known as his "proof": in a company liquidation, such a written claim is required in every case, whereas in a voluntary liquidation it is left to the discretion of the liquidator whether to require any person claiming to be a creditor to submit the claim in writing.[17] In a compulsory liquidation, forms of proof must be sent out by the liquidator to every creditor known to him, or identified in the company's statement of affairs.[18] The Rules provide that every creditor bears the cost of proving his own debt, including the cost of providing necessary documents or evidence.[19] The liquidator may, if he thinks it necessary, require a claim of debt to be verified by means of an affidavit, using a specially prescribed Form.[20]

The liquidator examines every proof, and may admit it for dividend either for the whole amount claimed, or for part of that amount, or he may reject it in its entirety.[21] If he rejects a proof in whole or in part, the liquidator must send the creditor a written statement of his reasons for doing so.[22] A creditor who is dissatisfied with the liquidator's decision respecting his proof may apply to the court for the decision to be reversed or varied. Such application must be made within 21 days of receiving the liquidator's statement of his reasons for the decision taken.[23] A more general right of appeal by application to the court is available to any contributory or any other creditor who is dissatisfied with the liquidator's decision admitting or rejecting the whole or part of any proof.[24] A hearing of such an application takes place upon due notice to the applicant, the liquidator, and the creditor whose proof is the subject of the application (if not himself the applicant).[25]

The Rules permit a creditor to withdraw his proof, or to vary it as to the amount claimed, at any time by agreement between himself and the liquidator.[26] Application may be made to the court to expunge a proof, or

---

[15] Insolvency Act 1986, s.153; *Butler v. Broadhead* [1975] Ch. 97.
[16] Insolvency Rules 1986, r. 4.182(2).
[17] *ibid.*, r. 4.73. For the prescribed form and contents of proof for use in a compulsory liquidation, see r. 4.75 and Form 4.25. In a voluntary liquidation, the proof may be accepted in any form, subject to the right of the liquidator to require more details: rr. 4.73(6), 4.76.
[18] *ibid.*, r. 4.74. See Practice Direction [1987] 1 All E.R. 107.
[19] *ibid.*, r. 4.78.
[20] *ibid.*, r. 4.77; Form 4.26.
[21] *ibid.*, r. 4.82(1).
[22] *ibid.*, r. 4.82(2).
[23] *ibid.*, r. 4.83(1).
[24] *ibid.*, r. 4.83(2).
[25] *ibid.*, r. 4.83(3).
[26] *ibid.*, r. 4.84.

to reduce the amount claimed, where it is alleged that the proof has been improperly admitted, or ought to be reduced. Application may be made by the liquidator himself, if he subsequently forms the view that his own decision in admitting the proof was incorrect, or by any creditor, if the liquidator declines to interfere in the matter.[27]

Set-off

In the winding up of an insolvent company, section 612 of the Companies Act 1985 (and its predecessors) formerly had the effect of causing the bankruptcy rules to apply as regards the rights of secured and unsecured creditors, debts provable, and the valuation of annuities and future and contingent liabilities. With effect from December 29, 1986 this ceased to be the case, although the substance of the pre-existing law remains essentially intact. The Insolvency Act 1985 effected the repeal of section 612 of the Companies Act,[28] without substituting any replacement provision. Accordingly, there is no statutory provision in force to require the application of any of the bankruptcy rules in company winding up. The latter thus becomes subject to the self-contained provisions of rule 4.90 of the Insolvency Rules 1986. However, the principles which are applicable to set-off in winding up under the Insolvency Rules do not differ materially from those which have hitherto been implanted from the law and practice in bankruptcy. The new provision in the Rules is identical in substance to section 323 of the Insolvency Act 1986, which contains the provisions regarding mutual credit and set-off in bankruptcy. Section 323 is a re-enactment, with amendments and modifications only with respect to drafting, of section 31 of the Bankruptcy Act 1914. Thus, the cases decided under the former legislation remain good law, and the identity of substance between bankruptcy and winding up has been maintained. The privileged position enjoyed by the Crown with regard to set-off, resulting from the application of the doctrine that the Crown is one and indivisible, has also been maintained. These matters were all discussed in Chapter 9 above, in relation to the operation of set-off in bankruptcy.[29] It will therefore suffice to refer the reader to the earlier discussion, with appropriate adjustments regarding the references there to "the bankrupt." One matter which needs to be explained however is that, in the case of set-off in a liquidation, the point in time at which sums due from the company to another party cease to be available for the purpose of set-off against liabilities due to the company from that same party is the time at which that other party had notice that a meeting of creditors had been summoned under section 98 of the Insolvency Act in consequence of the passing of a resolution for voluntary winding up or (as the case may be) that a petition for the winding up of the company was pending. Any sums which become due from the company after that time are not capable of

---

[27] *ibid.*, r. 4.85.
[28] Insolvency Act 1985, s.235 and Sched. 10, Pt. 2.
[29] See Chap. 9, *ante*, pp. 272–276.

inclusion in any taking of account for the purpose of set-off.[30] It should also be emphasised that the provisions relating to set-off are mandatory and cannot be waived by the company or the other party concerned, even by express contractual agreement.[31]

One further point to be noted concerning set-off is that it is only operative where the creditor in question actually lodges proof for the debt which is due from the company. This results from the express wording of rule 4.90(1), which refers to "mutual debts or other mutual dealings between the company and any creditor of the company *proving or claiming to prove for a debt in the liquidation*" (emphasis added). Therefore, if a secured creditor elects not to prove for the debt, it is excluded from the operation of any set-off in respect of a debt owed by that creditor to the company. Moreover, this position is not affected by the circumstance (if it should transpire) that the secured creditor may also have a separate, unsecured claim against the company, in respect of which proof is lodged: this does not compromise the creditor's situation in respect of the secured debt, although it is possible that (if the other requirements of the doctrine are satisfied) a set-off may operate in the case of the unsecured debt.[32]

Secured Creditors

The rules and principles applicable to the lodging of proof by secured creditors have already been discussed in relation to the lodging of proof for the purposes of voting at creditors' meetings, dealt with in Chapter 21.[33] It will suffice here to observe that, in relation to the lodging of proof for dividend purposes the options available to the secured creditor are fourfold, namely:

(1) To realise his security and prove for the balance (if any) outstanding after deducting the net amount realised;
(2) To assess the value of his security, and duly declare it to the liquidator, so as to receive dividends on the unsecured balance[34];
(3) To rely on the security for full satisfaction of the amount owing, and not to lodge proof at all; and
(4) To surrender the security to the liquidator, and thereupon prove for the whole debt as though unsecured.

---

[30] Insolvency Rules 1986, r. 4.90(3). *cf.* s.323(3) Insolvency Act 1986, discussed in Chap. 9, *ante*, p. 272.
[31] *National Westminster Bank Ltd v. Halesowen Presswork and Assemblies Ltd* [1972] A.C. 785 (H.L.).
[32] *Re Norman Holding Co. Ltd* [1990] 3 All E.R. 757; [1991] 1 W.L.R. 10.
[33] *Ante*, p. 574 *et seq.* See generally, Insolvency Rules 1986, rr. 4.95–4.99.
[34] This course of action is subject to the liquidator's right to redeem the security at the value put upon it in the creditor's proof: Insolvency Rules 1986, r. 4.97. See also r. 4.99.

Non-provable Debts

Certain debts are declared by the Insolvency Rules to be not provable in a liquidation.[35] These are:

(1) Any obligation arising under a confiscation order made under section 1 of the Drug Trafficking Offences Act 1986 or section 1 of the Criminal Justice (Scotland) Act 1987 or section 71 of the Criminal Justice Act 1988;

(2) (Except at a time when all other claims of creditors in the winding up have been paid in full with interest under section 189(2) of the Insolvency Act[36]), any claim arising by virtue of section 6(3)(a) or section 61(3)(a) of the Financial Services Act 1986, or by virtue of section 49 of the Banking Act 1987; and

(3) Subject to the same exception as in (2) above), any claim which by virtue of the Insolvency Act or any other enactment is a claim the payment of which in a bankruptcy or a winding up is to be postponed.[37]

---

[35] Insolvency Rules 1986, r. 12.3(2), (2A). The latter was inserted by (S.I. 1987, No. 1919). cf. *Woodley v. Woodley (No. 2)* [1994] 1 W.L.R. 1167 (C.A.), for discussion of the validity of r. 12.3.
[36] See Chap. 24, p. 611.
[37] For postponed creditors in bankruptcy, see Chap. 10, *ante*, section (A)(6) (p. 296).

CHAPTER 24

COLLECTION AND DISTRIBUTION OF ASSETS

Realisation and Disclaimer

It was stated in Chapter 22 above that one of the principal functions of the liquidator is his duty to secure that the assets of the company are got in, realised and distributed to the company's creditors according to the rules as to priority laid down in the Insolvency Act. The liquidator's powers in carrying out this task were also described in Chapter 22,[1] and the rules of priority of distribution will be explained below. Two matters which here require further consideration are the means of augmentation of the total body of assets available for distribution to creditors, and conversely the powers of the liquidator to disclaim, and thus relinquish the company's responsibility for, property which either has a negative value, or is not readily saleable.

Augmentation of the Available Assets

In addition to the assets remaining in the ownership of the company at the commencement of the liquidation (including debts due to the company from other parties), the liquidator enjoys extensive powers of retrieval of assets previously disposed of by the company, and may seek court orders to bring about the adjustment of prior transactions entered into by the company under circumstances whereby the assets have been diminished, to the detriment of the unpaid creditors.[2] These procedures for recovering property, including money, from third parties are described in Chapter 26 below. It is also possible that the investigation of the company's affairs during its descent into insolvent liquidation will reveal instances of misconduct on the part of directors and managers for which those persons may be made civilly liable to contribute to the company's

---

[1] *Ante*, p. 584.
[2] See especially, Insolvency Act 1986, ss.238–246, 423–425, discussed in Chap. 26, *post*. See also ss.234–237, *ante*, Chap. 22.

assets in addition to bearing possible criminal liability.[3] Civil and criminal liabilities of directors and officers of insolvent companies are described in Chapter 27.

Disclaimer of Onerous Property

Sections 178 to 182 inclusive of the Insolvency Act 1986 regulate the power of the trustee to disclaim any onerous property (as defined in section 178(3)), and thereby to extinguish the rights, interests and liabilities of the company in the property disclaimed.[4] Disclaimer does not, however, affect the rights or liabilities of any other person, except so far as is necessary for the purpose of releasing the company from any liability.[5]

The provisions of sections 178 to 182 inclusive of the Insolvency Act 1986 have replaced sections 618, 619 and 620 of the Companies Act 1985, all of which have been repealed. The impractical consequences of the previously restricted power of disclaimer were demonstrated in *Re Potters Oils Ltd (in liquidation)*,[6] in which Harman J. ruled that he had no jurisdiction to sanction a liquidator's application to disclaim an unsaleable chattel—a quantity of waste oil stored in tanks—because the unsaleability did not arise "by reason of its binding the possessor thereof to any onerous act," as formerly required by s.618(1) of the Companies Act. Not only is the law changed in several important respects, but the opportunity has been taken to harmonise the provisions on disclaimer in winding up with those applicable in bankruptcy, which are to be found in sections 315 to 321 of the Insolvency Act.[7] In view of the close correlation that now exists between disclaimer in bankruptcy and disclaimer in winding up, the reader is referred to the discussion of the sections pertaining to bankruptcy which is contained in Chapter 8 above, where the case decisions relating to disclaimer, arising under sections 178–182 and 315–321, are dealt with together. The following outline of the principles operative in winding up is provided as a convenient summary of the present law.

The most important change in the law of disclaimer is that the leave of the court is no longer required when the liquidator is a person other than the official receiver. Section 178(2) of the Insolvency Act enables the liquidator at his own initiative to disclaim any onerous property, as defined in subsection (3). The concept of onerous property is broader than that formerly embodied in section 618 of the Companies Act, and now means:

(1) any unprofitable contract; or
(2) any other property of the company which is unsaleable, or not readily saleable or is such that it may give rise to a liability to pay money or perform any other onerous act.

---

[3] See especially, Insolvency Act 1986, ss.212–217, *post*, Chap. 27.
[4] Insolvency Act 1986, s.178(4)(a).
[5] *ibid*; s.178(4)(b).
[6] [1985] BCLC 203, (1985) PCC 148; (1985) 1 BCC 99.
[7] See Chap. 8, *ante*, p. 235. For the recommendations of the *Cork Committee*, on which the present provisions are based, see Cmnd. 8558, Chap. 27.

It thus suffices if property is simply unsaleable, without there being a further necessity to show that the property is also subject to an onerous requirement. Conversely, if property is subject to an onerous requirement this will in itself suffice to render that property "onerous" for the purposes of section 178, even though it may be the case that the onerous requirement does not have the effect of rendering the property unsaleable or not readily saleable. Moreover, section 178(2) allows the liquidator to exercise the power of disclaimer notwithstanding that he has taken possession of the property, endeavoured to sell it or otherwise exercised rights of ownership in relation to it.

There is no longer any specified time limit within which the liquidator must exercise the power of disclaimer, the former restriction of 12 months under section 618(3) of the Companies Act having been omitted from the new provision. The liquidator may thus invoke the power of disclaimer at any time by the giving of notice in the manner prescribed in the Rules.[8] However, if a person interested in the property has made application in accordance with section 178(5), by serving written notice upon the liquidator for the time being requiring the latter to elect whether he will disclaim or not, and no notice of disclaimer has thereafter been served within the period of 28 days following the making of the application, the consequence is that the power of disclaimer ceases to be exercisable in respect of the property.[9]

Where the property to be disclaimed is of a leasehold nature, the liquidator is further required by section 179(1) of the Insolvency Act to serve a copy of the disclaimer on every person claiming under the company as underlessee or mortgagee, of whose address he is aware. In such cases, the disclaimer can only take effect provided that no application is made under section 181 of the Insolvency Act before the end of the period of 14 days beginning with the date of service of the last notice to be served under section 179(1), or alternatively, where such an application is made within the time permitted, if the court nevertheless directs that the disclaimer shall take effect.

The provisions of section 181 of the Insolvency Act, which replace those of section 619 of the Companies Act, enable any person who claims an interest in the disclaimed property, or any person who is under any liability in respect of the disclaimed property which will not be discharged by the disclaimer itself, to make application to the court for an order granting compensation or for a vesting order in respect of the property. It is further provided by section 178(6) of the Insolvency Act that any person sustaining loss or damage in consequence of the operation of a disclaimer is to be deemed to be a creditor of the company to the extent of the loss or damage, and accordingly may prove for that amount in the winding up. However, in assessing the extent of any loss or damage thus claimed, the court is empowered to take account of the effect of any order made under section 181.[10]

---

[8] Insolvency Rules 1986, rr. 4.187–4.194 inclusive.
[9] Insolvency Rules 1986, rr. 4.191; Form 4.54.
[10] Insolvency Act 1986, 181(5).

By virtue of section 182 of the Act, the court must not make an order under section 181 vesting property of a leasehold nature in any person claiming under the company as underlessee or mortgagee except on terms making that person subject to the same liabilities and obligations as the company was subject to under the lease at the commencement of the winding up, or alternatively, if the court thinks fit, subject to the same liabilities and obligations as that person would be subject to if the lease had been assigned to him at the commencement of the winding up.[11]

Priority of Distribution of Assets

The Insolvency Rules provide that whenever the liquidator has sufficient funds in hand he must declare and distribute dividends among the creditors in respect of the debts which they have respectively proved, but that he must do so subject to the retention of such sums as may be necessary for the expenses of the winding up.[12] Creditors must be notified of the declaration of a dividend, and must be given sufficient information to enable them to comprehend the calculation of the amount of the dividend and the manner of its distribution.[13] The requisite order of priority of distribution of the monies available from realisation of the assets is as follows:

(1) The costs and expenses of the liquidation, including the liquidator's own remuneration;
(2) Preferential debts;
(3) Debts secured by a floating charge;
(4) Ordinary debts;
(5) Post-insolvency interest on debts;
(6) Deferred debts;
(7) The balance (if any), to be returned to the contributories.

The fundamental principle to be followed is that all liabilities belonging to a higher category of priority must be fully discharged, or provided for, before any payment may take place in respect of a liability belonging to a lower category of priority. With regard to category (1), there is an internal order of priority of payment, specified in the Insolvency Rules,[14] while in the case of category (3) any questions of priority will be determined according to the rules regarding successive securities, based upon the requirements of registration and on the doctrine that the first in time

---

[11] See also s.182(3), for cases where no person claiming under the company is willing to accept an order in the required terms.
[12] Insolvency Rules 1986, r. 4.180(1).
[13] *ibid*; r. 4.180(2), (3).
[14] *ibid*; r. 4.218, *infra*.

prevails.[15] In relation to categories (2), (4) and (5), any shortfall between the totality of liabilities comprising a given category and the sum of money available to discharge those liabilities brings into operation the further principle of insolvency law, whereby debts of equal rank abate in equal proportions as between themselves.[16]

The foregoing observations serve to emphasise the advantageous character of fixed-charge security in the event of the insolvency of a corporate debtor. Whereas a floating-charge security is at any rate subordinated to categories (1) and (2), as listed above, a creditor who holds a validly created,[17] and properly registered, fixed charge over any company property may proceed to realise his security notwithstanding the onset of the winding up, and in this way may be spared the fate of the general creditors to whom little, if anything, may eventually be forthcoming by way of dividend.

1. The costs and expenses of the liquidation

In the case of a voluntary liquidation, section 115 of the Insolvency Act provides that all expenses properly incurred in the winding up, including the remuneration of the liquidator, are payable out of the company's assets in priority to all other claims. In the case of a winding up by the court, section 156 provides that the court may, in the event of the assets being insufficient to satisfy the liabilities, make an order as to the payment out of the assets of the expenses incurred in the winding up in such order of priority as it thinks just. Subject to this possibility in the case of a compulsory winding up, rule 4.218 of the Insolvency Rules provides that the expenses of the liquidation are payable out of the assets in the following order of priority:

(a) expenses properly[18] chargeable or incurred by the official receiver or the liquidator in preserving, realising or getting in any of the assets of the company including (where the company was already in voluntary liquidation) such remuneration of the voluntary liquidator and costs and expenses of the voluntary liquidation as the court may allow.[19]

---

[15] See Companies Act 1985, ss.395–409, and generally, *Palmer's Company Law* (25th ed. 1992, looseleaf), Part 13. See, *e.g. Re Woodroffe's (Musical Instruments) Ltd* [1985] 2 All E.R. 908; [1986] Ch. 366, for an example of successive floating charges. (*N.B.* the case was decided on the basis of pre-1986 legislation, and is no longer good law with respect to the actual decision reached).

[16] See Insolvency Act 1986, s.175(2)(a); Insolvency Rules 1986, r. 4.181.

[17] Note however the possibility that in certain circumstances a security may be rendered invalid by virtue of the further provisions of the Insolvency Act: *post*, Chap. 26.

[18] Note that this lays open the issue of whether a particular expense incurred by the liquidator was "properly" incurred, so as to be payable out of the assets under this primary head of priority. *cf. Re M C Bacon Ltd (No. 2)* [1991] Ch. 127 for an example of non-allowable expenses incurred through the bringing of an unsuccessful claim for avoidance of a floating charge as a transaction at an undervalue or as a preference (ss.238, 239).

[19] Insolvency Rules 1986, r. 4.219.

(b) any other expenses incurred or disbursement made by the official receiver or under his authority, including those incurred or made in carrying on the business of the company;
(c) the fees payable under any order made under section 414, including those payable to the official receiver (other than the fee referred to in sub-paragraph (d)(i) below), and any remuneration payable to him under general regulations;
(d) (i) the fee payable under any order made under section 414 for the performance by the official receiver of his general duties as official receiver;
 (ii) any repayable deposit lodged by the petitioner under any such order as security for the fee mentioned in sub-paragraph (i);
(e) the cost of any security provided by a provisional liquidator, liquidator or special manager in accordance with the Act or the Rules;
(f) the remuneration of the provisional liquidator (if any);
(g) any deposit lodged on an application for the appointment of a provisional liquidator;
(h) the costs of the petitioner, and of any person appearing on the petition whose costs are allowed by the court;
(j) the remuneration of the special manager (if any);
(k) any amount payable to a person employed or authorised, under Chapter 6 of Part 4 of the Rules, to assist in the preparation of a statement of affairs or of accounts,[20]
(l) any allowance made, by order of the court, towards costs on an application for release from the obligation to submit a statement of affairs, or for an extension of time for submitting such a statement;
(m) any necessary disbursements by the liquidator in the course of his administration (including any expenses incurred by members of the liquidation committee or their representatives and allowed by the liquidator under Rule 4.169, but not including any payment of corporation tax in circumstances referred to in sub-paragraph (p) below);
(n) the remuneration or emoluments of any person who has been employed by the liquidator to perform any services for the company, as required or authorised by or under the Act or the Rules;
(o) the remuneration of the liquidator, up to any amount not exceeding that which is payable to the official receiver under general regulations;
(p) the amount of any corporation tax on chargeable gains accruing on the realisation of any asset of the company (without regard to whether the realisation is effected by the liquidator, a secured creditor, or a receiver or manager appointed to deal with a security);

---

[20] See *ibid*; rr. 4.37, 4.41.

(q) the balance, after payment of any sums due under sub-paragraph (o) above, of any remuneration due to the liquidator.

The costs of employing a shorthand writer, if appointed by an order of the court made at the instance of the official receiver in connection with an examination, rank in priority with those specified in paragraph (a). The costs of employment of a shorthand writer so appointed in any other case rank after the allowance mentioned in paragraph (l) and before the disbursements mentioned in paragraph (m).[21] Any expenses incurred in holding an examination of a witness unfit for public examination, under rule 4.214, where the application for such examination is made by the official receiver, rank in priority with those specified in paragraph (a).[22]

2. Preferential debts

Section 175(1) of the Act states that in a winding up the company's preferential debts, within the meaning given by section 386, must be paid in priority to all other debts. Preferential debts rank equally among themselves after the expenses of the winding up.[23] The cross-reference to section 386 leads on in turn to Schedule 6 to the Act, which sets out the categories of preferential debts. In this way, a unified set of provisions regarding the nature and identity of preferential debts is made applicable to company and individual insolvency alike, since sections 175 and 328 of the Act make identical reference to section 386, and hence to Schedule 6 for the purpose of defining the debts which rank preferentially in both types of insolvency. The provisions of Schedule 6 were fully described in Chapter 10 above, in the context of discussing the sequence of distribution in bankruptcy, and it will suffice here to refer the reader to that earlier passage, with the advice that these provisions apply in both modes of insolvent winding up.[24]

Section 176 of the Act embodies a long-established rule of company insolvency law, whereby in cases where distress has been levied by any person within three months prior to the date of the winding up order, the claims of preferential creditors become a first charge upon the goods distrained on, or the proceeds of their sale. Section 176(3) also reproduces, in much clearer terms than under the former statutory enactments, the consequential rule whereby the person who is thereby obliged to surrender the fruits of his distraining actions is treated as a preferential creditor in respect of the amount surrendered or paid over to the company, albeit his preferential entitlement only attaches to the remainder of the company's property, apart from that which has become available by virtue of his own act of surrender of payment.

[21] *ibid*; r. 4.218(2).
[22] *ibid*; r. 4.218(3).
[23] Insolvency Act 1986, s.175(2)(*a*).
[24] See Chap. 10, *ante*, at pp. 291–295. See also Appendix II, *post*, p. 798, for the full text of Sched. 6.

3. Debts secured by a floating charge

Section 175(2)(b) of the Act provides that, so far as the assets of the company are insufficient to meet them, preferential debts have priority over the claims of holders of debentures secured by, or holders of, any floating charge created by the company, and are to be paid accordingly out of any property comprised in or subject to that charge. Thus, the rights of holders of floating-charge security are subordinated to the right of preferential creditors to be paid in full, but thereafter any remaining property comprised in the floating charge is available for the satisfaction of the claims of the creditors thereby secured. Mention has already been made of the possible need to resolve questions of priority as between holders of successively-created floating charges. It is also possible that questions of abatement may arise between holders of debentures of the same issue, in which case a presumption of equality will operate, and if the remaining assets are insufficient to satisfy all debenture holders' claims in full, they will receive proportional payment *pari passu*.

There was formerly a possibility that holders of a floating-charge security might contrive to enhance the potency of their protection still further through utilisation of the doctrine known as crystallisation.[25] By an express provision in the instrument creating the floating charge, certain events (including those typically occurring immediately prior to the commencement of insolvency proceedings) might be declared to have the effect of converting the charge into a fixed one which would hence be capable of enforcement independently of the winding up, and hence ahead of the satisfaction of the expenses of the liquidation and the claims of preferential creditors out of the assets affected by the crystallisation.[26] This particular form of increased protection for secured creditors has been eliminated by virtue of the amended definition of the expression "floating charge" now contained in section 251 of the Insolvency Act 1986,[27] namely "a charge which, as created, was a floating charge." The effect of this definition, in the context of section 175(2)(b), is that any charge which, as created, was a floating charge is permanently relegated behind the preferential creditors' claims in order of ranking against the assets in question, irrespective of whether the terms of the charge-creating instrument purport to cause it to crystallise into a fixed charge before the date of commencement of the liquidation.

It may be noted, finally, that the rights of creditors under a floating charge are preconditional upon the ultimate validity of the charge itself, and of the transaction to which it relates. The possibility that a floating charge may be avoided altogether, or that its terms may be subject to adjustment by the court in the exercise of its jurisdiction with respect to

---

[25] See, *e.g. Palmer's Company Law* (*supra*, n. 15) para. 13.129 *et seq*.
[26] For a vivid illustration, see *Re Brightlife Ltd* [1986] 3 All E.R. 673, decided shortly before the alteration of the law which is described in the text below, referred to in the judgment of Hoffmann, J. at p. 678.
[27] This provision was first enacted in s.108(3) of the Insolvency Act 1985.

prior transactions entered into by the company, is among the matters dealt with in Chapter 26 below.[28]

4. Ordinary debts

Once all the debts and expenses belonging to categories (1) to (3) above have been fully paid, the liquidator may proceed to distribute dividends to the general body of ordinary creditors. All creditors within this category stand on an equal footing, irrespective of the chronological order in which their claims originated, and so once again the principle of equally-proportioned abatement will operate if (as is frequently the case) the remaining funds are inadequate to enable all the ordinary creditors to receive payment in full.[29]

5. Post-insolvency interest on debts

Under the Insolvency Act 1986 a complete change has been brought about in the law concerning the payment of interest on debts proved in a winding up. Section 189 introduces new provisions in line with the recommendations of the *Cork Report*,[30] and provides for the payment of interest, at the rate prescribed in subsection (4), in respect of the period the debts have been outstanding since the company went into liquidation. Payment of post-insolvency interest under this provision can only occur if there is a surplus after all creditors' claims have been met in full, including claims for pre-insolvency interest which can be properly incorporated into the amount for which proof is lodged.[31]

All payment of interest under section 189 of the Insolvency Act is to be performed without any differentiation between preferential and non-preferential debts.[32] The rate of interest payable on any given debt, according to the formula contained in section 189(4), is whichever is the greater of:

(a) the rate specified in section 17 of the Judgments Act 1838 on the day on which the company went into liquidation; and
(b) the rate applicable to that debt apart from the winding up.

This ensures that a certain statutory minimum level of interest will be payable under section 189, regardless of whether a right to interest was reserved under the contract giving rise to the debt. Where, however, a rate greater than the currently applicable statutory rate has been specified in the contract, that rate will be payable in respect of the post-insolvency

---

[28] See Insolvency Act, ss.238–244, and also s.245 (avoidance of certain floating charges) *post*, pp. 640–651.
[29] Insolvency Rules 1986, r. 4.181.
[30] Cmnd. 8558, Chap. 31.
[31] Insolvency Act 1986, s.189(1), (2).
[32] *ibid*; s.189(3).

period, provided that the terms of the contract itself are not reopened and revised under section 244 of the Insolvency Act.[33]

The statutory rate of interest fixed under section 17 of the Judgments Act 1838 is periodically adjusted by means of a statutory instrument. The rate currently applicable (with effect from April 1, 1993) is 8 per cent.[34]

6. Deferred debts

There are certain classes of indebtedness which, by virtue of some statutory provision, are deferred for payment in a liquidation until the company's other debts and liabilities have all been paid in full. These are (in the order in which payment is to be made in case of a shortfall of funds to meet all such liabilities in full):

> (i) debts which fall within the provisions of sections 2 and 3 of the Partnership Act 1890, in that they represent loans made to the company at a rate of interest which is so expressed as to vary with the company's own profits, or loans made in consideration of a share in the company's profits in lieu of interest. Such loans themselves, together with any interest or share of profits accrued before the commencement of the winding up, are deferred debts;
> (ii) any amount payable by the company in respect of a failure on its part to redeem its own shares, or to implement an agreement to purchase its own shares[35];
> (iii) any sum due to a member of the company, in his character of a member, by way of dividends, profits, or otherwise. Such sums are by section 74(1)(f) of the Insolvency Act deemed not to be debts of the company, but that provision goes on to state that any such sum may be taken into account for the purpose of the final adjustment of the rights of the contributories among themselves.
> (iv) section 215(4) of the Act provides that where proceedings under section 213 or 214 have resulted in a finding of fraudulent or wrongful trading, the court may declare that any debts due from the company to the person in question, and any interest thereon, shall rank in priority after all other debts owed by the company and after any interest on those debts.

7. Return to contributories

In principle, any funds or assets remaining after all the expenses of the winding up have been met, and after all debts and liabilities falling within categories (2) to (6) inclusive have been paid, belong to the members of the

---

[33] See Chap. 26, *post.*
[34] Judgment Debts (Rate of Interest) Order 1993 (S.I. 1993, No. 564).
[35] Companies Act 1985, s.178(3), (4), (5) and (6).

company. The respective entitlement of each individual member to a proportion of any such surplus is determined by the provisions of the company's own constitution, namely its Articles of Association.

In a voluntary winding up, it is the duty of the liquidator to pay the company's debts and adjust the rights of the contributories among themselves.[36] In a winding up by the court, section 154 imposes upon the court the task of adjusting the rights of the contributories among themselves and of distributing any surplus among the persons entitled to it.

The *pari passu* Principle: Tradition and Reality

In the first Chapter of this book emphasis was placed on the collective nature of the majority of the insolvency procedures to be described.[37] This principle of collectivity is traditionally regarded as supplying the basis for the further principle of *pari passu* distribution of the assets of an insolvent company, or individual. However, as has been seen in the foregoing pages of the present Chapter, it would be a serious misconception to suppose that the *pari passu* principle operates in a comprehensive way with respect to every species of claim or liability accruing against the insolvent estate, or with respect to the distribution and destination of every item of property comprised within it. Instead, the distributive scheme which is actually established, under the legislative provisions described above, is essentially one in which the *pari passu* principle is applied *sequentially* in relation to certain, discrete groups of claims, ranked into categories according to a fixed system of priorities.[38] Moreover, in the case of the pre-preferential category comprising the costs and expenses of the liquidation, the *pari passu* principle is not applied.[39] Not only is it the case that the *pari passu* principle is applied in a non-unitary manner, but also there are significant, legally-established exceptions to its application in a variety of cases. Foremost among these are the cases of any creditors in whose favour some form of valid, real security has been created, whether of a fixed or of a floating character.[40] Additionally, the economic position of certain creditors may be enhanced through the operation of a reservation of title agreement, or by the use of a trust device.[41] Although it can be argued that security, and security-like, devices are not true exceptions to the *pari passu* principle, in that they relate to assets which, by definition, have either been removed from the debtor's ownership, or been prevented from passing into that ownership,[42] the net effect is that assets which formed an integral

---

[36] Insolvency Act 1986, s.165(5).
[37] *Supra*, p. 2. (The principal exception is administrative receivership, described in Chap. 14.)
[38] See, *e.g.* categories numbered 1–7.
[39] *Supra*, pp. 607–609 (category 1).
[40] *cf. supra*, p.600.
[41] These two forms of protective device are described in Chap. 26, *post*.
[42] See R.M. Goode, *Principles of Corporate Insolvency Law* (1990), Chap. IV, esp. at pp. 67–73.

part of the debtor's economic operation are excluded from the pool to which the collective distribution process does apply. Moreover, there are established, and indubitably genuine, exceptions to the *pari passu* principle in the form of the doctrine of set-off,[43] and also the instances of pre- and post-liquidation debts accorded a privileged entitlement to payment in the interests of enhancing the overall return to the general body of creditors,[44] and the further cases where the court exercises its discretion to allow a creditor to commence or continue an action or proceeding against the company, or to continue an execution or attachment which was incomplete at the commencement of winding up.[45]

The above description of the reality of the distributive régime operative under the current law of insolvency is scarcely such as to sustain credence in the traditional arguments to the effect that the *pari passu* principle is the very foundation of the entire system. Yet there are relatively modern pronouncements, carried in judicial decisions at the highest level, to the effect that the *pari passu* principle constitutes a mandatory code to be administered in an unswerving way as the embodiment of public policy, expressed through legislation, from which it is not open to parties to exclude themselves by means of any private arrangement, even in the form of a solemn, contractual agreement.[46] It must be submitted that the current position, in terms of policy and principle, is both muddled and confusing. It has resulted from the historic lack of a co-ordinated, thought-through approach to our law of credit, security and insolvency, amounting to a persistent failure (even in the context of the reforms of 1985–1986) to address the essentially interlocking and inter-dependent nature of these vital areas. Consequently, the law has become beset by anomalies and inconsistencies, particularly concerning the operation of the *pari passu* principle, which are in some instances squarely at odds with commercial and social realities (even though some of the anomalies themselves occur as a consequence of past attempts to respond to arguments for the creation of special exceptions to the principle of collectivity, in the name of justice and fairness).[47] The issues associated with this admittedly complex matter are much in need of a thorough re-examination. Not even the terms of reference of the *Cork Committee*, widely drawn though they were, conferred a remit of sufficient amplitude to permit its members to engage in a fundamental revision of the law of credit and security, to consider

---

[43] See *ante*, Chaps. 9 and 23.

[44] Such debts can be included in the costs and expenses of the liquidation, and as such are payable by the liquidator in the first instance, and then recovered out of the assets in the estate on a pre-preferential basis under I.R., r. 4.218(1)(a) (*supra*, p. 607). See also Goode, *op. cit. supra*, n. 42, at pp. 71–72.

[45] See ss.130(2) and 183(2)(c) of the Act, discussed in Chap. 22, *ante*.

[46] *National Westminster Bank Ltd v. Halesowen Presswork & Assemblies Ltd* [1972] A.C. 785 (H.L.); at p. 809 *per* Lord Simon and at p. 824 *per* Lord Kilbrandon; *British Eagle International Airlines Ltd v. Cie. Nationale Air France* [1975] 2 All E.R. 390; [1975] 1 W.L.R. 758 (H.L.): see [1975] 2 All E.R. at 409–411; [1975] 1 W.L.R. at 780–781 *per* Lord Cross.

[47] *e.g.* the preferential treatment accorded to claims for unpaid wages or salaries, and related entitlements, of the insolvent debtor's employees; the judicial nurturing of trust-like devices established for protection of the debtor's customers who paid in advance for goods or services.

whether long-established institutions such as the floating charge might be abolished or greatly modified.[48] Nevertheless, there is surely a compelling case for such a comprehensive review to be undertaken by an authoritative, and adequately resourced, committee at an early date in the future.[49]

Recent trends

While it remains to be seen whether there will be governmental initiatives towards further study and reform, there are emerging indications of a process of re-examination by the courts themselves of the received judicial wisdom concerning the possibility of parties contracting out of the *pari passu* rule. This has been prompted in large part by the need to reconcile legal doctrine and commercial reality, especially with regard to debt subordination agreements. In practice, it frequently happens that a company could only continue to trade and to incur credit with the support of a bank, or of a parent or subsidiary company, which is willing to conclude an agreement whereby the right to prove for or to receive payment of that party's debt is subordinated to the debts owed to other unsecured creditors. It may properly be pointed out that such an arrangement, far from being detrimental to the interests of the general body of creditors, is expressly designed to operate in their favour in the event of the debtor's insolvency. The assertion that such agreements contravene "the policy of the insolvency laws" appears to have been derived from dicta in cases concerning arrangements whose effect was, or could be, detrimental to the interests of the general body of creditors (such as attempts to circumvent the rules of set-off). Consequently, it is suggested, a valid distinction may be drawn between the latter type of agreement and one whereby a creditor freely consents to forego the rights which he would otherwise enjoy in relation to the debtor's estate, in such a way that no adverse effect is capable of resulting for parties who are strangers to the contract. This argument was accepted by Vinelott J. in *Re Maxwell Communications Corporation plc (No. 3)*,[50] a case concerning a subordination agreement concluded by a company which later went into administration proceedings under Part II of the Insolvency Act. Because of the context in which the case was decided, it remains distinguishable from those authorities referred to above, which bear upon insolvent liquidations, and by the same token Vinelott J. was in a position, despite sitting at first instance, to avoid having to regard himself as strictly bound by the authorities in question. Nevertheless, having carefully reviewed and analysed the English cases, and also those of Commonwealth and other overseas jurisdictions, the learned judge concluded that the true principle

---

[48] See Cmnd. 8558, Chap. 36, at paras. 1530–1531.
[49] See the comments and recommendations contained in the Report published in 1994 by "*Justice*": *Insolvency Law: An Agenda for Reform*, esp. at paras. 1.16–1.21; 5.1–5.6; 5.14–5.16; 6.4–6.8. See also D. Milman, *Priority Rights on Corporate Insolvency* in A. Clarke (ed.) *Current Issues in Insolvency Law* (1991), pp. 57–85.
[50] [1993] BCC 369. See also *Stotter v. Arimaru Holdings Ltd* [1994] 2 N.Z.L.R. 655, holding that subordinated debt does not offend against the *pari passu* principle.

to be extracted from the authorities is that a creditor cannot validly contract with his debtor that he will enjoy some advantage in a bankruptcy or winding up that is denied to other creditors, but that it is possible for a creditor freely to waive or postpone rights which he would otherwise personally enjoy, provided that the performance of this agreement does not upon insolvency adversely affect the right of third parties.[51] In view of the obvious importance of this question, it is to be hoped that an opportunity will arise for a reconsideration and restatement of the law to take place at the highest level.

Declaration and payment of dividend

The provisions of Part 11 of the Insolvency Rules are of common application in companies winding up and in bankruptcy. The reader is accordingly referred to the sections on the declaration and payment of dividend, and on the mode of payment, which are contained in Chapter 10 above.[52]

With regard to the final distribution in a winding up, rule 4.186 states that when the liquidator has realised all the company's assets or so much of them as can, in his opinion, be realised without needlessly protracting the liquidation, he must give notice, under Part 11 of the Rules, either:

(a) of his intention to declare a final dividend; or
(b) that no dividend, or no further dividend, will be declared.

After the date of giving such notice, the liquidator is to proceed to defray any outstanding expenses of the winding up out of the assets, and thereafter he must declare any final dividend which he is able to pay,[53] so laying the way open for the liquidation to enter into its concluding phase, which will be described in the next Chapter.

---

[51] *ibid.*, esp. at pp. 376, 380–383. The Australian case of *Horne v. Chester and Fein Property Developments Pty. Ltd* (1987) 5 ACLC 245, and the South African case *ex p. De Villiers, Re Carbon Developments (Pty.) Ltd* [1993] 1 SA 493(A), were cited with approval as persuasive examples of the upholding of the validity of subordination agreements.
[52] *Ante*, pp. 301–303.
[53] Insolvency Rules 1986, r. 4.186(3).

CHAPTER 25

THE CONCLUSION OF THE WINDING UP: DISSOLUTION AND AFTER

When the liquidator has completed the task of realising the company's assets, and has distributed them in accordance with the provisions described in the previous chapter, the winding up enters into its final phase. This consists of the formal dissolution of the company, whereby its existence as a legal person is terminated. The date of dissolution of the company constitutes the conclusion of the winding up, except that if at that date any assets or funds of the company remain unclaimed or undistributed and are in the hands of the liquidator or under his control, the winding up is not legally concluded until those funds have been either distributed or paid into the Insolvency Services Account.[1] Section 192 of the Insolvency Act imposes a duty upon the liquidator, if the winding up is not concluded within one year of its commencement, to send periodical statements to the registrar of companies explaining the progress of the proceedings and their current position.[2] Failure to comply with this requirement constitutes an offence for which the liquidator may be fined.[3]

Final Meeting Prior to Dissolution

Except in the case, described below, where an early dissolution takes place under section 202 of the Act, the advent of the dissolution of the company is signalled by the liquidator convening final meetings of the company and of its creditors, in the case of a voluntary winding up, and a final meeting of the company's creditors, in the case of a winding up by the court in which the liquidator is not the official receiver. These meetings are convened under section 106 and section 146 of the Act, respectively.

In a voluntary winding up the liquidator is required, as soon as the

---

[1] Insolvency Rules 1986, r. 4.223(2).
[2] Insolvency Act 1986, s.192(1); Insolvency Rules 1986, r. 4.223(1); Form 4.68: the reports must be sent at six-monthly intervals after the end of the first year. See also s.105 of the Act, on the summoning of meetings of the company and of its creditors annually until the liquidation is concluded (voluntary liquidations only).
[3] Insolvency Act 1986, ss.192(2), 430; Sched. 10.

company's affairs are fully wound up, to make up a final account showing how the winding up has been conducted and how the company's property has been disposed of, and he must thereupon call general meetings of the company and its creditors and lay the final account before them, and give an explanation of it. Each meeting must be advertised in the Gazette at least one month in advance, and all creditors who have proved their debts must be sent at least 28 days' notice of the final meeting.[4] Within one week after the date of the meetings (or of the later of them, when they are held on different dates) the liquidator must send a copy of the final account to the registrar of companies and make a return to the Registrar of the holding of the two meetings.[5] Failure by the liquidator to call the requisite meetings, or to send the copy of the final account together with the return to the registrar of companies, constitute offences for which the liquidator may be fined.[6] It is at the final meeting of creditors that a resolution may be passed against granting the liquidator his release, the effects of which were considered above in Chapter 22.[7] In the absence of such a resolution, the liquidator obtains his release when he makes the return to the registrar of companies of the holding of the final meetings, and the liquidator vacates office as soon as he has complied with the requirements of making that return and sending to the registrar the copy of his final account.[8] If the creditors resolve against granting him his release, the liquidator must obtain it from the Secretary of State, under conditions as to timing which the latter may determine.[9]

In a winding up by the court, the liquidator, if he is not the official receiver, is required by section 146(1) of the Act to summon a final general meeting of the company's creditors when it appears that the winding up is for practical purposes complete. The meeting must be summoned upon 28 days' notice given to all creditors who have proved their debts, and the notice must be gazetted at least one month prior to the holding of the meeting.[10] Section 146(2) enables the liquidator to economise upon the costs involved in communicating with creditors by giving the notice of the final meeting at the same time as giving notice of any final distribution, but in any case the liquidator is required to retain sufficient sums from the assets to cover the expenses of summoning and holding the final meeting.[11] As in the case of a voluntary liquidation, the final meeting of creditors in a winding up by the court has the dual functions of receiving the liquidator's final report, and of determining whether he shall have his release.[12] The report must contain an account of the liquidator's administration of the

---

[4] Insolvency Act, s.106(2); Insolvency Rules 1986, r. 4.126(1).
[5] Insolvency Act, s.106(3) If no quorum was present at either of the meetings, the liquidator must make a return to that effect, whereupon all requirements with respect to that meeting are deemed complied with: s.106(5).
[6] *ibid.*, ss.106(4), (6), 430, Sched. 10.
[7] *ante*, p. 580.
[8] Insolvency Act 1986, ss.171(6)(b), 173(2)(e). See also Insolvency Rules 1986, r. 4.126(2).
[9] Insolvency Act 1986, s.173(2)(e); Insolvency Rules 1986, r. 4.126(3).
[10] Insolvency Rules 1986, r. 4.125(1).
[11] Insolvency Act 1986, s.146(3).
[12] Insolvency Act 1986, ss.146(1), 172(8), 174(4)(d); Insolvency Rules 1986, r. 4.125(2), (3).

winding up, including a summary of his receipts and payments, and a statement by him that he has reconciled his account with that held by the Secretary of State: the creditors may question the liquidator with respect to any matter contained in his report, and may resolve against him having his release.[13] Where the final meeting has been held under section 146, the liquidator whose report was considered at the meeting vacates office as soon as he has given notice to the court and to the registrar of companies that the meeting has been held, and of any decisions there taken, including a statement whether or not he has been given his release.[14] The notice to the court must also be accompanied by a copy of the final report laid before the creditors' meeting, and a copy of the notice must be sent by the liquidator to the official receiver.[15] If there was no quorum present at the final meeting, the liquidator must report to the court that a final meeting was summoned in accordance with the Rules, but that there was no quorum present: thereupon, the final meeting is deemed to have been held, and the creditors not to have resolved against the liquidator having his release.[16] As with a voluntary liquidation, the release of the liquidator, in the sense and with the effect explained in Chapter 22, is effective from the time of his filing in court the notice of the holding of the final meeting, unless the creditors resolved against the granting of his release, in which case this again becomes a matter to be determined by the Secretary of State upon application by the liquidator.[17]

If the company is being wound up by the court, and the official receiver is the liquidator, no final meeting of creditors is convened but the official receiver gives notice to the Secretary of State that the winding up is complete for practical purposes, and is then released with effect from such time as the Secretary of State may determine.[18] The official receiver's giving of notice to the Secretary of State must be preceded by a notice of intention to do so, which must be sent to all creditors who have proved their debts, and must be accompanied by a summary of the receipts and payments made by the official receiver as liquidator.[19] When the Secretary of State has determined the date from which the official receiver is to have his release, he must give notice to the court that he has done so.[20]

Dissolution of the Company: Compulsory Winding Up

Under the provisions of the Insolvency Act 1986, the dissolution of a company at the conclusion of a winding up by the court is now accomplished by the Registrar of Companies in accordance with section

---

[13] Insolvency Rules 1986, r. 4.125(2), (3).
[14] Insolvency Act 1986, s.172(8), Insolvency Rules 1986, r. 4.125(4); Forms 4.42, 4.43.
[15] Insolvency Rules 1986, r. 4.125(4).
[16] *ibid.*, r. 4.125(5).
[17] Insolvency Act 1986, s.174(4)(d); Insolvency Rules, rr. 4.125(6), 4.121.
[18] Insolvency Act 1986, s.174(3).
[19] Insolvency Act 1986, r. 4.124(1), (2).
[20] *ibid.*, r. 4.124(3).

205 of the Act. The former procedure whereby the company was dissolved by order of the court, made under section 568 of the Companies Act, has been abolished and section 568 itself has been repealed. Under section 205, the dissolution of the company is brought about after notice of the holding of a final meeting of creditors has been sent to the Registrar, as is required to be done by section 172(8) of the Act.[21] Alternatively, this procedure is set in motion when the Registrar receives a notice from the official receiver, where the latter is serving as liquidator, that the winding up is complete.[22] The Registrar is obliged to register the notices upon receipt thereof, and the company will automatically be dissolved at the end of the period of three months beginning with the day of registration.[23] This is subject to the right of the official receiver, or any other person with a legitimate interest, to apply to the Secretary of State to give a direction deferring, for a period to be specified, the date at which the dissolution of the company is to take effect.[24] An appeal to the court lies from any decision of the Secretary of State on an application for a direction deferring the date of dissolution.[25]

Early Dissolution of Company: Compulsory Winding Up

When the Insolvency Act 1986 was brought into force, section 568 of the Companies Act was repealed and replaced by sections 202–205 of the Insolvency Act. Section 205 has been considered above. A new procedure is introduced under section 202, whereby the Official Receiver may apply to the Registrar of Companies at any time for an early dissolution of the company where he, as its liquidator, discovers that the realisable assets of the company are insufficient to cover the expenses of the winding up. It is also necessary, in order that the Official Receiver may be able to apply for an early dissolution, that he be of the opinion that the affairs of the company do not require further investigation. If it subsequently transpires that the assumptions upon which the official receiver's application to the Registrar was made were in any respect incorrect, or if there is any other reason to suggest that an early dissolution is inappropriate, the Official Receiver himself or other interested parties have a limited time in which to apply for directions to the Secretary of State under section 203(1). The period within which such an application may be made consists, effectively, of the 28 days' period of notice specified in section 202(3) as that which the Official Receiver must give to the creditors and contributories regarding his intention to make application for an early dissolution, plus the period of three months specified in section 202(5) as being the period, commencing with the date of registration of the application, at the end of which the company's dissolution is legally accomplished.

---

[21] Insolvency Act 1986, s.205(1)(a).
[22] *ibid.*, s.205(1)(b).
[23] *ibid.*, s.205(2).
[24] *ibid.*, s.205(3).
[25] *ibid.*, s.205(4). See also subsection (6) with regard to the giving of notice to the registrar of companies in cases where applications, or appeals, take place under subsection (3) and (4) respectively.

Dissolution of the Company: Compulsory Winding Up

The reason for the introduction of the new procedure for company dissolution is the statistically high incidence of companies which enter compulsory liquidation having either no assets at all, or so few as to be practically worthless. Up to one third of compulsory winding up cases involve companies which are in this condition, and the accelerated procedure for dissolution should save the time of the Official Receiver as well as the expenses of such futile operations as the sending out of final notice of the Official Receiver's intention to apply for his release. By virtue of section 202(4), the act of sending out the notice of his intention to apply for an early dissolution of the company simultaneously releases the Official Receiver from his duties in relation to the company, subject to any directions which may later be issued by the Secretary of State under section 203.

Dissolution of the Company: Voluntary Winding Up

Section 201 of the Insolvency Act 1986 governs the process of dissolution of the company in the case of a voluntary liquidation. Where the liquidator has sent to the registrar of companies his final account and return under section 106, the registrar must forthwith register them, and on the expiration of three months from the registration of the return the company is deemed to be dissolved.[26] Moreover, as in the case of a compulsory winding up, a procedure exists whereby the liquidator or any properly interested party may seek postponement of the dissolution, should a suitable ground for doing so be discovered in time. In this instance, application is to be made to the court for an order deferring the date at which the dissolution is to take effect for such time as the court thinks fit.[27] If an order is made, it is the duty of the person who applied for it to deliver to the registrar of companies, within seven days, an office copy of the order for registration: failure to comply constitutes an offence for which the person responsible may be fined.[28]

Official Notification: Dissolution by Striking Off

Section 711 of the Companies Act 1985 provides that the Registrar of Companies must cause to be published in the London Gazette notice of the receipt by him of any return by a liquidator of the final meeting of a company on a winding up, and of any order for the dissolution of a company on a winding up.[29] The latter provision refers to the alternative procedure for bringing about the dissolution of a company by striking it off the register, pursuant to section 652 of the Companies Act.[30] While this section is available for use against any company which is found to be

---

[26] *ibid.*, s.201(2).
[27] *ibid.*, s.201(3).
[28] *ibid.*, s.201(4), 430, Sched. 10.
[29] Companies Act 1985, s.711(1)(q), (r).
[30] *ibid.* s.652(1)–(3).

defunct, a special form of procedure is provided for use in cases where a company is being wound up, either compulsorily or voluntarily. According to section 652(4) if the registrar has reasonable cause to believe that no liquidator is acting, or that the affairs of the company are fully wound up, and the returns required to be made by the liquidator have not been made for a period of six consecutive months, the registrar must publish in the Gazette and send to the company or the liquidator (if any) a notice that at the expiration of three months from the date of that notice the name of the company mentioned in it will, unless cause is shown to the contrary, be struck off the register and the company will be dissolved. At the expiration of the declared time limit, the registrar may, unless cause to the contrary is previously shown, strike its name off the register, and if he elects to do so he must publish notice of this in the Gazette, and on publication of that notice the company is dissolved.[31] There is a special saving provision in section 652(6), whereby this mode of dissolution does not curtail the liability, if any, of every director, managing director and member of the company, and whereby also the court retains the power to wind up a company even though its name has been struck off the register. Accordingly, any contrivance whereby a voluntary liquidation is embarked upon, but subsequently left in abeyance, may be dealt with by striking off, but this will be without prejudice to the possibility that a properly conducted, compulsory winding up may be brought about at a later date, with consequential prospects that serious misconduct in relation both to the company's past affairs, and the former, abortive winding up, may be dealt with in the appropriate manner.[32]

Effect of Dissolution

The date when dissolution becomes effective marks the termination of the company's legal personality, and hence of its existence. It is this consequence of the winding up process—regardless of whether it is the voluntary or the compulsory mode which is employed—which constitutes the fundamental point of distinction between the insolvency of a corporation and that of an individual. In the case of the bankruptcy of an individual, the ultimate reinstatement of the debtor to full legal status and capacity is at all times in prospect through the eventual gaining of discharge from bankruptcy,[33] whereas no such outcome is possible through the completion of the winding up process. This is the case even though it may transpire that the company's realised assets, despite initial appearances to the contrary, are sufficient to discharge all liabilities which are eventually admitted to proof. Every creditor, and every person with a claim of any kind against the company, should therefore bear in mind that at the conclusion of the liquidation all liabilities will be extinguished

---

[31] *ibid.*, s.652(5).
[32] See further, Chap. 27, *post*.
[33] See Chap. 11, *ante*.

forever, since there will be no subsisting legal person by whom any liability is "owed," nor even (in contrast once again to the case of a discharged bankrupt) any prospect that unsatisfied liabilities may be settled out of a sense of moral obligation by a person against whom no legal enforcement is capable of taking place.

When a company is dissolved, all property and rights of any kind whatsoever which were vested in or held on trust for the company immediately before its dissolution (including leasehold property, but not including property held by the company on trust for any other person) are deemed to be *bona vacantia* (ownerless property), and accordingly belong to the Crown and vest, and may be dealt with, accordingly.[34] The Crown's title to such property may be disclaimed by a notice signed by the Treasury Solicitor within 12 months of the date on which the vesting of the property came to his notice, or within three months of receipt by him of a written application made by any person interested in the property, requiring him to decide whether he will or will not disclaim.[35] Where property is disclaimed by the Crown in this manner, it is deemed not to have vested in the Crown, and the court may then make a vesting order in respect of the property in favour of any person who either claims an interest in it or is under an undischarged liability in respect of it, and who makes application for this purpose.[36]

Dissolution Declared Void

Although dissolution, as explained above, has every appearance of finality of effect, the conceptual processes whereby a company may be first formed under law, and later wound up and dissolved, admit of one further cycle of operation. Under section 651 of the Companies Act 1985 the court enjoys a jurisdiction to entertain an application at any time within 2 years of the date of dissolution of a company, for a declaration to be made declaring the dissolution to have been void.[37] The persons eligible to apply for such a declaration are the liquidator of the company or any other person appearing to the court to be interested in the matter, and the granting or refusal of the declaration is governed by the court's discretion.[38] If the dissolution is declared void, section 651(2) provides that such proceedings may be taken as might have been taken if the company had not been dissolved. Thus, if very serious malpractices have taken place in relation to the management of the company's affairs, but these only come to light long after the conclusion of the winding up and the dissolution of the company, the latter may be reanimated for the purpose of pursuing the persons responsible, and possibly recovering assets

---

[34] Companies Act 1985, s.654(1).
[35] *ibid.*, s.656(1)–(3). The period of three months may be extended by the court.
[36] *ibid.* s.657.
[37] In consequence of amendments made to s.651 of the Companies Act 1985 by s.141 of the Companies Act 1989, the limit of two years is now imposed by s.651(4), subject to special exceptions governed by s.651(5)–(7): see *infra*.
[38] Companies Act 1985, s.651(1).

improperly disposed of, utilising the potent and far-reaching remedies of the insolvency law.[39] Conversely, the procedure for having a dissolution declared void may be utilised for the more congenial purpose of undertaking an orderly distribution, in accordance with the provisions of insolvency law, of any assets which fail to come to light until after the conclusion of the original liquidation process.[40] The procedure has its limits, however, and it does not provide a possibility for the resumption of claims by or against the company which were left incomplete before dissolution: the cause of action in such cases dies absolutely at the date of dissolution and cannot survive, nor be revived, to become effective again by order under section 651.[41] This is subject to a special exception under section 651(5), which allows an application to revive the company to be made at any time if it is for the purpose of bringing proceedings for damages for personal injuries, or for damages under the Fatal Accidents Act 1976, provided that the statutory limitation period for bringing the action has not expired.[42]

It has been held by the Court of Appeal that the jurisdiction under section 651 can be exercised to put the applicant for an order in a better position by enabling the company to meet a liability which would otherwise remain unpaid. In cases in which the order would directly affect the rights of third parties, for example by depriving them of the benefits which had accrued to them during the course of the liquidation or thereafter, such parties were entitled to be joined so as to allow them to argue in opposition.[43] However, apart from the specific power to make a limitation override order under section 651(6) in the limited circumstances contemplated by subsection (5), there is no general jurisdiction under section 651 to make an order overriding the impact of the statutes of limitation upon the position of any party who might otherwise be eligible to claim against the company whose dissolution is to be declared void.[44] This want of jurisdiction may not be a source of any widespread hardship in practice, since it is a fundamental principle of company insolvency law that periods of limitation cease to run once a winding up has commenced.[45] However, where a company had ceased to trade for many years prior to its dissolution, it may be that some parties' claims had already become time-barred before the commencement of the winding up, and hence the restoration of the company to its state

---

[39] See Chaps. 26 and 27, *post*.

[40] *cf.* the similar process whereby a company, whose dissolution under foreign law has been recognised by English law, may be revivified for the purpose of distributing assets situated in England, by means of a winding up by the English court: Chap. 30, *post*.

[41] *Foster, Yates and Thom Ltd v. H.W. Edgehill Equipment Ltd* (1978) 122 S.J. 860.

[42] Companies Act 1985, s.651(5), inserted by s.141(3) of the Companies Act 1989. This has the effect of overruling retrospectively (by virtue of s.141(4)) the decision in *Bradley v. Eagle Star Insurance Co. Ltd* [1989] 1 All E.R. 961; [1989] 2 W.L.R. 568. See also *Re Workvale Ltd* [1991] 1 W.L.R. 294.

[43] *Re Forte's (Manufacturing) Ltd; Stanhope Pension Trust Ltd v. Registrar of Companies* [1994] BCC 84 (where a Landlord's purpose in seeking avoidance of the dissolution of the original tenant was to make claims against still-solvent, intermediate assignees—the current tenant having gone into liquidation and its liquidator having disclaimed the lease).

[44] *Re Mixhurst Ltd* [1993] BCC 748.

[45] *cf.* Chap. 23, *ante*, p. 596.

immediately prior to dissolution will be of no avail, so far as they are concerned. This is but the inevitable consequence of those parties' failure to press their claims while they remained ripe, prior to the original dissolution.

When the period of 2 years specified in section 651(4) of the Companies Act 1985 has completely expired it ceases to be possible to revive the company's existence by declaring the dissolution to have been void. However, in the less-common situation where a company is dissolved through striking off, under the provisions of section 652 mentioned above, a longer period of 20 years is allowed for the bringing of any challenge to the striking off. This procedure is established under section 653, whereby if the company itself, or any member or creditor of it, feels aggrieved by the company having been struck off the register, the party in question may make application to the court at any time up to 20 years from the date of publication in the Gazette of the notice of striking off.[46] If the court is satisfied that the company was at the time of the striking off carrying on business or in operation, or otherwise that it is just that the company be restored to the register, the court enjoys a discretion to make an order to that effect.[47] On an office copy of the order being delivered to the registrar of companies for registration, the effect of section 653(3) is that the company is deemed to have continued in existence as if its name had not been struck off, and the court may make appropriate further orders for the purpose of placing the company, and all other persons, in the same position (as nearly as may be) as if the company's name had not been struck off. This can bring about the retrospective revival of liabilities of other parties, such as sureties, which had previously been discharged by the act of the Crown in disclaiming an interest in a lease which had become vested in the Crown as *bona vacantia* as a consequence of the company's dissolution.[48]

---

[46] Companies Act 1985, s.653(2). The Secretary of State also has *locus standi* to seek a restoration where he wishes to commence disqualification proceedings against the company's directors: *Re Townreach Ltd (No. 002081 of 1994)* [1994] 3 W.L.R. 983.
[47] *ibid.* In the case of striking off of a company during the course of its winding up, the latter ground, namely that it is just to do so, is logically the only one which can be invoked.
[48] *Allied Dunbar Assurance plc v. Fowle* [1994] BCC 422.

Chapter 26

THE EFFECTS OF WINDING UP ON CREDITORS AND THIRD PARTIES

Preliminary

In this examination of the effects of a winding up on the rights of creditors and other interested parties, it is as well to recall that the fundamental principle upon which winding up is based is the collective nature of the proceedings. The objective underlying the relevant legal provisions is to ensure that an orderly regime is imposed upon all interested parties, so that none of them individually may enhance his position by exploiting some fortuitous circumstance which may yield some personal advantage, in the form of a larger proportional return on debts which are due, or a direct and more rapid recovery of payment, than would result from participating in the processes of the winding up, and receiving dividend in common with all other creditors whose debts carry an equal ranking in the order of priority.[1]

In order to ensure that the above objective is achieved, the law establishes a series of barriers to the exercise of normal rights and remedies by or against a company when it is prospectively or actually in liquidation. By this means, the remaining assets of the company are maintained intact so that they may be administered in accordance with the principles of insolvency law. The law also goes further, in adopting a retrospective policy of scrutiny towards transactions to which the company was party during the months, or even years, prior to the commencement of liquidation. As in the case of personal insolvency,[2] the law here embraces the philosophy that certain transactions, even if entered into without iniquitous intent, are susceptible of avoidance in the event that the debtor (in this instance, the company now in liquidation) becomes insolvent either as a result of the transaction itself, or within a certain time thereafter. In such circumstances, it is argued, the party who has received a benefit, in cash or in kind, as a consequence of the transaction has actually done so at

---

[1] For the sequence and process of distribution of assets, see Chap. 24 *ante.*, and also Chap. 23 (Proof of Debts).
[2] See Chap. 8, *ante.*

the expense of the general body of creditors, who must perforce look to the assets of the company for ultimate satisfaction of their debts. Accordingly, the Insolvency Act provides a number of grounds on which prior transactions can be re-examined, and if necessary adjusted by the court so that, in effect, the lost assets are clawed back and put at the disposal of the liquidator, to be administered for the benefit of the company's creditors as a whole. These matters will be considered in turn.

The Advent of Winding Up: Preserving the Status Quo

It has already been explained that the technical moment of commencement of a winding up is either the date of the passing of a resolution for a voluntary winding up, or the date of the presentation of the petition in the case of a winding up by the court.[3] In the earlier discussions of the consequences of a winding up,[4] it was observed that several of the relevant provisions have the effect of preserving the status quo regarding the company's assets at and after the moment in question. Thus, with regard to a voluntary winding up, we may note the provisions in section 103 of the Act, with regard to the cesser of directors' powers; in sections 114 and 166, regarding dispositions of the company's property in the interval before a liquidator is duly appointed with the full participation of the company's creditors; and in sections 87 and 88, regarding the discontinuation of the company's business, and the invalidity of transfers of the company's shares or alterations in the status of its members.[5] Similarly, in a compulsory winding up, we may point to the conservational function of such provisions as sections 126 and 130(2), on staying or restraining of proceedings against the company and its property; section 127, rendering void any post-commencement disposition of the company's property and any transfer of shares or alteration in the status of its members; section 128, on the avoidance of any attachment, sequestration, distress or execution against the company's property; and the case-law rules governing the dismissal of the directors and the termination of the contracts of employment of the company's employees and agents.[6] Most of the statutory provisions just referred to were discussed in Chapter 22. However, section 127 will be considered here.

Dispositions and transfers after winding up: validation orders

Section 127 provides that in a winding up by the Court any disposition of the property of the company, and any transfer of shares, or alteration in the status of the members of the company, made after the commencement

---

[3] Insolvency Act 1986, ss.86, 129, discussed in Chaps. 19 and 22 respectively.
[4] See Chap. 19 at pp. 505–507, and Chap. 22 at pp. 554–558.
[5] See Chap. 19, *loc. cit. supra*, n. 4. Note also that, by virtue of s.112(1) of the Act, the court may upon application make any order, or exercise any powers, which it might exercise if the company were being wound up by the court. This may include the staying of any actions or proceedings brought against the company in voluntary liquidation.
[6] See Chap. 22, *loc. cit. supra*, n. 4.

of the winding up, is void unless the court otherwise orders. The practice of the court is to allow such payments or dispositions, pending the petition, if made honestly and for the benefit of the company and in the ordinary course of business.[7] The exercise of the discretion of the court under this section is controlled only by the general principles of justice and fairness.[8] Such an order may be made prior to the hearing of the winding up petition.[9] The fundamental principle influencing the court in the exercise of its discretion is that it will not validate any transaction which would result in a pre-liquidation creditor being paid in full at the expense of other creditors who will only receive dividends, unless to do so will benefit the unsecured creditors as a whole.[10]

Where the liquidator has had to resort to proceedings under section 127 to procure the avoidance of a transaction under which a proving creditor had gained an advantage, and the repayment of money which he would not voluntarily surrender for distribution in the winding up, it is lawful for the liquidator to deduct the costs of getting in that asset from any dividend which subsequently becomes payable to the creditor in question. This accords with the broad equitable principle that a person entitled to participate in and bound to contribute to the same fund cannot receive the benefit without discharging the obligation.[11]

If the directors of a solvent company show that they considered a particular disposition to have been necessary or expedient in the interests of the company and the court accepts that the reasons given were such as an intelligent and honest man could reasonably hold, the court will normally sanction the disposition, notwithstanding the opposition of a contributory.[12] Expenditure incurred in defending an unfair prejudice petition is not incurred "in the ordinary course of the company's business," because the principle is that the company's money should not be expended on disputes between shareholders.[13] On the other hand, the costs of defending a winding-up petition may be validated under section 127 as incurred in the ordinary course of business.[14]

In order to come within the ambit of section 127, it is essential that the transaction in question amounts to a *disposition* of the *company's* property. In the case of tangible property the key question is very often the determination of the actual ownership of the asset at the material time, particularly where aspects of sale of goods law, including reservation of

---

[7] *Re Oriental Bank Corporation* (1884) 28 Ch.D. 634; *Gorringe v. Irwell India Rubber Works* (1886) 34 Ch.D. 128; *Re Burton & Deakin Ltd* [1977] 1 All E.R. 631. See the useful article by Nigel Furey (1983) 46 M.L.R. 257. See also *Re Webb Electrical* (1988) 4 BCC 230.

[8] *Re Steane's (Bournemouth)* [1950] 1 All E.R. 21; *Re T. W. Construction Ltd* [1954] 1 W.L.R. 540; *Re Clifton Place Garage Ltd* [1970] Ch. 477 (C.A.).

[9] *Re Operator Control Cabs Ltd* [1970] 3 All E.R. 657n.

[10] *Re Gray's Inn Construction Co. Ltd* [1980] 1 All E.R. 814 (C.A.).

[11] *Re Davies Chemists Ltd* [1992] BCC 697.

[12] *Re Burton & Deakin Ltd* [1977] 1 W.L.R. 390 (where the opposing contributories were in fact also the petitioners alleging oppression).

[13] *Re Crossmore Electrical and Civil Engineering Ltd* (1989) 5 BCC 37. See *Practice Direction No. 1 of 1990* [1990] 1 W.L.R. 490; [1990] 1 All E.R. 1056 for the standard form of order under s.127 arising from a petition for winding up combined with an unfair practice application. See also *Re A Company (No. 00687 of 1991)* [1991] BCC 210, 212 (Harman, J.).

[14] *Re Crossmore Electrical and Civil Engineering Ltd, supra.*

title agreements, have been operative. In the case of intangible property—or choses in action—the same essential principles are applicable, and it may be necessary to establish the operative time of a transaction such as a purported assignment of a debt due to the company, for example in the case of a factoring arrangement.[15]

Special conceptual problems have been encountered in cases involving the payment of sums of money into or out of a bank account maintained by the company, particularly where the account is overdrawn at certain crucial periods.[16] It has been held at first instance that where a company's bank account is at all material times in credit, payments in the form of third party cheques accepted by the bank, collected by it on the company's behalf and credited to the company's account do not amount to a disposition of the company's property for the purposes of section 127. In contrast to the position where the company's account is overdrawn, there is no disposition of the company's property in favour of the bank when the essence of what is taking place is the increase of the amount standing to the credit of the customer in return for the surrender of the third party cheque. It is the drawer of the cheque whose property is disposed of.[17]

The invalidation of a disposition of the company's property under section 127 and the recovery of the property disposed of are two distinct matters. The section says nothing about recovery but merely avoids the disposition and gives discretionary power to the court to validate the transactions. Its object is that creditors should be paid *pari passu*. On a true construction the term "disposition" includes dispositions of a company's property whether made by the company or by a third party or whether made directly or indirectly. Thus where a director made out a "cash" cheque and bought money orders which were then sent to a creditor with intent to prefer him this was held to be a disposition within the section which must be repaid.[18]

The court has jurisdiction under section 127 to authorise a disposition of the company's property for the benefit of creditors, notwithstanding that a winding up order has not yet been made. Such an "anticipatory" validation can be of considerable practical value, both in enabling the company to continue to trade in a quasi-normal fashion pending the outcome of the winding up proceedings, and in enabling the safe completion of transactions of a time-critical character whose outcome will demonstrably enhance the net position of the general body of the

---

[15] *cf. Gorringe v. Irwell India Rubber Works* (1886) 34 Ch.D. 128 (whose outcome turned upon the rule that an equitable assignment of a legal chose in action is complete upon the giving of notice to the assignee, without there being further need (as with a statutory assignment) to give notice to the debtor).

[16] See, *e.g. Re Gray's Inn Construction Co. Ltd, supra*, n. 10.

[17] *Re Barn Crown Ltd* [1994] BCC 381 (His Honour Judge Rich, Q.C.), adopting the interpretation of the term "disposition" developed in the Australian decisions *Re Mal Bower's Macquarie Electrical Centre Pty Ltd* (1974) CLC 40–109, and *Re Loteka Pty Ltd* (1989) 7 A.C.L.C. 998.

[18] *Re J. Leslie Engineering Co. Ltd (in liquidation)* [1976] 1 W.L.R. 292. This case contains a useful analysis by Oliver J. of the way in which the court's discretion will be exercised.

company's creditors, in the event that its liquidation is subsequently ordered by the court.[19]

Where, before the presentation of a winding up petition, a company has entered into an unconditional contract for the sale of property which is specifically enforceable, the completion of the contract in accordance with its terms after the presentation of the petition does not constitute a disposition within the meaning of section 127.[20] The position might be otherwise if the contract itself was conditional or voidable, however, and as a general rule unless a contract entered into by the company is quite plainly specifically enforceable and there is no possible defence, it would be prudent to seek the prior approval of the court for the completion of the contract, particularly where the sums of money involved are substantial. The court may be prepared in certain circumstances retrospectively to validate a disposition made after the commencement of winding up, where it can be shown that the transaction would have been authorised if application had been made earlier, and that the usual principles of validation have been respected, namely that the transfer will not have the effect of reducing assets available to unsecured creditors.[21]

A shareholder of a company in liquidation has sufficient *locus standi* to make an application to the court under section 127 to validate a disposition of the company's property made after the commencement of the winding up.[22]

Contracts

Apart from contracts of employment already referred to, contracts to which the company is a party are not automatically terminated by liquidation, unless there is a term to that effect in the contract itself. If the effect of liquidation is to render the company incapable of performing any of its obligations under the contract, the other party may duly treat the contract as terminated by breach. Alternatively, the liquidator may expressly repudiate the contract, or may signify the company's repudiation by doing some act which is inconsistent with the company's continuing readiness to perform. The liquidator may find it expedient to confirm and sustain in being any contracts whose further performance is likely to yield benefits for the company, and hence for its general creditors. On the other hand, if the continuation of the contract is likely to prove disadvantageous, the liquidator may elect to invoke his right under section 178 to disclaim onerous property. The other party may force the liquidator's hand in this matter by serving notice under section 178(5) requiring the liquidator to decide whether he will disclaim or not, whereupon the liquidator must either serve notice of disclaimer within 28 days, or lose the right to do so

---

[19] *Re A.I. Levy (Holdings) Ltd* [1964] Ch. 19; see also *Carden v. Albert Palace Assocn.* (1886) 56 L.J. Ch. 166; *Re Douglas (Griggs) Engineering Ltd* [1963] Ch. 19; *cf. Re Miles Aircraft Ltd* [1948] Ch. 188.
[20] *Re French's (Wine Bar)* [1987] BCLC 499; (1987) 3 BCC 173.
[21] *Re Tramways Building and Construction Co. Ltd* [1988] Ch. 293; (1987) 3 BCC 443. See also *Re McGuinness Bros. (UK) Ltd* (1987) 3 BCC 571.
[22] *Re Argentum Reductions (UK) Ltd* [1975] 1 W.L.R. 186.

thereafter.[23] Another approach open to the other party to the contract is to apply to the court seeking an order under section 186 rescinding the contract on such terms as to payment by either party of damages for non-performance as the court thinks just. If the court awards damages against the company, these will constitute an ordinary debt in the liquidation, and may be proved for accordingly.[24]

Distress or Execution Levied

In Chapter 8 above,[25] an account was given of the application of section 346 of the Insolvency Act in cases where a creditor has commenced an execution against the goods or land of a person, or an attachment of a debt due to that person, before the commencement of bankruptcy of the person concerned. The basic rule embodied in the section is that the creditor is not entitled to retain the benefit of the execution or attachment, or any sums paid to avoid it, unless the execution or attachment, or the payment, in question was completed before the commencement of the bankruptcy. Provisions corresponding to those of section 346 but applicable in the case of winding up are contained in sections 183 and 184, with the commencement of winding up constituting the decisive point for completion of the execution or attachment, save when a creditor has had notice of a meeting having been called at which a resolution for voluntary winding up is to be proposed, when that date upon which he has notice is substituted for the date of commencement of winding up as the date by which the process of recovery of payment must be completed in order for it to be retainable by the creditor.[26] In other respects, the provisions of section 183 and 184 are parallel to those of section 346, and the reader is therefore referred to the earlier discussion of their effects.[27]

There is no reference in sections 183 or 184 to the exercise by a landlord of his right to levy distress for rent. Nor is there any section within the Parts of the Insolvency Act which govern corporate insolvency, to serve as a counterpart to section 347 which applies in bankruptcy, and which enables a landlord to levy distress, within prescribed limits, even after the commencement of bankruptcy.[28] In principle, therefore, a levying of distress for rent due before the winding up, and commenced but not completed before that date, may be completed, and the proceeds retained, unless there are special circumstances, such as fraud or unfair dealing, rendering it inequitable that the fruits of the distress should be retained.[29] The same approach is applicable in cases where distress is levied for unpaid taxes or non-domestic rates.[30] Thus, unless the court can be

---

[23] See Chap. 24, *ante*.
[24] Insolvency Act 1986, s.186(2).
[25] See p. 240, *ante*.
[26] Insolvency Act 1986, s.183(2)(a). See also Chap. 22 *ante*, at p. 555, *et seq*.
[27] See Chap. 8 *ante*, pp. 240–244.
[28] s.347 is discussed in Chap. 8, *ante*, p. 241.
[29] *Re Bellaglade* [1977] 1 All E.R. 319.
[30] *Herbert Berry Associates Ltd v. I.R.C.* [1978] 1 All E.R. 161 (H.L.).

The Advent of Winding Up: Preserving the Status Quo

persuaded to exercise its powers under section 112 or 126 to stay or restrain the distress which is in progress, it may be completed after the liquidation has commenced. However, the terms of section 128 are more widely and strongly drawn, and have the effect of rendering void any form of enforcement process which is put in force against the company's estate or effects after the commencement of winding up: distress is expressly listed in section 128(1), together with the processes of attachment, sequestration and execution, which are by that section declared to be void. Nevertheless, the position in section 130(2) should be noted, whereby the court is empowered to give leave for any "action or proceeding" to be proceeded with or commenced after the making of a winding up order or the appointment of a provisional liquidator. The court could therefore grant leave to distrain in respect of rent accrued due after winding up, for example where the liquidator has retained possession of the demised premises for the benefit of the winding up.[31]

Secured Creditors

In Chapter 24 above, the contrasting positions of the holders of fixed and floating securities were considered in relation to the distribution of the company's assets. Assuming that all the requisite formalities have been fulfilled, including proper registration of the security as a company charge under Part XII of the Companies Act 1985, it will be perceived that any holder of a valid, fixed charge over company assets is in a position of preeminent advantage in the event of the insolvent winding up of the company. This is because, under the established principles of the law of security applicable both to personal and corporate insolvency, the holder of a valid and subsisting, fixed security over any of his debtor's property is entitled to enforce his right of realisation of that security, and so may stand outside the insolvency process in satisfying the outstanding liability to such extent as the security is capable of yielding. Thereafter, if any unsatisfied balance remains due to the creditor in question, he may participate in the insolvent administration of the reminder of the debtor's estate, by proving for the balance and ranking for dividend according to the nature of the liability itself.[32] In effect, therefore, the assets within the insolvent estate which are comprised within any valid and unimpeachable fixed charge are predestined to remain outside the pool of assets available for distribution through the winding up process itself, except in so far as they may turn out upon realisation to yield a greater amount than is still outstanding upon the debt or liability in relation to which they serve as security. In that event, the secured creditor must pay over the surplus balance, either to the holder of any subsequent, fixed charge over the same property, or failing such, to the liquidator.

The different, but still appreciable, position occupied by the holder of a

---

[31] *Re Lundy Granite Co.* (1871) 6 Ch.App. 462; *Re North Yorkshire Iron Co.* (1878) 7 Ch.D. 661; contrast *Re Exchange Securities & Commodities Ltd* [1983] BCLC 186; *The Constellation* [1966] 1 W.L.R. 272; *Re Lancashire Cotton Spinning Co.* (1887) 35 Ch.D. 656 (C.A.). See also the discussion of s.130(2) in Chap. 22, *ante*, at p. 555, *et seq.*

[32] On proof of tests, and priority of distribution, in a winding up, see Chaps. 22 and 23, *ante*.

security which, as created, was a floating charge was explained in Chapter 24.[33]

In practice, of course, many creditors are not in a position to exact any formal security, whether of a fixed or a floating nature, from the company which becomes indebted to them. Viewed from the position of those unsecured creditors of the company, the advantages enjoyed by secured creditors, and also by preferential creditors,[34] appear especially poignant. Not unreasonably, it has been argued that an appreciable proportion of the assets which are destined to be claimed by, or distributed to, the secured or preferential creditors ahead of any payment to ordinary, unsecured creditors may in part represent the product of credit provided by the latter. The *Cork Report* included recommendations that would have brought about some redress in the present imbalance as between the unsecured creditors and the holders of floating charge security, but these were not implemented.[35] For the present, therefore, the plight of the ordinary, unsecured creditors—including trade creditors and suppliers, and customers who have paid in advance for goods or services not delivered or performed at the time of liquidation[36]—remains an unenviable one.

Reservation of Title Clauses

In the light of the foregoing remarks concerning the predicament of ordinary creditors in an insolvent liquidation, it is readily foreseeable that such creditors will search for ways of improving their prospects of achieving some measure of return upon the sums left owing to them by the company at the time of going into liquidation, or at the onset of any other insolvency procedure.[37] One such solution which has undergone considerable development, and been extensively used, in recent years has been the inclusion of a reservation of title clause in a contract under which goods of some kind—including materials for use in a manufacturing process—are supplied to the company on credit terms. By taking advantage of the freedom allowed by the law of sale of goods for the parties to the contract of sale to make express provision as to the time at which, and the conditions under which, property in the goods shall pass to the buyer,[38] it is possible to stipulate that the goods are not to become the property of the company, as their buyer, unless and until they have been fully paid for.

The use of such reservation of title clauses in contracts for the supply of goods to companies underwent a revolutionary transformation as a

---

[33] See p. 606, *ante*.
[34] See Chap. 24, *ante*, p. 609.
[35] See Cmnd. 8558, Chap. 36, at paras. 1538–1549. See generally, Chaps. 32–37 of the *Report*.
[36] The same disadvantage is shared by customers who have claims against the company in respect of unsatisfactory goods, or inadequately performed services, and by those (whether customers or not) who have claims arising from tortious injuries for which the company is responsible. See the discussion in Chap. 24, *ante*, of *The Pari Passu Principle: Tradition and Reality*, at p. 613, *et seq.*, and references in n. 49 on p. 615.
[37] The same difficulties are in prospect in the case of the appointment of an administrative receiver over the company, or even where an administration order is made (see Chap. 16, *ante*).
[38] Sale of Goods Act, 1979, ss.17, 19.

consequence of the decision of the Court of Appeal in *Aluminium Industrie Vaassen B. V. v. Romalpa Aluminium Ltd*[39] (whence is derived the sobriquet "*Romalpa Clause*"). In that case, it was held that the Dutch suppliers of aluminium foil under a contract whereby property in the foil was not to pass until payment, were entitled to recover the foil in the hands of the receiver of the English company by which it was bought, but not paid for. The Court held that as the foil was clearly identifiable it was recoverable by the assertion of a claim *in rem*, thereby enabling the suppliers to escape from the worst effects of being merely unsecured creditors of the insolvent buyer.

In a second, and more controversial, part of the *Romalpa* judgment the Court of Appeal also held that the terms of the agreement between the company and its supplier had the effect of conferring upon the latter the right to recover the proceeds of sub-sales of products made from the materials supplied but as yet unpaid for. The crux of the court's reasoning on this issue was that a fiduciary relationship of principle and agent arose between the company and its supplier in consequence of the terms embodied in their agreement.

In the ensuing development of the law and practice relating to reservation of title clauses, which occurred in a context of much controversy as to their implications for long-settled expectations in the area of credit and security, a dichotomy gradually emerged between those cases in which a relatively simple retention of title clause was employed, as in the *Romalpa* case itself with regard to the unsold aluminium still in the company's possession, and cases where the seller had inserted a more complex and sophisticated clause, aimed at achieving an even greater measure of protection in the event of the buyer's insolvency (along the lines employed by the further clauses of the *Romalpa* agreement). The latter type of clause—which would usually include some provision under which the seller reserved a right to recover the property even after it had become mixed with other property from a different source (as in a process of manufacture or construction), or to follow the proceeds of sale or disposal of the original goods themselves—has proved to be less successful in accomplishing its intended purpose. Unless the circumstances are such that, despite the mixing with other goods, the seller's goods have retained their physical identity so as to be retrievable,[40] the seller's rights against the goods themselves will generally be defeated through the process of mixing.[41] So, too, where the retention clause purports to extend the supplier's proprietary claims to the proceeds of any subsale which have been received by the buyer, the loss of identity of moneys through mixing can bring about the defeat of the supplier's claim.[42] If, in order to overcome this difficulty, the supplier sought to introduce even more subtle terms

---

[39] [1976] 2 All E.R. 552; [1976] 1 W.L.R. 676. This case is also referred to in Chap 8, *ante*, p. 216.
[40] As in *Hendy Lennox v. Puttick Ltd* [1984] 1 W.L.R. 485; *cf. Greenstone Shipping Co. S.A. v. Indian Oil Corp. Ltd, Financial Times*, March 20, 1987. (Mixed goods declared to be held in common with other suppliers or owners.)
[41] As in *Borden (U.K.) Ltd v. Scottish Timber Products Ltd* [1981] Ch. 25; [1979] 3 All E.R. 961 (C.A.); *Re Peachdart Ltd* [1984] Ch. 131.
[42] As in *Re Andrabell Ltd* [1984] 3 All E.R. 407.

purporting to bestow a right to trace property or proceeds on the basis of retention of equitable and beneficial rights of ownership,[43] a kind of Rubicon would be crossed in that the character of the clause would now become that of a floating charge created by the company, and as such would be void if unregistered.

Thus, the retention of title clause has evolved, and its validity in principle has been judicially acknowledged provided that its terms are drafted with sufficient care not to exceed certain limits. In the case of *Clough Mill Ltd. v. Martin*[44] the Court of Appeal reviewed the general principles applicable to *Romalpa*-type clauses, and were content that they should form an acceptable species of protection for unpaid sellers, if properly framed so as to operate within those limits. In the immediate aftermath of the *Romalpa* decision itself it was considered that the Court of Appeal had ushered in a new species of non-registrable security interest, capable of attaching to the goods supplied by the original seller and following them to their ultimate destination in the hands of an end-purchaser, or alternatively attaching to the proceeds of sub-sales. The judicial approach in subsequent cases has been to restrict the benefits of this protective device to those instances where goods sold under a "simple" reservation of title clause remain in an intact state in the hands of the original buyer. The House of Lords has confirmed the validity of an "all moneys" clause in relation to such an arrangement, and hence it is possible for the seller to render it a condition of sale that property in the goods shall not pass to the buyer until *all* moneys due from the buyer under past or future transactions have been fully paid.[45] This type of all-embracing proviso has the additional virtue, from the seller's point of view, of obviating the need to establish the identity of particular items kept and stored by the buyer, and linking them to a specific act of supply under contract.

Nevertheless, the economic protection obtained by the unpaid supplier by means of a reservation of title clause is tenuous at best. If the buyer proceeds to enter into a sub-sale with a third party—even if this is in contravention of the terms of the original contract of supply—the sub-buyer may well acquire a protected title as against the supplier,[46] unless the sub-sale is itself effected subject to a reservation of title by the intermediate buyer.[47] Potentially the most serious problem for the seller however is the possibility that the terms of the R.O.T. clause will be judicially construed as having given rise to the creation of a registrable charge by the buyer which is void against the liquidator or administrator or any creditor of the company, according to the provisions contained in Part XII of the Companies Act 1985.[48] Thus, unless the formalities and expense of regis-

---

[43] As in *Re Bond Worth Ltd* [1980] Ch. 228.
[44] [1984] 3 All E.R. 982; [1985] 1 W.L.R. 111.
[45] *Armour v. Thyssen Edelstahlwerke AG* [1991] 2 A.C. 339 (H.L.).
[46] *e.g.* by virtue of s.25 of the Sale of Goods Act 1929: *Four Point Garage Ltd v. Carter* [1985] 3 All E.R. 12.
[47] *cf. Re Highway Foods International Ltd* [1995] BCC 271.
[48] See esp. ss.395, 396. (Note: prospective amendments to Part XII of the Act of 1985 were enacted in Part IV of the Companies Act 1989. These amendments have not been brought into force.)

tration have been undertaken by the company, or by the seller personally,[49] the device will fail to achieve its objective of protecting the seller in the event of the buyer's inability to pay. Strictly speaking, a "pure" R.O.T. clause is not classifiable as a security interest, because it does not arise through the creation by a debtor company of a proprietary interest in or over property of which the company is owner, in favour of a creditor of the company. Instead, it consists of an act of *reservation* by the seller of his pre-existing, proprietary rights over the thing to be sold.[50] However, if there is the merest hint of an extension of the unpaid seller's rights of reclamation of property—and *a fortiori* where the proceeds of sub-sales are in issue—the appropriate way of analysing the provisions and effects of the clause is to regard them as amounting to a *grant* by the company of some type of right or interest over its own or some third party's property. As such, a registrable charge is likely to have been created within the meaning of section 396 of the Companies Act, with the consequences already described.[51]

Trust Devices

A further form of protection which has been developed in recent years, and which has enabled certain types of creditor to escape from the fate destined to be experienced by the other ordinary, unsecured creditors, involves the use of the trust device. Where the circumstances are such that the requisite elements necessary for the creation of a trust can be held to exist, funds which would otherwise have appeared to form part of the general assets of the company may be held to form part of a specially constituted trust, and as such to be held for the benefit of specific individuals, who may claim payment independently of the liquidation process.

One such case was *Barclays Bank Ltd v. Quistclose Investments Ltd*,[52] in which money was lent to a company for the specific purpose of enabling it to pay a dividend which had already been declared. The money was paid into a separate account at the company's bank, but was held in the company's name and remained untouched when liquidation commenced. The House of Lords held that the money was never intended to become part of the company's general funds, but was held on trust for a purpose which had now failed, and in consequence a resulting trust arose in favour of the respondents, by whom the original advance was made.

Further examples of successful impleading of the trust device have arisen where the company itself has consciously established a special,

---

[49] Companies Act 1985, s.399(1), (2).

[50] See R.M. Goode, *Legal Problems of Credit and Security* (2nd ed., 1988), esp. Chaps. 1, 3 and 5, for an illuminating discussion of the concept and legal nature of security.

[51] *Compaq Computer Ltd v. Abercorn Group Ltd* [1991] BCC 484; *Specialist Plant Services Ltd v. Braithwaite* [1987] BCLC 1 (C.A.); *Re Curtain Dream plc* [1991] BCC 484; *Welsh Development Agency v. Export Finance Co.* [1992] BCC 270 (C.A.); *Oditah* [1992] JBL 541. The last-named case, with its highly complex facts, is notable as having resulted in a judicial finding that no registrable charge had been created in the circumstances.

[52] [1970] A.C. 567 (H.L.) See also *Re Carreras Rothmans Ltd v. Freeman Mathews Treasure Ltd* [1985] Ch. 207.

separate fund for the purpose of guaranteeing repayment to an identified group of investors, or to provide benefits for the company's employees in such forms as health or pension or insurance schemes.[53] Similarly, where a company has endeavoured to protect its own customers, in the event of possible insolvency, by creating a special deposit account into which customers' deposits, and advance payments for goods or services, were to be paid and held until the transaction was fully performed, it has been held that such a distinctly maintained account can constitute a duly constituted trust fund whose proceeds are held for the benefit of those customers who, at the commencement of liquidation, can be shown to have contributed payments in respect of unfulfilled transactions.[54]

Not surprisingly, the validity of formation of an alleged trust under which a favoured sub-group would escape the fate otherwise in store for them according to the *pari passu* principle is seldom uncontested by those for whom the self same trust has detrimental implications. Sometimes the challenge may succeed on the basis of a straightforward application of the principles of trust law to the circumstances of the case, for example with respect to the need to establish the "three certainties" of intention, objects and subject-matter, in relation to the formation of the trust[55] (although, if the trust is of personalty, it should be noted that it is not a formal requirement that writing be employed, however desirable this may be as an aid of proof). Even where the constitutive requirements have been initially fulfilled, the operation of the trust may ultimately be prevented through the simple omission to ascertain or isolate the property intended to form the subject-matter of the trust, and to maintain it distinctly from other property of the company of a similar kind[56] (whether goods or money). In the case of money, which is the commonest example of this kind of trust device, the maintenance of a separate bank account, preferably bearing a distinctive name, is the safest practical course to adopt.

A further instance of the use of this type of protective device occurs in the form of trust retention provisions, used in various standard forms of building contracts. Either the party due to make payment may be required to constitute a separate trust in favour of the contractor or sub-contractor in question, with regard to retention moneys remaining in his control, or alternatively the payment of moneys due under such contracts can be contractually controlled so as to take place through an escrow account in the names of agreed representatives, thereby providing independent control over the moneys so that neither party can use them to exploit the other side's economic position in an opportunistic way. Such arrangements escape from the need for registration as charges, since the beneficial interest has been transferred to the party to whom payment is

---

[53] *Elkins v. Capital Guarantee Society* (1900) 16 T.L.R. 423; *Re Independent Air Travel Ltd* [1961] 1 Lloyd's Rep. 604; *Smith v. Liquidator of James Birrell Ltd* 1968 S.L.T. 174.

[54] *Re Kayford Ltd* [1975] 1 All E.R. 604; *Re Chelsea Cloisters Ltd* (1981) 131 N.L.J. 482; (1980) 41 P. & C.R. 98; *Re E. Dibbens & Sons Ltd* [1990] BCLC 577. cf. *Re Lewis's of Leicester Ltd* [1995] BCC 514 (an administration case).

[55] cf. *Re Multi Guarantee Co. Ltd* [1987] BCLC 257 (C.A.) (trust failed for want of certainty of intention and of words used).

[56] e.g. *Re London Wine Co. (Shippers) Ltd* (1986) PCC 121, dist. in *Re Stapylton Fletcher Ltd* [1994] 1 W.L.R. 1181.

destined in due course to be made, subject to satisfactory completion of the stage or stages of the work in progress.[57] There is the usual difficulty with this, as with other trust-type devices, that if the insolvent party, despite being under a contractual obligation to remit funds into an account where they would assume the character of trust moneys, has in fact failed to perform that undertaking, the other party is left without any right to call for that to be done which ought to have been done, since the essential basis of this claim against the insolvent party's estate is contractual rather than proprietary in nature.[58]

One further matter to be borne in mind in relation to the utilisation of trusts and trust-like devices as a prophylactic against the possibility of insolvency is that their efficacy in any given case is ultimately dependent upon them being held not to have contravened any overarching provisions of insolvency law regarding the avoidance of antecedent transactions to which the debtor has been a party. It should be noted that under some circumstances a court may well conclude that the constitution of a trust in favour of creditors amounted to the giving of a preference by the company within the meaning of section 239 of the Act, discussed below.

Supplies by Utilities

Section 233 of the Insolvency Act 1986 introduced an innovatory provision into the law of winding up, and is designed to prevent public utilities from exploiting their provision of near (or total) monopoly in relation to the supply of services vital to the continuation of a business activity. In Chapter 33 of the *Cork Report*, it was observed that such utilities were sometimes able retrospectively to gain for themselves a position tantamount to that of being a secured or preferential creditor in respect of charges for services supplied to the company prior to commencement of winding up. This may come about where the liquidator wishes to continue the business of the company for a period with a view to its being wound up in the most convenient way, or sold off on the most advantageous terms. In these circumstances, the public utilities may seek to impose special conditions before agreeing to renew or continue supply of commercially indispensable services such as water, electricity, gas and even the telephone. The conditions imposed may have the effect of ensuring that the utility recoups some or all of what is outstanding in respect of past supplies, as well as enjoying protection, in some form such as a personal guarantee furnished by the liquidator, in respect of payment for future supplies.

Section 233 of the Insolvency Act prohibits any supplier of gas, electricity, water or telecommunication services from making it a condition of the giving of a supply, or from doing anything which has the effect of making it a condition of the giving of a supply, that any

---

[57] *Lovell Construction Ltd v. Independent Estates plc* (unreported, June 25, 1992), discussed by Davis (1993) 6 Insolvency Intelligence, 25–27. See also Moss (1992) 5 Insolvency Intelligence 25–27.
[58] cf. *MacJordan Construction Ltd v. Brookmount Erostin Ltd* [1992] BCLC 350.

outstanding charges in respect of previous supplies given to the company are paid. Thus, the supplier may validly make it a condition that the liquidator personally guarantees payment of any charges in respect of subsequent services, but may not impose such a condition, whether directly or indirectly, in relation to previous supplies.

The provisions of section 233(1) of the Insolvency Act have the effect of making this section of the Act applicable not only in relation to requests for supply when made by a liquidator, but also when made by an administrator or an administrative receiver of a company, or by a provisional liquidator of the company or by the supervisor of a voluntary arrangement made under Part I of the Act.

Recovery of Assets Previously Disposed of by the Company: Adjustment of Antecedent Transactions

The proper conduct of an insolvent liquidation necessarily entails the carrying out of a progressive analysis of the conduct and affairs of the company over a considerable period prior to the commencement of liquidation. This investigation into the pathology of the company's failure will be undertaken by the liquidator in the course of his duties with respect to the getting in, realisation and distribution of the company's property, for only when he is in possession of the fullest available information about all matters relating to the insolvency can he properly discharge the tasks which are entrusted to him. In the case of a winding up by the court there is, as we have seen,[59] an express requirement in section 132 of the Act that the official Receiver must investigate and report upon the causes of the company's failure. These matters were discussed in Chapter 22 above, together with other provisions of the Act which facilitate the getting of the requisite information about the company's affairs.[60]

On the basis of the information thus obtained, it is possible that individual directors and managers of the company may face criminal or civil proceedings, as will be described in Chapter 27 below. It is also possible that evidence will be assembled which will enable the liquidator to augment the assets available for distribution in the liquidation by bringing about the avoidance, or adjustment, of prior transactions to which the company was party, whereby the company's assets were demonstrably depleted. The provisions of the Act which are relevant for this purpose are sections 238 to 241, 244 to 246, and 423 to 425 inclusive. These will now be considered in turn.

Transactions at an Undervalue and Preferences

Sections 614–616 of the Companies Act, together with section 44 of the

[59] See Chap. 22, *ante*, p. 560.
[60] See especially ss.131, 133, 143, 165–170, and 234–237, all discussed in Chap. 22, *ante*.

RECOVERY OF ASSETS PREVIOUSLY DISPOSED OF ETC.

Bankruptcy Act 1914, were repealed by the Insolvency Act 1985. Sections 238 to 243 inclusive of the Insolvency Act 1986 now contain the provisions to enable any of the company's previous transactions to be set aside in a winding up where it has amounted to the giving of a preference to any person, or where the transaction itself has consisted of the company's making a gift, or providing a consideration in return for a payment, or other consideration, which is significantly less in value than that which is provided by the company. Instead of the former terms "fraudulent preference" and "fraudulent conveyance," with their in-built connotations of fraud and moral turpitude, the new provisions in sections 238 to 243 of the Insolvency Act employ the more neutral terminology of "transaction at an undervalue" and "preference" (or, for Scotland, "gratuitous alienation" and "unfair preference"). In cases where a company has entered into a transaction defrauding creditors, under circumstances which would hitherto have been governed by section 172 of the Law of Property Act 1925, the relevant provisions can now be found in sections 423–425 of the Insolvency Act 1986.[61]

The two new concepts of "transaction at an undervalue" and "(voidable) preference" are distinct, although they are treated alongside each other in the same Part of the Insolvency Act. However, it is to be understood that a transaction may in some circumstances be voidable as a transaction at an undervalue, albeit it may not have amounted to a voidable preference.

Transactions at an undervalue

The statutory test for a transaction at an undervalue is contained in section 238(4), which states that a company enters into such a transaction with a person if:

(a) the company makes a gift to that person or otherwise enters into a transaction with that person on terms which provide for the company to receive no consideration; or

(b) the company enters into a transaction with that person for a consideration the value of which, in money or money's worth, is significantly less than the value, in money or money's worth, of the consideration provided by the company.

However, the provisions of section 238(5) must be further considered before it can be held that a transaction, though demonstrably at an undervalue, is voidable. This subsection is designed to enable the company to engage in genuine business transactions carried out in good faith in the reasonable belief that they will benefit the company. Such transactions may retain their validity by virtue of section 238(5), notwithstanding that in objective terms the criteria with respect to "undervalue" may have been satisfied.

[61] See *infra*, and also Chap. 8, *ante*, p. 232.

Preferences

The statutory test for the giving of a preference to any person by the company is contained in section 239(4). The drafting reflects the recommendation in the *Cork Report*[62] where it was argued that in the case of a voidable preference the burden of repayment should be borne by the party whom it was intended to prefer. Thus in the case where the party who has been preferred is the surety or guarantor of a debt owed to some other creditor, it is now possible to proceed directly against the surety or guarantor quite independently of any proceedings which may be taken against the creditor. The giving of a preference to a person who is one of the company's creditors, or to a person who is a surety or guarantor for any of the company's debts or other liabilities, will take place where the company does anything or suffers anything to be done which has the effect of putting that person into a position which, in the event of the company going into insolvent liquidation, will be better than the position he would have been in if that thing had not been done.

The provisions of section 239(4) are subject to the effects of subsection (5), which modifies the pre-existing law with regard to the relevant state of mind which must accompany the giving of the preference by the company. Previously, it was essential that the payment was made with dominant intention on the part of the company of preferring the creditor in question. What is henceforth required under section 239(5) is that the desire to produce the effect mentioned in section 239(4)(b) should have "influenced" the company in deciding to give the preference. This form of wording will ensure that a preference will be voidable provided that the desire to create an advantageous position for the creditor is at least present as an operative force in the minds of those who cause the company to confer the preference, even though it may not be the dominant intention under the circumstances. However, where directors yield to the application of genuine pressure by a creditor and accordingly make a payment, or perform some other act, which satisfies the test laid down in section 239(4)(b), it can nevertheless be argued that the preference is not a voidable one, since the company did not "desire" the effect which its action was destined to produce.

The above approach to the construction of the new provision, and in particular the assessment of the significance of the term "desire" in that context, was essentially that followed by Millet J. in *Re M. C. Bacon Ltd.*[63] The learned judge took the view that section 239 should be approached as a totally fresh enactment, and hence should not be interpreted with reference to authorities decided under previous legislation, save perhaps for the purpose of discerning a contrast between the former and the current intentions of Parliament as to the effect of the provision. He further emphasised that the use of word "desire" in the current provision connotes a far stronger and more positive state of mind on the part of the

---

[62] Cmnd. 8558, paras. 1270–1276. See also the discussion in Chap. 8, *ante* of the parallel provisions (ss.339–342) which are applicable in bankruptcy.
[63] [1990] BCC 78; [1990] BCLC 324. See Fletcher [1991] JBL 71.

company alleged to have given a preference, than was formerly signified by the word "intention". In the instant case, the company was found to be effectively dependent upon the maintenance of overdraft facilities by its bank, to enable it to continue its business. When finally prevailed upon, only a few weeks before going into liquidation, to give security in the form of a floating charge as a condition for the bank maintaining the overdraft, the company was held not to have given a voidable preference in the circumstances under which it acted. Such "desire" on the company's part as could be evinced from the evidence was characterised as a desire to sustain the company's business at a time of extreme financial difficulty, for which the maintenance of the bank overdraft was indispensable.[64] The material improvement in the bank's position through the giving of security was an inevitable consequence, but one which was incidental rather than being the "desired" effect, so far as the company was concerned.

Connected persons

Where the person to whom a preference has been given was connected with the company at the time the preference was given, section 239(6) creates a rebuttable presumption that the company was influenced by the desire to produce the effect mentioned in section 239(4)(b). Thus, a person connected with the company will be obliged to undertake the burden of proving that the company was not influenced by the relevant desire in making the payment in question. If he fails to persuade the court with regard to the company's "negative desire," the preference will be voidable. The meaning in this context of the expression "connected person" is supplied by the combined provisions of sections 249 and 435 of the Insolvency Act 1986. It refers to any person who is a director or shadow director of the company, or any person who is an associate of such a director or shadow director, or any person who is an associate of the company.[65] The special term "associate" is defined in elaborate detail in section 435 of the Insolvency Act,[66] and includes a wide range of relationships including that of employer and employee, but it is to be noted that, by virtue of section 239(6), a person is not to be deemed to be connected with a company for the purposes of section 239 if his sole connection arises from the fact of his being an employee of the company.[67] Despite the special exception in favour of employees of the company, the combined effect of sections 239(6), 249 and 435 is to create a wide range of

---

[64] [1990] BCC at 87; [1990] BCLC at pp. 335–336. See also the subsequent decision of the same judge in the same proceedings, where the liquidator who had unsuccessfully sought to impeach the floating charge as a preference was refused permission to recoup the costs of the bank, and his own costs in the proceedings, as an "expense properly incurred in the winding up": *Re M.C. Bacon Ltd (No. 2)* [1990] 3 W.L.R. 646.

[65] Insolvency Act 1986, s.249, reproduced in Appendix I, *post*. For cases concerning connected persons, see *Re Beacon Leisure Ltd* [1991] BCC 213 (which, however, is an unsafe decision which should not be followed); *Re Fairway Magazines Ltd* [1992] BCC 924; *Re D.K.G. Contractors Ltd* [1990] BCC 903.

[66] s.435 is reproduced in Appendix I, *post*.

[67] See however *Re Clasper Group Services Ltd* (1988) 4 BCC 673.

persons onto whom will be imposed the burden of disproving the company's desire to prefer.

The relevant time

A further aspect in which the law now operates more stringent rules against persons who contrive to gain an advantage as a result of their connection with the company arises under section 240. This section has the function of determining what periods of time will be operative so that any transaction entered into, or any preference given, within those periods will take place at "a relevant time" for the purposes of sections 238 and 239. In the case of a transaction at an undervalue or of a preference which is given to a person who is connected with the company, the operative period consists of two years ending with the date of the onset of the company's insolvency (the date of presentation of the petition for the making of the administration order, or the date of the commencement of the winding up, as the case may be).[68] By contrast, any preference which is not given to a connected person, provided that the preference does not simultaneously constitute a transaction at an undervalue, will only be given at "a relevant time" if it is given within the period of six months ending with the date of commencement of insolvency proceedings.[69]

One further statutory requirement must be fulfilled for a transaction or preference to be rendered voidable under sections 238 and 239 respectively. This arises by virtue of section 240(2), which states that the time at which a transaction is entered into, or at which a preference is given, shall not count as a "relevant time" for the purposes of section 238 or 239 unless the company:

(a) is unable to pay its debts within the meaning of section 123 of the Act at the time in question; or
(b) becomes unable to pay its debts within the meaning of section 123 in consequence of the transaction or preference.

Once again, a special, additional rule is included with reference to any person who is connected with the company: where the company enters into a transaction at an undervalue with a connected person (in the sense explained above), it is to be presumed unless the contrary is shown that the requirements of section 240(2) were satisfied with respect to the company at the time in question. The burden of proving that the company was solvent at the time of the undervalue transaction, and that it did not become insolvent as a result of the transaction itself, is thus cast upon the connected person with whom the transaction was entered into.

Avoidance of transactions at an undervalue or preference

Any transaction at an undervalue or preference rendered voidable by virtue of the provisions described above may be the subject of an

---

[68] Insolvency Act 1986, s.240(1)(a), (3).
[69] *ibid.* s.240(1)(b), (3).

application to the court for an order declaring the transaction or preference to be avoided and making whatever further order the court thinks fit for the restoration of the position to what it would otherwise have been. Section 241 of the Insolvency Act further elaborates upon the range of restitutional and consequential orders which the court may make at its discretion. According to section 238(1) and section 239(1), the right to make application to the court under each section, as appropriate, is conferred exclusively upon "the office holder," which in this context means either the administrator or the liquidator of the company, according to circumstances. It is therefore not possible for an administrative receiver of a company to invoke the provisions of sections 238 to 243 in relation to any transactions or preferences entered into or given by a company prior to going into receivership. If an administrative receiver considers that these provisions offer the most effective means of recovering assets which have been disposed of at an undervalue, or by way of a preference given, the proper recourse would seem to be for the appropriate steps to be taken to put the company into compulsory liquidation, or for an administration order to be applied for, so that a new office holder can be appointed with full standing to apply to the court for an order under sections 238 or 239, as the case may be.

Cross-border operation of the transaction adjustment provisions

A further possible limitation to the operation of the provisions of section 238 is a territorial one. To what extent is it a requirement that the person with whom the company has concluded the transaction should be resident, or in some sense present, in this country? In *Re Paramount Airways Ltd. (No. 2)* it was held at first instance that there was no jurisdiction to make an order under that section in respect of a person resident abroad, who had conducted no business within the jurisdiction of the English court, and with no place of business within the jurisdiction.[70] The Court of Appeal reversed this decision,[71] holding that the words "any person" in section 238 were unaccompanied by any qualifying expressions to limit the application of the section to cases where the person in question either was at the time of the transaction, or is at the time application is made, present in or otherwise personally connected with this country. The words "any person" were given their literal and natural meaning in the absence of any clear indication that Parliament had intended to impose any territorial restriction upon the operation of section 238. However, it was emphasised that the final decision whether to exercise this widely drawn jurisdiction is a matter for the discretion of the trial court, which must first give leave under rule 12.12(3) of the Insolvency Rules 1986 for service of process to take place out of the jurisdiction. If the court found that the overseas party had a minimal connection with England, this fact might lead it to conclude that it would be neither just nor proper to make

---

[70] [1991] 3 W.L.R. 318; [1991] 4 All E.R. 267.
[71] [1993] Ch. 223; [1992] 3 All E.R. 1; [1992] BCC 416.

an order against the party in question, and the judicial discretion would be exercised accordingly.

Protection of Third Party Purchasers: The Insolvency (No. 2) Act 1994

Section 241(2) of the Act is designed to meet the case where property which was the subject of a transaction which is later affected by an order made under section 238 or 239 has, in the meantime, been the subject of further transactions involving other parties. It is provided that the order of the court may affect the property of, or impose any obligation on, any person whether or not he is the person with whom the company in question entered into the transaction or (as the case may be) the person to whom the preference was given. Necessarily, provision had to be included to safeguard the position of innocent third parties acquiring property in good faith and for value, and without notice of the circumstances whereby the prior transaction was rendered impeachable. As originally enacted, these protective provisions in paragraphs (a) and (b) of section 241(2) were regarded as giving rise to a potential hazard for purchasers of unregistered land who might be taken to have had notice of "the relevant circumstances" without having in fact had knowledge of the actual or impending insolvency of the company. Such insecurity of title had inevitable commercial consequences for property transactions.

To remedy the perceived deficiencies in the drafting of section 241(2), the Insolvency (No. 2) Act amended the subsection, and inserted a new subsection (2A) after subsection (2). These reforms are non-retrospective, and have effect in relation to interests acquired and benefits received after July 26, 1994, the date on which the Act came into force.[72] Under the amended provisions of section 241(2), a party who has acquired an interest in property from a person other than the company and who acquired it in good faith and for value shall not suffer prejudice with respect to the interest so acquired. Section 241(2A) introduces a rebuttable presumption to the effect that, in either of the alternative cases mentioned in paragraphs (a) and (b) of the subsection, it is to be presumed for the purposes of section 241(2) that the interest was acquired or the benefit was received otherwise than in good faith. The alternative cases are: (a) that the third party in question had notice of the relevant surrounding circumstances and of the relevant proceedings; or (b) he was connected with, or was an associate of, either the company in question or the person with whom that company entered into the transaction or to whom that company gave the preference. The expression "the relevant surrounding circumstances" is defined in the newly substituted section 241(3) and means (according to context) either the fact that the company in question entered into the transaction at an undervalue; or the circumstances which amounted to the giving of the preference by the company in question.

---

[72] Insolvency (No. 2) Act 1994, s.6(2), (3).

Recovery of Assets Previously Disposed of Etc.

The requirement of notice of "the relevant proceedings", as embodied in section 241(2A)(a) is explained, in relation to the several possibilities involving the company going into liquidation or being made the subject of an administration order, by the further provisions of subsections (3A) to (3C). In each case, according to context, the requisite knowledge on the part of the third party is either of the fact that the petition has been presented on which the administration order, or winding-up order, is made, or of the fact that the administration order has been made or that the company has gone into liquidation, whether of a compulsory or of a voluntary nature.

Extortionate Credit Transactions

Section 244 of the Insolvency Act 1986 introduced a further remedy into the repertoire of the liquidator or administrator of a company.[73] The new provision, which is modelled on sections 137–139 inclusive of the Consumer Credit Act 1974, allows a liquidator or administrator to apply to the court for an order reopening any credit bargain which has been entered into by the company as debtor on terms which are extortionate. Section 244(2) is so drafted as to allow a credit bargain to be reopened whether or not the contract is still running and current at the date of the application to the court. Subsection (1) permits the reopening of any transaction for, or involving, the provision of credit to which the company "is, or has been a party" and in which the company occupies the role of debtor. By section 244(2) a transaction which is held to be, or to have been, extortionate may be made the subject of an order setting it aside in whole or in part, if the transaction was entered into in the period of three years ending with the day on which the company went into liquidation or, as the case may be, the administration order was made.

The definition of "extortionate credit transaction" for the purposes of section 244 is supplied in subsection (3), which provides that a transaction is extortionate if, having regard to the risk accepted by the person providing the credit,

(a) the terms of it are or were such as to require grossly exorbitant payments to be made (whether unconditionally or in certain contingencies) in respect of the provision of credit; or
(b) it otherwise grossly contravened ordinary principles of fair dealing.

The concluding words of subsection (3) serve to place the office holder in an advantageous position from a procedural point of view, by creating a rebuttable presumption that a transaction in respect of which an application is made under section 244 is or, as the case may be, was

---

[73] s.244 is a parallel provision to s.343 of the Act, applicable in bankruptcy: see Chap. 8, *ante*, p. 230.

extortionate. The mere act on the part of the office holder of making an application to reopen a credit transaction has the effect of imposing upon the party who occupies the role of creditor in the transaction a burden of proof consisting of a requirement to demonstrate a negative proposition, namely that the transaction was not extortionate within the meaning of subsection (3). The operation of this statutory presumption accords with the precedent set by section 171(7) of Consumer Credit Act 1974.

The range of possible provisions capable of inclusion in orders which the court may make under section 244 is set out in subsection (4), which authorises the court, at its discretion, to insert in its order one or more of the provisions therein listed. These include the setting aside of the whole or part of any obligation created by the transaction; the variation of any of the terms of the transaction or of the terms on which any related security is held; restitutional orders to be made against persons who have been party to the transaction or who hold property as security for the purposes of the transaction; and provisions directing the taking of accounts between persons.

Finally, it should be noted that, by virtue of subsection (5), the powers of section 244 are made exercisable in relation to any transaction concurrently with any powers exercisable in relation thereto as a transaction at an undervalue,[74] or under section 242 of the Act (gratuitous alienations in Scotland).

Avoidance of Certain Floating Charges

Section 245 of the Insolvency Act replaces the provision formerly contained in section 617 of the Companies Act 1985, and implements reforms proposed by the Cork Report.[75] The new section strengthens the rules under which a floating charge created by a company within 12 months prior to the commencement of insolvency proceedings (or, in the case of such a charge created in favour of a person who is connected with the company,[76] within two years prior to that date) is rendered invalid by the fact of the company's going into liquidation or becoming the subject of an administration order. Section 245(2) provides that a floating charge on the company's undertaking or property created at "a relevant time" (see below) is invalid except to the extent allowed by way of exception, according to the further provisions of the section itself.

A floating charge which comes within the operation of section 245 is invalid except to the extent of the aggregate of the value of:

(a) so much of the consideration for the creation of the charge as consists of money paid, or goods or services supplied, to the company at the same time as, or after, the creation of the charge (the so-called "new value" principle of pro rata validation);

(b) the value of so much of that consideration as consists of the

---

[74] See ss.238, 240 and 241 of the Act, discussed, *supra*.
[75] Cmnd. 8558, paras. 1551–1556.
[76] For the meaning of the expression "connected person," see Insolvency Act 1986, ss.249 and 435, reproduced in Appendix I, *post*.

discharge or reduction, at the same time as, or after, the creation of the charge of any debt of the company; and

(c) the amount of such interest (if any) as is payable on the amount falling within (*a*) and (*b*) in pursuance of any agreement under which the money was so paid, the goods or services were so supplied or the debt was so discharged or reduced.[77]

The time factor

In section 245(2)(a) and (b) the expression "at the same time as, or after, the creation of the charge" is used for the purpose of defining the boundary between "new" and "old" value with respect to payments, and other forms of provision of value to or on behalf of the company, which take place with reference to the floating charge security. In view of the fact that the formalities needed to complete the execution of a floating charge may take some time, and could be delayed due to extraneous factors, it can be of vital importance to establish the precise timing and sequence of events relating to the generation of any item of indebtedness alleged to enjoy the benefit of the "new value" exception established by section 245 (2). Equally important is the judicial approach to formulating the test of "contemporaneity" to be applied in cases where a payment was made at a time which chronologically preceded the moment of formal execution of the charge. In *Power v. Sharp Investments Ltd*[78] the Court of Appeal stipulated that the test of contemporaneity is to be a strict one, although an important point of distinction was embodied in the crucial passage of the leading judgment of Sir Christopher Slade. In his words:

> "In a case where no presently existing charge has been created by any agreement or company resolution preceding the execution of the formal debenture ... no moneys paid before the execution of the debenture will qualify for the exemption under [section 245(2)(a)], unless the interval between payment and execution is so short that it can be regarded as minimal and execution can be regarded as contemporaneous."[79]

The important distinction made by the Court of Appeal in its approach to the construction of section 245(2) concerns the situation where the company's promise to execute a debenture creates a present equitable right to a security, and moneys are advanced in reliance on it. In such a case, "the delay between the advances and the execution of the formal instrument of charge is immaterial; the charge has already been created and is immediately registrable, so that other creditors of the company will have had the opportunity to learn of its existence."[80] In equity, a floating

---

[77] Insolvency Act 1986, s.245(2).
[78] [1993] BCC 609, affirming on different and more strictly defined grounds the decision of Hoffmann J. *sub nom. Re Shoe Lace Ltd* [1992] BCC 367.
[79] [1993] BCC at 620. In an *obiter dictum* earlier, at p. 619, it was judicially suggested that an example of a "*de minimis*" interval of time might be a "coffee break".
[80] *ibid.*, at p. 619 *per* Sir Christopher Slade, adopting a distinction drawn by Buckley J. in *Re Jackson & Bassford Ltd* [1906] 2 Ch. 467 at p. 477.

charge is created by a contract evidenced in writing and for valuable consideration to execute, when required, a formal mortgage by way of floating charge.

The "relevant time" concept

Sections 245(3) and (4) have the effect of determining when the creation of a floating charge will take place at "a relevant time" for the purposes of determining its invalidity under subsection (2). By section 245(4) it is made a precondition to the operation of this invalidating provision that the company was either insolvent at the time of the creation of the floating charge or was rendered insolvent in consequence of the very transaction under which the floating charge was created. However, in any case in which the person in whose favour the charge was created was connected with the company,[81] the precondition as to the company's state of insolvency is not applicable, and hence all such charges are rendered invalid if the company goes into liquidation, or if an administration order is made against it, within two years of the date of their creation. This more stringent proviso is aimed particularly at preventing those who are directors or shadow directors of a company, and also other persons closely involved in its management, from conferring upon themselves an enhanced priority, as against the unsecured creditors of the company, by means of a floating charge which is mainly referable to finance which they have formerly provided to the company. Even if some fresh, additional capital or other consideration is furnished at or after the time of creation of the charge, it will only be valid to the extent of the actual value of that new consideration: the value of the past consideration is ignored and that portion of the debt remains unsecured.

The invalidation of a floating charge under section 245 does not affect the existence or validity of the actual debt which the charge purported to secure: the debt remains, but becomes an unsecured debt for which the person to whom it is owed must lodge proof, and rank for dividend, alongside the other creditors of equivalent rank.[82]

The provision in section 245(2)(b), which refers to the "discharge or reduction ... of any debt of the company" is intended to provide protection for cases where a company grants a floating charge in favour of a bank or finance house to secure further advances. Payments which are subsequently made by the bank to other creditors of the company in whose favour cheques have been drawn will qualify for exemption from the effects of the invalidating provision. This gives statutory confirmation of the case-law approach to the application of the previously applicable statutory provision.[83]

Transactions Defrauding Creditors

Where it can be established that a former transaction of the company

---

[81] See n. 76 *supra*.
[82] On priority of debts, see Chap. 24, *ante*.
[83] *Re Yeovil Glove Co. Ltd* [1965] Ch. 148.

was entered into for purposes which were essentially fraudulent, the transaction may be impeached under sections 423 to 425 of the Insolvency Act. These provisions, which form part of the general law, were discussed in Chapter 8 above, and the reader is referred to the previous account there given of their operation.[84]

---

[84] See Chap. 8, *ante*, p. 232.

CHAPTER 27

LIABILITY OF DIRECTORS AND OTHERS

Preliminary

Mention was made in the previous chapter of the investigative processes which take place during the course of an insolvent liquidation. As a more complete picture begins to emerge of the manner in which the company's affairs were managed during the period of its active trading existence, and particularly during the months immediately prior to the commencement of liquidation, it may become clear that one or more of the persons who effectively controlled the company's conduct of its affairs, or who managed its business, have at some time contravened the strict requirements of the law, whose provisions are designed to ensure that those who enjoy the privilege of trading with limited liability, using the medium of the corporate form, do not abuse that privilege. A series of statutory provisions establish a number of grounds of criminal or civil liability which may be incurred by the directors or managers of companies which undergo insolvency. These provisions are not only intended to serve as a deterrent against delinquent conduct on the part of those to whom they are applicable, but they also furnish further possibilities for the liquidator to cause additional assets to be made available for distribution to creditors. This is because, in the case of the civil liabilities described below, the loss of the privilege of limited liability can result in the director or manager in question being ordered to make restitution to the company, or to make a contribution to its assets, out of his or her personal estate.

(A) Criminal Offences Before and During Liquidation

Sections 206 to 211 inclusive of the Insolvency Act contain provisions whereby criminal offences are committed through malpractices on the part of past or present officers of the company, as follows.

(1) Fraud in anticipation of winding up

Section 206 of the Insolvency Act deals with fraud and other malpractices perpetrated by past or present officers of the company in the 12 months immediately preceding the commencement of the winding up (whether compulsory or voluntary) or at any time after the commencement. For the purposes of this section, and others to be discussed, the expression "officer of the company" includes a director, manager or secretary, and (except in cases (2) and (4) below) includes a shadow director, whilst the term "director" includes any person occupying the position of a director, no matter by what name he is called.[1] An offence under section 206 is committed by any officer who acts in any of the following ways[2]:

(a) concealing any part of the company's property to the value of £500 or more,[3] or concealing any debt due to or from the company; or

(b) fraudulently removing any part of the company's property to the value of £500 or more[3]; or

(c) concealing, destroying, mutilating or falsifying any book or paper affecting or relating to the company's property or affairs; or

(d) making any false entry in any book or paper affecting or relating to the company's property or affairs; or

(e) fraudulently parting with, altering or making any omission in any document affecting or relating to the company's property or affairs; or

(f) pawning, pledging or disposing of any property of the company which has been obtained on credit and has not been paid for (unless the pawning, pledging or disposal was in the ordinary way of the company's business). In the case of this mode of committing an offence, criminal liability is also incurred by any third party who knowingly takes the property in pawn or pledge, or who otherwise receives it.[4]

In the case of a person charged under paragraph (a) or (f) above, the onus of proving absence of *mens rea*, in the sense of proving that he had no intent to defraud, is cast upon the accused himself, while in cases falling under paragraphs (c) or (d) a similar onus is cast upon the accused, namely to prove that he had no intent to conceal the state of affairs of the company or to defeat the law.[5] It is submitted that the latter requirement is a compound one, and that the accused must establish both ingredients of the defence if he is to escape conviction.

---

[1] Insolvency Act 1986, ss.206(3), 251; Companies Act 1985, s.744. The terms "director" and "shadow director" are given statutory definition by s.741 of the Companies Act, and s.251 of the Insolvency Act 1986 incorporates that and other definitions into the Insolvency Act in the absence of any express, alternative definition supplied by the Insolvency Act 1986 itself.

[2] Insolvency Act 1986, s.206(1).

[3] The figure of £500 in Insolvency Act 1986, s.206(1)(a) and (b) was substituted by (S.I. 1986, No. 1996), pursuant to the enabling provision in s.206(7).

[4] Insolvency Act 1986, s.206(5).

[5] *ibid.*, s.206(4).

CRIMINAL OFFENCES BEFORE AND DURING LIQUIDATION

By virtue of section 206(2), persons are deemed to commit an offence if they are privy to the doing by others of any of the things mentioned in paragraphs (c), (d) and (e) above, and it is furthermore made an offence for a person to do any of the things mentioned in paragraphs (a) to (f) at any time after the commencement of the winding up, or to be privy to the doing by others of any of the things mentioned in paragraphs (c), (d) and (e) after that time.

Severe sanctions are prescribed for those found guilty of an offence under section 206: if tried upon indictment, the convicted person may be sentenced to seven years' imprisonment, or an unlimited fine, or both.[6]

(2) Transactions in fraud of creditors

Section 207 of the Act establishes a general offence in relation to transactions in fraud of creditors prior to the winding up. An offence is committed by any officer of the company who:

(1) Has made or caused to be made any gift or transfer of, or charge on, or has caused or connived at the levying of any execution against, the company's property; or

(2) Has concealed or removed any part of the company's property since, or within 2 months before, the date of any unsatisfied judgment or order for the payment of money obtained against the company.

It is a defence under this section to establish that the conduct constituting an offence under paragraph (a) occurred more than 5 years before the commencement of the winding up, or if the accused proves that, at the time of the conduct constituting the offence, he had no intention to defraud the company's creditors.[7] The punishments available in the event of conviction are identical to those under section 206, described above.[8]

(3) Misconduct in course of winding up

Under section 208 of the Act, any past or present officer of the company being wound up commits an offence in the following circumstances.[9] If he:

(a) does not make full and true disclosure and discovery to the liquidator of all the company's property, and of the circumstances and manner in which it was disposed of

---

[6] *ibid.*, ss.206(6), 430; Sched. 10.
[7] *ibid.*, s.207(2).
[8] *ibid.*, ss.207(3), 430; Sched 10.
[9] *ibid.*, s.208(1). For the purposes of this section, "officer" includes a shadow director: s.208(3).

otherwise than in the ordinary way of business (and to whom it was disposed of); or

(b) does not deliver up to the liquidator all such part of the company's property as is in his custody or under his control, and which he is legally required to deliver up; or

(c) does not deliver up to the liquidator all books and papers belonging to the company, of which he has custody or control and which he is legally required to deliver up; or

(d) knowing or believing that a false debt has been proved by any person in the winding up, fails to inform the liquidator as soon as practicable; or

(e) after the commencement of winding up, prevents the production of any book or paper affecting or relating to the company's property or affairs.

It is also an offence for any officer of the company after the commencement of winding up to attempt to account for any part of the company's property by fictitious losses or expenses, or if he has so attempted at any meeting of the company's creditors in the 12 months immediately preceding the commencement of winding up.[10]

The provisions of section 208(3) make it incumbent upon the accused to prove absence of *mens rea* in relation to any alleged offence under (a), (b) or (c) above, the requisite state of mind to be established being that he had no intent to defraud. If charged under paragraph (e), the accused must prove that he had no intent to conceal the state of affairs of the company or to defeat the law. The available punishments upon conviction are identical to those under section 206, described above.[11]

(4) Falsification of company's books

Section 209 of the Act provides that when a company is being wound up, any officer or contributory of the company commits an offence if he destroys, mutilates, alters or falsifies any books, papers or securities, or makes or is privy to the making of any false or fraudulent entry in any register, book of account or document belonging to the company. It is incumbent upon the prosecution to prove that the act in question was done with intent to defraud or deceive some person. The prescribed punishments on conviction are once again identical to those under section 206.[12]

(5) Material omissions from statement relating to company's affairs

Section 210 of the Act renders it an offence for any person who is a past

---

[10] *ibid.*, s.208(2).
[11] *ibid.*, ss.208(5), 430; Sched. 10.
[12] *ibid.*, ss.209(2), 430; Sched. 10.

or present officer (including a shadow director) of a company being wound up to make any material omission in any statement relating to the company's affairs. It is similarly an offence for such a person to have made a material omission in any such statement prior to the winding up, for example in the context of a receivership, administration procedure, or voluntary arrangement involving the company.[13] The onus of proving absence of intent to defraud is cast upon the accused, and the punishments in the case of conviction are identical to those under section 206.[14]

(6) False representations to creditors

It is an offence under section 211 of the Act for any past or present officer of the company, including a shadow director:

(a) to make any false representation or to commit any other fraud for the purpose of obtaining the consent of the company's creditors, or any of them, to an agreement with reference to the company's affairs or to the winding up; or
(b) to have made any false representation, or committed any other fraud, for that same purpose prior to the winding up.

In this instance, the onus of proving the existence of the requisite purpose is cast upon the prosecution. The same punishments are available as in the case of section 206, discussed above.[15]

(7) Criminal Liability for Fraudulent Trading

Section 458 of the Companies Act 1985 embodies a provision of general application which is not confined to situations where the company is in liquidation. It provides that if any business of the company is carried on with intent to defraud creditors of the company or creditors of any other person, or for any fraudulent purpose, every person who was knowingly a party to the carrying on of the business in that manner is guilty of a criminal offence. By Schedule 24 to the Companies Act, the punishments available in case of conviction on indictment are up to seven years' imprisonment, or an unlimited fine, or both.

(B) Civil Remedies and Penalties Applicable to Directors and Officers

Sections 212 to 217 inclusive of the Insolvency Act contain provisions

---

[13] *ibid.*, s.210(2). On the statement of affairs in winding up, see Chap. 21, *ante*; on the parallel requirements relating to voluntary arrangements and administration orders respectively, see Chaps. 14 and 15.
[14] *ibid.*, ss.210(4), (5), 430; Sched. 10.
[15] *ibid.*, ss.211(3), 430; Sched. 10.

under which civil liability may be imposed upon directors and officers of companies on account of their involvement in various types of malpractice.

(1) Summary remedy against delinquent directors and others

Section 212 of the Insolvency Act establishes a summary remedy against delinquent directors, and also against liquidators, administrators, administrative receivers, past or present officers of the company and other persons who are, or who have been, concerned or have taken part in the promotion, formation or management of the company. If in the course of the winding up of a company it appears that any of the persons just listed has misapplied or retained or become accountable for any money or other property of the company, or been guilty of any misfeasance or breach of any fiduciary or other duty in relation to the company, proceedings may be taken under section 212 against the person concerned.

The purpose of proceedings brought against a person under section 212 is to enable the court to examine the conduct of the person concerned, and thereupon to compel him to repay, restore or account for the money or property in whole or in part, plus interest at such rate as the court thinks just. A further consequence of such proceedings may be that the court will at its direction order the person to contribute a sum to the company's assets by way of compensation in respect of the misfeasance or breach of duty.[16] The right to make application under section 212 is conferred upon the official receiver or the liquidator, and upon any creditor or contributory of the company, subject to the limitation imposed by subsection (5) whereby a contributory is required to obtain the leave of the court before he may exercise the power to make an application. Nevertheless, subject to the obtaining of leave, a contributory may exercise the power to make application notwithstanding that he will not benefit from any order the court may make thereon.

It should be noted that there are no provisions within section 212 itself, nor in Schedule 9 to the Insolvency Act 1985, nor in Schedule 11 to the Insolvency Act 1986 (which contain transitional provisions relating to the implementation of the two Acts), to limit the effects of the section to acts of misfeasance or breaches of duty which occur after the section is brought into force. Hence, the summary remedy may be invoked against delinquent directors and others regardless of when the misconduct or misappropriation occurred. In some cases the liability of a director under section 212 may be concurrent with liability under some other provision, such as section 213 (fraudulent trading), 214 (wrongful trading), or 239 (giving of a preference), according to what has taken place.[17]

It is also to be emphasised that section 212 does not establish any new species of wrong, but merely provides a convenient and effective procedure for the recovery of money or property from a person who has

---

[16] *ibid.*, s.212(3).
[17] There are conflicting decisions as to whether or not cumulative liability may be imposed for violation of more than one provision, or whether "net" compensation should be determined: *cf. Re DKG Contractors Ltd* [1990] BCC 903; and *Re Purpoint Ltd* [1991] BCC 121.

committed a wrongful act according to established rules governing the conduct of company affairs. Examples of such acts include the making of secret profits by a promoter or director[18]; or the making of improper payments including the giving of a voidable (formerly a fraudulent) preference[19]; the sale of company assets at an undervalue[20]; the sale by a director of his own property to the company under circumstances which amount to a breach of fiduciary duty[21]; and for negligently causing loss to the company by failing to ensure that the company's premises were validly insured against fire.[22]

(2) Fraudulent Trading

Section 213 of the Act embodies the civil remedy in respect of fraudulent trading.[23] It is provided that if in the course of the winding up of the company it appears that any business of the company has been carried on with intent to defraud creditors of the company or creditors of any other person, or for any fraudulent purpose, the liquidator may apply to the court for an order under the section. The effect of the order is to declare that any persons who were knowingly parties to the fraudulent trading are to be liable to make such contributions (if any) to the company's assets as the court thinks proper. It is notable that this form of order does not involve the imposition of liability for the company's debts as such, but enables the court to form a judgment as to the extent to which it is appropriate to require each participant in a company's wrongful trading to contribute personally to the assets, so as to augment the funds available for distribution to unpaid creditors. Also to be noted is the use of the term "persons," which enables liability to be imposed upon a wider circle of participants in any such activity than merely the directors, officers and promoters of the company.

Of potential advantage from the standpoint of recovery of losses caused by wrongdoing is the fact that section 213 imposes no restriction in terms of the period of time prior to the company's winding up during which the events must have taken place in order for liability to be imposed.

There has been a lack of consistency over the years regarding the judicial approach to formulating the test of fraudulent conduct which is to be applied in cases falling under section 213 and its statutory antecedents. Prior to 1986 a somewhat indulgent approach, attributable to cases decided in the 1930s, was largely responsible for the civil remedy for fraudulent trading having become virtually a dormant provision in the Companies Act.[24] An element of judicial revisionism was manifested by

---

[18] *Gluckstein v. Barnes* [1900] A.C. 240 (H.L.).
[19] *Re Washington Diamond Mining Co.* [1893] 3 Ch. 95 (C.A.). For voidable preferences, see Chap. 26, *ante*.
[20] *Re Travellers' Chambers Ltd* (1895) 12 T.L.R. 529. For transactions at an undervalue, see Chap. 26, *ante*.
[21] *Gluckstein v. Barnes, supra*.
[22] *Re D'Jan of London Ltd* [1993] BCC 646.
[23] See also s.458 of the Companies Act 1985, discussed in (A)(7), *supra*.
[24] See *Re William C. Leitch Bros. Ltd* [1932] 2 Ch. 71; *Re Patrick and Lyon Ltd* [1933] Ch. 786; *Re White and Osmond (Parkstone) Ltd* (unreported, June 30, 1960). See the *Cork Report*, Cmnd. 8558, Chap. 44.

the Court of Appeal in 1984 in their judgment in *R. v. Grantham*,[25] in which the earlier cases were either distinguished or disapproved in the context of an appeal arising from the provision in what is now section 456 of the Companies Act 1985, imposing criminal liability for fraudulent trading.[26] The court there held that in order for a person to be guilty of the offence of fraudulent trading it is not necessary for the prosecution to prove that there was no reasonable prospect of the company's creditors *ever* receiving payment of their debts. Even if there was some hope or expectation in his mind that ultimately all debts would be paid, a person who takes part in the management of a company's affairs, and who obtains credit or further credit for the company when he knows there is no reason for thinking that funds will become available to pay the debt when it becomes due, or shortly thereafter, may be found guilty of the offence of "carrying on the company's affairs with intent to defraud creditors of the company".

Despite this more robust attitude signalled by the Court of Appeal with regard to the test of intent in relation to fraudulent trading, there have been further indications from rulings at first-instance that the previous tendency to look for evidence of "actual dishonesty involving, according to current notions of fair trading among commercial men, real moral blame"[27] has in certain cases remained embedded in the fabric of judicial thought processes even after the 1986 reforms.[28] Thus, in the absence of reasonably clear indications that the requisite intent to defraud was present at the time of the conduct in question, there remains a degree of uncertainty whether civil or criminal proceedings for fraudulent trading will prove to be successful in any given case. This reinforces the potential value of the alternative, civil remedy for wrongful trading discussed below.

Where civil proceedings for wrongful trading are brought by the liquidator under section 213, the current wording of the section is designed to make it clear that the application is brought on behalf of all creditors collectively, and not merely for the benefit of the actual victims themselves. The latter are therefore confined to receiving a pro rata dividend upon their aggregate claim for loss inflicted on them owing to the company's fraudulent behaviour.[29] In a case decided under the pre-1986 law it was held that where directors knew or had good grounds to suspect that there would not be sufficient assets to pay creditors in full, the act of preferring a creditor did not amount to an intention to defraud other creditors destined to be left unpaid.[30]

---

[25] [1984] Q.B. 675.

[26] See *supra*, (A)(7).

[27] This is the often-quoted expression, employed by Maugham J. in *Re Patrick and Lyon Ltd* [1933] Ch. 786, at p. 790.

[28] See, *e.g. Re L. Todd (Swanscombe) Ltd* [1990] BCC 125 (Harman J.); *Re a Company (No. 001418 of 1988)* [1990] BCC 526 (Judge Bromley, Q.C.).

[29] This is the consequence of the drafting of s.213(2), whereby persons may be made liable to make contribution to "the company's *assets*" (emphasis added). Former provisions (*e.g.* s.332(1), Companies Act 1948) referred to the imposition of unlimited personal responsibility for "all or any of the *liabilities* of the company" (emphasis again added). *cf. Re Cyona Distributors Ltd* [1967] Ch. 889 (C.A.).

[30] *Re Sarflax Ltd* [1979] 1 All E.R. 529 (Oliver J.).

(3) Wrongful Trading

A completely new basis of civil liability was created by section 214 of the Insolvency Act, which introduced a new concept of responsibility for wrongful trading. The origins of this section lie in the analysis in Chapter 44 of the *Cork Report* of the shortcomings of the existing law imposing criminal and civil responsibility for fraudulent trading. The Insolvency Law Review Committee proposed that a new and broader concept of "wrongful trading" should be introduced to overcome the combined obstacles presented by the developed law of fraudulent trading, which render it extremely difficult for a liquidator to succeed in an application for the imposition of personal liability for fraudulent trading.

The terms of what ultimately became section 214 of the Insolvency Act 1986 generated a considerable amount of controversy at every stage of the Parliamentary progress of the Insolvency Bill of 1984–1985. In particular, the Government steadfastly resisted every attempt to include any statutory definition of wrongful trading. Various proposed provisions were tabled, either embodying or based upon the draft definition clause included in the *Cork Report* itself,[31] but all these amendments were defeated,[32] As a consequence, the courts have been left with wide discretionary powers with which to formulate principles of liability applicable to directors of failed companies.

The imposition of responsibility for wrongful trading takes place through an order of the court by which the winding up order was made or, in the case of a company undergoing voluntary liquidation, a court with jurisdiction to wind up the company. The right to make application to the court for an order under section 214 is limited to the liquidator, and may only be exercised in cases where the company has gone into insolvent liquidation.[33] The purpose of the liquidator's application is to invite the court to declare that a person who is or has been a director of the company is to be liable to make such contribution (if any) to the company's assets as the court thinks proper.[34]

The "moment of truth" test

The basis upon which a person may be made personally liable to contribute towards the assets of a company which has gone into insolvent liquidation are as follows: it must be determined that at some time before the commencement of the winding up, the person in question knew or ought to have concluded that there was *no reasonable prospect* that the company would avoid going into insolvent liquidation, and it must also be the case that the person against whom the application is made was a director or shadow director of the company at the time when the probability of the company's eventual insolvency was or ought to have

---

[31] Cmnd.8558, para. 1806.
[32] See *Hansard* H.L. Vol. 461. cols. 742–753. Vol. 462. cols. 37–48; H.C. Standing Committee E. June 6, 1985, cols. 218–233; H.C. Vol. 83, cols. 559–570.
[33] Insolvency Act 1986, s.214(1) (2)(a).
[34] *ibid.*, s.214(1).

been known.[35] Therefore, no liability for wrongful trading can be imposed upon any person who has ceased to be a director at a time before either he had, or any reasonably diligent person could have had, a knowledge of the company's ultimate destiny or an awareness of facts from which that destiny could have been deduced.

In principle therefore, a director's responsibility for a company's wrongful trading commences from the moment when he has either actual or constructive knowledge that there is no reasonable prospect of the company's avoiding insolvent liquidation. Although the concept of wrongful trading has not been given statutory definition, it is apparent that the essence of the activity consists of the company's continuing to trade, and to incur liabilities, after the time when it was known, or ought to have been realised, by the directors, that an insolvent liquidation was inevitable, or, at least, would appear to be probable to a reasonable person in the place of the director sought to be held liable. In principle, therefore, the liabilities incurred from that time onwards should form the basis of the court's calculation of the quantum of contribution to be exacted from each of the present or past directors from whom the privilege and immunity of limited liability is, in effect, withdrawn by virtue of section 214 of the Insolvency Act. It must be conceded however that there are no restrictive words in the drafting of section 214 itself to preclude the imposition of personal liability for debts of the company whensoever incurred: the court has an unfettered discretion in this matter.

In the first reported case to have been decided under the new provision, Knox J. declared himself to be of the view that section 214 is primarily compensatory rather than penal, but was careful to avoid any suggestion that limits should be placed upon the very wide discretion conferred by Parliament on the court. He did however state that:

> "Prima facie the appropriate amount that a director is declared to be liable to contribute is the amount by which the company's assets can be discerned to have been depleted by the director's conduct which caused the discretion under section 214(1) to arise."[36]

The test of knowledge

For the purpose of determining what facts a director ought to know or ascertain, and what conclusions he ought to reach, section 214(4) lays down the test of the facts which would be known or ascertained, and the conclusions which would be reached, by a reasonably diligent person having both:

---

[35] *ibid.*, s.214(2)(b), (c), together with subsections (7) and (9). For indications of the judicial approach towards the determination of the "moment of truth" in relation to individual directors, for the purposes of s.214(2)(b), see *Re Produce Marketing Consortium Ltd* (No. 2) [1989] BCLC 520; noted [1989] J.B.L. 188–190, also discussed by Drake in [1989] J.B.L. 474 at pp. 487–490; *Re DKG Contractors Ltd* [1990] BCC 903; *Re Purpoint Ltd* [1991] BCC 121; *Re Sherborne Associates Ltd* [1995] BCC 40.

[36] *Re Produce Marketing Consortium Ltd* (No. 2) (*supra*) [1989] BCLC at p. 553.

(a) the general knowledge, skill and experience that may reasonably be expected of a person carrying out the same functions as are carried out by that director in relation to the company; and
(b) the general knowledge, skill and experience that that director has.

It is further provided by subsection (5) that the functions carried out by a director shall, for this purpose, be taken to include any functions which he does not carry out but which have been entrusted to him. The court is thus required to arrive at a conclusion as to the appropriate conduct and acumen of an hypothetical person assuming him to have possessed in combination the levels of general knowledge, skill and experience which the director in question subjectively did possess and which objectively he ought to have possessed in view of the position held. Therefore a director cannot derive any advantage from the fact that his personal qualities are inferior to those which may reasonably be expected of a director entrusted with the functions which actually repose in him, while at the same time a director who possesses above-average levels of knowledge, skill or experience will fall to be judged according to a commensurately higher standard. Above all, it will be impossible for any director to escape responsibility for the company's activities either because he conveniently neglected to ascertain the truth about the company's position, or because he honestly, but unreasonably, believed that the company would somehow avoid insolvency.

Defence to liability

Section 214(3) establishes a ground of defence for a director against whom a declaration of responsibility for a company's wrongful trading might otherwise be made. This subsection precludes the making of such a declaration in respect of any person if the court is satisfied that after the time when he became actually or constructively aware that the company was destined to undergo insolvent liquidation he took every step with a view to minimising the potential loss to the company's creditors as (assuming him to have known that there was no reasonable prospect that the company would avoid going into insolvent liquidation) he ought to have taken. Once again, subsection (4) requires the court to employ the test of the behaviour of a reasonably diligent person in deciding what were the steps which the director in question ought to have taken subsequent to the time established under the terms of subsection (2)(b). The same combined measure of the knowledge, skill and experience subjectively possessed by the director, and the objectively-determined requirements with regard to these three attributes which such a director may reasonably be expected to possess, again ensures that no director can successfully plead his personal inadequacies, or Micawberian optimism, as an exonerating reason for failure to take the steps which ought to have been taken. Thus, it will be relevant to ascertain whether, for example, the director in question consistently sought to persuade his fellow directors that the company should make application for an administration order, or should seek in some other way to engage its creditors in consultations about the possible course to pursue. A director may escape responsibility for wrongful trading, providing he has behaved both honestly and in a sound, businesslike manner in an effort to minimise the potential loss to creditors. So, too, may a "company doctor" who is taken onto the board when the company is manifestly *in extremis*, provided that his efforts to pull the company around are constantly addressed to the need to ensure that no step is taken which could result in a greater loss to creditors than that which they are already destined to suffer in consequence of the existing plight of the company.

Disqualification of directors

In addition to the imposition of personal liability upon present or former directors in accordance with the provisions of section 214 of the Insolvency Act, the court is further empowered by section 10 of the Company Directors Disqualification Act 1986 to make a disqualification order against any director who is so ordered to make a contribution to the company's assets.[37] The same power is exercisable in relation to a director found to have been party to fraudulent trading in proceedings brought under section 213 of the Insolvency Act.[38]

The court may make a disqualification order under section 10 of the Disqualification Act of its own motion and initiative, whether or not an application for such an order is made by any person eligible to do so. Therefore, although a liquidator other than the official receiver (who may only act in such matters upon the direction of the Secretary of State) does not have standing to make a direct application for a disqualification order under sections 6 and 7 of the Disqualification Act, the liquidator's application under section 213 or under section 214 of the Insolvency Act for a declaration of responsibility for fraudulent or wrongful trading (as the case may be), may indirectly lead to the making of a disqualification order against any director on whom such responsibility is imposed by the court.

(4) Restriction on the re-use of company names

Section 216 of the Insolvency Act is designed to tackle head on the phenomenon of the Phoenix syndrome[39] in its most blatant form, whereby a new company is created to carry on basically the same business, under the same coterie of directors, but under a slightly modified company name. Section 216 utilises the concept somewhat akin to 'guilt by association', whereby all persons who are or who have been directors or shadow directors of a company within the period of 12 months ending with the day before it goes into insolvent liquidation are, in a sense, contaminated by their connection with any name by which the failed company was known in that period of 12 months. Such a name is for this purpose termed a

---

[37] For disqualification orders, see section C, *infra*.
[38] See para. (ii) *supra*, in this section.
[39] See Chap. 19, *ante*, p. 500.

'prohibited name' in relation to the persons thus contaminated, and the concept of the 'prohibited name' also attaches to any other company name which is so similar to that borne by the failed company as to suggest an association with that company.[40] During the period of five years from the day on which the failed company went into liquidation it is a criminal offence of strict liability for any person to whom section 216 applies to be a director of, or to be in any way directly or indirectly involved with a company that is known by a prohibited name, or to be in any way involved with a business carried on under a prohibited name otherwise than by a company.[41] The only ways in which a person who is caught by the provisions of section 216 may avoid committing an offence through association with a company or business known by what is for him a prohibited name is either to obtain the prior leave of the court for this purpose, as section 216(3) provides, or alternatively to be sure that his case falls exactly within one of the three so-called 'excepted cases' which have been prescribed in the Insolvency Rules, and which enable a person to act without the leave of the court.[42]

The first excepted case (rule 4.228) arises where the office holder transfers the business of the failed company, or its assets, to a successor company one or more of the directors of which is or was formerly a member of the board of the failed company. An example of such a case would be a "management buy-out" concluded with the liquidator. In such cases rule 4.228 prescribes the procedure which must be followed, involving the giving of notice to all creditors of the insolvent company regarding the nature and circumstances of the transaction. If the successor company has effectively given notice under the rule, a person to whom section 216 applies and who has been named in the notice may act in relation to the successor company without committing an offence under section 216, notwithstanding that he has not the leave of the court to do so.

The second excepted case arises under rule 4.229,[43] and is essentially designed to cure the case where a person has acted as a director of a company with a prohibited name, and has accordingly contravened section 216, albeit he would have been granted leave by the court had an application for this purpose been made in time. An example would be where a person is already a director of two companies with closely similar names at the time when one of the companies goes into insolvent liquidation. Even where there are no attendant circumstances which would justify the refusal of leave to continue as a director of the surviving company, the person concerned will commit an offence under section 216(3) unless he is able to apply for and obtain leave of the court before the day on which the liquidating company goes into liquidation. The patent injustice, not to say absurdity, of such a state of affairs is capable of being averted by means of rule 4.229, whereby a person to whom section 216 applies will avoid committing an offence in these circumstances, provided that he applies to the court for leave to act in relation to the surviving

---

[40] Insolvency Act 1986, s.216(2).
[41] Insolvency Act 1986, s.216(3).
[42] Insolvency Rules 1986, rr. 4.228–4.230, as amended by (S.I. 1987, No. 1919).
[43] As substituted by (S.I. 1987, No. 1917).

company not later than seven days from the date on which the failed company went into liquidation, and provided also that leave is granted by the court not later than six weeks from that date.

The third excepted case is established by Rule 4.230, which provides that the court's leave under section 216 is not required where the company which is known by a prohibited name fulfils two express conditions:

   (a) it has been known by that name for the whole of the period of 12 months ending with the day before the liquidating company went into liquidation; and
   (b) it has not at any time within those 12 months been dormant within the meaning of section 252(5) of the Companies Act 1985.

This provision thus caters for cases where genuine businesses have been carried on on a group basis, with two or more of the companies concerned bearing closely similar names. The insolvent demise of one company within the group does not have the consequence that the directors must all either resign or seek authorisation from the court in order to carry on acting in relation to the surviving companies. On the other hand, the rule has been designed to prevent those directors who possess some degree of foresight from too easily evading the effects of section 216 by creating a dormant successor company ('a Phoenix in waiting') some time in advance of the expected date of the putting into liquidation of a company which is manifestly destined to fail at some time in the future.

Where leave of the court is applied for, the court will be concerned to assure itself that the transaction, under which the former director is to be associated with a company bearing a prohibited name, is essentially bona fide in nature. A further matter, which may be addressed by the imposition of specific conditions under which leave is granted, is the creation of adequate safeguards for the protection of the public, such as the maintenance of a proper capital base, and effective financial monitoring procedures.[44]

The consequences of contravention of section 216 are twofold. First, a criminal offence is committed by a person who acts in contravention of the section, punishable by imprisonment or a fine or both.[45] Secondly, section 217 imposes personal liability for company debts as a further consequence of contravention of section 216.[46] Section 217 deprives two kinds of person of the privileges normally associated with limited liability, and renders them personally liable for the 'relevant debts' of the company in relation to which they acted in a prohibited manner. The liability is cast upon the person who actually contravenes section 216 itself, and also upon any person who is involved in the management of the company and who acts or is willing to act on instructions given without leave of the court by a person

---

[44] cf. *Re Bonus Breaks Ltd* [1991] BCC 546.
[45] Insolvency Act 1986, ss.216(4), 430; Sched. 10. The punishments prescribed are: for conviction on indictment, up to two years' imprisonment or an unlimited fine, or both; for summary conviction, up to six months' imprisonment or a fine of up to £2,000, or both.
[46] cf. *Thorne v. Silverleaf* [1994] BCC 109 (C.A.).

Civil Remedies and Penalties

he knows at that time to be in contravention of section 216 in relation to the company. It should be noted that the 'secondary' liability of other persons is only incurred upon proof of the requisite knowledge on their part, but an important provision bearing upon the burden of proof in such cases is supplied by section 217(5), whereby a person who has at any time acted on instructions given without leave of the court by a person whom he knew to be in contravention of section 216 is presumed, unless he proves to the contrary, to have been willing at any time thereafter to act on any instructions given by that person. The definition of 'relevant debt' for the purpose of section 217 is supplied by section 217(3): in the case of the primary offender they are those debts and liabilities incurred by the company at a time when he was involved in its management, and in the case of a person 'secondarily' liable they are those incurred at a time when that person was acting or was willing to act on instructions given by the primary offender.

(C) Prosecution of Delinquent Officers and Members; Disqualification of Directors

(1) Prosecution of offenders

Attention was drawn by the *Cork Report*[47] to the need to ensure that the sanctions laid down by the law were actually applied in practice through the bringing of properly prepared prosecutions. In this way, a more effective deterrent is provided against delinquent behaviour on the part of those in charge of companies. Section 218 of the Insolvency Act deals with the procedure for prosecuting officers and members of companies being wound up. If it appears that any past or present officer, or any member, of the company has been guilty of an offence in relation to the company for which he is criminally liable, the court may direct the liquidator to refer the matter to the prosecuting authority. The court may give such direction upon the application of a person interested in the winding up, or of its own motion.[48]

Obligations are also laid upon the liquidator in every winding up (except where the official receiver is so acting) to report the discovery of evidence that any officer or member of the company has committed any criminal offence in relation to the company. In the case of a compulsory winding up, the liquidator must report the matter to the official receiver, and in the case of a voluntary winding up he must report the matter to the prosecuting authority and furnish that authority with further information, and allow access to documents, as required.[49]

Further provisions in section 218 are designed to produce a

---

[47] Cmnd. 8558, Chap. 48.
[48] Insolvency Act 1986, s.218(1). In England and Wales, "prosecuting authority" means the Director of Public Prosecutions: s.218(2)(a).
[49] *ibid.*, s.218(3), (4). The court may issue directions to a voluntary liquidator to report in the required manner, where the court is made aware of relevant facts which the liquidator has omitted to report as required: s.218(6).

co-ordinated flow of information between the prosecuting authority and the Department of Trade and Industry, so that the Secretary of State may further utilise his powers of investigation through the appointment of inspectors under sections 431 or 432 of the Companies Act 1985.[50] It is also made the duty of the liquidator and every officer and agent of the company past and present (other than any person who is actually accused of an offence) to give to the prosecuting authority or the Secretary of State all practicable assistance in connection with any criminal proceedings which are instituted by either of them.[51] For this purpose, the term "agent" includes any banker or solicitor of the company and any person employed by the company as auditor, whether that person is or is not an officer of the company.[52] Failure by any person to give such assistance as he is required by law to give may be met by the issue of a formal direction from the court to comply with the law's requirements, and in the case of non-compliance by a liquidator the court may direct that the costs shall be borne by him personally.[53]

(2) Disqualification of Directors

In Chapter 45 of the *Cork Report* a powerful case was advanced for the reform and strengthening of the court's powers of disqualification in cases where directors have shown themselves to be unfit to enjoy the privileges of limited liability. The application of more stringent standards to the conduct of company directors could not but enhance the general level of protection for the commercial community, and for the public at large, in their dealings with companies. The new legislative provisions concerning directors' disqualification are consolidated in the Company Directors Disqualification Act 1986 (hereafter, the Disqualification Act).[54] The original clause 7 of the Insolvency Bill 1984, from which the provisions currently contained in section 6 of the Disqualification Act finally evolved, was the most controversial provision in the Bill and underwent considerable alteration throughout all parliamentary stages.[55] The effects of section 6, and related sections applicable in cases of insolvency, will now be considered.

Section 1 of the Disqualification Act defines a disqualification order as one made by the court against a person whereby, for the period the order remains in force, that person may not, without the leave of the court,

    (a) be a director of a company; or
    (b) be a liquidator or administrator of a company; or

---

[50] *ibid.*, s.218(5).
[51] *ibid.*, s.219(3).
[52] *ibid.*
[53] *ibid.*, s.219(4).
[54] See ss.6–10, 15 and Sched. 1, The Disqualification Act is signified in footnotes below by the initials "C.D.D.A."
[55] For the original governmental proposals on disqualification, see the *White Paper* (Cmnd. 9175), paras. 12–14 and 46–51 inclusive. For discussion of the vicissitudes of the process of enactment of the relevant provisions, see Fletcher [1989] J.B.L. 365; also [1985] J.B.L. 1–4, 95–96, and 483–485.

(c) be a receiver or manager of a company's property; or
(d) in any way, either directly or indirectly, be concerned or take part in the promotion, formation, or management of a company.[56]

Disqualification for Unfitness

Section 6 of the Disqualification Act imposes upon the court a duty to disqualify any director of an insolvent company whom it finds to be unfit to be concerned in the management of a company. It is important to appreciate that, although the terms in which section 6 is drafted give rise to a mandatory obligation to disqualify, this is preconditional upon the court forming a judgment about the unfitness of the person concerned, based upon an appraisal of his conduct.[57] Thus, for disqualification to become obligatory, the court must be satisfied on two points. These are, first, that the person in question is or has been a director of a company which has at any time become insolvent (whether while he was a director or subsequently), and secondly, that his conduct as a director of that company (either taken alone or taken together with his conduct as a director of any other company or companies) makes him unfit to be concerned in the management of a company.[58] It is notable that, where reference is made to the person's conduct in relation to any other company, there is no requirement that that company also should be, or should have become, insolvent.

For the purposes of establishing the first precondition mentioned above, section 6(2) states that a company becomes insolvent if:

(a) the company goes into liquidation at a time when its assets are insufficient for the payment of its debts and other liabilities and the expenses of the winding up; or
(b) an administration order is made in relation to the company; or
(c) an administrative receiver of the company is appointed.

It is also specified that in the assessment of the conduct of the director whose disqualification is under consideration, account may be taken of his conduct in relation to any matter connected with or arising out of the liquidation. It is also relevant to note that the definition of "director" for this purpose includes a shadow director.[59]

By virtue of section 9(1) of the Disqualification Act, where it falls to a court to determine whether a person's conduct as a director or shadow director of a particular company or companies makes him unfit to be

---

[56] C.D.D.A., s.1(1). The nature of the mandatory requirement imposed by s.6 was analysed in detail by the Court of Appeal in *Secretary of State for Trade and Industry v. Gray* [1995] BCC 554.
[57] See C.D.D.A., s.6(1).
[58] *ibid.*
[59] *ibid.*, s.6(3), "Shadow director" is defined in s.741 of the Companies Act 1985.

concerned in the management of a company, the court must have regard to the matters mentioned in Schedule 1 to the Act. Part I of the schedule lists matters which are to be taken into account in all instances, while Part II lists matters which are to be taken into account where the company in question has become insolvent. The provisions of Schedule 1 (as amended)[60] are as follows:

MATTERS FOR DETERMINING UNFITNESS OF DIRECTORS

PART I

Matters Applicable in all Cases

(1) Any misfeasance or breach of any fiduciary or other duty by the director in relation to the company.
(2) Any misapplication or retention by the director of, or any conduct by the director giving rise to an obligation to account for, any money or other property of the company.
(3) The extent of the director's responsibility for the company entering into any transaction liable to be set aside under Part XVI of the Insolvency Act (provisions against debt avoidance).
(4) The extent of the director's responsibility for any failure by the company to comply with any of the following provisions of the Companies Act, namely—
  (a) section 221 (companies to keep accounting records);
  (b) section 222 (where and for how long records to be kept);
  (c) section 288 (register of directors and secretaries);
  (d) section 352 (obligation to keep and enter up register of members);
  (e) section 353 (location of register of members);
  (f) section 363 (company's duty to make annual returns); and

---

[60] Sched. 1 was amended by the Companies Act 1989, ss.23, 139(4) and Sched. 10, para. 35(1), (3).

(h) sections 399 and 415 (company's duty to register charges it creates).
(5) The extent of the director's responsibility for any failure by the directors of the company to comply with (a) section 226 or 227 of the Companies Act (duty to prepare annual accounts) or (b) section 233 of that Act (approval and signature of accounts).

Part II

Matters Applicable where Company has become Insolvent

(6) The extent of the director's responsibility for the causes of the company becoming insolvent.
(7) The extent of the director's responsibility for any failure by the company to supply any goods or services which have been paid for (in whole or in part).
(8) The extent of the director's responsibility for the company entering into any transaction or giving any preference, being a transaction or preference—
   (a) liable to be set aside under section 127 or sections 238 to 240 of the Insolvency Act, or
   (b) challengeable under section 242 or 243 of that Act or under any rule of law in Scotland.
(9) The extent of the director's responsibility for any failure by the directors of the company to comply with section 98 of the Insolvency Act (duty to call creditors' meeting in creditors' voluntary winding up).
(10) Any failure by the director to comply with any obligation imposed on him by or under any of the following provisions of the Insolvency Act—
   (a) section 22 (company's statement of affairs in administration);
   (b) section 47 (statement of affairs to administrative receiver);
   (c) section 66 (statement of affairs in Scottish receivership);
   (d) section 99 (directors' duty to attend meeting; statement of affairs in creditors' voluntary winding up);
   (e) section 131 (statement of affairs in winding up by the court);
   (f) section 234 (duty of any one with company property to deliver it up);
   (g) section 235 (duty to co-operate with liquidator, *etc.*).

Length of period of Disqualification; Evaluation of Directors' Conduct

Where the court forms the requisite conclusion as to the director's unfitness, section 6(4) imposes a minimum period of two years, and a maximum period of 15 years, for which the disqualification is to operate. Accordingly, considerable importance attaches to the development by the courts of clear indications, first, of the interpretative approach which they will adopt with regard to the provisions of Schedule 1, and to the concept of "unfitness" in section 6, and secondly, of the policy which they will pursue in selecting the period of disqualification, within the prescribed limits, according to the seriousness of the individual case.[61] It must be acknowledged that the canons of acceptable and unacceptable behaviour—in so far as these can be derived from the judicial pronouncements accompanying reported decisions—are neither defined nor deployed with the degree of clarity and consistency which is surely indispensable to the satisfactory operation of this vital element of insolvency law. In cases where the courts have been exercising powers of disqualification of a discretionary character, conferred under separate provisions of former or current legislation,[62] there have been occasions when a somewhat surprising degree of indulgence has been accorded towards directors whose defaults were judicially recognised as having been of a serious nature. Thus, even where there was persistent default in performing the obligations imposed on directors by the Companies Act with regard to the filing of documents, returns and accounts, the courts are capable at times of finding extenuating reasons for concluding that no disqualification order would be made.[63]

The notable feature of the disqualification process applicable to directors of insolvent companies under the freshly devised provisions of section 6 of the Company Directors Disqualification Act 1986,[64] is the mandatory nature of the court's duty to make a disqualification order in any case where a finding of unfitness is reached. Even though the court may be of the view that there is no *present* propensity on the part of the director to repeat past misdeeds, and that there is consequently no need to exclude that person from company management for the sake of protecting the public in the immediate future, the court has no discretion to exercise, once it has satisfied itself that the director's *past* conduct in relation to an insolvent company (either taken alone or taken in conjunction with his conduct as a director of any other company) amounts to a demonstration

---

[61] For reviews of the evolving case law see, *e.g.* Graham (1988) 1 Insolvency Intelligence 1–3; Dine (1988) 9 Co. Law. 213; Birds (1989) 10 Co. Law. 21; Dine [1994] J.B.L. 325. See L.S. Sealy, *Disqualification and Personal Liability of Directors* (4th ed.) for a thorough treatment of the subject.

[62] *e.g.* Companies Act 1948, s.188 (repealed), re-enacted as ss.295–302 of the Companies Act 1985 (repealed); C.D.D.A. 1986, ss.1–5, 8–11.

[63] *Re Civica Investments Ltd* [1983] BCLC 456; *Re Arctic Engineering Ltd (No. 2)* [1986] 1 W.L.R. 686; [1986] 2 All E.R. 346. *cf. Re Bath Glass Ltd* (1988) 4 BCC 130.

[64] *cf.* the repealed provision in s.300 of the Companies Act 1985, which was effectively replaced by s.6 C.D.D.A., where the court had a discretion whether to make a disqualification order.

of unfitness: section 6(1) unequivocally states that the court "shall" make a disqualification order. The Court of Appeal have affirmed that it was the intention of Parliament in enacting this provision to ensure that everyone whose conduct has fallen below the appropriate standard is disqualified for at least two years, irrespective of whether the court thinks it is currently necessary to do so.[65]

The above construction of the role and duty of the court leaves open the crucial question of the judicial standards deployed with regard to the determination of unfitness in a given case. While necessarily having regard to the matters mentioned in Schedule 1 to the Disqualification Act (reproduced above), as is required by section 9(1) of that Act, different judges have at times revealed a divergence of thinking as to the relative seriousness, as indicia of unfitness, of different types of conduct typically encountered in cases of this kind. One feature which is frequently present during the course of a company's financial decline is that various forms of fiscal and social security liabilities either fall into arrears or are not paid at all. The failure to pay Crown debts, while the company continues to trade, is a matter which is sometimes singled out for special censure by certain judges, as being essentially more culpable than the failure to pay commercial debts. The ancillary argument is sometimes advanced that the Crown is "an involuntary creditor" with respect to such debts and cannot protect itself in the same way as a creditor for unpaid goods or services.[66] A contrary approach was advanced by Hoffmann J. in *Re Dawson Print Group Ltd*,[67] where it was suggested that in the commercial world itself a failure to pay Crown debts was not regarded as an especially immoral breach of duty such as to lead, in itself, to the conclusion of unfitness. This pronouncement was made in the course of a judgment in which the wider question of the "test of culpability" to be applied in determining unfitness was also explored at some length. The learned judge advocated a test which, it is submitted, amounts to an intuitive and (ultimately) vague formulation of the standards to be applied, namely that there must be an infringement of commercial morality, or some really gross incompetence which persuades the court that it would be a danger to the public if that person were allowed to continue to be involved in the management of companies.

Both the general approach expressed by the "commercial morality" test formulated by Hoffmann J., and the particular view adopted by that judge in relation to the matter of non-payment of Crown debts, were expressly approved by the Court of Appeal in *Re Sevenoaks Stationers (Retail) Ltd*,[68] where it was stressed that each case must be closely assessed on its intrinsic merits so as to establish what was the significance of the non-payment in

---

[65] *Secretary of State for Trade and Industry v. Gray* [1995] BCC 554.
[66] *Re Stanford Services Ltd* [1987] BCLC 607; (1987) 3 BCC 326 (Vinelott, J.); *Re Lo-Line Electric Motors Ltd* [1988] Ch. 477 (Browne-Wilkinson, V.-C.); *Re Churchill Hotel (Plymouth) Ltd* (1988) 4 BCC 112 (Peter Gibson, J.); *Re Wedgecraft Ltd* (unreported, March 7, 1986) (Harman, J.).
[67] (1987) 3 BCC 322; [1987] BCLC 601.
[68] [1990] 3 W.L.R. 1165; [1991] 3 All E.R. 578; [1990] BCC 765 (Dillon, Butler-Sloss and Staughton, L.JJ.).

the context of the case. In principle, however, such non-payments could not "automatically" be treated as evidence of unfitness.[69] Significantly, in the case itself a disqualification of five years' duration was ultimately imposed. This reflected the serious view taken of the way in which the director had allowed the affairs of five separate companies to become hopelessly muddled and intertwined, and his failure to keep adequate records and accounts. There was no suggestion that the director had been "lining his own pockets" in the course of managing the companies, and indeed he had personally lost a substantial sum of money in consequence of their collapse. As Dillon, L.J. observed: "His trouble is not dishonesty, but incompetence or negligence in a very marked degree and that is enough to render him unfit."[70] In cases where there are more serious elements of corrupt or abusive conduct, such as fraudulent trading or the perpetration of so-called "Phoenix" operations,[71] not only will the court experience less difficulty in arriving at a determination of unfitness but also it is likely to reflect the degree of social harm posed by such behaviour when selecting the number of years for which the disqualification order will be in force. This was also the subject of guidance delivered by the Court of Appeal in *Re Sevenoaks Stationers (Retail) Ltd*,[72] where the following, three-tier approach was endorsed:

(i) the "top bracket" of disqualification for periods over 10 years should be reserved for "particularly serious cases," including those where a director has already previously had a disqualification order made against him;
(ii) the "middle bracket" of disqualification for from six to 10 years should apply for "serious cases which do not merit the top bracket"; and
(iii) the minimum bracket of two to five years' disqualification should be applied where, "though disqualification is mandatory, the case is, relatively, not very serious."[73]

The foregoing directives, while logically appropriate to the task in hand, do not seem to offer any much-needed indication as to the material factors which should finally distinguish cases from one another in terms of the degree of seriousness disclosed by their facts. The trial court is left with the responsibility of forming a view with regard to the relative seriousness of what has transpired, measured against a conception of "commercial morality" which is itself susceptible to subtle variations in interpretation, as the history of recent case law serves to show.

---

[69] [1991] 3 All E.R. at pp. 587–590, *per* Dillon, L.J. (the entire passage is instructive).
[70] *ibid.*, at p. 590.
[71] See, *e.g. Re Travel Mondial Ltd* [1991] BCC 224; *Re Swift 736 Ltd* [1993] BCC 312; *Re Keypack Homecare Ltd. (No. 2)* [1990] BCC 117; *Re Synthetic Technology Ltd., Secretary of State for Trade and Industry v. Joiner* [1993] BCC 549.
[72] *supra*, n. 68.
[73] [1991] 3 All E.R. at pp. 581–582, *per* Dillon, L.J.

Applications for Disqualification

Eligibility to make application to the court for a disqualification order is controlled by section 7 of the Disqualification Act. This section is designed to ensure that a centralised control is maintained over the making of all applications for a disqualification order under section 6. In principle, the right to make such applications is confined to the Secretary of State, in whose name such application may be made by virtue of section 7(1)(a). However, in the case of a person who is or has been a director of a company which is being wound up by the court in England and Wales, section 7(1)(b) enables the Secretary of State to direct the official receiver to make application for a disqualification order.

In order that the requisite information may be transmitted to the Department of Trade and Industry, so as to enable officials there to decide, on behalf of the Secretary of State and in his name, whether to apply for a disqualification order, a statutory obligation is cast upon every office holder in insolvency proceedings relating to companies to report forthwith to the Secretary of State if it appears that the ingredients of section 6(1) are satisfied as respects any director of the company concerned.[74]

An important time limit for the bringing of proceedings for disqualification is imposed by section 7(2). Except with the leave of the court, an application for the making of a disqualification order under section 6 against any person may not be made after the end of two years beginning with the day on which the company of which that person is or has been a director became insolvent.[75] It has been apparent since the enactment of the Disqualification Act that the limitation period of two years fixed by section 7(2) was unrealistically short, in view of the complexity of many of the cases in which directoral misconduct is most likely to have occurred. The prospect that the time limit may well expire before it is administratively possible to commence disqualification proceedings inevitably diminishes the capability of this potential sanction to serve as an effective deterrent against delinquent behaviour. No guidelines are furnished by section 7(2) as to the criteria on which the court is to base any decision to grant leave for an application for a disqualification order to be made after the end of the two-year period. In practice, the courts have developed a number of appropriate criteria, whose tendency is to limit the scope for mounting an out-of-time application unless the case for allowing it is strong and compelling. Factors to which the court will have regard are:

(i) the length of the delay;
(ii) the reasons for the delay;
(iii) the strength of the case against the director; and

---

[74] C.D.D.A., s.7(3), (4). See also the Insolvent Companies (Disqualification of Unfit Directors) (Proceedings) Rules 1987 (S.I. 1987, No. 2023), and the Insolvent Companies (Reports on Conduct of Directors) (No. 2) Rules 1986, (S.I. 1986, No. 2134).

[75] See C.D.D.A., s.6(2), described *supra*, for the meaning of the expression "becomes insolvent."

(iv) the degree of prejudice caused to the director by the delay.[76]

In assessing the factor of delay, and the reasons thereof, the court will distinguish between unexpected delays for which the applicant was not responsible, such as those caused by prevarication on the part of the director himself, and delays which cannot be so attributed and hence must be allowed for by the Secretary of State in framing operational procedures capable of being completed within the two-year period available for the purpose.[77] The Secretary of State cannot assume that any delay for which he is not responsible will automatically be added to the end of the two-year period by the court upon mere request.[78]

The possibility for the court to make a disqualification order of up to 15 years' duration, under section 10 of the Disqualification Act, against persons found liable for participation in fraudulent or wrongful trading, was considered earlier in this chapter.[79]

Personal Liability for Company's Debts of Person who Acts while Disqualified; Criminal Penalties for Contravention of Disqualification

When a disqualification order is made against any person, and also where a person is an undischarged bankrupt,[80] potent sanctions are imposed by sections 13 and 15 of the Disqualification Act in the event of any contravention of the consequent disqualification from involvement in company management. In the first place, such contravention amounts to a criminal offence for which the person responsible is liable to be punished under the terms of section 13. The available punishments are: on conviction on indictment, up to two years' imprisonment, or an unlimited fine, or both; and on summary conviction, up to six months' imprisonment, or up to £5,000 fine, or both.[81] The absence of any reference to a mental element in the statutory provisions formulating the criminal offences of acting in contravention of a disqualification order, or while an undischarged bankrupt, have the consequence that these are offences of strict, or absolute, liability without any requirement of *mens rea*.[82]

In addition to any criminal penalty to be imposed for contravention of a disqualification order, section 15 imposes a formidable civil sanction, in

---

[76] *Re Probe Data Systems Ltd. (No. 3), Secretary of State v. Desai* [1992] BCC 110, 118 (C.A.); *Re Tasbian Ltd. (No. 3)* [1992] BCC 358 (C.A.); *Re Polly Peck International plc, Secretary of State v. Ellis (No. 2)* [1993] BCC 890, 894.
[77] *cf. Re Copecrest Ltd.* [1993] BCC 844, 850 (C.A.) at 852, *per* Hoffmann, L.J.
[78] *ibid.*
[79] *Supra*, p. 525.
[80] C.D.D.A., s.11.
[81] *ibid.*, s.13(a), (b). The amount of £5,000, being the amount prescribed as "the statutory maximum," may be varied by statutory instrument. See Criminal Justice Act 1991, s.17, and S.I. 1992 No. 333; and Magistrates Courts Act 1980, ss.32(9), 143; Interpretation Act 1978, s.5, Sched. 1.
[82] *R. v. Brockley* [1994] BCC 131.

the form of the forfeiture of the protection of limited liability by the person or persons concerned. The section provides that any person who contravenes a disqualification order relating to himself (or who is an undischarged bankrupt involved in company management), and also any person who is involved in the management of a company and who acts or is willing to act on instructions given without the leave of the court by a person whom he knows at that time to be the subject of a disqualification order, or to be an undischarged bankrupt, shall be personally liable for all the relevant debts of the company in relation to which he or they act.[83] For the purpose of section 15, the "relevant debts" of a company are, in the case of a disqualified person, such debts and other liabilities of the company as are incurred at a time when that person was involved in the management of the company, and, in the case of a person whose liability arises from his acting as the medium through which a disqualified person influences the management of a company, such debts and other liabilities of the company as are incurred at a time when that person was acting or was willing to act on instructions given by the disqualified person.[84] In the case of the latter form of liability, incurred through acting on the instructions of another, section 15(5) establishes a presumption that any person who has at any time acted on instructions given without leave of the court by a person whom he knew at that time to be the subject of a disqualification order, or to be an undischarged bankrupt, is to be presumed, unless the contrary is shown, to have been willing at any time thereafter to act on any instructions given by that person.

The working of the new law on disqualification

The insolvency law reforms of 1985–86 undoubtedly contemplated that the recasting of the provisions relating to the disqualification of directors of insolvent companies would have a major impact upon the conduct of company affairs, and upon the entire ethos of directoral behaviour. As such, they may be said to have formed a crucial part of the strategic approach embodied in the *Cork Report* recommendations. On the basis of the statistical evidence which has accumulated since 1987, it is questionable whether the new provisions have succeeded in producing their intended effect. Certainly, the annual figures for proceedings actually brought under section 6, and of disqualification orders actually made, are significantly lower than those anticipated, particularly when set in the context of the high levels of company insolvencies during the years 1989–1994.[85] A report on the work of the Insolvency Service Executive Agency in carrying out its functions concerning company director disqualification was published in October 1993.[86] The report, produced by the National Audit Office, noted that since the introduction of the new legislation there had been approximately 153,000 corporate insolvencies in Great Britain, with findings of elements of unfit conduct by directors in some 28,000

[83] *ibid.*, s.15(1).
[84] C.D.D.A., s.15(3).
[85] See the statistical information in Appendix III, *post*.
[86] House of Commons papers, October 18, 1993, No. 907 (HMSO).

cases. By March 31, 1993, some 2,900 applications for disqualification had been made, of which 1,700 resulted in disqualification orders. Among the findings and conclusions of the report were indications that the resources available to handle the workload generated by this area of the law's operation were not adequate to meet the demands to be expected in a period of rapidly increasing insolvencies. In its recommendation that the Agency should strive to improve the processing of cases, prioritising as necessary, to ensure that as many proceedings as possible are taken where it is in the public interest to secure disqualification, the report effectively concedes that a large proportion of cases where elements of misconduct are discovered will in practice result in no active proceedings being taken against those responsible, because of lack of resources to process the cases within the limited time allowed by section 7(2) of the Disqualification Act. Not only does this amount to an acknowledgement that extensive resources are being wastefully expended by the private sector insolvency practitioners in fulfilling their reporting responsibilities, and by the Insolvency Service in processing and evaluating this paperwork, but it transmits a most unfortunate signal to errant directors that they probably need not fear the prospect of use of the disqualification sanction against them, unless they infringe commercial morality in a particularly gross way.

It is submitted that modifications are necessary to the law, and to the regulatory practices, applicable to disqualification of directors. One sensible reform would be the extension of the time limit imposed by section 7(2), so as to correspond more with the realities of gathering and processing the requisite information to enable a sensible judgment to be arrived at on whether to make application for a disqualification order. Considerable improvement in the rate of evaluation of the evidence of conduct of directors could be achieved through devolving to the office-holder the judgmental function of deciding whether the elements disclosed by his own investigation and administration of the case were such as to make it appropriate, in the public interest, to submit a report to the Insolvency Service. In this way, a substantial reduction could be effected in the generation of paperwork to be processed on both sides of the reporting relationship. Admittedly, this would be achieved at some risk of loss of objectivity of appraisal, and of the broadened consciousness of national levels of conduct that results from a centralised point of vantage. On balance, however, it seems preferable to aim at the maximum efficiency in deployment of the scarce—and costly—human resources needed to operate the disqualification process, so as to combine the fullest degree of enforcement of the law's provisions where the public interest demands it, with the fullest degree of deterrence in relation to those who have already become aware that the odds against their escaping from the law's attentions have been considerably lengthened.[87]

---

[87] In Part 4 of the National Audit Office Report (*supra*, n. 86), the results of a commissioned survey of representative samples of company directors and insolvency practitioners reveal a substantial lack of awareness, on the part of the former, of the C.D.D.A. itself and its relevance to them personally and to their business, together with a general belief that the disqualification arrangements were of little effect as a deterrent to misconduct, or as a means of protecting the public (see figures 7–9 inclusive, at pp. 16–18 of the report).

Part III

International Insolvency

CHAPTER 28

GENERAL PROBLEMS, AND ISSUES OF PRINCIPLE

Introduction

The first two Parts of this book have dealt with the provisions of the domestic law of England and Wales, as applicable to personal and to corporate insolvency respectively. That is to say, the account of the law there given is based upon the assumption that the case raises questions of a purely internal character, and that there are no elements within it which give rise to the need to refer to, or apply, the law of any foreign country, nor which establish the possibility that a foreign insolvency proceeding may properly take place in relation to the debtor. In practice, however, it can readily happen that the personal circumstances of an individual, or the corporate affairs of a company, include significant elements of contact with jurisdictions outside England and Wales. In such cases, questions of private international law (also known as Conflict of Laws) are likely to be encountered, either with respect to the entire conduct of the insolvency proceedings, or at any rate with respect to certain aspects of them.

The typical questions which arise in cases of international insolvency—or "cross-border" insolvency, as it is nowadays coming to be called—exemplify the usual characteristics of the conflict of laws process. These are, first, whether the courts of a given country can legitimately exercise jurisdiction in the case; secondly, if so, what rules of law they are to apply, either in the form of specially formulated provisions of the law of the *forum* or, through the operation of a choice of law process, in the form of provisions belonging to some foreign system of law. The third question to be considered concerns the recognition by the law of one country of the validity and effects of insolvency proceedings which have taken place in another. A related problem is the extent to which, and the means by which, some form of cross-border collaboration or mutual assistance may operate between courts, or between office holders, located in different jurisdictions but acting in relation to one and the same insolvent debtor.

As well as raising practical problems of considerable complexity, the above questions also involve major issues of principle, whose resolution is as yet far from perfect or satisfactory. In the final chapter of this book, a brief account will be given of the efforts taking place in modern times to achieve international agreements whereby the problem of cross-border insolvencies may be dealt with in a principled, and yet practical, way. The current provisions of English private international law in relation to personal and corporate insolvency respectively are considered in Chapters 29 and 30. In the remainder of the present chapter, we shall examine the general nature of the topic of international insolvency from the English law point of view, together with the issues of theory and principle which have provided the basis for international debate about this subject.

General Problems Associated with Bankruptcies Containing International Elements

In the law of bankruptcy, just as in other areas of law, some consideration of the possible implications of a conflict of laws becomes necessary whenever a case contains significant international elements. Such elements here consist, typically, of the debtor's being personally connected with one or more foreign countries (whether through nationality, through domicile, through residence, or through the conduct of business); or through owning assets (whether movable or immovable) which are physically located abroad; or through owing liabilities to creditors who themselves belong to politically foreign countries; or through having incurred liabilities abroad (whether tortious, contractual or of any other nature) under circumstances such that liability is properly regulated by foreign law.

Several important questions may arise when insolvency is attended by the presence of foreign elements. These are, first, whether the courts of England and Wales may competently exercise jurisdiction over the debtor, and if so, what rules of choice of law are to be applied in the circumstances. Secondly, assuming that the debtor is amenable to the bankruptcy jurisdiction of the English courts, whether the courts of one or more foreign countries may simultaneously have competence to open proceedings, and if so with what consequences. Thirdly, in view of the possibility that a debtor's assets, and also his liabilities, may be connected with or governed by the laws of a variety of different countries, whether the orders and decisions of a court in one jurisdiction may be effective in relation to property, and also persons, not currently within the territorial jurisdiction of that court. These questions of the international effectiveness of the judgments of the English bankruptcy court, and correspondingly of the effects accorded at English law to the judgments of foreign courts in bankruptcy matters, arise not only in relation to the original judgment or order whereby a debtor is adjudicated bankrupt, but also in relation to all subsequent judicial determinations arising out of or relating to the bankruptcy, up to and including the granting of an order of discharge from bankruptcy.

General Problems Associated with Liquidations Containing International Elements

There is a far greater probability that significant international elements will be present in the insolvency of a company than in a majority of cases of personal insolvency. The scale of corporate enterprise, as compared to the scale of the personal affairs of most individuals, together with the very nature of commercial activity render it highly probable that the affairs of a failed company will be associated with more than one jurisdiction or system of law. Thus, a company formed in one jurisdiction may engage in trade or pursue other corporate activities in one or more other jurisdictions. Liabilities may be incurred, or assets owned or acquired, in countries outside the company's "home" jurisdiction. Questions may arise concerning the *situs* of debts due to or from the company, or even concerning the *situs* of the company's shares. The possibility that the company's affairs may be widely spread between different jurisdictions may render it difficult, if not impracticable, for the winding up of the company to be performed in a single set of proceedings centered in one place.[1]

The above factors inevitably militate against a policy of outright adherence to the twin principles of unity and universality of liquidation which are sometimes advocated as constituting an ideal—or at least an idealised—solution.[2] On the other hand, it is fully in accord with both principle and authority, so far as English law is concerned, to regard all questions concerning the creation, continuing existence, and ultimate dissolution of a company as being primarily governed by the law of the place in which that company has undergone formation.[3] Hence the courts of that country are considered to constitute the proper *forum* for proceedings to bring about the insolvent liquidation of the company, and English law will recognise the effectiveness of any resultant decree whereby the company is declared to be dissolved, and its legal personality terminated. However, a distinction is made between the recognition of a foreign judicial decision affecting the status of a company, and the recognition of a decision purporting to affect the title or destination of its assets, or to discharge any legal liabilities to which the company is a party.[4] In these matters the principle of universality does not currently form the basis of approach adopted by English law, and as a further consequence of this a situation can arise in which a company is regarded by English law as having been duly dissolved, while property formerly owned by the erstwhile company remains undistributed, and debts due from it remain unsatisfied. Therefore, the practical necessity arises under English law for a separate liquidation to take place, whereby the company, despite its

---

[1] For a striking example of such a case of intertwined corporate structures linking with multiple jurisdictions, see *Re Bank of Credit and Commerce International SA (No. 2)* [1992] BCC 715 (C.A.). See also *Re Maxwell Communications Corporation plc (No. 2), Barclays Bank plc v. Homan* [1992] BCC 757 (Hoffmann J.), affd. C.A. [1992] BCC 767.
[2] See *infra*, next section.
[3] See Chap. 30, *post*.
[4] *ibid.*, p. 758 *et seq.*

having been dissolved abroad (or alternatively, while foreign proceedings to bring about its dissolution are still in progress), may be wound up in England. By this means any assets situate within the jurisdiction of the English courts may be administered in accordance with the rules applicable in an English winding up.[5] Such proceedings inevitably constitute an exception to the principle of unity of liquidation. A further exception to the same principle is permitted, on the grounds of overall convenience and the securing of fair and equal treatment for all creditors, in cases where the insolvent company has substantial material connections (in the form of assets or liabilities, or some combination of both) with two or more separate countries. In such cases concurrent liquidations may be allowed to take place, although it is the policy of English law at least to seek to promote co-operation between the respective liquidators, wherever this is practicable.[6]

With regard to the broad principles of justice and policy applicable to liquidations of an international character, much of what has already been said earlier in this chapter in relation to personal insolvencies of this kind can be reaffirmed, *mutatis mutandis*. Thus, the basic questions which arise include whether jurisdiction can and should be exercised; what rules of choice of law are to be applied during the course of the ensuing proceedings; whether the English proceedings will be acknowledged internationally as producing valid effects in relation to the company itself, and also in relation to its assets and liabilities; and conversely, whether equivalent recognition may be accorded in England in relation to the effects of liquidations which have taken place abroad. However, given that a company is a notional entity whose existence is dependent upon the application of relevant rules of law, the international insolvency of companies presents both theoretical and practical problems of a special order, which currently preclude the application of the fully common rules and practices that are satisfactorily employed in the insolvency of legal and natural persons. In essence, the response of English private international law to the problems posed by company liquidations containing international elements is a pragmatic one, whereby adherence to pure tenets of principle is sometimes relinquished in order to achieve results which are more closely in accordance with notions of common sense, and the ensuring of fairness to the parties concerned.

Conflicts of Principles: Unity Versus Plurality; Universality Versus Territoriality

Leaving aside for one moment the particular rules of English law, or those of any other given system of law, it can be stated that two primary issues of principle have tended to predominate in doctrinal arguments concerned with international insolvency law. These are: whether there should be only one set of proceedings in relation to a given debtor, or

[5] *ibid.*, p. 736.
[6] *ibid.*, p. 765.

whether it is admissible that there may be several sets of proceedings; and whether it should be accepted that one set of proceedings is effective in every other jurisdiction of the world, or should be limited in effects merely to its country of origin. The first of these issues is generally called the "unity of bankruptcy versus plurality", while the second, and closely related, issue is known as the "universality of bankruptcy versus territoriality".

Diversity of National Insolvency Laws

The fact that the world is subdivided, juridically as well as politically speaking, into a great many distinct entities is the very *raison d'être* of the subject of conflict of laws. The many different systems of law, even though capable of undergoing a generalised classification into a relatively small number of legal "families", nevertheless differ from one another in numerous details, with the consequence that the actual venue for proceedings can not infrequently assume a crucial significance in relation to the interests of the various parties concerned. The variations between the different national laws governing bankruptcy and company liquidations pertain not merely to the substantive and procedural aspects of the insolvency law itself, but are indeed seen to manifest themselves even in relation to the very basic question of the assumption of jurisdiction in insolvency matters. Thus, it can happen that one and the same person may be found simultaneously to be amenable to the bankruptcy laws of more than one country, partly on account of the diversity and spread of his activities but partly also because of the variety of jurisdictional criteria resorted to by the various legal systems concerned.

The same proposition is equally true in the case of a company. Under such circumstances the possibility arises that bankruptcy or winding up proceedings involving the same debtor may take place concurrently in different jurisdictions. Although each of such proceedings may purport to take effect in relation to the totality of the debtor's property wheresoever situate, the customary, practical limitations upon the extra-territorial effectiveness of judicial determinations will be reinforced in this instance by the logical impossibility that two or more concurrent adjudications, or orders for winding up, could simultaneously enjoy such universality of effect. Numerous additional problems immediately suggest themselves, including the possibility that the location and dispersal of the debtor's assets, as between the various jurisdictions in which proceedings are opened, may prove to be inconveniently disproportionate in relation to the dispersal of the creditors, having regard to the respective *fora* in which the latter may most conveniently seek to prove for their debts. Furthermore, in the event that some assets, and some creditors, are to be found in other countries in which no insolvency proceedings are actually taking place, the first vital question will be which, if any, of the concurrent proceedings will command recognition under the laws of those various countries so that the assets which are located there may be successfully claimed by the trustee or liquidator appointed under the proceedings in question. Secondly, and in many ways just as important, there will arise the question of the standing accorded to creditors from these third countries under the various concurrent administrations: will they be allowed to participate *pari passu* with the local creditors belonging to the *forum concursus,* or will their claims be in some way postponed? To what extent will account be taken, in the course of any given insolvent administration, of the amounts already recovered by foreign creditors either by means of private acts of diligence effected in jurisdictions in which, for some reason, the title of the trustee or liquidator is not judicially recognised, or through the expedient of separately lodging proof for the same debt in the other, concurrent administrations taking place elsewhere?[7]

Need to Resolve the Prevailing State of Confusion

The present, unco-ordinated state of affairs has further unhappy ramifications both from the aspect of the inevitable duplication of effort, and hence wastage of resources, entailed by multiple administrations of the insolvent's remaining assets, and also from the aspect of the defeat of legitimate expectations of creditors, both secured and unsecured, who may discover that their legal (and financial) interests are adversely affected by the fact that one or more sets of proceedings are opened against their debtor in jurisdictions other than the one whose laws have formed the anticipated basis of their rights of recourse in the event of insolvency.

The foregoing difficulties, amongst others, have led some writers[8] to advocate the conclusion of an international convention giving effect to the related principles of unity and universality of bankruptcy in place of the status quo whereby, in practice, when a debtor's affairs happen to be distributed between several distinct jurisdictions, plural bankruptcies or liquidations are capable of occurring with the result that in almost all cases the territorial effectiveness of each set of proceedings is confined within the jurisdictional limits of the country in which they are opened. Ideally, it may be argued that there should be a uniform international practice in relation to the exercise of insolvency jurisdiction, so that any given debtor would be

---

[7] *cf.* Nadelmann, (1946) 11 Law and Contemp. Prob. 696; Nadelmann, *Conflict of Laws, International and Interstate* (1972) at p. 340 *et seq.*; Hanisch in I.F. Fletcher (Ed.), *Cross-Border Insolvency: Comparative Dimensions (The Aberystwyth Insolvency Papers)*(1990), pp. 192–204. See also Hanisch (1993) 2 International Insolvency Review 151.

[8] See Nadelmann (1944) 93 U. of Pa.L.Rev. 58; (1943–4) 5 U. of Tor.L.J. 324; (1961) 10 I.C.L.Q. 70; Hirsch (1970) C.D.E. 50; Ganshof (1971) C.D.E. 146. See also Blom-Cooper, *Bankruptcy in Private International Law* (1954), also published in (1955) 4 I.C.L.Q. 170; Dalhuisen, *International Insolvency and Bankruptcy* (1980), Vol. I, Section 2.02(3); Trochu, *Conflits de lois et conflits de juridictions en matière de faillite* (1967, Paris), especially at pp. 1–65; Chaps. by Lipstein and by Dobson in I.F. Fletcher, *op. cit. supra* n. 7, at pp. 223–236 and 237–262 respectively; Chap. by Prior in H. Rajak (Ed.) *Insolvency Law Theory and Practice* (1993) at pp. 226–228. For the texts of bilateral conventions currently in force relating to bankruptcy, see Dalhuisen, *op. cit.,* Vol. II; for the texts of multilateral treaties incorporating bankruptcy provisions, see 155 L.N.T.S. (1935) 116 (Scandinavian Bankruptcy Convention of 1933); (1943) 37 A.J.I.L., Supp., at p. 138 (Montevideo Treaties of 1889–1939); 86 L.N.T.S. (1929) 112 (Havana Treaty of 1928, also known as the "Code Bustamante"). For previous, unsuccessful attempts to conclude a Bankruptcy Convention within the Hague Conference on Private International Law, see Actes de la 5e Conférence de d.i.p. (The Hague, 1925) and also Actes de la 6e Conférence (The Hague, 1928). See generally, Chap. 31, *post.*

amenable to the jurisdiction of only one country, or at most of a very restricted number of countries. The opening of insolvency proceedings in the country in question (or in any one of the countries in question, where the debtor happens at the outset to satisfy the agreed jurisdictional criteria in respect of more than one country) would thus constitute the primary insolvency administration for that particular debtor.[9] If, for suitably compelling reasons, it proved to be necessary to open one or more parallel proceedings in other countries where assets happened to be situate, these proceedings could be designated as secondary in nature, and of purely local effect, while at the same time remaining subject to the overarching authority of the primary proceedings. On the strength of such coordinated arrangements, the insolvency could then justifiably claim universal effectiveness, thereby eradicating virtually every one of the present difficulties outlined above.

In any given state throughout the world, in the absence of an international convention to regulate the law of insolvency, the separate national insolvency laws continue to be operated in conjunction with the locally-developed rules of private international law which the courts of that legal system employ whenever they encounter a problem of conflict of laws. Although a great deal of common ground exists in the realm of private international law, there are nevertheless important differences, in terms both of method and substance, between the conflicts rules developed by the various legal systems of the world. The English conflict of laws in relation to insolvency is presently in need of further development and modernisation. The relevant statutory provisions have been developed piecemeal over an extended stretch of time, and many of them still belong essentially to the nineteenth century in their substance, attitude and outlook. Hence, they belong also to an epoch when the theory and practice of private international law rested upon principles and doctrines which have undergone wholesale revision, often of a revolutionary nature, during the 20th century. Indeed, with regard to bankruptcy it may be said that the pre-1986 legislation failed almost entirely to make any provision for conflicts cases.[10] Accordingly, the English private international law of bankruptcy still rests for the most part upon judicial precedents, the majority of which are of no more recent date than the early years of the present century, while many 19th and 18th century cases still constitute the primary authorities on certain points of the law. In view of this, the account in Chapters 29 and 30 of the English private international law of insolvency is perforce a somewhat critical one, and is written in the expectation that several of the propositions which currently represent the law may soon undergo revision and reform.

Gulf between Theory and Reality

It is necessary to point out that there exists a notable discrepancy

---

[9] This is the approach adopted in the Istanbul Convention of the Council of Europe, and is also the basis proposed for use among members of the European Union under the Draft EEC Bankruptcy Convention. Both these texts are discussed in Chap. 31, *post*.

[10] See now Insolvency Act 1986, s.426, which applies to cases of bankruptcy and winding up, and in general to all forms of insolvency proceedings: *post*, Chap. 31.

between theory and reality in the matters of which we are currently speaking. It is one thing for a legal system unilaterally to advance the claim of universal effectiveness for the insolvency orders pronounced by its own courts; it is quite another thing for such judgments automatically to command that effectiveness internationally. Thus, while it may be possible for all courts within the country which constitutes the *forum concursus* to act on the assumption that the order enjoys effectiveness over persons and property both inside that jurisdiction and beyond it, there is no means of compelling the courts of other jurisdictions to concede that it enjoys the attribute of universality *proprio vigore*: such a contention flies in the face of the fundamental principle of the sovereign autonomy which must be accorded to the legal system of every independent country. Therefore the extent, if any, to which a given judgment or order made in insolvency proceedings will possess international effectiveness is a matter for determination by the foreign systems of law concerned. The recognition and effect which it will be accorded in other jurisdictions will be based upon the rules of private international law utilised by the systems in question, just as the recognition in England and Wales of the effects of a foreign judgment in comparable matters falls to be determined in accordance with our own practice in private international law.

Unless a principle of reciprocity is employed as the basis of recognition (as is the case under some countries' rules of private international law),[11] it may well transpire that a foreign court's order will be accorded certain effects by the courts of another country despite the fact that the comparable orders of the courts in the second country may fail to enjoy equivalent effectiveness under the rules of private international law of the former. But what is certainly true in all cases is that such international effectiveness as is enjoyed by a given insolvency order outside its jurisdiction of origin[12] is the consequence of the voluntary decision to accord it that effectiveness on the part of the other legal systems concerned. Therefore, whenever it transpires that property, whether movable or immovable, which is situate outside the jurisdiction of the *forum concursus* has devolved upon the trustee, or is claimable by the liquidator, by virtue of the order on which the proceedings are based, this consequence takes place, strictly speaking, by virtue of the legal rules in force in the country or countries of the *situs* of the property in question: it is impossible both in practical terms and also in terms of the doctrine of legal sovereignty, for such an effect to take place in the teeth of a contrary attitude maintained by the *lex situs*.

In the final analysis, it must be remembered that a court is likely to need to have regard for the practical realities inherent in any situation disclosed within proceedings. Thus, if an issue involves the turning over of assets,

---

[11] For description of the varying practices adopted in different countries, see *e.g.* Dalhuisen, *op. cit.*, Vol. I, Part III, Ch. 2.; Nadelmann (1967) 67 Colum.L.Rev. 995 (also in *Conflict of Laws, International and Interstate* (1972), p. 238); and (1964) 13 A.J.C.L. 72.

[12] Including of course such jurisdictions as may be constitutionally dependent upon the country of origin, or which may be associated therewith by the provisions of a previously-concluded treaty or convention regulating the enforcement of each other's judicial determinations.

currently located within the jurisdiction of the court, to a foreign-appointed trustee or liquidator, it is pertinent to reflect upon the practical consequences of such a turnover from the standpoint of creditors resident within the court's jurisdiction. Although in theory such creditors may be eligible to lodge their claims in the foreign administration, it may be demonstrable that their prospects of recovery are significantly less favourable than they would be if the assets were retained under the control of the court, and were made the subject of a separate insolvency proceeding governed by the local law. Hence, theories of the tidy and elegant solutions which are to be attained through fidelity to the twin principles of unity and universality of insolvency proceedings may prove to be unevenly applied in practice even by those courts which profess to subscribe to them. It is by no means unknown for a court, having duly acknowledged the importance of maintaining a respect for the principle of international comity, to discover pressing reasons for refraining from thus relinquishing its hold over the "bird in the hand."[13]

---

[13] See, e.g. *Felixstowe Dock and Railway Co. v. U.S. Lines Inc.* [1988] 2 All E.R. 77. For reflection on this decision, and its unfortunate legacy in terms of international judicial relations between the U.K. and the U.S.A., see Fletcher (1993) 6 Insolvency Intelligence 10–13, prompted by the decision in *Barclays Bank plc v. Homan*, referred to *supra*, n.1.

CHAPTER 29

BANKRUPTCIES WITH AN INTERNATIONAL ELEMENT: THE ENGLISH LAW AND PRACTICE

Jurisdiction to Adjudicate

The position at English Law

The legal requirements for a debtor to be capable of undergoing adjudication by a bankruptcy court in England and Wales have already been described.[1] We have seen that the requirements attaching to the presentation of a debtor's petition are relatively unexacting,[2] while in the case of a creditor's petition the essential prerequisites are that the debtor be "a debtor" both in the factual sense and also within the statutory sense employed by the Insolvency Act 1986,[3] and that the petition is presented by one or more creditors each of whom qualifies as a "good petitioning creditor" according to the criteria established by s.267 of the Act. What concerns us now is the significance of any foreign elements, whether pertaining to the debtor or to the petitioning creditor or to the relationship between them, from the aspect of the English court's jurisdictional competence.

The debtor

We have already seen that it is logically necessary for a person to be a "debtor" in the factual sense, in order for the bankruptcy law of England to be applicable to him or her in principle.[4] This entails that there should exist some legally enforceable indebtedness for money or money's worth, recoverable if necessary by means of legal proceedings brought before a court of competent jurisdiction. Therefore, if for any reason the indebtedness which is alleged to be the basis for a person's status as a

---

[1] See Chaps. 5 and 6, *ante*.
[2] See Insolvency Act, s.272, discussed in Chap. 6, *ante*, p. 117 *et seq*.
[3] See Insolvency Act, ss.267, 268, discussed in Chap. 6, *ante*, p. 101.
[4] See Chap. 5, *ante*, p. 70.

"debtor" is one which English law does not regard as being legally enforceable, it follows that the person ceases to be amenable to the English bankruptcy law. In addition to the example already considered, wherein the application of English domestic law gives rise to the conclusion that no enforceable indebtedness exists, it is necessary to consider further ways in which a similar conclusion may be arrived at in cases which contain some foreign element.

Debts discharged by prior bankruptcy

One of the ways in which a liability can be discharged is through the bankruptcy of the person owing it. Such a former bankruptcy may have taken place in England or in some foreign country. Unfortunately, the English private international law in relation to the discharge or cancellation of legal liabilities in this way is in a far from satisfactory state, and it can make a considerable difference, in cases of this kind, whether the discharge is alleged to have occurred as a result of a bankruptcy taking place within the jurisdiction of the English courts themselves, or within the jurisdiction which constitutes the "proper law" of the obligation in question (assuming that this happens not to be the law of England and Wales), or within some other foreign jurisdiction.

As will be explained in greater detail subsequently,[5] the effects which English law accords to a discharge from bankruptcy granted by a foreign court are markedly different from those which it claims for (and duly accords to) a discharge from bankruptcy granted by an English court. Therefore, if the ground upon which the debtor's liability towards his creditor is said to have been discharged is that he has undergone bankruptcy, and thereafter obtained his discharge, it is necessary to have regard to the jurisdiction in which those proceedings took place. If the bankruptcy proceedings took place within England and Wales, or in any other part of the United Kingdom and colonies, the debtor's discharge will be regarded by any English court as having discharged him from liability in respect of all debts provable in that bankruptcy, irrespective of which particular law happens to constitute the "proper law" of the debt in question.[6] Conversely, if the debtor's discharge has been obtained in foreign bankruptcy proceedings, the discharge will be recognised as effective under English private international law only if either it was granted by a court of the country whose law (again, according to English private international law) constitutes the proper law of the obligation in question[7]

---

[5] See *infra*.
[6] See *Odwin v. Forbes* (1817) Buck 57 (B.C.); *Royal Bank of Scotland v. Cuthbert* (1813) 1 Rose 462; *Edwards v. Ronald* (1830) 1 Knapp P.C. 259, 12 E.R. 317; *Quelin v. Moisson* (1828) 1 Knapp P.C. 265n., 12 E.R. 320; *Philpotts v. Read* (1819) 1 Brod. & B. 294, 129 E.R. 735; *Ferguson v. Spencer* (1840) 1 M. & G. 987, 133 E.R. 632; *Sidaway v. Hay* (1824) 3 B. & C. 12, 107 E.R. 639; *Armani v. Castrique* (1844) 13 M. & W. 443, 447 *per* Pollock, C.B., 153 E.R. 185, 186; *Gill v. Barron* (1868) L.R. 2 P.C. 157; *Simpson v. Mirabita* (1869) L.R. 4 Q.B. 257; *Ellis v. M'Henry* (1871) L.R. 6 C.P. 228. *cf. Re Nelson* [1918] 1 K.B. 459. See also Insolvency Act, s.281, and Chap. 11, *ante*, generally.
[7] *Burrows v. Jemino* (1726) 2 Str. 733, 93 E.R. 815; *Smith v. Buchanan* (1800) 1 East 6, 102 E.R. 3; *Potter v. Brown* (1804) 5 East 124, 102 E.R. 1016; *Phillips v. Allan* (1828) 8 B. & C. 477, 108 E.R. 1120; *Quelin v. Moisson* (*supra*); *Bartley v. Hodges* (1861) 1 B. & S. 375, 121 E.R. 745; *Gardiner v. Houghton* (1862) 2 B. & S. 743, 121 E.R. 1247; *Gibbs v. La Société*

or, alternatively, if it can at least be shown that the discharge, though not granted by the courts of the legal system which constitutes the proper law of the obligation, is recognised under the rules of private international law in force in that jurisdiction as having the effect of discharging the debtor's liability.[8]

It follows from what has just been stated that, if a discharge has been granted from a foreign bankruptcy occurring elsewhere than in the country whose law is the proper law of the obligation, and *a fortiori* where the proper law is the law of England and Wales,[9] English law will still regard the debtor as "a debtor" for the purposes of the potential exercise of its own bankruptcy jurisdiction. It will be noted that, in reaching the above conclusions, English private international law apparently takes no account of the question whether the foreign bankruptcy was pronounced by a court of competent jurisdiction.[10]

Debts based upon foreign judgments

Another ground on which English private international law may refuse to recognise that a state of indebtedness actually exists between the parties concerned is if the liability in question is based upon a foreign judgment which is unable to command recognition in England. The relevant rules of English law are divided between those applicable to judgments which are governed by the Brussels and Lugano Conventions on Jurisdiction and Enforcement of Judgments in Civil and Commercial Matters (concluded respectively between the Member States of the European Community and by the members of the European Free Trade Area and of the European Community),[11] and those applicable to judgments not governed by either

---

Industrielle et Commerciale des Métaux (1890) 25 Q.B.D. 399. If the effects of the foreign discharge itself, according to the law of the country in which it was granted, are not so extensive as to constitute a full discharge of the substantive liability with universal effect, it is possible that English law may still treat the debt as a subsisting one: see *infra*.

[8] So argued, *infra*. *cf. Armitage v. Attorney-General* [1906] p. 135.

[9] *Gibbs v. La Société Industrielle, etc.* (*supra*, n. 7).

[10] See further the criticisms voiced *infra*.

[11] Convention of September 27, 1968, subsequently amended and expanded: see the Civil Jurisdiction and Judgments Act 1982, which gives the Convention the force of law throughout the United Kingdom. A Convention of Accession to the Convention of 1968 was signed by the United Kingdom on October 9, 1978, and came into force on January 1, 1987. Further accessions, and amendments, were concluded in 1982 and 1989.

For the texts of the Accession Conventions, and of the original Convention as thereby amended, see O.J. 1978 L304/1 and L304/77; O.J. 1982 L388; and O.J. 1989 L285. The text is also published, together with an explanatory Note, in the Encyclopaedia of European Community Law, Volume BII. There is a full and up to date account of the effects of these Conventions on English Conflict of Laws in Dicey and Morris, *The Conflict of Laws* (12th ed., 1993), Chaps. 11 and 14. For other commentary upon the Convention, see Jenard, O.J. 1979 C59/1; Schlosser, O.J. 1979 C59/71; Fletcher, *Conflict of Laws and European Community Law* (1982), Chap. 4, and references therein cited, especially in nn. 18 and 23; Lasok and Stone, *Conflict of Laws in the European Community* (1987), Chaps. 5–7; Hartley, *Civil Jurisdiction and Judgments* (1984); Collins, *The Civil Jurisdiction and Judgments Act 1982* (1983); Dashwood, Hacon and White, *A Guide to the Civil Jurisdiction and Judgments Convention* (1986); Kaye, *Civil Jurisdiction and Enforcement of Foreign Judgments* (1987); O'Malley and Layton *European Civil Practice* (1989). A parallel convention to the Brussels Convention was signed at Lugano on September 16, 1988, and

convention. The latter kind of judgment is in turn subdivided into those foreign judgments pronounced by courts belonging to countries to which the Foreign Judgments (Reciprocal Enforcement) Act 1933 applies,[12] and those judgments of courts in countries to which the Act does not apply.[13] In cases governed by the Brussels Convention, the obligation to accord recognition is fundamental and the English Court is allowed only limited grounds on which to refuse to do so.[14] Where a case falls outside the operation of the Convention, however, it is a matter of primary consideration whether the foreign court enjoyed jurisdictional competence in an international, rather than in a merely domestic sense.[15] Even when the foreign court enjoyed jurisdiction in the international sense, its judgment may be denied recognition in England on a number of well-established grounds, such as the presence of active fraud whereby the original proceedings were tainted[16]; or of elements within the foreign judgment which contravene the principles of natural justice, or which render its recognition in England contrary to public policy.[17] The possibility of enforcing a foreign judgment may also become lost through reason of its becoming time-barred according to the provisions of the Limitation Act 1980.[18]

Jurisdiction over the debtor in personam

Assuming that the debtor is regarded by English law as being actually indebted, there are still a number of foreign elements the presence of any one of which in any given case is capable of precluding the exercise of bankruptcy jurisdiction *in personam*. Effectively, although applicable to

---

entered into force for the United Kingdom on May 1, 1992 (S.I. 1992 No. 745). It should eventually furnish a basis for recognition and enforcement of judgments between some 18 European states: O.J. 1988 L319/9.

[12] The Act currently applies to Austria, Belgium, Germany (Federal Republic), France, Israel, Italy, Holland, Norway, India, Suriname, Pakistan, Parts of Canada, Australian Capital Territory, Tonga, Guernsey, Jersey and the Isle of Man. Judgments of courts in those countries which are parties to the Brussels Convention (or the parallel, Lugano Convention) will usually be enforceable under that Convention.

[13] For a more complete account of the rules of English private international law concerning the recognition and enforcement of foreign money judgments, see: Dicey and Morris, *The Conflict of Laws* (12th ed., 1993), Chaps. 14, 15; Morris, *The Conflict of Laws* (4th ed., 1993), Chap. 9; *Cheshire and North's Private International Law* (12th ed., 1992), Chaps. 15, 16; Anton, *Private International Law* (2nd ed., 1990), Chap. 9; Wolff, *Private International Law* (2nd ed., 1950), Chap. 19; Read, *Recognition and Enforcement of Foreign Judgments* (1938).

[14] See Arts. 25–30 of the Brussels Convention, especially Art. 27.

[15] In the case of the Act of 1933, the relevant provisions are those of s.4(1)(a)(ii), (2) and (3). The leading cases on the common law meaning of the expression "jurisdiction in the international sense" are: *Buchanan v. Rucker* (1808) 9 East 192, 103 E.R. 546; *Schibsby v. Westenholz* (1870) L.R. 6 Q.B. 155; *Sirdar Gurdyal Singh v. Rajah of Faridkote* [1894] A.C. 670 (P.C.); *Pemberton v. Hughes* [1899] 1 Ch. 781; *Emanuel v. Symon* [1908] 1 K.B. 302.

[16] *Abouloff v. Oppenheimer* (1882) 10 Q.B.D. 295; *Vadala v. Lawes* (1890) 25 Q.B.D. 310; *Owens Bank Ltd v. Bracco* [1992] 2 W.L.R. 621 (H.L.); *cf.* Foreign Judgments (Reciprocal Enforcement) Act 1933, s.4(1)(a)(iv).

[17] *Jacobson v. Frachon* (1927) 138 L.T. 386; *Re Macartney* [1921] 1 Ch. 522; *Adams v. Cape Industries plc* [1990] Ch. 433 (C.A.); *cf.* Foreign Judgments (Reciprocal Enforcement) Act 1933, s.4(1)(a)(v).

[18] Limitation Act 1980, s.24.

debtors' and creditors' petitions alike, almost all of these elements are of relevance only in the case of a creditor's petition: where the debtor presents his own petition this very act of itself constitutes submission to the jurisdiction of the court, which suffices to confer upon the English court the requisite jurisdictional competence irrespective of the domicile or nationality of the debtor, and indeed irrespective of the fact that he may not even be resident in this country. The jurisdiction of the English court in the case of a debtor's petition is not affected by the fact that it may transpire that none of the creditors has any connection with this country, nor even by the fact that all of the debtor's assets are situated abroad. However, it is settled law that the English court will in practice refuse to make a bankruptcy order when it can be shown that the debtor has no assets within the jurisdiction of the English court,[19] and furthermore the courts are alert to the possibilities that the debtor may resort to the device of presenting his own petition as a means of defeating his creditors. Such abuses of the legal process may be readily thwarted by the court's exercising its discretion to refuse to make an adjudication,[20] or by its rescinding or annulling any orders which may have been made before the real position is exposed.[21] Where a debtor who has no prior personal association with this country, and whose creditors are all abroad, seeks to have recourse to English bankruptcy proceedings upon his own petition, the suspicion of abusiveness is readily aroused and the court will naturally be wary of exercising the jurisdiction which it nevertheless enjoys.[22]

Petitions by creditors

The greater number of legal strictures attaching to the initiation of bankruptcy proceedings based upon a creditor's petition give rise to numerous possibilities for the court's jurisdictional competence to be lost through the agency of a foreign element. In the first place it is important to recognise that although a person may be factually a debtor this alone is insufficient to render him amenable to the jurisdiction of the English court, whose jurisdiction is exercisable only over a person who is "a debtor" within the meaning of the Insolvency Act. This concept in turn consists of several components, most of which were considered earlier in Chapters 5 and 6 in their application to internal cases. The particular aspects of the statutory concept of "debtor" which are relevant to cases containing a foreign element are to be found in section 265(1) of the Insolvency Act, which provides that a bankruptcy petition shall not be presented to the court under section 264(1)(a) or (b) unless the debtor:

(a) is domiciled in England and Wales; or

---

[19] *Re Robinson* (1883) 22 Ch.D. 816. See also *Re Otway* [1895] 1 Q.B. 812; *Re Betts* [1897] 1 Q.B. 50; *Re Somers* (1897) 4 Mans 227.
[20] See *Re Bond* (1888) 21 Q.B.D. 17, especially at p. 20 *per* Cave, J.; *Re Betts* [1901] 2 K.B. 39.
[21] See Insolvency Act, ss.282, 375(1). See Chap. 11, *ante*.
[22] *cf. dicta* in *Re Pascal* (1876) 1 Ch.D. 509 (a case of a creditor's petition) in which the Court of Appeal indicated that English bankruptcy proceedings could be stayed if it later transpired that the debtor's estate was to be administered abroad.

(b) is personally present in England and Wales on the day on which the petition is presented; or
(c) at any time in the period of three years ending with that day:
   (i) has been ordinarily resident, or has had a place of residence, in England and Wales, or
   (ii) has carried on business in England and Wales.

Section 265(2) further provides that the reference in subsection (1)(c) to an individual carrying on business includes both the carrying on of business by a firm or partnership of which the individual is a member, and the carrying on of business by an agent or manager for the individual or for such a firm or partnership.

Although the foregoing provisions have the effect of limiting the *in personam* jurisdiction of the English bankruptcy courts, it should nevertheless be noted that their terms are still such as to be potentially very far-reaching. Thus, the applicability of our law of bankruptcy is not confined to those persons who are British subjects, or who are foreign subjects personally resident or trading in England[23]: a temporary presence here is in principle sufficient provided that it coincides with the date on which a creditor's petition is presented.[24] However, in cases where the debtor is normally absent from England and Wales, it must be borne in mind that the creditor may experience some difficulty in completing the formalities for service of a statutory demand, for the purpose of establishing the debtor's inability to pay the debt on which the petition is based.[25]

"Carrying on business"

The notion of "carrying on business," which is implanted in paragraph (c)(ii) of section 265, has received the attention of the courts particularly

---

[23] Such restrictions were formerly applicable, prior to the enactment of s.8 of the Bankruptcy and Deeds of Arrangement Act 1913, which was reproduced as s.1(2) of the Bankruptcy Act 1914 (repealed). On the limitations previously inherent in the English rules concerning jurisdiction, see *Re Crispin* (1873) L.R. 8 Ch.App. 374; *ex p. Blain* (1879) 12 Ch.D. 522; *Re Pearson* [1892] 2 Q.B. 263; *Re A.B. and Co.* [1900] 1 Q.B. 541, affirmed *sub nom. Cook v. C.A. Vogeler & Co.* [1901] A.C. 102 (H.L.). In *Re a Debtor (No. 2283 of 1976)* [1978] 1 W.L.R. 1512, Bridge L.J., at p. 1519, observed *ex abundante cautela* that, in the context of the case then before him (which involved a separate question of law), he would not venture to decide whether a person who is a British subject can be held to be "a debtor" within the meaning of s.1(2) of the Act of 1914. For further discussion of the application of pre-1986 English bankruptcy law to English citizens resident abroad, see *Re Tucker* [1990] Ch. 148 (C.A.), noted [1988] J.B.L. 168, 341. The *Tucker* case itself should not be regarded as a reliable authority for the purposes of the Insolvency Act 1986 in view of the changed character of the modern law, as acknowledged in *Re Seagull Manufacturing Co. Ltd* [1991] 4 All E.R. 257 (Mummery J.), affd. (C.A.) [1993] BCC 241; in *Bishopsgate Investment Management Ltd v. Maxwell* [1993] Ch. 1; [1992] 2 All E.R. 856 (C.A.), and in *Re Paramount Airways Ltd* [1993] Ch. 223; [1992] 3 All E.R. 1 (C.A.). See Fletcher (1992) 5 *Insolvency Intelligence* 27.
[24] Insolvency Act. s.265(1)(b). Note that there is no requirement that the petition must be served on the debtor *before* presentation, as is the case with proceedings commenced by means of a writ: see Chap. 6, *ante*.
[25] See Insolvency Act, ss.267(2)(c), 268, discussed in Chap. 6 *ante*.

from the aspect of the need to determine the precise time at which a business begins and ceases to be carried on. Although an isolated transaction of itself does not suffice to constitute the carrying on of a business, it is nevertheless established that even a single transaction can mark the commencement of business where it is accompanied by the intention that it shall form part of a regular means of earning a livelihood.[26] On the other hand, once a business has been commenced the precise moment of its discontinuation may be difficult to pinpoint, and it may become a nice question whether a business was still being carried on here at the material time, namely within the period of three years ending with the day on which the petition is presented. In *Theophile v. Solicitor-General*,[27] the House of Lords held that a debtor continues "carrying on business," for the purposes of amenability to the bankruptcy law of this country, until such time as all trade debts incurred during the course of that business have been paid. It was further held in the same case that the expression "trade debts" includes sums due to the petitioning creditor in respect of taxation levied on the income or profits of the business in question. There has been confirmation at First Instance that the decision in *Theophile* continues to serve as an authority for the purpose of interpreting the expression "has carried on business" as used in section 265(1)(c)(ii) of the Act of 1986.[28]

Where an individual utilises the device of incorporation as part of his system of conducting business activities, and thereafter purports to act as the agent or employee working on behalf of the company or companies so formed, it may appear superficially as though the statutory requirement that the debtor be "carrying on business" in England is not satisfied. However, in *Re Brauch*[29] the Court of Appeal held that an objective and realistic view must be taken of the actual business system which has been adopted in any given case. Having rejected the suggestion that proof that the debtor enjoyed complete effective control of the companies would of itself suffice for him to be "carrying on business," the Court nevertheless went on to hold that if the totality of evidence suggests that, (by means of the companies which he does in fact control) the individual concerned is operating in such a way that at some point he may expect to profit personally as a result of the activities carried on, as a matter of law, by or on behalf of those companies, then it may be possible to draw the conclusion that the person in question is conducting a separate business of his own, albeit in close association with that being carried on by companies.[30]

---

[26] See, *e.g. Re Mutton, ex p. Board of Trade* (1887) 19 Q.B.D. 102; *Re Wallis* (1885) 14 Q.B.D. 950.

[27] [1950] A.C. 186, followed and applied in *Re Bird* [1962] 2 All E.R. 406, [1962] 1 W.L.R. 686 (a case involving the interpretation of the same statutory expression, namely the carrying on of a business, when employed in s.4(1)(d) of the Bankruptcy Act 1914, *now repealed*). *cf.* also *Re Worsley* [1901] 1 Q.B. 309. (C.A.).

[28] *Re A Debtor (No. 784 of 1991)* [1992] Ch. 554; [1992] 3 W.L.R. 119; [1992] 3 All E.R. 376 (Hoffmann J.).

[29] [1978] Ch. 316 (the case was actually concerned with the construction of the concept of "carrying on business," as employed in s.4(1)(d) of the Bankruptcy Act 1914). See also *Graham v. Lewis* (1888) 22 Q.B.D. 1; *Re Clarke ex p. Pope and Knowles* [1914] 3 K.B. 1095.

[30] [1978] Ch. at 329, 330 *per* Goff, L.J., with whose judgment Orr, L.J. concurred. Buckley, L.J., also concurring, stated emphatically at p. 336 that "on a true view of the evidence it

Indeed, the very activity of promoting companies, taken together with the purposes for which such promotions are effected, may constitute one of the chief reasons for a conclusion that a person is "carrying on business" within the meaning of the Act.[31] It may be noted that the carrying on of "business" is the only activity mentioned in paragraph (c)(ii) of section 265(1). Hence, the question may arise whether the pursuit of a professional activity in England and Wales is of itself sufficient to found the jurisdiction of the bankruptcy courts here. The answer is supplied by section 436 of the Act, which states that the expression "business" includes a trade or profession, wherever the term is used in the Act.[32]

"Ordinarily resident"; "place of residence"

Another important concept from the aspect of the exercise of jurisdiction *in personam* is that of "ordinary residence" within the jurisdiction of the English courts. This expression is employed in section 265(1)(c)(i), together with the alternative connecting factor of the debtor's having "a place of residence" in England and Wales. In both cases, it is sufficient that the connecting factor was established in relation to the debtor at any time in the three years previous to petition. The meaning of each of these expressions is far from being precisely defined, and the decided cases tend to show that it is very much a question of fact and degree whether a person is considered to be "ordinarily resident," or to have a place of residence, in England. The concept of "ordinary residence" differs from that of domicile, as understood by English law, in that it is perfectly possible for one and the same person to be ordinarily resident in more than one jurisdiction at the same time.[33] In relation to tax liability it stated by Lord Cave that ordinary residence "connotes residence in a place with some degree of continuity and apart from accidental or temporary absences."[34] It should be noted that the term is not completely synonymous with habitual residence, a term of more recent origin, although the modern judicial tendency is to regard the two expressions as virtually interchangeable for many purposes.

A person can be ordinarily resident in this country despite the fact that, during the material period of time, he stays at not one address but several,[35]

---

would be more accurate to say that the companies were part of the machinery by which the debtor implemented his business projects."

[31] *cf.* [1978] Ch. at 329, *per* Goff, L.J. The learned Lord Justice also went on to assert that it was unnecessary, for this purpose, for the exact nature of the debtor's business to be precisely defined.

[32] *cf. Re A Debtor* [1927] 1 Ch. 97; *Re Williams' Will Trusts* [1953] 1 Ch. 138.

[33] *Re Norris* (1888) 4 T.L.R. 452; *Re Bright* (1901) 18 T.L.R. 37, reheard and affirmed (1903) 19 T.L.R. 203; *Re Brauch* [1978] Ch. 316. *cf. Re Erskine* (1893) 10 T.L.R. 32. (All the foregoing cases were decided under s.4(1)(d) of the Bankruptcy Act 1914 (repealed), or under equivalent provisions of earlier Bankruptcy Acts). Confirmation that "ordinary residence" is a non-exclusive concept was provided in the context of interpretation of a revenue statute in *I.R.C. v. Lysaght* [1928] A.C. 234. For further elaboration of the concept of ordinary residence, and related concepts, see Dicey and Morris, *op. cit. supra*, n. 13, at pp. 158–166.

[34] *Levene v. I.R.C.* [1928] A.C. 217 at p. 225.

[35] *cf. Re Bright* and *Re Brauch* (both *supra*).

and despite the fact that the places at which he stays are hotels, or other species of accommodation of which he may not be the legal owner.[36] Likewise, a single room, or other rented accommodation, may constitute a "place of residence" in view of the nature and quality of the use made of it by the debtor. Conversely, if the evidence is such as to show that the debtor's visits to England are of an intermittent character only, his status as a non-resident need not be jeopardised merely by the fact that when visiting he habitually stays at the same address.[37] But where a person pays for accommodation so as to have it at his disposal whether he occupies it or not, the fact that he may not have had occasion to occupy it at a material time, or during a material period, may not always be capable of averting a finding that he is ordinarily resident in England, or at any rate that he has a place of residence here.[38] Only where there is strong evidence to show that the debtor has, sometime previously, completely abandoned his established place of residence in England is the court likely to accept his contention that it no longer constitutes his place of residence despite the fact that he may retain title to it.[39]

The case of *Re Bright*[40] is illustrative of how far the courts are capable of going to reach a finding that a person is ordinarily resident in England. In that case the debtor, an American citizen domiciled in Argentina, spent extended periods in various hotels in London between January 1900 and May 1901. His primary reason for being in this country was his involvement in protracted litigation. The Court of Appeal, in two separate appeals entertained in respect of the same proceedings, twice held that the debtor was ordinarily resident, and thus amenable to the jurisdiction of the English bankruptcy court, during the period in question.[41] At the second hearing of the appeal, Collins M.R. said:

> "A long sojourn must not therefore be taken to be a *sine qua non*. There must, of course, be some duration, though not necessarily a very long one. Two or three days would not be sufficient. The question is one of fact. Various elements must be taken into consideration, and the purpose for which the man was here is one of the factors to be taken into account. If the man was here for a particular purpose which could not be conveniently disposed of

---

[36] In *Re Brauch, supra,* Goff, L.J. in the Court of Appeal went so far as to suggest, *obiter,* that a person might be held to have a "dwellinghouse" for the purposes of s.4(1)(d) of the Bankruptcy Act 1914 even though he was but the licensee with no legal or equitable interest in the property in question: see [1978] Ch. at 334.

[37] See *Re Erskine, supra.*

[38] *Re Hecquard* (1889) 24 Q.B.D. 71; *cf. Re Norris* and *Re Brauch* (both *supra*).

[39] As in *Re Nordenfeld* [1895] 1 Q.B. 151, distinguished in *Re Brauch, (supra).* The former case was decided, as was *Re Hecquard (supra),* under the equivalent provision to s.4(1)(d) of the Bankruptcy Act of 1914.

[40] (1901) 18 T.L.R. 37, reheard and affirmed (1903) 19 T.L.R. 203.

[41] It should again be noted that the case was decided under the equivalent provision to s.4(1)(d) of the Bankruptcy Act 1914, which required that the debtor must have been ordinarily resident in England within a year before the date of presentation of the petition. The period of time now specified in section 265(1) of the Insolvency Act 1986 is three years before petition, and it suffices that the residential criterion was fulfilled *at any time* within that period (emphasis added).

without his presence for a substantial time, and he had during that time been substantially resident in England, then it becomes a question of fact whether he was ordinarily resident or not. In my opinion there was abundant evidence to support the learned Registrar's conclusion."[42]

Perhaps the words of Lord Esher M.R., uttered in the course of his judgment in *Re Hecquard*, convey the essential spirit upon which the interpretation of this part of the law is based:

> "If within the year the debtor has had a dwelling-house in England, no time is limited during which he must have dwelt in it. If he is not a mere passing or casual visitor he has got such a hold on this country as is to make him liable to the English bankruptcy law."[43]

"Domiciled in England and Wales"

The jurisdictional provision which has the greatest capability of reaching persons who are physically absent from England and Wales at the time of presentation of the petition is that contained in section 265(1)(a) of the Act, whereby a petition may be presented against a debtor who is domiciled in England and Wales. The legal concept of domicile, which is not defined in the Insolvency Act, is one of considerable complexity. Although the term "domicile" is utilised by many legal systems of the world, and serves as a connecting factor for jurisdictional and choice of law purposes, the precise meaning of the term varies considerably between one legal system and another. The English law concept is in many respects unique,[44] although it has been exported into the legal systems of some Commonwealth countries. By English common law, it is established that a person can have but one domicile at any one time, although it is possible for a person to change his or her domicile in the course of a lifetime. Furthermore, it is held to be impossible for a person to be without a domicile at any time during life, no matter how difficult it may be to

---

[42] (1903) 19 T.L.R. 203 at p. 204.
[43] (1889) 24 Q.B.D. 71 at p. 74. As explained in n. 41, *supra*, the "catchment" period has been substantially lengthened from one year to three years under the Insolvency Act 1986.
[44] On the meaning of the term "domicile" at English law, see generally Dicey and Morris *The Conflict of Laws*, (12th ed., 1993) Chap. 7; Morris, *The Conflict of Laws*, (4th ed., 1993) Chap. 2; *Cheshire and North's Private International Law* (12th ed., 1992), Chap. 9. Among the leading cases, illustrative both of the artificiality and of the possible capriciousness of the concept of domicile at English law, see *e.g*: *Whicker v. Hume* (1858) 7 H.L.C. 124; *Bell v. Kennedy* (1868) L.R. 1 Sc. & Div. 307; *Udny v. Udny* (1869) L.R. 1 Sc. & Div. 441; *Winans v. Attorney-General* [1904] AC 287; *Ramsey v. Liverpool Royal Infirmary* [1930] AC 588. Note that, by s.1 of the Domicile and Matrimonial Proceedings Act 1973, a married woman became capable of acquiring a domicile of choice independent of the domicile of her husband. For the purposes of s.265(1)(a) of the Insolvency Act 1986, it must be established that the debtor has a domicile in England and Wales, as opposed to one in either Scotland or Northern Ireland, and the onus is on the petitioning creditor to prove the debtor's domicile where there is before the court evidence sufficient to place the issue in doubt: *cf. ex p. Cunningham* (1884) 13 Q.B.D. 418; *Re Barne* (1886) 16 Q.B.D. 522; *Re Duleep Singh* (1890) 7 Mor. 228.

ascertain precisely what that domicile may be. Domicile must therefore be distinguished from "nationality," or citizenship, for it is quite possible for a person to lack any nationality, and so belong to the category of "stateless" persons, while equally it is possible for a person to possess the status of citizen with regard to more than one country at a time—the phenomenon known as "dual nationality."

Basically, "domicile" at common law is associated with the idea of "home," in a permanent sense, so that English law generally regards a person as being domiciled in that country which constitutes his or her ultimate home, in a permanent and durable sense.[45] That is not to say however that a person need necessarily have a house, or even reside, within the country of his or her domicile, for the concept is essentially based upon a *subjective* association of the person with the country of domicile.

The idiosyncratic aspects of the "English law" formulation of the concept of domicile are of judicial creation,[46] and an important role is allocated to the subject's "domicile of origin," that is to say the domicile which attaches, for the purposes of English law, to every person at birth. This domicile is that of the father, if the child is legitimate and born in the father's lifetime, and that of the mother if the child is illegitimate or born after the father's death.[47] A person's domicile of origin is retained for life unless and until it is changed by the conscious acquisition of a different domicile of choice, either by the subject personally if of independent status, or otherwise by the person from whose domicile that of the subject is currently derived by dependence. It is incumbent upon the party who alleges that a change of domicile has been undergone by any given person, to prove this has occurred, since the law otherwise presumes the continuation of the existing domicile.[48] Even if the domicile of origin is validly displaced as a result of the acquisition of a domicile of choice, it remains in the background and will revive, and reattach to the subject, immediately the domicile of choice is abandoned, and until such time as a fresh domicile of choice is properly acquired.[49]

From the above remarks, it can readily be appreciated that a person may be domiciled in England and Wales, for the purposes of English law, even though he or she has neither resided in nor visited this country for a very substantial length of time. Indeed, in an extreme case it could occur that a person might be held to have an English domicile without ever having physically set foot in this country.[50] Conversely, of course, it can readily

---

[45] See *Whicker v. Hume* (1858) 7 H.L.C. 124, 160, *per* Lord Cranworth.
[46] The confusing use of the term "domicile," bearing a special statutory meaning, within the Civil Jurisdiction and Judgments Act 1982 (*supra*, n. 11) has brought further complication into this area of law (see ss.41–46 of the Act of 1982). In the discussion in the text above, however, the orthodox, common-law concept of "domicile" is in contemplation throughout.
[47] *Udny v. Udny* (1869) L.R. 1 Sc. & Div. 441, 547, *per* Lord Westbury.
[48] *Winans v. Attorney-General* [1904] A.C. 287 at 289.
[49] The Law Commission has proposed significant reforms of the law of domicile, including the abolition of the special doctrines associated with the domicile of origin: Law Commission Working Paper No. 88 (1985); final Report: The Law of Domicile (1987) (Law Com. No. 168; Scot. Law Com. No. 107; Cm. 200).
[50] *cf. Re O'Keefe* [1940] Ch. 124, for an extreme illustration of such a case.

arise that a person who was born in this country, and who has resided here ever since, may succeed in establishing that, under English law, he or she is domiciled in some foreign country in consequence of the operation of our rules for attribution of the domicile of origin. Given that the reference periods established by section 265(1)(c) in respect of the residential and business connecting factors are currently three years, it is perhaps unlikely that many occasions will arise in which the domiciliary connection with this country is the sole ground upon which the debtor's amenability to the bankruptcy jurisdiction of the English courts can be established. In such cases, rare though they may be, the long reach of the English bankruptcy jurisdiction based upon domicile may prove to be remarkably hard to shake off.

Finally, it may be noted that the fact that a debtor is domiciled in one of the other Member States of the European Union is no obstacle at present to the bringing of bankruptcy proceedings before the English courts (provided that one of the other grounds in section 265(1)(b), (c) or (d) can be established). This is because Article 1(2) of the Brussels Convention of 1968 (mentioned above) expressly excludes bankruptcy and other types of insolvency procedure from the scope of that convention, and of its rules for allocation of jurisdiction in civil or commercial matters. This holds true equally for the purposes of the Lugano Convention, also mentioned above.[51]

The limits of jurisdiction

We have seen above that the English law of bankruptcy in the present day is potentially applicable to a very wide number of people who, despite the fact that their primary legal and personal associations lie in other jurisdictions, nevertheless possess sufficient links with the jurisdiction of the English courts to render them potentially liable to undergo adjudication of bankruptcy through proceedings taking place in the English courts. In the absence of any internationally-concluded convention or treaty governing the exercise of jurisdiction in bankruptcy to which this country may become a party,[52] our courts retain very great freedom in relation to the actual exercise of their jurisdictional powers so liberally drawn. No self-imposed doctrines of jurisdictional restraint, based upon pleas of *forum non conveniens* or *lis alibi pendens*, have yet been developed in this country in relation to bankruptcy matters, so that it is not yet certain whether a debtor may successfully oppose the presentation of a petition by arguing that some other jurisdiction is logically or functionally the more appropriate *forum concursus*. In the general field of jurisdiction in civil and commercial matters, it is no exaggeration to state that the doctrine of *forum non conveniens* has undergone a revolutionary development in English law in recent years.[53] The leading cases did not

---

[51] See n. 11, *supra*, and text relating thereto.
[52] See Chap. 31, *post*.
[53] See P. Smart, *Cross-Border Insolvency* (1991), Ch. 2, and [1989] JBL 126, for a review of the case law and assessment of current possibilities. See also Dicey and Morris, *The Conflict of Laws* (12th ed., 1993), at p. 1159 (with particular reference to bankruptcy), and at Ch. 12 *passim* (pp. 395–438) on the general subject of *forum non conveniens* and related matters.

involve questions of bankruptcy or winding up, and it remains to be seen how far the impact of these cases will be carried across into the area of insolvency. However, it is at least arguable that courts will nowadays give serious consideration to a plea that insolvency proceedings would be more conveniently conducted elsewhere, and should be allowed to take place in that other jurisdiction, without the added complexity of a parallel English proceeding where no countervailing advantages are demonstrable.[54] Even where all the prescribed criteria for the making of a bankruptcy order are fully met, the English court has always had an ultimate discretion whether or not to make an order. This is expressly confirmed by section 266(3) of the current Act, whose terms are very widely drawn. It is submitted that the power conferred by this provision furnishes a suitable platform for the development of a doctrine of *forum non conveniens* (alternatively known as a doctrine of abstention) in relation to bankruptcy. This would not only be a continuation of the traditional notions of operating equitable standards in the context of bankruptcy jurisdiction, but also would be a logical development from the settled line of authority concerned with avoiding wasteful or pointless proceedings. This approach is encountered in such cases as those where it is shown that the debtor has no assets within the jurisdiction of the court, nor any prospect of having any, whereupon the court may deem it appropriate for recourse to be had to the somewhat pragmatically-exercised discretion not to adjudicate a debtor bankrupt here.[55]

International Effects of an English Adjudication

(i) Within the United Kingdom

According to the rules of private international law, the separate parts of the United Kingdom constitute separate "countries," or law districts. Consequently, provision needs to be made for enabling the bankruptcy orders (or their equivalents) made by the courts of one part of the Kingdom to be recognised and enforced in the other parts respectively. This is now accomplished through provisions contained in section 426 of the Insolvency Act 1986, which applies to England and Wales, to Scotland, and also to Northern Ireland.[56] Section 426(1) provides that an order made by a court in any part of the United Kingdom in the exercise of jurisdiction in relation to insolvency law shall be enforced in any other part

---

[54] *cf.* the instructive approach adopted successively by Hoffmann J. and by the Court of Appeal with regard to the related matter of the granting of an anti-suit injunction, at the court's discretion, to restrain the bringing of proceedings in a foreign court in a matter involving an insolvent company: *Re Maxwell Communications Corporation plc (No. 2), Barclays Bank plc v. Homan* [1992] BCC 757. See also *Re Harrods (Buenos Aires) Ltd* [1992] Ch. 72 (C.A.).

[55] See above, text to n. 19, and cases therein cited. See also Smart [1989] J.B.L. 126.

[56] Insolvency Act, ss.440(2)(c), 441(1)(a).

of the United Kingdom as if it were made by a court exercising the corresponding jurisdiction in the other part. The broad terms of this provision enable its effects to apply both to individual and also to corporate insolvency matters.

In framing the new provisions in the Insolvency Act, care was taken to avoid the anomalous and inelegant approach formerly embodied within the Bankruptcy Act 1914 and its predecessors, whereby it was declared that an English adjudication of bankruptcy brought about the automatic vesting of all the debtor's property, wherever situated, in his trustee in bankruptcy.[57] The new approach, expressed in subsections (2) and (3) of section 426, is to declare that nothing in subsection (1) requires a court in any part of the United Kingdom to enforce, in relation to property situated in that part, any order made by a court in any other part of the United Kingdom. The effect is thus that of allowing the courts of the *situs* of property their customary power of determining its proper destination, according to their own rules of private international law. The trustee (or liquidator) whose appointment arises under the law of a different part of the United Kingdom must therefore act under the local law of the place where any assets are situated, and must obtain the assistance of the local courts according to the provisions of section 426 itself. To facilitate this, section 426(3) contains an enabling provision to allow orders to be made so that the rights of a trustee or liquidator under the insolvency law of any part of the United Kingdom may be enjoyed with suitable modifications in relation to any property situated in another part of the United Kingdom, so as to correspond to the rights of an office holder appointed under the *lex situs*.

Any office holder appointed in any part of the United Kingdom is also at liberty to invoke the provisions for judicial assistance which are established by the further provisions of section 426.[58] These have the effect of rendering it obligatory for the courts of any part of the United Kingdom having jurisdiction in relation to insolvency law to assist the courts having the corresponding jurisdiction in any other part of the U.K. Although in many instances it is necessary for the office holder first to invoke the assistance of the court under whose jurisdiction his appointment arises, section 426(6) enables the office holder under the insolvency law of any part of the United Kingdom to address a direct request for assistance to the court exercising insolvency jurisdiction in another part, for the purpose of claiming property situated in that part. Any such request, whether made on an inter-judicial basis or, where permissible, directly by the office holder, empowers the requested court to apply, in relation to any matters specified in the request, the insolvency law which is applicable by *either*[59] court in relation to comparable matters falling within its jurisdiction, and in exercising its discretion in relation to such matters the requested court is

---

[57] *cf.* the combined effect produced by the provisions of ss.18, 53 and 167 of the Bankruptcy Act 1914 (repealed).

[58] See Insolvency Act, s.426(4)–(12), described more fully in Chap. 31, *post*.

[59] Emphasis added: see further, Chap. 31, *post*, where further consideration is given to the implications of Insolvency Act, s.426(5).

expressly commanded to have regard in particular to the rules of private international law.[60]

(ii) Outside the United Kingdom

In Chapter 8 above where the proprietary effects of an English bankruptcy order were explained, it was shown that the legal consequence of adjudication is that, apart from exempted property, all the bankrupt's property is automatically transferred to his trustee in bankruptcy, and vests in him immediately on his appointment.[61] The definition of "property" in section 436 of the Act is very broadly drawn, and includes "money, goods, things in action, land and every description of property *wherever situated* ..."[62] Thus, an English adjudication purports to have universal effect in relation to all the bankrupt's property, regardless of its location at the moment the bankruptcy order was made.

For very obvious reasons, the effect claimed for an English adjudication, and expressed above, cannot operate in any direct or literal sense outside the territorial limits of the jurisdiction of the English courts. In relation to property situated outside the United Kingdom, therefore, the trustee must establish his claim under the local law of the *situs*, and is dependent upon the validity of the English adjudication, and of his own appointment, being recognised according to the rules of private international law utilised by the courts of the *situs*. Even if his status, and entitlement to the property, are recognised in principle, the courts of the *situs* are likely to consider his rights to be subject to any real rights arising under the *lex situs* itself, and it is also possible that priority will be accorded to certain personal rights arising in favour of local creditors of the bankrupt.

Recognition by Commonwealth countries

In relation to those territories which retain their colonial status, or for whose affairs the United Kingdom has ultimate responsibility, the practical difficulties of international recognition and enforcement of insolvency orders may be overcome through the implementation of suitable provisions in the local legislation, whose effects will resemble those of section 426 of the Insolvency Act described above.

In the case of former colonies which now have independent status, and which now belong, for the most part, to the British Commonwealth, some degree of uncertainty exists concerning the exact basis upon which, if at all, an English adjudication enjoys the full legal effect claimed for it under the Insolvency Act. The earlier cases,[63] decided by English courts during the

---

[60] Insolvency Act, s.426(5).
[61] Insolvency Act, ss.283, 306, discussed in Chap. 8, *ante*.
[62] Emphasis added.
[63] See *Gill v. Barron* (1868) L.R. 2 P.C. 157; *Ellis v. M'Henry* (1871) L.R. 6 C.P. 228; *Callender, Sykes and Co. v. Colonial Secretary of Lagos* [1891] A.C. 460 (P.C.); *New Zealand Loan and Mercantile Agency Co. v. Morrison* [1898] A.C. 349 (P.C.). *cf. Re Eades Estate* (1917) 33 D.L.R. 335; *Re Graham (No. 2)* [1929] 3 D.L.R. 353. Contrast *dicta* in *Re Graham* [1928] 4 D.L.R. 375, 376 *per* Taylor, J.

colonial period, all utilise as the basis of decision a constitutional theory regarding the legislative competence of the "Imperial" Parliament which is no longer tenable since the granting of sovereign independence to the countries concerned. It is true that, as part of the formal process of according independence to former colonies, statutory provisions were often enacted for the purpose of ensuring that the legal arrangements which formerly obtained between them and the Mother Country should continue to survive after they attained independence.[64] However, the majority of such former colonies now enjoy full freedom to vary or repeal any such provisions which may have been effective in the past, and it is increasingly unlikely that the courts in such countries would be prepared to admit that an English bankruptcy order can enjoy full force in their jurisdiction *ratione imperii*. On the other hand, within the Commonwealth the spirit of legal co-operation, allied to the established provisions for the making of orders in aid between the courts of the various Member States, may enable an English trustee in bankruptcy to procure in practice many of the results which would formerly have ensued automatically from the debtor's adjudication. Therefore, in those countries of the Commonwealth with which such arrangements for judicial co-operation are in place, the English trustee may be able to obtain an appropriate order, pursuant to a request from the English court, vesting in the trustee such property of the bankrupt as may be found in the jurisdiction of the court thus requested.[65] Provision to enable such assistance to be accorded on a reciprocal basis is included in section 426 of the Insolvency Act, mentioned above.[66]

Recognition in the Republic of Ireland

One special example of domestic arrangements which have been made upon the initiative of the independent country itself so as to facilitate co-operation in legal matters by means of orders in aid, is to be found in the Republic of Ireland, where a constitutional provision enables the former *status quo* in relation to bankruptcy to continue in force despite the gaining of independence.[67] Hence, an English adjudication still enjoys immediate effectiveness in the Republic and the Irish courts are empowered to collaborate with their counterparts in the United Kingdom for the purposes of operating the system of orders in aid for which provision is currently made in section 426 of the Insolvency Act 1986 and in section 71 of the Bankruptcy (Ireland) Amendment Act 1872.[68]

---

[64] See, *e.g.* India (Consequential Provisions) Act 1949, s.1; Republic of the Gambia Act 1970, s.1.
[65] *cf. Re Graham (No. 2) (supra)*, and see also *Home's Trustee v. Home's Trustees*, 1926 S.L.T. 214.
[66] See Insolvency Act, s.426(4), (5), (11), further discussed in Chap. 31, *post*.
[67] See Article 73 of the Constitution of 1922, and Article 50 of the Constitution of 1937.
[68] *Re Bolton* [1920] 2 I.R. 324; *Re Bullen* [1930] I.R. 82; *Re Corballis* [1929] I.R. 266; *Re Reilly* [1942] I.R. 416; *Re Gibbons* (1960) 26 Ir.Jur. 60; *Re Jackson* [1973] N.Ir. 67. See also Insolvency Act, s.426(4), (5), (11), together with (S.I. 1986, No. 2123), discussed in Chap. 30, *post*.

Tax Bankruptcies

One logical limit to the operation of any arrangements for mutual assistance is encountered in cases where the debts in respect of which English bankruptcy has been occasioned include unpaid taxes due to the British Crown. According to a rule which enjoys widespread acceptance in private international law, the courts of one country will not enforce a foreign judgment or order which is penal in character or which is in substance an order for the payment, whether directly or indirectly, of taxes owed to a foreign sovereign.[69] There are recent indications of a readiness, in some parts of the commonwealth, to modify this doctrine in the light of present-day realities under which some fiscal liabilities are encountered in almost every case of insolvency. Hence, the doctrine of non-enforcement of revenue debts may be disapplied where the trustee or liquidator can be characterised as a collector of property on behalf of the ordinary creditors, as well as the foreign tax authorities.[70]

International recognition generally

Beyond the network of countries whose association with the United Kingdom is sufficiently close to enable collaborative arrangements to be maintained, the international effectiveness of an English adjudication is perforce dependent upon rules of private international law operated by the countries concerned. In spite of prolonged efforts to bring about the unification of private international law it is still true to say that in the world of today there remain numerous differences in approach to the solution of conflicts of law, so that no generalised assertion can be made regarding the extent to which recognition will be accorded to the claims of an English adjudication to take effect in relation to the bankrupt's property wheresoever situate. It usually proves to be the case that the rules of private international law which are in force in any given country will adopt a conservative attitude to acceptance of the full effectiveness of a foreign adjudication which purports to invest the trustee in bankruptcy with title to the debtor's immovable property situate in that jurisdiction, while on the other hand a more liberal attitude tends to prevail in questions concerning the title asserted by the foreign trustee to any of the debtor's movable property which happens to be there at the time of his adjudication.[71] Nevertheless, it must be conceded that, to whatever extent the trustee's title is acknowledged in any foreign country, his title is in reality dependent upon the operation of the rules and processes of the *lex*

---

[69] *Government of India v. Taylor* [1955] A.C. 491; *Buchanan v. McVey* [1954] I.R. 89; *Re Gibbons (supra)*; *Rossano v. Manufacturers' Life Insurance Co.* [1963] 2 Q.B. 352; *Schemmer v. Property Resources Ltd* [1974] 3 All E.R. 451. See also *Re Tucker (supra*, n. 23), and for further aspects of that case see D. Graham in I.F. Fletcher (Ed.) *Cross-Border Insolvency: Comparative Dimensions (The Aberystwyth Insolvency Papers)* (1990), Ch. 12 (pp. 205–215).

[70] *cf. Ayres v. Evans* (1981) 39 A.L.R. 129; *Priestley v. Clegg* (1985) (3) S.A. 955. See also *Re State of Norway's Application (Nos. 1 and 2)* [1989] 1 All E.R. 745; [1989] 2 W.L.R. 458 (H.L.).

[71] A similar dichotomy of approach is adopted by English private international law in its recognition of the effects of foreign adjudications: see below.

situs, including its rules of private international law, and is not attributable to the force of English law alone.

In assessing the trustee's legal standing, it is to be expected that foreign courts will take account of the position of local creditors from the jurisdiction in which they sit, will tend to give priority to any acts of diligence which may have been carried out in conformity with the local law, and above all will accord pre-eminence to the effect of any local bankruptcy which may have been opened.[72] If faced with the need to decide between the rival claims of two trustees in bankruptcy appointed in different jurisdictions beyond their own frontiers, foreign courts will generally adopt the solution which accords most with their own predilections in such matters as the connecting factor to which primary importance is to be attached. While the specially-formulated concept of domicile has hitherto been favoured in many jurisdictions belonging to the common law tradition, other factors such as nationality, residence and the doing of business are also utilised with varying degrees of preference in these and other countries. Some may accord priority of effect to the bankruptcy which is chronologically the first to be commenced, but such a solution can be criticised on the ground that it may yield arbitrary and unjust results under certain circumstances.[73] It must be acknowledged, at any rate, that the very breadth of the English rules for assuming jurisdiction to adjudicate necessarily entails that cases will arise in which, in the eyes of the international community of legal systems, England cannot be said to constitute the most appropriate *forum* in which the debtor's entire estate should be administered. In such cases, it is only to be expected that foreign courts may accord priority of effect to an adjudication undergone by the same debtor in the jurisdiction which, on an objective view of the case in its entirety, constitutes the most appropriate *forum concursus*, even though that adjudication may have been pronounced later in time than the English one.

Bankrupt's duty to assist in recovery of foreign assets

A bankrupt who has undergone adjudication in England is required by our law to assist his trustee in bankruptcy in his efforts to establish title to, and thereby recover for the estate, the bankrupt's assets abroad.[74] To this end, the debtor must execute any powers of attorney, conveyances, deeds or instruments as may reasonably be required by the trustee. In this way

---

[72] *cf.* the much-criticised actions of the English Court of Appeal in comparable circumstances in *Re Lorillard* [1922] 2 Ch. 638, criticised in (1922) 36 Harv.L.Rev. 608; (1951) 49 Mich.L.Rev. 1129, 1148. For cases illustrative of the attitudes displayed by some Commonwealth jurisdictions to the effects of foreign adjudications or analogous procedures, and to the status of trustees appointed thereunder, see *ex p. Bettle* (1895) 14 N.Z.L.R. 129; *Re Young* [1955] St.R.Qd. 254; *Re C.A. Kennedy Co. Ltd and Stibbe-Monk Ltd* (1977) 74 D.L.R. (3d) 87.

[73] This method of resolving conflicts between adjudications pronounced by the courts of co-ordinate jurisdiction was the one proposed in the First Draft EEC Bankruptcy Convention, described in Chap. 31, *post*.

[74] Insolvency Act, ss.291, 312, 333. The bankrupt's unreasonable failure to co-operate with his trustee is punishable as a contempt: *Re Harris* (1896) 74 L.T. 221. *cf. Royal Bank of Scotland v. Cuthbert* (1813) 1 Rose 462.

the trustee may succeed in recovering foreign assets situate in jurisdictions where the English adjudication would fail to be accorded the universality of effect which English law itself presumes to claim for it.[75]

Conclusions

The realities of international legal relationships therefore serve to deprive an English adjudication of full universality of effect in the literal sense. To the extent that such an adjudication is recognised and given effect within the territories of politically foreign countries, it must be acknowledged that these consequences are enjoyed through, and by virtue of, the legal systems of the countries concerned, and hence take place, if at all, *imperio rationis* rather than *ratione imperii*. However, it does not necessarily follow that the aspirations of English law that its adjudications shall enjoy universal effect are rendered altogether absurd or futile. Provided that the realities of the processes of private international law are properly acknowledged (and that due regard is paid to the need to preserve a consistency of approach in our own policies of recognition of foreign adjudications)[76] the fact that we declare an intention that an English adjudication shall be universally effective furnishes a helpful basis on which foreign legal systems may build in shaping their response. In particular, a clear signal concerning the substantive character of an English adjudication is given to those legal systems whose rules permit a foreign adjudication to be fully recognised and given effect. Were our aspirations to be expressed less unambiguously, the way would lie open for foreign courts to infer that an English bankruptcy was of territorial, not universal effect, or otherwise to resort to their preferred techniques of classification in appraising the legal character and effects of an English adjudication. If thereby certain aspects came to be classified as procedural in nature, the foreign court could omit to give effect to them by virtue of the widely-applied rule of private international law that all matters of procedure are governed by the *lex fori*, with the corollary that only such aspects of a foreign *lex causae* as are of a substantive nature will be applied by the *forum*.[77]

English law has indeed shown itself to be suitably realistic as regards the legitimate claims of the foreign law of the *situs* of the bankrupt's assets to regulate rights and interests in and against those assets, at least up until the date of commencement of the English bankruptcy.[78] On the basis of the traditional concept whereby, for historical reasons, the transmission of the

---

[75] For a realistic appraisal of the English court's true powers in relation to assets situate abroad, see Re Maudslay, Sons and Field [1900] 1 Ch. 602, at pp. 611–612, *per* Cozens-Hardy, J.

[76] See the further remarks *infra* regarding the international effects claimed for a discharge from an English bankruptcy.

[77] *cf.* Dicey and Morris, *The Conflict of Laws* (12th ed., 1993), Chaps. 2 and 8; Morris, *The Conflict of Laws* (4th ed., 1993), Chaps. 27 and 29; *Cheshire and North's Private International Law* (12th ed., 1992), Chaps. 3 and 6. See also *ex p. Melbourn* (1870) L.R. 6 Ch.App. 64 for an illustration of the practice of disregarding the procedural elements of foreign law, and of applying those of the *lex fori*.

[78] On commencement of bankruptcy, see Insolvency Act, s.278, discussed in Chap. 7, *ante*. For the proprietary effects of adjudication, see Chap. 8.

debtor's property on his bankruptcy is regarded as being analogous to an assignment of his property, it is also accepted that this analogy may be pursued as far as to admit the prevalence of "equities", in the form of prior charges legitimately created according to the *lex situs*, which take precedence over the title of the trustee in bankruptcy.[79] So, too, the ordinary English rules regarding the recognition of the paramount effectiveness of a foreign judgment *in rem* have the consequence that, in an English bankruptcy, the trustee's title may be defeated regardless, apparently, of whether the foreign judgment was pronounced before or after the commencement of bankruptcy.[80]

The international effects of an English discharge

According to section 281 of the Insolvency Act, when a bankrupt obtains his discharge from a bankruptcy pronounced under the Act the effect in law is to release the bankrupt, subject to certain limited exceptions, from all debts provable in his bankruptcy.[81] In the eyes of the English courts, this statutory discharge is of universal effect, and applies to all the bankrupt's liabilities, whether incurred in England or abroad and whether governed by English or by some foreign law.[82] The rationale traditionally advanced on behalf of this rule is based partly on the fact that, as is explained below, it is open to all creditors, whether domestic or foreign, to prove in the English bankruptcy, and partly on the fact that, since English law regards its own adjudications as enjoying universal effect, logic requires that an English discharge shall be of a complementary character. Nevertheless, the uncompromising formulation of the English rule flies in the face of the widely-accepted notion in private international law that the question of the discharge of a legal obligation is to be referred to the law by which that obligation is properly governed, a rule to which, as will be seen,[83] English private international law itself subscribes when determining the effects of a foreign discharge from bankruptcy. It may be observed that the principal authorities upon which this long-established rule of English law rests were all decided in the first half of the 19th century, at a time when the rules of private international law regarding the

---

[79] *Re Somes* (1896) 3 Mans. 131; *Re Sykes* (1932) 101 L.J. Ch. 298. For general discussion of the principle that the trustee takes subject to equities, see Chap. 8.

[80] *Cammell v. Sewell* (1860) 5 H. and N. 728, 157 E.R. 1371; *Minna Craig S.S. Co. v. Chartered Mercantile Bank of India, London and China* [1897] 1 Q.B. 460. *cf. Winkworth v. Christie, Manson and Woods* [1980] Ch. 496.

[81] For a full description of the law relating to discharge, see Chap. 11. For the meaning of the expression "debts provable in bankruptcy," see Chap. 9.

[82] *Royal Bank of Scotland v. Cuthbert* (1813) 1 Rose 462; *Odwin v. Forbes* (1817) Buck. 57 (P.C.); *Edwards v. Ronald* (1830) 1 Knapp P.C. 259, 12 E.R. 317; *Armani v. Castrique* (1844) 13 M. & W. 443, 447, 153 E.R. 185, 186 *per* Pollock, C.B. *arguendo*; *Gill v. Baron* (1868) L.R. 2 P.C. 157, 175–176 *per* Kelly L.C.B.; *Ellis v. M'Henry* (1871) L.R. 5 C.P. 228; *New Zealand Loan and Mercantile Agency Co. Ltd v. Morrison* [1898] A.C. 349 (P.C.), at 357–358, *per* Lord Davey. See also *Sidaway v. Hay* (1824) 3 B. & C. 12, 107 E.R. 639; *Re Nelson* [1918] 1 K.B. 459; *Swiss Bank Corp. v. Boehmische Industrial Bank* [1923] 1 K.B. 673, 678, *per* Bankes, L.J. and at 681, *per* Scrutton, L.J.

[83] See *infra*.

creation and extinction of obligations were in a primitive state. It is also surely not without significance that the cases in which were uttered the most forthright expressions of the effectiveness of an English discharge appear, on a strict appraisal of their facts, to have involved issues which were actually confined within the limits of the United Kingdom and the (then) British Empire. Hence, the language employed in key passages of the judgments would seem to have been not merely excessive but also unnecessary for the purposes of deciding the case at bar. It is submitted that this particular rule of English law is urgently in need of revision, and should be formulated in such a way as to accord with the commonly-accepted modern theory that the question of discharge of any legal obligation which is not governed by the law of the state in which bankruptcy occurs is to be referred to the law by which the obligation is considered to be governed.

The position of creditors in an English bankruptcy containing international elements

As a natural counterpart to the proposition that an English adjudication takes effect in relation to the bankrupt's entire estate in every part of the world, English law admits to proof all creditors to whom the bankrupt is indebted,[84] regardless of their nationality, domicile or country of primary residence, and also regardless of where the liability arose or was incurred, or of which country's law actually governs the obligation in question.[85] The ranking of any particular creditor for the purposes of receiving dividend during the process of distribution of the bankrupt's estate is therefore determined solely by reference to the nature of the debt itself, in accordance with the principles which have already been described.[86]

The operation of the principle *par est condicio omnium creditorum*, while commendable in itself on the grounds of equitable administration, nevertheless gives rise to certain difficulties both legal and practical in nature. These arise from the fact that, as has been explained above, the true international effectiveness of an English adjudication is necessarily dependent upon the extent to which the rules of law in force in other countries of the world actually accord it recognition and effect. It must be acknowledged that, in some jurisdictions at least, the title and standing of the trustee in bankruptcy may never be accorded recognition at all, while

---

[84] Subject only to exception in the case of those creditors whose debts belong to any of the categories of non-provable debts: see Chap. 9, *ante*. See also what is said at the beginning of this Chap. regarding the concept of indebtedness.

[85] *Re Kloebe* (1884) 28 Ch.D. 175; *Re Wiskemann* (1923) 92 L.J. Ch. 349; *Re Azoff-Don Commercial Bank* [1954] 1 Ch. 315, 333 per Wynn-Parry, J. *cf.* the much-criticized case of *Re Lorillard* [1922] 2 Ch. 638 (concerning the administration of the estate of a deceased insolvent) in which the foreign creditors' technical right to lodge claim in the English administration was rendered nugatory by the fact that, under English law, their claims were statute-barred, and hence their proofs would inevitably have been rejected.

[86] See Chap. 10. Note, however, the effect of the principle explained *supra* with regard to claims by the authorities of politically foreign countries for revenue and penal liabilities due from the bankrupt.

in others there may be a lengthy delay before such recognition can be gained through the appropriate local channels, whether administrative or judicial.[87] In such circumstances certain creditors may take action, either directly or through the courts, against both tangible and intangible assets presently situate within the jurisdictions in question. Such actions, which contravene the fundamental tenets upon which English bankruptcy law is based, give rise to problems of two kinds. The first question is to what extent, if at all, it is competent for the English courts to restrain such unilateral acts of diligence when effected beyond the courts' own jurisdiction, and the second is in what way such creditors may be dealt with subsequently in the event that their actions are initially successful?

Powers exercisable by English courts in relation to foreign proceedings

The possibility that English courts may restrain creditors from taking action against the bankrupt's foreign assets was explored in a small group of 19th century cases whose precise implications are not altogether easy to identify. Thus, in *Re Distin, ex parte Ormiston*,[88] it was held that the court would grant an injunction to restrain an "English creditor" from taking proceedings in a foreign court for a debt "incurred in England." It may be inferred from the brief report of the case that all the creditors, though described in the judgment as "British subjects", were also resident in England and hence were directly amenable to the *in personam* jurisdiction of the court granting the injunction. It may well also have been true that all the debts, as well as being incurred in England, were also governed by English law. The case was subsequently distinguished in *Re Chapman*[89] where the foreign actions were being undertaken by creditors who were resident abroad, albeit they were also citizens of the state in which they resided. It would seem safer to assert that, nowadays, the English courts would not normally issue an injunction against a creditor who did not reside or do business here. Indeed, the force of the maxim that "Equity does nothing in vain" should ensure that in practice the English courts will refrain from exercising their discretion to grant an injunction against a party who is personally beyond the reach of their jurisdiction. The factor of the creditor's nationality should, it is submitted, not nowadays be considered relevant to this question, nor indeed should the factor of domicile be so considered unless accompanied by some further factor such as residence or his doing business here. On the other hand, where the creditor in question has already become involved in the proceedings taking place in England—as by lodging proof in the bankruptcy, or even by presenting the petition himself—such action should in principle render him subject to the restraining jurisdiction of the English court regardless of whether he was previously amenable to the *in personam* jurisdiction of the English courts.[90]

---

[87] *cf.* remarks in the House of Lords, Hansard October 22, 1981, Cols. 864 (Lord Scarman) and 870 (Viscount Bledisloe).
[88] (1871) 24 L.T. 197.
[89] (1873) L.R. 15 Eq.75.
[90] *Re Tait and Co.* (1872) L.R. 13 Eq. 311 (see especially at p. 313 *per* Bacon, C.J., and see the

Trustee's powers to reclaim the fruits of foreign diligence by creditors

If the creditor's personal act of diligence against the bankrupt's foreign assets proves successful, the pertinent question is whether the trustee in bankruptcy may somehow retrieve the proceeds resulting therefrom, on behalf of the general body of creditors. If the creditor in question seeks also to prove in the bankruptcy for any outstanding balance of liabilities still alleged to be due to him from the bankrupt there is a long-settled rule to the effect that he must respect the equitable principles of equality of distribution which lie at the heart of our bankruptcy law. On the premiss that "he who seeks equity must do equity", the creditor may be excluded from lodging proof and receiving dividend unless and until he has duly accounted for and surrendered to the trustee all the fruits yielded by his private actions in any jurisdiction in the world.[91] It should be emphasised however that the principle of surrender into hotchpot as a precondition to the creditor's eligibility to lodge proof does not apply to the realisation of *bona fide*, pre-existing securities against the bankrupt's foreign assets, valid according to the law of the *situs* of the assets: such a creditor may prove for the balance of his claims against the bankrupt without being obliged to surrender his security, although he must of course account for and give credit for what he has received.[92] Where concurrent bankruptcies take place in this country and abroad in respect of the same debtor, the English court may conclude that the estate is in essence unitary, and if so will not permit a creditor who has obtained dividend in the foreign administration to receive dividend out of the English bankruptcy until all other creditors here have received dividend at the same rate as has been paid abroad.[93]

The "Hotchpot rule", as just described, is a sound and fair mechanism, apt to ensure that no creditor can take advantage of the extremely liberal policy operated by English law towards the claims of all creditors, while he simultaneously exploits the practical limitations which prevent an English adjudication from commanding in reality the universal effectiveness which

---

observations of the same learned Judge in *Re Morton* (1875) L.R. 20 Eq. 733 at 738. See also *Ord v. Barton* (1847) 9 D. 541). *cf. Moore v. Anglo-Italian Bank* (1879) 10 Ch.D. 681, where the fact that the foreign proceedings concerned the realisation of the creditor's security over immovable property situate in the foreign country, coupled with the clear evidence that all interested parties would be afforded notice and opportunity to be heard in those proceedings, seems to have influenced the English court in its decision not to restrain the petitioning creditor from maintaining the proceedings abroad. (This was a winding-up case, however.)

[91] *Selkrig v. Davies* (1814) 2 Dow. 230, 3 E.R. 848 (H.L.) (on appeal from the Court of Session); *Banco de Portugal v. Waddell* (1880) 5 App.Cas. 161 (H.L.); *Re Morton (supra)*; *Re Douglas, ex p. Wilson* (1872) L.R. 7 Ch.App. 490. The same principle is embodied in both Scots and English law: see *Lindsay v. Paterson* (1840) 2 D. 1373; *Stewart v. Auld* (1851) 13 D. 1337. See also *Re Bowes* (1889) W.N. 53, where the facts were somewhat special in view of the fact that the liability in respect of which the retention was permitted had become limitation-barred in England, and hence was not provable here. For a comparative survey of this subject, see H. Hanisch in I.F. Fletcher (Ed.) *op. cit. supra*, n. 69, Ch. 11 (pp. 192–204).

[92] *Re Somes* (1896) 3 Mans. 131; *Re Sykes* (1932) 101 L.J. Ch. 298. *cf. Re Bowes, (supra)*.

[93] *Stewart v. Auld (supra)*; *Re Douglas ex p. Wilson (supra)* especially at p. 493 *per* James, L.J. and at p. 494 *per* Mellish, L.J.

partially supplies the justification for the policy of according equal treatment to all creditors, regardless of their personal origins. In some cases, compliance with the Hotchpot rule necessarily entails a certain calculated risk on the part of the creditor, who may ultimately find that the dividend paid to him fails to match the *quantum* of what he has surrendered to the trustee. Hence, understandably, a creditor who is otherwise not personally subject to the jurisdiction of the English courts may conclude that it would be disadvantageous to become embroiled in the bankruptcy administration at all. If such a creditor prefers to pocket what he has recovered by his personal efforts, it is conceded that the English courts presently lack the power to compel him to lodge proof and thereby submit to English law on its full terms.[94] In the alternative, it has sometimes been suggested that the trustee's proper recourse in such circumstances lies by way of an action against the creditor for money had and received. This line of attack was explored in a series of early cases[95] whose authoritativeness for present day purposes is perhaps questionable. Ostensibly, those cases lay down a broad proposition to the effect that a creditor who attaches any foreign asset of the bankrupt after the latter has committed an act of bankruptcy upon which adjudication later takes place may be compelled to pay over the proceeds of attachment to the trustee as monies had and received to the trustee's use. On closer investigation, however, it transpires that in each instance the creditor was resident in England,[96] or in some other part of the United Kingdom,[97] and that he perpetrated the attachment knowing that the debtor had committed an act of bankruptcy, or had indeed already undergone adjudication. Moreover, the property involved in the foreign attachments appears to have been of a movable character, and hence some of the judicial decisions seem to have been heavily coloured by a consideration of the effects of the maxim "*mobilia personam sequuntur.*" The true scope of this particular remedy may therefore be a somewhat narrow one, since it would appear that no court has yet ventured to make an order for restitution against a creditor whose personal circumstances were not such as to render him subject to the *in personam* jurisdiction of the ordinary English courts, nor is it clear to what extent a creditor's lack of knowledge of the relevant events, or the possibility that immovable property might have undergone attachment, would affect the outcome of the action brought by the English trustee.

---

[94] *Selkrig v. Davies (supra)* at p. 249 *per* Lord Eldon, L.C. (3 E.R. at 854–855).

[95] *Neale v. Cottingham* (1764) 1 H.Bl. 132n, 126 E.R. 81 (also in Finley's Digest and Index of the Irish Reports (1830) 36n.; Wallis and Lyne, Irish Ch.Rep. (1839) 54); *Sill v. Worswick* (1791) 1 H.Bl. 665, 126 E.R. 379; *Hunter v. Potts* (1791) 4 Term Rep. 182, 100 E.R. 962; *Phillips v. Hunter* (1795) 2 H.Bl. 402, 126 E.R. 618. *cf. Brickwood v. Miller* (1817) 3 Mer. 279, 36 E.R. 108, where a distinction was drawn between those actions taken abroad to satisfy debts due from the bankrupt jointly with others, and those to satisfy debts due from the bankrupt alone.

[96] In the case of *Phillips v. Hunter (supra)* the creditor who attached the debtor's assets in America was residing abroad at the time, but was engaged in a partnership trading in England, with two partners who resided here. Moreover the attachment was effected in the name of himself and his partners, and the action for money had and received was brought by the trustee against all three partners together.

[97] In *Neale v. Cottingham (supra)*, the creditor was described as a "Dublin merchant." At the time, however, all of Ireland was subject to the sovereignty of the British Crown.

The attempt has sometimes been made to argue the case for a somewhat different basis for exercising this restitutionary remedy, namely that the creditor should be liable to an action for money had and received if, at the time he effected the attachment, he personally satisfied any of the jurisdictional requirements listed in the Insolvency Act (or its predecessors) as grounds to be satisfied in order that a debtor may be liable to undergo bankruptcy adjudication.[98] This seems, with respect, to be an unwarranted distortion of the meaning and purpose of the statutory provision in question which is, as we have seen, merely limitative of the liability of a debtor who is otherwise amenable to the bankruptcy jurisdiction of our courts to undergo bankruptcy here upon a creditor's petition. Of itself, section 265 of the Insolvency Act does not determine the question of the jurisdiction of the English bankruptcy courts over the debtor, much less does it do so with regard to the creditor. It is somewhat fanciful to conjure out of but one part of the rules governing a *debtor's* amenability to the bankruptcy law—relating moreover to circumstances which must be satisfied at the date of the petition—a rule to be applied to *creditors* at the date when they effect an attachment abroad.

The need for rationalisation of the rules of law

In truth, the general question of the jurisdiction of the English bankruptcy courts over creditors is nowhere the subject of systematic provision. Certain rules do indeed exist to enable the courts to exercise jurisdiction over any creditor who presents a petition against a debtor, or who endeavours to prove for his debt.[99] It is also accepted that the English bankruptcy law and its processes are available to creditors regardless of their personal origins or legal associations, should they wish to avail themselves of them. But beyond these principles, there is nothing to indicate that under English bankruptcy law persons who happen to be creditors are subject to any special jurisdictional rules differing from those which govern the exercise of *in personam* jurisdiction by English law generally.

It is submitted that hitherto there has been undue obsession with the question of the creditor's personal amenability to the jurisdiction of the English courts at the time of the foreign attachment,[1] while too little

---

[98] See now, Insolvency Act s.265, discussed earlier in this Chapter. See also *Cheshire and North's Private International Law* (12th ed., 1992), pp. 908–911; Dicey and Morris, *The Conflict of Laws* (12th ed., 1993) at pp. 1166–1168. *cf.* also *Re Paramount-Airways Ltd.* [1992] 3 All E.R. 1 (C.A.), at pp. 11–12, *per* Nicholls, V.-C. (a case involving reversal of a transaction entered into by an insolvent company with a person resident abroad).

[99] Insolvency Act s.266(2); Insolvency Rules, rr. 6.32; 6.96; 6.105. See also the cases cited *supra*, n. 85.

[1] One exception to this statement is to be found in Schmitthoff, *The English Conflict of Laws* (1954) at p. 270. On the other hand, Dicey and Morris, *The Conflict of Laws* (12th ed., 1993), at pp. 1167–1168, argue for a mid-way position in which the creditor's liability to disgorge would be conditional upon his having been resident in England at the time of carrying out the foreign attachment. This suggestion, which is less extreme than that advanced in the text above, is certainly a tenable one. It is submitted however that this approach is unduly restrictive of the English trustee's powers to act on behalf of the general body of creditors. *cf.* the position under Scots law, described by Anton, *Private International Law* (2nd ed., 1990) at p. 734.

attention has been paid to the question of ownership of the property attached, at the material time. Hence it is suggested that the proper approach in such cases is to enquire whether, at the time when the creditor carried out the attachment abroad, the property thus attached had already become vested in the trustee in bankruptcy in the eyes of English law. If such is the case, logic surely compels us to insist that the property which has been thus improperly acquired by the attaching creditor should be recoverable from any party into whose hands it can be traced, and whom the jurisdictional powers of English law are able to reach at the time when proceedings for recovery are instituted. The creditor's nationality, domicile or residence at the time of acting abroad should not be regarded as a material factor, nor should the matter of his knowledge or ignorance of the debtor's having undergone adjudication be considered relevant, since English law regards the divestiture of the bankrupt's property to be both automatic and universal without reference to the state of awareness of any other interested party. On the other hand, to compel a creditor thus to disgorge property which he may have obtained by means of a judicial award in his favour pronounced by some foreign court would necessarily entail the calling in question of the authoritativeness of the foreign court's judgment. In the case of foreign proceedings of an *in personam* character, English law has traditionally respected and given effect to the judgment of a foreign court which has enjoyed what English private international law terms "jurisdiction in the international sense."[2] Exceptions do exist however to the general rules concerning recognition of foreign judgments by the courts of this country, and it could well be argued that it would be contrary to English public policy to give effect to a foreign judgment pronounced in favour of a creditor at a time when, in the eyes of English law, title to the property in question had already become vested in the trustee in bankruptcy.[3] A further possible ground for non-recognition, which would be in point whenever a creditor had sought and obtained judgment in a foreign jurisdiction fully knowing of the debtor's adjudication, would be that the foreign judgment had been obtained by fraud,[4] in the sense that this highly material fact had not been brought to the notice of the foreign court, thereby preventing the latter from displaying such readiness as it might have to accord recognition and effect to the English adjudication.

It must be conceded that such an assertion of the paramount character of an English adjudication, over the claims of a foreign judgment delivered by a court enjoying jurisdiction in the international sense over the matter and parties before it, would be more acceptable if its use were reserved for those cases where England is indubitably the most appropriate *forum* in which the debtor should undergo bankruptcy, as would be the case where

---

[2] For the meaning of this term see references given in n. 15, *supra*.

[3] On non-recognition of foreign judgments on the ground that they contravene public policy, see *Re Macartney* [1921] 1 Ch. 522. See also Foreign Judgments (Reciprocal Enforcement) Act 1933, s.4(1)(a)(v); and also the Brussels Convention (*supra*, n. 11) Arts. 27(1), 28.

[4] *cf. Abouloff v. Oppenheimer* (1882) 10 Q.B.D. 295; *Vadala v. Lawes* (1890) 25 Q.B.D. 310 (not bankruptcy cases); Foreign Judgments (Reciprocal Enforcement) Act 1933, s.4(1)(a)(iv), and *cf.* also s.4(1)(b).

he is habitually resident, or has his principal place of business, here. In cases where the jurisdiction of the English bankruptcy court was based upon any of the more insubstantial types of connection with this country, it would seem a somewhat unprincipled proceeding to advance the claims of universality to the extent of overriding the determinations of foreign courts which, not unreasonably, might well have had difficulty in accepting the validity of the proposition that an English adjudication should invariably predominate, regardless of the circumstances in which the jurisdiction of the English bankruptcy court happens to have been exercised.[5] Admittedly, in the case of a foreign determination of an *in rem* character, English law has traditionally maintained a more absolute policy of recognition and respect.[6] However, in relation to movable property at any rate, it is tentatively suggested that the English practice of fully recognising the force of such determinations could be treated as being subject to exception in the case where England constitutes the most appropriate *forum* of bankruptcy, and where the English adjudication is pronounced earlier in time than the foreign determination in favour of the creditor.

Choice of law rules employed in bankruptcy proceedings in England

We have seen earlier that numerous issues may arise affecting the jurisdictional competence of the English bankruptcy courts over a debtor who is personally connected with one or more foreign countries by virtue of any of a variety of possible factors. In other cases, the necessity may sometimes arise for English courts to refer to foreign law, either to establish whether a given person has undergone a foreign adjudication whose effects would be recognised by English law, or to establish whether the effects of any foreign discharge are recognised in principle by the law which constitutes the proper law of some alleged obligation.[7] However, once an English bankruptcy has been declared, the present choice of law rule for the purposes of all matters pertaining to the administration of the bankrupt's estate, and its distribution among his creditors, is simply to the effect that all such questions are governed by English law as *lex fori*.[8] In so far as the majority of the rules which govern the minutiae of a bankruptcy administration may properly be classified as procedural in character, this is perfectly in accord with the widely-accepted principle of private international law that all matters of procedure are governed by the *lex fori*, with the corollary that no rule of foreign law which is of a procedural character may play any part in the processes of decision taking place at the *forum*.[9] Thus, the mode of lodging of proof for a debt is not affected by such

---

[5] The position would of course be further enhanced if English law were to accord to foreign adjudications of bankruptcy a degree of recognition fully comparable in its effects to those claimed by English law for its own adjudications.

[6] See *Cammell v. Sewell* (1860) 5 H. & N. 728, 157 E.R. 1371; *Minna Craig S.S. Co. v. Chartered Mercantile Bank of India, London and China* [1897] 1 Q.B. 460.

[7] See below.

[8] *Pardo v. Bingham* (1868) L.R. 6 Eq. 485; *Thurburn v. Steward* (1871) L.R. 3 (P.C.) 478; *cf. Re Kloebe* (1884) 28 Ch.D. 175.

[9] *ex p. Melbourn* (1870) L.R. 6 Ch.App. 64; *Re Doetsch* [1896] 2 Ch. 836.

factors as the creditor's domicile, nationality or residence, nor by the fact that the debt is regulated by foreign law. However, as has been indicated, it may be necessary to make incidental reference to the law by which any liability is properly regulated, in order to establish whether the debt is valid and provable, or whether it is to be regarded as having been discharged previously on any ground including, of course, any previous bankruptcy undergone by the debtor.[10] Where assets have been recovered abroad, it seems that any existing preferential rights enjoyed by certain creditors under the foreign *lex loci* will be respected by English law, but any advantage thereby gained by the creditors in question will be made the subject of an equalising exercise during the course of distribution of dividends, so that the foreign creditors will not receive any payments until the domestic creditors have received a proportionate amount in respect of their debts.[11]

The Recognition of Foreign Adjudications at English Law

The basic rule of recognition first developed at English law was, characteristically, to the effect that a foreign bankruptcy occurring in the jurisdiction in which the debtor was domiciled (in the English sense of that term) would be recognised here as valid.[12] To this narrow, even parochial, basis of recognition, a limited number of further grounds for recognition have been added in decided cases, namely that the jurisdiction of the foreign court of bankruptcy will be acknowledged where the debtor himself has submitted thereto, either by presenting his own petition,[13] or by appearing and participating in the foreign proceedings.[14] It would also seem reasonable to assert, despite the lack of clear authority upon the point, that a foreign adjudication will be recognised in England if it has taken place in a country in which the debtor is habitually resident, or in which he has been carrying on business.[15] In principle we ought to acknowledge the validity of any foreign adjudication based upon the exercise of a ground of jurisdiction which is utilised by English law itself,[16]

---

[10] See below.
[11] *Re Kloebe (supra)*, at p. 177, *per* Pearson, J. See also the effects of the "hotchpot" rule described above, p. 713.
[12] *Re Blithman* (1866) L.R. 2 Eq. 23.
[13] *Re Davidson's Settlement Trusts* (1873) L.R. 15 Eq. 383; *Re Lawson's Trusts* [1896] 1 Ch. 175; *Re Burke, King v. Terry* (1919) 54 L.Jo. 430, 148 L.T. Jo. 175.
[14] *Houlditch v. Donegall* (1834) 2 Cl. & F. 470 H.L., 6 E.R. 1232; *Re Anderson* [1911] 1 K.B. 896, especially at 902, *per* Phillimore, J.; *Re Craig* (1916) 86 L.J. Ch. 62; *Bergerem v. Marsh* (1921) 125 L.J. 630. See also *Schemmer v. Property Resources Ltd* [1975] Ch. 273, at 285–286, *per* Goulding, J.
[15] *cf.* the Scots cases of *Obers v. Paton's Trustees* (1897) 24 R.719, and *Home's Trustee v. Home's Trustees*, 1926 S.L.T. 214, which are to this effect.
[16] *cf.* (in the field of recognition of foreign divorce decrees) the now-superseded principle of recognition based on "reciprocity," established in *Travers v. Holley* [1953] P. 246. However, in his judgment in *Schemmer v. Property Resources Ltd (supra)* at p. 287, Goulding, J. observed that caution should be exercised nowadays in relation to the use of the rule in *Travers v. Holley* for purposes of analogy.

and indeed it would be reasonable to go further and assert that a foreign adjudication should be recognised where it is pronounced by the courts of a country with which the debtor is genuinely and substantially connected.[17] Probably, the fact that an adjudication of bankruptcy carries such important consequences affecting the bankrupt's legal status was a main reason why, historically, English private international law first utilised a rule of recognition closely resembling that which, at common law, used to be employed in questions concerning the validity of foreign decrees of divorce or nullity of marriage.[18] Just as the common law rules pertaining to questions of personal status generally have undergone revision and augmentation in order to meet modern needs and realities,[19] it is respectfully submitted that similar adjustment needs to take place in relation to recognition of foreign adjudications of bankruptcy. The old cases form a particularly unreliable basis for the modern law in this matter, not least because the very basis for the exercise of the *in personam* jurisdiction of the English bankruptcy courts has been radically altered during the present century. Prior to 1914, British subjects might be made bankrupt here regardless of whether or not they were present within the jurisdiction at the time of committing an act of bankruptcy while, conversely, foreigners might only be amenable to undergo adjudication if trading or at least resident here.[20] Moreover, under even earlier phases of our bankruptcy law, certain categories of person, such as non-traders or women, were altogether excluded from the application of the law *ratione personae*.[21] These and other alterations in our domestic policy concerning the assertion and exercise of bankruptcy jurisdiction surely necessitate a wholesale re-appraisal of our attitudes in response to the behaviour of foreign courts in comparable matters.

We have seen above[22] that where the "foreign" adjudication was actually pronounced by a court belonging to one of the other parts of the United Kingdom—that is to say Scotland or Northern Ireland—a mandatory obligation to recognise and enforce such an adjudication is imposed upon the English bankruptcy courts by section 426 of the Insolvency Act. By that section, any order made by a court having jurisdiction in bankruptcy in any of the three jurisdictions within the United Kingdom is required to be enforced by the bankruptcy courts of the other two sister jurisdictions as if the order had been made by the court required to enforce it in a case of

---

[17] See *Schemmer v. Property Resources Ltd* (*supra*) for a ruling that in the circumstances, an insufficient connection existed in relation to the foreign jurisdiction in question. (This was, however, a case concerned with recognition of the validity of the appointment of a receiver appointed by a foreign court).

[18] *cf. Le Mesurier v. Le Mesurier* [1895] A.C. 517; *Armitage v. Attorney-General* [1906] P. 135.

[19] See in particular the provisions first enacted by the Recognition of Divorces and Legal Separations Act 1971, now further reformed and replaced by Part II of the Family Law Act 1986.

[20] See *Re Crispin* (1873) L.R. 8 Ch.App. 374, 379 *per* Mellish, L.J.; *ex p. Blain* (1879) 12 Ch.D. 522, 532 *per* Cotton, L.J.

[21] The English bankruptcy law became applicable to non-traders for the first time in 1861: see Bankruptcy Act 1861, s.69. Married women, apart from women engaged in trade, were not amenable to the bankruptcy law until 1935: see Law Reform (Married Women and Tortfeasors) Act 1935, s.1(d) (further discussed in Ch. 1, *ante*).

[22] *Supra*, p. 703.

bankruptcy within its own jurisdiction.[23] The terms of section 426 are so expressed that it is thought to be incompetent for the court thus called upon to enforce an order in bankruptcy to enquire into or question the jurisdiction of the court from which the judgment has originated.[24] Any challenge to the assumption of jurisdiction by the originating court must therefore be pursued within that jurisdiction before the matter becomes final and unappealable under the law of that part of the United Kingdom.

Recognition in England of the Proprietary Effects of a Foreign Adjudication

With regard to the proprietary effects of a foreign adjudication of bankruptcy (other than one pronounced by a court elsewhere within the United Kingdom) English law utilises two rules of recognition, turning upon the distinction between movable and immovable property.

Movable property

In the case of movables English law has for over two centuries maintained the principle that the bankrupt's movable assets, situate within the jurisdiction of the English court, automatically vest in his foreign trustee in bankruptcy (or equivalent) from the moment of adjudication.[25] (This applies to both tangible and intangible forms of movable property). Accordingly, provided that under the law by which his appointment is regulated he has the right to sue in his own name to recover the assets formerly belonging to the bankrupt, the foreign trustee may enlist the aid of the English courts in his endeavours to recover those assets on behalf of the general body of creditors, and to repel any efforts by individual creditors to attach them for themselves.[26] Nevertheless, in accordance with the close affinity which exists between bankruptcy and assignments generally, the foreign trustee is considered at English law to acquire his title subject to equities existing at the moment of acquisition.[27] Therefore, if any creditor has completed an attachment here of any asset belonging to the bankrupt before the time when the trustee's appointment is regarded by English law as having taken effect, the trustee's title to the property will be *pro tanto* defeated.[28] This rule of English law is not immune from

---

[23] *cf.* the early case of *Houlditch v. Donegall (supra)* for a judicial ruling on the enforceability of judgments between the different jurisdictions within the United Kingdom.

[24] *cf.* the Scots cases of *Wilkie v. Cathcart* (1870) 9 M.168, and *Salaman v. Tod*, 1911 S.C. 1214.

[25] *Solomons v. Ross* (1764) 1 Hy.Bl. 131n., 126 E.R. 79; (also reported in Wallis & Lyne, Irish Chancery Reports 59, *note* (1839); *Jollet v. Deponthieu* (1769) 1 Hy.Bl. 132n., 126 E.R. 80; *Alivon v. Furnival* (1834) 1 C.M. & R. 277, 149 E.R. 1084. *cf. Araya v. Coghill*, 1921 S.L.T. 321.

[26] *Macaulay v. Guaranty Trust Co. of New York* [1927] W.N. 308, 44 T.L.R. 99; *cf. Re Young* [1955] St.R.Qd. 254, and contrast *Schemmer v. Property Resources Ltd* [1975] Ch. 273.

[27] *Levasseur v. Mason & Barry* [1891] 2 Q.B. 73. See above, with regard to the application of the same principle in the case of an English trustee in bankruptcy.

[28] *Galbraith v. Grimshaw* [1910] A.C. 508 H.L.; *Singer v. Fry* (1915) 84 L.J.K.B. 2025; *Anantapadmanabhaswami v. Official Receiver of Secunderabad* [1933] A.C. 394 (P.C.).

criticism on a matter of principle, since it operates to deny the foreign trustee a capacity to cut down individual creditors' acts of diligence by means of powers and remedies comparable to those with which an English trustee is clothed.[29] As the decided cases currently purport to express it, English law refuses to acknowledge the force of any rule under the foreign *lex concursus* whereby the effects of bankruptcy, or the title of the trustee, may be regarded as having commenced at a point in time anterior to the actual date when the order of adjudication was judicially pronounced. The main authority for this proposition is *Galbraith v. Grimshaw*,[30] in which the House of Lords held that a judgment creditor, who had commenced garnishee proceedings in England in order to satisfy a judgment obtained against his debtor in Scotland, was not to be deprived of the fruits of his attachment by reason of the judgment debtor's subsequently undergoing sequestration in Scotland. Their Lordships' decision had the effect of denying the Scottish trustee the right to exercise his usual powers to reduce prior diligences against the debtor's estate. The main reason offered by their Lordships for refusing to allow the Scottish trustee's title to escape from the impact of the "equity" created by the English garnishment was that the powers of the Scottish trustee in this respect were statutory in origin, and therefore could not claim to operate extraterritorially in relation to property situate outside the jurisdiction within which the statutory provisions were expressed to be operative. This somewhat unsophisticated, if not disingenuous, decision,[31] which purports to disallow any possibility that the rules of law in force in one jurisdiction may enjoy effect elsewhere by virtue of rules of private international law in force in the other countries concerned, is surely long overdue for reconsideration. Although the proposition which received supreme judicial endorsement in *Galbraith v. Grimshaw* is ostensibly complementary to a further, long-established rule that an English trustee is comparably bound by all equities which have become binding upon the debtor's foreign property prior to his adjudication,[32] the ends of justice would surely be better served if both rules were to be disaffirmed in the interests of affording maximum scope to the trustee to act as representative of the general body of creditors. It would surely be more in accordance with the principle that all creditors of an insolvent debtor should be treated on a basis of equality, if English private international law were fully to recognise the effects of any foreign rules for the retrospective avoidance of transactions, including individual acts of diligence by creditors, which form part of the system of law under which the bankruptcy has opened.

---

[29] *cf. Neale v. Cottingham* (1764) 1 H.Bl. 132n., 126 E.R. 81, wherein the English assignees in bankruptcy were enabled to recover from the defendant creditor, as moneys had and received to their use, the sum of £600 which the creditor had attached from persons indebted to the bankrupt by means of proceedings commenced more than 12 months before the date of the adjudication, and completed more than nine months before that date.

[30] [1910] A.C. 508.

[31] Castigated by Anton, *Private International Law* (2nd ed., 1990), p. 734 as "unfortunate." If pursued to its logical conclusion, of course, the thesis to which their Lordships subscribed would deprive the trustee of all legal claim to the bankrupt's foreign property, since in the last analysis his title is conferred by virtue of statutory provisions in force in the jurisdiction in which he was appointed.

[32] *Re Scheibler, ex p. Holthausen* (1874) L.R. 9 Ch.App. 722.

Immovable property

In the case of English immovable property belonging to a debtor adjudicated in any foreign country apart from Scotland or Northern Ireland, the established rule at English law is that such an adjudication is not of itself capable of effecting a transfer of title to the property in question.[33] This rule of English private international law is in line with the universal practice employed in relation to immovable property. It may be noted however that the rule itself is not balanced by a comparable curtailment of the claims for universal effectiveness against both movable and immovable property which are made, as we have seen,[34] in respect of an adjudication pronounced in England, or indeed in Scotland or Northern Ireland. However, in practice the English courts are likely to afford a foreign trustee a considerable degree of assistance in taking steps to obtain a vesting order in his favour, or to procure the formal conveyance to himself of the bankrupt's English immovable property. Indeed, the English court may empower the trustee to effect a sale of such property by formally appointing him a receiver of the bankrupt's property here, clothed with a power to sell the same and to deal with the proceeds in accordance with the provisions of the *lex concursus*.[35] Such co-operation from the English courts depends, as we have seen, upon a combination of factors. First, it is essential that the court be satisfied that, by the law under which he has obtained his appointment, the trustee is personally invested with title to the bankrupt's property, or at least that he is empowered to sell the same in his own name on behalf of the general body of creditors.[36] Secondly, it must be shown that the operation of the foreign law of bankruptcy purports to have application to the bankrupt's entire property wheresoever situate: if the *lex concursus* itself treats its effects as being confined within the limits of its own jurisdiction, the issue of recognition of the trustee's title to property situate in England does not even arise.[37] Thirdly, the foreign trustee's standing before the English courts depends upon the extent to which English private international law recognises the jurisdictional competence of the court which has made the order of adjudication upon which his appointment is consequently based. As has been explained above, English law is generally under-developed in this respect, and it remains to be seen how far the suggested tests of "reciprocity" or "genuine and substantial connection" will commend themselves to the courts in cases occurring in future.

---

[33] *Waite v. Bingley* (1882) 21 Ch.D. 674; *Re Levy's Trusts* (1885) 30 Ch.D. 119; *cf. Cockerell v. Dickens* (1840) 3 Moo. P.C. 98, 13 E.R. 45; *Phosphate Sewage Co. Ltd v. Molleson* (1878) 5 R. 1125; *ex p. Bettle* (1895) 14 N.Z.L.R. 129; *Australian Mutual Provident Society v. Gregory* (1908) 5 C.L.R. 615. The proposition stated in the text above should be distinguished from the question of whether an adjudication abroad may serve to work a forfeiture of an interest in real estate situate in England, by virtue of some provision in the will or settlement by which the bankrupt's interest is conferred: *Re Levy's Trusts* (*supra*); *Re Aylwin's Trusts* (1873) L.R. 16 Eq. 585. On forfeiture clauses generally, see Chap. 8.

[34] *Supra.*

[35] *Re Kooperman* [1928] W.N. 101, 72 Sol.Jo. 400; *Re Levy's Trusts* (*supra*) at p. 123, per Kay, J.; *Re Osborn* (1931–32) 15 B. & C.R. 189; *cf. Araya v. Coghill*, 1921 S.L.T. 321.

[36] *cf.* cases cited *supra*, n. 26.

[37] *cf. ex p. Melbourn* (1870) L.R. 6 Ch.App. 64.

The Effects in England of a Foreign Discharge from Bankruptcy

It would appear that, historically, English law has failed to regard an order of discharge from bankruptcy made by a foreign court as falling within the general principles of recognition applicable to foreign judgments pronounced in ordinary proceedings of an *in personam* character.[38] Hence, the question whether the foreign bankruptcy court may be said to have enjoyed jurisdiction in the international sense in relation to the bankrupt at the time of inception of proceedings seems never to have been employed as a basis for according recognition to any order of discharge subsequently granted by the court in question. The decided cases, such as they are, furnish authority only for the proposition that a foreign discharge from bankruptcy[39] will be recognised as a valid discharge of any contractual debt or liability provided that it operates as such under the proper law of the contract.[40] Although the point does not appear to have been pursued in any of the decided cases, it is herein assumed that English law would not adopt so narrowly rigid a view as to insist that the only instance in which a foreign discharge can be recognised as effective is one in which, coincidentally, the country of bankruptcy happens also to be the country of the proper law. It is submitted that it would be fully in accord with established practice under English private international law if England law were to recognise any foreign discharge which can be shown to be recognised by the law which does constitute the proper law of the obligation in question.[41] In the case of liabilities founded upon tort, it would appear that any discharge which is effective according to the law of the place where the tort was committed will preclude any action from being brought in England in respect of the same tort.[42]

Inconsistencies resulting from the current rules of English law

The above rule, which respects the widely-accepted principle that the

---

[38] See references *supra*, p. 694, n. 13, regarding the recognition of foreign judgments generally.

[39] That is, a discharge other than one pronounced by a court in Northern Ireland or Scotland, *q.v. infra*.

[40] *Burrows v. Jemino* (1726) 2 Str. 733, 93 E.R. 815; *Potter v. Brown* (1804) 5 East 124, 102 E.R. 1016; *Quelin v. Moisson* (1828) 1 Knapp P.C. 265n., 12 E.R. 320; *Gardiner v. Houghton* (1862) 2 B. & S. 743, 121 E.R. 1247; *Ellis v. M'Henry* (1871) L.R. 6 C.P. 228, 234 *et seq.*, *per* Bovill, C.J. *cf. Perry v. Equitable Life Assurance Society of U.S.A.* (1929) 45 T.L.R. 468.

[41] *cf. Armitage v. Attorney-General* [1906] P. 135 (a case on the recognition of foreign divorce decrees not granted by the courts of the matrimonial domicile, but recognised as valid according to the law there in force).

[42] Private International Law (Miscellaneous Provisions) Act 1995, Part III, which abolishes the common law rules based on *Phillips v. Eyre* (1870) L.R. 6 Q.B. 1, and *Boys v. Chaplin* [1971] A.C. 356 (H.L.). In exceptional cases, the applicable law will be that of the country whose law constitutes the "proper law" of the tort. In such cases, the statement in the text above would require to be modified so as to admit that a discharge effective under the *lex propria delicti* would preclude action in England. For further discussion, see Morris, *The Conflict of Laws* (4th ed., 1993), pp. 280–297; *Cheshire and North's Private International Law* (12th ed., 1992) pp. 529–550.

discharge of an obligation is a matter to be determined by the law by which the particular obligation is governed, is nevertheless impossible to reconcile with the corresponding rule, already described, whereby English law regards an English discharge from bankruptcy as possessing universal effect regardless of the proper law by which any of the bankrupt's obligations may originally have been governed.[43] The same rule of full, universal recognition is also applied by English private international law to any discharge pronounced by a bankruptcy court in Scotland[44] or Northern Ireland.[45] Various objections, in terms of both principle and logic, may be made to the unequal picture which thus emerges under English law as presently formulated. Thus, it seems absurd that English law will undoubtedly recognise the validity of the title of a foreign trustee to the bankrupt's English assets provided that the trustee derives his appointment under the law of the country where the bankrupt is domiciled, or to whose jurisdiction the bankrupt has submitted, yet will fail to apply the usual corollary that, in return for surrendering his available property to the trustee in bankruptcy for distribution among his creditors, the bankrupt becomes discharged from all his provable debts. The possibility might indeed arise that, despite his having so surrendered all of his property, and despite the fact that English private international law would recognise the validity of the adjudication, a discharged bankrupt might be held liable by an English court to fulfil some pre-existing obligation on the ground that the law by which the obligation is governed does not acknowledge the effectiveness of the discharge granted by the court of bankruptcy. This illogical dichotomy will persist until such time as there is established a common international practice both in relation to the identification of the proper law of an obligation, and also in relation to the grounds for international recognition of a bankruptcy adjudication. Since, at present, there is no widespread consensus in relation to either of these matters, the possibility always exists that a given adjudication may be recognised in one or more of the countries in which the bankrupt's assets may be found, but will not be recognised in some particular country whose law happens to constitute the proper law of an obligation to which the bankrupt was previously bound.

While the final solution to the foregoing problem is undoubtedly a long way off,[46] it may be said that some of the difficulties to be found in the English case law relating to the recognition of the effects of a foreign discharge appear to be of our own making. In a series of cases, in which the English courts concluded that English law constituted the proper law of the contract in question, it has been held that the debtor's adjudication

---

[43] See *supra*, p. 710, and criticisms there made.

[44] *Sidaway v. Hay* (1824) 3 B. & C. 12, 107 E.R. 639. *cf. Phillips v. Allan* (1828) 8 B. & C. 477, 108 E.R. 1120, where a distinction was drawn between the effects of discharge under the statutory procedure for sequestration, and those following upon the Scots procedure of *cessio bonorum*.

[45] *Ferguson v. Spencer* (1840) 1 M. & G. 987, 133 E.R. 632; *Simpson v. Mirabita* (1869) L.R. 4 Q.B. 257. *cf. Re Nelson* [1918] 1 K.B. 459, in which a distinction was drawn between the effects of a discharge from bankruptcy and those following upon the issue of a certificate of conformity to an arranging debtor.

[46] See however the developments taking place in recent times, discussed in Chap. 31.

abroad, and his subsequent discharge from that bankruptcy, did not have the effect of releasing him from his contractual liability.[47] It is submitted that the reasoning upon which these decisions were based is seriously defective, in that in each instance it was merely asserted that English law did not recognise the effectiveness of the foreign discharge from bankruptcy, whereas the appropriate question to have considered was whether English law, as the proper law of the contract, *ought* to recognise the exercise of bankruptcy jurisdiction by the courts of the foreign country in question. Thus, in what is perhaps the best-known example from this line of cases, the Court of Appeal in *Gibbs & Sons v. La Société Industrielle et Commercial des Métaux*[48] held that a French company could be sued in England in respect of a contract "made and to be performed in England", despite the fact that the defendants had undergone a judicial liquidation in France, the country which undoubtedly constituted the proper forum for such proceedings to take place. The plaintiffs had had the opportunity to lodge proof for their contractual claim in the French liquidation, but part of their claim had been rejected by the liquidator as inadmissible under French law. In the course of his judgment in favour of the plaintiffs, Lord Esher M.R. voiced the following rhetorical question:

> "Why should the plaintiffs be bound by the law of a country to which they do not belong, and by which they have not contracted to be bound?"[49]

and he went on to assert further that if the contract had been made in any foreign country other than France itself, the plaintiffs could sue upon it in this country and their action could not be affected by the law of France. With respect, if the judgment of Lord Esher M.R. must indeed be taken to express the position which obtains whenever English law is the proper law of a contract,[50] then English private international law in this respect is insular and xenophobic in the extreme, and is plainly guilty of maintaining dual standards with regard to the principle of universality of bankruptcy. It seems to be an assumption of the judgment of the learned Master of the Rolls that when English law is the proper law of the contract, no bankruptcy will have the slightest effect upon the parties' contractual rights unless the bankruptcy occurs in England itself, a condition which cannot be met in all cases because, for very obvious and proper reasons,

---

[47] *Smith v. Buchanan* (1800) 1 East 6, 102 E.R. 3; *Armani v. Castrique* (1844) 13 M. & W. 443, 153 E.R. 185, especially at p. 447 *per* Pollock, C.B.; *Bartley v. Hodges* (1861) 1 B. & S. 375, 121 E.R. 754; *Gibbs & Sons v. La Société Industrielle et Commercial des Métaux* (1890) 25 Q.B.D. 399; *National Bank of Greece v. Metliss* [1958] A.C. 509 (H.L.).
[48] (1890) 25 Q.B.D. 399.
[49] *ibid.*, at p. 406.
[50] It is noteworthy that the grounds upon which the Court of Appeal in 1890 deduced that the contract was governed by English law—namely that England was both the place of contracting and the place of performance of the contract—would not necessarily be so conclusive today, although in the circumstances of the particular contract in the *Gibbs* case, English law might still be held to be the proper law.

not every person who happens to enter into a contract governed by English law is capable of being made bankrupt in England.

While it is conceded that not every foreign adjudication is pronounced in circumstances which warrant the according of universal recognition to the bankruptcy and its subsequent resolution by discharge, it is undoubtedly the case that the vast majority do merit such recognition by the laws of other countries. English law should therefore formulate a properly-considered rule for recognition of foreign adjudications, which should be complemented by a further rule to the effect that any foreign bankruptcy which enjoys recognition by virtue of the rule of English private international law will also be considered as having the capability of discharging any contract of which English law happens to be the proper law, subject to the proviso that English creditors enjoy full rights to lodge proof in the foreign bankruptcy. It is further suggested that the test which English law ought to apply should be based upon criteria which are both more stable and more generally accepted than that of the debtor's domicile. Thus, a bankruptcy opened in the country of the debtor's habitual residence, or in which his principal centre of business is situated, should certainly merit such recognition. These two criteria, together with the possibility of the debtor's personal, voluntary submission to the bankruptcy jurisdiction of the *forum concursus*, could perhaps provide a widely acceptable basis for recognition. Alternatively, a less radical—and less satisfactory—solution, but one which it has already been suggested[51] may be reasonably in accord with common law rules developed as the basis for recognition of other types of status-determining decrees, would be to recognise any foreign adjudication pronounced by a court which has utilised a ground of jurisdiction known to the English domestic law of bankruptcy, or pronounced by a court with whose jurisdiction the debtor is genuinely and substantially associated.[52] It is furthermore submitted that, whichever rule is adopted for the purposes of recognising the effects of a foreign bankruptcy in relation to the discharge of the bankrupt's liabilities, the same rule should also be employed by English law for the purposes of recognising the title of the foreign trustee to the bankrupt's movable assets situate in England, and also his right to claim the bankrupt's English immovables.

Final limitations on the scope of recognition of discharge under foreign law

Finally, it must be remarked that the recognition in England of the effects of a foreign discharge is always conditioned by the nature of the legal effects which, under the *lex concursus* itself, follow upon a discharge granted in that jurisdiction. Thus, if by that law the effects of any discharge from bankruptcy are considered to be confined within the limits of that

---

[51] See *supra*.
[52] It may be noted, however, that the "reciprocal recognition" and "real and substantial connection" tests, formerly utilised at various times by English law for the purposes of according recognition to foreign divorce decrees, have now been supplanted by different, internationally-agreed tests now contained in the Family Law Act 1986.

country[53] or are considered to introduce a mere procedural bar to recovery of liabilities in that jurisdiction (as distinct from cancelling the substantive liabilities themselves)[54] English law will in either case continue to treat the debtor's liabilities as subsisting and enforceable by action.

Concurrent Bankruptcies

From the foregoing account of the English jurisdictional rules in bankruptcy, it is evident that there are at any given time a large number of persons who are in principle amenable to the jurisdiction of our courts. Of these, a not inconsiderable proportion will, by reason of various factors connecting them simultaneously with one or more foreign countries, also be amenable to the bankruptcy jurisdiction (or its counterpart) of the country or countries in question. Hence it may transpire that bankruptcy proceedings are commenced against one and the same debtor in more than one country virtually simultaneously. Alternatively, an attempt may be made to open bankruptcy proceedings in one country notwithstanding that the debtor has previously been adjudicated bankrupt in another jurisdiction where the processes of administration of his estate have already reached a fairly advanced stage. In either eventuality, the first issue of principle which arises is whether to pronounce an adjudication in a case where there are, or may be, concurrent bankruptcies in several different jurisdictions. Since the world has yet to enter into the idealised arrangements whereby each debtor would undergo bankruptcy only in the jurisdiction which by common agreement is recognised to be the most appropriate in the circumstances of the particular case (the principle of unity of bankruptcy),[55] it is customary for plurality of bankruptcies to be accepted in practice. In spite of this, some legal systems (including our own) have hitherto not been averse to claiming for their own adjudications the quality of universality which, logically speaking, is irreconcilable with the notion of plurality of bankruptcies.[56] This practice has given rise to several inconsistencies in our law regarding the recognition of foreign adjudications.[57]

Practice of the English Courts

So far as English law is concerned, it is no impediment to the exercise of bankruptcy jurisdiction by our courts that concurrent proceedings are pending abroad, or indeed that the debtor has undergone adjudication

---

[53] *cf. Philpotts v. Reed* (1819) 1 Brod. & B. 294, 129 E.R. 735, at p. 297, *per* Dallas, C.J. One prominent example of the application of the doctrine of territoriality is under Japanese law, where insolvency proceedings are not regarded as affecting the debtor's assets outside that country. See Makoto Ito in I. F. Fletcher (Ed.), *Cross-Border Insolvency: National and Comparative Studies* (1992), Ch. 9 (pp. 178–185), esp. at 180 and 182.
[54] *cf. ex p. Melbourn* (1870) LR 6 Ch.App. 64.
[55] Some current initiatives to create such arrangements, on a regionally-limited basis, in Europe and elsewhere are described in Chap. 31.
[56] See Chap. 28, *ante*.
[57] See *supra*.

abroad.[58] It is true that the English courts will exercise their usual discretion to decline to adjudicate a debtor if it can be shown that he has no assets in this country,[59] and it is also true that the proceedings here may founder if it transpires that the rules of English private international law require the English court to recognise that the petitioning creditor's debt has become discharged as a result of the foreign bankruptcy proceedings.[60] But in other respects, even as between the different parts of the United Kingdom, there is no set of mandatory rules in force to compel the courts in one part to renounce jurisdiction in favour of a court in another, even though the greater part of the debtor's assets, and perhaps the majority of the creditors, may be located in closer proximity to the latter. Indeed, the discrepancies between the insolvency laws of the three parts of the United Kingdom give rise to several situations in which the English court may discern that the interests of justice will be better served by permitting the English bankruptcy proceedings to continue concurrently with proceedings in some other part of the United Kingdom.[61] *A fortiori*, where the concurrent proceedings are taking place outside the United Kingdom there is no established procedure for procuring the consolidation of all proceedings within the particular jurisdiction which may objectively seem to be the most suitable one. Although some of the early cases contain *dicta* suggestive of a possible rule whereby English courts might renounce jurisdiction in favour of the courts of the debtor's domicile,[62] it cannot be supposed that any such principle could command the force of law today, in view of the fact that the domiciliary connecting factor has ceased to be employed as a primary basis for the exercise of bankruptcy jurisdiction even by our own courts.

Need for a rationalised approach

There is certainly a long-standing need for international bankruptcy law to be placed upon a rationalised, orderly footing by means of multilateral arrangements aimed at substituting the principle of unity for that of

---

[58] *Re McCulloch* (1880) 14 Ch.D. 716; *Re Artola Hermanos* (1890) 24 Q.B.D. 640; *Re a Debtor (No. 199 of 1922)* [1922] 2 Ch. 470; *Re a Debtor (No. 737 of 1928)* [1929] 1 Ch. 362. A contrary position is adopted by Scots law, whereby only one competent forum for sequestration is acknowledged. Accordingly, if a debtor amenable to the bankruptcy jurisdiction of the Scottish courts undergoes sequestration abroad, this event precludes the award of a sequestration in Scotland: *Strother v. Read* (1803), Morrison, "Forum Competens," Appendix 4; *Goetze v. Aders* (1874) 2 R. 150; *Phosphate Sewage Co. Ltd v. Molleson* (1878) 5 R. 1125.

[59] *Re Robinson* (1883) 22 Ch.D. 816, dist. in *Re a Debtor (No. 199 of 1922)*, supra.

[60] *cf. Re Pascal* (1876) 1 Ch.D. 509, 512, *per* James, L.J., For recognition of the effects of a foreign bankruptcy, see *supra*.

[61] As in *Re O'Reardon* (1873) L.R. 9 Ch.App. 74, and in *Re McCulloch* and *Re a Debtor (No. 199 of 1922)* (both *supra*). In the latter case the Court of Appeal found it an additional ground for allowing the English bankruptcy to proceed concurrently with the Scottish sequestration that the latter proceedings had been initiated by the debtor himself.

[62] *cf. Re Artola Hermanos*, (*supra*) at pp. 144–146, *per* Lord Coleridge, C.J., and at p. 649 *per* Fry, L.J. See also the remarks of Lord Westbury, L.C. in *Enohin v. Wylie* (1862) 10 H.L.C. 1, at p. 13, 11 E.R. 924 at p. 929, on the function of the court of the domicile as the *forum concursus* for the administration of estates in all cases of testate and intestate succession.

plurality.[63] In the meantime, it is submitted that more could be done than at present to save the duplication of effort and administrative costs which are the inevitable consequence of concurrent bankruptcies. Within the United Kingdom, at least, complementary provisions could be adopted with a view to ensuring that bankruptcy need only occur in one part of the Kingdom in any given case. On the wider international plane, some unilateral initiatives might be pursued, utilising the new opportunities made possible by section 426 of the Insolvency Act,[64] so that our courts might establish the practice of relinquishing jurisdiction in favour of some foreign *forum concursus* where the ends of justice and convenience would be demonstrably better served thereby. Where concurrent bankruptcies do take place, it may prove possible for the two trustees to collaborate in a constructive and beneficial way. An initiative of this kind was judicially sanctioned in *Re P. MacFadyen & Co.*,[65] in which the trustees in England and abroad resolved to pool all the assets and to distribute them rateably amongst the English and foreign creditors. By this means, much expense was spared and the possibility of costly litigation between the trustees themselves was avoided. Probably the most attractive feature of such an ad hoc arrangement was that it effectively surmounted the arbitrary inequities which might otherwise have resulted from the accidents of disposition of the assets at the moment of bankruptcy, as between the respective spheres of control of the two trustees.

---

[63] See Nadelmann (1944) 93 U.Pa.L.Rev. 58; (1946) 9 M.L.R. 154; (1943–4) 5 U.Tor. L.J. 324; (1961) 10 I.C.L.Q. 70. *cf. Re Paramount Airways Ltd. (No. 2)* [1992] BCC 416, at p. 424; [1992] 3 All E.R. 1, at p. 11, *per* Nicholls V.-C. ("There is a crying need for an international insolvency convention."). See further, Chap. 31, *post*.

[64] See suggestions in Chap. 31, *post*.

[65] [1908] 1 K.B. 675.

CHAPTER 30

LIQUIDATIONS WITH AN INTERNATIONAL ELEMENT

Jurisdiction to Wind Up Foreign Companies in England

An account was given in Chapter 20 of the general principles whereby a company which has not been formed and registered in England and Wales may be wound up by the court as an unregistered company under the provisions of Part V of the Insolvency Act.[1] The grounds on which an unregistered company may be wound up, as contained in section 221(5), were also described, and it was explained that these provisions are applicable to companies formed and registered under the law of a foreign country, and hence that they furnish the statutory basis for the exercise by courts in England and Wales of a jurisdiction to wind up foreign companies.[2] We will now examine the operation of this jurisdiction in more detail.

The meaning of "foreign company"

For the purposes of English company law, a foreign company is one which was incorporated under the law of any country outside Great Britain. Any such company which establishes or has a place of business in Great Britain is known as an "oversea company"[3] and, as such, is subject to special provisions of the Companies Act 1985 which impose a number of requirements upon the company with regard to registration of its presence, and nomination of one or more resident persons authorised to accept service of process and other formal notices on the company's behalf.[4] Where a company fulfils the conditions for being an oversea company, and duly complies with the ensuing statutory obligations, the company's

---

[1] See Chap. 20 *ante*, p. 528.
[2] *ibid.*, p. 531.
[3] Companies Act 1985, s.744.
[4] *ibid.*, Part XXIII (as amended), comprising ss.690A–703R inclusive. See especially ss.691, 695.

amenability to the jurisdiction of the English Courts is clearly and objectively established, and the procedural formalities for invoking that jurisdiction are greatly simplified. However, the jurisdictional competence of the English courts is not limited to those cases where a foreign company establishes a place of business here, nor even, where a place of business is established, to those cases where the oversea company has properly complied with the statutory requirements just referred to. Where an oversea company makes default in notifying the name and address of a person authorised to accept service of process, or where all such persons as have been so authorised are either dead, or for any reason cannot be served, a document may be served on the company at any place of business established by the company in Great Britain.[5] Furthermore, as will be seen below, there are instances in which the winding up jurisdiction of the English court has been successfully invoked, despite the fact that the foreign company had not established a place of business here, and so did not constitute an "oversea company" within the meaning of the Companies Act.

In the account which follows, the expression "foreign company" will serve to denote all companies incorporated under some foreign law whether or not they happen to qualify as "oversea companies" under English company law. It may be noted, however, that any company which has been incorporated under companies legislation in force in Great Britain is necessarily to be classified as a domestic company, even though the greater part—or indeed the entirety—of its business and other corporate activities take place overseas.[6] As such, the company will be liable to be wound up in accordance with the ordinary provisions of law contained in Part IV of the Insolvency Act, as described in Chapters 17 to 27 above.

The statutory definition of "unregistered company" supplied by section 220 of the Insolvency Act is so drafted as to be capable of applying, *inter alia*, to any company, partnership or association whose formation has occurred under foreign law. All such entities are in principle capable of being wound up by the English court as "unregistered companies."[7] A foreign company may be an unregistered company for the purposes of a winding up under Part V of the Insolvency Act despite the fact that a liquidation may be pending, or in progress, in its country of origin.[8] Indeed, as will be described below, the English courts are empowered to wind up a foreign company notwithstanding that the company may already have undergone liquidation and dissolution in its country of origin.[9] However, if it is the case that the company in question was never

---

[5] Companies Act 1985, s.695(2).
[6] *Reuss v. Bos* (1871) L.R. 5 (H.L.) 176; *cf.* Insolvency Act 1986, s.117(1): "The High Court has jurisdiction to wind up any company *registered in England and Wales*" (emphasis added). See also the definition of "company" contained in s.735 of the Companies Act 1985, discussed in Chap. 20, *ante*, p. 520.
[7] *Re Mercantile Bank of Australia* [1892] 2 Ch. 204 (decided under s.32(3) of the Companies (Winding Up) Act 1890).
[8] *Re Matheson Brothers* (1884) Ch.D. 225; *Re Commercial Bank of South Australia* (1886) 33 Ch.D. 174; *Re Federal Bank of Australia* [1893] W.N. 77.
[9] See Insolvency Act 1986, ss.221(5)(a), 225 discussed *infra*.

properly formed under the law of the country wherein it purports to have been incorporated, the position at English law is that there is not, and never has been, a legal entity in existence over which the jurisdiction of the English courts could be exercised, and hence no winding up can take place here.[10]

Winding up of foreign companies under section 221 of the Insolvency Act 1986

The main statutory basis for winding up of foreign companies is supplied by section 221 of the Insolvency Act, which effectively enables such a company to be wound up as an unregistered company under the Act. The general winding up provisions within Part IV of the Act are for this purpose specially modified by the provisions contained within Part V. Thus, the only form of winding up which is possible in the case of a foreign company is a compulsory winding up by the court: neither form of voluntary winding up is permissible in the case of a foreign company.[11]

The circumstances in which a foreign company may be wound up by the English court are listed in section 221(5) as follows:

(a) if the company is dissolved, or has ceased to carry on business, or is carrying on business only for the purpose of winding up its affairs;
(b) if the company is unable to pay its debts;
(c) if the court is of the opinion that it is just and equitable that the company should be wound up.

This section is but the latest embodiment of a provision which has been contained in the Companies Acts of this country since 1848.[12]

Section 221(5)(a): Company dissolved or having ceased to carry on business

The broad terms in which s.221(5)(a) of the Act is cast are such as to confer an extremely wide jurisdiction on the English courts to wind up foreign companies which have either entered into a state of financial difficulty or have actually undergone dissolution as a result of proceedings abroad. The opening words of the paragraph, ("if the company is dissolved ...") whose grammatical tense is somewhat less than clear, have been judicially construed to mean that the court has jurisdiction if the foreign

---

[10] *Re Imperial Anglo-German Bank* (1872) 26 L.T. 229; *cf. Maunder v. Lloyd* (1862) 2 J. and H. 718, 70 E.R. 1248 (decided on the basis of Common Law alone, and holding that the Court of Chancery had inherent jurisdiction to wind up a foreign partnership, initially validly formed, which might not have been fully wound up according to the law of its country of formation).

[11] Insolvency Act 1986, s.221(4).

[12] The provisions of s.221(5) were formerly enacted as: Joint Stock Companies Act 1848 s.5(7); Companies Act 1862, s.199(3); Companies Act 1908, s.268(1)(iii); Companies Act 1929, s.338(1)(*d*); Companies Act 1948, s.399(5); Companies Act 1985, s.666(5).

company "has been" dissolved abroad.[13] Whether such a dissolution has taken place is a question which, according to English rules of private international law, is referred to the law of the country under which the foreign company was incorporated.[14] This is a straightforward application of the principle that the personal, or domiciliary, law of a company formed under law is that of its State of incorporation, and that it is to the personal law that reference must be made regarding such matters as the validity of formation, status, powers and continued existence of the company as a legal person.[15] It is an established rule of English law that any question of foreign law must be proved as fact by means of the expert testimony of properly qualified persons.[16] In those cases where there is a general want of certainty as to the exact legal position under the foreign law in question, the English court of first instance will perforce have to evaluate the authority and credibility of the expert witnesses appearing before it, in order to determine whether a particular company shall be regarded as having undergone dissolution under the law of its state of incorporation.[17]

Problems inherent to the exercise of jurisdiction to wind up foreign companies

Each of the three different grounds mentioned in section 221(5)(a)

---

[13] *Re Family Endowment Society* (1870) L.R. 5 Ch.App. 118, 135–136 *per* Giffard L.J.; *Re Russian and English Bank* [1932] 1 Ch. 663; *Banque des Marchands de Moscou v. Kindersley* [1951] 1 Ch. 112 (C.A.).

[14] *Re Russian and English Bank* [1932] 1 Ch. 663; *Re Russian Bank for Foreign Trade* [1933] 1 Ch. 745; *Banque des Marchands de Moscou v. Kindersley* [1951] 1 Ch. 112 (C.A.); *Re Azoff-Don Commercial Bank* [1954] 1 Ch. 315.

[15] *Baroness Wenlock v. River Dee Co.* (1883) 36 Ch.D. 674, 685 *per* Bowen L.J.; *Lazard Bros. and Co. v. Midland Bank Ltd* [1933] A.C. 289 (H.L.) at 297 *per* Lord Wright; *cf. National Trust Co. Ltd v. Ebro Irrigation and Power Co. Ltd* [1954] 3 DLR 326, and also *Brown, Gow, Wilson v. Beleggings-Societeit N.V.* (1961) 29 D.L.R. (2d) 673. See also *General Steam Navigation v. Guillou* (1843) 11 M. and W. 877, 152 E.R. 1061; *Pickering v. Stephenson* (1872) L.R. 15 Eq. 322; *Gasque v. Commissioners of Inland Revenue* [1940] 2 K.B. 80; *Kuenigl v. Donnersmarck* [1955] 1 Q.B. 515; *Carl Zeiss Stiftung v. Rayner and Keeler Ltd* [1967] A.C. 853 (H.L.); *Adams v. National Bank of Greece S.A.* [1961] A.C. 255 (H.L.). See also Farnsworth, *The Residence and Domicile of Corporations* (1939) Chap. 6, especially pp. 225–235. For a modern assessment of the English case authorities and the principles to be deduced from them, see Dicey and Morris, *The Conflict of Laws* (12th ed. 1993), Ch. 30, esp. at pp. 1103–1116.

[16] See *e.g. Mostyn v. Fabrigas* (1774) 1 Cowp. 161, 98 E.R. 1021; *Nelson v. Bridport* (1845) 8 Beav. 527, 50 E.R. 207; *Lazard Bros. and Co. v. Midland Bank Ltd (supra)*. The rules concerning proof of foreign law have been modified by the provisions of the Civil Evidence Act 1972 s.4, but the general principle remains as stated in the text.

[17] The famous series of cases known as the "Russian Bank" cases, ensuing from the Russian Revolution of 1917, are the most familiar example of such a problem. *cf. Russian Commercial and Industrial Bank v. Comptoir d'Escompte de Mulhouse* [1925] A.C. 112 (H.L.), and *Lazard Bros. and Co. v. Midland Bank Ltd (supra)*. Since the latter case was decided by the House of Lords, it has generally been accepted by English courts that the various decrees of the revolutionary governments in Russia between December 1917 and January 1920 had the effect of dissolving the various private banking companies formerly established under Imperial Russian Law: see *Re Russian Bank for Foreign Trade* [1933] 1 Ch. 745; *Russian and English Bank and Florence Montefiore Guedalla v. Baring Bros. and Co. Ltd* [1936] A.C. 405 (H.L.); *Banque des Marchands de Moscou v. Kindersley (supra)*; *Re Banque Industrielle de Moscou* [1952] 1 Ch. 919; *Re Banque des Marchands de Moscou (Koupetschesky) (No. 2)* [1954] 1 W.L.R. 1108; *Re Russian Commercial Bank* [1955] Ch. 148. For judicial comments upon the authority and credibility of the expert testimony adduced on such occasions, see *e.g.*

constitutes an alternative, self-sufficient basis for the winding up of a foreign company.[18] Once it is established that the foreign company has either undergone dissolution under the law of its State of incorporation, or has ceased to carry on business, or that it is carrying it on only for the purpose of winding up its affairs, the English court's jurisdiction to wind up the company is properly constituted according to the provisions of the statute. This seemingly wide, and unqualified, jurisdiction enjoyed by the English court gives rise to certain difficulties, both in terms of principle and also in terms of logic.

Apparent conflicts with established principle

As a matter of principle, it may be argued that the assertion of a jurisdiction to wind up a company by means of proceedings taking place outside the State of its incorporation runs counter to the maxim which has just been stated above, whereby English law regards the domiciliary law of a company—namely the law of its state of incorporation—as supplying the proper legal regime to control the vital questions of the company's legal personality and status.[19] This, in combination with the principle of unity of liquidation,[20] if rigidly adhered to, would necessarily preclude the English courts from exercising jurisdiction to wind up any company not formed under the laws of the United Kingdom itself. The justification for creating a statutory exception whereby the English courts are nevertheless empowered to wind up a foreign company is to be found in the overriding necessity to safeguard the legitimate interests of parties in this country, and especially those whose dealings with the foreign company have taken place within the jurisdiction of the English courts. Such persons might well suffer prejudice if their fate were subjected exclusively to the law of the state of incorporation, and to such processes as might take place within that jurisdiction. For one thing, the rules of law applied within the foreign legal system might prove to be unfair and discriminatory from the point of view of any creditor who is not personally attached to the country in question.[21] On the other hand, an English creditor with an unsatisfied claim against a foreign company might well have no prospect of recovery whatsoever if the company is already considered to be dissolved according to the law of its State of incorporation or, alternatively, if there are other technical reasons why the company cannot be put into liquidation in that

---

Lazard Bros. and Co. v. Midland Bank Ltd [1933] A.C. 289 at 300–302, *per* Lord Wright; *Re Russian Bank for Foreign Trade* [1933] 1 Ch. 745 at 759–760, *per* Maugham J.; *Re Banque des Marchands de Moscou (Koupetschesky)* [1958] Ch. 182 at 193–202, *per* Roxburgh J.; and *cf. Russian Commercial and Industrial Bank v. Comptoir d'Escompte de Mulhouse* [1925] A.C. 112 at 125–128, *per* Lord Cave.

[18] *Inland Revenue v. Highland Engineering Ltd* 1975 S.L.T. 203.
[19] See cases cited *supra*, n. 15.
[20] On the principle of unity of insolvency, see Chap. 28, *ante*.
[21] On the problems of discriminatory rules in international insolvency cases, see K. Nadelmann, *Conflict of Laws, International and Interstate* (1972) at p. 340 *et seq.*; and by the same author: (1946) 9 M.L.R. 154; (1946) 11 Law and Contemp. Problems 696. For a reassessment of the position from the standpoint of Argentine law in its present-day setting, see J. Dobson in I.F. Fletcher (ed.) *Cross-Border Insolvency: Comparative Dimensions (The Aberystwyth Insolvency Papers)* (1990), Ch. 7 at pp. 124–130.

State. Thus, in the interests of justice and expediency, a statutory exception has been created to the principle that the law of the State of incorporation is alone competent to regulate any question concerning the company's status and continued existence.

Potential scope of the jurisdictional rule, and its application in practice

The ambit of the jurisdiction conferred on the English courts by section 221(5) of the Insolvency Act is indeed extensive, and is such as to empower the court to wind up as unregistered any foreign company which either has been dissolved or has ceased to carry on business, even where the company has not previously carried on business, nor had a place of business in this country. In practice however the English courts have shown a cautious and pragmatic approach to the exercise of the exceptional jurisdiction which they thereby enjoy.

Where the foreign company has established only minimal connections with this country, and has not even established any place of business here, the courts have until recently confined the exercise of their jurisdiction to wind up a company which in other respects fulfils the requirements laid down by section 221(5)(a) of the Act to those cases where the petitioning creditor can show that the company has assets within the jurisdiction of the English court and also that there is at least one person here over whom the jurisdiction is exercisable, and with a legitimate interest in obtaining an order for winding up.[22] In this context the local asset whose presence may well prove decisive with regard to the exercise of the court's discretion to order a winding up may be of any kind, tangible or intangible. In particular, the requirements of section 221(5)(a) have been held to be satisfied where the company's sole asset within the jurisdiction of the English court consisted of a claim against an insurance company which would, if met, be payable in England,[23] or of some right of action maintainable here with a reasonable possibility of success.[24]

In the most recent phase of the case-law evolution the courts have been

---

[22] *Banque des Marchands de Moscou v. Kindersley* [1951] 1 Ch. 112 (C.A.), especially at 126–127, *per* Lord Evershed M.R.; *Re Azoff-Don Commercial Bank* [1954] 1 Ch. 315; *Inland Revenue v. Highland Engineering Ltd* 1975 S.L.T. 203; *Re Compania Merabello San Nicholas S.A.* [1973] 1 Ch. 75, especially at 91–92, *per* Megarry J.; *Re Allobrogia Steamship Corp.* [1978] 3 All E.R. 423; *Re Eloc Electro-Optieck and Communicatie B.V.* [1981] 2 All E.R. 1111, note (Farrar) [1982] J.B.L. 225. The apparently contrary rulings in *Re Lloyd Generale Italiano* (1885) 29 Ch.D. 219, and in *Re Tovarishestvo Manufactur Liudvig-Rabenek* [1944] Ch. 404 should, it is submitted, be regarded as unsound. The decision in the former case has more than once been judicially distinguished on the ground that the company in that case had no assets, as well as no place of business, within the jurisdiction of the English Court, so that the case cannot furnish authority for the proposition that there is no jurisdiction to wind up a foreign company which has no branch office in this country. The *ratio decidendi* of the latter case (the *Rabenek* case), although not the actual result of the case itself, was effectively refuted in the course of judgment by the Court of Appeal in *Banque des Marchands de Moscou v. Kindersley (supra)*.

[23] *Re Compania Merabello San Nicholas S.A. (supra)*.

[24] *Re Allobrogia Steamship Corp.*; *Re Eloc Electro-Optieck and Communicatie B.V.* (both *supra*).

prepared to adopt an even more liberal approach, under which the presence of assets within the jurisdiction of the English court does not constitute an indispensable, minimum requirement for the purpose of enabling a winding up order to be made. In one decision, at first instance, it was held that the English court has jurisdiction to wind up a foreign company with no assets in the jurisdiction, provided that a sufficiently close connection is established between the company's business and this country.[25] Such a connection was considered to be established by virtue of the fact that the Liberian debtor company had obtained a substantial loan from an English bank (the petitioner). Despite the lack of assets here, the existence of a substantial debt governed by English law and repayable in England, together with the lack of any alternative jurisdiction in which a winding up could more appropriately take place, led the English court to exercise jurisdiction. A similar approach was adopted in a subsequent case of a company which had been incorporated in Guernsey and maintained its registered office there. Despite the fact that there were not, and never had been, any assets in England (though there were assets in other countries, including Portugal) there was ample evidence to indicate that the company's business had been controlled and conducted from England using an hotel to the North of London as the base. Very substantial loans—including one of £16.6 million borrowed from the petitioner—had been negotiated and drawn down in this country. Harman J. considered that there was plainly a close business connection with England, and that neither Guernsey nor Portugal was a more appropriate jurisdiction in which a winding up might take place, the former being rendered unsuitable by virtue of its archaic and outmoded processes despite being the country of incorporation.[26]

The above cases indicate that a sufficient connection with this country, for winding up purposes, may be established through the fact that a substantial portion of the foreign company's business activities have been conducted from England, or with English creditors, even though the company has no assets here. *A fortiori*, where the company's associations with this country are of a substantial nature, and there are also assets here, a winding up in England may be regarded as highly appropriate.[27] Significantly, it is not essential that the local asset should be one which would pass under the liquidator's control in the event of a winding up, provided that it can be shown that the asset will be of benefit to a creditor in some way.[28] Hence, the possibility that such an asset may pass directly to the petitioning creditor or to some other creditor by virtue of the operation of a rule of subrogation will not have the consequence of disentitling the

---

[25] *International Westminster Bank v. Okeanos* (also reported *sub nom. Re a Company (No. 00359 of 1987)*) [1988] Ch. 210; [1987] BCLC 450; [1987] 3 All E.R. 137; [1987] 3 W.L.R. 339, note (Dine) (1988) 9 Co.Law 30.

[26] *Re a Company (No. 003102 of 1991) ex p. Nyckeln Finance Co. Ltd* [1991] BCLC 539.

[27] *Re Syria Ottoman Railway Co.* (1904) 20 T.L.R. 217; *Re Azoff–Don Commercial Bank* (*supra*).

[28] *Re Compania Merabello San Nicholas S.A.*; *Re Allobrogia Steamship Corp.*; *Re Eloc Electro-Optieck and Communicatie B.V.*; *Re a Company (No. 00359 of 1987)* (*Okeanos*); *Re a Company (No. 003102 of 1991)* (all *supra*).

petitioning creditor from initiating proceedings for the winding up of the company.

It is submitted that a flexible and pragmatic approach to the exercise of jurisdiction to wind up foreign companies is to be welcomed, given the present day opportunities for conducting business on a multi-jurisdictional basis using a company formed in a country chosen mainly, if not wholly, on account of its relaxed regime in respect of company law matters. Nevertheless, there needs to be a principled basis for the application of jurisdictional rules which are framed in a liberal manner, lest they lend themselves in turn to other forms of abuse or oppression. The decision of Knox J. in *Re Real Estate Development Co.*[29] is an instructive example of the judicial approach to the question of how far the jurisdiction under section 221(5) can legitimately be extended before it incurs the charge of being exorbitant in its application. In that case, which concerned a Kuwaiti company, not only were there no assets within the jurisdiction, but the company itself had never traded within this country and it transpired that the principal basis of the petitioner's claim was a French judgment in favour of a French bank against the company, which had been rendered enforceable in England by the requisite process of registration of foreign judgments. The only other, tangential contact with this jurisdiction was a transaction whereby the company had disposed of shares in an English-formed company to another Kuwaiti company in circumstances which might render the transaction voidable under English law as a fraudulent conveyance. The learned judge held that these factors did not amount to a sufficient connection with this country to justify the court's exercise of its winding up jurisdiction.

"Any association"

The opening words of section 220 of the Act, which supplies the definition of "unregistered company" for the purposes of Part V, are seemingly very wide in their scope, since they state that the expression "includes any association and any company", with the exception of a company registered in any part of the United Kingdom under past or present legislation relating to companies. Judicial interpretation has served to narrow the meaning of the word "association" so that it is confined to associations formed for gain or profit, and does not apply to such entities as sporting or social clubs or societies not conducted in the form of partnerships nor in such a way as to render the members liable except for their subscriptions.[30] In the case of the *International Tin Council*,[31] an international organisation established by treaty and with its headquarters in London, the fact that the treaty provided that the ITC "shall have legal personality", and that secondary legislation in the United Kingdom had provided that the ITC was to have "the legal capacities of a

---

[29] [1991] BCLC 210.

[30] *Re St. James' Club* (1852) 2 De G.M. & G. 383; 42 E.R. 920; *Re International Tin Council* [1989] Ch. 309 (C.A.) (see *per* Nourse L.J. at pp. 329–330); *Re Witney Town Football and Social Club* [1993] BCC 874.

[31] *supra*, n. 30, affirming the decision of Millett J. reported at [1987] Chap. 419.

body corporate" was held not to render it subject to the jurisdiction of the English court to make a winding up order or to appoint a receiver. The further provisions of the ITC agreement, and of the secondary legislation, conferred "immunity from suit and legal process" upon the ITC, and so matters arising from its operations that would ordinarily have led to unpaid creditors having recourse to insolvency proceedings could not have that consequence, but were non-justiciable in the English courts.

"Any company"

Section 220 of the Act further provides that the expression "unregistered company" includes "any company", with the exception of "a company registered in any part of the United Kingdom under the Joint Stock Companies Acts or under the legislation (past or present) relating to companies in Great Britain".[32] As already stated, this supplies the basis for a winding up order to be made under section 221 in respect of a "foreign" company, meaning one whose incorporation has taken place under the laws of a foreign state. The question arises however, whether a company which has been formed under the companies legislation in force in Northern Ireland can be considered to come within the definition of "unregistered company" as quoted above, since Northern Ireland is within the United Kingdom but is not included in the expression "Great Britain".[33] Section 441 has the effect of limiting the extent to which the provisions of the Insolvency Act 1986 apply to Northern Ireland, and indicates that most of the Act's provisions will not so extend. However, this is subject to the proviso in section 441(2) which refers to "any provision expressly relating to companies incorporated elsewhere than in Great Britain".

In *Re Normandy Marketing Ltd*,[34] Morritt J. held that the words "expressly relating to" are not the same as "expressly *referring* to", and that it was possible to construe the words "any company" in section 220 as expressly relating to companies incorporated in Northern Ireland, since the words are unlimited and include companies incorporated elsewhere than in Great Britain.[35] Accordingly, Morritt J. held that a company incorporated in Northern Ireland can be wound up in England as an unregistered company under section 221 of the Act. The learned judge drew attention to the explicit limitation imported by section 221(2) into the operation of the section in the case of an unregistered company which has a principal place of business in Northern Ireland: such a company cannot be wound up under Part V of the Act unless it has a principal place

---

[32] Insolvency Act 1986, s.220(1)(*b*).
[33] The formal title of the state of which Northern Ireland forms a part is: "the United Kingdom of Great Britain and Northern Ireland".
[34] [1993] BCC 879. The case is also reported *sub nom. Re a Company (No. 007946 of 1993)* [1994] 2 W.L.R. 438.
[35] [1993] BCC at pp. 882–883. The passage includes a discreet disapproval of statements in the 11th edition of *Dicey and Morris on the Conflict of Laws*, at pp. 1144 and 1145, to the effect that a company incorporated in Northern Ireland cannot be wound up under s.221 of the Act. The same statements appear in the 12th edition of the work (published 1993 prior to the decision in the case under discussion) at p. 1128.

of business situated in England and Wales or Scotland, or in both England and Wales and Scotland. Hence, for the purposes of any case where a company has been incorporated in Northern Ireland and also has a principal place of business there, the conditions imposed by section 221 (3) would have to be met before any winding up could take place in England or in Scotland under that section. However, if a company has been incorporated in Northern Ireland but has no principal place of business there, no such limitation will be operative.

Logical difficulties associated with the operation of the English jurisdictional rule in relation to dissolved companies

As a matter of logic, the notion that an English court may proceed to exercise a jurisdiction to wind up a foreign company which has already undergone dissolution in its state of origin may be said to contain an essential absurdity, in that our rules of recognition of the legal effect of such a foreign dissolution[36] necessarily produce the effect that the dissolved company has already become a non-entity in the eyes of English law, and hence there is nothing in existence, legally speaking, which could form the subject matter of an English winding up. Once again, the necessary rejoinder to this essentially conceptual, but nevertheless powerful, objection is found to be based upon expediency and common sense, in that it would be ultimately perverse and unjust, if the legitimate interests of parties within the jurisdiction of the English court were to be denied any effective protection as a result of the dogmatic adherence to a rule of recognition of the effects of processes occurring under foreign systems of law, regardless of the inherent quality or fairness of the processes in question.

In order to surmount the logical objection to the practice of apparently exercising the jurisdiction to wind up an already non-existent legal person, the English courts have evolved the fiction that in cases of this kind the dissolved foreign company is deemed to be revivified for the sole purpose of enabling it to undergo a winding-up in England.[37] A related question which has at times given rise to the keenest controversy in the course of argument in cases of this kind concerns the implications of such a notional revivification from the standpoint of the Crown's entitlement to the undistributed assets of a dissolved foreign company, by virtue of the doctrine of *bona vacantia*. Once again, judicial resourcefulness has ensured that the overall purpose of procuring a winding-up of a dissolved foreign company is not frustrated as a consequence of the operation of the rule that, as a matter of prerogative, all the company's assets within the jurisdiction of the English court pass to the Crown as *bona vacantia* from the moment of its dissolution abroad. This doctrine, if applied without modification, would render it impossible to carry out a winding-up in

---

[36] See further, *infra*.
[37] *Russian and English Bank and Florence Montefiore Guedalla v. Baring Bros. and Co. Ltd* [1936] A.C. 405 (H.L.), especially at 425–428, *per* Lord Atkin. *cf.* Lipstein (1952) 11 C.L.J. 198; F.A. Mann (1962) 11 I.C.L.Q. 471; M. Mann (1952) 15 M.L.R. 479, (1955) 18 M.L.R. 8.

JURISDICTION TO WIND UP FOREIGN COMPANIES IN ENGLAND

England because by the time any attempt was made to present a petition for the winding up of a dissolved company there would be no assets available for distribution to creditors. The rejoinder to such arguments, when these have been advanced on behalf of the Crown itself on certain occasions, has been presented by way of a reformulation of the doctrine of *bona vacantia* as applied to such situations, so that the title of the Crown is treated as a defeasible one whose defeat is brought about by the notional reanimation of the company occurring, as we have seen, upon the making of an order for winding up in England.[38]

Thus it is settled that a dissolved foreign company may be wound up in England, and that the proceedings may be rendered purposeful by virtue of the fact that assets which, during the interregnum, have been vested in the Crown may be retrieved on behalf of the company for distribution to those creditors whose debts are not considered to have been discharged by the company's original dissolution.[39] Likewise, any liabilities which were due to the company at the time of its dissolution and which were not, according to English private international law, discharged thereby may be sued for, and anything which is thereby recovered is added to the other assets available for distribution in the English winding-up. But what is considerably less than clear is the exact position under English law with regard to the status to be ascribed to the company during the interregnum between its initial dissolution abroad and its reanimation by virtue of the English winding-up. It has twice been held at first instance that the company's reanimation is not retrospective, and hence that any acts, performed during the period between the original dissolution of the company abroad and the subsequent making of the winding up order by the English court, whereby persons purported to represent or act on behalf of the dissolved company, remain invalid since they took place at a time when the company was non-existent in law.[40] On the other hand, there are two reported cases in which it has been suggested in the House of Lords, and actually held at first instance, that the consequences of the operation of the doctrine of reanimation of the company must be pursued to their logical conclusion, so that operations supposedly conducted on behalf of the company, subsequent to the latter's dissolution, may be treated as having given rise to liabilities which are capable of being included in the English winding up as though the dissolution of the company had not in fact taken place.[41] On the general grounds of convenience and fairness, it is submitted that the latter view is to be preferred since it at least avoids the

---

[38] *Russian and English Bank and Florence Montefiore Guedalla v. Baring Bros. and Co. Ltd* (*supra*) at 426–427, *per* Lord Atkin; *Re Azoff-Don Commercial Bank* (*supra*); *cf.*, *Re Banque Industrielle de Moscou* [1952] 1 Ch. 919, and observations thereon in *Re Banque des Marchands de Moscou (Koupetschesky)* [1958] 1 Ch. 182 at 192–193 *per* Roxburgh J.

[39] See *infra*.

[40] *Re Banque des Marchands de Moscou (Koupetschesky), Wilenkin v. The Liquidator* [1952] 1 All E.R. 1269 (Vaisey, J.); *Re Russian Commercial and Industrial Bank* (1963) 107 S.J. 415, 416, *per* Buckley J. (possibly *obiter*; *cf.* also *Russian and English Bank v. Baring Bros. and Co. Ltd* [1934] Ch. 276 (Bennett J.); *ibid.* [1935] Ch. 120 at 123–124 (Clauson J.).

[41] *Re Russian Commercial and Industrial Bank* [1955] Ch. 148 (Wynn-Parry J.), applying the *dictum* of Lord Atkin in *Russian and English Bank and Florence Montefiore Guedalla v. Baring Bros. and Co. Ltd* [1936] A.C. 405, 427–429.

invidious distinctions that would otherwise fall to be made as between the claims of different creditors who have had dealings with the company at various phases of its life and after-life.

Section 221(5)(b): Company unable to pay its debts

This ground for making a winding up order is relatively straightforward, and corresponds to that laid down in section 122(1)(f) of the Act as one of the grounds on which a company registered under the Companies Acts may be wound up by the court.[42] As in the case of section 122(1)(f), the provision contained in section 221(5)(b) of the Act is supplemented by further provisions to facilitate the fulfilment by the petitioner of the task of establishing, for the purpose in hand, that the company is unable to pay its debts. In this instance sections 222 and 224 contain provisions which closely resemble those embodied in section 123 of the Act with regard to internal cases,[43] whereby the inability of the company to pay its debts is deemed to be established upon proof of any one of seven specified matters. The alternative situations in which a foreign company can be deemed to be unable to pay its debts, and may thereupon be wound up by the English courts, are as follows:

(i) if a creditor, by assignment or otherwise, to whom the company is indebted by a sum exceeding £750 then due, has served on the company, by leaving at its principal place of business or by delivering to the secretary or some director, manager or principal officer of the company, or by otherwise serving in such manner as the court may approve or direct, a written demand in the prescribed form requiring the company to pay the sum due, and the company has for three weeks after the service of the demand neglected to pay the sum or to secure or compound for it to the creditor's satisfaction[44];

(ii) if an action or other proceeding has been instituted against any member for any debt or demand due, or claimed to be due, from the company, or from him in his character of member, and notice in writing of the institution of the action or proceeding having been served on the company by leaving it at the company's principal place of business, or by delivering it to the secretary, or some director, manager or principal officer of the company, or by otherwise serving it in such manner as the court may approve or direct, the company has not within three weeks after service of the notice paid, secured or compounded for the debt or demand, or procured the action or proceeding to be stayed, or indemnified the defendant to his reasonable satisfaction against the action or proceeding, and against all costs, damages and expenses to be incurred by him because of it[45];

---

[42] See generally, Chap. 20, *ante*.
[43] See Chap. 20, *ante*. The provision contained in s.223 is not analogous to any of those contained in s.123, however.
[44] Insolvency Act 1986, s.222(1).
[45] *ibid*, s.223.

(iii) if in England and Wales execution or other process issued on a judgment, decree or order obtained in any court in favour of a creditor against the company, or any member of it as such, or any person authorised to be sued as nominal defendant on behalf of the company, is returned unsatisfied[46];

(iv) if in Scotland the *induciae* of a charge for payment on an extract decree, or an extract registered bond, or an extract registered protest, have expired without payment being made[47];

(v) if in Northern Ireland a certificate of unenforceability has been granted in respect of any judgment, decree or order obtained as mentioned in paragraph (iii)[48];

(vi) if it is otherwise proved to the satisfaction of the court that the company is unable to pay its debts as they fall due[49];

(vii) if it is proved to the satisfaction of the court that the value of the company's assets is less than the amount of its liabilities, taking into account its contingent and prospective liabilities.[50]

Section 221(5)(c): the Just and Equitable ground

Section 221(5)(c) of the Act enables the English court to wind up a foreign company "if the court is of opinion that it is just and equitable that the company should be wound up." This potentially very wide discretion to wind up a foreign company is expressed in terms identical to those employed in s.122(1)(g) of the Act with regard to the winding up of companies registered in England and Wales or in Scotland, and it may be said that the principles which have been developed with regard to the application of s.122(1)(g) could, if appropriate, be invoked in cases falling under section 221(5)(c). However, in practice the latter sub-section has seldom if ever been employed in isolation as a ground for the exercise by an English court of its jurisdiction to wind up a foreign company, but has tended to furnish an additional basis for doing so in conjunction with one of the other grounds expressed in paragraph (a) or (b) of section 221(5).[51] The apparently sparing use which has been made of section 221(5)(c) is perhaps explicable in view of the fact that, as has been explained, the very concept of an English court's assuming jurisdiction to wind up a foreign company represents a direct exception to the general principle followed by English law in such matters, and is thus only to be undertaken when the court is satisfied that, in the circumstances, this is defensible in terms of justice and expediency. It is notable moreover that the introductory words of section 221(5) itself are permissive, rather than mandatory, and that by providing that an unregistered company *may* be wound up in the

---

[46] *ibid*, s.224(1)(a).
[47] *ibid*, s.224(1)(b).
[48] *ibid*, s.224(1)(c).
[49] *ibid*, s.224(1)(d).
[50] *ibid*, s.224(2).
[51] *cf.*, *e.g. Re Compania Merabello San Nicholas S.A.* [1973] 1 Ch. 75 (just and equitable ground invoked in conjunction with company's inability to pay its debts, and also with the grounds specified in s.399(5)(a) of the Companies Act 1948, equivalent to Insolvency Act 1986, s.221(5)(a)).

circumstances therein specified they accordingly clothe the English court with a discretionary jurisdiction which, it may be said, effectively ensures that in practice no winding up order is made under section 221(5) unless the court is satisfied that it is just and equitable that this should be done.

Winding Up of Foreign Companies under Section 225 of the Insolvency Act 1986

In addition to the winding up jurisdiction conferred by section 221(5) of the Act, and totally independent from it,[52] a special jurisdictional rule is contained in section 225 of the Act, in the following terms:

> "Where a company incorporated outside Great Britain which has been carrying on business in Great Britain ceases to carry on business in Great Britain, it may be wound up as an unregistered company under this Act, notwithstanding that it has been dissolved or otherwise ceased to exist as a company under or by virtue of the laws of the country under which it was incorporated."

This provision, first enacted as section 91 of the Companies Act 1928, was devised for the particular purpose of removing doubts which had arisen in relation to the English courts' exercise of jurisdiction to wind up companies originally formed under the laws of Imperial Russia, and subsequently dissolved during or shortly after the Revolution of 1917. Those doubts, based in large part upon the considerations of logic and of principle mentioned above, were in the event judicially answered and allayed by means of a series of judgments confirming that the scope of the successive statutory predecessors of the provision now contained in section 221(5) of the Insolvency Act was already sufficiently broad to serve the purposes of justice since it actually empowered the English courts to wind up a dissolved foreign company regardless of whether the latter had ever done business in Great Britain.[53] Thus the ground of jurisdiction now contained in section 225 was destined to be a somewhat redundant provision of our company insolvency law, since it embodies preconditions to the effect that the foreign company must have previously carried on business here, and must also have ceased to do so, prior to the presentation of the petition for winding up. As though this were not sufficient of itself to render the provision a dead letter, the courts at an early stage effectively delivered the *coup de grâce* to its prospects of serving any useful purpose by apparently forming the view that the effects of what was

---

[52] *Inland Revenue v. Highland Engineering Ltd* 1975 S.L.T. 203, 204–205, *per* Lord Grieve; *cf. Re Russian and English Bank* [1932] 1 Ch. 663.

[53] *Re Russian and English Bank* (*supra*); *Russian and English Bank and Florence Montefiore Guedalla v. Baring Bros. and Co. Ltd* [1936] A.C. 405 (H.L.); *Banque des Marchands de Moscou v. Kindersley* [1951] 1 Ch. 112 (C.A.); *Re Azoff-Don Commercial Bank* [1954] 1 Ch. 315; *Inland Revenue v. Highland Engineering Ltd* (*supra*); *Re Compania Merabello San Nicholas S.A.* [1973] 1 Ch. 75; *Re Allobrogia Steamship Corp.* [1978] 3 All E.R. 423; *Re Eloc Electro-Optieck and Communicatie B.V.* [1981] 2 All E.R. 1111; *cf. Re Family Endowment Society* (1870) L.R. 5 Ch.App. 118 (decided under s.199 of the Companies Act 1862), and see in general the discussion of s.221(5)(a) of the Insolvency Act 1986, *supra*.

then section 338(2) of the Companies Act 1929 were limited to the case of companies which had ceased to do business in Great Britain only *after* the section was first given the force of law.[54] The view was almost certainly an incorrect interpretation of the true intentions of the legislature in framing the original section 91 of the Companies Act 1928, and may also be said to have been based on a misunderstanding of the precise effect of the judgment of Bennett J. in *Re Russian and English Bank*.[55] That case is generally invoked as authority for the proposition that the then section 338(2) of the Companies Act 1929 (currently section 225 of the Insolvency Act 1986) was not retrospective in effect. However it is clear that in the key passage of his judgment in that case,[56] Bennett J. was concerned to establish whether the passing of section 338(2) of the Companies Act 1929 could have had the purpose, or at any rate the consequence, of cutting down the separate jurisdiction to wind up a dissolved foreign company by virtue of the long-established statutory provision under which in fact the winding up order in that case was actually made, and which was re-enacted as section 338(1)(d) of that same Act of 1929. This was the provision, previously embodied in the Companies Acts of 1862 and 1908, which is currently contained in section 221(5) of the Insolvency Act. In ruling that the legislature had had no such intention of cutting down the effects of section 338(1)(d), it is submitted that Bennett J. did not furnish a conclusive interpretation of the precise legal force of section 338(2), taken in isolation. It is furthermore submitted that the views subsequently uttered, albeit as *obiter dicta*, by members of the House of Lords in an appeal which arose at a subsequent stage of the same liquidation,[57] are strongly persuasive authority for a contrary reading of the

---

[54] This has been presumed by, *e.g.*, successive learned editors of *Dicey's Conflict of Laws*, to have been the effect of *Re Russian and English Bank* [1932] 1 Ch. 663 (Bennett J.) but, as is submitted in the text on this page, this interpretation of the decision is at least questionable. See also *Russian and English Bank v. Baring Bros.* [1921 R. 806][1934] Ch. 276 (Bennett J.); and *cf. Russian and English Bank v. Baring Bros.* [1932] 1 Ch. 435 (Eve J.); *ibid.* [1935] Ch. 120, especially at 124 and 126 (Clauson J.); *ibid.* [1935] Ch. 127 (C.A.), especially at 131–132 (Slesser L.J.); in all four of these reported judgments, it is submitted, the question which was exercising the Court on each occasion was not the possible retrospective effect of s.338(2) of the Act of 1929, but the issue of the notional reanimation of the company by virtue of the English winding up, and whether that consequence enjoyed retrospective effect.

[55] [1932] 1 Ch. 663 (*cf.* the statement in Dicey and Morris, *Conflict of Laws* (10th ed., 1980) p. 735, n. 77). The case is discussed in the 12th edition of the work (1993) at p. 1124 with the submission that it ought not to be followed.

[56] *ibid.*, at [1932] 1 Ch. 668–669. It is true that the learned Judge posed the general question "whether [s.338] *as a whole* has any retrospective operation" (emphasis added). But in the passage referred to he proceeded to answer his own question by arguments leading to the conclusion that the legislature in 1929 had not in any way cut down or encroached upon the long-established jurisdiction to wind up a dissolved foreign company, conferred on the English courts by s.338(1)(d) of the Act of 1929.

[57] *Russian and English Bank and Florence Montefiore Guedalla v. Baring Bros. and Co. Ltd* [1936] A.C. 405 (H.L.) at 415–416, *per* Lord Blanesburgh, and at 424–425, *per* Lord Atkin. In this decision the House of Lords, by a majority of three to two, overturned the judgments of Clauson J. and the Court of Appeal referred to in n. 54 *supra*. It is also noteworthy that Eve J., in yet another phase of these same proceedings generated by the liquidation of the Russian and English Bank, expressed the view *obiter* that s.338(2) "would appear to fit the circumstances," and that a winding up order could be sought under that subsection: see [1932] 1 Ch. 435 at 444.

effects of section 338(2), and hence of its current counterpart. In practice, however, the point has never undergone judicial reconsideration in view of the more ample scope of its sister section, formerly section 338(1)(d), currently re-enacted in the Insolvency Act as section 221(5).[58]

Procedural matters

The precise steps to be followed in initiating proceedings for the winding up of a foreign company by the English court are determined by the answers to two distinct, but in some respects related, questions. First, did the company ever establish a place of business, or alternatively did the company ever do business, within the jurisdiction of the English courts? Secondly, if the company previously established a place of business here, were the necessary steps taken for the purpose of complying with the requirements of section 691 of the Companies Act 1985? These possibilities will be considered in turn.

(a) Company neither having a place of business, nor having done business, within the jurisdiction of the English courts

In this instance, although the company may have only tenuous links with this country, there exists as we have seen a jurisdiction to wind up the company here under certain circumstances.[59] This jurisdiction must be properly grounded through the petitioning creditor's effecting service of the petition in the appropriate manner. Rule 12.12 of the Insolvency Rules provides that the Rules of the Supreme Court (and County Court Rules, respectively) do not apply in insolvency proceedings. Rule 12.12 goes on to provide that where, for the purposes of insolvency proceedings, any order of the court, or other document, is required to be served on a person who is not in England and Wales, the court may order service to be effected within such time, on such person, at such place and in such manner as it thinks fit.[60] Alternatively, substituted service may be authorised where personal service cannot be effected, as may well be the case where a foreign company has already undergone dissolution in its country of origin so that there exists no person on whom, nor even any place at which, the service of the petition may be effected in a direct manner. In such cases the English court may make an order for substituted service either within or out of the jurisdiction of the court.[61] Such an order will contain directions to be followed by the petitioner so as to make it reasonably possible that the advent of the English proceedings will come to the notice of parties who may be potentially interested therein. Where the company has been

---

[58] See however *Re Tea Trading Co. K. and C. Popoff Bros.* [1933] Ch. 647; *Dairen Kisen Kabushiki v. Shiang Kee* [1941] A.C. 373 (P.C.), (the latter case was decided under provisions of the Hong Kong Companies Ordinance 1932, s.313(2), whose terms are identical to those of (now) s.225 of the Insolvency Act 1986).

[59] See *supra*, especially in paragraph (a), in which the effects of s.221(5)(a) of the Insolvency Act 1986 are explained.

[60] Insolvency Rules 1986, r. 12.12(3).

[61] *ibid.*; rr. 4.8(4), (5), (6), (7), 4.21(2).

dissolved abroad, with the consequence that the English Crown may have become entitled to assets here as *bona vacantia*, the Treasury Solicitor should also be notified of the proceedings.[62]

(b) Company having done business in England, but not having a place of business here

In this instance the company's contacts with England are still not sufficiently strong for it to be possible to identify some person, or some place, within the jurisdiction as that on whom, or at which, direct service of the petition may be effected. The appropriate procedure is accordingly for substituted service to be carried out in accordance with the court's instructions or for leave to be obtained for the petition to be served abroad,[63] with notice to the Treasury Solicitor in appropriate cases.[64]

(c) Company which has had a place of business in England and which has complied with the requirements of section 691 of the Companies Act 1985

Section 691 of the Companies Act 1985 makes it obligatory for all oversea companies which establish a place of business within Great Britain to deliver a number of items to the registrar of companies for registration, within one month of the establishment of the place of business. Besides various documents pertaining to the company's constitution and management, section 691(1)(b)(ii) specifies that the company must register the names and addresses of some one or more persons, resident in Great Britain, who are authorised to accept on behalf of the company service of process and any notices required to be served on the company. If such registration has properly taken place, section 695 further provides that any process or notice required to be served on an oversea company shall be sufficiently served if addressed to any person whose name has been thus delivered to the registrar, and left at or sent by post to the address which has been so delivered.[65] Fulfilment by the foreign company of the formalities prescribed by the Companies Act thus greatly simplifies and facilitates the process of initiating a winding up of such a company by the English courts. This formal act of submission to the jurisdiction is not without its drawbacks, however, because there appears to be a *lacuna* in the statutory provisions, whereby no procedure has been established for the formal cancellation of the registration of any particular person as the company's authorised agent for receipt of service.[66] Thus, at any rate so

---

[62] Practice Note [1952] W.N. 170. Relevant aspects of the doctrine of *bona vacantia* are discussed *supra*, and also, *infra*.
[63] See *supra*, n. 60 and 61.
[64] *ibid.*, n. 62.
[65] See also s.694A, inserted (together with other amendments and insertions relating to Part XXIII of the Companies Act 1985) by the Oversea Companies and Credit and Financial Institutions (Branch Disclosure) Regulations 1992, S.I. 1992 No. 3179.
[66] See *Employers' Liability Assurance Corp. Ltd v. Sedgwick, Collins and Co. Ltd* [1927] A.C. 95 (H.L.) at 103–104, *per* Lord Cave; *Sabatier v. The Trading Company* [1927] 1 Ch. 495. See also *Rome v. Punjab National Bank (No. 2)*, (C.A.) [1989] BCLC 328.

long as such a person remains alive and resides at the registered address, the jurisdiction of the English court may apparently be established by following the simple procedure specified in section 695 of the Companies Act, even though the company itself may long since have ceased to trade within this country.[67] Such an unsatisfactory state of affairs is long overdue for rectification and it is submitted that proper procedures should be established whereby a foreign company may formally apply to cancel, or alter, a registration previously made in compliance with section 691, on proof that all existing liabilities payable to persons within this country (including the Crown) have been fully discharged.

The "doing of business" test

Considerable importance is thus seen to attach to the question whether an oversea company may properly be said to have established a "place of business" within Great Britain, such that the provisions of section 691 of the Companies Act become applicable. Plainly, in order for it to be found that a foreign company has a "place of business" in Great Britain it is first necessary to establish that the company carries on business in this country. This in turn introduces the possibility that, with the help of local agents whose authority is carefully circumscribed, a foreign company may contrive to do business *with* England without, in law, doing business *in* England. This distinction has long been maintained by English law,[68] with consequences which may perhaps appear less than felicitous from the standpoint of the English courts' capability to exercise jurisdiction in relation to foreign companies which, by an astute manipulation of the doctrine of agency and the general rules of contract law, effectively earn business revenue from dealings with parties in Great Britain while nevertheless ensuring that they are technically not carrying out their business "inside" this jurisdiction.[69] Although some revision of the current doctrine of English law in this matter is perhaps desirable in view of its propensity for impairing the jurisdictional capacity of the English courts, the fact remains that under the present state of the law it is necessary to establish first that the foreign company in question carries on its business in this country, either directly or by means of a duly-authorised representative, and secondly that the business of the company is carried on at some identifiable location which may thus be held to constitute a "place of business" for the purpose, *inter alia*, of rendering the provisions of s.691 applicable to the company.

(d) Company which has had a place of business in England, but which has not complied with the requirements of section 691 of the Companies Act 1985

By section 695(2) of the Companies Act, where an oversea company

---

[67] See cases cited in n. 66 *supra*, and also the provisions of s.695(2)(b), discussed *infra*.
[68] See, *e.g. La Bourgogne* [1899] A.C. 431 (H.L.); *Okura v. Forsbacka Jernverks A/B* [1914] 1 K.B. 715, distinguishing *Saccharin Corp. Ltd v. Chemische Fabrik A.G.* [1911] 2 K.B. 516.
[69] *cf.* the more liberal philosophy adopted by the courts of the U.S.A. in formulating a "doing of business" test in relation to the exercise of jurisdiction over out-of-state corporations, as

fails to effect the registration required by the provisions of section 691, a document may be served on the company by leaving it at, or sending it by post to, any place of business established by the company in Great Britain. The same procedure is specified in the case where one or more persons' names and addresses have previously been registered pursuant to section 691, but at the time of inception of proceedings all such persons are either dead or have ceased to reside at the address which was delivered to the registrar, and also where all such persons refuse to accept service on behalf of the company, or for any reason cannot be served.[70] It is essential that the "place of business" utilised for this purpose is one at which the company is carrying on business at the time when service of process takes place: it is not sufficient to show that the company may at some former time have carried on its business at the place in question, if the evidence shows that no such activity was being pursued there at the date of service.[71] It has been suggested judicially, by way of an *obiter dictum*, that a company might under some circumstances be estopped from denying that a particular address constituted its place of business for this purpose, for example if the company has held itself out as carrying on business at that address and has done nothing in the way of giving notice to the contrary to persons having dealings with it.[72]

International Effects of an English Winding Up

General principles

In real terms, the international effectiveness of any winding up order is ultimately dependent upon the net result of applying the relevant rules of private international law of all the countries which are in any way concerned. No universally-accepted rules of private international law exist to govern questions concerning the recognition of foreign orders for the winding up of companies or other legal persons, a state of affairs which may under some circumstances give rise to a considerable degree of practical difficulty and inconvenience.[73] However, in the light of the general principles already explained above, which are associated with the exercise of jurisdiction to wind up companies, it must perforce be acknowledged that it is not every winding up order which should necessarily command full international effectiveness. Thus, while it is fully in accord with principle to assert that such effectiveness should be accorded to a winding up order made by a court for the jurisdiction under the laws of which the company in question has undergone formation, it would be less acceptable to advance the same claims on behalf of certain other types of order. For example, a winding up order may be made by a

exemplified in such cases as *International Harvester Co. v. Kentucky*, 234 U.S. 579 (1914); *International Shoe Co. v. State of Washington*, 326 U.S. 310 (1945).
[70] Companies Ct 1985, s.695(2)(b).
[71] *Deverall v. Grant Advertising Inc.* [1955] Ch. 111.
[72] *Deverall v. Grant Advertising Inc., supra*, at 119, *per* Jenkins, L.J.
[73] For an account of initiatives towards the elimination of such problems, see Chap. 31, *post*.

court in the exercise of special jurisdictional powers conferred by provisions of its domestic law, whereby relatively slight contacts between the company and the country in question may be deemed sufficient for this purpose. In such cases, while arguments on the grounds of convenience and expediency may furnish a compelling justification for encroaching upon the basic principle that a company's legal existence is a matter to be controlled by the law of its state of incorporation, it is necessary nevertheless to concede that orders of this kind may in practice be restricted to a purely local effect. As such they may serve perfectly legitimate purposes, such as the administration and distribution of assets located within the jurisdiction of the court concerned.

In cases where the contacts between the company and the country of the *forum* are of subsidiary importance to those existing between the company and its country of formation, or the country in which its main centre of operations is located, it would be jurisdictionally improper, as well as unrealistic in practical terms, to insist that the order of a court of the former country should be effective with respect to assets situate in other jurisdictions.[74] In particular, it may be anticipated that a winding up order made by an English court against a foreign company will not normally be accorded recognition by the courts of the country in which that company was incorporated, and any attempt by the English *forum* to purport to administer or dispose of assets located outside its jurisdiction is unlikely to be recognised as internationally valid.[75]

Foreign courts' rules of recognition are ultimately decisive

Despite the distinction which has been made above between the principles which should govern the international effectiveness of a winding up order made by an English court with regard to an English-formed company, and those which should apply with regard to an order for the winding up of a foreign company, it must be conceded that no hard and fast rule of universal application exists with regard to either species of order. National practice in matters of private international law in the field of the recognition of foreign judgments or orders varies from the liberal to the restrictive, and (in the absence of any international convention to which the State concerned may be a party) the policy adopted by any given country will be determined locally. Therefore, when one or more foreign

---

[74] See however *Re International Tin Council* [1987] Ch. 419 at 446; [1987] 1 All E.R. 890 at 899, *per* Millett J., where it is stated that "in theory, the effect of [an English winding up] order is worldwide", even when made in relation to a foreign company. The learned judge conceded however that other countries, in accordance with their own rules of private international law, may not recognise the English winding up order or the title of the liquidator appointed by our courts.

[75] *cf. National Trust Co. Ltd v. Ebro Irrigation and Power Co. Ltd* [1954] 3 D.L.R. 326. The very fraught question of the attitude of the courts of the state of incorporation, under whose laws a foreign company has already been wound up, towards the English courts' assertion of jurisdiction over the English assets of such companies, has seldom been openly explored. In the Russian Bank Cases for example (discussed at length, *supra*) the Soviet Government habitually refrained from laying claim to commercial assets remaining in the hands of parties outside the Soviet Union. Hence the English courts were left free to determine the ultimate destination of these assets according to the rules of English law.

jurisdictions have been identified whose recognition or non-recognition of the English winding up order may be of crucial significance it is essential to consult the rules and practice in relation to the recognition of foreign judgments which operate within the jurisdictions concerned, in order to anticipate the likelihood that the English order will command recognition in those countries.

Effect on foreign assets of an English winding up

Unlike the position under the English law of bankruptcy, whereby it is declared that upon his adjudication substantially the whole of the bankrupt's property, wherever situate, becomes vested in his trustee in bankruptcy for the benefit of his creditors,[76] the making of an order for the winding up of a company does not purport to cause the company to be automatically divested of its assets.[77] Even within the British Commonwealth therefore there is no suggestion that the making of a winding up order has the effect, by itself, of altering the legal title to the company's assets.[78] Instead the winding up order is regarded by English law as impressing the company's assets with a trust in favour of those persons interested, whether as creditors or as contributories, in the winding up. The company is thus divested of beneficial ownership of its assets which are thereafter required to be applied in discharge of its liabilities.[79] It becomes the duty of the liquidator, and the person charged by law with the task of conducting the winding up, to take into his custody or under his control all the tangible and intangible property to which the company is entitled, and of which it remains the legal owner.[80]

As a matter of law, an English winding up order is not regarded as being limited in its effect to the company's English assets and affairs. The liquidator is authorised to accept proofs lodged by foreign creditors in respect of the company's liabilities incurred overseas, or governed by foreign law. Thus in the English winding up the general principle to be observed is that the company's assets are to be distributed rateably among the *whole* body of creditors,[81] but subject to any overriding rule of public policy whereby certain categories of claim may be excluded from enforcement in England either by direct or indirect means.[82] Correspondingly, the effects of the order may legitimately purport to extend to the company's

---

[76] See Insolvency Act 1986, ss.306, 283 discussed in Chap. 8, *ante*.
[77] See *New Zealand Loan and Mercantile Agency Co. Ltd v. Morrison* [1898] A.C. 349 (P.C.).
[78] *ibid*.
[79] *Re Oriental Inland Steam Co.* (1874) L.R. 9 Ch.App. 557; *Ayerst v. C. and K. (Construction) Ltd* [1976] A.C. 167 (H.L.). See *Re International Tin Council, loc. cit. supra*, n. 74, *per* Millett J.
[80] For the liquidator's duties, see Chap. 22, *ante*.
[81] *Re Azoff-Don Commercial Bank* [1954] 1 Ch. 315, 333, *per* Wynn-Parry J., referring to *Re Kloebe* (1884) 28 Ch.D. 175 (a bankruptcy case).
[82] *e.g.* claims on behalf of representatives of a foreign state to recover revenues, or penal impositions, which are not enforceable in England: *Re Delhi Electric Supply and Traction Co. Ltd* [1954] Ch. 131 (C.A.), affirmed *sub nom Government of India v. Taylor* [1955] A.C. 491 (H.L.). For indications of a changing attitude towards tax bankruptcies from the standpoint of international recognition and enforcement, see Chap. 29, *ante*, at p. 707 (text to nn. 69 and 70).

foreign assets unless the order of the court itself introduces some restrictive limitations upon the liquidator's powers in relation to assets located overseas. Such restrictions, though not common nowadays, have been inserted on occasions in anticipation of there being concurrent liquidations of the same company, and in the interests of averting conflict between liquidators appointed in separate jurisdictions.[83]

Competing claims to assets

Since it is only the beneficial, and not the legal, title of the company's assets which is affected by the English order for winding up, it is necessary whenever assets are located outside the jurisdiction of the English courts for the liquidator to exercise his statutory power to sue in the name and on behalf of the company,[84] and thus to utilise the appropriate processes of the local law of the *situs* in order to assert and maintain control over the assets in question. The House of Lords has held that, by virtue of the doctrine of reanimation, a liquidator appointed in an English winding up may maintain such action on behalf of a foreign company even where that company has additionally undergone dissolution in its country of formation.[85] In so invoking and submitting to the legal process of the *situs*, the liquidator must perforce concede that the resolution of competing claims against those assets is a matter to be resolved by application of the rules of private international law of the *lex situs*.

Competing claims are likely to emerge from two quarters in particular. The first source consists of any rival liquidator, or other official purporting to have been invested with powers of administration over the company's assets, whose appointment has been made by the court of some jurisdiction outside England and Wales. This can of course include a liquidator or other official appointed by a court of the *situs* of the asset in question. In all such cases the extent to which the claim of the English liquidator to the assets will be upheld, as against that of any rival claimant, is directly dependent upon the rules of private international law utilised by the courts of the *situs* for the purpose of recognising the validity of the appointment of a foreign trustee or liquidator.[86] Where the foreign court encounters a problem regarding the relative priority of two such rival appointments, one of which has been made by a court of the *situs* itself, it may generally be expected that the foreign *forum* will exhibit a preference for upholding the priority of claim of that liquidator whose appointment is of local origin. Where the conflict of priorities arises between liquidators none of whom has been appointed locally by the court of the *situs* itself, pre-eminence will usually be accorded to the one whose appointment

---

[83] *Re Commercial Bank of South Australia* (1886) 33 Ch.D. 174; *Re Federal Bank of Australia* [1893] W.N. 77; *Re Hibernian Merchants Ltd* [1958] 1 Ch. 76. On concurrent liquidations, see *infra*.

[84] See Insolvency Act 1986, Sched. 4, para. 4.

[85] *Russian and English Bank and Florence Montefiore Guedalla v. Baring Bros. and Co. Ltd* [1936] A.C. 405 (H.L.). The doctrine of reanimation is discussed *supra*.

[86] For the rules of law applicable by an English court in such circumstances see *infra*.

originated in the jurisdiction with which the company has the more significant or substantial legal association, measured according to the traditional approaches of the private international law of the *situs* of the assets. If upon application of these rules the courts of the countries in question appear to have enjoyed co-ordinate jurisdiction, priority may be accorded to the liquidator whose claim was established earlier in terms of time, measured either from the date of his original appointment or from the date at which a claim to the assets was first lodged for the courts of the *situs* itself.

The second source of competition which an English liquidator may encounter consists of claims asserted by creditors of the company, acting either in the exercise of existing rights of security created in their favour over specific assets, or in the exercise of such remedies of diligence as the law of the *situs* may make available to them in their capacity as creditors of the company. Victory in such a race may again go ultimately to the party who has been first in time to act, but is also dependent upon the extent to which the rules of private international law of the *lex situs* recognise the validity of the respective legal bases upon which the rival parties' claims are founded. Thus, in the case of foreign assets, the application of the rules of private international law of the *lex situs* imports an additional dimension to the generally-accepted rule that the rights of a liquidator, like those of a trustee in bankruptcy, are subject to equities which have taken effect against assets of the company at a date prior to that of the order on which his own appointment is based.

Restraining creditors from taking proceedings abroad

If the English liquidator experiences competition from creditors of the company in his attempt to acquire control of the company's foreign assets, he may in certain situations be able to invoke the assistance of the English courts in order to restrain the creditors in question from pursuing their claims in other jurisdictions. By virtue of express provisions in the Insolvency Act, the making of an English winding up order has the immediate effect of staying all actions or proceedings against the company or its assets.[87] Thereafter, no such actions or proceedings may be commenced or continued unless this is done by leave of the English court itself, and subject to such terms as the court may impose.[88] This statutory "freezing" of other actions is operative throughout the United Kingdom, and the courts of all three jurisdictions comprising the United Kingdom are obliged to give effect to it.[89] However the effects of the statute are

---

[87] Insolvency Act 1986, s.130(2). See also s.126 for the possibility of a stay of action or proceedings being obtained between the time of presentation of a winding up petition and the making of an order pursuant thereto.

[88] *cf. Re Thurso New Gas Co. Ltd* (1889) 42 Ch.D. 486.

[89] Insolvency Act 1986, s.426(1), (2). *Re International Pulp and Paper Co.* (1876) 3 Ch.D. 594; *Re Hermann Loog Ltd* (1887) 36 Ch.D. 502; *Re Thurso New Gas Co. Ltd (supra)*; *Martin v. Port of Manchester Insurance Co. Ltd* 1934 S.C. 143; *Boyd v. Lee Guinness Ltd* [1963] N.Ir. 49; *Re Dynamics Corporation of America* [1973] 1 W.L.R. 63. For the different position of secured creditors see *Re West Cumberland Iron and Steel Co.* [1893] 1 Ch. 713, and *infra*.

necessarily confined to the territorial limits of the sovereign jurisdiction of the United Kingdom legislature, and no foreign court could be said to be affected by a restraint thus imposed as a consequence of the making of an English order for winding up.[90] Hence foreign proceedings *per se* are not affected by the English order.

Nevertheless, an alternative line of approach may be taken on an *in personam* basis against any of the creditors to the foreign proceedings who may be personally amenable to the jurisdiction of the English courts so that judicial control may be exercised over them. Such control may be imposed by means of an injunction restraining the creditor or creditors personally from commencing or continuing proceedings outside the jurisdiction of the English court—generally known as an "anti-suit injunction."[91] It must be remembered however that the equitable remedy of injunction is one whose availability is always a matter of discretion so far as the English court is concerned. In addition to overall considerations of fairness in the circumstances of the case itself, the court will inevitably have regard to the practical utility of the injunction and will not issue one where to do so would be plainly a futile or hollow gesture.

On the one hand therefore, a creditor who is resident in this country can readily be subjected to the court's subsequent exercise of the sanction of punishment for contempt, and it is equally the case that an overseas creditor who has voluntarily submitted to the English process of winding up by lodging proof therein can be treated as thereby becoming subject to the overall control of the English court.[92] But where the creditor is personally beyond the reach of the English court's powers of personal enforcement of its order, even though he may be a British subject or may have a technical domicile in this country, the court will refrain from taking a course of action which would be in vain.[93] On the other hand where the circumstances are otherwise appropriate for the issue of an injunction the position of the party to be enjoined is not affected by whether he has or has not elected to lodge proof in the English winding up. While it is true that there is no power to compel him to come in to proof, the court will not allow him to escape from the application of the common regime ordained for all creditors in the English winding up by the expedient of refraining from participating therein on a voluntary basis. Thus, an injunction may be issued regardless of whether the creditor is bound by proof or not.[94] Where any unsecured creditor, in defiance of the statutory rules specified above or any injunction which the English court may have issued, has

---

[90] *Re Vocalion (Foreign) Ltd* [1932] 2 Ch. 196.

[91] *cf. Midland Bank plc v. Laker Airways Ltd* [1986] 1 Q.B. 689 (C.A.); *Re North Carolina Estate Co.* (1889) 5 TLR 328. For an instructive survey of the jurisdiction to issue anti-suit injunctions, see the judgment of Hoffmann J. in *Re Maxwell Communications Corporation plc (No. 2), Barclays Bank plc v. Homan* [1992] BCC 757 at pp. 761-763 (affd., C.A., *ibid.*, p. 767).

[92] *cf. Selkrig v. Davies* (1814) 2 Dow 230, 3 E.R. 848 (H.L.); *Re Douglas* (1872) L.R. 7 Ch.App. 490; *Banco de Portugal v. Waddell* (1880) 5 App.Cas. 161 (H.L.). See also *Re Maudslay, Sons and Field* [1900] 1 Ch. 602, 611-612, per Cozens-Hardy, J.; *Re Oriental Inland Steam Co.* (1874) L.R. 9 Ch.App. 557.

[93] *Re North Carolina Estate Co. Ltd* (1889) 5 T.L.R. 328; *cf. Re Vocalion (Foreign) Ltd (supra)*.

[94] *Re Central Sugar Factories of Brazil (Flack's Case)* [1894] 1 Ch. 369.

proceeded to carry through an attachment or execution against the company's foreign assets he may be compelled to surrender into hotchpot the fruits of his private diligence.[95]

The delicate issues of policy and principle associated with the granting of anti-suit injunctions in relation to insolvency proceedings were carefully examined by the Court of Appeal in *Re Maxwell Communications Corporation plc (No. 2), Barclays Bank plc v. Homan*.[96] The case arose from administration order proceedings in which the administrators wished to initiate proceedings in New York in order to impeach as a preference a transaction which had resulted in a payment of funds being made to the Bank in reduction of the company's overdraft. It was anticipated that there would be better prospects of bringing about avoidance of that transaction under the United States Bankruptcy Code than under the equivalent provisions of the United Kingdom Insolvency Act 1986. The Bank's application for an anti-suit injunction was unsuccessful, the Court of Appeal being of the view that such an injunction would inevitably be regarded by the foreign court as an interference with the process of justice in a matter properly residing within its own jurisdictional competence and discretion.[97] For that reason, the jurisdiction to restrain foreign proceedings was one to be exercised rarely, and with proper recognition of comity (that is to say, of the respect owed to the foreign court). In the view of the Court of Appeal, the principles to be applied in such cases were those confirmed in the sequence of recent decisions of the House of Lords and the Privy Council in relation to the doctrine of *forum non conveniens*,[98] from which it emerged that the established line of English cases dealing with injunctions restraining foreign proceedings retains its authority, and is based on principles distinct from those involving the staying of English proceedings.[99] The principles applicable where application is made for an anti-suit injunction were summarised thus:

> "(1) If the only issue is whether an English or a foreign court is the more appropriate forum for the trial of an action, that question should normally be decided by the foreign court on the principle of *forum non conveniens*, and an English court should not seek to interfere with that decision.
>
> (2) However, if, exceptionally, the English court concludes that the pursuit of the action in the foreign court would be vexatious and

---

[95] *Re Oriental Inland Steam Co.* (*supra*) and other cases cited *supra*, n. 92. *Cf. Re Suidair International Airways Ltd* [1951] Ch. 165, for a case where the creditor was allowed to retain the fruits of an execution which would have been completed prior to commencement of winding up, but for the evasive and obstructive tactics of the debtor company itself.

[96] [1992] BCC 767, affirming the judgment of Hoffmann J., *ibid.*, p. 757 (see n. 91 *supra*).

[97] [1992] BCC at 773, *per* Glidewell L.J., citing the comments of Lord Scarman in *British Airways Board v. Laker Airways Ltd* [1985] A.C. 58 at p. 95, and of Judge Harold Greene in *Laker Airways Ltd v. Pan American World Airways*, 559 F.Supp. 1124 (1983) at p. 1128.

[98] The principal authorities are: *The Abidin Daver* [1984] A.C. 398 H.L.; *Spiliada Maritime Corp. v. Cansulex Ltd* [1987] A.C. 460 H.L.; and *Société Nationale Industrielle Aerospatiale v. Lee Kui Jak* [1987] A.C. 871 P.C. For a full account of the modern case law, see Dicey and Morris, *op. cit. supra*, n. 15, Chap. 12, esp. at pp. 408–411.

[99] See [1992] BCC at pp. 770–774, *per* Glidewell L.J.

oppressive, and that the English court is the natural forum (*i.e.* the more appropriate forum for the trial of the action) it can properly grant an injunction preventing the plaintiff from pursuing his action in the foreign court.

(3) In deciding whether the action in the foreign court is vexatious and oppressive, account must be taken of the possible injustice to the defendant if the injunction be not granted, and the possible injustice to the plaintiff if it is. In other words, the English court must strike a balance."[1]

In the circumstances of the case, the Court of Appeal concluded that no injunction should be granted.[2] It is submitted that, in a case where the applicant for an anti-suit injunction is the liquidator (or other office-holder) appointed in English insolvency proceedings, and the party whom it is sought to enjoin is a creditor whose foreign legal action may be characterised as a contravention of the *pari passu* principle, the arguments in favour of granting an injunction are somewhat more forceful, since the office-holder will otherwise be put to the expense of contesting the issue of jurisdiction in the foreign proceedings, with inevitable depletion of the assets available to the general body of proving creditors. This situation is distinguishable from one where it is the office-holder who is accused, in effect, of forum-shopping overseas in order to gain a juridical advantage over some party desirous of retaining property previously obtained from the company. Nevertheless, it seems likely that the spirit of comity which was openly espoused by the Court of Appeal in *Barclays Bank plc v. Homan* will be respected and endorsed in future cases, save where it can be argued that there are grounds for suspecting that the same spirit, and comparable standards of judicial objectivity towards questions of *forum non conveniens*, cannot be relied upon on the part of the foreign court where the proceedings are destined to take place.

Special position of secured creditors

What has been said above in relation to the restraining of actions by creditors is subject to the special exception concerning the rights of secured creditors to enforce their security even after the commencement of winding up by means of such processes as may be appropriate according to the law of the *situs* of the asset against which the security has been created. A secured creditor will not be restrained from pursuing such action as may be necessary to enable him to complete the enforcement of his rights, and realisation of his security, and this is true irrespective of whether the asset in question is situate within or outside the jurisdiction of

---

[1] *ibid.*, at pp. 773–774.

[2] In a subsequent hearing before the Bankruptcy Court of the Southern District of New York, the administrators' preference action was dismissed at the motion of the defendants, challenging the appropriateness of the venue of the proceedings on the basis that the U.K. law of preference avoidance should properly apply: *Re Maxwell Communications Corporation plc* (Case No. 91 B 1574 1), 170 Bankr. 800; 25 Bankr. Ct. Dec. CRR 1567 (August 5, 1994, Judge T. Brozman).

the English court.³ In many cases the crucial question may well be whether the particular creditor has, before the commencement of winding up, attained the status of secured creditor through the taking of such steps or proceedings as may be necessary to constitute him as such.⁴ Once the winding up has commenced however all processes of attachment, sequestration, distress or execution which are subsequently put into force against the estate or effects of the company are rendered void by statute,⁵ and hence no creditor whose security is dependent upon the completion of any of those procedures may enjoy the status of secured creditor, or retain the fruits of any such process, unless he had completed the execution or attachment in question before the commencement of the winding up.⁶

Choice of Law

In every winding up taking place in England pursuant to the Insolvency Act 1986 English law is applicable both as to matters of procedure and as to matters of substance. The former rule is in accordance with the well established principle that matters of procedure are governed by the *lex fori* while the latter rule is considered to be the inevitable consequence of the exclusively statutory basis of the proceedings in question. Since the winding up provisions in the Insolvency Act itself, and the statutory predecessors from which its relevant provisions are derived, make no reference to the application of any foreign rules of substantive law in relation to the winding up it had long been accepted that the English statutory rules are exclusively applicable.⁷ This proposition remains broadly true even where the English liquidation is taking place simultaneously with a winding up conducted in some foreign jurisdiction, both in circumstances where the English proceedings can properly be regarded as being ancillary in nature, and *a fortiori* where the converse is true.⁸ In the words of that learned and experienced judge, Vaughan-Williams J,

> "... the desire to act as ancillary to the court where the main liquidation is going on will not ever make the court give up the forensic rules which govern the conduct of its own liquidation."⁹

---

³ *Moore v. Anglo-Italian Bank* (1879) 10 Ch.D. 681; *Re West Cumberland Iron and Steel Co.* [1893] 1 Ch. 713; *Minna Craig Steamship Co. v. Chartered Mercantile Bank of India, London and China* [1897] 1 Q.B. 460.

⁴ *cf. Re Derwent Rolling Mills Co.* (1904) 21 T.L.R. 81, *affirmed* (C.A.) *ibid.* 701; *Minna Craig Steamship Co. v. Chartered Mercantile Bank of India, London and China* (*supra*).

⁵ Insolvency Act 1986, s.128.

⁶ *ibid.*, ss.183, 185. *cf.*, *Re Suidair International Airways Ltd* [1951] Ch. 165.

⁷ *Re English, Scottish and Australian Chartered Bank* [1893] 3 Ch. 385, 394, *per* Vaughan-Williams J. (*affirmed* C.A., *ibid.*); *Re Suidair International Airways Ltd* [1951] Ch. 165, 173, *per* Wynn-Parry J.

⁸ *Re English, Scottish and Australian Chartered Bank* (*supra*); *Re Commercial Bank of South Australia* (1886) 33 Ch.D. 174; *North Australian Territory Co. Ltd v. Goldsborough, Mort and Co. Ltd* (1889) 61 L.T. 716; *Re Suidair International Airways Ltd* (*supra*).

⁹ *Re English, Scottish and Australian Chartered Bank*, *loc. cit. supra*, n. 7.

However, when acting under section 426 of the Insolvency Act in response to a request for assistance addressed by a foreign court, English courts now have express authority to apply foreign, as well as English, insolvency law.[10]

The accepted notion of the controlling role assumed by the *lex fori* in an English winding up has never precluded the possibility of specific reference being made to foreign law during the course of the winding up for the purpose of establishing some matter whose ultimate determination will nevertheless take place subject to the rules of English law. Thus, if any indebtedness allegedly due to or from the company is properly governed by foreign law the validity of the debt, for such purposes as the lodging of proof, must be established by reference to its proper law.[11] Similarly any questions regarding the status or rights of legal or natural persons may require to be referred to the foreign law by which, in the eyes of English private international law, these matters are properly considered to be regulated in the circumstances in question. Thus, in an English liquidation of a company incorporated under foreign law the very validity, and legal nature and consequences, of that formation may first have to be determined by reference to the law of corporate formations of the foreign country in question,[12] while such questions as the liability of any particular persons to contribute to the payment of the company's debts in accordance with the provisions of section 226(1) of the Insolvency Act, or the entitlement of those persons by virtue of section 154 of the Act to any surplus resulting from the liquidation, will in some cases have to be resolved by reference to the law of the company's state of incorporation.[13] So, too, questions regarding the validity of the appointment of directors of the company, or of acts which the directors have purported to carry out in the company's name with binding effect, may have to be answered on the basis of the appropriate provisions of the law of the country under whose jurisdiction the company's formation and conduct properly fell to be governed at the time or period in question.[14]

Recognition of Foreign Liquidations

General principles

As already explained above, the fundamental principle long accepted by

---

[10] Insolvency Act 1986, s.426(5). See further, Chap. 31, *post.*
[11] *Gibbs and Sons v. La Société Industrielle et Commerciale des Métaux* (1890) 25 Q.B.D. 399 C.A.; *Re Higginson and Dean* [1899] 1 Q.B. 325; *National Bank of Greece v. Metliss* [1958] A.C. 509; *Adams v. National Bank of Greece* [1961] A.C. 255 (H.L.); *Re Banque des Marchands de Moscou (Koupetschesky), Royal Exchange Assurance v. The Liquidator* [1952] 1 All E.R. 1269; *Re Banque des Marchands de Moscou (Koupetschesky) (No. 2)* [1954] 1 W.L.R. 1108 (C.A.).
[12] *Maunder v. Lloyd* (1862) 2 J. and H. 718, 70 E.R. 1248; *Von Hellfield v. E. Rechnitzer and Mayer Frères and Co.* [1914] 1 Ch. 748 (C.A.). *cf. Skyline Associates v. Small* (1974) 50 D.L.R. (3d) 217.
[13] *General Steam Navigation Co. v. Guillou* (1843) 11 M. and W. 877, 152 E.R. 1061; *Re Banque des Marchands de Moscou* [1958] Ch. 182.
[14] *Risdon Iron and Locomotive Works v. Furness* [1906] 1 K.B. 49 (C.A.); *Banco de Bilbao v. Sancha* [1938] 2 K.B. 176 (C.A.); *National Trust Co. Ltd v. Ebro Irrigation and Power Co. Ltd* [1954] 3 D.L.R. 326.

RECOGNITION OF FOREIGN LIQUIDATIONS

English law is that the law of the company's domicile is primarily competent to control all questions concerning the company's initial formation, and subsequent existence, as a legal person.[15] As was also explained above,[16] the domicile of a company is for this purpose treated as being, possibly immutably, located in the country under the laws of which the company originally underwent formal incorporation and registration so as to attain a legal identity and status.[17] From this fundamental principle it follows that English private international law will accord recognition to a foreign dissolution of a company which has taken place under the law of the company's domicile, as understood by English law: if the true construction of the effect of the winding up according to the foreign legal system is to bring to an end the company's legal existence, that consequence will be accepted and recognised at English law.[18] Where the company has been wound up under the law of some foreign country other than that in which the company is considered to have been domiciled during the period of its existence, the English law approach to recognition is far less dogmatic. It would be in accordance with principle if English law were to refer to the law of the domicile to establish whether by that law the liquidation is considered to have any effect upon the company's legal status. If, in the eyes of the company's domiciliary law, its continued existence is considered to be unaffected by the purported winding up which has taken place under the law of some other jurisdiction, it is not to be expected that English law would accord recognition to the winding up, save where it had taken place under the law of some other part of the United Kingdom.[19] There is now a statutory requirement comparable to

---

[15] *Bank of Ethiopia v. National Bank of Egypt* [1937] 1 Ch. 513; *Banco de Bilbao v. Sancha* [1938] 2 K.B. 176 (C.A.). See also cases cited *supra*, p. 734, nn. 14–17 inclusive.

[16] *Supra* p. 734.

[17] See cases cited at p. 734 *supra* n. 14–17 inclusive, especially *Gasque v. Commissioners of Inland Revenue* [1940] 2 K.B. 80; *Keunigl v. Donnersmarck* [1955] 1 Q.B. 515; *Carl Zeiss Stiftung v. Rayner and Keeler Ltd* [1967] A.C. 853 (H.L.). It may be noted that although ss.42 and 43 of the Civil Jurisdiction and Judgments Act 1982 contain special rules for determining the domicile and seat of a corporation, these rules are confined in their application to matters regulated by the Act itself, and by the Brussels Convention of September 27, 1968 to which the Act of 1982 gives effect within the United Kingdom. The Convention, by virtue of A.1(2), is expressly precluded from having application to "proceedings relating to the winding up of insolvent companies or other legal persons," and hence neither the Convention nor the Act of 1982 should at this stage be considered to have established a new general test for determining the domicile of a company for the purposes of English private international law.

[18] *Lazard Bros. and Co. v. Midland Bank Ltd* [1933] A.C. 289 (H.L.) at 297, *per* Lord Wright. *cf. National Trust Co. Ltd v. Ebro Irrigation and Power Co. Ltd* [1954] 3 D.L.R. 326. See also the results attained in the earlier phase of the "Russian Bank Cases" (described *supra*) on the basis of the English courts' original tendency to conclude that the banking companies had not undergone dissolution under Soviet law: *Russian Commercial and Industrial Bank v. Comptoir d'Escompte de Mulhouse* [1925] A.C. 112 (H.L.); *Banque International de Commerce de Petrograd v. Goukassow* [1925] A.C. 150 (H.L.); *Employers' Liability Assurance Corp. Ltd v. Sedgwick, Collins and Co. Ltd* [1927] A.C. 95 (H.L.); *Sabatier v. The Trading Company* [1927] 1 Ch. 495.

[19] For enforcement throughout the United Kingdom of the winding up orders made by courts in the several parts thereof, see Insolvency Act 1986, s.426, discussed (in relation to its application to bankruptcy) in Chap. 28 *ante*.

the legal rules long applicable in the case of bankruptcy that the courts of this country accord recognition to, and assist in the enforcement of, orders for winding up made by the courts of a number of countries belonging to the British Commonwealth.[20]

In those cases where the foreign court, by which the winding up order was made, was exercising a special jurisdictional power comparable to that described above with regard to the competence of the English courts to wind up a foreign company under certain specified circumstances,[21] there is a superficial attraction in the argument that English law should recognise an act of a foreign court performed under circumstances in which, *mutatis mutandis*, an English court would have been competent to make an order for winding up. However, although such a "reciprocal" basis of recognition has been accepted in relation to some types of foreign judgment affecting matrimonial status,[22] the weight of judicial opinion is decidedly against the expansion of this practice into the claim of commercial judgments, or judgments affecting the status of legal persons such as companies.[23]

Extent of recognition of a foreign liquidation

From the general principles stated in the previous section it follows that a liquidator appointed under the law of the company's place of incorporation will be recognised at English law as having authority to wind up the company, and to represent it in legal proceedings brought either against or on behalf of the company, provided that such representative authority is conferred upon him by the law governing his appointment.[24] Conversely there is no reported incidence of recognition having been accorded in England to a liquidator appointed under the law of some other jurisdiction than that in which the company underwent incorporation. With respect to liquidations of this kind, the inference which most readily suggests itself is that, the effects of such a liquidation being regarded as of

---

[20] Insolvency Act 1986, s.426(4), (5), (11), together with S.I. 1986, No. 2123 and S.I. 1989, No. 2409. For the former position, see *New Zealand Loan and Mercantile Co. v. Morrison* [1898] A.C. 349 (P.C.).

[21] See *supra*, describing the provisions contained in s.221(5)(a) of the Companies Act 1948.

[22] See, *e.g. Travers v. Holley* [1953] P. 246; *Merker v. Merker* [1963] P. 283, 296 (application of the doctrine of reciprocal recognition to foreign divorce decrees and nullity decrees respectively).

[23] *cf. Re Trepca Mines Ltd* [1960] 1 W.L.R. 1273 C.A. at 1281, per Hodson L.J.; *Société Co-opérative Sidmetal v. Titan International Ltd* [1966] 1 Q.B. 828, 838–841, per Widgery J.; *Schemmer v. Property Resources Ltd* [1975] Ch. 273. Contrary views were expressed by Denning L.J. in *Re Dulles' Settlement (No. 2)* [1951] Ch. 842, 851. It may be further noted that the doctrine of recognition of foreign divorce decrees on the basis of reciprocity of rules of jurisdiction, established by the decision of the Court of Appeal in *Travers v. Holley* (*supra*), was subsequently abrogated by the Recognition of Divorces and Legal Separations Act 1971, s.6.

[24] *Banco de Bilbao v. Sancha* [1938] 2 K.B. 176 (C.A.); *Bank of Ethiopia v. National Bank of Egypt* [1937] 1 Ch. 513; *Macaulay v. Guaranty Trust Co. of New York* [1927] W.N. 308; (1927) 44 T.L.R. 99; *Burr v. Anglo-French Banking Corp. Ltd* (1933) 49 T.L.R. 405; *Sea Insurance Co. v. Rossia Insurance Co. of Petrograd* (1924) 20 Lloyd's Rep. 308; *Onassis v. Drewry* (1949) 83 Lloyd's Rep. 249; *Re I.I.T.* (1975) 58 D.L.R. (3d) 55.

necessity confined to the territorial limits of the jurisdiction in which the winding up is taking place, the liquidator's capacity to act on the company's behalf and to deal with its assets must be deemed to be similarly restricted so as to be limited to property situate within the jurisdiction of the foreign court.[25]

While the company is still in the course of being wound up by means of a liquidation conducted abroad, and indeed right up until such time as the company's legal existence is considered to have terminated according to the provisions of the company's own domiciliary law, it remains possible for the company, through the liquidator, to perform legally valid acts (such as the conclusion of contracts) and to sue and be sued in proceedings initiated before the English courts.[26] However once the company's legal personality has ended through dissolution according to its own personal law, no further acts may thereafter be validly performed by the company as such, nor may actions or proceedings taken against the company be regarded as legally effective.[27]

Position of English branch of foreign parent company

Where there exists an English branch of a foreign-incorporated company, the dissolution of the parent company according to the latter's personal law is considered to bring about the simultaneous dissolution of the legal personality of the English branch.[28] However, the possibility that such a branch may continue to enjoy a *de facto* existence for some time after the dissolution *de iure* of both its parent company and (consequently) itself, may give rise to a number of problems, especially when allied to the fact that, as is explained below, the foreign liquidation is not considered to have any direct legal effect upon the company's assets in England. For these reasons the necessity may arise to invoke the statutory jurisdiction conferred upon the courts here[29] to wind up the English branch of a foreign company which has already been dissolved, or which has entered into liquidation, in the country of its domicile.[30] By this means, assets situate

---

[25] *North Australian Territory Co. Ltd v. Goldsborough, Mort and Co. Ltd* (1889) 61 L.T. 716; *National Trust Co. Ltd v. Ebro Irrigation and Power Co. Ltd* [1954] 3 D.L.R. 326.

[26] This statement of principle appears to be supported by the decision in: *Bank of Ethiopia v. National Bank of Egypt (supra)*; *Onassis v. Drewry (supra)*; *Russian Commercial and Industrial Bank v. Comptoir d'Escompte de Mulhouse* [1925] A.C. 112 (H.L.); *Banque Internationale de Commerce de Petrograd v. Goukassow* [1925] A.C. 150 (H.L.); and *Employers' Liability Assurance Corp. v. Sedgwick, Collins and Co. Ltd* [1927] A.C. 95 (H.L.).

[27] *Lazard Bros. & Co. v. Banque Industrielle de Moscou* [1932] 1 K.B. 617 (C.A.); *Lazard Bros. & Co. v. Midland Bank Ltd* [1933] A.C. 289 (H.L.); *Burr v. Anglo-French Banking Corp. Ltd* (1933) 49 T.L.R. 405; *Russian and English Bank and Florence Montefiore Guedalla v. Baring Bros. and Co. Ltd* [1936] A.C. 405 (H.L.).

[28] *Russian and English Bank and Florence Montefiore Guedalla v. Baring Bros. and Co. Ltd (supra)*.

[29] See Insolvency Act 1986, ss.221(5), 225 discussed *supra*.

[30] *Russian and English Bank and Florence Montefiore Guedalla v. Baring Bros. and Co. Ltd (supra)*; *Re Russian and English Bank* [1932] 1 Ch. 663; *Re Tea Trading Company K. and C. Popoff Brothers* [1933] Ch. 647; *Re Russian Bank for Foreign Trade* [1933] Ch. 745; *Re Tovarishestvo Manufactur Liudvig-Rabenek* [1944] Ch. 404 (still good law, it is submitted on this point); *Banque des Marchands de Moscou v. Kindersley* [1951] 1 Ch. 112 (C.A.); *Re Azoff-Don Commercial Bank* [1954] 1 Ch. 315.

within the control of the English court may be made available to creditors in the English winding up, but it must be emphasised that proof may be admitted only in respect of those debts which are regarded as having been validly incurred by the branch during the time that it was possessed of full legal capacity to function as the legitimate branch of its overseas parent.[31]

It must be borne in mind that the debt in respect of which proof is lodged in the English winding up must be one which is not considered by English private international law to have been discharged by virtue of the foreign liquidation of the parent company. With regard to debts incurred between the foreign dissolution of the company and the commencement of the English winding up, it will be recalled that earlier in this chapter a description was provided of the special doctrine of notional resurrection of the legal personality of a dissolved foreign company which is wound up in this country under the appropriate provisions of the Insolvency Act.[32] In view of this doctrine it is as well to emphasise that the preponderance of judicial and academic opinion favours an application of the concept of revivification of the company such that its legal personality, and hence its capacity to perform legally binding acts, is fully reinstated with retrospective effect so that it may be applicable to a point in time earlier even than the date of commencement of the English winding up.[33]

Discharge of debts under a foreign liquidation

According to English law a foreign liquidation is considered to effect the discharge only of such of a company's liabilities as are properly governed by the law of the country in which the liquidation takes place or, alternatively, of such as are governed by some other foreign law under which the liquidation is accorded the same effect.[34] Consequently whatever may be the purported effect of the liquidation according to the law of the country in which it has been conducted, the position at English law is that a debt owed to or by a dissolved company is not considered to be extinguished unless that is the effect according to the law which, in the eyes of English private international law, constitutes the proper law of the debt in question.[35] In the application of the foregoing rule English law considers

---

[31] *Sea Insurance Co. v. Rossia Insurance Co. of Petrograd* (*supra*); *Re Russian Bank for Foreign Trade* (*supra*); *Re Banque des Marchands de Moscou (Koupetschesky) (No. 2)* [1954] 1 W.L.R. 1108. *cf. Russian Commercial and Industrial Bank v. Comptoir d'Escompte de Mulhouse*, and *Banque Internationale de Commerce de Petrograd v. Goukassow* (both *supra*, n. 26; both cases were decided upon the premise that, in the circumstances, the respective companies had not undergone dissolution according to their Soviet personal law at the time when the material events took place).
[32] See *supra*, p. 740.
[33] See cases cited on p. 740, *supra*, at nn. 40 and 41.
[34] See p. 758, *supra*, especially cases cited at n. 11.
[35] *Gibbs and Sons v. La Société Industrielle et Commerciale des Métaux* (1890) 25 Q.B.D. 399 (C.A.); *Re Higginson and Dean* [1899] 1 Q.B. 325; *National Bank of Greece v. Metliss* [1958] A.C. 509 (H.L.); *Adams v. National Bank of Greece* [1961] A.C. 255 (H.L.) (both the latter two cases involved the amalgamation of one company with another under the law of Greece, which was the place of incorporation). *cf.* the general formulation of principle in *Russian and English Bank and Florence Montefiore Guedalla v. Baring Bros. and Co. Ltd* [1936] A.C. 405 (H.L.), at 428, *per* Lord Atkin.

Recognition of Foreign Liquidations

a debt to be situate in the place where payment is due, in the sense that action may be brought in the courts of that country utilising orthodox rules of jurisdiction in order to enforce payment, regard being had where appropriate to such factors as the residence of the debtor, the proper law of the contract, and the terms thereof with regard to payment.[36] Similarly the shares of a company are regarded as situate in the country where they can be effectively dealt with, and hence any debt in the form of dividend due in respect of such shares will be locally situate in the same place as the shares themselves.[37]

Effect of foreign liquidation over English assets

In contrast to the rules of recognition applied by English private international law in relation to the proprietary effects of a foreign adjudication of bankruptcy,[38] there is no rule of English law whereby the proprietary effects of a foreign liquidation are recognised as extending beyond the territorial limits of the jurisdiction in which the foreign liquidation has taken place.[39] Thus regardless of the effects claimed for its own orders of liquidation and dissolution by the provisions of the foreign legal system itself, English law insists upon maintaining with respect to the foreign liquidation of legal persons the same conceptual and practical distinctions which have historically developed in our domestic law, between the adjudication in bankruptcy of natural persons and the winding up of insolvent companies. On this basis a company in winding up is not divested of its assets, which remain legally the property of the company, although the beneficial interest in them is transferred to the company's creditors, assessed collectively, and the company's affairs are required to be administered with a view to satisfying their claims so far as is practicable. When, upon completion of the winding up, the company undergoes formal dissolution one consequence is that any undistributed assets of the dissolved company are left without any legal owner, and therefore pass to the Crown as *bona vacantia*.[40] In a similar way any English

---

[36] *Spiller v. Turner* [1897] 1 Ch. 911; *Indian and General Investment Trust Ltd v. Borax Consolidated Ltd* [1920] 1 K.B. 539; *London and South American Investment Trust Ltd v. British Tobacco Co. (Australia) Ltd* [1927] 1 Ch. 107; *Deutsche Bank and Disconto Gesellschaft v. Banque des Marchands de Moscou* (C.A. December 14, 1931 unreported); *Re Russian Bank for Foreign Trade* [1933] 1 Ch. 745, 766–767, per Maugham J.; *Adelaide Electric Supply Co. Ltd v. Prudential Assurance Co. Ltd* [1934] A.C. 122 (H.L.); *R. v. International Trustee for the Protection of Bondholders A.G.* [1937] A.C. 500; *Re Banque des Marchands de Moscou (Koupetschesky), Wilenkin v. The Liquidator* [1952] 1 All E.R. 1269, 1271, per Vaisey J.; *Re Banque des Marchands de Moscou (Koupetschesky) (No. 2)* [1954] 1 W.L.R. 1108, 1113, per Roxburgh J.; *Brown, Gow, Wilson v. Beleggings-Societeit N.V.* (1961) 29 D.L.R. (2d) 673; *Libyan Arab Foreign Bank v. Bankers Trust Co.* [1989] Q.B. 728.

[37] *Brassard v. Smith* [1925] A.C. 371 (P.C.); *R. v. Williams* [1942] A.C. 541 (P.C.); *Standard Chartered Bank Ltd v. Inland Revenue Commissioners* [1978] 1 W.L.R. 1160.

[38] See Chap. 29, *ante*.

[39] *cf. New Zealand Loan and Mercantile Agency Co. Ltd v. Morrison* [1898] A.C. 349 (P.C.), in which the basic distinction is drawn between the bankruptcy of an individual and the winding up of a company.

[40] *Re Higginson and Dean* [1899] 1 Q.B. 325; *Re Wells, Swinburne-Hanham v. Howard* [1933] 1 Ch. 29 (C.A.).

assets of a foreign company which undergoes liquidation will pass to the Crown as *bona vacantia* from the moment when, according to the rules of English private international law explained above,[41] the company's legal existence is recognised as having been extinguished.[42] This doctrine, it has already been explained, is flexibly applied so that if an application is made for the winding up in England of a company which has already undergone dissolution abroad, the Crown's title to the company's assets as *bona vacantia* is treated as a defeasible one, and the English assets are thereupon made available for distribution in the English winding up.[43]

A further consequence of the notional reanimation of a dissolved foreign company is that the liquidator appointed in the English winding up is empowered to take proceedings in the company's name to recover any debts and liabilities which may be outstanding in the company's favour, and which have been left in abeyance by reason of the company's previous dissolution.[44] By the same token, proof may be lodged in England in respect of any debts left unpaid by the foreign company at the time of its former dissolution, provided that the debt in question is not one which, according to English private international law, is considered to have been discharged by virtue of the foreign liquidation. Indeed it has been held that the petition for a winding up in England may be presented by a creditor whose debt, on which the petition is founded, is actually in dispute.[45] This exception to the general rule that a disputed debt may not form the basis of a creditor's petition for winding up has been judicially created in order to avert the unwelcome consequence that such creditors would otherwise be left without a remedy in the wake of the foreign liquidation, despite the fact that there might be assets in England to which they could legitimately look for satisfaction of their claims. Furthermore it has been held that the initial termination of the company's legal existence under the foreign liquidation proceedings has the effect of preventing the running of time for the purposes of the Limitation Acts, since from the date of the dissolution of the company there was no debtor who could be sued.[46]

From the foregoing description of the rules applied by English law in determining the effects of a foreign liquidation upon assets situate here, it follows that the foreign liquidator will have to make formal application to the English courts in order to recover and realise on behalf of the company any English assets which he wishes to claim for the benefit of the creditors in the foreign liquidation. In so doing the liquidator will be affected by any equities which have risen in relation to the assets in question prior to the

---

[41] See p. 758 *et seq.*, *supra*.

[42] *Lazard Bros. and Co. v. Banque Industrielle de Moscou* [1932] 1 K.B. 617, 641, *per* Scrutton L.J.; *Re Banque Industrielle de Moscou* [1952] 1 Ch. 919; *Re Azoff-Don Commercial Bank* [1954] 1 Ch. 315; *Re Banque des Marchands de Moscou (Koupetschesky)* [1958] 1 Ch. 182, 192–193, *per* Roxburgh J.; *Re Usines de Melle's Patent* (1954) 91 C.L.R. 42.

[43] See pp. 740–741, *supra*, and cases cited *ibid.*, in nn. 37 and 38.

[44] *Russian and English Bank and Florence Montefiore Guedalla v. Baring Bros. and Co. Ltd* [1936] A.C. 405 (H.L.).

[45] *Re Russian and English Bank* [1932] 1 Ch. 663; *Re Russian Bank for Foreign Trade* [1933] 1 Ch. 745; *cf.* also *Re Azoff-Don Commercial Bank* [1954] 1 Ch. 315.

[46] *Re Russo-Asiatic Bank* [1934] 1 Ch. 720; *cf. Re Banque des Marchands de Moscou (Koupetschesky) (No. 2)* [1954] 1 W.L.R. 1108, where claims were held to be maintainable in an English winding up, begun in 1932, of a company dissolved under Soviet law in 1918.

date at which his own application is instituted before the English courts. Moreover it is apparent that all such applications by the liquidator of a foreign company may be made only for so long as the company itself continues to exist according to its personal law, because thereafter the assets will have vested in the Crown as *bona vacantia*. In responding to any such application brought by a foreign liquidator the English courts will first have regard to the question whether the validity of the liquidator's own appointment is recognised by English law,[47] and if so whether the effect of enabling the asset in question to be employed in the course of the foreign liquidation will work to the prejudice, or inconvenience, of creditors in this country who might naturally expect to have recourse against any such asset in partial or entire satisfaction of their outstanding claims against the company. The problem will be especially acute in cases where the insolvency laws of the place of liquidation contain provisions which effectively discriminate against creditors from outside the country in question, or where they will otherwise be disadvantaged through the circumstances under which the foreign proceedings are destined to take place. If it transpires that such undesirable consequences would result from a release of assets into the disposition of the foreign liquidator, the appropriate recourse is for a qualified party to present a petition for the company to be wound up in England so that the English assets can be administered here in accordance with the English rules for company liquidations.[48]

Concurrent Liquidations

The foregoing sections of this Chapter make it abundantly clear that English law has accepted the proposition that although in principle a company should be wound up in the jurisdiction from which its legal existence is derived, in practice there may be compelling reasons why this either cannot be done at all, or at least cannot be done in a fully satisfactory way. In particular English law places paramount emphasis upon the need to ensure that all creditors enjoy equality of treatment (*par condicio creditorum*) so far as that can be legally secured. Accordingly if assets are located within the jurisdiction of the English courts the latter have been prepared to respond to arguments founded upon equity and reason, and to bring about an English winding up whereby those assets may be made available to English and other creditors who would encounter inconvenience or—worse—inequitable and unjust treatment in seeking to pursue their claims via the medium of foreign liquidation proceedings which are either taking place or are in contemplation.[49] *A fortiori*, where the

---

[47] See *supra*.
[48] See *Felixstowe Dock and Railway Co. v. U.S. Lines Inc.* [1988] 2 All E.R. 77, for a lengthy discussion of these issues, by Hirst J. The learned judge concluded that the English assets should not be released to the American liquidator. For reflections on the wider impact of this decision on the spirit of judicial co-operation between the U.K. and the U.S.A., see Fletcher (1993) 6 Insolvency Intelligence 10–13. See, generally, Chap. 31, *post*.
[49] *Re Matheson Brothers* (1884) 27 Ch.D. 225; *Sedgwick, Collins and Co. v. Rossia Insurance Company of Petrograd* [1926] 1 K.B. 1.

foreign liquidation has already been concluded the plight of any unsatisfied creditors is more readily appreciated in its true extent. The chosen mode of making English assets available to creditors in all such cases is through the initiation of a separate winding up which may, according to circumstances, be administered concurrently with the foreign proceedings, or even subsequent thereto.[50] Where there exists a reasonable prospect of open and even-handed co-operation between the persons administering two concurrent liquidations the courts have readily embraced the notion that the English winding up may be regarded as ancillary to the one taking place in the company's state of incorporation.[51] Thus, judicial care will be taken to ensure that so far as is possible no unnecessary conflict arises between the two liquidators. For example, the concept of equality of treatment for *all* creditors will be respected wherever possible, and this may entail the relinquishing of funds or assets to the foreign trustee or liquidator without first insisting that all creditors in the English liquidation shall have been paid in full.[52] Thus, although the holding of an English winding up may achieve several useful purposes—such as ensuring that English assets are not syphoned away abroad purely to meet the privileged claims of certain foreign creditors (for example State or public authorities) whose claims would not be directly enforceable in England—the overriding concept of justice in such circumstances will nevertheless be respected, and the English winding up will not be allowed to furnish an opportunity for English creditors to reap a windfall in the form of a higher proportional return upon their claims than is enjoyed by their foreign counterparts, purely as a result of the fortuitous location within the jurisdiction of the English courts of assets bearing a high value in relation to the total sum of the unmet claims of the company's English creditors.

---

[50] The latter situation will necessarily arise when the company has already been dissolved by virtue of the foreign proceedings: *q.v. supra*.

[51] *Re Commercial Bank of South Australia* (1886) 33 Ch.D. 174; *Re Federal Bank of Australia* [1893] WN 77 C.A.; *Re Vocalion (Foreign) Ltd* [1932] 2 Ch. 196; *Re Hibernian Merchants Ltd* [1958] 1 Ch. 76.

[52] See cases cited in n. 49, *supra. cf. Re Standard Insurance Co. Ltd* [1968] Qd.R. 118; *Re Air Express Foods Pty. Ltd* [1977] Qd.R. 107. But note the judicial observations made in *Felixstowe Dock and Railway Co. v. U.S. Lines Inc., supra*, n. 48. For consideration of the prospects for enhanced cross-border cooperation using the provisions of the Insolvency Act 1986 s.426, and by other means, see Chap. 31, *post*.

CHAPTER 31

INTERNATIONAL REGULATION OF CROSS-BORDER INSOLVENCY

From the account already given, in Chapters 28 to 30, of the problems encountered in cases of insolvency containing cross-border implications, it may readily be appreciated that this is an area in which there is an urgent need for the development of some kind of framework for international co-operation and mutual assistance. Thus, we have seen above that the unilateral initiatives taken in our own legal system, using rules and doctrines of private international law, not only seem to give rise in their present form to logical difficulties and inconsistencies, but also encounter serious limitations in the realm of their practical application. This is because, in a world of some 150 sovereign states, (many of which are internally subdivided into a number of separate "law districts") no one country is in a position to impose upon the others its own rules and methods for solving legal problems, however admirably the solutions may appear to have been devised. Therefore, whenever the assets of an insolvent debtor are dispersed between two or more jurisdictions the effectiveness and efficiency of any insolvency proceedings centred in one country will be dependent upon the degree of recognition and co-operation accorded by the laws of the other jurisdictions involved. These are vital matters from the point of view of the insolvency practitioner who, as office holder in the proceedings, faces the task of tracing, collecting and realising the debtor's assets, and distributing the proceeds in a fair and orderly way among all those who can properly be regarded as creditors entitled to share in that distribution.

It is not only the trustee or liquidator who experiences, when appointed, acute problems both of a legal and of a practical nature. Even before any insolvency proceedings have commenced, the creditors and their debtor alike face the need to discover the exact nature of their respective legal rights, in order to plan their affairs properly. The parties will therefore need to know in which jurisdiction, or in which jurisdictions, insolvency proceedings may be capable of taking place; what would be the force and effect of such proceedings; and to what extent the proceedings may enjoy international effectiveness through the workings of private international law as practised by the countries concerned. All of this requires much research into questions of comparative law, as well as of private international law, and the answers are seldom likely to be as precise and clear-cut as might be desired.

In modern times there has been an increasing tendency to regard international conventions as providing the most suitable vehicle for the solution, or at least the simplification, of problems experienced in the field of private international law.[1] International insolvency has been no exception to this, and a number of such initiatives have been undertaken during the last hundred years, both in Europe and elsewhere.[2] Such conventions prove in practice to be extremely difficult to produce and carry into effect, because the normal problems of finding an acceptable *via media* between the different legal systems involved are compounded, in the case of insolvency, by reason of the profound and widespread implications carried by insolvency proceedings, which bear upon matters of personal status and capacity, property rights, security rights, preferential entitlements, and further issues of civil and criminal liability for offences and malpractices relating to debt and insolvency. In the course of negotiations bearing upon such complex and socially sensitive issues, there is a natural reluctance on the part of most countries to abandon the principles and values embodied within their own legal systems. This is partly due to the very real difficulties which would be posed for the states concerned from the aspect of their internal legal system, if substantial changes were to be made necessary by reason of such international agreements. In part, also, it must be acknowledged that at the level of such international negotiations it is often felt that national honour and prestige are at stake.

Early attempts to establish an international, multilateral bankruptcy convention were unsuccessful,[3] and at present the most concrete achievements in international co-operation in this field are the bi-lateral and tri-lateral treaties concluded between a number of European States.[4] A more ambitious treaty framework has been concluded between five Scandinavian countries, whose sense of affinity has enabled them to

---

[1] Of foremost significance in this field is the Hague Conference on Private International Law. Other organisations actively working for the unification of private and commercial law through international conventions include the Council of Europe; the United Nations Commission on International Trade Law (UNCITRAL); the International Institute for the Unification of Private Law (UNIDROIT); and the European Union (evolving from the European Economic Community). See Fletcher *Conflict of Laws and European Community Law* (1982), Chaps. 1 and 3, and references there cited.

[2] For a survey of the history of these developments, see K. H. Nadelmann, (1943–44) 5 U. of Toronto L.J. 324; (1944) 93 U. of Pennsylvania L.Rev. 58 (the latter article is also reprinted in Nadelmann, *Conflict of Laws, International and Interstate* (1972), p. 299. See also the same author (1961) 10 I.C.L.Q. 70, and further references in Chap. 28, *ante*, n. 8.

[3] Such attempts were those of the Hague Conference of 1925–1928 and of the International Law Association during 1954–1956.

[4] Examples are the Franco-Belgian convention of 1899; the Franco-Italian convention of 1930; that between Belgium, the Netherlands and Luxembourg of 1961; and that between the Netherlands and Germany of 1962. For fuller details, see references in n. 8 of Chap. 28, *ante*.

collaborate closely in this and in other legal matters,[5] and as a further example of regional co-operation between states sharing a common heritage in legal and historical terms, one may cite the provisions on bankruptcy contained in the Montevideo Treaties of 1889 and 1940, to which a number of Latin American states are ratifying parties.[6] Canada and the United States of America negotiated a bankruptcy treaty on a bilateral basis in 1979, but to date it has been neither signed nor ratified.[7] The formation in 1994 of the North American Free Trade Area (NAFTA), comprising Canada, Mexico and the U.S.A. reinforced the need to regulate cross-border insolvency matters in the North American hemisphere. Work was commenced in that same year under the auspices of the American Law Institute, to develop a framework within which such regulation could be accomplished.

The Draft Bankruptcy Convention of the European Union/Economic Community

One development with the potential to achieve significant results in this field of international treaty law is the project undertaken from 1960 onwards among the states belonging to the European Economic Community, and more recently known as the European Union.[8] The motivation for this project is derived from the requirement imposed upon the member states of the Union by Article 220 of the Treaty Establishing the EEC,[9] the fourth paragraph of which necessitates the conclusion of a convention to secure, for the benefit of nationals of the member states, "the simplification of formalities governing the reciprocal recognition and enforcement of judgments of courts or tribunals." At an early stage, it was decided to sever the topic of insolvency from the rest of the field of civil and commercial judgments covered by the remit in Article 220(4), and the latter became the subject of a separate convention, already concluded and

---

[5] See the Nordic Bankruptcy Convention, concluded between Denmark, Finland, Iceland, Norway and Sweden on November 7, 1933, 155 L.N.T.S. (1935) 116; Bogdan (1985) 34 I.C.L.Q. 49.

[6] See the Treaty of 1889, Articles 35–48; Treaty of 1940, Articles 40–53. For the full text, see (1943) 37 A.J.I.L. supplement p. 138. The 1889 Treaty is ratified by Argentina, Bolivia, Colombia, Paraguay, Peru and Uruguay; the 1940 Treaty by Argentina, Paraguay and Uruguay. See also the Havana Treaty of 1928: 86 L.N.T.S. (1929) 112, 362.

[7] For the text, see Dalhuisen, *International Insolvency and Bankruptcy*, (1980) Vol. 2, Appendix D; Honsberger, The negotiation of a Bankruptcy Treaty: 1985 Meredith Memorial Lectures, University of McGill.

[8] 15 European states are currently members of the European Union. Negotiations for the Bankruptcy Treaty were commenced between representatives of the six founding member states (Belgium, France, West Germany, Italy, Luxembourg and the Netherlands), and were expanded after January 1973 to include the three additional members who acceded from that date (Denmark, the Irish Republic, and the United Kingdom). The accessions of Greece (1981), of Portugal and Spain (1986) and of Austria, Finland and Sweden (1995) added to the complexity of the final process of concluding the convention.

[9] Signed in Rome on March 25, 1957, and hence often known as "The Treaty of Rome." The Treaty entered into force on January 1, 1958. The Treaty remains in force, though much amended.

in force since February 1973.[10] Work continued separately on the Bankruptcy Project whose progress may be divided into two principal phases. *Phase I* saw the tortuous, and overly-secretive, elaboration of a complex and controversial text which was tacitly abandoned some time after the submission of a Draft Convention to the Council of Ministers in April 1980. The full title of the Draft, and its opening Article, indicated that it was to apply to every sort of insolvency proceeding: "bankruptcy, winding up, arrangements, compositions and similar proceedings." *Phase II*, amounting to a relaunch of the project, commenced in April 1990 with the creation of an ad hoc working party under an initiative inspired by the success of the Council of Europe in concluding the Istanbul Convention, which was subsequently opened for signature on June 5, 1990 (see below).[11]

Phase I occupied the negotiators for some 20 years or so in which the project passed through two distinct stages of evolution. The first stage, conducted by a committee of experts drawn from the then six member states working together with officials of the Commission, resulted in a Preliminary Draft Convention, published in February 1970.[12] This draft was accorded a generally critical reception in view of its highly ambitious structure and consequent complexity.[13] These criticisms were partially met in the course of the second stage of work between 1970 and 1980, in which representatives of the three additional member states also participated, and which resulted in the amended Draft of April 1980.[14] The basic conception of the Draft of 1980 was however essentially the same as that of the Preliminary Draft, despite numerous changes in matters of detail. The indications are that sufficiently strong opposition to the adoption of the Draft Convention was expressed by certain member state governments, so as to render it impossible for it to be adopted by the Community as a whole. The project was therefore discontinued, without ever having been formally or publicly renounced. In the circumstances, it would seem unnecessary here to engage in any detailed discussion of the Draft

---

[10] See the Convention of September 27, 1968 on Jurisdiction and Enforcement of Judgments in Civil and Commercial Matters ("The Brussels Convention"), referred to in Chap. 29, *ante*, at p. 693: see references there given in n. 11.

[11] Answer of Commissioner Bangemann to Question No. 3128/91 in the European Parliament: O.J. 1992, C141/38.

[12] E.Comm.Doc. 3.327/1/XIV/70–F, dated February 16, 1970, together with Explanatory Report (the Noël–Lemontey Report), E.Comm.Doc. 16.775/XIV/70–F. English translations of the two documents were subsequently published under the same coded reference number, substituting the suffix-letter "E" in place of "F."

[13] See Hunter (1972) 21 I.C.L.Q. 682, and (1976) 25 I.C.L.Q. 310; Nadelmann (1970) Riv.Dir.Int.Priv. e Proc. 501 (also in English in Nadelmann, *Conflict of Laws, International and Interstate* (1972) p. 340); same author, (1977) 52 N.Y.U.L.R. 1, at 27–32; Fletcher in K. Lipstein (Ed.) *Harmonisation of Private International Law by the E.E.C.* (1978), p. 119 (also published in (1977) E.L. Rev. 15); Report of the Bankruptcy Convention Advisory Committee (1972) (Cmnd. 6602), *passim*, especially the note of reservations by A.E. Anton, pp. 105–128.

[14] The text was published in English by the Department of Trade as Text of the EEC Draft Bankruptcy Convention, with explanatory notes, April 1980. For analysis and comment, see Fletcher, *supra*, n. 1, Chap. 6 (with text of Draft printed as Appendix C); Thieme, (1981) 45 Rabels Z. 459; Trautman, Westbrook and Gaillard, 41 AJCL 573 (1993), at pp. 578–586.

Convention of 1980, save for the purpose of commenting upon the shortcomings which may have contributed to its ultimate failure. Since it is quite likely that there will be future projects for concluding international conventions in this field, it is important that the lessons of the *Phase I* EC Draft should be properly learnt, in the hope that the same errors and miscalculations are not repeated.

The Phase I Draft of 1980—main features

The first feature to be noted is the ambitious choice of the type of convention to be developed, namely a "double" or "direct" convention. This type of international instrument transcends the characteristics of the more usually encountered "simple" or "indirect" type, which merely lays down criteria with regard to the assumption and exercise of jurisdiction which, if met in the jurisdiction of origin, will render the judgment or order eligible to be recognised and enforced in the other participating jurisdictions. In a "direct" convention, on the other hand, mandatory rules of jurisdiction are laid down which must be complied with by courts in the convention states whenever they are seized of matters falling within the ambit of the convention. Then, on the assumption that jurisdiction was properly exercised in conformity with these requirements, judgments may be enforced elsewhere in the participating states with a minimum of formalities, and in a virtually automatic manner.[15] If such a convention is to work properly, the rules for taking jurisdiction must be soundly devised, and clearly drafted, so that all parties may readily ascertain their implications for any matter which concerns them. Unfortunately, the provisions implanted in the 1980 Draft fell considerably short of this ideal, and would have given rise in practice to results which, at best, could have been capricious and arbitrary, and at worst, unjust and even farcical. In effect, a three-tier hierarchy of jurisdictional norms was to have been created, with supremacy of competence being accorded to the courts of the Contracting State in which the debtor's "centre of administration" was situated.[16] Although this key connecting factor was defined in the Draft, the definition was by no means free from ambiguity and obscurity, and could have led to much confusion in practice.[17] In the absence of a centre of administration in any contracting state, a secondary ground of jurisdiction was to be the existence of any "establishment" of the debtor in any of the states concerned. This could give rise to concurrent jurisdictional competence if the debtor had more than one "establishment" in different contracting states.[18] To overcome the possibility of conflicting

---

[15] This is also the case under the Brussels Convention, another "double" convention of the type described: see Chap. 29, *ante*, references in n. 11.

[16] 1980 Draft Art. 3 (see n. 14, *supra*).

[17] 1980 Draft, Art. 3(2) states: "The centre of administration means the place where the debtor usually administers his main interests. In the case of firms, companies or legal persons that place shall be presumed, for the purposes of this Convention and until the contrary is proved, to be their registered office, if any." Problems of secondary definition are numerous, and unresolved.

[18] 1980 Draft, Art. 4(2) states: "an establishment exists in a place where an activity of the debtor comprising a series of transactions is carried on by him or on his behalf." Again, there are unresolved problems of secondary definition of the terms employed.

adjudications, and with a view to supplying a clear means of identifying the court whose order was to predominate, the Draft contained two further rules. First, priority was to be accorded to the first proceedings which were actually opened in chronological order.[19] Secondly, if two rival proceedings were opened on the same day, precedence was to be enjoyed by the judgment of that court which sits in a place whose name is first alphabetically.[20] The former sub-rule is unfortunate, in that it plainly offers temptation to local creditors to act preemptively, and thus ensure that the insolvency will be administered in their locality and according to the law of that place. The latter sub-rule is an absurd example of a mechanical solution, quite unworthy of the serious interests to which it was intended to apply. The third, and lowest, tier of jurisdictional competence would arise in the absence of the centre of administration or any establishment anywhere in the contracting states: each would then be at liberty to open proceedings according to its local law, but these would be of purely local effect and would fall outside the scope of the Convention.

The other primary feature of the principles upon which the 1980 Draft Convention was based was the overt espousal of the twin ideals of unity and universality of bankruptcy,[21] as proclaimed through the terms of Article 2:

> "The proceedings to which this Convention applies, when opened in one of the contracting states, have effect *ipso iure* in the other contracting states and so long as they have not closed, shall preclude the opening of any other such proceedings in those other states."

This bold proclamation was reinforced by the provisions of Article 34(1), whereby such bankruptcies would take effect in relation to the whole of the debtor's assets situated within the contracting states. This seemingly forthright commitment to the academic ideal of a "pure," unified régime for the administration of an insolvent debtor's estate, was accompanied by further provisions governing choice of law, which would have had the effect of making the internal law of the *forum concursus* the applicable law in relation to many matters arising within, and related to, the insolvency.[22] Therefore, the law of the state in which any insolvency proceedings were concentrated would be destined to enjoy a dominant role, not merely administratively and procedurally but also substantively, with profound consequences, inevitably, for parties' previously settled expectations.

It was at this point that the scheme of the Draft Convention began to fall victim to the reactionary pressures aroused by its own highly potent implications. At the heart of the system of distribution of the debtor's assets that is contained in every country's insolvency law, lie the rules for determining the different categories of preferential creditors and their

---

[19] 1980 Draft, Arts. 13(2), 58(1).
[20] *ibid.*, Art. 58(2).
[21] See Chap. 28, *ante*.
[22] 1980 Draft, Arts. 15–18.

relative ranking *inter se*, and the rules for determining the rights of secured creditors in relation to various assets within the estate.[23] These rules differ widely from one legal system to another, and are at the same time intimately linked to an entire infrastructure of legal provisions, and social and commercial expectations, which it would be invidious to overturn by a sidewind, as it were. Hence, in these matters, the Draft Convention actually abandoned the logic inherent in the universality principle, and allowed the rights of creditors within each contracting state to be maintained in accordance with local law, but only as against those assets situated in the jurisdiction in question.[24] This approach, termed "localisation of assets," whereby as many sub-estates would become established as there were contracting states in which assets were located at the opening of proceedings, would have been extremely cumbersome to operate in practice, and was also tantamount to an acknowledgement that the time was not yet ripe for a wholehearted acceptance of the principles of unity and universality, even as between states so closely linked as the partners belonging to the EEC. A final demonstration of cynical inconsistency was given through the provisions for dealing with assets located outside the territory of the contracting states, but recovered by the office holder and available for distribution. In this instance, the universality principle was readily reasserted, so that the assets recovered or realised in non-contracting states were to be aggregated with those forming the sub-estate within the *forum concursus* itself, and destined to be administered according to its rules of law.[25] Thus did the authors of the 1980 Draft reveal their willingness to apply against claimants resident in non-contracting states the full rigours of the universality doctrine, while yet shrinking from applying that same doctrine to those resident inside their own Community.

In the light of the above deficiencies and inconsistencies, as well as others not detailed here, it is perhaps as well that this particular instance of *folie de grandeur* was destined never to be adopted or put into force. As a lesson of history, however, it may serve as an example of the errors to be avoided by those who seek to negotiate future conventions of this kind.

The Phase II Draft Convention—features and prospects

Although the political momentum for concluding an EEC Bankruptcy Convention was lacking during the decade after 1980, the legal and commercial necessity for such a convention within the progressively integrated economic environment of the European Union was undiminished. Rather, the need for a convention was greatly enhanced by the developments of that period. This was recognised, albeit belatedly, by the creation of a fresh working party in May 1989, an event which inaugurated *Phase II* of the convention project which, at the time of writing, appears to have a reasonable prospect of giving rise to a completed

---

[23] See Chaps. 10 and 24, *ante*.
[24] 1980 Draft, Arts. 43–52. For description and criticism, see Fletcher, *op. cit. supra*, n. 1, at pp. 222–234.
[25] *ibid.*, Art. 43(2).

text for signature by the Member States. Although the ensuing period of ratification and implementation by the individual states could well extend over a number of years, so that entry into force may be several years away, there is at least room for cautious optimism that the deficiency of uniform legal provision to regulate cross-border insolvency within the European Union is about to be remedied.

At present, the text of the Draft EEC Bankruptcy Convention retains the status of work in progress at the level of the committee of experts which has met under the chairmanship of Dr Manfred Balz. The text has not yet progressed to being a finalised text submitted to the Council of Ministers for potential adoption. The remarks which follow are therefore intended only to provide an outline account of what have emerged as the principal tendencies of the *Phase II Draft*, recognising that there is no firm guarantee that all of these will be retained in the final version of the text. Still less would it be appropriate to engage in analysis of the details of the draft provisions at this stage of their gestation.

Study of the successive versions of the working text prepared between 1990 and 1995 reveal certain "core" concepts, amounting to an amalgamation of elements derived from different sources.[26] Some aspects of the *Phase I Draft* of 1980 are still discernible, although considerable selectivity has been exercised in eliminating many of the unhappy excesses that have been noted above. Other elements clearly owe their inspiration to the Istanbul Convention,[27] notably with regard to the facility in Chapter III for opening secondary bankruptcies and the provisions in Chapter IV concerning provision of information to creditors and the manner of lodging their claims. Other elements are altogether new. A fundamental principle employed in the Draft is that it is conceived as a "double" or "direct" convention, containing jurisdictional rules which must be followed by the courts of all contracting states in matters falling within the ambit of the convention and which simultaneously displace any domestic rules which are inconsistent with them. In this respect, the basic approach of the 1980 Draft is resurrected as forming a necessary part of any scheme for regulating legal matters in a uniform way throughout the European Union. This leads in turn to the vital question of the jurisdictional criteria to be employed in determining which state's courts are competent to open insolvency proceedings in any given case. A hierarchy of primary and secondary levels of competence is employed, with primary competence accorded to the courts of the contracting state in which the centre of the debtor's main interests is situated.[28] Although no complete definition of

---

[26] The latest versions of the text seen by the author are Documents 11013/94, representing the state of the text as at December 1994 and Document 6497/95, of April 12, 1995. Interesting comparisons may be made with a much earlier version, dated March 25, 1991, Doc.25419/91, which relates to an Explanatory Memorandum dated June 28, 1991 which reveals the origins and aims of the provisions then contained in the text. The usual practice with regard to EC conventions is to accompany the finished text with an explanatory report written by members of the drafting committee which is published in the *Official Journal* so as to furnish a formal aid to interpretation. For an extended analysis of the draft provisions at a pre-final stage, see Trautman, Westbrook and Gaillard, *loc. cit. supra*, n. 14, at pp. 602–609.

[27] See below.

[28] Draft (1994), Art. 2(1).

this concept is supplied, there is a further provision to the effect that in the case of a company or legal person the place of the registered office shall be presumed to be the centre of its main interests in the absence of proof to the contrary. The secondary criterion, for cases where the debtor's centre of main interests is not in any of the contracting states, allows the courts of a state in which the debtor possesses an establishment or other assets to exercise jurisdiction to open insolvency proceedings, with the proviso that these shall not affect an establishment or other assets of the debtor situated in another contracting state.[29] No guidance was provided in the earlier versions of the Draft as to the meaning of the term "establishment", which raised the spectre that there could be some problems in the light of different interpretations encountered within domestic legal traditions, although these should be curable in time through the interpretative activity of the European Court of Justice. In the later versions of the Draft, a proposed definition of "establishment" for the purposes of the convention has begun to evolve, giving it the meaning of "any place where the debtor carries out a non-transitory economic activity with human means and goods". Some further refinement may be expected before the final version is concluded. To be commended is the absence from the evolved text of provisions whose effect would have been to create an incentive to creditors to act pre-emptively in cases where parallel competence is possessed by courts of more than one state. The profound importance of the jurisdictional provisions is obvious upon observing that the terms of the articles dealing with applicable law ensure that, with only limited exceptions, the law of the contracting state in which insolvency proceedings are opened (*lex fori concursus*) shall apply both in matters of procedure and likewise in matters of substantive law.[30]

In Chapter III of the Draft there are provisions to enable secondary insolvency proceedings to be opened in other states than that in which proceedings are opened on the basis of the centre of the debtor's main interests.[31] The purpose of such secondary proceedings will usually be to enable local creditors to retain any special advantages which they enjoy according to the local law of insolvency, such as preferential status or security over property, which may not be treated as favourably with respect to themselves under the *lex fori concursus*. Typical examples include the rights of employees with respect to arrears of salary, and claims of tax authorities to unpaid fiscal obligations. Under a secondary insolvency proceeding, any local assets may be administered according to the local insolvency law, and thereby the local creditors' position will be sustained to the extent that the realised value of those assets will permit. Nevertheless, an overarching principle of universality of bankruptcy is respected through the provision that all creditors' claims are eligible to be lodged in both the main and in any secondary proceedings, so that it is not conceded that the assets comprised in the secondary proceedings are

---

[29] *ibid.*, Art. 2(2). (*Note*: in the 1995 version of the Draft, the words "or other assets" are omitted from Art. 2(2), leaving only the possession by the debtor of "an establishment" within the territory of a contracting state to serve as a basis for secondary jurisdiction.)
[30] *ibid.*, Art. 3. Excepted cases are set out in Arts. 4, 4a, 5, 6, 7, 7a, 8, 8a and 8b.
[31] Draft (1994), Art. 19. Further provisions are set out in Arts. 20–30 inclusive.

"ring-fenced" for the exclusive benefit of local creditors, even though in practice their advantaged position may result in exhaustion of the funds ahead of any distributions to out-of state claimants. The vital proposition is that the *total* estate of the debtor is to be administered on a basis of universal collectivity, so that creditors who have received payment from one source are not enabled to duplicate their recovery out of funds being administered elsewhere: their participation in the parallel proceedings will be subject to the proviso that they can only receive what would constitute their pro rata entitlement according to the distributional rules of the *lex concursus*, taking into account for this purpose the proportion which has already been paid elsewhere.

One of the main practical consequences of the entry into force of a properly designed international bankruptcy convention should be the facilitation of the taking of timely and effective steps by the liquidator or trustee to preserve value for the benefit of all creditors collectively, in relation to assets dispersed in different jurisdictions. To counteract the "race of diligence", and to neutralise the advantages enjoyed by local creditors in terms of space and time, it is vital to ensure that the office-holder's status and rights are recognised internationally with minimal formalities needed to establish credentials, and that the rights and powers exercisable in other jurisdictions should be those conferred by the law of the state of the opening of proceedings. Moreover, the defining moment in terms of the time from which the judgment opening proceedings becomes internationally effective, and the office-holder's powers are exercisable, should be the time that it becomes effective in the state of opening of proceedings. All these *desiderata* are currently met under the terms of the *Phase II* draft.[32] While the liquidator appointed by a court of the contracting state in which the centre of the debtor's main interests is situated thus enjoys the capability to exercise in other contracting states all the powers conferred by the law of the state of appointment, including the right to remove the debtor's assets from the territory in which they are situated, this is subject to certain qualifications and exceptions. These are that in exercising his powers the liquidator must comply with the law of the contracting state within whose territory he wishes to take action, in particular with regard to procedures for the realisation of assets, and secondly that the exercise of powers in another state is possible only so long as no secondary proceedings have been opened in that state in accordance with the procedure established by Chapter III.[33] The latter exception provides further insight into the potential function of the secondary insolvency procedure, since it will serve as a tactical tool in any contest between creditors outside the state where primary proceedings are opened, and the office-holder who is there appointed. The important consequence however of foreign creditors resorting to secondary proceedings linked to the presence of local assets, is that the character of those proceedings becomes firmly established as belonging to the realm of

---

[32] *ibid.*, Arts. 9, 9a, 10, 11, and 12. Arts. 13–18 are also relevant, particularly Art. 18 which creates the familiar exception to recognition on the grounds of manifest incompatibility with the public policy of the recognising state.

[33] *ibid.*, Art. 10(1), (3). See also Arts. 4 and 5.

insolvency law, and they are thereby imbued with the principles of collectivity and universality, instead of it being possible for local creditors to engage in acts of private diligence aimed at enabling them to remain outside the framework of insolvency.[34]

Chapter IV of the Draft Convention contains useful provisions to facilitate the provision of information to creditors in multi-jurisdictional insolvencies, and to simplify the procedure for lodging claims where the creditor's preferred working language is not that of the state under whose law the insolvency is being administered. The contents of this Chapter are directly inspired by those of Chapter IV of the Istanbul Convention, whose terms are virtually identical in substance, *mutatis mutandis*.[35] In consequence of the fact that the European Union has a far greater number of official languages than the Council of Europe—12 as from January 1995, in contrast to just two for the Council of Europe—the EEC Draft offers a very practical solution to the creditor's linguistic dilemma by proposing the development of a standard form entitled "Invitation to lodge a claim", to be prepared in all the official languages of the Union and stating the time limits to be observed. Any creditor who has his habitual residence, domicile or registered office in a contracting state other than that in which the proceedings have opened would be entitled to lodge claim in an official language of his "home" state, but may be required to provide a translation into an official language of the state in which the proceedings are being conducted.[36]

The EEC Convention would be non-retrospective, in the sense that its provisions would not apply to proceedings opened before its entry into force. That date could be at some considerable distance into the future, since the current terms of entry into force would require ratification on the part of all the signatory states.[37] Thereafter, alteration to the main text of the convention would involve the cumbersome process of convening a revision conference, but fortunately this would not be necessary merely for the purpose of adjusting the schedules of proceedings, state by state, to which the convention's provisions will apply. This is because the latter are listed in separate Annexes to the convention which may, by virtue of Article 44, be amended unilaterally at any time by the contracting states through notification to the Secretary-General of the Council of the European Union. Following circulation of notice to the other contracting states, the desired amendment will be deemed accepted if no objections are raised within the ensuing three months.

The European Bankruptcy Convention of the Council of Europe: The Istanbul Convention

As *Phase I* of the EEC project for an international insolvency convention

---

[34] See Hanisch (1993) 2 *International Insolvency Review 151–164*.
[35] *Phase II Draft*, Arts. 31–34. *cf.* Istanbul Convention, discussed *infra*, Arts. 29–32.
[36] *ibid.*, Art. 34. See also Art. 33 on contents of the lodgement of claim. (*cf.* Istanbul Convention, Arts. 31 and 32).
[37] *ibid.*, Art. 38. See also Art. 35.

lost momentum after 1980, so the centre of attention in this field was transferred from Brussels to Strasbourg. The Council of Europe, whose headquarters is in the latter city, has a far larger participating membership—currently 34 strong—than the European Union, but it so happens that all 15 members of the Union are simultaneously members of the Council of Europe. From 1981 onwards, under the aegis of the European Committee on Legal Co-operation, successive draft versions of a European Convention on Certain International Aspects of Bankruptcy were elaborated. The concluded convention was opened for signature in Istanbul on June 5, 1990 and hence is generally known as the *Istanbul Convention*, and will be referred to as such in this chapter.[38]

Initially, the intention was to draw up a relatively modest international convention to allow the office holder in insolvency proceedings to act in other jurisdictions on behalf of the body of creditors and to enable him to take protective measures and to institute legal proceedings abroad. It was also proposed that clear provisions should be made to ensure the right of foreign creditors to prove their claims in, and to receive adequate information about, insolvency proceedings concerning their debtor. Such a convention would have very limited effects, of course, but its practical utility would be considerable, given that it proves most difficult presently for a trustee or liquidator even to bring or defend foreign proceedings concerning the insolvent's estate. Moreover, if the practical results of such a simple convention were positive and attractive, a series of further projects could be envisaged, covering a further range of matters.

As work on the Draft European Convention progressed, however, its ambitions began to proliferate. Additional purposes were included, necessitating a far more elaborate structure for the text as a whole. The jurisdictional criteria, formulated for the purpose of determining the competence of the courts or other authorities in a given state to open insolvency proceedings, bear a close resemblance to those which were included in the EEC Draft Convention of 1980, and are indeed virtually identical to the somewhat differently worded provisions of the *Phase II* EEC Draft, as described above. These include the concept of the "state in which the debtor has the centre of his main interests," as the basis for allocating primary jurisdictional competence, and the state in whose territory the debtor has "an establishment," as the secondary basis for competence where the "centre of main interests" is not located in the territory of any of the contracting states.[39] The same perils of want of clarity and uniformity of meaning, as were noted in the case of the EEC Drafts, may therefore resurface with regard to the Istanbul Convention. In that case, the problems may prove to be particularly intractable because, unlike the European Union, the Council of Europe has no existing court of international competence to which questions of interpretation of this kind

---

[38] E.T.S., No. 136; text published (in English only) in I.F. Fletcher (Ed.), *Cross-Border Insolvency: Comparative Dimensions (The Aberystwyth Insolvency Papers)* (1990), Appendix II (pp. 297–313).
[39] Istanbul Convention, Arts. 3, 4.

might be referred under the terms of the Convention itself.[40] Moreover, further complexities have resulted from the inclusion of new provisions to allow the possibility of opening secondary bankruptcies in other contracting states at the request of the office holder in the main bankruptcy or of other parties granted that right under the local law.

An important point to note is that the Istanbul Convention is designed as a "simple" or "indirect" type, that is to say it merely specifies criteria which, if met in any given case of the opening of insolvency proceedings in one contracting state, enable the proceedings to be recognised and enjoy other effects in the territory of the other States Parties. There is no requirement that states amend their existing law and practice regarding the exercise of jurisdiction in matters within the ambit of the convention, but as a corollary to that there is no obligation to recognise or enforce a judgment or order which does not meet the specified criteria, even though it was made by a court of a contracting state.

Article 1 indicates that the scope of the convention is confined to "collective insolvency proceedings which entail a disinvestment of the debtor and the appointment of a liquidator, and which may entail the liquidation of the assets". The term "disinvestment of the debtor" is explained in Article 1(3)(b) as meaning "the placing of power to manage, control and dispose of assets in the hands of a liquidator", while the latter term is defined by sub-paragraph (a) as meaning any person or body whose function is to administer or liquidate the assets of the bankrupt or to supervise the activities of the debtor. A list of the persons or bodies which qualify as "Liquidator" for the purposes of the convention is provided in Appendix B to the text, while a similar list, state by state, is supplied by Appendix A to indicate all the types of proceedings which fall within the ambit of the convention.

The criteria for determining indirect international competence to open insolvency proceedings are set out in Article 4, under which primary competence is accorded to the courts or other authorities of the Party in which the debtor has the centre of his main interests. In the case of companies and legal persons, unless the contrary is proved, this is presumed to be at the place of their registered office. Secondary competence, in cases where the centre of the debtor's main interests is not located in the territory of any Party or where a bankruptcy cannot be opened in such a Party because of provisions of its national law, is accorded to the courts or other authorities of the Party in whose territory the debtor has an establishment.[41] Where the occasion for resorting to the secondary

---

[40] The European Court of Justice is competent to receive references for interpretation of the Brussels Convention of September 27, 1968, by virtue of a Protocol on Interpretation signed on June 3, 1971 and would acquire a further jurisdiction to interpret the EEC Bankruptcy Convention under the terms of the *Phase II* Draft (Art. 34a–e). The only existing court of a permanent nature established under the auspices on the Council of Europe is the European Court of Human Rights, established specifically for the purposes of the European Convention on Human Rights of November 4, 1950 (see Articles 19(2), and 38 to 56 of that Convention).

[41] Note that there is no further basis of jurisdiction derived from the presence of "other assets" apart from "an establishment". *cf.* early versions of the *Phase II EEC Draft*, Art. 2(2), discussed *supra*.

basis of jurisdiction is the debtor's immunity from undergoing bankruptcy by the law of the centre of main interests, the latter Party is not obliged to apply the convention *in casu*, and hence assets located in that state may remain outside the framework of the convention.

The Istanbul Convention has as its main purpose to guarantee a minimum of legal co-operation in matters such as the power of administrators and liquidators to act outside their national territory. To qualify for such co-operation, article 3 requires that the decision to open the bankruptcy must: (a) emanate from a court or other authority having competence under Article 4; (b) be effective in the territory of the party where the bankruptcy is opened; and (c) not be manifestly contrary to the public policy of the Party in which the liquidator intends to exercise his powers under the terms of Chapter II or in which the opening of a secondary bankruptcy is requested under the terms of Chapter III. The latter condition would render it possible for one Party to decline to accord co-operation under the convention in a case where the foreign proceedings can be characterised as a "tax bankruptcy", for reasons which have already been discussed.[42] It follows from the restricted aims of the convention that there can be no question of any international effects taking place in relation to assets of the debtor as a direct consequence of insolvency proceedings, even where the latter meet the criteria laid down by Articles 3 and 4. Moreover, Article 40 allows any ratifying State to enter a reservation to the effect that it will not apply either Chapter II or Chapter III, a facility which, if utilised to any large extent by the states which eventually ratify it, will render the Istanbul Convention a somewhat symbolic gesture, with little practical value.

Chapter II itself appears somewhat promising as a vehicle for advancing the cause of cross-border cooperation by means of gradual and limited steps. Article 7, in conjunction with Articles 2 and 3, enables the liquidator to act in other jurisdictions simply on the basis of exhibiting a copy of the order of his appointment to the relevant authorities of the state of acting. Article 8 further enables him to take any necessary steps to protect or preserve the value of the assets of the debtor, in the place of their *situs*, with effect from the date of his original appointment. Such steps are however required to be taken in accordance with the law of the *situs*, and the liquidator is not allowed to remove assets from the territory of that state. The powers of administration, management and disposal of assets, and also the power to remove them from the territory of their *situs*, is accorded under Articles 10 and 11, but these acts must be carried out subject to the local law, and must be preceded by public advertisement followed by a suspension of two months, during which time any interested party may request the opening of a local bankruptcy, or of proceedings to prevent bankruptcy, which thereupon gives rise to a further period of delay in the exercise of the liquidator's powers pending determination of the request.[43] A further outcome of the suspension can be the lodging of objections

---

[42] See Chap. 29, *ante*, p. 707.

[43] Note the provisions of Art. 11(2) regarding the taking of actions by preferential creditors, or those with public law claims or with claims arising from the operation of an establishment of the debtor or from employment locally, during the period of suspension.

under Article 12 to the liquidator's proposed exercise of powers, placing the onus on the liquidator to persuade the court of his entitlement to exercise those powers under the convention. Above all, the opening of local bankruptcy proceedings can take place, and thereby preclude the liquidator from exercising his powers in the state in question.[44] Such a bankruptcy would be a secondary bankruptcy according to the provisions of Chapter III, which enables such proceedings to be opened in any state in which an establishment of the debtor is situated, or in which assets of the debtor are situated.[45] The fact that a bankruptcy has previously been opened in accordance with Articles 4(1) and 3(b) and (c) is sufficient basis for the opening of a secondary bankruptcy, without regard to whether the debtor is insolvent in the state where secondary proceedings take place.[46] Standing to apply for the opening of secondary proceedings is accorded under Article 18 to both the liquidator in the main bankruptcy and any other person granted the right to make such request under the local law. The essential purposes underlying the system of secondary bankruptcies, and the principle of interrelationship between main and secondary proceedings, have already been rehearsed in the earlier discussion of the same solution to the "universality problem" that is proposed under the latest version of the EEC Draft Convention, which is actually modelled upon the Istanbul Convention in this aspect.[47] Similarly, the useful provisions in Chapter IV concerning the provision of information to creditors and the convenient method of lodging their claims have been closely borrowed by the EEC Draft and were referred to above, the major point of contrast being that, since the Council of Europe operates with only two official languages (English and French), Articles 31 and 32 of the Istanbul Convention together enable creditors to lodge their claims in writing in their own language with the proviso that if this is not also an official language of the state which has opened the procedure the creditor must attach a translation in that language or in one of the official languages of the Council of Europe. Similarly, notices sent by the liquidator to creditors informing them of the opening of proceedings and inviting them to lodge claims within a specified time limit are required to be accompanied by a translation in either English or French where the original is expressed in some other language.[48] However, Article 39 enables ratifying states to derogate from this convenient provision by a declaration requiring notices and claims to be drawn up exclusively in one of the official languages of the state in question.

Article 34 sets a requirement of a minimum of three ratifications to enable the Istanbul Convention to enter into force between those states which ratify it. Since the date of opening the convention in 1990, eight

[44] Art. 14.
[45] Art. 17.
[46] Art. 16.
[47] See *supra*, p. 775. See the further provisions of the Istanbul Convention, Arts. 19–28. For a more detailed comparison of the two conventions see I.F. Fletcher in J.S. Ziegel (Ed.), *Current Developments in International and Comparative Corporate Insolvency Law* (1994), Chap. 32 (pp. 709–727), and also Trautman, Westbrook and Gaillard, *loc. cit. supra*, n. 14, esp. at 586–609.
[48] Arts. 30, 32(1).

states have signed but so far only one of those (Cyprus) has lodged ratification.[49] The convention has thus not yet entered into force. The government of the United Kingdom has given no public indication of its intentions with regard to the possibility that it may become a party to the convention. Participation in the forthcoming EEC Convention on bankruptcy is not incompatible with ratification of the Istanbul Convention, since provisions inserted in the two texts have the effect that, as between the members of the European Union, the EEC Convention shall take precedence in any case of overlap.[50] Despite its inbuilt limitations, whereby the states which become parties to it may elect to cut down its effects to a bare minimum with regard to themselves, the Istanbul Convention helps to symbolise an emergent spirit of international co-operation at regional level. As such, it could serve as a bridging device on the road towards more globally constituted arrangements for cross-border collaboration in urgent and practical matters arising from insolvency.

Judicial Co-operation in Cross-Border Insolvencies: the Way Ahead?

In the absence, currently, of any formal arrangements, on a truly international basis, for the regulation of cross-border insolvency problems, courts—and office holders and practitioners—must necessarily resort to more traditional techniques in devising workable solutions to the difficulties they encounter. We have already seen that the English courts have shown their readiness to sanction collaborative agreements between English and foreign trustees or liquidators, in cases where there are concurrent proceedings and where the proposed agreement is clearly in the best interests of achieving fairness and justice.[51] Thus, given an appropriate degree of willingness on the part of the judiciary to adopt a fairly "activist" stance in relation to the giving of practical assistance, coupled with a display of initiative tempered by a sense of equity and proportion on the part of practitioners, much may be accomplished in individual cases on the basis of the existing provisions of domestic law.[52]

Established judicial tendencies in some jurisdictions to work towards the solution of familiar difficulties in international cases have been reinforced in recent years through the enactment of more clear and positive provisions in national insolvency legislation, directing courts as to

---

[49] The signatory states thus far are: France; Germany; Greece; Luxembourg; Turkey; Belgium; Italy; Cyprus.

[50] Istanbul Convention, Art. 38; EEC Draft, Art. 36.

[51] See *Re. P. MacFadyen & Co.* [1908] 1 K.B. 675; *Re McCulloch* (1880) 14 Ch.D. 716; *Re Commercial Bank of South Australia* (1886) 33 Ch.D. 174; *Re Federal Bank of Australia* [1893] W.N. 77; *Re English, Scottish and Australian Chartered Bank* [1893] 3 Ch. 385, considered in Chaps. 29 and 30, *ante*.

[52] See, *e.g.*, the initiatives taken in the celebrated *Herstatt* case: Nadelmann (1977) 52 N.Y.U.L.R. 1; (1984) 33 I.C.L.Q. 431; Becker (1976) 62 A.B.A.J. 1292. See also the comparative survey of the status of foreign administrators of insolvent estates, by S. Riesenfeld, (1976) 24 A.J.C.L. 288. *cf.* Fletcher (1993) 2 International Insolvency Review 7, esp. at pp. 21–25.

the manner in which they may respond to overseas requests for assistance, whether from other courts or from office holders in the foreign proceedings. A prominent example of such a provision is to be found in section 304 of the United States Bankruptcy Code of 1978.[53] Under this section, a case ancillary to a foreign proceeding may be commenced by a foreign representative filing a petition under the section in the American bankruptcy court. The court is then enabled to provide active assistance to the foreign representative in such forms as—enjoining the commencement or continuation of any action against the debtor with respect to property involved in the foreign proceedings, or against the property itself; the enforcement of any judgment against the debtor with respect to the property; ordering turnover of the property of the estate, or the proceeds of the property, to the foreign representative; or ordering other appropriate relief.

Section 304 of the United States Bankruptcy Code has proved to be a successful innovation, and has inspired law reformers, and legislators, in other common law jurisdictions to explore similar models of co-operation. An unadopted Bill presented to the Canadian Parliament in 1984 would have provided for requests to be made to the courts of that country from foreign courts with jurisdiction in insolvency matters, whereupon the Canadian court could have acted in aid through the exercise of its own parallel powers.[54] More recently, the Australian Law Reform Commission in the Final Report of its General Insolvency Inquiry advocated the amendment of Australian insolvency laws to permit insolvency administrations which have originated and are being conducted in an overseas country to be recognised and enforced in Australia.[55] The Commission further recommended the enactment of provisions to enable Australian courts to give aid to the administrator in foreign insolvencies. These proposals were subsequently implemented by means of a provision, currently contained in section 581 of the Corporations Act, which provides that in all matters relating to the insolvency administration of a foreign company the Australian courts with jurisdiction in relation to company matters: (a) shall act in aid of, and be auxiliary to, the courts of prescribed countries that have jurisdiction in such matters; and (b) may act in aid of, and be auxiliary to, the courts of other countries that have jurisdiction in such matters. The prescribed countries for this purpose are currently: Jersey; Canada; Papua New Guinea; Malaysia; New Zealand;

---

[53] 11 U.S.C. §304. For comments, see Boshkoff (1987) 36 I.C.L.Q. 729; Unger (1985) 19 Int.L. 1153; Morales and Deutsch (1984) 39 Bus.Law. 1573; Honsberger (1980) 30 Case W.Res.L.Rev. 631. See also R. A. Gitlin, E.D. Flaschen and D.M. Grimes, United States Treatment of Foreign Insolvency Proceedings, published as Chap. 19 of *Norton Bankruptcy Law and Practice* (1989 ed.), also published in I.F. Fletcher (Ed.), *op. cit. supra*, n. 38, Chap. 4(b) (pp. 69–94). See also: Boshkoff in J.S. Ziegel (Ed.), *op. cit. supra*, n. 47, Chap. 29 (pp. 677–686), and the same author in 72 Wash. U.L.Q. 931 (1994); Westbrook, 65 Am.Bankr.L.J. 457 (1991); Trautman, Westbrook and Gaillard, *loc. cit. supra*, n. 14, at pp. 609–622; Gitlin and Flaschen, 42 Bus. Law 307 (1987); Westbrook in A. Clarke (Ed.) *Current Issues in Insolvency Law* (1991), pp. 27–57; Booth, 66 A.Bankr.L.J. 135 (1992).

[54] Bill c. 17, an Act respecting bankruptcy and insolvency, Canada, 1st reading January 31, 1984: clause 315.

[55] Australian Law Reform Commission, Report No. 45 (1988), Vol. 1, paras. 967–975.

Singapore; Switzerland; the United Kingdom, and the U.S.A. Thus recognition of insolvency proceedings originating before the courts of any of those countries is a matter of obligation for Australian courts, which are likewise required to give assistance in response to a formal request to do so from the foreign court in question. The according of recognition and assistance to courts not located in the prescribed countries is a matter for the discretion of the Australian court, which is therefore able to exercise its own judgment with regard to the nature and quality of the foreign insolvency process and its conformity to accepted standards and principles. In all cases, the nature of the powers exercisable by the Australian court in response to a letter of request from a foreign court is restricted to the powers which it could exercise if the matter had arisen within its own jurisdiction.[56]

Co-operation by United Kingdom Courts: Section 426 of the Insolvency Act 1986

Section 426 of the Insolvency Act 1986 offers considerable potential for the development of a network of arrangements for reciprocal assistance between insolvency courts in this country and overseas. It is a large and complex section, whose provisions were earlier considered with regard to their effect upon the recognition and enforcement of insolvency orders between the different parts of the United Kingdom, and also between countries belonging to the Commonwealth.[57] The key provision in section 426, from the genuinely international point of view, is subsection (4), which provides that:

> "The courts having jurisdiction in relation to insolvency law in any part of the United Kingdom shall assist the courts having the corresponding jurisdiction in any other part of the United Kingdom *or any relevant country or territory*" (emphasis added).

The meaning of the expression "relevant country or territory" is supplied by subsection (10), so as to denote:

> (a) "any of the Channel Islands or the Isle of Man, or
> (b) any country or territory designated for the purposes of this section by the Secretary of State by order made by statutory instrument."

The way is thus prepared for the gradual extension of the facility afforded by section 426, whenever the Secretary of State is satisfied that appropriate arrangements are in place on a reciprocal basis, to justify the designation of a given state or territory for the purposes of section 426. To

---

[56] Corporations Act (Australia), s.581(3). *cf.* the more extensive scope accorded to the courts of the United Kingdom under s.426(5) of the Insolvency Act 1986, discussed, *infra*.
[57] See Chap. 29, *ante*, at p. 703, and also Chap. 30 at pp. 759–760.

date, one order has been made in which 17 countries or territories, all but one of them within the Commonwealth, are so designated.[58]

The nature of the assistance available

The further provisions of section 426 give rise to intriguing possibilities as to the nature of the assistance which may be provided by the United Kingdom courts in response to a request made by a court in any of the Channel Islands or the Isle of Man, or in a jurisdiction which has been duly designated for this purpose, and is thus a "relevant country or territory." Section 426(5) states that a request made to a court in any part of the United Kingdom by a court in any such jurisdiction is authority for the court to which the request is made to apply, in relation to the matters specified in the request, the insolvency law which is applicable by *either* court in relation to comparable matters falling within its jurisdiction.[59] The concluding words of subsection (5) are of special significance:

> "In exercising its discretion under this subsection, a court shall have regard, in particular, to the rules of private international law."

Thus, the principles embodied in the private international law of this country, and described in Chapters 29 and 30 above, with regard to the recognition of foreign insolvency proceedings, and the degree of effectiveness to be accorded to them, are of relevance, as are the rules belonging to the general body of English conflict of laws concerning choice of law in matters of all kinds. These supply the basis on which the English court can decide in what way it will exercise its discretion as to the mode of assistance to be accorded in fulfilment of the court's statutory obligation, under subsection (4), to render assistance of some kind. One striking illustration of the scope of the discretionary powers conferred on the United Kingdom courts by section 426(5) is *Re Dallhold Estates (UK) Pty. Ltd,*[60] in which a company incorporated under the companies legislation of Australia was subject to application for a winding up order before the Federal Court in that country, and a provisional liquidator had been appointed. It was perceived that the optimum way of preserving the value of a leasehold asset of the company situate in England would be by means of an administration order under Part II of the Insolvency Act 1986. If a petition for an administration order had come before the English court by way of original proceedings it would probably have been outside the

---

[58] The Co-operation of Insolvency Courts (Designation of Relevant Countries and Territories) order 1986, (S.I. 1986, No. 2123). The countries and territories so designated are: Anguilla, Australia, the Bahamas, Bermuda, Botswana, Canada, Cayman Islands, Falkland Islands, Gibraltar, Hong Kong, Republic of Ireland, Montserrat, New Zealand, St. Helena, Turks and Caicos Islands, Tuvalu, and the Virgin Islands. The provisions of s.426 have been made applicable, with appropriate modifications, to the Bailiwick of Guernsey and to Northern Ireland. See, respectively, S.I. 1989, No. 2409; and S.I. 1989, No. 2405 (N.I. 19), Art. 381 and Sched. 9, para. 41(b).

[59] Emphasis added. See s.426(10), as amended, for the statutory meaning of the expression "insolvency law" in this context.

[60] [1992] BCC 394.

jurisdictional competence of the court to make such an order in relation to a company not formed and registered under domestic legislation.[61] However, in hearing the matter pursuant to a letter of request issued by the Federal Court, Chadwick J. concluded that it was clearly part of the purpose of section 426(5) to give the requested court a jurisdiction it might otherwise not have had in order that it can give assistance to the requesting court in the way directed by subsection (4). He therefore responded by making an administration order, on the basis that this was part of the insolvency law which the English court could apply to comparable matters falling within its own jurisdiction.[62]

In another case, this time arising from the liquidation of a company incorporated in the Cayman Islands and ordered to be wound up by the Islands' Grand Court, Rattee J. responded to a letter of request from that court, submitted under section 426, by making declarations under sections 213, 214 and 238 of the 1986 Act, all three of which had no statutory counterparts under the companies laws of the Cayman Islands themselves.[63] The case arose out of the complex, multi-jurisdictional proceedings concerning the collapse of the *BCCI* corporate banking "empire" which had had extensive business involvement with the United Kingdom through various subsidiaries incorporated under different foreign laws. Having regard to the fact that the companies' affairs were "hopelessly intertwined",[64] the learned judge stated that it was desirable for the courts having insolvency jurisdiction in respect of the various companies respectively to co-operate to the fullest extent possible. In the instant case, this could best be attained by the English court trying the claims of the liquidators of the Cayman company against parties alleged to have been parties to fraudulent or wrongful trading, giving rise to potential liability under sections 213 and 214, or to have been the recipients of payments constituting transactions at an undervalue capable of being impeached by the liquidators under section 238.[65] In the course of arriving at this conclusion, Rattee J. helpfully observed that the "discretion" conferred by the words of the concluding paragraph of section 426(5) (quoted above) was to be understood as being a discretion on the part of the *requested* court (*i.e.* the court in some part of the United Kingdom) to decide whether to apply its own law or the law of the requesting court to the matters specified in the request and that it is in respect of that discretion that the requirement is imposed whereby the court must have regard to the rules of private international law.[66]

---

[61] *cf. Re Devon and Somerset Farmers Ltd.* [1993] BCC 410, distinguishing *Re International Bulk Commodities Ltd.* [1993] Ch. 77; [1992] BCC 463. See Moss (1993) 6 Insolvency Intelligence 19. See Chap. 16, *ante*, esp. p. 431.

[62] [1992] BCC at pp. 398–399.

[63] *Re Bank of Credit and Commerce International SA* [1993] BCC 787. (A further declaration was made under s.212, which had some counterpart in Cayman law.)

[64] See *Re Bank of Credit and Commerce International SA (No. 2)* [1992] BCC 715, 719, *per* Nicholls V.-C.

[65] [1993] BCC at pp. 790–791, and 803.

[66] *ibid.*, at p. 801. Rattee J. expressed his dissent from the contrary view on this point stated by Chadwick J. in *Re Dallhold Estates (U.K.) Pty. Ltd.* [1992] BCC 394 at p. 398. It is respectfully submitted that the analysis of Rattee J. is correct.

atmosphere of relative calm and dignity, reflected in the passages to be found in judgments delivered by the courts on both sides of the Atlantic at various stages in the process, wherein a spirit of mutual trust and respect is expressed through the language of comity.[69] Although the *Maxwell* case may prove to be a unique product of its own highly specialised facts, its value as a harbinger of enhanced judicial readiness to act as facilitators of constructive solutions to the problems posed by cross-border insolvencies is very great, and is to be welcomed.

The future

A development which has drawn close inspiration from the *Maxwell* case, as well as from other recent examples of international judicial co-operation in recent years, has been the initiative towards the creation of an international convention to provide an established framework for such co-operation to take place among as many countries as possible. This initiative is being pursued jointly under the auspices of INSOL International and UNCITRAL.[70] The benefits of such a convention could be substantial, given the current difficulty in achieving a sensible balance between principle and expediency in cross-border insolvencies: while in principle it is desirable to trace and retrieve every asset on behalf of the general body of creditors, in practice it may give rise to disproportionately high expenditure of costs in a frequently uncertain cause. Only in cases of the magnitude of *BCCI* or *MCC*, where the total asset values are still substantial, may it prove a cost-effective exercise to enlist the skills of highly paid insolvency practitioners and lawyers for the sake of achieving the theoretical ideal of a near-universal administration of the debtor's estate.

The examples to date of international co-operation may be said to be heavily dependent upon the degree of confidence and trust built up through experience among practitioners and judges at a personal level. The challenge for the future is to reduce the degree of dependence upon individuals, and to develop a framework of co-operation based upon reciprocal acceptance of the standards and integrity of national insolvency laws themselves, and of the judiciary and practitioners by which they are administered. If in due course an UNCITRAL convention is concluded to enable such a framework to be adopted between a growing number of states, transcending merely regional or historic groupings and affinities, the benefits should be considerable and, simultaneously, the evolution of international insolvency will have been greatly advanced.

[69] See *Re Maxwell Communications Corporation plc (No. 2), Barclays Bank plc v. Homan* [1992] BCC 757, at pp. 759–760 and at p. 767 *per* Hoffmann J. (Ch.D.) and at p. 769 *per* Glidewell L.J. and at pp. 777–778 *per* Leggatt L.J. (both C.A.); *Re A.W. Brierley*, 145 B.R. 151 (Bankr.S.D.N.Y. 1992), Judge Tina Brozman; *Re Maxwell Communications Corporation plc* (Case No. 91 B 15741) 170 Bankr. 800; 25 Bankr. Ct. Dec. (CRR) 1567. (Bankr.S.D.N.Y., August 5, 1994) (also Judge Brozman). For comment, see Fletcher (1993) 6 Insolvency Intelligence 10–13; Flaschen and Silverman in J.S. Ziegel (Ed.), *op. cit. supra*, n. 47, Chap. 25 (pp. 621–645).

[70] See the proceedings of the inaugural, joint Colloquium on Cross-Border Insolvency, held in Vienna in April 1994, published in (1995) 4 International Insolvency Review (Special Conference Issue) 1–115.

Appendix I

STATUTORY MEANINGS OF "CONNECTED PERSON" AND "ASSOCIATE" WHERE USED IN THE INSOLVENCY ACT 1986

Section 249 "Connected" with a company

249. For the purposes of any provision in this Group of Parts,[1] a person is connected with a company if:

(a) he is a director or shadow director of the company or an associate of such a director or shadow director, or
(b) he is an associate of the company;

and "associate" has the meaning given by section 435 in Part XVIII of this Act.

Part XVIII

Interpretation

Section 435 Meaning of "associate"

435.—(1) For the purposes of this Act any question whether a person is an associate of another person is to be determined in accordance with the following provisions of this section (any provision that a person is an

---

[1] The First Group of Parts of the Insolvency Act 1986 comprises Pts. I to VII inclusive (ss.1–251).

Appendix I

associate of another person being taken to mean that they are associates of each other).

(2) A person is an associate of an individual if that person is the individual's husband or wife, or is a relative, or the husband or wife of a relative, of the individual or of the individual's husband or wife.

(3) A person is an associate of any person with whom he is in partnership, and of the husband or wife or a relative of any individual with whom he is in partnership; and a Scottish firm is an associate of any person who is a member of the firm.

(4) A person is an associate of any person whom he employs or by whom he is employed.

(5) A person in his capacity as trustee of a trust other than:

(a) a trust arising under any of the second Group of Parts or the Bankruptcy (Scotland) Act 1985, or
(b) a pension scheme or an employees' share scheme (within the meaning of the Companies Act),

is an associate of another person if the beneficiaries of the trust include, or the terms of the trust confer a power that may be exercised for the benefit of, that other person or an associate of that other person.

(6) A company is an associate of another company:

(a) if the same person has control of both, or a person has control of one and persons who are his associates, or he and persons who are his associates, have control of the other, or
(b) if a group of two or more persons has control of each company, and the groups either consist of the same persons or could be regarded as consisting of the same persons by treating (in one or more cases) a member of either group as replaced by a person of whom he is an associate.

(7) A company is an associate of another person if that person has control of it or if that person and persons who are his associates together have control of it.

(8) For the purposes of this section a person is a relative of an individual if he is that individual's brother, sister, uncle, aunt, nephew, niece, lineal ancestor or lineal descendant, treating:

(a) any relationship of the half blood as a relationship of the whole blood and the stepchild or adopted child of any person as his child, and
(b) an illegitimate child as the legitimate child of his mother and reputed father;

and references in this section to a husband or wife include a former husband or wife and a reputed husband or wife.

(9) For the purposes of this section any director or other officer of a company is to be treated as employed by that company.

Appendix I

(10) For the purposes of this section a person is to be taken as having control of a company if:

(a) the directors of the company or of another company which has control of it (or any of them) are accustomed to act in accordance with his directions or instructions, or

(b) he is entitled to exercise, or control the exercise of, one third or more of the voting power at any general meeting of the company or of another company which has control of it;

and where two or more persons together satisfy either of the above conditions, they are to be taken as having control of the company.

(11) In this section "company" includes any body corporate (whether incorporated in Great Britain or elsewhere); and references to directors and other officers of a company and to voting power at any general meeting of a company have effect with any necessary modifications.

Appendix II

PROVISIONS OF THE INSOLVENCY ACT 1986 CONCERNING THE SEQUENCE OF DISTRIBUTION OF ASSETS OF AN INSOLVENT DEBTOR, AND DEFINING THE CATEGORIES OF PREFERENTIAL DEBTS[1]

Part IV—Winding up of Companies registered under the Companies Acts

Section 175 Preferential debts (general provision)

175(1) In a winding up the company's preferential debts (within the meaning given by section 386 in Part XII) shall be paid in priority to all other debts.

175(2) Preferential debts—

(a) rank equally among themselves after the expenses of the winding up and shall be paid in full, unless the assets are insufficient to meet them, in which case they abate in equal proportions; and

(b) so far as the assets of the company available for payment of general creditors are insufficient to meet them, have priority over the claims of holders of debentures secured by, or holders of, any floating charge created by the company, and shall be paid accordingly out of any property comprised in or subject to that charge.

---

[1] Preferential debts are dealt with in Chaps. 10 and 24, *ante*.

APPENDIX II

PART IX—BANKRUPTCY

Section 328 Priority of debts (Bankruptcy)

328(1) In the distribution of the bankrupt's estate, his preferential debts (within the meaning given by section 386 in Part XII) shall be paid in priority to other debts.

328(2) Preferential debts rank equally between themselves after the expenses of the bankruptcy and shall be paid in full unless the bankrupt's estate is insufficient for meeting them, in which case they abate in equal proportions between themselves.

328(3) Debts which are neither preferential debts nor debts to which the next section applies also rank equally between themselves and, after the preferential debts, shall be paid in full unless the bankrupt's estate is insufficient for meeting them, in which case they abate in equal proportions between themselves.

328(4) Any surplus remaining after the payment of the debts that are preferential or rank equally under subsection (3) shall be applied in paying interest on those debts in respect of the periods during which they have been outstanding since the commencement of the bankruptcy; and interest on preferential debts ranks equally with interest on debts other than preferential debts.

328(5) The rate of interest payable under subsection (4) in respect of any debt is whichever is the greater of the following—

(a) the rate specified in section 17 of the Judgments Act 1838 at the commencement of the bankruptcy, and
(b) the rate applicable to that debt apart from the bankruptcy.

328(6) This section and the next are without prejudice to any provision of this Act or any other Act under which the payment of any debt or the making of any other payment is, in the event of bankruptcy, to have a particular priority or to be postponed.

Section 329 Debts to spouse

329(1) This section applies to bankruptcy debts owed in respect of credit provided by a person who (whether or not the bankrupt's spouse at the time the credit was provided) was the bankrupt's spouse at the commencement of the bankruptcy.

329(2) Such debts—

(a) rank in priority after the debts and interest required to be paid in pursuance of section 328(3) and (4), and
(b) are payable with interest at the rate specified in section 328(5) in respect of the period during which they have been outstanding since the commencement of the bankrupty;

and the interest payable under paragraph (b) has the same priority as the debts on which it is payable.

Part XII—Preferential Debts in Company and Individual Insolvency

Section 386 Categories of preferential debts

386(1) A reference in this Act to the preferential debts of a company or an individual is to the debts listed in Schedule 6 to this Act (money owed to the Inland Revenue for income tax deducted at source; VAT, insurance premium tax, car tax, betting and gaming duties, beer duty, lottery duty; social security and pension scheme contributions; remuneration etc. of employees; levies on coal and steel production); and references to preferential creditors are to be read accordingly.

386(2) In that Schedule **"the debtor"** means the company or the individual concerned.

386(3) Schedule 6 is to be read with Schedule 4 to the Pensions Schemes Act 1993 (occupational pension scheme contributions).

Section 387 "The relevant date"

387(1) This section explains references in Schedule 6 to the relevant date (being the date which determines the existence and amount of a preferential debt).

387(2) For the purposes of section 4 in Part I (meetings to consider company voluntary arrangement), the relevant date in relation to a company which is not being wound up is—

(a) where an administration order is in force in relation to the company, the date of the making of that order, and
(b) where no such order has been made, the date of the approval of the voluntary arrangement.

387(3) In relation to a company which is being wound up, the following applies—

(a) if the winding up is by the court, and the winding-up order was made immediately upon the discharge of an administration order, the relevant date is the date of the making of the administration order;

APPENDIX II

    (b) if the case does not fall within paragraph (a) and the company—
        (i) is being wound up by the court, and
        (ii) had not commenced to be wound up voluntarily before the date of the making of the winding-up order,
    the relevant date is the date of the appointment (or first appointment) of a provisional liquidator or, if no such appointment has been made, the date of the winding-up order;
    (c) if the case does not fall within either paragraph (a) or (b), the relevant date is the date of the passing of the resolution for the winding up of the company.

387(4) In relation to a company in receivership (where section 40 or, as the case may be, section 59 applies), the relevant date is—

    (a) in England and Wales, the date of the appointment of the receiver by debenture-holders, and
    (b) in Scotland, the date of the appointment of the receiver under section 53(6) or (as the case may be) 54(5).

387(5) For the purposes of section 258 in Part VIII (individual voluntary arrangements), the relevant date is, in relation to a debtor who is not an undischarged bankrupt, the date of the interim order made under section 252 with respect to his proposal.

387(6) In relation to a bankrupt, the following applies—

    (a) where at the time the bankruptcy order was made there was an interim receiver appointed under section 286, the relevant date is the date on which the interim receiver was first appointed after the presentation of the bankruptcy petition;
    (b) otherwise, the relevant date is the date of the making of the bankruptcy order.

Schedule 6   The Categories of Preferential Debts

Section 386

CATEGORY 1: DEBTS DUE TO INLAND REVENUE

1 Sums due at the relevant date from the debtor on account of deductions of income tax from emoluments paid during the period of 12 months next before that date.

    The deductions here referred to are those which the debtor was liable to make under section 203 of the Income and Corporation Taxes Act 1988 (pay as you earn), less the amount of the repayments of income tax which the debtor was liable to make during that period.

2 Sums due at the relevant date from the debtor in respect of such

APPENDIX II

deductions as are required to be made by the debtor for that period under section 559 of the Income and Corporation Taxes Act 1988 (sub-contractors in the construction industry).

CATEGORY 2: DEBTS DUE TO CUSTOMS AND EXCISE

3 Any value added tax which is referable to the period of 6 months next before the relevant date (which period is referred to below as **"the 6-month period"**).

For the purposes of this paragraph—

(a) where the whole of the accounting period to which any value added tax is attributable falls within the 6-month period, the whole amount of that tax is referable to that period; and

(b) in any other case the amount of any value added tax which is referable to the 6-month period is the proportion of the tax which is equal to such proportion (if any) of the accounting period in question as falls within the 6-month period;

and in sub-paragraph (a) **"prescribed"** means prescribed by regulations under the Value Added Tax Act 1983.

3A Any insurance premium tax which is referable to the period of 6 months next before the relevant date (which period is referred to below as **"the 6-month period"**).

For the purposes of this paragraph—

(a) where the whole of the prescribed accounting period to which any insurance premium tax is attributable falls within the 6-month period, the whole amount of that tax is referable to that period; and

(b) in any other case the amount of any insurance premium tax which is referable to the 6-month period is the proportion of the tax which is equal to such proportion (if any) of the accounting reference period in question as falls within the 6-month period:

and references here to accounting periods shall be construed in accordance with Part III of the Finance Act 1994.

4 The amount of any car tax which is due at the relevant date from the debtor and which became due within a period of 12 months next before that date.

5 Any amount which is due—

(a) by way of general betting duty or bingo duty, or

(b) under section 12(1) of the Betting and Gaming Duties Act 1981 (general betting duty and pool betting duty recoverable from agent collecting stakes), or

(c) under section 14 of, or Schedule 2 to, that Act (gaming licence duty).

from the debtor at the relevant date and which became due within the period of 12 months next before that date.

5A The amount of any excise duty on beer which is due at the relevant date from the debtor and which became due within a period of 6 months next before that date.

5B Any amount which is due by way of lottery duty from the debtor at the relevant date and which became due within the period of 12 months next before that date.

5C Any amount which is due by way of air passenger duty from the debtor at the relevant date and which became due within the period of six months next before that date.

CATEGORY 3: SOCIAL SECURITY CONTRIBUTIONS

6 All sums which on the relevant date are due from the debtor on account of Class 1 or Class 2 contributions under the Social Security Contributions and Benefits Act 1992 or the Social Security (Northern Ireland) Act 1975 and which became due from the debtor in the 12 months next before the relevant date.

7 All sums which on the relevant date have been assessed on and are due from the debtor on account of Class 4 contributions under either of those Acts of 1975, being sums which—

(a) are due to the Commissioners of Inland Revenue (rather than to the Secretary of State or a Northern Ireland department), and
(b) are assessed on the debtor up to 5th April next before the relevant date, but not exceeding, in the whole, any one year's assessment.

CATEGORY 4: CONTRIBUTIONS TO OCCUPATIONAL PENSION SCHEMES, ETC.

8 Any sum which is owed by the debtor and is a sum to which Schedule 4 to the Pensions Schemes Act 1993 applies (contributions to occupational pension schemes and state scheme premiums).

CATEGORY 5: REMUNERATION, ETC., OF EMPLOYEES

9 So much of any amount which—

(a) is owed by the debtor to a person who is or has been an employee of the debtor, and
(b) is payable by way of remuneration in respect of the whole or any part of the period of 4 months next before the relevant date,

Appendix II

as does not exceed so much as may be prescribed by order made by the Secretary of State.[2]

10 An amount owed by way of accrued holiday remuneration, in respect of any period of employment before the relevant date, to a person whose employment by the debtor has been terminated, whether before, on or after that date.

11 So much of any sum owed in respect of money advanced for the purpose as has been applied for the payment of a debt which, if it had not been paid, would have been a debt falling within paragraph 9 or 10.

12 So much of any amount which—

(a) is ordered (whether before or after the relevant date) to be paid by the debtor under the Reserve Forces (Safeguard of Employment) Act 1985, and

(b) is so ordered in respect of a default made by the debtor before that date in the discharge of his obligations under that Act.

as does not exceed such amount as may be prescribed by order made by the Secretary of State.[2]

INTERPRETATION FOR CATEGORY 5

13(1) For the purposes of paragraphs 9 to 12, a sum is payable by the debtor to a person by way of remuneration in respect of any period if—

(a) it is paid as wages or salary (whether payable for time or for piece work or earned wholly or partly by way of commission) in respect of services rendered to the debtor in that period, or

(b) it is an amount falling within the following sub-paragraph and is payable by the debtor in respect of that period.

13(2) An amount falls within this sub-paragraph if it is—

(a) a guarantee payment under section 12(1) of the Employment Protection (Consolidation) Act 1978 (employee without work to do for a day or part of a day);

(b) remuneration on suspension on medical grounds under section 19 of that Act or remuneration on suspension on maternity grounds under section 47 of that Act;

(c) any payment for time off under section 31(3) or 31A(4) of that Act (looking for work, etc.; ante-natal care) or under section 169 of the Trade Union and Labour Relations (Consolidation) Act 1992 (trade union duties); or

(d) remuneration under a protective award made by an industrial tribunal under section 189 of the latter Act (redundancy dismissal with compensation).

---

[2] The amount prescribed is currently £800: Insolvency Proceedings (Monetary Limits) Order 1986, (S.I. 1986, No. 1996), Art 4.

Appendix II

14(1) This paragraph relates to a case in which a person's employment has been terminated by or in consequence of his employer going into liquidation or being adjudged bankrupt or (his employer being a company not in liquidation) by or in consequence of—

    (a) a receiver being appointed as mentioned in section 40 of this Act (debenture-holders secured by floating charge), or
    (b) the appointment of a receiver under section 53(6) or 54(5) of this Act (Scottish company with property subject to floating charge), or
    (c) the taking of possession by debenture-holders (so secured), as mentioned in section 196 of the Companies Act.

14(2) For the purposes of paragraphs 9 to 12, holiday remuneration is deemed to have accrued to that person in respect of any period of employment if, by virtue of his contract of employment or of any enactment, that remuneration would have accrued in respect of that period if his employment had continued until he became entitled to be allowed the holiday.

14(3) The reference in sub-paragraph (2) to any enactment includes an order or direction made under an enactment.

15 Without prejudice to paragraphs 13 and 14—

    (a) any remuneration payable by the debtor to a person in respect of a period of holiday or of absence from work through sickness or other good cause is deemed to be wages or (as the case may be) salary in respect of services rendered to the debtor in that period, and
    (b) references here and in those paragraphs to remuneration in respect of a period of holiday include any sums which, if they had been paid, would have been treated for the purposes of the enactments relating to social security as earnings in respect of that period.

CATEGORY 6: LEVIES ON COAL AND STEEL PRODUCTION

15A Any sums due at the relevant date from the debtor in respect of—

    (a) the levies on the production of coal and steel referred to in Article 49 and 50 of the E.C.S.C. Treaty, or
    (b) any surcharge for delay provided for in Article 50(3) of that Treaty and Article 6 of Decision 3/52 of the High Authority of the Coal and Steel Community.

Appendix II

ORDERS

16 An order under paragraph 9 or 12—

(a) may contain such transitional provisions as may appear to the Secretary of State necessary or expedient;
(b) shall be made by statutory instrument subject to annulment in pursuance of a resolution of either House of Parliament.

Appendix III

INSOLVENCY STATISTICS

(Sources: Department of Trade and Industry; KPMG Peat Marwick).

Table A
Insolvencies in England and Wales 1960–1986

Year	(1) Bankruptcies	(2) Deeds of Arrangement	(3) Company Liquidations[1]	(4) Compulsory Liquidations	(5) Creditors' Voluntary Liquidations
1960	2944	276	1563	525	1038
1961	3642	299	1846	612	1234
1962	4273	329	2196	718	1478
1963	4129	241	2154	729	1425
1964	3552	214	2104	724	1380
1965	3556	206	2595	805	1790
1966	3862	200	3250	934	2316
1967	4224	162	3535	1230	2305
1968	4150	148	3165	1108	2057
1969	4552	220	3510	1181	2329
1970	4907	180	3689	1269	2420
1971	4643	150	3506	1166	2340

[1] The figure in Column 3 comprises both compulsory liquidations and creditors' voluntary liquidations. The separate figures for these are given in Columns 4 and 5 respectively.

APPENDIX III

Table A
Insolvencies in England and Wales 1960–1986—continued

Year	(1) Bankruptcies	(2) Deeds of Arrangement	(3) Company Liquidations[1]	(4) Compulsory Liquidations	(5) Creditors' Voluntary Liquidations
1972	4244	93	3063	1150	1913
1973	3817	100	2575	1080	1495
1974	5608	110	3270	1395	2325
1975	7143	128	5398	2287	3111
1976	7108	99	5939	2511	3428
1977	4403	82	5831	2425	3406
1978	3826	76	5086	2265	2821
1979	3456	44	4537	2064	2473
1980	3986	52	6890	2935	3955
1981	5075	76	8596	2771	5825
1982	5654	46	12067	3745	8322
1983	6981	51	13406	4807	8599
1984	8178	51	13721	5260	8461
1985	6730	48	14898	5761	9137
1986	7093	62	14405	5204	9201

[1] The figure in Column 3 comprises both compulsory liquidations and creditors' voluntary liquidations. The separate figures for these are given in Columns 4 and 5 respectively.

APPENDIX III

Table B
Insolvencies in England and Wales 1987–1994

Year	(1) Bankruptcies	(2) Deeds of Arrangement	(3) Individual Voluntary Arrangements	(4) Company Liquidations[2]	(5) Compulsory Liquidations	(6) Creditors' Voluntary Liquidations	(7) Administration Orders	(8) Company Voluntary Arrangements	(9) Administrative Receiverships	(10) Directors Disqualified
1987	6994	29	404	11439	4116	7323	131	21	950	145
1988	7717	11	779	9427	3667	5760	198	47	858	257
1989	8138	3	1224	10456	4020	6436	135	43	1187	270
1990	12058	2	1927	15051	5977	9074	211	58	2634	286
1991	22632	6	3002	21827	8368	13459	206	137	4112	317
1992	32106	2	4686	24425	9734	14691	179	76	4333	409
1993	31016	8	5679	20708	8244	12464	112	134	2854	419
1994	25634	2	5103	16728	6597	10131	159	264	2040	(355)

[2] The figure in Column 4 comprises both compulsory liquidations and creditors' voluntary liquidations. The separate figures for these are given in Columns 5 and 6 respectively.

Appendix III

Insolvencies in England and Wales, 1960–1986

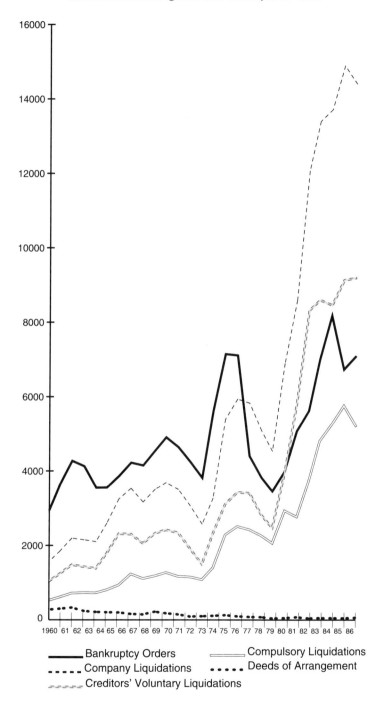

Appendix III

(a) Bankruptcy Orders in England and Wales, 1987–1994

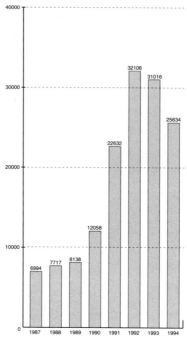

(b) Individaul Voluntary Arrangements in England and Wales, 1987–1994

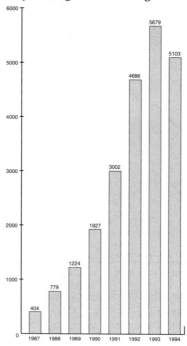

Appendix III

(c) Company Liquidations in England and Wales, 1987–1994

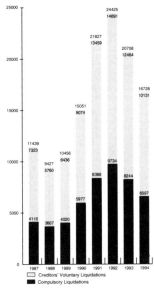

(d) Administative Receiverships in England and Wales, 1987–1994*

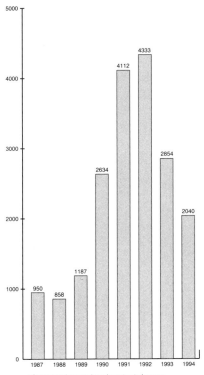

* Group appointments have been treated as one

APPENDIX III

(e) Company Administrative Orders in England and Wales, 1987–1994★

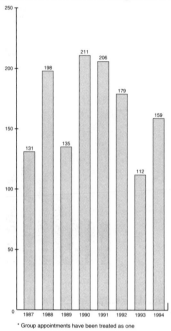

★ Group appointments have been treated as one

(f) Company Voluntary Arrangements in England and Wales, 1987–1994

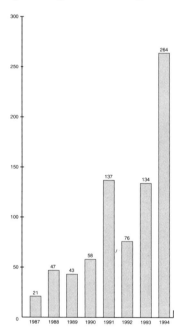

INDEX

ABSCONDING,
  bankruptcy offences,
    bankrupt's conduct in the initial period, 347
    conduct prior to presentation of petition, 340
ACT OF BANKRUPTCY,
  abolition of the concept, 69
ADMINISTRATION ORDERS, 61, 65
  Bankruptcy Act 1883, 60
  Cork Report recommendations, 60
  debtor's request, 61
  effects of the order, 62
  hearing of the request, 62
  implementation, 64
  partnerships, 79
  statutory provisions, 60
ADMINISTRATIVE RECEIVER, 380
  adoption, meaning of, 375
  annual and final accounts, 381
  appointment of, 380
  creditors' committee, 381
  employees' contracts, 383
  expenses incurred by, 382
  Insolvency Act 1994, 379
  liability on contracts,
    contracts of employment adopted by, 373
    pre-receivership contracts, 373
  power to dispose of charged property, 381
  powers of, 373
  remuneration, 382
  report to Registrar, 380
  statutory provisions applicable to, 373
  supplies of utilities, 379
  vacation of office, 382
ADMINISTRATOR OF A COMPANY,
  administration order discharged,
    vacation of office, 469
  adoption of contracts of employment, 471
  antecedent transactions,
    avoidance of, 458–459
  appointment of, 449
  charged property,
    power to deal with, 456
  creditors' meeting, 464

ADMINISTRATOR OF A COMPANY—*cont.*
  deemed to be acting as an agent of company, 452
  general duties,
    company's, 460
    investigate company's affairs, 460
    manage affairs, business and property, 461
    sending out notice of order, 461
    statement of affairs, 462
  general powers, 454
  joint appointments, 449
  legal status, 452
  liquidation expenses, 470
  nominations submitted for appointment, 449
  powers of, 452
  release of, 468
  removal from office by court,
    unfair prejudice application, 451
  replacement, 450–451
  resignation of,
    circumstances necessary, 450
  revision of proposals, 465
  statement of proposals, 463
  vacation of office, 469
ANNUITIES,
  calculation of liability,
    proof of debts, 264
ANNULMENT OF BANKRUPTCY,
  effect of, 325
  principal grounds for, 322
  procedure, 324
APPEALS,
  Chancery Court Division, 24
  Court of Appeal, 24
  termination of bankruptcy,
    discharge by order of the court, 314
APPELLATE JURISDICTION,
  termination of bankruptcy,
    discharge by order of the court, 314
ASSETS,
  collection and distribution of,
    augmentation of available assets, 603
    declaration and payment of dividend, 616

INDEX

ASSETS—*cont.*
  collection and distribution of—*cont.*
    disclaimer of onerous property, 604
    law of disclaimer, change in, 604
    pari passu principle, 613
    priority of distribution of assets, 606
    realisation and disclaimer, 603
    requisite order of priority, 606
  priority of distribution,
    costs and expenses of liquidation, 607
    debts secured by floating charge, 610
    deferred debts, 612
    ordinary debts, 611
    post-insolvency interest on debts, 611
    preferential debts, 609
    return to contributories, 612
ASSIGNEES,
  capacity to present a bankruptcy petition, 86
  equitable assignment, 86
  legal chose in action, 86
  powers of,
    non statutory assignment, under a, 86
ASSOCIATE,
  statutory meaning of, 791
AUTOMATIC DISCHARGE,
  bankrupt's conduct,
    prior to commencement of bankruptcy, 309
  Cork report recommendations, 308
  deserving debtor, 308
  discharge of the order, 308
  elapse of three years, bankruptcy order, 307
  establishing the 15-year clean sheet, 308
  first time bankrupts, 307
  honest but unfortunate debtor, 309
  official receiver's duties, 308
  undischarged bankrupt,
    failed with the obligations, 308

BANK OF ENGLAND,
  Insolvency Services Account, 176
BANKRUPT'S ESTATE,
  after-acquired property, 199
  bankrupt's home,
    Cork report recommendations, 196
    dependent children, 199
    dwelling house, occupational interest in, 197
    family home, postponement of sale, 196
    joint owners, 195
    Law of Property Act 1925, 195
    sole owner, 195
    transfer of his interest to spouse, 198
  bankrupt's income,
    after acquired property, claimable as, 203
    income defined, 203–204
    income payments order, 203
    reasonable domestic needs of family, 204

BANKRUPT'S ESTATE—*cont.*
  choses in action,
    bankrupt's right to sue, 191–192
    classic definition, 191
    contract of a continuous nature, 193
    European Court of Human Rights, 192
    injury to credit or wounded feelings, 191
    passed to his trustee, 191
    rights of action, 191
    torts of a personal character, 191
  commencement of bankruptcy,
    property belonging to bankrupt, 189
  composition of,
    basic principles, 188–189
  doctrine of reputed ownership, abolition of, 208
  equitable interests, 190
  exempt property,
    categories of, 219
    concept of necessity, 219
    family assets, 218
    items necessary for basic domestic needs, 219
  family assets,
    exempt property, 218
    items necessary for basic domestic needs, 219
  forfeiture clauses,
    conditions necessary, 213
  inalienable pension rights,
    private pension fund, 220
  insurance,
    potential liabilities to third parties, 194
  intangible property,
    licence fees, 190
    patents, 190
    royalties, entitlement to, 190
    trademarks, 190
  mixed funds, 211
  power of examination,
    people who can be summoned, 208
  powers of appointment,
    advowson, 212
    bankrupt settlor, 211
    settled property, 211
  private pension fund, 22
  property,
    formulation of concept of, 188
  property bankrupt ceased to own, 212–213
  property held on trust,
    bare trustee of any property, 209
    express trust, 209
  property not vesting in the trustee,
    bankrupt ceased to own, 212
    exempt property and family assets, 218
    forfeiture clauses, 213
    inalienable pension rights, 220

INDEX

BANKRUPT'S ESTATE—*cont.*
property not vesting in the trustee—*cont.*
  mixed funds, 210
  powers of appointment, 211
  property held on trust, 209
  reservation of title clauses, 216
  rule in *ex parte Waring*, 210
property vesting in the trustee,
  after-acquired property, 199
  bankrupt's home, 194
  bankrupt's income, 203
  choses in action, 191
  commencement of bankruptcy, 189
  doctrine of reputed ownership,
    abolition of, 208
  equitable interests, 190
  insurance, 194
  intangible property, 190
  power of examination, 208
  property defined, 188
  rule in *ex parte James*, 207
  trustee takes subject to equities, 205
  vesting, meaning, 188
reservation of title clauses,
  doctrine of reputed ownership, 216
  preference, definition, 218
  properly drafted, 216
rule in *ex parte James*, 207
rule in *ex parte Waring*,
  holder of a bill of exchange, 210
subject to equities, trustee takes title, 205
title clauses,
  reservation of, 216
BANKRUPT'S HOME,
  court's discretion, 197
  family home,
    postponement of sale up to one year, 196
  joint owner, 195
  matrimonial home,
    treatment of, 195
  Matrimonial Homes Act 1983, 196
  non-bankrupt spouse, 196
  sole beneficial owner, 196
  sole owner, 195
BANKRUPT'S INCOME,
  bankrupt's former spouse,
    maintenance order, 204
  concept of income, 204
  earnings, constitution of, 204
  family, definition, 204
  income payment order, 203
  income, definition of, 203
  reasonable domestic needs of family,
    income payment meeting, 204
  retention of a proportion of his income, 203
BANKRUPTCIES WITH
  INTERNATIONAL ELEMENTS,
  bankruptcy proceedings in England,
    choice of law rules, 717

BANKRUPTCIES WITH
  INTERNATIONAL ELEMENTS—
  cont.
  bankrupt's foreign assets,
    creditor's personal act of diligence
      against, 713
  concurrent bankruptcies,
    practice of English courts, 727
  English adjudication,
    international effects of, 703
    rationalisation of the rules of law, 715
  English bankruptcy,
    position of creditors in, 711
  English discharge,
    international effects of, 710
  English law and practice, 691
  foreign adjudication,
    recognition in England of proprietary
      effects, 720
  foreign adjudications at English Law,
    recognition of, 718
  foreign discharge from bankruptcy,
    effects in England, 723
  general problems associated with, 682
  international effects of English
    Adjudication,
    outside the United Kingdom, 705
    recognition by Commonwealth
      countries, 705
    Republic of Ireland, recognition by, 706
    within the United Kingdom, 703
  jurisdiction to adjudicate,
    carrying on business, 696
    debtor in personam, 694
    debtor, the, 691
    debts discharged by prior bankruptcy, 692
    domiciled in England and Wales, 700
    foreign judgements, debts based upon, 693
    limits of jurisdiction, 702
    ordinarily resident, 698
    petitions by creditors, 695
    place of residence, 698
    position at English Law, 691
  powers exercisable by English courts,
    foreign proceedings, 712
  proprietary effects of foreign
    adjudication,
    immovable property, 722
    movable property, 720
  tax bankruptcies,
    bankrupt's duty to recover foreign
      assets, 708
    international recognition, generally, 707
BANKRUPTCIES,
  international element,
    general problems with, 682
BANKRUPTCY ACT 1883,
  Court mergers, 23

813

INDEX

BANKRUPTCY AND INSOLVENCY,
  distinction between, 4
BANKRUPTCY COURT,
  establishment of, 23
BANKRUPTCY DEBT,
  definition, 83
BANKRUPTCY LAW,
  a debtor,
    meaning, within Insolvency Act, 37
  alternatives to bankruptcy,
    formal procedures, 41 *et seq.*
    informal procedures, 66–67
  bankrupt's estate,
    composition of, 188
  bankruptcy adjudication, undergoing,
    determining which individuals, 69
    summary administration, 40
  bankruptcy order,
    effect of, 145
    petition presented to court, 37
  Bankruptcy Petition, *see*
      BANKRUPTCY PETITION
  bankrupt's discharge, 39
  contract, general law of, 71
  County Court Administration Order,
    statutory procedure for payment of
      debts, 37
  creditor's petition, 38
  creditors, conduct of, 36
  criminal offences by bankrupt, 40
  debt counselling, 37
  debtor,
    citizen or resident abroad, 40
    English Bankruptcy Court,
      jurisdiction of, 38
    indebted to petitioning creditor for
      £750, 73
    insolvent, death of, 40
    undischarged from previous
      bankruptcy, 40
  debtor-creditor relationship,
    legal parameters of, 36
  debtor's nationality, 74
  Debtors Act 1869, 99
  Deeds of Arrangement Act 1914,
    voluntary procedures, 37
  dividends, payment of, 39
  English Bankruptcy Court, jurisdiction
    of, 38
  estate fully administered, 39
  extortionate credit transactions,
    court empowered to re-open
      transaction, 230
  formal alternatives,
    voluntary arrangements, 36
  formal alternatives to,
    composition arrangement, 36
    scheme of arrangement, 36
  honest, unfortunate debtor,
    protection of, 36
  informal alternatives to, 37
  informal moratorium, 37

BANKRUPTCY LAW—*cont.*
  jurisdiction of English Courts,
    debtor's personal amenability, 74
  liquidated sum,
    requirements that debt is, 103
  official receiver, 39
    ascertaining reasons for insolvency, 38
    bankrupt's conduct and affairs
      investigated, 38
    bankrupt's creditors, meeting of, 38
    main responsibilities, 39
    public examination, holding of, 39
    validity and size of liabilities, 38
  outline, 35 *et seq.*
  partnerships,
    legal background, 77
    present law, 78
  Payne Committee,
    judgement debts, 73
  petitioning creditor's debt, 101
  popular conception of, 35
  powers of the trustees, 171
  provable debts, 39
  rehabiliatative philosophy, 36
  trustee in bankruptcy,
    appointment of, 39
  trustee in bankruptcy appointed, 39
  undischarged bankrupts, 80
BANKRUPTCY LEVEL,
  statutory minimum level of £750, 102
BANKRUPTCY NOTICE,
  formal device, now obsolete, 110
BANKRUPTCY OFFENCES,
  bankrupt's conduct in the initial period,
    347
    absconding, 347
    concealment or removal of property,
      346
    failure to explain losses, 350
    failure to reveal improper proof, 349
    false statements to creditors, 347
    fraudulent disposal of property, 346
    gambling, 348
    non-delivery of books and papers, 349
    non-disclosure of property, 348
    omission in statement of affairs, 349
    property obtained on credit, 347
    removal of property, 346
    undischarged bankrupt engaging in
      trade, 354
    undischarged bankrupt obtaining
      credit, 350
  books and papers,
    conceal, destroy or falsify, 339, 347
    innocent intention, defence of, 340,
      347
    offences relating to, 339, 347
  computer records,
    offences relating to bankrupts, 339
  conduct prior to presentation of petition,
    absconding, 340

INDEX

BANKRUPTCY OFFENCES—*cont.*
conduct prior to presentation of petition—*cont.*
books and papers, 339
concealment of records, 343
concealment or removal of property, 337
deception, 344
destruction or falsification of records, 343
dishonestly obtaining services, 345
evasion of liability by deception, 345
false accounting, 345
false statements to creditors, 340
fraudulent disposal of property, 339
gambling and irresponsible conduct, 343
proper business accounts, failure to keep, 342
property obtained on credit, 341
removal of property, 337
undischarged bankrupt,
obtaining credit, 350–354
BANKRUPTCY ORDER, 38
advertised in newspapers, 143
bankrupt,
criminal liability, 150
official receiver's duties, 150–151
personal liberty, risk of losing, 151
personal situation of, 150
redirection of mail to official receiver, 152
set of duties imposed, 151
bankrupt's estate, 241
after-acquired property, 199
bankrupt's income, 203
basic principles governing the composition of, 188
choses in action, 191
composition of, 189
equitable interests, 190
forfeiture clauses, 213
insurance, 194
intangible property, 190
matrimonial home, 196
property vesting in the trustee, 188
reservation of title clauses, 216
subject to equities, trustee takes, 205
bankrupt's income, 203–205
Chief Land Registrar,
notification by official receiver, 143
commencement of, 145
consequential proceedings,
appointment of a trustee, 160
creditors' committee, 182
creditors' meetings, 160–162
first meeting of creditors, 160
private examination, 152
resolutions and voting, 163
special manager, 185
statement of affairs, 155
trustee, appointment of, 166

BANKRUPTCY ORDER—*cont.*
creditors' committee,
appointment of, 182
functions of, 182
purpose of, 182
creditors' meeting,
chairman's duties, 165
deposit as security, 162
expenses of summoning, 162
first meeting, 160–162
forms of proxy, 165
majority in value of those present, 163
minimum quorum, 166
nature of business transacted, 162
notice of meeting, 21 days, 162
official receiver's duties, 161
period of 12 weeks, 160
proxy voting, 165
quorum requirements, 166
record of proceedings, 165
representation by proxy, 166
requisitioning a, 161
resolutions, passing of, 163
summary administration certificate, 160
trustee, appointment of, 160–162
useful purpose of summoning, 161
value of debt owing to voting creditors, 163
voting rules, 163
date of presentation of petition, 143
date, time and making of, 143
debtor's intention to appeal against, 144
distress for rent, 241
drawn up in requisite form, 143
effects of, 145
estranged spouse,
position of, 148
immediate effect, 145
landlord power to levy distress, 148
London Gazette, officially published in, 143
making of, 143
official receiver,
duty of, 38
function of, 146
receiver and manager of bankrupt's property, 38
private examination,
become part of file of proceedings, 154
court's discretion in excluding people, 153
documents to be produced, 153
foreign resident, 154
place of examination, 154
proceedings recorded, 154
refusal to submit to, 153
stop order, 154
ultra vires argument, 154
proprietary effects,
bankrupt's estate, 188

815

INDEX

BANKRUPTCY ORDER—*cont.*
  proprietary effects—*cont.*
    curtailment of trustee's title, 234
    trustee's title, extension of, 221
  public examination,
    alternative procedure, 159
    formal procedure, 158
    legal representation of bankrupt, 160
    main purpose of, 157
    money offered to purchase silence, 158
    obligation by bankrupt to attend, 159
    official receiver's duties, 157–160
    questions answered upon oath, 157
    Registrar of court presides at, 160
    third parties, answers not admissable, 158
    written record maintained, 158
  register of writs and orders, 143
  Registrar of court,
    duties of, 143
  registration of order, 143
  secured creditors,
    debtor's adjudication, 149
  special manager appointed by court, 146
  statement of affairs,
    filed in court, 157
    filing of the statement, 157
    material omissions from, 156
    official receiver's duties, 156
    omitting to furnish information in full, 156
    period covered, 155
    pre-bankruptcy period, 155
    scheduled lists, 155
  summary administration, certificate of, 160
  termination of bankruptcy,
    annulment of, 322
    automatic discharge, 307
    discharge by order of the court, 309
  third parties at risk,
    statutory provisions to protect, 145
  transactions at an undervalue, 221
  trustee in bankruptcy,
    commencement of appointment, 168
    duties, 175
    powers of, 171
    records and accounts, 176
    removal or vacation of office, 180
    remuneration, 170
    resignation of, 180
    validity of appointment, 168–169
  trustee's title, curtailment of,
    court protected transactions, 244
    disclaimer of leasehold interests, 237
    dispositions or payments made by bankrupt, 244
    distress or execution levied, 240
    payments designed to avert bankruptcy, 246

BANKRUPTCY ORDER—*cont.*
  trustee's title, curtailment of—*cont.*
    property disclaimed by the trustee, 235
    protected transaction, 245
  trustee's title, extension of,
    associates, 223–225
    book debts, 231
    burden of proof, 223
    effects test, 227
    extortionate credit transactions, 230
    motive, 227
    nature of the remedy, 225
    preference to a particular creditor, 226
    relevant time, 223
    relevant time, 229
    remedies available for use by court, 229
    transactions at an undervalue, 221
    transactions defrauding creditors, 232
    two-to-five year case, 223
    two-year case, 223
    unregistered general assignments of book debt, 231
  trustee, appointment of,
    official receiver's duties, 160
    person appointed from private sector, 161
    summary administration certificate of, 160
  unsecured creditors,
    debtor's judication, 149
  voting rules of creditor's meeting, 163
BANKRUPTCY PETITION,
  bankruptcy level,
    adjusted by statutory instrument, 102
  bankruptcy notice,
    obsolete formal device, 110
  bankrupts,
    exempted property, 92
    sue in tort, 92
    torts of a personal character, 92
  commercial morality, 97
  Consumer Credit Act 1974,
    judgment debt, 136
  creditor's abuse of process,
    debtor's remedies for, 99
  creditor's petition,
    application to set aside statutory demand, 113
    assets, lack of, 136
    assignees, 86
    bankruptcy debt, 83
    bankruptcy level, 102
    companies, 84
    creditors guilty of impropriety, 97
    creditors ineligible to petition, 94
    creditor, statutory definition, 82
    debtor's apparent inability to pay, 110
    expedited petition, 112
    hearing of the petition, 130
    joint creditors, 94
    liability for rates, 92

INDEX

BANKRUPTCY PETITION—*cont.*
  creditor's petition—*cont.*
    liquidated sum, 103
    minors, 83
    partnerships, 84
    presentation of, procedural requirements, 127
    properly qualified creditor, 83
    statutory demand, 110
    trustee of a debt, 84
    unsatisfied execution, 116
  debtor's inability to pay, 110
  debtor's petition,
    abuse of the right of, 118
    advantages of, 117
    hearing of petition, 138
  eligibility to present,
    creditor's petition, 82
    debtor's petition, 117
    petition following default, 122
  garnishee orders, 90
  petition following default,
    voluntary arrangement, in connection with, 122
  petitioning creditor's debt,
    conditions relating to debt, 101
    debt must be unsecured, 106
  powers of the court, 135
  presentation of petition,
    procedural requirements, 127
  procedure and jurisdiction,
    allocation of jurisdiction, 125
    County Courts, 125
    court districts, 124
    debtor's petition, 129
    debtor's place of residence, 124
    High Court, 124
    London Insolvency District, 124
    power of transfer of proceedings, 126
    principal place of business, 124
    proper court for bringing proceedings, 124
    requirements for presentation of petition, 127
    transfer of proceedings between courts, 126
    voluntary arrangement in force for debtor, 126
  secured creditor, definition, 107
  statutory demand,
    application to set aside, 113
    Cork Report recommendation, 110
    formal procedure, 110
  tainted petition, 98
  trustees in bankruptcy,
    assignments by, 90
BANKRUPTCY (SCOTLAND) ACT 1985,
  insolvency practitioners, 28

BANKRUPTCY,
  alternatives to,
    administration orders, 60
    deeds of arrangement, 59–60
    formal procedures, 41 *et seq.*
    individual voluntary arrangements, 41 *et seq.*
    informal procedures, 66 *et seq.*
  formal alternatives to, 36
  legal condition or status, 4
  technical meaning, 35
  termination of,
    automatic discharge, 307
BANKRUPT'S DISCHARGE,
  application to the court, 40
  effect of, 39
  first time bankrupts, 39
BANKRUPT,
  conduct prior to presentation of petition, criminal offences, 337 *et seq.*
  dwelling house,
    occupational interest in, 197
  meaning, 35
  private examination, application for, 152
  property belonging to,
    commencement of bankruptcy, 189
    redirection of mail to official receiver, 152
  release conditions,
    bankruptcy order annulled, 38
    discharge gained, 38
  termination of bankruptcy,
    situation of, 320
BARRISTERS' FEES,
  Bar Council rule, 255
  Council of the Law Society,
  Law Society Compensation Fund, 255
  non-recoverability of, 255
BILLS OF EXCHANGE,
  given as security for payment of a debt, 262
  liability on the Bill, 260
BILLS OF SALE ACT 1878,
  book debts, 231
BLAGDEN COMMITTEE,
  preferential debts, 293
BOOK DEBTS,
  avoidance of unregistered general assignments, 231
  Bills of Sale Act 1878, 231
BUSINESS ACCOUNTS,
  failure to keep,
    bankruptcy offence, 342

CERTIFICATE OF DISCHARGE,
  date on which discharge effective, 317
CHANCERY DIVISION,
  Judges, 24
  Masters of, 24

Index

CHIEF LAND REGISTRAR,
creditor's petition,
notice of petition sent to, 128
debtor's petition,
notice of petition sent to, 129
CHOSES IN ACTION,
bankrupt's estate,
classic definition, 191
CO-SURETY,
bankruptcy of, 268
COLLECTION AND DISTRIBUTION OF ASSETS,
augmentation of available assets,
commencement of liquidation, 603
disclaimer of onerous property,
change in law of disclaimer, 604
concept of onerous property, 604
no specified time limit to exercise power of, 605
property of a leasehold nature, 605
provisions in winding up, 604
dividend,
declaration and payment of, 616
priority of distribution of assets,
categories of priority, 606
realisation and disclaimer,
liquidator's powers, 603
COLLECTIVITY PRINCIPLE, 2
COMMENCEMENT OF BANKRUPTCY,
making of bankruptcy order, 189
property belonging to bankrupt at, 189
relation back doctrine, 189
COMMON LAW COURTS,
assignments, 86
COMPANIES (CONSOLIDATION) ACT 1908,
former Companies Acts, 520
COMPANY ADMINISTRATION ORDERS,
administration expenses, 469
administration procedure,
conditions necessary, 421
administrator of a company,
antecedent transactions, avoidance of, 458
appointment of, 449
circumstances for resignation, 450
different nominations submitted, 449
fees and expenses, 469
general duties, 460
general powers, 454
legal status, 452
powers of, 452
release of, 468
removal of, 451
resignation of, 450
revision of proposals, 465
unfair prejudice application, 451

COMPANY ADMINISTRATION ORDERS—*cont.*
administrator's proposals,
creditors' committee, 466
creditors' meeting, 463
creditors' and members' interests, protection, 466
adoption of contracts of employment, 471
advertisement of order, 441
antecedent transactions,
avoidance of, 458
appeals against decision of court, 441
attainment of an authorised purpose,
likelihood of, 423
authorised purposes,
additional purpose, 425
likely to achieve one or more, 424
list of, 423
real prospect of attainment, 424
test of likelihood, 424
charged property,
power to deal with, 456
commencement of moratorium,
postponement of, 437
company going into liquidation,
time factor, 427
company's affairs, statement of, 462
company's inability to pay its debts, 422
conditions when order not made, 426–430
Consultative Document,
Company Voluntary Arrangements and, 479
contracts of employment,
adoption of, 471
Paramount Case, 472
Cork report proposals, 419–421
court's power,
discretionary, 426
creditors' meeting,
administrator's proposals, 463
conclusion of, 464
voting on a resolution, 464
debenture holder, status of, 428
directors' personal liability,
administration procedure, 421
directors to act collectively, 430
discharge of, 468
administrator's remuneration, 469
vacation of office by administrator, 469
effect of, 442
effects of application,
administrative receiver appointed, 437
commencement of statutory moratorium, 435
restraint on advertising, 436
floating charge,
debenture, 420

INDEX

COMPANY ADMINISTRATION
ORDERS—*cont.*
floating charge holder, 429
general effects of,
  directors, position of, 448
hearing of the petition,
  procedure, 438
historical background, 419
Insolvency Act 1994,
  contracts of employment, 476
insurance company,
  excluded from order being made, 426
Irish counterpart,
  Examinership, 481
lifting the moratorium,
  relief against stay, 443
low incidence of usage,
  reasons for, 479
making of the order,
  procedure, 438
notification of order,
  complying with requirement, 447
persons eligible to present a petition, 430
position of directors,
  Company Directors Disqualification Act, 448
  disqualification from company management, 448
  power suspended for duration of order, 448
presentation of petition,
  administrator's role, 440
procedural requirements, 432
procedure,
  administrative receiver appointed, 438
  floating charge holder, position of, 438
  guidelines to make order, 439
  interim orders, 439
  persons represented, 438
  purposes for whose achievement it is made, 439
procedure on application,
  court to which petition presented, 432
  floating charge holder, position of, 432
  prescribed deposit payable by petitioner, 435
  procedural requirements, 432
  requirements imposed, 432
rehabiliatative procedure, 420
review and reform of law, 478
secured creditor,
  granting of leave, 444
  restraints imposed upon, 429
statutory moratorium,
  commencement of, 435
suitability of administration to be used, 430
supplies by utilities, 459
transmission of order, 441
unfair prejudice applications, 451

COMPANY DIRECTORS
DISQUALIFICATION ACT 1986, 79, 431
insolvency practitioners disqualifying order, 28
COMPANY INSOLVENCY,
alternatives to winding up,
  company administration orders, 419
  company voluntary arrangements, 401
compulsory winding up,
  winding up by the court, 519
creditors' voluntary winding up, 491
creditors and third parties,
  effects of winding up on, 627
insolvent liquidations,
  aspects common to both forms of, 593
liability of directors, 653
non-liquidation procedures,
  receivers, 359 *et seq.*
winding up of insolvent companies, 485 *et seq.*
COMPANY NAMES,
restriction on the re-use,
  excepted cases, 665–666
  guilt by association, 664
  management buy-outs, 665
  Phoenix syndrome, 664
  prohibited name, 665
COMPANY VOLUNTARY
ARRANGEMENTS,
approval of the proposal, 411
background to, 401
challenging the arrangement,
  grounds on which application made, 412
completion of,
  expenses of the administration, 414
  notice and report, 414
creditor's claim of his entitlement to vote, 408
creditors' meeting, 407
effect of approval, 411
implementation of the proposal, 413
meetings of the company and creditors,
  purpose of, 407
near negligible usage,
  reasons for, 415
nominee, function of, 404
persons eligible to make proposal, 402
proposal for, 402
reform of the law, 415
requisite majority for passing resolutions, 410
review of the law, 415
revised proposals for, 416
statement of affairs, 406
statutory moratorium, lack of, 415
terms of the proposal, 403
voting rights of creditors, 408

819

INDEX

COMPULSORY WINDING UP,
  Companies Act 1929, 520
  Companies Act 1985,
    company, meaning, 520
    existing companies, definition, 520
  company's assets,
    control and preservation of, 488
    distribution of, 489
  company, meaning, 520
  disqualification orders, 489
  dissolved companies, 521
  early dissolution of company, 620
  exercisable in two kinds of company, 519
  existing companies, meaning, 520
  field of application of law, 519
  final meeting prior to dissolution, 618
  former Companies Acts, 520
  grounds to take place,
    registered companies, 521
    unregistered companies, 528
  illegal associations, 521
  initiated by court order, 487
  insolvent partnership, 521
  Joint Stock Companies Act, 520
  liquidator,
    principal tasks of, 489
  minimum level of indebtedness, 488
  official receiver's duties, 488
  outside the ambit of provisions, 521
  re-use of the names of companies,
    Phoenix syndrome, 489
    restrictions on, 489
  registered companies,
    balance sheet test, 523
    cash-flow test, 523, 526, 527
    classification as, 519–521
    company unable to pay its debts, 523
    Financial Services Act 1986, 522
    grounds for, 522
    proof of inability to pay debts falling due, 527
    statutory demand, 524
    unsatisfied execution, 526
  service of a statutory demand for payment, 488
  special register bodies, 521
  trade unions, 521
  unregistered companies,
    classification as, 519–521
    company unable to pay its debts, 530
    foreign companies, application to, 531
    grounds for, 528
    grounds for, 529
CONCURRENT BANKRUPTCIES,
  practice of the English courts, 727
  rationalised approach, need for, 728
CONNECTED PERSONS,
  winding up law,
    creditors and third parties, effect of, 643

CONNECTED PERSON,
  statutory meaning of, 791
CONSOLIDATED FUND,
  Insolvency Services Account, 177
CONSUMER CREDIT ACT 1974R,
  judgment debt, 136
CONSUMER CREDIT ACT 1974, 71
CONTRACTS OF EMPLOYMENT,
  administrative receiver, 373
  adopted by administrators,
    Insolvency Act 1994, 476
    Paramount Case, 472
  adopting, 376
  adoption of,
    administrator of a company, 471
    Paramount Case, 472
  legislation, background to, 373
  receivers appointed out of court, 371
CORK REPORT,
  abusive practices, eradicating, 26
  floating charge receivership,
    abusive practices, eradicating, 26
  insolvency practitioners,
    standardised regulation, 26
  statutory demand, 110
  voluntary liquidation,
    abusive practices, eradicating, 26
COUNTY COURTS ACT 1846,
  County Courts, establishment of, 24
COUNTY COURT,
  Administration Order,
    gradual payment of debts, 37
  Bankruptcy Petition,
    proper court for bringing proceedings, 125
COURT OF EQUITY,
  assignments, 86
CREDIT TRANSACTIONS,
  extortionate,
    concept of grossness, 230
    court's powers to re-open transaction, 230
    meaning of, 230
CREDITORS' COMMITTEE,
  appointment, 182
  first meeting, 183
  functions of, 182
  meeting, first, 183
  membership of, 183
  purpose of, 182
  resignation of members, 184
  travelling expenses, 185
CREDITORS' MEETING,
  administrator's proposals, 464
  majority in value vote, 163, 464
  resolutions, passing of, 163, 464
  trustee, appointment of, 163
  voting procedure, 163
CREDITOR'S PETITION,
  abuse of process,
    debtor's remedies for, 99
  assets, lack of, 136

820

INDEX

CREDITOR'S PETITION—*cont.*
  assignees,
    choses in action, 86
    joinder of the assignor, 88
    joined as a party, 87
    part of larger debt assigned, 89
    petion alone, eligibilty of, 89
    powers of, 86
  assignments by trustees in bankruptcy,
    equivalent provision, 91
    third parties, 91
  bankruptcy debt,
    definition, 83
  bankruptcy level,
    statutory minimum figure of £750, 102
    statutory threshold adjusted, 102
  companies,
    authorised agent, 85
    officer of the company, 85
    petitioning company enters liquidation, 85
  creditors ineligible to petition,
    co-surety, 95
    deed of arrangement, 95
    person has become surety for another, 94
    principle of estoppel, 96
    valid voluntary arrangement, 95
  creditor, statutory definition, 82
  debtor,
    apparent inability to pay, 110
    creditors guilty of impropriety towards, 97
    maliciously abused legal proceedings, 100
  debtor's apparent inability to pay, 110
  debtor's inability to pay,
    unsatisfied execution, 116
  expedited petition,
    deterioration in debtor's financial position, 112
    three week period, 112
  hearing of the petition,
    advertising hearing publicly, 131
    creditors give notice of intention to appear, 131
    debtor absconded, 130
    debtor opposes petition, 130
    debtor's requirement to appear, 131
    dismissing petition, reasons for, 132
    expedited hearing, 130
    minimum time elapse, 130
  joint creditors, 94
  liability for rates, 92
  liquidated claim,
    classification of claims, 104
  liquidated sum,
    payable to petitioning creditor, 103
  malicious proceedings, 100

CREDITOR'S PETITION—*cont.*
  minors, 83
  partnerships,
    co-petitioners, 85
  petitioning creditor's debt,
    conditions relating to debt, 101
    debt must be unsecured, 106
    sum payable immediately, 105
  powers of the court, 134
  presentation of petition,
    procedural requirements, 127
  procedural requirements,
    act of service, 129
    affidavit to verify statements, 128
    amount of debt, the consideration for it, 127
    appropriate Form, 127
    copy for service on debtor, 128
    debtor identified by name, 127
    files application, 128
    main steps necessary, 128
    notice sent to Chief Land Registrar, 128
    occupation of debtor, 127
    official receipt for deposit, 128
    petitioning creditor's debt, 128
    place of residence of debtor, 127
  properly qualified creditor, 83
  secured creditor,
    elects to retain security, 109
    estimate of value of security, 108
    give up own security, 109
  statutory demand,
    affidavit proving service of demand, 112
    alternative types of, 111
    application to set aside, 113
    Cork Report recommendation, 110
    prescribed forms for use in serving, 112
  tainted petition, 98
  trustee of a debt, 84
  trustees in bankruptcy,
    assignments by, 90
CREDITORS' VOLUNTARY WINDING UP,
  assets and liabilities,
    statement of, 494
  centrebinding operations, 501
  commencement of,
    appointment of liquidator, 509
    consequences of, 505
    meeting of creditors, 507
    powers of directors cease, 506
    selling business as going concern, 506
    transfer of shares, 507
  conversion from members' to, 495
  conversion from voluntary to compulsory, 496

INDEX

CREDITORS' VOLUNTARY WINDING UP—*cont.*
copy of the resolution,
  advertised in London Gazette, 505
  lodged with registrar of companies, 505
corporate insolvency,
  Cork report recommendations, 499
declaration of solvency,
  delivered to registrar of companies, 495
formal declaration of solvency,
  statutory requirements, 494
implementation of major reforms, 500
liquidation committee,
  appointment of, 514
liquidator,
  appointed from private sector, 499
  appointment of, 509
  powers and duties of, 513
  remuneration, 512
  resignation, 511
  vacation of office, 512
liquidator, appointment of,
  legal requirements, 509
meeting of creditors,
  advertisement of meeting, 507
  appointment of liquidation committee, 509
  company's, 508
  postal notice of at least seven days, 507
  proof of debts for voting purposes, 510
members' and creditors',
  distinction between, 493
misuse of company names,
  Phoenix operations, 500
new law and major reforms, 500 *et seq.*
petition presented by official receiver, 497
proof of debts for voting purposes, 510
resolution for, 504
subsequent course of liquidation, 514

CREDITORS, 107
bankruptcy order,
  first meeting, 160
false statements to,
  bankruptcy offences, 340
  bankruptcy offences, 347
statutory definition, 82
transactions defrauding,
  bankruptcy offences, 232
trust devices, 637

CRIMINAL BANKRUPTCY,
abolition of, 355
generally, 355

CRIMINAL COURTS ACT 1973, 356

CRIMINAL JUSTICE ACT 1988,
criminal bankruptcy, 356

CRIMINAL LAW,
bankruptcy offences,
  Theft Act 1968, 344
offences under general, 344
provisions of, in relation to bankruptcy, 336

CROSS-BORDER INSOLVENCY,
international regulation,
  bi-lateral treaties, 768
  co-operation by United Kingdom courts, 784
  draft bankruptcy convention, 769
  European Bankruptcy Convention, 777
  European Union/Economic Community Convention, 769
  Istanbul Convention, 777
  judicial co-operation, 782
  judicial co-operation outside section, 426, 787
  Maxwell case, 789
  multilateral bankruptcy convention, 768
  nature of assistance available, 785
  private international law, 785
  tri-lateral treaties, 768
judicial co-operation,
  international convention, 789

DEBTOR'S PETITION,
abuse of the right of, 118
  ability to buy time restricted, 118
  appeal to allege impropriety, 119
  court's power to review, rescind or vary, 119
  court's residuary discretion to refuse, 118
advantages of, 117
debtor's estate, protection of, 140
hearing of the petition,
  findings to not make bankruptcy order, 138
  presenting own petition, 138
  procedural steps, 138
  summary administration procedure, 138
  voluntary arrangement with creditor, 138
indebtedness,
  no minimum figure of, 122
interim receiver appointed, 140
powers of the court, 140
presentation of petition,
  procedural requirements, 129
procedural requirements,
  Chief Land Registrar sent notice of petition, 130
  debtor's affairs verified by affidavit, 130

822

INDEX

DEBTOR'S PETITION—*cont.*
  procedural requirements—*cont.*
    debtor's name and residence
      identified, 129
    occupation of debtor, 129
    receipt for deposit of £135, 130
    request for bankruptcy order, 129
    statement that debtor unable to pay
      debts, 129
DEBTORS ACT 1869, 99
DEBTOR,
  absconded before hearing of petition,
    130
  bankruptcy level,
    claiming a set-off against amount
      owed, 103
  concept of a debt, 70
  creditor and, relationship of, 70
  creditor's abuse of process,
    debtor's remedies for, 99
  creditors guilty of impropriety towards,
    97
  Debtors Act 1869, 99
  English Courts, jurisdiction of,
    domiciled in England or Wales, 75
    jurisdictional criteria, 74
    ordinary residence, 75
  establishing if person qualifies, 37
  estate, protection of, 140
  general characteristics of term, 70
  inability to pay, 110
  jurisdiction of English Courts,
    personal amenability to, 74
  maliciously abused legal proceedings,
    100
  nationality of, 74
  natural obligation concept, 70
  petition served personally by court
    officer, 128
  petitioning creditor,
    indebted for unsecured amount of
      £750, 73
  place of residence, 698
    determining proper court for
      proceedings, 124
  principal, 267
  public examination,
    process of, 157
  special categories of,
    married women, 76
    Members of Parliament, 76
    members of the peerage, 76
    mentally disordered person, 77
    minors, 76
    unsound mind, person of, 76
  status of,
    applicability of bankruptcy law, 72
  status of, applicability of bankruptcy law,
    72
  writ of sequestration against, 149

DEBTS,
  mutual, 274
  non-provable, 251
  pre-preferential, 290
  preferential, 291, 797
  provable, 250–251
DEBT,
  assignment, 86
  bankruptcy, definition, 82
  judgment, 113
  preferential, 797
  secured, 106
  secured creditor, definition, 107
  statutory demand, 111
  unsecured, 106
DECEASED PERSONS,
  insolvent estates,
    administration of, 330
DEEDS OF ARRANGEMENT ACT
  1914,
  alternatives to bankruptcy, 37, 59
DEEDS OF ARRANGEMENT,
  Cork Report,
    voluntary arrangement, new form, 59
  Deeds of Arrangement Act 1914,
    use governed by, 59
  registration of deeds, 59
DEFERRED DEBTS,
  liquidation, for payment in, 612
DEPARTMENT OF TRADE AND
  INDUSTRY,
  administration of Insolvency Law, 25
  Insolvency Service, 25
  Inspector General, 25
  trustee in bankruptcy,
    appointment of, 167
DIRECTORS,
  contract of employment, 384
  determination of unfitness,
    matters for, 670
    three-tier approach, 674
  disqualification of,
    applications for, 675
    criminal penalties for contravention
      of, 676
    length of period of, 672
    unfitness, matters for determining,
      670
  evaluation of conduct, 672
  liability of, during liquidation,
    criminal offences, 653 *et seq.*
  officer of company, 384
DISCLAIMER, LAW OF,
  important changes, 604
DISSOLUTION OF THE COMPANY,
  compulsory winding up,
    accomplished by Registrar of
      Companies, 619
  dissolution declared void, 623

Index

DISSOLUTION OF THE COMPANY—*cont.*
  effect of, 622
  official notification,
    London Gazette, published in, 621
  striking company off the register, 621
  voluntary winding up, 621
DISTRIBUTION OF ASSETS,
  bankruptcy, expenses of,
    payable out of the estate, 288
  categories of liabilities,
    order of priority, 288
  declaration and payment of dividend,
    trustee's notice of intention, 301
  declaration of dividends, 301
  final distribution,
    trustee must give notice in prescribed manner, 303
  final dividend, 304
  final meeting of creditors, 304
  interest,
    accrued since commencement of bankruptcy, 295
  ordinary debts, 295
  payment of dividend,
    mode of payment, 303
  post-final dividends, 304
  postponed debts, 296
  pre-preferential debts, 290
  preferential debts,
    Blagden Committee, 293
    categories of, 291, 797
    Cork Committee, 293
  priority of,
    costs and expenses of liquidation, 607
    debts secured by a floating charge, 610
    deferred debts, 612
    expenses of the bankruptcy, 288
    interest, 295
    ordinary debts, 295, 611
    post-insolvency interest on debts, 611
    postponed debts, 296
    pre-preferential debts, 290
    preferential debts, 291, 609, 797
    requisite order, 606
    return to contributories, 612
    surplus, payable to bankrupt, 298
  second bankruptcy,
    Blagden committee recommendations, 299
  surplus payable to bankrupt, 298
  unclaimed dividends, 304
DIVIDENDS,
  payments of, 301
  post-final, 304
  unclaimed, 304
DOCTRINE OF REPUTED OWNERSHIP,
  abolition of, 208

DOMICILE,
  English law concept of, 75
DWELLING HOUSE,
  bankrupt has occupational interest in, 197

EMPLOYMENT PROTECTION (CONSOLIDATION) ACT 1978,
  pre-preferential debts, 290
ENGLISH BANKRUPTCY COURT,
  debtor is personally amenable to jurisdiction, 38
ENGLISH BANKRUPTCY LAW,
  philosophical foundations, 35
ENGLISH WINDING UP,
  international effects of,
    choice of law, 757
    competing claims to assets, 752
    creditor taking proceedings abroad, restraint, 753
    foreign assets, 751
    foreign courts rule of recognition, 750
    general principles, 749
    secured creditors, special position of, 756
EQUITABLE ASSIGNMENT,
  legal chose in action, 86
EQUITABLE INTERESTS,
  bankrupt's estate, 190
EQUITABLE SET-OFF,
  doctrine of, 278
EUROPEAN BANKRUPTCY CONVENTION,
  Council of Europe,
    Istanbul Convention, 777
EUROPEAN COURT OF HUMAN RIGHTS,
  violation of rights, 192
EUROPEAN UNION/ECONOMIC COMMUNITY,
  Draft Bankruptcy Convention,
    phase 1 draft 1980-main features, 771
    phase 11-features and prospects, 773
EXAMINERSHIP,
  Irish counterpart of administration order, 481
EXTORTIONATE CREDIT TRANSACTIONS,
  definition of, 647
  winding up law,
    creditors and third parties, effect of, 647

FIDELITY BOND,
  insolvency practitioners, 30
FINAL DIVIDEND,
  distribution of assets, 304
FIRST TIME BANKRUPTS,
  discharge of, 39

INDEX

FLOATING CHARGE RECEIVERSHIP,
Cork Report, 26
FLOATING CHARGE,
debts secured by, 610
FOREIGN ADJUDICATIONS AT ENGLISH LAW,
recognition in England of proprietary effects,
movable property, 720
recognition of, 718
FOREIGN ADJUDICATIONS OF ENGLISH LAW,
recognition in England of proprietary effects,
immovable property, 722
FOREIGN COMPANIES IN ENGLAND,
jurisdiction to wind up,
any association, meaning, 738
any company, meaning, 739
company ceased to carry on business, 733
company dissolved, 733
company having or not having done business, 746–747
company not having a place of business here, 746
company unable to pay its debts, 742
dissolved companies, 740
dissolved foreign company, 741
doing of business test, 748
English winding up, International effects, 749
foreign company, meaning, 731
just and equitable ground, 743
potential scope of jurisdictional rule, 736
procedural matters, 746
section 225, Insolvency Act, 744
FOREIGN CURRENCY DEBTS,
proof of debts, 597
sterling equivalent of debt, 258
FOREIGN DISCHARGE FROM BANKRUPTCY,
effects in England,
final limitations on the scope of recognition, 726
inconsistencies from current rules of law, 723
FOREIGN LAW,
procedural incapacity under,
proof of debts, 254
FOREIGN LIQUIDATIONS,
discharge of debts under, 762
English assets, effect of, 763
English branch of foreign parent company,
position of, 761
recognition of, 758

FOREIGN TAX LIABILITIES,
proof of debts, 254
FORMAL PROCEDURES,
administration orders,
commencement of procedure, 61
discharge, revocation or variation, 65
effects of, 62
implementation, 64
deeds of arrangement, 59
individual voluntary arrangements,
cases decided under earlier legislation, 56
prior to adjudication, 42
subsequent to adjudication, 53
FRIENDLY SOCIETIES ACT 1974, 291
FRIENDLY SOCIETIES,
claims of trustees of, 291

GAMBLING,
bankruptcy offence, 343, 348
GARNISHEE ORDERS,
bankruptcy order against garnishee, 90
rights of,
garnishee, 90
garnishor, 90

HIGH COURT,
Bankruptcy Petition,
procedure and jurisdiction, 124

IMMOVABLE PROPERTY,
proprietary effects of foreign adjudication, 722
INDIVIDUAL INSOLVENCY,
See PERSONAL INSOLVENCY & BANKRUPTCY LAW
INDIVIDUAL VOLUNTARY ARRANGEMENTS,
cases decided under earlier legislation, current validity, 56
prior to adjudication,
accountability of supervisor, 52
completion of arrangement, 52
creditors' meeting, 47
effect of approval, after creditors' meeting, 50
first steps, 42
interim order, procedure following, 45
supervisor of arrangement, 51
subsequent to adjudication,
approval of proposal, 55
creditors' meeting, 55
first steps, 54
interim order, procedure following, 54
INFORMAL MORATORIUM,
informal alternative to bankruptcy, 37
INFORMAL PROCEDURES,
informal moratorium, 66
multi-party contract, 67
non statutory, contractual composition, 66

INDEX

INSOLVENCY ACT 1984,
  administrative receiverships, 379
INSOLVENCY ACT 1986,
  company winding up,
    County Courts jurisdiction, 24
  criminal offences,
    established by, 335
  insolvency practitioners, 31
    disqualifying factors, 28
    granting authorisation, 31
    withdrawal of authorisation, 31
INSOLVENCY ACT 1994,
  contracts of employment,
    adopted by administrators, 476
INSOLVENCY AND BANKRUPTCY,
  distinction between, 4
INSOLVENCY LAW,
  administration,
    Chancery Division, 24
    Chancery Divisional Court, 24
    County Courts Act 1846, 24
    Court of Appeal, 24
    Department of Trade and Industry, 24, 25
    High Court Registrars, 24
    insolvency practitioners, 25
    Insolvency Service, 25
    London Bankruptcy Court, 23
    London Bankruptcy District, 24
    London Insolvency District, 24
    official receivers, 25
    present arrangement, 23 et seq.
    Supreme Court of Judicature, 23
INSOLVENCY PRACTITIONERS REGULATIONS 1986, 29
INSOLVENCY PRACTITIONERS TRIBUNAL,
  refusal or withdrawal of authorisation, 32
INSOLVENCY PRACTITIONERS,
  administrative receivers, 26
  applicant a 'fit and proper person', 29
  Company Directors Disqualification Act 1986, 28
  conflict of interest, 29
  Cork Report recommendations, 26
  criminal sanction, 27
  disqualifying factors, 28
  education and practical training, 29
  eligibility to act as office holder, 27
  fidelity bond, 30
  general penalty sum, 30
  granting of authorisation, 31
  Insolvency Act 1986, 27
  Insolvency Practitioners Regulations 1986, 29
  Insolvency Practitioners Tribunal, 32
  liquidator or provisional liquidator, 26
  negative criteria for qualification as, 28

INSOLVENCY PRACTITIONERS—
    cont.
  partnerships, 79
  personal licence requirement, 26
  present regulation of, 27
  primary requirement of, 26
  private sector appointment, 25
  professional body, 29
  recognised professional body, member of, 26
  refusal of authorisation, 31
  requisite qualification, 28
  trustee in bankruptcy, 26
  valid authorisation, 28
  withdrawal of authorisation, 31–32
INSOLVENCY SERVICE EXECUTIVE AGENCY,
  company director disqualifications, 677
INSOLVENCY SERVICES ACCOUNT,
  trustee must pay all money received into, 176
INSOLVENCY SERVICE,
  Department of Trade and Industry, 25
INSOLVENCY,
  distinction with bankruptcy, and, 4
  historical development of the Law, 6
INSOLVENT DEBTOR,
  death of, 40
INSOLVENT ESTATES OF DECEASED PERSONS,
  administration of,
    date of commencement of bankruptcy, 331
    debtor's petition, 330
    deceased's liabilities discharged in priority, 330
    insolvency administration petition, 330
    jurisdiction, 333
    statement of affairs prepared, 331
INSOLVENT PARTNERSHIPS ORDER 1986,
INSOLVENT PARTNERSHIPS ORDER 1994,
  insolvency practitioners, 27
INSOLVENT PARTNERSHIPS,
  modifications to standard procedures, 40
  wound up as unregistered company, 521
INSPECTOR GENERAL,
  controlling and supervisory function, 25
  Department of Trade and Industry, 25
INSURANCE COMPANIES ACT 1982,
  company administration orders, 426
INTANGIBLE PROPERTY,
  bankrupt's estate, 190
INTELLECTUAL PROPERTY,
  bankrupt's estate, 190

INDEX

INTERNATIONAL INSOLVENCY,
  bankruptcy jurisdiction in personam, 694
  Brussels and Lugano Conventions, 693
  conflicts of principles,
    unity versus plurality, 684
    universality versus territoriality, 684
  cross-border insolvency,
    international regulation, 767
  domiciled in England and Wales, 700
  domicile, concept of, 701
  general problems, 681
  issues of principle, 681 *et seq.*
  liquidations with international element, 731
  National Insolvency Laws,
    diversity of, 685
  state of confusion,
    need to resolve the prevailing, 686
  theory and reality,
    gulf between, 687
INTERNATIONAL JUDICIAL CO-OPERATION,
  INSOL International,
    international convention, 789
  international convention,
    initiative towards creation of, 789
  Maxwell case, 789
  UNCITRAL,
    international convention, 789
IRRESPONSIBLE CONDUCT,
  bankruptcy offence, 343

JOINT CREDITORS,
  creditor's petition, 94
JOINT STOCK COMPANIES ACT,
  company, meaning, 520
JUDGEMENT DEBT,
  grounds for rejection of, 136
  statutory demand, 112
JURISDICTION OF THE ENGLISH COURTS,
  debtor's personal amenability to, 74–76

LAW OF PROPERTY ACT 1925, 86
LIABILITY OF DIRECTORS,
  civil remedies and penalties,
    fraudulent trading, 659
    restriction on the re-use of company names, 664
    summary remedy against delinquent directors, 658
    wrongful trading, 661
  delinquent directors, summary remedy against, 658
  disqualification of,
    Company Directors Disqualification Act 1986, 668
    criminal penalties for contravention of, 676

LIABILITY OF DIRECTORS—cont.
  disqualification of—*cont.*
    evaluation of directors' conduct, 672
    length of period of, 672
    unfitness, matters for determining, 670
    working of new law on, 677
  liquidation, criminal offences during,
    false representations to creditors, 657
    falsification of company's books, 656
    fraud in anticipation of winding up, 653
    fraudulent trading, criminal liability, 657
    material omissions from statement of affairs, 656
    misconduct in course of winding up, 655
    transactions in fraud of creditors, 655
  prosecution of delinquent directors,
    disqualification of directors, 668
  wrongful trading,
    defence to liability, 663
    disqualification of directors, 664
    disqualification order, 664
    moment of truth test, 661
    new concept of responsibility for, 661
    test of knowledge, 662
LIMITATION ACT 1980, 70
LIMITED PARTNERSHIPS ACT 1907, 79
LIQUIDATED SUM,
  petitioning creditor, payable to, 103
LIQUIDATION COMMITTEE,
  Committee of Inspection, no longer known as, 589
  functions to be performed by, 590
  membership of, 590
  resignation of members, 591
  suspended from performing functions,
    official receiver is the liquidator, 592
LIQUIDATIONS WITH INTERNATIONAL ELEMENT,
  concurrent liquidations, 765
  English winding up,
    choice of law, 757
    competing claims to assets, 752
    creditor taking proceedings abroad, restraint, 753
    effect on foreign assets, 751
    foreign court's rules of recognition, 750
    general principles, 749
    secured creditors, special position of, 756
  foreign companies in England,
    company ceased to carry on business, 733
    company dissolved, 733
    company unable to pay its debts, 742

LIQUIDATIONS WITH
  INTERNATIONAL ELEMENT—
  cont.
  foreign companies in England—cont.
    conflicts with established principle, 735
    dissolved foreign company, 741
    jurisdiction to wind up, 731
    just and equitable ground, 743
    meaning of foreign company, 731
    potential scope of jurisdictional rule, 736
    procedural matters, 746
    section 225, Insolvency Act 1986, 744
    unregistered company, 738
    winding up under section 221, Insolvency Act, 733
  foreign liquidations,
    discharge of debts under, 762
    English Assets, effect of, 763
    English branch of foreign parent company, 761
    extent of recognition of, 760
    general principles, 758
    recognition of, 758
LIQUIDATION,
  costs and expenses of the,
    payable out of assets in order of priority, 607
  criminal offences before and during,
    false representations to creditors, 657
    falsification of company's books, 656
    fraud in anticipation of winding up, 653
    fraudulent trading, criminal liability for, 657
    material omissions from statement, 656
    misconduct in course of winding up, 655
    transactions in fraud of creditors, 655
  international elements,
    general problems associated with, 683
LIQUIDATOR'S BOOKS AND ACCOUNTS,
  Cork report recommendations, 589
  details of books and records to be kept, 587
  records retained for six years, 588
LOCAL GOVERNMENT FINANCE ACT 1992, 93
LONDON BANKRUPTCY COURT,
  Supreme Court of Judicature, merger with, 23
LONDON BANKRUPTCY DISTRICT, 24
LONDON GAZETTE,
  bankruptcy order officially published, 143

LONDON INSOLVENCY DISTRICT,
  High Court jurisdiction, 24
  jurisdiction exercised by High Court, 124
LOSSES,
  bankrupt's failure to explain, criminal offence, 350

MALICIOUS PROCEEDINGS,
  creditor's abuse of process,
  debtor's remedies for, 100
MATRIMONIAL CAUSES ACT 1973, 198
MATRIMONIAL HOMES ACT 1983, 196
MATRIMONIAL HOME,
  bankrupt's estate, 195
  bankrupt, sole beneficial owner, 196
  Cork Report recommendations, 196
  Matrimonial Homes Act 1983, 196
  sale of family home to be postponed, 196
MEMBERS OF PARLIAMENT,
  special category of debtor, 76
MEMBERS OF PEERAGE,
  special categories of debtor, 76
MINORS CONTRACTS ACT 1987,
  minors as special category of debtor, 76
MINORS,
  creditor's petition, 83
  special categories of debtor,
    enforceable contracts, 76
    Minors Contracts Acts 1987, 76
    rule of qualified enforceability, 76
    service contracts, 76
MISUSE OF COMPANY NAMES,
  Phoenix operations, 500
MOVABLE PROPERTY,
  proprietary effects of foreign adjudication, 720

NATIONAL INSOLVENCY LAWS,
  diversity of, 685
NON-LIQUIDATION PROCEDURES,
  receivers,
    appointed by the court, 362
    appointed out of court, 368
    general issues affecting, 382
    types of, 360
NON-PROVABLE DEBTS,
  bankruptcy, in, 251
  liquidation,
    debts declared not provable, 601

OCCUPATIONAL PENSION SCHEMES,
  preferential debts, 800

INDEX

OFFICIAL RECEIVER,
  administrative receiver, 361
    annual and final accounts, 381
    appointment of, 380
    company's affairs, investigation of, 380
    creditor's committee, 381
    power to dispose of charged property, 381
    remuneration and expenses, 382
    report to registrar, 380
    vacation of office, 382
  administrative receivers,
    liability on contracts, 373
    powers of, 373
  appointed by the court,
    administrative receiver, 368
    contracts, 366
    directors, 384
    duties, 367
    employees automatically dismissed, 382
    indemnity out of the assets, 367
    powers of, 365
    status of, 364
    supervision, 364
  appointed out of court,
    administrative receivers, 373
    adopting a contract, 376–378
    agent of company, 395
    contracts of employment adopted by, 371
    directors, 384
    employees, contracts of employment, 383
    Insolvency Act 1994, 379
    liability on contracts, 371
    pre-receivership contracts, 371
    receivership accounts, 372
    statutory liability, extent of, 378
    statutory provisions applicable to, 369
    supplies of utilities, 379
  appointment of, 25
  bankrupt,
    general meeting of creditors, 151
    investigation into conduct and affairs of, 150
    redirection of mail, 152
  bankruptcy order,
    function of, 146
    receiver and manager of bankrupts estate, 146
  bankrupt's statement of affairs submitted to, 38
  ceasing to hold office, 25
  company insolvency,
    types of receiver, 360
  death of, provisions, 25
  deputy, appointment of, 26
  duties of, 38
  equitable duties, 397
  existing contracts, not liable for, 388

OFFICIAL RECEIVER—*cont.*
  floating charge, 361
  function of, 25
  general issues affecting, 382
  Insolvency Act 1986,
    provisions relating to, 25
  investigatory functions, 25
  LPA receiver, 360
  managerial function transferred, 146
  post-receivership supplies, 394
  pre-receivership supplies,
    amounts due in respect of, 390
  public examination,
    discretion, excercise in, 159
    duties of, 157
  responsibilities of, 25
  statement of affairs,
    requirement to assist bankrupt, 156
  status, 25
  supplies of services, 390
  types of, 360
  winding up petition by, 539
ONEROUS PROPERTY,
  concept of, Companies Act 1985, 604
ORDER OF DISCHARGE,
  certificate of discharge, 317
  copies of order sent to bankrupt, 317
  date on which made, 316
  drawn up by court,
    effective date, 316
  effect of, 317
  Secretary of State to give notice of, 317
  situation of bankrupt, 320
ORDINARY DEBTS,
  distribution of assets, 295
  priority of distribution of assets, 611

PARAMOUNT CASE,
  contracts of employment, adoption of, 472
PARI PASSU PRINCIPLE, 2
  collection and distribution of assets,
    insolvent company, 613
  recent trends, 615
  tradition and reality, 613
PARTNERSHIP ACT 1890, 78
PARTNERSHIP VOLUNTARY ARRANGEMENTS, 79
PARTNERSHIPS ORDER 1994, 78
PARTNERSHIPS,
  Administration Order, 79
  legal background,
    collective proceedings, 78
    disclosure of partners' names, 77
    Partnership Act 1890, 78
  Partnership Voluntary Arrangements, 79
  present law,
    collective insolvency procedure, 78
    Company Directors Disqualification Act 1986, 79

INDEX

PARTNERSHIPS—*cont.*
present law—*cont.*
    Insolvency Act 1986, 78
    insolvent partnerships wound up, 78
    joint debtors' petition, 79
    Partnership Voluntary Arrangements, 79
    Partnerships Order 1994, 78
    petitions against more than one partner, 79
    unregistered companies, 78

PAYNE COMMITTEE,
  judgement debts, 73

PERSONAL INSOLVENCY,
  alternatives to bankruptcy,
    formal procedures, 41
  Bankrupt's estate,
    composition of, 188
  bankruptcy law, outline of, 35 *et seq.*
  bankruptcy order,
    commencement of bankruptcy, 38
    creditors' committee, 182
    making of, 143
    public examination, 157
    special manager, 185
  bankruptcy petition,
    eligibility to present, 81 *et seq.*
  bankruptcy, technical meaning, 35
  bankrupt, who can be made?, 69 *et seq.*
  creditor's abuse of process,
    debtor's remedies for, 99
  creditor's petition, 82 *et seq.*
  creditor's petition,
    commercial morality, 97
  debtor's petition, 117
    advantages of, 117
  dividends, payment of, 39
  formal alternatives to, 36
  formal alternatives to bankruptcy,
    voluntary arrangements, 36
  garnishee orders, 90
  honest debtor, protectection, 36
  informal moratorium, 37
  informal procedures, 66
  liability for rates, 92
  liquidated sum,
    payable to petitioning creditor, 103
  official receiver,
    duties of, 38
    investigation of bankrupts conduct, 38
  partnerships,
    legal background, 77
    present law, 78
  petition following default,
    voluntary arrangement, 122
  powers of the trustee,
    ancillary powers, 175
    general, 174
    subject to permission, 171

PERSONAL INSOLVENCY—*cont.*
  proof of debts, 249
  provable debts, 39
  termination of bankruptcy,
    annulment of bankruptcy, 322
    annulment of bankruptcy, 322
    discharge by order of the court, 309
  transactions defrauding creditors, 232
  trustee in bankruptcy,
    appointment of, 166–168
    assignments by, 90

PETITIONING CREDITOR'S DEBT,
  competent petitioning creditor,
    status of, 101
  conditions relating to debt, 101
  debt must be unsecured, 106
  debt not unsecured,
    conditions necessary, 106
  debtor's inability to pay, 110
  judgment debt, 134
  liquidated sum,
    species of claim classified as, 104
  precise identification necessary, 101
  secured creditor,
    definition, 107
  statutory demand, 128
    alternative statutory demands, 111
  sum payable immediately, 105

PHOENIX SYNDROME,
  company's directors' liability, 664
  misuse of company names, 500
  special new provisions to combat, 489

POST-INSOLVENCY INTEREST ON DEBTS,
  winding up law,
    priority on distribution of assets, 611

POSTPONED DEBTS,
  categories of, 297
  distribution of assets, 296

PRE-PREFERENTIAL DEBTS,
  distribution of assets, 290
  Friendly Societies,
    claims of trustees of, 291

PRE-RECEIVERSHIP CONTRACTS,
  administrative receivers, 373
  receivers, general issues affecting, 371

PREFERENCES,
  winding up law,
    connected persons, 643
    Cork report recommendations, 642
    statutory test for the giving of, 642

PREFERENTIAL DEBTS,
  bankruptcy,
    priority of debts, 796
  categories of, 291
    customs and excise, debts due to, 799
    Inland Revenue debts, 798
    levies on coal and steel production, 802
    occupational pension schemes, 800

INDEX

PREFERENTIAL DEBTS—*cont.*
 categories of—*cont.*
  remuneration of employee, 800
  Social Security Contributions, 800
 company and individual insolvency, 797
 debts to spouses, 796
 paid in priority to all other debts, 795
 priority of distribution of assets, 609
 qualification as, 292
 qualifying periods, 292
 relevant date, 797
PRINCIPAL DEBTOR,
 bankruptcy of, 267
PRINCIPLE OF COLLECTIVITY,
 pari passu principle,
  distribution of assets, insolvent company, 4, 613
PRIVATE EXAMINATIONS,
 application to court to conduct, 567
 confidential statements, 569
 custody and inspection of documents, court's powers, 567
 disclosure of information, 569
 discretion influencing factors, 565
 officers of the company and others, 561
 reserved material,
  inspection of, 570
 section 235,
  non-judicial examinations, 564
 section 236,
  principles of application, 562
 self-incrimination, 565
PROOF OF DEBTS,
 annuities,
  calculation of, for purposes of proof, 264
 barristers' fees,
  non-recoverability of, 255
 cheques and Bills of Exchange,
  Bill used as security, 262
  liability on the Bill, 260
 contingent liabilities,
  general features, 262–264
 costs, 269
 costs, liability for, 269
 debts which may be proved,
  deed of covenant, claims based upon, 257
  double proof, rule against, 255
  foreign currency debts, 258
  interest, 279
  procedural incapacity under Foreign Law, 254
  provable and non-provable debts, 250
  shares, 258
  tort claims, 256
 equitable set-off,
  doctrine of, 278
 foreign currency debts, 597
 foreign tax liabilities, 254

PROOF OF DEBTS—*cont.*
 guarantors,
  co-surety, bankruptcy of, 268
  principal debtor, bankruptcy, 267
 mode of proof,
  admission of proofs, 285
  claims in respect of interest, 285
  company liquidation, written claim, 598
  creditor can withdraw his proof, 598
  debts payable in the future, 285
  expunging of proof, 286, 598
  ordinary cases, 280
  periodical payments, 284
  rejection of proof, 285
  secured creditors, 281
  time limit, court fixes, 598
  written claim required, 598
 non-provable debts, 251
  debts not provable in a liquidation, 601
 proof,
  creditor's task, 249
 proof for interest, 279
 provable debts,
  estimated value, 597
  which debts may be proved, 250
  winding up of a company, 596
  winding up petition, 596
 Rule in *Cherry v. Boultbee*, 276
 secured creditors,
  lodging of proof for dividend purposes, 600
  options available, 600
 separation agreement,
  periodical payments under a, 265
 set-off,
  liquidation, 599
  mutual credits, 274
  mutual debts, 274
  mutuality, requirement of, 273
  possibility of effecting, 272
  Rule in *Cherry v. Boultbee*, 276
 surety, bankruptcy of, 269
 trustee in bankruptcy,
  functions of, 249
 trustee's powers, 253
 winding up,
  liability must exist at commencement, 597
PROPERTY,
 bankrupt's,
  belonging to, commencement of bankruptcy, 189
  vesting in the trustee, 188
 bankrupt's conduct in the initial period,
  concealment or removal of, 346
  non-disclosure of, 348
 bankrupt's conduct prior to petition,
  concealment of, 337
  obtained on credit, fraudulent dealing, 341
  removal of, 337

831

Index

PROPERTY—*cont.*
  broad definition, 188
  fraudulent disposal of,
    bankruptcy offence, 339
    bankruptcy offence, 346
  intellectual, 190
  obtained on credit, fraudulent dealing, 347
  removal or concealment of,
    bankruptcy offence, 337
PROVABLE DEBTS,
  legally recoverable debts, 39
  winding up of a company,
    provisions applicable, 595
PROVISIONAL LIQUIDATOR,
  appointment of, 550
  primary object for, 551
PUBLIC EXAMINATIONS,
  officers of the company,
    application to court for, 570
    failure to attend, warrant of arrest issued, 570
    former liquidator of company, 572

RATES,
  liability for, 92
RATING LIABILITY,
  bankruptcy petition,
    preferential status, removal of, 93
  Local Authority enforcement powers, 94
  local authority, presented by, 93
RECEIVERSHIP ACCOUNTS,
  registrar of companies, 373
RECEIVERS,
  appointed by the court, 362
  appointed out of court, 368
  general issues affecting, 382
  See also OFFICIAL RECEIVER
RECOVERY OF ASSETS,
  previously disposed of
    by the company,
      connected persons, 643
      extortionate credit transactions, 647
      floating charges, avoidance of certain, 648
      preferences, 642
      transactions at an undervalue, 641
REMUNERATION,
  trustee in bankruptcy, 170
RESERVATION OF TITLE CLAUSES,
  contracts for the supply of goods, 634
RULE IN *Cherry v. Boultbee*
  proof of debts, 276

SECOND BANKRUPTCY,
  Blagden committee recommendations, 299
  Cork committee endorsement, 299
  distribution of assets, 299–300

SECRETARY OF STATE,
  winding up petition by, 539
SECURED CREDITORS,
  definition, 107
  lodging of proof,
    dividend purposes, 600
  proof of debt, 281
SECURED DEBT,
  petitioning creditor's debt,
    conditions necessary, 106
SEPARATION AGREEMENT,
  periodical payments under,
    provable debts, 265
SERIOUS FRAUD OFFICE,
  investigative powers,
    right to silence, 566
SHARES,
  shareholder become bankrupt,
    provable debt, 258
SMALL BANKRUPTCIES,
  summary administration,
    bankrupt's discharge automatic after two years, 329
    certificate for, 327
    hearing of debtor's petition, 327
    notice to creditors, 329
    official receivers duties, 328
    procedure, 327
    small bankruptcies level, 328
    value of assets in bankrupt's estate, 328
SOCIAL SECURITY CONTRIBUTIONS,
  preferential debts, 800
SPECIAL MANAGER,
  bankruptcy order, 185
STATUTORY DEMAND,
  affidavit proving service of demand, 112
  application to set aside, 113
    award of costs, 116
    contra proferentem rule of construction, 116
    court hearing, 114
    filing an, running of time limit ceases, 113
    grounds for, 114
    other grounds, 115
  bankruptcy notice, 110
  foreign currency, 112
  formal procedure, 110
  Government departments, issued by, 113
  Insolvency Rules 1986,
    essential information needed, 111
  Minister of the Crown, issued by, 113
  running of the time limit, 114
STATUTORY MORATORIUM,
  presentation of petition,
    commencement of, 435

INDEX

SUBJECT TO EQUITIES,
  trustee takes, 205
SUMMARY ADMINISTRATION PROCEDURE,
  small bankruptcies, 327
SUPREME COURT OF JUDICATURE ACTS 1873–1875,
  structure of courts, reorganisation, 23
SURETY,
  bankruptcy of, 269

TAX BANKRUPTCIES,
  international element,
    bankrupt's duty to recover foreign assets, 708
TERMINATION OF BANKRUPTCY,
  annulment of bankruptcy,
    effect of, 325
    principal grounds for, 322
    procedure, 324
  automatic discharge,
    first time bankrupts, 307
  commencement of, 307
  discharge by order of the court,
    appeals, 314
    appellate jurisdiction, 314
    application for, 310
    bankrupt's conduct, 309
    discretionary powers of court, 313
    hearing of the application, 311
    official receiver given notice of application, 310
    order of discharge, 316
    powers of the court, 311
    previous state of bankruptcy, 309
    removal of legal restraints, 321
    report on bankrupt's conduct, 310
    situation of the bankrupt, 320
    unconditional refusal of discharge, 313
  Insolvency Act 1986, 307
  small bankruptcies,
    summary administration procedure, 327
TERMINATION OF DISCHARGE,
  discharge by order of the court, 317
  effect of discharge, 317
THEFT ACT 1968,
  criminal law,
    offences under general, 344
TORT CLAIMS,
  provable debts, 256
TRANSACTIONS AT AN UNDERVALUE,
  court's powers to order restitution of property, 225
  relevant time, 222
  two-to-five year case, 223
  two-year case, 223

TRANSACTIONS AT AN UNDERVALUE—*cont.*
  winding up law,
    creditors and third parties, effect of, 641
  relevant time, 644
  statutory test for, 641
TRANSACTIONS DEFRAUDING CREDITORS,
  applications under section 423,
    victim of the transaction, 233
  court's discretionary powers, 234
  intent to defraud, 232
  transaction at an undervalue, 232
TRIBUNALS AND INQUIRIES ACT 1971,
  insolvency practitioners,
    refusal or withdrawal of authorisation, 32
TRUSTEE IN BANKRUPTCY,
  appointment of, 39
    commencement of, 168–169
    Department of Trade, 167
    first meeting of creditors, 167
    insolvency practitioner, 168
    official receiver's duties, 167
    private sector, from, 167
    summary administration, certificate for, 168
    validity of, 168–169
  assignments by, 90
    third parties, 91
  control of,
    court jurisdiction, 178
    creditors' committee, 178
    discretionary powers of court, 179
  dividends, payments made to proving creditors, 39
  duties of, 175
  financial records maintained, 176
  Insolvency Services Account, 176
  money realised by, 39
  payments made to proving creditors, 39
  powers enjoyed by, 90
  powers of, 39
    ancillary powers, 175
    creditors' committee, permission of, 171
    exercisable with sanction, 171
    general powers, 174
    subject to permission, 171
  records and accounts, 176
    Consolidated Fund, 177
  removal or vacation of office,
    reasons for, 180
  remuneration,
    basis to be used for fixing, 170
    challenging the, 170
    disallowment, reasons for, 171
    dissatisfaction with rate, 170

833

TRUSTEE IN BANKRUPTCY—*cont.*
  resignation of, 180
TRUSTEE,
  appointment of, in bankruptcy, 160

UNCLAIMED DIVIDENDS,
  distribution of assets, 304
UNDISCHARGED BANKRUPT,
  engaging in trade,
    bankruptcy offence, 354
  further bankruptcy proceedings, 80
  obtaining credit,
    criminal offence, 350
  personal disqualifications, 150
  personal situation of, 150
  post-adjudication debts, 80
  removal of legal restraints, 321
UNSECURED DEBT,
  petitioning creditor's debt, 106

VOLUNTARY LIQUIDATION,
  Cork Report, 26
VOLUNTARY PROCEDURES,
  formal procedures,
    administration order, 60
    deeds of arrangement, 59
    individual voluntary arrangements, 41–58
  informal procedures, 66
VOLUNTARY WINDING UP,
  appointment of liquidator, 487
  commencement of, 487
  creditors', 487, 493
  dissolution of the company, 621
  final meeting prior to dissolution, 617
  members' and creditors',
    distinction between, 493
  procedure, 487

WINDING UP LAW,
  advent of, 628
  alternatives to,
    company administration orders, 419
    company voluntary arrangements, 401
  civil remedies and penalties for directors,
    fraudulent trading, 659
    restriction on the re-use of company names, 664
    summary remedy against delinquent directors, 658
    wrongful trading, 661
  collection and distribution of assets, 603 *et seq.*
  commencement of, 628
  company's assets,
    preserving the status quo, 628
  company's books,
    falsification of, 656

WINDING UP LAW—*cont.*
  compulsory winding up,
    assembling of accurate statement, 488
    company's affairs, statement of, 488, 489
    company's assets, distribution of, 489
    early dissolution of company, 620
    field of application,
    final meeting prior to dissolution, 618
    initiated by means of court order, 487
    investigation into company's affairs, 488
    official receiver's duties, 488
    Phoenix syndrome, 489
    principal tasks of liquidator, 489
    service of a statutory demand for payment, 488
    winding up by court, 485
  conversion of mode, 495
  creditors' voluntary winding up,
    assets and liabilities, statements of, 494
    commencement of, 505
    conversion from members' to, 495
    declaration of solvency, 486, 494
    formal declaration of solvency, 494
    major reforms implemented, 500
    meeting of directors, 494
    misuse of company names, 500
  creditors and third parties, effect of, 627
    adjustment of antecedent transactions, 640
    connected persons, 643
    contracts, 631
    cross-border operation, 645
    dispositions and transfers, 628
    distress or execution levied, 632
    extortionate credit transactions, 647
    preferences, 640, 642
    preserving the status quo, 628
    protection of third party purchasers, 646
    recovery of assets previously disposed of, 640
    relevant time, 644
    reservation of title clauses, 634
    secured creditors, 633
    supplies by utilities, 639
    transaction adjustment provisions, 645
    transactions at an undervalue, 640, 641
    transactions defrauding creditors, 650
    trust devices, 637
    trust retention device, 638
    validation orders, 628
  dispositions and transfers,
    after winding up, 628
  disqualification of directors,
    Company Directors Disqualification Act 1986, 668
    unfitness, matters for determining, 670

INDEX

WINDING UP LAW—*cont.*
  dissolution,
    early, 617
    final meeting prior to, 617
  dissolution of the company,
    compulsory winding up, 619
    dissolution declared void, 623
    effect of, 622
    striking out of the register, 621
  effects of on creditors and third parties, 627
  final meeting prior to dissolution, 617
  floating charges,
    avoidance of certain, 648
    concept of relevant time, 650
    time factor, 649
  floating charges, avoidance of certain, 648
  liability of directors,
    civil remedies, 657
    criminal liability for fraudulent trading, 657
    criminal offences before / during liquidation, 653
    disqualification of directors, 668
    falsification of company's books, 656
    fraud in anticipation of winding up, 653
    material omissions from statement of affairs, 656
    misconduct in course of winding up, 655
    penalties applicable to directors and officer, 657
    transactions in fraud of creditors, 655
  members' voluntary winding up, 485
  proof of debts,
    foreign currency debts, 597
    mode of proving, 598
    non-provable debts, 601
    provable debts, 595
    secured creditors, 600
    set-off in liquidation, 599
  protection of third party purchasers, Insolvency (No 2) Act 1994, 646
  qualified insolvency practitioner, liquidator of company, 485
  recovery of assets,
    previously disposed of by company, 640
  reservation of title clauses, 634
  supplies by utilities, 639
  third party purchasers,
    protection of, 646
  transaction adjustment provisions, cross-border operation, 645
  transactions at an undervalue, 640
    relevant time, 644
  transactions defrauding creditors, 650
  two separate modes of procedure, 485

WINDING UP LAW—*cont.*
  voluntary winding up,
    appointment of liquidator, 487
    commencement of, 487
    conversion from, to compulsory, 496
    creditors', 487
    dissolution of the company, 621
    final meeting prior to dissolution, 617
    most frequently used in practice, 486
    procedure, 487
    solvent and insolvent companies, 485
    timing of, 486
  winding up order, *see* WINDING UP ORDER
  winding up petition, *see* WINDING UP PETITION

WINDING UP OF COMPANIES,
  registered under Companies Act, preferential debts, 795

WINDING UP ORDER,
  action or proceeding,
    commencement or continuation of, 557
    distress as, 557
  appointment of liquidator,
    certification of appointment, 578
    steps to, 558
  commencement of winding up, 554
  creditors and contributories,
    first meeting of, 572
  discretion influencing factors, 565
  discretionary powers of court, 556
  effects of,
    company's, 555
    directors dismissed, 555
    terminating employment of employees and agent, 555
    validation order, 555
  execution or attachment, 557
  first meeting of creditors and contributories,
    conduct of meeting, 574–575
    Cork report recommendations, 572–574
    entitlement to vote, 575
    nomination of liquidator, 572–574
    official receiver designated chairman, 574
    procedural requirements, 574
    resolutions allowed, 577
    voting on basis of majority in value, 573
  investigation by official receiver,
    company's, 560
    company's, 561
    private examinations of officers of company, 561
    section 235—non-judicial examinations, 564
    section 236—principles of application, 562

INDEX

WINDING UP ORDER—*cont.*
  liquidation committee,
    committee of inspection, 589
    functions to be performed by, 590
    membership of, 590
    resignation of members, 591
  liquidator,
    appointment of, 577–580
    books and accounts, 587
    general duties, 583
    legal status, 582
    nature of the role played by, 583
    powers exercisable with and without sanction, 585–586
    principal, specific functions of, 584
    release of, 582
    removal of, 580
    remuneration, 582
    resignation of, 580
    vacation of office, 581
  liquidator's powers exercisable,
    with sanction, 585
    with sanction in winding up by court, 585
    without sanction in any winding up, 586
    without sanction in voluntary, 585
  liquidator, appointment of,
    first meeting of creditors and contributories, 578
  nomination of liquidator,
    first meeting of creditors and contributories, 572
  non-judicial examinations,
    section 235, 564
  officers of the company,
    private examination of, 561
    public examination of, 570
  official receiver,
    company's, 561
    duties of, 558
    initial duties, 558
    investigation by, 560
    investigation of company, 558
    provisional liquidator, as, 558
    statement of affairs, 558
  pari passu principle, 556
  private examinations,
    access to information, 568–569
    application to court to conduct, 567
    confidential statements, 569
    confidentiality, grounds of, 566
    custody and inspection of documents, 567
    disclosure of information, 569
    discretion influencing factors, 565
    informally obtained information, 567
    interviews used as material evidence, 566
    officers of the company, 561

WINDING UP ORDER—*cont.*
  private examinations—*cont.*
    reserved material, inspection of, 570
    section 235—non-judicial examinations, 564
    section 236—principles of application, 562
    self-incriminations, 565
    transcripts of formal examinations, 567
  proceedings against the company,
    leave to commence or continue, 555–556
  provisional liquidator appointed, 555
  public examinations of officers of company,
    application for, 570
    failure to attend, warrant of arrest issued, 570
    former liquidator of company, 572
    self-incrimination, privilege against, 571
    statement of affairs, 571
  publicity to third parties, 557–558
  remedy of distress, 557
  section 236, principles of application, investigation by official receiver, 562
  Serious Fraud Office,
    right to silence, 566
  statement of affairs, 558
  staying of all proceedings, 555
WINDING UP PETITION,
  advertisement of,
    concept of, 546
    copy lodged at court,
    reasons to restrain, 545
    seven clear days in Gazette, 544
  appeals against, 549–550
  certificate of compliance, 547
  Companies Court, 541
  company registered in Scotland, 542
  contributory's petition,
    conditions to present, 535
    contributory, meaning, 535
  costs,
    petition dismissed, 549
    successful petition, 549
  County Court, 541
  courts having jurisdiction, 541
  creditor's petition,
    eligible to present, 536
    minimum amount of indebtedness, 536
  directors, petition by, 534
  District Registries, 541
  hearing of,
    opposed petition, 548
    unopposed petitions, 548
  interlocutory appeal, 550
  notice of appearance, 547
  opposition by other creditors, 537
  payment or tender, 537

INDEX

WINDING UP PETITION—*cont.*
  persons eligible to present, 533
  petition by official receiver, 539
  petition by Secretary of State,
    company in voluntary winding up, 540
  petition dismissed,
    costs, 549
  petitions by the company, 534
  presentation of,
    filed at court where it will be heard, 543
    prescribed form, 543
    verified by an affidavit, 543
  provisional liquidator,
    appointment of, 550
    authority of, 551
    object of appointing, 551
  rescission of, 550

WINDING UP PETITION—*cont.*
  service of, 543
  special manager,
    appointment of, 551
    functions of, 551
    powers of, 551
    termination of power, 552
  successful petition,
    costs, 549
  withdrawal of,
    conditions for, 547

WRONGFUL TRADING,
  defence to liability, 663
  moment of truth test, 661
  new concept of responsibility for, 661
  test of knowledge, 662